P9-ELQ-077

www.letsgo.com

SPAIN, PORTUGAL & MOROCCO

researcher-writers
Christa Hartsock
Jocelyn Karlan
Grace Sun
Mark Warren

staff writers
Simone Gonzalez
Adrienne Y. Lee
_____ McLeod

Maya Shwayder
Sara Joe Wolansky

research man
Anna E. Bo

editor
Jonathan Rossi

managing editor
Marykate Jasper

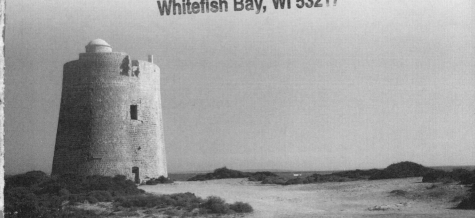

CONTENTS

RESEARCHER-WRITERS

CHRISTA HARTSOCK. Christa's love affair with Barcelona began with her extensive research on the city's urban planning for her senior thesis. An art and architecture scholar, she was powerless to resist the likes of Gaudí's Manzana de Discordia. After her immaculate research was finished, Christa embarked on an epic biking trip to Amsterdam, where she snored loud enough to wake up the whole town.

JOCELYN KARLAN. After spending part of last summer stranded on top of a mountain in Ecuador, Jocey chalks up her time with Let's Go as a success. A student of psychology, Jocey may have used hypnosis to charm the locals—or maybe she's just incredibly amiable. Her editors think it's the latter; Jocey's enthusiasm to research every nook and cranny (and cave) in Andalusia made her indispensable.

GRACE SUN. Grace explored the heart of Spain—Madrid—and mastered the inner workings of its atria (discotecas) and ventricles (endless tapas bars). Starting off her route with a nasty case of bronchitis did nothing to dampen Grace's spirits—and neither did encountering a bunkmate doing meth in southern Portugal. Grace's willingness to try new things (except meth) made her research shine.

JOE TOBIAS. Hailing from the Great White North, Joe is a mountain man with a poet's soul. When he isn't writing sonnets, he can be found somewhere in the wilderness of the Northeastern US. His travels for Let's Go took him to Morocco and southwestern France, allowing him to master snake charming and wine tasting.

MARK WARREN. Traipsing along the Camino in northern Spain and scooting south into Portugal, Mark circumnavigated nearly half of the Iberian Peninsula. This modern-day Magellan's route was a whirlwind of port wine, seafood, and learning that Portuguese is really not that similar to Spanish.

SPAIN, PORTUGAL & MOROCCO

Forget *Lost* and its enchanted island—the Iberian Peninsula has seen more drama than ABC's entire Thursday night lineup. Isolated from Europe and Africa by mountain and sea, Spain and Portugal are themselves cultural mosaics of time. Despite being fiercely proud of their individuality, Spain's regions share a common rhythm. From the lull of afternoon siestas to the riotous tapas bars and *discotecas*, Spain harbors an invigorating lifestyle that galvanizes any traveler. For daring backpackers looking to elevate their adventures, rock climbing in El Chorro can provide history lessons laced with continental views. If the flatlands are more your cup of tea, check out the beaches of Sitges in Catalonia or the chic northern city of San Sebastian to soak up rays and see local birthday suits. If the only buff part of your body is your brain, head north to Madrid's Museo del Prado: with almost 10,000 pieces of art, they don't have enough room to display their entire collection.

Portugal draws hordes of backpackers by fusing its timeless inland towns and majestic castles with industrialized cities like Lisbon, whose graffiti-covered walls separate bustling bars from posh *fado* restaurants. The original backpackers, Portuguese patriarchs like Vasco da Gama, pioneered the exploration of Asia, Africa, and South America, and the country continues to foster such discovery within its borders, with wine regions like the Douro Valley, immaculate forests and mountains in its wild northern region, and 2000km of coastline for tourists to traverse.

While Morocco rests only 13km from the southern tip of Spain, it's a world apart from Europe. Travelers interested in Muslim heritage, spicy Moroccan cuisine, or merely the historical significance of that misunderstood Fès hat consistently agree that Morocco's inventive combination of African and European culture makes the short visit south from Iberia the perfect worldly experience.

when to go

Summer is **high season** (*temporada alta*) for most of Spain and Portugal, when tons of tourists come to live *la vida loca*. Winter is high season for ski resorts in the Pyrenees, Sierra Nevada, and Atlas mountain ranges. In many areas, high season begins during **Semana Santa** (Holy Week; April 17-24 in 2011) and includes festival days like Pamplona's **Running of the Bulls** (p. 321). July and August bring some serious heat, especially to the central plains and southern coasts. When the locals take vacation in other parts of Europe in August, tourism peaks on the Iberian Peninsula, leaving behind closed offices, restaurants, and empty lodgings for travelers. To be safe, make sure to book **reservations** if you plan to travel in June, July, and August.

Taking advantage of the **low season** (*temporada baja*) has many advantages, most notably lighter crowds, longer days, and lower prices. Some lodgings drastically cut their prices, and there's no need for reservations. Call restaurants and sights before your trip for their off-season schedule before including them in your itinerary. Even as major cities and university towns exude energy during these months due in part to study abroad students, smaller coastal towns are empty, and sights almost everywhere cut their prices.

what to do

For the last two millennia, invaders ranging from hordes of European tribes to overzealous study-abroad students have swept over these countries, leaving their own mark on a culture already ripe with customs, tradition, history, and an undeniable fervor. Witness this excitement in Madrid's famous nightlife (p. 47), in the historic Alfama district in Lisbon (p. 361), or even in the hectic Moroccan medinas (p. 426). There are countless ways to see Spain, Portugal, and Morocco: some tourists binge on sightseeing, getting through multiple churches and monuments every hour, while others spend weeks trekking through small towns, trying to find that *authentic* way of life unaffected by globalization. Whatever your travel desires, these countries will not disappoint.

SMALL PLATES, BIG OPTIONS

Your mother would scold Spain for maintaining a national dinnertime after 9pm—that is, until she tried the country's delectable tapas. Spain tides itself over before dinner with appetizing starters called tapas. Derived from the Spanish verb *tapar*, meaning "to cover," tapas are a ubiquitous treat flavored with garlic, chilies, and blends of spices like paprika and cumin. From cold vegetable medleys to roasted meat slathered in original sauces, these small plates are a perfect sampling of regional and national cuisine. As a traveler, you can almost tell your whereabouts with just one look at your plate. In Madrid and parts of Andalucia, tapas bars serve small tapas free with drinks, and certain areas like Logrono's **Calle Laurel** and Leon's **Barrio**

Humédo are filled with finger-food havens dedicated to these tasty tidbits. In parts of northern Spain like Salamanca, chefs cook up *pinchos*, or tapas on toothpicks, that keep the snack from falling off its bread. Regardless of where you find yourself, don't miss out on a sampling of the nation's favorite little antipasto that could.

- **CASA ALBERTO:** Home to eclectic tapas like lamb's knuckles and pig's ears, this bar also serves up regional favorites like salted cod and oxtail. (Madrid, Spain; p. 37.)

- **TABERNA DE ANTONIO SANCHEZ:** Opened in 1830 by a Spanish bullfighter, this bar serves up piping hot *tapas calientes*; it's rumored that two of these bad boys together rival any dinner option in Madrid. (Madrid, Spain; p. 36.)

- **EL XAMPANYET:** While named after the house wine, this place should be named after its deliciously varied tapas selection. (Barcelona, Spain; p. 252.)

- **GATZ:** Despite sharing the surname of the famous Great Gatsby, this tapas bar is not a sham. With pinchos prizes lining its walls, Gatz serves up some seriously tasty dishes like fried *froie* and potato *pinchos* and salmon wrapped around cream cheese and capers. (Bilbao, Spain; p. 311.)

- **A FUEGO NEGRO:** Let's Go's choice for tapas with some 'tude, A Fuego Negro serves up some heavy rock and even heavier tapas plates. (San Sebastian, Spain; p. 305.)

top five sweets for your sweetie

5. TANGIER: Head to Cafe de Paris, a Moroccan cafe that has served mint tea to everyone from WWII spies to Matt Damon. Don't worry, overprotective boyfriend—he's not a regular.

4. SEVILLA: Impress your lover with sticky buns made by gifted nuns in the Santa Cruz district at El Torno bakery.

3. PORTO: Bring your love muffin to a Croft tasting tour to try some of the Douro region's best Port, a sweet dessert wine.

2. GRANADA: Fall in love with your *amorcito* one more time over some *pinono*s, sugary cookies covered in baked cream at Lopez Mezquita.

1. CÓRDOBA: Share the *hojas con chocolate*, a Spanish puff pastry longer than your forearm, at the Pasteleria-Cafeteria San Pedro.

FROM DUSK 'TIL DAWN

Taking the etymology of the term "nightlife" to its extreme, Spain and Portugal help make the Iberian the peninsula that never sleeps. Barcelona's eat-late-but-party-later attitude creates an edgy nightlife that reflects the city's distinct sense of style. With intoxicating energy flowing from an array of *discotecas* and *tablaos*, Madrid has become internationally recognized as one of the greatest party cities in the world. Sevilla's **La Macarena** district is the perfect meeting ground for travelers looking to booze with locals, and **Ibiza** houses some of the world's largest clubs. Bring out your inner bro in the student-packed **Salamanca**, an international frat-star haven, or head out on the town in Portugal's **Lagos**, a city with more bars and backpackers per square meter than any other place in the world. Off the peninsula in nearby Morocco, visitors breath in aromatic mint tea as they spend hours enjoying the summer breeze in quiet cafes and lounge on neighborhood rooftops before heading out for late nights in the country's discos. Even if your days are packed with that next art history lesson, make sure to take advantage of all these countries have to offer 24 hours a day.

- **MADRID:** Find the next big *discoteca* in Madrid's Chueca district (p. 52), a nightlife sanctuary home to some of the trendiest and sleek clubs and bars.

- **BARCELONA:** For alternative music and some of Spain's most eclectic party people, head to Barcelona's El Raval district to move to the beat of your own drum. (p. 272)

- **SALAMANCA:** Students and the young at heart don't think about heading to clubs until well after midnight in this party 'til the break of dawn locale. (p. 75)

- **LAGOS:** Turn your surfboard into a giant shotboard by surfing the beaches until dusk and starting the night early in one of the city's bars dotting the coastline. (p. 393)

- **IBIZA:** Sand might not be the only thing you get in your pants after a night on this debauched island. (p. 207)

SOUQ-CESSFUL SHOPPING

If there's only one thing Let's Go enjoys on this green earth, it's finding a great deal on the road. If there's another thing Let's Go enjoys, it's *making* a great deal on the road. No, aspiring capitalists looking to exploit foreign laws with sketchy transactions, we're not advocating anything illegal—especially not in a foreign country where the word misdemeanor isn't in the national vocabulary. Instead, we're telling you to get your frugal selves over to the Moroccan cities of Fès and Marrakesh to explore their outdoor bazaars and find the best deals on everything from trinkets and baubles to fresh produce and livestock. In Fès, watch out for a mixed thoroughfare of donkeys wielding refrigerators on their backs, old men weaving carpets and baskets along corridors, and unmarked leather dye pits that could turn you into an Oompa Loompa with just one misstep. In old Marrakesh, enjoy the snake charmers, mystics, and charlatans all looking to impress you into forking over some dirhams. However, before bringing out your wallet, make sure to haggle your way to a price within your budget—because nothing makes a purchase better than a bargain.

- **FÈS MEDINA:** Fès, the artisanal capital of Morocco, houses this outdoor bazaar specializing in everything from authentic blue pottery to henna tattoos to daggers. (p.429)

- **MARRAKESH SOUQ:** Offering virtually everything under the Sun, this *souq* is never-ending, timeless, and potentially dangerous if you lose your friends. (p. 461)

- **DJEMA'A AL-FNA:** Head to this incredible outdoor spectacle in old Marrakesh (p. 457) to barter and buy your way into some Moroccan culture.

BEYOND TOURISM

That last guided tour put you to sleep? Need to take a break from schlepping your baggage around cobblestone streets? Or maybe you're broke beyond belief and in need of some spare cash to prolong your trip? Whatever the case may be, use our Beyond Tourism section that shows how to study, work, or volunteer in these countries to spice up your trip and help you get closer to the local way of life.

- **ACADEMIC STUDIES ABROAD:** Use this one-stop shop to find a study abroad program in Spain that fits your specific needs and wants. (p. 506)

- **DON QUIJOTE:** With schools in both Spain and Morocco, don Quijote offers courses for students with all levels of language ability. (p. 510)

- **QUERCUS:** Volunteer with this Portuguese activist group and focus on issues like water contamination and nuclear waste. (p. 510)

- **SUNNY AU PAIRS:** Enroll with this network and land a job taking care of Spanish niños for a few months. (p. 513)

student superlatives

- **BEST PLACE TO FULFILL YOUR PIPE DREAMS:** Head to Barcelona's Pipa Club, an unmarked bar and lounge specializing in tobacco products.

- **BEST ROCK AND SOL:** Come to Puerta del Sol, the "gateway of the sun" and soul of Madrid's shopping, people-watching, and partying.

- **BEST MIXTURE OF THE SACRED AND THE PROFANE:** Imbibe in all kinds of sin at Porto's Festa de São João in commemeration of John the Baptist.

- **BEST PLACE TO PARTY LIKE ITS 1755:** At the Palacio Real, you'll live like a king—at least until the end of the one-hour walking tour.

- **BEST PLACE TO RETIRE:** Even if your 401K hasn't kicked in yet, head to Madrid's Parque del Retiro for rest and relaxation in the city's best green space.

- **BEST USE OF PIGEON POOP AND COW URINE:** Don't let these ingredients stop you from buying the dyed leather from Fès's famous tanneries.

- **BEST PLACE TO BRANCH OUT:** Head to Ifrane's Cascade de la Vierge, home to the oldest cedar tree in all of Africa.

suggested itineraries

BEST OF SPAIN, PORTUGAL & MOROCCO (1 MONTH)

Discover the Iberian Peninsula and then some by traveling first through Portugal and southwestern Spain and then into Morocco.

1. **LISBON:** Visit Portugal's capital city, where hilltop castles and Roman arches overlook a modern metropolis.

2. **PORTO:** Imbibe the city's namesake wine along the impressive Douro River.

3. **SALAMANCA:** Rage with study abroad students from around the world at this internationally-recognized college town.

4. **MADRID:** The beating heart of Spain, Madrid is the political and geographic center of the country and offers countless opportunities to partake in Spanish culture.

5. **GRANADA:** Play king of the hill for a day in the Alhambra, the crowning jewel of this city found at the foot of the Sierra Nevadas.

6. **SEVILLA:** Dance the flamenco late into the night in Spain's third-largest city.

7. **CADIZ:** Housing the Spanish Navy since the 1700's, this port city offers tourists breathtaking vistas and is arguably the oldest city on the Iberian Peninsula.

8. **GIBRALTAR:** Whether you want to sip a Guinness or swing with Barbary apes, a daytrip to the UK's Mediterranean gem won't disappoint.

9. **TANGIER:** Sample tea at one of the cozy cafes in this gateway to Africa.

10. **CHEFCHAOUEN:** Take a load off and chillax in the gorgeous mountain town of Chefchaouen nestled high up in the Rif.

11. **FÈS:** Have a sensory overload in the medinas and open-air markets of this imperial city.

12. **MARRAKESH:** At the gateway to the Atlas Mountains, Marrakesh's old world allure and proximity to nature make it Morocco's southern gem.

Best of Spain, Portugal & Morocco

FRANCE

Porto

2

Salamanca

3 **4**

1

Lisbon

Madrid

Barcelona

5

SPAIN

Sevilla

7 **6**

8 Cadiz

Grenada

Tangier **10**

9 Gibraltar

Chefchaouen **11**

12

MOROCCO

Fez

ALGERIA

13

Marrakesh

BRONZING AND BURNING ON THE IBERIAN PENINSULA (2 WEEKS)

Pale—why wait? Grab a few train tickets and be on your way to UV heaven with this fortnight of fun along the Iberian Peninsula's sunniest beaches.

1. ALGARVE: Head to the white sand beaches of Lagos for year-round sunshine on Portugal's west coast.

2. LISBON: Travel to the beaches of Cascais to shred some waves with the local surfing community.

3. PORTO: Be careful when mixing sun and sherry in this Portuguese paradise.

4. BILBAO: With some of the best beaches in Spain, Bilbao offers a myriad of water sports and activities that attracts countless tourists to its sandy beaches.

5. SAN SEBASTIAN: A resort destination for the European bourgeoisie on holiday, this beach town comes equipped with kayaking and surfing lessons for all levels.

6. VALENCIA: With less inhabited beaches and palm-tree-studded plazas than the rest of Spain, soak up some sun and even some Spanish skills in this beach region.

7. ALICANTE: Spend nights fist-pumping in this party town's discos and days recuperating along its white sand beaches.

8. IBIZA: Get baked on Ibiza's warm sands in more ways than one before heading to its crazy clubs and downright dirty discos.

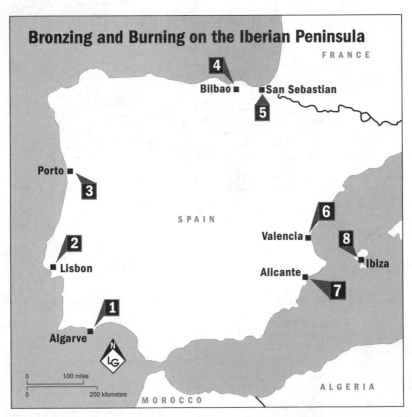

Bronzing and Burning on the Iberian Peninsula

WINES OF THE WEST (1 WEEK)

Cultured connoisseurs and crazy college kids alike will enjoy a week of western wine tasting in the best regions of Spain and Portugal.

1. SANTIAGO DE COMPOSTELA (1 DAY): This city is a great starting point for ☑**wine-tasting** in the Galicia region known for its Albariño wine.

2. PORTO (2 DAYS): With various international imposters attempting to steal its name, this city's port wine remains the original tawny dessert masterpiece.

3. JEREZ (2 DAYS): Made from white grapes grown near this town, Jerez's sherry is an underappreciated post-dinner treat.

4. RONDA (1 DAY): Learn the secrets, smells, and processes behind the age-old winemaking in this Andalucian city.

Wines of the West

FRANCE

1 ■ Santiago de Compostela

■ **Porto**
2

SPAIN

4
■ **Ronda**
Jerez ■
3

Tangier ■
5

0   100 miles
0   200 kilometers

N
LG

MOROCCO

ALGERIA

MOROCCO BY METROPOLIS

Take a crash course in Moroccan culture with a 14-day trip to the country's most historically important cities.

1. TANGIER: Home to several imperial powers over its tumultuous history, Tangier provides backpackers a doorway into the historic relationship between Europe and Africa.

2. FÈS: The great-grandaddy of urban empires, Morocco's oldest imperial city is home to one of the world's oldest universities—and namesake of one of its coolest fashion statements.

3. RABAT: This political capital full of bureaucrats also houses some of Morocco's best traditional food selections.

4. CASABLANCA: Here's looking at you, kid—and in Morocco's largest city and biggest port, there's a lot to look at.

5. MARRAKESH: Snake charmers, storytellers, and steaming night markets make this "Red City" a bustling blast from the past.

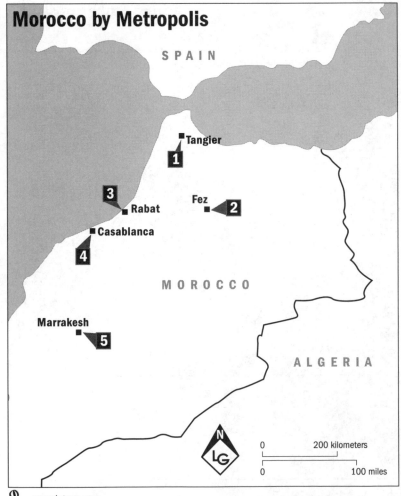

Morocco by Metropolis

SPAIN

Tangier
1

3
Rabat
Fez **2**

Casablanca
4

MOROCCO

Marrakesh
5

ALGERIA

0   200 kilometers

0   100 miles

how to use this book

CHAPTERS

In the next few pages, the travel coverage chapters—the meat of any Let's Go book—begin with Madrid. We then move through the rest of Spain, west into Portugal, and finish across the strait in Morocco.

But that's not all, folks. We also have a few extra chapters for you to peruse:

CHAPTER	DESCRIPTION
Discover Spain, Portugal & Morocco	Discover tells you what to do, when to do it, and where to go for it. The absolute coolest things about any destination get highlighted in this chapter at the front of all *Let's Go* books.
Essentials	Essentials contains the practical info you need before, during, and after your trip–visas, regional transportation, health and safety, phrasebooks, and more.
Spain, Portugal & Morocco 101	Spain, Portugal & Morocco 101 is just what it sounds like–a crash course in where you're traveling. This short chapter on Spain, Portugal, and Morocco's history and culture makes great reading on a long plane ride.
Beyond Tourism	As students ourselves, we at *Let's Go* encourage studying abroad, or going beyond tourism more generally, every chance we get. This chapter lists ideas for how to study, volunteer, or work abroad with other young travelers in Spain, Portugal, and Morocco to get more out of your trip.

LISTINGS

Listings—a.k.a. reviews of individual establishments—constitute a majority of *Let's Go* coverage. Our Researcher-Writers list establishments in order from **best to worst value**—not necessarily quality. (Obviously a five-star hotel is nicer than a hostel, but it would probably be ranked lower because it's not as good a value.) Listings pack in a lot of information, but it's easy to digest if you know how they're constructed:

ESTABLISHMENT NAME 💳💵♿🚫📶🍸❄⛅▼ type of establishment ❶

Address ☎phone number 🖥website

Editorial review goes here.

🧭 Directions to the establishment. ℹ Other practical information about the establishment, like age restrictions at a club or whether breakfast is included at a hostel. $ Prices for goods or services. ⏰ Hours or schedules.

ICONS

First things first: places and things that we absolutely love, sappily cherish, generally obsess over, and wholeheartedly endorse are denoted by the all-empowering **👍Let's Go thumbs-up.** In addition, the icons scattered throughout a listing (as you saw in the sample above) can tell you a lot about an establishment. The following icons answer a series of yes-no questions about a place:

💳	Credit cards accepted	💵	Cash only	♿	Wheelchair-accessible
🚫	Not wheelchair-accessible	📶	Internet access available	🍸	Alcohol served
❄	Air-conditioned	⛅	Outdoor seating available	▼	GLBT or GLBT-friendly

The rest are visual cues to help you navigate each listing:

☎	Phone numbers	🖥	Websites	🧭	Directions
ℹ	Other hard info	$	Prices	⏰	Hours

OTHER USEFUL STUFF

Area codes for each destination appear opposite the name of the city and are denoted by the ☎ icon. Finally, in order to pack the book with as much information as possible, we have used a few **standard abbreviations.** In Spain, c. stands for *calle*, or street. Av. stands for *avenida*, or avenue. In Portugal, r. stands for *rua*, or road, and Plaça is used in place of *plaça*, or street. In Morocco, bld. stands for boulevard. Pl. represents place.

PRICE DIVERSITY

A final set of icons corresponds to what we call our "price diversity" scale, which approximates how much money you can expect to spend at a given establishment. For **accommodations,** we base our range on the cheapest price for which a single traveler can stay for one night. For **food,** we estimate the average amount one traveler will spend in one sitting. The table below tells you what you'll typically find in Spain, Portugal, and Morocco at the corresponding price range, but keep in mind that no system can allow for the quirks of individual establishments.

SPAIN AND PORTUGAL	ACCOMMODATIONS	FOOD	WHAT YOU'RE LIKELY TO FIND
❶	under 20	under 6	Campgrounds and dorm rooms, both in hostels and actual universities. Expect bunk beds and a communal bath. You may have to provide or rent towels and sheets.
❷	20-29	6-12	Upper-end hostels or lower-end hotels. You may have a private bathroom, or there may be a sink in your room and a communal shower in the hall.
❸	30-37	13-17	A small room with a private bath. Should have decent amenities, such as phone and TV. Breakfast may be included.
❹	38-50	18-25	Should have bigger rooms than a ❸, with more amenities or in a more convenient location. Breakfast probably included.
❺	over 50	over 25	Large hotels or upscale chains. If it's a ❺ and it doesn't have the perks you want (and more), you've paid too much.
MOROCCO	ACCOMMODATIONS	FOOD	WHAT YOU'RE LIKELY TO FIND
❶	100dh	20-60dh	Probably street food or a fast-food joint, but also university cafeterias and bakeries (yum). Usually takeout, but you may have the option of sitting down.
❷	100-200dh	61-90dh	Sandwiches, pizza, appetizers at a bar, or low-priced entrees. Most ethnic eateries are a ❷. Either takeout or a sit-down meal, but only slightly more fashionable decor.
❸	201-300dh	91-130dh	Mid-priced entrees, seafood, and exotic pasta dishes. More upscale ethnic eateries. Since you'll have the luxury of a waiter, tip will set you back a little extra.
❹	301-400dh	131-180dh	A somewhat fancy restaurant. Entrees tend to be heartier or more elaborate, but you're really paying for decor and ambience. Few restaurants in this range have a dress code, but some may look down on T-shirts and sandals.
❺	over 400dh	over 180dh	Your meal might cost more than your room, but there's a reason—it's something fabulous, famous, or both. Slacks and dress shirts may be expected. Offers foreign-sounding food and a decent wine list.

SPAIN

MADRID

In 1561, King Felipe II made Madrid the capital of what would become the world's biggest empire. Located in the center of the country, Spain's pulsing heart never stands still. Part of this dynamism is due to the city's cultural diversity. *Madrileños* and tourists alike frequent the thousands of restaurants, bars, and clubs packed throughout each of the city's diverse neighborhoods. As an international melting pot, Madrid is a place where you can walk into almost any venue and meet someone from the opposite corner of the world. By day, Madrid has two of the best art museums in the world: **Museo del Prado** and **Museo Nacional Reina Sofía,** the national museum of modern art. Some other must-sees are the **Palacio Real,** a vast 18th-century royal palace, and the **Catedral de la Almuena.**

Don't let all this culture talk make you think Madrid is all museums all the time. On the contrary, Madrid is filled with fun-loving people who love to lounge, eat great food, drink, and dance. Take a break from touring in gorgeous **Parque del Retiro,** the former retreat of the kings. To see Madrid's quirky side, head to the indie **Malasaña** neighborhood for one-of-a-kind cafes and bars, or check out **Chueca,** Madrid's vivacious gay district. Adopt the *madrileño* lifestyle and take an afternoon siesta to gather energy for after the sun sets, when Madrid's true character comes to life. Dine at 10pm with the locals or better yet, go (tapas) barhopping along **Calle de las Huertas** or any of the streets near **Plaza Santa Ana.** Consider yourself warned—big discos don't really get going until 2am or later, and partygoers stay out until the user-friendly metro opens at 6am, stumbling back home in a sea of commuters as the sun rises.

greatest hits

- **SEE *GUERNICA* AT THE MUSEO NACIONAL REINA SOFÍA.** This painting by Picasso immortalized the atrocities of the Franco regime and is one of the best pieces of modern art (p. 29).

- **RENT A ROWBOAT.** Float around on Parque del Buen Retiro's large man-made lake (p. 18).

- **PARTY LIKE A ROYAL.** Pretend you're nobility at this restored mansion-turned-*discoteca* but shimmy without shame with thoroughly modern go-go dancers (p. 47).

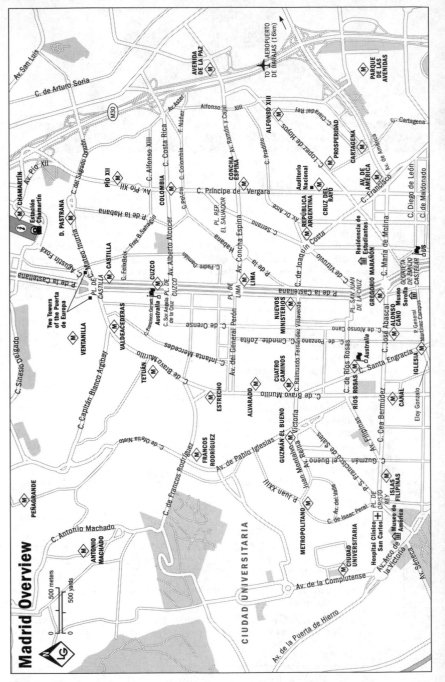

Madrid Overview

madrid

500 meters
500 yards

TO AEROPUERTO
DE BARAJAS (16km)

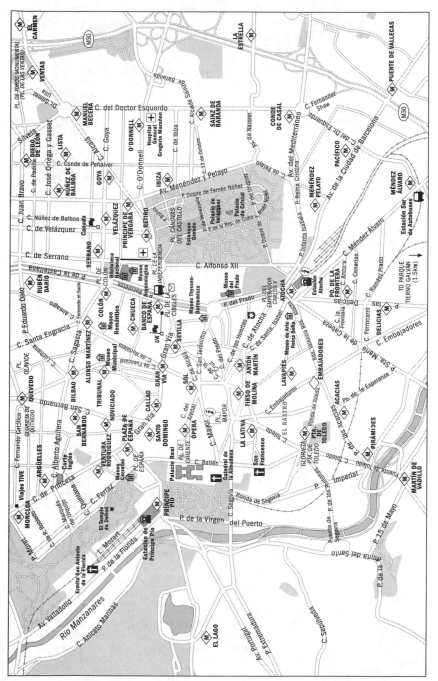

madrid

orientation

EL CENTRO

Bordered by the beautiful Palacio Real in the west and the relaxing Parque del Retiro in the east, El Centro, the heart of Madrid, and it encompasses the city's most famous historical sites and modern venues. Ancient churches, plazas, and winding cobblestone streets are set beside hip clubs and lively bars. In the middle is **Puerta del Sol,** the "soul of Madrid," where thousands descend to ring in each New Year. By day it is filled with tourists and locals checking out the restaurants and shopping that fill the eight streets meeting at Sol, and by night clubbers continue the party until 6am or later. Also in El Centro is **Plaza Mayor,** a vibrant square bordered by restaurants and filled with street performers and vendors. Finally, **Plaza Santa Ana** provides a popular meeting place where locals and tourists can escape for lunch and pre-club drinks. If you only have a few days in Madrid, El Centro gives a great taste of Madrid's culture and people. You can get around quickly with the Metro, but the area is also easily walkable, as the main sites are close to one another. When in doubt, stick to the main streets: **Calle de Alcalá, Calle Mayor, Calle de las Huertas,** and **Calle de Atocha** for great restaurants, nightlife, hostels, and cafes.

LA LATINA AND LAVAPIÉS

Known as the multicultural center of Madrid, La Latina and Lavapiés burst at the seams with international restaurants, bars, and cafes. Less frequented than the Sol or Plaza Mayor areas, these districts are where the locals go to drink and eat before heading out to enjoy more popular nightlife in other quarters. If you find yourself in La Latina, be sure to barhop on **Cava Baja,** a narrow street packed with enough cocktail bars, beer stops, restaurants, and tapas bars to suit any taste. With a relatively recent influx of immigrants from North Africa, the Middle East, and India, Lavapiés is a great place to eat if you're looking for an alternative to Spanish tapas. **Calle de Lavapiés** is filled with Indian restaurants, many specializing in tasty tandoori dishes.

HUERTAS

Huertas street's walls are etched with quotes from writers like Cervantes and Calderón de la Barca who lived in this historically literary neighborhood during its Golden Age. Today, the neighborhood centers itself on **Plaza Santa Ana** and **C. de las Huertas** and is bordered by C. Alcalá (north), Pasea del Prado (east), and C. Atocha (south). Get rid of your writer's block with Huertas' many tapas bars, lively nightlife, and delicious food along Plaza Santa Ana, Calle del Principe, and Calle de Echegaray.

THE AVENIDA DEL ARTE AND RETIRO

Once reserved for royalty, the beautiful **Parque del Buen Retiro** is a peaceful gem in the middle of hectic Madrid—much like a Spanish Central Park. Full of wide walkways, gardens, cafes, and entertainers, this is the perfect place to exercise or take a load off and people watch. Rent a rowboat for 45min. for €5 and paddle around the lovely man-made lake near the northern entrance to the park. Next door to these grounds is the **Paseo del Prado,** home to some of the world's best art museums including the **Museo Nacional del Prado** and the **Reina Sophia** modern art museum. Walk along this tree-lined boulevard to see some of the best sights that Madrid has to offer.

GRAN VÍA

Though it celebrated its centennial in 2010, Gran Vía isn't ready for retirement yet. The bustling "Broadway Madrileño" has evolved from a musical mecca to a bustling thoroughfare full of theaters, fast-food restaurants, shopping, and nightlife. Indeed, Gran Vía has just gotten younger with age. It may once have been where grandma came to see the opera, but now it's where the young and the trendy come for international shopping and clubbing.

madrid

CHUECA AND MALASAÑA

Madrid's famous gay neighborhood **Chueca** is centered on [M]Chueca and encompasses **Hortaleza, Infantas, Barquillo,** and **San Lucas** streets. Packed with modern restaurants, a wide variety of bars, and some of the best nightlife in Madrid, the district is a go-to neighborhood for anyone—regardless of orientation. The **Malasaña** area is named after **Manuela Malasaña,** a seamstress who became an unwilling martyr for Spain in the Peninsula War when she was executed by French forces for holding scissors that were interpreted as a weapon. Today, Malasaña is home to the city's hipster crowd and attracts hard-rock and grunge fans to its many venues. Both neighborhoods are funky and colorful and maintain a paddle-your-own-canoe mentality.

ARGÜELLES AND MONCLOA

Just north of Plaza España is Argüelles, a series of crisscrossing streets centered around shopping-filled **C. de la Princesa.** The neighborhood is highly residential and not really geared toward tourists, but the beautiful **Templo de Debod** is worth any traveler's time. The lookout points behind this temple present a scenic view of western Madrid. The **Paseo del Pinto Rosales** on the border of the beautiful **Parque del Oeste** offers excellent cafes and a quiet atmosphere in which to enjoy lunch. To the north of Argüelles is Moncloa, which is right beside the university area. Although not as touristy as the center, **Moncloa** has some worthwhile stops, including the **Arco de La Victoria** and the **Museo de America.**

SALAMANCA

The poshest neighborhood in Madrid, Salamanca is a high-end residential area filled with luxury shopping. Walk down **C. de Serrano** or **C. Jose Ortega y Gasset** and find yourself surrounded by Gucci, Prada, and Louis Vuitton. This shaded area is calmer than the city center and a nice place to get away from the throngs of tourists.

accommodations

EL CENTRO

👍 HOSTAL IVOR

💳⊗📶❄ HOSTAL ❹

C. Arenal, 24, 2nd fl. ☎91 547 10 54 🖥www.hostal-ivor.com

This beautiful hostal, located between Puerta del Sol and Plaza Mayor, home to many of El Centro's most prominent restaurants, cafes, clubs, and bars, is more like a mid-range hotel in terms of accommodations and service. Bright, clean, and well-decorated, Ivor's 25 rooms are comfortable but pricey. Extremely friendly service sets Hostel Ivor apart from its competition, with free Wi-Fi, ensuite bathrooms, and a cozy room make for a pleasant stay.

 # From Puerta del Sol, walk down C. del Arenal a little bit past C. de las Hileras. $ Singles €44; doubles €65. ⏰ Reception 24hr.

LOS AMIGOS HOSTEL

💳⊗📶❄ HOSTEL ❶

C. Arenal, 26, 4th fl. ☎91 559 2472 🖥www.losamigoshostel.com

Located a short walk away from Puerta del Sol, Los Amigos Hostel is smack dab in the center of C. Arenal. Rooms are shared, but unbunked beds provide a nice alternative to usually cramped hostel living, especially for those with *grande* neighbors and fears of even the smallest heights. Amenities include Wi-Fi, a communal kitchen, and complimentary continental breakfast.

*# From Puerta del Sol walk down C. del Arenal until you pass C. de las Hilerias; Los Amigos will be on your right. **i** Breakfast included. Extra large lockers and towels available for rent. Linens included. Free Wi-Fi. $ Dorms €17-19; doubles €45-50. ⏰ Multilingual reception 8am-midnight.*

HOSTAL CERVANTES
🗝⊗📶❄ HOSTAL ④

C. Cervantes, 34 ☎91 429 83 65 🖥www.hostal-cervantes.com

A beautiful walk from the Prado or Thyssen-Bornemisza, Hostal Cervantes is located in the same neighborhood as some of the city's finest hotels. With friendly service and clean, spacious rooms in a relatively quiet area of El Centro, Cervantes is a great place to stay. Be sure to book ahead, as most travelers jump at the chance to stay at this perfectly located hostel.

➔ From the Museo Thyssen-Bornemisza, walk toward the Plaza Canovas del Castillo and make a right onto C. de Cervantes. $ Singles €40-45; doubles €50-55; triples €65-70.

HOSTAL RESIDENCIA MARTIN
🗝⊗📶❄ HOSTEL ③

C. Atocha, 43 ☎91 429 95 79 🖥hostalmartin.com/en

This hostal is located between the bars and clubs of Puerta del Sol and the museums of Paseo del Prado. Amenities include ensuite bathrooms, free Wi-Fi, safety boxes, and a daily change of towels. While it does not provide the social life of a youth hostel, it does have the comfort and privacy of a small hotel.

➔ From Ⓜ Antón Martín, walk straight down C. de Atocha. Right before you hit C. Cañizares, the hostel will be on your right. $ Singles €29; doubles €39; triples €49.

HUERTAS

✎ WAY HOSTEL
🗝⊗📶❄ HOSTEL ②

C. Relatores, 17 ☎91 42 005 83 🖥www.wayhostel.com

This new, modern-but-homey hostel charges the same prices as youth and backpackers' hostels without the cramped bunk beds. Each of these 6- to 10-bed dorms is clean, spacious, and well decorated. The welcoming kitchen and TV room feel like upscale college common areas—perfect for your next beer.

➔ Ⓜ Tirso de Molina. From the station, walk towards the museum district and make a left up C. Relatores. The hostel will be on your right. ℹ Breakfast included. Book online. $ €18-24 depending on room and time. ⏰ Reception 24hr.

HOSTEL MONTALOYA
📶🗝⊗❄ HOSTAL ③

Plaza Tirso de Molina, 20 ☎91 360 03 05 🖥www.hostalmontaloya.blogspot.com

While pricier than dorm-style living, Montaloya is more of a small hotel than a youth hostel with comfortable beds, TVs, ensuite baths, and even desks in all rooms. Though the front desk only speaks Spanish, the hostal's comfortable beds and proximity to restaurants, bars, and stores along the Plaza Tirso De Molina make it a convenient choice for travelers.

➔ Ⓜ Tirso de Molina. Located just outside Tirso de Molina. ℹ Elevator available; call ahead for wheelchair-accessible accommodations. $ Singles €45; doubles €58; triples €80. ⏰ Reception 24hr.

CAT'S HOSTEL
📶🗝⊗❄ HOSTEL ①

C. Cañizares, 6 ☎91 369 28 07 🖥www.catshostel.com

This popular hostel is mostly comprised of basic dorms (2-14 beds) with shared bathrooms. There are some doubles with private baths, but availability is decided upon arrival. A colorful bar area with beer barrel tables, the "Cat's cave" social basement, and a restored Moorish patio provide travelers with spaces to mingle. Organized tapas tours and pub crawls often meet here. The staff is friendly, but you might have to wait a while to check in during peak hours. Reserve a room ahead of time as it often fills up quickly.

➔ From Ⓜ Antón Martín, walk one block down C. de la Magdalena and make a right onto C. Cañizares. Cat's will be on your left. ℹ Breakfast included. Laundry €5. $ Dorms €17-22; doubles €38-42 ⏰ Reception 24hr.

INTERNATIONAL YOUTH HOSTEL
🗝⊗📶❄ HOSTEL ①

C. de las Huertas, 21 ☎ 91 429 55 26🖥www.posadadehuertas.com

Located right on the drinking hub of C. de Huertas, this brightly painted, social hostel is ideal for groups of backpackers looking for other people to join their

madrid

wolfpack. With various food and sights tours as well as pub crawls that leave from IYH, you won't have any trouble meeting people—even your bedroom can have up to 10 people in bunk-bed-style accommodations complete with shared bathrooms.

✦ ⓂAntón Martín. Walk north up C. de Leon, make a right on Huertas. *i* Breakfast included. Luggage storage. Free Wi-Fi. Ⓢ Dorms €16-22. 🕐 Reception 24hr.

MAD HOSTEL
⬥⊗⁽ᵠ⁾❄ HOSTAL ❶

C. de la Cabeza, 24   ☎91 506 48 40 🖳www.madhostel.com

Mere minutes from the party people at Plaza Santa Ana, this hostal is great for travelers on a budget. Standard but clean rooms vary with 4-6 bunk beds that may or may not be single-sex. Bottom bunkers should beware of smacking their heads on the relatively low top bunks. Pick up a drink and play a game of pool in Mad's social space to meet fellow travelers.

✦ ⓂAntón Martín. From the station, walk forward down C. Magdalena then take C. Olivar, the second street on the left. Walk until you see C. Cabeza and turn right. Look for the Mad Hostel signboards on the left side of the street. *i* Breakfast, safe, and linens included. Towels available for €5 deposit. Laundry machines available. Small 4-piece gym and rooftop terrace. €10 key deposit. Reserve ahead. Ⓢ €16-23. 🕐 24 hours.

HOSTAL VETUSTA
⬥⊗⁽ᵠ⁾❄ HOSTAL ❷

C. de las Huertas, 3   ☎91 429 64 04 🖳www.hostalvetusta.com

This comfortable and friendly hostel puts you at the intersection of two bastions of nightlife—Plaza Santa Ana and C. de las Huertas. Hostal Vetusta offers standard decor. Be sure to ask staff members about ensuite bathrooms and other possible amenities—just be ready to put hand gestures to good use unless your Spanish is better than their English.

✦ ⓂAntón Martín. Across the street from Plaza Del Angel. *i* Rooms have working desks. ⓈDorms €25-30 depending on room. 🕐 Reception 24hr.

HOSTAL LOPEZ
⬥⊗⁽ᵠ⁾❄ HOSTAL ❷

C. de las Huertas, 54   ☎91 429 43 49 🖳www.hostallopez.com

Hostal Lopez's yellow walls, wood paneling, and super friendly service are located just three minutes from the Prado. You'll feel right at home here with the front desk staff that speaks perfect English and Italian.

✦ ⓂAntón Martín. From the station walk north up C. de Leon until you get to C. de las Huertas. Ⓢ Singles and doubles €25-40. 🕐 Reception 24hr.

HOSTAL RIVERA
⬥⊗⁽ᵠ⁾❄ HOSTAL ❸

C. Atocha, 79   ☎91 429 01 17 🖳ocio.arrakis.es/hostalrivera

Although the front desk looks more like a kitchen table than a check-in area (make a left from the door to get there), this hostel has comfortable rooms complete with full baths. While bubbles and bath salts are not included in the price of your stay, every room at least has a TV.

✦ ⓂAtocha. Walk straight up C. Atocha from the Atocha metro stop. Ⓢ Singles with bath €30; doubles with bath €45. 🕐 Reception 24hr.

HOSTAL EDREIRA
⬥⊗⁽ᵠ⁾❄ HOSTAL ❸

Atocha, 75   ☎91 429 01 83 🖳www.hostaledreira.com

Steps from ⓂAntón Martín, Hostal Edreira puts you smack dab between nightlife hotspots and the museum district, allowing you to get your drink on while maintaining some semblance of culture. As Edreira is a popular destination, make sure to book early.

✦ Right outside of the Antón Martín metro station. *i* Ensuite bathrooms. Ⓢ Singles €40; doubles €55; triples €70. 🕐 Reception 24hr.

accommodations • huertas

tooth mouse

Most countries have some tradition involving children's baby teeth. In America, we're used to a tooth fairy replacing them with coins as we sleep. However, in Spain (and other Spanish-speaking countries like Argentina), the agent of tooth-to-coin transformation is actually a mouse! His name, in the legend, is Ratoncito Pérez. Ratoncito translates to "cute little mouse," and Pérez is a generic last name (think Smith). The tooth-mouse story came into being—allegedly—when the royal Prince Alfonso XIII lost one of his first baby teeth. The royal parents, in an effort to reassure him, asked a certain priest to formulate some sort of nice story for the toothless prince. So, as he didn't have much of a choice, the priest wrote a book about a boy, Bubi (the prince's nickname), who loses a tooth but is later rewarded by a mouse. It probably had a bunch of priestly morals thrown in there as well, but what really stuck was the idea of a mouse swapping teeth for presents. You might think it's a bit of a one-sided deal, but rumor has it that Ratoncito Pérez is actually building a modernista mansion out of all the baby teeth.

HOSTAL BIANCO III
C. Echegaray, 5

☎91 369 13 32 ▪www.hostalbianco.com

This hostel in the middle of nightlife central C. Echegaray puts you between Puerta del Sol and C. de la Huertas, two places equally ideal for a crazy night. Beautifully decorated and comfortable, Bianco almost looks like a hotel—complete with marble paneling.

✠ *From ⓂSol, walk east down Carrera de San Jeronimo and make a right onto C. Echegaray.* ⓘ *Ensuite bathrooms. Free Wi-Fi.* Ⓢ *Singles €38; doubles €45; triples €65.* Ⓒ *Reception 24hr.*

HOSTAL AGUILAR
Carrera de San Jeronimo, 32

☎34 91 429 59 26 ▪www.hostalaguilar.com

With a huge lobby area, swipe access, modern furniture, and private bathrooms, Aguilar is more hotel than hostal (and the prices definitely reflect this fact). You'll have to splurge to stay at the Hostal Aguilar, but depending on your budget, it might be worth it for a one-night hotel experience.

✠ *From Puerta del Sol, walk east along Carrera de San Jeronimo towards Paseo del Prado.* Ⓢ *Singles €44; doubles €57; triples €94.* Ⓒ *Reception 24hr.*

HOSTAL LEON
Carrera de San Jerónimo, 32

☎91 429 67 78

Located in the same building as the Hostal Aguilar, the Hostal Leon provides a cheaper option that still provides more comfort and privacy than a youth hostel. The presence of the owner's fluffy white dog give you a homey feel that you would not find at another chain hotel.

✠ Ⓜ *Sol. From Puerta del Sol, walk east along Carrera de San Jeronimo towards Paseo del Prado.* ⓘ *Ensuite sinks.* Ⓢ *Singles €20; doubles €40.* Ⓒ *Reception 24hr.*

HOSTAL MADRID CENTRO
Carrera de San Jeronimo, 32

☎91 429 68 13

Somewhere in between Hostal Leon and Hostal Aguilar, both figuratively and literally, as it is the top of the same building, the Hostal Madrid Centro is family-owned and perfect for a traveling family or group.

✠ Ⓜ*Sol. From Puerta del Sol, walk east along Carrera de San Jeronimo towards Paseo del Prado.* Ⓢ *Singles €20; doubles €35-40; triples €60; quads €75-80.* Ⓒ *Reception 24hr.*

CHIC AND BASIC COLORS
➳⊗⟨ᵖ⟩❄ HOTEL ❺
C. de las Huertas, 14 ☎91 429 69 35 ▣www.chicandbasic.com

Tired of the grayscale offered in most other hostels? Chic and Basic will smack you in the face with bright color-coordination distinct to each one of its well-decorated rooms. After a great night's sleep, make yourself breakfast or lunch from their stocked pantry in the posh living room area. Check online for various discounts and special offers.

⌖ Ⓜ*Anton Martin. From Plaza del Angel, walk straight down C. Huertas toward the museum district. Chic and Basic Colors will be on your right.* ⓘ *Ensuite bathrooms. Same company has a high-end hotel called Chic and Basic on Atocha.* Ⓢ *Singles €60-90.* ⌚ *Reception 24hr.*

GRAN VÍA

▧ LA PLATA
➳⊗⟨ᵖ⟩❄ HOSTAL ❺
Gran Vía, 15 ☎34 91 521 17 25 ▣www.hostal-laplata.com

Owned and operated by the Garrido brothers, this hostel exudes quirky charm, from its brightly painted lobby to the unnecessary chandeliers in every room. Thanks to this place's incredibly helpful and friendly staff, *Let's Go* recommends this hostal out of all the options in this building.

⌖ Ⓜ*Gran Vía. Walk straight east; building will be on your right.* Ⓢ *Singles €45; doubles €60.* ⌚ *Reception 24hr.*

▧ HOSTAL FELIPE V
➳⊗⟨ᵖ⟩❄ HOSTAL❺
Gran Vía, 15 - 4th fl. ☎91 522 61 43 ▣www.hostalfelipev.com

Felipe V runs itself like a hotel with spacious rooms and friendly service. Family owned and operated, this hostal has been recently renovated and offers guests a daily newspaper and concierge-like services in its lobby.

⌖ Ⓜ*Gran Vía. Walk east; building will be on your right.* ⓘ *Breakfast €4.50. Offers travel agency service and reservations for airport shuttles.* Ⓢ *Singles €46; doubles €64; triples €78.* ⌚ *Reception 24hr.*

HOSTAL SPLENDID
➳⊗⟨ᵖ⟩❄ HOSTAL ❸
Gran Vía, 15 ☎91 522 47 37 ▣www.hostalsplendid.com

With wood paneling like an old ship, this splendid hostal almost seems nautically inspired. Speaking Spanish will help you navigate the front desk, but the service is friendly regardless of your language skills.

⌖ Ⓜ*Gran Vía. Walk straight east; building will be on your right.* Ⓢ *Singles €32; doubles €47; triples €65.* ⌚ *Reception 24hr.*

HOSTAL ANDORRA
➳⊗⟨ᵖ⟩❄ HOSTAL ❺
Gran Vía, 33, 7th fl. ☎91 532 31 16 ▣www.hostalandorra.com

Complete with a cushy and well-furnished TV room, this hostal looks more like a cozy bed and breakfast than its more corporate neighbors. The rooms here are somewhat expensive for a solo backpacker, but the doubles are well priced and reminiscent of your childhood friend's beautiful house in the 'burbs.

⌖ Ⓜ*Callao. Walk east down Gran Vía.* Ⓢ *Singles €47; doubles €62.* ⌚ *Reception 24hr.*

HISPANO ARGENTINO HOSTAL
➳⊗⟨ᵖ⟩❄ HOSTAL ❺
Gran Vía, 15, 6th fl. ☎91 532 24 48 ▣www.hispano-argentino.com

Standing out from the rest of the hostals within this building with a gigantic glass door, this place proves to be a painful optical illusion for some first-time patrons. While a night's stay might break the bank for some travelers, the rooftop terrace provides a beautiful view of Gran Vía, and the rooms include amenities like mini-fridges and hairdryers.

⌖ Ⓜ*Gran Vía. Walk straight east; building will be on your right.* Ⓢ *Singles €55-65; doubles €85.* ⌚ *Reception 24hr.*

HOSTAL SANTILLAN
💳🚭📶❄ HOSTAL [3]

C. Gran Vía, 64 ☎91 548 23 28 💻www.hostalsantillan.com

Operated by the same family for over four generations, Hostal Santillan features well-decorated rooms for a decent price. Make sure to ask one of the owners about hostal-sponsored excursions to Toledo and the Palacio Real.

🧭 [M]Plaza de España. ℹ Laundry service. Ensuite bathrooms and daily room cleaning, and laundry service. Ask about scheduled excursions and free baggage storage. [$] Singles €30-35; doubles €50-55; triples €70-75. ⏰ Reception 24hr.

HOSTAL A. NEBRIJA
💳🚭📶❄ HOSTAL [3]

Gran Vía, 67 - 8th fl. ☎91 547 73 19 💻www.hostalanebrija.com

The best part of this hostal is its spectacular views of the Palacio Real, the cathedral, and the nearby gardens. The second-best part is the eclectic collection of religious paintings and porcelain decorations in its lobby. With attractive prices in this neighborhood of expensive hostels, Hostal A. Nebrija is hard to turn down.

🧭 [M]Plaza de España. [$] Singles €28; doubles €36; triples €55. ⏰ Reception 24hr.

HOSTAL AVENIDA
💳🚭📶❄ HOSTAL [4]

Gran Vía, 15 - 4th fl. ☎91 521 27 28💻www.hostalavenidamadrid.com

Avenida claims to be a 20min. walk away from over 200 tourist attractions, and the same can be said for all the hostels within this building complex. With so many options in this neighborhood (and even just in this building), there is nothing special about Avenida except for its supremely comfortable beds.

🧭 [M]Gran Vía. Walk straight east; building will be on your right. [$] Singles €40; doubles €60. ⏰ Reception 24hr.

madrid

CHUECA AND MALASAÑA

HOSTAL LOS ALPES
💳🚭📶❄ HOSTAL [4]

C. de Fuencarral, 17 - 3rd and 4th fl. ☎91 531 70 71💻www.hostallosalpes.com

Located on one of the best shopping streets in Madrid, Hostal Los Alpes is a great place for you and your wallet to rest after a day of shopping. You'll breathe easy large rooms, spacious bathrooms, and nice common area with leather seating and a community computer. Your wallet will stay pleasantly plump, as the prices here are remarkably reasonable for the service provided.

🧭 [M]Chueca. Make a right onto C. de Gravina and a right onto C. de Hortaleza. [$] Singles €28; doubles €50. ⏰ Reception 24hr.

HOSTAL AMERICA
💳🚭📶❄ HOSTAL [4]

C. de Hortaleza, 19 5th fl. ☎91 522 64 48 💻www.hostalamerica.net

Located in the top floor's penthouse suite, Hostal America is the best in the building. Rooms feature big windows, new furniture, spacious bathrooms, and paintings on the wall. Service is friendly, quick, and mostly English-speaking. Be sure to check out the outdoor terrace's great view.

🧭 [M]Chueca. Make a right on C. de Gravina and a right on C. de Hortaleza. [$] Singles €43; doubles €55; triples €70. ⏰ Reception 24hr.

HOSTAL CAMINO
💳📶 HOSTEL [3]

C. de Hortaleza, 78 ☎91 308 14 95 💻www.hostalcamino.es

The basic Hostal Camino is ideally located between the best of Chueca shopping and nightlife, but be prepared to hike up a hill of stairs for this convenience. Once you reach the summit, rooms feature simple furnishings and basic amenities at a bargain rate for this neighborhood. While the friendly staff only speaks Spanish, they go out of their way to make your stay mountains above the rest.

🧭 [M]Chueca. Make a right on C. de Gravina and a right on C. de Hortaleza. [$] Singles €30; doubles €40. ⏰ Reception 24hr.

HOSTAL MARIA LUISA
💳🚭📶❄ HOSTAL [4]

C. de Hortaleza, 19 2nd fl. ☎91 521 16 30 💻www.hostalmarialuisa.com

This well-kept hostal has all the amenities of a small hotel at a much lower price. Nightstands, patterned bed coverings, and wooden wardrobes make the rooms look like they belong in someone's house, and the common area includes living-room-style couches with TV and pictures on the wall. All it's missing is a mom and some meatloaf.

➜ *ⓂChueca. Make a right on C. de Gravina and a right on C. de Hortaleza.* $ *Singles €39; doubles €50; triples €69; quads €85.* ⏰ *Reception 24hr.*

HOSTAL PRADA
💳🚭📶❄ HOSTAL [4]

C. de Hortaleza, 19 3rd fl. ☎91 521 20 04 💻www.hostalprada.com

Equidistant from Gran Vía and the Chueca neighborhood, Hostal Prada provides a great location among some of the city's best dining and nightlife options. Recently renovated, the hostal's hardwood floors, white furniture, and squeaky clean bathrooms make for an enjoyable stay.

➜ *ⓂChueca. Make a right on C. de Gravina and a right on C. de Hortaleza.* $ *Singles €38; doubles €48.* ⏰ *Reception 24hr.*

ARGÜELLES AND MONCLOA

HOSTAL ANGELINES
🔘🚭📶❄ HOSTAL [4]

Hilarion Eslava, 12 ☎91 543 21 52

This well-kept hostal puts you near Madrid's university district. Although several metro stops away from the city center, it's a better value than closer hostals and will save you some money. Big, sparkling white bathrooms and huge beds make it an excellent place to take refuge after a long day exploring the city.

➜ *ⓂMoncloa. Walk south down C. de la Princesa and make a left on C. de Romero Robledo. Keep walking until you reach Hilarion Eslava, then make a left.* $ *Singles €40; doubles €45.* ⏰ *Reception 24hr.*

HOSTAL MONCLOA
💳🚭📶❄ HOSTAL [4]

C. de Hilarión Eslava, 16 ☎91 544 91 95 💻www.hostalmoncloa.com

For the comfort of a hotel at the price of a hostal, splurge and come to Hostal Moncloa. Rooms and ensuite bathrooms are huge and include large flatscreen TVs. Rooms tend to be a bit dark, but size and excellent service make up for it.

➜ *ⓂMoncloa. Walk south down C. de la Princesa and make a left onto C. de Romero Robledo. Keep walking until you reach Hilarion Eslava, then make a left.* $ *Singles €45; doubles €50.* ⏰ *Reception 24hr.*

ALBERGUE JUVENIL SANTA CRUZ DE MARCENADO (HI)
💳🚭📶❄ HOSTEL [1]

C. de Santa Cruz de Marcendado, 28 ☎91 547 45 32

At only €12 per night for dorms, you'll be hard-pressed to find livable accommodations at a lower price. Dorms are formatted in typical hostel style with bunk beds and adjacent lockers. Common area is relaxed, with colored couches and vending machines. Be sure to reserve well in advance, as rooms for this cheap hostel go quickly.

➜ *ⓂArgüelles. Walk 1 block down C. de Alberto Aguilera way from C. de la Princesa, turn right onto C. de Serrano Jover, then left onto C. de Santa Cruz de Marcenado.* $ *Dorms €12. Discounts available for HI members.* ⏰ *Reception 9am-9:45pm. Curfew 1:30am.*

OUTSIDE THE CITY CENTER

CAMPING ALPHA
🚭⛅ CAMPING [1]

12.4km down Ctra. de Andalicia in Getafe ☎91 695 80 69 💻www.campingalpha.com

This clean and welcoming campsite features paved roads, pool, tennis courts, showers, laundry and internet center. Outside, it might get uncomfortable in the middle of Madrid's infamously hot summers.

✠ *Walk down Vada Santa Catalina, cross the bridge, and bear right. Take bus #447, which stops across from the Museo de Jamón. Cross the footbridge and walk 1½km back toward Madrid along the busy highway following the signs.* ⑤ *Apr-Sept €7 per person; €7.10 per tent. Oct-Mar €5.56 per person; €5.68 per tent. 2- to 5-person bungalows €51-100.*

sights

EL CENTRO

🎖 PALACIO REAL ♣⊗❋ MONUMENT
C. de Baillén ☎91 454 87 00 ◪www.patrimonionacional.es

After the previous Muslim fortress was destroyed in a fire, Philip V began building the almost entirely marble Palacio Real. Its size and opulence are overwhelming, with each displayed room filled with vast collections of priceless furniture, tapestries, paintings, porcelain, and other things you'd expect to find in a house made of marble. Go on the 1hr. tour (in English or Spanish) that takes you through the palace's most richly decorated and renovated rooms and gives you behind-the-scenes stories about palace quirks. One can't-miss room is the Salón del Trono, where the king and queen used to greet visitors (today the palace is only used by the royal family on official state occasions). Still want more after the palace tour? Check out the **Real Armeria** (Armory) with an awesome collection of knights' armor and the **Oficina de Farmacia** (Royal Pharmacy), which features crystal and porcelain medicine receptacles. If you're in town on the first Wednesday of the month between September and May, check out the changing of the guard at noon.

✠ ⓜ*Opera. Walk west down C. de Arrieta. Palacio Real will be at the end of the road.* *i* *Come early to avoid long lines.* ⑤ *€8, with tour €10, students, seniors, and children 5-16 €3.50.* 🕐 *Open Apr-Sept M-Sa 9am-6pm, Su 9am-3pm; Oct-Mar M-Sa 9:30am-5pm, Su 9am-2pm.*

PLAZA MAYOR ⊗⸸🍴 PLAZA
Plaza Mayor

Built in the 15th century as a market square and home to important members of the court during the 17th century, the Plaza Mayor is steeped in history and architectural beauty. Today, it keeps the flavor of both its historic uses. By day, its hundreds of restaurants, shops, and street performers function as a modern-day market square. By night, live flamenco and music performances provide entertainment fit for a king's court. During the week-long **Fiesta de San Isidro** that begins on May 15, the plaza comes alive in celebration to honor Madrid's patron saint. The tourist office located in the plaza is quite helpful for free maps and suggestions for activities and other sights.

✠ ⓜ*Sol or* ⓜ*Opera. From Puerta del Sol, walk 2min. down C. Mayor towards the Palacio Real. It will be on your left.*

PUERTA DEL SOL ⊗⸸🍴 PLAZA
C. de Cedaceros, 10

Located in Puerta Del Sol is Spain's *Kilometre Zero*, the point from which all distances in Spain are measured. The Esquilache mutiny of 1766 began here in 1808, when *madrileños* took up arms against French troops in a historic resistance captured in Goya's *Dos de Mayo* and *Tres de Mayo*. Today, it is the headquarters of Madrid's regional government, hundreds of restaurants and cafes, and some of the best shopping in the city. This common meeting spot for *fútbol* game celebrations, protests, and celebrations is the true "soul" of the city.

✠ ⓜ*Sol.*

madrid

la corrida de toros

Bullfighting has an ancient pedigree: it stems from the Roman tradition of making things fight other things for fun. Back in the day, there were man versus man fights, tiger versus man fights, tiger versus bull fights, and any number of other permutations. While a tiger versus man fight in this day and age would likely cause a small riot, for some reason bullfights are still quite popular. Bullfighting has had its detractors throughout the ages: Pope Pius X declared bullfighting forbidden, but not for the reason you might think. No, the Pope was worried about the immortal souls of the matadors who were voluntarily risking their lives. Later in Spain's history, Dictator Francisco Franco deemed bullfighting one of the true Spanish sports and greatly fostered its growth. Most people believed that Franco's support would be the death knell of the bullfighting following after the end of his rule: however, for some reason it continued on, bloody as ever. Today, the president of Spain, Jose Luis Rodriguez Zapatero, has banned children younger than 14 from even viewing the bullfights, and banned its broadcasts on public television. Since the bull is traditionally killed within the ring in Spain, this seems a valid opposition.

If you're really squeamish about this kind of thing, you could go to Portugal, where the bulls are never killed in the arena—they're moved off-site first. If you're just kind of squeamish, we would suggest leaving before the matador is awarded his trophy of an ear, a hoof, or perhaps a tail—the skill of the matador is positively correlated with the number of body parts awarded. On a related note, bull tail is a delicacy in Spain, said to be of a consistency resembling gelatin.

sights · el centro

CATEDRAL DE LA ALMUDENA
🔨ⓑ❂ CATHEDRAL
C. Bailen
☎91 542 22 00

Located right next to the Palacio Real, this cathedral has an incredible cavernous marble interior. Walk in for free and take in the 66ft. diameter dome and featured statues and artwork. In the 11th century, the image of the Virgin over the entrance was hidden by Mozarabs. When Madrid was reconquered by King Alfonso VI of Castile, the soldiers endeavored to find the statue to no avail. According to legend, after days of prayer, the spot on the wall hiding the icon crumbled to reveal this magnificent statue.

✿ *Right next to Palacio Real.* Ⓢ *Free.* 🕐 *Open daily 10am-2pm and 5-8pm.*

PLAZA DE ORIENTE
ⓒ✀ PLAZA
Plaza de Oriente, 2

This beautiful plaza is filled with perfectly manicured hedges, fountains, and statues in honor of former Spanish kings and queens that surround the equestrian statue of Philip IV by Montañes. Lovers, tourists, sunbathers, and sunbathing tourist-lovers all lounge around the plaza.

✿ *Across from the Palacio Real.* Ⓢ *Free.*

JARDINES DE SABATINI
ⓒ✀ GARDEN
C. de Baillen, 9
☎91 588 53 42

Jardines de Sabatini is an outdoor reflection of the wealth and opulence of the royal palace. Immaculately kept trees, hedges, and fountains create a relaxing atmosphere, and tourists with children stroll through this soccer-mom haven during the day. Buy a gelato at one of the many cafes across the street and come here for a mid-afternoon break from reality.

✿ *Right next to the Palacio Real.* Ⓢ *Free.* 🕐 *Open until dusk.*

PLAZA DE LA VILLA
@⌀ PLAZA

Plaza de la Villa, 5

This tiny plaza is easy to overlook, but it's certainly worth a few minutes of your time. A mixture of Spanish architectural styles, this Castilian square provides a pleasant place to rest while walking along the busy C. Major—offering a nice break from the other super touristy plazas nearby.

✦ *From the Palacio Real, walk down C. Mayor towards Puerta Del Sol; the plaza will be on your right.* ⓢ *Free.*

LA LATINA AND LAVAPIÉS

BASILICA DE SAN FRANCISCO EL GRANDE
@ CATHEDRAL

C. de San Buenaventura, 1
☎91 365 38 00

This Roman Catholic Church is one of the most distinctive structures in La Latina. The basilica was designed in a Neoclassical style in the second half of the 18th century and comes to life when lit up at night. The cathedral has three chapels, including the Chapel of San Bernardino de Siena, where Goya's magnificent painting of the chapel's namesake rests. Pay close attention to the picture and you will see that the figure on the right not looking up is Goya himself. Don't forget to check out the adjacent gardens outside that hold spectacular views of western Madrid.

✦ *From ⓜLa Latina, walk straight west down Carrera S. Francisco.* ⓢ *Free. Guided tours €3.* 🕐 *Open Tu-F 11am-12:30pm and 4-6:30pm, Sa 11am-noon.*

LA IGLESIA DE SAN ANDRÉS
@ CHURCH

Plaza de San Andrés

One of the oldest parishes in Madrid, La Iglesia de San Andrés used to be *the* go-to church for La Latina local San Isidro Labrador, the patron saint of Madrid. Much of the original interior was destroyed during the Spanish Civil War, but the structure still showcases a Baroque style crafted by designer José de Villarreal. Pay specific attention to the 15th-century cupola stationed above the sanctuary of the San Andrés Chapel.

✦ *ⓜLa Latina. Make a left onto C. de la Cava and walk until you see the church.* ⓢ *Free.*

HUERTAS

REAL ACADEMIA DE BELLAS ARTES DE SAN FERNANDO
✦@✦ MUSEUM

C. de Alcalá, 13
☎91 524 08 64 ✉rabasf.insde.es

The oldest permanent art institute in Madrid, the Real Academia de Bellas Artes is a short walk away from bustling Puerta del Sol. With a small collection, it can be comfortably visited in a couple of hours. If you need to blast through this museum, don't forget to check out the Goyas in room 20.

✦ *From Puerta del Sol, walk east down C. de Alcalá. Real Academia de Bellas Artes de San Fernando will be on your left.* ⓢ *€5; groups of 15-25 €2.50; students, under 18, and over 65 free.* 🕐 *Open M 9am-2:30pm, Tu-F 9am-7pm, Sa-Su 9am-2:30pm.*

CAIXAFORUM
✦@✦ CONCERT HALL ❶

Paseo del Prado, 36
☎91 389 65 45

The Caixaforum exhibition space and concert hall features a "vertical garden" of greenery, vines, and ivy covering what would otherwise be a plain wall. Stop by on your way from the museums along Paseo del Prado for a quick picture in this beautiful architectural spot.

✦ *From ⓜAtocha, walk north up Paseo del Prado; the Caixaforum will be on your right.* ⓢ *Free. Charges for concerts.*

AVENIDA DEL ARTE

MUSEO NACIONAL REINA SOFÍA

C. Santa Isabel, 52

☎91 774 10 00 ▣www.museoreinasofia.es

💥⊗ ART MUSEUM

This public collection of 20th-century art has burgeoned since Juan Carlos I declared the building a national museum in 1988 and named it after his wife. The building is a work of art in itself, with two futuristic-looking glass elevators ferrying visitors up and down the museum as they look north over the skyline. The museum's 10,000-piece collection of paintings, sculptures, installation pieces, and film is amazing by anyone's standards. The second and fourth floors are mazes of permanent exhibits charting the Spanish avant-garde and contemporary movements. If that's not for you, the second-floor galleries dedicated to **Juan Gris, Joan Miró,** and **Salvador Dalí** display Spain's vital contributions to the Surrealist movement. If you're pressed for time, make sure not to miss Pablo Picasso's ▣*Guernica*, the highlight of the Reina Sofía's permanent collection and the centerpiece of its knockout Gallery 206. Make sure to read about this paintings symbolic ties to the Spanish Civil War.

⚡ ⓂAtocha. *i* €6, ages 17 and under and over 65 free Sa afternoon and Su. Temporary exhibits €3 Ⓢ €6, temporary exhibitions €3. Ⓞ Open M 10am-9pm, W-Sa 10am-9pm, Su 10am-2:30pm.

MUSEO THYSSEN-BORNEMISZA

Paseo del Prado, 8

☎91 369 01 51 ▣www.museothyssen.org

💥⊗ ART MUSEUM

Unlike the Prado and the Reina Sofía, the Thyssen-Bornemisza covers international art from many periods: exhibits range from 14th-century canvases to 20th-century sculptures, and its collection encompasses periods of art overlooked by the other two. The museum is housed in the 19th-century **Palacio de Villahermosa** and contains the collection of the late Baron Henrich Thyssen-Bornemisza. Today, the museum is the world's most extensive private showcase. Take advantage of the spread by checking out its **Baroque** collection that includes pieces by **Caravaggio, Riber,** and **Claude Lorraine.** Also, don't forget to explore the **Impressionist, Fauvist,** and early **avant-garde** pieces that paved the way to modern art as we know it today. To be honest, there's too many famous artists to namedrop—just come here to be wowed and won over by its gigantic collection.

⚡ From the Prado, walk straight north up the Paseo Del Prado. Museum is at the corner of Carrera de San Jeronimo and Paseo Del Prado. Ⓢ €7, children under 12 free. ⓄOpen Tu-Su 10am-7pm.

MUSEO NACIONAL DEL PRADO

C. Ruiz de Alarcón, 23

☎34 91 330 2800 ▣www.museodelprado.es

💥⊗ MUSEUM

With its Goyas and El Grecos, Rembrandts, Raphaels, and Rubens, the Prado has enough alliterative artistic awesomeness to make the Louvre look not so special after all. Organized by country, the ground floor houses Spanish (12th to 16th century), French, Dutch, and Italian (17th-19th century) works. While *Let's Go* recommends that you spend a few hours here, if you're in a rush, be sure to catch the can't-miss works. **Velázquez's** masterpiece ▣*Las Meninas*, considered one of the finest paintings in the world, captures a studio scene centered on the Infanta Margarita. Velásquez himself stares out from behind his easel in the left side of the painting. It may look like just another picture of wealthy Spaniards in big dresses, but this piece has been praised as the culmination of Velázquez's career—a meditation on reality, art, illusion, and the power of easel painting. That pouting dog in the corner looks a lot more profound now, doesn't it? **Goya's** ▣*Majas*—two paintings with differing states of clothing side-by-side of a woman believed to be the Duchess of Alba—wows audiences with its intricate brushstrokes. Take a free museum map and get the English audio tour (€3.50) for background information on the museum's 1500+ displayed paintings. To get the most masterwork for your moola, try to make it during free entrance.

⚏ Ⓜ*Banco de España* and Ⓜ*Atocha. From* Ⓜ*Atocha, walk north up Paseo del Prado; the museum will be on your right just past the gardens.* ⓘ *Free entry Tu-Sa 6-8pm, Su 5-8pm. Consult website for up-to-date schedule.* Ⓢ *€8, students €4, under 18 and over 65 free.* ⌚ *Open Tu-Su 9am-8pm.*

REAL JARDÍN BOTÁNICO ⬤ⓧ⌂ GARDEN

Plaza de Murillo, 2 ☎91 420 30 17 🖳www.rjb.csic.es/jardinbotanico/jardin

The perfect place to rest after a visit to the Prado, this small garden is full of well-kept flowers and exotic collections. Sit in the shade on one of the many benches of this oasis in the middle of Madrid's museum district as you ruminate on the countless pieces of art you just cranially ingested.

⚏ *Next door to the Prado.* Ⓢ *€2.50, students €1.25, groups €0.50.* ⌚ *Open daily Jan-Feb 10am-6pm; Mar 10am-7pm; Apr 10am-8pm; May-Aug 10am-9pm; Sept 10am-8pm; Oct 10am-7pm; Nov-Dec 10am-6pm.*

CHUECA AND MALASAÑA

CONVENTO DE LAS SALESAS REALES ⓧ CATHEDRAL

C. Barbara de Braganza ☎91 319 48 11

This mostly empty church is a calm getaway from the hustle and bustle of Chueca. Next door to some of the district's classiest shopping, its beautiful monastery was designed by Francois Carlier and is worth a pit-stop and a photo. Go inside to see the dome, which features painted biblical scenes and the tombs of Fernando VI and Barbara de Braganza, constructed by Francesco Sabatini and Francisco Gutierrez.

⚏ Ⓜ*Colon. From Pl. Colon, go down Po. de Recoletos and take a right onto C. de Barbara de Braganza.* Ⓢ *Free.* ⌚ *Open M-F 9:30am-1pm and 5:30-8pm, Sa 9:30am-2pm and 5-9pm, Su 9:30am-2pm and 6-9pm. Closed to tourists during mass.*

MUSEO DE HISTORIA ⬤ⓧ MUSEUM

C. Fuencarral, 78 ☎91 588 86 72 🖳www.munimadrid.es/museodehistoria

This renovated 18th-century building built during the reign of Felipe V now holds a collection of sketches, models, paintings, drawings, and documents that showcase the history of Madrid. Saved from destruction in 1919 by the Spanish Society of Friends of Art, the museum is now considered one of Madrid's historical-artistic monuments. Come for a cultural break from all the shopping on C. Fuencarral.

⚏ Ⓜ*Tribunal. Walk straight north up C. Fuencarral.* Ⓢ *Free.* ⌚ *Open Tu-Sa 10am-9pm, Su 11am-2:30pm.*

GRAN VÍA

▨ PLAZA DE ESPAÑA ⓧ⌂ PLAZA

On a sunny day the Plaza de España is filled with street performers, vendors, sunbathers, and Spanish couples showcasing some serious PDA. In the middle of the plaza, look for the statues of Don Quixote and Sancho Panza, and then head west to scope out the statue of celebrated wordsmith Cervantes.

⚏*The western end of Gran Vía.* Ⓢ *Free.*

TELEFÓNICA BUILDING ⓧ❄ LANDMARK

C. Gran Vía, 28 ☎01 055 50 22

Completed in 1920 by Ignacio de Cardena and over 1,000 workers, this building inspired by the work of American architect Lewis S. Weeks was the first skyscraper in Madrid and arguably the first in all of Europe. Used during the Spanish Civil War as a lookout by the Republicans, it was a target of many bombings and reportedly housed Ernest Hemingway on several occasions.

⚏ Ⓜ*Gran Vía.*

madrid

ARGÜELLES AND MONCLOA

👍 TEMPLO DE DEBOD ⊗☀ TEMPLE, PARK

C. de Ferraz, 1 ☎91 366 74 15 💻www.munimadrid.es/templodebod

On a nice day, this is one of the most beautiful spots in Madrid. In the '60s, when massive flooding threatened to destroy the ancient temple complex at Au Simbel, Egypt, a team of Spanish archaeologists helped to rescue these national treasures. In appreciation, the Egyptian government shipped the Templo de Debod to Madrid's Parque de la Montana, where you can now see the small archaeology exhibit housed inside. Outside of the temple is a series of original archways that are even more impressive at night, lit up and reflected in the adjacent pool. The park surrounding the temple teems with families, runners, tourists, and locals lounging in the afternoon sun. Go to the lookout point behind the temple for one of the most beautiful views of Madrid.

➜ ⓂPl. de Espana. Walk to the far side of Pl. de Espana, cross the street, walk a couple of blocks right, and it will be on the left. $ Free. ⏰ Open Apr-Sept Tu-F 10am-2pm and 6-8pm, Sa-Su 10am-2pm; Oct-Mar Tu-F 9:45am-1:45pm and 4:15-6:15pm, Sa-Su 10am-2pm. Rose garden open daily 10am-8pm.

MUSEO DE AMÉRICA 🎫⊗☀ MUSEUM

Av. de los Reyes Catolicos, 6 ☎91 549 26 41 💻www.museodeamerica.mcu.es

In 1771, Carlos III started a collection that brought together pieces from the first archaeological excavations carried out in America with ethnographic objects collected from scientific expeditions. Today, the modern Museo de América holds a collection that encompasses American cultures from the tip of South America to the tundra of Alaska. Some of the most interesting artifacts are treasures from the pre-Columbian cultures conquered by the Spanish, including Mayan hieroglyphic documents.

➜ ⓂMoncloa. Cross the street, make a left, and walk straight. $ €3, EU citizens €1.50, under 18, over 65, and students free. ⏰ Open Tu-W 9:30am-3pm, Th 9:30am-3pm and 4-7pm, F-Sa 9:30am-3pm, Su 10am-3pm.

ARCO DE LA VICTORIA 🎫♿☀ ARCH

Near Parque Del Oeste

If you're getting off at the Moncloa stop, be sure to snap a picture by the Arco de la Victoria, a monument built in 1956 by order of General Franco to commemorate the rebel army's victory in the Spanish Civil War. Of course, judging by the monument, you'd think that Franco and his friends came to power stomping through the country Julius-Caesar-style, but that glorious horse and chariot at the top of the arco is unfortunately just a few centuries too anachronistic. Surrounded by traffic, it looks almost like Madrid's version of the Arc de Triomphe.

➜ ⓂMoncloa.

PARQUE DEL OESTE 🎫⊗☀ PARK

C. de Francisco y Jacinto Alcântara

A nice shaded place to come exercise during hot summer months, the Parque del Oeste is popular with families and tourists looking to take a nice stroll after a day of museum-hopping. Less crowded than the popular Retiro Park, Parque del Oeste is a lush break from the concrete jungle of western Madrid. If you're parched, plenty of tiny cafes line Paseo del Pinto Rosales near the park. However, exercise caution as nighttime approaches, as the park gets a lot less charming and a lot more alarming after sunset.

➜ ⓂMoncloa. ℹ Let's Go does not advise walking here after dark. $ Free. ⏰ Open 24hr.

CASA DE CAMPO 🎫⊗☀ PARK

Avenida de Portugal

Madrid's biggest park, the sprawling Casa de Campo is a popular sight for locals and tourists alike. The park offers various exercise options, including long running and biking trails as well as kayak and rowboat rentals in its lake. For another type of heartrate booster, the amusement park **Parque de Atracciones** has roller coasters and more cotton candy than you could ever eat. (✝ ⓂBatan or bus #33 or 65. *From the metro station, turn right and walk up the paved street away from the lake.* ☎91 463 29 00 🖥www.parquedeatracciones.es ⌚ *Open M-Sa 9am-7pm.)* To hang out with some new feathered friends, look no further than the park's **zoo and aquarium.** (☎91 512 37 70 🖥www.zoomadrid.com. ⌚ *Open daily, but check website for hours as schedule changes.)*

✝ ⓂLago, Batan, and Casa de Campo are all within the park. *i* Let's Go does not advise walking here after dark. ⑤ Free. ⌚ Open 24hr.

SALAMANCA

🏛 BIBLIOTECA NACIONAL

⊗� NATIONAL LIBRARY

Paseo de Recoletos, 20-22

☎91 883 24 02 🖥www.bne.es

With an intricately carved marble exterior, the massive Biblioteca Nacional is an impressive sight. It's not your typical books-and-bar-codes library, but rather a host to various temporary exhibitions (usually on literary topics) and cultural performances. Usually the gates are closed, so you can't get too close to this building. On your way here, check out the beautiful adjacent **Jardines del Descubrimiento,** a grassy public plaza that spans the street and is smattered with trees and (expensive) outdoor cafes.

✝ ⓂColon. ⑤ Free. ⌚ Usually closed to the public. Check online for special visitor times.

MUSEO SOROLLOA

●⊗❀ ART MUSEUM

Po. General Martinez Campos, 47

☎91 310 15 84 🖥www.museosorolla.mcu.es

This museum, the former residence of Valencian painter **Joaquin Sorolla Bastida,** displays the work of painters and sculptures from the late 19th century. Some of Bastida's famous pieces include *La Siesta* and *Mis Hijos.* The adjacent garden features myrtle taken from the Alhambra and a series of fountains.

✝ ⓂIglesia. Turn right on Plaça General Martinez Campos. ⑤ €3. Free Su. ⌚ Open Tu-Sa 9:30am-8pm, Su 10am-3pm.

MUSEO LAZARO GALDIANO

●⊗❀ ART MUSEUM

C. Serrano, 122

☎91 561 60 84 🖥www.fig.es

This former palace includes paintings by El Greco, Goya, and Velazquez, as well as works from the Italian Renaissance and Celtic and Visigoth periods. Some notable works include *Young Christ,* unofficially attributed to Leonardo da Vinci and Hieronymus' *Ecce Homo.*

✝ ⓂGregorio Maranon. ⑤ €4, students €3, EU citizens free. ⌚ Open M 10am-4:30pm, W-Su 10am-4:30pm.

MUSEO DE CIENCAS NATURALES

●⊗❀ NATURAL HISTORY MUSEUM

C. Jose Gutierrez Abascal, 2

☎91 411 13 28 🖥www.mncn.csic.es

A nice departure from the many art museums that flood Madrid, the Museo de Ciencas Naturales features sparkling minerals, stuffed animals, and dinosaur bones. A shrine to all things science, it has something for visitors of all ages.

✝ From ⓂGregorio Maranon, walk 2 blocks north on Po. de la Castellana. ⑤ €5, students and under 14 €3, under 4 free. ⌚ Open Tu-F 10am-6pm, Sa 10am-3pm, Su 10am-2:30pm.

OUTSIDE THE CITY CENTER

🏛 EL PRADO

●⊗❀ PALACE

Paseo del Prado

☎91 376 15 00

Originally built in the 15th century as a hunting lodge for Enrique IV, El Prado was also the permanent residence of Franco, who remained there until his death in 1975. On display are Franco's bathroom, private prayer room, and bedroom cabinet where he kept Saint Teresa's silver-encrusted petrified arm, one of his most treasured possessions. The palace also holds a Velázquez painting and Ribera's *Techo de los Hombres Ilustres (Ceiling of the Illustrious Men)*.

✚ ⓂMoncloa. *Take bus #601 from the underground bus station adjacent to Moncloa.* Ⓢ €4, *students and over 65 €2.30.* ⓒ *Open Apr.-Sept M-Sa 10:30am-5:45pm, Su 9:30am-1:30pm; Oct-Mar. M-Sa 10:30am-4:45pm, Su 10am-1:30pm. Mandatory 45min. guided tour in Spanish; last tour leaves 45min. before closing.*

un-spanish spanish languages

It seems odd, but Spaniards actually speak a variety of languages, usually in addition to regular (Castilian) Spanish. The Spanish government officially recognizes three additional languages: Euskara, spoken in the Basque country; Catalan, spoken in northeastern Spain—and therefore Barcelona; and Gallego, spoken in northwestern Spain.

Of the three, Euskara is undoubtedly the most unusual: in fact, it hasn't actually been found to be related to any other language. Fortunately, even if you're visiting the Basque Country, knowledge of Euskara is not essential; you can usually get by with straight-up Spanish. However, if you're really interested, here are some key words: *kaixo* (hello), *eskerrik asko* (thank you), *bai* (yes) and *ez* (no).

Catalan is usually perceived as a mixture of French and Spanish, which makes sense considering the region where it is spoken—the corner of Spain that borders France. You can see the French influence in action in these Catalan words: *si us plau* (please), and *l'home* (the man). This language also uses an egregious number of x's, pronounced as one would the English "ch."

Finally, the Galician language is extremely similar to Portuguese: the two languages developed together all the way up until the 14th century, when some political tension resulted in a split. However, the necessary travel words resemble Spanish as well as Portuguese: *ola* (hello), *baño* (bathroom), and *polo* (chicken).

food . el centro

food

EL CENTRO

Food in El Centro tends to be on the pricey side, as the area is rampant with tourists. If you're sitting outside on the terrace, just grab a seat and the waiter will come to you. Many places will charge you for table bread, so don't touch it if you don't want to pinch pennies. Most restaurants in El Centro don't provide free water, either, but will instead bring you their most expensive bottled mineral water with a fine vintage year—so stick to the house wine or explicitly ask for beverage prices. If you go down a winding cobblestone street, you're bound to find a hole-in-the-wall restaurant with more reasonable prices. For those on an even tighter food budget, a nice alternative to eating out is to go to a local grocery store such as **Dia** or **Carrefour** or a small shop labeled *alimentaciones* to buy sandwich fixings and fruit for a bargain. You'll find even better bargains at the Plaza de San Miguel marketplace.

👍 EL ANCIANO REY DE LOS VINOS
💳 🚭 🍸 ❄ SPANISH 3

C. de Bailén, 19 ☎91 559 53 32 💻www.elancianoreydelosvinos.es

Right across the street from the Catedral de la Almudena, this is the perfect place to relax after a tour of the cathedral or Palacio Real. Sit outside on the terrace and sip an afternoon drink *(€3.50)*. Try the *Tinto de Verano*, a refreshing wine-based drink similar to sangria. El Anciano offers *canapés (€6.50)*, salads *(€10-15)*, a variety of tapas *(€6-13)*, and sandwiches *(€6)* that all can be topped off with dessert *(€5)*.

🚏 Walk across the C. de Bailén from the Catedral de la Almudena. ⏰ Open daily 10am-midnight.

EL MADRONO
🚭 💳 ⛅ SPANISH 2

Plaza Puerta Cerrada, 7 ☎91 364 56 29

Steps away from Plaza Mayor, El Madrono provides traditional Spanish fare. Split the special of four tapas and a main course *(€16.50)* between two, but buy your own cocktail *(€2-5)*. Entrees *(€10-20)* are also big enough to be shared. If there's a wait, try the sangria at the bar. Make sure to order the Meatballs of the Grandmother, and go next door for mindblowing gelato.

🚏 Right by the main entrance to the Plaza Mayor. El Madrono's green paint and Spanish murals make it stand out. $ Entrees €10-20.

CHOCOLATERÍA SAN GINÉS
💳 🚭 🍸 ❄ CHOCOLATERÍA 1

Plaza de San Ginés, 5 ☎91 366 54 31

An absolute late-night must for clubbers and early risers, this chocolatería is famous for its classic chocolate *con churros (€4)*. After dancing off just as many calories, come here around 5 or 6am to cap your night off with a sweet treat.

🚏 From Puerta Del Sol, walk down C. Arenal until you get to Joy nightclub. It will be tucked in the tiny Plaza de San Ginés. $ Chocolates from €4. ⏰ Open 24hr.

RESTAURANTE SABATINI
💳 🚭 🍸 ❄ SPANISH 2

C. Bailén, 15 ☎91 547 92 40

Restaurante Sabatini's motto, *"Disfruta como un rey,"* or where you can "eat like a king" is appropriate, as it is located directly across the street from Madrid's famous royal palace. Get the gelato before walking through the palace gardens, or get their menu of the day *(€9.50)*. Tapas run around €3.60 and *raciones calientes*, or hot dishes, are €8.

🚏 Directly across C. Bailen from the Palacio Real. $ Tapas €3-12. ⏰ Open daily 7:30am-11:30pm.

spanish snails

Most people believe that the French are the initiators of snail consumption; however, gastropods are also a food of choice in many parts of Spain. The snails, called *caracoles*, are usually common ground-snails and appear much smaller than the French escargot. They are usually served in their own shells, cooked in a special sauce and served as an appetizer. However, you may also find them outside the shell in paella or in certain soups. If you're up for the challenge, here's how to eat your snail: grab a shell from the serving bowl and pull your little snack out of his home by the head, using your teeth. Though the Spanish are all for utensil use, *caracoles* are generally considered acceptable finger food. Finally, chew very, very thoroughly. *Buen provecho!* (Bon appetit!)

CERVECERÍA LA PLAZA 💳⊗🍸❄ TAPAS [2]

Plaza de San Miguel, 3 ☎91 548 41 11

Locals and tourists come here to get relatively cheap tapas and entrees *(under €10)* to go with their *cerveza*. Hugely popular, Cervecería la Plaza has two locations, one in the Plaza de San Miguel and one in Plaza de Santa Ana. Both with packed outdoor terraces shaded by large umbrellas to protect against intense sun, they offer lively atmospheres with generous portions.

➜ From the Palacio Real, walk down C. Mayor toward Puerta del Sol. Plaza de San Miguel will be on your right. $ Beers €3. Entrees and tapas under €10.

FABORIT 💳⊗🍸📶❄ CAFE, FAST FOOD [1]

Alcalá 21 🖥www.faborit.com

The Starbucks of Spain, Faborit is near almost every major tourist site in Madrid. Their *shakerettes*, or fresh juice mixes, are delicious. Try the orange and strawberry juice mix or go for a frappe iced coffee drink. Buy a medium *(€3.25)* and large drink *(€4.25)*, and enjoy the modern furniture and young cool vibe. If you can't wait for your next meal, grab a dessert or sandwich *(€5)*.

➜ [M]Sol. Walk down Alalá. It will be on your left next to Starbucks. ℹ Most locations offer free Wi-Fi. $ Juices, desserts, and sandwiches €3-6.

DEHESA SANTA MARIA 💳⊗🍸❄☀ TAPAS [2]

C. Mayor, 88 ☎93 367 00 52 🖥www.dehesasantamaria.com

This chain restaurant with locations throughout Madrid features traditional Spanish tapas such as *Tapa de Tortilla Rellena Con Jamon*, a mini tortilla pastry with ham. It's also known for its meats and cheeses, so try the *Ibéricos y Quesos*. If you're in the mood for just a snack, go for the special—beer and a tapa for €1.

➜ At the corner of C. de Bailén and C. Mayor. $ Tapas €3-12.

LA LATINA AND LAVAPIÉS

👍 **MANO A MANO** 💳⊗🍸❄ SPANISH [3]

C. Lavapiés, 16 ☎91 468 70 42

This small restaurant in Lavapiés cooks up authentic Spanish favorites in family-style portions. Bringing a family or a few friends who can seriously chow down? Go splitsies on one of their gigantic rice dishes packed with seafood and vegetables, or order solo and try one of their *raciones* like the Iberian ham *(€12)*.

➜ [M]Lavapiés. Walk straight uphill up C. Lavapiés. $ Raciones €7-12. Rice dishes for 4 to 6 people €28. ⏰ Open daily 2-5pm and 9pm-1am.

MARIMBA 💳⊗📶🍸☀ CAFE, BAR [1]

C. de Lavapiés, 11

Marimba is one of the more modern cafes in the Lavapiés district, offering beverages accompanied by tapas during the day and cocktails at night. You might have to stand with your drink next to Marimba's sparse seating, but super attentive service makes up for the lack of space.

➜ [M]Lavapiés. Walk uphill on C. Lavapiés. $ Tapas €3.50. Coffee and tea €2. Cocktails €6. ⏰ Open daily 11am-2am.

SAN SAPORI 📶💳⊗🍸☀ CAFE, BAR [2]

C. Lavapiés, 31 ☎91 530 89 96

With orange and green paint covering the wall, this funky little gelateria is a nice place to please your sweet tooth after dinner in Lavapiés. Get one of the delicious gelato flavors, or spring for coffee, tea, cake, or a pastry.

➜ [M]Lavapiés. Walk uphill on C. Lavapiés. $ Coffee €2-5. Gelato €3-6. ⏰ Open daily 11am-midnight.

LA BULLA TAKEOUT ❷

C. Lavapiés, 44

If you're looking for something quick to eat, come to La Bulla for a takeout meal. Take your pick of empanadas, pizza, pies, sushi, salads, cereals and meats. You can also try one of their many coffees and teas. Try their specials of the day advertised on signs throughout the restaurant.

[M]Lavapiés. Walk uphill on C. Lavapiés. $ Entrees €5-10. ⏰ Open daily 10am-9pm.

CALCUTA INDIAN ❷

C. Lavapiés, 48 ☎91 530 66 76

One of the staples of Lavapiés is the variety of ethnic restaurants lining C. Lavapiés. If you're in the mood for Indian food, come to Calcuta, which specializes in typical tandoori dishes. Get the vegetable menu for two *(€20)* or the meat menu for two *(€32)*. If you're ridin' solo, go for the menu of the day: your choice of an appetizer (like a vegetable samosa), entree (like chicken tikki masala), and naan *(€8)*. You can also try one of their typical vegetable dishes like *Saag Aloo, (potatoes with spices and onions; €4.95).*

[M]Lavapiés. Walk uphill on C. Lavapiés $ Meals €8-20. ⏰ Open daily 12pm-5pm and 8pm-midnight.

EL PALADAR CAFE ❶

C. Argumosa, 5 ☎91 467 85 35

This tiny place only offers outdoor seating, but it's a local favorite and a nice place to sit and relax in Lavapiés. Get a small snack *(€3.50)* or a larger *racion (€6.50)* of one of their regional specialties. If you've never had it, be sure to try *horchata*, a sweet refreshing summertime milk-like drink made from tigernuts.

[M]Lavapiés. Walk east down C. Argumosa. $ Tapas €2-5. Raciones €5-10. ⏰ Open daily 11am-midnight.

madrid

HUERTAS

DIBOCCA RESTAURANTE ITALIANO ITALIAN ❷

Paseo de los Olmos, 28 ☎91 517 22 19 www.dibocca.com

If you're sick of tapas and craving some Italian in the middle of Espagne, look no further than DiBocca, upscale environment without the pricetag. Try one of their regular or stuffed pastas *(€10)*, salads *(€8)*, meats and fish *(€11)*, or desserts *(€4.65)* to get a taste even Snookie would enjoy.

From Puerta del Sol walk straight south down Pasea de los Olmos (tiny street). i English menus available. $ Entrees €5-12.

LA NEGRA TOMASA CUBAN ❷

C. de Cádiz, 9 ☎91 523 58 30 www.lanegratomasa.es/

Come to this fun Cuban restaurant for big portions, big drinks, and a raucous good time. Waitresses in Cuban garb serve up traditional Cuban fare in a restaurant with walls lined floor to ceiling with memorabilia. Try one of the main dishes like the *Ropa Vieja Habanera (€8-12)*. Order *para picar*, tiny appetizers to share *(€3-7)*, and while you're there be sure to get a cocktails *(€6-7)*.

From Puerta del Sol, walk south down C. de Espoz y Mlna, restaurant will be on your right. $ Entrees €8-12. ⏰ Day prices for drinks: 1:30-11pm.

TABERNA DE ANTONIO SANCHEZ TAPAS ❷

Meson de paredes, 13 ☎91 539 78 26

Founded in 1830 by bullfighter Antonio Sanchez, this taberna has had a lot of time to perfect its delicious tapas and entrees. Get a variety of tapas *(€1-3)* to share as two *tapas calientes* are filling enough for dinner. If you can find this restaurant, the inside covered in dark-wooded walls and Spanish paintings feels like a step back in time. Make sure to try the *Mortados Calientes de Chizo* or the

Escalipines à la Madrilena for a taste of the old world.
🪧 *From Ⓜ Tirso De Molina, walk past the Plaza de Tirso de Molina until you get to C. del Meson de Paredes. It will be on your left.* $ *Entrees €3-15.*

CASA PATAS — 💳 TRADITIONAL, FLAMENCO [3]

C. de los Cañizares, 10 — ☎91 369 04 96 💻www.casapatas.com

For a perfectly Spanish cultural experience, come to Casa Patas for a flamenco show at 9pm or midnight *(€30, includes one drink, around 1.5hr).* With unbelievably talented dancers, the show is fun and fast-paced. Make a reservation in advance, and stay afterwards for a nice but pricey dinner.
🪧 *From Ⓜ Antón Martín, walk up Atocha and turn left onto C. del Olivar. Casa Patas will be on your right after Cat's Hostel.* $ *Entrees €10-30.* ⏰ *Open M-Th 1-4:30pm and 8pm-midnight, F-Sa 7:30-1am.*

👍 **CASA ALBERTO** — ❄🍸 TRADITIONAL [2]

the art of *tapear*-ing

You may be under the (very common) impression that tapas are a type of Spanish food. However, it would be better to say that tapas are a Spanish way of eating.

Tapas are said to have been invented out of necessity. According to *The Joy of Cooking,* the original tapas were the slices of bread or meat which sherry drinkers in Andalusian taverns used to cover their glasses between sips, explaining the verb's origin: *tapar*, to cover. The reasoning behind this was protection from the fruit flies that abound during hot Spanish summers, and their penchant for sherry. Eventually, the bartenders realized that by diversifying their food offerings, they would net more customers, and the idea of tapas came into being. Today the tapas themselves may be any type of Spanish food, served in small portions. The verb tapear contains the essence of tapas, as it means, colloquially: to go out to several bars and order a drink and a few tapas at each. It's the quintessential method of Spanish socializing: similar to a pub crawl, but with way more food.

C. de las Huertas, 18 — ☎91 429 93 56 💻www.casaalberto.es

Founded in 1827, Casa Alberto is one of the oldest taverns in Madrid. Come for a taste of some of the best tapas in the city, made from carefully selected ingredients and true to the recipes of past generations. Lancers and *banderilleros* used to come here to imbibe a "cup of courage" before entering the bullring. Feeling adventurous? Enter your own bullring of fear by trying tripe (stomach...yum), or pig's ear. If you'd rather stay in your comfort zone, go with customer favorites such as snails, lamb's knuckles, oxtail, veal meatballs, or Madrid-style salt cod.
🪧 *From Plaza del Ángel, walk down C. de las Huertas towards the Prado. It will be on your right.* $ *Entrees €5-20.* ⏰ *Open daily noon-1:30am.*

CAFETERIA MARAZUL — 💳❄ TRADITIONAL [2]

Plaza del Ángel, 11 — ☎91 369 19 43

Cafeteria Marazul is conveniently located right outside of the Hostel Persal in Plaza del Ángel. This cafe offers good food and even better service. Get a typical Spanish warm entree like *patatas bravas (€8-14)* or a *bocadillo*, a Spanish sandwich *(€6-7).*
🪧 *From Ⓜ Anton Martin, walk right down C. Atocha, and make a right on C. Olivar. Walk until you see Plaza del Ángel on your left right before Plaza Santa Ana.* $ *Entrees €5-12.*

TAHONA PETER-PAN
🍴 CAFE ❶

C. Atocha, 45 ☎91 429 56 60

Tahona Peter-Pan is just steps from Cat's Hostel and the boatloads of hostels on C. del Atocha. This small bakery and coffee shop serves up tasty pastries and coffee. Be sure to check out their filling lunch special: a salad, sandwich, and Pepsi *(€5.95)*.

 # From [M]Anton Martin, turn right down C. Atocha; before you hit C. Olivar, it will be on your right. $ Entrees €3-10. ⏰ Open daily 7:30am-8pm.

LATERAL
🍴 TRADITIONAL ❸

Pl. Santa Ana, ☎91 420 15 82 🖥www.cadenalateral.es

Although this restaurant in tourist-heavy Plaza Santa Ana caters to foreigners, it is a great place to get a taste of gourmet local fare. Share various *pinchos* (tiny appetizer-like morsels) to share like the Sirloin with Caramelized Onion or the Mushroom Crêpes *(€3.20)*. Don't know what to get? Order from the "suggestions" part of the menu or get one of their many side dishes *(€6)*, salads *(€6.50)*, or desserts *(€4)* at a reasonable price.

 # If you face the ME Madrid Reina Victorial Hotel in Plaza Santa Ana, Lateral will be on your left. $ Entrees €5-15. ⏰ Open daily noon-midnight.

O'PULPO MESON RESTAURANTE
🍴 TAPAS ❷

C. de los Cañizares, 8 ☎91 369 02 46 🖥www.opulpo.com

Right next door to Cat's Hostel, O'Pulpo serves up traditional local tapas with a one-big-family attitude. Try the Tortilla Tapa—a mixture of potatoes, eggs, and onion, with the *Tinto de Verrano*, a beverage made with wine and lemon Fanta.

#From Plaza Santa Ana, walk south down C. Olivar and pass C. Magdalena. It will be on your right. $ €5-15. ⏰ Open daily 10am-4:30pm and 8:30pm-midnight.

madrid

LA TAPA DEL MUNDO
🍴🍸 INTERNATIONAL ❷

C. de la Magdalena 1 ☎91 369 36 47

If you're craving food from back home, this place will probably have something for you no matter where you began your trip. Get entrees *(€10)* from hamburgers to nachos with guacamole to complement their specialty cocktails *(€6)*. Feeling that morning hangover? Try the traditional Spanish *churros con chocolate (€2.40)* or an American breakfast *(€4.20)*.

 # Right outside [M]Tirso De Molina. $ Entrees €3-15.

FATIGAS DEL QUERER
🍴🍸 TAPAS ❶

C. de la Cruz, 17 ☎91 523 21 31 🖥www.fatigasdelquerer.es

Come to this restaurant/bar combination on tiny C. de la Cruz for authentic Spanish tapas and drinks. In traditional Spanish style, meat is shaved off fresh by the order. Salads *(€4-8)*, tapas caliente *(€2)*, large meat dishes *(€8)*, and desserts *(€2.50)* are complemented by a great beer and wine selection *(€2-3)*.

 # From Plaza del Angel, go north up C. Espoz y Mina, bear right so that the street turns into C. de la Cruz. $€4-12. ⏰ Open M-F 11am-1:30am, Sa-Su 11am-2:30am or 3am. Kitchen closes 1am.

LA SOBERINA
🍴🍸 TAPAS ❷

C. Espoz y Mina ☎91 531 05 76 🖥www.lasoberbia.es/

For a traditional Spanish dish try the *Arroz Abanda* at La Soberina. Originally a way to use up leftovers from the week, *Arroz Abanda* is a gumbo-like seafood rice dish. From 1-5pm get the special: an appetizer and entree *(€9.50)*. *Tapas calientes (€4)* and drinks *(€1.90)* also served.

 # From Plaza de Santa Ana head down C. Espoz y Mina towards Puerta Del Sol. $ Entrees €4-12. ⏰ Open daily 8:45am-2am.

EL TIGRE
🍴🍸 TAPAS BAR ❶

C. de las Infantas, 30

El Tigre is crowded, hectic, loud, and fun. Buy a round of drinks (try one of their big mojitos) and get free plates full of tapas to go with them. Enough to fill you up, the tapas here are deep fried and delicious. Prepare to fight your way through the crowd to grab a ledge to perch your food and drink. Originally a local favorite, El Tigre has been discovered by travelers who now make up a large part of their clientele.

From [M]Gran Vía, walk north up C. de Hortaleza and make a right onto C. de las Infantas. It will be on your right. $ Entrees and drinks €3-10 ⏰ Open late.

MESON CINCO JOTAS — TAPAS ❷

Serrano, 118 ☎91 563 27 10 🖥www.mesoncincojotas.com

Touting the "best ham in the world," Meson Cinco Jotas is known for its genuine Iberian ham. With English picture menus available, Meson Cinco Jotas aims to please anglophiles. Order a variety of *tostas* to share like the goat cheese with caramelized onion. *Tapas calientes (€2.50-3.60);* raciones *(€10-12.50).*

In the Plaza Santa Ana. $ €5-20. ⏰ Open daily 8am-2am.

GIUSEPPE RICCI GELATO AND CAFFÉ — ❄ GELATO ❶

C. Huertas, 9 ☎91 429 33 45 🖥www.heladeriaricci.com

This is the perfect place to grab a delicious gelato snack and chill after a day at the museums. Get a tiny cup of gelato as a pick-me-up in the middle of the day... the cookie dough is *delicioso.*

Walk down C. Huertas from Plaza del Angel. It will be almost immediately on your left. $ Smalls €2.20; medium €2.70; large €3.20.

EL INTI DE ORO — ❄🍸 PERUVIAN ❸

C. Amour de Dios, 9 ☎91 429 19 58 🖥www.intideoro.com

Craving authentic Peruvian food? Wanting to try it for the first time? This Peruvian restaurant with English menus (with pictures) is a great way to take a break from tapas-heavy Spanish fare. Try the traditional *Arroz Chaufa con Pollo (€9.50).* One of the best parts of the meal is the specialty dessert drink brought with the check—with Bailey's, milk, cinnamon, and secret ingredients, it may make you want to leave a bigger tip.

Steps away from [M]Anton Martin down C. Amour de Dios. $ Entrees €5-15. ⏰ Open daily 1pm-midnight.

MIRANDA — ❄ INTERNATIONAL ❷

C. de las Huertas, 29 ☎34 913 691 025

This cute and classy restaurant offers a break from the steady stream of tapas bars along C. de las Huertas. Miranda offers some classic Spanish fare but also dishes up food from around the world. Sit down for a yummy mixed salad *(€9-10),* an entree *(€12-14),* tapas *(€7-10),* or *tostas (€4).* Looking for a steal? Try their special: an appetizer, main course, and dessert *(€12).*

From Plaza Santa Ana walk down C. de las Huertas towards the museum district. Miranda will be on your left. $ Entrees €5-15. ⏰ Open 9am-2am.

extra virgin

A little-known fact about Spain is that it is the world's leading producer of olive oil, squeezing out about 44% of the world's oil. Therefore, you'll find a lot of foods are cooked in the stuff: meats, potatoes, toast—whatever we in America might put butter on. In fact, it is estimated that each Spaniard consumes an average of 14 liters of olive oil per year.

VIVA LA VIDA
✔ VEGETARIAN ❷

Huertas, 57 ☎91 369 72 54 ▪www.vivalavida.vg

One of the few vegetarian options in Huertas is Viva La Vida, a tiny buffet-style to-go locale that also sells organic fruits, veggies, and dairy. The food is priced based upon weight, so don't overload but instead get small samplings of each tasty dish. Eat it in a nearby park like the Parque Del Retiro.

✴ *C. de la Huertas between C. de San Jose and C. del Fucar.* Ⓢ *Buffet €21 per kg of food.* ☒ *Open daily 11am-midnight.*

EL BASHA
✔ MIDDLE EASTERN ❷

Estamos en Plaza Matute, 7 ☎91 429 96 10 ▪www.restauranteelbasha.com

With cushions for chairs and hookahs available on request, this authentic Middle Eastern restaurant is a nice break from the row of tapas bars along C. de la Huertas. Try their huge selection of tea in the afternoon or a variety of Arab dishes such as *arayes* with meat and couscous. Go in on Saturday nights for a belly dancing show.

✴ *C. de la Huertas between C. de San Jose and C. del Fucar.* Ⓢ *Entrees €5-15.*

LIZARRAN
✔ TAPAS ❸

C. del Prado, 4 ☎91 429 33 61 ▪www.lizarran.es

Come to this upscale tapas restaurant and choose from a huge variety of cold and warm designer tapas. Keep your toothpicks, as you are charged based on the number you have on your plate at the end of the meal. Not in the mood for tapas? Lizzarran also provides a variety of cold cuts, salads, meats, and desserts.

✴ *From Plaza de Santa Ana, make a left onto C. de Echegaray.* Ⓢ *Entrees €10-25.*

LA FINCA DE SUSANA RESTAURANT
✔❄✌ MEDITERRANEAN ❸

C. de Arlabán, 4 ☎91 429 76 78 ▪www.lafinca-restaurant.com/

Although it looks forebodingly expensive from the outside, this white-tabled Mediterranean restaurant serves some reasonably priced meals. Come here for a date or a night out with friends and choose between various appetizers *(€7)*, fish *(€8)*, and other meats *(€6-10)*. To be safe, go for something in the "suggestions" part of the menu.

✴ *From the* Ⓜ*Seville, walk south down C. del Principe and make a left on C. de Arlabán.* Ⓢ *Entrees €6-20.* ☒ *Open M-W 1-3:45pm and 8:30-11:30pm, F-Sa 1-3:45pm and 8:30-midnight, Su 1-3:45pm and 8:30-11:30pm.*

GRAN VÍA

▨ RESTAURANTE LA ALHAMBRA DE SANTO DOMINGO
✔⊗✌ MEDITERRANEAN ❷

Jacometrezo, 15 ☎91 548 43 31

Come to La Alhambra de Santo Domingo to order cheap and fast Mediterranean food. Their menú of the day includes an appetizer, entree, bread, drink, and dessert *(€8)* and is a great deal for backpackers looking to fill up for cheap. For a smaller meal, explore their kebab plates *(€4)*, pizzas *(€3)*, or desserts *(€3.50)*.

✴ Ⓜ*Callao. Walk east down Jacometrezo, restaurant will be on your left.* Ⓢ *Meals around €10.*

[H]ARINA
✔⊗✌❄ SANDWICHES, DESSERTS, COFFEE ❷

Plaza de la Independencia, 10 ☎91 522 87 85 ▪www.harinamadrid.com

Go through the sliding glass doors of this chic bakery for a delicious dessert and drink or a small salad before visiting nearby Retiro Park.

✴ *Outside the entrance to Retiro park in the Plaza de la Independencia.* Ⓢ *Food €5-15.* ☒ *Open M-Su 9am-9pm.*

OTOTOI
✔⊗✌(♥)☕ FUSION ❸

C. Alcalá 35 ☎91 522 64 39 ▪www.ototoi.es

Craving food from the East in the middle of Madrid? Put down that MSG-laden General Gao's chicken and head to Ototoi, a Japanese and Mediterranean fusion restaurant steps away from Gran Vía. With a chic decor inspired by Japanese wood-block prints, you'll feel thrown back in time to a Spanish version of the Edo period. Try a sushi mix, a warm Mediterranean dish, or some combination of both.

☘ ⓂSevilla. *Walk straight east up C. Alcalá.* ⓈEntrees €5-20. ⌚ *Open M-Th 8:30am-2am, F 8:30am-3am, Sa noon-3am, Su noon-5pm.*

GINO'S ☞⊗♨❄⑴ ITALIAN ❸

C. de Alcalá, 23 ☎91 522 96 74 ▣www.grupovips.com

Head to Gino's for reasonably priced Italian favorites. Get their *menú del día (€10.95)* to eat like an Italian king, or try their salads *(€8-9)*, panini *(€3-8)*, or anti-pasto *(€7.95)* to sample standard motherland fare.

☘ ⓂSeville. Ⓢ *€5-15.* ⌚ *Open M-Th 1:30-3:30pm and 8:30pm-midnight, F-Sa 1:30-3:30pm and 8:30pm-1am.*

THE WOK ☞⊗⟡❄⑴ ASIAN FUSION ❸

C. de la Virgen de los Peligros, 1, ☎912 758 125 ▣www.grupovips.com

This restaurant offers a break from Spanish tapas and a taste of Asian fusion food in a modern, Eastern-inspired environment. Entrees are full of interesting flavors and pay tribute to Japanese, Chinese, and Thai cooking. Get appetizers to share like their dumplings *(€6.70)*, or dine solo with an individual wok dish *(€11)*. Natural fruit juice offerings like the papaya, passion, and orange juice mix *(€2.75)* highlight their diverse menu.

☘ ⓂSeville. Ⓢ *Food €7-20.* ⌚ *Open daily M-Su 10am-10pm.*

VITAMINA ☞⊗⟡❄ DINER, AMERICAN ❷

C. Gran Vía, 47 ☎91 541 55 23 ▣www.vitaminass.es/

If a diner married a buffet but was simultaneously meeting a passionate juice bar on the side, that love triangle would be Vitamina, a restaurant perfect for big groups and families that can't agree on their fare. For lunch, take advantage of their full buffet and drink *(€8.90)*, or try one of their salads, sandwiches, hamburgers, pizzas, or pastas *(€7-10)*. One full page of the menu is dedicated to fruit shakes of every combination *(€3-€4)*, so tame that oppressive heat with a pre-made concoction or choose three fruits and design a drink of your own.

☘ ⓂGran Vía. Ⓢ *Food €5-10.* ⌚ *M-Su 8am-1am.*

MERCADO DE LA REINA ☞⊗⟡❄ TAPAS ❸

C. Gran Vía, 12 ☎91 521 31 98 ▣www.mercadodelareina.es

The classy Mercado de la Reina is an upscale break from Gran Vía shopping. Business suits flock to this mercado's back tables during their lunch breaks, so plop down into one of the high stools in the front of the restaurant to taste *pinchos* made from organic ingredients that come paired with wine.

☘ *From* ⓂGran Vía metro stop walk straight east down Gran Vía, restaurant will be on your right. Ⓢ *Entrees €10-20.* ⌚ *Open M-Th 9am-midnight, Sa-Su 10am-1am.*

CHUECA

▦ BAZAAR ☞⊗⟡❄ MEDITERRANEAN ❷

C. de la Libertad, 21 ☎91 523 39 05 ▣www.restaurantbazaar.com

With immaculate white tablecloths, plush seats, and romantic candles, you'd expect this restaurant to be forebodingly expensive. Think again. Bazaar boasts cheap dishes *(€8-10)* in a ritzy atmosphere, but some portions are on the smaller side.

☘ ⓂChueca. Make a left on C. Augusto Figuroa, and a right on C. de la Libertad, 21. Ⓢ *Entrees €8-10.* ⌚ *Open daily 1:15-4pm and 8:30-11:45pm.*

▦ MAGASAND ☞⊗⟡⑴❄ CAFE, SMOOTHIES ❶

Travesía de San Mateo, 16 ☎91 319 68 25 ▣www.magasand.com

With an advertising slogan like, "incredible sandwiches, impossible magazines," Magasand is a cafe you need to experience to understand. Have one of their

food · chueca

fresh sandwiches, salads, smoothies, or coffees made-to-order by the jovial staff, and then move upstairs to lounge on hip couches and colorful stools as you read one of their many alternative artsy magazines.

🪧 [M]Chueca. Make a right on C. Augusto Figuroa, and another right on C. Hortaleza. Turn right onto Travesía de San Mateo (there's a sign on Hortaleza pointing you in the right direction). [$] Sandwiches €5-8. Salads €4-7. ⏰ Open daily 9:30am-1:30pm and 4-9pm.

IL PIZZAIOLO 💳🚭💳 ITALIAN [2]

C. de Hortaleza, 84 ☎91 319 29 64 💻www.pizzaiolo.es

With bright murals of Italian landmarks on the wall and amicable service, this eatery is a great place to come and enjoy a little Italiano in the middle of Chueca. Try an antipasta or salad served in handmade bread bowls, or splurge on one of their made-to-order thin-crust personal pizzas *(€8-10)*.

🪧 [M]Chueca. Make a right on C. de Gravina and a right on C. de Hortaleza; restaurant will be on your right. [$] Pizzas €8-10. ⏰ Open M-Th 1:30pm-midnight, F-Sa 1:30pm-12:30am, Su 1:30pm-midnight.

MAOZ 💳🚭❄ VEGETARIAN [1]

C. de Hortaleza, 5 ☎64 740 87 31 💻www.maozusa.com

This tiny restaurant serves affordable vegetarian to the meatless masses. Although there are a few chairs and stools, most people order one of Maoz' falafel sandwiches or salads for the road. Don't expect the best salad you've ever tasted, but this fast food spot gives a bang for your buck.

🪧 [M]Gran Vía. Walk straight up C. de Hortaleza, and the restaurant will be on your left. [$] Entrees €6. ⏰ Open daily noon-2am.

STOP MADRID 💳🚭🍸❄ TAPAS [1]

C. de Hortaleza, 11 ☎91 521 88 87 💻www.stopmadrid.es

Founded in 1929, this traditional Madrid tavern offers Iberian ham, Spanish cheeses, and 70 different kinds of wine. Marble walls, wine bottle decor, and wooden stools make this place feel like you've hot-tub-time-machined your way back to the old country.

🪧 [M]Gran Vía. From the Gran Vía stop, walk straight up C. de Hortaleza. [$] Entrees €5-10. ⏰ Open daily noon-2am.

MAMA INES CAFE 💳🚭🍸❄ COFFEE [1]

C. de Hortaleza, 22 ☎91 523 23 33 💻www.mamaines.com

Advertised as a "meeting place for people from all over the world," Mama Ines cafe certainly borrows from a variety of cultures. Try coffee from Hawaii, Kenya, Ethiopia, or Tanzania, and then pair it with one of their sandwiches like the classic *jamón y queso* (ham and cheese).

🪧 [M]Gran Vía. Walk straight up C. de Hortaleza. [$] Sandwiches €5-10. ⏰ Open daily 10am-2am.

NURIELLE 💳🚭🍸❄ DESSERT, COFFEE, COCKTAILS [1]

C. de Hortaleza 38 ☎91 523 53 23 💻www.nurielle.es

Take a break from shopping on Gran Vía or in Chueca and come to NuRielle for gelato, sandwiches, coffee, or cocktails. White leather chairs and chic black tabletops give this place a classy feel without the high prices, and their menú combos *(drink, sandwich, and dessert; €5.50)* are a steal.

🪧 [M]Gran Vía. Walk straight up C. de Hortaleza. [$] Menú €5.50. cocktails €3-6. ⏰ Open M-Th 8am-1pm, F 8am-1:30am, Sa 9am-1:30am, Su 10am-1:30am.

VIVARES 37 💳🚭🍸❄ FUSION [2]

C. de Hortaleza, 52 ☎91 531 58 13

Labeled as "homemade food with a modern touch," Vivares 37 offers Asian-Spanish fusion cuisine. The bright orange walls and leather seats vaguely reminds us of something out of a Harley Davidson commercial. Nonetheless, this place is fancy enough for a dinner out with friends and casual enough for a quick lunch all by your lonesome self. Enjoy their menú of the day *(appetizer, entree, and dessert; €11.90)*.

✢ ⓂGran Vía. Walk straight up C. de Hortaleza. ⑤ Entrees €5-15. ⓩ Open daily 12:30-5:30pm and 8:30pm-12:30am.

stop worrying and love the nap

The afternoon nap is hardly an alien concept to the typical American college student, but out in the real world, dropping off for an hour or two in the middle of the day is a tough feat to pull off—if you live in the boring, nine-to-five United States, that is. Spain, on the other hand, has it all figured out: after waking up to a big bowl of *cafe con leche* and heading off to work for four or five hours, the Spanish come back home around 1pm for lunch, immediately followed by that most glorious of Iberian traditions, the *siesta*. The *siesta* doesn't have to be a nap; it's quite common instead to just tumbarse (lie down) on the sofa and slip into a dazed stupor in front of one of the popular game shows that daily grace the Spanish airwaves (or the Spanish-dubbed Los Simpson, whose afternoon broadcast consistently ranks among the top-rated programs). Yes, there are still another few hours of work in the afternoon, but the break helps divide and conquer the workday in a way that makes those last few hours between *siesta* and fiesta manageable.

PIÙ DI PRIMA
●⊗❣❈ ITALIAN ❺

C. de Hortaleza, 100 ☎91 308 33 72 ▣www.piudiprima.com

For an upscale meal, put on your fancy shoes and come to Più di Prima for some of the best Italian food in the city. In the evening, dim candles, white table clothes, and sparkling white lights make this a picture-perfect date spot. Have a fancy dinner for two, but make sure you're breaking the bank for someone special.

✢ ⓂChueca. Turn around, make a right on C. Augusto Figuroa, and another right on C. de Hortaleza. ⑤ Entrees €10-25. ⓩ Open daily 1:30-4pm and 9pm-midnight.

BAIRES CAFE
●⊗❣⁽ᵖ⁾❈ CAFE ❷

C. de Gravina, 4 ☎91 532 98 79

With floral artwork and plastic chairs, this cafe is a good place to grab a coffee and check your email during the day and throw back a few cocktails with friends at night. With black plastic chairs and simple furnishings, the cafe is casual with an energetic atmosphere. Check out the local art adorning the walls—most of it is on sale.

✢ ⓂChueca. Turn left on C. de Gravina towards C. Hortaleza. ⑤ Drinks €5-10. ⓩ Open daily 9:30am-midnight.

ISOLÉE
●⊗❣❈ CAFE ❷

C. de las Infantas, 19 ☎91 522 81 38 ▣www.isolee.com

With white leather seats and minimalist grass decor, Isolée serves up "fashion, food, and lifestyle" with trendy flair. Feel sophisticated as you sip on chocolate cappuccinos and windowshop the store in the back for all your posh, overpriced food items, drinks, and even clothing and accessories.

✢ ⓂGran Vía. Walk north up C. de Hortaleza and make a right on C. de las Infantas. ⑤ Entrees €5-10. ⓩ Open M-Tu 10am-10pm, F-Sa 11am-1am, and Su 4-10pm.

DIURNO
●⊗❣❈ CAFE, VIDEO RENTAL ❶

San Marcos, 37 ☎91 522 00 09 ▣www.diurno.com

Get your freshly prepared sandwiches, desserts, pastas, and more at this yuppie haven reminiscent of an iPod commercial. With a huge selections of DVDs for you to rent and buy, take your food to-go and catch up on the last season of *Modern Family*.

✇ ⓂChueca. Make a left onto C. Augusto Figueroa, and a right onto C. de la Libertad, 21. Diurno is across from Bazaar. Ⓢ Sandwiches €5-10. ◷ Open daily 10am-midnight.

EL TIGRE
➡⊗⌇❄⌂ TAPAS ❶

C. de las Infantas, 30 ☎91 532 00 72

El Tigre is crowded, hectic, loud, and fun. Buy a round of drinks (try one of their big mojitos) and get free plates full of tapas to go with it. Enough to fill you up, the tapas here are deep fried and delicious, and even hardy eaters can fill up for under €5. Prepare to fight your way through the crowd to grab a ledge to perch your food and drink. Originally a local favorite, El Tigre was recently discovered by travelers who now make up a large part of their clientele.

✇ ⓂGran Vía. Walk north up C. de Hortaleza and make a right on C. de las Infantas. It will be on your right. Ⓢ Beer €1.50. Drinks with tapas €3-10. ◷ Open daily 10am-2am.

WAGABOO
➡⊗⌇❄ FUSION ❹

C. Gravina, 18 ☎91 531 65 67 🖳www.wagaboo.com

Wagaboo delivers on its motto of "fun eating." You can't miss this Italian-Asian fusion restaurant's neon pink sign and well-decorated interior. Even its menu is unique, boasting a "fun, cheerful, and very light start" with appetizers, a "choice of surprising specialties" for main offers, and "supremely creamy ice creams" to finish off your meal.

✇ ⓂChueca. Make a right onto C. Gravina. Ⓢ Appetizers €5-10; entrees €10-20. ◷ Open daily 1-5pm and 9pm-1am.

MALASAÑA

🅝 LA DOMINGA
➡⊗⌇❄ SPANISH ❸

C. del Espíritu Santo, 15 ☎91 524 48 09 🖳www.ladominga.com

Come to this upscale restaurant for fancy Spanish food even the pickiest of eaters can enjoy. With wood furnishings, a large bar, and dark red walls, this is the perfect place to try conservative Spanish fare for the first time. On weekdays, go for their *menú* of the day (€10.90).

✇ ⓂTribunal. Go west on C. de San Vincente Ferrer, make a left on C. del Barco, and make a right on C. del Espíritu Santo. Ⓢ Entrees €10-15. ◷ Open daily 1pm-4:30pm and 8:30pm-noon.

HOME BURGER BAR
➡⊗⌇❄ BURGERS ❷

C. del Espíritu Santo, 12 ☎91 522 97 28 🖳www.homeburgerbar.com

With tunes from the '50s, bright booths, and menus printed on paper bags, Home Burger Bar is a retro burger joint in the middle of Malasaña. Try one of their famous gourmet burgers (€10-13), salads, or club sandwiches.

✇ ⓂTribunal. Go west on C. de San Vincente Ferrer, make a left on C. del Barco, and make a right on C. del Espíritu Santo. Ⓢ Burgers €10-13. Sandwiches €8-15. ◷ Open M-Sa 1:30-4pm and 8:30pm-midnight, Su 1-4pm and 8:30-11pm.

HAPPY DAY
➡⊗⌇❄ CAFE ❶

C. del Espíritu Santo 11 ☎66 720 11 69

As the name suggests, this happy-go-lucky bakery serves up its adorably decorated gourmet cupcakes, pastries, and hot chocolate with a smile. With big windows, handwritten menus in colorful chalk, and brightly wrapped chocolates, everything about this place politely says, "Have a nice day."

✇ ⓂTribunal. Go west on C. de San Vincente Ferrer, make a left onto C. del Barco, and make a right on C. del Espíritu Santo. Ⓢ Pastries €2-6. ◷ Open daily 9am-11:30pm.

LA VITA É BELLA
➡⊗⌇❄ ITALIAN ❶

Plaza de San Ildefonso, 5 ☎91 521 41 09 🖳www.lavitaebella.com.es

With limited seating, La Vita é Bella is more like a delicious Italian deli than actual restaurant. Try their lasagna or alfredo pasta *(€2.50-5)*, or go for one of their many vegetarian options. Best for a quick takeout dinner or lunch.

🚏 [M]Tribunal. Go west on C. de San Vincente Ferrer, make a left onto C. del Barco, and make a right onto C. del Espíritu Santo $ Entrees €2.50-5. ⏰ Open daily noon-2am.

LOLINA VINTAGE CAFE 💳🚭🍸❄ CAFE ❶

C. del Espiritu Santo, 9 ☎66 720 11 69 💻www.lolinacafe.com

Filled with '50s memorabilia like album covers and movie stills, mismatched armchairs, and vintage lamps, this quirky cafe looks like it was assembled from knick-knacks in a Brooklyn thrift store but fits perfectly into the trendy Malasaña scene. Great selection of teas (try the Green Earl Grey) in super-cool pots that detach to reveal cups hidden underneath *(€2)*.

🚏 [M]Tribunal. Go west on C. de San Vincente Ferrer, make a left onto C. del Barco, then make a right onto C. del Espíritu Santo. $ Salads €8. Cocktails €6. Coffee and tea €2-5. ⏰ Open M-Tu 9:30am-1am, W-Th 9:30am-2am, F-Sa 9:30am-2:30am, Su 9:30-1am.

LA ZARA 💳🚭🍸❄ SPANISH ❷

Jesús de Valle, 31 ☎91 522 07 03

Come to La Zara for a quick meal to take a break from exploring the Malasaña district. Try the menú of the day that includes salad, two *tostas*, dessert or coffee, and drink *(€9)* to get a better deal than its clothing-brand equivalent. Unfortunately, there are no clearance sales.

🚏 [M]Tribunal. Go west on C. de San Vincente Ferrer, make a left onto C. del Barco, and make a right onto C. del Espíritu Santo. Walk down the street, and Jesús de Valle will be on your left. $ Menú €9. ⏰ Open daily 11am-1am.

BANZAI 💳🚭🍸❄ JAPANESE ❸

C. del Espiritu Santo, 16 ☎91 521 70 81

Craving Japanese food in the middle of *España?* With dozens of sushi options and warm traditional dishes, modern Japanese restaurant Banzai might just have the perfect roll for you. Not into raw fish? Try their express menú *(warm entree and salad of the day: €10)*.

🚏 [M]Tribunal. Go west on C. de San Vincente Ferrer, make a left onto C. del Barco, and make a right onto C. del Espíritu Santo. $ Sushi €10-15. ⏰ Open daily 12:30-4:30pm and 8:30pm-1am.

CRÊPERIE LA RUE 💳🚭🍸❄ CRÊPERIE ❷

C. Espíritu Santo, 18

This tiny crêperie calls itself a "un pedacito de Francia en el centro de Madrid," or a little bit of France in the center of Madrid. We agree. French music, paintings of Parisian landmarks, and the delicious smell of savory and sweet crêpes make this place seem like the set from *Amélie* and the perfect stop for a mid-afternoon snack. Order your crêpe to go as there is limited seating.

🚏 [M]Tribunal. Go west on C. de San Vincente Ferrer, make a left onto C. del Barco, and make a right onto C. del Espíritu Santo. $ Crêpes €4-8. ⏰ Open daily 11:30am-midnight.

ALQAMARU - EL CAFE DE LA LUNA 💳🚭🍸❄ CAFE ❷

C. del Espíritu Santo, 15 ☎91 521 95 66 💻cafe-de-la-luna.iespana.es

With orange walls and chalk-written menus, this simple cafe offers coffee, tea, *tostas*, and cocktails. Try their goat cheese and candied red pepper tosta *(€3.80)*, or go for their two-for-one mojito deal *(€7)*.

🚏 [M]Tribunal. Go west on C. de San Vincente Ferrer, make a left onto C. del Barco, and make a right onto C. del Espíritu Santo. $ Tostas €3.80. Cocktails €7. Tea €2.80. ⏰ Open daily 12:30pm-2am.

EL RINCÓN 💳🚭🍸❄ CAFE ❶

C. del Espíritu Santo, 26 ☎91 522 19 86

Funky wall decor, mismatched furniture, and interesting knick-knacks like homemade metal jewelry make El Rincón a caricature of bohemian Malasaña.

Grab a midday coffee or tea for a pick-me-up, and pair it with a sandwich or fresh-baked pastry like the chocolate filled croissant *(€2)*.

✠ Ⓜ*Tribunal. Go west on C. de San Vincente Ferrer, make a left onto C. del Barco, and make a right onto C. del Espíritu Santo.* Ⓢ *Sandwiches €5-10.* Ⓒ *Open daily 11am-2am.*

OLOKUN
⬥⊗✆✿ CUBAN ❸

C. Fuencarral, 105 ☎91 445 69 16

If you'd like to taste classic Cuban food, look no further than Olokun. Get a tropical drink *(€5-7)* to go along with the beach scenes on the walls. Try Cuban classics like *tostones (€6)* or *Ropa Vieja (shredded beef served over rice; €10)*. For a little taste of everything, go for the menú *(€11.90)*. If you get bored waiting for your meal, you can always go play with the foosball table in the basement.

✠ Ⓜ *Tribunal. From the Tribunal metro stop walk straight north up C. Fuencarral. Restaurant will be on your left.* Ⓢ *Entrees €10-15.* Ⓒ *Open daily noon-5pm and 9pm-2am.*

ARGÜELLES AND MONCLOA

▦ LA TABERNA DE LIERIA
⬥⊗✆✿ SPANISH ❹

C. del Duque de Liria, 9 ☎91 541 45 19 ▣www.latabernadeliria.com

This offbeat restaurant serves up classy Basque food in interesting flavor combinations in an atmosphere that seems like your distant relative's living room. To get a taste of everything, try their preset menu combinations made for two or more people. Wine and cheese tastings as well as lessons in how to cook duck *foie gras* are offered periodically, so consult their website for a schedule of these tasty exhibitions.

✠ Ⓜ*Ventura Rodriguez. Walk forward, take the left fork in the road (C. San Bernardino), and walk straight forward.* Ⓢ *Entrees €15-20.* Ⓒ *Open daily 10am-2am.*

EL JARDÍN SECRETO
⬥⊗✆✿ CAFE ❶

C. de Conde Duque, 2 ☎91 541 80 23

Tucked away in a tiny street close to C. de la Princesa, El Jardín Secreto is Arguelles's best-kept secret. Walk into this eclectic cafe filled with beaded window coverings, wooden ceiling canopies, and crystal-ball table lights to enjoy one of their dozens of coffees, hot chocolates, and snacks. For a real taste of the varied treats Secreto has to offer, try the Chocolate El Jardín served with chocolate Teddy Grahams and dark chocolate at the bottom of your cup *(€6)* or the George Clooney cocktail with *horchata*, crème de cocoa, and cointreau *(€7.25)*.

✠ Ⓜ*Ventura Rodriguez. Walk straight, take the left fork in the road (C. San Bernardino) and walk forward.* Ⓢ *Coffee and tea €3-6. Cocktails €7.25. Desserts €4.20.* Ⓒ *Open M-Th 6:30pm-1:30am, F-Sa 6:30pm-2:30am, Su 6:30pm-1:30am.*

NEBRASKA
⬥⊗✆✿ SPANISH, AMERICAN ❷

C. de la Princesa, 3 ☎91 542 64 97 ▣www.gruponebraska.com

This chain with eight locations around the city serves up Spanish and American fare such as ham dishes, hamburgers, and steak—we'd say it's close to Tex-Mex, but somehow that seems geographically wrong. Their best deals are the *menú del día (€10)* or breakfast special that comes with coffee and a *churro (€2.10)*.

✠ Ⓜ*Plaza de España.* Ⓢ *Meals €3-12.* Ⓒ *Open M-Th 8am-11:30pm, F-Sa 8am-1:15am, Su 8am-11:30pm.*

CASCARAS
⬥⊗✆✿ SPANISH ❷

C. Ventura Rodriguez, 7 ☎91 542 83 36 ▣www.restaurantecascaras.com

With cityscapes decorating the walls, bookshelves filled with novels and ceramic pots, and chic lighting fixtures near the bar, Cascaras walks a fine, friendly line between homey and modern. Come to watch the game on one of the many TVs that are placed throughout the sprawling two-level restaurant, or simply enjoy one of

madrid

their specialty vegetarian dishes like the pumpkin ravioli with mushroom sauce.
🧭 ⓂVentura Rodriguez. Walk south down C. de la Princesa and make a right onto Ventura Rodriguez. $ Meals €5-15. ⏰ Open M-F 7:30am-1am, Sa-Su 7:30am-2am.

LAS CUEVAS DEL DUQUE 💳🚭🍸❄ SPANISH ❹

C. del Duque de Liria, 9 ☎91 559 50 37 💻www.cuevasdelduque.galeon.com

With a motto that roughly translates to "the nobility and art of the good eat," Las Cuevas del Duque features typical Spanish fare as well as unique hunting dishes like boiled deer with mixed vegetables and pickled quail. If you're going with a group, split their tasting menu for a three-course meal to share, a high-quality meat dish, a "fresh and good" fish tasting, dessert, and a regional wine.
🧭 ⓂVentura Rodriguez. Walk forward, take the left fork in the road (C. San Bernardino), and walk straight. The restaurant will be on a tiny street to your right. $ Entrees €15-30. ⏰ Open daily 7-11pm.

KURTO AL PLATO 💳🚭🍸❄ SPANISH ❺

Serrano Jover, 1 ☎91 758 59 46 💻www.kultoalplato.com

Described as Basque haute cuisine in miniature, Kurto al Plato is a great place to try designer tapas in a swanky atmosphere. Located right next to the El Corte Ingles department store, Kurto al Plato is your perfect stop for a post-shopping dinner, but make sure your wallet isn't wiped before you order. High black chairs, funky plates, and a colorful chalk drink menu all add to the upscale but slightly offbeat decor.
🧭 ⓂArgüelles. Walk straight south down C. de la Princesa. $ Meals €12-20. ⏰ Open M-Th 8:30-11:30pm, F-Sa noon-1am, Su 8:30-11:30pm.

nightlife

EL CENTRO AND GRAN VÍA

👍 **OHM/BASH LINE** 💳🚭🍸❄ CLUB

Plaza de Callao, 4 ☎91 532 01 32 💻www.pacha-madrid.com

Known as Bash Line on weekdays and Sundays and Ohm on Fridays and Saturdays, this lively club has drag queens out front and DJs who keep the beats going until the sun comes up. Organized themed parties are regular features.
🧭 ⓂTribunal. $ Cover M-F €10-15; Sa €10-14; Su €10-15. ⏰ Open W-Su midnight-6am.

👍 **PALACIO GAVIRIA** 🚭🍸❄ CLUB

C. del Arenal, 9 ☎ 91 526 60 69 💻www.palaciogaviria.com

Built in 1850 and inspired by the Italian Renaissance, the Palacio Gaviria is a beautiful palace turned nightlife hotspot. Make your royal entrance by heading down the grand marble staircase onto the dance floor powered by techno beats and electric dance moves. Be on the lookout for promoters of Palacio Gaviria in Puerta del Sol, as they will often have vouchers for free entry or drinks.
🧭 From Puerta del Sol walk straight down C. del Arenal. $ Cover M-Th €10, F-Sa €15, Su €10. ⏰ Opens at 11pm.

CAFE DEL PRÍNCIPE 💳🚭🍸❄ BAR

Plaza de Canalejas, 5 ☎ 91 531 81 83

A 2min. walk away from Puerta del Sol, this bar and restaurant offers the "best mojitos in Madrid" as well as a variety of entrees and beverages. Come to take a tranquil break from the noisy Sol without going too far to get back to all the clubs.
🧭 Right at the corner of C. de la Cruz and C. de Principe. $ Mixed drinks €5-15.

JOY ESLAVA 🍸❄ CLUB

Arenal, 11 ☎91 366 37 33 💻www.joy-eslava.com

An old standby, this converted theater has stayed strong amid Madrid's rapidly changing nightlife scene. Number one among study-abroad students and travelers, this club plays an eclectic mix of music and features scantily clad models (of both sexes) dancing on the theater stage. Balloons and confetti periodically fall from the ceiling New-Year's-Eve-style.

ⓢ *Cover M-W €12; Th €15; F-Su €18.* ⓩ *Open M-Th 11:30pm-5:30am, F-Sa 11:30pm-6am, Su 11:30pm-5:30am.*

all night long

Ever since dictator Franco's death in 1975, the *madrileños* have been going out like it's going out of style. *La movida*, the youth countercultural movement post-1975, broke all those pesky Franco-era taboos by over-indulging in everything from booze to knocking boots. While few places are as countercultural as they were in the '70s, the student nightlife scene is just as jammin'—but maybe with fewer drugs. Start your night off at **Kiyo** in Chueca and sip a kiwi, vodka and *sake* concoction in the heart of Madrid's gay nightlife. Next, head to **Kapital,** a classic huge disco that will please any clubgoer with four levels of themed dance floors, go-go dancers of both genders, and enough fog to give you asthma. Don't stop grinding until sunrise, and then cap off the evening with *chocolate con churros,* fried dough dipped in thick, molten hot chocolate at **Chocolateria San Ginés.**

madrid

ORANGE CAFE
◆⊗❞✲ CAFE, BAR
Serrano Jover, 5
▣www.soyorangecafe.com

Come to Orange Cafe for a rock concert in the evening and a packed club at night. Filled with many tourists and travelers, the club plays mostly American pop music. Come on Wednesday nights between 11:30pm and 12:30am for free drinks and entry for ladies. Check online for concert times.

⌕ *Across the street from the ⓜArguelles.* ⓢ *Cover €10-15.* ⓩ *Open daily 11:30pm-2am.*

EL CHAMPANDEZ
◆⊗❞✲ BAR
C. de Fernando, 77
☎91 54 29 68 ▣www.chapandaz.com

With manmade stalactites hanging from the ceiling, this unique bar is designed to look like a cave (complete with a specialty drink that bartenders drip from the ceiling). Although it's pretty quiet earlier in the evening, it starts getting packed with pre-clubbers fast.

⌕ *From ⓜMoncloa, get to the intersection of C. de Fernando and C. de la Princesa and walk straight east down Fernando.* ⓢ *Drinks €10.* ⓩ *Open daily 10pm-3am.*

DEL DIEGO COCKTAIL BAR
◆⊗❞✲ BAR
C. de la Reina, 12
☎91 523 31 06

With classy drinks and a comfortable atmosphere, Del Diego is a local favorite. Try the apple martini or cosmopolitan *(€10)* for one of the bartender's favorite drinks.

⌕ *From the Gran Vía metro station walk north up C. de Hortaleza, make a right onto C. de la Reina.* ⓢ *Cocktails €10.* ⓩ *Open daily 7pm-3am.*

LOLA
◆⊗❞✲ BAR
C. de la Reina, 25
☎91 522 34 83

With mostly white decor and twinkling Christmas lights, Lola is swanky but by no means pretentious. Come to relax or to drunkenly spell out Lola's name through song.

⌕ *From ⓜGran Vía, walk north up C. de Hortaleza. Take a right on C. de la Reina.* ⓢ *Cocktails €9-10.* ⓩ *Open M-Th noon-2am, F-Sa noon-2:30am.*

BAR COCK

♦⊗Ұ❀ BAR

C. de la Reina, 16

◼www.barcock.com

We really like the idea that this place has been a walking penis joke since its opening in 1921. Today, with its rooster-covered walls and large selection of cocktails (€9), the joke lives on.

⚑ *From ⓂGran Vía, walk north up C. de Hortaleza, make a right on C. de la Reina.* ⑤ *Cocktails €9.* ⚅ *Open M-Th 8pm-3am, F-Sa 3:30pm-4am.*

POUSS

♦⊗Ұ❀ BAR

C. de las Infantas, 19

☎91 521 63 01

Recently renovated, this bar features music from '70s pop to '40s hits to contemporary Italian chart toppers. A cocktail bar, runway, and round seats make this a nice place to grab a drink before heading out to a *discoteca* in Gran Vía or El Centro.

⚑ *From ⓂGran Vía, walk north up C. de Hortaleza, then make a right on C. de las Infantas.* ⑤ *Cover €10.* ⚅ *Open M-Sa 10pm-2am.*

REINABRUJA

♦⊗Ұ❀ CLUB

C. Jacometrezo, 6

☎91 542 81 93 ◼www.reinabruja.com

With color-changing illuminated walls and stenciled pillars, this club is full of 20- to 30-somethings jamming to a mix of Spanish and American pop music.

⚑ *Next to ⓂCallao.* ⑤ *Cover €12; includes 1 drink. Wine €7. Mixed drinks €9.* ⚅ *Open Th-Sa 11pm-6am.*

LA LATINA AND LAVAPIÉS

▨ SHOKO

♦Ұ⊗ DISCOTECA

C. de Toledo, 86

☎91 354 16 91 ◼www.shokomadrid.com

With massive "bamboo" shoots that reach to the ceiling, a huge stage featuring internationally acclaimed acts, and a swanky VIP section *Let's Go* wishes it could live in, Shoko is an Oriental-inspired *discoteca* that follows the rules of Feng Shui and breaks any rules against a good time.

⚑ *ⓂLa Latina. Head straight south down C. de Toledo.* ⑤ *Cover €10-15.* ⚅ *Open daily 11:30pm-late.*

CASA LUCAS

♦⊗Ұ♨ BAR

Cava Baja, 30

☎91 365 08 04 ◼www.casalucas.es

The inviting orange walls, paintings, and corked wine bottles create a friendly vibe, and once you've opened that wine bottle, you'll never want to leave this mellow, comfortable *casa*. Casa Lucas is a comfortable place to grab a glass of wine. Calmer than some of La Latina's rowdy options, Casa Lucas also has tapas and *raciones*—just pay attention to the prices, as some expensive *raciones* can turn into a brutal bill.

⚑ *ⓂLa Latina. Walk west down Plaza de la Cebada. Make a right onto C. de Humilladero and continue right on Cava Baja.* ⑤ *Raciones €5-20.* ⚅ *Open daily 8:30pm-midnight.*

ANGELIKA COCKTAIL BAR

♦⊗Ұ♨ BAR

C. Cava Baja, 24

☎91 364 55 31 ◼www.angelika.es

Come to this sleek cocktail bar for a classy cocktail in an all-white lounge. Glowing purple lights and well-dressed patrons add to this ultra-cool environment that actually rents DVDs. We can't decide if this is the drunkest Blockbuster or the most cinema-friendly bar in Madrid.

⚑ *ⓂLa Latina. Walk west down Plaza de la Cebada. Make a right onto C. de Humilladero and continue right on Cava Baja.* ⑤ *Cocktails €5-10.* ⚅ *Open daily 3pm-1am.*

EL BONANNO

♦⊗Ұ♨ BAR

Plaza del Humilladero, 4

☎91 366 68 86 ◼www.elbonanno.com

Located at the southern end of hoppin' Cava Baja, El Bonanno is a fun place to grab a beer or cocktail before heading out to a *discoteca*. With no real place to sit, patrons sip their drinks standing up in this lively bar.

➜ ⓂLa Latina. Walk east toward Plaza del Humilladero. If you've reached Igl. S. Andrés, you've gone too far. $ Cocktails €3-10. ⏰ Open daily 12:30pm-2:30am.

LA PEREJILA
💳🚭🍸⛅ TAPAS, BAR

C. Cava Baja, 25 ☎91 364 28 55

This place immediately stands out because of the live parakeets out front. The tropical theme continues inside with green walls, fake shrubbery, and quirky knick-knacks that make this feel like a themed restaurant at an amusement park. Come to see the eclectic decor, stay for a taste of their homemade tapas, and spend the night for *cerveza* and sangria.

➜ ⓂLa Latina. Walk west down Plaza de la Cebada. Make a right onto C. de Humilladero, and continue right on Cava Baja. $ Cocktails €5-10. ⏰ Open daily 1-4pm and 8:15pm-12:30am.

AROCA XI
💳🚭🍸⛅ SPANISH, COCKTAIL BAR

Plaza de los Carros ☎91 366 54 75 💻www.grupoaroca.com

Quieter than many of the bar options on nearby Cava Baja, Aroca XI provides a nice restaurant and bar for conversation and cocktails before a big night on the town. High metal chairs, candlelight, and friendly service make for a posh start to your evening.

➜ ⓂLa Latina. Walk west down C. de Humilladero until you see Igl. S. Andres on your right. As you face the church, Aroca XI will be on your left. $ Entrees €5-15. Cocktails €6-8. ⏰ Open daily noon-midnight.

HUERTAS

👍 KAPITAL
💳🚭🍸💳 CLUB

Atocha, 125 ☎91 420 29 06

If you only have one night in Madrid, be sure to make it to Kapital, one of the biggest clubs in Spain (if not the world). With seven different floors of music and a huge variety of drinks to encounter, this sprawling *discoteca* has something for every party animal—even you, Mom. Don't come too early; the place starts going strong around 2am.

➜ 2min. walk up Atocha street from ⓂAtocha. $ Cover €15; includes 1 free drink. Drinks €10-15. ⏰ Open Th-Sun 11:30pm-5:30am.

SWEET
🚭🍸💳 CLUB

C. del Doctor Cortezo, 1 ☎918 694 038

Suspended cages, a disco-ball dance floor, and men and women in daring apparel are staples of this hot nightclub. Whips may be confiscated upon entrance.

➜ From ⓂAnton Martin, walk uphill on Atocha and make a left on C. del Doctor Cortezo. $ Cover €10-14 cover; includes one drink ⏰ Open F-Sa 11pm-daybreak.

EL IMPERFECTO
💳🚭🍸 BAR

Plaza de Matute, 2 ☎91 366 72 11

Despite the name, this is the perfect place in Huertas to grab dessert or a drink. In most bars it is nicer to drink outside weather permitting, but this bar's intricately decorated interior makes it the exception. With a huge variety of cocktails, try the mojito *(€6.50)*. Coffee, hot chocolate, and other non-alcoholic drinks *(€4)*.

➜ From ⓂAnton Martin, walk uphill until you reach Plaza de Matitute. Make a right towards C. de las Huertas. It will be on your right. $ Drinks €4-10.

THE VARIETY TAVERN
🍸 CLUB

C. de las Huertas, 63 ☎91 369 10 46 💻www.varietytavern.com

Wish you could dance like a true Spaniard? On Mondays this tavern offers free dance lessons from 2:30-7:30pm. Incurable case of two left feet? One of the tavern's excellent beers or cocktails *(€4-8)* could make you feel like your name is Fred Astaire.

➜ C. de las Huertas by C. del Fucar. $ Drinks €3-10.

EL SECRETO DE RITA

✈🍸 BAR

C. Echegaray , 10

A restaurant and bar with feminine embellishments in the decor (think pink, crystal, and any other look from your little sister's room), El Secreto de Rita is a peaceful venue in the middle of noisy Huertas for a pre-club drink.

🍴 *From Plaza Santa Ana walk north up C. Echegaray toward Puerta el Sol. It will be on your left.* Ⓢ *Drinks €3-10.* 🕙 *Open M-W 6pm-2am, F-Sa 6pm-2:30am.*

DUBLINERS

✈❄🍸 BAR

C. Espoz y Mina, 7

☎91 522 75 09

Come to this Irish bar for a bucket of beers *(€15),* a huge screen for sporting events, and a good ol' time. Filled with travelers from all over the world, Dubliners has a fun, international vibe and gets packed and crazy during major sports games. Ever seen grown men from around the world attempt their own drunken rendition of "We are the Champions"? You can even go in for the Dubliners' breakfast *(€5.70).*

🍴 *From Puerta del Sol walk straight south down C. Espoz y Mina. Bar will be on your left.* Ⓢ *Drinks €5-10.* 🕙 *Open M-Th 11am-3am, F-Sa until 11am-3:30am, Su 11am-3am.*

the *botellón*

The *al fresco* method of Spanish socializing, the *botellón* has lately gotten a lot of negative attention from older generations of Spaniards. The word basically means a giant, public pregame, in which the youths of Spain buy cheap alcohol, bags of ice, and plastic cups and then drink in the street. Many people believe the tradition arose because of the steep drink prices in bars and the former lack of real open container laws in Spain. However, another possible cause is the Spanish custom of not inviting guests over to the home just to get wasted, which does seem to make pregaming a necessarily public activity. However, the *botellón*'s noisiness and (some would say) moral questionability have led the government to take extreme measures: some cities have considered passing laws forbidding any drink to be consumed in the street.

IREAL

❄🍸 BAR

C. Echegaray, 16

With flashing laser lights, a mixture of Spanish and American pop music, and speedy bartenders, iReal should be on your upcoming playlist. Come here for a drink with friends before going big at one of the nearby *discotecas.*

🍴 *From Plaza Santa Ana walk straight up C. Echegaray towards Puerta del Sol.* Ⓢ *Drinks €5-10.* 🕙 *Open daily 11pm-3am.*

MIDNIGHT ROSE

✆⊗🍸✈ BAR

Plaza de Santa Ana , 14.

☎ 91 701 60 20 ✉midnightrose.es

Feeling elegant? Put on your fancy pants and go to this lounge and restaurant for chic decor and drinks to match. Low lighting, a huge selection of fancy cocktails *(€5-15),* and a swanky setting make this the perfect place for a sumptuous night out. The view from the rooftop terrace is rumored to be among the most beautiful in Madrid, but you'll have to wait in line to see this beauty.

🍴 *Most prominent building in Plaza Santa Ana (lit purple at night).* Ⓢ *Cocktail €5-15.*

nightlife . huertas

VINOTECA BARBECHERA 🍴🍸 BAR, RESTAURANT

C. del Principe, 27 ☎91 420 04 78 🖥www.vinoteca-barbechera.com/

With tables and chairs made out of beer barrels, Vinoteca Barchechera is a fun place to grab a reasonably priced drink while still enjoying the bustle of Plaza Santa Ana. Part of a chain of wine bars, Vinoteca Barbechera also serves a good range of tapas, including rolls stuffed with chorizo, ham or anchovies, smoked tuna and trout, and a range of desserts.

🚏 Plaza Santa Ana. $ Drinks €5-15. ⏰ Open daily 10am-midnight.

VIVA MADRID 🍸 BAR

C. de Manuel Fernández y González, 7 ☎91 429 36 40

Students, travelers, artists, and artists who sometimes travel as students come to party in this crowded and noisy bar, decorated in turn-of-the-century decor. It is rumored that during the 1950s, Ava Gardner and the bullfighter Manolete got handsy here—watch out for some perverted Picasso looking to buy you a drink.

🚏 From [M]Sol, walk towards the museum district on Carrera de San Jeronmino; make a right onto C. de Manuel Fernandez y Gonzalez. $ Beer €4. Other drinks €6. ⏰ Open F noon-1am, Sa noon-2am.

SOL Y SOMBRA 🚭🍸🍴 CLUB

C. de Echegaray, 18 ☎915 428 193

Friendly bouncers, Spanish disco music, and paper flowers at the entrance make this an exhilarating club to back, back, back it up. Although smaller than most of Madrid's *discotecas*, the lively vibe makes Sol seem bigger than it is. All the single ladies should come early to get in for free.

🚏 From [M]Sol, walk towards the museum district on Carrera de San Jeronmino, make a right onto C. de Echegaray. $ Drinks €10-15.

SALA STELLA 🚭🍸🍴 CLUB

Arlabán, 7 ☎91 523 86 54

A local favorite, Sala Stella's '70s disco decor and techno beats make this weekends-only club a stylish all-night spot. Come for the mosaic ceiling tiles, beautiful people, and a packed dance floor.

🚏 From [M]Sevilla, go south down C. de Cedaceros and make a right on Arlabán. $ Cover €10-14; includes one drink. ⏰ Open F-Sa 1am-7am.

madrid

CHUECA

✓ KIYO 🍴🚭🍸🍴 BAR

C. de Barbieri, 15 ☎91 522 01 82

This lime green bar stands out even in the eclectic Chueca district. Come in for their signature kiwi cocktail drink made with fresh crushed kiwi, vodka, and sake *(€7)* served by bartenders passionate about this newly opened spot—just don't be surprised when pop like Lady Gaga is blasting on replay.

🚏 [M]Chueca. Walk straight south down C. Barbieri towards Gran Vía. Discoteca will be on your right. $ Cocktails €5-9. ⏰ Open daily 9pm-3am.

EL51 🍴🚭🍸❄ BAR

C. de Hortaleza, 51

With white leather chairs and purple underlighting, EL51 is steps away from some of Chueca's best nightclubs, and a good stop for classy cocktails and conversation before going out. Get two for one cocktails until 1am.

🚏 [M]Chueca. Make a right on C. Augusto Figuroa, then a right onto C. de Hortaleza. $ Cocktails €8-10. ⏰ Open daily 6pm-3am.

AREIA 🍴🚭🍸🍴 BAR

C. de Hortaleza, 92 ☎91 310 03 07 🖥www.areiachillout.com

With crimson drapes, wood benches, and embroidered pillows and couches, this Moroccan-themed cocktail bar is a romantic place for drinks with a date. Try a margarita or martini served in fancy glassware with fresh fruit.

⚑ ⓂChueca. *Make a right onto C. Augusto Figuroa, then a right on C. de Hortaleza; bar will be on your right.* Ⓢ *Cocktails €6-9.* ⌚ *Open daily 1pm-3am.*

SHORT BUS ◆⊗Ψ◆ BAR
C. Pelayo, 45

The motto of this funky bar is "open your mind and everything else," and we're sure they mean just about everything. With questionable cartoons on the walls and bright colors everywhere, this is a haven for the weird and wonderful.

⚑ ⓂChueca. *Walk straight north up C. Pelayo; bar will be on your left.* Ⓢ *Cocktails €5-10.* ⌚ *Open daily 11am-2pm and 9pm-3am.*

STUDIO 54 ◆⊗Ψ◆ DISCOTECA
C. Barbieri, 7 ☎61 512 68 07 ▪www.studio54madrid.com

Steps away from ⓂChueca, this packed *discoteca* has enough beautiful people, booze, and beats to do the original Studio 54 proud. Filled with a mostly gay clientele dressed to the nines, this place is fun for anybody with an open mind. Women even get in for free sometimes, depending on the time and night.

⚑ ⓂChueca. *Walk straight south down C. Barbieri towards Gran Vía. Discoteca will be on your right.* Ⓢ *Cover €10.* ⌚ *Open Th-Sa 11:30pm-3:30am.*

LONG PLAY ◆⊗Ψ❄ DISCOTECA
Plaza de Vázquez de Mella, 2 ☎91 532 20 66

The DJ at Long Play spins upbeat Lady Gaga, Rihanna, and Spanish pop that gets the packed dance floor moving. Most clubgoers are gay, but great jams and a lively atmosphere make it a fun time for everyone. Go to the upstairs bar for a break from sweaty dancing.

⚑ ⓂGran Vía. *Go north up C. Hortaleza, make a right onto C. de las Infantas, and a left to Plaza de Vázquez de Mella.* Ⓢ *Cover €10, includes one drink. Drinks €8.* ⌚ *Open daily midnight-7am.*

MUSEO CHICOTE ◆⊗Ψ❄ BAR
Gran Vía, 12 ☎91 532 67 37 ▪www.museo-chicote.com

Longtime favorite of artists and writers, this retro-chic cocktail bar maintains its original 1930s design. During the Spanish Civil War, the foreign press came here to wait out the various battles, and during the late Franco era it became a haven for prostitutes. Today this bar continues to make headlines as one of Madrid's most talked about hotspots.

⚑ ⓂGran Vía. *Walk east from the metro stop. Museo Chicote will be on the left side of the street.* Ⓢ *Cocktails €7-9.* ⌚ *Open daily 8am-3am.*

MALASAÑA

▨ LA VÍA LÁCTEA ◆⊗Ψ◆ DISCOTECA
Velarde, 18 ☎91 446 75 81

This *discoteca* dates back to the beginning of the *movida* era and has the bric-a-brac to prove it. It's covered floor to ceiling with pop music memorabilia like album covers, concert posters, photographs, and more. Jams from the '50s through the '80s prove to be a popular mix and continue to delight young, international ravers more than 30 years after the club's inception.

⚑ ⓂTribunal. *Walk north up C. Fuencarral and make a left onto Velarde.* Ⓢ *Cover €8-12.* ⌚ *Open daily 7:30pm-3:30am.*

LA SUECA ◆⊗Ψ❄ COCKTAIL BAR
C. de Hortaleza, 67 ☎91 319 04 87

Great for cocktails and conversations with friends, this Nordic-style modern bar serves Swedish finger food like herring and salmon if you get the munchies. Come early for a calmer atmosphere.

⚑ ⓂChueca. *Make a right onto C. Augusto Figuroa, and another right onto C. Hortaleza.* Ⓢ *Cocktails €5-10.* ⌚ *Open daily 8pm-2am.*

CAFE COMERCIAL

Glorieta de Bilbao, 7

🍴⊗♿Y🍷 CAFE, BAR

☎91 521 56 55

Although it founded in 1887, the cavernous Cafe Commercial has kept up with the times, so look elsewhere for old world charm. Still, this place is an institution, serving up coffee and snacks by day and tapas and mixed drinks by night on marble tabletops surrounded by mirrored walls.

⚥ ⓂBilbao. Ⓢ *Internet access €1.80 per hr. on 2nd fl. Drinks and tapas €3-7.* ⏰ *Open M 7:30am-midnight, Tu-Th 7:30am-1am, F 7:30am-2am, Sa 8:30am-2am, Su 9am-midnight.*

CLUB NASTI

San Vicente Ferrer, 33

🍴⊗Y🍷 DISCOTECA

💻www.nasti.es

Come to Club Nasti on Saturday nights for a hipster heaven of synthesized pop, electro beats, and punk jams. For a lighter touch try Friday nights, when house DJs spin indie rock like The Strokes, The Artic Monkeys, and The Ramones. Small dance floor gets packed as the night progresses, and you might end up wanting to shimmy out of your sweaty plaid shirt to dance only in your Ray Bans. Just remember: what happens at Nasti stays at Nasti.

⚥ ⓂTribunal. *Walk south down C. de Fuencarral and make a right onto San Vicente Ferrer.* Ⓢ *Drinks €8-12.* ⏰ *Open Th 2-5am, F 1-6am, Sa 2-6am.*

CAFE-BOTILLERIA MANUELA

C. de San Vicente Ferrer, 29

🍴⊗Y❄ CAFE, BAR

☎91 531 70 37

Want to pretend like you're in pre-Franco Spain, when the closest thing to a *discoteca* was a rowdy Gypsy flamenco show? With flowers, candles, marble, and mirrors, Cafe-Botilleria Manuela exudes old world charm. Enjoy a coffee or cocktail while playing one of their many available board games. A Chopin sonata or two may lilt over to your table, thanks to impromptu piano playing in this cafe.

⚥ ⓂTribunal. *Walk south down C. de Fuencarral and make a right onto San Vicente Ferrer.* Ⓢ *Cocktails €8-12.* ⏰ *Open daily June-Aug 6pm-2am; Sept-May 4pm-2am.*

ARGÜELLES AND MONCLOA

MI BOHIO

C. Luisa Fernada, 9

🍴⊗Y❄ BAR, CUBAN

☎915 41 58 91

A small bar and Cuban restaurant tucked away near C. de la Princesa, Mi Bohio looks like the place in this neighborhood where everybody knows the locals' names. Since nightlife is slim in this area, head to this watering hole for some drinks and a game on its large TV.

⚥ ⓂVentura Rodriguez. *Walk north up C. de la Princesa and make a left onto C. Luisa Fernanda.* Ⓢ *Beer €1.50. Cocktails €7.50.* ⏰ *Open daily 11am-1am.*

ORANGE CAFE

Serrano Jover, 5

🍴⊗Y❄ BAR, CLUB

💻www.soyorangecafe.com

Orange Cafe is a venue for local rock acts in the evening and a packed dance club later at night. Filled with many tourists and travelers, the club plays mostly American pop music. Ladies should take advantage of free drinks and free entry Wednesday nights between 11:30pm and 12:30am. For a list of concerts and cover charges, consult their website.

⚥ ⓂArgüelles. Ⓢ *Cover €10-15, depending on night.* ⏰ *Open F-Sa 11:30pm-6am.*

arts and culture

With some of the best art museums, public festivals, and performing arts groups in the world, Madrid's arts and culture scene is thriving. From street performers in Retiro Park to Broadway musicals, you can find anything you're looking for in this metropolis. Come for traditional entertainment such as **classic flamenco,** or push the envelope at one of Madrid's contemporary art, music, or theater venues.

CORRIDAS DE TOROS *Bullfights*

Whether you see it as animal torture or as national sport, the spectacle of *la corrida,* or bullfighting, is a cherished Spanish tradition. Although it has its origins in earlier Roman and Moorish practices, today it's considered Spain's sport, and some of the top *toreros*, or bullfighters, are true celebrities in Spain. The bullfight has three stages. First, the *picadores*, lancers on horseback, pierce the bull's neck muscles. Then, assistants thrust decorated darts called *banderillas* into the bull's back to slightly injure and tire it. Finally, the *matador* kills his large opposition with a sword in between the bull's shoulder blades, instantly causing its demise. Animal rights activists call the activities savage, cruel, and violent, but aficionados see it as an art and a sport requiring quick thinking and skill. The best place to see bullfighting in Madrid is at the country's biggest arena, **Plaza de las Ventas,** where you can buy tickets in *sol* or *sombra* (sun or shade) sections. Get your tickets at the arena the Friday and Saturday leading up to the bullfight. *(C. Alcalá 237 ☎913 56 22 00 🖥www.las-ventas.com ↗ ⓂVentas ⏰ Ticket office open 10am-2pm and 5-8pm.)* You'll pay more to sit out of the sun, but either way you'll have a good view of the feverish crowds who cheer on the matador and wave white handkerchiefs called *pañuelos* after a particularly good fight. Rent a seat cushion at the stadium or bring your own, as the stone seats tend to be uncomfortable. Bullfights are held on Sundays and holidays throughout most of the year. During the **Fiesta de San Isidro** in May, fights are held almost every day, and the top bullfighters come face to face with the fiercest bulls.

MUSIC

👍 SOL Y SOMBRA — 💳🚭🍸❄ PUERTA DEL SOL

C. de Echegaray, 18 — ☎91 542 81 93 🖥www.solysombra.name

Located next door to nightlife hub Plaza Santa Ana, this part-nightclub, part-live-music venue has fresh sounds that include live jazz, R and B, and soul. Come for the music and stay for the dancing until the morning. Friendly bouncers and polite club promoters set this place apart from the string of overzealous bars and clubs along C. de Echegaray.

↗ ⓂSol. Walk east toward Plaza de las Cortes and make a right onto C. de Echegaray. $ Cover €5-10. ⏰ Open Tu-Sa 10pm-3:30am.

👍 HONKY TONK — 💳🚭🍸❄ SALAMANCA

C. de Covarrubias, 24 — ☎91 445 68 86 🖥www.clubhonky.com

This lively bar is a hangout for rock fans of all ages. Best on weekends when rowdy crowds keep the place rockin' until early in the morning, Honky Tonk puts its weekly schedule online. Find an act you like, bring that special someone, and spend the evening gettin', gettin', gettin' those honky-tonk blues.

↗ ⓂAlonso Martinez. Go north up C. de Sta. Engracia. Make a left onto C. de Nicasio Gallego and make a right on C. de Covarrubias. $ Cover €5-10. ⏰ Open M-Th 9pm-5am, F-Sa 9pm-5:30am, Su 10pm-5am.

CAFE CENTRAL — 💳🚭🍸❄ EL CENTRO

Plaza del Ángel 10 — ☎91 369 41 43 🖥cafecentralmadrid.com

Cafe Central features classic jazz as well as acts ranging from Latin to fusion. Located conveniently in Plaza del Angel, this venue is the perfect place to watch a great show, then head out to explore Huertas, one of Madrid's nightlife hot spots. Check online for a list of performance times.

➔ Ⓜ Antón Martín. Walk uphill on Atocha and make a right at the 1st traffic light. Plaza del Angel will be the plaza on your left. $ Cover €8-12.

CLAMORES
💳🚭🍸❄ GRAN VÍA

C. de Albuquerque, 14 ☎91 445 79 38 💻www.salaclamores.com

With performances ranging from pop to soul to classical jazz, Clamores has something that's music to everyone's ears.

➔ Ⓜ Bilbao. Walk north up C. de Fuencarral, and make a right on C. de Alburquerque. $ Cover €5-12. ⏰ Check online for showtimes.

CAFE POPULART
💳🚭🍸❄ EL CENTRO

C. Huertas, 22 ☎91 429 84 07 💻www.populart.es

As its name suggests, this cafe is a popular spot for jazz lovers in Madrid. Smoky, small, and intimate, Cafe Populart has small black marble tables where groups gather to listen, gossip, and drink.

➔ Ⓜ Antón Martín. Walk north up C. Leon and make a left onto C. Huertas. $ Cover €5; includes 1 drink. ⏰ Nightly shows 9pm-2am.

FLAMENCO

👍 CARDAMOMO
💳🚭🍸❄ PUERTA DEL SOL

C. de Echegaray, 15 ☎91 369 07 57 💻www.cardamomo.es

For classic flamenco in the middle of a nightlife hub, check out Cardamomo. Offering nightly shows at 10:30pm, Cardamomo is a great place to start an evening of barhopping on C. de Echegaray. Check online for show times, performers, and special events.

➔ Ⓜ Sol. Walk east toward Plaza de las Cortes, and make a right on C. de Echegaray. $ Tickets €10-15. Check with your hostel for discounts. ⏰ Nightly shows 10:30pm.

CASA PATAS
💳🚭🍸❄ EL CENTRO

C. de los Cañizares, 10 ☎91 369 04 96 💻www.casapatas.com

Offering a perfect Spanish experience, Casa Patas holds flamenco shows each night at 9pm and midnight. With unbelievably talented dancers, the shows are fun and fast-paced. Make a reservation in advance and stay afterward for a nice but pricey dinner.

➔ Ⓜ Antón Martín. Walk up Atocha and turn left on C. del Olivar. Casa Patas will be on your right, after Cat's Hostel. $ Tickets €30; includes 1 drink. Dinner €10-30. ⏰ Open M-Th 1-4:30pm and 8pm-midnight, F-Sa 7:30pm-1am.

LAS TABLAS
💳🚭🍸❄ GRAN VÍA

Plaza de España, 9 ☎91 542 05 20 💻www.lastablasmadrid.com

Las Tablas offers authentic flamenco at lower prices than some of the other nearby establishments. Located at the corner of C. Bailen and Cuesta San Vicente, it's the perfect place to stop and experience some Spanish culture after a day shopping along Gran Vía.

➔ Ⓜ Pl. de España. Head to the far end of the plaza. $ Tickets €24; includes 1 drink. ⏰ Shows M-Th 10:30pm, F-Sa at 8pm and 10pm, Su 10:30pm.

THEATER

👍 TEATRO COLISEUM
💳🚭🍸❄ GRAN VÍA

Gran Vía, 78 ☎91 523 82 83

Since Gran Vía is often referred to as the Broadway of Madrid, it makes sense that the sprawling Teatro Coliseum, currently home to the smash hit *Chicago, El Musical*, is located there. One of the biggest theaters in the city, Teatro Coliseum has hosted some of Broadway's best, including *Beauty and the Beast* and *Mamma Mia!*

🚇 [M]Plaza de España. From the plaza walk east down Gran Vía. Theater will be on your left. $ Prices vary depending on seat location. ⏰ Check online for showtimes.

TEATRO ESPAÑOL
AVENIDA DEL ARTE

C. del Principe, 25 ☎91 360 14 80

Funded by Madrid's municipal government, Teatro Español features a range of classic Spanish plays and performances. Watch a show, then relax and have dinner at one of the many restaurants and bars in Plaza Santa Ana.

🚇 [M]Antón Martín. Walk uphill on Atocha. Make a right at the 1st light and keep walking until you see Plaza Santa Ana. $ Tickets €3-20; half-price on W. ⏰ Box office open daily 11:30am-1-:30pm and 5-6pm.

TEATRO HÄAGEN-DAZS CALDERÓN
EL CENTRO

C. de Atocha, 18 ☎91 200 66 17 💻www.teatrohaagen-dazs.es

Named for its recent takeover by **Häagen-Dazs,** this massive theater has a seating capacity of 2000 and features modern musicals, dance, and theater performances. Recent shows include *Cómplices*, *El Musical*, *Rafael Amargo*, *Princesas Del Flamen*, and *Diary of Anne Frank—The Musical.*

🚇 [M]Tirso de Molina. From Tirso, walk straight north up C. del Doctor Cortezo. $ Tickets €25-60. ⏰ Shows begin most evenings at 8pm.

TEATRE BELLAS ARTES
EL CENTRO

Marqués de Casa Riera, 2 ☎91 532 44 37 💻www.teatrobellasartes.es

Putting on 10 plays a year, Teatre Bellas Artes has been a huge cultural center since the 19th century in Madrid. Recent productions includes *Fedra*, *El Rey de Algeciras*, and a performance of Ingmar Bergman's *Autumn Sonata.*

🚇 [M]Banco de España. Walk west down C. de Alcalá and make a left onto Marqués de Casa Riera. $ Tickets €16-25. ⏰ Box office open Tu-Su 11:30am-1:30pm and 5pm-curtain.

FÚTBOL

Fútbol games are a beloved tradition throughout Spain but especially in Madrid. Fans of **Real Madrid** line the streets and pack into bars to watch the match. If the team wins, celebrations continue until early the next morning. For the best fútbol experience, head to Estadio Santiago Bernabeu. Tickets to games in this massive stadium will be steep *(€50-100)* unless you can find discounts. Tickets for **Atlético** and **Getafe,** two other local teams, are a bit cheaper.

ESTADIO SANTIAGO BERNABEU
MODA

Av. Cochina Espina, 1 ☎91 364 22 34 💻www.santiagobernabeu.com, www.realmadrid.com

Site of the 2010 European Final Cup, Estadio Santiago Bernabeu is also home to the Real Madrid fútbol team, named the greatest club of the 20th century by FIFA. Come watch a match and feel the tumultuous energy of the crowd as it cheers on its beloved home team. Come early, as navigating your way through this humongous stadium is almost impossible. During the summer, tours of this massive stadium are available.

🚇 [M]Santiago Bernabeu. Stadium is across the street from the metro station. $ Tours €15, under 14 €10. ⏰ Check online for tour times and dates.

ESTADIO VICENTE CALDERÓN
OUTSKIRTS

Po. de la Virgen del Puerto, 67 ☎91 364 22 34 💻www.clubatleticodemadrid.com

Estadio Vicente Calderón is home to the Atlético fútbol team (red and white stripes). With a storied past that includes European Cups and international recognition, this Madrid-based club participates in the esteemed *Primera* Division of *La Liga.*

🚇 [M]Pirámides or [M]Marqués. $ Price varies. ⏰ Check online for game times and dates.

COLISEUM ALFONSO PÉREZ
OUTSKIRTS

Av. Teresa de Calcuta ☎91 695 97 71

Coliseum Alfonso Pérez is home to the Getafe fútbol team that participates in La

Liga. Although the club was founded in 1946, it was re-established in 1983 after a merger with another local club. Despite offering spectators some great soccer, this club pales in comparison to its local rivals.
[M]Los Espartales. $ Price varies.

FESTIVALS

FIESTAS DE SAN ISIDRO
SALAMANCA
C. de Alcalá, 237
www.esmadrid.com/sanisidro
From mid-May to early June there are bullfights almost every day at **Plaza de las Ventas,** where some of the best bullfighters in Spain come to battle some of the country's fiercest bulls.
⏰ *May 15-early June.*

ORGULLO GAY
www.orgullogay.org
During Orgullo Gay, one of the biggest pride parades in Europe, Madrid explodes with GLBT-friendly celebrations, parades, parties, and more. Chueca, Madrid's gay district, is particularly lively.
⏰ *Last week of June.*

BOLLYMADRID
LA LATINA AND LAVAPIÉS
www.bollymadrid.com
During the first week of June, Lavapiés features Bollywood dance performances, movies, and amazingly cheap Indian food. Get a sampling of Indian food from one of the many food stands surrounding [M]Lavapiés, then watch a Bollywood movie or see a dance show. Check online for dance performance venues and times.
[M] Lavapies. $ Performances free. Food €1-5. ⏰ *1st week of June.*

MADRID CARNIVAL
The week before Lent, Madrid celebrates with a Mardi Gras-esque spectacle of parades, costume parties, and extravagant masks. There is also a tradition called "The Burial of the Sardine," in which participants decked out in black cloaks and hats walk through the streets with a coffin containing an effigy of a dead sardine. Don't understand? Neither do we, but it's seriously awesome.
⏰ *Feb 18-25, 2011.*

FIESTAS DE SAN LORENZO
www.fiestasdesanlorenzo.com
August is the traditional month for festivals in Madrid. During the Fiestas de San Lorenzo in mid-August, *madrileños* celebrate with dancing in the streets, processions, and outdoor concerts. Check online for specific activities and times.
⏰ *Varies.*

DOS DE MAYO
MALASAÑA
On May 2, 1808, the people of Madrid rose up against Joseph Bonaparte, Napoleon's brother, to fight for their freedom against French rule. The battle began the six-year War of Independence. Today, *madrileños* celebrate that battle in Malasaña.
⏰ *May 2.*

NOCHEVIEJA
PUERTA DEL SOL
To ring in the new year, hundreds of *madrileños* gather at Madrid's version of Times Square, Puerta del Sol, to watch the ball drop from the clock tower. Instead of counting down, the clock chimes 12 times to represent good fortune for the 12 upcoming months of the year. According to tradition, you're supposed to eat a grape at every toll and drink at midnight.
[M]Sol. ⏰ *Dec 31.*

THREE KINGS PROCESSION EL CENTRO

During the procession of Three Kings in Madrid, around 30 carriages filled with 7000kg of sweets proceed from Retiro Park to Plaza Mayor via Sol. During the procession the "Kings" and various helpers shower sweets on the huge crowds who gather on the streets of Madrid, and local establishments host theatrical antics for children.

⏰ *Jan 5.*

MADRID EN DANZA

From mid-March to late April, Madrid plays host to a flurry of dance performances from around the world. From ballet to modern dance, there's something for everyone at this festival that celebrates movement, not Tony Danza.

$ *Tickets vary by venue.* ⏰ *March-April.*

shopping

Madrid has enough flea markets, department stores, upscale boutiques, and chain stores to satisfy the addictions of the most serious shopaholics. Each street radiating north from **Puerta del Sol** is filled with clothing, accessories, and souvenir shops. **Gran Vía**, **Plaza Mayor**, and Northwest Madrid near **C. de la Princesa** are shopping meccas with an eclectic mix of options perfect for retail therapy. The **Salamanca** district northeast of the center is home to the exclusive and the expensive, acting as the Rodeo Drive of Madrid by housing Burberry, Gucci, Prada, and other stores your backpacking self can't afford.

UPSCALE

ABC SERRANO SALAMANCA

Serrano, 61 ☎91 577 50 31 www.abcserrano.com

This small complex of upscale boutiques and chain stores sells high fashion, jewelry, cosmetics, art, housewares, and more to Spaniards and tourists willing to shell out some serious cash. Set in what used to be a *Madrileno* newspaper office, ABC Serrano is home to cafes and restaurants for pick-me-up snacks during your epic day of materialism.

[M]Serrano. Walk north; ABC will be on your left. ⏰ *Varies; most stores open M-Sa 10am-midnight.*

EL CORTE INGLÉS EL CENTRO

Preciados, 3 ☎91 379 80 00 www.elcorteingles.es

Selling everything from clothing, shoes, and accessories to housewares, books, electronics, and perfumes, El Corte Inglés is almost like the illegitimate Spanish lovechild of a Macy's and a Borders. Steps away from Puerta del Sol, the flagship store of this large chain spans multiple buildings, harboring enough options to exhaust even the most tireless international shopaholic.

[M]Sol. ⏰ *Open M-Sa 10am-10pm; some locations Su noon-8pm.*

ZARA ARGUELLES

Princesa, 45 ☎91 541 09 02 www.zara.es

One of the most popular chain stores in Madrid, there is at least one Zara in every major shopping district inside of the city limits. With stylish and professional outfits at reasonable prices, Zara is perfect for acquiring modern European threads to hit the clubs with at night. Blend into the native population by toting your blue Zara bag during your trip.

[M]Arguelles. ⏰ *Open M-Sa 10am-8:30pm.*

EL RASTRO

If you're in town on a Sunday, don't miss El Rastro, the biggest and most frantic flea market in Madrid. Beginning at **Pl. Cascorro** off **C. Toledo** and ending at the bottom of **C. Ribera de Cortidores,** rows of vendors in makeshift stalls set up outside permanent shops to pawn off their goods. From modern art and handmade trinkets to international clothing and knock-off jewelry and fragrance, *Let's Go* imagines you can pretty much buy anything your heart desires at this Spanish bazaar. Locals and tourists swarm this market, so come in the early hours to beat the heat and avoid the crowds from 9am-3pm. Buyers beware: this market is notorious for **pickpockets.** Stay alert, don't bring anything flashy, and guard your valuables. Always keep your hand on your bag while walking. After haggling for that used paella recipe book, drift to the **Plaza Mayor** for lunch and more shopping or the **Plaza de Tirso de Molina** for cheerful flower stands and fountains.

BOUTIQUES

◙ OH MY GOD   ✦ SALAMANCA

C. Serrano, 70   ☎91 435 44 12◙www.ohmygod.com.es
Like, oh my God! Come to Oh my GOd boutique in the upscale Salamanca district for funky, chunky, one-of-a-kind jewelry pieces. While you may not be able to take your eyes off these fancy baubles, keep in mind that they're about 3 times as much as a backpacker's daily budget. Internet buyers beware: make sure to type in the web address correctly or run the risk of ending up at a ◙**Russian bride site.**
⚑ Ⓜ*Serrano. Walk north up Serrano street.* ⓢ *Items from around €100.* ⌚ *M-Sa 10:30am-8pm.*

POÈTE   SALAMANCA

C. de Castelló, 32   ☎91 577 60 62 ◙www.tiendapoete.com
Come to the Poète for flirty and feminine tops, skirts, and dresses. Covered in pinks, yellows, and various flower prints, this is very much a girly-girl's boutique wo-manned by a friendly staff.
⚑ Ⓜ*Velázquez. Go east on C. de Goya and make a left onto C. de Castelló.* ⓢ *Clothing €40-200.*

MARKETPLACES

PLAZA DE SAN MIGUEL   ✦⊗⚑✿ EL CENTRO

Plaza de San Miguel, 2   ◙www.mercadodesanmiguel.es
This almost-open-air market sells fine meats, cheeses, flowers, wine, and miscellaneous gifts for an arm and a leg. The partially indoor A/C makes for a beautiful place to have a glass of wine and enjoy blue skies away from Madrid's summer heat, but inside the vibe is a bit like a Whole Foods, with produce that's every bit as expensive.
⚑ *At the Pl. de San Miguel, off the northwest corner of Pl. Mayor right beside the cerveceria.* ⓢ *Prices vary.* ⌚ *Open M-W 10am-midnight, Th-Sa 10am-2am, Su 10am-midnight.*

CUESTA DE MOYANO   ⊛⊗ AVENIDA DEL ARTE

If you're looking for Spanish books, head to Cuesta de Moyano, the book marketplace on the southern edge of Retiro Park. Around 30 stalls set up shop every Sunday to sell secondhand finds and antique books. Come and browse the stalls to find some Spanish first editions or that new Clive Cussler book in foreign print before heading to an afternoon picnic in the park.
⚑ Ⓜ*Atocha. Cross Paseo del Prado and walk uphill. Retiro will be on your left.* ⌚ *Open Su 10:30am-sunset.*

BOOKS

Finding English books in Madrid can be difficult unless you're willing to pay a bundle. If you're looking for a specific English title, the mega-chain book stores like **El Corte Inglés** or **Casa del Libro** will be your best bets. If you're just browsing, check out some of the smaller bookstores located throughout **C. Huertas,** or at the **Cuesta de Moyano** Sunday marketplace.

👍 CASA DEL LIBRO — 💳⊗❄ GRAN VÍA

Gran Vía, 29 — ☎90 202 64 02 💻www.casadellibra.com

This sprawling bookstore is your best bet for English titles. With three floors and multiple sections, Casa del Libro has the latest bestsellers and hundreds of titles. As Spain's largest bookstore chain, it also has locations nearby at C. Fuencarral, 119 and C. Alcalá, 96.

⇄ [M]Gran Vía. Walk west down Gran Vía. $ Prices vary. ⏰ Open M-Sa 9:30am-9:30pm, Su 11am-9pm.

BERKANA LIBRERIA GAY Y LESBIANA — 💳⊗❄▼ CHUECA

C. Hortalez, 64 — ☎91 522 55 99 💻www.libreriaberkana.com

This gay and lesbian bookstore in the heart of Chueca is an excellent source of information about GLBT events and parties throughout Madrid. Some titles focus on sexuality, but there are other options including poetry, religion, education, and even GLBT-friendly comics.

⇄ [M]Chueca. From the Chueca stop, turn around, make a right on C. Augusto Figuroa, and make another right onto C. Hortaleza. $ Prices vary. ⏰ Open M-F 10am-9pm, Sa 11:30am-9pm, Su noon-2pm and 5-9pm.

ALTAIR — 💳⊗❄ GRAN VÍA

C. Gaztambide, 31 — ☎91 543 53 00 💻www.altair.es

If you're looking for excellent travel guides, Altair is your best bet. This travel bookstore with titles of locations from all over the world has a friendly and knowledgeable staff.

⇄ [M]Argüelles. Walk north up C. de Hilarion Eslava, make a right onto C. de Melendez Valdes, and make a left onto C. Gaztambide. $ Prices vary. ⏰ Open M-F 10am-2pm and 4:30-8:30pm, Sa 10:30am-2:30pm.

EL CORTE INGLÉS — 💳⊗❄ EL CENTRO

Preciados, 2 — ☎ 91 379 80 00 💻www.elcorteingles.es

Conveniently located in the middle of Puerta del Sol, El Corte Inglés, a giant department store, holds tons of books primarily in Spanish. During the summer, the store often puts stalls of discounted books along its exterior.

⇄ [M]Sol. Bookstore is facing the middle of Sol right by the massive guy-on-a-horse statue. $ Prices vary. ⏰ Open daily 10am-10pm.

essentials

PRACTICALITIES

- **TOURIST OFFICES:** Start off at the **Madrid Tourism Centre** in Plaza Mayor *(☎91 588 16 36 💻www.esmadrid.com),* where you can get city and transit maps as well as suggestions for activities, food, and accommodations. English and French are spoken at most tourist offices located throughout the city and can be incredibly helpful in planning your day. Additional tourist offices and stands are all over the city, labeled by large orange stands with exclamation marks: **Calle del Duque de Medinaceli 2** *(☎91 429 49 51 ⏰ Open M-Sat 9:30am-8:30pm, Su and holidays 9:30am-2pm);* **Estacion de Atocha** *(☎91 528 46 30 ⏰ Open Mon-Sat*

9:30am-8:30pm, Su and holidays 9:30am-2pm); **Madrid-Barajas Airport Terminal 1** *(☎91 305 86 56)* and **Terminal 4** *(☎90 210 00 07 ⏰ Open daily 9:30am-8:30pm).* Also, there is a tourist office at the **train station** *(☎91 315 99 76 ⏰ Open M-Sa 8am-8pm, Su 9am-2pm).*

- **TOURS:** Different themed tours leave regularly from the Madrid Tourism Centre. For dates, times, and more information visit 💻www.esmadrid.com. Also, many youth hostels host tapas tours, pub crawls, and walking tours for reasonable prices and are great for meeting people and finding awesome food in the process. Check out www.toursnonstop.com for tours *($€10 tapas and pub tours).* **LeTango Tours** is run by a Spanish-American husband-wife team, with tours that take you to local bars, give you fun city facts, and explain Spanish traditions *(☎91 369 47 52 💻www.letango.com).* Run by historian and writer Stephen Drake-Jones, the **Wellington Society** offers different themed tours of Madrid and day excursions to places like Toledo and Segovia *(☎609 143 203 💻www.wellsoc.org).* Another option is **Madrid Vision** *(☎917 79 18 88 💻www.madridvision.es),* which runs the double-decker red buses that you see throughout the city. You can choose between the *historicó* and *moderno* routes, each making 15-20 stops throughout the city *($ €17; certain discounts available online).*
- **CURRENCY EXCHANGE:** The easiest place to change your money is the airport. You can also change your money in stations in both Puerta Del Sol and Gran Vía (see booths that say "change"), but try to use these as a last resort, as rates are bad and commission charges are high. Most hostals and hotels will also be able to change your money, with rates varying by location. Another option is **Banco Santader Central Hispano,** which charges €12-15 commission on non-American Express Travelers Cheques *(max. exchange €300).* Wherever you go, be sure to bring your passport as identification.
- **LUGGAGE STORAGE:** Store your luggage at the **Aeropuerto Internacional de Barajas** (☎913 936 805 $ 1-day €3.70; 2-15 days €4.78 per day. ⏰ Open 24hr.) or at the **bus station** *($ €1.40 per bag per day; open M-F 6:30am-10:30pm, Sa 6:30am-3pm).*
- **POST OFFICES:** Buy stamps (*sellos*) from a post office or tobacco stand (yellow/brown sign). Madrid's **central post office** is at Plaza de Cibeles *(☎91 523 06 94; 90 219 71 97 ⏰ Open M-F 8:30am-9:30pm).* Post boxes are usually yellow with one slot for "Madrid" and another for everywhere else.
- **POSTAL CODE:** 28008

EMERGENCY!

- **EMERGENCY NUMBERS:** In case of a **medical emergency**, dial ☎061 or ☎112. For non-emergency medical concerns, go to **Unidad Medica Angloamericana,** which has English speaking personnel on duty by appointment. *(C. del Conde de Aranda, 1, 1st fl. ☎914 35 18 23 ⏰ Open M-F 9am-8pm, Sa 10am-1pm.)*
- **POLICE: Servicio de Atención al Turista Extrarijero** (SATE) are police who deal exclusively with tourists and help with contacting embassies, reporting crimes, and canceling credit cards. *(C. Legantos, 19 ☎91 548 85 27; 90 210 21 12 ⏰ Open daily 9am-midnight.)*

GETTING THERE ✈

By Plane

All flights come in through the **Aeropuerto Internacional de Barajas** *(☎902 404 704 💻www.aena.es).* The **Barajas** metro stop connects the airport to the rest of Madrid. *($ €2.)* The **Bus-Aeropeurto 200** leaves from the national terminal T2 and runs to the city center through the **Avenida de America** metro station *(☎902 50 78 50 ⏰ Every 15min. 5:20am-11:30pm).* **Taxis** are readily available outside of the airport, and it takes about 30min. and €35 to get to the city center. For more information on ground transport, check out 💻**www.metromadrid.es.**

By Train

Trains *(☎902 24 02 02 💻www.refe.es)* from northern Europe, France, and **Barcelona** (including the high-speed AVE train) arrive on the north side of the city at Chamartin. Trains to and from the south of Spain and Portugal use **Atocha.** Buy tickets at the station or online. There is a **RENFE** information office located in the main terminal. *(☎902 24 02 02 ⏰ Open daily 7am-7pm.)*

By Bus

AVE trains offer high-speed service to southern Spain, including **Barcelona** and **Sevilla.** *(Estacion Chamartin, C. Agustin de Foxa ☎91 300 69 69; 91 506 63 29.)* Be sure to keep your ticket, or you won't be able to pass the turnstiles. Call **RENFE** for both international destinations and domestic travel. *(☎90 224 34 02 for international destinations; 902 24 02 02 for domestic.)* Ticket windows open daily 6:30am-9pm; buy tickets at vending machines outside of these hours. Check online for prices, as plane tickets may be cheaper depending on season. If you prefer four wheels, any private bus company runs through Madrid, and most pass through **Estación Sur de Autobuses** *(C. Mendez Alvaro ☎914 68 42 00 💻www.estacionautobusesmadrid.com. ℹ Info booth open daily 6:30am-1am).* National destinations include **Algeciras, Alicante, Oviedo,** and **Toledo,** among others. Inquire at the station, online, or by phone for specific information on routes and schedules.

GETTING AROUND

By Metro

The Madrid metro system is by far the easiest, cheapest way to get you almost anywhere you need to go in the city. Service begins at 6am (7am on Sunday) and ends around 1:30am. Try to avoid rush hours at 8-10am, 1-2pm, and 4-6pm. The fare is **€1** for a one way trip. If you're making multiple trips, you can save by purchasing a combined **10-in-one metrobus ticket** for €7. Madrid's metro system is clean, safe and recently renovated. Trains run frequently, and green timers above most platforms show increments of five minutes or less between trains. Be sure to grab a **free metro map** (available at any ticket booth or tourist office). **Abonos mensuales,** or monthly passes, grant unlimited travel within the city proper for €46, while **abonos turisticos** (tourist passes) come in various lengths (1, 2, 3, 4, or 7 days) and sell for €5-24 at the metro stations or online. For metro information go to 💻**www.metromadrid.es**.

By Bus

Buses cover areas that are inaccessible by metro and are a great way to see the city. Try the nifty handout "Visiting the Downtown on Public Transport" to find routes and stops. *($ Free at any tourist office or downloadable at 💻www.madrid.org.)* Tickets for the bus and metro are interchangeable. From midnight-6am, the *Búho* (owl), or night bus, travels from Pl. de Cibeles and other marked routes along the outskirts of the city. *(M-Th every 30min. midnight-3am, every 1hr. 3-6am; F-Sa every 20min; Su every 30 min. midnight-3am.)* These buses, marked on the essential **Red de Autobuses Nocturnos** *(available at any tourist office)* run along 26 lines covering regular daytime routes. For info, call **Empresa Municipal de Transportes** *(☎902 50 78 50 💻www.emtmadrid.es).* **Estacion Sur** *(C. Mendez Alvaro ☎91 468 42 00)* covers mainly southern and southeastern destinations out of Madrid such as **Granada, Sevilla, Málaga,** and **Valencia.** Go to 💻**avanzabus.com** for timetables and routes.

By Taxi

Registered Madrid taxis are black or white and have red bands and small insignias of a bear and madroño tree (symbols of Madrid). Hail them in the street or at taxi stands all over the city. A green light means they're free. The fare starts at €1.75 and increases by €1 every kilometer thereafter. To call a city taxi, dial ☎91 447 51 80.

By Moped and Bike

You can hire a bike from **Karacol Sport** for €18 per day. *(C. Tortosa 8 ☎91 539 9733 **i** Cash deposit of €50 and photocopy of your passport required ◼www.karacol.com ☒ Open M-W 10:30am-3pm and 5-8pm, Th 10:30am-3pm and 5-9:30pm, F-Su 10:30am 3pm and 5-8pm.)* Biking in the city is ill-advised, but Casa de Campo and Dehesa de la Villa both have easily navigable bike trails. **Motocicletas Antonio Castro** rents mopeds from €23-95 per day including unlimited mileage and insurance, but you'll need your own lock and helmet—you just need to be 25 years old and have a driver's license for motorcycles. *(C. Clara del Rey, 17 ☎914 1300 47 ◼www.blafermotos.com ☒ Open M-F 8am-6pm, Sa 10am-1:30pm.)*

madrid

CENTRAL SPAIN

Anywhere that's most famous for its monasteries might sound pretty boring, but central Spain is tricky like that—from pubs named after museums to festivals named for saints, nothing is ever as lame as it sounds. Sure, they've traded in their discotecas for a bubbling bar culture and left Lady Gaga and 50 Cent for El Greco and *los reyes católicos*, but this is also the land of Salamanca, one of the three best university towns in Spain. It's where Jewish, Muslim, and Christian cultures have intersected for centuries—we all know those interactions were certainly not "boring"— as well as a place where nuns make *mazapán* and religious holidays make people go nuts. In short, it's a place that's just as quintessentially Spanish as those bigger, more bragged-about cities. Maybe even more so.

greatest hits

- **MONK-EY BUSINESS.** Who knew that cells could be so swanky? The monasteries in Toledo and San Lorenzo de El Escorial are seriously tricked out, with palaces, pantheons, and intricate carvings.
- **GOLD DIGGERS.** Salamanca is called Spain's "Golden City," but it isn't shaped from the shiny stuff. Instead, it's carved out of golden Villamayor stone.

student life

Central Spain lacks the bass-thumping beats of Madrid's *discotecas*, but give your eardrums a rest and give your eyes a workout. San Lorenzo and Toledo offer beautiful sights, from El Greco's famous paintings to views of the austere royal Monasterio. If people are more your thing than inaminate objects, head to Salamanca, one of the three best university towns in Spain. The University has been around since 1218, and it's got the battle scars of a survivor (bull's blood stains left by graduates—we're serious). The bars are better here than the *discotecas*, so order up a beer at the **British Museum** (n.b. not a museum) and prove to the local intellectuals that you know a thing or two about Don Quijote.

toledo ☎925

Known as the "Ciudad de las Tres Culturas" (City of Three Cultures), this small town was the medieval home of **Muslims, Jews,** and **Christians.** El Greco's hometown has remained largely unchanged since the 16th century, when it inspired his much admired *View of Toledo* featured in New York's Metropolitan Museum of Art. Today, you can walk around winding cobblestone streets to take in beautiful Gothic sights and views of the surrounding river. The city center has become rather commercial, filled with souvenir shops selling knight's armor, Damascene swords (à la *Lord of the Rings*) and **marzipan**, a sweet almond treat.

ORIENTATION

Toledo is a web of cobblestone streets that fork at every opportunity. A wrong turn is almost inevitable, but the entire city is very walkable, so you'll find yourself back on the right path in no time. The **Monasterio de S. Juan de los Reyes** on the western edge of the city, the **Alcázar** on the eastern side, and the central **Catedral** are can't-miss stops on any tour of Toledo. To get your bearings straight, start your trip with the **Zocotren** tour which leaves from **Plaza Zocodover** and takes you on a ride through some of Toledo's most important sights *(☎925 23 22 10 💻www.zocotren.com $ €4.25, children €1.85, group €2.50)*. The train also takes you slightly outside the center of the city across the river for a panoramic view.

ACCOMMODATIONS

ALBERGUE JUVENIL CASTILLO DE SAN SERVANDO — HOSTEL ❶

Subida al Castillo ☎925 22 45 54

This awesome hostel is in a castle. Enough said. One of the dominant features on the Toledo skyline, this fortress once gave refuge to El Cid Campeador. Located an uphill 10-15min. walk away from the middle of town, this HI hostel features spacious common rooms, a pool with a panoramic view of the center of Toledo in the summer, and the cheapest accommodation prices in the city. Book way in advance, as spaces tend to fill up quickly.

*➔ From the city center, cross the river using Puente Acantara. You'll be able to see it from afar. It's the only castle in the area. **i** Wi-Fi €1 per hr. $ Dorms €10.40, ages over 30 €13.65. ⏰ Lockout 11am-2pm.*

HOTEL IMPERIO — BUDGET HOTEL ❸

C. Cadenas, 5 ☎925 22 76 50 💻www.hotelimperio.es

Long a budget favorite in Toledo, the Hotel Imperio has basic hotel amenities, friendly service, and an excellent location. Just north of the Catedral and the

Alcázar, Hotel Imperio is also next door to some of Toledo's best restaurants and bars along **Pícaro Cafe-Teatro,** one of the few nightlife locations in the heart of the city. Rooms feature large, comfortable beds and sparkling clean ensuite bathrooms with temperamental showerheads.

➡ From the Catedral walk straight north. Hotel is located right beside the Iglesia S. Nicolas. ℹ Free Wi-Fi in lobby. $ Singles €30; doubles €45, with extra bed €60. Groups of 3 or more check availability and prices online. ⏰ Reception 24hr.

LA POSADA DE MANOLO 💳🚭📶❄ HOSTAL [4]

Calle de Sixto Ramón Parro, 8 ☎925 282 250 💻www.laposadademanolo.com

Located directly next door to the Catedral, La Posada de Monolo is a quaint hostal complete with exposed brick finishings and rustic wooden doors. Filled with medieval cottage decor (including old school wooden tools on the wall), this spacious hostal is the perfect place to rest after a day of conquest and pillaging—or at least exploring Toledo.

➡ Located in a small street directly southeast of the cathedral. $ Singles €42; doubles €66. ⏰ Reception 24hr.

HOSTAL PALACIO 💳🚭📶❄ HOSTAL [3]

Calle de Alfonso X 'El Sabio', 3 ☎925 215 972 💻www.hostalpalacios.net

With comfortable beds and yellow walls, the rooms in this conveniently located hostal look like the guestroom in someone's house. Adjacent to the hostal is Restaurante Palacio, where you can choose from Iberian or other European fare.

➡ From the cathedral, walk northeast up C. Nuncio Viejo. ℹ Breakfast €2. $ Singles €30-35; doubles €50. ⏰ Reception 24hr.

SIGHTS 👁

👍 ANTIGUOS INSTRUMENTOS DE TORTURA ♿🚭❄ EXHIBITION

C. Alfonso XII ☎92 525 38 56

With nooses, wooden cages, and crushing 👍**wheels** galore, this exhibition of ancient torture devices is an eerie but interesting glimpse into the Spanish Inquisition and medieval justice. Wooden cases seem tame next to a head crusher, thumbscrews, heretic's fork, scold's bridle, and chastity belt. The interrogation chair, a seat made entirely of iron spikes that can also be warmed up via fire underneath, is particularly interesting and morbid. Fun fact: modern neurology shows that after being cut off, a severed head realizes what has happened for several seconds afterward. Talk about a retrospective.

➡ Just south of Iglesia de S. Roman. $ €4, children €3, families €12. ⏰ Open daily 9am-8pm.

👍 MONASTERIO DE LOS REYES ♿🚭❄ MONASTERY

Av. Constitución 284 ☎92 522 38 02

Located on the western edge of the city, the Monasterio de los Reyes was commissioned by Ferdinand and Isabella to commemorate their victory in the Battle of Toro over the Portuguese. This beautiful church has intricate stone details and is largely empty and peaceful. Go to the second floor for a bird's eye view of the adjacent cloister in the shape of a square surrounding a beautiful garden filled with orange trees and colorful flowers.

➡ Located along the western edge of the city center. Follow the signs. $ €2.30, students €2. ⏰ Open daily 10am-6:45pm.

IGLESIA DE SAN ILDEFONSO ♿🚭 CHURCH

Plaza del Padre Juan de Mariana, 1 ☎925 251 507

Advertised as the "View from Heaven," the lookout point from the top of Iglesia de San Ildefonso features some truly spectacular panoramic views that include the Cathedral and Alcázar. Fair warning: you'll have to hike up quite a few stairs to get to this **Kodak** moment, but the view from the top makes it worth it.

From the Catedral, go north up C. del Nuncio Viejo. i If touring times happen to coincide with mass or other religious ceremonies, the latter takes precedence. $ €2.30, students €2. ⏰ Open daily May-Aug 10am-6:45pm; Sept-Apr 10am-5:45pm.

MUSEO DE SANTA CRUZ — MUSEUM

C. Miguel de Cervantes, 4 ☎925 221 036 www.jccm.es

Built in 1504, the Museo de Santa Cruz is fittingly laid out in the shape of a cross. Inside, it holds a collection of impressive embroidered tapestries, a handful of El Greco paintings, and portraits of Spanish historical figures. It's a nice break from the beating Toledo sun during summertime, and the basement holding remains from local archaeological digs is open intermittently.

Right next to Plaza Zocodover. $ Free. ⏰ Open M-Sa 10am-6pm, Su 10am-2pm.

HOSPITAL DE TAVERNA — MUSEUM

C. Cardenal Taverna, 2 ☎925 220 451

Don't be alarmed by the name; Hospital de Taverna is a converted 16th-century Greco-Roman palace, not an actual hospital. The private art collection on display features five paintings by El Greco: The **Holy Family, The Baptism of Christ,** and portraits of St. Francis, St. Peter, and Cardinal Taverna. Also in the collection is Ribera's **The Bearded Woman.** On the way back, sit and enjoy a *horchata* or *limon* in the adjacent Paseo de Merchan (La Vega), a park with various cafes and ice cream stands.

Directly north of the city wall. From Puerta Nueva de Bisagra, go north up C. de Cardenal Taverna. ⏰ Open daily 10am-1:30pm and 3-5:30pm.

PUENTE DE ALCÁNTARA — BRIDGE

East of Museo de Santa Cruz

Originally Roman, this footbridge with two half point arches leads you to the Castillo de San Servando from the center of Toledo. Walk across this bridge for some of the best panoramic views of Toledo, and take a quick pic between the gorgeous skyline and lush river.

Located on the eastern edge of the city, east of Museo de Santa Cruz. Follow the stairs down. $ Free. ⏰ Open 24hr.

ALCÁZAR — PALACE, MUSEUM

C. General Moscardo, 4 ☎92 522 16 73

Dominating the Toledo skyline, the Alcázar was built in the 3rd century and served as a Roman and later Visigoth palace. At the beginning of the Spanish Civil War, it became famous as the site of a 70-day siege that almost destroyed it. After sustaining several fires, it was reconstructed in the fifties. Today, it houses the Army Museum, which exhibits items such as the electronic equipment used during the siege, models of the former Alcázar, and photographs taken during battle. It is closed indefinitely for renovation.

It's a 2min. walk from Plaza Zocodover (you can see it from the plaza). $ €4, under 9 free. ⏰ Open Tu-Su 9:30am-2pm.

FOOD

Food in Toledo tends to be expensive, but there are some great dining options smattered throughout the many tourist traps. Go to a cafe for breakfast or a mid-afternoon coffee break from sightseeing. Try some *mazapán* from one of the dozens of bakeries lining each street. Traditionally made by nuns, *mazapán* is a sweet treat made from almond paste and sugar that comes in a huge variety of shapes and sizes, from cookies to nuggets to colossal chunks. For a huge range of choices, stop by **Plaza Zocodover** on the eastern side of the center or **Plaza Mayor** right beside the Catedral.

DAR AL-CHAI
◆⊗(( ))♈✱☾ CAFE ❷

Pl. de Barrio Nueva, 6   ☎925 225 625 ▉www.daraichai.com

Complete with Moorish arches, colorful tiling, and floor cushions, this cafe is the perfect place to relax and grab a specialty tea before heading to one of Toledo's sights. Try one of the fruit, flora, or *con leche* teas, or go for a specialty coffee. If you have the munchies, try one of the crepes served with fruity syrup toppings and mounds of whipped cream. If you're not in the mood for something sweet, try one of their many *tostas*. Great for breakfast or an afternoon snack.

⚑ *From Monasterio de S. Juan de los Reyes, walk south down C. de los Reyes Católicos. Plaza will be in a nook on your left.* Ⓢ *Coffee and tea €2-4. Crepes and tostas €4-6.* ☒ *Open M-Th 9:30am-10pm, F-Sa 4pm-1am, Su 9:30am-10pm.*

CAFE DEL FIN
◆⊗(( ))♈✱☾ CAFE ❷

C. Taller del Moro 1   ☎925 251 052 ▉www.cafedelfin.com

With bright colors and dim candle lighting, Cafe del Fin is a fun hangout and a solid place to grab lunch or a coffee. Go for a typical Spanish dish, or try one of the many cocktails or coffees.

⚑ *From the monastery walk straight east down C. del Angel. Make a right onto C. Taller del Moro.* Ⓢ *Salads €8.50-€10. Entrees €12-14. Raciones €8-10.* ☒ *Open M-W 8:30am-6pm, Th 8:30am-1am, F 8:30am-2am, Sa 9am-2am, Su 9am-12:30am.*

LA FLOR DE LA ESQUINA
◆⊗♈✱☾ SPANISH ❸

Plaza Juan de Mariana, 2   ☎925 253 801

With white-washed fence decor and a handwritten chalk menu on the wall, this adorable tapas restaurant is the perfect place to grab a drink and mid-afternoon snack. The menu includes classic Spanish food and a large selection of tapas. Come for a break after touring nearby Iglesia de Los Jesuitas.

⚑ *With your back to Iglesia de Los Jesuitas, the restaurant will be on your left.* Ⓢ *Entrees €5-15.* ☒ *Open daily noon-4pm and 6:30pm-midnight.*

TABERNA ALFERITOS 24
◆⊗♈✱☾ SPANISH ❸

C. Alfertos, 24   ☎902 106 577 ▉www.alfileritos24.com

Come to this sprawling restaurant for tapas on the first floor or dinner in the upscale restaurant upstairs. White stone decor, sleek wooden furniture, and low lighting make for a fun and casual tapas location by day and romantic date location by night. For a delicious lunch, try the marinated chicken sautéed with assorted vegetables.

⚑ *From Iglesia S. Nicoles, make a left onto C. Alfertos. Restaurant will be on your left.* Ⓢ *Entrees €5-15.* ☒ *Open M-Sa 10am-1am, Su 10am-midnight.*

NIGHTLIFE

Toledo's nightlife pales in comparison to Madrid's 24/7 party-animal lifestyle, but you can still find some good bars to sit, relax, and enjoy the medieval atmosphere.

PICARO CAFE TEATRO
◆⊗(( ))♈✱☾ COCKTAIL BAR

C. Cadenas, 6   ☎627 526 076 ▉www.picarocafeteatro.com

Across the street from Hotel Imperio, Picaro Cafe Teatro is an unassuming but undeniably solid choice for a night out on the town. And we mean solid in both ways: with wood-and-metal benches, this cocktail bar almost looks like a warehouse at night, but as the evening progresses, it fills up with good people and good music. Colorful lights mix with abstract art to create a mysterious but lively atmosphere, especially when guest DJs spin new sets.

⚑ *From the Catedral, walk straight north up C. de Tornerias. Veer right onto C. del Cornercio. Make a left onto C. de la Plata, and then a right onto C. Cadenas.* Ⓢ *Mixed drinks €4-6.* ☒ *Open M-F 4pm-3am, Sa-Su 4pm-6am.*

central spain (side tab)

LA TABERNA DE LIVINGSTON COCKTAIL BAR [2]

C. Alfertios, 4

With zebra-print chairs, grayscale pictures of Africa, hunting memorabilia, and British posters, this place screams colonialism. Despite the decor, the establishment is a good stop for a coffee or cocktail after exploring Toledo—and a once-in-a-lifetime opportunity to pester everyone on the premises with, "Dr. Livingston, I presume?" Try the mojito, strawberry daiquiri, or cosmo *(€6)*.

From Iglesia S. Nicoles, make a left onto C. Alfertos. $ Salads and entrees €7-10. Drinks €4-6. ⏰ Open Tu-F 10am-2:30am, Sa-Su noon-2:30am.

ARTS AND CULTURE

CIRCULO DE ARTE TOLEDO

Pl. de San Vicente, 2 ☎925 214 329 www.circuloartetoledo.org

This venue is a cafe, art gallery, and concert hall all rolled into one. With Moorish decorative arches, white brick, and modern paintings covering the walls, it's a cool place to grab a hot or cold coffee. Try the Cafe Bombon Creme *(€2.50)*, a sweet coffee served in a large shot glass with different strata of delights: chocolate syrup on the bottom, coffee in the middle, and cream on top. For breakfast, go for one of their combo deals of a pastry and coffee *(€2)*. Wines are relatively cheap *(glasses €1.80-2, bottles €9-15)*, and other options like tapas *(€5)* and desserts *(€4)* are reasonably priced. Check online for concerts and theater times.

Right next to Convento Agustinas Gaitanas. $ Coffee and cocktails €4-8. ⏰ Hours vary depending on performance times. Check online.

SINAGOGA DE SANTE MARIA

C. Reyes Católicos, 4 ☎925 227 257

Built in 1180, this converted synagogue (now owned by the Catholic Church) is considered to be one of the oldest Jewish worship centers in Europe. Built by Moorish architects, this converted art gallery held up by plain white columns with intricate stone details features religious art and Toledo landscapes.

From the monastery, walk east down C. Reyes Católicos. Gallery will be on your left. $ €2.30. ⏰ Open daily 10am-2pm and 3:30-6pm.

SHOPPING

LA CURE GOURMANDE

C. Comercio, 23 ☎925 258 990 www.la-cure-gourmande.com

For the perfect gift for just about anyone, head to La Cure Gourmande. This chocolate chain with locations throughout Spain, France, and Belgium serves up a huge variety of chocolates, candies, and cookies. Some are Toledo- and Spanish-themed and make a delicious treat for friends and family back home, especially marzipan, a sweet cookie-like confection made from sugar and almond meal.

Directly north of Mezquita de las Tornerias. $ Chocolates €1-10. ⏰ Open daily 10am-10pm.

ESSENTIALS

Practicalities

- **TOURIST OFFICES:** There is a tourist office located in the **train station** which provides free indispensable maps of Toledo in English and Spanish. Grab one on your way from the station to the city. Another option is the **tourist information office.** *(Puerta de Bisagra ☎ 92 522 08 43 ⏰ Open M-F 9am-6pm, Sa 9am-7pm, Su 9am-3pm.)* You can also go to the office at the **Casa de Mapa** *(Pl. de Zocodover ⏰ Open daily 11am-7pm)*.

- **CURRENCY EXCHANGE:** For a 24hr. ATM with no commission, try the **Banco Santander Central Hispano** *(C. del Comercio, 47 ☎925 229 800 ⏰ Open Apr-Sept M-F 8:30am-2pm; Oct-Mar M-F 8:30am-2pm, Sa 8:30am-1pm).*
- **LUGGAGE STORAGE:** Stash your stuff at the bus station *($ €1.80-3 per day. ⏰ Open daily 7am-11pm).*
- **INTERNET ACCESS:** Try Locutoriao El Casco across from the post office *(C. La Plata, 2 ☎925 22 61 65 $ €1.50 per hr. ⏰ Open daily 11am-11pm).*
- **POST OFFICE:** For mailings, contact the **post office** *(C. de la Plata, 1 ☎925 223 611 ⏰ Open M-F 8:30am-2pm and 5pm-8:30pm, Sa 9:30am-2pm).*

Emergency!

- **PHARMACIES:** Pharmacies are located throughout the city, including one at Pl. de Zocodover *(☎ 925 221 768 ⏰ Open daily 9:30am-2pm and 5-8pm).*
- **HOSPITAL:** For medical assistance, contact the **Hospital Virgen de la Salud** *(Av. de Barber ☎925 269 200).*
- **POLICE:** The police station is at the corner of Av. de la Reconquista and Av. de Carlos III (☎925 250 412).

Getting There

By Train

The **RENFE** high speed train from **Atocha** is probably the best way to get to Toledo. Trains take about 30 minutes and take you to the Toledo RENFE station *(Po. de la Rosa, 2. ☎902 240 202)* where a bus or taxi can take you to the center of town. There are 12 trains per day *($ Around €8. ⏰ Arriving and departing at 6:50am, 7:50am, 9:20am, 10:20am, 10:50am, 12:20pm, 1:50pm, 3:50pm, 5:50pm, 6:50pm, 7:50pm, and 9:50pm).* Not all trains run everyday. Consult **www.renfe.com** for details or pick up a pamphlet at the train station. It is probably best to buy your tickets one day prior as lines to buy tickets day-of can be long and unpredictable.

By Bus

Buses run from **Estación Sur** in Madrid. *(⏰ 1hr., every 30min. M-F 6am-10:30pm, Sa 6:30am-10:30pm, Su 8am-11:30pm. $ Around €5.)* Buses take you to **Av. Castille La Mancha** *(☎925 215 810 ⏰ 7am-11pm),* 10min. away from Puerta de Bisagra. **Alsina Graelis** *(☎925 215 850 or 963 497 230)* has buses to and from **Valencia** *(⏰ 5hr., M-F 3pm. $ €25; buy ticket on board).*

Getting Around

Walking is the easiest way to get to all the major sights in Toledo. Be sure to pick up a **free map** at the train station or tourist office. Keep in mind that the city's many steep cobblestone streets may be difficult to navigate for visitors in wheelchairs. The most important **buses** are the 8.1 and 8.2 that travel from the bus station to the center of town. Buses #1-7 leave from Pl. de Zocodover on various routes throughout town. *($ €0.95 per day, €1.25 per night).* For a mixture of transportation and touring, hop on one of the double-decker tour buses smattered throughout the city. For **taxis,** call Radio Taxi *(☎925 227 070)* or Gruas de Toledo *(☎925 255 050).*

san lorenzo de el escorial ☎91

A day trip to El Escorial's monastery, mausoleum, and royal headquarters is a great excuse to get out of the city. Walk through the complex's magnificent stone exterior to find tranquil gardens, libraries filled with tapestries, and magnificent paintings. Afterwards, grab a coffee at one of the cafes at the plaza across the street. In August, the **Fiestas de San Lorenzo,** fill the streets with not-so-monastic parades, dancing, and fireworks. Whatever you do, don't come on a Monday: the entire city (including restaurants and attractions) is closed.

ORIENTATION

The biggest attraction in San Lorenzo is the **Monasterio**. If you have time, you can also go to the nearby **Prince's Cottage** or the **Santa Cruz del Valle de Los Caidos** (the Holy Cross of the Valley of the Fallen), which was built as a monument to those who lost their lives in the Spanish Civil War. Bus #660 runs from **Pl. de la Virgen de Gracia** to the monument *(☎918 904 125; Tu-Su 3:15pm, returns 5:30pm; round-trip and admission, €8.30).*

ACCOMMODATIONS

HOSTAL CRISTINA — HOSTAL [3]

C. Juan de Toledo, 6 — ☎918 901 961 www.hostalcristina.es

Although most people go to El Escorial as a daytrip, if you do decide to stay overnight, your best budget option is the Hostal Cristina, located 10min. from the monastery. The hostal isn't anything to write home about, but it does have ensuite bathrooms and safety deposit boxes.

From the bus station, walk downhill towards the monastery; hostel will be on your left. $ Doubles €47.20; triples €53.20. Reception 24hr.

SIGHTS

El Escorial Monastery — ☎918 90 59 03

Built with the instructions, "Simplicity in the construction, severity in the whole, nobility without arrogance, majesty without ostentation," El Escorial follows this minimal but awe-inspiring building plan. Four towers surround the **central basilica** in a perfect rectangle, and the architects **Juan Bautista de Toledo** (followed by his pupil **Juan de Herrera,** who took over after Toledo's death) concentrated on straight lines instead of decorative patterns. Completed in 21 years, the complex has 16 patios, 88 fountains, 1200 doors, and 2700 windows. Felipe II commissioned the monastery as a final resting place for the Spanish royal family, possibly attempting to alleviate his guilt for sacking a French church at the Battle of San Quentín in 1557.

FELIPE II PALACE

East side of complex

The Habsburg Apartments are on the east side of the basilica and are used by the King and the royal family during their stay at El Escorial. The bedroom where Felipe II died in 1598 is preserved almost exactly as it was four centuries ago and features the adjustable bed that Felipe II used to observe Sunday mass while he was bedridden.

ROYAL PANTHEON

Stairs begin at ante-sacristy

One of the most impressive and creepiest rooms in El Escorial is the Royal Pantheon, the final resting place of four centuries worth of Spanish kings and queens that gave birth to them. This circular room is black and gold, and the walls are filled with labeled caskets in a kind of royal filing system. Walk out the hallways towards the Basilica that hold the caskets of royal children.

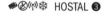

BASILICA

Center of monastery

The sheer size of the Basilica, especially the dome itself, is breathtaking. The massive Greek cross-shaped basilica features 45 altars, hundreds of statues and paintings of saints, and ceiling frescos by Cambiasso and Giordano. Once seen as a direct link between the Spanish kings and God, the basilica is the most impressive part of El Escorial.

BOURBON PALACE

Northeast corner of the complex

During the reign of Carlos III in the 18th century, a section of the building was remodeled to house the Bourbon apartments. Today, these rooms feature a collection of tapestries based on the works of Goya.

FOOD

CROCHÉ CAFETÍN

CAFE, BAR [1]

C. de San Lorenzo, 6 ☎918 905 282 www.crochécafetín.com

With chandeliers hanging over dark wood and marble tabletops, Croché Cafetín exudes old world charm befitting this city. Come for one of their many cocktails or "cafes muy especiales," special coffees from around the world mixed with liquor after taking the monastery tour.

From the monastery entrance, walk straight uphill past the tourist office and past C. Floridablanca. When you get to the square, the cafe will be on your left. $ Coffees and cocktails €4-10 ⏰ Open daily 10am-midnight.

LA CHISTERA

SPANISH [2]

Plaza de Jacinto Benavente, 5 ☎918 903 726

La Chistera is the best lunch or dinner option near the monastery thanks to its family-style service, strong flavors, and classic Spanish dishes. Order the menú *(a large appetizer, entree, and coffee or dessert; €9)* to help energize you through a day of sightseeing.

Walk 2min. straight uphill from the monastery entrance; restaurant will be on your left. $ Entrees €5-10. ⏰ Open daily 9am-midnight.

ARTS AND CULTURE

FIESTAS DE SAN LORENZO

Begins at Town Hall www.fiestasdesanlorenzo.com

Visits to San Lorenzo are popular during the second week in August when the town holds a host of fiestas in honor of **San Lorenzo,** the city's patron saint. The city begins this celebration by setting off a rocket from the balcony of the Town Hall, and nine days of traditional dance, religious events, concerts, sports, *vaquillas* (bullfights with young bulls), and other activities follow. For a complete list of events, check out the city's website.

$ Free. ⏰ Aug 10-16, 2011.

ESSENTIALS

Practicalities

- **TOURIST OFFICES:** The central **tourist office** has information about public transportation and local sights. *(C. Grimaldi, 4 ☎918 90 5 313; www.sanlorenzoturismo.org. With your back facing the monastery entrance, walk uphill to the tourist office on your right. ⏰ Open Tu-F 11am-6pm, Sa-Su 10am-3pm.)*

Emergency!

- **POLICE:** For emergencies, contact the **police** *(Pl. de la Constitución, 3 ☎918 905 223).*

Getting There
By Train
Trains run to El Escorial from the Atocha and Chamartín stations in **Madrid.** (⑤ €2.90 🕙 1hr., 30 per day M-F and Su 5:47am-10:15pm; Sa 19 per day 5:47am-1015pm.) Buy tickets at the station the day of your trip. El Escorial's train station (☎918 900 015) is 2km outside the center of town, but a shuttle runs between the bus and train stations. (⑤ €1.15.🕙 M-F every 20min. 7:23am-10:38pm, Sa-Su every 20min.-1hr. 9:44am-10:38pm.)
By Bus
Bus #661 runs from Madrid's Ⓜ Moncloa. (☎918 96 90 28 ⑤ €3.20. 🕙 50 min.; every 10-30min. M-F 6:15am-10pm, Sa 8am-9:30pm, Su 9am-11pm.)
Getting Around
It's at max a 10min. walk from the bus stop to the monastery, so you can walk virtually anywhere in this city without the need of a taxi or bus.

salamanca ☎922

Dubbed Spain's "Golden City", Salamanca radiates with beautiful landmarks carved of yellow Villamayor stone. However, pretty plazas and cathedrals aside, this city's a college town at heart, famous for its **Universidad de Salamanca,** one of the oldest in Europe. Once a battleground for Arabs and Christians, Salamanca no longer needs to worry about rampaging armies but raging students. At any time, Salamanca's streets are filled with students going to and from classes, sitting at outdoor cafes, and partying at the city's many bars and clubs.

ORIENTATION

The major sights of Salamanca center around the **Plaza Major** area. The streets from Plaza Mayor to the north are full of great clothing, shoe, and accessory chains. While you are in Salamanca, a must-see is the **Universidad**, steps away from Plaza Mayor. Once you've seen the university, be sure to check out the stunning old and new **Cathedrals** (directly south of the university). Every Monday and Wednesday, an English **walking tour** leaves from the tourist information office in Plaza Mayor (min. 10 people). The sights in the tour include Plaza Mayor, Casa de las Conchas, Cleriecia, Universidad Civil, and Catedrales, with admission to the monuments included in the price (€15). The full tour lasts about 2 hours (☎653 759 602).

ACCOMMODATIONS

HOSTAL SARA
&Ⓧ((ɣ))❄ HOSTAL ❹

C. de Meléndez, 11 ☎923 28 11 40 🖥www.hostalsara.org

Prettily decorated with floral bed coverings and light wood floors, Hostal Sara is a great option between Plaza Mayor and the University. Rooms look like hotel rooms and include a mini-fridge and full bath. Hostal is also easily wheelchair accessible with a larger-than-standard elevator.

✚ From the university, walk northeast up C. de Meléndez toward Plaza Mayor. ⑤ Singles €38; doubles €45-48. 🕙 Reception 24hr.

HOSTAL LAS VEGAS
&Ⓧ((ɣ))❄ HOSTAL ❷

C. Melendez, 13 ☎923 21 87 49 🖥www.lasvegascentro.net

Despite the neon sign out front, Hostal Las Vegas is the opposite of luxurious Sin City. Accommodations are super basic (sink in the bedroom area, small adjacent bathroom) but cheap. It has random decor—the hallway looks like something you'd find inside a *discoteca*, but it puts you in right in the middle of Salamanca sights and close to the clubs.

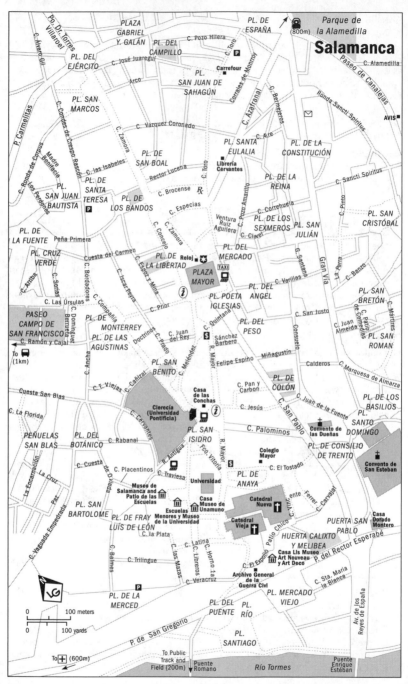

Salamanca

From the university walk northeast up C. de Meléndez toward Plaza Mayor. ⑨ Singles €24; doubles €36-45. ⊠ Reception 24hr.

HOSTAL CATEDRAL
♥⊗(๑)❋ HOSTAL ❸

C. de Rua Mayor, 46-48
☎923 27 06 14

Next door to the beautiful Salamanca cathedral, Hostal Catedral is owned by a friendly landlady who treats each visitor like visiting family. Rooms have personal touches like crocheted bed linens. This isn't your grandma's hostal, though—it's located near the boisterous, noisy Pl. de Anaya.

Next door to the Cathedral. ⑨ Singles €30; doubles €48. ⊠ Reception 24hr.

HOSTAL CONCEJO
♥⊗(๑)❋ HOSTAL ❹

Pl. de la Libertad, 1
☎923 21 47 37 ▣www.hconcejo.com

With flowered white linens, light hardwood floors, and full baths, these beautifully decorated, modern rooms at the Hostal Concejo resemble those of a boutique hotel. Steps away from Plaza Mayor, many rooms have excellent balconies with furniture and views of the winding cobblestone streets and beautiful buildings outside. Check online for special discounts and deals.

Right next to Plaza Mayor. ⑨ Singles €45-49; doubles €56-69; triples €79-83. ⊠ Reception 24hr.

SIGHTS
◉

UNIVERSIDAD
⊛⊗❋ UNIVERSITY

C. Libreros
☎923 27 71 00

The heart of Salamanca, the university is one of the most important buildings in the city and a jewel of the Spanish Renaissance. One of the oldest universities in Europe, it was founded by Alphonse IX of Leon in 1218. Legend has it that if you can find the frog (perched atop a skull) in the front facade of the university without assistance you will receive good luck and marriage. Inside the university you can view the historical library which holds 40,000 precious volumes including priceless manuscripts like *El Libro de Buen Amor* by the archpriest of Hita. You can also see the classroom where Fray Luis de Leon used to teach. While you're here, look for the red marks covering the sides of the building. When students graduated and became doctors, they used to stamp the walls with a mixture of bull's blood and oil.

Right next to Plaza Mayor. ⑨ €4, students and over 65 €2, under 12 free. Free M morning. ⊠ Open Tu-F 10:30am-12:45pm and 5-7pm, Sa 9:30am-1:30pm and 3-7pm, Su 10am-1:30pm.

CATHEDRAL
⊛⊗❋ CATHEDRAL

Pl. de Anaya
☎923 21 74 76

The new and old cathedrals are attached to one another (although you have to pay a fee to see the old cathedral). During the construction of the new cathedral, the old one was kept intact so that residents of Salamanca would still have a place to attend services. Built over two centuries, the new cathedral incorporates Gothic, Baroque, and Renaissance styles and is stunning in its beauty and grandeur. When you enter, be sure to look for the astronaut and lion with an ice cream cone carved into the stone by mischievous artisans during the cathedral's renovation. One of the unusual features of the new cathedral is the choir stand in the middle, built to optimize acoustics. In the old cathedral, be sure to go to ⊠ Santa Barbara chapel where legend has it if you put your feet on the tombstone of the bishop Juan Lucero, wisdom will transfer from your feet to your head.

Just south of Plaza Mayor ⑨ New cathedral free. Old cathedral €4.75, students €3.25; free to all Tu 10am-noon. ⊠ New cathedral open daily 9am-8pm. Old cathedral open daily 10am-7:30pm.

salamanca · sights

PLAZA MAYOR

⊛⊘❊ PLAZA

Right in the center of the city is Plaza Mayor, one of the most beautiful plazas in all of Spain. Built by Alberto de Churriguera in 1775, the plaza is a popular social hub and has been the centerpoint of Salamanca's political, economic, and religious activities. At different times in its history it has served as a market, concert hall, bullring, and theater. Today it is home to dozens of restaurants and tourist shops.

✣ *Just east of the University.* Ⓢ *Free.*

CASA DE LAS CONCHAS

⊛⊘❊ CONVERTED HOUSE

C. Compania, 2

☎923 26 93 17

Built by Rodrigo Arias Maldonado at the end of the 15th century, the "House of Shells" is dotted with 365 shells on its outward facade, one for each day of the year. They represent Maldonaldo's love for his wife (her family symbol was the shell) and his dedication to the Order of Santiago to which he belonged.

✣ *Across the street from the university.* Ⓢ *Free.* ⌚ *Open M-F 9am-9pm, Sa 9am-2pm and 3-7pm, Su 10am-2pm and 3-7pm.*

MUSEO DE LA HISTORIA DE LA AUTOMOCION

⊛⊘❊ MUSEUM

Pl. Mercado Viejo

☎923 26 02 93 ▣www.museoautomocion.com

Opened in 2002, this relatively new museum showcases a car collection mostly belonging to Gomez Planche. With over one hundred vehicles, thousands of parts, and scores of car accessories, the collection is an impressive ode to the car's place in history. From awkwardly-looking spoke wheel contraptions to fancy, shiny sports cars worthy of *2 Fast 2 Furious*, this museum has it all.

✣ *Just south of the cathedral.* Ⓢ *€3, students and over 65 €2. Free on 1st Tu of each month 5-8pm.* ⌚ *Open Tu-Su 10am-2pm and 5-8pm.*

FOOD

◨

▨ PONEY PISADOR

➨⊘(ⁱ)❊ FUSION ❷

Plaza San Juan Bautista, 7

☎923 26 38 55 ▣www.elponeypisador.com

An adorable little restaurant in a century-old house, Poney Pisador is the perfect place to go for a reasonably priced, unique meal. Each room is eccentrically decorated and different. Think bright, colorful table settings, mismatched chairs, knick-knacks on the walls, and funky light fixtures. Menus change with the seasons and include a large appetizer, entree, and dessert.

✣ *On the east side of Plaza San Juan Bautista.* Ⓢ *Menu €15.* ⌚ *Open daily 1:30-4pm and 9pm-2am.*

DELICATESSEN AND CAFE

➨⊘(ⁱ)❊ MEDITERRANEAN ❷

C. de Meléndez, 25

☎923 28 03 09

Steps away from Plaza Mayor, this restaurant and cafe offers a variety of fusion cuisine at a fraction of the cost of restaurants in the plaza. Get their menu of the day *(€11 day, €15 night),* and sit in a cool, comfortable, but hip atmosphere. In the back of the restaurant is an outdoor heated terrace with faux tropical plants and a massive skylight. At night, local DJs spin pop tunes and music videos play on the big screen projector.

✣ *From the southwest corner of Plaza Mayor walk straight south.* Ⓢ *Entrees €5-20.* ⌚ *Open daily 10am-3am. Kitchen open 1-4pm and 8:30pm-midnight.*

CAFE BAR MANDALA

➨⊘(ⁱ)❊ CAFE, BAR ❶

C. de Serranos, 9

☎923 12 33 42

Right across the street from the university, Cafe Bar Mandala is a popular hangout for students and visitors. Take a break from touring Salamanca and kick back with a drink from one of their five different drink menus. Hot day outside? Get a fruity Italian ice drink (menu is translated in six different languages so you know exactly what you're getting) or one of their 12 flavored ice teas like melon, peach or watermelon *(€2.50 small, €2.70 large)*. If you want to warm up, there's an entire menu dedicated to teas *(€2)* and a separate one for different kinds of hot chocolates. In case that isn't enough, fill up on one of their many milkshakes, ice cream sundae combos, or fresh juice mixes.

❦ *Next door to the university.* Ⓢ *Tea €3. Strawberry beer €3.50 .* Ⓩ *Open daily 9am-1am.*

NIGHTLIFE

BRITISH MUSEUM
🌐🚫♿ ♈ BAR, CLUB

C. San Justo, 36

Don't be fooled by the nerdy name: this "museum's" patrons are laid back local students who love jammin' to The Beatles, Duffy, and a host of good ol' American pop. This bar's vibe is relaxed, but lively and fun. Don't expect a whole lotta dancing; it's mostly kids hanging out enjoying their brews.

❦ *From the intersection of San Justo and Gran Vía, walk east; the bar will be at the corner of the street on your right.* Ⓢ *Beer and mixed drinks €3-8.* Ⓩ *Open M-Th 7pm-3am, F-Sa 7pm-4:30am.*

GATSBY
🌐🚫♿ ♈ BAR, DISCO

C. de los Bordadores, 16
☎923 21 72 74

With old farming tools, tribal masks, and wooden chandeliers hanging from the ceiling, Gatsby is themed more like Westphalia than West Egg. However, you can live out a little of the indulgence from Fitzgerald's novel: with friendly bartenders, a large bar area, and a dance floor, you get your pick of what you want to do. With a good mix of Spanish and American clientele and music, Gatsby is loved by everyone (except maybe Daisy).

❦ *From Pl. Mayor, walk west down C. del Prior and make a right onto C. de los Bordadores.* Ⓢ *Beer and mixed drinks €3-8.* Ⓩ *Open M-Th 5:30pm-4am, F-Sa 5:30pm-5am.*

CAMELOT
🌐🚫♿ ♈ BAR, DISCO

C. de los Bordadores, 3
☎923 21 21 82

Decorated to look like an ancient castle, Camelot is your best bet for a pre-modern pregame or dark (ages) dancefloor. With a wrought-iron balcony, the second floor is a perfect place to party like its 1299. Some nights there are free flamenco *tablaos* that get the crowd moving early in the night.

❦ *From the university, walk north up C. de la Comopania.* Ⓢ *Beer and mixed drinks €3-8.*

ARTS AND CULTURE

Named European Capital of Culture in 2002, Salamanca has an infinite mix of excellent museums, stunning architecture, and music and art venues. If you're lucky enough to be in Salamanca during one its many yearly festivals, soak in all the Spanish art, music, bullfighting, and partying you can get. Check out an outdoor concert, go to an awesome art museum, or see a play or Spanish movie at one of the many theaters that are interspersed throughout the city.

Theater and Music

During the summers, there are theater and music performances in the streets. Some notable performances are "Jazz in the Street," "Lives and Fictions of the City of Salamanca," "Theatre in the Street," and local festivities like "Etnohelmanitica—international festival of roots music."

TEATRO LICEO
♠🚫♿❄

Plaza de Liceo, s/n
☎923 27 22 90

Built on the area that used to be the ruins of the convent of San Antonio del Real, this theater hosts drama, dance, and opera.

Ⓩ *Performances throughout Jan.*

TEATRO JUAN DE ENZINA 📽⊗❀

C. Tostado ☎923 29 45 42

This university-sponsored theater offers some of the cheapest seats in all of Spain and focuses on contemporary theater, dance, and music performances.

🕐 *Year-round shows.*

Corridas de Toros

PLAZA DE TOROS DE SALAMANCA "LA GLORIETA" 📽⊗♨ PLAZA MAYOR

La Glorieta Bullring of Salamanca

Plaza de la Glorieta ☎923 22 12 99

As the area around Salamanca is the most prominent bull-breeding territory in Spain, you can expect some wicked fights and even wilder fans. During June and September, the famous Plaza de Toros de Salamanca, also known as "La Glorieta," hosts the most famous matadors and fiercest bulls during these festival months. Bullfights used to happen in Plaza Mayor, until La Glorieta was completed in 1893. Today it holds up to 10,000 spectators and hosts cultural events and concerts when bullfighting isn't in season. If you happen to be in Salamanca during February, make the 30min. trip to Ciudad Rodrigo, where the Carnaval del Toro shakes the city up with street dancing, carnival festivities, music, and bullfighting.

⚘ *Just north of the main part of town.*

MUSEO TAURINO 📽⬥ PLAZA MAYOR

C. del Doctor Piñuela, 5-7 ☎923 21 94 25 🖥www.museotaurinosalamanca.es

To learn more about this fierce and fraught sport, check out the bullfighting museum, Museo Taurino. Go check out matador fashion, bullfighting in Spanish popular culture, and some mad fighting facts.

⚘ *Pl. Mayor.* 🕐 *Open Tu-F 6-9pm, Sa noon-2pm and 6-9pm, Su noon-2pm.*

Festivals

REYES MAGOS

Like most Spanish cities, Salamanca needs very little reason to party. Every year on January 5th, residents, students, and tourists celebrate the arrival of the Three Kings during Cabalgata de los Reyes Magos, an evening parade that features dancing, music, and costumes. The day after is similar to Christmas day in the United States, when presents and large meals combine for an excellent day.

🕐 *Jan. 5-6.*

CORPUS CHRISTI

On June 18th, the Corpus Christi celebration occurs in full force around the Old Cathedral (Catedral Vieja). Salamanca residents celebrate with street performers and parties in the streets.

🕐 *June 18th.*

ESSENTIALS

Practicalities

- **TOURIST OFFICES:** The **Municipal Tourist Office** hands out free maps and pamphlets. *(Plaza Mayor, 32 ☎923 21 83 42* 🕐 *Open June-Sept M-F 9am-2pm and 4:30-8pm, Sa 10am-8pm, Su 10am-2pm; Oct-May M-F 9am-2pm and 4-6:30pm, Sa 10am-6:30pm, Su 10am-2pm.)* The **Regional Tourist Office** also has free information. *(R. Mayor ☎ 923 26 85 71* 🕐 *Open July-Sept M-Th 9am-8pm, F-Sa 9am-9pm, Su 9am-8pm; Oct.-June daily 9am-2pm and 5-8pm.)* Look out for **DGratis,** a free listing of goings-on distributed every Friday, available at tourist offices and distributors in Pl. Mayor. See 🖥www.salamanca.es for details.

- **CURRENCY EXCHANGE: EuroDivisas** has ATMs and currency exchange. *(R. Mayor, 2 ☎923 21 21 80* 🕐 *Open M-F 8:30am-10pm, Sa-Su 10am-7pm.)*
- **LUGGAGE STORAGE:** Store bags at the train station *(Ⓢ €3-4.50)* and bus station *(Ⓢ €2.* 🕐 *7am-7:45pm).*
- **LAUNDROMAT:** *(Pasaje Azafranal, 18 ☎923 36 02 16* Ⓢ *Wash and dry €4.* 🕐 *Open M-F 9:30am-2pm and 4-8pm, Sa 9:30am-2pm.)*
- **INTERNET ACCESS:** The **Biblioteca Pública** *(Casa de Las Conchas, C. Compañía, 2 ☎923 26 93 17* 🕐 *Open July-Aug M-F 9am-3pm, Sa 9am-2pm; Sept-June M-F 9am-9pm, Sa 9am-2pm)* offers free internet access and a modern, comfortable reading room. **Cyber Place Internet** *(Pl. Mayor, 10, 1st fl.* Ⓢ *€1 per hr.* 🕐 *Open M-F 11am-midnight, Sa-Su noon-midnight)* is flooded with foreign students calling mom, but has good rates for internet access. **Cyber Anuario** *(C. Traviesa, 16* ☎ *923 26 13 54* 🕐 *Open M-Sa 11am-2:30pm and 4:30-11pm)* offers internet at €1.50 per hr.
- **POST OFFICE:** *(Gran Vía, 25-29 ☎923 28 14 57; fax 923 28 14 57* 🕐 *Open M-F 8:30am-8:30pm, Sa 9:30am-2pm.)*
- **POSTAL CODE:** 37001.

Emergency!

- **EMERGENCY NUMBER:** ☎112.
- **POLICE:** *(Ayuntamiento, Pl. Mayor, 2* ☎923 19 44 40)*
- **CRISIS LINES:** Red Cross *(C. Cruz Roja, 1* ☎923 22 22 22)*

Getting There

By Plane

Flights arrive at the **Aeropuerto de Salamanca.** *(Ctra. Madrid, km 14 ☎923 32 96 00)*

By Train

The **Vialia Estación de Salamanca** *(Po. de la Estación ☎902 24 02 02)* has trains arriving from: **Lisbon** *(Ⓢ €47.* 🕐 *6hr., 1 per day 4:51am)* and **Madrid** *(Ⓢ €15.* 🕐 *2½hr., 6-7 per day 6am-7:53pm).*

Getting Around

Since most of the sights are packed in the center of the city around Plaza Mayor, Salamanca is easily walkable. The train station is a 15-20min. walk from the middle. If you are carrying a lot of luggage, flag down one of the taxis that roam around the main streets.

SEVILLA

They always say that two heads are better than one. Well, how about three or four heads? And what if we stick some crowns on those heads, and stick the bodies of those heads on horseback, and equip them with guns, spears, and catapults? Sevilla's history is far from simple and definitely far from boring. Since just after the Phoenetian settlement of Cadiz around 1110 BCE, this capital city of Andalucia has passed through the hands of the Romans, the Moors, and the Catholics. Take one peek at such major structures as the Alcázar and Catedral to get a perfect visual of the alterations of purpose and design at each of these buildings.

Modern Sevilla has by no means abandoned its value of integrated culture. This hot spot (literally and figuratively) rakes in energy, tradition, style, and creativity from all over the world. Take flamenco for example—this sexy dance style will get your heart bumping and your foot tapping through its Caribbean, Indian, Greek, African, and Spanish folk roots.

Maybe it's this mix of cultures that's made Sevillians so welcoming. Whether a local is pointing out directions, lending you a few euro for a bus ticket, or begging you to try their favorite item on a menu, you'll feel right at home the second you encounter your first fragrant orange tree. You'll pack more tapas into your belly than you ever thought possible and sip on the fruity and refreshing tinto de verano to cool yourself down. So get here already, and pack your walking shoes!

greatest hits

- **GO GOTH.** Witness the sheer size of Santa Cruz's La Catedral, the world's largest Gothic building—dark eyeliner not included with admission (p. 91).
- **HIP-SHAKING HISTORY.** Shimmy on down to El Centro's *Museo del Baile Flamenco,* home to all things flamenco (p. 93).
- **SWEET TREATS.** Head to Confiteria la Campaña for specialty desserts with recipes dating back to the shop's opening in 1885 (p. 98).

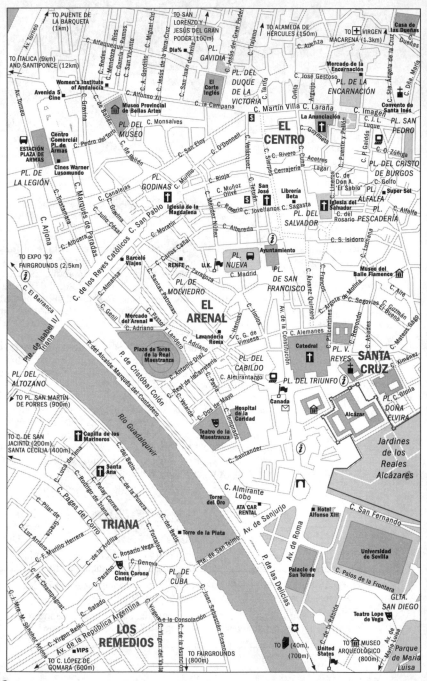

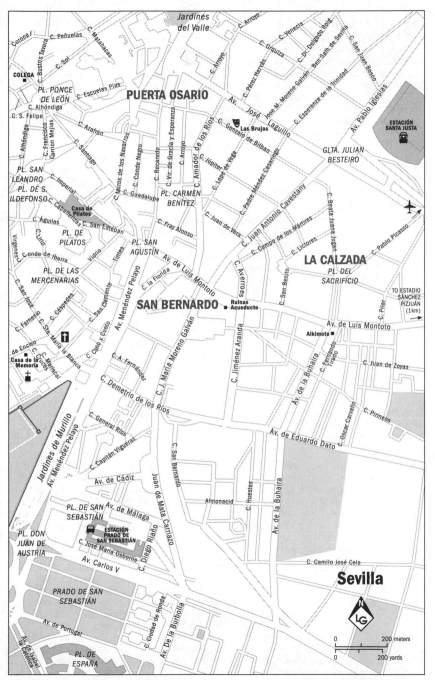

Sevilla

orientation

orientation

Sevilla can be divided into a few loosely separated neighborhoods. While the areas of **Arenal** and **Santa Cruz** are decently designated and the canal provides a fairly obvious dividing line into Triana, knowing at which point you step into **El Centro** or **La Macarena** depends upon who you ask. Some locals will swear that a site is a devout member of El Centro, and others may describe the same area as being "nearby Plaza de Armas." Some friends from across the canal may strongly hold that they are Trianans, rather than Sevillaños. Most generally, the **Alcazar** and **Catedral** are the biggest historical landmarks in Santa Cruz, the **Alameda de Hercules** denotes La Macarena, and the dominant shopping trio of **Calle Sierpes, Calle Cuna,** and **Calle Velazquez Tetuan** hold strong in El Centro.

The divisions aren't merely geographic—you'll quickly dub Santa Cruz as tourist-filled, El Centro as commercial, La Macarena as a mix of religious and reckless, and Triana as slow-paced and mellow. No matter what personality you prefer, you'll fit in anywhere in this welcoming capital city.

SANTA CRUZ

Santa Cruz can be divided into two main hubs: the transportation center and the cultural center. The **Prado de San Sebastian** is home to the main bus station and a metro stop, so you're likely to arrive at this large park when you first enter the area. The Prado is adjacent to the university and only a stone's throw away from the **Cathedral** and **Alcazar,** the main cultural centers of Santa Cruz. Surrounded by an array of small and slightly confusing streets inaccessible to any vehicle wider than a Vespa, this area definitely requires a map. Keep in mind that Santa Cruz is only a very small neighborhood of Sevilla, so you can walk across it, from the Cathedral to the **Plaza de Espana,** in under 20min. (assuming you're the fit traveler we know you are).

EL CENTRO

El Centro (literally, "the center" for you stubborn anglophones) is the largest neighborhood in Sevilla and can be ambiguously designated as all areas that are not part of Santa Cruz, Triana, El Arenal, or Macarena. The heart of El Centro is the **Plaza de la Encarnación.** As El Centro happens to be the commercial focus of Sevilla, the three shopping streets of **Calle Cuna, Calle Sierpes,** and **Calle Velazquez Tetuan** are valuable landmarks to know when traversing this window-shopping haven. **Plaza Alfalfa** is the core of the local social scene, packed with bars and outdoor patios. A southern boundary for this neighborhood is the **Estación de Autobuses Plaza de Armas,** located along the canal, where you can find buses to neighboring province Cádiz.

LA MACARENA

The biggest landmarks to keep in mind for getting around La Macarena are the **Alameda de Hercules,** a center for eating, clubbing, and getting a drink, and **C. Feria,** a street lined with smaller shops and restaurants along with the occasional local bar. **C. Torneo** and **C. Resolana** border La Macarena and are major streets for bus routes and transport, and Torneo has quite a few hot clubs in its repertoire. Otherwise, the slew of convents and churches splashed all over La Macarena are useful landmarks for a personal pilgrimage to this area.

EL ARENAL AND TRIANA

Sandwiching the canal between the **Puente de San Telmo** and **Puente de Triana** lie these two neighborhoods of Sevilla. On the northern side of the canal, El Arenal's main street is **Paseo de Cristobal Colon** along the canal, and its main center is the **Plaza de Armas,** located at the base of the Puente de Triana. Once making your way to the "other side of the tracks," per se, you'll find the neighborhood of Triana. While the main streets, **Avenida de la Reublica Argentina** and **Calle San Jacinto** will be useful landmarks, the layout of Triana is generally much less confusing compared to the rest of Sevilla. **Calle Betis** along the water is home to some of the nicest seafood restaurants and best bars and clubs in Sevilla. **Calle de Salado** is another useful spot to check out, as it is lined with inexpensive, multi-cultural restaurants.

sevilla

accommodations

Save money. Make friends. These should be two of your top goals in picking somewhere to stay in Sevilla. You can find quite the array of backpacker's hostels that will provide great prices as well as plenty of social, fun activities to keep you occupied, just in case the amazing city around you isn't enough to fill up your days.

SANTA CRUZ

Santa Cruz is the most touristed region of Sevilla. The accommodations definitely reflect this fact, so you have tons of options when choosing where to stay. Because of this competition, the hostels here are some of the best-priced and most conveniently located in Spain. At most hostels, you'll find yourself in the center of Sevillian history and not too far from shopping or the canal.

SAMAY SEVILLA HOSTAL — HOSTAL [1]

Menendez Pelayo, 13 ☎955 215 668 www.samayhostals.com

Probably one of the nicest hostels in the Santa Cruz region, Samay provides all the essentials at great rates. Upon entering the hostel, you'll be welcomed by an English-speaking staff member (or three) ready to help you to your room. While the patterned walls and loud furniture in the first-floor lobby are a little too retro for comfort, these minor decorative issues are worth overlooking. The rooms are comfortable and clean with ensuite bathrooms. They also offer an almost overwhelming slew of entertainment, including free walking tours, tapas tours, and flamenco and *discoteca* nights. Feel the comfort of Samay by relaxing on the top-floor terrace or making breakfast in the open kitchen. While the maximum stay is officially one week, some travelers report that if you flash a smile at the guy at the desk, he'll let you stay longer.

7min. from Prado de San Sebastian, on the left-hand side of the street if leaving the Prado. [i] Lockers and towels included. $ 8-person dorm €15; 6-person €18; 4-person €20. Reception 24hr.

HOSTAL FLORIDA — HOSTAL [4]

Menendez Pelayo, 27 ☎954 422 557 www.hostalfloridasevilla.com

Although it has hostel in it's name, Hostal Florida would be much better described as a cheap hotel. While private rooms, TVs, and no bunk beds at all sound great on paper, the cramped bedrooms and total lack of common space eliminate the social feel of a backpackers' hostel. Such a sentiment is reflected in the staff as well: though friendly, they lack the energy and warmth seen at other local hostels. If you'd rather watch Spanish reruns on TV than imbibe in a pitcher of sangria with fellow travelers coming through Santa Cruz, then maybe this spot is for you.

Located about a 10min. walk from Prado de San Sebastian, on the left-hand side of the street if leaving the Prado. [i] Ensuite safes and bathrooms. $ Doubles and triples €45.

PICASSO BACKPACKER — HOSTEL [1]

San Gregario, 1 ☎954 210 864 www.piramide.com

This smaller, inexpensive hostel is hidden in a small courtyard only meters from the Peurta de Jerez fountain and minutes from the Cathedral and Alcazar. It maintains an authentic Spanish feel with colorful Moorish-style tiles and greenery in the entryway but caters to foreign travelers. The older woman at the desk is extremely friendly and speaks clear English. The rooms are equipped with clean sheets, and the large windows and small balconies do wonders for the aesthetically minded. While Picasso "usually" offers Wi-Fi, some visitors complain that the service was shut down during their stay, without any specific date of return. Despite such complications, if you're looking for convenience, the location is hard to beat.

If following the gaze of the statue at Puerta de Jerez, follow a small block and make a sharp right. The hostel is located in a small courtyard. [i] Complimentary tea and coffee. Female-only housing available. $ 6-person dorms €10.50; doubles €44; triples €39; quads €33.

SEVILLA INN BACKPACKERS

HOSTEL [1]

C. Angeles, 11 ☎954 219 541 🖥www.sevillabackpackers.es

One of the newer hostels on the Santa Cruz scene, Sevilla Inn Backpackers provides a prime location and all the necessary amenities. Don't let this silver lining pull you in too quickly, though. Prices can get pretty steep for private housing, and charges for usually free services such as clean towels *(€1)* and clean linens *(€2)* add to the bill. If you're willing to pay the extra charges, you will be rewarded with free continental breakfast, a TV lounge, free Wi-Fi, an open kitchen, and a patio on the roof. Working closely with Samay hostels, Sevilla Inn offers many of the same tours and shows. The friendly staff not only works at the front desk but also prepares BBQ and paella on the top-floor terrace every evening *(€5).*

5min. from the Cathedral. [i] Walking tours M-Sa 4pm. Tapas tours M and Th 8pm. Night tours M, T, Th, F, and Sa. $ 8-person dorm €15; 6-person €17. Singles €50; quads €80.

EL CENTRO

Accommodations in El Centro are wonderfully convenient, but near impossible to find. The tiny streets and sharp corners could leave you lugging heavy baggage around for much longer than you want. To be safe, look up a map online in advance, and be confident in asking the locals for help. Sevillians will battle over a chance to point you in the right direction.

OASIS BACKPACKERS' HOSTEL

HOSTEL [2]

Plaza de la Encarnacion 29 1-2. ☎954 293 777 🖥www.hostelsoasis.com

If there was a competition to think of every possible accommodation a backpacker would request, Oasis could defeat even the neediest of travelers. From a roof-top pool (more of a pond, but in the Sevillian heat, any body of water is appreciated) to an in-hostel happy hour (2 beers, wines, sangrias, or shots for €2) to bike rentals and Spanish lessons, Oasis has it all. The rooms are the biggest seen in Sevilla with tons of additional shelving and space for those of you who are still working out the kinks of "light packing." The location also can't be beat: the Plaza de la Encarnacion is the center of El Centro, and Oasis is smack in the Plaza. While the hostel has three buildings of housing, try to get a room in the building with the reception because it houses the pool and the kitchen where breakfast is served.

At the corner of Plaza de la Encarnacion. If looking at the more visible #29, turning right into the alley and the entrance is on the left-hand side where the alley curves. [i] Pool, breakfast included 8am-11am daily. $ All rooms (4, 6, or 8-bed) €20. ⏰ Reception 24hr.

HOSTEL NUEVO SUIZO

HOSTEL [2]

C. Azofaifo 7 ☎954 229 147 🖥www.nuevosuizo.com

Located right off the main shopping streets of El Centro, Hostel Nuevo Suizo puts in a full effort to provide a classy establishment, from the skylight and stone columns in the entryway to the flowers resting on the pillows of each bed. By providing free breakfast, free Wi-Fi, a phone for free international calling, a terrace, and all the coffee and tea you can drink until you wet your pants or OD on caffeine (whichever comes first), this hostel brings the goods. But be mindful that Nuevo Suizo is a bit pricier than other local hostels, and they find ways to sneak the prices up a bit higher. While private suites range from €27-€31, even the public suites are €23-€25 for 2-3 people and €17 for 9 people. Keep in mind that the higher the floor, the higher the price because, as the girl at the desk explains, "you get the bonus of extra quiet."

In a small alley off C. las Sierpes right by C. Vargas Campos. $ 9-bed dorms €17, 2-3 bed €23-25. Singles €27-31. ⏰ Reception 24hr.

SEVILLA URBANY HOSTEL

HOSTEL [1]

Doña Maria Coronel 12 ☎954 227 949 🖥bookings@sevillaurbany.com

Although it's located only a block from Iglesia San Pedro, the religious vibes aren't enough to keep you feeling entirely safe traveling to Sevilla Urbany. The small winding roads leading to the hostel are confusing and uncomfortable.

Once inside the hostel, you may even still feel a bit on-edge. Unlike other hostels in the area, the patrons suggest locking up all your luggage when leaving the room. This hostel seems to have invested more into its spacious, tiled bathrooms than its actual sleeping quarters, which have the bottom bunks frameless on the floor. While the prices are competitive and the free breakfast is tempting, you may be best off scoping out some other options.

*On the left hand side if traveling from Plaza San Pedro on C. Doña Maria Coronel. **i** €2 extra charge for credit card use. €2 charge for towel. Breakfast included. $ 8-bed dorms €16-18, 6-bed €18-€20, 4-bed €21-23. ⏰ Reception 24hr.*

TRAVELLER'S INN BACKPACKERS — HOSTEL [1]

C. Augosto Plasencia 5 ☎954 216 724 🖥www.sevillabackpackers.com

Squeezed into a small plot of land not far from Plaza Alfansa, Traveler's Inn Backpackers packs floor-upon-floor of pristine facilities, perfect as long as you're not intending to spend much time in your bedroom. While the dorms are clean and safe, you may need to inhale before entering, as they're so cramped that it's often difficult to even open the door. Aside from the not-so-spacious bedrooms, Traveler's Inn does provide free breakfast, free Wi-Fi, a spacious, marble kitchen, and 2 rooftop terraces. The colorful painted tiles and sky lighting both contribute to the welcoming aesthetics of the establishment.

*If leaving Plaza de Alfalfa turn right at the intersection of Odreros and Luchana Rojas; it will be on the left-hand side. **i** Breakfast included. Some bathrooms ensuite, some on the hall. $ 8-bed dorm €16, 6-bed €16-18, 4-bed room €19. ⏰ Reception 24hr.*

LA MACARENA

La Macarena lacks the social backpacker's hostels found in other areas of Sevilla. While the *pensiones* are decently priced (especially for groups of 2 or 3), the only friend you'll make will be the receptionist happily accepting your payment. El Centro isn't a far walk and may be your best option to visit La Macarena. We promise—even walking back from a wild night on the Alameda is manageable.

PENSIÓN ALAMEDA — PENSIÓN [2]

Alameda de Hércules 31 ☎954 900 191 🖥www.hostalalameda.es

Although Pensión Alameda's location right in the heart of La Macarena may be tempting, you're probably better off staying at one of the backpackers' hostels in El Centro. The rooms aren't cheap, even if you split them with your posse, and you completely miss out on the social aspect of hostel living. The older woman who works at the desk lives at Alameda as well, but doesn't give you access to the kitchen or living room, despite leaving the doors wide open to tempt you with the TV you can't watch.

*On the right side of the Alameda if walking from C. Calatrava. **i** All rooms with bath. $ Singles €25; doubles €40-45; triples €60.*

PENSIÓN MACARENA — PENSIÓN [2]

C. San Louis 91 ☎954 370 141

Pensión Macarena is as neat and tidy as they come—walking into the tiled entryway, you'll smell the cleaning supplies glistening off the floors and walls, and the whole *pensión* is kept just as spotless. The rooms aren't huge but are adequately sized, and some have ensuite bathrooms. Although the staff doesn't speak much English, they're extremely friendly and accommodating. Even their little gray terrier will come lick your feet as you book a room. This is a great option for a quiet, secluded stay away from other backpackers.

At Plaza Pumarejo along C. San Louis, toward El Centro from the Basilica Macarena. $ Singles €20; doubles €30, with bath €40; triples €45/51. ⏰ Reception 24hr.

TRIANA AND EL ARENAL

Aside from a few streets right along the canal, Triana is an area for finding a flat, settling down, and enjoying the mellow life south of the Guadalquivir. This means hostel selection is a bit limited, as they expect backpackers to be staying in El Centro where life is faster. You *will* find a strong selection of nice hotels, so just decide how much you want to splurge.

TRIANA BACKPACKERS — HOSTEL ❷

C. Rodrigo de Triana 69 ☎954 459 960 www.trianabackpackers.com

This peaceful, traditional looking hostel takes on the true Triana spirit—from the hammocks and jacuzzi on the terrace to the board games and couches in the lounge to the Spanish radio playing through the halls, it's the perfect place for a relaxing stay. You won't find the same hustle and bustle of other backpacker's hostels but rather a safe, pristinely-clean abode to just chill out. If you want to enjoy a walk, you're located just meters from the canal, or you could choose to just turn on the reading lamp at your bunk and lounge all evening. Mellow by no means implies boring—sign up for a 1.5hr. *(€5)* or 2.5hr. *(€6)* bike excursion to Cartuja or Italica, or head out for a free Flamenco show with your new hostel friends. The go-with-the-flow style has one drawback: the receptionists are sometimes missing from the desks and take their time coming back. But remember, patience is a virtue.

*From Puente de Triana, take C. de San Jacinto and make a left onto Rodrigo de Triana; the hostel is on the left side of the street. **i** Breakfast included. Female-only suites available. $ 10-bed dorms €15-18; 6-bed dorms €16-19; 4-bed dorms €17-20. Doubles €50. Reception 24hr.*

LA POSADA DE TRIANA S.L. — PENSIÓN ❹

C. Pages del Corro 53 ☎954 332 100 www.laposadadetriana.com

Within a recently-renovated 19th century building lies a small, welcoming hotel, La Posada de Triana. The friendly older woman at the desk will use her best English to greet you with a smile, and then lead you to your small, but colorfully decorated room equipped with artwork, closet space, a (very) compact bathroom, and your own fan. There aren't any bells and whistles, like breakfast or organized social events—just a simple place to sleep with a great location. You are going to be paying a heavier bill *(€23-30 per person)*, but at least there aren't any ridiculous charges for towels, sheets, credit card use, running water, or a hug (you know how some backpackers' hostels can get).

*From Puente de Triana, take C. de San Jacinto, and make a right onto C. de Pages del Corro; the pensión is on the right side of the street. **i** TV available. $ Singles €45; doubles €60; triples €70. Reception 24hr.*

OUTSIDE THE CENTER

If visiting Sevilla, there's no law that says you have to stay smack in the center of the city (well, we actually aren't particularly familiar with Andalucian law, but we're just guessing).

ALBERGUE INTURJOVEN SEVILLA (HI) — HOSTEL ❷

C. Isaac Peral 2 ☎955 035 886 www.inturjoven.com

Located just 7 or 8 minutes from the Prado, Inturjoven provides open, modern, large spaces for a generally under-25 crowd. The large patios, snack rooms, all-you-can-eat buffet meals, and TV rooms makes this the perfect option for the high school or college-aged backpacker just looking to chill out and maybe open up a deck of cards at their hostel. The rooms are large and clean, although completely undecorated, and provide ample closet space. Price doesn't vary based on whether rooms have balconies or ensuite bathrooms, so do your best to score one of the nicer rooms.

*Take Bus 34 from C. del Cid to Isaac Peral Stop (about 7-8min, €1.20). **i** Breakfast included. All other meals €8 buffet. Wi-Fi €1 per hr., €6 per day. Laundry: €2.50 wash, €2 dry. $ 25 and under €22.50; over 26 €28.50. €3.50 discount with HI card. Reception 24hr.*

sights

With a history of violent battle, valiant conquest, and devout religion, Sevilla is bound to have quite a few sights worth seeing. Whether preserved or honored, the historic places all around this capital city are worth your time and energy. Even with this rich history, you'll find spicy hotspots for an evening out and perfect places to lounge.

SANTA CRUZ

Santa Cruz is the most historic portion of Sevilla, and it's got some sights to show for it. Join the other swarms of tourists checking out the most famous buildings, gardens, and establishments to take in all the Sevillian history.

👍 PLAZA DE ESPAÑA — HISTORIC SIGHT, MONUMENT

Avda. Isabel la Católica

Constructed for the Iberian Exposition of 1929, you'd be shocked to see how well modern architecture can mock traditional Moorish style. Being a bit anachronistic is a common theme for the Plaza de España—George Lucas even filmed part of *Star Wars: Return of the Clones* on the bridges of the site. The Plaza was built as an apology to the nations of the world who had fallen to the violence of Spanish colonialism and takes on this request for forgiveness in full force–the plaza itself is constructed in the shape of a heart. The details of the Plaza are the perfect Spanish history study guide: the seating surrounding the main area is decorated with colorful, hand-made tiles, with each booth honoring one of the principal cities of Spain. All major Spanish leaders are preserved in statue form, so don't worry, you won't forget anyone important next Double Jeopardy round.

🧭 Directly across Avenida de Portugal from the Prado of San Sebastian. $ Free. ⏰ Open daily 7am-11pm.

LA CATEDRAL — CHURCH

Entrance by Pl. de la Virgen de los Reyes — ☎954 214 971

This isn't just any old church. The Cathedral happens to be the world's largest Gothic building and the third-largest church, holding these literally huge distinctions with pride. The city restricts any construction project from exceeding 100m to ensure that the Jiralda Tower of the Cathedral remains the highest point in Sevilla. The church itself has a rich history of the Sevillian shift from Moorish to Catholic control. The tall, thin Jiralda Tower was mysteriously the only portion of the Islamic mosque to survive an earthquake in 1365. The stained-glass windows and gold-plated religious scenes lining the interior are worth checking out, as they have a Moorish-Catholic flare that traditional Renaissance churches lack. Watch out for the ambush of "religious" palm readers at the exit: they'll grab you, tell you how many kids you're bound to have, and then guilt you into tipping.

🧭 Located off Avenida de la Constitucion next to the Alcazar. $ €7.50, students €2. ⏰ Open July-Aug M-Sa 11am-5pm, Su 9:30am-4pm; Sept-June M-Sa 11am-5pm, Su 2:30pm-6pm.

untraditional catholicism

On July 3rd, 2005, Spain became the third country worldwide to legalize marriage between two men or two women. Even though almost 73% of Spaniards identify as Roman Catholic, an affiliation that officially condemns homosexuality, it was reported that the legalization received around 66% public approval. The law's passing can be attributed to José Luis Rodríguez Zapatero, the country's socialist President who was first elected in 2004. Zapatero is also behind laws limiting bullfighting, and another record-breakingly liberal move: placing more women than men in his presidential cabinet.

THE ALCAZAR

HISTORIC SIGHT, FORTRESS

Patio de Bandera ☎954 502 323 🖥direccion@patronato-alcazarsevilla.es

Don't stress about getting your black tie back from the dry cleaners before visiting the Alcazar. While it does double as the summer palace for Spanish royalty, it also makes a great casual stop on any visit to Santa Cruz. After the Romans originally constructed the walls to protect the city, the Moors then expanded them into an all-out fortress to protect against enemy advances on Sevilla. Once the Catholics took over, they converted the fortress into a palace, somehow overcoming the irony of being peace-loving Christian monarchs residing in a Muslim establishment. Rich with honorary sites for icons such as Dona Maria de Padilla, the woman who threw boiling oil in her face to stop King Frederic from making moves on her (you'd think she would've just stopped showering), the Alacazar has a new story around every corner. The orange trees lining the outdoor plazas provide a picture-perfect splash of color.

🧭 Located off the back corner of La Catedral, off Plaza de Triunfo. $ €7.50, students free. ⏰ Open April-Sept M-Sa 9:30am-7pm; Oct-Mar daily 9:30am-5pm.

UNIVERSIDAD DE SEVILLA

☁ UNIVERSITY

C. San Fernando, 4 ☎954 551 000 🖥http://www.us.es

If every college in the world looked like this, we'd probably have far more productive youth. The *Universidad de Sevilla* is the second-largest building in all of Spain and uses every square inch to saturate you with impressive and breathtaking architecture. While the library and computers are only available to students and university personnel, the open stone courtyards lined with statues of religious and historic Spanish figures are the perfect place for some reading, writing, or a siesta. If you think you're too cool for school, consider that this university has quite the rebellious history. Originally built as a tobacco factory, the establishment once employed the "deadly sexy" Carmen, namesake of the traditional Sevillian song. And if you're interested in gaining some knowledge while spending time in Sevilla, the university offers a variety of extension classes.

🧭 Down the block from Prado de San Sebastian. 3min. walk from Estacion de Prado. $ Free. ⏰ M-Sa 7am-9:45pm.

JARDINES DE MURILLO

♿☁ GARDEN, PARK

Avenida de San Francisco Javier, 24 ☎954 932 475

So maybe you haven't heard of Bartholomew Murillo, the not-so-world-renowned Sevillian artist. But since Diego Velazquez ditched his roots to spend most of his life in Madrid, the people of Sevilla hold proudly to their back-up plan. The *Jardines de Murillo* (Gardens of Murillo) are lined with Moorish-influenced tile seating areas, and the array of giant ficus trees, towering well overhead with a girth that would intimidate any tree-hugger, provide ample shade. The Fountain of Christopher Columbus, located in the center of the gardens, honors the adventurer himself (who is rumored to have been born in Catalonia and buried in the Cathedral), as well as his historic sugar daddys, Ferdinand and Isabella. The white stone columns and metallic ship of Isabella prove who truly wore the pants in the 15th-century Spanish empire, while Ferdinand's death by indigestion is commemorated by his name surrounded by carved foods at base of the statue.

🧭 Enter at Christopher Columbus fountain off Menendez de Pelayo. It's on the left if leaving the Prado. $ Free. ⏰ Open 24hr.

EL CENTRO

While many of the sights may be hidden on tiny side streets that require an additional 20 minutes (we're being optimistic) to find, this bunch is surely worth the hunt. El Centro has some of the best museums and cultural centers in town, all of which have definitely mastered the art of giving a tour.

MUSEO DEL BAILE FLAMENCO
MUSEUM

Manuel Rojas Marcos 3 ☎954 340 311 💻www.museoflamenco.com

This museum is the one-stop shop for all things flamenco. Walking through the halls of this high-tech, automated museum, you'll be bombarded by movies, photography, and artifacts explaining the rich history of flamenco in Sevilla. Be sure to check out the dress worn during the opening ceremonies of the 1992 Barcelona Olympics for a piece of hip-shaking history. After you're done with the techy side of this museum's entertainment, look at the 300-year-old, underground Moorish gallery that holds classic flamenco photographs. The museum offers live flamenco performances in the evenings, and, if you're not too shy, try your hand at some dancing with the professionals and get your groove on, Sevillian style. The performers from the evening shows teach a quick, 20 minute class open to the public at 7:30pm M-Th.

From the Catedral, take C. Argote de Molina, turn left onto C. Estrella, and then turn left onto Manuel Rojas Marcos; the museum will be on the right. i Exhibits in English and Spanish. $ €10, students €8. Flamenco performances M-Th €15, students €12; F-Sa €23/20. Flamenco classes €10. ⏰ Museum open daily 9:30am-7pm. Flamenco performances M-Th 7pm, F-Sa 7:30pm. Flamenco classes M-Th 6:30pm.

MUSEO DE BELLAS ARTES
MUSEUM

Plaza del Museo 9 ☎954 786 500 💻www.museodeandalucia.es

The most user-friendly museum you'll ever encounter, the Museo de Bellas Artes is organized in such a way that you walk from room to room through a chronological journey of the history of Sevillian and Spanish art. Starting in the medieval period and progressing to the 20th century, the museum even devotes entire rooms to its favorite artists, including Murillo, Valdés Leal, and Zurbarán. The courtyards are also definitely worth exploring.

At intersection of C. Alfonso XII and C. San Vicente. i Lockers available €1. Exhibitions rotated throughout the year. $ €1.50, free with EU passport. ⏰ Open Tu-Sa 9am-8:30pm, Su 9am-2:30pm.

virgin statue

La Macarena is the Virigin of Hope, praised and represented in the form of the large wooden statue in the center of Basílica La Macarena. The popular mid-90s song, "Macarena" by Los del Rio is only related in that it is about a girl named Macarena. So don't go trying any hip-shaking 8-counts in the middle of any Sevillan churches.

AYUNTAMIENTO
GOVERNMENT BUILDING, MONUMENT

C. Pajaritos 14 ☎954 590 600 💻www.sevilla.org

If you're looking to get a strong grasp of the political history and development of Sevilla, there's no better source than the government itself. The Ayuntamiento offers free tours twice a day Tuesday through Thursday (don't forget your passport), but keep in mind that they're conducted entirely in Spanish. Even if a few details are lost in translation, you'll get to check out the Sevillian State House—constructed in the 16th century and completed in the 19th century—much of which is still in use today by the governing bodies of Sevilla. The entire building is open to the public on May 28 to celebrate *Día de Fernando*, the day for the Catholic Castillian king who helped establish Spain.

Travel from Puerta de Jerez down Avenida de la Constitucion, 1min. from the Catedral. i Passport required for entry. $ Free. ⏰ Tours Tu-Th 5:30pm and 6pm.

CASA DE PILATOS
PALACE

Plaza de Pilatos 1 ☎954 225 298 💻casapilatos@fundacionmedinaceli.org

This ancient palace named after Pontius Pilate himself gives any visitor a perfect taste of life among the historic Sevillian royalty. From frescoes to classic artwork to international gifts from China, Japan, England, and Germany, the Casa de Pilatos is stuffed with symbols of luxury, religion, and history in Andalucia. The tours run every half hour from 10am until closing and are worth the extra €3, since they include the upstairs of the palace and descriptions of many of the wonderfully preserved artifacts dating back to the 16th and 17th centuries. Pay close attention to the story of the palace being used as a hospital during Spain's civil war.

Turn off Av. Menendez Pelayo onto C. St. Esteban and keep left. Casa de Pilatos will be on the right-hand side. $ Entry to ground floor €5, complete tour €8. ⏰ Open daily Apr-Oct 9am-7pm; Nov-Mar 9am-6pm. Tours every 30min. 10am-closing.

LA MACARENA

On paper, La Macarena may look like church upon church (with maybe a convent or basilica thrown in for variety), and that's just what you'll find. That's not to say that the religious history found in La Macarena is not unique at each of its sights. With some exploration, you'll come away with a much better understanding of **Semana Santa** and **Feria de Abril,** two of Sevilla's most important festivals.

BASÍLICA DE SAN LORENZO Y JESUS DE GRAN PODER — CHURCH

Plaza de San Lorenzo, 13 ☎954 915 686 🖥www.gran-poder.es

This church combo is one of the most ornate and impressive around. When facing the duo, the Basílica de San Lorenzo is on the left and is filled with golden artwork, glistening altars, and wall-covering frescos. The Basílica de Jesus de Gran Poder sticks to its name—it's one powerful place. Even the entirely marble, circular main room pales in comparison to the massive altar in the center. The tall golden statue of Jesus adorned with purple robes and carrying the cross is the main sight of this basilica. People from all over line up to pass behind the statue, showing reverence by kissing the ankle and saying a quick prayer—just make sure not to leave any lipstick stains!

From Alameda, take C. Santa Ana and turn left onto C. Santa Clara; the Plaza and churches are on the right. $ Free. ⏰ Basilica open M-Th 8am-1:30pm and 6-9pm, F 7:30am-10pm, Sa-Su 8am-2pm and 6-9pm. Mass M-Th 9:30am, 10:30am, 12:30pm, 6:30pm, 7:30pm, 8:30pm; Sa 9:30am, 10:30am, 1:15pm, 7:30pm, 8:30pm; Su 9:30am, 11am, 12:30pm, 1:30pm, 7:30pm, 8:30pm.

BASÍLICA LA MACARENA AND HERMANDAD DE LA MACARENA MUSEUM — CHURCH

C. Becker 1, 3 ☎954 901 800 🖥www.hermandaddelamacarena.es

Upon walking into the Basílica La Macarena, you will be immediately impressed by the highly ornate altars and stunning artwork decorating the ceiling. But let's be honest—if you've been traveling through La Macarena, you've seen a bunch of awe-inspiring churches at this point. What makes this one special is the history connected to this namesake of the neighborhood. Upon visiting the museum attached to the basilica, you'll learn all about the history of the **Semana Santa** (holy week) festivities in Sevilla. You'll hear tales of the **Hermandad,** or religious brotherhood, that has now become a main icon of this holy week. Perfectly preserved documents, books, tapestries, and ancient flags are great eye candy as you walk the museum halls. The massive, decorated floats once used during Semana Santa nearly 100 years ago will leave you with an appreciation for the magnitude and significance of the historic festival. You can also browse the crystal rosaries and bracelets being sold in the museum shop by the entrance.

At the intersection of C. San Louis and C. Resolana; the entrance is on C. Resolana. $ Museum €5, under 16 €3. Basilica free. ⏰ Basilica open M-Sa 9am-2pm and 5-9pm, Su 9am-2pm and 5-9:30pm. Museum open daily 9am-1:30pm and 5-8:30pm. Mass M-F 9am, 11:30am, 8pm, 8:30pm; Sa 9am, 8pm; Su 10:15am, 12:15pm, 8pm.

CONVENTO SANTA PAULA — MUSEUM, RELIGIOUS SIGHT

C. Santa Paula, 11 ☎954 536 330 🖥www.santapaula.es

While you may feel like you're sneaking into the land of Oz when ringing the doorbell at the tiny, brown door toward the right corner of the convent, you'll soon be greeted by a slew of nuns and all feelings of rebellion will probably vanish (along with that dream of a scarecrow, tin man, and lion at your side). You can visit the small convent museum *(€3)* and browse the collection of artifacts stored in this 15th-century establishment. While none of the items are labeled, your own private nun will guide you through the three museum rooms, pointing out her favorite parts. She may have even helped to make the marmalade sold on the bottom floor *(small €3, large €4.35)*. Pick up a bottle of any flavor you can imagine (what does an orange blossom even taste like?)

↗ *Located near C. Siete Dolores, neighboring Plaza Santa Isabel and Iglesia San Marcos.* $ *Tour €3.* ⏰ *Museum open T-Su 10am-1pm. Shop open T-Su 10am-1:30pm, 4:30-7pm.*

EL ARENAL AND TRIANA

PLAZA DE TOROS DE MAESTRANZA — MONUMENT

Paseo de Cristóbal Colón, 12 ☎954 210 315 💻www.realmaestranza.com

Constructed between 1761 and 1881, Plaza de Toros de Maestranza is one of the oldest bullfighting rings in the world. The Maestranza offers a tours of the ring, stables, and museum (conducted in both English and Spanish) that will leave you feeling like a true master of the almost 300 years of bullfighting history. You can walk in right before the tours, conducted every 20min., and get in without a problem. The bullfights themselves, occurring on about 40 Sundays between April and October, are a true taste of Sevillian culture. Aside from during the *Feria de Abril,* when the best matadors are in town, you're fine grabbing a ticket the day before or even hours before the fight.

↗ *Off Paseo de Cristóbal Colón between Plaza de Armas and Torre de Oro.* $ *Tours €6, students €4. Bullfights €25-150 depending on seat.* ⏰ *Museum open daily May-Oct 9:30am-8pm; Nov-Apr 9:30am-7pm. 40min. tours run every 20min. Bullfights select Su Apr-Oct 7pm, 7:30pm.*

TORRE DE ORO — MUSEUM, VIEWS

Paseo de Cristóbal Colón s/n, near the intersection with Almirante Lobo ☎954 222 419

While it may no longer be filled with gold (sorry to burst your bubble), the Torre de Oro is still worth a visit. The now-maritime-museum can be covered in a maximum of 20min., at no cost with a student ID. But even if you come for some history, you'll stay for the views. Climb the spiraling marble steps to the top of the tour (yes, you should go all the way to the top) and you'll be able to see all of Triana to one side of the canal as well as great views of the Cathedral and Alcazar if looking toward Santa Cruz.

↗ *On the canal side of the street at the intersection of Cristóbal Colón and Almirante Lobo.* **i** *Cameras permitted.* $ *€2, students free. Automated tour free upon request.* ⏰ *Open Tu-F 9:30am-1:30pm, Sa-Su 10:30am-1:30pm.*

PARQUE DE LOS PRINCIPES — PARK

Intersection of Avenida de la Republica Argentina and C. Santa Fe

Bridges, fountains, pathways—no, it's not your favorite miniature golf course, but Parque de los Principes. Situated about a 10min. walk from the Canal, this park is the perfect place to relax, lie out, or go for a run or bike ride. Between the orange trees and hyacinths, you'll find yourself in one picturesque spot (beware: those pretty purple flowers may look nice, but they're viciously sticky and always seem to find themselves stuck right to your *trasero*). The city must have noticed that once you settle down, you'll probably never want to leave the park—hence that particularly practical food option. **Kiosko Bar**, located in the back right corner if entering from C. Santa Fe, offers home-made tapas *(€2.20)*, coffee *(€1.20)*, and a slew of drinks ranging from beer *(€1.20)* to whiskey *(€5)*.

↗ *From Puente de San Telmo take Av. de la Republica Argentina until you see the park on your left.*

NEAR ESTACIÓN PLAZA DE ARMAS

CENTRO ANDALUZ DE ARTE CONTEMPORÁNEO MUSEUM

Avenida Américo Vespucio 2 ☎955 037 070 💻www.caac.es

Embedded into the grounds of **Monasterio de la Cartuja de Santa Maria de las Cuevas** lies this oasis of modern Sevillian art. And that's quite a pairing to have–the classic, Moorish-style monastery grounds provide a harsh contrast with the bright white walls and mutli-media art collection found in the hallways of the museum. From movies, to slideshows, to music, and even interactive pieces, you'll find some of the most creative, colorful, and shocking artwork on the Sevillian scene. Make an afternoon of the treck across the river and spend some time lunching in the monastery gardens after a bit of cultural exposure at the museum.

About a 10 minute walk west from Estacion Plaza de Armas and then cross Puente de la Cartuja and make a right after crossing the bridge. **i** *Credit Card not accepted. Tours available.* $ *Museum admission €1.80, free on Tuesdays.* ⏰ *Apr-Sept Tu-Fr 10am-9pm, Sa 11am-9pm, Su 10am-3pm. Tours Su 12:30pm.*

the great outdoors

PARQUE DOÑANA

PARQUE DOÑANA — PARK

Las Carretas, 10 ☎630 978 216 🖥www.donana-nature.com

One of the largest national parks in all of Europe, Parque Doñana provides you with a good dose of nature and a strong urge to purchase a pair of binoculars and the complete set of an *Indiana Jones* movie. The excursions led out of **El Rocío** can be described as "safari-lite"—bouncing around in the back of a 4x4, try to hold your camera steady enough to catch a photo or two (or 200). The park itself is bordered by three cities that proudly share rights to its territory (**Huelva**, **Cadiz**, and **Sevilla**) and is composed of three main ecosystems: **forest**, **marshland**, and **beach.** Such a variety of untouched natural conditions provides for the exciting diversity of flora and fauna found in the park. While the friendly tour guides will provide a disclaimer that they can't promise you'll see any animals (it's a national park, not a zoo), we'd be shocked if you went through a whole visit without getting sight of something with a heartbeat. There are eagles, horses, and red deer to name a few. And don't forget the swarms of pink flamingos (did you know they get their color from a shrimp-only diet? You'd know if you took the tour!). Doñana also offers free entrance for unguided hiking routes throughout the park, but we think the excursion services are worth the extra price—from diagrams to maps, your guide will have the knowledge to make sure you don't miss an inch of Parque Doñana. However, don't think it's all about nature—you'll hear myths and stories about of the park, too. Don't the tomb of **Duchess Doña Ana** and the park's 13th-century identity as a **hunting ground** pique your interest?

From Estación Plaza de Armas, take a 1½hr. bus to Matalascañas (€6.61), and then take a 20min. bus to El Rocío/El Almonte (€1.17) and get off at the El Rocío stop. The visitor center for excursions to the park is to the left of the main church at El Rocío. **i** *Tours led in Spanish.* $ *Excursion through the park via van and bus €25 per schedule.* ⏰ *Excursions daily 8:30am and 5:30pm; 3-3½ hr. long.*

food

SANTA CRUZ

Because Santa Cruz draws in the most tourists of Sevilla, restaurants in the area are typically a bit larger and a bit done-up. You'll find many eateries with multiple floors of seating, bright lighting, and more English-speaking staff members.

HORNO DE SAN BUENAVENTURA — TRADITIONAL, CAFE [2]

28 Carlos Canal ☎954 221 829

Perfect for those exhausted by a day of travel in the Sevillian sun. Horno is located a hop, skip, and a jump (assuming all three of these are conducted with extensive force) away from the Cathedral and serves up a variety of perfect "cool down" foods at low prices. Utilize the overwhelming smell of the fresh bakery portion of the restaurant to help you ignore the line of pigs' legs hanging over the bar. The gazpacho *(€4.50)* is served chilled, with three large ice cubes floating atop this traditional tomato treat. If you're looking to further relieve the downpour of sweat streaming from your brow, try the wide selection of gelatos—the classic Málaga flavor of the region (actually rum-raisin) is the perfect sweet treat to end any meal. A historic relic originally established in 1385, Horno has had 5 different names and many more years of practice perfecting a wide selection of inexpensive dishes.

Located directly across Avenida de Constitución from the Cathedral. *i* *Outdoor table, and bar seating available.* $ *Tapas €2.25-€4.50. Sandwiches €3.50-€8.50. Ice cream €1.10.* ⏰ *Open daily 7:30am-11pm.*

EL TORNO ♿ BAKERY [1]

Plaza del Cabildo, 2 ☎954 219 190 eltonosl@terra.es

Thought the lack of street address might make it hard to find, El Torno is a bakery you don't want to miss—just cross Avenida de Constitución one block beyond C. del Mar (if your back is to the Cathedral) and you'll find the small plaza just steps away. The nuns of the Clausura Convent bake a fresh assortment of cookies, pastries, and marmalades each day. While the cookies aren't necessarily cheap, if you split a box of 12 *(€5.50-6.50)* with some friends, it's well worth the price—come on, you're supporting nuns. Made with whole hazelnuts and sweet jelly, the *galletas de almendras* taste like divine inspiration, and the nuns claim their orange marmalade is the best in town.

i *Credit card accepted for purchases over €10.* $ *Cookies €5.50-6.50 per box.* ⏰ *Open M-F 10am-1:30pm and 5pm-7:30pm, Sa-Su 10:30am-2pm.*

TABERNA COLONIALES TRADITIONAL, TAPAS [2]

Plaza Cristo de Burgos, 19 ☎954 501 137

C. Fernandez y Gonzalez, 36-38 ☎954 229 281, info@tabernacoloniales.es

The biggest complaint to make about Taberna Coloniales is that it's just too busy for its own good, but lucky for you they've expanded to two locations to ease the congestion. Even for lunch there's a chance that you'll need to wait for a table, but it's worth it. While most dishes—aside from the more expensive country bread platters or *tablas* (€5.05-10.75)—don't expect some tiny tapa to come out of the kitchen. Each helping is like a tapa on steroids, filling a whole face-sized plate. The *pollo con salsa de almendras* *(€2.50)* and the daily specials are both worth a try. Keep in mind that these waiters are pretty savvy: while they put bread on the table, it isn't free *(€1.70)*. If you're not going to eat it, ask them to take it away.

Located across Avenida de Constitución from the Cathedral down Plaza Cristo de Burgos. $ *Plates €1.55-€3.55. Tablas €5.05-10.75* ⏰ *Open daily 1:30-4:30pm and 8:30pm-12:15am.*

LEVIES TRADITIONAL, INTERNATIONAL [2]

C. San Jose, 15 ☎954 215 308 cafelevies@hotmail.com

Levies is the ideal dinner spot for the not-so-adventurous traveler. With colorful word art on its menu and outdoor seating, this spot is essentially a lite tapas bar. Expect traditional names prepared in a way that makes life as easy as possible for the chef—uninspired gazpacho, potato chips, and chilled red wine. This isn't to say that the establishment is touristy. Rather, they just redid the place and are hoping to bring in tourists by leaving coupons in all the main hostels. Pick one up for a free sangria with your meal. If you're a picky eater, the vegetarian section or non-Spanish offerings such as couscous and curry could be a nice curveball during your trip.

If leaving the Prado, turn left of Menendez Pelayo after the Diputacion Provincial de Sevilla. *i* *Bar has outdoor patio seating; tavern and terrace are indoors.* $ *Tapas €2.60-3.30. Wine by the bottle €8-12.* ⏰ *Bar open daily 7:30am-2am. Tavern and terrace open daily 7:30am-5pm and 8pm-2am.*

EL CENTRO

There are a few different types of places you'll find to dine in El Centro. Along the merchant area, eateries focus on speed and tourist appeal—getting you in, out, and back to stuffing shopping bags. At Plaza Alfalfa, you'll find patios jammed with locals snacking on their daily plate of *caracoles*, or snails. Otherwise, the small, winding streets of El Centro house some of the oldest, most classic tapas joints in all of Sevilla.

🖼 CONFITERIA LA CAMPAÑA   🍴🏛 BAKERY ❶
C. Sierpes, 1-3   ☎954 223 570

If you've got a sweet tooth, we've found your kryptonite. La Campaña has been serving up desserts since 1885 and has definitely mastered the task. The staff, dressed in parlor-esque aprons with headbands for the women and striped vests and bowties for the men, welcomes you and indulges your cravings. Served since the restaurant's opening, the *cervantinas* and *ingleses* are classics you've got to try. The *ingleses (€2.20)*, their most popular dessert, provides a sweet flan-like flavor without the gooey texture. Not feeling so adventurous? La Campaña also sells meringues, éclairs, truffles, cakes, and tarts *(€1.80-2.20)*. If you're looking for a real meal (although we can't imagine why you'd turn down a couple different courses of dessert), La Campaña also serves some fancier savory items such as smoked salmon and fresh cheese sandwiches—in short, you're gonna want to use your get-out-of-diet free card to go *loco*.

🔆 *If walking from the Ayuntamiento down C. Sierpes, it will be on the right.* Ⓢ *All desserts €1.80-2.20.* 🕐 *Open daily in summer 8am-11pm; in fall, winter, and spring 8am-10pm.*

🖼 LA BODEGA DE LA ALFALFA   🍴♿🍸❄ TRADITIONAL, TAPAS ❷
C. Alfalfa, 4   ☎954 227 362

For those who want their food fast but also want to hang out, La Bodega offers the tastiest, most traditional tapas around, serving it before you can even pick out which barrel along the wall you'll use as a table. The restaurant, centered around a bar that serves up all its food and drinks, has some of the friendliest, most enthusiastic waiters around, ready to gush about their favorite traditional dishes. The *mambru carmelo (€2.10)*, made of a brie-like cheese topped with sugar and honey and then baked to carmelize the sugar, combines sweet and savory like you've never experienced before. The *bacaloa al estilo la viuda (€2.20)*, a house specialty seafood, will have you licking your plate to get every drop of the tomato sauce garnish (maybe use some bread to scoop it up for the sake of looking less savage). The regulars tend to order a side of olives and one of the beers on tap, so maybe try that if you're trying to live like the locals.

🔆 *Located right off Plaza de Alfalfa at the base of C. Alfalfa.* Ⓢ *Tapas €1.80-2.20. Entrees €5-9.* 🕐 *Open daily 2:30-4pm and 8pm-midnight.*

EL RINCONCILLO   🍴🍸 TRADITIONAL, TAPAS ❶
C. Gerona 40-Alhóndiga, 2   ☎954 223 183🖥elrinconcillo.es

Opened in 1670, El Rinconcillo is the oldest tapas bar in Sevilla, and the tiled walls and warm lighting are clear relics of this historic past. Rinconcillo has definitely used its experience to get its staff in perfect working order—they serve so many people that they manage to keep tabs chalked on the bar without getting even a speck of white powder on their dressy uniforms. This place is even swanky enough for your senior prom (well, maybe a prom 25 years ago). Ask anyone for the house special and they'll tell you to try the *Pavia*—deep fried *bacaloa* served straight from the frier.

🔆 *Located on a tiny street behind Iglesia Santa Catalina if coming from the Plaza de Ponce de Leon.* Ⓢ *Tapas €1.80-2.80.* 🕐 *Open daily 1pm-1:30am.*

TABERNA DE LOS TERCEROS   🍴♿🍸🏛 TRADITIONAL, TAPAS, BREAKFAST❷
Plaza de Terceros, 11   ☎954 228 417

Taberna de los Terceros presents a perfectly Sevillian dinnertime atmosphere. Packing the place to the brim at 10pm, Taberna's local clientele takes full advantage of the establishment's outdoor patio, wooden tables, and colorful array of traditional tapas (€2.40-3.60). However, keep in mind that an afternoon *siesta* may be necessary to control your appetite and keep you mellow enough to withstand the not-so-speedy service. While much of the staff stands strongly behind the *camambert frito con mermelada de frambusa* (fried Spanish cheese served over fresh jam) as the best the house has to offer, try to branch out into some of the heartier meat and seafood tapas. Taberna de los Terceros also offers an extensive list of *desayunos*, or breakfast combos. The house special includes coffee, orange juice, and a traditional tostada *(toast served with olive oil and tomato; €4)*.

✪ *Located at the intersection of C. del Sol and C. Busto Tavera, in sight of the Church of Santa Catalina.* Ⓢ *Tapas €2.40-3.60. Desayunos €1.50-4.* 🕐 *Open daily 8:30am-midnight.*

HABANITA   🕶️👌♈❆ INTERNATIONAL, VEGETARIAN ❸
C. Golfo 3   ☎606 716 456 🖳www.habanita.es

Habanita represents the antithesis of typical Sevillian eating. While the secluded courtyard and mellow atmosphere could be a relaxing break from the party scene booming in nearby Plaza Alfalfa, the service is frustratingly slow and the prices continue to add up from the expensive courses and extra "service and bread" charge. We've yet to decide whether the combination of yucca, bolognese, cous cous, and ratatouille on one menu is a case of healthy variety or an identity crisis. While we'd suggest you save this option until you just can't even *look* at another tapa, we also recognize that the vegetarian and vegan distinctions on the menu will be extremely helpful to our more diet-specific travelers.

✪ *Off the far right corner of Plaza Alfalfa when entering the plaza from C. Alfalfa.* Ⓢ *Half-portions €4.15-8.25. Cocktails €4.50-5.75.* 🕐 *Open daily 12:30-4:30pm and 8pm-12:30am.*

LA MACARENA

Throughout most of La Macarena, you'll find small tapas bars packed with local regulars. Things get a bit classier (and a bit costlier) if you eat along the Alameda, but the open patio seating and centralized location make it worth the extra cash.

📓 ESLAVA   🕶️♈❆ TAPAS ❷
C. Eslava, 5   ☎954 906 568 🖳rb@restauranteeslava.es

Although the restaurant's pricier options will probably burn a hole in your wallet before you finish your meal, you should definitely try the delicious food at Eslava—even if it's only one plate of tapas. While it's filled to the brim in both the late afternoon and evening, try to squeeze your way through the crowd to place an order. All the ingredients are totally fresh, from the wide selection of raw shellfish *(half €6-8, full €12-17)* to the produce brought in straight from the owner's farm between June and October. Get your hands on those veggies by ordering the *strudel de verduras (€2.20)*. You'd be crazy to skip the over-easy egg served on top of a mushroom cake with mushroom sauce and honey *(€2.20)*—it won first prize for Sevilla's best tapa in 2010. Eslava is by no means a touristy establishment, but it rakes in locals and tourists alike.

✪ *Take C. Santa Ana from the Alameda and turn left once you see C. Santa Clara.* 𝒊 *Bar and restaurant separate.* Ⓢ *Tapas €2.20. Drinks €1-2.* 🕐 *Bar open daily 12:30-4:30pm and 8pm-midnight. Restaurant open daily 1-4pm and 9-11pm.*

CASA PACO   🕶️👌♈❆ TRADITIONAL ❷
Alameda de Hércules, 23   ☎663 959 266

While Casa Paco serves an array of classic Sevillian dishes from *salmorejo (€2.50)*, a chilled soup similar to gazpacho, to *carrillada (€3.50)*, pig's cheek, its general ambience is a nice break from the typical dark, divey Sevillian tapas bar. The prices are a little higher than the competition nearby, but it's clearly worth it—the place is packed on any summer night starting at 9pm. Even the pharmacist next door promotes Casa Paco to her customers (after bagging your prescription, of course). Her favorite *revuelto de papas (€2.50)*, a Spanish-style egg and potato omelette, is a unique version of the classic Spanish tortilla.

✪ *If coming from the Torneo, turn right off C. Santa Ana at the Alameda.* Ⓢ *Tapas €2.50-4. Entrees €7-12. Wine and beer €1.50-2.50.* 🕐 *Open daily 1:30-4:30pm and 8:30pm-midnight.*

ALMANARA

🍴♿🍸❄☁ VEGETARIAN ❷

Alameda de Hercules, 85 ☎954 372 897 💻www.restaurantealmanara.es

After a couple days of tapas bars and bodegas, you may start to find that your bread, cheese, and serrano ham intake is through the roof. And that's where Almanara comes in, offering the best vegetarian food in Sevilla. The salad Alamanara is refreshing and sweet, overflowing with dried fruit, nuts, avocado, and cherry tomatoes. You can even try some meat substitutes if the full cross-over to vegetarianism is out of your league—they swear by their soy burgers and bolognese. Located right on the Alameda de Hercules, this sleek restaurant with a spacious patio is the perfect way to fill up before a night out on the town. Enjoy some veggies and save the caloric intake for the sangria!

➔ Located on the right of the Alameda from El Centro. ℹ Special vegetarian menu M-F 1:30-4pm. $ Salads €7.50-9. Entrees €7.50-12. ⏰ Open daily 1:30pm-midnight.

TRIANA AND EL ARENAL

As Triana and Arenal border the Guadalquivir Canal running right through Sevilla, it's only natural that they'd specialize in fish and seafood. Any restaurant located along the canal will tell you that they make the very best fish *frito* (fried) or *a la plancha* (grilled). That isn't to say that this neighborhood has given up on the classic tapas culture. Branch beyond the major canal-side streets to find some of the cleanest, classiest tapas bars serving up all the classics with an extra splash of seafood. Triana is also unique in its offering of some ethnic foods, entirely non-Spanish. While **Calle Salado** may not look like much, you'll find some well-priced establishments ready to ship you off to Japan, Thailand, India, or the other side of the Mediterranean.

✔ FARO DE TRIANA

🍴❄☁ TRADITIONAL, SEAFOOD, VIEWS ❸

Puente Isabel II (Puente de Triana) ☎954 336 192

You may get a bit discouraged walking down C. Betis and seeing restaurant after restaurant offering fresh seafood at painfully expensive prices. What's the backpacker to do? Faro de Triana may be your solution. While not cheap, Faro provides slightly lower prices without any loss of quality. You can keep it casual and still get the freshest fish around. Like most of the restaurants along the canal, Faro specializes in its fried *(½ portion €9, full €15)* and whole grilled *(€15-18)* fish options. The heaping half portions are large enough to fill you up and maybe even take you out of commission for your next meal. Even the location and seating options can't be beat: for great views and some A/C, eat at the bar; for a classier dining experience, try the lower dining room; and for some snacking along the canal, take your meal to the outdoor patio.

➔ Immediately to the left once you cross Puente de Triana. $ Half portions €9, full €15-18. ⏰ Open M-Sa 8am-midnight. Open later on the weekends.

BLANCA PALOMA

🍴🍸❄ TAPAS, TRADITIONAL, SEAFOOD ❷

San Jacinto, 49 ☎605 816 187

Upon entering Blanca Paloma, you'll be immediately impressed by this clean, classy restaurant with a stunning wooden bar and charming red curtains. While Trianans love their larger fish platters, Blanca Paloma proves that they haven't neglected the tapas culture. You can still get top seafood—their eggplant stuffed with shrimp *(€2.10)* and shrimp with garlic *(½ portion €6, full €12)* are highly recommended—but you've also got the option to enjoy more classic tapas and meat dishes. While the staff will be happy to recommend their favorite dishes, just grab one of the many local regulars sitting at the bar, and they'll pour their hearts out on the best way to fill your belly.

➔ At the intersection of San Jacinto and C. Pajes del Corro. On the farther right corner if coming from Puente de Triana. $ Tapas €1.80-3, ½ portions €5.40-9, full €9-15. ⏰ Open M-F 8:30am-4:30pm and 7pm-midnight, Sa 12:30-4:30pm and 8:30pm-12:30am, Su 8:30am-4:30pm and 7pm-midnight.

MERCADO DE TRIANA

♿❄ MARKETPLACE ❷

Intersection of San Jorge and Altozano

The cleanest, best organized, air-conditioned marketplace you'll find in Sevilla. Hop between vendors, checking out the freshest produce, meats, and pastries, and stop at the souvenir shop on your way out. **Bar La Muralla** *(Mercado de Triana 72 ☎954 344 302 ☺ Open M-Sa 6:30am-3pm.)* in the back of the Mercado uses all the products offered in the marketplace to serve lunch and breakfast to its enthusiastic local customers. You'll get laughed at if you ask for a menu—they don't even have one! Just ask for a recommendation and they'll tell you about all the fresh products that have come in that day *(tapas €2.20-3, ½ portions €6).* La Muralla is a particularly perfect place to grab a breakfast of *churros con chocolate* or a lunch to go.

�« *On the right-hand side at the base of the Puente de Triana.* ⑤ *Prices vary based on vendor.* ☺ *Open M-Sa 7:30am-3pm. Hours for specific vendors vary.*

nightlife

Sevilla's nightlife takes into account its two main forces: the hip, young locals looking for some good wine and snails to snack on and the swarms of study abroad students and visitors learning to best coordinate their sweat-stained T-shirts with their newest pair of stilettos. Keep in mind that most local Sevillians make their way to the coasts in the summer, so the winter night scene is far busier than summer.

SANTA CRUZ

Not necessarily the party capital of Sevilla, Santa Cruz still has some nice spots to get your drink on, see a show, and enjoy some late-night tapas. Most of the hotspots retain their local flair despite the loads of tourists frequently this district. If you're looking for where the locals are spending their nights in the Santa Cruz area, make your way to **Plaza de Alfalfa** and the small surrounding streets. You'll find Sevillians dominating the outdoor patios of the bars and restaurants, snacking on *caracoles*, snails, and enjoying an inexpensive pitcher of sangria or tall glass of beer.

BAR ALFALFA   ⴲ BAR
C. Candilejo, 1   ☎954 222 344 ▨baralfalfa@hotmail.com
When traveling to the locals' hotspot in Sevilla, Plaza de Alfalfa, you might as well go to the Plaza's namesake. While this small, wooden tavern keeps things traditional, offering only Spanish and Italian wines and liquors (sorry Tom Cruise, no cocktails!) and specializing in classic Sevillian *brusquettas* (locally made bread topped with different meat, seasoning, and vegetable combinations), it's by no means outdated. If you're willing to get adventurous and step out of the backpacker bubble to see what Sevillan 20-somethings are up to (or maybe use this for an early pregame), get ready to test out your Spanish, listen to the local music, and chat over a glass of vino.

�« *Located right at the tip of Plaza Alfalfa, off C. Alfalfa.* ⑤ *Drinks €1.60-€2.80, brusquetta €2.30-€2.90.* ☺ *Open daily 9am-2:30am.*

ANTIGUEDADES   ⴲ⚅ BAR
Argote de Molina, 40   ▨www.tapearensevilla.com
Stepping into Antiguedades, you may be a little confused as to whether you're in a bar or a Halloween shop. With mannequins dressed as clowns draping the walls and fake bloodied hands and feet adorning the ceiling, let's hope you're a happy drunk who can get through the night without freaking out. And if the decor isn't enough to get you on your toes, maybe the Spanish covers of '80s American hits (Video le Mató la Estrella del Radio, anyone?), or mashups between classic Spanish songs and American hip hop will freak you out. The bar itself caters to a mix of mostly locals and some tourists, mostly popular for pre-dinner drinks around 5-9pm. While the cocktails are a bit pricey, they offer all the classics from *mojitos* to *caipiriñas* (a Barcelonian lemony, sweet drink). The pitcher of sangria has a special splash of coconut rum and the perfect refreshing treat for 3-4 people to split.

�« *From Plaza Virgen de los Reyes, take Placentines to Argote de Molina and the bar will be on your left.* **i** *Drinks discounted from 5-9pm.* ⑤ *Wine and beer €2. Cocktails €6. Pitchers €12.* ☺ *Open daily 5pm-3am.*

CARBONERÍA
🍺🍸 BAR, FLAMENCO

C. Levies, 18 ☎954 229 954

While you may at first feel uncomfortable walking down the slim, curving alleyway of C. Levies to the Carbonería, you'll soon realize that the few other stragglers on the street are also sneaking peaks at their maps. This large establishment packs itself chock full of young backpackers looking for high-energy fun. Carbonería offers competitive drink prices *(1L of sangria; €8)* and free performances every evening, including Flamenco and a Spanish singing style called *Copla*. While the people sitting beside you at the long tables in the main hall will not be Sevillians, chances are you'll meet citizens from at least a few different countries around the globe.

🪧 Turn off C. Santa Maria onto C. Levies and follow the road as it starts to curve. $ Beer and wine €1.50-4. Cocktails €5.50. ⏰ Open daily 8pm-2am. Flamenco show M-F 11pm, Sa-Su 11pm and midnight.

EL CENTRO

NOVECCENTO
🎟🍸⛅▼ BAR

C. Julio Cesar, 10 ☎954 229 102 💻www.noveccento.com

While this small GLBT-friendly bar in the southern portion of El Centro may not look like much—the rusting, rainbow-neon sign out front and patio of all of 3 tables aren't exactly in pristine condition—its simplicity brings in the locals night after night. Noveccento only serves beer, wine, sodas, and a limited collection of cocktails, yet you won't hear a complaint in the crowd. Come chill out to the relaxing soundtrack of both Spanish and English tunes, and sit along the small bar (but be prepared to endure thick clouds of cigarette smoke—there's not one open window in the place). While fairly empty around opening time, Noveccento is packed by 11:30pm, and you'd be lucky to get a seat on a Sunday in the winter.

🪧 C. Julio Cesar links C. Reyes Catolicos and C. Marques de Paradas on the diagonal. $ Wine, beer, and soda €2. Cocktails €6. ⏰ Open in summer M-Th 8:30pm-3am, F-Sa 8:30pm-4am, Su 8:30pm-3am; open in winter M-Th 5pm-3am, F-Sa 5pm-4am, Su 5pm-3am.

LA MACARENA AND WEST

La Macarena and the area further west may very well be the best place to set out for an evening in Sevilla. You'll find everything from open patio dining to relaxed bars and classy clubs. Your best bet is to start on the Alameda, exploring the side streets branching off this central parkway. If you're looking for the most massive, high-end clubs around, make the trek across the bridge to the intersection of the Torneo and C. Resolana—just be ready to spend as much for a beer as you did for your last meal.

✓ THEATRO ANTIQUE
🎟🍸❄⛅ CLUB

C. Matematicas Rey Pastor y Castro s/n ☎954 462 207 💻www.antiquetheatro.com

1200 square meters, a 1400 person capacity, 3 outdoor bars, *and* a swimming pool? We don't want to get you all flustered with the math, but the full magnitude of Theatro Antique can't even be comprehended without a visit. This upscale club is the place to see and be seen, catering to a few famous faces and thousands of trendsters looking for the snazziest evening around. You'll hear the booming music from all the way across the river, putting some of the smaller clubs along the Torneo to shame. In the summer, take relaxation to a whole new level by sitting around the pool on the Aqua Antique patio in your personal cabana, hanging with friends and sipping your overpriced *caipiriña (€8)*. Antique continues to outperform even with it's schedule: it stays open so late that, upon leaving, you could stumble right over to a nearby breakfast joint for some *churros con chocolate*...and a giant cup of coffee.

🪧 From the Alameda, take C. Calatrava and cross the bridge; the club is on the left. $ Beer €4. Sangria €6. Mojitos and caipirinas €8. ⏰ Open in summer Tu-Su midnight-7am; in winter Th-Sa midnight-7am.

BODEGA VIZCAÍNO
🍺🍸 BAR, LOCALS

C. Feria 27 ☎954 386 057

Even with only two guys behind the counter, Bodega Vizcaíno manages to cater to its overflowing, riotous clientele. Busiest with locals in their 20s and 30s around

9:30pm, it's still completely packed for an afternoon drink. Grab a cold beer *(€1.10)* or local wine *(€1-1.30)* served straight out of the barrels resting behind the bar, or try a local specialty, the *Tinto de Verano*, a fruity drink offered with your choice of white, orange, or lemon liqueur *(€1.10)*. If you're feeling really adventurous, don't just snack on the complimentary green olives but order up some fresh, chilled *bacalao* like a local. Maybe you'll impress a Sevillian or two.

Located near the intersection of C.Feria and C. Correduría. $ Beer €1.10. Wine €1-1.30. ⏰ Open M-Sa 8am-11:30pm.

JACKSON CLUB

C. Relator 21

From the front door, Jackson may not look like much—it lurks in a dark corner with a cheesy icon as a sign—but don't pass judgment just yet. Walk down the slim hallway on any night of the week around 2am and you'll find a packed dance floor lined with colorful, patterned walls (which change multiple times a year for the sake of variety) booming with 80s funk. The bartenders joke about how the standard patron is what they describe as "pijippie," a combination of *pijos*, or trendy fashionistas, and a free spirited hippie youth, between the ages of 20 and 35. While they must advertise that they close at 3am, locals describe their schedule as "111pm through the rest of the week." So grab a beer *(€2-3)*, and rely on that next morning's latte to wake you up after a night of hip-shaking heaven.

Off to the far left corner of the Alameda from El Centro; the bar is on the left. $ Beer €2-3. Mixed drinks €6-7. ⏰ Open daily 11:30pm-3am.

EL BARON RAMPANTE BAR

Arias Montaro, 3 ☎647 249 537

There may not be a beach in Sevilla, but so what? You can have a tropical evening, beachy music, and a bamboo-decorated bar any day by making your way into the colorfully lit El Baron Rampante. You can chill out, grab a mojito, and just enjoy this casual, upbeat bar environment without the nasty sea gulls or sticky sand (save that for Costa del Sol). The owner can't be older than 25, and his youth seems to bring in an equally hip staff and clientele. Located right on the Alameda, this GLBT-friendly spot is absolutely packed on weekend nights. You can also catch some flamenco at 8pm every Su.

Located on the left-hand side of a small street branching off the Alameda between C. Recreo and C. Santa Ana. $ Beer and wine €2. Mojitos and caipirinhas €6. ⏰ Open daily 4pm-1am.

BOSQUE ANIMADO BAR

Arias Montaro, 5 ☎954 916 862

Escape the noisy, crowded patios of the Alameda and experience the relief of entering into this fairy-tale cave setting—and it's GLBT-friendly to boot. The earth-toned walls, brass bar, and woody seating will provide you with a comfort and sense of secrecy that you haven't experienced since you built pillow forts out of your living room cushions. With your *cubata (€6)* in hand, grab any seat at the bar aside from the one at the corner—it's permanently occupied by a gnome statue, signature to Bosque Animado. Surrounded by a mix of 20- and 30-something tourists and locals, enjoy the mellow music early in the early evening, and hear the playlist shift to prep for the party around midnight. If you're in town at the right time, definitely don't miss Halloween in October and Carnivales in February.

Located on the left-hand side of a small street branching off the Alameda between C. Recreo and C. Santa Ana. $ Beer €1.50-2.50. Cocktails €6. ⏰ Open daily 4pm-2am.

EL ARENAL AND TRIANA

Triana may be a laid-back, low-key neighborhood, but that doesn't mean Trianans don't know how to have fun. The streets bordering the canal will offer up all the classic drinks and some of the best playlists around. Generally, the clubs attract a younger crowd of late-teens and 20-somethings, jazzed up on hormones and soda pop and ready for a good time.

KUDÉTA CAFE CHILLOUT DISCOTECA (AKA BUDDHA) ♥♥❄♨ CLUB

Plaza de la Legión   ☎954 089 095 ▤www.kudetasevilla.es

If you ask a local how to get to Kudéta, they'll likely shrug their shoulders. But if you drop the name Buddha, you'll get an immediate sly smirk—they've probably been there, and they've probably had some crazy nights. Kudéta is one of the largest clubs in all of Sevilla, packing its three stories so full that they even expand into the Centro Commercial during their busiest weekend hours. They know they'll fill up, so they have no problem offering prices far higher than much of their competition. While the 1st floor remains pretty mellow (how can you not be mellow with pictures of Siddhartha on every wall and silky pillows and drapes everywhere?), offering hookah and a selection of wines and beers, things get rowdy on the upstairs dance floor and outdoor terrace. Thursday nights are reserved for enormous study-abroad student parties of about 1000 visitors, so you'll probably fit in quite easily.

⚢ *Located within the Centro Comercial de Plaza de Armas, in the portion closest to Av. de la Expiración.* Ⓢ *Bottles of beer €4. Cocktails €7.50.* ⏲ *Open in summer daily 3pm-6am; in winter M-W 3pm-4am (only lounge open), Th-Sa 3pm-6am, Su 3pm-4am (only lounge open).*

ISBILIYYA ♥♨♥▼ BAR, CLUB

Paseo de Cristobal Colon, 2   ☎954 210 460

With a canalfront terrace absolutely packed on any summer night and a booming dance floor all year round, Isbiliyya may be Sevilla's greatest hotspot for GLBT nightlife. Cross the Puente de Triana and be welcomed by the friendly staff, as open and congenial as the crowds of locals (young and old) ready to meet and mingle. Enjoy the cafe during the evening, the bar a bit later *(discounted drinks until 1am—beers are just €2 and mixed drinks €4)*, and the party until the early mornings. The combo of '80s dance and pop house music can't be beat. Did we mention the pride of Isbiliyya—every night at 1:30am the bar holds a drag show on its main stage, bringing out some of the most colorful and creative costumes that this city has ever seen. Grab a caipirina or mojito *(€3.50)* and enjoy the music, dance, and maybe even return that wink you get from the guy singing in the spotlight.

⚢*Located on Paseo de Colon, right at the base of Puente de Triana.* Ⓢ *Beer €3. Cocktails €3.50.* ⏲ *Open daily 8pm-4am. Drag show daily 1:30am.*

FLAMINGO LOUNGE ♥♿♥ BAR, CLUB

Paseo de Cristobal Colón 4

Don't be discouraged if you feel like the bartender is a little distracted, or even looking right past you. He's probably just trying to sneak a peek at the Sevilla soccer game projected onto a screen on the front patio of Flamingo Lounge. The bar and club broadcast all the local soccer games and put up a slide show if no one is playing. Such activities bring in all the young locals for the early part of the night, but when the club gets going later on, it becomes an even mix of locals and tourists. The pitchers of sangria *(€15)* can satisfy you and four friends (or three thirstier friends), and the extra minty mojitos *(€6)* do the classic drink proud. While the salted seeds and nuts on the table are free, keep in mind how thirsty you already are after a day in the Sevillian sun—upping your sodium just ups your orders (and hurts your hangover).

⚢ *Located on Paseo Colón between Plaza de Armas and Plaza de Toros.* Ⓢ *Cocktails €6. Beer €2. Jar of sangria €15.* ⏲ *Open daily approx. 4pm-3am; closing time depends on how busy the club is.*

arts and culture

As the capital of **Andalucia,** Sevilla attracts the best and brightest on the artistic and cultural scene. Sevilla's got the money, the motivation, and the spirit of possibility flowing through the streets. Don't just think you're gonna find macarenas and castanets—Sevilla provides traditional flamenco, opera, dance, and performance, as well as a slew of avant-garde theaters and smaller concert halls to be enjoyed by young and old alike. The arts are by no means limited to velvet chairs and golf claps, though—scream your lungs out from the sidelines of a soccer match and try not to cover your eyes at the **Plaza de Toros.**

THEATER

Theater culture in Sevilla caters to those looking for big, extravagant performances as well as smaller, private experiences. Apart from the listings below you can find indie and alternative concerts at **Sala Fun Club** *(Alameda de Hercules, 86* ☎*954 218 064* 🖥*www.funclubsevilla.com* 🕐 *Th-Sa 9:30-10pm)*, or folk and blues shows at **Cafe Lisboa** *(Alhóndiga* ☎*983 291 615* 🕐 *M-Sa 3pm-3am, Su 1pm-3am.)* or **El Hobbit.** *(C. Regina, 20* 🕐 *Shows around 10pm, Th Jazz, Sa Folk)* If you want to catch a flick, **Avenida 5 Cines** *(C. Marques de Paradas 15)* shows international films with Spanish subtitles for €5.50, while **Cinesa** *(Plaza de la Legion, 8* ☎*902 333 231)* in the mall at Plaza de Armas, shows flicks dubbed in Spanish *(€6.50)* and even 3D movies *(€9.50).*

TEATRO LOPE DE VEGA ◆ SANTA CRUZ

Av. María Luisa s/n ☎955 472 828 🖥www.teatrolopedevega.org

Teatro Lope de Vega is the main theatrical stage in all of Sevilla, and it fits any stereotype you'd hold of a classic theater—red velvet chairs and curtains with golden trim. Run and orchestrated by the city government, this theater is located just behind the Universidad de Sevilla. Shows usually start around 9pm; depending on the performance, tickets can range from €4 to €45.

⚓ *Located off Parque Maria Luisa near the Universidad and the Plaza de España.* Ⓢ *Tickets €4-45.* 🕐 *Box office open Tu-Sa 11am-2pm and 6-9pm, Su 11am-2pm.*

TEATRO DE LA MAESTRANZA ◆ ARENAL

Paseo de Colon 22 ☎954 223 344 🖥www.teatromaestranza.com

Teatro de la Mestranza holds operas, flamenco shows, and dance and piano recitals for a classier, more formal crowd. Don't be troubled by the statue of the non-Spanish Mozart out front—the theater is merely thanking him for including the city of Sevilla in his *Marriage of Figueroa* through the character Barbaro.

⚓ *Located right next to the Plaza de Toros on Paseo de Colon.* Ⓢ *Tickets €17-39.* 🕐 *Open Th-F 8:30pm.*

LA IMPERDIBLE ◆ OSUNA

Plaza del Duque s/n ☎954 905 458 🖥www.imperdible.org

The first independent theater in all of Sevilla, La Imperdible puts on smaller plays, flamenco shows, concerts, and even child productions, priding itself on its originality and diversity of performance style. The shows are created "on demand," ready to serve the local interest. Stop here to get a taste of some less classical Sevillian theater.

⚓ *Branching off C. Alfonso VII, make a left if coming from the Torneo.* Ⓢ *General admission €12, student €9. Concerts €6.* 🕐 *Performances Th-Sa 7-11pm, Su 6-8pm.*

SALA CERO ◆ EL CENTRO

C. Sol, 5 ☎954 225 165 🖥www.salacero.com

Since its creation in 1999, Sala Cero has stood strongly by its philosophy of promoting local creativity and literary promise. Over the years the theater has put on eight performances, all but one of which were original comedies written by Andalucian playwrights.

⚓ *Right near the church of Santa Catalina, at the base of Plaza de Terceros.* Ⓢ *Tickets €11.* 🕐 *Performances W-Th 11am-2pm and 6:30-8:30pm, F 11am-2pm and 6:30pm-curtain, Sa 6:30pm-curtain, Su 6:30-8:30pm.*

FLAMENCO

🖼 TARDES DE FLAMENCO EN LA CASA DE LA MEMORIA ◆♈☁ SANTA CRUZ

C. Ximenez de Enciso 28 ☎954 560 670 🖥www.casadelamemoria.es

Hidden away in a small, tented garden plaza, Tardes de Flamenco knows how to set the scene and pack the house. The show is performed by four artists, all of whom couldn't be older than 25. Try not to scrape your chin on the floor when your jaw drops—these kids know their stuff. Running through two centuries of flamenco, they layer on the components, starting with just a guitar before adding in the male and female dancers one at a time. The dancers aren't the only ones getting their heart rate up—you'll get so sucked into the drama that you'll feel your chest pounding. Hands down the best deal for classic flamenco around. Buy tickets in advance and arrive at least 30min. early, as every show tends to sell out.

C. Ximenez crosses C. Santa Maria la Blanca and extends into Plaza Alianza, right in between the Alcazar and Convento de la Encarnacion. $ €15, students €13. ⏰ Daily shows at 9pm and 10:30pm. Arrive at least 30min. early to get a seat.

TABLAO EL ARENAL

🎫🍸 ARENAL

C. Rono, 7 ☎954 216 492 💻www.tablaoarenal.com

Tablao de Arenal requires an investment of time and money but has been rumored to host the very best classic Flamenco in town. If you don't want to take our word for it, even the **New York Times** called it the best place in the world to experience flamenco. The show goes for about two hours and the prices range from €37-€72 depending on how much you want to be eating and drinking with the performance.

Between the bullring and Hospital de Caridad. $ Show and 1 drink €37. Show with tapas, drink, and dessert €59. Show with full dinner €72. ⏰ Shows daily 8pm and 10pm.

EL PATIO SEVILLANO

🎫🍸 ARENAL

Paseo de Cristobal Colón, 11A ☎954 214 120 💻www.elpatiosevillano.com

One of the oldest flamenco bars in town, El Patio Sevillano provides another classic Flamenco performance with a meal included at a steep price. Compared to Tablao de Arenal (whose prices are about the same), you're getting a shorter show (1½hr.) at a less famous establishment. That said, the colorful, cool, underground tiled dining room does set the tone for some traditional Spanish culture.

On Cristobal Colón, only meters from the bullring. $ Show €37. Show with tapas €59. Show with full dinner €70. ⏰ Shows daily at 7pm and 9:30pm.

FESTIVALS

SEMANA SANTA

SPRING

💻www.semana-santa.org

Semana Santa, or **Holy Week,** is the annual period between Palm Sunday and Easter Sunday, and thus the last week of Lent. During these seven days, all 57 religious brotherhoods of the city adorn hooded robes and guide two candlelit floats honoring Jesus and the Virgin Mary along the tiny, winding Sevillian streets. As they make their way to the Catedral, they grab the attention of around one million spectators year after year. You don't need to be a religious person to be awed by the history and picturesque spectacle that is Semana Santa. Hotels and hostels fill far in advance but are slightly less busy if you come during the first portion of the week, as Semana Santa culminates on **Good Friday.** If you're going to stay for the end of the week, you may also consider extending your trip until **Feria de Abril**—you may be due for the shift from pious patron to partier. The tourist offices of the city are well-equipped to answer any questions about accommodations and dining during this busy time in Sevilla. You can also visit the museum at the **Basílica La Macarena** to learn more about the history of Semana Santa. *(C. Becker 1, 3 ☎954 901 800 💻www.hermandaddelamacarena.es)*

FERIA DE ABRIL

Los Remedios District of Sevilla 💻www.feriadesevilla.andalunet.com

Following the holy week of Semana Santa each year, Feria de Abril is the time for Sevilla to let its hair down and celebrate its rich culture and history. Started in 1847 as a **cattle-trade expo** in the Prado de San Sebastian, this week of festivities has made great strides ever since—the Feria today takes up one million sq. m of Sevillian territory! The celebrations take place in three main parts: the 15-block **Real de la Feria,** the colorful amusement park at **Calle de Infierno,** and the main entrance, or **Posada.** The Real is the heart of the Feria—the asphalt is covered in golden sand to match the bullring, the sidewalks are lined with *casetas*, (canvas houses where you can spend the week drinking and eating with friends and family), and horse-drawn carriages and flamenco dancers pass through the streets. Don't forget the biggest event lineup of the week. Each day, six bulls are set into the ring at **Plaza de Toros de la Maestranza** to face off against the most famous matadors Spain has to offer. Tickets go way in advance, so call the office for reservations (☎*954 210 315)*.

From the moment thousands of Chinese-style lanterns light up the city in unison at midnight of the first night to when Sevilla cuts to black at the closing of the festivities at midnight on the last night, you are in for quite the treat. But remember, the secret's out about this Spanish tradition. Hostels book fast, and you should expect higher prices. As far as suggestions, turn to the **information offices** throughout the city or the **kiosks** located on the Feria grounds. Special, direct buses run from the Prado and Charco de la Pava to the Real, and the C1, C2, and 41 bus lines stay running throughout the day *(€1.50)*. Both ends of Metro Line 1 are located smack in the middle of the excitement. The city government recommends that you monitor your alcohol consumption and designate meeting locations before going out for the day, as the streets become extremely packed and dangerous for inebriated wanderers.

futbol

Two main soccer teams, Sevilla and Betis, dominate this region, and you better determine your loyalties fast. Even the local newspaper website has separate tabs for the fans of each of these two teams. But the rivalry has died down a bit in recent years, as Betis had to get bumped down to a lower league than Sevilla, and it doesn't look like they'll be bumping back up any time soon. The Estadio Ramón Sánchez Pizjuan (Av. de Eduardo Dato s/n ☎902 510 011 wwww.sevillafc.es) houses Sevilla in the northeast corner of the city, and is said to be one of the snazziest stadiums in all of Spain. The current capacity of 45,500 guests is actually a reduced version of the original 70,000 before FIFA restrictions kicked in. With such claims to fame as having hosted the World Cup Semifinal in 1982 and being the only stadium where the Spanish national team is undefeated, the feeling of pride and history is even stronger than the smell of freshly mowed grass. Real Betis, across the river, calls Estadio Manuel Ruiz de Lopera (Av. Heliópolis s/n ☎902 19 1907 wwww. realbetisbalompie.es) its home. This stadium, even larger than that of the Sevilla team, is Betis' best compensation for their poor showing in recent seasons.

shopping

Whether it's losing yourself in an open-air market, window-browsing until you buy that authentic souvenir, or simply taking in a mall, you can find all the shopping styles Sevilla has to offer throughout its neighborhoods. While **El Centro** is probably the best place to start, especially along C. Sierpes, C. Cuna, and C. Velazquez Tetuan, that doesn't mean you should neglect the many options offered at the mall at **Plaza de Armas** or in the markets around **Triana** and **Santa Cruz.** As for souvenir shops, you'll find them around every corner—offering all the cheesy keepsakes you could dream of. Hope you left room in your pack!

EL CENTRO

Yeah, it's the center of the city geographically, but who cares about longitude and latitude when you have fashion on your mind? El Centro is the center for stuffing shopping bags, swiping credit cards, and marching the packed streets between Santa Cruz and La Macarena.

CALLE VELÁZQUEZ TETUÁN, CALLE LAS SIERPES, AND CALLE CUNA

The best way to get your shopping fix while in Sevilla is to visit three main streets right in the middle of town. C. Velázquez Tetuán, C. las Sierpes, and C. Cuna are smaller roads, lined end to end with every type of shopping you can imagine. With the **Ayuntamiento** and **Calle Martin Villa** as bookends, you get a nice chunk of space for hours of browsing all the colorful, product-packed displays. There are also many outdoor seating areas if you want to rest your shoulders from the weight of all those shopping bags and lots of small cafes to grab a bite. While the roads are packed throughout the day with high-paced tourists and locals, they're empty in the evenings when the stores close and are lit enough to offer a safe place for an evening stroll. Prices and hours vary depending on the store.

Between the Ayuntamiento and C. Martin Villa.

CENTRO COMERCIAL Y DE OCIO DE PLAZA DE ARMAS — MALL

Plaza de la Legión, 8 ☎954 908 282 www.ccplazadearmas.com

When your craving to shop and your need for A/C come into conflict, we have a solution for you: Centro Comercial is a glowing beacon of climate-controlled hope at the bottom tip of El Centro. The glass walls and tin ceiling enclose this small, two-story mall that somehow manages to pack in all the essentials. From clothing to sporting goods to fast food and bars, you can get all you need without the overwhelming feeling of the mall metropolises found across the globe. The five-screen movie theater *(tickets €6)* on the second floor is also a great option to avoid the summer sun. Check out the dinner-and-a-movie deals offered at many of the restaurants to save a couple bucks.

*Located directly across C. Arjona from the Estación de Autobuses Plaza de Armas. **i** ATM available. Parking in public lot, adjacent to mall. $ Movie theater ticket €6. ⏰ Mall open daily 9am-1:30am. Stores open M-Sa 10am-10pm.*

SANTA CRUZ

MERCADO PUERTA DE LA CARNE — MARKET

Av. de Cadiz

While it may not look too impressive from the outside, the rusting, high, tin roof of Mercado Puerta de la Carne houses one of the largest fruit and meat markets of Sevilla. From pineapples and peaches to sardines and pork slabs, you can find all the freshest, cheapest food items in town. It also happens to be a one-stop shop to prep for a hot date: you could get a haircut *(Peluqueria Eligia Camacho ☎654 967 762 ⏰Open M-Sa 8:30am-3pm),* buy your significant other some jewelry *(Joyeria Carmen Martinez ☎954 426 344 ⏰ Open M-Sa 9am-2:30pm.),* and even pick up a bouquet of flowers all without leaving the Mercado. Just hope that the fish stench of the establishment doesn't stick to your clothes.

*Cut under the bridge on C. Demetrio de los Rios and turn left. **i** Many of the establishments take credit cards, but it depends on which vendor you ask. Peluqueria does not take credit card. $ Fruits from €0.90-1.50 per kg. Meats €6.80-8.20 per kg. ⏰ Open daily 8am-3pm (although times depend on vendors' arrival).*

FELIX CARTELISMO — POSTERS

Av. de la Constitucion 26, Galeria at Plaza de Cabilido Local D ☎954 218 026 www.poster-felix.com

For the collectors and artists out there, Felix Cartelismo is definitely worth stopping at. Those of you who just want to decorate your dorm room with something other than Bob Marley's or Audrey Hepburn's face may also want to browse. Walking among a pricey selection of collectibles including original prints by local artists and vintage tins and posters from old Sevillian establishments *(€30-250),* you may get a chance to bring home something historic and unique. Or you could take the path of just buying a reproduction (who's gonna know, right?) and save the extra cash *(€6-9).* They'll give you a storage tube and point you to the post office around the corner if you don't want to lug your purchase around in your pack.

↔ *On Av. de la Constitución, opposite side of the street from the Catedral.* $ *Reproductions €6-9. Originals €30-250. Classic originals up to €1000.* ⏰ *Open M-F 10am-3pm and 5-8:30pm, Sa-Su 10am-3pm.*

OUTSKIRTS

C. FERIA FLEA MARKET — FLEA MARKET

C. Feria

Unless you're looking to buy a new set of headlights, a used action figure, or a bootleg Spanish-dubbed DVD (which you very well may be interested in doing—who are we do judge?), you likely won't actually buy anything at the C. Feria Flea Market. But that's not to say that you shouldn't visit. You'll get a kick at all the junk they try to sell off, and maybe the most diligent of you will discover a diamond in the rough (not literally).

↔ *Between the Iglesia San Gil and Plaza de Monte-sion. Turn off C. Resblana onto C. Feria to start at the beginning of the market.* $ *Prices vary according to vendor.* ⏰ *Open approximately Th 8am-2pm.*

essentials

PRACTICALITIES

- **TOURIST OFFICES:** The **Centro de Información de Sevilla Laredo** has extensive information for tourists in Sevilla. *(Pl. de San Francisco, 19 ☎954 595 288 💻www.sevilla.org/turismo ⏰ Open M-F 9am-7:30pm, Sa-Su 10am-2pm.)* **Turismo de la Provincia** also has tourist information and gives out special discounts at some of the newer and more popular restaurants in the area. *(Pl. del Turinfo, 1-3 ☎954 210 005 💻www.tourismosevilla.org ⏰ Open daily 10:30am-2:30pm and 3:30-7:30pm.)*
- **LAUNDROMAT: Vera Tintoreria** provides self-service wash and dry at two different locations. *(☎954 534 495 for Aceituna 6; ☎954 541 148 for Menendez Pelayo, 11. $ Wash and dry €10. ⏰ Open M-F 9:30am-2pm and 5:30-8pm, Sa 10am-1:30pm.)*
- **INTERNET : Internetia** internet cafes offer Wi-Fi and computers. *(Menendez Pelayo 43-45 ☎954 534 003 $ €2.20 per hr.)*
- **POST OFFICE:** The main post office has a bank and also helps with international cell phones. *(Av. de la Constitución 32 ☎902 197 197 💻www.correos.es.)*

GETTING THERE

By Train

To get to Sevilla, your best option is to hop on a train. The main train station, Estación Santa Justa *(Av. de Kansas City ☎902 240 202)* offers luggage storage, car rentals, and an ATM. You can catch a train from the airport in Madrid to Sevilla via the **AVE** train *($ €80.70. ⏰ 2½hr., every 30min. daily 6:15am-11pm)* or the **Alvia** train *($ €63.30. ⏰ 2hr. 45 min., 2 per day).*

By Bus

Take the C-1 bus to Prado de San Sebastian to get to the city center. If traveling by bus from the Estación Prado de San Sebastian, there are three major lines from which to choose: **Los Amarillos** *(☎902 210 317 💻www.touristbuses.es)*, **Alsina Graells** *(☎902 422 242 💻www.alsa.es)*, and **Transportes Comes** *(☎902 199 208 💻www.tgcomes.es)*.Estación Prado de San Sebastian also happens to be a stop on the city metro, a major local bus stop, and a tram stop. To purchase tickets to leave the city from the Estacion Prado, look for salesmen under yellow archways, behind the hustle and bustle of all the local buses on the street. The other major bus station in the southern part of the city, the Estación Plaza de Armas, receives every bus from **Portugal** and sends buses going to **Valencia, Salamanca, Leon,** and **Asturias.**

By Train

For booking regional travel by train, contact **Alsa** (☎*902 422 242* 💻*www.alsa.es)* or **Damas** (☎*954 907 737* 💻*www.damas-sa.es).*

GETTING AROUND

As far as getting around Sevilla goes, the only major restriction to walking is the temperature. The region itself is not very large and is easily manageable on foot. That being said, the city is well-equipped with buses, trams, a Metro line, and bike rentals. If you're not willing to withstand the heat (especially in those summer months), grab yourself a cold Fanta and hop on some public transit.

By Bus

The **Tussam** buses blanket the city. (💲 *€1.20.)* The **C-3** and **C-4** buses, running every 10 min., are particularly helpful, as they circle the border of the city clockwise and counterclockwise, respectively.

By Metro

The **Metro** is also extremely useful. **Metro Line 1** (💲 *One-way €1.30, day pass €4.50.* 🕐 *M-Th 6:30am-11pm, F 6:30am-2am, Sa 7:30am-2am, Su 7:30am-11pm)* ends in Ciudad Expo and Olivar de Quintos, making stops in Prado de San Sebastian, San Bernardo, Gran Plaza, and Parque de los Principales.

By Bike

As far as biking goes, you'll quickly notice that the locals are all about this mode of transport. You'll find lines of **Sevici** (💻*www.sevici.es)* bicycles around the city. Set up a year-long (💲 *€10)* or week-long (💲 *€5)* subscription at any kiosk with your credit card.

By Taxi

If you do decide to call a cab, **Radio Taxi** (☎*954 580 000)* and **Tele Taxi** (☎*954 622 222)* are the two lines recommended by city officials.A popular song goes, "*Sevilla tiene un color especial,*" literally, "Sevilla has a special color." For students, that color is *tapas al fresco* with beer. Locals and international students alike spend every night that's above 60°F outside drinking wine or beer while munching on plate after plate of tapas. But don't shovel the delicious food and bolt— Spanish dining is all about relaxation and conversation. Order a glass of *jerez*, sherry, and soak up the Andalusian night as you sip on the good life.

ANDALUCIA

The saying goes that while Madrid and Barcelona are the face of Spain, Andalucia is the soul. This southern region may have a rich history of Roman and Arab rule, with many cultural remnants and sights to enjoy, but it's also home to many of those things that you'd call distinctly Spanish. The major cities like Granada, Córdoba, and Sevilla will forever argue for the rights to the founding of flamenco, bullfighting, and even those delicious tapas, but there's little doubt that it all blossomed out of Andalucia.

From the cliffsides and cascades of Ronda to the endless vineyards of Jerez to the turquoise waters of Nerja, you'll never want to end your trek though this southern region. There's a reason that Ferdinand and Isabella decided to move into the Alhambra in Granada and why the Moorish kings wanted to set up their capital in Córdoba. These cities are an unbeatable source of history and hold a distinctly Spanish flare.

We're not trying to say that Andalucia's only great for the historian or cultural anthropologist. It can feed your belly just as well as your brain. You'll enjoy the cool refreshment of a fresh bowl of *gazpacho* or *salmorejo* (chilled tomato based soups and sauces), sip a *tinto de verano* (red wine and carbonated lemon soda), and take a massive helping of *rabo de toro* (bull's tail). Treat that dessert craving to a Granadan *pinono*, a Sevillian *inglese*, or a Córdoban *pastel cordobes*. You'll find some of the world's sweetest wines and freshest olive oils. After that late-night dinner, hit the town for salsa, merengue, flamenco, and jazz. As the bars and clubs like to say, they open their doors late, and keep them open into *la madrugada* (the rest of the week).

greatest hits

- **GET THE PICTURE.** Really, don't miss a single shot of gorgeous Ronda. Even the bus ride is picturesque (p. 126).
- **WALKING ON SUNSHINE.** Come stroll on the Costa del Sol, home to Spain's most beautiful beaches (p. 168).
- **TWICE AS NICE.** With decorations from two different dynasties and influences from two continents, you know the Alhambra's going to be gorgeous (p. 157).

The Muslims' beautiful *la Alhambra* is matched by the architectural beauty and splendor of the rest of the city. Can't quite afford to stay in such high quality digs? Can't really afford to stay anywhere? If you don't have the cash for a hostel, head for the hills, literally. If you're okay with no running water or electricity, you can join the legions of student travelers and others who take up residence in the **caves of Sacromonte.** Obviously, this is not the safest option, but if you want to relive the lives of cave-painting ancestors, go ahead. Just know that at this point the stuff on the cave walls probably isn't paint.

jerez de la frontera ☎956

While *"jerez"* may be the Spanish word for ⚐sherry, this small city is not confined to this one alcoholic area of expertise (although it does excel, above and beyond, with its wide array of wineries and bodegas). Rather, Jerez has quite the array of interests, but we don't recommend that they all be combined at once—any mix of sherry, brandy, flamenco, horseback riding, and speed car racing would not turn out so pretty. However, if utilized and appreciated individually, any of these fascinating pastimes will be top-quality, outshining almost any other place on the globe.

And while it may be slightly less tangible, there is definitely one other quality in which Jerez should take pride—**hospitality.** Don't be surprised if you get stopped on the street by a local because you're looking a bit lost. He or she will likely offer to walk you all the way to the Alcazar, Centro Andaluz de Flamenco, or even to his or her favorite bar for a chilled glass of **fino** (one of the most popular local sherries). And on the way, the Jerezian will probably wave to some friends who are enjoying their regular seat on the patio of one of the many tapas bars.

This peaceful little town proudly situates itself smack dab between Europe and Africa, thus providing for a unique natural beauty (something you'd never expect while passing the giant Michelin man and the massive industrial complex on the way here). So grab a horse, do a dance, watch a race, drink a cup, and enjoy all that Jerez has to offer—just don't do it all at once.

ORIENTATION

Jerez is not a particularly large or complicated city. Upon exiting the bus and train station on the edge of town, you're only about a 10min. walk from the city center, found at **Plaza del Arenal.** Major streets like **Calle Corredera** and **Calle Large** branch off the plaza and can guide you to loads of hotels and major shopping and sights, respectively. Further north in the city, beyond **Plaza Mamelon,** you'll find some of the best museums and the main equestrian center of Jerez. Jerez is also particularly tourist-friendly with signs all over the city pointing you in the direction of the main sights and hot spots, whether wineries, museums, tourist offices, or restaurants.

ACCOMMODATIONS

NUEVO HOTEL   ⚐⚡(ꞌꞌ)❄   HOTEL ❶

C. Caballeros 23   ☎956 331 600 ▣www.nuevohotel.com

It may be marble, it may be shiny, and the rooms may be pretty darn big (with tasteful, pleasant decorations along the walls and pristinely clean bathrooms), but you're still going to get a surprisingly low price at Nuevo Hotel. Located a straight shot from Plaza del Arenal, the center of the city, you definitely can't beat

andalucia

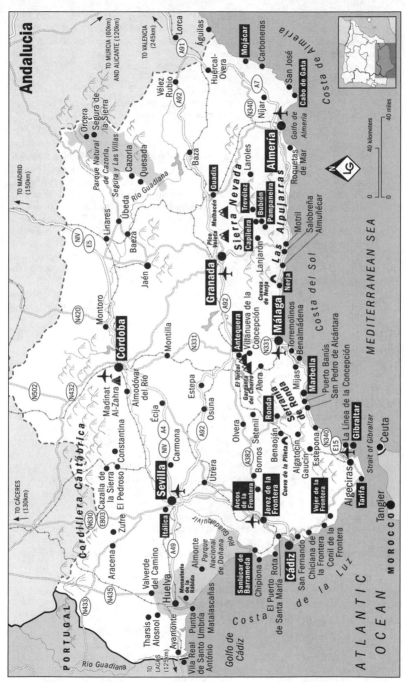

the location (and you also can't beat the included breakfast and free Wi-Fi). The entire place smells like a cross between lavender and Pine-Sol (so like washing a flower pot?), and the small sitting areas hidden all about the multi-floor hotel are the perfect place to chat with a new friend or curl up to read a book. The staff will greet you in Spanish, but they'll pull together some simple English phrases if need be to make you feel more at home. Let's be real: it's *nuevo* (new)—clearly, they're up to date with your visiting needs.

 # C. Caballeros branches off from the Plaza del Arenal. The hostel is on your left if coming from the plaza. $ Singles €25; doubles €40; triples €50. ⏰ Reception 24hr.

HOSTAL LAS PALOMAS HOSTAL [2]

C. Higueras, 17 ☎956 343 773 🖥www.hostal-las-palomas.com

Walk into this classic, Andalucian hostel and be greeted by the friendly Spanish-speaking staff. The guy at the desk may spice up your welcome with some sarcasm, jokes, and even a cold glass of *tinto de verano*, but we're confident you can handle it (he might also throw in some English slang so he seems up with the Joneses). Hostal Las Palomas is one of the closest quality hostels to the bus station, making that heavy pack of yours much less of a concern, and it's only a few minutes walk from the **Plaza del Arenal** at the city center. Enjoy the decently spacious rooms that are simple but clean. While the lower-priced rooms don't have bathrooms, you at least get a small sink to wipe the summer sweat off your face—and keep up with that dental hygiene. They also sell sodas, water, and coffee in the lobby *(€0.50-1)* to make sure you're refreshed upon heading out for the day.

 # Between C. Corredera and C. Medina, just past the Plaza de las Angustias, about a 10min. walk from the bus/train station. $ Singles €20, with bath €25; doubles €30/35; triples €50; quads €60. ⏰ Reception 24hr.

SIGHTS

Jerez offers a wide variety of sights to show off its many prides and interests, but just as the bars close early in the evenings, the sights close early in the afternoons. Most of the big spots are opened only in the mornings (closing around 2pm), so use your grandad's bedtime to help you get up before the afternoon heat.

Real Escuela Andaluza del Arte Ecuestre

The **Real Escuela Andaluza del Arte Ecuestre** *(Av. Duque de Abrantes s/n ☎956 318 008 🖥www.realescuela.org ⏰Open M-Sa 10am-2pm)* is Jerez's gem—a royal equestrian facility, dubbed as such by King Juan Carlos I in 1987. The facility controls the academy grounds, including the stables, saddlery, palace, training rings, and performance arena, as well as the Museo del Arte Ecuestre and Museo del Engache. When visiting the Real Escuela, you can purchase a ticket for €10 to allow access to all of these sights or a €4 ticket to see just the Museo del Enganche. **Tours** are run at the academy grounds and at the Museo del Enganche Monday through Saturday at 10:30am and 2:30pm *(English and Spanish, 1-1½hr.)*, but they depend on demand and organized groups—oftentimes tours are run at additional hours as well. Upon entering, just ask the greeter behind the security check-in about tours and he can inform you of the day's schedule. Exhibitions are open Tuesdays and Thursdays (and Fridays in August) at noon, and you can sit-in on training sessions from 11am-1pm on Mondays, Wednesdays, and Fridays. During the **Feria de Caballos** in early May, there are additional exhibitions on Friday and Saturday evenings for higher prices, but the museum and grounds visits remain at the same price.

MUSEO DEL ARTE ECUESTRE MUSEUM

Av. Duque de Abrantes s/n ☎956 318 008 🖥www.realescuela.org

A gold mine of information on all things equestrian. Whether you're curious about training, competition, horse selection, or performance, it's all here. And not just here, but here in a high-tech, multimedia fashion that includes movies, models, music, and slideshows. Whether you're for evolution or creationism, you can learn about the history of the horse in both a scientific and mythological sense, and even learn a bit of "horse speak" (if you know how to read your pony's ears, you can become the next horse whisperer). This is the perfect stop on a visit to the Real Escuela—it will give you all the background you need before seeing the horses in action at an exhibition or training session.

Ticket office at the corner of Av. Duque de Abrantes and C. Hijuela de la Zorra. i All exhibits in English and Spanish. $ €10. Open M-Sa 10am-2pm.

MUSEO DEL ENGANCHE — MUSEUM

C. Pizarro, 17 ☎956 319 635 www.realescuela.org

The Museo del Enganche, or the horse-drawn carriage museum, hones in on the artful and traditional qualities unique to regal equestrian culture (how high-brow can we sound in one listing?). Exploring the grounds of this small museum, you will see the carriages, harnesses, and saddles used over the centuries as well as the costumes worn by top equestrian competitors. The museum prides itself on its 3D exhibit, but the best part about Museo del Enganche are those things that are actually 3D because they are living—you'll come across stables, washing areas, and leather workshops where you can see horses and humans getting through their day's work.

When C. Ponce branches into Av. Duque de Abrantes and C. Pizarro, stay left. i Tours and exhibits in English and Spanish. $ Museum €4. Escuela Real €10. Open M-Sa 10am-3pm.

Elsewhere

ALCAZAR AND CAMARA OSCURA — MONUMENT

Alameda Vieja s/n ☎956 149 555 www.jerez.es

This fantastically preserved mixture of Almohade and Christian influence dates all the way back to the 12th century. With the combination of palaces, octagonal protection towers, mosques (which can become churches with a few simple alterations), and some pretty sweet baths, you can see why the Spanish royalty under Alfonso X put up such a fight to take over the Alcazar. In the main tower of the **Palacio de Villavicencio,** which happens to be highest point of the city, you'll be so high that you'll probably feel like you're stuck with the birds at the tops of the hyacinth trees (and probably trying to find a way to un-pop your ears). But then you'll get a glimpse of the **Camara Oscura** and your whole world will be turned upside down. One peek through this pinhole camera and you can get a bird's-eye view of all of Jerez.

Open July 16-Sept 15 M-F 10am-7:30pm, Sa-Su 10am-2:30pm; Sept 16-Oct M-Sa 10am-5:30pm; Nov-Jan daily 10am-2:30pm; Feb-July 15 M-Sa 10am-5:30pm.

ZOCO DE ARTESANIA DE JEREZ — MARKET

Plaza de Peones s/n ☎956 344 534

We know that you're loving the pure Spanish culture, from tapas to flamenco (and, of course, local liquors), but it's always good to spice things up and recognize the other influences that make Jerez the city it is today. The Zoco de Artesania is a crafts market that does just that—over 22 vendors come to the Zoco, representing a combination of locals and visitors from Northern Morocco. Feel that Moorish influence as you walk the halls, see the mosque murals on the walls, and smell the delicious incense coming from shop windows. The Zoco has it all—jewelry, textiles, books, honey, spices, teas, leathers, metals, ceramics—and provides good prices for original, handmade products. Take your time browsing the shops in this three-story complex and maybe even grab a bite to eat or a tea infusion at Bar Restaurante La Medina, located on the second floor.

Located in the Plaza de Peones in the center of the old part of the city, about a 1-2min. walk from the police station. $ Prices vary based on vendor. Open M-F 9:30am-2pm and 6-9:30pm, Sa 10:30am-2pm.

MUSEO MISTERIO DE JEREZ AND PALACIO DEL TIEMPO ✦ MUSEUM, CHURCH

C. Cervantes, 3 ☎956 182 100 🖳info@elmisteriodejerez.org

A two-in-one deal? This is better than ice-cream discounts at the supermarket! The Museo Misterio de Jerez and Palacio del Tiempo are perfect ways to see two very different aspects of Jerez's history. At the Museo Misterio, you'll see projection films explaining the history of the city's wine culture and bodegas. We promise it'll be easier to solve the mystery of these delicious wines while you're still sober. And if you cross the yard to the Palacio del Tiempo, you'll find Europe's top (and Spain's only) collection of antique watches. While this topic probably attracts a particular breed, you can pass through as quickly or slowly as you like, taking time to scope out antique watches that date back all the way to the 17th century.

✢ Entrance to the left of the Museo del Enganche along C. Pizarro. Just walk through the botanical gardens and the ticket office is on the right. **i** *Tours to the Museo Misterio de Jerez must be organized with a group, although individuals can join group tours.* $ *€6, students €3 per museum.* ⏰ *Museo Misterio tours Tu-F 10am, noon. Palacio del Tiempo tours Tu-F 9:30, 10:30, 11:30am, 12:30, 1:15pm.*

WINERIES

Sherry is the pride and joy (and namesake) of Jerez. All over the city, you'll find bodegas large and small ready to show you around and sell you the best wines and brandies they've got. *Jerez*, the Spanish word for sherry, has been grown in the area since the 11th century BCE, when the Phoenicians discovered that their grapes were looking plumper than ever due to the special chalky soil and strong summer and winter climate of the region. Today, Jerez has perfected a unique production system in which the companies extract their wines and brandies from the lowest barrels, or *soleras*, which contain drink from many different harvests from the above barrels, or *criaderas*. They'll claim that each sip you get has the perfect balance of experience and youth (and you're an experienced youth, right?). While the winery tours are fairly standardized, you'd be crazy to skip the chance to try at least one—Tio Pepe is the largest exporter in Jerez, but **Domecq** *(⏰ Tours M-F 10, 11am, noon, 1, 5, 6, 7pm, Sa noon; tour and tastings only Tu, Th, and Sa)* and **Harvey's** *(⏰ Tours M-F noon)* are strong competitors.

BODEGA TIO PEPE ✦

C. Manuel Maria Gonzalez, 12 ☎902 440 077 🖳bodgastiopepe.com

Manuel Maria Gonzalez was living the dream in 1835—he was 23 years old when he took all his savings to invest in opening up a winery in one of the most picturesque, peaceful areas of southern Spain. That one major risk turned into Jerez's biggest winery, exporting to 115 countries worldwide and accepting such special visitors as the Spanish royal family, Pablo Picasso, and Steven Spielberg. Taking a tour at Bodega Tio Pepe, you'll get a chance to learn about the history of sherry production in the region, see the major cellars of the bodega (aging 80,000 barrels of sherry and brandy at any given time!), and even taste a few sips yourself. The fruity smell of the cool cellars is the perfect break from the sweaty summer heat.

✢ Located about 5-10min. walking from the Plaza del Arenal, at the intersection of Alameda Vieja and C. Manuel Maria Gonzalez. **i** *Tours in Spanish, English, or German.* $ *Tour and wine tasting €10. Tour, wine tasting, and tapas €16.* ⏰ *Tours in English M-Sa noon, 1, 2, 5, 6:30pm, Su noon, 1, 2pm.*

THE GREAT OUTDOORS

As Jerez is located halfway between Africa and Europe, it's a central starting point for many outdoor excursion routes. The four main routes that branch out from the city include the **Southern Forests Route** (through Los Alcomocales Natural Park), the **Southern Mountains Route** (through the Sierra de Grazalema Natural Park), the **Donana Area and Marshes Route** (through the Guadalquivir River estuary), and the **Lagoons and Jerez Countryside Route.** All of these can be done on horseback or on foot. More information can be found in the detailed pamphlets provided at the information center. If you're not feeling like totally giving into those tent and sleeping-bag tendencies, there are plenty of other options in and around Jerez that combine accommodation with nature.

CLUB ECUESTRE LA ARBOLEDA AND A CAMPO ABIERTO 🎫 HORSEBACK RIDING

La Arboleda: Camino La Jara ☎630 867 672 💻www.clubecuestrelaarboleda.com

A Campo Abierto: A-381 exit 31 or A-396 km 1 ☎649 958 446 💻www.acampoabierto.com

If the Real Escuela de Arte Ecuestre isn't enough for you, there are definitely other options to get your full dose of horse time. At La Arboleda you can take guided horseback-riding tours along the beaches and pine groves of the outskirts of Jerez. And at A Campo Abierto you can see the breeding grounds for the horses and bulls used in equestrian competitions and bullfights. A Campo Abierto also offers exhibition shows on Monday, Wednesday, and Saturday at 11:30am. As there are no direct buses to either of these sights, you're best off taking a cab.

FOOD

Jerez eating involves outdoor patios, a chilled glass of wine, and a social setting packed with local regulars. While the city offers a good variety of classic Spanish cuisine, you'll also come across some sneaky Jerez alterations to many of your dishes. Don't be surprised to find a hint of sherry in a sauce, in your *salmorejo*, and, ultimately, in your belly. Jerez also prides itself on its proximity to Northern Africa, so you may find some Moorish and Mediterranean influences in your dining as well.

RESTAURANTE GAITAN 🎫🍸 SPANISH, CAFE 3

C. Gaitan, 3 ☎956 168 021 💻www.restaurantegaitan.es

Here's your chance to get adventurous, whether you want to splurge at the restaurant *(about €25-30 per person)* or stay stingy at the cafe. Restaurante Gaitan is one of the best in Jerez—and clearly one of the best in Spain, winning the Premio Nacional de Gastronomia—and will leave your mouth watering from its combination of traditional and unique menu items. The house specialty, bull's tail in a classic "Jerez sauce" *(tapa €3, ½ ration €6, full ration €12)* will help heal your scarred mental state from that recent bullfight, as you'll finally be grateful for the meal you got out of it. For the more adventurous among you, leave the basic *bacaloa* behind and try some new sea critters like the squid served in ink *(½ ration €6, full ration €10)* or the Galician octopus stew *(½ ration €6, full ration €12)*. You'll feel like royalty as the friendly, smiling waiters serve you complimentary olives and bread beside your cloth napkin and clean glass (so don't look around to see every other table getting the same treatment), and relish the chance to enjoy a meal without having to fight to order at a crammed tapas bar.

Turn right off C. Porvera onto C. Gaitan, just before the 24hr. pharmacy. The restaurant is on the right. $ *Bar/cafe tapas €2-3, ½ rations €4-7, full rations €8-13. Restaurant about €25-30 per person.* ⏰ *Open daily 8am-11:30pm.*

MESON ALCAZABA 🎫🍸❄ SPANISH 2

C. San Francisco de Paula, 6 ☎956 332 960

Ask anyone in town—the manager of the tourist office, the receptionist at the hostel, the old drunkard sitting outside the bodega—and they'll all tell you that Meson Alcazaba serves up the best local, classic Jerez cuisine in town. And what does Jerez-style cooking entail, you may ask? Sherry with everything, of course! Whether it's the *salmorejo* *(€3)*, served with a splash of *fino* mixed in, or the house specialty, *bacalao al pil pil* *(tapa €2.50, ration €12)* topped with a sherry reduction sauce, this city knows how to use its namesake to enhance every dish it serves. Whether you're looking for some quick tapas (make sure to ask for the tapas menu if that's your intention) or a more slow-paced dining room (with tablecloths), Alcazaba can provide it at a reasonable price. Check the menu of the day to get a combo of bread, dessert, a full ration, and a drink *(€8.50)*, or keep an eye out for local advertised deals that could make it cheaper to get a drink pairing with a tapa than to get the tapa alone.

C. San Francisco de Paula runs parallel to C. Medina, branching off to the left between C. Evora and C. Higueras if coming from the city center. $ Tapas €1.70-3, ½ rations €5-7, full rations €6-12. Open M-F 9am-midnight, Sa 10am-midnight, Su noon-midnight.

CEFETERIA LA VEGA TAPAS [1]

Plaza Esteve, s/n ☎956 337 748

This hot spot may have one of the simplest menus you'll ever find (just tapas, *bocadillos*, and *montaditos*), but with this simplicity you don't lose quality. Cafeteria La Vega is one of the largest establishments in Jerez, offering a pit stop in its high-ceiling dining room, indoor balcony with cushioned, loungey seating, rooftop terrace, and outdoor patio, but it somehow finds a way to pack the place every morning. If you can get a seat before noon, make your way over for some of the most competitive prices in town *(tapas €2, breakfasts €1.40)* for a simple, classic breakfast toast or tapa. Chat with the local regulars that will be waving good morning (or *buenos dias?*) to all of their friends and maybe even indulge in some of the special bakery treats tempting you from behind the glass counter.

Located on the corner of Plaza Esteve, less than 1min. from the Plaza del Arenal if you follow C. Lanceria. $ Tapas €2, ½ rations €6, full rations €8-12. Open daily 7am-9:30pm.

NIGHTLIFE

Disclaimer: Jerez is not a party town—it's actually pretty far from it. The nightlife culture in this peaceful town (which largely attracts an older crowd of tourists) centers around social, outdoor patios that crowd the streets with locals and tourists enjoying the great prices of the city's wines and liquors. Walking through the Plaza del Arenal, C. Largas, or Plaza Plateros, just follow the sound and you'll come across some of the best spots around. Most of the best bar-restaurants are open all day, so you can enjoy your drinks in the afternoon, the evening, and maybe even the morning if you are looking to have a long night. Some of the flamenco *tablaos* are also notorious for not just showing you some dance but getting you dancing and offering evening beverages—you can try Tablao del Berber, which the locals kindly call "Beri Beri," near the Plaza del Mercado as one such option. Keep in mind that "nightlife" in Jerez refers to an earlier night than the rest of Spain. Most of your options (even the late night ones) will close by 1:30am.

EL GALLO AZUL TAPAS BAR

Carretera de Cortes km 3,5 (Plaza Esteve) ☎956 337 529 www.casajuancarlos.com

This higher-end bar and restaurant knows how to keep things classy without killing you with the price. The packed outdoor patio right on Plaza Esteve outshines the other bars in the area, as the cute indoor kitchen area decorated with robin's-egg-blue walls and paintings of roosters (it's not that weird—the direct translation of *gallo azul* is "blue rooster") experiences quite a bit of foot traffic from the staff. But even though it's busy, and even though the waiters are frantically running around, Gallo Azul knows how to be efficient—the electronic ordering system keeps everything in line from the perfectly-presented, mouthwatering desserts *(€3.50-5)* to your *fino* on ice. Locals will tell you that it's one of the nicest places to spend an evening in Jerez, and your tastebuds shout cockadoodle-doo in agreement. While they are scheduled to close at 12:30am, some regulars describe this time as a "loose estimate."

Located in Plaza Esteve, on the corner with C. Larga. $ Tapas €2.40. Desserts €3.50-5. Beer €1.40. Wine €1.50. Open in summer M-Sa 11:30am-4:30pm and 8pm-12:30am; in winter M-Sa 11:30am-12am, Su during festivals.

BAR BARBIANA

🍷🍸☀ BAR

Plaza del Banco ☎956 321 248

Sit back, relax, and enjoy the music on the patio as you sip wine, beer, or even a cup of tea and watch those kids studying in the public library across the way. Bar Barbiana is a casual, typical, and popular Jerez bar—the drinks are cheap, the clientele is mixed and mellow, and you can find it bustling at any time of day. On a warm summer night, there's nothing better than spending less than €5 on a glass of some of the finest local sherry, a classic *montadito*, and a simple pastry, all while huddled around a small table, chatting with your closest friends.

🚏 Plaza del Banco branches off C. Larga. The bar is on the corner of the plaza, across from the public library. $ Tapas €1.30-2.20. Beer €1.20. Wine €1.50. Mixed drinks €1.50. ⏰ Open daily 7am-midnight.

ARTS AND CULTURE

Flamenco

LA TABERNA FLAMENCO

🍷

C. Angostillo de Santiago ☎956 323 693 💻www.latabernaflamenca.com

Jerez is a city of many interests, and flamenco is one that they do not take lightly. La Taberna Flamenco offers shows year-round featuring local dancers that will perform a style of flamenco with a bit of a Jerez twist. This large, air-conditioned, indoor patio will provide a delicious and filling meal (appetizer, two courses, dessert, and drink) if you go with the dinner option, but it also provides a wide selection of drinks from it's full bar if you save a bit of money and take the €15 ticket. The small, wooden stage at the corner of the dining room may not look like much, but it's the perfect setting for a classic and intimate performance of the best flamenco Jerez has to offer.

🚏 Located off C. Ancha at the Plaza de Santiago. About a 10min. walk from the information office. $ Dinner and show €35. Tapas and show €20. Drink and show €15. ⏰ Flamenco performances July-Sept daily 10:30pm; Oct and Mar-June Tu-Sa 10:30pm; Nov-Feb Tu-Sa 10pm.

CENTRO ANDALUZ DE FLAMENCO

🍷

Plaza San Juan, 1 ☎856 814 132 💻caf.cica.es

This educational facility is the top dog for official flamenco facilities in all of Andalucia, and as the boss, it knows its stuff. Spend one afternoon at the Centro Andaluz de Flamenco (free of charge) and enjoy access to the libraries, photos, archives, audio recordings, and videos stored within the facility. The center also broadcasts short films *(30min.)* from its comfy, big-screen movie theater *(daily 10, 11am, noon, 1pm; additional evening shows on W at 5 and 6pm)*. If you want to become a regular and stop in at a different film every day, just remember to bring your own popcorn and slushie.

🚏 Located in Plaza San Juan near the Palacio San Martin. Take C. Chancilleria from C. Provera, and the center is on the right. $ Free. ⏰ Open June 15-Sept 1 M-F 9am-2pm; Sept 2-June 14 M-Tu 9am-2pm, W 9am-2pm and 4:30-7pm, Th-F 9am-2pm.

Festivals

While Jerez celebrates the Semana Santa and Christmas with quite a bit of spirit (like almost any city throughout Spain), it is also home to some unique festivals and celebrations that you can only find within the borders of this eclectic city.

FERIA DE CABALLO AND THE MOTORCYCLE GRAND PRIX

During those first weeks of May, the quiet little town of Jerez will grab an international spotlight—well, two spotlights, actually. Each year during the spring, Jerez hosts its Feria de Caballo, a celebration of the city's equestrian culture, and it happens to coincide with the world motorcycle championships, held in Jerez's own **Cicuito de Jerez** *(Ctra. Arcos Km. 10 ☎956 151 100 💻www.circuitodejerez.com)*. At the Feria, which centers on **Parque González Hontoria,** you'll find hundreds of canvas tents, or *casetas*, ready to welcome you to enjoy the parades, costumes, and competitions of the week. Unlike the Feria de Abril in Sevilla, these *casetas* are open to even tourists, so head on in to try a *rebujito*, the popular Feria combo of lemonade and *fino*. When you get tired of horses, move on to horsepower with some speed racing—over 250,000 people may crowd into the Circuito for any day of competition. You can arrive early to sit in on training and the classifying sessions, or just head over in time to catch that green light.

🧭 The Circuito is located on the outskirts of the city (about 10km from the center) and will need to be accessed by car or taxi. $ Hotels and hostels will typically offer "low-season" prices as well as higher "moto" or "feria" prices.

HARVEST FESTIVAL

If Jerez is the city of sherry, what can be more important than the annual grape harvest, taking place each year during the first two weeks of September? And take our word for it—this isn't simply a juice commercial with guys in wellies stomping fruit. Jerez does it up big for the harvest as the city not only celebrates its thriving sherry culture but also makes this event more exciting by incorporating two of its other strengths, flamenco and horses. Enjoy parades, performances, and even the public blessing of the grapes, held in front of the main cathedral of the old city. Eat and drink better than you ever had as the bodegas bring out their top products, and the city hosts a slew of tapas competitions. If you'd like to tour a bodega (or even stay in Jerez at a hostel), make sure to call and reserve a spot far in advance, as these will fill up quickly.

$ Restaurants, wineries, and accommodations generally raise their prices during the Harvest Festival. ⏰ 1st 2 weeks of Sept. Blessing of the grapes usually around midday on the 1st day of the festival.

ESSENTIALS

Practicalities

- **TOURIST OFFICES:** The main information center for the city is the perfect place to start any visit: they'll provide you with the best maps, the best recommendations, and all the help you need in English, French, German, or Spanish. The website is extremely helpful and well-organized, and it can be entirely translated into English with the click of a button. *(C. Media Cristina, s/n ☎956 341 711 💻www.turismojerez.com ⏰ Open M-F 9am-3pm and 5-7pm, Sa-Su 9:30am-2:30pm.)*
- **INTERNET:** The municipal **library** is open to the public free of charge and also offers Wi-Fi if you ask for the password at the front desk. *(⏰ Open M-F 9:15am-2:15pm and 4:30-8:15pm, Sa 9:30am-1:15pm.)* Jerez has **city Wi-Fi** *(☎902 509 951 💻www.wifijerez.net)* that covers a large portion of the area including Plaza del Arenal, C. Larga, C. Sevilla, and Alameda Vieja—just stop into any store advertising "wifijerez" and purchase a pre-paid access card.

Emergency!

- **POLICE:** *(Plaza de Arroyo, s/n ☎091)*
- **EMERGENCY: Ambulance:** ☎061.
- **HOSPITAL:** *(Carretera Circumvalocion, s/n ☎956 032 000)*
- **24HR. PHARMACY:** While many of the pharmacies in town are locally owned and therefore close fairly early, there are some 24hr. pharmacies available—try the one at C. Provera 32. *(☎956 342 323 🧭 At the intersection with C. Gaitan. ℹ Credit cards accepted.)*

Getting There

Jerez makes visiting fairly painless. Whether you want to arrive by plane, train, or bus, the option is there. The **Jerez International Airport** *(Ctra. N-IV, Conexión A-4 Sevilla-Cádiz ☎956 150 000)* is located on the edge of town and accommodates flights from such major European Airlines as Iberia, Spanair, and Ryanair. Renfe **trains** arrive at the main bus and train station *(Plaza de la Estación, s/n ☎902 240 202 for trains; 956 149 990 for buses)* and take about 4hr. from Madrid and 1hr. from Sevilla. Comes *(☎956 321 464 ✉www.tgcomes.es)* and Linesur *(☎956 341 063 ✉www.linesur.com)* **buses** can both get you from Sevilla in about 1½hr. for under €10 on multiple buses a day.

Getting Around

Jerez is not a very large city and is therefore easily manageable by foot. You'll find that you can get almost anywhere from the **Plaza del Arenal** in a 10min. walk or less. There are also **signs** pointing out all the main restaurants, sights, bodegas, museums, and other necessities that are put up by the city of Jerez that will guide you in the proper direction. If you would rather take one of the pink city **buses,** especially to some of the sights on the outskirts of the city, there are over 19 bus lines that run from 7am-11pm (depending on the line) for €1.10 per trip. The most popular **taxi** company is Radio Taxi *(☎956 344 860),* and they have stops in multiple locations all over the city, designated by a sign.

gibraltar ☎350

This **strait,** jutting out from the base of the Iberian Peninsula, may only be about 3 mi. long and 1 mi. wide, but what it lacks in size it makes up for in culture, character, and history—and quite a long history at that! Not only was the strait settled by the Moors, Romans, Catholic monarchs, and the British crown, but it also has been proven to be the stomping grounds of at least a few of our Neanderthal ancestors. It has even survived a violent seige and various World War II battles to get to its status today. As you cross through customs, turn in your **euro** and Spanish theta for some **pounds** and a nice English drawl—the lively pub culture and abundance of fish-and-chips shops all over the land mass will immediately clue you into Gibraltar's proud membership in the **United Kingdom.** You'll also find thriving Jewish, Indian, and Moroccan populations, so feel free to enjoy their culture and delicious eats as well. While **Main Street** and **Casemate's Square** may bring back fond memories of amusement parks and world's fairs—flashy, fast, and stuffed with tourists—the Rock of Gibraltar will introduce you to a side of nature unlike anything you have ever seen. So whether you want to sip a Guinness or swing with the Barbary apes, be ready for one intense day trip to Gibraltar.

ORIENTATION

Gibraltar is a single, tiny strip of land and is therefore extremely easy to navigate. **Casemate's Square,** packed with pubs and fish-and-chips shops, will be the first thing you encounter beyond the airport runways. When you see signs in the area pointing toward "city center," you're getting led to Casemate's. **Main Street** continues out from Casemate's and will guide you all the way to the tip of the Gib. This street, supplemented by the small side streets branching off it, has all the shopping and restaurants you'll need in the area. The **Rock of Gibraltar** is to the left of Main St. if facing the tip of the strait and takes up nearly 50% of Gibraltar itself.

ACCOMMODATIONS

Accommodations in Gibraltar are generally fancy resorts and villas, designed for wealthier vacationers hoping to enjoy the beaches for a week or so (and keep in mind that pounds make these hotels even pricier than their Spanish equivalents). While there are a few less expensive options on Gibraltar, you may also consider staying in one of the hotels, hostels, or pensions located in **La Linea,** the city directly on the Spanish side of the border. Nearby, these accommodations are typically inexpensive and provide quiet, private rooms. The extra 10-15min. walk to Casemate's Square is worth the €10-15 per night.

HOSTAL CARLOS I
(((•))) 🌱 ❄ 🖥 HOSTAL ❶

C. Carboneros 6   ☎956 762 135 🖳www.hostalcarlos.es

Only a 5min. walk from the Spain-Gibraltar border, Hostal Carlos is one of your best options when visiting the Gib. The prices are lower than nearly any accommodation on the strait, and you'll enjoy the simple, spacious rooms with small but clean bathrooms ensuite. While breakfast is not included in the price, the restaurant attached to the hotel provides a convenient meal option for the busy traveler. While the street traffic may be a bit noisy if you get a room toward the front of the hotel, just tune it out with your personal satellite TV. You may still be in Spain, but this is a great way to visit Gibraltar.

⚡ *Located in the center of La Linea, about 5min. from the Gibraltar border and a 3min. cab ride from the bus station. Towels included.* Ⓢ *Singles €28-35; doubles €36-45.* ⏰ *Reception 24hr. Preferred check in by 6pm.*

EMILE YOUTH HOSTEL
◉ HOSTEL ❶

Montagu Bastion, Line Wall Rd.   ☎200 51106 🖳www.emilehostel.net

If you're only staying for a night or two, Emile Youth Hostel may be the perfect, inexpensive accommodation. Emile Youth Hostel is functional but lacks many of the simple luxuries found elsewhere—the mattresses are thin, the showers are communal, and the cafeteria is a work in progress. The owner himself is a bit rough around the edges and may not be particularly friendly upon your arrival, but if you rub him the right way, he warms up immediately. To the travelers he really likes, he'll probably offer a coffee or tea and chat them up about his philosophies on life (some of which are that no hostel should accept credit cards, and that communal bathrooms are the way to go).

⚡ *Along the wall of Line Wall Rd., to the right of the International Commercial Center upon entering Casemates.* **i** *Breakfast included. Towels £1. Communal, gender-separated showers. Cafeteria available.* Ⓢ *Dorms £17; doubles £40.*

SIGHTS

While the main thing to see in Gibraltar is obviously the Rock (and boy is it worth it), that doesn't mean that the rest of the city should be overlooked. There are a few smaller, lower-budget sights that may be worth a visit if you have the time to spare before your cable car heads up.

GIBRALTAR MUSEUM
🌱 ⚘ ❄ MUSEUM

18-20 Bomb House Ln.   ☎200 74289 🖳www.gibmuseum.gi

If you want to be spoon-fed some history about Gibraltar and the Rock, this is a quick and easy way to get information. The Gibraltar Museum is fairly simple and low-budget (the fake cave-like decorations and outdated model soldiers go together like peanut butter and hot dogs—essentially, not at all), but that by no means detracts from its informative nature. Enjoy a brief film about the natural and political history of Gibraltar, and you'll be all set to appreciate the city with a newfound palate of knowledge. The preserved Moorish baths dating back to 700 CE reside in the basement and are definitely worth even a quick peek. While we wouldn't call this a "must-see," it's a relaxed, air-conditioned option to educate you a bit during your visit.

⚡ *Bomb House Ln. branches off from Main St. to the right if heading toward the tip of the strait. Museum is on your right.* Ⓢ *£2.* ⏰ *Open M-F 10am-6pm and Sa 10am-2pm.*

THE ALAMEDA, GIBRALTAR BOTANICAL GARDENS
GARDEN

Europa Rd.

Just beyond the cable-car office, the stone steps of the Alameda Botanical Gardens will beckon you in to explore the grounds. While it may at first seem like a simple spot to rest your legs after a hike around the Rock (and sitting in one of the gazebos along the small bridges may suit this desire), there's much more to be seen than just cactuses and stones. The gardens curve and branch up

andalucia

and down their stone paths, ultimately unveiling the extensive flora and fauna available to you, plus a full outdoor theater and wildlife park. You'll see bats, birds, and quite a few bugs once deeper in the gardens. Follow the arrows to find your way out—that is, once you feel like you've gotten to see all that these surprisingly extensive gardens have to offer. Remember, the Rock isn't the only natural item that Gibraltar has to offer.

Entrance on Europe Rd., just beyond the cable-car office. $ Free.

THE GREAT OUTDOORS

The Rock of Gibraltar

For the sake of this book, putting about 100 thumbs-up symbols before this listing just wouldn't be economical. But we will let you know that visiting the Rock of Gibraltar will be one of the most fascinating, awe-inspiring, stunning, spectacular, exciting, and overall fun things you ever do. The Rock takes up about 50% of Gibraltar and probably contributes about 85% of what this strait has to offer. Millions of years of tectonic plates, earthquakes, and volcanoes helped create this 426m tall landmass, reaching about as high as the **Eiffel Tower with a Ferris Wheel sitting on top of it.** The climate on the Rock has changed significantly over time, but today this limestone body perfectly houses caves, tunnels, greenery, birds, and those adorable little monkeys. The **Barbary Macaques** won't be sitting in any cages as you climb to the top of the Rock; instead, they'll be roaming completely free, so make sure to be careful opening up any snacks—they have grabby hands and aren't afraid to make new friends. You can get so close to these fuzzy friends that you can stare eye-to-eye with mama, papa, or baby macaque, and maybe even reach out to pet them. They'll accompany you as you hike or drive the paths going steeply up and down this Jurassic land mass. Feel like Indiana Jones, stepping carefully around the stalactites and stalagmites taller than you in **Saint Michael's Cave.** Ignore all you learned at middle-school cotillion as you crouch and hunch through the kilometers of tunnels used during the 1782 Siege of Gibraltar. Embrace your inner royalty while exploring the grounds of the ancient Moorish Castle and looking out onto the Mediterranean Sea and all of Gibraltar.

There are a couple ways to go about visiting the Rock of Gibraltar. If you're up for it, we'd recommend taking the **cable car** and walking between the sights. While you may need to commit about three hours to this style of travel, you'll save the most money, see the most things, and get the most one-on-one monkey time. You can take a cable car to the top of the rock to start your hike (and it is a hike—although manageable in flip-flops, you will be most comfortable in walking shoes) by purchasing a ticket at the **Cable Car Gibraltar** booth *(☎200 42683 🖳www.gibraltarinfo.com ⏰ Open daily Apr-Oct 9:30am-7:15pm, Nov-Mar 9:30am-5:15pm. Cars every 15min., 6min. trip to the top)* off **Europa Road,** next to the botanical gardens. Cable Car Gibraltar offers multiple packages for visiting the Rock: just views *(£9);* views and Nature Reserve, which includes monkey dens, St. Michaels' cave, Great Siege tunnels, and Moorish castle *(£19);* views and a dolphin-watching cruise to be conducted after you visit the Rock *(£23.50);* or views, dolphin watching, and Nature Reserve *(£33.50).* All tickets are £1.50 less if you decide to purchase a one-way cable car ticket and take the extra 10min. walk down the Rock. If you decide you'd rather take a shorter visit to the Rock, the local **Gibraltar Taxi Service** *(☎200 70027 🖳gibtaxiass@gibtelecom.net i 4-person min.)* runs tours of the Rock as well. They run a 1½hr., four-stop tour for £12 and a 2½hr., six-stop tour for £16. Beware of marketing tactics: while these prices may seem like a bargain, you will have to pay the additional entrance fees at each of the sites on the Rock, some of which are as high as £10.

FOOD

It won't take you long to realize that Gibraltar is a British territory, and any obvious differences between here and the rest of the peninsula are in the cuisine. Everywhere you turn, you'll find pubs or fish-and-chips joints, interspersed with the fast-foodie's dream selection of everything from Subway to Pizza Hut to Burger King. You'll also find a strong Indian and Moroccan influence in many of the restaurants. While Main St. and Casemates Sq. are lined with the major stereotypes, try **Queensway Quay** for some classier seafood options or the **Ocean Village** for some nicer, larger establishments.

WATERFRONT RESTAURANT — BAR, INTERNATIONAL ❸

Queensway Quay Unit 4, 5 ☎200 45666 www.gibwaterfront.com

Waterfront is the largest restaurant in Gibraltar with the most square footage and the biggest name around. Whether a dignitary, a businessman, or a committed local, anyone who's anyone will be dining at Waterfront. Located right on the Quay, you'll enjoy harborside views from the outdoor patio or dining room, or you can relax in the wood-framed, lodgey interior bar and dining area. Either way, this is the perfect break from the intense, touristy vibe of Main St. and Casemates Sq. (and the standard clientele is composed of less than 25% tourists). You can save your wallet by picking and choosing from the bar menu, or just splurge on one of the world-class steaks *(£17.50-24.50)* or curry options *(£12-17)*. Since you're already giving into your deepest desires, don't skip out on dessert—the banana splits and milkshakes are the perfect way to cool off *(£3-6)*.

Located on Queensway Quay, at the far end closest to Casemates Sq. $ Bar menu: Sandwiches £4.25-7; main courses £7.50-11. Restaurant: vegetarian £12-16; seafood £13-18; steaks £17.50-24.50; salads £9-15. ⏰ Open daily 9am-11:30pm. Kitchen open 10am-11pm.

ORGANICS PLUS — ORGANIC ❶

256 Main St.

When the smell of deep-fried cod and potatoes is getting to be too much, Organics Plus is the health nut's savior. This inexpensive, tiny restaurant offers the best prices in town for their homemade options, all organic and made from scratch. The British owner will proudly tell you his story of importing top-notch meats from Wales and fresh produce from Spain while picking up one of his freshly baked quiches or pizzas *(£1.50-3)*. He'll also offer you the daily selection of vegetarian and meat options and create a hefty combo platter with your choice of risotto, rice, or potatoes *(vegetarian £4, meat £5)*. Join the health-minded locals who rush in and out during lunchtime with their Tupperware, and even grab some of the organic cakes and puddings before you go.

On the right side of Main St. as you head toward the tip of the strait. $ Salads £1.75, large £3.50. Vegetarian combo plates £4. Meat combo plates £5. Pies and pizzas £1.50-3. ⏰ Open M-F 11am-5:30pm, Sa noon-4pm.

ROY'S COD PALACE — FISH AND CHIPS ❷

2/2 Watergate House, Casemate's Sq ☎200 76662

We know there are tons of fish-and-chips options blanketing this tiny strait, but we at least thought we'd clue you in to the best one around. Roy's is a top-notch classic that any local would be able to point out in an instant (and any keen nose could smell out in an instant—it's like an oily heaven). While Roy may not be behind the counter serving up heaping helpings of deep-fried, freshly caught cod, his son's there, ready to welcome you into this family gem. Whether your appetite is small *(£6)*, medium *(£7.50)*, or large *(£12)*, you can dive into this greasy treat and thank that British flag waving out in Casemate's Square.

Located in the corner of Casemate's Square, by the Information Office. $ Fish and chips £6.25, £7.50, or £11.95. Burgers £5. Salads £5-8. ⏰ Open M-Sa 10am-10pm.

NIGHTLIFE

Nightlife in Gibraltar is definitely hottest in the summers and on the weekends, and after a week of quiet nights, Gibraltar's ready with some late-night action. Most of the nightlife options open fairly early, serving as restaurants during the day and turning things up once the sun goes down (and almost until it comes right back up). You'll find high-end clubs in the new **Ocean Village Complex** and tons of pubs in the corner of **Casemate's Square** and **Irish Town.**

👍 ALLSWELL — BAR

Casemate's Sq. Unit 4 ☎200 72987

Allswell is the epitome of the Gibraltar pub scene. With karaoke M and W 9pm-1am, daily happy hours with discount shots *(£1.50)* 10pm-12am, and foaming pints of classic British beers *(£3)*, it may very well be the hottest spot in town, especially on a Friday in the summer.

⏰ Open M-Th 10am-2am, F-Sa 10am-3am, Su 10am-2am.

👍 SAVANAH — 💳🍸❄☁ CLUB

27 Leisure Island, Ocean Village Complex ☎200 66666 🖥www.savanah.gi

The hottest new club in town definitely knows how to please the young and lively. This sleek, two-story club glistening with disco balls and light shows has all the specialties you can imagine: student-only Thursdays in the summer, band-tribute nights for dinnertime, and international DJ performances once a month. You can grab some friends to share a jug of sangria or Pimm's *(£10.50)*, or pick something off the long list of signature cocktails *(£4.50)*. You can use the springtime happy hour to try the most popular Passion-Mint and Chili Margarita and Turkish Delight (vodka, limoncello, chocolate liqueur, rose liqueur) for the price of one. While the club gets going around 1am on Fridays and Saturdays, you can also enjoy the daytime patio lounge all week long. Grab one of the small, secluded tables with some friends and take in the marina view under a giant green umbrella.

➜ Located at the end of the Ocean Village Complex near the casino. $ Cover £5 (but higher on nights with guest performances). Mixed drinks £4.50-5.50. Jugs £9.50-10.50. ⏰ Open M-Th noon-1am, F-Sa noon-6am, Su noon-1am.

GALA CASINO — 💳❄🍸 CASINO, BAR

Ocean Village Complex ☎200 76666 🖥www.galacasinogibraltar.com

Gala Casino is a lot like Gibraltar—it may not be very large, but it has the character to outdo even some of its bigger competitors. This two-story bar, restaurant, and casino is one of the newer additions to the Gib and really brings out a lively late-night (slash early-morning) culture. From colorful light displays to flashing slot machines, the energy is always high. And hopefully your hands are always hot—take your shot at poker *(M 8pm, T-Th 9pm, F 8pm, Sa-Su 9pm)*, blackjack, roulette, or even bingo *(£2 for 10 games)*. Spend your winnings on a classy cosmopolitan *(£6)* or a jumbo platter *(£8-12)* to split with at least a friend or two. They're themed to fit your cravings, whether you want Texas wings, Bombay samosas, or Mediterranean flatbreads. And even if it's not your lucky night, you can still enjoy the mellow lounges and friendly staff, ready to comfort you while trying to loosen your grip on your now-empty bag of poker chips.

➜ Located at the far end of the Ocean Village Complex, away from Casemate's Square. ℹ 18+. $ Beer £3. Mixed drinks £6. Burgers £6-6.50. Sharing platters £8-12. ⏰ Open M-Th 10am-4am, F-Sa 10am-6am, Su noon-5am.

ESSENTIALS

Practicalities

The biggest thing to keep in mind when visiting Gibraltar is that **you're leaving Spain and entering Britain.** Bring your **passport!** You will not be able to get through customs without it.

- **TOURIST OFFICE:** The **Information Center** *(☎350 74950 🖳www.gibraltar.gov.gi)* at the corner of Casemate's Sq. can give you pamphlets and information on any questions or concerns you have about the strait.
- **CURRENCY EXCHANGE:** While any establishment will accept both euro and pounds, restaurants are notorious for creating their own personal exchange rates. You can find official exchange offices at customs or all along Main St., but it may just be easiest to withdraw pounds from an ATM and exchange back to euro once you're back in Spain and the rates are more reliable.

Emergency!

- **POLICE:** *(New Mole House Rosia Rd. ☎200 40918; 200 72500)*
- **HOSPITAL:** **St. Bernard's Hospital.** *(Harbour Views Rd. ☎200 79700)*

Getting There

If arriving by bus to Gibraltar, you will actually be arriving at the **La Linea Bus Station** on the Spanish side of the border. The station provides services from **Comes** from Cadiz, or from **Portillo** along the Costa del Sol. Once in La Linea, you will need to pass through customs at the Gibraltar border, but this process is always open and very simple. Customs is fastest on foot, as you simply show your passport and walk down a hallway. The car line can get a bit longer, but is generally efficient. **Taxis** cannot cross the border, so you may need to leave your cabbie in La Linea, cross the border by foot, and then hop into a Gibraltar taxi. You can fly directly into the Gibraltar Airport from the UK on **EasyJet, British Airways,** or **Monarch** *(2½hr.).*

Getting Around

Gibraltar itself is only about 3mi. long and thus most easily navigated on foot. If you are traveling around a bit, especially toward the beaches, the Rock, Queensway Quay, or the airport, hop on one of the city **buses** or vans that run every 15-30min. *($ £0.60 one way, round-trip £0.90, day pass £1.50. 🕐 M-F 6:30am-9pm, Sa 7am-9pm, Su 8am-9pm.)* The Gibraltar Taxi Service *(☎200 70027🖳gibtaxiass@gibtelecom.net)* will take you anywhere on the Gib or offer you a guided tour of the rock. **Taxis** are stationed all along the airport terminal and at designated stops throughout the city.

ronda ☎952

The best piece of advice *Let's Go* can give you before visiting Ronda: charge your camera. We're not kidding. Even the bus ride there is a scenic smorgasbord: you'll be shocked and inspired by the spectacular cliff views. But, don't snap too many pics on the bus—'cuz baby, you ain't seen nothing yet. Make it around the bend for the main event. The white houses of Ronda straddle a steep and spectacular gorge, splitting the new and old city in epic fashion. The three bridges across the gorge—Puente Nuevo, Puente Romano, and Puente Arabe—laud and link the historic influences of Romans, Moors, and Christians in Ronda. Just keep reminding yourself that you're not actually in a fairy tale—it just looks like one.

Once you're on foot and ready to explore, you'll find a sleepy, peaceful town blessed with the interesting contrast between its old and new regions. In the new city, you'll find commercial streets, noisy restaurants, and an active nightlife. In the old one, you'll come across crafts markets and tanneries, some quiet, fancy dining options, and, of course, all the spectacular, historic sights that Ronda has to offer.

You'll probably be able to master every inch of this tiny town within a day or two, but even a short daytrip is worth your time. Grab a quick bus from Costa del Sol or more central regions, and maybe you'll get lucky enough to kiss a Spanish frog and meet Prince or Princess Charming in the fairy-tale setting that awaits you.

ORIENTATION

In the new city, **Calle Espinel** will take you down to the **Puente Nuevo,** providing you with the city's best shopping and greatest excitement along the way. Keep in mind that locals often refer to C. Espinel as C. Labola. **Calle Sevilla** and **Calle Jerez** are strong choices to seek out nightlife and restaurants as well. The **Plaza de España** is at the base of Puente Nuevo, which links to the old city of Jerez. Once across, **Calle Arminan** runs down the middle of the old city, lined with crafts shops and tanneries. There are signs all around the old city pointing you toward the main sights, which are clustered within meters of each other.

ACCOMMODATIONS

Ronda typically caters to young daytrippers and older, wealthier travelers looking for a longer vacation in this peaceful town. This combination of sightseers leaves Ronda with a strong selection of three- and four-star hotels and pricey bed and breakfasts around the picturesque old city. But that doesn't leave the rest of us without hope! You'll come across inexpensive hostels, pensions, and hotels surrounding the bus station in the new city.

👍 HOTEL ARUNDA II

HOSTAL [3]

C. José María Castelló, 10-12 ☎615 233 877 💻www.hotelesarunda.com

After a long bus trip, there's nothing nicer than being able to fall into a comfy, wood-framed, white-sheeted bed or shower in your large, tiled, sparkling, bathroom. Well, we can't get you these things the moment you step off your bus (maybe it'll be possible with a few more years of technological development), but Hotel Arunda II won't make you wait long. Located just steps from the bus station and just a few blocks from all the city action, this hotel will get you settled in a jiffy. Even if there's a bit of a wait due to the smaller staff, enjoy the cozy plaid couches and local bullfighting posters in the lobby until you get your key. If you're lucky, you could even get the special surprise of a double room for a single price, depending on availability. Wake up to a Spanish breakfast of cereals and toasts in its cute cafeteria (included with price of room), where they don't just leave out a pot of coffee but instead brew up fresh lattes to make sure you're awake for a day of exploration.

➡ Located just meters from the bus station; signs point you to the hotel. ℹ Breakfast included. $ Singles €29; doubles €47; triples €60. ⏰ Reception 24hr. Breakfast served 8-10:15am.

HOTEL MORALES

HOTEL [3]

C. Sevilla, 51 ☎952 871 538 💻www.hotelmorales.es

Hotel Morales fully embraces the need for a refreshing visit to Ronda. With posters honoring the local scenery and national parks all along the hallways, and white-walled, bright rooms with large windows, you will definitely feel like a vacationer in its scenic vibe. To keep with the natural feel, get ready for a bit of a hike—while Hotel Morales has an elevator, the owner will always direct you to the rose-toned staircase to make your way up this five-story establishment. Once you turn your key in the door, turn on that TV and enjoy your spacious single or double with an ensuite tiled bathroom. When making your reservation, keep in mind that Wi-Fi tends to work best on the lower floors.

➡ From the bus station, take C. San Jose to C. Sevilla and turn left. ℹ Free Wi-Fi. $ Singles €30; doubles €45. ⏰ Reception 24hr.

SIGHTS

If visiting the information center or the tourist website, you'll come across quite the lengthy list of sights to see in Ronda. But don't be alarmed: most of these locations are packed tightly together around the old city. While most do not offer guided tours, feel free to walk in and look around. When planning your trip, also keep in mind that many sights offer free admission on Sundays.

MUSEO DEL BANDELERO — MUSEUM

C. Armiñan, 65 ☎952 877 785 www.museobandelero.com

One visit here will have you rooting for the bad guys. This museum of bandits, pillagers, and rebels is the only one of its kind in Spain. It presents the long legacy of myth and reality that surrounds the *bandeleros* who have wreaked havoc on the Iberian Peninsula since the time of the Romans. You learn about the weapons, the lifestyle, and the men behind the bandana and brimmed hat—Jose Maria, or "El Tempranillo," for example, was so notorious that he often didn't even need to pillage. He'd simply write polite letters requesting often wealthy landowners provide him with some cash, and they'd hand it right over. While they do have a small corner devoted to honoring the Civil Guard that helped to end banditry over the course the 19th century, *Let's Go* recommends the bad guys.

Along C. Armiñan, the main street in the old city. [i] Information mostly in Spanish and French, some English supplements. $ €3, students €2.50. Open daily 10:30am-8pm.

PLAZA DE TOROS — MONUMENT

C. Virgen de la Paz 15 ☎952 871 539 www.rmcr.org

Bullfighting is something to be taken seriously, and the Plaza de Toros is the best place to see that attitude in action. When visiting the oldest bullfighting ring in all of Spain, you'll be immediately impressed by the remarkable two-story sandstone structure. The people of Ronda want to make sure you know they're the oldest and most classic, so their museum calls out the Sevillian "ostentatious swerves." Since its opening in 1785, the Plaza de Toros has housed two of the biggest legacies in Spanish bullfighting: the Romeros of the 18th century and the Ordoñezes of the 20th. Pedro Romero, the head of the Romero Dynasty, actually fought the premier fight at the plaza, and is still honored today at the annual **Feria de Pedro Romero**, the biggest festival in all of Ronda. When visiting the Plaza de Toros, you'll see the bullring as well as collections of firearms, costumes, horse carriages, harnesses, and saddles. By the end of your visit, you'll feel like an expert in all things—just don't get to thinking that means you know how to fight one.

At the base of C. Espinel, across from the Information Office. $ €6. Open daily Mar 10am-7pm, Apr-Sept 10am-8pm; Oct 10am-7pm; Nov-Feb 10am-6pm. Closed on days of bullfights.

MUSEO JUAQUIN PEINADO — MUSEUM

Plaza del Gigante, s/n ☎952 871 585 www.museojuaquinpeinado.com

Born and raised as a loyal local, Juaquin Peinado loved his home town. His pride and passion for Ronda's culture made it all the more difficult for him to travel to France and pursue his artistic talents. But, we will admit, we're glad he took such a leap of faith. Peinado, a close friend and student of Pablo Picasso, was clearly influenced by his mentor. The bold colors, harsh lines, and abstract style will definitely trigger memories of Art History 101. This museum pays tribute to the artist, one of the most talented men to come out of Ronda, through hall after hall of his work, including pro-form, Neo-Cubism, and nude sketch sections. Housed in the Motezuma Palace, once inhabited by the last heirs of the Mayan royalty themselves, the Museo Juanquin Peinado wonderfully portrays and explains all that Peinado accomplished in those homesick years until his death.

Right by Casa del Gigante, the plaza branches off from C. Armiñan. [i] Call in advance for guided tours. $ €4, students €1. Free on Su. Open in summer M-F 10am-7pm, Sa-Su 10am-3pm; in winter M-F 10am-6pm.

THE GREAT OUTDOORS ⚠

Take a look at Ronda. You've got countryside, gorges, rivers, and plain old nature all around you. This cliffside city is perfect for those of you looking to step out of your cushy hotel room or that air-conditioned museum (although we know both are great) and get out into the natural world. Ronda is surrounded by three national parks: **Parque Natural Sierra de las Nieves** *(☎902 111 166* 🖳*www.sierranieves.com)*, **Parque Natural Sierra de Grazalema** *(☎956 727 029* 🖳*www.grazalema.info)*, and **Parque Natural Los Alcornocales** *(☎956 709 703* 🖳*www.alcornocales.org)*, all of which have unique ecosystems and settings. If you're looking for some more action-packed outdoor activity, **Pangea** *(C. Pasaje 10 ☎952 873 496* 🖳*www.pangeacentral.com)* runs guided excursions in the surrounding areas including kayaking *(€22)*, canyoning *(€39-60)*, mountain biking *(€22-40)*, and spelunking *(€40-80)*, with prices varying based on duration and difficulty of the trip.

FOOD 📖

You will not have a hard time finding a spot to eat in Ronda: main streets like **Calle Espinel** are lined with tapas bars looking to rake in tourists. **Calle Nueva**, branching off Plaza de España, is packed with restaurant after restaurant, offering mid-range prices for large plates. If you're willing to spend the extra cash, Ronda also has an extensive selection of high-quality restaurants, and even one with a Michelin Star.

Desserts

Keep in mind that one of the pride and joys of Ronda dining is their mastery of sweets— this is one city that values sugars, honeys, and flours and puts those values to use.

DAVER
CONFITERÍA, DESSERTS ❶

C. Espinel, 58 ☎952 879 161

Recommended by the city as a top tourist destination, Daver is a sleek and shiny desserterie specializing in homemade ice cream *(€1.10-1.70)* and *miloja caramelizada (€1.75)*, a sweet, layered pastry with cream filling.

⑤ *Ice cream €1.10-1.70.* 🕐 *Open daily 9am-9pm.*

Meals

🍽 CAFETERÍA DON MIGUEL
💨 🍴 ❄ SPANISH, VIEWS, DATE SPOT ❶

Plaza de Espana 4, 5 ☎952 871 090 🖳www.dmiguel.com

Descend the tiled stairway from Plaza de España into the Hotel Don Miguel and find yourself with one of the best views Ronda has to offer. The multi-tier, outdoor terrace is carved right into the wall of cliffs beside Puente Nuevo, and all these views are included in the prices at Cafetería Don Miguel. The "snack shop" attached to the fancier Restaurante Don Miguel *(€20-25 per person)*, can provide you with quite the hearty, lunch. Grab a seat at one of the small, marble coffee tables and enjoy some light and refreshing treats or heavier fare. The vegetarian sandwich topped with an avocado and asparagus salad, tomatoes, and eggs on crispy toast *(€3.40)* is one delicious option. Try to keep your nose from going too high in the air when requesting a taste of the home-made pâtés *(€9.15)* or classic cured sausages *(€10)*, both prepared in the traditional fashion. Also, make sure that your pinkie finger is appropriately pointed out as you sip the selection of coffees, teas, and fresh juices and munch on Don Miguel's artisan desserts *(€2.90-4.10)*. You may also want to find a seat in the shade, as the service is far from speedy—they probably think you're too lost in the Rondeñan countryside to notice.

🍴 *Located in the corner of Plaza de Espana, to the left if facing Puente Nuevo.* ⑤ *Cafeteria: breakfast €2.90-4.10, sandwiches €3.20-4.20, fish/meat €3.70-8.80. Restaurant: appetizers €6.45-17.50, fish €10.75-15.85, meat €11.25-18.20.* 🕐 *Cafeteria open daily 12:30-8pm. Restaurant open June-Aug M-Sa 12:30-4pm and 8-11pm, Su 8-11pm; Sept-May daily 12:30-4pm and 8-11pm.*

ronda . food

LA SACRISTÍA

Comte Salvador Carrasco, s/n

🍴♈️⏱ TAPAS ❷
☎617 369 763

On the tiny street corner of Comte Salvador Carrasco, you'll come across three or four inexpensive tapas bars with barrelled tables out front. How will you ever choose between them? Take our advice and try La Sacristía. At the end of the tapas-bar stretch, it's the classiest and cleanest on the street, with tiled floors and dark-wood framing, but it still keeps its prices unbelievably low. Take a peek at their tapas menu—you won't find anything over €2. If you're not exactly sure what you want, the friendly staff will make some swanky suggestions like *foie de pato* (duck liver) with a liquor reduction sauce *(€6.80),* but you can also consult the chalkboard to see what the daily dish *(€3),* tapa *(€1),* and fish *(€1)* specials are. Whether you come to start your day with a sweet or savory breakfast tosta *(€2-3),* or end the night with one of the local wines of the week *(€1.50 per glass),* you'll always find this small bar full of locals.

🍴 *Near the bus station at the corner of Comte Salvador Carrasco and Pasaje El Cante.* Ⓢ *Tapas €1-2. Toasts €2-3. Raciones €6-12.* ☎ *Open Tu-Sa noon-1am, Su noon-4pm.*

LOS CÁNTAROS

C. Sevilla 66

🍴♿️♈️❄ ANDALUCIAN ❷
☎952 876 323

Walk into this homey Andalucian kitchen and learn what tradition is all about. From the clay walls to the wooden ceiling beams to the plaid table cloths, there's no question that Los Cántaros is authentic. You'll find the best of the fresh, local Rondeña specialities from *rabo de toro (bull's tail; €10),* with the meat falling right off the bone, to *manitas de cerdo (pig's feet; €8.50),* prepared to succulent perfection. Beyond the scope of just Ronda, they take pride in their general Andalucian classics, providing an extensive list of *tortillas espanolas,* scrambled full of fish, meat, or vegetarian ingredients *(€3-6).* The helpings are big on their own, but if you're really hungry, the *prix-fixe* menu is a total steal, serving up two courses, bread, and dessert *(€8)* with extensive options in case you're not feeling brave enough to try those more obscure, body parts.

🍴 *On C. Sevilla between C. Laurina and C. San Jose.* Ⓢ *Daily menu €8. Totillas €3-6. Ractiones €6-12.* ☎ *Open Tu-Su 8:30am-noon and 8pm-late.*

NIGHTLIFE

Ronda may seem like a quiet little town, but it knows how to have a good time. The standard Ronda evening begins with conversation over drinks and some cheap tapas on an outdoor patio, and you'll find late-night bar-restaurants filling **Plaza del Sorcerro** and **Plaza Carmen Abela** with tables, chairs, and noisy conversation. **Calle Jerez** and the surrounding side streets offer bars and clubs for a younger crowd looking to get on their feet.

DULCINEA

C. Rios Rosa 3

🍴♈️⏱ BAR
☎952 871 003

This tavern-tastic watering hole definitely doesn't look like a party hot spot: 30- to 50-somethings listening to classic rock or live piano dominate the bar area, where they've been loyal regulars since Dulcinea opened in the '60s. While they'll welcome you with open arms, better pull a reverse Cinderella and wait until midnight to show up at this ball. When the clock strikes 12, the dance floor opens and the young crowd floods in. The tiled dance floor with high pillars lit by skylights and Chinese lamps is one magical scene, but this not-so-Disney dance floor can get down and dirty. The DJ claims that he'll play anything popular and commercial but loves blasting whatever the crowd requests. Grab a generous glass of beer *(€2)* and make a request for Top 40, Spanish, Flamenco, Hip Hop, or even Pirate Folk (well, maybe not that last one).

🍴 *C. Rios Rosa links Plaza Carmen Abela to C. Los Romedios.* Ⓢ *Wine or beer €2. Mixed drinks €5.* ☎ *Open M-Th 4pm-3am, F-Sa 4pm-4am, Su 4pm-3am. Dance floor opens F-Sa after midnight.*

EL TEMPLO 🔞🍸♿❄ DISCOTECA

C. Jerez, 6

No, we're not suggesting you spend your evening at another ancient, Moorish ruin, but El Templo is a bit of a Rondeñan shrine. The sanctum of the party pilgrimage, this discoteca is packed to the gates with 20- to 25-year-olds at around 2am on the weekends, but if you arrive by 1:30am you'll enjoy discounted mixed drinks and cocktails. If it's summertime, you can even score a spot on the outdoor terrace and down their delicious summer mojitos *(€3)*. Once you've laced up your dancing shoes, you'll be drawn to the dance floor's disco balls, slideshows, and light display like flies to a bug zapper. The atmosphere will shock you into party mode with the loud, upbeat hip hop and R and B. All the med students are invited for Thursday parties, so take advantage of the chance to get smarter by grinding up on your future orthopedic surgeon.

⇄ Located on C. Jerez between C. San Jose and C. Pozo. $ Beer €2. Mixed €3, after 1:30am €4. ⏰ Open Th-Sa 11:30pm-4am.

FESTIVALS

FERIA DE PEDRO ROMERO

On May 19, 1785, Spain opened its first bullfighting ring in Ronda, and **Pedro Romero** valiantly inaugurated the historic structure. Now, over 200 years later, the city of Ronda is still honoring this bullfighter's name with the annual Feria de Pedro Romero, the most important celebration in the city. Even though we've jumped from the 18th to the 21st century, many locals say that during the *feria*, it's like those few hundred years never happened. All obligations and stresses are set aside; it's not until the closing of the final festivities that the city returns to a life of 3G, 3D, and 3oh!3.

Turns out Rondeñans don't just travel back in time—they also head back to the future come festival time. Although the *feria's* officially held in early September each year, celebrations like the fair's opening speech and the Flamenco singing festival already begin by late August. When that ninth month comes around, the real action starts with a parade, the ceremonial turning-on of all the decorative city lights, and the opening up of the *peñas* and *casetas* at the **Feria del Centro**, the 20-somethings' party center of the week. But let's get back to the roots and focus of this celebration—the bullfighting. Saturday and Sunday are packed with the year's most spectacular and long-awaited traditional **Goyaesquo bullfights**, a style sacred to Ronda's history, and you can catch the artistry of the **Carriage Contest** and the new perspective of **horse bullfighting** later in the evenings.

As this is the city's most significant festival, and recommended by the Andalucian government as one of the best celebrations for tourists, you'll need to book your accommodations well in advance if arriving before or during the festivities throughout the late summer. While some would recommend finding a hotel or hostel as close to the bullring as possible, Ronda is an easy city to navigate, so just check out the elevated festival prices and see what you can find in your budget.

ESSENTIALS

Practicalities

- **TOURIST OFFICES:** You are probably best off beginning any visit to Ronda at the **Information Office** *(Paseo San Blas Infante, s/n ☎952 187 119 🖥www.tourismoronda.com ⏰ Open M-F 10am-7pm, Sa 10am-2pm and 3-5pm, Su 10am-2:30pm)*. This office and its helpful website offer clear schedules and calendars explaining prices and opening times for all the main sights, lists of the top restaurants, and a compilation of the top tour guides in the area with all the necessary contact information.
- **CURRENCY EXCHANGE:** The one **money exchange** center is located around the corner at C. Virgen de la Paz 2 *(Open daily 10:30am-2pm and 4-8:30pm)*.

- **INTERNET:** The **municipal library** *(Plaza de Merced 2 ☎952 874 142 🖥www.bibliotecaronda.blogspot.com)* is open to the public and provides free Wi-Fi. You can also get internet access at **Ciber-locutorio.** *(Calle Cruz Verde 44 ☎669 984 562 ⏰ Open M-Sa 10am-2pm, 4-10pm, Su 4-10pm. $ €1.20 per hr.)* There are also other internet cafes along C. Cruz Verde.

Emergency!

Emergency Numbers: **Police:** ☎092 *(Palacio de Justicia, C. Carlos Cano, s/n).*
Medical Services: **Hospital General Basico** *(Caretera El Burgo, s/n* ☎951 065 001; *Emergency Room ☎951 065 218).*

Getting There

Taking a bus or train through the mountains to Ronda may seem tough, but like we told you before, the route's scenic and both modes of transit are equally convenient. The **bus station** *(Plaza Concepcion Garcia Redondo, 2 ☎952 872 260)* runs trips from Costa del Sol on **Portillo** *(☎952 872 262 🖥www.ctsa-portillo.com)*, getting you from **Málaga** *($10.31 ⏰ 2¾hr.)* or **Marbella** *($ €5.35 ⏰ 1¼hr.)*. Comes *(☎952 871 992 🖥www.tgcomes.es)* runs a line from **Cadiz** *($ €13.84 ⏰ 3¼hr.)* that stops in **Jerez de la Frontera** and **Arcos de la Frontera**. Los Amarillos *(☎952 187 061 🖥www.losamarillos.es)* will get you to Ronda from **Sevilla** *($ €10.86 ⏰ 2hr.)* or **Granada** *(⏰ 4hr. $ €20)*. You can also arrive at the **train station** *(Avenida de Andalucia, s/n ☎952 871 673)* on a Renfe tain *(☎902 320 320 🖥www.renfe.es)* from **Madrid** *($ €65.30 ⏰ 4hr.)* or **Córdoba** *($ €31.80 ⏰ 1¾hr.)*.

Getting Around

Walking around the city of Ronda can take less than half an hour, assuming you don't stop for ice cream or a long gaze into the countryside along the way. Locals and tourists alike navigate the city on foot. There is only one bus line that covers the outskirts of the area; it runs hourly and is primarily used by local commuters to get to work. So, for your visit, just stick to the cobblestone paths of the old city and neatly organized grid of the new.

córdoba ☎957

If you spent centuries under Moorish rule as the capital of the Western world, you'd have a bit of a complex, too. It may be over 700 years since Córdoba was held to such high acclaim, but this city continues to maintain its individuality from the surrounding Andalucian region. You'll find yourself experiencing thousands of years of history and learning about Jewish, Islamic, Roman, and Catholic cultures as you make your way through the alleyways of **La Juderia.** You'll fill your belly with the classics of the *cocina cordobes* (Córdoban kitchen) while you sip an infused tea. You'll relax in an ancient Arab bath to rest up before a night on the town in one's of Avandia de America's massive clubs. Córdoba combines a slew of interests that you'd never expect as the highlights of this historic city: the classic patios decorated with stunning tiles, plants, and fountains, the traditional and modern guitar music resonating throughout the city, and the slew of *Ximenez* grapes that produce the sweet wines of the region. Córdoba may have fallen from massive international attention, but don't worry, it's not bitter. You'll still receive the warm hospitality of a city packed with sights, activities, and good eats.

ORIENTATION

While the northern part of the city is fairly modern, the southern section, especially **La Judería,** is plagued by ancient, inconvenient street planning. You'll find most of your historic sights packed into this Jewish Quarter, including the top dogs like the **Mezquita** and the **Alcazar. Calle San Fernando** runs from the Guadelquivir River up between two of the main plazas of the city, **Plaza Corredera** and **Plaza de las Tendillas**. Plaza Corredera is packed with outdoor patio restaurants open late, and you'll find all your commercial and shopping needs, an information office, multiple pharmacies and ATMs, as well as a few restaurants and desserteries in and around **Plaza de las Tendillas.** Geographically and socially, this plaza is a city center.

ACCOMMODATIONS

Córdoba is absolutely covered in accommodations. Whether in or out of La Judería, you won't need to take more than a few steps to find a sign pointing you to at least three or four hostels and hotels. These signs will also designate the number of stars for the accommodation—most hostels, aside from a very few nicer ones like **Hostal El Triunfo,** are one star, while hotels in Córdoba range from one to five stars. You'll find that prices vary greatly based on season, sometimes by as much as €35. The "low season" is generally November through August, the "middle" from March to October, and the "high" on the weekends in April and May and during festivals and holidays.

HOSTAL EL TRIUNFO

HOSTAL ❷

C. Corregidor Luis la Cerda, 79 ☎957 498 484 www.hostaltriunfo.com

Attention all students: this may be the best deal in town if you're coming during the low season. You can get up to three meals included with your stay, a spacious, well-decorated room with wire-framed bed and marble floors, and even have the kitchen pack you a picnic basket *(€10)* for a day on the town. The massive, shaded plaza-restaurant where breakfast, lunch, and dinner are served is a comfortable spot regardless of whether you come to just relax or to stuff your face at the bar or buffet. Your neighbors may not be stopping over to ask for a cup of sugar, considering they're the Mezquita and the Puente Romano (two of the most significant sights in Córdoba!), but the vested, tie and clip-adorning receptionists will provide you with all the information you need to know.

At the base of the Puente Romano, C. Corregidor is located right behind the Mezquita. ***i*** *1-3 meals included. Free Wi-Fi.* *High-season singles €80-100; non-student doubles €120-140; student doubles with 1 meal €57, with 2 €70, with 3 €83. Mid-season singles €42-62; non-student doubles €67-82; student doubles €30/33/41. Low-season singles €33; non-student doubles €58; student doubles €17/23/30. Safes €3 per day; luggage storage €2 per day.* *Reception 24hr. Breakfast 8-11am; lunch 12:30-4pm; dinner 7:30-11pm.*

TERRACE BACKPACKERS

HOSTEL ❷

C. Lucano 12 ☎957 492 966

Terrace Backpackers may be the perfect stop for any young traveler on the go. It's impossible to not feel upbeat when entering the lobby and seeing every wall painted a different bold color and covered with fun facts and interesting star-shaped lamps. Plus, the staff (and a welcome board with your name on it) will welcome you with a big smile and enthusiasm about all that Córdoba has to offer. And let's admit it, as young travelers, we can be a bit lazy during lulls in the trip. No problem—Terrace Backpackers will spoon-feed you all the information you need without even leaving the lobby. The chalkboards around the hostel provide the daily weather report, tips for local discounts, and maps pointing out the hottest restaurants and clubs. While you'll have to get a little active to climb up to the rooftop terrace, it's worth the hike. You'll find a fully accessible kitchen where you can cook up some lunches and dinners, and a comfy seating area to meet fellow travelers. Although breakfast isn't included, you'll get big discounts at the Cafeteria el Pilar del Porto next door *(breakfast €1.50-5).*

From the bus station, take bus #3 to C. San Fernando and turn left onto C. Lucano. ***i*** *Female-only dorms available.* *Low-season dorms €11-17; private doubles €36. High-season dorms €15-23; private doubles €60. Laundry €5. Towels €2 for dorms.* *Reception 24hr.*

HOSTAL LA FUENTE

HOSTAL ❷

C. San Fernando 51 ☎957 487 827 www.hostallafuente.com

Walking by Hostal la Fuente in the evenings, it's hard to miss the green glow coming from the classic Andaluz patio. *La fuente,* or its fountain, may not be much,

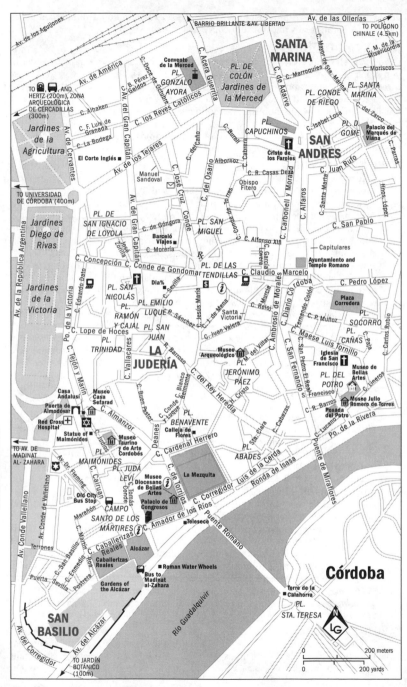

Córdoba

but its shaded area with hanging plants and marble tables is one classy hangout. Once you get into the hallways, you don't lose even an ounce of class. You'll find surprisingly (considering its low prices) tasteful artwork, fancy couches, and giant wood-framed mirrors as you make your way up this four-story building. The red-and-white-striped matching comforters and curtains may sound circus-esque, but they actually balance well with the wall's soothing floral print and the small glass study table in the corner—believe us, we're not clowning around.

 # Take bus #3 to C. San Fernando. The hostel is on the right. ***i*** *Towels €2. Wi-Fi €1 per hr.* [$] *High-season singles €30-38; doubles €41-50; triples €55-60; quads €70-80. Prices around €5 lower in low season.* ⏰ *Reception 24hr.*

HOTEL BOSTON

🛏 📶 ❄ HOTEL [3]

C. Málaga, 2 ☎957 474 176 🖥www.hotel-boston.com

Climbing the marble steps toward the second-story reception at Hotel Boston, you'll probably be expecting some snazzy, high-priced hotel stay. We hate to break it to you, but this hotel is not the Four Seasons Boston. Although Hotel Boston may not be your dream 5-star resort, it definitely provides a good stay for the price tag. Your spacious yellow room decorated with painted flowers will be clean and bright, and while your bathroom may be small enough to brush your teeth, shower, and do other bathroom-y things simultaneously, Boston compensates with full beds, spacious closets, and desk space in all rooms. While the man at the front desk may not provide a warm welcome, the reception area is still a popular and quiet place to read, relax, or grab a coffee.

 # C. Málaga branches off Pl. de las Tendillas. ***i*** *Breakfast €4.50.* [$] *Singles €33-35; doubles €42-49; triples €55-60.* ⏰ *Reception 24hr.*

HOSTAL SENECA SENSES Y COLOURS

☺ 📶 ❄ HOSTAL [3]

C. Conde y Luque, 7 ☎957 473 234 🖥senses@colours.com

Hostal Seneca was most likely designed by a group of free-spirited hippies. From the makeshift "reception desk" to the patterned tapestries hanging in each dorm to the wonderfully cozy and laid-back common spaces in the plant-covered patio and shaded rooftop terrace, everything decorating this *hostal* would be a hit with Cheech and Chong. And come on: senses and colors? It even sounds like a mellow, flower-power-esque stay. Stay in one of the colorful dorm rooms equipped with balconies to hang your clothes and large, clean, hallway bathrooms. The beds are extra-long and extra-wide if you're lucky enough to score a non-bunk, so try to browse the vacancies before taking that key. While they don't offer breakfast, they do have vending machines, coffee machines, and a fully functional kitchen on the first floor.

 # C. Conde y Luque is in La Judería between C. Deanes and Plaza Benavente. ***i*** *Towels included.* [$] *8-bed dorms €14-24; 6-bed dorms €15-25. Singles €27-40; doubles €33-65; triples €55-80.* ⏰ *Reception 8am-midnight.*

ALBERQUE INTURJOVEN DE LA CREATIVIDAD HI

🛏 📶 ❄ HOSTEL [1]

Plaza Judá Leví s/n ☎957 355 040 🖥www.inturjoven.com

Take in two main aspects of the title when considering this accommodation: *creatividad* (creativity) and *joven* (young), because this HI hostel embraces both of those things quite well. As you walk up to the automatic, sliding-glass doors at the entry, you're welcomed into a massive, marble lobby that looks like a combination of a spa and doctor's office, with large pamphlet-covered tables surrounded by lofty couches. While the modern tire-swing art piece at the entrance isn't ready to play on just yet, feel free to let loose in the 24hr. TV lounge or start an international game of Red Rover on the spacious outdoor patio. As you walk toward your room, catch a glimpse of the unique, colorful graffiti decorating each door. It doesn't exactly match the hostel's ceilings, white walls, and blue columns elsewhere, but the tagging provides a youthful touch.

🚏 In the Judería near the Museo Taurino and C. Manriquez. $ High-season dorms €19 for guests, over 26 €25; low-season dorms €14/20. €3.50 discount with HI card. i Towels €2. Wi-Fi €1 per hr. ⏰ Reception 24hr.

SIGHTS

This is one city with quite a few things to see. Luckily, most of the sights are concentrated in and around **La Judería** and can be easily accessed with a short walk. Make sure to check schedules ahead of time (💻www.turismodeCórdoba.org offers an organized and updated schedule of sights), as many are closed on Mondays, open only one day a week, or free at specific times. Organize and plan accordingly, and you should be able to hit up sight after sight without too much difficulty.

MUSEO DE BELLAS ARTES — MUSEUM

Plaza de Porto, 1 ☎957 355 550 💻www.museosdeandalucia.es

Looking for a cure for your artistic deprivation? Well, this building was the Hospital de la Caridad until 1837, and today though you'll have to look elsewhere for help with that head cold, this museo is definitely capable of attending to any creativity-killing ailment. At the Museo de Bellas Artes, you'll get a quick trip through 15th- to 20th-century Spanish and Córdoban culture with some of the world's most spectacular pieces of art. The museum is organized by era and denotes not just the birth and death of each artist but also the Spanish cities where they lived, studied, and worked. While the museum includes artists from all over Spain, it prides itself on its extensive Córdoban representation through drawing and painting exhibits as well as its modern art collection. You'll find all types of media at the Museo de Bellas Artes, from engravings to sculptures to oil on canvas, and you'll find yourself consistently impressed by the various mediums of expression. The massive pieces in the Baroque chapel will stun you with their bold colors and powerful subject matter, and the bright, contemporary sculptures will leave you perplexed and intrigued.

🚏 You can reach Plaza de Porto by taking C. Lucano from C. San Fernando. i Pamphlets available in English but exhibits only in Spanish. $ €1.50, EU citizens free. ⏰ Open Tu 2:30-8:30pm, W-Sa 9am-8:30pm, Su 9am-2:30pm.

LA MEZQUITA — MUSEUM

C. Cardenal Herrero s/n ☎957 470 512 💻www.turismodeCórdoba.org

You've seen the pictures, you've heard the stories, and you've noticed that it's listed at number one on any map you pick up of the city. La Mezquita is Córdoba's top sight and one of the most important relics in the world. Originally the Visigoths' Christian Church of San Vicente, the structure was knocked down under Moorish rule and converted into a mosque in the year 785. From its opening, La Mezquita was the most important Islamic structure in the West and turned Córdoba into a world capital. You'll see the strong Moorish design in the striped (red-brick and white-stone) archways that decorate the entire interior of La Mezquita, but even the traditional mosque had a bit of Christian twist when builders frugally used pieces of the San Vicente church in its construction. Eventually, during the Reconquista in 1236, this splash of Christian influence became more of a tidal wave. King Ferdinand III ordered the development of chapels, transepts, and choirs to re-Christianize the structure and turned the palm-tree courtyard into the more Spanish orange-tree courtyard. Today, La Mezquita stands as a symbol of the blending Muslim and Christian influence found throughout Córdoba. Many suggest that, despite its tumultuous history, the consistent value placed on the structure, whether by Moors or Spaniards, allowed for its wonderful preservation into the modern era.

🚏 From Puente Romano, take C. Torrijos along the southern wall and turn right at the front of the building. i Information available in English and Spanish. $ €8; free 8:30am-10am. ⏰ Open M-Sa 8:30am-7pm, Su 8:30am-10am and 2-7pm. Mass Su 11am-1pm.

andalucia

CASA ANDALUSÍ
C. Judios 12

MONUMENT

☎957 290 642 ▪www.lacasaandalusi.es

The people of the 12th century definitely knew how to relax. Come live the high (High Middle Ages, that is) life at this preserved patio and house, where you can enjoy fountains, floating flowers, and fresh scents. Inspect the replica of the 10th-century Arab paper factory, one of the first known means of printing in the world. Feel free to buy some of the printed Córdoban poetry, translated into the language of that special someone. You can take a look through the Muslim-Andaluz coin collection (no, you can't use them to pay the entrance fee) in the classic-style tea room equipped with traditional leather stools and stained glasses. In the basement you'll find the house's cool, moist tunnels and the well-preserved original tile floors.

⚑ *Take C. Tomas Conde from the Alcazar and follow C. Judios. Located near the Sinagoga.* ⓘ *Information available in English and Spanish.* Ⓢ *€2.50.* ⏰ *Open daily 10:30am-7pm.*

CASA DE SEFARAD
Intersection of C. Judios and C. Averroes

CULTURAL CENTER

☎957 421 404 ▪www.casasefarad.es

This cultural center will take you through the history of the Jewish people in Córdoba and explain their lasting influence in the city today. The Sephardic Jews represented a combination of Arab, Spanish, and Jewish traditions that found a way to survive despite the brutality of the 14th Century Spanish Inquisitions. Walking through the 14th-century first floor, you'll learn the basics of Jewish culture: holidays, music, important rabbis and leaders, and even an explanation of the philosophy behind kosher dining. Three brand-new exhibits were also recently added upstairs, detailing the Sinagoga, the Inquisition, and Maimonides, a top thinker and philosopher in Sephardic-Jewish history. As this is a cultural center and not just a museum, there's always room for some more hands-on fun: Casa de Sefarad holds weekly evening activities like concerts and flamenco shows *(8:30pm)* that help to depict how even classic Spanish traditions have a splash of Sephardic influence. Keep an eye out for **Casa Mazal** *(C. Tomas Conde 3* ☎957 203 605 ▪*www.casamazal.es.* Ⓢ *Dinner €15-20 per person),* the new restaurant opened by the Casa de Sefarad to share Sephardic heritage in its most delicious form—homemade kosher dining.

⚑ *From the Alcazar, take C. Tomas Conde to C. Judios until you hit C. Averroes.* ⓘ *Information in English and Spanish.* Ⓢ *€4, students €3.* ⏰ *Open M-Sa 10am-6pm, Su 11am-2pm. Tours noon or upon request with group.*

CAPILLA MUDEJAR DE SAN BARTOLOME
Facultad Filosofia y Letras

MONUMENT

☎902 210 774 ▪www.tourismodeCórdoba.org

After the 1391 Inquisition attacks on Córdoba, the Jewish and Muslim people were running low on options. The Mudejar traditions—a combination of Christian, Jewish, and Muslim—found a safe haven in the Capilla Mudejar. Although particularly small, especially in comparison to the impressive Sinagoga, the collection of 15th-century floors, walls, and mosaics is worth your time. The *zocalo* tile stylings (the zig-zag patterns you'll find on the walls) are an example of an advanced design technique preserved in the Capilla. On your way out, you can also take a look at the mysterious crypt set beside the Capilla, thought to be dedicated to St. James.

⚑ *Near the Sinagoga off Plaza Maimonides.* ⓘ *Information in English and Spanish.* Ⓢ *Free.* ⏰ *Open daily mid-June to mid-Sept 10:30am-1:30pm and 5:30pm-8:30pm; mid-Sept to mid-June 10:30am-1:30pm and 3:30-6:30pm.*

TORRE DE LA CALAHORRA AND MUSEO VIVO DE AL-ANDALUS
Puente Romano, s/n

MUSEUM

☎957 293 929 ▪www.torrecalahorra.com

The Museo Vivo de Al-Andalus prides itself on its ability to take you back in time to the period between the ninth and the 13th centuries, when Córdoba was the world's cultural center and more than one million people walked its streets. Passing room to room of the museum, you'll encounter many points of pride in the Córdoban heritage, including the advanced surgical technology of Abulcasis,

córdoba . sights

whose methods were still being cited until the 20th century, or the musical stylings of the *rebab*, a wooden string-and-bow instrument that produces traditional tunes. In the hall of thinkers, you'll be addressed by some of the best and brightest: Alfonso X will tell you about opening the world's first school where Jews, Christians, and Muslims studied in tandem while Ibn Arabi will tell you about the power of love and the importance of individual thought. You can inspect scale models of such major sights at the Alhambra and Mezquita and learn about the Córdoban lifestyle during its heyday from hygiene to dining to education.

✔ *Located across the Guadalquivir, at the base of Puente Romano.* ℹ *Automated tour available in English and Spanish.* Ⓢ *€4.50, students €3.* Ⓚ *Open daily May-Sept 10am-2pm and 4:30-8:30pm; Oct-Apr 10am-6pm.*

ALCÁZAR DE LOS REYES CRISTIANOS ✒♿♨ MUSEUM
C. Caballerizas, s/n ☎957 420 151 ▦www.turismodeCórdoba.org

When King Alfonso XI ordered the construction in 1328 of a visitors' palace for the Spanish royalty visiting Córdoba, we doubt he had any idea how many purposes the structure would take on over the years. The Alcázar has served as a planning headquarters for the discovery of America and reconquest of Granada, an outpost for the Inquisition, a 19th-century prison, a 20th-century town council, and, today, a top tourist destination with artistic gardens and fountains. As you explore the grounds, feel free to climb the towers of the Alcázar (some are original, while others were added in the 15th and 18th centuries) or explore the collections of second- and third-century Roman mosaics, discovered during the 1950s excavations of Plaza Corredera. These mosaics are the most beautiful pop quiz you will ever take: What geometric pattern is that? Which Greek God is Neptune? (The water one.) Which woman is Medusa? (The snake-haired one.)

✔ *Located beside the Mezquita, near Campo Santo de los Mártines.* ℹ *Information in Spanish only.* Ⓢ *€4, students €2; all free on W.* Ⓚ *Open Tu-F 8:30am-7:30pm, Sa 9:30am-4:30pm, Su 9:30am-2:30pm.*

SINAGOGA ✒♿♨ SYNAGOGUE
C. Judios, s/n ☎957 290 642 ▦www.turismodeCórdoba.org

When the Jews were expelled from Spain in 1492, all but three synagogues in the entire country were destroyed, and only one survived in Andalucia—the Sinagoga. Although it wasn't knocked down, the Jewish religious center was converted into a hermitage and hospital in 1492 and later into a factory. It wasn't until 1884 when a piece of falling plaster gave a clue to the rich artistic design hidden in the ceiling that the building was converted into a national monument and the restoration began. Today, while you can't explore the entirety of the synagogue, you can enjoy the historic beauty of the main prayer room's walls engraved with Hebrew biblical inscriptions, translated on posters around the museum.

✔ *From the Alcazar, take C. Tomas Conde to C. Judios.* ℹ *Information available in English and Spanish.* Ⓢ *Free.* Ⓚ *Open Tu-Sa 9:30am-2pm and 3:30-5:30pm, Su 9:30am-1:30pm.*

MUSEO CARBONELL DEL ACEITE DE OLIVA ✒♿♨ MUSEUM, TASTING TOUR
Caretera N-IV Km, 388 ☎957 320 400 ▦visitas.alcolea@gruposos.com

A guided visit to Carbonell will teach you everything you ever needed to know about olives and olive oil. From 3D projection films to flamenco dancers to shelf upon shelf of olive-oil secrets (yes, there are plentiful secrets to this tasty topping), you'll be enthralled throughout the entirety of your visit. You'll get to take a train through the groves themselves, where your guide will explain the different types of trees and plants grown by Carbonell, the biggest olive-oil producer in Spain. And what's a visit without a tasting? The guided tasting session will clue you in on the most minute details that make different types of oils uniquely delicious. While you'll find many Carbonell products in the gift shop, browse around Córdoba hostels for coupons and big discounts.

andalucia

➔ About 2-3km outside of Córdoba. Take Crta. N-IVa all the way. Taxi €15 or more each way. ℹ Ages 8 and older. Visits must be booked in advance. $ Free. ⏰ Tours M-F at 10am, noon, and 4pm.

CASA MUSEO ARTE SOBRE PIEL ♿ MUSEUM

Plaza de Agrupacion de Colfradias, 2 ☎957 050 131 💻www.artesobrepiel.com

To understand this museum, we should first get some vocab out of the way (you can make flash cards later): *Omeyan* refers to 10th-century Arabic culture, and *Guademeci* refers to leather-embossed artwork. Now you can truly appreciate this privately owned museum that displays the fruits of 50 years' worth of devoted labor by the artist Ramon Garcia Romero. Romero spent this time working to recreate the lost products of the *Omeyan* culture and later opened this house to showcase his work. He presents both the traditional *Omeyan* geometric works focusing on birds and vegetables as well as the later 13th-century works that feature religious and historic figures. The museum displays different manufacturing methods of embossing and studding the leather as well as the necessary tools (it looks more like a dentist's workplace than an art studio) used to create these stunning, colorful products.

➔ From the Mezquita, take C. Cespedes and make a right. ℹ Information available in English and Spanish. $ €3. ⏰ Open Tu-Sa 11am-2pm and 4:30-8pm, Su 11am-2pm.

FOOD

Upon arriving in Córdoba, you won't be saying goodbye to any of the Andalusian classics like *revueltos*, *tortillas*, or *espinacas con garbanzos*. However, it's definitely worth taking a bite of some of the dishes distinct to the Córdoban kitchen. Taste a crispy, hot *flamenquin*, a rolled log of ham served deep-fried, or a cool, refreshing bowl of *salmorejo*, a tomato-based soup or sauce topped with ham and honey. If your sweet tooth is calling, the *pastel cordobés* is best when eaten in its namesake, and this thin cake with jelly filling is sweet, flaky, and topped with powdered sugar. Rather than just simple tapas, this city is big on pre-set menus offering a couple courses, bread, and a dessert *(€8-20)*. You'll find a lot of touristy spots around **La Judería,** late-night patios at **Plaza Corredera,** and ice-cream parlors, desserteries, and bigger establishments at **Plaza de las Tendillas.** To save money, pick a picnic from the large produce section and shelves packed with unbeatable grocery deals at **Maxi Dia Supermercado** *(C. Sevilla, 4 ⏰ Open M-Sa 9:30am-9:30pm)*, just off the **Plaza de Tendillas** that is lined with numerous pharmacies.

SOUL FOOD ♿ MODERN [3]

C. San Fernando, 39 ☎957 471 404

We don't want to knock traditional culinary styles, but there's something to be said for the most creative, modern menu in town. Soul Food offers international fare that values unique pairings of flavors and textures. The entrees, or "half rations" *(€7-10.50)* are a good size for a lighter lunch or for dinner if paired with an appetizer. The asparagus and smoked prawn risotto *(€9.75)* and grilled duck topped with dates, corn, and spiced bread *(€8.50)* bring the young regulars back over and over again. They definitely don't neglect dessert: the molten chocolate cake *(€6.50)* and coconut mousse topped with mango and green tea *(€5.50)* are tasty treats that speak to your soul and waistline. Even though this sleek, colorful restaurant is equipped with a bar, two dining rooms, and an outdoor patio, expect a wait on the weekends unless you call ahead. Avoid this wait and cut the price with the midday menu (Tu-F) that allows you to pick two entrees, a drink, and dessert just for €9.

➔ Bus #3 stops at the base of C. San Fernando. If walking from the bus stop, the restaurant is on the right. ℹ Vegetarian options available. $ Appetizers €4.50-7; ½ rations €7-10.50. Desserts €5-6.50. ⏰ Open in summer Tu-Sa 1-6pm and 8pm-1am, Su 1pm-7pm; in winter Tu-Sa 1pm-1am, Su 1-7pm.

TABERNA SALINAS TRADITIONAL [2]

C. Tundidores, 3 ☎957 480 135 www.tabernasalinas.com

There are a few mysteries about Taberna Salinas: How is it that the manager has the energy to greet every customer who enters with a warm smile? How do they cover entire walls in traditional Andalusian art and ceramics and still present a tasteful decor? And most importantly, how do they serve face-sized plates, overflowing with traditional cuisine at such low prices *(€6.20-6.70)*? We must not be the only ones wondering such things about Taberna Salinas—the main, shaded, plant-filled patio and small side dining rooms are always packed with locals and tourists chatting away over a filling meal. Originally opened as a wine tavern in 1879, Salinas made the switch to the restaurant world 45 years after its founding. You'll find a menu of house specialties like the *naranjas picas con aceite y bacalao (orange slices with local fish and olive oil; €6.70)*, homemade *chorizo (spicy sausage; €6.70)*, and *morcilla (black pudding; €6.20)*. But don't think that Taberna Salinas neglects its native Córdoba: they have the crispiest *flamenquin (€6.70)*, the most refreshing *salmorejo (€6.20)*, and the most melt-off-the-bone *rabo de toro (€6.70)* in town. Don't forget Salinas's slew of wines in barrels and bottles kept right on site.

Near Plaza Corredera. Make a left off C. Marin. $ Raciones €6.20-6.70. Open Sept-July M-Sa 12:30-4pm and 8-11:30pm.

PASTELERÍA-CAFETERÍA SAN PEDRO BAKERY, ICE CREAM [1]

C. Escultor Juan Mesa, 10 ☎957 474 482

Córdoba prides itself on a slew of delicious mealtime portions, but don't overlook dessert. Pastelería San Pedro definitely embraces this philosophy, making its pastries and desserts *(€1.25-1.50)* so big that you probably won't be able to even look at another *flamenquin* for at least a few hours. The *hojas con chocolate*, puff pastries dipped in dark chocolate *(€1.35)*, will be longer than your forearm. If you're looking to taste the traditional *pastel cordobéz (€1.25)*, a thin, flaky, sweet cake with a jelly centerhead here to take a bite. You could also stop in for a sizable, savory *empenada (€1.30)* or a chilly scoop of homemade ice cream *(regular or sugar free; €1.20-€2.15)*. The prices are equally low in the market portion of the shop, which sells basic cereals, breads, and kitchen goods.

In front of the Parroquía de San Pedro, near the Plaza Corredera. $ Desserts €1.25-1.50. Ice cream €1.20-2.15. Empenadas €1.30. Open daily 7:30am-9pm.

NIGHTLIFE

We know you've spent your entire afternoon navigating the small streets of **La Judería,** but when the sun goes down, it's time to make your way out of there. Córdoba is a city that's always down for a good time and out for a long time. In the area near **Plaza Corredera** and **Calle Alfaros,** you'll find smaller cafe-bars open day and night, catering to a young, mellow clientele. Following **Avenida del Gran Capitan** away from the city center, the bars and clubs keep getting bigger and more extravagant. By the time you hit **Avenida de America** and further outward, it's just massive establishment after massive establishment packed with glowing lights, pricey drinks, and a flashy crowd. Many bars and clubs host live performances on the weekends around 9 or 10pm. These shows are great when they're free, but around the city outskirts, these performances often drive covers through the roof.

BAMBUDDHA BAR

Avenida del Gran Capitan, 46

Bambuddha is impossible to miss and even more difficult to pass up. From first glance, you'll notice the tented front patio, hidden away under low-draped white sheets that glow with green and red lights and paper lanterns. The dark windows make the Indian-themed interior seem even more exclusive. Depending on when you walk into this bar and club, you will immediately feel welcomed, in one of a few ways. If it's early evening on a Tuesday night, you could stumble in on a salsa dancing class *(€5)*. If it's midnight during the week, you'll find young locals sipping mixed drinks and coffees, sitting around on couches and cushioned stools, and if it's around 1:30am on a weekend, you'll find yourself at a packed dance floor, pushing your way through the sweaty masses to order a summer mojito or caipirinha from a member of the attractive bar staff.

🪧 *At the intersection of Gran Capitan and Avenida de America.* $ *Beer €3. Cocktails €6-7. Dance classes €5-20 per month.* ⏰ *Open M-W 3pm-3am, Th-Sa 3pm-4am, Su 3pm-3am.*

LA ESPIGA 💳🍸📶 BAR

C. San Pablo, 4 🖥www.laespigaCórdoba.com

La Espiga is able to bring out the inner hippie in anyone. Felt flowers decorate the pastel walls and low-beamed ceilings, beatniks and singers perform on weekends, and the folk soundtrack provides the perfect environment in which to enjoy the incense and an infused tea *(€1)*. While it does get packed after midnight on the weekends, especially during performances, La Espiga is not the place for mosh pits. Instead, the clientele is ready to grab a cocktail *(€5-7)* and a large, homemade *empanada* *(€2)* and just enjoy the show. This two-story bar-cafe fills every nook and cranny with cozy wood-framed furniture so you can snuggle up in your own private abode to work with the Wi-Fi or have a drink with a friend.

🪧 *Near Plaza Corredera. Take C. Capituales to C. San Pablo and make a right; Espiga is on the right.* $ *Tea €1. Beer €1.50. Cocktails €5-7. Empanadas €2.* ⏰ *Open in summer M-F 9am-3-:30pm and 6pm-3am, Sa 6pm-3am, Su 8pm-3am; in winter daily 9am-3:30pm and 5pm-3am. Performances after 10pm.*

AUTOMÁTICO 🚫❄🍸 CAFE, CLUB, BAR

C. Alfaros, 4 🖥www.myspace.com/automaticomuzikbar

Automático can be described kind of like a mullet: business in the front, party in the back. The front of Automático is a cafe area, with a bar equipped with a cappuccino and latte machine that can muster up any caffeinated drink you can think of *(€1-2)*. As you make your way further into this late-night hangout, you'll find yourself at the modern bar and elevated dance floor, glistening under the disco ball and jamming to dance beats. Whether these tunes are part of the Thursday night live shows *(10pm)* or the DJ-produced weekend parties, you'll definitely want to get moving with the young, casual crowd into the early morning. Take your pick of cocktails *(€4-5.50)*, as Automático serves up all the classics—martinis, bloody Marys, mai-tais, and white Russians—and extra fruity surprises like the *cielito lindo* (vodka, blue curasao, and pina colada), named after the classic Spanish song, or the *sgroppino* (vodka, limoncello, and vanilla ice cream), named after something with an insufficient amount of vowels.

🪧 *Near Plaza Corredera, take C. Capituales to C. Alfaros; Automático is on the right.* $ *Tea €1.50. Coffee drinks €1-2. Cocktails €4-5.50.* ⏰ *Open M-W 5pm-2am, Th 5pm-3am, F-Sa 5pm-4am, Su 5pm-2am. Concerts Th 10pm.*

ARTS AND CULTURE ♫

Between flamenco and festivals, you may have a pretty packed cultural agenda when visiting Córdoba, but you should still consider making time for a few other cultural options that the city has to offer. If looking for live performances, the **Orquesta de Córdoba** *(C. Cruz Conde 13 ☎957 491 767 🖥www.orquestadeCórdoba.org)* and the **Gran Teatro** *(Av. Gran Capitan 3 ☎957 480 237 🖥www.teatroCórdoba.com $ Tickets €3-20)* are two great starting points. The **Zoco** *(C. Judios, s/n ☎957 204 033 🖥www.aretensiadeCórdoba.com ⏰ Open M-F 10am-8pm.)*, or crafts market, was founded in 1960 and today houses workshops and stores that sell one-of-a-kind ceramics, metalwork, leather products, and wood crafts with a Moroccan and Córdoban-Arabic influence. The **Hammams de Al-Andalus** *(C. Corregidor Luis de la Cerda 51 ☎902 333 334 🖥www.hamman.es ⏰ Open daily* *every 2hr. 10am-midnight)* is a pricier cultural experience but is a perfect way to feel like you're vacationing. Duck into their original Arab baths to soak in the culture *(€26)* and enjoy a soothing massage on the side *(€33-48)*.

Flamenco

Flamenco in Córdoba is much more reasonably priced than other cities in Andalucia like Sevilla. While Tablao Flamenco Cardenal is definitely the main spot that you'll come across, there are multiple options around the city that offer their own spin on this classic dance. The **Casa de Sefarad** hosts flamenco performances about twice a month *(8:30pm in its small, 50-person patio)* that emphasize the mix of Spanish, Islamic, and Jewish cultures that helped to develop the dance. **Perol Flamenco** *(C. Julio Romero de Torres 4* ☎*647 711 266)* combines a simpler show *(8pm)* with a hearty, traditional dinner including *salmorejo, fino, perol,* and a surprise dessert *(€20)*.

TABLAO FLAMENCO CARDENAL ✦❦❀ THEATER
C. Torrijos, 10   ☎957 483 320 ◼www.tablaocardenal.com
Check out any tourism website or city promotion, and this is the spot they'll suggest. Tablao Flamenco Cardenal puts on six 2hr. shows a week *(10:35pm)* featuring 11 performers, five of which have received national acclaim. You'll get a taste of many different types of flamenco from different time periods and regions of Spain including *sevillanas, allegrías, seguilladas,* and *bulerías*. Whether you're looking for the classic show or some modern variations, Tablao Flamenco Cardenal will give you a taste of everything. Your €20 will include the show and one drink, but feel free to help yourself at the bar.
✦ *C. Torrijos runs alongside the Mezquita near C. Judería.* Ⓢ *Show and 1 drink €20.* Ⓚ *Open M-Sa 10:35pm-12:20am.*

Festivals

FESTIVAL DE LA GUITARRA MUSIC FESTIVAL
Gran Teatro, Avenida Gran Capitan, 3   ☎957 480 237 ◼www.guitarraCórdoba.com
Held for over two weeks every July, the Festival de la Guitarra is one of the biggest events of the summer in Córdoba. The festival celebrates the music, history, and culture of the guitar in Spain and over recent years has gained international exposure. While the focus of the festival is the flamenco guitar, jazz and modern guitar also make bold showings and impress the crowds. The first portion of the festival is the Training Program, in which top musicians and artists teach courses on different guitar styles *(€25-315)*, construction processes, musical composition, and flamenco dancing *(€85)* and singing *(€175)* classes. You can download the tuition form on the festival website. Classes are open but limited in size, so you should apply early. Prices range depending on the type and duration of the course. The second half of the festival is devoted to public concerts and performances held all over the city at the Gran Teatro, the Alcázar, the Palacio de Congresos, and the Plaza Corredera, with tickets ranging from free to €55. The city also hosts a ton of film screenings, book signings, and educational discussions, all focused around the star of this very special festival: the guitar.
Ⓢ *Music lessons €25-315.* Ⓚ *July 6-25th.*

ESSENTIALS

Practicalities

- **TOURIST OFFICES: Turismo de Córdoba** has information points all over the city in addition to their central office at C. Rey Heredia *(*☎*22 957 201 774* ◼*informacion@ turismodeCórdoba.org* Ⓚ *Open daily M-F 8:30am-2:30pm):* in the **Renfe-AVE station** *(C. Estación AVE-RENFE* ☎*902 201 774* ◼*infoave@turismodeCórdoba.org* Ⓚ *Open daily 9:30am-2pm and 5-8pm),* in front of the **Alcazar** *(C. Campo Santo de los Mártires, s/n* ☎*902 201 774* ◼*infoalcazar@turismodeCórdoba.org* Ⓚ *Open*

M-Sa 9:30am-2pm and 4:30-7:30pm, Su 9am-2pm and 4:30-7pm), and in the **Plaza de Tendillas** *(Plaza de Tendillas, s/n ☎902 201 774 💻infotendillas@turismodeCórdoba.org ⏰ Open daily 9:30am-2pm and 5:30-8:30pm).* Their website *(💻www.turismodeCórdoba.org)* is extremely useful and can be translated into English. Turismo de Córdoba also offers evening walking tours that include a tapa and a drink *(☎902 201 774 $ 2hr. tour €15 ⏰ Mar-Nov F-Sa; July-Oct M-Su.).* You'll find free Wi-Fi at the **Biblioteca Publica Provincial** *(C. Amador del Rios, s/n ☎957 355 480 ⏰ Open M-F 9am-9pm, Sa 9am-2pm),* inside the Junta de Andalucia.

Emergency!

- **EMERGENCY NUMBERS:** General Emergencies ☎112
- **POLICE:** National ☎091, Local ☎092
- **FIRE:** ☎080
- **PHARMACIES:** There's one 24hr. pharmacy just off the plaza, **Farmacia y Labrotorio El Globo** *(C. Marmol de Banuelos 4 ☎957 474 024),* that you can reach by taking C. Leon. **CajaSur** banks *(☎901 247 247 💻www.cajasur.es ⏰ Open M-F 8:30am-2:30pm)* around the city (two found near Plaza de las Tendillas and one at the intersection of C. San Fernando and C. Lucano) offer money exchange services as well as ATM.

Getting There

Renfe AVE trains *(💻www.renfe.es)* run in and out of the **Córdoba train station** *(Plaza de las Tres Culturas ☎902 240 202)* from **Sevilla** *(⏰ 45min., 16 per day 7:15am-11pm $ €32.10),* **Málaga** *(⏰ 50min., 9 per day 9am-9:15pm $ €44),* **Madrid** *(⏰ 1hr. 40min., 21 per day 9am-10pm $ €66.30),* and **Barcelona** *(⏰ 4hr. 40min., 8:15am, 10:20am $ €133.70).* Altria runs a train from **Granada** *(⏰ 2hr. 20min., 9:45am, 6:05pm $ €34.30)* and Alvia runs trains from **Cadiz** *(⏰ 2hr. 40min., 8:45am, 4:25pm $ €38.20).*

The main **Bus Station** *(Plaza de las Tres Culturas ☎957 404 040),* located in front of the Train Station, runs **Alsina** buses *(💻www.alsinagraells.es ☎957 278 100)* to and from **Málaga** *(⏰ 2hr. 30min., 4 per day 8:30am-5pm $ €12.72),* **Marbella** *(⏰ 4hr. 15min., 8:30am $ €17.91),* **Sevilla** *(⏰ 1hr. 45min., 6 per day 7:35am-6pm $ €10.36),* and **Barcelona** *(⏰ 3hr. 30min., 6pm, 12:20am $ €67.07-€76.68),* and **Sercobus buses** *(☎902 229 292)* to and from **Madrid** *(⏰ 4hr. 45min, 6 per day 1am-6:20pm $ €14.25)* and **Cadiz** *(⏰ 3hr. 15min., 2:50pm, 6:50pm $ €8.90).*

Getting Around

Aucorsa *(☎957 764 199 💻www.aucorsa.net)* runs 17 urban bus lines around Córdoba, M-Sa 6am-11pm, Su 6:30am-11pm for €1.10 or €1.50 on soccer and Feria days. The **#3** bus runs from the **train and bus stations** through Plaza de las Tendillas, down to the river, and back up C. San Fernando and is particularly useful for getting into and around La Judería. There's a direct bus line to the **Medina Azahara** *(☎902 201 774 💻informacion@turismodeCórdoba.org)* from two bus stops on Paseo de la Victoria, one near the Red Cross Hospital roundabout and one opposite the Roman Mausoleum. The line runs Tu-Sa 10:30am and 5pm, Su 9:30am-10:15pm for €6.50. You will also find **taxis** *(☎957 764 444)* between the bus and train stations and around the city. Generally, all the sights are clustered around **La Judería.** The streets are tiny and interconnected, so you're probably best off on foot. Even a walk from the Guadalquivir to the bus and train stations won't take you more than 25min. Outside La Judería, the main plazas like **Plaza Corredera** and **Plaza de las Tendillas** are only 5min. apart on foot.

málaga ☎968

Málaga may be located right on the water, but don't show up looking for pooka shells, ukuleles, or any muppets singing *Kokomo*. With an airport, bus and train stations, and a major coastal port, Málaga has become a center for both tourists and urban living. If you turn your back to the waves, you'll get lost in the tall buildings, popular plazas, and wide avenues. With so many people coming down to Málaga, you can benefit from a wonderful array of restaurants, some of the most comfortable accommodations around, and the hopping variety of student-filled late-night destinations.

The hometown of Pablo Picasso, this city takes a great deal of pride in their Cubist, and you can enjoy plenty of sights and references to the artist around every corner. The rich Moorish and Roman history may not be as prevalent as in the nearby cities of Granada or Córdoba, but the combination of Arab, Christian, and Jewish cultures still provides a richness and variety that can only be found in Andalucia.

Málaga essentially wraps up a nice collection of vacation destinations all in one. Get a tan, stuff a shopping bag, and sip some sangria—this is the real deal.

ORIENTATION 🛈

The city center of Málaga is bordered by the **Río Guedalmedina** to the west, the **Alameda Principal** to the south, the **Alcazaba** and **Catedral** to the east, and **Plaza de la Merced** to the north. The main shopping and commercial part of the city, where you'll also encounter many banks and ATMs, branches off around **Calle Marques de Larios.** The primary sights generally cluster around **Calle San Augustin** and **Calle Alcazabilla.** You'll find a strong selection of restaurants, bars, and clubs, generally populated by a younger crowd, near **Plaza de la Merced** and **Calle Alamios.** The **Tunnel Alcazaba** will take you from Plaza de la Merced to the popular **Malagueta Beach,** or you can take a bus to the quieter, more family-oriented **Padregalejo Beach.**

ACCOMMODATIONS 🏠

🏨 CASA BABYLON ✈(((•))) ❄❋ HOSTEL ❷

C. Pedro de Quejana, 3 ☎952 267 228 🖳www.casababylonhostel.com

Only a 7min. walk from Plaza de la Merced, Casa Babylon is a glowing beacon of hope for the free-spirited backpacker. The shirtless, gaucho-pant-wearing receptionist will greet you warmly at the front gates and happily sit you down in the "chill out" lounge, where you'll sink into the big leather couches beside a collection of guitars and psychedelic murals. But just because the hostel has this hippie vibe doesn't mean you need to fully give in to that persona—shower in your spacious bathroom and snuggle up in your sleeping bag in the large, pristinely clean, tiled dorm rooms. At Casa Babylon, you can grab a drink at the bar, make dinner in the spacious kitchen, take some "you time" in the hammocks out front, or even watch local soccer games with the young staff.

⚥ *From Plaza de la Merced, take C. Victoria to C. Compas de la Victoria and make a right onto C. Louis Maceda and continue onto Pedro de Quejana.* 🛈 *Breakfast, towels, and linens included. Laundry €2.* Ⓢ *2- to 8-bed dorms €18-19.* ⏰ *Reception 24hr.*

🏨 PICASSO'S CORNER BACKPACKERS ✈♿(((•)))❄☂ HOSTEL ❷

C. San Juan de Letran, 9 ☎952 212 287 🖳www.picassoscorner.com

The name isn't just a tourist ploy—this backpacker's getaway is located smack dab in the center of the main sights of Málaga (we're talking minutes from Picasso's house, the Picasso Museum, and the Catedral) and right in the middle of the hottest nightlife. It honors the artist with colorful, bright rooms all equipped with balconies overlooking good ol' Pablo's beloved hometown. Picasso's corner knows how to make you comfy at home and informed while out and about. Feel free to browse its massive amount of information on all the local sights and restaurants, or just make conversation with the all-knowing bartenders behind the large, tiled bar in the lounge. You can make yourself dinner on the rooftop BBQ or in the well-equipped communal kitchen, or enjoy nightly homemade meals *(€5)*. Keep in mind the 10% discount if you've stayed at Funky or Pilar in Córdoba.

C. San Juan de Letran branches off Plaza de la Merced near the information point. i Breakfast and sheets included. Female-only dorms available. Laundry €3. Luggage storage available. $ 6-bed dorms €18; 4-bed dorms €19. Doubles €44. Towels €2. Beach umbrella €3. ⏰ Reception 24hr.

HOSTEL BABIA HOSTEL [2]

Plaza de los Martires, 6 ☎952 222 730 www.babiahostel.com

Sometimes even the smallest of conveniences can brighten your day—isn't it nice to have a full restaurant at your feet, a foosball table in your giant living room, and some friendly Spaniards offering to teach you how to SCUBA dive *(€50)?* Hostel Babia has clean, modern, and bright facilities, from it's fully equipped kitchen with colored picnic tables to its sizable TV screen in the lounge. Even if the communal bathrooms (curtained stalls) aren't a point of full luxury, the high-ceilinged rooms with colorful walls, metal-framed bunks, and small balconies will definitely provide a good night's sleep for the tired traveler.

From C. Carreteria, take C. Andres Perez to Plaza de los Martires. i Breakfast, towels, and sheets included. Luggage storage available. $ 10-bed dorms €16; 8-bed €17; 6-bed €18. Doubles €44.

SIGHTS

While Málaga is a top beach destination, there's definitely more to it than just sun and sand. As the birthplace of **Pablo Picasso,** it had to have quite a few sights dedicated to the artist. You'll also find traces of the Roman, Phoenician, and Moorish heritage of the city, whether you're just passing by the **Roman Amphitheater** or roaming the paths of the **Alcazaba.** Most of the major sights are clustered around **Plaza Obispo, Calle San Augustin,** and **Calle Alcazabilla,** but there are also many smaller, special spots worth seeking out.

ALCAZABA FORTRESS

C. Alcazabilla ☎630 932 287 www.ayto-malaga.es

If you've been to Granada, you'll probably view the Alcazaba as a smaller version of the Alhambra. From the views to the gardens to the fountained passageways, there's no doubt that this building is another flavor of Moorish fortress. But even if you've seen the Alhambra (and also if you haven't), Málaga's Alcazaba is still worth a visit. Walking between the numbered stops on the grounds, you'll visit sights like the **Puerta de las Columnas** (Gate of the Columns) that perfectly signal the Arab additions to Roman structures. In the **Nazarith Palace,** built between the 11th and 14th centuries, you'll see three main courtyards, including the **Torre de Maldonado,** which is decorated with manmade marble columns. If you're a real go-getter (and have good walking shoes), you can make the trek up to the **Gibralforo** *(combined ticket €3.95),* the additional hideout and viewpoint used by Moorish royalty.

Next to Roman Amphitheater off C. Alcazabilla. i Tour pamphlets in English and Spanish. $ €2.10, students €0.60. Free Su after 2pm. Combined ticket with Gibralforo €3.95. ⏰ Open daily in summer 9:30am-8pm; in winter 8:30am-7pm.

CATEDRAL MÁLAGA CHURCH

C. Molina Lario s/n ☎952 228 491

The Catedral Málaga is often facetiously called the "one-armed lady" because one of its towers was never completed, but you can't really blame them for not finishing—this structure is enormous! After knocking down a mosque and a smaller church, the city took on the huge task of constructing this Renaissance-style cathedral in 1527. While they were able to build enough by 1588 to open up for mass, the financial struggle, including failed harbor taxes and cancellations, continued over the next two centuries. Even though the church may never be an emblem of architectural perfection, you can still stare in awe at the massive, green organs overlooking the choir, the Chapel of the Incarnation dedicated to the patron saint of Málaga, and the main altar decorated with marble podiums and stained glass.

➤ *Entrance at Plaza del Obispo.* ℹ *Audio tour available in English included in ticket price.* $ *€4.* ⏰ *Open M-F 10am-6:45pm, Sa 10am-5:45pm.*

👍 MUSEO DE PICASSO — 🎟♿ MUSEUM

C. San Augustin, 8 ☎902 443 377 💻www.museopicassomalaga.org

While you can feel the presence and history of Pablo Picasso throughout the city of Málaga, there is no better place to truly capture the aura of the artist than the museum dedicated to the man himself. The building's pale marble floors and white walls allow the creative and wonderful collection to speak for itself. The rooms are organized in chronological order, allowing you to trace the changes and stages of the artist's style to better understand his passionate views on politics, education, the human body, bullfighting, and (of course) women. You'll find quotes along the walls by Picasso with repeated examples of that oh-so-famous signature. Aside from the main collection, you can enjoy the permanent basement archaeological sight of 7th- and 8th-century Phoenician, Roman, and Moorish constructions, and the temporary exhibitions that hone in on one aspect of Picasso's work and supplement his art with media from modern artists.

➤ *Off C. San Augustin between the Catedral and Plaza de la Merced.* ℹ *All information in English and Spanish.* $ *Collection €6. Temporary exposition €4.50. Combined ticket €8, students €4.* ⏰ *Open Tu-Th 10am-8pm, F-Sa 10am-9pm, Su 10am-8pm.*

MUSEO DE ARTES Y COSTUMBRES POPULARES — 🎟♿ MUSEUM

Pasillo de Santa Isabel, 10 ☎952 217 137 💻www.museoartespopulares.com

The world is full of museums detailing ancient history and modern developments, but sometimes those guys in the middle get overlooked. The Museo de Artes y Costumbres Populares is a traditional 17th-century inn converted into a museum honoring Málaga lifestyle. It's organized a bit like a game of *Clue*—learn about the blacksmith in the stable with the carriages, or the bourgeois in the bedroom with the wooden birthing chair. You'll get a glimpse of all the top professions from every social class and learn the folklore and religion that flooded their minds. You can even trace back time through posters for the *Grandes Fiestas en Málaga*, still celebrated every August to date.

➤ *Make a left off C. Cisneros onto Pasillo de Santa Isabel and the museum is on the left.* ℹ *Information in English and Spanish.* $ *€2, students €1.* ⏰ *Open in summer M-F 10am-1:30pm and 5-8pm, Sa 10am-1:30pm; in winter M-F 10am-1:30pm and 4-7pm, Sa 10am-1:30pm.*

BEACHES

While the beaches closest to the city center are generally very crowded and not necessarily picturesque, you'll find more peaceful terrain and better photo ops as you move east along the coast. While we know you want to show off those washboard abs in your swimsuit, you'll really have to struggle to resist the freshly grilled and fried local seafood, or the steaming paellas, restaurants lining the boardwalks.

👍 PLAYA DE PEDROGALEJOS — ♿📶🍸☀ BEACH

While it may require a little extra travel to get there, the quick bus ride is definitely worth the trip down to Playa de Pedrogalejos. This lengthy, 1200m strip of beach has finer sand and finer views along the small, curled up, *w*-shaped of coves that protect you from the bigger waves and colder water. You can rent a lounge chair *(€2.50-3.50)* and enjoy a free drink or snack with the rental, or just picnic like a local under the clusters of colorful beach umbrellas. The boardwalk is packed with restaurants of varying prices, grilling up fresh fish right on the sand out of old tin boats converted into fire pits. You can even burn off those paella calories with some pickup soccer on the enclosed, sand pitches. As you make your way further east toward **Playa de Palo-Pedrogalejos** and **Playa Palo,** you'll encounter the *caseta* (canvas booth) flea market, selling everything from *Dora the Explorer* towels to fresh fruits and discounted underwear—Christmas shopping, anyone?

�" *Take bus #11 or 34 to Avenida Juan Sebastian Elcano and make a right onto any side street down to the beach.* ℹ *Information kiosk, showers, and bathrooms available.* ⑤ *Lounge chairs €2.50-3.50.* ◻ *Lifeguards on duty 11am-8pm. Lounge chair rentals 9:30am-8:30pm.*

FOOD

As you're never more than about 20min. from the ocean, it's no surprise that coming across fresh seafood is pretty easy in Málaga. Whether you want a thick tuna steak *a la plancha* (grilled), or some *calamaritos fritos* (fried calamari), the options are seemingly endless. But Málaga doesn't stop at seafood—this industrial tourist center also offers a wide selection of international, modern, and creative cuisine that will satiate even the most critical of foodies. If you're looking for something fresh and simple, the M-Sa **marketplace** (8am-3pm) offers a wide selection of local fish, produce, meat, cheese, and baked goods.

RUCALA   🍽♿❖ MODERN, INTERNATIONAL ❷

C. Carreteria, 73   ☎952 222 883 🖳www.rucala.es

Who needs a gym? Take one step into Rucala, and you'll immediately feel refreshed and healthy (it's named after a type of lettuce for goodness sake!). The green walls, plants, and nature decor are constant reminders of the literal freshness of the food, and the modern, international menu is a constant reminder of the stylistic freshness of the kitchen staff. Their extensive salad selection, starring the popular goat cheese, raisin, apple, and honey mustard option (€6.50), is based in a collection of crisp mixed greens, but the rest of the menu is ready to hit any ingredient from anywhere on the planet. Warm up with duck confit with risotto and mango chutney (€12) or a teriyaki chicken wok with coconut milk and rice (€8). The *menú* of the day (€8) is an awesome deal and constantly changing to include funky variations of world classics—ever seen a "caprese" prepared with mozzarella pearls floating in chilled tomato soup with basil leaves and honey? Yeah, neither had we.

�‘ *On the right if coming from the river on C. Carreteria.* ℹ *Vegetarian options available.* ⑤ *Appetizers €4-7. Salads €6.50-7; entrees €8-€12. Desserts €4-4.50. Menú of the day €8. Wine €2.40-2.60.* ◻ *Open daily 1:30pm-12:30am.*

TAPERIA PEPA Y PEPE   🍴♿❖⏚ TAPAS, TRADITIONAL ❶

C. Caldereria, 9   ☎650 821 316

Pepa and Pepe must have made a lovely match if they were going to spearhead their own timeless Andalucian restaurant. The menu is filled with a great selection of inexpensive wine and beer, fried and grilled seafood (ration €4.80-5.50, half-ration €2.90-3.80), and classic dishes at shockingly low prices. Walk into this small restaurant, and you'll be able to see the entire kitchen staff working under the brick archway in the corner next to the ham, sausage, and wine bottles that decorate the walls. Feel free to grab a rickety wooden table inside or a barrel and stool in the Plaza, and order up some traditional bacon-wrapped dates (ration €4.80, half-ration €2.90) or chicken, shrimp, or pork *pinchos* (skewers; €1.80 each), marinated and grilled to perfection. Because it's small, Pepa y Pepe is always overflowing with locals pouring out of the open glass doors. Just be glad for the lightning-fast service—spots open up quick!

🌘 *Cross Plaza de Uncibay from C. Mendez Munez and make a left.* ⑤ *Rations €3-7.50; half rations €1.80-3.80. Tapa €1-1.80. Beer €1-1.60. Wine €1.20-1.80.* ◻ *Open M-Th 1-4pm and 7:30pm-midnight, F-Sa 1-4pm and 7:30pm-12:30am, Su 1-4pm and 7:30pm-midnight.*

CLANDESTINO   🍽♿❖❖ INTERNATIONAL ❸

C. Nino de Guevara, 3   ☎952 219 390 🖳www.clandestino.com

Clandestino just puts you in a sharing mood. Maybe it's because of the friendly waitstaff or the warm, homey feeling of yellow walls decorated with kitchen-

málaga • food

themed paintings. Maybe it's the 12-page drink menu of quality, international wines *(€2.20-2.60)*, beers *(€1.60-4.50)*, and mixed drinks *(€4-6)* that may require you to team up to make a selection, or maybe it's the absolutely massive portions of fresh, unique, and delicious dishes that will stuff a solo eater to the brim. Consider splitting some comfort food like the pumpkin ravioli stuffed with foie gras and goat cheese *(€11)* or a huge, refreshing Kazuo Salad overflowing with grilled asparagus, bamboo shoots, avocado, tomato, buffalo mozzarella, and topped with a light, soy vinaigrette *(€10)*.

From C. Mendez Nunez, take C. Belgrano and make a right onto Nino de Guevara. $ Appetizers €9.90-14.90. Pasta €10-11.40. Salads €10-11.20. Meat and Fish entrees €15-18. Desserts €5.50-5.60. Menu of the day €9. ⏰ Open daily 1pm-1am. Menu of the day available M-F 1-5pm.

NIGHTLIFE

Nightlife in Málaga is clustered into the area between **Calle Mendez Nunez** and **Calle Alamios** near **Plaza de la Merced,** but that doesn't mean your options are limited. You'll find a wide selection of student-populated bars and clubs, all with their own musical tastes and types of patrons. Don't even think of requesting *Baby One More Time* at a rock club or some Zeppelin at a commercial club, or risk receiving derisive laughter. Pick your mood and your spot, and let the good times roll.

SALA CAIRO — CLUB, BAR

C. Juan de Padilla, 15 — www.salacairo.es

Sala Cairo is Málaga's spot for your high-profile night out. Sit on their shiny, patent-leather stools, watch videos on one of their multiple flatscreen TVs, sip pricey mixed drinks *(€6)* at one of the two glowing bars, and maybe even reserve a spot at the elevated VIP area equipped with sleek white couches. Coming here means you'll be hanging out with the hottest, most stylish 20-somethings in town, all dressed and ready to dance to Sala Cairo's poppy, '80s Spanish music into the early hours. If you're ready to go out a bit earlier, you can enjoy €2 off any drink until 1:30am or even catch the Thursday night concerts around midnight.

Juan de Padilla is between Mendez Nunez and Beatas. $ Cover Sa night €6-7. Beer €4. Mixed drinks €6. ⏰ Open Th-Sa 11pm-4am.

BUNKER BAR — BAR, CLUB

C. Mariblanca, 9

You don't need to duck and cover to enter this bunker, but you should be ready for something a little rougher around the edges. Walk into this small bar and club and lean up against the metal grating on the walls and funky, dark murals in the corners. Bunker says they play a little bit of everything from anywhere in the world, but they maintain a strict policy against playing commercial pop or anything that could be found on *Perez Hilton*. Instead, Bunker is the place to rock out to some alternative beats and grab a beer *(€2-2.50)* with a mix of tourists and local students. You can party hard at the bi-monthly Saturday night concerts and DJ sets, or chill during Tuesday movies and Wednesday night storytelling.

From Plaza de la Merced, take C. Alamios and make a right onto Mariblanca. $ Beer €2-2.50, half-liters €3.50. Mixed drinks €5-6. ⏰ Open M-Th 11pm-3am, F-Sa 11pm-4am. Movies and storytelling 9:30pm.

LA BOTELLITA — CLUB

C. Alamos, 36 — www.labotellita.com

La Botellita is any MTV viewer's dream, offering pop and commercial hits on its dance floors as four flatscreens display music videos. This club knows how to rake in the students with flashy, silver-and-black patterned walls and namesake bottles along its bar. Early birds beware: La Botellita wouldn't even consider getting a crowd until after 2:30am. You can sit and drink at the tables along the walls, or get grooving down in the center of the dance floor. Thursday nights during the school year are student-only, so get ready to release your academic stress with all the other bookworms.

Take C. Alamos from Plaza de la Merced and the club is on the left. $ Beer €3. Mixed drinks €3.50. ⏰ Open Th-Sa 11pm-4am.

ESSENTIALS

Practicalities

- **TOURIST OFFICES:** There are multiple tourist information points throughout the city, including the **central municipal tourist office** *(Plaza de La Marina, 11 ☎952 122 020 💻www.malagaturismo.com ⏰ Open daily Oct-Feb 9am-6pm; Mar-Sept 9am-8pm).* There are also smaller information points throughout the city at Plaza de la Merced *(⏰ Open daily 10am-2pm.),* near the Post Office *(⏰ Open daily 10am-2pm.),* and at the train and bus stations *(⏰ Open daily 10am-8pm),* and near the Picasso Museum *(C. Granada, 70 ⏰ Open daily 9am-6pm).*
- **TOURS:** The city runs **guided walking tours** from the Info Office *(Plaza de la Marina ⏰ Nov-Mar M-Sa 10am, 12pm, 5pm; Apr-Oct M-Sa 9am, 11am, 6pm $ €5)* that stop at such sights as the Cathedral, Picasso Museum, Alcazaba, and Roman Theater. You can also rent a **audio tours** from the Plaza de la Marina tourist office on one of eight themes including traditional, religious, Picasso, and contemporary. **Málaga Bike Tours** *(C. Trinidad Grund, 1 ☎606 978 513 💻www.malagabiketours.eu $ €23. ⏰ 4hr., 10am)* will show you the city and offer a free drink. Tour in a *bicitaxi* (rickshaw) with **Tricosol** *(☎657 440 605 💻www.tricosol.com $ Full tour €18, half tour €10. ⏰ Open daily 8am-10pm; duration varies upon request)* from Plaza de la Constitución, the Cathedral, or the Roman Theatre, or even get picked up from your accommodation.
- **CURRENCY EXCHANGE:** You can **exchange money** at Barclay's Bank *(C. Marques de Larios, s/n ☎952 220 425 ⏰ Open M-F 8:30am-2:30pm)* or at El Corte Ingles *(Av. Andalucia, 4-6 ☎952 076 500 ⏰ Open M-Sa 10am-10pm)* department store, which also has one of the city's largest **supermarkets** and a post office point.
- **INTERNET:** The **public library** *(C. Ollerias, 34 ☎952 133 950 ⏰ Open M-F 9:30am-8pm)* is also a cultural center, restaurant, and a **free Wi-Fi** point. Many restaurants and cafes around the city also supply free **Wi-Fi**.
- **POST OFFICE:** The main **post office** *(Av. Andalucia, 1 ☎902 197 197 💻www.correos.es ⏰ Open M-F 8:30am-8:30pm, Sa 9:30am-2pm)* also has an ATM and photocopy services.

Emergency!

- **EMERGENCY NUMBERS:** ☎012. Ambulance and Emergency Healthcare: ☎061. Red Cross: ☎952 222 222. Information: ☎010.
- **POLICE:** National ☎091 or ☎952 046 200. Local: ☎092 or ☎952 126 551. The police station is located at Av. de la Rosaleda, 19.
- **LATE-NIGHT PHARMACIES:** There's a **24hr. pharmacy** *(Alameda Principal, 2 ☎952 212 858)* that closes its doors in the evening but will open if you ring the bell.

Getting There

By Plane

The **Málaga Airport** *(Avenida García Morato ☎902 404 704 💻www.aena.es)* is located about 8km outside the city and runs international and domestic flights on many airlines including **Air Berlin** *(☎952 105 520 💻www.airberlin.com),* **Air France** *(☎952 048 192 💻www.airfrance.com),* **Aer Lingus** *(☎952 105 488 💻www.aerlingus.com),* **British Airways** *(☎902 111 333 💻www.britishairways.com),* **Iberia** *(☎952 136 166 💻www.iberia.com),* and **Virgin Airlines**

(☎952 048 349 💻www.virgin-atlantic.com). **Bus #19** from Plaza del General Torrijos is a direct airport shuttle that runs every 30min. from 6:30am-12am. You can also take a Renfe train to the airport on line C-1 from Málaga-Centro Station or Málaga Railway Station every 30min. from 5:45am-11:45pm.

By Train

The **Málaga Railway Station** *(Explanada de la Estación, s/n ☎902 24 02 02 ⏰ 6:10am-11pm)* runs **Renfe** trains *(💻www.renfe.com)* from: **Barcelona** *($ €138.80. ⏰ 5hr. 50min; 10:20am, 3:50pm),* **Córdoba** *($ €39.60. ⏰ 1hr.; 11 per day 8:30am-12:25am),* **Sevilla** *($ €36.40. ⏰ 2hr.; 6 per day 6:50am-7:35pm),* **Madrid** *($ €76.40. ⏰ 2hr. 50min; 12 per day 9:25am-12:25am),* and **Valencia.** *($ €54.80. ⏰ 9hr. 40min; 11:30am).* You can take either of the circular routes or buses #1, #3, or #4 to the train station.

By Bus

The **bus station** *(Paseo de los Tilos, s/n ☎952 350 061 💻www.estabus.emtsam.es)* is located near Plaza de la Marina and en route to the airport. It runs lines from multiple companies to destinations all over Spain, and connecting throughout Europe and North Africa. **Diabus** *(☎902 277 999 💻www.daibus.es)* runs from **Madrid** *($ €21.80. ⏰ 6hr. 7 per day 7:30am-12am).* **Alsa** *(☎913 270 540 💻www.alsa.es)* runs from: **Sevilla** *($ €15.80. ⏰ 3hr. 30min, 7 per day 7am-8:30pm);* **Córdoba** *($ €12.70. ⏰ 2hr. 30min, 4 per day 8:30am-5pm);* **Granada** *($ €9.80. ⏰ 2hr. 17 per day 7am-9:30pm);* and **Barcelona** *($ €77.81. ⏰ 17hr., 3 per day 5:30pm-12am).* **Los Amarillos** *(☎952 363 024 💻www.losamarillos.es)* runs from **Ronda** *($ €9.20. ⏰ 1hr. 45min, 8 per day 8am-8pm).*

Getting Around

By Taxi

Much of Málaga, especially in the historic quarter, is composed of small passway streets accessible only by foot. But don't fret: walking is extremely manageable. Even from the bus station to the nightlife center around Plaza de la Merced is only a 15min. walk. Taxis are better at navigating the small streets than the public buses. **Unitaxi** *(☎952 333 333)* and the **Taxi Union** *(☎952 040 804)* are the city's recommended companies. It costs about €20 to take a cab to the airport. *(⏰ 15min.)* If you're traveling the larger streets and longer distances, the city buses run by **Empresa Municipal de Transportes** *(Alameda Principal, 15 ☎902 527 200 💻www.emtmalaga.es $ Single ride €1.10, 10 rides €7)* can easily get you to all points in the city. Buses **#11** and **#34** from Paseo de los Curas are perfect for getting to the more eastern beaches farther from the city center, **C-1** and **C-2** run circular routes around the city, and **N-1, N-2,** and **N-3** are the "noctural," late-night lines. From Paseo del Parque **#4, #3,** and **#19** run to the bus and train stations and **#19** *(⏰ 40 min.; M-F 6:25am-11:30pm, Sa-Su 6:30am-11:30pm)* runs to the airport. The **A Express** *($ €2)* runs more directly to the airport, getting you from the train station to the airport in about 15min. All city buses stop on the **Alameda Principal**.

By Bike

You can also **rent bikes** from **Cyclo Point** *(Avenida Juan Sebastián Elcano 50 ☎952 297 324 💻www.cyclo-point.com ⏰ Open T-F 10am-8pm, Sa 10am-5pm. $ €10 per day, €50 per week)* or **Bike 2 Málaga** *(C. Victoria, 15 ☎952 211 296 💻www.bike2malaga.com $ €5 per half day, €10 per day. ⏰ Open daily10am-2pm and 4-8pm).*

granada ☎858 or 958

So *Let's Go* rents a time machine, and it's the 15th century. You're the queen of Spain (a queen who supposedly wore the same dress for the entire extent of her reign, no less), and you can live anywhere in your kingdom. Where do you choose to reside? If you're **Isabela la Catolica**, the Spanish queen who, with the help of her far-less-powerful husband, **Ferdinand**, gobbled up the Iberian peninsula for the sake of the kingdom and the church, then you're picking Granada. In 1492, Granada had spent centuries under Moorish Rule, and **Boabdil**, the last sultan on the Iberian Peninsula, was holding strong to his city while his brethren fell left and right. However, with a little persuasion and a whole lot of gold, Isabela was one persuasive lady. It may look like she's holding a grenade in all the city statues, but the city got taken without a drip of bloodshed, and she's really just gripping a pomegranate. This city symbol was part of Granada's draw—the citrus fruits like figs, oranges, and pomegranates were making bank for Boabdil, so the Spaniards wanted the goods.

Now let's fast-forward a good couple hundred years. Today, you have a city still glowing with a North African influence, including stunning remnants of Boabdil's crown like the Alhambra. You have a combination of Mediterranean, Moroccan, and Spanish cuisine on every block. Excitement from the urban, commercial city center, all the way into the hippie-inhabited caves of Sacromonte give this city an energy unlike any other. Granada may have a population under 250,000, but you pack that crowd into a small city without anything but mountains for hours, and it can feel like NYC. So enjoy the high-speed lifestyle in Realejo and by the university, and then get in touch with the nearby nature.

And just like it packs in its people, Granada also bundles it's culture and pizzazz together. Your bar is your restaurant, your restaurant is your flamenco or jazz show, and your show is your place to meet the locals. So grab some free tapas and a dancing partner, and enjoy the ride.

ORIENTATION

Plaza Nueva
The area around Plaza Nueva connects main street **Calle Gran Vía** to the more northern **Albacin** region that holds **La Alhambra.** All the Moroccan restaurants, tea stops, shops, and hookah bars can be found around **Calle Cria Nueva** and **Calderería Vieja,** and there are plenty of falafel options and tapas bars on **Calle Elvira.** Follow **Calle Santa Ana** up towards the Alhambra, and you'll travel along old, picturesque streets. Generally, the streets are small and winding, so make sure to bring a map. One of the main squares of the city is **Plaza San Nicolas;** and the adjacent **Mirador Nicolas** is one of the best places to get a view of the Alhambra. You'll also find a fresh produce market in **Plaza Larga.** Furthest north, the **Sacromonte** region is generally classified as the hippie and gypsy area of Granada.

Catedral and University
South of **Calle Gran Vía,** the streets become much more organized and manageable. This area is right by the university, and the student vibe is strong. School-supply shops, bookstores, and cafes with internet can be found on nearly every corner. **Plaza Trinidad** and **Plaza Bib Rambia** are lined with restaurants and small shops, and they're great places to stop for relaxing meals or some retail therapy. **Calle Pedro Antonio de Alarcon** is a great street for late-night tapas and drinks, especially if you're looking to run into the student crowd. If you're looking to just relax with some reading or a picnic, **Parque Fuente Nueva** (*Open daily 8am-10pm)* is a student favorite, located right around university grounds.

Elsewhere

You'll find Granada's commercial district along **Calle Reyes Catolicos** and **Arcera del Darro**—the shops get bigger, the streets get wider, and the general effort of the city grows with decorations, fountains, and landscaping as you walk closer to the intersection. This area, **Realejo,** is a wonderful spot to explore on a weekend stroll. You'll find families brunching and relaxing on **Carrera del Genil,** some of the city's most traditional tapas along **Calle Navas,** and a major square with lots of food options at **Campo Principe.**

Located around the outskirts of the city clockwise from the Alhambra, you'll find the **Sierra Nevada** mountain range, the major science center **Parque de las Ciencias,** the **Parque Garcia Lorca,** the **Renfe** and **bus stations,** and **La Cartuja.**

ACCOMMODATIONS

Plaza Nueva

OASIS GRANADA HOSTEL ❷

Pl. Correo Viejo, 3 ☎958 215 848 🖳www.oasisgranada.com

This hostel chain definitely has hostel living down to a science. Arriving at Oasis Granada, you're guaranteed one of the most luxurious, convenient, and generally pleasant hostel stays around. With top-notch facilities including a massive cafeteria (where your free breakfast is served), full bar (with a free drink upon arrival and nightly happy hour), and a rooftop terrace to soak up some sun, this place really delivers on the promise of its name. If you can get yourself to leave, Oasis will make sure you're acquainted with the city in a variety of ways. Check out the welcome board in front to get the daily list of activities, including themed tours. Socialize at the evening dinner parties or tapas outings, use their friendly staff to get some nightlife tips, and then come home to your multi-room dorm suite with a thick mattress, clean sheets, and a fuzzy blanket to keep you cozy. The only drawback of living in an oasis is that you won't be alone: this busy accommodation is always overflowing with partiers on the weekends.

From the bus station, take bus #3 or 33 to Gran Vía de Colon 1, make a right onto Carcel Baja and a left onto Placeta Correo Viejo. ℹ *Breakfast included. Free activities and tours. Towel rental €1.* [$] *Dorms €15-18.* ⏰ *Reception 24hr. Breakfast 8-11am.*

arab baths

Feeling tense from all that travel? Granada is a great place to enjoy a traditional Arabic bath. Although it's not cheap, there's no better way to find true relaxation than in the ancient, historic banuelos of Granada. Hammams de Al Andalus (C. Santa Ana 16 ☎958 229 978 🖳www.granada.hammamspain.com ⏰ Open daily 10am-12am with appointments every 2 hr.) is a larger company that offers packages of bathing (€21), different massages (€30-40), and a full Al-Andalus ritual service (€47) that incorporates the traditional exfoliation techniques used by the Moorish before prayer. They offer reduced student rates Monday through Thursday during their low season at less popular times. Aljibe de San Miguel (C. San Miguel Alta 41 ☎958 522 867 🖳www.aljibsanmiguel.es ⏰ Open daily 10am-12am with appointments every two hr.) offers slightly lower rates (baths €19, bath and massage €28-37; exfoliation and massage €45) and a different variety of services including chocolate massages (€39), "skiers" massages (€39), and a "tired legs" specialty (€29).

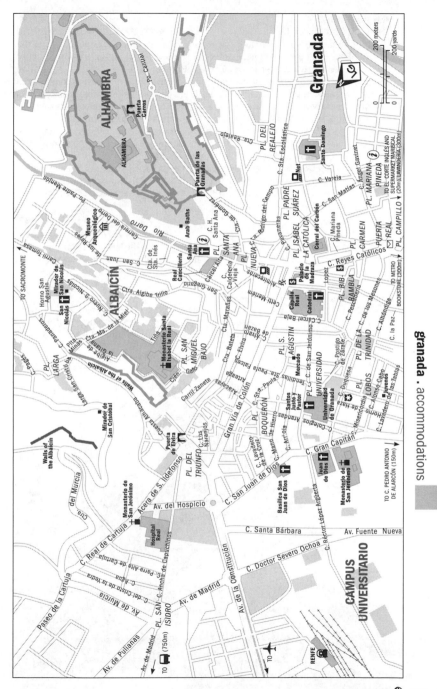

ALHAMBRA

Puerta
Carros

ALHAMBRA

200 meters

200 yards

0

0

PL. DEL
REALEJO

Ctra. Realejo

C. Sta. Escolástica

Santo Domingo

Net

TO EL CORTE INGLÉS AND
SUPERMARKET MERCASOL
(20m); LAVANDERÍA (300m)

C. Varela

C. San Matías

C. Angel Ganivet

PL. PADRE

Po. Padre Manjón

PL. ISABEL
LA CATÓLICA

PL.
SUÁREZ

PL. MARIANA
PINEDA

Museo
Arqueológico

Carrera del Darro

Río Darro

Arab Baths

C. H.
Santa Ana

C. Pavaneras

C. Mariana
Pineda

TO METRO
BOOKSTORE (300m)

Cta. de Sta. Inés

C. Navas

C. Rodrigo del Campo

Corral del Carbón

Santa
Ana

Real
Cancillería

PL.
SANTA
ANA

NUEVA

C. Almireceros

Cetti Meriém

Palacio
de la
Madraza

PL. REAL

PUERTA
REAL

PL. CAMPILLO

TO C. PEDRO ANTONIO
DE ALARCÓN (150m)

C. Reyes Católicos

PL. BIB-

RAMBLA

C. Pescadería

Mirador de
San Nicolás

San
Nicolás

ALBAICÍN

Calderería
Vieja

San Gregorio

San Juan de los Reyes

Capilla
Real

Catedral

C. Cárcel Baja

C. Mesones

C. de los Mesones

Horno San
Agustín

Trillo

Cta. Algibe

Cta. Marañas

C. Álvaro
de Bazán

PL. S.
AGUSTÍN

Mercado

C. de San Jerónimo

PL. DE LA
TRINIDAD

C. Alhóndiga

C. la Paz

TO SACROMONTE

C. Nuevo S. Nicolás

Camino Nuevo de San Cristóbal

Cta. de
las Minas

Monasterio Santa
Isabel la Real

Cta. Ma. de la Miel

Aljibe de
la Gitana

PL. SAN
MIGUEL
BAJO

Cta. Bateta

Cmón. Gato

Ctra. Elvira

Carril Zenete

C. Sta. Paula

PL. C.
BOQUERÓN

Arteaga

Santos
Justo y
Pastor

Universidad
de Granada

C. Misericordia

C. Duquesa

PL.
UNIVERSIDAD

C. Postigo de Zárate

TRINIDAD

LOBOS

Jovenes

C. Cobertizo Cabo

C. Alonso Cano

C. Lavadero de las Tablas

PL.
LARGA

Walls of the Albaicín

Cuesta Alhacaba

Mirador de
San Cristóbal

Puerta
de Elvira

Ctas. Naranjos

Gran Vía de Colón

Sta. Paula Falces

Colegios

Arandas

C. Arriola

C. Lavadero
de la Cruz

C. Mano de Hierro

C. de
la Haza

PL. DEL
TRUNFO

C. Gran Capitán

Walls of
the Albaicín

Ctra.
del Murcia

Ctra.
del Murcia

Monasterio de
San Jerónimo

Hospital
Real

Acera de S. Ildefonso

Av. del Hospicio

C. San Juan de Dios

Basílica San
Juan de Dios

Juan
de Dios

Monasterio de
San Jerónimo

C. Rector López Argüeta

Ferra Alta de Capuchinos

C. Real de Cartuja

C. Santa Bárbara

Av. Fuente Nueva

Paseo de la Cartuja

Av. de Murcia

C. del Cristo de la Yedra

C. Agua

Av. de Madrid

PL. SAN
ISIDRO

C. Ancha de Capuchinos

Av. de la Constitución

C. Doctor Severo Ochoa

C. de Madrid

C. Alta de Cartuja

TO
(750m)

Av. de Pulianas

Av. de Madrid

CAMPUS
UNIVERSITARIO

RENFE

TO

PENSIÓN BRITZ 📶 PENSIÓN ❷

C. Cuesta de Gomerez, 1 ☎958 223 652 🖥www.lisboaweb.com

While high-quality backpackers' hostels can be found all around the area, that type of stay isn't for everyone. For the more selective voyager, Pensión Britz provides a great private alternative. You'll find your quiet room with large armoir, checkered comforter and drapes, and particularly springy mattress to be a great place to relax in peace. The rooms with ensuite bathrooms are definitely a bit more expensive, but they are larger and brighter than the other rooms that only have a sink in the corner of the room. The spunky Spanish staff will hop out of their seats to help you plan reservations and tours at all the sights and fight to get you special offers around town. If you're planning a longer stay, they may even offer to include breakfast if you ask nicely enough.

⇆ C. Reyes Católicos becomes Pl. Santa Ana and Cuesta Romerez branches off to the right. ***i*** *Ventilation in rooms. Washing machine available.* Ⓢ *Singles €17-25, with bath €33-38; doubles €30-36, with bath €40-48; triples €45-48, with bath €51-57; quads €50-55, with bath €60-68.* ⏰ *Reception 24hr.*

WHITE NEST HOSTEL 📶 HOSTEL ❷

C. Santisimo 4 ☎958 994 714 🖥www.nesthostels.com

This hostel may be called the "white nest," but white is the last color you'll be seeing in its bright, modern interior. From the flower decals around the entryway to the

andalucia

psychedelic mural in the cafeteria and pop art in the private rooms, you're forced to feel lively and awake during your stay. The color-coded dorm rooms are cool and quiet, so even in this hustling hostel you can definitely get a good night's rest. Enjoy the extensive amounts of common space, including a full kitchen and multiple lounges, all located just minutes away from Plaza Nueva and the Alhambra. The White Nest is one of the newer hostels on the market, but it's quickly gaining in popularity and receiving acclaim left and right—so book fast and book early.

After Pl. Santa Ana becomes Carrera del Darro, make a right onto C. Santisimo. Buses #31, #32, and #35 also stop at C. Banuelo night near C. Santisimo. ℹ *Rooms ventilated. Computers €1.50 per hr. Free tea and coffee.* $ *10-bed dorms €15; 8-bed €16; 4-bed €17-19; female-dorm €17-18. Doubles €45-49.* ⏰ *Reception 24hr.*

Catedral and University

FUNKY BACKPACKERS

HOSTEL ❷

C. Conde de las Infantes ☎958 800 058 funky@alternativeacc.com

Funky Backpackers describes itself as the "multicultural" hostel of Granada, and we couldn't agree more. You'll find murals from all over the world all over the walls, nightly dinners of international cuisine *(€4-5)*, and a full cultural activity agenda including salsa dancing, flamenco shows, inter-language discussions, and music jam sessions. Regardless of your cultural background, it's impossible to not be stunned and impressed by the dorm living—each room has a kitchen, sofa, and lockable private closet. The English-speaking staff has the knowledge to answer even the most difficult tourist questions, and there are schedules and travel ideas posted around the lobby. If you've stayed or plan to stay at Picasso's Corner in Málaga or Terrace Backpackers in Córdoba, you'll get a 10% discount off the already shockingly low prices.

Conde de las Infantes intersects with Plaza Trinidad. ℹ *Credit card min. €50; €1 charge for smaller sums. Breakfast included. Female-only dorms available.* $ *7-bed dorm €12.75; 6-bed €13.35-€15.75; 4-bed €16.75; female-only €16.75. Doubles €38.* ⏰ *Reception 24hr.*

EL GRANADO

HOSTEL ❷

C. Conde de Tendillas, 7 ☎958 049 767 www.elgranado.com

This hostel may only be a year old, but after one step into the large, marble entryway, you won't be surprised to hear that it's already racking up awards for cleanliness and all-around atmosphere. While the triple bunks "on-hall" aren't the most private way to stay, you'll still enjoy a private, lockable closet and a sparkling bathroom. The dorms, bright and happy with their polka-dot sheets, are not huge but are comfortable (at least after you climb your way to your third-story bunk). The entire staff lives within the hostel, and this bunch of English-speaking international misfits is ready and willing to hang out and grab a drink on the terrace overlooking the tiled rooftops of Granada.

Take C. Duquesa from Plaza Trinidad and make a left onto Conde de Tendillas. ℹ *Breakfast included. Female floor available.* $ *On-hall beds €16; dorms €18.* ⏰ *Reception 24hr.*

Elsewhere

HOSTELONE

HOSTEL ❷

C. Azhuma, 30 ☎958 521 346 hostelonegranada@gmail.com

Although a bit out of the way from the main hustle and bustle of the city (15min. to the Catedral on foot), HostelOne is a quieter option than many backpackers' hostels—but that's just because the word hasn't gotten out yet! Only in operation since February 2010, the accommodations are clean, modern, and up to date. Simple rooms of wooden bunks and white sheets are bright and tidy, the kitchen is fully stocked with all cooking necessities, and the rooftop pool (to be completed by summer 2011) isn't going to provide a workout but is spacious enough for some splashes.

Take C. San Anton to C. Alhamar and turn left at C. Mulhacen. ℹ *Breakfast included. Laundry €4. Towels €1.* $ *6-bed dorms €14-18; 3-bed €15-22. Doubles €22-24.* ⏰ *Reception 8am-midnight.*

ALBERQUE INTURJOVEN GRANADA (HI)

📶 ((•)) ❄ HOSTEL ❷

C. Ramon y Cajal, 2   ☎958 002 900 ▣www.inturjoven.com

Run by the Andalucian government, Inturjoven hostels like this gem always feel particularly safe and organized. Even though Alberque Inturjoven Granada is situated in a more industrial area south of the university that has quite the assortment of graffiti, the hostel is a nice escape from the surroundings. Rooms are big and simple, each with large closets and tons of space. Even though it's not centrally located, the nearby Camino Ronda bus stops catch a wide array of city lines. Despite the hostel not having a public kitchen, daily meals are offered and vending machines line every floor.

⚑ *Take the circular bus lines (#11, 21, or 23) to Camino Ronda 10 and turn right at Ramon y Cajal.* **i** *Parking available. Towels €2. Breakfast €2; lunch and dinner €8.* Ⓢ *Under-25 singles €16-19; doubles €16-19; triples €16-19. Over-25 singles €22-25; doubles €22-25; triples €22-25.* ⚑ *Reception 24hr.*

SIGHTS

🔘

The sights of Granada are unlike any other you'll visit in Spain. Rather than a simple checklist of museums, churches, and monuments (although Granada does have quite the impressive array of those as well), Granada's history can be explored by just grabbing a map and wandering around the different historic *barrios* of the city. You'll find a unique vibe in the **Albaicin** and **Sacramonte**, get a taste of the Spanish history around the **Cathedral**, and find yourself in complete awe as you make your way around **the Alhambra.**

Elsewhere

PARQUE DE LAS CIENCIAS

MUSEUM

Av. de la Ciencia, s/n   ☎958 131 900 ▣www.parqueciencias.com

Although catered to the young, the Parque de las Ciencias is the perfect spot for the curious and young at heart. Just look at the name—this isn't any old science museum but rather a park with science, including enormous learning facilities and tons of options for exploration. The exhibits are multimedia and interactive, so slide down a double helix, ride to the top of the observation tower, and compete with your friends to see whose brain conducts the most electricity—all in one afternoon. While major exhibits on Darwin, Al-Andalus scientific history, and all the happenings inside your body (yes, yours) are always there to educate and entertain, Parque de las Ciencias is also constantly putting in a tireless effort to introduce newer exhibits to keep you up to date on what's going on in the world of science.

⚑ *End of the #1 bus line.* **i** *Information available in English and Spanish.* Ⓢ *€6. Planetarium €2.50.* ⚑ *Open Tu-Sa 10am-7pm, Su 10am-3pm. Planetarium sessions held every hr.*

CASA-MUSEO FREDERICO GARCIA LORCA

MUSEUM, PARK

C. Virgen Blanca s/n   ☎958 258 466 ▣www.huertadesanvicente.com

Probably one of Granada's best spots for a picnic or a morning jog (there are signs posted all around recommending stretching and toning exercises), the entirety of Parque Frederico Garcia Lorca smells of the roses that line its paths. Whether you want to sit at the duck pond or enjoy one of the two restaurants in the park, you cannot leave without stopping at the main event. The Casa-Museo Frederico Garcia Lorca is the original summer house of the famous Spanish poet, playwright, and director who was devastatingly assassinated after his disappearance during the Spanish Civil War. This emblem of Granadan culture is now honored in the home where he found some of his greatest inspiration. You can tour his kitchen, his grand piano, and his desk of work and even see his high-school diploma, which rats out his barely passing grades.

⚑ *Take the circular bus to the intersection of C. Recogidas and Camino de Ronda and follow the signs.* **i** *Tours available in English and Spanish.* Ⓢ *€3, students €1. Free on W.* ⚑ *Open Tu-Su July-Aug 10am-2:30pm; Oct-Mar 10am-12:30pm and 4-6:30pm; Apr-June and Sept 10am-12:30pm and 5-7:30pm.*

HIKING

You can get a serious workout hiking in Granada. Wander the **aqueducts** in the hills above the Alhambra or even the **old city wall** up in Sacromonte (if you're not too afraid of heights, it's also fun to climb up and stand on the wall itself) to get great views of the Darro River Valley. The best way to get to the aqueducts is to make a right through the parking lots at the intersection of **Carrera del Darro** and **Cuesta de Chapiz** until you see a pink, paved path going up the hill. Trails branch off the path to the right and will lead you to some of the city's best picnic and sunset spots. If you're feeling like getting out of town, Granada is situated just minutes from nearby mountain ranges. Take a visit to the **Monachil** pueblo and hike to its waterfalls. A bus leaves from **Paseo de los Basillos,** near its intersection with Acera del Darro. *($ €1.10 each way. ⏰ Every 30min. 8am-10pm.)* Monachil is the end of the line, and just follow the river to the falls for this 2-3hr. hike.

Alhambra

In 1238, **Sultan Al-Ahmar** of the Nasrid Dynasty took a look around Granada and realized that he had an opportunity to make something of the old **alcazaba** in the Albayzin area, an already centuries-old fortress with foundations constructed by the Romans. Al-Ahmar had a vision of turning this protective city wall into a palace and getaway for Arab royalty and top government officials. However, by 1491, Granada wasn't a princely paradise but a scrappy survivor. It was all that remained of the kingdom of al-Andalus, and *los reyes Católicos* were sieging the city in what would become the final act of the 780-year *Reconquista*. By 1492, Granada belonged to Ferdinand and Isabella, and we're sure that once all-powerful Isabella saw the this city's Alhambra, she decided that the couple was never going to leave this place.

Today, we definitely need to give a big thank you to good old Al-Ahmar (much more interesting than Weird Al or that creepy Uncle Al) for creating the Alhambra, one of the most historic and symbolic sights in all of Spain. It's the government's biggest moneymaker (Sagrada Familia has a higher income, but it loses tons to renovations), and it will soon be one of your favorite spots on the map. When visiting the Alhambra, be prepared to devote a good 3½-4hr. to your visit, as there is a ton to see. The Alhambra isn't simply a single sight—it's a fortified city full of gardens, museums, towers, and baths, not to mention a UNESCO World Heritage Site.

There are a few ways to get tickets to the Alhambra. *(C. Real s/n ☎902 441 221 💻www.alhambra-patronato.es $ €12.)* To purchase your ticket in advance, inquire at any of the La Caixa dispensers around the city, including one at the **Tienda de la Alhambra** *(C. Reyes Católicos, 40 ☎902 888 001 💻www.alhambra-tickets.es).* Many hostels will also book tickets for you at an additional charge of €2. You can buy tickets on the day of your visit at the entrance, either at the ticket office or the automated machines in the **Access Pavilion.** The ticket office is open from 8am until 1hr. before close.

The general daytime tickets allow access to all sights on the grounds—either in the morning *(⏰ 8:30am-2pm)* or in the afternoon. *(⏰ Mar 15-Oct 14 2-8pm; Oct 15-Mar 14 2-6pm.)* An evening ticket includes access to the gardens or Nasrid palaces, but not both, for €12 as well. *(⏰ Evenings Mar 15-May 31 and Sept 1-Oct 14 Th-Sa 10-11:30pm; Oct 16-Nov 14 F-Sa 8-9:30pm.)* These later visits allow you to see the Alhambra when the grounds are lit up against the night sky.

NASRID PALACES

Once on the grounds, the **Nasrid Palaces** are definitely the hot spot of the Alhambra. They're so hot, in fact, that you have to pick a specific time slot upon which to enter when purchasing your ticket to the Alhambra. You're limited to 1hr. of exploration, and there's a ton to see, so be ready for quite the journey through these remarkable grounds. Making your way through the **Sala de la Barca, Salon de Comares,** and **Sala de las Albencerrajes,** you'll be shocked and impressed by the detailed original plasterwork, curving and winding its way up to the tall pointed ceilings of the rooms. The turquoise, yellow, and green tiles add a splash of lovely color to these once-royal rooms. Remember that the lion is king of the jungle, and the **Patio de los Leones** is definitely the ruling architectural spot in the entire Alhambra. A complex system of aqueducts used gravity to power this fountain (and all the plumbing of the Alhambra), and such creativity and technical prowess blew the conquering Catholic royalty "out of the water." (Yeah, we went there.)

PALACIO DE CARLOS V

Museo de Bellas Artes   ☎958 895 430 ▧www.museosdeandalucia.es
Museo del Alhambra   ☎902 441 221 ▧museo.pag@juntadeandalucia.es

While the Palacio de Carlos V is often referred to as the "unfinished" and thus "forgotten" palace, there are definitely memories to be made here. At this 16th-century Renaissance-style palace, you'll not only get to explore the striking circular courtyard with two stories of marble columns, but you can also enjoy the two museums on the grounds.

The **Museo de Bellas Artes** is Granada's main art museum and actually the oldest public museum in Spain. The exhibitions begin in the historic year of 1492—yes, yes, it's the year when Columbus █**sailed the ocean blue**, but it's also the year that Granada shifted from Arab to Catholic control—and make their way into the modern day. There's a lot of local pride going on, from works by Granada natives to works inspired by the city itself. The museum also holds temporary rotating multimedia exhibits.

Also in the palace is the **Museo del Alhambra,** which holds a wide breadth of information and objects from the Alhambra itself. Luckily, since Ferdinand and Isabella settled into the Alhambra in the 15th century, all of the decorations, building elements, and possessions of the royal couple have been preserved and moved around the palaces. But now it's come time to share the spotlight—the museum, in development since 1940, now houses one of the world's best collections of Spanish-Moorish and Nasrid art.

Ⓢ *Museo de Bellas Artes €1.50, EU students free. Museo del Alhambra free.* ☒ *Palacio box office open daily Mar-Oct 8am-7pm; Nov-Feb 8am-5pm. Museo de Bellas Artes open Mar-Oct Tu 2:30-8pm, W-Sa 9am-8pm, Su 9am-2:30pm; Nov-Feb Tu 2:30-6pm, W-Sa 9am-6pm, Su 9am-2:30pm. Museo del Alhambra open July 1-Sept 15 T-Su 8:30am-2pm; Sept 16-June 30 Tu-Su 8:30am-2:30pm.*

ALCAZABA

The **Alcazaba** is largely to thank for the survival of the sight you're enjoying today. This fortress was definitely hard to get around (especially when traveling by donkey and wearing cloth slippers), and it protected the Alhambra for hundreds of years. However, today you can go where all those would-be conquerors wanted to be. Climb the Torre del Cubo, Torre de Homenaje, and Torre de la Vela to survey your kingdom: you'll be lost in the panoramic views of all of Granada, snapping pictures of the hundreds of thousands of tiled rooftops extending into the horizon.

GENERALIFE

The **Generalife** was definitely built for a king—or should we say a sultan? Constructed between the 12th and 14th centuries, this maze of gardens, patios, and fountains was intended to be the sultan's place of rest. And it's not all just nature up here. You'll also enter the stunning royal villa, decorated with the beautifully detailed plasterwork, as well as the outdoor theater where the dance portion of the annual **Festival Internacional de Música y Danza** is held. You'll climb the **escalera de agua,** a staircase lined with laurel trees and streams of water running down either handrail, and exit through the **Promenades of Oldeander and Cypress Trees.** And in case your eyes weren't already aesthetically overwhelmed, you can also look down over the entire Alhambra below.

Albaicín *Albayzín*

The history and conceptualization of the Albaicín barrio may seem a little conflicted: some say that the name of this ancient Muslim barrio could translate to "the miserables" in Arabic; others proudly explain that this quarter is actually the oldest, most historic portion of Granada, where the first Muslim court of the city was established in the 11th century. Today, the romantic Albaicín area, dipping into a valley that will send back a booming **echo** if you shout from the right place along **Calle Santa Ana**, still holds strong remnants of its Muslim past. Despite later alterations by Ferdinand and Isabella, this UNESCO World Heritage Site still has a Nasrid-style flair.

OLD MUSLIM BARRIO — NEIGHBORHOOD

The signs that you've entered this area are subtle at first. Walking the streets, you'll start to notice churches like the **Iglesia de Santa Anat** that have oddly mosque-like entrances. Walking up C. Carmen de Darro, you can enter the **buñuelos,** or Arab baths. *(☎958 027 800 ⏰ Open T-Sa 10am-2pm. $ Free.)* These are now a public monument. You can freely explore the **carmens,** or classic patio-gardens of the wealthy, at **Casa del Chapiz** on C. Cuesta del Chapiz and discover a whole new way of showing off your wealth (nothing was flashier than a snazzy garden with citrus trees and a few bamboo shoots). Along Carmen de Darro or Cuesta de Acahaba, you can visit the **original city walls** of Granada that once protected last sultan Boabdil's five Granadan castles. In the marketplace of Plaza Larga, you'll encounter the **Puerta de Pesa**. Notice the remaining weights hanging from this entryway--they were once used as a warning and reminder to merchants that consequences awaited if they were to cheat the customers of the marketplace. While a few remain to sustain the warning (so yes, you really did just buy 3 kilos of pomegranates), most of the weights have today been moved to the Albaicín's **Archeological Museum**, along with many other pieces of Granada's history (C. del Darro, 41 ☎958 225 640 $ €1.50, EU citizens free. ⏰ Open Tu 2:30-8:30pm, W-Sa 9:30am-8:30pm, Su 9:30am-2pm).

PLAZA ST. NICOLAS — VIEW, PLAZA

Beside the Church of St. Nicolas

The best thing to see *in* the Albaicín is actually the best thing to see *from* the Albaicín. Make your way to **Plaza St. Nicolas** alongside the Church of St. Nicolas and you can get the best views of the Alhambra found anywhere in Granada. They're especially great on those night when the Alhambra is open for evening visits, as the entire fortified city will be glowing with lights.

Sacromonte

Let's look at those monthly bills: rent, electricity, plumbing, heat. It all really adds up. But you know what's a cheaper option? Digging yourself a cave in the mountains across from the Alhambra. That must have been the thought process (more or less) of the Indian gypsies who dug into the mountainside when arriving on the Iberian peninsula in the 15th century. While they were living comfortably for centuries along the Río del Darro, the boom came when the lower classes packed their bags for Sacromonte between the late 19th and mid-20th century—by 1950 there were 3682 known cave dwellings along the mountainside.

But a genius for economical living wasn't the only talent these gypsies had. Walking the **Camino del Sacromonte,** you'll come across flamenco bar after flamenco bar, all ready to present the gypsy *zambra* style of this famous dance. You can also stop in at the museum honoring *zambra* and one of its top performers, **Cueva Maria la Canastera** *(Camino de Sacromonte, 89 ☎958 121 183 🖳cuevacanastera@yahoo.es).*

MUSEO CUEVAS DE SACROMONTE — MUSEUM, CAVES

Barranco de los Negros s/n ☎958 215 120 🖳www.sacromontegranada.com

In this museum, you'll get to see many of the original, although restored, cave dwellings that look surprisingly cozy. They might be dug-in holes, but you'll see stables, kitchens, bedrooms, and workspaces all comfortably kept up in these small, manmade caves. You'll also learn about the unique ecology of the **Darro River Valley,** which houses La Alhambra on one bank and Sacromonte on the other, and get an awesome view of this unbeatable duo.

$ *€5.* ⏰ *Open daily Apr-Oct 10am-2pm and 5-9pm; Nov-Mar 10am-2pm and 4-7pm.*

HOLY CAVE — CAVE, RELIGIOUS SITE

At the Abadía del Sacromonte

Sacromonte, or "holy mountain," is named such because of years of myth and legend. The holiest of these myths centers on the appropriately named **Holy Cave,** where a pile of ashes, supposedly being those of Granada's patron saint, San Cecilio, were discovered along with some leaden books suggesting the best means of converting Muslims to Catholicism. It was thought that the books were written by the saint. When Ferdinand and Isabella got word of this cave, they invested huge sums to create the *via crucis,* a line of over 1000 crosses along the mountain. Today, even though the legends have been proven false—the leaden books were actually written by a random Moorish scholar and are now stored in the **Abadía del Sacromonte**—the mountain remains a religious emblem and the **Procession to Sacromonte** is held on the first Sunday in February each year to honor San Cecilio.

Cathedral Quarter

CATEDRAL DE GRANADA — ★♿☁ CHURCH

C. Gran Vía de Colon, 5 — ☎958 222 959

Queen Isabella grew up in a nunnery, so it only makes sense that she'd put one hell of a church in her favorite city (should we not be saying "hell" in the same sentence as "church"?). The Catedral de Granada, formerly connected to the Capilla Real where Isabella is actually buried, is a massive, circular building lined with 13 golden *capillas,* or chapels, all of which are completely outshone by the Capilla Mayor in the center of the church. This sanctuary, surrounded by multiple organs and thick marble pillars (you'd need at least three people to give them a good hug), was definitely made for presentation's sake. It looks more like a theater than a church—two levels of balconies and stained-glass windows are the backdrop for the enormous red-carpeted altar in front. You'll also get to visit the Sacristía when entering the Catedral, which stores religious artwork and artifacts from centuries of Catholic royalty in Granada.

✦ *Entrance on C. Oficios.* ℹ *Information in Spanish only.* $ *€3.50. Audio tour €3.* ⏰ *Open M-Sa 10:45am-1:30pm and 4-8pm, Su 4-8pm. Ticket office closes 15min. before close.*

CAPILLA REAL — ★♿☁ CHURCH

C. Oficios, 3 — ☎958 227 848 🖥www.capillarealgranada.com

Here, you'll come across the tombs of King Ferdinand and Queen Isabella, the leaders that acquired Granada from the Muslim sultans and then decided that they never wanted to move out (and when we say never, we mean never). Their massive marble tomb sits beside the tomb of Phillip the Handsome and Joanna I—but of course it's elevated a good foot or two higher. And at the base of these tombs lies not only a forever-burning wax candle, but also the crypt, where you can actually see the coffins of all four of these rulers, along with Isabella's grandson, Prince Michael. The main altar of the room not only has the standard religious figures and statues of Isabella and Ferdinand on either side, but also contains images depicting the acquisition of Granada from Bilbao in 1492, as well as the Muslim christenings of 1509. In the Sacristía, you'll see the collection of Isabella's preserved artwork and possessions, including her crown and scepter.

✦ *Located beside the entrance to the Catedral.* ℹ *Informative pamphlets available in English for €0.10.* ⑤ *€3.50.* ⌚ *Open M-Sa 10:15am-1:30pm and 4-7:30pm, Su 11am-1:30pm and 4-7:30pm. Ticket office closes 15min. before close.*

FOOD

Food in Granada takes on three main types: Spanish-Granadan (think bold cuisine— *tortilla sacramonte* is scrambled up with marrow, brains, and bull's testicles), North African, and Mediterranean. Everyone will have their favorite falafel spot that they can't name but can loosely direct you toward as well as their idea of the best *teteria*, or Arabic tea shop, packed with people sitting on cushions and sharing puffs of hookah. The tapas of Granada are what will really make you never want to leave—order a drink at any tapas bar and they'll bring it out with a selection of free small plates of food.

Plaza Nueva

🕮 BAR KIKI   ♥✌☺ TAPAS, BAR ❸

Pl. de San Nicolas 9   ☎958 276 715

You're sitting enjoying your view from Pl. de San Nicolas when you notice booming conversation from your peripheral. That's definitely Bar Kiki—unless some hippie vendors are getting extra chatty. The huge tented patio out front is always packed with locals, who come for the creative menu that uses fresh products purchased at the local Mercado Daria. Kiki serves up massive rations intended to be split between two people *(€14-20).* Their specialty, Solomillo Nacional, celebrates Granada's Moorish influence with a hefty slab of tenderloin topped with almonds, apples, dates, raisins, and a reduction of sweet Pedro Ximenez wine *(€20).* If the market has fresh tuna that day, you'll be lucky to get a free tapa of *Atun de Barbate*, fish marinated with olive oil, white wine, onions, and almonds, alongside a big mug of beer *(€2)* or a glass of Spanish wine *(€3).*

🍴 *Located right behind the viewpoint at Plaza de San Nicolas.* ⑤ *Plates for 2 €14-20. Beer €2. Wine €3.* ⌚ *Open M-Tu 10am-midnight, Th-Su 10am-midnight.*

🕮 CASA LOPEZ CORREA   ♥✌ TAPAS ❸

C. de los Molinos, 5   ☎958 223 775

You might be caught off-guard when walking into Casa Lopez Correa. It smells Spanish, but it looks Granadan. It's serving free tapas, but most of the patrons are speaking English. First off: this is not a tourist trap! Casa Lopez Correa just happens to be the stand-in "town bar" for all the Aussies, Brits, Kiwis, and Americans who decided to settle down in Granada. The crowd is likely inspired by the British owners: the wife works behind the stove and the husband works the bar, each preparing the house specialties. The worldly options are homemade and include Italian, English, Moroccan, and Spanish dishes. The *menú* of the day *(2 courses €10; 3 courses €12)* involves massive portions whose fragrances pour out from the open kitchen into the small restaurant. The extensive cocktail selection is especially impressive as there's not a syrup in sight, and all the mojitos, *caipirinhas*, and margaritas are made with fresh fruits and quality liquors *(€6).* The tapa you get alongside these beverages is a hefty sampling of the menú's daily special.

🍴 *From Pl. Isabel La Catolica, take C. Pavaneras until it curves into C. de los Molinos to the right.* ⑤ *Appetizers €3.50-7.50; entrees €7.50-9.50. Mid-size rations €5-10. Beer €1.70. Wine €2.10.* ⌚ *Open M-F noon-4pm and 8pm-1am, Sa 8pm-1am, Su 1-5pm with reservation only.*

Catedral and University

🕮 POE   ♥✌ OPEN LATE ❶

C. Verónica de la Magdelena, 40   🖵www.barpoe.com

Poe may very well be the destination for the most delicious and least expensive meal in Granada. Walk in and snag a spot at the small loungey tables or at the wooden bar stools, then check out the warm yellow walls, woven grass lamps, and eclectic collection of African art. Chat with the British owner if you can catch him between his conversations with all the university regulars who come in and report about their recent exams, the latest soccer game, and even that special someone who's stealing their heart. Order a beer *(€1.50-4)* or glass of wine *(€1.50-2.70)*, both of which are available in non-alcoholic versions *(€1.50)*, and take your pick of free tapas. The chicken with a sweet and spicy Thai sauce is their most popular option, but the Portuguese *bacaloa* and Brazilian black bean and pork stew are both pretty irresistible. If you can't stop eating, just tack on an extra tapa for €1.20, a half-ration for €3.50, or a full ration for €6.

From Plaza Trinidad, take C. Alhondiaga to C. La Paz and turn right. *i* *Vegetarian options available.* $ *Beer €1.50-4. Wine €1.50-2.70. Extra tapa €1.20. ½-ration €3.50, ration €6.* ⏰ *Open Tu-Su 8pm-2am.*

LA CAMPERERIA 🍴🍸 BAR 2

C. Duquesa, 3 ☎958 294 173

Walking down C. Duquesa, it's impossible to miss the sleek, metallic sign denoting La Campereria in all-bold caps—that, and the crowd of loud, young, socializing students overflowing out of its front door. This restaurant-bar has an extensive menu of meat, fish, and salad options but specializes in its *camperos*, or round, pressed sandwiches sliced up pizza-style for sharing. Although they're pressed, it's hard to flatten out these absolutely stuffed savories. The vegetarian *(tomato, corn, pineapple, heart of palm, lettuce, fried onion, and mayo; €7.50)* and the chef special *(tomato, York-style ham, cheese, chicken or beef, egg, herbs, fried onion, lettuce, and mayo; €9)* are two irresistible favorites. Order your drink at the white bar that glows with red lights and is lined with beer taps and bottles of champagne and get a free slice of *campero* matched with a hearty, hot side dish like fresh spinach tortellini.

From Plaza Trinidad, follow C. Duquesa and the restaurant is on the left. $ *Camperos €6-9. Meat €10.50-18. Fish €12-14. Menú of the day €9.50. Dessert €2-4. Beer €1.90. Wine €2.50. Mixed drinks €4.* ⏰ *Open M-Th 8am-1am, F-Sa 8am-2am, Su 8am-1am.*

LOPEZ MEZQUITA 🍴 BAKERY 1

Av. Reyes Católicos, 39 ☎958 221 205

Walking along Reyes Católicos and Av. del Darro, you'll find tons of sweets shops and ice cream parlors advertising the years they opened (some even toting the ancient 2004 establishment date). Wherever you look, it's going to be hard to beat out Lopez Mezquita bakery, which has cooked up the classics since 1862. Sit down at the parlor counter where vested waiters who look like they're from a barbershop quartet serve you coffee and breakfast, or go browse the main display of goodies in the front. You can't leave Granada before trying the city's classic *pinono*, a sugary cookie covered in baked cream *(€1.10)*, or munching on the wide selection of meal-sized *empanadas* with such creative options as bacon-and-date stuffing *(€1.40)*.

On Reyes Católicos, near the intersection with Gran Via. $ *Pastries €0.70-1.70. Breakfasts €1.20-2.85.* ⏰ *Open M-F 9am-2:30pm and 5-9pm, Sa 10:30am-2:30pm.*

andalucia

Elsewhere

CASA JUANILLO 🍴🍸☀ TRADITIONAL 2

Camino del Sacramonte, 81-83 ☎958 223 094

This one is definitely worth the hike up Sacramonte. Casa Juanillo serves some of the most traditional Granadan dishes with one of the best views in the city. While the owner and his children will greet you at the street-level terrace, walk up to the classic Andalucian patio for a real treat. The brick and clay construction borders the dollhouse-esque blue panes and huge windows that give you the perfect view of the Alhambra and Darro River Valley below. And it's not just the design that's classic: whether you go with tapas and share a big jar of sangria *(€9)* with your free small plates (cross your fingers for the top knotch *albondigas*) or taste the *tortilla al monte*, full of the traditional pig's brains and purple peppers

(€9), you will leave stuffed and smiling.

🚌 Take bus #34 or 35 to Camino del Sacramonte. $ Entrees €7-14. Beer €1.80. Wine €2-3. Free tapa with drink. 🕐 Open Tu-Sa noon-4:30pm and 8pm-midnight, Su noon-4:30pm.

LA CHICOTÁ — TAPAS ❷

C. Naves, 20 ☎958 220 349 💻www.lachicota.es

We know it can be overwhelming to choose a place to eat on C. Navas; the street is lined with restaurants and packed with locals trying to take their pick. Should you draw straws? Spin a wheel? Have your llama sniff it out? While all three of those could work, you may just be better off taking our word for it and sitting down at La Chicotá. The meant-to-be-shared rations and oversized tapas taste as good as they look. Even the waiters are excited about the stunning presentation—some store pictures on their cell phones of the house favorite *cremoso de queso con miel* *(€10)*, a plate of hefty cheese pieces dripping in fresh honey and accompanied by fresh veggies. The stuffed potatoes *(€5.50)* are cheap, filling, and always ordered. The *patata relleno Chicotá* is overflowing with ham, mushrooms, and the secret spicy sauce. Even if it requires a little squirming or a mid-meal jog, make room for the homemade profiteroles doused in chocolate and hazelnut sauce and freckled with powdered sugar *(€5)*. While you can't make reservations for those busy dinner hours, the speedy waiters won't leave you hanging for more than a few minutes.

🚌 From C. Reyes Catolicos, walk through Plaza Carmen to C. Naves. $ Vegetable plates €7-12. Entrees €7.50-14. Desserts €2-5. Beer €1.70. Wine €2.50-3. 🕐 Open daily noon-midnight.

OLEUM GASTROBAR — MODERN ❸

C. San Anton, 81 ☎958 295 357 💻www.restauranteoleum.com

While we can't necessarily define "gastrobar" in the general sense, we can say that, in the case of Oleum, it's a dining option with sophistication and creativity. This bright, modern restaurant with a huge marble bar and patterned green and white walls glows with a fresh feeling that complements its organic food. The chefs in the kitchen know how to have some fun with the menu, so every free tapa will be presented in a brand-new way. Sip *salmorejo* out of a beaker through a straw, get your *brocheta* suspended on a small wooden boat, or, if you're feeling ready for a whole meal, try the house specialty *cordero a la lata* *(€14.10)*, a heaping portion of flavorful meat and veggies.

🚌 C. San Anton branches off C. Recogidas near the intersection with Reyes Catolicos. $ Salads €5.70-10.15. Entrees €6-19. Desserts €4-4.50. Beer €1.80. Wine €3. Coffee €1.20. 🕐 Open daily 7am-1am.

NIGHTLIFE

Plaza Nueva

LA FONTANA — BAR

C. Carrera del Darro, 19 ☎958 227 759

The decorations around La Fontana are a little disjointed. With eclectic modern paintings, alcohol in glass displays, and an adorable hanging hot-air-balloon statue over the bar, there's a lot going on aesthetically—but this little splash of everything is part of the appeal. Whether you want to use the free Wi-Fi to sit quietly in a private corner, shoot a few games of pool with a friend, or cheer your heart out at the Spanish soccer games being screened on multiple TVs and a huge projector, there's something for everybody in this eclectic watering hole. With all these activities to keep you busy, hopefully you won't get too frustrated with the slow service at the bar. You may get quite a few apologetic looks from overwhelmed bartenders, but they do mean well—they'll be chugging beers between runs to the kitchen, so you know why they're always so smiley and conversational once they finally pass you that free tapa.

🚌 From Plaza Nueva, take C. Santa Ana to Carrera del Darro. $ Beer €1.80. Wine €2-3. Cocktails €5. Coffee €1.50. 🕐 Open M-Th noon-3am, F-Sa noon-4am, Su noon-3am.

Catedral and University

If you're looking for some real late-night fun in Granada, there's no better place than near the university. Stressed, overworked 20-somethings need somewhere to let loose, and they can't even get started until they finish that last assignment. You'll find all the hottest dance clubs south of Gran Vía and tons of bars packed with regulars throwing up waves, blowing kisses, and getting friendly.

CLUB AFRODESIA — CLUB

C. Almona del Boqueron s/n — www.afrodesiaclub.com

Time to shake your groove thing! Club Afrodesia, brought to you by the same owners as local favorite **Booga Club** *(C. Santa Barbara 3 www.boogaclub.com)*, is one of Granada's top spots to bump and grind without twiddling your thumbs until that 2am opening time. Check out hip hop Tuesdays, Jamaican Club Wednesdays, or the Thursday through Saturday funk nights that energize the crowds. The party doesn't really get started until 2 or 3am (even later in the summers), but come early and relax on leather couches near swanky wood paneling and a leopard-print DJ booth. Go for a simple beer *(€3)* or take the Afrodesia route and just mix something with a Redbull *(€4.50)*.

Almona del Boqueron branches off Gran Vía at C. Cedran. $ Shots €2.50. Beer €2.50-3. Redbull €3. Mixed drinks €5-5.50. Open Tu-Th 11pm-3am, F-Sa 11pm-4am.

BAR RECA — BAR, ROMANTIC

C. Conde de Infantes, Pl. Trinidad — ☎958 225 182 www.eltrillodereca.com

Bar Reca is the perfect place for that mellow, classy drinker with a progressive palate. Sip your large glass of wine *(€2.50)*, munch on some beef carpaccio *(€15)* or breaded goat cheese with tomato marmalade *(€10)*, and order from your handsome young waiter wearing a hot pink polo. (Disclaimer: this is definitely a date spot and always packed with smooching couples, but guys better be suave enough to compete with the hunky staff.) The tapa of the day *(free with a drink)* and the secret ingredients behind the house sauce *(served with tuna or pork cheeks; €15)* may always be changing, but the regulars keep coming back no matter what's on the menu.

On the corner of Pl. Trinidad. $ Rations €10-15. Beer €1.80. Wine €2.50. Open M-Th 10am-2am, F-Sa 11am-3am.

PERRA GORDA — CLUB

C. Almonda del Boqueron, s/n

It's time to whip out those ripped jeans and studded leather jackets, because Perra Gorda is Granada's hot spot for rock and roll. This dark, red-and-black-themed club centers on the massive square bar ringed by posters for local concerts. Whether you're enjoying your cheap mojito *(€3)*, taking advantage of the three Buds for €5, or making it in time for the happy hour where all mixed drinks are two for €3, your wallet will catch a ton of breaks. Check out Perra Gorda's weekly entertainment—from throwing up your index and pinkie fingers at the Wednesday acoustic concerts, to playing your heart out in the Monday night foosball tourney (winner gets a free bottle of gin or rum in the fall), or dancing along the hallway with the late-night local crowd.

Almona del Boqueron branches off Gran Vía at C. Cedran. $ Shots €1-2. Beer €1.20-2.50. Mojitos €3. Mixed drinks €4. Open M-Th 10pm-3am, F-Sa 10pm-4am, Su 10pm-3am. Happy hour 10pm-midnight.

SALA VOGUE — CLUB

C. Duquesa, 35 — www.salavogue.es

Sala Vogue is a double-trouble student favorite: you've got two dance floors, two DJs, and two absolutely massive bars surrounding each dance floor. With all these options, Vogue can feed your partier soul no matter what mood you're in. *Sala 1* will be spinning indie, pop, rock, and '80s hits, while *Sala 2* can soothe

andalucia

your cravings for electronic and house. While you may have to pay a little extra for the guest DJs (Vogue rakes in some international hot shots), you can enjoy the 3 beers for €5 during the week, or the one-mixed-drink or two-beer deal with your cover on the weekends. You'll bump into your university buddies like Lucy from Psych 101 and Ricky from Rocks for Jocks year-round, and the tourists swarm in during the summer months. However, don't expect a crowd until 3 or 4am at least—they'll be finishing their homework first, right?

On C. Duquesa between Gran Capitan and Horno de Abad Málaga. $ Cover Th-Sa €6; includes 1 mixed drink or 2 beers. Beer €3. Mixed drink €5. ⏰ Open M-Th midnight-6am, F-Sa midnight-7am, Su midnight-6am.

Elsewhere

Along Camino del Sacromonte in the evenings, you'll find bar upon bar offering cheap drinks (with free tapas, of course) and even cheaper flamenco, jazz, and poetry readings. **Pena las Cuevas de Sacromonte** *(Camino de Sacromonte, 21 ☎920 182 663 💻www.erasmusgranada.com)* has free shows every night *(11pm)* and special flamenco-poetry combos on Fridays and Saturdays *(10pm)*. **Museo Cuevas del Sacromonte** screens open-air independent films Tuesdays and Thursdays *(10pm; €3)* and has flamenco shows on Wednesdays *(10pm; €12)* throughout July and August.

MAMBRU

🍴🍸 BAR, RESTAURANT

C. San Anton, 85 ☎958 255 362

Mambru describes itself as a place of food and music, and *Let's Go* recommends both of these specialties. The Spanish tunes include a mix of salsa, merengue, jazz, and reggae and only get louder as the day goes on—it might be hard to compete with the volume for a conversation, so just munch on a warm, freshly made tapa with your beer *(€1.80)*. They're always whipping up *paella*, even though it's not on the menu, so you may get real lucky with that free taste. You can start the night in the upstairs Zen dining room that holds long wooden tables and a woven grass carpet, but once you're ready for a little dancing and a lot of conversation, the huge bar with an extensive liquor selection is the place to be.

C. San Anton branches off C. Recogidas near the intersection with Reyes Catolicos. $ Appetizers €8-13; meat dishes €10-19.50; fish dishes €12.50-15; dessert €3-5.50. Beer €1.80. Wine €2.20-2.80. Mixed drinks €4-6. ⏰ Restaurant open M-W 2-4pm and 8:30-11:30pm, Th 2-4pm and 8:30pm-1:30am, F-Sa 2-4:30pm and 8:30pm-1:30am, Su 2-4pm and 8:30-11:30pm. Bar open M-Th 8am-2am, F-Su 8am-4am.

ARTS AND CULTURE

Flamenco And Jazz

VENTA EL GALLO

🍴🍸 BAR, RESTAURANT, FLAMENCO

Barranco Los Negros, 5 ☎958 228 476 💻www.ventaelgallo.com

Though pricier than many of the divier flamenco-jazz bars around Granada, Venta el Gallo is known for being one of the highest-quality options for traditional Granadan flamenco. Since it's located in Sacromonte, you know you're getting the authentic thing—you're where the *zambra* dance style started, for goodness's sake! This classic Andalucian house has an arched clay stage decorated with hanging pots and pans that supports a full band and multiple performers. You and over 100 other audience members can enjoy the show with a classy drink or stuff yourself with the multi-course menu of classic Granadan recipes and "El Gallo" specialty preparations. Since they know their location is only convenient for cave dwellers, they offer a pickup and dropoff service *(€6)* if you don't feel like taking the bus.

Take bus #34 or 35 to the base of C. del Sacromonte and follow the signs. i Pickup and dropoff €6. $ Dinner and show €52. Drink and show €22. ⏰ Restaurant open daily 1-4:30pm and 7:30pm-midnight. Dinner with show 8:30pm. Shows 9:30 and 10:30pm.

ESHAVIRA CLUB DE JAZZ 🍸 JAZZ CLUB, BAR

C. Postigo de la Cuna, 2 ☎958 290 829 🖥www.eshavira.es

This underground music club is a local favorite and a Granadan classic (so classic that the owner will be kissing the cheeks of all the regulars as they walk in). Eshavira puts on jazz shows every Thursday, Flamenco shows every Sunday *(€6-10 depending on the size and notoriety of the group performing)*, and holds open Jam sessions every Tuesday *(€3)*. Since its 1989 opening, this two-room club has done up what was once a deteriorating pair of Arab houses (and by "done up" we mean kept the dimly lit, heavy-iron-door look but added posters of jazz legends). The owners worked hard, and now the club has become a bustling hotspot of Granadan flare that rakes in talented artists from all over the world. It even hosts its own winter Jazz and Flamenco Festival in November and December. They distribute their monthly schedule to all of the local hostels, so ask at the nearest front desk—that is, if the young local working there hasn't already recommended it.

➜ In alley off C. Azacayas between C. Elvira and Gran Vía. $ Concerts €6-10. Jam sessions €3-4. Beer €2. Wine €2. Mixed drinks €2. ⏰ Open Tu-Th 9pm-3:30am, F-Sa 9pm-4am, Su 9pm-3:30am.

LE CHIEN ANDALOU 🍸 BAR, FLAMENCO, JAZZ CLUB

Carrera de Darro, 7 ☎646 741 996

Le Chien Andalou is all about bringing different styles and cultures together: it's got a French name (meaning "the Andalusian Dog," the title of a famous modernist Buñel film), Arabic, Mediterranean, and Spanish tapas (their large helpings of *tabbouleh* are one lucky find and come free with drink), and a combo of flamenco and jazz. Shows go on every night at 10pm, but make sure to get there at least 30min. early to get a seat–the low tables leading up to the arched stage fill up long before curtain call. Try not to miss the special Wednesday night flamenco fusion show that brings together the best of jazz and flamenco with classic dancers, tons of percussion, and a full band of guitars, violins, and saxophones.

➜ From Plaza Nueva, take C. Santa Ana to Carrera del Darro. $ Shows M-Th €5, F-Sa €6, Su €5. Beer €2. Wine €2-3. Cocktails €5. ⏰ Open M-Th 7pm-3am, F-Su 4pm-4am. Shows daily 10pm.

Festivals

CORPUS CHRISTI SPRING

While this citywide party is technically intended to celebrate the presence of Jesus Christ in Holy Communion, Corpus Christi has become more debaucherous than religious over the years. The Catholic monarchs brought the festivities to Granada hoping to use the excitement to win over the large Muslim and Jewish populations. Some say that the royalty even urged the local government to invest huge sums of money in the celebrations and make this party as wild, crazy, and fun as possible–you'll be glad that these "suggestions" were taken seriously. The Thursday of the festival, when the **Corpus Christi Parade** is held and the throne created by Miguel Moreno is carried through the streets, is the most important day of the event and is always 60 days after Easter. In its entirety, the festival lasts from the *Encendio*, or lighting of all the city lights Monday at midnight, until the **fireworks** extravaganza the following Sunday. Over the course of the week, *casetas* and a fun fair are set up on the outskirts of the city, and *Carocas*, or satirical cartoons depicting the events of the past year, are played in **Plaza Bibrambla.** Direct bus lines run to the festival grounds for €1.40. Hostels and hotels tend to fill up, so book in advance.

⏰ 60 days after Easter.

FESTIVAL INTERNACIONAL DE MÚSICA Y DANZA SUMMER

The Festival Internacional de Música y Danza is one of Granada's most prized events. Held now for over 50 years, this summertime festivity brings together a wide variety of music and dance forms, including flamenco, piano, zarzuela, orchestral, and vocals. Performances are held all over the city, including such awe-inspiring spots as the outdoor theater of the **Generalife** and the Alhambra's **Palacio de Carlos V.** For tickets and the festival program of events, contact the festival box office at the **Corral del Carbón** *(C. Mariana Pineda, s/n ☎958 221 844 💻taquilla@granadafestival.org)* or **Ticketmaster** *(☎902 150 025 💻www.ticketmaster.es/granadafestival).*

ESSENTIALS [i]

Practicalities

- **TOURIST OFFICES:** There are over 25 tourist offices in the greater Granada area, including one at the airport *(☎958 245 269 💻iturismo.aeropuerto@dipgra.es),* at Plaza del Carmen *(☎958 248 280 💻informacion@granadatur.com),* and in the Alhambra *(Avda. Generalife, s/n ☎958 544 002 💻www.andalucia.org).*
- **TOURS:** The tourist bus line for Granada runs year-round English tours *(💻www.citysightseeing-spain.com/html/es/tour $ €10. ⏰ 1hr. 15min., every 15min.)* that stop at 10 major sights. You can also hop on the free walking tour, officially run out of Oasis Granada, that leaves from the fountain at Plaza Nueva every day at 11am (€3-5 tip recommended).
- **CURRENCY EXCHANGE: Interchange** *(C. Reyes Católicos 31 ☎958 224 512 ⏰ Open M-Sa 9am-10pm, Su 11am-3pm and 4-9pm)* is a money-exchange office that provides services with all major credit cards, including American Express.
- **INTERNET:** The **Biblioteca de Andalucía** *(Profesor Sainz Cantero, 6 ☎958 026 900 💻www.juntadeandalucia.es/cultura/ba ⏰ Open M-F 9am-9pm, Sa 9am-2pm)* has eight computers that you can use for free for up to an hour. You can also use the facilities at the **university,** including the free Wi-Fi. **Idolos and Fans** is an internet cafe *(Camino de Ronda, 80 ☎958 265 725 ⏰ Open daily 10am-midnight. $ €1.80 per hr., €9 per 6hr., €12 per 10hr)* that has facilities for photocopying, fax, scanning, video chat, computer use, Wi-Fi, and even a Playstation 3.
- **POST OFFICE:** The closest post office is at Puerta Real *(intersection of C. Reyes Católicos and Acera del Darro ☎958 224 835 ⏰ Open M-F 8:30am-8:30pm, Sa 9:30am-2pm).*

Emergency!

- **EMERGENCY NUMBERS: Municipal police:** ☎092. National police: ☎091.
- **LATE-NIGHT PHARMACIES:** You'll find a few 24hr. pharmacies around the intersection of C. Reyes Catolicos and C. Acera del Darro, including **Farmacia Martin Valverde** *(C. Reyes Catolicos, 5 ☎958 262 664).*
- **HOSPITALS/MEDICAL SERVICES:** Call the **Hospital Universitario Vírgen de las Nieves** *(Av. Fuerza de las Armadas, 2 ☎958 020 002)* or the **Hospital San Juan de Dios** *(C. San Juan de Dios s/n ☎958 022 904).* For an ambulance, contact a local emergency team *(☎958 282 000).*

Getting There ✈

By Air

Airport Federico García Lorca *(☎958 245 200)* is located about 15km outside the city in Chauchina and can be accessed along the A-92 highway. It connects to the **Madrid, Barcelona,** and **Majorca** airports domestically as well as Britain's **London-Stansted** and **Liverpool** Airports, Germany's **Frankfurt-Hahn Airport,** and Italy's **Bologna** and **Milano Bergamo** Airports. Air Europa, Iberia, SpainAir, RyanAir, and Vueling Airlines all fly through Granada.

By Train

The main **train station** *(Av. de Andaluces, s/n ☎958 204 000)* runs Renfe trains *(💻www. renfe.es)* to and from **Barcelona** *(💲 €60.50. ⏰ 11½hr.; 8am, 9:30pm.)*, **Madrid** *(💲 €66.80. ⏰ 4hr. 25min.; 9:05am, 5:05pm.)*, **Sevilla** *(💲 €23.90. ⏰ 3hr., 4 per day 7am-6pm.)*, and **Algeciras** *(💲 €20.40. ⏰ 4½hr.; 7am, 12:15, 3:45pm.)*, as well as many other smaller cities.

By Bus

The **bus station** *(Caretera Jaén s/n ☎958 185 480)* runs Alsa buses *(💻 www.alsa.es)* around Andalucia *(☎958 185 480 for the regional line)*, as well as connecting to **Madrid** *(☎958 185 480)* and the **Valencia-Barcelona** *(☎902 422 242)* lines. You can arrive from **Sevilla** *(💲 €20. ⏰ 3hr., 9 per day 8am-11pm)*, **Cadiz** *(💲 €31. ⏰ 5hr., 4 per day 9am-9pm)*, **Madrid Estación Sur** *(💲 €17. ⏰ 5hr., 15 per day 1am-11:30pm)*, or **Málaga** *(💲 €10. ⏰ 1½hr., 15 per day 7am-9:30pm)*, as well as many other destinations. Autocares Bonal *(☎958 46 50 22)* also runs a direct route to and from **Sierra Nevada** ski resorts *(⏰ 25min.; M-F 3 per day, Sa-Su 4 per day)* during ski season.

Getting Around

Transportes Rober *(☎900 710 900 💻www.transportesrober.com)* runs almost 40 bus lines around the city *(💲 €1.20, 7 rides €5)*, as well as smaller direct buses to the **Alhambra,** the **Albaicín,** and the **Sacromonte.** These **tourist lines** are #30, 31, 32, and 34, and the **circular lines** (#11, 21, and 23) make full loops around the city. Rober also runs a special Feria line. *(💲 €1.40.)* While most lines generally run between 6:30am and 11:30pm every day, the **Buho lines** *(#111 and 121 💲 €1.30.)* operates from midnight to 5:15am. Lines #3 and 33 from the **bus station** and lines #3, 6, 9, and 11 from the **train station** take you to **Gran Vía de Colon.** Also, there's an airport shuttle from the 2nd stop on Gran Vía. *(💲 €3. ⏰ 45min.; 11-13 per day.)*

nerja ☎952

The tourist capital of the Costa del Sol, Nerja clearly knows how to entertain with the awe-inspiring Cueva de Nerja, the high-energy party harbor at Plaza Tutti Frutti, and over 13km of Spain's hottest beaches. Even though Nerja may seem more amusement park than historical sightseeing haven, its culture is far better than its cotton candy. This ancient Moorish town is actually named for the Arab word *narixa*, meaning "abundant spring," describing the beautiful but menacing limestone waterfalls pouring down from the surrounding Sierra. Nerja prides itself on its untouched ocean coves, temperate and sunny climate, and relaxed, beachy attitude. This small town is the perfect place to get a tan, snack on the catch of the day, and rejuvenate in a Spanish paradise.

ORIENTATION

Avenida de la Pescia is the street you'll take upon entering Nerja and that you'll use to visit the Cueva de Nerja. It has more of an industrial feel, but it's also extremely efficient, packing in a police station, multiple supermarkets, a gas station, and bus stops all within a 5-10min. walk. **Calle Pintada** and **Calle Almirante Fernandiz** take you from Av. la Pescia down to the beach, and you'll find lots of shops, accommodations, and restaurants along them. C. Almirante Fernandiz, with the help of **Calle Los Huertes** and **Calle Rodriguez Acosta,** also borders the historic center of the city. The "beach town" part of Nerja is found near the **Balcón de Europa, Plaza Cavana,** and **Calle El Barrio** and **Calle Diputación.**

ACCOMMODATIONS

👍 HOSTAL MARISSAL — 📶🍸❄ HOSTAL [3]

Paseo Balcon de Europa, 3 — ☎952 520 199 💻www.hostalmarissal.com

Hostal Marissal puts you smack-dab in the beach center of Nerja. Your room's sea-foam green sheets and curtains and dark wooden furniture will leave you thinking it's time for sunshine and sand, and the bustling cafeteria-style restaurant on the ground floor will keep you (and every other beachgoer around) happily fed. Located on the boardwalk to the Balcon de Europa, Hostal Marissal also provides unbeatable views and an ocean breeze. If you're lucky enough, your room's balcony will face the sea and be a perfect spot to reenact some Kate and Leo moments.

On the boardwalk to Balcon de Europa. *i* *Towels and sheets included. TV and bathroom ensuite.* [$] *Singles €30-45; doubles €40-60.* ⏰ *Reception 9am-midnight.*

HOSTAL ABRIL

HOSTAL ❷

C. Pintada, 124 ☎952 526 124 www.hostalabril.com

Hostal Abril is the perfect way to relax on your beach getaway. This family-run establishment will make you feel right at home as the young kids come kiss Mom goodbye while she checks you in at reception. The bright, spacious rooms with white sheets, marble floors, and sunflowers will provide you with some rest (and with some free tea on the side table), while the patio-garden with full lounge chairs and benches will give you some sun without the sand. It's located just steps from the bus stop, so you can drop off your belongings and take a trip to the Cueva de Nerja without any hassle. For a slightly higher price, you can also check out of the **Apartamentos Abril** *(C. Cristo esquina C. San Juan 1),* whose rooms come equipped with full kitchen and living room space.

From the bus stop and facing the beach, C. Pintada is to the left of the park; the hostal is on the left. *i* *Towels and sheets included. TV, safes, and bathroom ensuite.* [$] *Singles €25-33; doubles €33-42; triples €36-55; quads €43-75; quints €47-82.* ⏰ *Reception 9am-11pm.*

SIGHTS

As Nerja is detached from the **caves,** aqueduct, and small historic towns beyond the city border, many of the sights are just that—things you will see from afar. The **Balcón de Europa** was used as a fortress in the ninth century but today is a great spot to catch some ocean views and grab a bite to eat with all your fellow tourists. The **Barco de Chanquete** featured all over the popular '80s TV series *Verano Azul* symbolizes the recent increase in Nerja's tourism. The **La Dorada I** boat housed the character Chanquete on the show and would do Gilligan, the Professor, and even the Millionaire proud.

CUEVA DE NERJA

CAVE

Caretera de Maro, s/n ☎952 529 520 www.cuevadenerja.es

You've got two million years of rainwater and bicarbonate to thank for this puppy. The 264,279 cu. m Cueva de Nerja (Cave of Nerja) is one of Spain's best tools for studying the prehistoric era on the Iberian Peninsula and has become one of the largest draws to the tourist capital of Costa del Sol. The caves' history sounds like Steven Spielberg's 1985 classic *The Goonies*, but we promise this is no Hollywood feature. Five young boys discovered the Cueva in 1959, and within two years the sight was converted into a national point of historic interest. Today, there exist three primary cavities of the cave, including the touristic **lower gallery** as well as the upper and new gallery only open to speleologists for research. Don't be disappointed by the security, though. The touristic cave boasts massive stalagmites, threatening stalactites, and a ton of other forms like "soda straws," "pearls," and "pineapples," whose names may remind you more of a beach resort than of the cool shadows you'll be exploring. While the Shaquille O'Neals of the world may have to crouch a tiny bit to descend down the steps, everyone will find an open, underground, natural palace that's perfect for getting a cheesy tourist photo taken *(€8).* Hopefully you won't encounter any of your childhood nightmares in the **Sala de las Fantasmas** (Hall of Ghosts), and you can get a flashless photo with the world-record-holding **Gran Columna del Catacismo** (central column of the Hall of Catacism). You'll walk by the main stage where the annual **Festival de Cueva de Nerja** *(mid-July; shows at 10pm; €50)* holds its ballet, orchestra, tango, and flamenco performances. You can also visit the **Centro de Interpretacion** *(open daily 10am-2pm and 4-6:30pm)*, where you'll find further details about the history and structure of the cave as well as a full-scale model and various films. Ready for some relaxation? Enjoy a picnic on the shaded tables at **Plaza de los Descubridores** or head into the **restaurant** *(Plaza de los Descubridores, 1 ☎952 529 558 🖳www.lorenzoreche.net $ Buffet €8.80)*, where you can get a table on the patio overlooking the beach and the picturesque town of Maro.

➜ Take the Nerja-Cuevas bus or drive to Exit 295 off Autovia del Mediterraneo or Hwy. N-340. i Cave info in English and Spanish; interpretation center only in Spanish. $ €8.50. ⏰ Open daily in summer 10am-7:30pm; in winter 10am-2pm and 4-6:30pm.

EL AGUILA AQUEDUCT — LANDMARK

Hwy. N-340

While the El Aguila (The Eagle) Aqueduct may look like it was built in Roman times, this 19th-century structure with four stories and 37 arches is actually a mere stylistic model—but that doesn't mean it's not awesome! The aqueduct was originally intended to irrigate the orchards around Maro and Nerja and provide water to the city's old sugar factory. Today, much of its practical use has been shut down, but it still holds some irrigation purpose, and its original "pure and clean contraception" inscription on one of the lower arches makes for an awesome photo op. Whether you're walking back from the Cave of Nerja or making the drive into the city, it's definitely worth pulling over to snap a shot or two.

➜ Off Hwy. N-340 between Nerja and the Cueva along the panoramic pull-over point.

MARO — HISTORIC TOWN

The tiny town of Maro (if you can even call it a town—city maps refer to it as an "Andalucian corner") is only a few steps from the Cueva de Nerja and even closer to the beaches and farmland surrounding it. Walking the streets among the white houses, blue waters, and green orchards, you won't hear much other than chirping birds, flowing fountains, and maybe a tourist or two blasting Bob Marley from a parked car taking in the **panoramic viewpoints.** While there are a few small accommodations and scarcely populated restaurants, Maro is more about picturesque relaxation than five-star establishments. The **beaches** are smaller than those found within the city lines of Nerja, and this same simplicity carries over into the town's main sight, **Iglesia Nuestra Senora de las Maravillas** (Church of Our Lady of Wonders). This small church was completed in the 17th century, but its structure holds remnants of a much older design. The eclectic architectural stylings, including wooden beams and pointed arches, house some cluttered religious artwork and small electric fans, all honoring the patron saint of Maro.

➜ Off Autovia del Mediterraneo of Hwy. N-340, adjacent to the Cueva de Nerja. Take the Nerja-Cuevas bus or drive to Exit 295 off Autovia del Mediterraneo or Hwy. N-340. It's a 5min. walk from Cueva de Nerja along the green path.

THE GREAT OUTDOORS

Scuba Diving

BUCEO COSTA NERJA

Playa Burriana ☎952 528 610 🖳www.nerjadiving.com

This family-run diving company is Nerja's only dive center and is equipped to take you out for a quick dive trip or teach you all you need to know for certification. PADI courses for one to four people are available for many types of snorkel, scuba, emergency, and rescue certification for both adults (over 14) and teens (over 12), and TDI technical diving courses are offered for those trying to test their limits. Rent all the necessary equipment for a daytime or evening dive or snorkel session. While the shop itself is located on Playa Burriana, the dive sights extend further east along the Costa del Sol, handpicked to bring you the best chance of seeing an octopus, dolphin, or swordfish face-to-face (or face-to-fin). ♣ *Office on Playa Burriana.* **i** *Medical forms to be completed available on website. All guides speak English.* Ⓢ *PADI courses €100-420; PADI Professional €180-625. Snorkel tours €30. Scuba with guide and equipment tours €50, night €62 (10% off if 3 or more). Scuba with just guide €35/42. Insurance €6 per day, €24 per month.* 🕐 *Regular dives at 9:30am, 1:30, 4pm. Night dives after 7pm. Make reservations a few days in advance.*

Beaches

PLAYA BURRIANA

☎952 522 156

This stretch of sand along **Paseo Maritimo Antonio Mercero** is one of Nerja's most popular beaches and one of the main tools for raking in all the summer visitors to this sunny city. The boardwalk is packed with **gift shops, snack stands,** and **ice cream parlors** that are ready to soothe that sweet tooth or equip you with a new umbrella or boogie board. Tons of **restaurants** and **bars** serve up any type of cuisine you could imagine, with a heavy emphasis on fried fish and barbecue. Most of the restaurants are large with busy outdoor patios, generally offering Wi-Fi and plenty of TV screens. There are also a few nicer restaurants along C. **Filipinas,** all with their own bit of character—some have ridiculous, decorative flags draping their ceilings, some present the most luxurious breakfast options in town, and others hold dance performances on a nightly basis. On the sandy shore, you'll find everything from volleyball courts and playgrounds to a **police station** and **public changing rooms.** You can rent a **lounge chair** *(€4)* from any of the small, umbrella-shaded podiums along the beach. Before you head back to your car or your hotel, make sure to check out the **viewpoints** along the switchbacks branching off **Calle Bajamar.**

i *Pets and loud music are not permitted.* 🕐 *Lifeguard station and police station open daily 11:30am-8pm. Beach open June 15-Sept 15.*

Hiking

The Sierra Almijara and the Sierra de Tejada mountain ranges, including the 1832m peak of Navachica, overlook Nerja. The most eastern part of the Sierra Almijara is referred to by locals, maybe a bit self-obsessively, as the **Sierra de Nerja.** Even if the people of Nerja are vain in naming their mountain range, we can't blame them for wanting to establish this namesake because of the beautiful hiking options through these sierras. One of the most popular full-day hikes passes through the **Rio Chillar,** giving you the chance to swim in the Vado de los Patos (Ford of the Ducks), explore the Cueva de las Palomas (Cave of the Doves), smell the eucalyptus forests and apricot trees, and catch sight of the main dam and irrigation channels. You'll find the start of the route and base of the riverbed at **Calle El Picasso,** near the sports complex, or at **El Playazo Beach.** You'll find multiple other routes starting from the **Fuente del Esparto.** From the fountain, the two most popular routes are the challenging, 36km (round-trip) climb to the top of **Navachica** and the shorter half-day trip to the **Almendron Cliff.** Both hikes are notorious for their spectacular views and memorable visits to two of the old city mines, **Mina del Uno** (Mine of One) and **La Fruia** (The Fury).

Updated and more detailed information on hiking routes is available from the **information center,** but even those pamphlets warn that trails are often a bit ambiguous and that permanent, natural structures are your best bet as directions. **Adventura** also leads guided hiking trips *(€35 per person)* along Rio Chillar and through the Sierra Almijara.

Other Outdoor Activities

ADVENTURA

Paseo Burriana, 2 or C. Mediterraneo, 3   ☎952 520 471 🖳www.adventuranerja.com

Adventura is ready to find you all that its name describes: an adventure. Whether by mountain, land, or sea, this company has the facilities and guides to help you

nerja • the great outdoors

get your adventurous fix. Their land department offers such activities as horseback riding *(€25 per hr., €45 per 2hr.)* and off-road biking *(€20 for bike, €40 with guide)*, the mountain department can get you hiking *(½ day €35 per person)* or canyoning *(€60 per perşon; min. 4 people; 4-5hr.)*, and the water section will get you drenched with a windsurf *(from €10 per hr.)* or a kayak trip *(€20 per person; 3hr. guided tour)*. They also serve as a scuba booking agent for **Buceo Costa Nerja,** but they don't provide guides, equipment, or facilities of their own. Even if you don't decide to set out into the world, the Adventura Clubhouse is still worth a stop. Enjoy a drink or tapa at the bar, watch an activity slideshow, chat up the instructors, or enjoy the customer Wi-Fi service. Ask about their activity packages that last up to a week.

Office at the far end of Playa Buriana. **i** *Insurance forms and packed lunches available upon request. Free Wi-Fi; computers €4 per hr. Headsets and webcams also available.* ⏰ *Office and clubhouse open daily in summer 10am-8pm; in winter 10am-6pm.*

FOOD

Since Nerja is a beach town, all traditional Spanish restaurants feature tons of fresh seafood at great prices. Since Nerja is also a top tourist destination, you'll come across various international cuisine options, especially British and Italian restaurants. Along **Playa Buriana** and **Plaza Fabrica de los Cangrejos,** you'll find great views and outdoor patios but few things authentically Spanish. Don't be turned off by restaurants run out of hotels and *hostals*—with such a bustling tourist industry, many of these spots will be the most established, popular dining destinations in town.

LAS PEINATAS — MODERN, SPANISH ❷

C. San Miguel, 18 ☎952 526 397 www.peinatablanca.com

Las Peinatas is kind of like MTV's *Pimp My Ride*—it's all about taking something classic and making it new and fresh (without the fuzzy dice or flame decals). With the decor, you'll immediately notice the glistening *peinatas* (traditional hairpins often worn for flamenco) decorating almost every inch of wall space in this modern restaurant. The menu follows this vibe as well, including the sweet cherry gazpacho *(€4.50)* and the *pastel de rabo de toro con foie y setas*, or bull's-tail pie with *foie gras* and mushrooms *(€9.50)*, which both take a unique spin on Andalucian classics. Take advantage of some timeless money-savers like a free tapa with any drink off the extensive wine list *(€1.80-2.20 per glass)* or the tasty, marinated olives and warm bread that come with your meal. Many of the rations are easily large enough to split, so don't be thrown off by the surprisingly low prices—this place is just a steal.

From the bus stop, make a right on C. San Miguel and walk about 3min.; the restaurant is on the left. $ *Rations €3.50-11.50. Desserts €4.50-5.90.* ⏰ *Open daily 10am-4pm and 7pm-midnight.*

ANAHI — DINER ❷

Puerta del Mar, 6 ☎952 521 457

Don't fret—you may be getting some of the best ocean views off Balcon de Europa, but your wallet won't feel a thing. Anahi is one of Nerja's top diners, and its simple, inexpensive menu will make you smile almost as much as the sea breeze off the small patio or the beautiful view through the huge glass doors of its interior dining room. If you're sick of standard Spanish breakfasts like toast and jam (or just looking for some gluttony), Anahi will make sure you're too full to function. Try the savory asparagus omelet *(€5.20)* or steak-and-eggs platter *(€7)*. Or give into temptation and order the waffles topped with chocolate and vanilla ice cream, chopped walnuts, and honey *(€4.20)*. The fresh-fruit tarts, croissants, and quiches *(€1-2)* can easily be taken to go for a sightseeing snack. Anahi also boasts an array of toasty sandwiches *(€1.60-3.50)*, including their signature Anahi burger, piled high with lettuce, tomato, onion, bacon, and eggs *(€3.50)*.

Located to the left of Balcon de Europa as you face the water. **i** *Ocean-view balcony.* $

Pastries €1-2. Eggs €3.70-7. Pancakes and waffles €3.50-4.20. Sandwiches €1.60-3.50. Lunch and dinner entrees €6.30-11. ☼ Open daily 8am-12:30am.

AYO
Playa Buriana s/n

⊛ ❡ ⬭ BEACH RESTAURANT ❷
☎952 522 289 ▪www.ayonerja.com

Everyone in Nerja has heard of Ayo—this restaurant owner not only opened up one of Playa Buriana's top eateries over 40 years ago, but he also was one of the first people to ever explore the Cueva de Nerja (he'll humbly tell you how he wasn't one of the five *descubridores* honored at the sight, but will make sure you know that it was Ayo and comrades who first came across the entirety of the cave). Don't think Ayo's personal celebrity is what rakes in the clientele to the checkered tablecloths right on the sand. While Ayo has a full menu of entrees, with some of the best freshly grilled fish (*€12.75*) and lamb (*€13.75*) in town, this spot is famous for its overflowing plates of *paella* (*€6*). In the corner of the sandy plot, it's impossible to miss the massive iron pan atop a wooden fire being attended to by multiple chefs. They'll be making up fresh seafood-and-chicken *paella* all day long, so stop in at any time and get one of the warmest, freshest, and tastiest samplings on the Costa del Sol.

✴ At the end of the Antonia Mercero boardwalk. ℹ Flamenco July-Sept W 9-11pm. Ⓢ Appetizers and eggs €2-8.25. Paella €6. Meat and fish €5-14.50. Beer €1.80. House wine €7 per bottle. ☼ Open daily noon-10pm.

NIGHTLIFE

Nightlife in Nerja, like all other aspects of the city, changes from season to season. The sunnier it is, the more tourists you'll find. As far as lingo goes, keep in mind that the "pubs" will have lengthy drink menus but aren't just for sitting and sipping—they'll often have dance floors in addition to their large, outdoor terraces. Along **Playa Buriana**, you'll come across lots of English-run pubs that are popular but overflowing with every tourist in town. **Plaza Tutti Frutti** is the heart of the night scene, lined with pubs and clubs on all sides. Keep your eyes peeled for promoters handing out **two-for-one drink deals** and other specials along the plaza. All establishments on the plaza open at 10pm and close between 3 and 4:30am. There are a few designated *discotecas* just outside the plaza, the most popular of which is **Jimmy's** (C. de Antonio Millón), but these dance havens don't even open until 2am.

⬛ LA EMBAJADA
Plaza Tutti Frutti 2

⊛ ❡ ✳ ⬭ PUB,DISCOTECA
▪www.publaembajada.com

Walking around Plaza Tutti Frutti, you'll notice that La Embajada is one of the few places bringing in more locals than tourists. The reason's simple: this card-themed, black-and-red bar and dance floor is a total ace. You can enjoy the comfy white couches on the outdoor terrace while checking out the flatscreen TV or make your way inside (where you'll find yet another bar, another flatscreen, and an elevated DJ booth) to dance, and maybe find that lucky king or queen (or jack?). While the drinks aren't necessarily cheap, you do get to choose from quite the cocktail selection (*€5*)—the sex on *la embajada* (vodka, grenadine, peach liquor, and orange juice) is one of the biggest sellers. If you're visiting in July or August, the Friday-night themed parties make La Embajada one of the hottest spots in town.

✴ If entering Plaza Tutti Frutti from Av. Castilla Perez, it's one of the 1st bars on the right. Ⓢ Beer €3. Cocktails €5. ☼ Open daily 10pm-4:30am.

ESSENTIALS

Practicalities

- **TOURIST OFFICES:** The tourist information office is located on the ground floor of the Ayuntamiento (C. Carmen 1 ☎952 521 531 ▪tourismo@nerja.org ☼ Open M-Sa 10am-2pm and 5-9pm, Su 10am-2pm) and can provide maps, guides, schedules, and general information in English and Spanish.

- **CURRENCY EXCHANGE:** You can exchange money at the **La Caixa Bank** *(i 24hr. ATM available. ⏰ Open M-F 8:15am-2pm)* at Plaza Cavana or visit the exchange office a few doors down *(C. El Bario s/n ☎670 035 922 💻www.easynerja.com ⏰ Open M-Sa 10:15am-1:30pm and 5:30-8:30pm),* which will also help you to book a taxi *(€65)* or minibus *(€100)* to the **Málaga Airport.**
- **INTERNET:** The **public library Salvador Rueda** *(☎952 528 252 💻biblioteca@nerja.es ⏰ Open M-F 10am-2pm and 5-8pm)* is located at Plaza la Ermita, behind the church, and offers free Wi-Fi and three computers. There is a **Time Sport Fitness Center** *(Av. de Pescia, 21 ☎952 522 882 $ 1-day pass €8, 1-week €38; sauna free Tu for men, Th for women. ⏰ Open M-F 8am-11pm, Sa 9am-2pm)* on Av. la Pescia just beyond the intersection with C. Rodriguez Acosta that offers equipment, classes, sauna, and internet access.
- **POST OFFICE:** The post office *(C. Almirante Fernandiz, 6 ☎902 197 197 💻www.corres.es ⏰ Open M-F 8:30am-8:30pm and Sa 9:30am-1pm),* also offers a bank, a **Western Union,** and **Telecor** phone services.

Emergency!

- **EMERGENCY NUMBER:** Ambulance. *(☎902 505 061)*
- **POLICE:** Local police. *(C. Virgen de Pilar, 1 ☎091, 952 521 545 💻policialocal@nerja.org)*
- **LATE-NIGHT PHARMACIES:** While there is not a specific 24hr. pharmacy in Nerja, the six city pharmacies rotate staying open 24hr. on a six-day cycle.

Getting There

Traveling directly to Nerja is limited to buses and cabs. If you need to fly, the nearest **airport** is in Málaga, and you can then take a bus from there. *($ €4. ⏰ Every 30min. 7am-midnight.)* You can also take a RadioTaxi cab *(€70)* between Nerja and the airport. The tourist website *(💻www.nerja.org)* has time tables for trips to and from all nearby cities.

By Bus

You can connect from the bus station *(Av. Pescia s/n ☎902 422 242),* which is actually more of a busline stop, on **Alsa** buses *(💻www.alsa.es)* to: **Málaga** *($ €4. ⏰ 1hr., 23 per day 7am-11pm);* **Granada** *($ €9. ⏰ 2hr., 7 per day 7am-8pm);* **Almeria** *($ €12. ⏰ 4hr., 6 per day 7:45am-7pm);* **Córdoba** *($ €16. ⏰ 4hr. 30min.; 3, 5pm);* **Sevilla** *($ €20. ⏰ 5hr.; 7, 8am, 6pm);* **Madrid** *($ €20. ⏰ 7hr. 30min.; 8, 8:30am, 3, 3:30pm);* or **Barcelona** *($ €75. ⏰ 15hr., 9:30pm).*

Getting Around

Nerja is easily small enough to travel corner to corner on foot. You'll find that many of the winding streets are actually far easier to travel while walking, and you also get to opportunity to window-shop and restaurant-hop along the way. If you decide to hop on a **bus,** there are three main lines around the central part of Nerja. The year-round bus line stops along **Avenida Pescia,** makes a loop around the beach-town center at **Plaza de Ermita, Calle Chaparil,** and back up **Avenida Castilla Perez** *(⏰ M-F 9am-10pm, Sa-Su 10am-10pm),* and is supplemented by an additional summer line *(⏰ M-F 9:30am-2pm).* There is also a line that just circulates the **marina** *(⏰ Daily 9:45am-9:45pm).* Buses run about every 30min. during the summer and every hour during the winter. There are taxi stops at **Plaza Ermita** and at the intersection of **Avenida Castilla Perez** and **Calle Jaen.** The **RadioTaxi Nerja** office *(C. Pintada, 81 ☎952 520 537)* is open 24hr. a day. If visiting by car, there are parking structures all around the city, the largest of which is located at Huertos de Carabeo between **Calle Los Huertos** and **Calle Carabeo.**

VALENCIA AND ALICANTE

From the craggy mountain backdrop of Alicante to the hypermodern playground of Valencia and everywhere along the Costa Blanca in between, the Mediterranean Coast boasts exactly what you would expect—beautiful sandy beaches peppered by hidden alcoves, stretches of water as blue as lapus lazuli, and practically endless white umbrellas. However, the coast is more than a place where you'll have to empty some sand from your shoes. The southwest corner of Spain boasts a little bit of everything, including cheap museums, thriving contemporary culture, booming nightlife, and serene mountain views. With a history dominated by Phoenicians, Carthaginians, Greeks, Romans, and Moors, the area offers a surprising mix of influences that invade plates, palaces, and parties everywhere you turn. A Moorish stronghold from 1094 until 1238 when it was reconquered by Castile, the area still has an Arab influence that sets it apart from its northern neighbors. The next conquest came in the 1930s, when the *Valencianos* became the last region incorporated into Franco's Spanish empire.

Since regaining its autonomy in 1977, Valencia and its surrounding areas have experienced a resurgence of local pride and culture. All along the middle Mediterranean Coast signs and pamphlets sport the local dialect, *valencià*, and killer **paella** and **agua de Valencia** brighten every menu. Charming **cascos antiguos** brim with small, quirky bars, while the brilliant architecture of churches and palatial abodes are converted into sleek new museums. Though Valencia and Alicante are the metropolises along the coast, party destinations such as **Benidorm** and **Sitges** attract hordes of clubhoppers looking to party on the waterfront until the break of dawn.

No matter your destination, expect the possibility of a relatively cheap stay, and plan to use both your Spanish skills and your *siesta* wisely.

greatest hits

- **GARDEN STATE OF MIND.** Valencia's got a great group of gardens where you can escape from the heat and hustle of city life (p. 181).
- **THE REST IS HISTORY.** The archaeological and art museums in Alicante might not help with your tan, but they'll make you look a lot more cultured (p. 190).

Since Spaniards who work regularly take at least a month off in August, it should come as no surprise that students have even more time off, often beginning in July and going through September. And when they're off, they're off—no resumé-padding internships here. Thus, many students go down to the Costa Blanca beaches in Valencia and Alicante to enjoy the virtually rain-free weather, delicious seafood, and beautiful beaches. While on vacation, students wake up late and head to the beach, often lunching on *paella*, a dish emblematic of Spain that originated in Valencia. Watersports are available for the active types, or you can just sleep off your hangover in the sand. During the summer, the party goes all night long at the discos.

valencia ☎96

With the energy of Madrid, the warmth of Sevilla, and the artsy spunk of Barcelona, Valencia is a smaller city that combines the best of its neighbors through a mix of extremes. Layers of history unfold with a short walk through the city, whether from the almost year-round extravagant costumes and sword slinging of the Moors-and-Christians celebrations or from the menus dotted with regional dialect Valencià, both of which are remnants from the clash of Moorish invaders and Catalan crusaders that left an indelible mark both on the city's culture and architectural landscape. Old city gates overlook the plethora of church belltowers scattered throughout the city, while incredible ever-changing street art and quirky architecture like the Art Deco theater shake up the antique charm of plazas in the **Ciutat Vella.** Winding around the northern boundary of the old city is the lush **Jardín del Turia,** and it's hard to believe that not long ago these grassy paths were instead the Río Turia, which was diverted after the river flooded the city with 2m of water in 1957. Located along its former banks is a mix of the best of the old city's artistic treasures, a young and hip university area bustling with student life, and the ultramodern, ultra-contrasting architectural marvel of the **City of the Arts and Sciences.** Despite its beauty and respectable pedigree, the town is anything but a reliquary of heartwarming buildings. Cuisine and culture are matched with incredible beaches, and oranges and Valencian tomatoes will have any produce-lover in rapture for weeks. Sticky paella dots nearly every table in town (as it should; Valencia is its birthplace), while flamenco fills the smallest clubs. With all of this authentic flair, be prepared to practice your Spanish—fewer tourists means fewer English menus.

ORIENTATION

The most convenient way to enter the city is via the Metro to the **Xátiva** or **C. Colon** Metro stations or the train to **Estación del Norte. Avenida Marqués de Sotelo** runs from the train station and **Plaza del Toros** through the **Plaça del Ajuntament,** the center of town. Taking a slight right once you get to the end of this triangle-shaped plaza will have you walking along **C. San Vicente Martir,** leading you to the most bustling areas of town, including the center of architecture, restaurants, and tourism, **Plaza Reina.** To the left upon entering this plaza is a land of shops and pedestrians around **Pl. Doctor Collado,** and continuing inward will take you past the **Mercat Central** into the old city. Plan on bringing a map if you'll be spending time on these confusing streets. To the right upon entering Plaza Reina is **C. Paz,** a big and bright road leading to impressively ritzy architecture and higher-end shops. Continuing straight to the end of the Plaza Reina, past the cathedral, will eventually get you to the old riverbed-now-turned-park **Jardín**

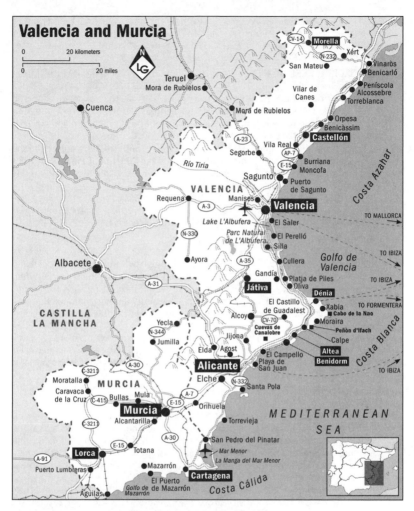

Valencia and Murcia

0 20 kilometers
0 20 miles

TO MALLORCA
TO IBIZA
TO IBIZA
TO FORMENTERA
TO IBIZA

Golfo de Valencia

MEDITERRANEAN SEA

Costa Azahar
Costa Blanca
Costa Cálida

CASTILLA LA MANCHA

VALENCIA
MURCIA

del Turia, and with a right and a 3km walk (or bike or bus ride) you'll make your way along the university area to the modern marvel of the **City of Arts and Sciences.**

ACCOMMODATIONS

RED NEST HOSTEL   ◆�599♥❄ HOSTEL ❶
C. La Paz, 36   ☎96 342 71 68 ■www.nesthostelsvalencia.com

Bright and vibrant, this hostel is so popular—and rightfully so—that it has two locations within a 5min. walk. A mix of large private and dormitory-style rooms features modern decor, windows with beautiful views to the street, and even a convenient cubby for the upper bunks. The inside of the hostel is decorated like a cheery Rubik's cube, only with copious bathrooms and a fully stocked kitchen. A/C in the rooms is sometimes spotty, but a huge fifth-floor lounge keeps things chilly for those afraid of melting away.

🚶 From the train station, walk along Marqués de Sotelo and follow it as it takes a slight right and turns into C. San Vicente Martir. Once you enter the Plaza Reina, take a right onto C. Paz. Red Nest is a 5-10min. walk. ***i*** *Sheets included. Free Wi-Fi; computer with internet €1 per 15min. Kitchen available.* [$] *Dorms €18-25; doubles €60-65. Towel and padlock deposit €5 each.*

HOME BACKPACKERS HOSTEL 💳♿📶 HOSTEL ❶

Pl. Vicente Iborra, 46 ☎96 391 37 97 🖥www.likeathome.net

Four floors of rooms range from cozy six-person dorms to expansive 12-person jungle gyms. The social life centers on the equipped kitchen and the sunny terrace. Though the price is bare-bones, it includes everything you need—sheets, towel, Wi-Fi, and a safebox, as well as a vibrant social scene and pop-art murals to link it to its slightly more mature brother, Home Youth Hostel. Centered in the Old City, the hostel is a little bit farther from the bustling life of Plaza Reina, but this just means more authentic places and cheaper prices for those not already swayed by an entirely English-speaking staff.

🚶 From C. de Caballeros turn onto C. de San Miguel. Take the 2nd left onto C. del Doctor Beltran Bigorra and look for Home Backpackers sign. ***i*** *Linens and towels included. Lockers and safety boxes available.* [$] *12-bed dorms €12.50; 6-bed €16.* ⏰ *Reception 24hr.*

HOME YOUTH HOSTEL 💳🚭📶❄ HOSTEL ❷

C. de la Lonja, 4 ☎96 391 62 29 🖥www.likeathome.net

All the perks of a *pensión* (large, private rooms without having to climb up to the top bunk) with the perks of a youth hostel (a crowd that's actually fun, an equipped kitchen, and punchy decor that will amuse rather than lull you to sleep). Young and social clientele populate the funky leather chairs of the pop-art-clad living room. Rooms facing outward offer an incredible in-your-face view of the Baroque La Lonja across the street.

🚶 From the train station, walk along Av. del Marqués de Sotelo and follow it to take a slight right onto C. Vicente Martir. Take the 3rd left onto C. de los Derechos. Home Youth is located in the plaza. ***i*** *Linens and towels included. Luggage storage and security boxes. Equipped kitchen available.* [$] *3- to 4-bed dorms in summer €23; in winter €15-17. Doubles €30.*

HOSTAL EL CID 💳🚭❄ HOSTAL ❸

C. Cerrajeros, 13 ☎96 392 23 23 🖥www.hostalelcid.es

Besides the charming tiled staircase leading to reception, nothing in this quaint, stylish pension is befitting of the rustic plaster and dark-wood imagery that the name provokes. Homey doubles are decorated with everything from German design magazines to wire dress forms and old card catalogs. Recently transferred to new management, the hostel may be undergoing renovation in the near future.

🚶 From the train station, walk along Av. del Marqués de Sotelo and follow it to take a slight right onto C. Vicente Martir. Take the 2nd left onto C. Cerrajeros and look for El Cid's sign. ***i*** *Linens and towels included.* [$] *Doubles €30-37, with bath €35-47.* ⏰ *Reception 9am-7pm.*

PENSIÓN PARIS 💳🚭📶 PENSIÓN ❷

C. Salvá, 12 ☎96 352 67 66 🖥www.pensionparis.com

Sleep like you're in a crib in the large, immaculately kept rooms with a color palette befitting a cheesy baby shower at Pensión Paris. Quiet rooms with some huge corner suits (think two sets of windows) are perfect for those looking for a calm, cheap, and private refuge from the city while still being in the middle of it all.

🚶 From the train station, walk along C. Marqués de Sotelo. Take a right onto C. de las Barcas halfway through the Plaza del Ayuntament. Take a hard right onto C. del Poeta Querol at the theater and the 1st right onto C. de Miñana. Pensión Paris will be on the left, as the street dead-ends onto C. de Salvá. [$] *Singles €23; doubles with sink €34, with shower €40, with bathroom €42; triples with sink €50, with shower €54.*

RESIDENCIA ALICANTE

PENSIÓN ❸

C. de Ribera, 8

☎96 351 22 96

Standard *pensión*-style rooms with TV. Think twice before opting to pay more for a private bathroom—you might have to climb over the toilet to get to the shower. ⚑ *From the train station, walk along C. Marqués de Sotelo and take the 1st right onto C. del Convento de Santa Clara. Take a left onto C. de Ribera—Residencia Alicante is located next to a busy cafe.* ⓢ *Singles €25-35; doubles €35-45; triples €60.*

SIGHTS

The old city and the area around **Plaza Reina** are dotted with beautiful architectural works and older sites. Lovers of early architecture should be sure to visit **La Lonja** and tour the various **churches** scattered throughout the area, all of which have free admission. The steel and ceramic wonder of the **Mercat Central**, Europe's largest food market, is not to be missed, while the city's top-rated (and dirt-cheap, often free) museums are worth the lost beach time. Of those not listed here, the **Museu de les Bells Arts** and **Ceramic Museum** are top-notch.

CIUDAD DE LAS ARTES Y LAS CIENCIAS

ARCHITECTURE, MUSEUM

Avenida Autopista del Saler, 1

☎90 210 00 31 ◻www.cac.es.

Like a set from a science-fiction film, the futuristic blue and white citadel that comprises the City of the Arts and Sciences may feel like a world away from the rest of the antique charms, winding streets, and shaded plazas of Valencia. And, in all seriousness, it is—designed almost entirely by architect Santiago Calatrava, the white near-algorithmic designs and eerily blue reflecting pool encase a 350,000 sq. m mini-city entirely of its own. The Boba Fett-helmet-esque **Palau de les Arts** begins the complex, housing opera, dance, and musical performances, and is only available with tickets to a performance or through one of their infrequently offered guided tours. Next is the eye-shaped **l'Hemispheric,** housing an IMAX theater, laser shows, and a planetarium. From here, to the left is the honeycomb-meets-postmodernism crib of the hands-on **Museu de les Ciències Princip Felipe,** while the expansive white spine of the **Umbracle** stretches along the street to the right, innocuous by day, but springing into a thriving club at night. Last but not least is Spain's largest aquarium, **L'Oceanographic,** with over 45,500 aquatic creatures. Prices for admission to the ocean complex are steep, but the dolphin shows are top-notch. ⚑ *Bus #35 runs from near Plaza de Toros.* ⓢ *Museum entrance €7.50, students and children €5.80; special exhibits €2 more. L'Hemispheric tickets €7.50, students and children €5.80. L'Oceanographic €23.30, students and children €17.20. Combination tickets €19-30.50; can be bought at train station through Cercanias trains or at box office.* ⓤ *Museum open daily Sept 13-June 30 10am-7pm; July 1-Sept 12 10am-9pm. L'Hemispheric runs shows daily every 45-60min. 10am-midnight except during siesta (2:30-4pm). L'Oceanographic open in high season daily 10am-midnight. Guided tours of Palau de les Arts M-F at 11am, noon, 2pm.*

SANTA IGLESIA CATEDRAL DE VALENCIA

ARCHITECTURE

Pl. de la Reuina

Cathedral ☎96 391 01 89, Museum ☎96 392 43 02

Though many bell towers dot the skyline of Valencia, the Catedral's 70m **Micalet** (cathedral tower) is the biggest and baddest of them all. For €2 you can make the 202-stair trek to the top and see the view from above—Victor Hugo once counted 300 bell towers from the city, and if you stick around until the top of the hour then you will get to hear them in surround sound. The Catedral itself was begun in 1238, after the original Catedral was replaced by a mosque during Muslim rule in the eighth century. Though stepping inside is free, getting an up-close view of the ornate Gothic **Capilla de Sant Caliz** will cost you. It's a small price to pay for getting up close and personal with a chalice purported to be the **Holy Grail** used by Christ at the Last Supper.

➜ Located at the northern end of Plaza de la Reina. $ €4.50 (includes audio tour and museum), children and seniors €3. Tower €2, under 14 €1. ⏰ Cathedral open daily 7:30am-1pm and 4:30-8:30pm. Tower open daily 10am-7pm. Museum open Mar-Nov M-Sa 10am-1pm and 4:30-7pm, Su 10am-1pm and 4:30-5:30pm. Guided visits of cathedral in high season daily 10am-6:30pm; in low season M-F 10am-5:30pm, Su 2-5:30pm.

INSTITUT VALENCIÀ D'ART MODERN (IVAM) 🎟♿❄ MUSEUM

C. Guillém de Castro, 118 ☎96 386 30 00 🖥www.ivam.es

Come see a huge amount of contemporary art for less than you'd pay to rent a towel at your hostel. Permanent galleries house a famed collection of abstract works by 20th-century sculptor Julio Gonzalez and artist Ignacio Pinazo, while temporary exhibits fill the remaining galleries with avant-garde works from the 20th and 21st centuries, including sculpture, painting, video, and architectural works. Even if only a few galleries are open during your visit (which may happen—this museum's exhibits are constantly in flux), it's well worth the trip.

➜ Leaving the Basilica, take C. Caballeros until it turns into C. Quart. Walk under the Torres de Quart and take a right down C. Guillem de Castro; the museum is on the right. Bus #5 from Pl. del Ajuntament. $ €2, students €1; free on Su. ⏰ Open Tu-Su 10am-10pm. Library open M-Th 10am-2pm, F 10am-3pm.

PLAZA DE TOROS AND MUSEO TAURINO DE VALENCIA 🎟 MUSEUM

C. Xàtiva ☎96 388 37 38 🖥www.museotaurinovalencia.es

A permanent exhibition offers a peek both behind and in front of the scenes of Valencian bullfighting. Articles in the permanent collection range from *El Morenillo* Juan Jimenez's 1852 waistcoat to a life-size stuffed bull ready to spring into action. Look for the multilingual briefers on the history, traditions, and methods of the sport, from the training of a young *picador* to the path of a bull from birth to (possible) pardoning in the ring. If you're not planning on attending a show, sneak peeks of the ring are also offered every half hour.

➜ [M]Xàtiva. In covered area to left of Plaza de Torros when facing the rink from C. Xátiva; museum is halfway down to the right. $ Free. ⏰ Open Tu-Su 10am-8pm. Guided tours of bullring every 30min.

THE GREAT OUTDOORS

Beaches

Chances are if it's summer and you're in Valencia, then your hostel will empty out midday as beach bums make the pilgrimage to the city's shores. The cream-colored sand fills with white umbrellas during the peak season, with sunbathers and outdoor enthusiasts splashing in the azure water and walking, biking, and running along the boardwalk that creeps along the expansive beach. If you're planning on walking or biking to the beach, **Avenida del Puerto** runs from the riverbed to the port, after which the beach is just a few blocks north; otherwise, buses #20, 21, and 22 will drop you off seaside. (*⏰ About 15min. from city center.*) **Las Arenas** is the most popular beach and is connected by the boardwalk to **La Malvarossa,** which provides water to the sea creatures of L'Oceanographic in the **City of Arts and Sciences.** Although you won't get any alone time by heading the 14km south to **Salér,** the view will be much more attractive, including a beautiful pebbled beach, white sand dunes, and a calm lagoon. The **Autocares Herca** bus runs to **Salér** (*➜ On the way to El Perello. ⏰ 30min., every hr. 7am-9pm. $ €1-1.10, depending on destination*) from the intersection of Gran Vía de Germanías and C. Sueca. To get to the bus stop, exit the train station and take a right down C. Xàtiva, then turn right onto C. Ruzafa to Gran Vía. Look for a yellow MetroBus post. The ride to Salér can be jammed on weekends, and be sure to leave an entire day to make it worth the trip. For those adventurers seeking the beauty of Salér without the crowds, continue 10min. further on the bus for Salér and walk for another half hour along the shore—the undeveloped **La Devesa** sports a luxurious beach with a nudist section, as well as an incredible forest and lake. However, don't expect the beach bars and capitalist comforts of the city beaches—be sure to bring your own food, and be prepared to use the forest to take care of business. When looking for the return bus, look toward the intersection of the main road and the beginning of the forest trail.

Parks

JARDÍN DEL TURIA ♿

Jardín del Turia is easy to stumble upon, wrapping around the northern portion of the old city where the river used to be before being diverted. Lined with lush grass, pedestrian paths, and stray kittens, this park is now a favorite with casual athletes and bike tours.

➜ Just north of the cathedral.

JARDINES DEL REAL ♿

Near the Museo de Bellas Artes and off C. Sant Pío are the Jardines del Real, with maze-like paths dotted by modern sculpture, equally abstract ponds, and a fountain resembling a big rubber ducky dedicated to Walt Disney to keep things from getting too intellectual.

➜ Walk to the river on C. del Salvador behind the cathedral and continue to Ptg. Trinidad. Take a right onto C. Sant Pio V and enter just past the museum.

JARDÍN BOTÀNIC ♿

C. Quart, 80 ☎96 315 68 17 🖥www.uv.es/jardibotanic

Jardín Botànic is the most impressive of the parks, with over 43,000 kinds of plants of 300 international species blossoming with reckless abandon. Budding horticulturists should be sure to bring along your dichotomy chart, while others can simply kick back and relax under the shade on one of their many benches.

➜ Go left out of the Po. de Pechina, exit down Gran Via, and take a left onto C. Quart—the gardens are on the western end of Río Turia near Gran Vía Fernando el Católico. $ €0.60. ⏰ Open Tu-Su May-Aug 10am-9pm, Sept-Oct and Mar-Apr 10am-8pm; Nov-Feb 10am-6pm.

FOOD

Paella, paella, paella, *agua de Valencia*. These are the words that will be pounded into your skull as you trek the paths of the city, with large black pans of yellow rice and seafood splayed out on nearly every table and jars of the area's famed alcoholic drink being offered at every bar. If you're looking for something lighter, try grabbing some fresh fruits and veggies from the gorgeous Art Nouveau **Mercat Central,** the largest food market in Europe since 1928. *(☎96 382 91 00 ⏰ Open M-Sa 6am-2:30pm.)* For **groceries,** try **El Corte Ingles** *(C. Pintor Sorolla ☎96 315 95 00)* or the smaller **Mercadona** *(C. el Poeta ⏰ Open M-Sa 9:15am-9:15pm).*

✓ SAGARDI — TAPAS ❷

C. San Vicente Martir, 6 ☎96 391 06 68 🖥www.sagardi.com

Delectable Basque-inspired tapas wallpaper the bar—be prepared to fight for a seat, or join the locals and stand as you fill your plate with *pinxos*. Inventive bread-bottomed boats of love float into your mouth on a sea of nectarly sangria.

➜ On San Vicente Martir on the left shortly before Plaza Reina. $ Pinxos €1.80. Sangria €3. ⏰ Open daily 11:30am-3:30pm and 7:30pm-1:30am.

✓ SOL I LLUNA — CAFE ❷

C. del Mar, 29 ☎96 392 22 16 🖥www.solilluna.net

A two-story interior with A/C offers a relaxed, shabby-chic alternative to the peaceful but sunny plaza seating outside. White wooden wicker chairs and black tables provide the perfect place to take advantage of free Wi-Fi during slower hours. Delectable tapas and smaller entrees please business lunchers, while a bustling nightlife scene brings a crowd of laid-back locals. Get the falafel if it's on the menu for the day—you'll never want to eat from another kebab stand again.

Take a right onto C. del Mar from Plaza Reina when facing the cathedral from the far end near C. San Vicente Martir. Sol i Lluna is located in the small plaza. $ Tapas €3.50-5.50. Entrees €6.50-13.50. Midday menú half €7, full €10. ⏰ Open M 2-4pm, Tu-Sa 2-4pm and 9pm-last customer.

LA LLUNA — VEGETARIAN, VALENCIAN ❷

C. San Ramón, 23 — ☎96 392 21 46

A taste of traditional Valencia, *sin carne*. This tucked-away vegetarian eatery serves fresh, delicious seafood-less paella, gazpacho, *creama catalana*, and more to a pack of dedicated locals and map-carting travelers. A bohemian, dark-raftered interior is splattered with moon memorabilia, while the lone waiter struggles to stay afloat in the crowded sea of tables.

From Plaza Tossal in the old city, walk on C. Alta and take a left onto C. Corona. Follow C. San Ramon as it curves to the right; La Lluna is on the left. $ Appetizers €4-6; entrees €4-6. Dessert €3.50-4. Midday menú €7.20. ⏰ Hours vary; call for weekly schedule.

ZUMERIA NATURALIA — CAFE ❶

C. del Mar, 2 — ☎96 141 45 03

Incredible crepes and *bocadillos* spotlight the thing that keeps customers coming back—over 50 fresh, tasty fruit drinks are at your disposal, served in huge crystal goblets. Perfect for a light dinner. Get the night started with a smoothie mixed drink *(€5-6.50)*, and don't be surprised if you can't stop at just one. Outdoor seating on the calm street outside provides overflow for when the tightly packed wicker chairs get too full for comfort.

When facing the cathedral in Plaza Reina, C. del Mar is about halfway through the square on the right. Zumeria Naturalia is immediately on the right, tucked into the lower level on the marble facade. Look for chairs and their sign. $ Juices €3-4, with alcohol €5-6.50. ⏰ Open M-Th 5pm-1am, F-Sa 5pm-3am, Su 5pm-midnight.

EL RALL — VALENCIAN ❸

C. Tundidores, 2 — ☎96 392 20 90 www.elrall.es

A popular paella eatery with a lively crowd that spills out onto their secluded plaza. Rice dishes are brought out in skillets based on the size of the group, though parties of one will be left ordering a la carte. If the passing guitar and accordion players aren't properly setting the mood, intimate seating is also available inside.

From the Mercado Central, take the road to the right of Lonja de la Seda (C. Pere Compte) and follow as it becomes Estameñería Vieja. Once in the plaza, El Rall is to the right, on C. Tundidores. i Reservations recommended. $ Appetizers €8.50-15; meat and fish entrees €13-16. Paella €12-15 per person (min. 2 people). Picaditas €8.50-15. ⏰ Open daily 1-4:30pm and 8-11:30pm.

LA PAPPARDELLA — ITALIAN ❸

C. Bordadores, 5 — ☎96 391 89 15 www.ciciositalianos.com

A huge selection of tasty pastas from gnocchi to rigatoni, as well as the crostini-like *piadine*, offer a taste of something (comparatively) exotic in the tourist haven around Plaza de la Reina. Two levels with bright modern decor and wooden floors offer ample seating and sometimes impeccable views, though if you fight for an outdoor spot, you'll likely be serenaded by accordion songs from next door while looking out over the construction site behind the cathedral.

When facing the cathedral in Plaza Reina, take the road to the left that runs in front of the church, C. de la Correjería. The first right is C. Bordadores—turn onto it, Pappardella is on the left. i Gluten-free options available. $ Salads €6.80-10. Entrees €7-13. Midday menú €14. ⏰ Open daily 2-4pm and 9pm-midnight.

NIGHTLIFE

There is a reason why hostels are littered with bodies sleeping through the siestas during midday. Valencia's nightlife starts off late, with bars and pubs not hitting their stride until around midnight. Check the pedestrian areas around **Plaza de la Virgen** and **C. de Caballeros** for big, bright places and crowds of fellow travelers to start off the night with the region's famed *agua de Valencia*. The old city hides a plethora of smaller, quirkier bars and nightclubs, especially around **Plaza Tossal** and **Collado**, attracting hordes of clubhoppers. **Dance clubs** remain painfully empty until 1 or 2am and become packed shortly thereafter. For calmer destinations, check around plazas in the old quarter, and for some more intense action, scout out the university area around **Avinguda Blasco Ibañez**. For a list of events, check out *Valencia City (€0.50)*, available at newsstands and tourist offices, and the free monthly *24/7 Valencia* available at internet cafes, tourist booths, and some hostels.

CAFE DEL DUENDE ◆👌♈❀ BAR, FLAMENCO

C. Turia, 62 ☎63 045 52 89 💻www.cafedelduende.com

Intimate, upbeat bar dedicated to its dance and drink. This local favorite gives the best deal in town, bringing together flamenco so close you can touch the performers, a crowd that knows how to clap and sing along, and beer, all for just €7. Show up early to get a seat; otherwise, stand, stomp, and join the show.

🍴 *From the center of town, take a left onto C. de Quart and a right onto C. del Turia at the Jardín Botànic. Cafe del Duende is at the far end of the garden.* 👆 *Flamenco Th-F, some Sa at 11:30pm. Distributes Alma 100 and Flama, free monthly publications about flamenco. Schedule of performances on website.* 💲 *Flamenco show €7; includes 1 drink.* 🕐 *Open Th 10pm-2:30am, F-Sa 10pm-3:30am, Su 6-11pm.*

RADIO CITY 👌♈❀ CLUB

C. Santa Teresa, 19 ☎96 391 41 51 💻www.radiocityvalencia.com

One bar up front and two on the dance floor keep the youth moving to alternative American pop like Gnarls Barkley and Gorillaz with cheap mini-mojitos flowing freely. Kitschy painted tiles cover the ceiling, and a small border running around the club gives free kama sutra lessons for those looking to pick up some moves.

🍴 *From the Mercado Central, take a left onto C. de Belluga across from the church. Take a right onto C. Santa Teresa.* 👆 *Flamenco Tu 11pm, Bass City W nights 12:30am.* 💲 *€7 min. drink purchase. Cocktails €5-7. Beer €3-4.* 🕐 *Open daily 10pm-2:30am.*

L'UMBRACLE TERRAZA ◆👌♈△ CLUB, BAR

Av. de Saler, 5 ☎67 166 80 00 💻www.umbracleterrazza.com

Nestled right next to the dazzling white and geometric modern architecture of the City of Arts and Sciences, the open-air L'Umbracle Terraza offers dazzling views of the city's unnaturally striking (and illuminated) setting. The nightclub is more than just a place to do some sightseeing—swanky white tables and chairs dot the patio, while lower couch-beds invite bedazzled guests to kick back, relax, take in some hookah, and prepare for the move to **Mya**, the bustling nightclub below.

🍴 *#35 bus to City of Arts and Sciences from near Xàtiva. Located in outside garden parallel to the city.* 👆 *List of events available on website.* 💲 *Cover €15.* 🕐 *L'Umbracle open Apr-Sept M-Sa 11:30pm-late. Mya open daily Th-Sa 1am-later.*

JOHNNY MARACAS ◆👌♈❀ BAR, CLUB

C. de Caballeros, 39 ☎96 391 52 66

The maracas and miniature bongos lining the bamboo walls aren't just for show—you might hear a beat from the bartenders if the feeling is right. A relaxing cave-dweller-meets-Havana-chic atmosphere that's more classy than kitsch provides a chill alternative to the often-suffocating bar dance floors elsewhere, with killer mojitos and a fish tank under your drink to sweeten the deal. Latin beats serenade drinkers every night of the week, and don't be surprised if you stumble across a salsa lesson.

From the Mercado Central, follow C. de Maria Cristina past the church and take a slight right onto C. Bolsería. At the plaza, take a right onto C. Caballeros and walk just a few seconds. Johnny Maracas is on the right before Fox Congo. $ Beer €3-4. Mixed drinks €6-7. ⏰ Open M-Th 7pm-3am, F-Su 7pm-4am.

AKUARELA CLUB, BAR

Pub at C. Juan Llorens, 48; disco at Eugenia Viñes, 152 ☎96 385 93 85 🖥www.akuarela.es

Located along Malvarrosa Beach, Akuarela isn't an easy stumble from your hostel—plan on paying for a ride to get to the party. Once you arrive on your magical steed, plan to stay the night (and morning). During the summer this party center boasts a pub, club, and a beachside party zone, and during the winter the pub and club still wait at your disposal. Four floors of dancing with remarkably classy decor, complete with bars and plush seating at each level, make for a hard but tasteful night, with a huge rooftop terrace to catch a breather. Expect a mix of every danceable music imaginable, with a focus on Spanish styles—from Valencia's own artists to electronica, R and B, and salsa.

Taxi ride to Plaza Malvarossa. i Flyer gains free entrance until 3am and €3 discounts on drinks after. $ No cover at pub, but 1-drink min. Free entrance to club with €7 purchase at pub; otherwise Th-Sa €13, after 3am €16. ⏰ Pub open daily 6pm-3:30am. Club open Sa midnight-7-:30am. Beach club open daily in summer midnight-7:30am.

BOLSERIA CAFE CAFE

C. Bolsería, 41 ☎96 391 89 03

Terraced seating hosts an upscale cafe and a chic bar by night—expect button-up shirts, shiny tops, and dismissal at the door if you're wearing a threadbare, ratty T-shirt. Dancing takes place in the nautical-themed, steel-clad, and rose-decked back room, though you will be lucky if there is standing room as the cafe gets packed later in the night.

From the Mercado Central, follow C. de Maria Cristina past the church and take a slight right onto C. Bolsería. The cafe is on the corner in the plaza. i Free agua de Valencia before 12:30am. Salsa on M, 1-drink min. Americana night on W. $ Beer €4.50. Mixed drinks €6. ⏰ Open daily 7pm-3:30am.

FOX CONGO CLUB

C. Caballeros, 35 ☎96 391 85 67

Hop up onto the back benches and shimmy your hips to get the night started off right. Fox Congo fills up quick and early for those looking to get into their groove before others have stopped their barhopping. Chemically lit marble and metal walls set the stage while dancey pop plays to an open, international crowd of hostelers and locals who move to equally diverse (and sometimes clashing) rhythms.

From the Mercado Central, follow C. de Maria Cristina past the church and take a slight right onto C. Bolsería. At the plaza, take a right onto C. Caballeros and walk just a few seconds. Fox Congo is on the right. $ Beer €4. Mixed drinks €7. ⏰ Open Tu-Sa 8pm-3:30am.

CAFE NEGRITO BAR

Pl. Negrito, 1 ☎96 391 42 33

Popular cafe and even more popular late night hangout, Negrito draws a younger crowd with industrial metal walls and a pop-art mentality. A wide selection of reasonably priced drinks keeps things interesting—if you arrive early, grab one of their silver tables out in the calm courtyard, but if you show up late, plan to fight for a spot even to stand.

From in front of La Lonja, take the road to the right (C. Pere Compte) and continue as it becomes C. Estameñerá Vieja, C. de la Purísima, and then C. de Calatrava. When you enter the plaza, the cafe is on the right. $ Beer €2-3. Mixed drinks €4-6. Agua de Valencia €7. ⏰ Open daily 3pm-3:30am.

FESTIVALS

Like virtually any Spanish city, Valencia literally lights up during the **Fogueres de San Juan** with bonfires, fireworks, and all the other sorts of fires you can imagine. The **Semana Santa,** in the week preceding Easter, litters the city with children's theater and monks reenacting biblical scenes, while **Virgin de los Desamparados (Our Lady of the Forsaken)** (May 11) brings masses of worshippers to follow the flower-blanketed path of the Virgin Mary's likeness from the Basilica in the Plaza de la Virgen to the cathedral.

LAS FALLAS — SPRING

Spaniards love their fire, so how could a festival dedicated San José, the patron saint of carpenters, disappoint? Reportedly following the tradition of local 16th-century carpenters burning wood that had accumulated over the year, Valencia's citizens erect *fallas* (huge wooden cardboard and papier-mâché figures) across the city just to burn them down. The real party begins the last Sunday in February just outside of the Torres de Serranos, after which *mascletas* (fireworks displays) are shown daily at 2am in the Pl. del Ayuntamiento until the festival's conclusion. Nightly showers of light illuminate the Turia Gardens, culminating in the appropriately named *Nit del Foc* (night of fire) on March 18 and the burning of the *fallas* at midnight, ringing in San José's day with a bang.

⏰ *Mar 12-19.*

BATTLE OF THE TOMATOES — SUMMER

This isn't your average middle-school food fight. Now in its 65th year, the Battle of the Tomatoes in nearby Buñol brings a flock of locals and travelers alike armed with goggles, strong arms, and a change of clothes. The day kicks off on the last Wednesday in August at 11am with a brave soul snatching a ham from the top of a greased pole, after which hundreds of tons of tomatoes pour from the back of a truck and the hurling begins. Parades of the city's *gigantes* (giants) and *cabezudos* (masked figures who carry a stick or pig bladder and chase people) add a regal spin to the veritable mess.

⇆ *Train to Buñol from Estación del Norte.* ⏰ *Last W in Aug.*

FIESTIU DE JULIOL — SUMMER

Originally a flower and produce fair devised in 1871, Fiestiu de Juliol (July Fest) has come a long way from old ladies and fruit stands. Concerts and open-air cinema dot the city's gardens and the Palau de la Música, while regular events on beaches and parties keep the festivities rolling well into the night. Bullfights occur daily, and the festival concludes with a float-filled parade along Paseo de la Alameda and the 120-year-old *batalla dels flors* (battle of the flowers), in which young girls shower the crowd with flowers from their stately carriages.

⏰ *July 8-24.*

ESSENTIALS

Practicalities

- **TOURIST OFFICES:** The **Regional Office** provides information on events, lodging, and other points of interest and can also help you find a place to stay. *(C. de la Paz, 48 ☎96 398 64 22 🖥www.comunitatvalenciana.com ⏰ Open M-F 9am-8pm, Sa 10am-8pm, Su 10am-2pm.)* **Branch at Estación del Nord.** *(C. Xátiva, 24 ☎96 352 85 73 🖥www.turisvalencia.es ⏰ Open M-Sa 9am-7pm, Su 10am-2pm.)* **Branch at Plaza Reina.** *(Pl. Reina, 19 ☎96 315 39 31 ⏰ Open M-Sa 9am-7pm, Su 10am-2pm.)*
- **LUGGAGE STORAGE: The bus and train stations** provide 24hr. storage of your stuff for a small fee. *($ €2.50-5, depending on size of luggage. ⏰ Open daily 5am-1am.)*

- **LAUNDROMAT: The L@undry Stop** provides internet so you can Facebook away the hours while your clothes get clean. *(C. Baja, 17 ☎96 391 35 28* ◼*www.myspace. com/thelaundrystop* ⓲ *Wi-Fi available.* ⓢ *Wash €4. Dry €3. Soap €0.50. Internet €.50 for 20min.* ⓺ *Open daily 9:30am-10pm.)*

- **INTERNET ACCESS:** The **Work Center** provides an entire range of services and supplies for any businessperson or rogue backpacker, from printing to pens to computer stations. *(C. Xàtiva, 19 ☎96 112 08 30* ◼*www.workcenter.es* ⓢ *Internet access €3 per hr. Wi-Fi available.* ⓺ *Open M-Th 24hr., F 7am-11pm, Sa 10am-2pm and 5-9pm, Su noon-2pm and 5-11pm.)*

- **POST OFFICE:** The main branch offers a step above the normal services, with Western Union and call center in a locale fit for a king. *(Pl. del Ajuntament, 24 ☎96 351 23 70* ◼*www.correos.es* ⓺ *Open M-F 8:30am-8:30pm, Sa 9:30am-2pm.)*

- **POSTAL CODE: Center** 46002; **Renfe** 46007; **Ruzafa** 46005.

Emergency!

- **EMERGENCY NUMBERS:** ☎112 or ☎96 152 51 59.

- **POLICE:** Contact the **police** near Pg. de Alameda *(Pg. de Alameda, 17 ☎96 360 03 50* ⚓ ⓶*Alameda)* or C. Maestre *(C. Maestre, 2 ☎96 315 56 90* ⚓ ⓶*Av. del Cid).*

- **CRISIS LINES:** Call the **Red Cross Ambulance.** *(☎96 367 73 75.)*

- **LATE-NIGHT PHARMACIES:** **Late-night pharmacies** rotate by night—check listing in local paper *Levante (€1)* or the *farmacias de guardia* schedule posted outside any pharmacy around the Pl. de la Reina and Pl. de la Virgen *(☎96 391 68 21).* **Info Salud** provides health info *(☎96 391 68 21).*

- **HOSPITAL/MEDICAL SERVICES:** Contact the **Hospital Clínico Universitario** *(Av. Blasco Ibáñez, 17 ☎96 386 39 00).*

Getting There

By Plane

If you are flying to Valencia, you are probably flying on **Aena** into the **Aeropuerto de Manises/Airport of Valencia** *(☎96 159 85 00* ◼*www.aena.es)*, 8km from the city. **Bus #150** *(☎96 150 00 82)* runs between the airport and the bus station. *(*ⓢ *€1.20.*⓺ *35min., every 30min. 5:25am-11:55pm.)* The **Metro** line #3 or #5 goes straight from the airport to C. Xàtiva, on the outskirts of Valencia by the *Ajuntament.* *(*ⓢ *€1.80.)* You can also take a **taxi** from the airport to city center. *(*ⓢ *About €15.)*

By Train

RENFE runs from **Estación del Norte.** *(C. Xátiva, 24 ☎96 352 02 02* ◼*www.renfe.es)* Trains from: **Alicante** *(*ⓢ *€13-28.* ⓺ *2hr., 11 per day 7am-9pm);* **Barcelona** *(*ⓢ *€24-43.* ⓺ *3-5hr., every 1-2hr. 5am-8pm);* **Granada** *(*ⓢ *€51.* ⓺ *8hr., 12:44am);* **Madrid** *(*ⓢ *€25-48.* ⓺ *3½-6hr., every hr. 6:50am-8:20pm).* Allot time to go through security.

By Bus

Take buses to the **Estación Terminal d'Autobuses.** *(Av. Menéndez Pidal, 11 ☎96 346 62 66* ⚓ *Across the riverbed, a 20min. walk from the city center.)* Municipal bus #8 runs from Pl. del Ajuntament and the bus station. *(*ⓢ *€1.10.)* **ALSA** *(☎90 242 22 42* ◼*www.alsa.es)* has bus services from **Alicante** *(* ⓢ *€18-21.* ⓺ *2½-5hr., every hr. 6am-9pm),* **Barcelona** *(*ⓢ *€25-30.* ⓺ *4-6hr., every 2-3hr. 7am-8pm),* and **Málaga** *(*ⓢ *€52.* ⓺ *11-13hr., 5 per day 8am-11:30pm).* **Autores** *(☎96 349 22 30* ◼*www.auto-res.net)* goes to **Madrid.** *(*ⓢ *€23.* ⓺*4hr., 10 per day 10:30am-3am.)*

By Ferry

Trasmediterránea offers a ferry service to Valencia *(Muelle de Poniente ☎90 245 46 45 🖳www.trasmediterranea.es).* Take bus #4 from Pl. del Ajuntament or #1 or 2 from the bus station. Reserve through a travel agency or risk inconvenience by buying tickets at the port on the day of departure.

Getting Around

For complete information and routes for Valencia's public transportation, contact the **Municipal Transport of Valencia (EMT) Office.** *(Pl. Correo Viejo, 5 ☎96 315 85 15; 96 315 85 25 🖳www.emtvalencia.es ⏰ Open M-F 9am-2pm and 4:30-7:30pm.)*

By Bus

Bus schedules depend on day and route. The **tourist routes** are 5, 5B, 25, and 95, while **Bus #8** *(⏰ Every 9-11min. 6am-10:30pm)* runs to the bus station. Buses #20, 21, and 22 *(⏰ Every 10-12 min. 9am-8:40pm)* go to **Las Arenas** and **Malvarrosa** along Pg. Marítim. Buy tickets *(€1.25)* on board or a one-day pass at newsstands *(€3.50).* **Late-night buses** N1, N2, N3, N4, N5, N6, and N7 go through **Pl. del Ajuntament** *(⏰ Every 45 min. M-W 11pm-1am, Th-Sa 11pm-3am, Su 11pm-1am).*

By Metro

The Metro *(P. de Xirivelleta ☎96 397 40 40 🖳www.metrovalencia.com)* service loops around the *casco antiguo* (old quarter) and into the outskirts. The most central stop is on C. Xàtiva across the street from the train station or on C. Colón by El Corte Inglés. Buy tickets from machines in any station. *($ €1.25-1.70 depending on distance. 10-ride pass €7.45-10.)*

By Taxi

Contact **Radio Taxi** *(☎96 370 33 33),* **Tele Taxi** *(☎96 357 13 13),* **Onda Taxi** *(☎96 347 52 52),* and **Buscataxi** *(☎90 274 77 47)* for pickup and rates.

By Bike

Rent bikes from **Orange Bikes** *(C. Santa Teresa, 8 ☎96 391 75 51 🖳www.orangebikes.net ⇄ From the main entrance of the Mercado Central, walk down Av. María Cristina away from Pl. Ajuntamiento and turn down the 2nd street, continuing on to the end. From Pl. de la Virgen, take C. Caballeros until it turns into C. Santa Teresa. $ Bikes €9-12 per day, €45-55 per week. ⏰ Open M-F 9:30am-2:30pm and 4:30-8pm, Sa 10am-2pm and 7-7:30pm)* or **Doyoubike** *(Corner of C. Musico Magenti and Puebla Larga ☎96 337 40 24 🖳www.doyoubike.com $ M-Th €2 per hr., €10 per day, F-Su €4 per hr., €15 per day. Weekend €25, week €40).*

alicante ☎96

The most iconic image of Alicante—the craggy Castillo Santa Barbara rising above the bustling nightlife and brilliant beaches of the modern city—is also the reason Alicante's become such a huge tourist destination. Surrounding mountains and lush pine forests make an outdoorsy complement to lazy days in the sand, while loads of free museums and attractions grab those looking to pack up their beach bags and beat the heat—the only site that charges admission is the world-famous **MARQ,** which is well worth the €3 price tag.

Just after sunset, the streets in the old city teem with groups of young things crawling to fill restaurants, cozy bars, and hopping clubs, while the bright *discotecas* of the port fill with tourists and locals as the night marches on. Though a busy party and sunbathing destination in its own right, Alicante has also become the home base for those looking to tap all of the summer resources of the **Costa Blanca,** or "White Coast," that stretches from Dènia to Alicante, named for the color of the fine sand that pads its shores. While the other towns along the water, such as Altea and Dénia,

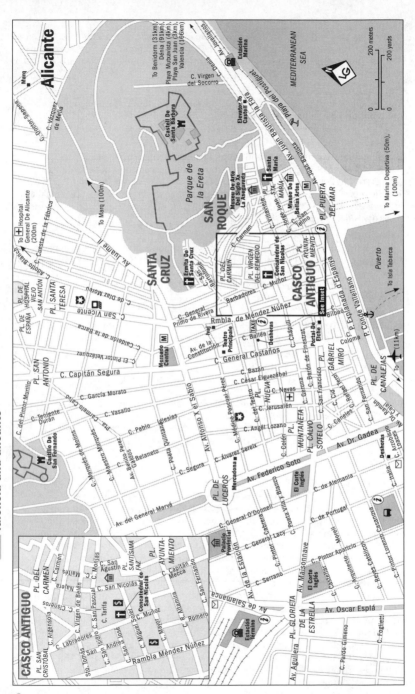

valencia and alicante

Alicante

make for more relaxed, secluded, and clean beachgoing, Alicante boasts cheap, sometimes quirky, and incredibly social accommodations just a short TRAM ride away that trump the rising prices of those developing resort destinations.

ORIENTATION

For those traveling from afar, trains arrive at the **Estación Central,** located on the western edge of the city on **Avenida Salamanca.** A short walk down this road will take you to **Pl. Luceros,** which intersects with **Avenida Federico Soto,** which runs straight to the beach (becoming **Av. Doctor Gadea** near the water) and close to the **bus station** on C. Portugal. Continuing straight through Pl. Luceros will have you walking along **Avenida Alfonso X el Sabio,** the main artery of the city. Walking 10-15min. will drop you off in front of the Mercat Central and **TRAM Station** (where trains from Costa Blanca arrive), while a right just past the market onto **Rambla Méndez Núñez,** known simply as La Rambla, provides a plethora of huge shops and restaurants as well as easy access to the cozier and more interesting options of the *casco antiquo.* If you decide to take the pedestrian **C. Casaños** between La Rambla and Av. Frederico Soto, a world of ritzy restaurants awaits, with cheap shops and food located on any of the side streets. If sand and sun is your destination, the red marble floors and shop-laden path of the **Explanada d'Espanya** run nearly 2km across the port, linking the **Parque de las Canalejas** to the beach and providing access to the looming **Castillo Santa Barbara's** elevator.

ACCOMMODATIONS

Quality hostels and pensions with good prices abound in the *casco antiguo*—if you feel overwhelmed by the selection, stop by the tourist office to get an extensive brochure on accommodations in the area. If you have a specific place in mind, be sure to book at least a week ahead of time, as the appeal of sandy beaches fills up the better hostels during the summer months. If arriving during the **Fogueres de Sant Joan** *(June 18-25)*, be sure to book well in advance or risk sleeping on the beach.

PENSIÓN VERSAILLES

⊕Ⓧ⒯⌂ PENSIÓN ❷

C. Villavieja, 3 ☎96 521 47 93, 93 96 532 98 00

A laid-back, beach-appropriate tropical paradise just minutes from the water and in the heart of the old city's bumping nightlife. Pensión Versailles mixes the two perfectly—12 quirky, bare-bones rooms sport bright, breezy decor while lacking work-related things like outlets. A communal kitchen and gorgeous open terrace contribute to a family feel, with an owner that seems more like a fun-loving grandpa than a business owner. Like any family arrangement, he'll be sure to know your name before you leave (and will be sure to greet you by it when you return on your next trip).

⚑ *From La Rambla, walk toward the mountain on C. San Isidro and follow it as it becomes C. San Pascua and then C. Villavieja; it's on your left.* ⓘ *Linens and towels included. Free Wi-Fi, but it doesn't often work. Free internet.* ⑤ *4-bed dorms €23; singles €25; doubles €50.* ⌚ *Terrace open until midnight.*

HOSTAL LES MONGES PALACE

Ⓧ⒯❋ HOSTAL ❸

C. San Agustín, 4 ☎96 521 50 46 ▣www.lesmonges.es

With a name like "Les Monges Palace," you should expect nothing less than palatial, and that's exactly what Les Monges provides. Chic rooms with modern decor, low Japanese-style beds, and anti-kitsch wicker furniture make for a world away from the ascetic monastery it faces. All rooms include A/C, plush towels, and sleek TVs, and for those willing to splurge, two of the doubles even come with an ensuite sauna and hot tub.

⚑ *From La Rambla, walk toward the mountain on C. San Isidro and follow it as it becomes C. San Pascual. The hostal is on the corner of C. San Pascual and C. San Agostin.* ⓘ *Continental breakfast €6. Towels included. Internet €3 per hr.* ⑤ *Singles €36; doubles €52, with private bath €59, with sauna and hot tub €98; triples €68, with bath €70.* ⌚ *Reception 24hr.*

CALDERON 41 ⊗⊗📶 HOSTEL [1]

C. Calderon, 41 💻www.hostelworld.com

You get what you pay for, and, considering the comfy beds, clean rooms, and pleasant, youthful decor, Calderon is allowed to have its faults. A helpful, accommodating staff will lend you whatever they lack, whether a hotplate for a makeshift kitchen, a spot in their room to store your bag, or time on their laptop. Just don't expect them to make another shower magically appear—one is all they have for the whole hostel—and be sure to insist on a room with a window.

➜ *Face the front of the Mercado and take the road that runs to its left (C. Calderón de la Barca). Follow as it bends to the right and continue walking until just before the Plaza Espanya. The hostel is behind an unmarked door immediately after the casino Calderon 41.* ***i*** *Linens included. Luggage storage available. Free Wi-Fi.* $ *Dorms €15.*

HOSTAL-PENSIÓN LA MILAGROSA 💳♿📶❄ HOSTAL [1]

C. Villavieja, 8 ☎96 5216 918 💻www.hostallamilagrosa.com

Pristine rooms with minimal decoration (hope you enjoy looking at yourself; only a mirror serves to spruce things up), but the view speaks for itself—ask for a room facing the Baroque Basilica Santa Maria. Even if you don't get your pick, you can always scope out the view (and a fantastic shot of the craggy fortress looming overhead) from the roomy rooftop terrace, complete with sun, shade, and an impressively equipped kitchen.

➜ *From La Rambla, walk toward the mountain on C. San Isidro and follow it as it becomes C. San Pascua and then C. Villavieja; the hostel is on your right.* ***i*** *Towels included. Laundry wash €3, dry €2. Kitchen and terrace available.* $ *Singles €20, with private bath €30; doubles €35/45; triples €45/60; 2-person apartment €60.* ⏰ *Reception 24hr.*

SIGHTS 👁

👍 MUSEO ARQUEOLÓGICO DE ALICANTE (MARQ) 💳♿❄ MUSEUM

Plaza del Doctor Gómez Ulla ☎96 514 90 00 💻www.marqalicante.com

Inside this pristine and expansive villa lays the ultramodern exhibition halls of the Museo Arqueológico Provincial de Alicante (MARQ)—named European Museum of the Year in 2004. Step inside to see the beautifully arranged and catalogued collections from the Paleolithic, Iberian, Roman, Islamic, and modern periods that are brought to life with tasteful murals, audio, and videos. More than a moratorium for a distant past, the MARQ includes informative and interactive dioramas on methodology and the practice of archaeology, transporting visitors via time capsule to a shipwreck, through the years of a church's architectural evolution, and even to a modern dig site. Temporary traveling exhibits give you a reason to keep coming back. Snag an audio tour for a comprehensive experience, complete with appropriately dramatic music, or tag along on a guided tour if your *castellano* is up to par. If the fake dig sites have struck your fancy, arrange to head out to one of the museum's real ones—tickets to nearby **Tossal de Manises,** site of ancient Lucentum, come cheap, and the realm of the ancients is just a short TRAM ride away.

➜ *Take the TRAM to the MARQ stop for the museum and to Lucentum for the dig site.* ***i*** *Tickets can be purchased in advance through ServiCAM (☎90 244 43 00 💻www.servicam.com).* $ *€3, students €1.50. Tossal entrance €2, students €1.20. Combined MARQ-Tossal entrance €4; good for 1 month. Guided tour €1.50.* ⏰ *Museum open July-Aug Tu-Sa 11am-2pm and 6pm-midnight, Su 11am-2pm; Sept-June 15 Tu-Sa 10am-7pm, Su 10am-2pm. Tossal open June 15-Sept 14 Tu-Sa 9am-noon and 7-10pm, Su 9am-noon; Sept 18-June 15 Tu-Sa 10am-2pm and 4-6pm, Su 10am-2pm.*

👍 MUSEO DEL BELLES ARTES GRAVINA (MUBAG) ♿❄ MUSEUM

C. Gravina, 13-15 ☎96 514 67 80 💻www.mubag.org

The 18th-century Palacio Gravina has housed the Museo del Belles Artes Gravina (MUBAG) since the palace's restoration in 2001. Two floors house over 500 paintings, sculpture, drawings, and ephemera from the 2000-piece collection of the local Diputacion (provincial council) from in and around Alicante. High ceilings and dark-wood floors organized around a grand central staircase play host to occasional concerts and more informal exhibits, while the upper two floors house the real goods. Up one set of stairs will land you among religious works, portraiture, and lots of still-lifes from the 16th to 19th centuries, while the upper floor houses the modern collection, often featuring temporary themed exhibits. Nestled in between the Postiguet city walls and the Santa Maria basilica, the museum is just a short walk from the heart of the *barrio*, and the price (free) can't be beat. Sacrifice an hour or two at the beach to soak in some local culture from the time before tourists flocked to the umbrella-ed shore.

Walk along the Esplanade toward the castle. Take a left onto the road right after the Luxembourg Consulate and a right onto the next road, C. Gravina. The museum is on the left. $ Free. ⏰ Open May-Sept Tu-Sa 10am-2pm and 5-9pm, Su 10am-2pm; Oct-Apr Tu-Sa 10am-2pm and 4-8pm, Su 10am-2pm.

CASTILLO SANTA BARBARA

CASTLE
☎96 516 21 28

Perched above the city, the Castillo Santa Barbara may be one of two castles in the city, but it's the only one you'll remember after you leave. Although the structure as a whole dates as far back as the 10th century under Moorish rule, the primary portions visitable today were constructed in the 15th century and have seen their fair share of conflict since, including a damaging blow during the Spanish Civil War that threatened to tumble its now-flag-bearing side off the mountain. Today, the castle itself offers breathtaking panoramic views of the city and the devastatingly blue water, with the cannon-sprinkled top offering the best comprehensive panorama over the narrow streets and stony plazas of the *casco antiguo*. A more direct route to the top is the sometimes functioning elevator located just across from Postiguet Beach. However, if you make the climb to the top, a splattering of cafes and a museum exhibit await to provide some shade, sustenance, hydration, and maybe even a stiff drink.

Walk along the Esplanade along the beach to reach the elevator (on the left), or climb to the top via the pedestrian path that snakes up the mountain. $ Free. ⏰ Open Apr-Sept daily 10am-10pm with elevator running 10am-7:40pm, last ride up 7:20pm; Oct-Mar daily 10am-8pm with elevator running 10am-7:40pm, last ride up 7:20pm; exhibition halls open daily 10am-2:30pm and 4-8pm.

BEACHES

Alicante's **Playa del Postiguet** is just a stumble away from the *casco antiguo*, located directly across from the Ajuntament and running by the base of the mountain. The picturesque beach is a fan favorite and always crowded during the summer months, but it's usually possible to find a spot to plant your umbrella. Restaurants, ice cream shops, and makeshift tents line the Esplanada just minutes away, leaving the consumer world at the fingertips of swimmers and sunbathers. To get a little further away from civilization (and the crowds and litter that accompany it), consider taking the TRAM out to the more tranquil **Playa de Sant Joan** or **Playa del Mutxavista.** (*For Playa de Sant Joan or Playa del Mutxavista, take the TRAM to the stops of the same name. ⏰ Runs every 20min. in summer; every hr. in winter. $ €1.20.*)

FOOD

RESTAURANTE VILLAHEMY

VALENCIAN [3]

C. Major, 37
☎96 521 25 29 www.villahemy.com

With an interior this loud, an eatery needs to cook up some serious cuisine for the bite to match up to the bark. Luckily, Villahemy follows through (and then some)—their daily *menú* will have you wishing you'd taken it easy on the bread beforehand, with delectable, mindblowing specialties including cold melon soup, paella, and the local favorite—*bacalao*.

From La Rambla, turn onto C. Major, a few blocks away from the water. Restaurant is right after the plaza. $ Appetizers €5-10.50; entrees €10-18. Menú midday on weekdays €11, midday on weekends €13, nights €15. Open Tu-Sa 1-4pm and 8pm-midnight, Su 1-4pm.

KEBAP KEBAB ❶

Av. Dr. Gadea, 5 ☎96 514 10 20

Chances are, if you've been traveling, you've probably succumbed to questionable döner kebabs for a cheap meal, and Kebap manages to right these wrongs in one fell swoop. Seriously fresh ingredients make for huge, tasty wraps with perfect ergonomics for the haul. Though locations are scattered throughout the city, the one right next to the port is the most welcoming, with a kitschy neon sign and a lush, warm interior.

Walk down Av. Federico Soto or Av. Dr Gadea toward the sea. Kebap is near the start of the boulevard. i Other location at C. San Fernando, 12. $ Salads €2.90-3.40. Appetizers €2.90-4.20; entrees €5-7.30. Wraps €3-3.50. Open daily 1:30-4pm and 8pm-midnight.

LA BARRA DE CÉSAR ANCA TAPAS ❷

Plaza Gabriel Miró at C. Ojeda ☎96 520 15 80

La Barra de César Anca pleases fat and slim wallets alike—snag some cheap *pinxos* (€1.50) to fill up before ordering one of their signature tapas. Inventive dishes like artichoke stuffed with cuttlefish in their ink with garlic aioli, or tart apple *millefeuilles* with foie, smoked cod, and goat cheese (both €3.90) are artfully served on little slate tablets, a step above the normal white plate. Locals and tastefully dressed beachgoers fill its lively bar below, while seating above caters to those desiring a more reserved setting.

Walk down Av. de Ferederico Soto or Av. Dr. Gadea toward the water and take a left onto C. del Cid. Take a right to enter Plaza Gabriel Miró; the restaurant is on the side closest to the water. $ Pinxos €1.50. Appetizers €6.50-12.50; entrees €8.50-10. Inventive tapas €3.75-8.50. Open M 1-4pm, Tu-W 1-4pm and 9-11pm, Th-Sa 1-4pm and 9pm-midnight.

MAMMA LOLA ITALIAN ❸

C. Castaños, 16 ☎96 514 40 69 www.restaurantemammalola.es

Of the ritzy restaurants lining the pedestrian C. Castaños, Mamma Lola will give you the most chic for your money, with a tiered interior of bright wood, stone walls, lush couches, and exposed duct work. The loving Mamma herself keeps watch over waiters serving fresh, mouthwatering gourmet pasta, pizza, and salad.

Walk toward the water on La Rambla and take a right onto C. de Girona about halfway down. Take another right onto the pedestrian C. Castaños. $ Appetizers €5-11; entrees €10-18. Salads €9-13. Open M-Th 8-11:30pm, F-Sa 8pm-12:30am, Su 8pm-11:30pm.

NIGHTLIFE

The most popular area in the evenings is **El Barrio,** a spot full of crooked pedestrian-filled streets between La Rambla and the base of the mountain in the *casco antiguo.* Intimate bars and enormous clubs pack nearly every street as confused hoards of foreign clubhoppers fill whatever place suits their fancy for the night. Interestingly, a ragingly popular place one night may be embarrassingly empty the next.

Bars get bigger and brighter as you near the water, with a range of restaurants and bars with floor-to-ceiling windows lining the tent-lined Esplanade after sunset. To the left of the **Port** at the water's edge sits a huge complex of bars and raging *discotecas,* almost all of which don't charge a cover (though some may require a minimum order). Though it's mostly a top destination on weekends, a decent following fills the places that remain open during weekdays as well. Plan to show up late—most places don't get moving until 2am.

👍 EL COSCORRÓN — ♿̸ 🍸 ❄ BAR

C. Tarifa, 2 — ☎96 521 27 27

Head through the miniature door and past the padded rafter (there's a good reason why the bar is named after the Spanish word for "bump on the head") and into this den that time seems to have forgotten. Cave-painting-like graffiti covers every possible surface, from windowsills to plaster to cigarette machines, and jazz flows over two floors of buzzing chatter. Grab one of their mojitos *(€3)* from the mint-stuffed watering can—just be sure to ask for some sugar if you fear sour pucker.

➡ From La Rambla facing the water, take a left onto C. San José and another left onto the narrow C. Tarifa. Coscorrón is the miniature door to the left. $ Beer €2. Mojitos €3. Mixed drinks €5-6. ⏰ Open daily 7pm-last customer.

ARTESPIRITU — ♿ 🍸 ☀ BAR

C. Labradores, 26 — ☎67 501 99 94

Since you'll probably trip over their sea of outdoor seating while swimming from C. Labaradores to Plaza San Cristobal, you may as well pull up a seat while they're free. A crowd of locals sporting tattoos and Chelsea cuts fill this bohemian joint as reggae and groove hits play over the stereo. Drink specials for students draw in barcrawlers early, with dancing erupting later in the night.

➡ Take a left when facing the water where La Rambla joins with C. Tomas Lopez Torregrosa to enter the plaza. Artespiritu is up the stairs and to the right on C. Labradores. $ Teas €2. Beer €3, students 1L for €3.50. Mixed drinks €5. ⏰ Open daily 10am-4am.

ASTRONÓMO — 🍸 ❄ ☀ CLUB, BAR

C. Virgen de Belén at C. Padre Maltés — ☎96 514 35 22

Spanish pop, dance, and electronica pound through two floors in this ever-popular club in the *casco antiguo*. Although crowds can be unpredictable in the area, Astrónomo is a safe bet. Recharge with a Red Bull and vodka at their chill gated terrace across the street, filled with little tables and wrapped in greenery.

➡ Walking along La Rambla toward the sea, take a left onto C. Miguel Soler to run by the Cathedral of Saint Nicolas. Continue and take the left at the elbow, then take the 1st right and the 1st left onto C. Padre Maltés. $ Beer €3. Mixed drinks €5-8. ⏰ Open Th-Sa 11pm-4am.

LA BIBLIOTECA — ♿̸ 🍸 ❄ CLUB

C. Muelle de Poniente, 6

One of the many nightlife hotspots in the port's Panoramis complex, La Biblioteca packs its three floors with college students that have put away the books for the night to dance to a mix of Spanish pop, reggaeton, and electronica. If you show up too late, be prepared to perform a canonization-worthy miracle to get to the bar—shoving through the stifling crowds will be more difficult than trying to part the Red Sea.

➡ Face the sea and walk along the Esplanade to the right until reaching the port. Located within the huge Panoramis complex. $ Beer €4. Mixed drinks €5-6. ⏰ Open F-Sa midnight-6am.

BAR SUPPORTER — ♿ 🍸 ❄ BAR

C. San Nicolas, 14

With the Ramones on the stereo and anti-fascism stickers on the walls, this bar has repped the real underground since its opening in 1989. Friendly bartenders will chat with you about everything from Nico to Cuba, as small groups of 👍**Commie** 20-somethings trickle in for a cheap pint throughout the night.

➡ Walking along La Rambla toward the sea, take a left onto C. Miguel Soler to run by the Cathedral of Saint Nicolas. Continue and take the left at the elbow onto C. San Nicolas. Bar is on the right. $ Beer €2-3. Mixed drinks €5. ⏰ Open F-Sa 10:30pm-4am.

JOPLIN ⊛♿🍸 BAR

C. Tarifa, 7

Work your way through the crowd lining the little path in front of this small alternative club and its saucy sister La Jarana. A disco ball sprinkles light over a crowd of music-loving youth, and upstairs past a mural of the bar's namesake, Janis Joplin, is another more sparsely populated bar—perfect for chatting about that killer show you just missed. A mix of '60s, pop, rock, hip hop, and whatever else strikes the bartender's fancy spins throughout the night.

⇄ From La Rambla facing the water, take a left onto C. San José and another left onto the narrow C. Tarifa. $ Beer €2-3. Mixed drinks €4-6. ⏰ Open daily 10pm-3am.

LA JARANA ⊛⊗🍸❄ BAR

C. Tarifa, 9

Stop into this little bar on any night of the week and you might find Latin beats, body paint, fake dreads, or some mix of the three. A brightly muraled *mestizaje*, or meeting point, La Jarana boasts a small crew dedicated to dancing in a decor unabashedly geared toward the younger set.

⇄ From La Rambla facing the water, take a left onto C. San José and another left onto the narrow C. Tarifa. i Samba every Th at 11pm. $ Beer €2-3. Mixed drinks €4-6. ⏰ Open daily 10pm-3am.

ROUTE 66 ⊛♿🍸☕ BAR

C. Labradores, 5 — 💻www.facebook.com/routesixtysixbarrio

Though a far cry from the tough-as-nails biker bar it half-heartedly attempts to emulate, this small bar offers a hard-rock alternative to the pop and electronica of surrounding bars. The eagle-clad walls and vintage advertisements mimic the legendary badboy trail that gives the bar its name, with blackhaired bartenders singing along to alt rock hits providing the entertainment until barhopping travelers start to trickle in.

⇄ Take a left when facing the water where La Rambla joins with C. Tomas Lopez Torregrosa to enter the plaza. Walk up the stairs and take a right onto C. Labradores. $ Beer €2. Mojitos €3. Cocktails €5. ⏰ Open M-Th 4pm-3am, F-Sa 4pm-4am, Su 4pm-3am.

UNDERGROUND ⊛♿🍸 BAR

C. Padre Maltés, 2

Out of the ashes of reggae bar Marley rose Underground, *casco antiguo's* den-like home to house and trance. A miniscule dance floor lets you get up close and intimate, and the music will never leave you looking for a dance partner.

⇄ Walking along La Rambla toward the sea, take a left onto C. Miguel Soler to run by the Cathedral of Saint Nicolas. Continue and take the left at the elbow, then take the 1st right and the 1st left, near Astronomo's beer garden. Underground is on the right. $ Beer €2. Mixed drinks €5. ⏰ Open M-Th 10pm-3am, F-Sa 10pm-4am, Su 10pm-3am.

FESTIVALS

MOORS AND CHRISTIANS — SPRING, SUMMER

Though Alicante is not the only city in Spain to celebrate the *Reconquista*, its almost endless festivities make it one of the best. Each district throws its own festival throughout the months between March and August, with the largest taking place in mid-June in the San Blas district. Townspeople don elaborate period dress and take up arms, fireworks, and their skirts for a reenactment of the capture of the castle, with parades, parties, and feasts filling the streets before the dust even settles.

FOGUERES DE SANT JOAN — FALL

Pyromaniacs delight in Alicante's Fogeres de San Joan, as fireworks, firecrackers, bonfires, and effigies on fire light the streets, plazas, and beaches. The city

prepares itself starting September 20, with a parade in traditional clothing to start off the festivities. Daily firework shows in the Plaza de los Luceros *(2pm)* prep the crowd until the arrival of the evening of September 23, when locals and internationals take part in parades and gorge themselves on open-air feasts. With stuffed tummies and a good buzz, the crowds gather to watch midnight fireworks displayed atop Mt. Benacantil, and then they come to watch the *cremàs* (giant bonfires) in Pl. de Ayuntamiento burn the *fogueras* (giant papier-mâché creatures). After some serious pyrotechnics, the drunken masses move to the beach for the *banyà* (group swim) before partying until sunrise.
⏰ *Sept 20-23.*

LA VIRGEN DEL REMEDIO SUMMER

On August 5, the city joins to celebrate their matron saint, Virgen del Remedio (Our Lady of Remedy), with parades and music. Festivities are kicked off on August 3, with the *Alborada*, a traditional choral concert.
⏰ *Aug 3-5.*

ESSENTIALS ℹ

Practicalities

- **TOURIST OFFICES:** The **Main Tourism Office-Bus Station** provides tourist information, including brochures and event guides. *(Estación de Autobuses, C. Portugal, 17 ☎96 592 98 02 💻www.alicanteturismo.com ℹ Other branches by Esplanada d'Espanya and Playa San Juan. ⏰ Open M-F 9am-2pm and 5-8pm, Sa 10am-2pm.)* For more information, check with **Tourist Info Rambla** *(Rambla Méndez Núñez, 23 ☎96 520 00 00 ⏰ Open M-F 9am-8pm, Sa 10am-8pm, Su 10am-2pm)*, **Tourist Info RENFE** *(Estación de Tren RENFE, Ava. Salamanca ☎96 513 56 33 ⏰ Open M-F 9am-2pm and 5-8pm, Sa 10am-2pm)*, and **Tourist Info Airport** *(⇆ Airport ☎96 528 50 11 ⏰ Open M 9am-3pm, Tu-F 9am-8pm, Sa 10am-8pm).*
- **LUGGAGE STORAGE:** *(C. Portugal, 17 ☎96 510 72 00. ⇆ At the bus station. $ €4-8 per bag. ⏰ Open daily 8am-9pm.)*
- **INTERNET:** **Internet Cafe Xplorer** provides access to 30 computers, printing, fax, Skype, and breakfast. *(C. San Vicente, 47 ☎96 521 46 24 $ €0.70 per 30min. ⏰ Open daily 10am-2am.)*
- **POST OFFICE:** *(C. Bono Guarner, 2 ☎96 522 78 71 💻www.correos.es ℹ Branch on corner of C. Arzobispo Loaces and C. Alemania ☎96 513 18 87 ⏰ Open M-F 8:30am-8:30pm, Sa 9:30am-1pm.)*
- **POSTAL CODE:** 03002.

Emergency!

- **POLICE:** *(Av. Julián Besteiro, 15; C. Médico Pascual Pérez, 21 ☎091; 96 510 72 00.)*
- **CRISIS LINES:** **Red Cross.** *(☎96 525 25 25)* **Hope Hotline.** *(☎96 513 11 22)*
- **HOSPITAL/MEDICAL SERVICES:** **Hospital General.** *(C. Maestro Alonso, 109 ☎96 593 83 00 💻www.dep19.san.gva.es)* **Emergency Medical Services.** *(☎96 524 76 00)*

Getting There ✈

By Plane

If you are flying, you will land at the **Aeroport Internacional de El Altet** *(☎96 691 91 00, 96 691 94 00 💻www.aena.es)*, 11km south of the city center. **Iberia** *(☎90 240 05 00)* and **Air Europa** *(☎90 240 15 01)* have daily flights from **Madrid, Barcelona,** and the **Islas Baleares,** among other destinations. **Alcoyana** *(☎96 526 84 00)* bus #C-6 runs to the airport from Pl. Luceros. *($ €1.20. ⏰ Every 40min.)* Buses also leave from Pl. Puerta Mar.

By Train

RENFE trains run from Estación Central *(Av. de Salamanca ☎90 224 02 02 💻www.renfe.es ⏰ Open daily 7am-midnight)* to **Barcelona** *($ €50-55. ⏰ 5-5½hr., every 1-2hr. 7am-6:20pm)*, **Madrid** *($ €44.70. ⏰ 4hr., every 2-4hr. 7am-8pm)*, and **Valencia** *($ €14-28. ⏰ 1½-2hr., every 1-2hr. 7am-7pm)*. The **Ferrocarrils de la Generalitat Valenciana (TRAM)** to the right of the Mercado Central has service along the *Costa Blanca*. *(Estació Marina, Av. Villajoyosa, 2 ☎90 072 04 72 💻www.fgvalicante.com.)* In summer, the **Transnochador** runs to beaches including **Altea** and **Benidorm.** *($ €1.20-5.60. ⏰ Every hr. 11:25pm-3am.)*

By Bus

Estación d'Autobuses *(C. Portugal, 17 ☎96 5 13 07 00 💻www.alicante-ayto.es/trafico)* has bus lines running to Alicante. **ALSA** *(☎90 242 22 42; 96 598 50 03 💻www.alsa.es)* to: **Altea** *($ €4.80. ⏰ 1½hr., every hr. 7am-7pm)*; **Barcelona** *($ €41-46. ⏰ 7-9hr., 6 per day 1-10pm)*; **Benidorm** *($ €4-5. ⏰ 45min-1hr., every 30min. 6:30am-10:30pm)*; **Denía** *($ €10. ⏰ 2-3hr., 13 per day 7am-9pm)*; **Granada** *($ €28. ⏰ 5½-7hr., 3 per day 11:36am-9:46pm)*; **Madrid** *($ €27-38. ⏰ 5-6hr., every hr. 10:45am-7:45pm)*; **Málaga** *($ €38. ⏰ 7½-9½hr., 11:35am-9:46pm)*; **Sevilla** *($ €37. ⏰ 9½hr., 9:25am)*; **Valencia** *($ €18-21. ⏰ 2½-5hr., every 30min-1hr. 6:30am-10:30pm)*.

Getting Around

The easiest way to get around in Alicante is with the **TAM-Alicante Metropolitan Transport** *(C. Díaz Moreau, 6 ☎96 514 09 36; 90 072 04 72 💻www.subus.es)*. Buses **#21** and **22** run from near the train station in Alicante to Playa San Juan. *($ €1.20.)* The **TRAM** also provides access to the MARQ and various places within the city. *($ €1.20.)* **Taxis** are also a popular way to get around town, so contact Radio Taxi *(☎96 525 25 11)*, Tele Taxi *(☎96 510 16 11)*, or Área Taxi *(☎96 591 05 91)* for estimates.

LAS ISLAS BALEARES

This Western-Mediterranean archipelago is the perfect place for any summer vacationer. The primary islands of the Balearics—Majorca, Menorca, Ibiza, and Formentera—may lie only a short flight or boat ride apart, but each island maintains a unique personality and culture that complements the others in exciting and wonderful ways. Witness the industry and commerce of Majorca's capital **Palma**, the peace and quiet of **Formentera's** small villages and resorts, the pride of **Menorca's** traditional summer festivals and rich wildlife, and the shamelessness of **Ibiza's** crazy club scene.

While you're welcome to visit during any time of year, your best bet for fun is from June to August. While the accommodations may be pricier, they'll at least be open, and you'll get clear skies, warm waters, and tons of traditional foods and fresh fish to enjoy. While you may not have the convenience of hopping on a bus to get between these hotspots, you can save tons of money by booking flights and ferries in advance.

Since pre-historic times, the islands have been home to countless travelers who have stopped over off Africa and the Iberian Peninsula to see what all the talk is about on the Balearic Islands. Now it's your turn.

greatest hits

- **PARTY PEOPLE, PUT YOUR HANDS IN THE AIR.** Head to Ibiza for the best seaside celebration in the Mediterranean (p. 207).
- **GOODNESS GRACIOUS, GREAT BALLS OF FIRE!** The island of Majorca lights up with bonfires and barbeques during the Fiestas de Sant Sebastià every year (p. 205).

majorca *mallorca* ☎971

Since 7000 BCE, people have been using Majorca as an island pit stop in the Mediterranean. Whether it was the Romans, the Byzantines, the Arabs, or the Catalonians, it was always take, take, and more take. Majorca was convenient. It was the biggest island of the Balearics. It had a varied landscape. But over the past 9000 years or so, Majorca has taken a stand, and it isn't going to be pushed around any longer.

We're not going to suggest that Majorca is a spiteful up-and-comer. On the contrary, its rich, multicultural history contributes to the island culture today. Sights like the **Catedral** and **Castell de Bellver** are glowing reminders of all the people who were lucky enough to visit centuries ago, while museums like the **Fundacio Pilar i Joan Miró** suggest that even some of the most talented greats of our time proudly called Majorca home. This "island of calm," as famous Spanish poet Ruben Dario described it, now offers luxurious resorts, delicious local cuisine, abundant shopping options, and a thriving athletic culture centered around biking and aquatic sports. You can tan beside the turquoise waters of this summertime gem by day, and check out the clubs, bars, and restaurants around Palma's port all night. Majorca is mature—it wants to give you relaxation and fun, with some education along the way.

ORIENTATION

The city of Palma is organized around its major plazas. **Plaza Espanya** is the major transit center where the train and metro stations can be accessed and where many of the tour buses congregate. **Plaza Mayor** has some patio restaurants, street performers, and small kiosk shops, and is surrounded by small streets open only to traffic. **Calle San Miguel** and **Calle Sindicat** near the plaza are packed with small restaurants, cafes, and shops. **Plaza Rei Joan Carles I** is the center of the high-end, expensive shopping in Palma that extends onto **Avenida Jaime III, Calle Unio,** and **Passeig des Born.** The **Paseo Maritimo** curves around the port, where you'll find many of the most popular clubs and nightlife destinations.

ACCOMMODATIONS

While the city of Palma is definitely the center of the island, this center isn't necessarily catering to budget travel. If you're looking for cheaper rooms, inexpensive and thriving nightlife, and some beach time, the nearby town of **Arenal** is only a 25min. bus ride out of Palma on the Playa de Palma.

In Arenal

HOSTAL TIERRAMAR HOSTAL ❸
C. Berlin, 9 ☎971 262 751 ▪www.hostaltierramar.com
One of the most popular accommodations in Arenal (and that's saying something—this whole town is packed with hostels), Hostal Tierramar knows how to

las islas baleares

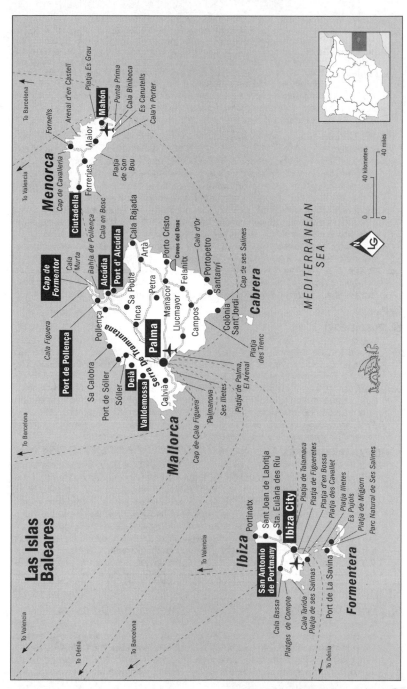

Las Islas Baleares

Menorca
Cap de Cavalleria

Mahón

Fornells
Alaior
Arenal d'en Castell
Platja Es Grau
Punta Prima
Cala Binibeca
Es Canutells
Cala'n Porter

Ciutadella

Ferreries
Cala en Bosc
Platja de Son Bou

Mallorca

Cap de Formentor

Alcúdia
Port d' Alcúdia

Cala Rajada
Porto Cristo
Coves del Drac
Cala d'Or
Portopetro
Santanyí
Cap de ses Salines

Cala Murta
Bahía de Pollença
Cala
Sa Pobla
Inca
Artà
Felanitx

Petra
Manacor
Llucmayor
Campos
Colònia
Sant Jordi

Cabrera

Port de Pollença

Cala Figuera
Pollença

Serra de Tramuntana

Sa Calobra
Port de Sóller
Sóller

Deià
Valldemossa

Palma

Calvià
Palmanova
Ses Illetes
Platja de Palma,
El Arenal
Platja des Trenc

Cap de Cala Figuera

MEDITERRANEAN SEA

Ibiza

Portinatx
Sant Joan de Labritja
Sta. Eulària des Ríu

Ibiza City

San Antonio de Portmany

Cala Bassa
Platges de Compte
Cala Tarida
Platja de ses Salines
Port de La Savina

Platja de Talamaca
Platja de Figueretes
Platja d'en Bossa
Platja des Cavallet
Platja Illetes
Es Pujols
Platja de Migjorn
Parc Natural de Ses Salines

Formentera

To Valencia
To Barcelona
To Dénia
To Valencia
To Barcelona
To Dénia
To Barcelona
To Valencia

0 40 kilometers
0 40 miles

majorca . accommodations

provide a comfortable stay for the beach-minded. Enjoy sizable rooms with tiled floors and colorful sheets that light up when you open up your window to the ocean views. Your massive bathroom is the perfect place to scrub the sand and sunscreen from your body, and the first-floor cafeteria will give you the opportunity to get a book from the library, shoot some pool, or enjoy basic snacks and sandwiches 24hr. a day. At Tierramar, you're steps from the shining blue waters of the Playa de Palma—as well as a direct bus ride into the city (lines #15 and #25).

Take bus #21 from the airport to the last stop at Playa de Palma and walk back two blocks from the stop to C. Berlin. i Breakfast, sheets, towels included. $ Singles €26-32; doubles €38-47; triples €57. ⏰ Reception 24hr.

HOTEL LEBLON BUDGET HOTEL ❷

C. Trasimero, 67 ☎971 490 200 hotel-leblon@hotmail.com

Hotel Leblon would be an easy bet in a boxing match—it's a hotel-quality accommodation that keeps its prices competing in the budget ring. The rose-colored sheets near your large closet and decorative art is just the beginning. Make your way down to the first-floor bar, colorfully decorated with liquors and syrups, and order up a cocktail *(€3.50)* or snack all day long. The pool out back is decorated with nautical tiles and overflowing with neon floatie toys, so hopefully you'll still have time to swim a lap or two after spending the day at the nearby Playa de Palma. You can also stay at the nearby **Sol de Mallorca** that shares the reception at Leblon, but offers even cheaper singles *(€30)*, doubles *(€34)*, triples *(€39)*, quads *(€45)*, and quints *(€65)*.

Take bus #21 from the airport to the last stop at Playa de Palma and walk back two blocks from the stop to C. Berlin, which intersects C. Trasimero. i Breakfast, sheets, and towels included. Pool available. Restaurant. Bike rentals €6. $ Doubles €40; triples €45. ⏰ Reception 24hr.

In Palma

HOSTAL RITZI HOSTAL ❸

C. Apuntadores, 6 ☎971 714 610 www.hostalritzi.com

Hostal Ritzi is a prime cut of convenience—you're steps from one of Palma's main plazas and paying a price that's more suited for a room in Arenal. This hostal totally embraces the bed-and-breakfast vibe: you'll get a warm welcome from the friendly staff, a spacious but homey room, and comfy green couches in the common area. Enjoy a full breakfast in the morning in the bright dining room or on the outdoor patio, and then make your way out onto the town.

C. Apuntadores branches off Plaza Reina. i Breakfast, sheets, and towels included. $ Singles €30; doubles €55-70. Extra bed €20. ⏰ Reception 8:30am-midnight.

HOSTAL APUNTADORES HOSTAL ❹

C. Apuntadores, 8 ☎971 713 491 www.palma-hostales.com

Although the prices are getting a bit higher, Hostal Apuntadores definitely provides you with a comfortable stay. Your neat and tidy room will smell fresh, the green-and-beige sheets and wood panels provide a classy and traditional look, and the spacious closet will be manna from heaven for you not-so-light packers. You can grab a coffee or snack from the first-floor cafe and enjoy it on the leather couch, or take the elevator up eight stories to sip and chat on the rooftop terrace that overlooks beautiful city sights like the port and Catedral.

C. Apuntadores branches off Plaza Reina. i Sheets and towels included. Rooftop terrace. $ Singles €35, with bath €50; doubles €50/€64; triples €75. ⏰ Reception 24hr.

SIGHTS

CASTELL DE BELLVER HISTORICAL SIGHT, CASTLE, PRISON

C. Camilo Jose Cela, 17 ☎971 735 065

Every kid dreams of visiting a castle—especially one nestled up in the mountains with stone towers, a deep moat, and high ceilings. However, the Castell de Bellver didn't last as a castle for long. Although intended to be a royal residence for the Catholic kings when visiting the island, this structure has actually spent much of its history serving as a fortified, high-security prison. Exploring the grounds, you'll enjoy the best views of all of Majorca, the colorful tapestries and marble statues filling the rooms, and a fascinating exhibit about one of Bellver's most famous prisoners, Gaspar Melchor Jovellanos, the Enlightenment thinker locked up for simply being "different." While this Euro-Gothic sight may require quite the hike to arrive at the main gates (unless you take the bus which drops you at the doorstep), enjoy the exercise and climb the steps—we promise it's worth the trek.

Take bus #3 or #46 to Plaza Gomila and take C. Bellver to the top. Tour bus takes you directly to the sight. i Information in English and Spanish. $ €2.50, students under 18 €1. ⏰ Open June-Sept M-Sa 8:30am-8:30pm, Su 10am-5pm; Oct-May M-Sa 8am-7:30pm, Su 10am-5pm.

FUNDACIO PILAR I JOAN MIRÓ — MUSEUM

C. Saridakis, 29 ☎971 701 420 🖥miro.palma.cat

There are many people in this world who have a strong pride in their home town—how else would we end up with songs like *I Love LA* or *Cleveland Rocks?*—but not many people can turn that pride into something as fascinating and beautiful as the Fundacio Pilar. Creator Juan Miró spent his childhood summers in Majorca with his grandmother, escaped to the island during the Nazi invasion of France, and permanently moved to Palma in 1956. Even though he wasn't a resident until later in life, Miró still had an attachment to the capital and decided to donate his entire studio space and much of his collection to the city. Today, the Fundacio Pilar i Joan Miró not only holds about 2500 pieces by the artist, but also provides you with the chance to see his studios. You'll see easels and paintings in the *Taller Sert*, designed by exiled architect and close friend Josep Sert, as well as a large collection of original graffiti in the *San Boter*.

Take bus #3 or #46 to Marivent and then follow the signs up to the Fundacio. i Information in English and Spanish. $ €6, students €3, free on Sa. ⏰ Open May 16-Sept 15 T-Sa 10am-7pm, Su 10am-3pm; Sept 16-May 15 T-Sa 10am-6pm, Su 10am-3pm.

PALACIO REAL DE LA ALMUDIANA — PALACE

C. Palau Reyal ☎971 214 134 🖥www.patrimonionacional.es

Although this massive stone structure right on the shores of Majorca was originally constructed for Muslim royalty during the 10th century, Jaime II's arrival in Majorca marked a time for change. This first Catholic monarch of the island left a few remnants of the Arab constructions, but from the second he placed the cross-holding angel on top of *Torre de Angel*, it was clear that no one would be praying towards Mecca in this house. While many couples settle for the his-and-hers towels or coffee mugs, Spanish monarchs took things a step further—the Palacio Real has separate residences, orchards, and chapels for the Queen and King, all wonderfully decorated with pointed ceilings, colorful tapestries, and furniture. You can even wander through the original Arab baths used more for luxury than hygiene.

Take the steps near Plaza Reyna. Entrance is between the palace and the Catedral. i Information available in English and Spanish. Tours arranged based on demand. $ €3.20, students €2.30. Tours €4. Audio tours €2.50. ⏰ Open Apr-Sept M-F 10am-5:45pm, Sa 10am-1:15pm; Oct-Mar M-F 10am-1:15pm and 4-5:15pm, Sa 10am-1:15pm.

CATEDRAL MUSEU — CHURCH

Plaza Almoina ☎902 022 445

Unlike many other Mediterranean and Iberian cities, Majorca has a strong Christian heritage dating back to the 5th century. While such tolerance was definitely not reciprocated in the years of the Inquisition, the Arab monarchs of Majorca allowed the Catalonian bishops to maintain the Christian community of the island throughout the years of Muslim rule. Such tolerance was the savior of the enormous and picturesque main Catedral. Whether you're entering Palma by bus, bike, or foot, it's impossible to miss this massive structure, with thick stone columns up to 24m tall and over 60 stained glass windows. Fifteen centuries of wear and tear definitely warrant some renovation, so during the 20th century,

Antonio Guadí arrived to save the day. This famous Spanish architect and designer constructed the stunningly beautiful canopy at the front of the church which hangs from the ceiling, glowing with lanterns.

Take the steps from Plaza Reyna and the entrance is around the back of the Catedral. ***i*** *Informational pamphlets in English and Spanish.* $ *€4.* ⏰ *Open June-Sept M-F 10am-6:15pm, Sa 10am-2:15pm; Nov-Mar M-F 10am-3:15pm, Sa 10am-2:15pm; Apr-May M-F 10am-5:15pm, Sa 10am-2:15pm.*

FOOD

Majorca has quite the selection of international cuisine. Walking the streets of Palma, you'll come across many tapas bars and Spanish restaurants, but there are also tons of ethnic options. This island makes the most of its coastline—if you're looking for fresh seafood, just explore the larger restaurants on the **Paseo Maritimo** or leading up to **Plaza Reina.** You should also take advantage of the traditional Majorcan dishes. Fried *mallorqui* (fried offal, potatoes, tomatoes, and onions), vegetable *trumbet* (eggplant, peppers, potatoes, tomatoes, and onions), toasty *pa amb oli* (bread topped with tomato, oil, and salt with cheese, fish, or meats), and savory *sabrosada* (pork and pepper pâté) are some of the local specialities.

LA CUEVA — TRADITIONAL ❸

C. Apuntadores, 5 ☎971 724 422

While La Cueva (the cave) lives up to its name with an underground location and low ceilings, this bright, traditional destination wouldn't suit any stalactites, pirates, or even Batman. La Cueva's menu is simple, with a long list of classic Spanish *tapas* served up at full *ración* sizes. You can see all your options sitting behind the bar, and the chef constantly cooks up more food to refill these deep-dish platters. Locals devour the *gambas al ajillo*, *(shrimp with garlic sauce; €12)* and massive platters of traditional *jamon jagubo* *(€14, large €22).* You may have to fight your way through the crowd congregating outside the door, but it's worth the wait.

C. Apuntadores branches off Plaza Reina. $ *Raciones €5-18.* ⏰ *Open M-Sa noon-midnight.*

CAFE COTO — INTERNATIONAL, MAJORCAN ❷

Plaza Drassana, 12 ☎636 096 126 www.bar-coto.com

Cafe Coto certainly knows how to be bold—the hot pink exterior, massive flowers growing up the gates, burning red interior walls, golden tables, and giant Frida Kahlo paintings certainly make a statement. However, the decor isn't the only thing making a statement at this cute patio-cafe. The international menu provides a wide array of homemade options to cure any craving. Indian dishes like the goat cheese with homemade mango chutney *(€6.50)* and Sri Lankan soups *(€5.50)* can transport you to anywhere on the globe. If you'd prefer some local flavor classic Majorcan *pa amb olis* *(€6.50)* or a Spanish tapa tasting platters *(small €8; large €15).* Freshly baked desserts like the warm apple strudel make the daily *menú* *(€10)* even more tempting.

From Plaza Reyna, take C. Apuntadores and make a left into the Plaza. $ *Entrees €5.50-9.50. Salads €8.50. Sandwiches €3-4. Desserts €2-8. Menú of the day €10.* ⏰ *Open M-F 8am-1am, Sa-Su 9am-1am.*

SAMBAL — ORIENTAL ❸

Plaza Progress, 15 ☎971 220 122 www.restaurantesambal.com

Sambal describes itself as a "kitchen with emotion," and we bet your tastebuds will get pretty emotional after experiencing their food. This Asian fusion restaurant featuring Thai, Japanese, Chinese, and Mediterranean fare is a prime example of Majorca's thriving multicultural cuisine options. The menu is overflowing with tempting dishes designated with symbols of spiciness and meat-content. Hopefully the golden Siddhartha sitting cross-legged in the corner will help guide you to a decision, as choosing three styles of curry with 5 options of meat and veggies *(€11.90-16.90)* can cause quite the existential crisis.

Take bus #3 to Plaza de Progress. ***i*** *Vegetarian options available.* $ *Appetizers €1.90-5.90.; entrees €8.90-16.90. Salads €6.90-10.90.* ⏰ *Open M-Sa 11am-4pm and 8-11:30pm.*

FORN DES TEATRE

🍴📶🍸❄☁ TRADITIONAL [2]

Plaza de Weyler, 8 ☎971 727 383

Forn des Teatre is the perfect place to grab some traditional Spanish cuisine while staying smack in the city center. You can enjoy those warm summer nights on an outdoor patio overflowing with locals and bustling with the combination of conversation and tunes played by the street performers standing steps away, or make your way into the relaxed, two-story restaurant with Wi-Fi access and televisions. While you can enjoy the long list of *tapas*-style *raciones (€3.50-10.90)* or Majorcan classic *pa amb olis (€6.50),* the signature of Forn des Teatre is the wide selection of *pinxtos (€1.50).* The 14 daily options do change, but the classics hold strong. The *sobrasada* is a spicy pâté, classic to the island and one of the most popular *pinxtos* at the bar, but the smoked salmon, eggplant, tortilla, and serrano-and-sunny-side-up-egg varieties are equally tantalizing.

🧭 In front of the Theater between Plaza Rei Juan Carles I and Plaza Mayor. $ Raciones €3.50-10.90. Salads €6.95-€9.25. Entrees €9.75-12.90. Desserts €2.95-4.50. ⏰ Open daily 9am-1am.

THE GUINESS HOUSE

🍴♿🍸❄☁ CAFE, BAR [2]

Parc de la Mar

Disclaimer: we understand that The Guiness House is innately touristy and that the menu isn't exactly creative, but the location and ambience make this spot one that you just can't skip. Located right on the waters of the Parc de la Mar with the city's best view of the Catedral, there's no better place to enjoy a summer afternoon snack. Busiest during the open hours of the Catedral, as visitors work up quite the appetite after gazing at Gaudi's glorious canopy, it also draws a crowd in summer evenings with open-air movies *(9pm July-Aug).* For all you beer connoisseurs out there, The Guinness House lives up to its name with a lengthy list of international *cervesas* on tap or by the bottle *(€2.60-4.60),* served up at the outdoor patio bar or the even larger tavern bar inside the restaurant.

🧭 On Parc de la Mar across from the Cathedral. ℹ Outdoor movies available July-Aug. $ Sandwiches €4.85-5.90. Entrees €6.70-12.90 Salads €6.50-7.80. Pizzas €6.50. Burgers €4.75-7.25. ⏰ Open daily 8am-2am.

ECO-VEGETARIA

🍴♿📶🍸❄ VEGETARIAN [3]

C. Industria, 12 ☎971 282 562

Eco-Vegetaria may very well be Palma's best destination for a fresh, creative, vegetarian meal. While your only option is the multi-course menú, which changes on a daily basis, you get some freedom of selection with the appetizer, two entrees, and dessert *(€13.50).* You'll feel its comfortable ambience in the toasty pumpernickel bread, the refreshing A/C, and the mellow soundtrack. Don't be embarrassed if you find yourself coming back for more. You'll fit right in with the local regulars waiting to get their frequent visitor cards stamped while they pay the bill *(buy 5 meals, get one free).*

🧭 Take C. Industria from Plaza Progress toward C. Argentina. $ Menú of the day €13.50. ⏰ Open M-Th 1:15-4pm, F-Sa 1:15-4pm, and 8:30-11pm.

NIGHTLIFE

Around the streets of Palma, near the main plazas and city center, you'll come across a few late-night, loungey cafes and mellow bars, but the real nightlife is concentrated along the **Paseo Maritimo.** Take a walk along this pathway, checking out all those fancy yachts in the harbor as you go, and 10min. away from the Catedral, things will start to heat up.

MOJITO SOUL

🍴♿🍸❄☁ BAR

Paseo Maritimo, 27 🖥www.mojitosoul.com

You may currently associate nature, envy, and marshmallow breakfast cereals with the color green, but one night out on the Paseo Maritimo and you may start to think of Mojito Soul every time you encounter that portion of the color wheel. That's because the entire place is lit by glowing green lights. The DJ spins a mix of soul and R and B hits to entertain the young, international crowd as they try to answer the eternal question—another daiquiri *(€8)* or another dance. While 75% of bars and clubs in Spain will tell you that they specialize in *mojitos* and *caipirinas*, here's a spot that actually deserves that accolade. You can try 7 varieties of each of these drinks *(€8)*, whether in their classic form or with a fruity twist like strawberry, peach, or passionfruit.

 # On Paseo Maritimo on the inland side. $ Cocktails €8. ⏰ Open daily in summer 9pm-4am; in winter 10pm-3am.

GIBSON BAR

Plaza Mercat, 18 ☎971 716 404

Unless you've spent quite a few years at bartending school, Gibson will likely be a learning experience. The lengthy menu (5 pages of whiskeys alone) lists drinks in varieties you never knew existed, but at least it features detailed explanations and histories at the bottom of each page. The house specialty dry martinis come in 14 styles, but the Gibson Dry is definitely the most popular, combining gin, vermouth, a small onion, and lemon zest *(€6.50)*. Cocktails like the "bull shot" *(€7)* may be a test of testosterone levels, but you can also enjoy a simple caipirinha with or without alcohol *(€7)*. Gibson's open all day long, and we won't judge if you're looking for that 8am Bloody Mary *(€7)*, but you can also enjoy a simple coffee *(€1.50)* on the outdoor patio.

 # Plaza Mercat branches off C. Unio between Plaza Rei Joan Carles I and Plaza Weyler. i Non-smoking area available. $ Mixed Drinks €6-7. Beer €2. Coffee €1.50. ⏰ Open daily 8am-3am.

SA RIBELLETA BAR, CAFE

C. Boteria, 1 ☎971 722 489

Sa Ribelleta may be small, but it rakes in locals and tourists of all ages with a vengeance. This mellow, outdoor bar simply screams Majorca—you have the laid back island attitude from the chill waitstaff to the loungey chairs, the simple menu of all the classic snacks including *pa amb olis (€4-€8)*, fried *mallorquines*, refreshing *trampo* (salad with oil, tomato, onion, and green peppers), and healthy *tumbet* (vegetables), and a selection of exclusive house wines and island cocktails. From your small, candle-lit wooden table, order up any dish in a small *(€4.50)* or large *(€8)* size (accompanied with bread), and sip the shockingly sweet, alcoholic, Majorcan *hierbas (€4)*. While the closing time is technically 1am, they often stay open later on the weekends to enjoy the warm evening into the late night hours.

 # On C. Boteria, off Plaza Llotja. $ Beer €2.50-4.80. Wine €3. Hierbas €4. Cocktails €7.50. Snacks €4-8. Coffee €1.90-3. ⏰ Open M-Th 11am-1am, F-Su 8pm-1am.

THE SOHO BAR

Avenida Argentina 5

You're not having a hallucination of Doc Brown picking you up in the De Lorean. You're not reliving your mom's senior prom. You've just stepped into The Soho, Palma's indie bar with quite the '50s decor. From the velvet couches to the bar cluttered with Rubik's Cubes and big sunglasses, to the patterned wallpaper and old-school TV's, you may subconsciously feel your pants tightening in the thighs and belling out at the ankles. Such novelty themes aren't to be enjoyed by the people who actually lived through the '60s; instead, you'll find yourself cozying up at one of the low coffee tables and watching projections of black-and-white TV shows with a student-dominated crowd. Depending on your mood, you can order up a "Woodstock 1969," with vodka, spring, soda, and lemon *(€7)*, an "Audrey Hepburn," with vodka, *cava*, Bailey's, milk, and canela *(€7)*, or one of the many others off the long list of house cocktails. Bring a student ID on Tuesdays to grab a €5 cocktail, or just show up on Thursdays for €1.50 beers.

 # Off Paseo Maritimo on Avenida Argentina on the left side. i Credit card min.€10. $ Beer €2-4.80. Cocktails €7. ⏰ Open M-Th 6:30pm-2:30am, F-Sa 6:30pm-3am, Su 6:30pm-2:30am.

MISTRAL BAR, CLUB

Paseo Maritimo, 28

You'll have tons of club options along Paseo Maritimo, but Mistral isn't one to skip. You'll know just from walking by and scoping out the attractive locals on the outdoor patio that this is a crowd you want to be dancing against. The dark navy walls, accented by the two glistening, silver bars, may portray a night sky, but this doesn't signal bedtime—it signals a long night of groovin' and movin' to blasting mash-ups of commercial hits. Prismatic cocktails and colorful strobe lights will keep your energy up until the sun comes up to help you with a tan on your walk home.

On Paseo Maritimo on the inland side. $ Beer €4. Mixed drinks €7. Open daily 10pm-5am.

FESTIVALS

Most of the events and festivities held in Palma are music and art festivals. While they are greatly attended and enjoyed, these aren't saints' days or folk festivals: they are modern, changing celebrations that don't necessarily hold much historical significance. One of the most popular is the **Fira del Ram** in March and April, which brings in the newest, most high-tech amusement park rides to the city. The most historical event of the year (and one of the most historical in all of Spain) is the **Festa de l'Estendard,** or Banner Day, that honors Majorca's inclusion into the Christian Spanish kingdom under King James in 1229. The *Ayuntamiento* publishes pamphlets and also has an online calendar detailing the city festivities, with a special calendar for the **Fiestas de Sant Sebastià.**

FIESTAS DE SANT SEBASTIÀ

This festival, beginning annually in mid-January, is Palma's biggest party of the year. It honors the patron saint of the city, Sant Sebastia, who took on his honorable role as the plague ended in 1524. Millions of people are suddenly no longer dying—there's gotta be someone to thank, right? Taking over all the major plazas of Palma, including the **Plaza Mayor, Plaza Rei Carles I,** and **Plaza Espanya,** this celebration is filled with constant concerts and performances, bike and foot races, guided tours, and parties. At the start of the week on January 16, the festivities begin with the lighting of bonfires and barbeques and the procession of dancing devils through the streets. The festivities build until January 20th, the day good old Sebastia was actually dubbed a saint. A grand mass is held in the **Catedral,** major artistic and musical awards are presented at the **Teatre Principal,** competition brews at the *diada* cycling race, and a spectacular fireworks display is set off in the evening.

ESSENTIALS

The official language of Majorca is **Catalan,** not Spanish, and so the city's streets, plazas, and structures have Catalonian names. Luckily, almost everything is translated into Spanish, and often English as well.

Practicalities

- **TOURIST OFFICES:** There are 4 main tourist offices available in Palma. The **Majorca Tourist Information** service has two locations, the Head Office at Parc de las Estacions and the Casal Solleric Office at Passeig des Born, 27 (☎902 102 365 palmainfo@a-palma.es). The **Palma City Council** has also established two offices, one at **Placa de la Reina 2** *(☎971 712 216)* and one at the **Airport** *(☎971 789 556).*
- **TOURS:** The **Town Council** runs walking tours from Plaça de Cort, next to the olive tree *(☎971 720 720 i Given in English and Spanish M-Sa 9am-6pm).* Other city tours are available from **Palma on Bike** *(3hr. 30min.; M-Su 10am from Avenida Gabriel Roca, 15 and 10:30am from Avenida Antoni Maura, 10 $ €25).* There are also **taxi tours.** *(Look for designated signs on city cabs $ €30 per hr.)* The **tourist bus** picks up from 16 stops all over the city. *(Tours last 1hr. 20min. Leave every 20min. Mar-Oct 10am-8pm, Nov-Feb 10am-6pm. $ €13).*

- **CURRENCY EXCHANGE:** There's a currency exchange office with an admittedly inconsistent schedule. *(Avenida d'Antoni Maura, 28 ⏰ Usually open in summer daily 10am-5pm; in winter M-F 10am-5pm.)*
- **INTERNET:** Free city Wi-Fi is available at Plaça Joan Carles I, the Parc de Llevant, S'Escorxador, and the Cultural Centre Flassaders. It can be accessed in 30min. increments by activating your computer's bluetooth. Many restaurants and cafes also offer Wi-Fi with more forgiving time limits. The **public library** also has Wi-Fi. *(Palau Reial, 18 ☎971 711 122 ⏰ Open M 9:30am-2pm, T 4-8pm, W 9:30am-2pm, Th 4-8pm, F 9:30am-2pm.)*
- **POST OFFICE:** The **central post office** is located at C. Constitucion 6 *(☎902 197 197 💻www.correos.es ⏰ Open M-F 8:30am-8:30pm, Sa 9:30am-2pm).*

Emergency!

- **POLICE: Local police** can be found at C. Sant Fernan *(☎971 225 500 💻www.palmademallorca.es).* **National police** are at C. Ruiz de Alda, 8 *(☎971 225 200 💻www.policia.es).*
- **HOSPITAL:** The **general hospital** is located at Plaza Hospital, 3 *(☎971 212 000 💻www.gesma.org).*
- **LATE-NIGHT PHARMACY:** You'll find pharmacies all over the city, and a **24-hour pharmacy Bagur** at C. Aragon, 70 *(☎971 272 501).*

Getting There

By Plane

The **Palma de Mallorca Airport** *(☎971 789 000)* is located 11km southeast of Palma and runs flights from tons of international and domestic airlines including **Air Berlin** *(☎902 320 737 💻www.airberlin.com),* **Easy Jet** *(☎08 712 882 236 💻www.easyjet.com),* **Iberia** *(☎902 400 500 💻www.iberia.com),* **Lufthansa** *(☎49 696 960 💻www.lufthansa.com),* **Spanair** *(☎971 916 047 💻www.spanair.com),* and **Vueling Airlines** *(☎807 001 717 💻www.vueling.com).* The **Aena** website *(💻www.aena.es)* and **Amadeus** website *(💻www.amadeus.net)* are particularly helpful in consolidating information from all the major airlines. As many of the flights are short and run very consistently, prices vary immensely depending on booking, day of the week, and time of day of the flight. The **Empresa Municipal de Transportes** runs an **airport bus line** (*$ €2 [i] #1, every 12-15min. ⏰ M-F 6am-1:50am, Sa-Su 6am-1:10am*) taking your right into Palma, stopping along C. Gabriel Alomar, Porta de Camp, and Avenida Alexandre Rosello. You can use busline **#21** if you're staying in Arenal.

By Ferry

You can also travel to Mallorca on a boat *(general information Autoritat Portuària de Balears 💻www.portsdebalears.com)* from the Spanish mainland or between Islands. **Acciona-Trasmediterranea** *(☎902 454 645 💻www.trasmediterranea.es)* runs to Palma from **Barcelona** *(⏰ 7½hr., M-Th 1pm, 11pm, F-Su 11pm)* and **Valencia** *(⏰ 7hr., M-Sa 11:45am, Su 11:59pm)* on the mainland, as well as to **Ibiza** *(⏰ 4 hr., F, Su, M 7pm)* and **Menorca** *(⏰ 5.5hr., Su 5:30pm).* **Baleària Eurolínies Marítimes** *(☎902 160 180 💻www.balearia.com)* runs to **Ibiza** *($ €52.20-65.40 ⏰ 3½hr., Sa-M 2:45am, 8pm, Tu, Th, F 12:30am, 8pm, W 12:30am, 2:45am, 8pm)* or **Formentera** *($ €52.20 ⏰ 4hr., M-Su 1:15pm).*

Getting Around

By Bus

Public buses within the city of Palma are run by the **Empresa Municipal de Transportes (EMT)** Urbanas de Palma de Mallorca *(C. Josep Anselm Clave, 5 ☎971 214 444).* There are 35 lines *($ €1.25, €8 for 10 rides)* that run M-Su from as early as 6am until as late as 2am. Lines **#1** and **#21** run to the **airport** (*$ €2 ⏰ May-Oct 6am-1:50am, every 12min; Nov-Apr 6am-1:10am, every 15min*), and line **#50** runs a circular route *(⏰ May-Oct 9:30am-7pm, Nov-Apr 10am-4:40pm; stops every 20min.).* Line **#41** is the overnight line *($€1 ⏰ F-Sa*

11:45pm-7am; every 15min). Also useful are lines **#15** *(💲 €1.25 ⏰ Daily 5:45am-1:20am, every 10min)* and the faster **#25** *(💲 €1.25 ⏰ M-F 6:25am-9:25pm, Sa-Su 6:30am-9:30pm; every 10-13min)* to Playa de Palma, and lines **#3** *(💲 €1.25 ⏰ Daily 5:45am-12:35am, every 9-10min)* and **#46** *(💲 €1.25 ⏰ M-Sa 6:30am-11:10pm, Su 7:18am-11:30pm, every 20-35min)* which travel along the port, stopping at major sights like Castell de Bellver and Fundacio Pilar i Joan Miró.

By Taxi

You can also take the city taxis *(⏰ M-F 9pm-7am and weekends 💲 €4 plus €1 per km)*, designated as available by a green light on the top of the car from **Taxi Palma Radio** *(☎971 755 440)* or **Radio Taxi** *(☎971 755 414)*. There are major taxi stops at **Plaza Weyler, Plaza Forti, Avenida Jaime III, Plaza Reina,** and **Passieg de Sagrera.**

To get to other parts of Majorca beyond Palma, **Transport de les Illes Balears (TIB)** *(☎900 177 777 🖥tib.caib.es)*, or TIB, runs 5 series of bus lines *(#100, #200, #300, #400, and #500)* from Palma that go clockwise around the island. They are notorious for running late, and their timetables vary significantly, but they are technically scheduled to begin running as early at 6am and until as late as 11pm. TIB also runs a Palma to **Pobles** train *(⏰ M-F 5:45am-11:15pm, Sa-Su 6:05am-11:15pm)* and a metro line between the **Estación Intermodal** and the **Estación UIB.** *(⏰ M-F every half hr. 6:30am-10:30pm; every 15 minutes 6:30am-7am, 8:30pm-10:30pm; Sa-Su every hour 6:30am-10pm, every 30 minutes 6:30am-7:30am, 9pm-10pm.)* Tren de Sóller runs the scenic "Western Highlights" route along the coast to **Soller** from **Plaça d'Espanya** *(💲 €10 ☎971 752 051 🖥www.trendesoller.com ⏰ 8am-7:30pm)* enjoyed by tourists and locals alike.

By Bike

Palma is also a major center for cyclotourism, and getting around on a **bike** is extremely popular, whether on your own or in a guided tour. **Palma On Bike** *(Avenida Antoni Maura 10 and Avenida Gabriel Roca 15 ☎971 918 988 🖥www.palmaonbike.com 💲 Bike rental for 1-2 days €12 per day, 3-7 days €10 per day. Kayak rental doubles €50 per day, singles €30 per day. Rollerblades rental €10 per day)*.

ibiza ☎971

We won't tell Mom and Dad, but we know why you're making the trip to Ibiza. You want the whitest sands, the clearest waters, the hottest sun, and the sexiest clubs. This small, Mediterranean island has a rich history of settlement and exploration, but it's modern status is the real draw. You'll be wearing as little clothing at the beach as is acceptable, stuffing your face with the delicious selection of international eats, and reaping the benefits of the commercial tourist industry.

This is where the young and beautiful come to get tanner and more beautiful on their summer vacations. Take that summer designation seriously—this packed party scene turns into a quaint and empty town during the winter months, so work hard all year to save the cash for this trip. You'll be encountering pricey accommodations, ridiculous covers, and expensive *mojitos*, but memories (assuming you can remember all that goes down on this debauchery-filled island) are priceless. Test your limits and see how many nights straight you can go beaching by day and clubbing by night. You're in for a ride!

ORIENTATION

Ibiza City is not very large and can be traversed with just a short walk. The main avenues running across the city are **Avenida d'Isidor Macabich,** where you'll encounter the bus station, and **Avenida de España,** where you'll find a slew of different markets, restaurants, internet cafes, and small shops. The **Passeig Vara de Rei** and the **Plaza de Parque** both branch off Avenida de España and are frequented by all the city visitors. The commercial shopping area is most developed on and around **Avenida Bartolome Roselo,** and the most interesting restaurants line the port along **Avenida Andenes** and **Avenida de Santa Eularia del Riu.** The historical centers of Ibiza are the World Heritage sight of **d'Alt Vila** and the ruins of **Puig des Molins.**

ACCOMMODATIONS

Accommodations in Ibiza City are few and far between and generally pricey. If you're coming to the island to party, **Sant Antoni** may be your best bet. The hotels and hostals are less expensive, you're right on the beach, and you're in prime location to see some of the hottest clubs and the **Sunset Strip.** Also keep in mind that Ibiza is a highly seasonal island—summer prices will be significantly higher than anything in the winter (if the accommodation even stays open after September).

Sant Antoni

👍 HOTEL OROSOL 💳♿📶🍸❄⛅ HOTEL [3]

Cami General, 1 ☎971 340 712 💻www.orosolhotel.com

For these prices (especially if you're traveling with a group), the luxury you find at Hotel Orosol is unbelievable. This larger hotel is scooting its way up to 3-star status and is stacked with all those fine facilities that your hostel may be missing from all the hostel-hopping. Your massive room's red sheets, TV, and balcony are only some of the amenities—the full continental breakfast buffet, big pool (290m away), and bright, modern lobby add to the luxury. The welcoming receptionists will provide you with slews of information on local travel and give you tons of activity suggestions—need a bike? Want a discount club ticket? Care to visit Formentera? They'll organize it all for no additional cost. Just take it easy and relax. You're on vacation, remember?

🧭 From the bus station, take Ramon y Cajal to the first intersection to the right. ℹ Breakfast, sheets, and towels included. Pool. Cafeteria. A/C €3-12. Laundry €7 wash, €4 dry. $ Singles €26-53; doubles €40-92; triples €57-120; quads €70-172. ⏰ Reception 24hr.

👍 HOSTAL VALENCIA 💳🚭📶🍸❄⛅ HOSTAL [2]

C. Valencia, 23 ☎971 341 035 💻www.ibizahostalvalencia.com

Hostal Valencia looks more like a home than a hostal—and we're talking about a home that you're dying to own. From the comfy couches and warm living room area to the full cafeteria-restaurant with orange-cushioned chairs and stocked bar to the porch-patio and lush garden, this is one little oasis that you won't want to leave. The forest-green sheets in your bedroom and small, yellow-tiled bathroom are pristinely clean and organized. Plus, the pool out back beckons. You can also find all the information necessary about Ibiza in the lobby, equipped with a whole kiosk of pamphlets and ideas to make your vacation much more interesting.

🧭 At the intersection of Carrer de Mosen and C. Valencia. ℹ Sheets and towels included. Pool. Cafeteria. $ Singles €25-70; doubles €40-80; triples €54-105. ⏰ Reception 24hr.

HOSTAL MONTANA 💳🚭📶🍸 HOSTAL [2]

C. Roma, 8 ☎971 340 490 💻www.montanamarino.com

Hostal Montana knows how to help you make the most of your stay in San Antonio—the friendly staff will point out the best beaches, direct you to the pool at their sister-hostel, **Hostal Marino,** sell you discount tickets to the hottest clubs, or organize a ferry trip to Formentera. You'll enjoy your complimentary breakfast in the morning, but if that night of partying has you sleeping until the afternoon, you can always fight that hangover by grabbing a snack in the cafeteria-bar or wake yourself up with a game of foosball between *bocadillos.* The rooms will make you feel like you've scored a snazzy hotel room, as they come equipped with a mini-fridge (store the mixers), full closet (unpack the stilettos), small balcony (toast to the sunset), and clean, comfy beds (maybe get some—sleep, that is).

🧭 From the bus station, take C. Ramon y Cajal and make a left on C. Roma. ℹ Breakfast, sheets, towels, mini-fridge, and safe included. $ Singles €17-35; doubles €28-70; triples €42-105. ⏰ Reception 24hr.

Ibiza City

👍 HOSTAL LAS NIEVES/JUANITO 💳🚭 HOSTAL [2]

C. Juan de Austria, 17/18 ☎971 190 819 💻www.hostalibiza.com

Located in the middle of the city center, a short walk from the historic d'Alt Villa

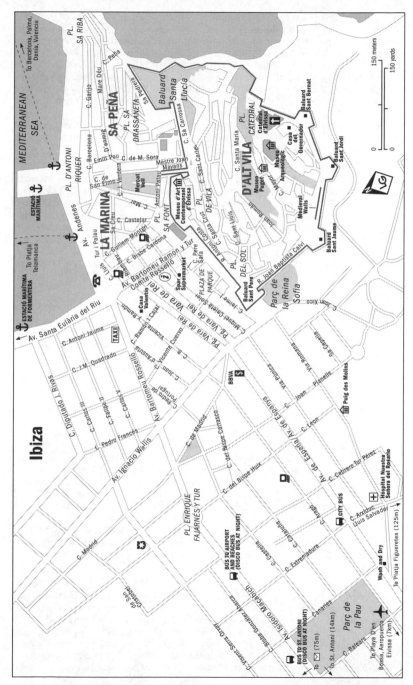

Ibiza

MEDITERRANEAN SEA

To Barcelona, Palma, Denia, Valencia

PL. SA RIBA

C. Peña

ESTACIÓ MARÍTIMA

PL. D'ANTONI RIQUER

Andenes

ESTACIÓ MARÍTIMA DE FORMENTERA

To Platja Talamanca

AV. Santa Eulària del Riu

SA PEÑA

C. Gargo

C. Barcelona

C. d'enmig

C. Emili Pou

C. de San Elmo

C. de M. Sora

C. de M. Verdera

C. Sa Creu

C. Mar

C. Castelar

LA MARINA

C. Guillem Monteri

Tur i Palau

Lluís

Ramblo

C. Bisbe Cardona

Av. Bartomeu Ramon y Tur

Comte Rosselló

Casa Valentín

Mestre Joan Mayans

Merrat Vell

C. Antoni Palau

Museu d'Art Contemporani d'Eivissa

PL. SA FONT

C. Pere Sala

Vara de Rei

PLAÇA DE SA FONT

PARQUE

Spar Supermarket

Pg. Vara de Rei

Miquel Caleta Soler

C. Jaime I

C. Antoni Jaume

C. J.M. Quadrado

C. Dipurado J. Rivas

C. Cardos III

C. Felipe II

C. Cardos V

Pedro Frances

Av. Ignacio Walls

Av. Bartomeu Rosselló

Ramón

C. Ramón Tur

Vicente F. Cuervo

Vicente, P. Ausuló

C. Joan

C. Portugal

C. de Madrid

TAXI

PL. ENRIQUE FAJARNÉS Y TUR

C. de San Cristóbal

C. Madrid

C. del Bispe Carrasco

C. de Madrid

C. del Bispe Huix

BUS TO AIRPORT AND BEACHES (DISCO BUS AT NIGHT)

AV. Isidoro Macabich

V. Isent Serra Orvay

Bisse González Abarca

BUS TO ST. ANTONI (DISCO BUS AT NIGHT)

To (75m)

To St. Antoni (14km)

Canaries

C. Balears

Parc de la Pau

C. Castelló

C. Extremadura

To Platja D'en Bossa, Aeroporto Eivissa (7km)

To Platja Figueretes (125m)

Wash and Dry

Hospital Nuestra Señora del Rosario

C. Antxuri Lluís Salvador

CITY BUS

Av. de España

C. Planells

Via punta

Via romana

C. Joan

C. León

C. Cabrera Tur Pérez

Puig des Molins

Baluard Santa Lucía

Baluard Sant Bernat

CATEDRAL

Catedral d'Eivissa

Casa del Governador

Museu Arqueològic

Baluard Sant Jordi

D'ALT VILA

Museu Puget

Medieval Walls

Baluard Sant Jaume

C. Santa Maria

C. Sant Ciutat

C. Sant Lluís

C. Antoni Costa

DE VILA

DEL SOL

R. Antoni Costa

Joan Román

Baluard Sant Pere

R. Joan Baptista Calvi

Parc de la Reina Sofia

R. de

Sta. Cecília

C. Joan Xico

Via punta

Sa Carrossa

Sa Drassaneta

DRASSANETA

C. Sa petrera

BBVA

150 meters
150 yards

and the history-making Playa d'en Bossa, this hostal pair is run out of the same reception on C. Juan de Austuria and gives you a bit of freedom in deciding how much you're going to spend. Simply put, Hostal Juanito is probably the best price you'll find in Ibiza city, but it isn't a point of luxury. You'll enjoy a spacious and clean room but will have to sleep through the heat with no A/C. Las Nieves provides some ventilation and the possibility of ensuite bathrooms, which ups the ante a bit. Either way, they both have the same best feature—the couple that owns the place is one of the nicest you'll encounter on the island, and they are ready to help you plan out your trip.

From the bus stop, take Avenida d'Isidor Macabich, turn right onto Avenida Ignac Wallis and left onto Juan de Austria. $ Nieves singles €30; doubles €60, with bath €75. Juanito singles €25; doubles €50. ⏰ Reception open daily 9am-1pm and 4-8pm.

EUROPA PUNICO — HOSTAL [3]

Carrer de Aragon, 28 ☎971 303 428 💻www.hostaleuropapunico.com

This quiet and peaceful hostal, conveniently located near the Parc de la Pau and Avenida d'Espanya, may be one of the best deals you'll find in Ibiza City (and believe us, accommodation deals are few and far between). Your bright room with wooden floors and cream sheets only brightens when you open up your sizable window or small balcony. You can pile your plate high at the breakfast buffet, and take your meal out onto the lush patio with shaded picnic tables and comfy seats.

From the bus stop, take C. Extremadura to Carrer de Aragon. ℹ Breakfast, linens, and towels included. $ Singles €33-66; doubles €40-103; triples €55-139. ⏰ Reception 24hr.

SIGHTS

The most historic part of Ibiza City is **d'Alt Vila** ("the Walled City"), a UNESCO World Heritage sight. Walking the small, winding streets (or rather climbing, as it's pretty steep), you can enjoy the major sights or follow one of the designated routes described in pamphlets available at the **information offices.** The **bastions** around d'Alt Vila are the perfect look-out points, and the **Baluarte des Porta Neu Sant Pere** holds a small museum exhibit explaining the construction of the city. Also, while the **Museum of Contemporary Art** is currently being renovated (as of summer 2010), the exhibits are available in the Ayuntamiento.

CATEDRAL D'EIVISSA — CHURCH

Plaza de la Catedral, 1

In the year 1234, a group of Catholic monarchs sat down and realized what Ibiza was missing—no, not a new *discoteca*, but a cathedral dedicated to the Virgin Mary. Plans for this classic, Gothic-style Catedral began, and construction continued all the way until the 16th century. The Catedral d'Eivissa takes particular pride in its collection of 14th- and 15th-century artwork and its 16th- and 17th-century bells, which are still rung today. Just a few years back, in 2006, yet another change was made. The small museum in the side of the cathedral now holds paintings and sculptures from Ibiza's religious history.

Across from the information office. Follow signs upon entering d'Alt Vila. ℹ Information available in English and Spanish. $ Catedral free. Museum €1. ⏰ Open in summer T-Sa 9:30am-1:30pm and 5-8pm; in winter T-Sa 9:30am-1:30pm and 4-7pm.

MUSEU PUGET — ❄ MUSEUM

C. Major, 18 ☎971 392 147

Like father, like son—the Museu Puget is dedicated to papa Narcis Puget Vinas and son Narcis Puget Rique, two artists from the island of Ibiza who together compiled quite the collection. The permanent exhibition is composed of 130 pieces by this talented pair, including Vinas' drawings and oil paintings and Rique's watercolors. If this isn't enough island pride for you, the building itself has been a point of interest on the island since the 15th century. This classic Ibizan house passed through the hands of some of the island's most powerful families over the years, including the Laudes of the 1700s and the Comasemas of the 1800s, before becoming a museum in 2007.

Near the information office. Follow signs upon entering d'Alt Vila. Information available in English and Spanish. $ Free. Open May-Sept T-F 10am-1:30pm and 5-8pm, Sa-Su 10am-1:30pm; Oct-Apr T-F 10am-1:30pm and 4-6pm, Sa-Su 10am-1:30pm.

MUSEU ARQUEOLOGIC — MUSEUM

Plaza de la Catedral, 3 — ☎971 301 231

You think Ibiza rakes in international visitors today? It only got so good at filling its beaches and clubs because it has 3000 years of practice. The Archaeological Museum takes you through six major periods in Ibiza and Formentera's history: Prehistoric, Phoenician, Punic, Early Roman, Late Roman and Late Antiquity, and the Islamic Medieval. Each exhibit provides a clear timeline, maps, and images to really send you back in time—and of course lots of ceramics, statues, and currency.

Next to the information office. Follow signs upon entering d'Alt Vila. Information available in English and Spanish. $ €2.40, students €1.20. Open Apr-Sept T-Sa 10am-2pm and 6-8pm, Su 10am-2pm; Oct-Mar T-Sa 9am-3pm, Su 10am-2pm.

BEACHES

While it depends on how you divide it up, there are at least 50 distinct beaches surrounding the island of Ibiza. They all have their own character and pros and cons. You can endure the biggest crowds and enjoy the biggest parties at beaches closer to the city, or you can battle the bus schedule to reach Ibiza's nature reserves and smaller coves. Pick your poison, pick your pleasure. No matter what you choose, you'll be under that same Mediterranean sun, sipping the (essentially) same *mojitos*.

PLATJA DE SES SALINES — BEACH

10min. drive from Ibiza Town in the Salines Nature Reserve

There's a reason Platja de Ses Salines is one of Ibiza's most popular beaches. Here in the Salines Nature Reserve, you'll find clean, soft sands, and warm, clear waters. With barely any waves, you'll see tourists and locals wading out into the sea to test their skills at paddleball or just floating around on an inflatable tube. While Ses Salines is the perfect place to relax and work on that summer tan, it's also going to provide you with some of the biggest, most-established beach restaurants on the island. **The Jockey Club** and **Malibu** will serve cocktails right to your lounge chair, spray you with their mist machines, and have their DJs spinning hot tunes all day long.

Take Bus #11 from Ibiza City to Salines. First aid available. $ Lounge chair and umbrella rentals €6-10. Lifeguard on duty daily noon-7pm.

CALA BASSA — BEACH

Near Sant Antoni

If you say its name fast, "Cala Bassa" may remind you a touch of *The Teenage Mutant Ninja Turtles'* "cowabunga!" While you can definitely enjoy pizza and sea creatures (and a life free of bad guys) while relaxing at this small cove getaway, there's way more to the Cala Bassa than any '80s cartoon can provide. Whether you want to leap off the rocky cliffs into the warm waters below, play some paddle ball right on the waveless shore, or enjoy the multi-tiered sand levels under the shade of the trees, you'll reap the benefits of smooth sand and clear waters. Cala Bassa is also perfect to test your wits at some water sports—**Ski Pormany** (*11am-7pm, summers only*) offers waterskiing (*€20*), banana-boating (*€10*), and tubing (*€15*), and **Pheonix Dive Center** (*☎971 806 374 www.pheonixdive.de 10am-6pm, summers only*) offers snorkeling (*from €15*) and SCUBA (*€34*) adventures. Both companies work best with walk-ins, so just show up and hop in the water!

Take the #7 bus from Sant Antoni. Showers and bathrooms available. No camping. $ Chair rentals €4. Lifeguard on duty daily July-Sept 11am-7pm; Oct 1-15 noon-6pm; June 15-30 noon-6pm.

PLATJA D'ES CAVALLET 🍸⛅ BEACH

A short walk from Salines to the coast.

Platja d'es Cavallet's free-spirited vibe stems from a few factors: groups of locals frequently make the switch from swimsuits to birthday suits, masseuses perform aggressive and artistic massages right on the sand, the few restaurants sprinkled along the beach (like the huge **Chiringay**) play mellower tunes than the average Ibizan beach-bar, and any tourists who arrive via public transit have just made the 30min. walk through the stunning Salines Nature Reserve to arrive at this peaceful paradise. Along the coast you'll find tons of rocky coves being settled by savvy locals looking for some private tanning and even pass by the 15th-century **Torre de ses Portes.**

➤ Take bus #11 from Ibiza City to Salines and then walk on the coast to D'es Cavallet. ℹ First Aid available. Nudity permitted. ⏰ Lifeguards on duty daily 11am-7pm.

FOOD 🍎

👍 BAR 43 TAPAS 💳🍸❄ INTERNATIONAL, OPEN LATE [2]

Avenida de Espana, 43 ☎971 300 992 💻www.ibiza-43.com

Some numbers hog all the attention: lucky (or unlucky) 13, fab 4, and sweet 16. But what ever happened to good old 43? Luckily, Bar 43 Tapas is here to boost this poor, neglected number's self-esteem by serving 43 varieties of international tapas to an equally international clientele. You can test your knowledge of international flags or chat with the owners about the decorations on the walls, all of which have been collected over the course of their world travels. These tapas are the perfect size for sharing, so grab a group to try some Spanish *albondigas* in mustard sauce *(€5)*, a Mexican *quesadilla* *(€4.50)*, a Greek salad *(€4.80)*, and some Indian chicken curry *(€6.50)*. You can add to the party by tasting one of their refreshing cocktails, like the fruity, tropical "Ibiza 43" that mixes rum, apricot brandy, various juices, and blackberry liqueur *(€7)*.

➤ Near the bus stop on Avenida de Espana. $ Tapas €4-6.50. ⏰ Open Tu-Sa 1-5pm and 8pm-1am.

👍 BON PROFIT 💳♿🍸❄ TRADITIONAL [2]

Plaza del Parque 5

If we learned anything from David and Goliath, *Stuart Little*, or *The Princess and the Pea*, it's that even the little guy can have a huge impact—and Bon Profit fits right in with those small-but-strong competitors. Located right on the Plaza del Parque, this classic Spanish restaurant may only cover a small space, but it serves up huge portions at shockingly low prices. You can enjoy a full plate of steaming *paella* *(€3.80)* for lunch any day of the week, or the selection of local fish like the specialty *dorada* *(€9.50)*. Even any selection off the lengthy wine list will only cost you €1.90 per glass. The friendly staff will serve you with a smile in this old-time establishment, where the plaster has been artistically removed from parts of the walls to uncover the warm brick below.

➤ On the Plaza del Parque, on the side closest to d'Alt Vila. ℹ No smoking. $ Entrees €3.80-10.90. Desserts €1.20-€2.70. ⏰ Open daily 1-3pm and 8-10pm.

BAR SAN JUAN 💳🍸❄ TRADITIONAL [3]

C. de Montgri, 8 ☎971 311 603

This Ibiza classic is a family establishment, passed down through three generations over the past 60 years. Just don't think that Bar San Juan is stuck in some outdated ways. You'll find a lengthy list of daily options every time you walk in to this small restaurant packed with chatty locals. It may not look too exciting from the outside, but the moment you walk in and see the massive portions passing under your nose, you'll understand why you're lost in the sound of bustling conversation and clinking glasses. On a menu that's all about choices, you'll find a slew of fresh options like dorada, salmon, sepia *(€5-10.80)*, 6 different types of tortillas *(€3.50-5)*, and a hefty mixed paella *(€4.80)*.

From Passeig Vara de Rei, take either of the side streets to C. de Montgri. ℹ *Smoking and non-smoking areas available.* $ *Appetizers €4.50-8. Salads €3-6.50. Fish and meat €4-12. Desserts €1.80-2.50. Wine €1-1.70.* ⏰ *Open M-Sa 1-3:30pm and 8:30-11:30pm.*

KE KAFE FUSION, MEDITERRANEAN, INDIAN, MOROCCAN ❸

C. Bisbe Azara, 5 ☎971 194 004 www.kekafe-ibiza.com

Ke Kafe is truly international—you'll find a menu full of Mediterranean, Spanish, Moroccan, Indian, and Thai classics—but it also understands the multicultural universal of good eats. No matter what you're in the mood for, whether its warm cous cous with veggies, chicken, or lamb *(€11-14)*, or a refreshing "7 Pekados" salad *(€7)* topped with fresh strawberries, goat cheese, nuts, and a fruity vinaigrette, Ke Kafe will soothe your cravings. It will also soothe your mind with a mellow soundtrack, Tibetan peace flags on the walls, and the warm glow of orange lamps.

On one of the small side streets between C. Compte Rossello and C. de Montgri. $ *Salads €7. Appetizers €6-7; entrees €10-15.* ⏰ *Open M-Sa 1-4pm and 9pm-midnight.*

ANCIENT PEOPLE INDIAN, OPEN LATE ❷

Avenida de Espana, 32 ☎971 306 687 www.ancientpeopleibiza.com

You've spent the day climbing the streets of D'alt Vila, and now we're throwing more ancient people at you? Don't fret—we're giving you a break from cathedrals and museums (for the moment). This traditional Indian restaurant and tea shop overflows with the smell of classic spices and booming conversation. Take a seat on one of the sequined pillows, among the colorful drapes, or even lie down at a low table on the small platform in back. You'll find all those classics you've missed while traveling Spain: one part of the menu allows you to select chicken *(€8.95)*, lamb *(€9.95)*, or prawns *(€10.50)* and match that up with a preparation of your liking, whether it be *korma*, *kashmiri*, or *vindaloo*. The reasonably priced vegetarian section of the menu, including the recommended veggie curry *(€6.50)*, will definitely not disappoint.

On Avenida de Espana near the intersection with Carrer Extremadura. ℹ *Vegetarian options available. Wait possible on weekend.* $ *Appetizers €3.95-5.75; entrees €8.95-12. Vegetarian dishes €5.50-6.75. Desserts €3.25.* ⏰ *Open M-Th 1pm-midnight, F-Sa 1pm-2am, Su 6pm-midnight.*

NIGHTLIFE

Nightlife is Ibiza's pride and joy. Whether you're an Ibiza virgin or a proud veteran, the enormous, packed *discotecas* will never cease to shock and impress. While you need to be prepared for big covers and pricey drinks, you can find discounts from the street promoters in all the city centers and along the beaches as well as at many hostel receptions. The major clubs are generally located outside the cities, splashed all over the island, including **Eden** and **Es Paradis** in Sant Antoni, **Pacha** at the Ibiza port, and **Privilege** and **Amnesia** near San Rafael. But don't fret, as Ibiza has made club transport particularly convenient with the **discobus** *(€3)* which runs lines from midnight to 6:30am, dropping you right at the doors to the major clubs. There are also options for some less expensive partying. The **Sunset Cafes** and smaller clubs along **Calle Santa Anges** in Sant Antoni are some favorite spots, and there are also late night bars all over Ibiza City.

SPACE CLUB

Playa d'en Bossa ☎971 304 432 www.spaceibiza.com

You may be wondering how they came up with the name Space. Maybe it's because this enormous club with over 4 dance floors, a bar around every corner, and various lounges will move the crowds to new spaces as the night gets busier and busier. Maybe it's because while you're dancing on the crowded dance floor among go-go girls and costumed performers on stilts, a little extra room would be desirable. Or maybe it's just because this club is out of this world. This top Ibiza disco is ready to party any night of the week, but you should make sure to check out the "We Love Sundays" parties and top DJ Carl Cox's hard techno beats every Tuesday.

Take the Discobus from the Ibiza port to Space, or bus #14 during the day to Playa d'en Bossa. $ Beer €10. Mixed drinks €13-17. ⏰ Open M 10pm-6am, Tu 8pm-6am, W 10pm-6am, Th 8pm-6am, F-Sa 10pm-6am, Su 4pm-6am.

👍 EDEN — CLUB

C. Salvador Espriu, 1 ☎971 340 212 🖥www.edenibiza.com

This is one debauchery-filled garden of Eden that could only have been created by the party gods—you've got massive flatscreens playing the hottest music videos, a giant warehouse-sized space, multiple levels of circular dance floors, and a VIP guest list stacked with some of the world's hottest DJs and celebs. Eden is all about temptation, and the glistening red apples all over the dance floor just remind you of all those things that you're dying to have, from that sexy dance partner across the room to those pricey spirits behind the bar. As major clubs on Ibiza go, every night is something special. For the past decade, Eden has created a name for itself with its "Judgment Sundays" of intense techno, and more recently, the "Wonderland" Fridays with world-class DJ sets that bring in stars like Lady Gaga. That apple's just sitting there—take a bite.

Take Disco Bus line #1 or #4 to Sant Antoni or take C. Ramon y Cajal to the rotunda and follow C. Dr. Fleming. $ Cover €20-55. Beer €10. Mixed drinks €12. ⏰ Open daily midnight-6am.

👍 ES PARADIS — CLUB

C. Salvador Espriu, 2 ☎971 346 600 🖥www.esparadis.com

The title doesn't lie—you have found Ibiza's party paradise (and we doubt it was hard, considering its ad posters absolutely blanket the island). Take one step inside this enormous pyramid of party glory and scope out the multiple levels of circular dancefloors and stages decorated with sparkling discoballs and spiraling vined terraces. The fog and strobe lights will get you lost in the line-up of house and electronic hits, and you'll dance until your feet are sore at Wednesday's "Clubland," whip out that leather for Tuesday's "Ibiza Rocks," bob your head along on the calmer Sunday "Jukebox," and then make use of Es Paradis' signature, deep dancefloor-gone-pool at the Monday and Friday "Fiesta del Agua" (pool fills up at 5am).

Discobus line #1 or #4 to Sant Antoni or take C. Ramon y Cajal to the rotunda and follow C. Dr. Fleming. i GLAS (gay, lesbian, and straight) night on Th. $ Cover €30-€45. Beer €6-7. Mixed drinks €11-12. Cocktail €12-13. ⏰ Open daily midnight-6am.

CAFE DEL MAR — BAR

C. Vara de Rey, 27 ☎971 342 516 🖥www.cafedelmarmusic.com

There seems to be a striking similarity between the vibe in *Aladdin*'s "A Whole New World" and that in Cafe del Mar. This bar makes you feel like you're soaring through the clouds with its pillowed ceiling, white, pink, and blue decor, mellow tunes, and amorphous design. The cafe is a classic that's been around way longer than that street rat and his monkey friend (since 1980 to be exact). Head down on any summer night around sunset, and there's no doubt that you'll find an absolutely packed outdoor patio right on the water. Don't let all this talk of dreams and genies get you sleepy—while Cafe del Mar may be the perfect, laid-back alternative to the Ibiza club scene, it also is one of the island's most popular pre-clubbing spots.

Sunset Strip. Take Vara de Rey in Sant Antoni down to the water. $ Coffee €4-10. Beer €4.50-7.50. Wine €5.50. Liquors €5-15. Cocktails €10-11. ⏰ Open daily 5pm-1am.

CAFE SAVANNAH — CAFE, BAR, CLUB

C. Balanzat, 38 ☎971 348 031 🖥www.savannahibiza.com

Coming to Ibiza, your priorities are likely partying, tanning, drinking, and eating—and Savannah can give you everything that you're looking for. This chic cafe-bar-club, right on Sant Antoni's sunset strip, is impossible to miss—from its hot pink drapes to its white globe lamps to its tiled, arching interior and pink bar. You can enjoy the large, beautifully presented portions off their menu, including international hits like Asian woks *(€13-14),* Spanish Iberian pork *(€16),* or the multicultural mini-burger combo *(€13)* with lamb-mint, beef-cheddar, and chicken-curry varieties for you to taste. Once you've filled up and watched the Ibiza sunset on the outdoor patio, the whole mood changes. The DJs' mellow tunes turn into commercial dance beats, and the club in back opens up to get you moving, whether hosting their notoriously popular pre-club parties *(W-Sa),* or holding their own until the early morning *(M-Th, Sa).*

⚑ *Sunset Strip. Take Vara de Rey in Sant Antoni down to the water.* Ⓢ *Wine €4. Mixed drinks €8. Cocktails €9. Appetizers €8.50-10.50; entrees €13-22. Desserts €6.50-7.50.* ✉ *Cafe open daily 11am-midnight. Bar open M-Th midnight-6am, Sa midnight-6am.*

ESSENTIALS

Practicalities

- **TOURIST OFFICES:** There are **information offices** (✉*www.ibiza.travel)* all around the island, including at the **port** *(C. Antoni Riquer 2* ☎*971 191 195* ✉ *Apr-Oct M-Sa 9:30am-6pm, Su 10am-1pm; Nov-Mar M-F 9:30am-3:30pm, Sa 9:30am-2:30pm).* Another convenient location is at the **airport** *(*☎*971 809 118* ✉ *Open May-Oct M-F 9am-8pm, Sa 9am-7pm; Nov-Apr M-F 9am-3pm, Sa 8am-1pm).* There are multiple offices in Ibiza City, including at **Vara de Rey** *(Passeig Vara de Rey 1* ☎*971 301 900* ✉*info@ibiza.travel* ✉ *Open Apr-Oct M-Sa 9am-8pm, Su 9am-3pm; Nov-Mar M-F 9am-7pm, Sa 10am-6pm, Su 10am-2pm),* in **Dalt Vila** *(Plaza Catedal s/n* ☎*971 399 232* ✉ *Open June-Sept M-Sa 10am-2pm, 5pm-9pm, Su 10am-2pm; Oct-Mar M-Su 10am-3pm),* and at **Parc de la Pau** *(Avenida d'Isidor Macabich* ✉ *Open Apr-Oct M-Sa 10am-1:30pm, 5pm-8pm, Su 10am-2pm; Nov-Mar M-Sa 10am-2pm).* There are also offices in **Sant Anotoni** *(Passeig de Ses Fonts s/n* ☎*971 343 363* ✉ *Open May-Oct M-F 9:30am-8:30pm, Sa 9am-1pm, Su 9:30am-1:30pm; Oct-Apr M-F 9:30am-2:30pm, Sa 9:30am-1:30pm),* **Santa Eularia des Rui** *(C. Caria Riquer Wallis* ☎*971 330 728* ✉ *Open May-Oct M-F 9:30am-1:30pm, 5pm-7:30pm, Sa 9:30am-1:30pm; Nov-Apr M-F 9am-2pm, Sa 9am-1:30pm),* and beaches **Cala Llonga** *(*✉ *Open May-Oct daily 9:30am-2pm, 3:30pm-8pm)* and **Es Canar** *(*✉ *May-Oct daily 9:30am-2pm and 3:30-8pm).*

- **INTERNET:** You can get **Wi-Fi** access at the **public library** in the Espacio Cultural Can Ventosa *(C. Ignasio Wallis, 26* ✉ *Open M-F 8am-3pm; in summer Tu 8am-3pm),* or at **Telecentro** internet cafe *(Carrer de Castilla, 10* ☎*971 394 269* ✉ *daily 10am-11:30pm)* that offers internet for €1 per hour and printing and copying for €.20 per page.

- **LAUNDROMATS:** You can do your laundry at **Wash and Dry Ibiza** *(Avenida de Espana, 53* ☎*971 394 822),* which also has ironing services and internet access.

- **POST OFFICE:** The central **Post Office** of Ibiza City *(Avenida Isodor Macabich 67* ☎*971 399 769* ✉ *Open M-F 8:30am-8:30pm, Sa 9:30am-2pm)* also has an ATM, photocopy and fax services, and an Ebay desk.

Emergency!

- **EMERGENCY NUMBER:** ☎112.

- **POLICE: National** (☎091; 971 398 831). **Local** (☎092; 971 315 861 for Ibiza).

- **HOSPITALS: Can Misses** (☎971 397 000). **Red Cross Ibiza** (☎971 390 303).

- **LATE-NIGHT PHARMACIES: Pharmacies** around each city rotate being open 24hr. You can visit any pharmacy during the day, and they can give you the schedule of which pharmacies are next in line to stay open. Within Ibiza City, there are pharmacies all over, including at **Parque de la Pau,** at **Paseo Vara de Rey,** along **Avenida Espanya,** and three near the border of **D'alt Vila.**

Getting There

By Plane

The **Ibiza Airport**, Sant Jordi *(☎971 809 900)*, is located 7km from Ibiza City and 5km from Sant Jordi. Over 50 airlines connect through the airport including **Air Berlin** *(☎902 320 737 🖳www.airberlin.com)*, **Air Europa** *(☎902 401 501 🖳www.aireuropa.com)*, **British Airways** *(☎902 111 333 🖳www.britishairways.com)*, **Aer Lingus** *(☎952 105 488 🖳www.aerlingus.com)*, **Iberia** *(☎902 400 500 🖳www.iberia.com)*, **Ryan Air** *(☎353 124 80 856 🖳www.ryanair.com)*, **SpanAir** *(☎971 916 047 🖳www.spanair.com)*, and **Vueling** *(☎807 001 717 🖳www.vueling.com)*. There is also Wi-Fi access throughout the airport. From the airport, city bus line **#9** *($ €3.20 ⏰ June and Sept only every 1hr. 30min., 7am-11:30pm)* runs to Sant Antoni, and **#10** *($ €3.20 ⏰ Apr-Oct 6am-12am, every 20min., Nov-Mar 7am-11:30pm, every 30min)* and **#10B** *($ €3.20 ⏰ July-Aug 12:30am-5:30am, every hour)* run to the Ibiza City. **Radiotaxi** *(☎971 800 080)* can take you by cab for €.90/km during the day and €1.10 over night, plus a €1.50 airport supplement fee. Cabs from the airport to Sant Antoni are generally €25-€30, and €15-€20 to Ibiza City. The Aena website *(🖳www.aena.es)* and Amadeus website *(🖳www.amadeus.net)* are particularly helpful in consolidating information from all the major airlines. As many of the flights are short and run very consistently, prices vary immensely depending on how far in advance you book, and the day of the week and time of day of the flight.

By Ferry

You can arrive via boat to Ibiza from the Spanish mainland or between other islands in the Mediterranean. **Acciona-Trasmediterranea** can take you from **Barcelona** *(⏰ 8hr., Su-Tu, Th-Sa 1 per day at varying times from 9:30am-10:30pm)*, **Valencia** *(⏰ 4hr. 20min., F-Sa 5pm)*, and **Majorca** *(⏰ 3hr. 45min., M, F, Su 7pm)*. **Baleària Eurolínies Marítimes** can also take you from **Barcelona** *(⏰ 8hr., M, W 10:30pm, F 10:30pm, 11pm, Su 11pm $ €62.40)*, **Valencia** *(⏰ 3-5hr., M, W 4:30pm, Tu, Sa 9pm, F, Su 4:30pm, 9pm $ €78)*, and **Majorca** *(⏰ 2-3hr., M-Sa 8am and 10am, Su 8am and 9am $ €52.20-65.40)*, but also offers travel from **Fromentera** *(⏰ M-F 12 per day 7:30am-9pm, Sa-Su 17 per day 7:30am-9pm $ €23)*.

Getting Around

By Bus

Izabus is the main bus company for the city, running 34 lines to all different parts of the island. Lines **#9** *($ €3.20. ⏰ June and Sept only every 1hr. 30min., 7am-11:30pm)*, **#10** *($ €3.20. ⏰ Apr-Oct every 20min., 6am-12am; Nov-Mar every 30min., 7am-11:30pm)*, and **#10B** *($ €3.20. ⏰ July-Aug every hr., 12:30am-5:30am)* run to the airport from Sant Antoni and Ibiza city, respectively. Line **#0** *(⏰ Sept-June M-Sa every 15min., 7:30am-9am, 1:30-3:30pm, 7-8:30pm; July-Aug last leg runs until 2am)* circles the Ibiza City and **#3** *(⏰ June-Oct 15 every 30min., 7am-11:30pm; Oct 15-May every 30min., 7am-10:30pm)* runs between Ibiza and Sant Antoni. Fares and line schedules vary, but generally range between €1 and €2.50. The main **bus stop** in Ibiza City is located on Avenida d'Isidor Macabich, near the Pac de la Pau. As far as nightlife travel goes, the summer **Discobus** *(☎971 313 447 🖳www.discobus.es)* runs 4 lines that stop at Ibiza's major clubs, including **Space, Pacha, Amnesia,** and **Privilege,** from approximately 12am-6:30am *($ €3)*.

By Taxi

There are also multiple **taxi companies** on the island, including Radio Taxi Ibiza *(Ibiza City ☎971 398 483)* and Radio Taxi Sant Antoni *(☎971 343 764)*. There are taxi points in Ibiza City along the **port,** near **Parque de la Pau,** off **C. Galicia,** and off **Avenida Bartomeu Rossello.** You can rent a **motor scooter** *($ €38-65 per day)* or **bike** *($ €6-10 per day)* from **Extra Rent A Car** in Ibiza City *(Avenida Santa Eulalia s/n ☎971 190 160 🖳www.extrarent.com)*. **Top Moto** also rents scooters. *(☎971 344 266 $ €24-29 per day.)*

BARCELONA

Ask any local and they'll readily tell you—Catalonia is not Spain. As the fiesty gem and burbling metroplis of the area, Barcelona fervently defends its region's status as a nation despite cries from the rest of Spain, and the resurgence of Catalan language (a mix of French and Castilian), culture, and pride after its violent repression by Franco sets it a world apart from its *castellano*-speaking countrymen. Don't worry, though; Spanish in a general sense is still spoken across the area, and even those whose Spanish doesn't extend beyond *cerveza* will find it relatively easy to be understood.

You don't need to sip from the famed fountain of **Canaletes** to fall forever in love with the city. Nestled in between the Montserrat mountains, Mediterranean waves, and the Rivers Bésos and Llobregat, the city offers a bit of the best of everything—incredible parks dotted by surreal architecture, mindblowing (and sleep-depriving) nightlife, mouthwatering tapas, quirky nooks and crannies, and culture oozing from every pore. And, if somehow the promise of **Gaudí's architecture,** incredible museums, quirky bars, raging clubs, human towers, views from mountaintops, and free music galore wasn't cnough, there's always the 🏖**beach.**

greatest hits

- **CAVA WITH A VIEW.** Grab a glass of the bubbly stuff while soaking in the view from Mirablau (p. 284).
- **CITY AT YOUR FEET.** Climb up the Columbus Monument at the end of La Rambla and gaze out over the entirety of Barcelona (p. 233).
- **ART IS FOR LOVERS.** Stroll with your sweetheart along the *Manzana de la Discordia* (p. 242) and then through the sculpture garden at the Fundació Miró (p. 245).

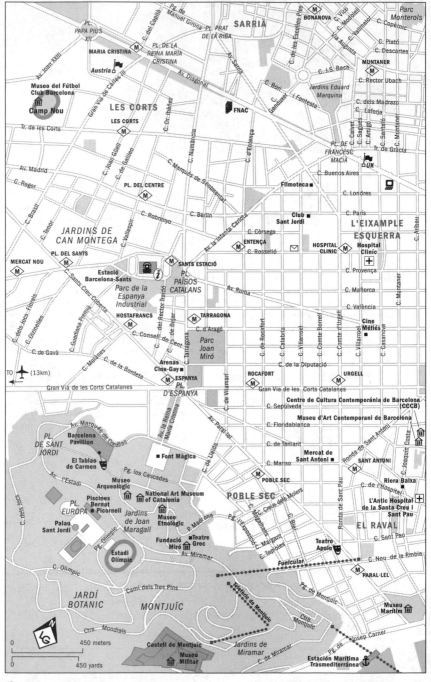

barcelona

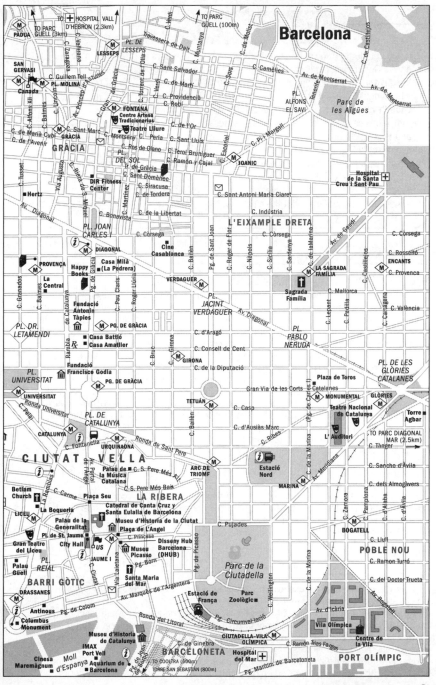

Barcelona

orientation

(art) student life

It doesn't matter if you're not a student of art history; everyone should learn about Antoni Gaudí's work in Barcelona. This isn't another boring church builder—this is the guy who decided a church needs bowls of fruit atop its spires. He tried to build a housing subdivision on a bare hill with a giant lizard fountain that did not attract enough buyers (Parc Güell); he designed whimsical, incredibly detailed houses with mosaics galore for Barcelona's business tycoons (Manzana de Discordia); and he began construction his most well-known work, an exultant expression of his personal Roman Catholicism (Sagrada Familia). Gaudí's vision has proved so inspiring that construction has continued on the Sagrada Familia since its beginning in 1882 and may be completed in 2026, the centennial of Gaudí's death. Students often sketch Gaudí's creations, and Parc Güell is the perfect location for a picnic and beautiful view of the city.

orientation

BARRI GÒTIC AND LAS RAMBLAS

If there is one thing to know about Barri Gòtic, it's this: you will get lost. Knowing this, the best way to properly orient yourself to the neighborhood is to spend an entire day learning your way around. **Las Ramblas** provides the western boundary of the neighborhood, stretching from the waterfront north to Plaça Catalonia. **Vía Laietana** cuts through the city nearly parallel to Las Ramblas, running directly in front of the Catedral, through **Plaça del' Angel**, and marks the eastern border of the Barri. The primary east-west artery, **Carrer de Ferran**, runs perpendicular to Las Ramblas and Via Laeitana, separating the Barri Gòtic into the **lower** (from C. de Ferran to the water) and **upper portions** (C. de Ferran to Carrer de Fontanella). Street names are located on plaques located on the upper stories of buildings, facing the main street, along with names of the squares. For these areas, the **L3 and L4 lines** of the metro will be most helpful, with Ⓜ**Drassanes**, Ⓜ**Liceu**, and Ⓜ**Catalonia** dropping along Las Ramblas (L4), and Ⓜ**Jaume I** located in the heart of the Barri Gòtic, at the intersection of **C. Ferran** and **Via Laietana**.

LA RIBERA

If you're looking for fashion-forward boutiques or cavernous *botegas* housed in medieval stone, Ribera is the place for you. For everyone else, the area may be incredibly frustrating for its lack of cheap options and tourist accessibility, but it does provide a more authentic alternative to the Barri Gòtic's crowded streets. For those looking for the most bang for their buck, **Passeig del Born** offers some cheap eats, as well as enough bars to make any pub crawl a night to remember—or to drunkenly forget.

EL RAVAL

Notorious as Barcelona's rougher neighborhood, Raval shouldn't be missed because of its bad rap. A healthy student population makes for quirky (and cheap) eateries as well as vibrant nightlife. Areas around **Rambla del Raval** and **Carrer Joaquim Costa** boast lots of smaller bars and late-night cafes frequented by Barcelona's alternative crowd. For daytime shopping, check out **Riera Baixa**, a street lined entirely with secondhand shops that also hosts a fleamarket on Saturdays, and the neighborhood around **Carrer Dr. Dou** and **Carrer Elisabets** for higher-end (though still reasonably priced) shops. Be sure to take heed of the locals' warning: watch out for deserted streets and aggressive prostitutes during the night, and be aware that sometimes streets may still be eerily empty and filled with equally aggressive men or sneaky pickpockets during daylight hours.

L'EIXAMPLE

In this vibrant neighborhood, pronounced *eh-sham-plah*, big blocks and dazzling architecture means lots of walking and tons of exciting storefronts. The modernista building-lined **Passeig de Gràcia** runs from north to south, with the **Eixample Dreta** encompassing the area around **Sagrada Família** and **Eixample Esquerra** comprising the area closer to the University. Though the former contains the notorious **Sagrada Família**, as well as some surprisingly cheap accommodations for those willing to make the hike, the more pedestrian-friendly area is the Esquerra. While this neighborhood is notoriously posh, there are some cheaper and more interesting options as you get closer to **Plaça Universitat**. The stretch of **Carrer de Consell de Cent** boasts vibrant nightlife, where many "hetero-friendly" bars, clubs, and hotels help give "Gay-xample" its fitting nickname.

BARCELONETA

Barceloneta is a land of beaches and tourist traps that capitalizes on sunbathers flocking to beaches. A short walk from the Barri Gòtic along the water on **Passeig de Colon** will bring you to ⓜ**Barceloneta**. **Passieg de Joan de Borbó** is the main road curving along the water toward the **beach**, housing museums and restaurants you want to avoid like the plague. Venture onto any of the streets off of **Psg. Joan de Borbó**, and you'll find a tight grid of little shops and more authentic (though by no means cheaper) haunts, with the plaza around **C. del Baluart** being particularly lucrative. A 10-15min. walk along the packed beaches heading away from the **Gothic Quarter** will get you to the ritzy clubs and restaurants of **Port Olímpic**.

GRÀCIA

Gràcia is hard to navigate by metro. While this may at first seem like a negative, this poor municipal planning is actually a bonus. Filled with artsy locals and a few drunken travelers, Gràcia is best approached on foot. ⓜ**Diagonal** will drop you off at the start of **C. Gran de Gràcia**, which creates the eastern border of Gràcia up until ⓜ**Fontana**. Take a right onto any road along this walk, and you'll be navigating Gràcia's plaza-centric **C. de Ros de Olano/C. de Terol**, which runs perpendicular to C. Gran de Gràcia, intersecting the restaurant and student-laden **C. Verdi**. For bustling plazas both day and night, your best bets are **Pl. del Sol** and **Pl. de la Revolución de Septiembre de 1868**, both off of C. de Ros de Olano.

accommodations

BARRI GÒTIC AND LAS RAMBLAS

▨ **HOSTAL MALDÀ**   ☻⊘⑺ HOSTAL ❶

C. Pi, 5   ☎93 3317 30 02 ▧www.hostalmalda.jimdo.com

Hostal Maldà provides a dirt-cheap home away from home, complete with your mother's cat, kitschy clocks, ceramics, and confusing knickknacks. A comfy lounge with books and TV feels more like a living room than a dorm common space. Unlike many hostels, the price does not change with the season, nor will this hostal be booked months beforehand during the summer months—knowing their audience and popularity, the owners only accept sixty percent of capacity through reservations, so try stopping by if you're stranded or weren't quick enough to snag a room beforehand.

⚐ ⓜ*Liceu. Begin walking in front of the house with the dragon and take an immediate left onto C. Casañas. Stay on this road as it passes in front of the church and through the Plaça del Pi. Enter the Galerias Maldà (interior shopping mall) and follow the signs to the hostel.* **i** *Sheets included. Luggage storage available. All rooms have shared bath.* ⓢ *Singles €15; doubles €30; triples €45; quads €60.* ⚐ *Reception 24hr.*

YOUTH HOSTEL ALBERGUE
HOSTEL [1]

C. Palau, 6 ☎93 319 53 25 www.bcnalbergue.com

Clean dormitory-style rooms fitting 4-8 people with pleasant views onto the street and courtyard below. All rooms include cheerily colored ceilings and wooden floors, and some include balconies—perfect for scoping out fellow travelers, restaurants, or even the nearby trinket store. Common space provides a bright, albeit sterile seating area to veg out and watch TV, grab snacks from the vending machine, and even challenge fellow hostelers to a riveting game of chess.

 # [M]Liceu. Walk down C. Ferran toward Las Ramblas. Take the first left once reaching the Plaça Sant Jaume, onto C. de la Ciudad. Right onto C. d'Arai. Second left, onto C. del Palau. i Free breakfast 8-9:30am. Lockers included. Sheets €2. Kitchen open 7-10pm. $ 4- to 8-bed dorms €13-24.50. ⏰ Reception 24hr.

HOSTAL-RESIDÈNCIA REMBRANDT
HOSTAL [2]

C. de la Portaferissa, 23 www.hostalrembrandt.com

Unlike most hostels, which only offer a practically infinite number of small, dark rooms that look exactly the same, the Hostal-Residència has a variety of large, spacious rooms with pleasant quirks and details. Many rooms include multiple large windows or balconies looking out over the corner of the street or into the courtyard, and one triple even has a loft. For once, it's worth the price to have a bathroom ensuite—even the ones that aren't equipped with jacuzzis are still big enough to spend an entire week in relaxing. The rooms are a real steal in the low season, and the location and charm are still worth it in the high season.

 # [M]Liceu. Walk down Las Ramblas toward Plaça Catalonia and take a right onto C. Portaferissa; the hostal is by Galerias Maldà. i Linens and towels included. $ Singles €20-30, with bath €20-35. ⏰ Reception 9am-11pm.

HOSTAL-RESIDENCA LAUSANNE
HOSTAL [3]

Avinguda del Portal de l'Àngel, 14 ☎ 933 02 11 39 www.hostallausanne.es

An incredibly classy stairwell (marble stairs, blue- and gold-glazed tile) leads to an equally classy hostel. Each room sports excellent views, but try getting one that faces the patio—the view is better and it will be quieter at night, so long as your hostelmates aren't total hooligans. Enjoy the view from your own room, chat up some fellow travelers in the bohemian common space with free internet, microwave, and TV, or chill out on the back patio and look out over the neighboring rooftops.

 # [M]Catalonia. Exit the metro and walk along the street toward the Corte Ingles, the rounded building with horizontal bands. Upon reaching the far corner of the square, turn right onto Avinguda del Portal de l'Àngel. i Towels, sheets, and toiletries included. Fridge and luggage storage available. $ Singles €28-35; doubles €47-54; triples €68-75. Call for most up-to-date prices. ⏰ Reception 24hr.

QUARTIER GOTHIC
HOSTEL [2]

C. Avinyó, 42 ☎93 318 79 45 www.hotelquartiergothic.com

Flags from many countries and the hostel's own propaganda and regalia deck the walls and halls of Quartier Gothic. Rooms overlooking the courtyard have the best views and the least noise from the nightlong babbling of the Gothic Quarter. Though the attached baths are more spacious than in comparable hostels in the area, the shared bath is practically a room of its own (though only intended for one person at a time). With some rooms including TV and DVD players and a relatively impressive breakfast (selection of juices, coffee, tea, bread, and pastries), this hostel shows up many in its price range in terms of amenities while still being in a central location. Short-term apartment by Casa Milà also available through informal arrangement with one of the employees.

 # [M]Drassanes. Head toward Plaça de Catalonia on Las Ramblas. Turn right onto C. dels Escudellers, then right onto C. Avinyó. i Breakfast €3. Safety box in room, lockers available for day

after checkout for €2. Linens included. Rooms with private bath also have TV and DVD player. ⑤
Singles €19-27; doubles €32-57; triples €42-75. Discount for booking online. ② *Reception 24hr.*

PENSIÓN CANADIENSE
✈(ᵗ)❄ PENSIÓN ❸

Baixada de San Miquel, 1   ☎93 301 74 61 ▣www.pensioncanadiense.com

Tucked away in the Gothic Quarter, the nine rooms of the Pensión Canadiense tempt the budget traveler with quiet rooms just seconds away from the bustling nightlife of the Barri Gottíc. Each room has a private bath that will make you feel like backpacking royalty as well as balconies that face the street and interior courtyard for you to hold court.

✻ Ⓜ*Jaume I. Walk on C. Ferran towards Las Ramblas. Turn left on C. de Avinyó and take the first left onto Baixada de San Miquel. Hostel is immediately on your left. Upon entering building, take the right stairwell.* ⅰ *Sheets and towels included.* ⑤ *Doubles €60-70, triples €95.* ② *Reception 24hr. 4-night min. stay.*

PENSIÓN LA CALMA
✈Ⓧ(ᵗ) PENSIÓN ❷

C. Lleona, 8-10   ☎93 318 15 21 ▣www.pensionlacalma.com

Ask to see the rooms yourself to find the one sporting the most beautiful balcony view in all of the cheap hostels in the Gothic Quarter—hanging laundry, latticed gardens, terraced roofs, and all. A refreshing break from the nondescript, chain-like interiors being adopted by many hostels with private rooms, the Pensión La Calma instead promises sheets that look like they came out of the '70s, tile from the '80s, and paintings that would look at home in any secondhand store.

✻ Ⓜ*Liceu. Head toward the sea on Las Ramblas. Turn left onto C. Ferran, then right onto C. Raurich. Take the second left, C. Lleona.* ⅰ *Towels and linens included. Microwave and fridge available.* ⑤ *Doubles €42, with bath €50, triples €63/€75.* ② *Reception 24hr.*

ARCO YOUTH HOSTEL (ALBERGUE ARCO)
✈Ⓧ(ᵗ) HOSTEL ❷

Arco de Santa Eulalia, 1.   ☎93 412 54 68

Offering rooms for 6, 8, and 18 people with lockers ensuite, the Arco Youth Hostel provides a bunk in which to crash and food to wake up to in the morning. There's a communal kitchen with fridges, microwaves, a stove, and cookware for those looking to impress with culinary prowess. The smaller common space has couches, books, and a television for enjoyment—just hope that no one is using their "gym," a.k.a. the exercise bike squeezed confusingly along the wall. Decent prices for the area, but be sure to abide by their extensive check-in and cancellation policies to avoid fees.

✻ Ⓜ*Liceu. Walk down C. Boqueria. Arco de Santa Eulalia is the third right. Breakfast included. Lockers available with €10 key deposit. Towels included; sheets €1.70. Kitchen. Call if arrival time is different than originally noted. Fee for cancellation of reservation less than 48 hours in advance or no show, only accepts cancellation through email (not phone or fax).* ⑤ *Dorms €20-23.* ② *Reception 24hr.*

HOSTAL CAMPI
✈Ⓧ(ᵗ)❄ HOSTAL ❸

C. Canuda, 4   ☎933 01 35 45 ▣www.hostalcampi.com

Upon entering Hostal Campi, be prepared to navigate the labyrinth of well-lit, breezy social spaces—complete with balconies and sculpture-like bamboo shoots—to get to your room. Rooms are average size for the price and area, with singles, doubles, triples, and quads available for rent (for the latter, just ask them to add a bed to a triple). The more people staying, the better the deal, and with almost limitless common space, there's no need to worry about being stuck with your bros in an overcrowded room.

✻ Ⓜ*Catalonia. Walk toward the sea on Las Ramblas and take a left onto C. Canuda.* ⅰ *Internet €1 per hr. TV and computers available in living room.* ⑤ *Singles without bath €30-34; doubles €52-67; triples €67-87.* ② *Reception 24hr.*

PENSÍON MARI-LUZ

♠⊗(((•)))❄ PENSIÓN ❷

C. Palau, 4   ☎933 17 34 63 ▣www.pensionmariluz.com

Pensión Mari-luz offers large, spacious rooms at a modest price and is the one of the most fashionably decorated hostels in its price range. Well-matched paint, bedspreads, and artwork (seems that the owners have a penchant for Dalí) offer a lively feeling that the nearly nonexistent social space lacks. With just a few chairs positioned in the alley-like foyer and a TV the size of a netbook, don't expect much socializing in this *pensión*.

✳ Ⓜ*Jaume I. Walk down C. Ferran toward Las Ramblas. Take the first left upon reaching the Plaça Sant Jaume, onto C. de la Ciudad. Right onto C. d'Arai. Second left onto C. Palau.* ⓘ *Lockers in dorm rooms; security boxes in doubles. Sheets and towels included. Kitchen, phone, and fax available.* Ⓢ *Dorms €15-23, with bath €16-24; doubles €50-60; triples €48-72; quads €60-92 (all with hall shower); quads with bath €64-96.* ⓩ *Reception 24hr. Min. stay depends on season.*

HOSTAL LEVANTE

♠❄ HOSTAL ❸

Baixada de San Miquel, 2   ☎933 17 95 65 ▣www.hostallevante.com

Considering the rumors that the place used to be a haunt of Picasso when it was previously a whorehouse, Hostal Levante is now almost eerily clean and upstanding, with only a few stained chairs hinting dirtier days. Spacious yet simple private rooms cater to an older (or at least older acting) crowd than most similarly priced places in the area, and the hostel is much calmer as a result. If you don't mind shared facilities, save the €10 for the closet-sized bathroom.

✳ Ⓜ*Liceu. Walk down Las Ramblas toward the sea. Take a left onto C. Ferran and a right onto C. Avinyó. Baixada de San Miquel is on the left, and Hostal Levante is right at the corner.* ⓘ *Lock box in room. Towels and linens included.* Ⓢ *Singles €35, with bath €45, doubles€55/65; triples €90.*

barcelona

KABUL YOUTH HOSTEL 💳♿📶🍸❄ HOSTEL [1]

P. Reial, 17 ☎93 318 51 90 💻www.kabul.es

One of the biggest and most popular hostels in Barcelona, the Kabul Youth Hostel has hosted nearly one million backpackers since its establishment in 1985. The hostel offers bare-bones, dormitory-style accommodations and a rooftop terrace. Lower-capacity rooms are often cramped and more expensive, but if you can get one with a balcony (just ask), then it's worth the added expense. The common space boasts backpacker photo galleries, a pool table, other table games, music, and a never-ending swarm of chatty younger travelers that are genuinely excited about meeting other travelers. Free breakfast and dinner make the price of a room here a steal.

➡ ⓂLiceu. Walk toward the sea along Las Ramblas and turn left onto C. Ferran. Take the first right and enter the Plaça Reial. Kabul Youth Hostel will be on the far left, with well-marked glass doors. ℹ Complimentary breakfast (8-10am) and dinner (8:30pm) first come, first served. Lockers included with €15 key deposit. Luggage storage available. Blanket included; sheets €2. Laundry facilities available. 20min. free internet per day. Guestlist access to local clubs. Ⓢ Dorms €15-29. ⏰ Reception 24hr.

HOSTAL FERNANDO 💳♿📶❄ HOSTAL [2]

C. Ferran, 31 ☎93 301 79 93 💻www.hfernando.com

A bright, open reception area with friendly staff accurately portrays what travelers will find inside. While Hostal Fernando offers clean, spacious rooms, the decor of the private rooms feels almost like a Holiday Inn. Common room with TV, kitchen, and dining space on 3rd floor.

➡ ⓂLiceu. Left onto C. Ferran from Las Ramblas. On left. ℹ Complimentary breakfast and linens. Towels €1.50. Internet €1 per 30min. Lockers included for dorms; safe box for private rooms. Credit card required for first night reservation. All private rooms have bath, dorms available with or without bath. Ⓢ Dorms €18-25; singles €45-55; doubles €60-75; triples €75-90; family rooms (fit 4-6) €90-160. ⏰ Reception 24hr.

HOSTAL SANTA ANNA 🚫💳🚫♿ HOSTAL [2]

C. Santa Anna, 23 ☎93 301 22 46

Small, dark rooms, and almost medieval offerings—no internet, no wheelchair access, and cash only—mean you're paying almost exclusively for the location and customer service (which, barring technological progress, is superb). The shared baths are barely big enough to turn around in, so it's worth investing in one that's attached to the room. Besides having a helpful staff, you're also guaranteed to make some new friends—though there are no common spaces, there are a few friendly cats and small dogs ready and willing to receive your love if you can find them.

➡ ⓂCatalonia. Walk down las Ramblas toward the water. Take a left onto C. Santa Anna. Ⓢ Doubles €50-60; triples €60. ⏰ Reception 24hr.

HOSTAL PARISIEN 🚫💳❄📶 HOSTAL [3]

La Rambla, 114 ☎93 301 62 83

High ceilings and rooms that actually remind you that you're in the old city, complete with a parrot that will greet you in every language imaginable. Rooms are simple and somewhat pricey for the area (with bathrooms the size of small closets), but some have balconies that open onto La Rambla.

➡ ⓂLiceu. Walk toward Plaça Catalonia on La Rambla. On right. ℹ No alcohol permitted. Ⓢ Doubles €60, with partial or complete bath €65. ⏰ Short-term apartment also available. Prices may vary, call 7-10 days ahead to secure price for stay.

HOSTEL SUN + MOON 💳📶❄ HOSTEL [2]

C. Ferran, 19 ☎932 70 20 60 💻www.sunandmoonhostel.com

Though the crowded dormitory-style rooms seem like an utter sham price-wise, with travelers needing to rent sheets, blankets, and towels, the private rooms and apartments can be relatively economical and a fun place for larger groups to stay, provided you don't mind staying somewhere with the charm and decor of a kindergarten classroom. The hostel sports an incredibly lively atmosphere, filled with an endless stream of young travelers and located on one of the busiest streets in the Gothic Quarter. The common area feels more like a cafeteria than a living room, though, so you may want to take your revelries to the streets.

→ [M]Liceu. Walk toward the water on Las Ramblas. Take a left onto C. Ferran. ℹ Free breakfast 8-9am. Sheets €2; towels €2; blankets €3. Luggage room €2. Free internet from 8am-midnight. $ Apartments from €130. Dorms €25-28. ⏰ Reception 24hr.

LA RIBERA

👍 PENSIÓ 2000
✉📶 PENSIÓN [2]

C. Sant Pere Més Alt, 6 ☎93 310 74 66 💻www.pensio2000.com

Brightly colored and well-lit rooms provide excellent views of the Palau de la Música Catalana across the street (and, reportedly, some complementary music performances on louder nights). High ceilings and a relaxed, college-living-room-like common space (without the empty beer cans and hookah, of course) make for a friendly home away from home, complete with concerned and super helpful hostel-owners-cum-parents.

→ [M]Jaume I. Walk on Via Laietana toward the Cathedral and take a right onto C. Sant Pere Més Alt, 6. Pensió 2000 is located directly across from the Palau. ℹ Breakfast €5. Internet €1 per day. $ Doubles €55, with private bath €60. Extra bed €20, second extra bed €16. ⏰ Reception 24hr.

barcelona

👍 GOTHIC POINT YOUTH HOSTEL
✉📶❄ HOSTEL [1]

C. dels Vigatans, 5 ☎932 68 78 08 💻www.gothicpoint.com

This youth hostel sports a social life as vibrant as its nearly fluorescent lime green walls, with a ping-pong table along the huge terrace for those nights when you just need to duke it out. The chutes-and-ladders-esque bedrooms provide standard youth hostel fare with one significant improvement: most are enclosed in their own wall of curtains for some semblance of privacy.

→ [M]Jaume I. Walk down C. Argenteria and take a left onto C. dels Vigatans. ℹ Kitchen available. Inquire about working to pay for your stay. Sheets €2. Towels €2. $ Dorms €15-23. ⏰ Reception 24hr.

HOTEL TRIUNFO
✉📶❄ HOTEL [4]

Pg. de Picasso, 22 ☎933 10 40 85 💻www.atriumhotels.com

Chic upscale rooms with curtains that actually match the covers, luxurious bathrooms with slick black tubs, and flatscreen TVs on the wall make this expensive option worth its price tag. A small common room with black leather couches, a contrasting white sculpture, and posters of worldwide art exhibitions provide the perfect place to prep before heading across the street to catch a classical performance in the Parc de la Ciutadella.

→ [M]Arc de Triumf. Walk on Passeig de Lluís Companys through the arch and toward the Parc. Follow the curve to the right once it meets the park to walk onto Pg. de Picasso. Hotel Triunfo is on the right underneath the arcade. ℹ All rooms have private bathroom. $ Singles €40-45; doubles €60-70; triples €80-95. Discounts M-F. ⏰ Reception 24hr.

HOSTAL RIBAGORZA
✉📶❄ PENSIÓN [2]

C. de Trafalgar, 39 ☎933 19 19 68 💻www.hostalribagorza.com

Brown- and blue-tiled floors paired with orange covers make for a funky color palette ensuite, while knick-knack ceramics make you feel as if you're staying with your Spanish grandmother. Let this place spoil you with clean rooms, balconies, and surprisingly large shared bathrooms.

→ [M]Arc de Triumf. Stand on the far side of the Arc farthest from the Parc with your back to the arch. C. Trafalgar is the first street on your left. $ Doubles €45, with bath €55-62; triples €60/€75. ⏰ Reception 24hr.

HOSTAL DOS REINOS
💳⃠♿⃠ PENSIÓN ❷

C. de Trafalgar, 39, 4th fl. ☎60 618 54 98

Cheap private rooms compensate for the fact that some of the hostel's other amenities are hit-or-miss—be prepared for a reportedly weak Wi-Fi signal and the possibility of a non-functioning toilet covered by a sheet in one of the shared bathrooms. However, the price is rarely beat, and the place provides a clean spot to lay your head. Be sure to use the elevator unless you're training to climb Everest—Dos Reinos is located on the fourth floor.

➜ ⓂArc de Triumf. Stand on the far side of the Arc farthest from the Parc with your back to the arch. C. Trafalgar is the 1st street on your left. $ Doubles €40; triples €60; quads €80. 10% additional fee for booking online, so call to make reservation. ⏰ Reception 24hr.

HOSTAL NEW ORLEANS
💳♿⃠📶 HOSTAL ❸

Av. del Marquès de l'Argentera, 13 ☎933 19 73 82 💻www.hostalorleans.com

Large rooms with ensuite bathrooms boast the nicest flatscreen TVs for a hostel in this price range—perfect for inviting your friends over to watch the game, since there isn't a common space.

➜ ⓂBarceloneta. Walk on Plà de Palau away from the water and take a right onto Av. del Marquès de l'Argentera. ℹ Communal microwave and fridge available. $ Doubles €60-65; triples €70-75; quads €80-85. ⏰ Reception 24hr.

PENSIÓN CIUDADELA
💳♿📶❄ PENSIÓN ❸

C. del Comerç, 33 ☎933 19 62 03 💻www.pension-ciudadela.com

Large air-conditioned rooms provide a pleasant retreat from the busy streets. There's no common room, so head to the Parc for socializing or make sure you get a room with a balcony to lounge on instead.

➜ ⓂBarceloneta. Walk on Plà de Palau away from the water and take a right onto Av. del Marquès de l'Argentera. The pensión is on the left at the corner of C. Comerç. $ Doubles €66; triples €72. ⏰ Reception 24hr.

PENSION PORT-BOU
💳♿⃠ PENSIÓN ❷

C. del Comerç, 29 ☎933 19 23 67

With no kitchen or Wi-Fi and a TV that will leave you feeling as if you stepped back into the '80s, Port-Bou is a no-frills pension. Clean, sometimes spacious accommodations provide a retro feel for those tired of glitz, glam, and the last few decades. If renting a room with an ensuite bathroom, just be sure it's one you can fit inside. Luckily, rooms come relatively cheap, so this is an affordable option if you're just looking to crash.

➜ ⓂBarceloneta. Walk on Plà de Palau away from the water and take a right onto Av. del Marquès de l'Argentera. Take a left onto C. Comerç. $ Doubles €45, with private bath €55; triples €55/€60. ⏰ Reception 24hr.

HOSTAL NUEVO COLÓN
💳♿📶 HOSTAL ❷

Av. del Marquès de l'Argentera, 19 ☎933 19 50 77 💻www.hostalnuevocolon.com

Newly renovated rooms provide motel-level charm without the underage drinkers partying illegally next door. Rooms range widely in size, so be sure to scope out the selection if you are claustrophobic.

➜ ⓂBarceloneta. Walk on Plà de Palau away from the water and take a right onto Av. del Marquès de l'Argentera. $ Doubles €47; triples €87. ⏰ Reception 24hr.

BARCELONA 4 FUN
💳♿⃠📶 HOSTAL ❷

C. Ample, 24 ☎93 268 41 50 💻www.barcelona4fun.com

An unmarked door in an unmarked building hides private rooms with the social life (and shared bathrooms) of a hostel (if you can find the place, anyway). Young travelers pack this hostal's 2- and 3-person rooms, though most time is spent either in the kitchen or in the living room with a sunny view to the street, comfy furniture, and computers with free internet. Close to Barceloneta if you can't stay too far from the clubs.

✇ ⓂBarceloneta. While facing the water, walk to your right along Psg. Isabel II/Psg. Colom. Walk for 5min. and turn right onto C. Avinyó. At the 2nd street (C. Ample), take a right. Look for a huge stone doorway on your left and doors leading into black-and-white checkered marble hallway. Go up grand staircase–door is unmarked, but it's door #2 on the 1st floor. *i* Free internet and Wi-Fi. Breakfast included. Towels €1. ⑤ Doubles €54-60; triples €81-90.

EL RAVAL

▧ HOTEL PENINSULAR
⊜ & (ꞵ) ❄ HOTEL ❸

C. Sant Pau, 34   ☎93 302 31 38 ▣www.hpeninsular.com

Four stories of rooms wrap around a well-lit courtyard with hanging plants. Comfortable rooms with little desks, and windows overlooking the picturesque surroundings make for a gigglishly quaint place to rest your head.

✇ ⓂLiceu. On Las Ramblas, turn your back to Plaça Catalonia. C. Sant Pau will be on your right. *i* Free Wi-Fi and toiletries. ⑤ Doubles €60; triples €85; quads €100. ♨ Reception 24hr.

IDEAL YOUTH HOSTEL
⊜ & (ꞵ) ❄ HOSTEL ❶

C. la Unió, 12   ☎933 42 61 77 ▣www.idealhostel.com

An industrial-chic common space with foosball and amoeba-like couches hosts to a revolving door of vibrant backpacking youth. The bathroom facilities in this standard youth hostel smell so soapy you know they're clean. Young, helpful staff will point you in the right direction and may even end up going with you to show you the ropes.

✇ ⓂLiceu. Walk toward the water on Las Ramblas and take a right onto C. de la Unió. *i* Breakfast included. Safebox available. ⑤ Dorms €18. €9.50 deposit. ♨ Reception 24hr.

HOSTAL GAT XINO
⬗ & (ꞵ) ❄ ⊿ HOSTAL ❸

C. l'Hospital, 155   ☎93 324 88 33 ▣www.gatrooms.com

The super modern and stylish rooms with a white, black, and lime green color code will have you begging to buy one of their T-shirts to blend into the colorful surroundings. The actual presence of interior decor even extends into the hotel's cafe and bathrooms. If you end up craving a chromatic world beyond this souped-up checkerboard, feel free to lounge in their woodbenched courtyard.

✇ ⓂSant Antoni. Walk down C. de Sant Antoni Abat, which runs diagonally from the corner of the plaça. Stay right onto C. l'Hospital at the fork. *i* Breakfast, towels, and toiletries included. Ensuite bathrooms. ⑤ Doubles €66-86.

CENTER-RAMBLAS YOUTH HOSTEL
⬗ & (ꞵ) HOSTEL ❷

C. l'Hospital, 63   ☎93 412 40 69 ▣www.center-ramblas.com

Though you won't be aching to call this place home, the social atmosphere and clean rooms make this place an attractive stay for a few nights. Industrial metal walls filled with photo murals of Barcelona will persuade you to head into the city with newly made friends in tow.

✇ ⓂLiceu. Walk down C. l'Hospital. *i* Breakfast and sheets included. Lockers €2. Towels €2. Washer €2. Dryer €2. ⑤ Dorms in summer €25, in winter €17-21. ♨ Breakfast 8:15-10am.

L'EIXAMPLE

▧ SANT JORDI: HOSTEL ARAGO
⬗ (ꞵ) HOSTEL ❸

C. Aragó, 268   ☎93 215 67 43 ▣www.santjordihostels.com/hostel-arago

Sit back in their gloriously bright, home-like kitchen and common space, or gather round on one of the couches and listen to hostelmates play covers of Bob Dylan and Andrew Bird on the communal guitar. Any hostel with quotes from Guy Debord, Wittgenstein, and Nietzsche on its board has to be a little different, and this one is in the best way. Modern wooden and steel bunks offer a little more privacy and comfort than most hostels, though with nightly outings and a

solid, exciting community, chances are you'll be spending little time in them.
 # Ⓜ Passeig de Gràcia. Walk along Psg. de Gràcia away from Plaça Catalonia and the Corte Ingles. Take a left onto C. d'Aragó. i Lockers and luggage storage included. Sheets and blankets included. Laundry available. Kitchen and computers with internet. $ Dorms €30-35. ⏰ Reception 24hr.

SANT JORDI: APARTMENTS SAGRADA FAMILIA — HOSTEL ❷

C. del Freser, 5 ☎93 446 05 17 www.santjordihostels.com/apt-sagrada-familia/

For those sick of dining on takeout, coffee, and beer, Sant Jordi's apartment-style lodging offers the chain's characteristic laid-back style, communal guitar, employee dedicated to arranging nightly parties, and guarantee of social hostel-mates as cool as you (or as cool as you want to be). Each apartment includes a private bath (or two), a stylish and comfy living room, free washing machine, and stocked kitchen. With rooms for one, two, or four people, you can pick your privacy without *pension*-style isolation.

 # Ⓜ Hospital Sant Pau. Walk along C. del Dos de Maig toward C. Corsega. Take a left onto C. Rosselló and stay left as the road splits to C. del Freser. i Apartments include living room, TV, washing machine, ensuite bathrooms, and kitchen. Free Wi-Fi. Lockers, sheets, and blankets included. $ 4-bed dorms €16-28; singles €20-38; doubles €36-64. Towels €2. ⏰ Quiet hours after 10pm.

HOSTEL SOMNIO — HOSTEL, HOSTAL ❸

C. de la Diputació, 251 ☎93 272 308 www.somniohostels.com

This ultra-sleek hostel offers the best of both worlds—beautifully decorated private rooms and cost-efficient and dorm-style bunking. Cool wooden floors and modern decor will leave you expecting to pay the price, but you'll be thankfully disappointed. Super helpful and friendly staff will direct you to the best little tapas bar or the only cost-efficient driving tour in Barcelona. Watch for more locations in the near future, as they look to expand throughout Spain.

 # Ⓜ Passeig de Gràcia. Walk along Gran Vía toward the University and take the first right onto Rambla de Catalonia. Somnio is on the corner of C. Diputacio and the Rambla. i Breakfast €2. Locker, towel, and bedding included. Free Wi-Fi. $ Dorms €26; singles €44; doubles €78, with bath €87.

HOSTAL RESIDENCIA OLIVA — HOSTAL ❹

Passeig de Gràcia, 32 ☎93 488 01 62 www.hostaloliva.com

If you think the interior view of this modernista building from the wood-framed elevator is something, just ask for a room facing the street. Large windows facing the grandiose Passeig de Gràcia offer peep shows of the architectural orgasm of the Manzana de Discordia. Though lacking the fantastic views, interior rooms make up for their shortcomings with more room to move around. Large, bright rooms with marble floors and class suit the price range for amenities alone, and the near private view of Gaudí makes it well worth the extra cash.

 # Ⓜ Passeig de Gràcia. Walk along Psg. de Gràcia away from Plaça Catalonia and the Corte Inglés. Hostal Residencia Oliva is on the corner of C. Diputacio and Psg. de Gràcia, on your right. i Free Wi-Fi. $ Singles €38; doubles €66-85; triples €120.

EQUITY POINT CENTRIC — HOSTEL ❷

Psg. de Gràcia, 33 ☎93 215 65 38 www.equity-point.com

Equity Point's location can't be beat, especially for its price. Though the expansive number of rooms and the gargantuan, but beautiful, reception area in this modernista building might intimidate you, their website puts it most accurately when it states that this hostel is "like a cuckoo that's muscled into the very plushest of nests." Great views from the bunk-style rooms and a ton of amenities, including a terrace and bar, provide the perfect reprieve if somehow you don't feel like spending the day out front along Passeig de Gràcia.

 # Ⓜ Passeig de Gràcia. Walk along Psg. de Gràcia away from Plaça Catalonia and the Corte Ingés. Equity Point is on the corner of C. Consell de Cent and Psg. de Gràcia. i Lockers available. Free Wi-Fi; computers with internet free for 20min. Top sheet and blanket €2 each. Towel €2 with €2 deposit. $ Dorms €18.50-30. ⏰ Kitchen open until 10pm.

GRAFFITI HOSTAL HOSTEL [1]
C. Aragó, 527 ☎93 288 24 99

True to its name, this hostel has graffiti, ranging from impressive works of art spanning entire walls to incredibly mundane scratchings by drunk hostelmates. An unmarked door hides the cheapest rooms in Barcelona complete with lockers, two outdoor terraces, and a common room. If you've visited before, be sure to stop by again—the hostel is under new management and has a facelift to show for it.

[M]Clot or [M]Encants. From Clot, face the rocket-shaped Agbar Tower and head directly to your right along C. d'Aragó. From Encants, walk along C. del Dos de Mag toward Agbar Tower and take a left onto C. d'Aragó. $ Dorms €10-13. ⏰ Common areas closed midnight-8am.

BARCELONA URBANY HOSTEL HOSTEL [2]
Avinguda Meridiana, 97 ☎93 503 60 04 www.barcelonaurbany.com

The tons of young people flocking to this hostel guarantee a fun, social experience, and the free gym access and nightly clubbing outings provided by Barcelona Urbany simply greaten the potential. Rooms are supermodern, but don't be surprised if you want to spend most of your night on the terrace bar sipping super cheap beer and sangria *(€1)* instead.

[M]Clot. Walk along Av. Meridiana toward the rocket-shaped Agbar Tower. Urbany will be on your right, on the corner of Meridiana and C. de la Corunya. i Breakfast included. Luggage storage. Laundry available. $ All-female dorms €23-34; mixed dorms €20-31. Singles and doubles €68-94. ⏰ Reception 24hr.

HOSTAL GIMÓN HOSTAL [2]
C. Mallorca, 557 ☎93 455 44 32 www.hostalgimon.es

Bright white modern rooms with wooden floors and furniture, each with a good-size attached bathroom. A comfortable and quiet place to return for the night, though not much more. While each room includes a TV, you'll need to head across the street to the Locutori in search of internet access.

[M]Clot. Walk along Meridiana with your back to the rocket-shaped Agbar Tower and take a hard left onto C. de Mallorca. i Private bathrooms and TV. $ Doubles €50; triples €65.

HOSTAL EDEN HOSTAL [2]
C. Balmes, 55 ☎93 452 66 20 www.hostaleden.net

Don't expect another white-walled sleeping box—bright, pastel colored walls mimic the vivid blues, greens, yellows, and reds of the covers. The interior bathrooms are just big enough to get around in easily, and each comes with a hair dryer for when the windblown look isn't cutting it. The rooms aren't incredibly spacious, but also aren't closet-sized—just be nimble if you take the far side of the bed.

[M]Passeig de Gràcia. Walk along Passeig de Gràcia away from Plaça Catalonia and the Corte Ingles. Take a left onto C. d'Aragó just after Casa Battló. Take a left onto C. Balmes. i Towels, safety boxes, and fans included. $ Singles €25-30, with bath €35-55; doubles €35-45/€50-60.

BARCELONETA

There are very few budget accommodations in Barceloneta—it's better to stay in La Ribera or Barri Gòtic if you want to be near Barceloneta and all its clubs and beachfront.

PENSIÓN PALACIO PENSIÓN [1]
Pg. Isabel II, 10 ☎93 319 36 09 www.pensionpalacio.com

Bright, cheerful private rooms with dormitory-cheap prices. Just a few minutes' walk from the beach, this *pension* with a deceiving laundry list of rules and fees (they're actually laid-back, we promise) is just a 5min. walk from both the hip neighborhood of Born and the sandy beaches of Barceloneta.

[M]Barceloneta. With your back to the beach, walk to the left on Pg. Isabel II. Pensión Palacio is under the arcade on the left side. i Safety box included in each room. Laundry wash €5, dry €2. Kitchen €1 per day. Computers with internet available. $ Singles €15-22; doubles €30-44; triples €45-66. ⏰ Computer room open 8am-11pm.

SEA POINT
✦✿(🏠) HOSTEL ❶

P. del Mar, 1-3 ☎93 231 20 45 🖳www.equity-point.com

Offering Equity Point feel for an Equity Price Sea Point is just seconds from San Sebastian beach, making it the only youth hostel bordering the water this side of Barceloneta. Tumble out of one of their solid metal bunk beds (no annoying midnight squeaks here) and onto the sand—though clean, bright, and lively, the accommodations aren't as spiffy as other Barcelona hostels in the chain.

✦ Ⓜ*Barceloneta. Follow Pg. Joan de Borbó until Pl. del Mar (near the beach) and enter the hostel through the cafe on the right side of the building.* ⓘ *Breakfast included. Lockers €3. Sheets €2. Luggage storage. 20min. free internet access. Kitchen.* ⓢ *Dorms €15-25.*

GRÀCIA

ALBERGUE-RESIDENCIA LA CIUTAT
✦✿(🏠)✲ HOSTEL ❶

C. de ca l'Alegre de Dalt, 66 ☎93 213 03 00 🖳www.laciutat.com

Colorful dorm-style rooms for offer a cheerily saturated, modern place to rest your head. Useful facilities dot every floor, including a fully-equipped kitchen, common room with TV, and showers. Single and double rooms are also available, with discounts given to those who stay longer than seven days. The Disney-meets-graffiti murals lining the corridors exemplify the vibrant and young social atmosphere, and the terrace provides a welcome break for a breath of fresh air. Getting there from the city center may be a pain, but the bustling student-friendly (and cheap) nightlife of Gràcia is just a short walk away.

✦ Ⓜ*Joanic. Walk along C de l'Escorial through the plaza and follow for 5-10min. Take a right onto C. de Marti before the Clinic and take the first left onto C. de ca l'Alegre de Dalt.* ⓘ *Lockers and towels included. Sheets €1.80. Free internet at public computers. Equipped kitchens and shared bathrooms on each floor. Laundry service available.* ⓢ *4- to 10-bed dorms €17-20; singles €35-50; doubles €26-30. First night deposit required for online booking.* 🔯 *Reception 24hr.*

HOSTAL LESSEPS
✦⊗(🏠) PENSIÓN ❸

C. Gran de Gràcia, 239 ☎93 218 44 34 🖳www.hostallesseps.com

Recently renovated, this *pension* boasts 16 larger rooms, all with huge baths and sleek flatscreen TVs. With these amenities, some people decide to not leave their rooms. Even for the area, this hostel is surprisingly quiet.

✦ Ⓜ*Lesseps. Walk away from the giant road along C. Gran de Gràcia. Hostal Lesseps is a few blocks down on the right.* ⓘ *All rooms with ensuite bath. Free internet at public computers.* ⓢ *Singles €40; doubles €65; triples €80.*

HOSTAL SAN MEDÍN
✦⊗(🏠) HOSTAL ❸

C. Gran de Gràcia, 125 ☎93 217 30 68 🖳www.sanmedin.com

Big beds and spacious rooms make this hostal feel more like a bed and break-fast than a budget *pensión*. Pictures of Barcelona's famous architecture dot the newly wallpapered walls, and mini chandeliers add some sparkle to your sleeping space. Snag a room with a balcony; otherwise you'll be looking out into a drab scene (though quiet) lightwell.

✦ Ⓜ*Fontana. Take a right onto C. Gran de Gràcia. San Medin is a block down on the right, just after Rambla de Prat.* ⓘ *All rooms have a fan.* ⓢ *Singles €30, with bath €45; doubles €50/60; triples €70/80.*

PENSIÓN NORMA
🚫⊗(🏠) PENSIÓN ❸

C. Gran de Gràcia, 87 ☎93 237 44 78

Meticulously maintained but somewhat bland rooms in an unbeatable location provide a relaxing place to return for the night after marching the *modernista*-studded Passeig de Gràcia nearby. To be safe, don't leave valuables in your room. Although the pension is in a safe area, you'll need to turn in your keys before you leave, and at times the staff is less than diligent about watching guard over them at the reception desk.

➜ [M]Fontana. Take a right onto C. Gran de Gràcia. Pensión Norma is a few blocks down on the right. ℹ Sheets included. $ Singles €30; doubles with sink €45, with bathroom €55; triples €66. ⏰ Reception 24hr.

OUTSKIRTS

Surrounded almost entirely by beautiful parks, Barcelona welcomes those adventurous backpackers who shy away from the touristy haunts of Las Ramblas. A number of camping sites and youth hostels are available, both of which are normally accessible by bus or metro. For camping, the **Associació de Càmpings de Barcelona** *(Gran Vía de les Corts Catalanes, 608 ☎93 412 59 55 💻www.campingsbcn.com)* has more info, while the **Youth Hostel Network of Catalonia** *(C. Calàbria, 147 ☎93 483 83 41 💻www.xanascat.cat)* features information about a few government-sponsored youth hostels in the city and surrounding areas.

The Great Outdoors

Almost all of Barcelona's campsites come equipped with baffling amenities, and even the more reserved campsites have basic bathing and laundry facilities as well as a supermarket and restaurant. If you're not the tenting type, affordable 4- to 6-person bungalows are usually available with kitchens and complete bathrooms. Many have minimum stay requirements, so be prepared to kick back and settle down for a few days.

CÀMPING TRES ESTRELLAS ♿📶 CAMPSITE [1]

Autovía de Castelldefells, km. 186.2, Gavá ☎93 633 06 37 💻www.camping3estrellas.com

If you got any closer to the beach, you'd be washed out to sea at high tide. Camping facilities dot the beautiful beach of Gavá, 12km from the city center *(35min. by bus)*. Extensive facilities boast not one but two swimming pools (in case you're afraid of sharks), volleyball nets, and a grill area, along with the expected supermarket, bar, and restaurant.

➜ Gavá stop on bus L94 or L95 from Plaça Catalonia. Campsite 5min walk from station. ℹ Pools, restaurant, supermarket, and BBQ area available. $ Camping €6-8 per person; €7.50-9 for tent. 2-person cabin €26-38; 4-person cabin €38-60. ⏰ Open Mar 15-Oct 15.

CÀMPING BARCELONA 💳♿📶 CAMPSITE [1]

Carretera N-11Km 650, Mataró ☎93 790 47 20 💻www.campingbarcelona.com

A coastal campsite along Martaró beach about 45min. from Barcelona by train boasts enough facilities to have you considering staying in some nights. A beachside restaurant doubles as a club at night, and shady grassy plots give views of the nearby shore. The campsite covers all of the bases with a swimming pool, internet cafe, laundromat, restaurant, supermarket, and even a farm for those looking for a little animal companionship (by the way, pets are allowed so you can also bring your own).

➜ [M]Mataró and free shuttle bus from station to campsite outside the train station every 10 min. N82 bus picks up outside of campsite each hour. Free bus to Plaça Catalonia from campsite Mar-June and Sept-Nov (35min.). ℹ 6A power supply access. Pet-friendly. Swimming pool, restaurant, supermarket, laundry facilities, and bike rental available. Free shuttle to Martaró Beach every 15-30min. $ Camping €5-9 per person. 4-person bungalow and car €85-165; 6-person bungalow and car €110-165. Down payment of 35% and a deposit of €150 for bungalows. ⏰ Open Mar 27-Nov. Check website for full availability.

CÀMPING MASNOU ♿ CAMPSITE [1]

Carretera. N-II km 633 Camil Fabra, 33. ☎93 555 15 03 💻www.campingsonline.com

A more rustic and down-to-earth alternative to many of the resort-esque campsites. Camping Masnou is close to the water, recommended for those looking to indulge in the outdoors or just rest their head inside a tent after sightseeing in the city. Cheap bungalows provide a warmer alternative to your frigid tent during the winter months.

➜ [M]Masnou or N80 bus from Plaça Catalonia. Campsite 5min. walk from station. ℹ Bike rental, laundry, supermarket, pool, and restaurant available. Pet-friendly. $ Camping €5.20 per person. 4-to 6-person bungalows €60-90. ⏰ Open year-round.

BARRI GÒTIC AND LAS RAMBLAS

Barri Gòtic

COLUMBUS MONUMENT TOWER

Portal de la Pau ☎93 302 52 24

Located where Las Ramblas meets the water, the Columbus Monument offers an unbeatable view of the city and a certain heart attack for those afraid of heights for just €3. The 60m statue was constructed from 1882-1888 in time for Barcelona's World's Fair in order to commemorate Barcelona's role when Christopher Columbus met with King Ferdinand and Queen Isabella upon his return from the New World. Though it is said that the 7.2m statue at the top of the tower points west to the Americas, it actually points east, supposedly to his hometown of Genoa. Around the base of the column are reliefs depicting the journey, as well as bronze lions that are guaranteed to be mounted by tourists on any given hour.

[M]Drassanes. Entrance located in base facing water. $ €3, seniors and children €2. ⏰ Open daily May-Oct 9am-7:30pm, Nov-Apr 9am-6:30pm.

MUSEU D'HISTORIA DE LA CIUTAT ♿ HISTORY

Pl. del Rei ☎93 256 21 00 💻www.museuhistoria.bcn.es

If you thought the winding streets of the Barri Gotíc were old school, check out the Museu d'Historia de la Ciutat nestled 20m underneath Pl. de Reial. Underneath this unassuming plaza lies the excavation site of **archaeological remains** of ancient Barcino, the Roman city from which Barcelona sprouted. One thing has remained the same—the people of this area love their booze, and huge ceramic wine flasks can be seen dotting the site, as well as intricate floor mosaics and strikingly well-preserved ruins ranging from the first to 6th centuries AD. The second part of the museum in the area features the comparatively new **Palacio Reial Major,** a 14th-century palace for Catalan-Aragonese monarchs that was built in part using the fourth-century Roman walls. Inside the palace, the expansive and impressively empty Gothic **Saló de Tinell** (Throne Room) is the seat of legend: here Columbus was received by Fernando and Isabel after his journey to the New World, while the **Capilla de Santa Àgata** avoids the fame of kitschy tales and goes right for the goods, hosting rotating exhibits about modern and contemporary Barcelona.

[M]Jaume I. i Free multilingual audio guides. $ Museum and exhibition €7, students and under 25 €5, under 16 free. Museum €6, students €4. Exhibition €1.80/1.10. ⏰ Open Apr-Sept Tu-Sa 10am-8pm, Su 10am-3pm; Oct-Mar Tu-Sa 10am-2pm and 4-7pm, Su 10am-3pm.

CITY HALL ♿ GOVERNMENT

P. de Sant Jaume—Ciutat, 2 ☎93 402 70 00 💻www.bcn.es

The government-appropriate 18th century Neoclassical facade facing the Plaça hides a more interesting 15th century Gothic facade located at the old entrance to the left of the building (which is now also the tourist entrance). Inside City Hall are a myriad of treasures, both fantastical and more somber—the lower level is home to many pieces of sculpture from the Catalan masters (many of these same artists have work in the Museu Nacional d'Art de Catalonia), while the upper level boasts impressively lavish architecture and interiors such as the *Saló de Cent*, where the *Consell de Cent* (Council of One Hundred) ruled the city from 1372-1714. Around certain holidays, the Giants of the Old City may be seen lurking the halls, towering figurines representing past kings and queens, horses, indecipherable monsters, and dragons.

[M]Jaume I. Take a right onto C. de Jaume I after exiting the station. Once in Plaça de Jaume I, City Hall is on your left. i Tourist info available at entrance. To enter, take alley to the left of City Hall

and take a right onto C. Sant Miquel. $ *Free.* ⏰ *Tourist info open M-F 9am-8pm, Sa 10am-8pm, Su and holidays 10am-2pm. City Hall open to public Su 10am-2pm.*

👍 LA BOQUERIA (MERCAT DE SANT JOSEP) — MARKET

La Rambla, 89

If you're looking for the freshest tomatoes, leeks the size of a well-fed child's arm, fruit prickly enough that it could second as a shirukin, sheep's head (eyes included), or maybe just some nuts, the Boqueria has you covered in the most strikingly beautiful way. Though each neighborhood in Barcelona lays claim to its own *mercado*, Mercat de Sant Josep is not only the biggest and impressive in the city, but it also claims the title of largest-open air market in all of Spain. As a consequence, expect to have to fight your way through wildebeest-like hordes of locals and tourists alike to get those cherished lychee for your picnic on the beach. If filling your stomach from the glowing rows of perfectly arranged, perfectly ripe produce doesn't satisfy your famished gut, restaurants surrounding the market offer meals made of fresh produce straight from the nearby vendors. For the frustrated vegans in the city, the market will be your godsend—just turn a blind eye to the ham legs hanging on the outskirts.

➜ *[M]Liceu. Walk on Las Ramblas toward Plaça Catalonia and take a left onto Plaça de Sant Josep.* ⏰ *Open M-Sa 8am-8pm, though some individual stands stay open after 9pm.*

CATEDRAL DE CANTA CRUZ Y SANTA EULALIA DE BARCELONA — ♿ CATHEDRAL

P. de la Seu ☎93 315 15 54 🖥www.catedralbcn.org

Behold: the Cathedral of the Holy Cross and Santa Eulalia (La Seu, for short) and its ever-present construction-related accoutrements, Barcelona's only cathedral and a marvel of beauty and perseverance. The impressive scaffolding rig and skeletal spire drawing attention away from the Gothic facade are actually signs of what you'll see advertised with the "Sponsor a Stone" campaign in the interior—costly renovations that began in 2005. The cathedral is no stranger to drawn out projects, however. Although construction on the cathedral began in 1298, the main building wasn't finished until 1460, the front facade until 1889, and the central spire until 1913.

Once you've been funneled through the scaffolding and into the main building's interior, almost all signs of construction disappear. Soaring vaulted ceilings mark the nave, and decadently decorated chapels—28 in all—line the central space. Most important, however, is the *cathedra* (bishop's throne) that designates this building as a cathedral and is found on the altar. Don't miss the crypt of Saint Eulalia, located at the bottom of the stairs in front of the altar.

To the right of the altar (through a door marked "Exit") is the entrance to the cloister, a chapel-laden courtyard enclosing palm trees and thirteen white ducks that are intended to remind visitors of Saint Eulalia's age at the time of her martyrdom. Here you will find the cathedral's museum, which hides various religious paintings and altarpieces in various stages of needing to be cleaned, a very gold monstrance (used during communion), and, in the Sala Capitular, Bartolomé Bermejo's *Pietà*. If you only have €2 to spend, pay to take the lift instead—you'll get up close and personal with one of the church's spirals and find yourself with a breathtaking view of the city.

➜ *[M]Jaume I. Left onto Via Laietana and then left onto Av. de la Catedral.* $ *Catedral free. Museum €2. Elevator €2.50. Tours €5.* ⏰ *Free admission M-F 8am-12:45pm and 5:15-7:30pm, Sa 8am-12:45pm and 5:15-8pm, Su 8am-1:45pm and 5:15-8pm. Visitor admission M-Sa 1-4:30pm. Inquire about guided visit to museum, choir, rooftop terraces, and towers.*

PALAU DE LA GENERALITAT — GOVERNMENT

☎902 400 012 🖥www.gencat.cat/generalitat/eng/guia/palau/index.htm

Facing the Plaça Sant Jaume I and the Ajuntament, the Palau de la Generalitat provides a second reason this plaza is incredibly popular with protestors and petitioners. The Renaissance facade dates from the early 17th century, hiding a Gothic structure that was obtained by the Catalan government in 1400. Although the majority of visitors will be stuck admiring its wonderfully authoritative feel from the exterior, with a bit of magic in the way of good timing it is possible to see the interior. Inside, visitors will find a Gothic gallery, an orange tree courtyard, St. George's Chapel, a bridge to the house of the President, many historic sculptures and paintings, and the **Palau's carillon**, a 4898 kg instrument consisting of 49 bells that is played on holidays and for special events.

✢ Ⓜ*Jaume. Take a right onto C. de Jaume I after exiting the station. Once in Plaça de Jaume I, Palau is on your right.* Ⓢ *Free.* ☼ *Open to the public on Apr 23, Sep 11, and Sep 24, and on 2nd and 4th Su of each month from 10am-2pm.*

GRAN TEATRE DEL LICEU   ⴲ❋ THEATER

Las Ramblas, 51-59   ☎934 85 99 00 🖥www.liceubarcelona.com

Along the sometimes dirty paths, animal cages, and peddlers of Las Ramblas is one of the Europe's grandest stages that specializes in opera and classical performances. The Baroque interior of the auditorium will leave you gawking at the fact that it dates back only to 1999 when the interior was reconstructed after a 1995 fire (though, to be fair, it is an exact reconstruction of the previous auditorium). A 20min. tour provides a glimpse of the ornate *Sala de Espejos* (Room of Mirrors), where Apollo and the Muses look down upon opera-goers during intermission, and the five-layered bedazzled auditorium, where you may catch a director yelling furiously during a rehearsal if you are lucky. For a more in-depth tour that won't leave you spending half of your time looking at stackable chairs in the foyer or being told about the donors list (though it does include Placido Domingo), be sure to either come for the 1hr. tour at 10am, arrange a behind-the-scenes tour with the box office, or attend a performance in person.

✢ Ⓜ*Liceu.* ℹ *Discount tickets available.* Ⓢ *20min. tour €4, 1hr. tour €8.* ☼ *Box office open M-F 10am-2pm and 2-6pm. 20min. tours start every 30min. daily 11:30am-1pm; 1hr. tour daily at 10am.*

P. DE L'ANGEL   ⴲ☝ HISTORY

Corner of Via Laietana and C. de la Princessa

The square immediately surrounding the Ⓜ Jaume I may now seem like nothing but a place to grab a good pastry, but in the days of Roman Barcino this spot was the main gate into the city. To revel in some of this seemingly absent history, simply walk parallel to **Via Laietana**, the busy street forming one side of the square's border. For a more contemporary piece of history (though still dating from the triple digits CE), look no further than the angel statue facing the street that happens to be pointing to her toe. This sculpture commemorates the event from which the plaza got its name—reportedly when carrying the remains of Saint Eulalia to the cathedral from Santa Maria del Mar, the caravan came to the plaça. Suddenly, the remains became to heavy to carry, and upon setting down the remains, an angel appeared and pointed to her own toe, alerting the carriers that one of the church officials had stolen Santa Eulalia's little digit.

✢ Ⓜ*Jaume I.* Ⓢ *Free.*

ROMAN WALLS   ⴲ HISTORY

Scattered throughout the Ciutat Vella, portions of the Roman remains are marked clearly with orange and black info plaques by the city, and it's hard not to run into at least one of them. For those history buffs looking for the most bang for their buck, walk down C. Tapineria (it's to your back as you exit the metro station), a narrow street connecting Plaça de l'Angel and Plaça Ramon Berenguer. This street holds the most concentrated number of fourth-century wall remains, though they may be hard to spot, as they are entirely incorporated into the base of the 14th-century Palau Reial Major. The second area of interest is the **Plaça Seu** in front of the Cathedral. To the left of the Cathedral is the only remaining octagonal tower, and to the right are a reconstruction of the Roman aqueduct and other smaller remains.

✠ ⓂJamue I. Ⓢ Free.

Las Ramblas

Beginning along the sea and cutting straight through to Plaça Catalonia, Las Ramblas is Barcelona's world-famous main pedestrian thoroughfare that attracts flocks of visitors and flocks of people attempting to draw money from said visitors. Lined with trees, cafes, tourist traps, human statues, beautiful buildings, and pickpockets, the five distinct promenades combine seamlessly to create the most lively and exciting pedestrian area in the city. The **Ramblas**, in order from Plaça Catalonia to the Columbus Monument are: **La Rambla de les Canaletes**, **La Rambla dels Estudis**, **La Rambla de Sant Josep**, **La Rambla dels Cataputxins**, and **La Rambla de Santa Mònica**.

LA RAMBLA DELS ESTUDIS   ♿ PROMENADE
Las Ramblas

Named for the university that was once located here (*estudis* means "studies" in Catalan), the path is now closer to a lesson in animal taxonomy than scholarly topics. Known as "Las Ramblas dels Ocells" (literally, of the birds), the shops along this stretch of pavement sell everything from rabbits to guinea pigs, iguanas to turtles, ducks to parrots, and much more. Here is your place to pick up a pigeon, and with some good training, you may soon be able to sidestep Spain's postal service. This area justifiably becomes the target of Barcelona's active and outraged animal rights proponents, but there seems to be no indication that Las Ramblas will be any less furry, fluffy, or feathery anytime soon.

✠ ⓂCatalonia. Walk toward the water.

LA RAMBLA DE SANT JOSEP   ♿ PROMENADE
Las Ramblas

If you're looking for a bouquet for that special someone, or you've just decided that your hostel bathroom could really benefit from a few rose petals, La Rambla de Sant Josep is your place. Flower shops line this stretch of the pedestrian avenue, giving it the nickname "La Rambla de les Flors." Following the theme of living things now dead, the impressive Boqueria is found along this stretch, along with the once-grand and now practically gutted **Betlem Church**. The end of this promenade is marked by Miró's mosaic in the pavement at Plaça Boqueria.

✠ ⓂLiceu. Walk toward Plaça Catalonia.

LA RAMBLA DELS CATAPUTXINS   ♿ PROMENADE
Las Ramblas

La Rambla dels Cataputxins boasts access to ⓂLiceu and a straight shot to Plaça Sant Jaume I via C. Ferran, which runs directly through the center of the Gothic Quarter. Cafes and restaurants line this portion of Las Ramblas, and eager business owners will try desperately to pull you into their lair—if "tapas" and specials listed in English don't do it first. Littered with eye candy such as the **Casa Bruno Cuadros** (corner of C. Boqueria and Las Ramblas, the one with the 🐉dragon in front), Teatre Liceu, and a mosaic by Joan Miró, this portion of Las Ramblas is often the busiest.

✠ ⓂLiceu. Walk toward the sea.

LA RAMBLA DE SANTA MÒNICA   ♿ PROMENADE
Las Ramblas

Ending at the feet of Christopher Columbus himself, La Rambla de Santa Monica leads the boulevard to the waterfront. This portion of the path is the widest and, unlike its saintly name would suggest, the most packed with vices and temptation. Though filled with artists peddling their takes on Miró, your face, or dolphins in the shape of letters during the day, at night the area becomes thick with prostitutes aggressively looking for confused potential clients.

⇞ [M]Drassanes.

LA RAMBLA DE LES CANALETES ♿ PROMENADE

Las Ramblas

The head of Las Ramblas when walking from Plaça Catalonia to the water, this rambla is named after the fountain that marks its start—Font de les Canaletes. Surprisingly unceremonious, the fountain is not a spewing spectacle of lights and water jets but instead a fancy drinking fountain with four spouts, rumored to make those who drink its water fall in love with the city. These days the fountain has amusingly run dry, so be sure to fill your Nalgene elsewhere.

⇞ [M]Catalonia.

LA RIBERA

DISSENY HUB BARCELONA (DHUB) ♿ DESIGN, ART

C. Montcada, 12; Av. Diagonal, 686 ☎93 256 23 00; 93 256 34 65 🖳www.dhub-bcn.cat

Ever dream of making a chair simply with a beam of light? Chances are you haven't, but just in case you have (or you're curious how it's even possible), Disseny Hub Barcelona will show you said chair, let you touch it, and even explain every single step of its magical creation. Split over two buildings nearly a town apart, Disseny Hub Barcelona focuses on showcasing Barcelona's cutting edge contemporary art with a commercial edge through amazing historical displays, video supplements, and a creative laboratory that fosters the budding designer in even the least creative visitor. The **Montcada branch,** located across from the Museu Picasso, houses temporary exhibitions and study galleries that test the limits of the imagination, including everything from heat sensitive wallpaper to an automated dessert printer. Just across town, the Palau de Pedralbes hosts the **Museu de les Arts Decoratives** and the **Museu Tèxtil i d 'Indumentària,** both highlighting the evolution of art objects and fashion from the Romanesque to the Industrial Revolution with enough quirky artifacts and period dress to make it worth the trek. Currently, the price of admission provides access to both museums, but look for both to be housed under the same roof in the upcoming year as the primary home of the Disseny Hub Barcelona is finished in Plaça de les Gloriès Catalanes in 2011.

⇞ *Montcada: [M]Jaume I. From Metro, walk down C. de la Princesa and turn right onto C. de Montacada. Pedralbes: [M]Palau Reial.* ℹ *New combined museum to be opened in 2011 in Plaça de les Glories.* $ *Admission to both centers €5. Free Su 3-8pm.* ⏰ *Montcada open Tu-Sa 11am-7pm, Su 11am-8pm. Pedralbes open Tu-Su 10am-6pm.*

PICASSO MUSEUM ♿ ARCHITECTURE, ART

C. Montcada, 15-23 ☎93 256 30 00 🖳www.museupicasso.bcn.es

Tucked away amongst the *bodegas* and medieval charms of Ribera is the Museu Picasso—five connected mansions dedicated to showcasing what Picasso's work was like before he was cool. His early years' collection is organized chronologically, providing insight into his development into the international star of Cubism. However, the collection is not completely Barça-centric. Paintings from after his time in Paris show the influence of the Impressionists he encountered, while several works from his Blue and Rose periods help to literally paint a picture of his past. The most sweeping gesture of influence is easily the room of the artist's 58 renditions of Velázquez's *Las Meninas*, where the iconic Spanish painter's work is spiked and contorted into a nightmare landscape of Cubist forms. Temporary exhibits highlight the work of Picasso's contemporaries, though the museum would easily attract the same droves of visitors without them. Expect a long wait along the crowded street of Montcada during any day of the week, especially on Sundays when the museum is free. To beat the throngs of people, try hitting up the museum early or waiting until the later hours.

🚇 [M]Jaume I. From the Metro, walk down C. de la Princesa and turn right onto C. de Montacada. ℹ Free entrance on first Su of each month. $ €8.50 (valid for 2 days, only for permanent exhibits). Annual subscription (permanent and temporary exhibits included) €14. ⏰ Open Tu-Sa 10am-7-pm, Su 10am-2:30pm.

PARC DE LA CIUTADELLA ♿📶 PARK, MUSEUMS

Between Psg. de Picasso, C. Pujades, and C. Wellington

Once the site of the Spanish fortress built by King Felipe V in the 18th century, the park was transformed into its current state after the citadel was destroyed in preparation for the Universal Exhibition of 1888. This sprawling complex designed by Josep Fontserè includes copious green space as well as various *modernista* buildings from the period. Points of architectural interest span from two areas: the antique fort holds the governor's palace, arsenal, and *capilla*, and the Exhibition in 1888 area showcases century-old gems, many of which are still in use today. The steel and glass **Hivernacle,** a greenhouse-turned-civic-space near the Pujades entrance, maintains its original function as well as its newer one as a concert venue. The **Natural History Museum** *(☎93 319 69 12)* continues educating crowds and completing conservation work between its two locations. The **Museu Martorell** functions as a geology museum, and the 📷**Castillo de los Tres Dragones,** designed by Lluís Domènech i Montaner (of Palau de Música Catalana and Hospital de Santa Creu fame) comprises the **Zoological Museum** building and the entrance to the **Barcelona Zoo** *(☎90 245 75 45💻www.zoobarcelona.cat).* The extravagant **Cascada Monumental** fountain located in the center of the park, designed in part by Antoni Gaudí, still provides a spectacle for any visitor. Though a newer addition, the 📷**mastodon** near the entrance of the zoo makes for an excellent photo opportunity.

For those just looking to use the park as, well, a park, bike trails run around the exterior walls, and dirt pedestrian paths break up the lush grass and tree-shaded pockets. Expect to see nearly every corner covered in picnickers during the summer months, and be sure to stop by and join the locals for a bath in the fountain.

🚇 [M]Arc de Triomf. Walk through the arch and down the boulevard to enter the park. ℹ Free Wi-Fi available at the Geological Museum, Parliament building, and Zoological Museum. $ Park free. Museum €4.10-5.60, Su 3-8pm free. Zoo €16. ⏰ Park open daily 10am-dusk. Natural History Museum open Tu-Sa 10am-6:30pm, Su 10am-8pm. Zoo open May 16-Sep 15 10am-7pm; Oct 10am-6pm; Nov-Dec 10am-5pm; Jan-Feb 10am-5pm; Mar-May 15 10am-6pm.

SANTA MARÍA DEL MAR ♿ CHURCH

C. Canvis Vells, 1 ☎93 319 23 90 💻www.santamariadelmar.es

Ribera is dominated by this church's stoic presence, but it's nearly impossible to get a good glimpse of the Santa Maria. Nearby streets only allow remotely satisfactory views of the exterior from the Fossar de les Moreres at the end of Passeig del Born. The Plaça Santa Maria, located at the west entrance of the church, holds the best views of the church's impressive rose window (dating back to 1459) and the intricate relief and sculptural work of the main entrance. Constructed between 1329 and 1838, this church exemplifies Catalan Gothic style—tough on the outside, light and airy on the inside. The inside is perplexingly spacious and open, with tall, slim octagonal pillars lining the main nave and no constructed boundaries between the nave and the altar area. Although there are three naves, it feels as if the interior is made of only one. Despite the beautiful proportions and effect of the architecture, the interior has little decoration, due to a conflagration there in 1936 during the Spanish Civil War.

🚇 [M]Jaume I. Walk down C. de l'Argenteria to enter the plaza. Santa Maria del Mar will be in front of you to your right. $ Free. ⏰ Open M-Sa 9am-1:30pm and 4:30-8:30pm, Su 10am-1:30pm and 4:30-8:30pm.

ARC DE TRIOMF   ♿ ARCHITECTURE

Between Passeig de Lluís Companys and Passeig de Sant Joan

For a proper greeting from the city of Barcelona, be sure to arrive by bus and get dropped off at the **Arc de Trimof Station.** If you're coming by other means, cheat and come here anyway. Situated at the beginning of a wide boulevard leading to the **Parc de la Ciutadella,** the arch not only picturesquely frames the palm tree- and *modernista* building-lined road and its incredible terminating point, but also literally embraces visitors with a sculptural frieze by Josep Reynés with the inscribed phrase "Barcelona rep les nacions," or *"Barcelona welcomes the nations."* This seemingly incongruous ceremonious declaration stems from its construction for the 1888 Universal Exhibition, when the arc served as the main entrance to the fairgrounds in the Parc.

Nowadays the arc serves as little more than a historical artifact but is worth a gander if you are in the area. The triumphant brick arch was designed by Josep Jilaseca i Cassanovas in the Moorish revival style. Its exterior is decked out with sculptures of 12 women representing fame and a relief by Josep Lllimona depicting the award ceremony.

✙ Ⓜ*Arc de Triomf.* Ⓡ *Free.* ⓗ *Open 24hr.*

EL RAVAL

CENTRE DE CULTURA CONTEMPORÀNIA DE BARCELONA (CCCB)   ⎈♿ ART

C. de Montalegre, 5   ☎93 306 41 00 🔗www.cccb.org

A literal hub for anything involving the more contemplative ideas of the city, the Centre de Cultural Contemporània de Barcelona boasts everything from art exhibitions to lectures on Gilles Deleuze to theater to literature to help trying to figure out what the hell public and private space really means. Three exhibition galleries, two lecture halls, an auditorium, and a bookstore fill the striking architectural complex, consisting of an early 20th-century theater-turned-supersleek glass-expansion-wing. Paired with the thought-provoking collections of nearby MACBA, the CCCB offers everything you'll need to inspire that next existential crisis.

✙ Ⓜ*Universitat. Walk down C. Pelai and take the 1st right and then a left onto C. Tallers. Take a right onto C. Valldonzella and a left onto C. Montalegre, which will place you in front of the Museum complex.* 𝏟 *Guided visits in Spanish Th 6pm, Sa 11:30am.* Ⓡ *One exhibition €4.50. Two or more exhibitions €6, under 25 €3.40, under 15 free. €3.40 on W; free on 1st W of month, Th from 8-10pm and Su 3-8pm.* ⓗ *Open Tu-W 11am-8pm, Th 11am-8pm, F-Su 11am-8pm. Last entry 30min. before close.*

MUSEU D'ART CONTEMPORANI DE BARCELONA (MACBA)⎈♿ ARCHITECTURE, ART

P. dels Angels, 1   ☎93 412 08 10 🔗www.macba.cat

If the teeny art galleries and student-studded eateries around El Raval have struck your fancy, consider checking out the culture hub that helped to spawn them all. Bursting out of the narrow streets and into its own spacious plaza, the bright white geometries of American architect Richard Meier's 1995 building have made an indelible mark on the land, both architecturally and culturally, by almost single-handedly turning the area into a regional cultural and artistic center. The stark, simple interior plays host to an impressive collection of contemporary art, with particular emphasis on Spanish and Catalan artists, including a world-renowned collection of interwar avant-garde art. Due to its prime location near the Universitat and its undeniable appeal to local youth, MACBA prides itself on hip happenings. During the summer, "Nits de MACBA" keeps the doors open until midnight on Thursday and Friday nights, with free guided tours and reduced admission. Students and art afficionados alike flock to the popular hangout to catch one of the more experimental rotating exhibits, exciting complements to the static permanent collection. As if this weren't enough, the museum completely transforms during Barcelona's Sonar music festival every year, magically converting into the Sonar Complex stage and denying admittance to all those without a festival ticket.

✈ ⓜUniversitat. *Walk down C. Pelai and take the 1st right and then a left onto C. Tallers. Take a right onto C. Valldonzella and a left onto C. Montalegre, which will place you in front of the Museum complex.* **i** *Guided tours in English included in ticket purchase.* ⑤ *Entrance to all exhibits €7.50, students €6; temporary exhibits €6/4.50. One-year pass €12.* 🕐 *Open June 24-Sept 24 M 11am-8pm, W 11am-8pm, Th-F 11am-midnight, Sa 10am-8pm, Su 10am-3pm; Sept 25-June 23 M 11am-7:30pm, W-F 11am-7:30pm, Sa 10am-8pm, Su 10am-3pm.*

L'ANTIC HOSPITAL DE LA SANTA CREU I SANT PAU   ♿ ARCHITECTURE
C. de l'Hospital, 56

Not to be confused with Lluís Domènech i Montaner's Hospital de la Santa Creu in the Eixample, L'Antic Hospital de la Santa Crue i Sant Pau (or Old Hospital of Santa Cruz and Saint Paul) is a 15th-century Gothic building located in the middle of Raval. Although the main core no longer functions as a hospital, it does house an interior courtyard bedecked with beautiful trees, benches, and a restaurant. The interior theater rocks a rotating marble dissection table, and the archives boast a recording of famous Catalan architect Antoni Gaudí's death in 1926. At this time, the hospital was used to treat the poor, and Gaudí was mistaken for a homeless man and brought to the premises after being hit by a tram. The hospital also now houses the Reial Acadèmia de Farmàcia de Catalonia, the National Library of Catalonia, and an art museum in its chapel, the latter two of which are open to the public.

✈ ⓜLiceu. *Walk down C. de l'Hospital.* ⑤ *Free.*

LA CAPELLA DE L'ANTIC HOSPITAL DE LA SANTA CREU I SANT PAU ♿❋ MUSEUM
C. de l'Hospital, 56   ☎93 442 71 71 ▤elnostremuseu.blogspot.com

The chapel of the Antique Hospital of Santa Cruz's rustic stone walls and arches provide fantastic views of the building's interior Gothic architecture. Though mostly gutted of all decoration, the upper balcony and dilapidated organ are still on view above the main entrance. The chapel now serves as a center for contemporary and experimental art with smaller rotating exhibitions.

✈ ⓜLiceu. *Walk down C. de l'Hospital.* ⑤ *Free.* 🕐 *Open Tu-Sa noon-2pm and 4-8pm, Su 11am-2pm.*

NATIONAL LIBRARY OF CATALONIA   ♿❋ LIBRARY, ARCHITECTURE
C. de l'Hospital, 56   ☎932 70 23 00 ▤www.bnc.cat

Although once housed in the Palau de la Generalitat de Catalonia, the collection now known as the National Library of Catalonia found its home in the Old Hospital in 1940. The library was considered a general-use library during the Franco years and was declared the national library of Catalonia after his fall. Today, over 20,000 volumes are open to the public, including the soaring vaults of the general reading room.

✈ ⓜLiceu. *Walk down C. de l'Hospital.* ⑤ *Free.* 🕐 *Open M-Th 9am-8pm, Sa 9am-2pm.*

RIERA BAIXA   ⊛♿♲ FLEA MARKET, SECONDHAND
C. de la Riera Baixa   ▤www.facebook.com/pages/Riera-Baixa

A street lined entirely with secondhand shops, Riera Baixa is a mecca for any bargain or vintage shopper. The main attraction happens on Saturdays when clothes, records, trinkets, cameras, and an unfathomable amount of other stuff combine with Raval's largely student population, giving birth to the most exciting flea market in the city.

✈ ⓜLiceu. *Walk down C. de l'Hospital and take a slight right onto C. de la Riera Baixa.* 🕐 *Flea-market Sa 11am-9pm. Shops open daily.*

L'EIXAMPLE

📷 FUNDACIÓ ANTONI TAPIES 🎫♿ ARCHITECTURE, ART

C. Aragó, 255 ☎93 487 03 15 💻www.fundaciotapies.org

Housed in a building by *modernista* architect Lluis Domenech i Montaner, the Fundació Antoni Tapies is made unmissable by its mess of wire and steel atop a low brick roofline, a sculpture by its namesake Antoni Tapies entitled "Núvol i Cadira," or "Cloud and Chair" (1990) that supposedly shows a chair jutting out of a large cloud. Once inside, the lower two levels are dedicated to temporary exhibitions on incredible modern and contemporary artists and themes, recently holding work by Eva Hesse and Steve McQueen. Ascend to the top floor to find the gallery space dedicated to famous Catalan artists, including Antoni Tapies himself. Paintings and sculpture using found materials shed new light on Catalonia's turbulent past, while summer nights light up with DJ nights, free drinks, and after-hours galleries.

⇄ [M]Passeig de Gràcia. Walk toward the mountain on Psg. de Gràcia and take a left onto C. Aragó. The museum has a funky mess of wire on top. $ €7, reduced €5.60. Free May 18 and Sept. 24. ⏰ Open Tu-Su 10am-8pm.

📷 SAGRADA FAMILIA 🎫♿ ARCHITECTURE

C. Mallorca, 401 ☎93 208 04 14 💻www.sagradafamilia.cat

If you know Barcelona, you know Sagrada Familia—its eight completed towers and fanciful forms befitting of its Gaudí nametag have been plastered on tourist magazines, highlighted in movie advertisements, and featured in every panorama of the city ever photographed in the modern era. And with over 120 years of construction, the cranes surrounding the Sagrada Familia complex have become as iconic as the temple itself.

Although still a work in progress, Sagrada Familia's construction began way back in 1882. The super-pious, super-conservative **Spiritual Association for Devotion to St. Joseph (or the Josephines)** commissioned the building as a reaction to the liberal ideas spreading through Europe in the decades prior. It was intended as an Expiatory Temple for Barcelona in commemoration of the Sacred Family—Mary, Jesus, and Joseph. When searching for an architect, the Josephines looked in-house and picked Diocesan architect Francisco de Paula del Villar as their main man, but the relationship quickly turned sour, and one year later the church replaced him with Gaudí after only the Gothic foundations had been laid.

At the time of employment, Gaudí was just 30 years of age, and he would continue to work on the building until his death over forty years later. Modest private donations founded the construction of the church in the beginning, but after the completion of the **crypt** in 1889, the church received an incredibly generous private donation allowing Gaudí to step up his game. This extra cash gave birth to the design that would make the building both the most ambitious and the most impossible to complete in the city. After building the **Nativity Facade,** a drop in private donations slowed construction, and in 1909 temporary schools were built next to the church for workers' children. Gaudí set up shop on-site a few years later, living next to his incomplete masterpiece until his brutal death by tram just outside of the church's walls in 1926. Fittingly, he was buried inside the **Carmen Chapel** of the crypt.

Gaudí's bizarre demise marked the start of a tragic period for the temple. The Civil War brought construction entirely to a hault, and in 1936 arsonists raided Gaudí's tomb, mashed the plaster models of the site, and burned every document in the workshop, effectively destroying all artifacts of the architect's original intention. Since then, plans for the construction have been based off of the remaining reconstructed plaster models, with computers only recently being used to help understand their complex mathematics.

Currently, the building remains under the auspices of the Josephines, and architect Jordi Bonet, whose father worked directly with Gaudí, remains in charge of the overall direction. The Cubist **Passion Facade** (Passion being the crucifixion, death, and resurrection of Christ) faces Pl. de la Sagrada Família, and was completed by Josep Marià Subirachs in 1998. Its angular and abstracted forms are a far cry from Gaudí's original plans for the facade in 1911 and provide a stark contrast to his own more traditional Nativity Facade on the opposite face. The first mass was held inside the gutted church in 2000 for celebration of the millennium, and the church's apse is projected for completion in the upcoming year thanks to a continuous stream of popular donations (read: your ticket price).

If all goes well, the projected completion date is 2026, coincidentally both the 100th anniversary of Gaudí's death and the date that hell is predicted to freeze over. Until then, paintings of the completed building line the adjacent **Casa Museu Gaudí,** and an exhibition dedicated to the mathematical models let you imagine the completed building that you'll probably never get to experience.

🚏 Ⓜ Sagrada Familia. ***i*** *Guided tours in English May-Oct at 11am, 1pm, 3pm, and 4pm; Nov-Apr at 11am and 1pm. $ €11, students €9, under 10 free. Elevator €2.50. Combined ticket with Casa-Museu Gaudí €13, students €11. ⏰ Open daily Apr-Sept 9am-8pm, Oct-Mar 9am-6pm. Last elevator to the tower 15min. before close.*

CASA BATTLÓ ✎♿ ARCHITECTURE

Pg. de Gràcia, 43 ☎93 216 03 06 💻www.casabatllo.es

From the spine-like stairwell wrapping around the scaled building's interior to the undulating 📷**dragon-esque** curve of the ceramic rooftop, the Casa Battló will have you wondering what kinds of drugs Gaudí was rectally injecting. This architectural wonderland was once the home of the fantastically rich and is now the most heavily frequented of the three *modernista* marvels in the **Manzana de la Discordia** lining Passieg de Gràcia. A self-guided audio tour lets you navigate the dream-like environs at your own pace, so be sure to spend some time with the curved wood and two-toned stained glass of each of the doors (from both sides—the glass changes color), the soft scale-like pattern of the softly bowed walls, and the charybdis-esque light fixture that pulls the entire ceiling rippling into its center. Gaudí's design spans from the incredibly logical to the seemingly insane, including a blue lightwell that passes from deep navy to sky as you descend in order to distribute light more evenly.

If you're having a problem parting with the cash to get in, just try this logic, heard in line at the box office: if your flight to Barcelona had cost €18 more than you paid, would you still have taken it? Then why miss this gem for the same price? Like the guy who needed convincing, you won't be disappointed.

🚏 Ⓜ Passeig de Gràcia. Walk away from Plaza Catalonia on Passeig de Gràcia. Casa Battló is 2½ blocks down on the left. ***i*** *Tickets available at box office or through TelEntrada. Entrance includes free self-guided audio tour. $ Tours €17.80, students and BCN cardholders €13. ⏰ Open daily 9am-8pm.*

CASA MILÀ (LA PEDRERA) ✎♿ ARCHITECTURE

Pg. de Gràcia, 92 ☎93 484 59 00 💻www.lapedreraeducacio.org

No, this building's facade didn't melt in the Barcelona sun, though it has garnered some equally unflattering comparisons. Its nickname "La Pedrera" literally means "the quarry," and stems from popular jokes, criticism, and caricatures about the house upon its construction 100 years ago. Although wealthy businessman Pere Milà hired Gaudí after being impressed by his Casa Battló a few blocks away, his wife began to loathe her version of Gaudí's signature style as construction progressed, and eventually refused to let the costly venture proceed. Not one to let the difficult couple have the last word, Gaudí sued the rich pair over fees and gave his winnings from the suit to the poor. Not ones to have Gaudí have the last say, the couple then looked elsewhere to complete their home interior, making La Pedrera the only house designed by Gaudí that isn't graced by his furniture.

La Pedrera still functions as a home to the rich, famous, and patient—the wait list for an apartment is over 20 years long—as well as offices of the Caixa Catalonia. Many portions of the building are open to the public, including an apartment decorated with period furniture (and, true to the house, not designed by Gaudí) and the main floor. The attic, a space known as **Espai Gaudí**, boasts a mini-museum to the man himself, including helpful exhibits explaining the science behind his beloved caternary arches and what exactly it means for the architect to be "inspired by natural structures." Up top, a terrace holds the perfect photo opportunity, whether with the desert-like sculptural outcroppings or the view overlooking Barcelona to Gaudí's Sagrada Familia. During the summer the terrace lights up both literally and metaphorically with jazz performances on Friday and Saturday nights in a series known as *La Nit de Pedrera*.

✦ ⓂDiagonal. Walk on C. Rosselló toward Passeig de Gràcia and take a right. La Pedrera is on the left at the corner of C. Provença. *i* Free audio tour with entrance. Ⓢ €9.50, students and seniors €5.50. Concerts €12; glass of cava included. ◷ Open daily Mar-Oct 9am-8pm; Nov-Feb 9am-6:30pm. Last entry 30min. before close. Concerts last weekend of June and July F-Sa 9pm-midnight.

CASA AMATLLER   ✦ ARCHITECTURE, CHOCOLATE
Pg. de Gràcia, 41   ☎93 4487 72 17 ▨www.amatller.com

The severe, rational counterpart to Gaudí's neighboring acid trip **Casa Batlló**, Casa Amatller was the first of the trio of buildings that has come to be known as the **Manzana de la Discordia.** In 1898, chocolate mogul Antoni Amattler commissioned **Josep Puig i Cadafalch** to spruce up the facade of his prominent home along Passieg de Gràcia, and out popped a mix of Catalan, neo-Gothic, Islamic, and Dutch architecture in a strict geometric plane. A carving of Sant Jordi battling the pesky ▧dragon appears over the front door, accompanied by four figures engaged in painting, sculpting, and architecture. Amattler's peddling in the muses is more than just decorative. Inside the building, find the **Amattler Institute of Hispanic Art,** including a library accessible to visiting scholars and students of art history. Although the house is currently undergoing renovations, the main floor is still open to visitors by reservation every Friday at noon, though times will change as the work progresses. If you're in the area and feel like stopping by to take a look at this gem, the lower level gift shop includes a free exhibition of the house and its sculpture and informs you as to exactly how Amattler got so filthy rich, with bars of the company's delicious chocolate for sale on your way out the door.

✦ ⓂPasseig de Gràcia. Walk away from Plaza Catalonia on Passeig de Gràcia. Casa Amatller is two and a half blocks down on the left. *i* Reservation by phone or email required for tour. Ⓢ Tours €10; includes chocolate tasting. ◷ Guided tours F at noon.

HOSPITAL DE LA SANTA CREU I SANT PAU   ⚐ ARCHITECTURE
C. Sant Antoni Maria Claret, 167   ☎90 207 66 21 ▨www.santpau.es

Notoriously the most important piece of *modernista* public architecture, this hospital's practice is anything but *nouveau*. Dating back to 1401, the Hospital de la Santa Creu i Sant Pau is the newest embodiment of the medical practice formerly housed in the Antique Hospital de la Santa Creu in Raval. Wealthy benefactor Pau Gil bequested funds for the building upon his death with strict instructions, including the name appendage. Construction then began in 1902 under the design of **Lluís Domènech i Montaner,** who in almost Gaudían fashion (only made more appropriate by Gaudí's anonymous death in the old hospital), died before its completion. His son then saw the work to fruition, giving the hospital 48 large pavilions connected by underground tunnels and bedazzled with luxurious modernist sculptures and paintings. Although the hospital still functions as a world class medical facility today, you won't need to break a leg to appreciate its beauty. Guided tours are offered daily as a part of Barcelona's Ruta de Modernisme.

☆ ⓂHospital Sant Pau. ☏ Guided tours in English daily at 10am, 11am, noon and 1pm. Information desk open daily 9:30am-1:30pm.

GRÀCIA

⬛ PARC GÜELL   ⊛⟁ PARK, ARCHITECTURE
Gràcia

Now a mecca for countless tourists and outdoor-loving locals alike, Parc Güell was originally intended for the eyes of a select few. Catalan industrialist, patron of the arts, and all-around man of disgusting wealth Eusebi Güell called upon his right-hand man **Antoni Gaudí** in 1900 to collaborate on an endeavor completely unlike the previous Güell Palau. The patron envisioned a luxurious community of 60 lavish homes wrapped around an English-inspired, Ebenezer-Howard-esque garden paradise overlooking Barcelona—rich, elite, and pleasantly removed from the mundane realities of the city and its plebian people. Unfortunately for the complex, other members of Barcelona's upper class weren't convinced; they weren't about to abandon the amenities of the city for a cut-off hunk of grass dotted by Gaudí's seemingly deranged buildings, which that at the time lacked even basic living luxuries. Construction came to a halt in 1914, and in 1918 the area became a park when the Barcelona City Council bought the property.

The park was opened to the public in 1923 and has since been declared a UNESCO World Heritage Site. Buses bring flocks of visitors directly to the **Palmetto Gate,** a structure flanked by a guardhouse-turned-museum and giftshop. Hand-drummers stationed outside of the facing alcove often provide a dream-like soundtrack for walking through the gingerbread-esque architecture. Those with sturdy shoes lacking a fear of heights often choose to take the metro and climb the escalators to the nature-clad side entrance. The main attractions of the park (and, consequently, the areas most packed with people) are the brightly-colored mosaics and fountains, like the **salamander fountain** just across from Palmetto Gate. The pillar forest of the **Hall of One Hundred Columns (Teatre Griego),** dotted with sculptural pendants by **Josep Maria Jujol,** musicians, and people peddling fake handbags. The intricate vaults of the hall support **Plaça de la Nautralesa** above, enclosed by the winding **serpentine bench,** decked in colorful ceramics, including 21 distinct shades of white that were castoffs from the **Casa Milà.** If you catch yourself wondering how a ceramic bench can be so comfortable, thank the woman rumored to have sat bare-bottomed in clay for Jujol to provide the form.

Paths to the park's summit provide amazing views, and one in particular showcases what the park has left to offer: walk to the right when facing the salamander fountain from its base. Follow the wide path and veer right toward the shaded benches and continue climbing uphill to come across the **Casa-Museu Gaudí** (C. d 'Olot, 7 ☎93 284 64 46 🖳www.casamuseuGaudí.org). As you continue, the third and last original building of the complex, **Juli Batllevell's Casa Trías** lays inconspicuously ahead, still privately owned by the Doménech family. **El Turo de Les Tres Creus** greets visitors at the top of the wide path. This, the park's highest point with appropriately incredible views, was originally intended to be the residents' church and now serves instead to mark the end of the ascent.

☆ ⓂLesseps. Walk uphill on Travessera de Dalt and take a left to ride escalators to safety. Bus #24 from Plaça Catalonia stops directly in front of the park. Ⓢ Free. Museum €5.50, students €4.50. ☏ Open daily Oct-Mar 10am-6pm; Apr-Sept 10am-8pm.

BARCELONETA

MUSEU D'HISTÒRIA DE CATALUNYA   ⬥♿ ARCHITECTURE, ART
Pl. de Pau Vila, 3   ☎93 225 47 00 🖳www.es.mhcat.net

If you're finally tired of having "Catalonia is not Spain" pounded into your head without a proper explanation as to what that could even possibly mean, stop by the Museu d'Història de Catalonia and be converted to the Catalan cause. Settled right before where the old city becomes the tourist-lined Barceloneta (purposefully so, perhaps?), this informative museum doubles as regional propaganda, attempting to inform anyone and everyone about Catalonia's history, politics, and culture in a way that is both inspiringly patriotic and amazingly informative. Detailed displays recount the city's history, complete with English captions and vivid dioramas, and shed light on the layers of history and ruins that you've seen throughout the city. But more than being a simple supplement to your tour guide, the museum provides something more helpful—a historical briefer as to what makes Barcelona and Catalonia as a whole just so unique. The museum recounts its history from flint tools to the harrowing, rollercoaster days of Castillian relations to the Catalan beatdown by Franco and the subsequent rise after his demise. One foot in the door and you'll be ready to track down your own independentist flag to take home.

❖ Ⓜ*Barceloneta. Museum is located along the water on Psg. Joan de Borbó.* ⓘ *Free admission on first Su of month.* Ⓢ *€4, students and under 18 €3.* ⓧ *Open Tu 10am-7pm, W 10am-8pm, Th-Sa 10am-7pm, Su 10am-2:30pm. Last entry 30min. before close.*

MONTJUÏC AND POBLE SEC

⬛ FUNDACIÓ MIRÓ
Parc de Montjuïc

❖♿ ARCHITECTURE, ART
☎93 443 94 70 ▣www.fundaciomiro-bcn.org

From the outside in, the Fundació serves as both a shrine to and a celebration of the life and work of Joan Miró, one of both Catalonia and Spain's most beloved contemporary artists. The bright white angles and curves of the Lego-esque Rationalist building were designed by Josep Lluís Sert, a close friend of Joan Miró. Since its first opening, the museum's holdings have expanded beyond Miró's original collection, with many works by those inspired personally by the artist being donated or acquired in the years after his death. A rotating collection of over 14,000 works now fills the open galleries with views to the grassy exterior and adjacent **Sculpture Park.** Highlights of the collection include paintings and gargantuine *sobreteixims* (paintings on tapestry) by Miró, as well as works by Calder, Duchamp, Oldenburg, and Léger. Like much of Barcelona, the foundation refuses to be stuck in its past— although an impressive relic of a previous era, the foundation continues to support the contemporary arts in the present day. Temporary exhibitions have recently included names such as Olafur Eliasson, Pipllotti Rist, and Kiki Smith, while the more experimental **Espai 13** houses exhibitions by emerging artists selected by freelance curators. Overwhelmed? You should be. This is one of the few times we recommend paying for the audio tour *(€4).*

❖ Ⓜ*Parallel and then take the Funicular to the museum.* Ⓢ *€8.50, students €6. Audio tour €4. Sculpture garden free.* ⓧ *Open July-Sept Tu-Sa 10am-8pm, Su 10am-2:30pm; Oct-June Tu-Sa 10am-7pm.*

NATIONAL ART MUSEUM OF CATALONIA
Palau Nacional, Parc de Montjuïc

❖♿ ARCHITECTURE, ART
☎93 622 03 76 ▣www.mnac.es

This majestic building perched atop the escalator summit of Montjuïc isn't quite as royal as it would at first appear. Designed by Enric Català and Pedro Cendoya for the 1929 International Exhibition, the Palau Nacional has housed the Museu Nacional d'art de Catalonia (MNAC) since 1934. Though the sculpture-framed view over Barcelona from the museum's front can't be beat, more treasures await inside. Upon entrance you'll be dumped into the gargantuan colonnaded **Oval Hall,** which, although empty, gets your jaw appropriately loose to prepare for its drop in the galleries. The wing to your right houses a collection of Catalan Gothic art, complete with wood-paneled paintings and sculptures Pier 1 would die to duplicate. To your left in the main hall is the wing housing the museum's impressive collection of Catalan Romanesque art and frescoes, removed from their original settings in the '20s and installed in the museum space—a move for the best considering the amount of churches devastated during the Civil War just a decade later. Upstairs are the more modern attractions, with MNAC's collections of modern art to the left, numismatics (coins, for you non-collectors) to the slight right, and drawings, prints, and posters to the far right. For those intoxicated by the quirky architecture of the city, Catalan *modernisme* and *noucentisme* works dot the galleries, from Gaudí's 1907 "Confidant from the Batlló House" chair to Picasso's Cubist "Woman in Fur Hat and Collar." Ranging from 1800-1940, the collection highlights both the shape of Barcelona's avant-garde movements at the time and paints a pictures as to how they got that way. If art isn't your thing, check out the currency collection—though beauty may be in the eye of the beholder, this 140,000-piece brief in the history of Catalan coin will hardly have any detractors.

☦ ⓂEspanya. *Walk through the towers and ride the escalators to the top—the museum is the palace-like structure.* ⓲ *Free entrance on first Su of each month.* ⓢ *Permanent exhibits €8.50 (valid for two days). Annual subscription (permanent and temporary exhibits) €14.* ⌚ *Open Tu-Sa 10am-7pm, Su 10am-2:30pm.*

POBLE ESPANYOL

➟♿❀ ARCHITECTURE, ART

Av. de Francesc Ferrer i Guàrdia, 13   ☎93 508 63 00 ▣www.poble-espanyol.com

One of the few original relics from the 1929 International Exhibition still dotting the mountain, the Poble Espanyol first aimed to present a unified Spanish village from its disparate, disjointed parts. Inspired by *modernista* celebrity Josep Puig i Cadafalch's original idea, the four architects and artists in charge of its design visited over 1600 villages and towns throughout the country to construct its 117 full-scale buildings, streets, and squares. Though intended simply as a temporary arts pavilion, the outdoor architectural museum was so popular that it was kept open as a shrine (or challenge) to the ideal of a united Spain that never was and never will be. Nowadays, the Poble Espanyol is all of this and more, with artists' workshops lining the winding roads peddling goods, spectacles during the day, and Terrazza and other parties raging on during the night.

☦ ⓂEspanya. *Walk through the towers and take a right after climbing the escalators to the top.* ⓢ *€8.90, students €6.60. Night entrance €5.50.* ⌚ *Open M 9am-8pm, Tu-Th 9am-2am, F 9am-4am, Sa 9am-5am, Su 9am-midnight. Shops open daily in summer 10am-8pm; in winter 10am-6pm.*

the great outdoors

BEACHES

Let's talk ▣*platges*—that's beaches in Catalan. For basic information on all of the city beaches, contact the **city beach office** (☎932 21 03 48 ▣*www.bcn.cat/platges*). Tents, motorcycles, soap, loud music, littering, and dogs (though we've only seen dogs and trash) are all prohibited. Showers, bathrooms, police, first aid, and basic info are available at each individual beach June-Sept 10am-7pm. Lifeguards are present at all beaches June-Sept daily 10am-7pm; Mar-June Sa-Su 10am-7pm. Lockers are available at the police station during certain hours. For the gym rats and juice heads, almost all beaches have some sort of outdoor workout facility.

PLATJA SAN SEBASTIÀ

♿ BEACH

Mouth of the Port to C. del Almirall Cervera   ▣www.bcn.cat/platges

The first of Barcelona's public beaches when stumbling out of the Ciutat Vella, Platja San Sebastià, along with Barceloneta, is one of the oldest beaches in the city. Older residents of the Barri Gòtic fill the available sand and are joined by a mix of tourists attracted to its convenient location. Like all beaches closer to Las

Ramblas and the center of the city, San Sebastià will fill up quickly, especially on weekends. If you're looking for a place a little more private, the end furthest from Barceloneta—near Torre San Sebastià—promises something at least remotely resembling peace and quiet. ✻ ⓂBarceloneta. *i* Bathrooms, swimming area, and showers available. ⓈFree. ♿ Wheelchair-accessible bathing services available June and second half of Sept on holidays and weekends. Open daily July-1st week of Sept 11am-6pm.

PLATJA BARCELONETA   BEACH
From C. del almirall Cervera to Port Olimpic   🖥www.bcn.cat/platges

The most popular (read: crowded) beach in Barcelona, Barceloneta attracts a vibrant mix of visitors, tourists, and brave locals regardless of the weather. In short, good luck finding a place to sunbathe even when there's no sun to be seen. With three volleyball courts, an outdoor gym, information center, various restaurants, a boardwalk, skating area, ping pong, and a *bibloplaya* (beach-centric library), Barceloneta offers (nearly) everything but a spot to lay your towel. ✻ ⓂBarceloneta or ⓂCiutadella *i* Info center. Book rental. Showers, public restrooms, volleyball courts, ping pong tables, and gym available. ⓈFree. ♿ Open 24hr.

PLATJA DEL BOGATELL   BEACH
From Bogatell Pier to Mar Bella Pier   🖥www.bcn.cat/platges

A rock wall protects a portion of Platja del Bogatell from the sea's sometimes perilous waves; however, the sport of choice here is not swimming, but marathon sunbathing on sand that resembles kitty litter when it gets wet. As with Platja San Sebastià, expect this beach to be frequented more heavily by an older crowd as teenagers and young adults flock to the busier Platja Barceloneta and more secluded Platja Nova Mar Bella. The adjacent Parc del Poblenou also offers a pleasantly green haven for those few that have grown tired of sand and waves. ✻ ⓂPoblenou or ⓂLlacuna. *i* Swimming area, showers, volleyball courts, and ping pong tables available. ⓈFree. ♿ Open 24hr.

PLATJA MAR BELLA   BEACH
From Mar Bella Pier to Bac de la Roda   🖥www.bcn.cat/platges

Past the Bogatell naval base, rocky outcroppings provide cover for Barcelona's only designated portion of nude beach. Past this short stretch of plentiful skin is a gay beach, marked by a rainbow flag flying at the beachside restaurant. Mostly frequented by younger and local people, the two sections provide a perfect place to shed some inhibitions (among other things). ✻ ⓂSelva del Mar. *i* Showers, public restrooms, ping pong tables, skating area, and basketball available. ⓈFree. ♿ Open 24hr.

PLATJA NOVA MAR BELLA   ♿ BEACH
Bac de Roda Pier to Selva de Mar Pier   🖥www.bcn.cat/platges

The furthest of all the beaches and consequently the least crowded, Platja Nova Mar Bella is the stomping ground of local youth, teenagers, and students. Still easily accessible by metro, this beach boasts a more relaxing alternative to the tourist-pushing match of Barceloneta, especially on weekends. ✻ ⓂSelva de Mar and ⓂEl Marisme. *i* Showers and public restrooms available. ⓈFree. ♿ Wheelchair-accessible bathing services available on holidays and weekends during June and second half of Sept. Open daily July-1st week of Sept 11am-6pm.

PARKS

PARC DE COLLSEROLA   ♿ PARK
Crta. de l'Esglèsia, 92   ☎93 280 35 52 🖥www.parccollserola.net

Just twenty minutes outside the center of Barcelona by train lies the largest metropolitan park in the world. At 84.65sq. km, Parc de Collserola makes Paris' Bois de

Boulogne look like a playground and New York's Central Park like a grade school shoebox diorama. The park stretches along the **Collserola mountain range** from the **Besos River** to the **Llobregat River**, with **Barcelona** and the **Vallés basin** forming its southern and northern boundaries, respectively. Although the park is easily accessible by public transportation, few people from outside of Barcelona and its environs make the short trek, so expect to find all signs and informational material in Catalan.

Collserola isn't your typical "city park." The city grid is nowhere to be seen, and there are more than pigeons and squirrels here. The park offers a refreshing dose of fresh air and wildlife that the gridded city misses. Due in part to straddling two distinct climates, the coastal **Mediterranean** and the more deciduous **Euro-Siberian,** Collserola shelters a wide range of flora and fauna, including the occasional wild boar. For a greatest hits showcase of the variety that the park has to offer, the trail from **Parc del Laberint** ([M]Mundet) to **Sant Cugat** is highly recommended. Besides a relaxing place to birdwatch and improve your classification skills, the park also offers many opportunities for exercise, with a ton of hiking trails and the **Carrertera de les Aigües** (Water Road), a cycling track that follows the ridge of the mountain range.

For those who do not find never-ending delight in the birds and the bees, the park is littered with places to eat, benches to relax on, and historic pieces of architecture and ruins to mentally digest. History buffs will want to check out the 12th-century **Sant Adjutori** and **Sant Medir,** while modernists should be sure to make a stop at the **Collserola Tower,** a telecommunications tower designed by architect Normal Foster for the 1992 Olympic Games. Although the games have long past, its 10th-floor observation room and unbeatable location on Vilana hill make it an ideal place to look out over all of Barcelona, Montserrat, and, if the day is clear, even the Pyrenees.

➹ [M]Baixador de Valividvera for Information Center (S1, S2), [M]Peu de Funicular (S1, S2), [M]Les Planes (S1, S2), [M]La Floresta (S1, S2, S5, S55), or [M]Mundet (L3). ℹ Tourist information center, museum, and restaurant near [M]Baixador de Valvidvera entrance. Other museums and restaurants scattered throughout; see website for full listing. $ Free. ⏰ Tours daily 10am-2pm. Info center open daily 10am-3pm.

food

BARRI GÒTIC AND LAS RAMBLAS

ATTIC ♿🍸❄ FANCY ❸

La Rambla, 120 ☎933 02 48 66 💻www.angrup.com

After a long day along Las Ramblas, Attic provides a soothing and incredibly orange world away from the performers, pickpockets, and never-ending construction. Serving fresh and utterly delectable food with prices downright reasonable for the quality of cuisine and mere presence of cloth napkins, Attic has no dress code, but it may be best to leave that pit-stained T-shirt and the pair of Tevas behind for the day.

➹ [M]Liceu. On La Rambla toward Plaça Catalonia. $ Appetizers €4.60-11; meat entrees €8-16.50, fish €10-13. ⏰ Open daily 1-4:30pm and 7pm-12:30am.

LA COLMENA ♿🍸 PASTRY SHOP ❶

P. de l'Angel, 12 ☎933 15 13 56

Directly facing the Plaça l'Angel, *pastelería* and *bombonería* La Colmena sweetly greets visitors as they appear bleary-eyed from the labyrinth of the Barri Gòtic and the Catalonian Sun. La Colmena offers a variety of pastries, chocolates, sweets, and hard drinks (of the dessert variety) to take the buzz off a day of continually getting lost. Mirrored walls and marble inlaid floors covered with confectioneries make you feel as if you've suddenly walked into an old-time mix between the shop in *Charlie and the Chocolate Factory* and the gingerbread house of Hansel and Gretel. Offerings range from the expected—chocolate *(€1.30)* and truffles *(€2)*—to those specific to Cataluña, like the *pastellitas de l 'Angel (€1.25),* a small and flaky pastry shell with sugary pumpkin filling. If you're overwhelmed (as you should be), just ask the knowledgeable staff.

[M]Jaume I. La Colmena is at your back after exiting the metro. $ Sweets €1.30-4. ⏰ Open daily 9am-9pm.

ESCRIBÀ DESSERT ❶

La Rambla, 83 ☎933 01 60 27 www.escriba.es

Grab a coffee and ogle the stained-glass peacock or one of the many just as impressive works of art waiting to be devoured in the front display case. With tarts, croissants, cakes, and deceivingly beautiful and life like rings made of caramel, Escribà is waiting to tempt you from every corner of the store. If you're not in the mood for sweets, select one of their savory dishes, such as the croissant with blue cheese, carmelized apple, and walnuts *(€4.50)* or the "bikini" bread mold with ham and brie *(€3.50)*.

[M]Liceu. Walk toward Plaça Catalonia. Escribà is almost immediately on the left. $ Sandwiches €3.50. Salads €3. Menú €5.90. i Open Tu-Su 9am-9pm.

L'ANTIC BOCOI DEL GÒTIC CATALAN ❸

Baixada de Viladecols, 3 ☎933 10 50 67 www.bocoi.net

Enter the lair of L'Antic Bocoi del Gòtic, where walls of rustic stone are somehow made impressively classy. The restaurant specializes in Catalan cuisine with fresh, seasonal ingredients and prides itself on bringing new ideas to traditional food. The staff recommends their selection of cheeses and their own take on the *coques de recapte*, a traditional regional dish made of a thin dough with delicious fresh produce and thickly layered meats. This hip joint fills up quickly after opening.

[M]Jaume I. i Reservations recommended. $ Appetizers €7-10, entrees €9-20. ⏰ Open M-Sa 8:30pm-midnight.

CAJ CHAI TEA ❶

Sant Domenech del Call, 12 ☎610 33 47 12 www.cajchai.com

Pronounced Chai Chai and named after the Czech"caj", or teahouse, the interior gives off more of a pseudo-Japanese zen vibe than any eastern European bohemian affectations. Beg the waitstaff to help guide you through their overwhelming list of teas from around the globe, and be sure to ask if there are any teas that are particular to the season. A variety of Arab, Indian, and Japanese pastries *(€1.50-2)* provide the perfect complement to the international array of teas. Luckily, all teas come in a personal pot, so you'll have an excuse to lounge in the good vibes for awhile longer. Morning specials for chai and pastries also available.

[M]Jaume I. Exit the metro station and take a right onto C. Jaume I, walking through the square with administrative buildings. After passing through the square, the road becomes to C. Ferran. Walk briefly down C. Ferran and take a right onto the narrow Sant Domenech del Call. $ Personal teas €2.50-7, pot for four €12-15, snacks €1.50-2. Cash only. ⏰ M 3-10pm, Tu-Su 10:30am-10pm.

ARC CAFE FUSION, THAI ❷

C. Carabassa, 19 ☎933 02 52 04 www.arccafe.com

Down the narrow Carrer d'en Carabassa, Arc Cafe is easy to miss. For this reason, it's a great place to stop in when you're sick of the fanny packs and sneakers that crowd Las Ramblas—it's virtually guaranteed to be tourist-and bustle-free. The restaurant boasts a vegetarian-friendly menu that rotates every three months as well as popular Thai nights Th-F (regular menu still available). Luckily, their curries are always available—choose between chicken, bean curd, and jasmine rice *(€10.50-11.50)*—just be sure to order a mojito with Malibu to cool off *(€6)* if you're brave enough to go for spice. Cheaper midday menu also offered daily *(€9.60)*.

🍽 Ⓜ*Drassanes. Walk toward the Sea on Las Ramblas, take a left onto Carrer de Josep Anselm Clavé. Walk 5 min. and stay on this road as it changes names to Carrer Ample. Take a left onto Carabassa. Arc Cafe on right.* 𝒊 *Reservations recommended on weekends.* Ⓢ *Appetizers €4.90-7.90; entrees €8.50-11.90. Wine €2. Beer €2-3.* 🕐 *Open M-Th noon-1am, F-Sa noon-2am.*

LES QUINZE NITS
P. Real 6

🍴♿♈☕❄ MEDITERRANEAN ❷
☎933 17 30 75 ▣www.lesquinzenits.com

Despite the restaurant's white tablecloths, leather chairs, and fabulous view of the Plaça Reial, the line outside of Les Quinze Nits is enough to make any weary traveler looking for a classier dinner reconsider their priorities. Where else would you woo your most recent roadside romantic acquisition on a backpacker's budget? Try the duck confit with triaxat and pesto sauce *(€10)* or the leek pie with tomato and arugula *(€6.31)*. Expect a 30min. wait upon opening, but reportedly the line diminishes around 9pm.

🍽 Ⓜ*Liceu, walk down Las Ramblas toward the Sea and take a right on C. Ferran, then right onto Passeig Madoz. Restaurant on the left as you enter Plaça Reial.* 𝒊 *No reservations.* Ⓢ*Appetizers €3-6; entrees €6-10. Bread €.85.* 🕐 *Open daily 1-3:45pm and 8:30-11:30pm.*

GOPAL
C. Escudeller, 42

🍴♿(🛜) VEGAN, DELI ❶
☎933 189 215

Located in the same plaça as Vegetalia, Gopal is a vegan deli that doesn't leave you guessing where its allegiances lie. Animal rights propaganda lines the walls, and a waitress in an Animal Liberation T-shirt mans the deli case filled with beautiful burgers of beans, lentils, seitan, and tempeh, as well as a variety of pre-packaged veggie proteins and dairy substitutes for customers' home use. This spot is the perfect place to find more information on veggie-friendly restaurants and related events in the city as well as some dirt-cheap chow—€5.90 will get you a first and second course, soup, bread, and dessert. For a dessert that will leave you wondering why you ever bothered with other animals' secretions in the first place, be sure to pick up one of Gopal's cakes or muffins from Lujuria Vegana on your way out the door.

🍽 Ⓜ*Liceu. Walk down Las Ramblas toward the sea. Take a left onto Carrer dels Escudellers and walk for about 5min. Gopal is on the right once you enter Plaça George Orwell.* Ⓢ*Sandwiches €3.50. Produce and salads €3. Menú €5.90.* 🕐 *Open daily 10am-midnight.*

XALOC
C. de la Palla 13-17

🍴♿♈❄ TAPAS, MEAT ❷
☎933 01 19 90

"Tapas, Mediterranean cuisine, Iberian Meats, Cheeses." What you see is what you get, and this phrase emblazoned across their menu header (combined with an entire epic wall of Iberian ham legs) does not disappoint. They know where they excel: high quality meats serve as the primary focus of simple dishes. Try one of their sampler plates of Catalan sausages *(€7)* or anything including *jamón* (ham). And, of course, vegetarians and vegans beware—you may be stuck with bread and salad.

🍽 Ⓜ*Liceu. Walk down C. de la Boqueria and take an immediate left onto C. del Cardenal Casañas. Stay on this road in front of the church and through the Plaça del Pi, following it right as it leaves the square and becomes C. Palla. Xaloc is located where C. Palla merges with C. Banys Nous.* Ⓢ *Tapas €2-7.* 🕐 *Open daily noon-midnight.*

TUCCO
C. d'Aglà, 6

🍴⊗♈ PASTA ❶
☎933 01 51 91

True to its name, Tucco "fresh pasta" offers just that—a selection of fresh pastas topped with your choice of sauce and cheese *(€3.95)*. The limited seating in the teeny store serves as a revolving door for hip, young locals and internationals wandering far off the beaten paths of the Gothic Quarter. If pasta isn't your thing, a selection of wallet-and veggie-friendly sandwiches, pizzas, desserts, salads, and snacks fill the nutritional void a meal of carbs creates. Don't expect to sit if you come at mealtime; instead, take your plasticware and hit the road.

✚ Ⓜ*Licue. Walk on Las Ramblas toward the water. Take a left onto C. Escudellers. Left onto C. d'Aglà.* Ⓢ *Pasta €3.95. Pizza from €9.* 🕑 *Open M-F 1-11:30pm, Sa 1-6pm.*

VENUS DELICATESSAN
Ⓜ &♿ (ᵗ) ¥   MEDITERRANEAN ❷

C. Vinyó, 25
☎93 301 15 85

Ever-changing colorful local art and a laid-back staff make for a relaxed atmosphere, perfect for taking advantage of the free Wi-Fi. The deli is dotted both by laptop-and-book toting students as well as small groups looking for a calm place to relax and enjoy the afternoon. Though many of their salads are adventurous and refreshing, fresher fare for a similar price can be found in the area. If looking for something more substantial, there's always the gazpacho *(€5.50)* or moussaka *(€7.80)*, or go big with the day's *menú (€10)*.

✚ Ⓜ*Liceu. Right off of C. Ferran coming from Las Ramblas.* ⓘ *Free Wi-Fi for customers.* Ⓢ *Salads €5.50-8. Entrees €6.60-9.90. Menú €10.* 🕑 *Open daily noon-midnight.*

CAFE DE L'OPERA
♿ &♿ ¥   CAFE ❷

La Rambla, 74
☎93 317 75 85 🖥www.afeoperabcn.com

Beginning in the 18th century as a boarding tavern and later a chocolate shop, the cafe assumed its current form in 1929, adopting the amusing mix of modernist curves, Grecian women, and pastel paint colors that can be seen today. Don't be fooled by the fancy Parisian facade or the impressive historical pedigree—although famous as a Barcelonan post-opera institution, Cafe l'Opera offers affordable fare and a wide list of beers (including "Cannabis Club," *(€3.60)* which purportedly tastes like, well, you can guess), wines, drinks, and tapas.

✚ Ⓜ*Liceu. On La Rambla when walking toward the water.* ⓘ *Credit card only over €20.* Ⓢ *Tapas €2-4. Sandwiches €3-6.70. Specials €10.50-13.* 🕑 *Open daily 8:30am-2:30am.*

MAOZ VEGETARIAN
♿&   VEGETARIAN/FALAFEL ❶

C.Ferran,13 and La Rambla, 95
☎653 84 76 53 🖥www.maozusa.com

Short on time, cash, and patience? Stop into Maoz and grab a falafel with toppings buffet *(€4.20)* or fries *(€2.20)*. Don't expect to linger, though—this little corner restaurant barely has room for you to order. Instead, take your meal out onto the streets and walk proud knowing that even if it's chain fast food, at least it's not McDonald's.

Ⓢ *Falafel €4.20. Fries €2.20.* 🕑 *Open daily 11am-3am.*

TRAVEL BAR
♿&♿ (ᵗ) ¥ ❄☂   BAR ❷

C. de Boqueria, 27
☎933 42 52 52 🖥www.travelbar.com

Predictably, this bar unabashedly caters to travelers. Unpredictably, it's a fantastic outside-the-hostel resource for people on the road, whether to meet fellow backpackers, chow down on a cheap meal, watch the game on the big screen, indulge in free internet, or browse their collection of travel books. Empty pockets? Stop in at 8pm for their €1 meals and to peruse their community bulletin board for deals on tours, rentals, and flamenco dance lessons. Older readers take note: complete with an endorsement from MTV, this place seems to cater almost exclusively to the college crowd. Menu is uncreative, overpriced, and downright cruel to vegetarians, but luckily it's near many delicious (and cheap) culinary alternatives.

✚ Ⓜ*Liceu. Exit and walk down C. de Boqueria. Bar on the left.* Ⓢ *Tapas €2-3. Entrees €6-12.50. Beer €3-5. €1 meals nightly at 8pm. 10% charge to sit on terrace.* 🕑 *Open daily 12:30pm-11:30pm.*

food • barri gòtic and las ramblas

LA RIBERA

EL XAMPANYET — TAPAS [2]

C. de Montcada, 22 — ☎933 19 70 03

The cup doeseth overfloweth, with sheepskin wine bags, an overwhelming selection of *cava*, and crunchy old locals spilling out the door and onto the street at all hours. Inside is a museum of casks, blackened bottles, and kitschy bottle openers displayed against a handpainted ceramic tile background. We recommend you try their cask-fresh *cerveza* *(€3.50)* or their house wine *xampanyet* *(€2)*, and pad your stomach with some of their delicious tapas *(€1.10-12.50)*.

[M]Jaume I. Walk down C. de la Princesa and take a right onto C. de Montcada, towards the Museu Picaso. Xampanyet is on the right before reaching Plaçeta Montcada. $ Tapas €1.10-12.50. Beer €3.50. Wine and cava from €2. Open Tu-Sa noon-4pm and 7-11pm, Su noon-4pm.

PETRA — RESTAURANT [2]

C. dels Sombrerers, 13 — ☎933 19 99 99

With dark wood, stained glass, art nouveau prints, menus decaled onto wine bottles, and chandeliers made of silverware, Petra will have you expecting a high price for its eccentricity. Luckily, the bohemian feel is matched by bohemian prices. Pastas like the delicious gnocchi with blue cheese and asparagus *(€5.15)* and entrees *(€7.85)* are nice on the wallet.

[M]Jaume I. Walk on C. Princesa and take a right onto C. del Pou de la Cadena. Take an immediate left onto C. de la Barra de Ferro and a right onto C. dels Banys Vells. Petra is located where C. dels Banys Vells terminates at C. dels Sombrerers. $ Menú €6.50. Appetizers €4.85-7.05; entrees €7.85. Open Tu-Sa 1:30-4pm and 9-11:30pm, Su 1:30-4pm.

barcelona

LA BÁSCULA — VEGETARIAN CAFE [2]

C. dels Flassanders, 30 — ☎933 19 98 66

A working cooperative that serves cheap vegetarian sandwiches, *empanadas*, and salads. Doors serve as tables and a mixture of art, environmentally-friendly sodas, and protest flyers hanging up around the walls set this restaurant apart from the rest. Though discreetly robed in the same antique exterior as more expensive places, Báscula provides a cheaper alternative to the upscale eateries in other stone hideaways surrounding Ribera. Hours and seating availability may change as the restaurant fights for its right to serve in-house, but takeout is available no matter the outcome.

[M]Jaume I. Walk down C. de la Princesa and take a right onto C. dels Flassanders. $ Entrees and salads €7-9. Sandwiches €4-4.50. Piadinas €6. Open W-Su 1-11pm.

HOFMANN PASTISSERIA — PASTRY SHOP [1]

C. dels Flassaders, 44 — ☎932 68 82 21 www.hofmann-bcn.com

Pastry school meets storefront in this Seussian mindbender in a French countryside setting. Artisans work on delectable goods in clear view on the mind-bending spiral staircase above, while glass cases and wooden cabinets filled with adorable gelatos *(€3.50)*, precious marmalade jars *(€8)*, and a selection of not-so-sickeningly-cute-but-utterly-delectable tarts and cakes wait below. For breakfast, try a coffee and one of the fresh croissants.

[M]Jaume I. Walk down C. de la Princesa and take a right onto C. dels Flassanders. Hofmann is located immediately before crossing Passeig del Born. $ Croissants €1-1.50. Gelato €3.50. Marmalades €8. Chocolates €1-5. Coffee €1.20-1.50. Open Tu-W 9am-2pm and 3:30-8pm, Th-Sa 9am-2pm and 3:30-8:30pm, Su 9am-2:30pm.

LA LLAVOR DELS ORIGENS — CATALAN [2]

C. Vidriería, 6 — ☎934 53 11 20 www.lallavordelsorigens.com

La Llavor dels Origins serves typical Catalan fare with a picture menu that lets you see in almost excruciating detail what you will soon be eating. Seasonal menus rotate every two months, while the regular menu changes every six, ensuring that there will always be something new to scrutinize (and maybe cook on your own—all recipes are available on the website). Drawings from customers young and not-so-young deck the walls, belying the sleek, modern decor with homey charm.

✠ Ⓜ*Jaume I. Walk down C. de la Princesa and take a right onto C. Montcada. Upon crossing the Passeig del Born, C. Vidriería is the street directly in front of you.* *i* *Organic meat available on request.* Ⓢ *Entrees €5.84-9.20. Beer €3. Wine €3.50. 15% discount for takeout.* ⓧ *Open daily 12:30pm-1am.*

BUBÓ ⬦♿♈❄⬥ BAKERY, CAFE ❶
C. Caputxes, 10 ☎932 68 72 24

Whether you're chilling in the outdoor seating with an up-close and personal view of Santa Maria del Mar or just gazing through the display case of the bakery next door, Bubó is sure to delight the eyes. Heartier fare includes reasonably priced sandwiches from its "world sandwich tour," while the perfectly glazed tarts and a rainbow of macaroons promise to deliciously tempt any sweet tooth.

✠ Ⓜ*Jaume I, Exit to C. de l'Argenteria and walk down C. de l'Argenteria away from Via Laietana. Once entering the plaza surrounding the church, take an immediate right onto C. dels Sombrerers and the first left onto C. Caputxes.* Ⓢ *Sandwiches €3.25-4. Tapas €2-6. Desserts €1-3.50. Cakes €20-30. Cocktails €4-8.* ⓧ *Open M 4-10pm, Tu-Th 11am-10pm, F-Sa 10am-1am, Su 10am-10pm.*

BODEGA LA TINAJA ⬦♿♈❄ WINERY, RESTAURANT ❸
C. de l'Esparteria, 9 ☎933 10 22 50 🖳www.bodegalastinajas.com

With so much wine lining the walls that you'll feel tipsy just looking in, this dark, earthy den behind a huge Gothic door provides bottle after bottle, ⌐jug after jug, and even barrel after barrel for whatever your thirst (or just eyes) may desire. The smell of seasoned meat fills the air with typical Catalan entrees *(€10-21).*

✠ Ⓜ*Barceloneta. Walk away from the water on Plà del Palau and turn right onto folo Plà del Palau at the end of the plaza. Turn left onto Plaça de les Olles and follow it as it veers into C. de les Dames. Turn right onto C. de l'Esparteria.* *i* *Large selection of wine. Sometimes hosts guitar and flamenco concerts.* Ⓢ *Salads €7.25-8.75. Full entrees €10-21, half €4.25-11.* ⓧ *Open Tu-Su 8am-midnight.*

EL ROVELL ⬦♿♈❄ CATALAN ❸
C. de l'Argenteria, 6 ☎932 69 04 58 🖳www.elrovelldelborn.com

Literally "the yolk" and not so literally "the place to meet," El Rovell satisfies both claims with a special egg-centric menu section and a large TV for congregating around the game. Don't be fooled by the screen in the back and the buckets hanging from the tables—this is no spit-your-shells-on-the-floor sports bar. Classy red leather stools and a clean wood interior match equally refined clientele and cuisine, like *huevos rotos* (scrambled eggs) with *foie gras* *(€9.25).*

✠ Ⓜ*Jaume I. Exit to C. de l'Argenteria and walk down C. de l'Argenteria away from Via Laietana.* Ⓢ *Entrees €7.50-24. Salads €6.50-14. Tapas €5.50-11.* ⓧ *Open daily 1-4pm and 7pm-midnight.*

VA DE VI ⬦♿♈ CATALAN ❸
C. dels Banys Vells, 16 ☎933 19 29 00

This 15th-century tavern was once home to Christopher Columbus, though nowadays the rustic, earthy interior is caught in a decorating rift between 19th-century cellos and random fluorescent lightning bolts ripping through the main room. The menu hearkens back to its historic past with a selection of traditional Catalan dishes, cheeses from France and Spain, and enough wine and *cava* to get you to believe you discovered the 🔁New World.

✠ Ⓜ*Jaume I. Walk down C. de l'Argenteria and take a left onto C. Rossic. Take a right onto C. dels Banys Vells.* Ⓢ *Meats €4-14.20. Cheeses €4-9. Tapas €1.50-6.50. Wine €2. Cava €2.50. Beer €1.50.* ⓧ *Open M-Th 6pm-2:30am, F-Sa 6pm-3am, Su 6pm-2:30am.*

food · la ribera

GADES FONDUES

♠♿♈❅ FONDUE ❸

C. l'Esparteria, 10

☎933 10 44 55 🖳www.gadesfondues.com

For those who just can't get enough of sticking food in other food, Gades Fondues steps up to fill a role often neglected. A choice of chocolate, meat, and cheese fondues *(€14-16 per person)* lets you pick it and stick it in a much classier setting than the phrase would imply. Salads, carpaccio, and a selection of other dishes fill out the menu for those looking for a less interactive meal.

✱ Ⓜ*Jaume I. Walk down C. Princesa and take a right onto C. Montcada. Cross Passeig del Born and follow C. de la Vidrieria until you reach C. de l'Esparteria.* ✦ *Fondues require min. 2 people.* Ⓢ *Salads €9.95. Fondues €14-16 per person. Tapas €5.95-12. Entrees €9.95-18. Menú €20-22.* ☒ *Open M-Th 8:30pm-midnight, F-Sa 8:30pm-1am.*

LONJA DE TAPAS

♠♿♈❅ TAPAS ❸

Placeta Montcada, 5

☎93 315 14 47 🖳www.cellerdelaribera.com

A long dining room with an arched arcade and dark wooden tables may appear like the cleaned-up, posh brother of every other tapas bar in the area. Lonja serves incredibly fresh, beautifully prepared Mediterranean-style tapas that range in price, and the pricey but comprehensive *menú de gustació* awaits if you can't make a decision on your own.

✱ Ⓜ*Jaume I. Walk down C. Princesa and take a right onto C. Montcada. Placeta Montcada is the small plaza at the end of C. Montcada.* ✦ *Other location at Pla de Palau, 7 with same hours.* Ⓢ *Tapas €4-11. Menú de gustació €36.* ☒ *Open M-Th noon-midnight, F-Sa noon-1am, and Su noon-midnight.*

EL RAVAL

◼ SOHO

♠♿♈ PITA, HOOKAH ❶

C. Ramelleres, 26

One of the most recent additions to Raval, Soho is also one of the most welcome, serving cheap and simple eats like pitas and pastas with meat and vegetarian options *(€1.95)* without sending you off in a rush. Low-slung seats with smaller, intimate rooms make the perfect setting for test-driving a hookah from the impressive wall of smoking paraphernalia *(€10).*

✱ Ⓜ*Universitat. Walk down C. Tallers and take a right onto C. de les Ramelleres.* Ⓢ *Pitas €1.95. Pasta €2.95. Hookah €10.* ☒ *Open M-Sa 1pm-midnight.*

◼ JUICY JONES

♠♿♈❅ VEGETARIAN ❷

C. Hospital, 74

☎934 43 90 82 🖳www.juicyjones.com

The big brother of the Juicy Jones in the Barri Gotíc, this version of the vegetarian eatery offers a Raval-inspired twist—daily specials of Indian dahl and curries spice up the normal selection of sandwiches, plates, and an impressive selection of juices. If you have ever wondered what M.C. Escher's art would have looked like in the times of LSD, the interior will satisfy your curiosity.

✱ Ⓜ*Liceu. Walk down C. de l'Hospital. Juicy Jones is on your right on the corner of C. Hospital and C. d'En Roig, before you hit Rambla del Raval.* Ⓢ *Menú €8.50. Daily thali plate €5.95. Tapas €1.95-3.50. Sandwiches €3.85-4.50.* ☒ *Open daily 1-11:30pm.*

◼ NARIN

◉♿♈ MEDITERRANEAN ❶

C. Tallers, 80

☎933 01 90 04

Sitting discretely along the shops and cafes of C. Tallers, Narin is hiding the best baklava in Barcelona and equally scrumptious falafel, *shawarma*, and kebabs. If you can't stand the heat, get out of the kitchen—the inside feels like a sauna with wooden walls and sweaty people. Luckily, beers come cold and cheap *(€1.80)* for those looking to brave the bar area, and a tiled dining room provides a reprieve from the buzz of the kebab shaver.

✱ Ⓜ*Universitat. Walk down C. dels Tallers.* Ⓢ *Pitas €2.90-4. Snacks €2.50-4.80. Baklava €1. Beer €1.80.* ☒ *Open M-Th 11am-2am, F-Sa 11am-3am, Su 11am-2am.*

HELLO SUSHI
C. Junta de Comerç, 14

👤♿⚏ SUSHI ❸

☎934 12 08 30 ■www.hello-sushi.com

The vaguely oriental interior with a modern, artsy twist provides sushi platters for a reasonable price, enticing a young clientele into its dark, pillow-padded lair. Dine at the bar, grab a table, or sit on the floor in the foyer and admire the paintings while the smell of *tempura* and *teriyaki* entice you to stay for another round.

✦ Ⓜ*Liceu. Walk down C. l'Hospital and take a left onto C. Junta de Comerç.* **i** *Live music at times; check website for schedule.* ⑤ *Daily menú €8.50 or €14.50. Salad €4. Entrees €8-14. Sushi combos €12-32.* 🕐 *Open Tu-Sa 12:30-4:30pm and 8:30pm-12:30am, Su 8:30pm-12:30am.*

SHALIMAR
C. Carme, 71

👤♿⚏ PAKISTANI, INDIAN ❷

☎933 29 34 96

Shalimar serves authentic Pakistani and Indian dishes tandoori style. Generous portions and delicious meat-based curries including chicken *(€7)*, lamb *(€8.20)*, and shrimp *(€9)* punctuate a menu that would make any vegetarian happy. Hand-painted tiles and warm lighting perk up the interior as lace curtains block out the busy streets of Raval.

✦ Ⓜ*Liceu. Walk down C. de l'Hospital and take a right onto C. d'En Roig. Left onto C. del Carme. Shalimar is on the left before the fork in the road.* ⑤ *Appetizers €2-8. Veggie specials €3.70-4. Shrimp curry €9.30. Chicken €7. Beer €2.* 🕐 *Open M-Tu 8pm-midnight, W-Su 1-4pm and 8pm-midnight.*

MADAME JASMINE
Rambla del Raval, 22

♿⚏ CAFE ❶

Allow yourself to be seduced either by the 19th-century French-brothel-chic interior or the scrumptious *bocadillos*. Orange and red lighting sets the mood, incense fills the nostrils, and a selection of sultry Latin, electro, and lounge music will get you in the mood to partake in the less literal red light activities lining the streets of Raval.

✦ Ⓜ*Liceu. Walk down C. de l'Hospital and take a right onto Rambla del Raval. Madame Jasmine will be on your left nearly two thirds down.* ⑤ *Sandwiches and salads €4.75. House vermouth €2.20. Cocktails €5.50. Shots €2.* 🕐 *Open M-F 5:30pm-2:30am, Sa-Su 1:30pm-2:30am. Kitchen open daily until midnight.*

MENDIZABAL
C. Junta de Comerç, 2

Ⓢ♿⚁ FOODSTAND ❶

A crowd of young, artsy students out front and vibrant multicolored tiles in the back make this otherwise inconspicuous foodstand hard to miss. Take your cheap eats to go, or grab a seat on the terrace in the neighboring plaza for an extra 10% (look for the coordinating chairs). Some veggie-friendly options are available—we recommend the tomato, brie, and avocado sandwich *(€3.60)*.

✦ Ⓜ*Liceu. Walk down C. l'Hospital. Mendizabal is at the corner of C. l'Hospital and C. Junta de Comerç.* **i** *Terrace seating located in plaça across the street, but will cost 10% extra.* ⑤ *Bocadillos €3.60-4.10. Beer €2.50. Postres €1.30-2.80.* 🕐 *Open daily 8am-12:30am.*

KASPARO
Pl. Vincenç Martorell

Ⓢ♿⚏⚁ CAFE ❷

☎933 02 20 72

A veggie-friendly menu lays host to an incredibly busy indoor diner with enough outdoor seating to compensate for the handful of seats available inside at the bar. Sit on the metal-clad seating of the terrace to partially escape the clatter of dishes and silverware inside, and grab one of their veggie-friendly *platos del día* *(€4.55-8.50)* or just a beer *(€2.70-3.35)* to satisfy whichever appetite you've mustered.

✦ Ⓜ*Catalonia. When facing Las Ramblas, take the road to your right (C. de Petal) along the plaza. Turn left onto C. de Jovellanos at the end of the plaza. Follow C. de Jovellanos as it becomes C. de les Ramelleres, and Plaça de Vincenç Martorell is on the left.* ⑤ *Tapas €2.55-11.10. Appetizers €1.35-5.30; entrees €4.55-8.50.* 🕐 *Open daily 9am-midnight.*

food . el raval

ORGANIC
♦ ♿ ♈ ✿ CAFE, MEDITERRANEAN ❷

C. Junta de Comerç, 11   ☎933 01 09 02 ▣www.antoniaorganickitchen.com

For once, you won't have to worry about space for seating—organic has enough room to fit an entire youth hostel and their luggage. A vegan buffet *(€7)* surprises and delights with croquettes, pasta, and salad fixings, while all vegetarian Mediterranean dishes will please even the most outspoken carnivores. Be sure to say thanks to Mother Earth as you leave—she'll be looking down on you approvingly, surrounded by peas, earth, and fire, to your left.

EN VILLE
♦ ♿ ♈ ✿ ♋ BISTRO ❸

C. Doctor Dou, 14   ☎933 02 84 67 ▣www.envillebarcelona.es

Marble-topped tables, terra-cotta floors, wicker chairs, and lamps that mimic the posts outside combine for a charming bistro-style restaurant that brings the outside in while still serving impressive dishes like the roasted pig with melon and cantaloupe tartare *(€14.50)*. Actual outdoor seating is available as well, if that's your thing, but be sure to sit inside to be serenaded by live flamenco, jazz, or bosanova on Tuesday and Wednesday nights.

✚ Ⓜ*Liceu. Walk toward Plaça Catalonia on Las Ramblas. Take a left onto C. del Carme and a right onto C. Doctor Dou.* *i* *Live music on Tu and W nights.* Ⓢ *Tapas €3.50-19.70. Appetizers €6.90-11.80; entrees €12.50-19.70.* ⏰ *Open M 1-4pm, Tu-Sa 1-4:30pm and 8pm-midnight.*

L'HORTET
♦ ♿ ♈ ✿ VEGETARIAN ❸

C. Pintor Fortuny, 32   ☎ 933 17 61 89 ▣www.hortet.es

An upscale vegan and vegetarian eatery for when Maoz and Gopal just aren't cutting it. Understated interior details will leave you guessing where its allegiances lie, with red faux-leather tablecloths and abstract paper lights that only vaguely resemble produce. Come hungry during the day—only the entire *menú* is available *(M-F €9.80, Sa €12.95, Su €14.95)*, while the restaurant offers up lighter fare a la carte on nights and Sundays.

✚ Ⓜ*Liceu. Walk on las Ramblas toward Plaça Catalonia and take a left onto C. del Pintor Fortuny.* *i* *A la carte items only available on nights and Sundays midday.* Ⓢ *M-F midday menú €9.80, Sa €12.95, Su €14.95; night menú €14.95. A la carte items €4.50-9.50.* ⏰ *Open M-W 1-4pm, Th-Sa 8-11pm.*

BIOCENTER
♦ ♿ ♈ ✿ VEGETARIAN ❷

C. Pintor Fortuny, 25   ☎933 01 45 83 ▣www.vegetarianobarcelona.com

Bright white walls and a modular grid make the perfect gallery-like setting for its rotating selection of paintings, sculptures, and dusty-looking antique books. Relaxing piano music contributes to the feel, and an entirely vegetarian menu specializing in healthy and ecologically friendly cuisine waits to please your inner, socially conscious yuppie.

✚ Ⓜ*Liceu. Walk on las Ramblas toward Plaça Catalonia and take a left onto C. del Pintor Fortuny.* Ⓢ *Menú €15. Appetizers €5-7.50; entrees €7.50-9.25. Dessert €3.50-4.25.* ⏰ *Open daily 1-11pm.*

CHULO
♦ ♿ ♈ ♋ CAFE ❶

Pl. Vincenç Martorell   ☎933 02 40 95

Gold indoor couches and painted cherry trees inject a shabby chic upscale twist into the interior of this little cafe, but the real life is outside on the terrace in Plaça Vincenç Martorell, where it helps form the trifecta of cafes lining the side of the courtyard. Cheap breakfasts like the *toasta* with brie and tomato *(€3.50)* and *bocadillos*, like salmon and cream cheese *(€4.90)*, make this cafe the best of the bunch.

✚ Ⓜ*Catalonia. When facing Las Ramblas, take the road to your right (C. de Petal) along the plaza. Turn left onto C. de Jovellanos at the end of the plaza. Follow C. de Jovellanos as it becomes C. de les Ramelleres, and Plaça de Vincenç Martorell is on the left.* Ⓢ *Breakfast €1.90-4.20. Sandwiches €4.50-5.50. Salad €5.75-7.* ⏰ *Open daily 10am-midnight.*

barcelona

CAFE D'ANNUNZIO 💳♿🍸❄⛅ CAFE [2]

Pl. Vincenç Martorell ☎933 02 40 95

Rainbow stickers mark the glass doors of the last of the three cafes that line the arcade of Plaça Vincenç Martorell. Pictures of Venice and sculptures of Roman heads dress up the otherwise generic interior that sells delicious coffee supplied by Cafe del Dog. Sit inside to find an anachronistic, ill-fitting mix of '80s alternative hits playing over the stereo.

🪧 *Ⓜ Catalonia. When facing Las Ramblas, take the road to your right (C. de Petal) along the plaza. Turn left onto C. de Jovellanos at the end of the plaza. Follow C. de Jovellanos as it becomes C. de les Ramelleres, and Plaça de Vincenç Martorell is on the left.* Ⓢ *Appetizers €1.60-4. Platters €10-15. Beer €2.70-3. Sandwiches €5-8, small €3.25-5.50.* ⏰ *Open daily 9:30am-1am.*

CAFETARIUM 💳♿🍸❄ CAFE [2]

C. Tallers, 76 ☎667 64 01 11 🖥www.cafetarium.com

Much classier and less horror-movie-esque than the name would imply, Cafetarium serves a mix of cheaper sandwiches and more filling *platos del día* for when the *bocadillos* and coffee aren't cutting it. For those missing the greasy comforts of home, a double hamburger *(€5.15)* will remind your arteries of the good old days. Quirky frames and cheap vintage-chic chandeliers make those creature comforts just hip enough to stomach.

🪧 *Ⓜ Universitat. Walk down C. dels Tallers.* Ⓢ *Sandwiches €3.30-5.15. Menú €7.45. Tapas €4.10-6.10.* ⏰ *Open M-Sa 8am-1am.*

L'EIXAMPLE

👍 **OMEÍA** ♿🍸❄ JORDANIAN [2]

C. Aragó, 211 ☎934 52 31 79

When you're (literally) sick of gorging yourself on cheap shawarma from stands, stop in to Omeía for some authentic Middle Eastern fare that will only make you regret not having a bigger stomach. Start off with their roasted red pepper soup *(€6.50)* and fill up with one of their traditional Jordanian dishes *(€9-13)*. A word of advice: be prepared to take a long walk around the long blocks of l'Eixample after you finish to ease digestion.

🪧 *Ⓜ Universitat. Walk on C. d'Aribau to the left of the University. Take a right onto C. Aragó.* Ⓢ *Starters €5.95-7. Entrees €6-13. Menú €7.50.* ⏰ *Open daily 10am-4pm and 8pm-midnght.*

👍 **EL JAPONES** 💳♿🍸❄ JAPANESE, SUSHI [3]

Passatge de la Concepció, 2 ☎934 87 25 92 🖥www.grupotragaluz.com

This sushi costs more than the price of your hostel for the night, but it's more than worth shortening your trip. Bulk up on noodles or rice and order a mixed sushi platter *(€10.50-21.80)* for a cheaper (though by no means cheap) alternative. A sleek interior and romantic ambience makes for the perfect place to bring a date or make new friends.

🪧 *Ⓜ Diagonal. Walk toward Passeig de Gràcia and take a right onto it. Take a right onto Passatge de la Concepció, the first smaller road on the right.* Ⓢ *Appetizers €5.70-10.20. Noodles €5.90-6.40. Sushi €4.90-9.90. Sushi platters €10.50-21.80.* ⏰ *Open M-W 1:30-4pm and 8:30pm-midnight, Th-Sa 1:30-4pm and 8:30pm-1am, Su 1:30-4pm and 8:30pm-midnight.*

CERVESERIA CATALANA 💳♿🍸❄⛅ TAPAS, CATALAN [3]

C. Mallorca, 236 ☎932 16 03 68

Tapas, *flautas*, seafood, burgers, beer, wine, and more—it's easy to see why locals flock to Cerveseria Catalana's warmly lit interior in the dark of night. During the evening hours, the bar and outdoor seats are abuzz with the lively chatter of 20-somethings, while the crowd gets older (though no less lively) as you move back through the proper tables. Plan on waiting to get a seat, or give in and join the barside party.

🪧 *Ⓜ Diagonal. Walk away from Passeig de Gràcia and take a right onto Rambla de Catalonia. Take a right onto C. Mallorca.* Ⓢ *Starters €3.85. Salads €3.10-6.10. Tapas €3-12.* ⏰ *Open daily 8am-1:30am.*

CAFE CHAPULTAPEC

♨♿(((•)))♈❄☂ MEXICAN ❷

C. Comte Borrell, 152

☎934 51 92 85 🖳www.cafechapultepec.com

Cheap, veggie-friendly burritos (*€4.15*) and other Mexican platters as well as free internet and an inside reminiscent of a coastal Mondrian painting make this cafe a pleasant retreat from the rest of the overpriced Eixample. Grab some *chilaquiles polls verdes* or *rojos* (*€5.90*), or try one of their flavored hotcakes with tocino, ham, or maple syrup (*€3.80-4.50*). Following its namesake, it's located a bit outside of the most heavily frequented areas, so it may require some traveling. But hey—isn't that what you're doing all this for?

✦ ⓂUrgell. *Walk along Gran Vía with your back to the rocket-shaped Agbar Tower and take a right onto C. Comte Borrell.* Ⓢ *Starters €3.30-4.60. Entrees €4.15-5.25. Dishes €5.90-7.90.* ⓩ *Open Tu-F 10am-4pm and 7-11pm, Sa 12:30-4:30pm and 7-11pm, Su 12:30-4:30pm.*

FRIDA'S MEXICAN RESTAURANT

♨♿☂❄ MEXICAN ❷

C. Bruc, 119

☎93 457 54 09

Reportedly the most authentic Mexican restaurant in Barcelona, Frida's serves anti-TexMex quesadillas, *tostadas*, and a range of platos, including *cochinita pibil* (*€11.65*) and *michoacan carnitas* (*€11.35*), generally for much less than they're worth. Kick back with a Jamaican-flavored margarita (*€5.70*) at the bar, sit under a fitting picture of Frida Kahlo, or take your food to go and picnic along nearby Passeig de Gràcia.

✦ ⓂGirona. *Walk on C. Girona toward C. Aragó and take a left onto C. de Mallorca. Frida's is on the corner of Mallorca and Bruc.* Ⓢ *5 tacos €8.90 Th and F. Salads €5.90-6.30. Tostadas and quesadillas €2.85-2.95. Entrees €7.80-11.35. Margaritas €5.70.* ⓩ *Open Tu-Sa 1-4pm and 8:15pm-midnight.*

GINZA

♨♿☂ JAPANESE ❸

C. Provença, 205

☎934 51 71 93

A tastier alternative to the multitude of all-you-can-eat Japanese-style restaurants in the area for a similar (or better) price. Fresh ingredients and delicious dishes are served in a somewhat bland but homey interior, though the portrait of Sumo wrestlers in a rainbow variety of suits is worth a look. Start with a miso soup (*€3*), fill up on *tempanyaki* (*€6-12*), and finish it all off with a shot of *sake*.

✦ ⓂDiagonal. *Walk on C. del Rosselló away from Passeig de Gràcia. Take a left onto C. Balmes and a right onto C. de Provenca.* Ⓢ *Appetizers €3-9.60; entrees €6-12. Sushi €6.50. Weekday lunch menú €9.89; weekends and nights €10.85.* ⓩ *Open M-Sa 1-4pm and 8pm-midnight, Su 1-4pm.*

MAURI

♨♿☂❄ PASTRY SHOP, TEA SHOP, DELI ❶

Rambla del Catalonia, 102 and 103

☎932 15 10 20🖳www.pasteleriasmauri.com

This tripartite pastry-deli-dessert shop has something to enchant whatever your hunger. Dine in the 102 shop over little sandwiches, croquettes, and croissants, or order something from the deli next door and dine in the wood and plaster salon. Across the street you'll find their *bomboneria* and tearoom, offering adorable giftbaskets in case you're looking to woo a fellow traveler.

✦ ⓂDiagonal. *Walk away from Passeig de Gràcia and take a right onto Rambla de Catalonia. The pastisseria is on the right and the tea shop on the left.* Ⓢ *Pastries and snacks €1.50-2.50. Lunch menú €13.* ⓩ *Open M-F 9am-9pm, Sa 9am-9pm, Su 9am-3pm.*

CAFE PARC BELMONT

♿☂❄☂ CAFE, TAPAS ❷

C. Lepant, 256

☎932 31 13 58

The friendly ex-pat staff, collection of '60s hits from across the world (California Dreamin', anyone?), and pictures from Paris, New York, Barcelona, and more create the perfect setting to surround yourself in the idealized cultures you never knew. A selection of cheap sandwiches (*€2.55-3.10*) and delicious tapas keeps even the poorest starving artist happy.

🚇 [M]Sagrada Familia. Walk downhill on C. Lepant. Cafe Park Belmont is on the left. Entrees €6.25-9.95. Sandwiches €2.55-3.10. Tapas €.95-3.45. Salads €4-6.20. ⏰ Open M-Sa 9am-11pm.

LAIE BOOKSTORE CAFE CAFE, CATALAN [3]

C. Pau Claris, 85 ☎933 18 17 39 💻www.laie.es

Laie's is the perfect place to curl up with a purchased book after impressing your friends with your memorization of one of their literary quotes along the windows. Choose from a sunny yellow backroom with palm trees and burlap shades or chill out in the dark, shaded couches of the front. A veggie-friendly snack bar with gourmet mini sandwiches and pastries provides snacks during the odd hours, while an all-you-can-eat lunch buffet satisfies the hunger knowledge can't fill.

🚇 [M]Gràcia. ℹ Internet €1 per 15min. $ Coffee and snacks €1.35-4.50. Beer €2-2.60. Wine €1.55-3. Lunch menú M-F €14; Sa-Su €17. ⏰ Open M-F 9am-1am, Sa 10am-1am.

COLMADO DE SOL BEER, CAFE [2]

C. Consell de Cent, 383 ☎935 33 19 47 💻www.colmadodelsol.com

Although this little cafe offers a variety of deli-style items for takeout or enjoyment at one of their few tables, the real attraction is in their almost limitless selection of beer. Over 300 different types line the walls, all chilled and ready for your stomach. Knock back a few before heading to their tapas bar next door, or pick up a couple of classy brews so you're not stuck paying €1 for Estrella from a six-pack later in the night.

🚇 [M]Girona. Walk along C. Consell de Cent toward C. del Bruc. Colmado de Sol will be right after the intersection. $ Plates of the day €7.90. Dinner menú €9.90. ⏰ Open M-Sa noon-10pm.

EL ÚLTIMO AGAVE MEXICAN [3]

C. Aragó, 193 ☎934 54 93 43 💻www.elultimoagave.com

Wrapped in brick and tastefully crumbling red plaster, this humbly named Mexican *rincón*, or corner, whips up tacos, *enchiladas*, and the *Último Agave (€14)*, which they claim are better (and more expensive) than most *fajitas*. Let the pole of *coronita* caps guide your path through their selection of Mexican beers, or simply opt for a margarita.

🚇 [M]Universitat. Take C. Aribau, to the left of the University. Turn left onto C. Aragó. $ Appetizers €7-10.50; entrees €10-18. Desserts €4.50-5. ⏰ Open M-Th 7pm-2:30am, F-Sa 7pm-3am, Su 7pm-2:30am.

BARCELONA-MADRID (PA AMB TOMÀQUET) CATALAN [3]

C. Aragó, 282 ☎93 215 70 27

Named after the railroad line that used to run here, Barcelona-Madrid is the destination for delicious Catalan dishes and classy decor without the exclusivity imposed by lack of seating. Two floors of dark wood and bright plaster (and some little birdies) play host to shoppers and local businessmen during the lunchtime hours. Try the preserved duck with figs *(€10.20)* or the more adventurous marinated oxtail with herbs *(€9.90)*.

🚇 [M]Girona. Walk toward C. d'Aragó and take a left onto the street. La Rita is a flew blocks down on your left. $ Appetizers €7-11; entrees €9-16. ⏰ Open daily 1-4pm and 8:30-11:30pm.

LA FLAUTA TAPAS, SANDWICHES [2]

C. Aribau, 23 ☎93 323 70 38

La Flauta takes its name from the long, thin crusty Catalan sandwich that puts other *bocadillos* to shame. Bearing no resemblance to the stale bread and two slices of cheese you drunkenly paid €4 for at 3am, these sandwiches are stuffed full of mouth-watering veggies, meat, and cheese *(half €3.65-6.90; whole €4.75-8.75)*. Lots of veggie options, tapas, and other plates fill out the menu in a decor that would never leave you believing that they're known for two pieces of bread and some filling.

🚇 [M]Universitat. Walk down C. d'Aribau, the road to the left of the University. La Flauta is 1 block down on the left. $ Weekday lunch menú €10.50. Entrees €4.50-7.90. Sandwiches €3.65-7.90. ⏰ Open M-Sa 7am-1:30am.

THAI GARDENS 🚬♿🍸❄ THAI [3]

C. Diputació, 273 ☎93 487 98 98 🖥www.thaigardensgroup.com

If you're just looking for some Thai food, grab their takeaway menu. If you're looking to impress, bring your date to the sprawling, city-like, overtly Thai interior, complete with a robed hostess and wooden bridge to greet you—in case you weren't already convinced you were walking into a parallel universe. To complete the experience, call ahead to sit at one of their traditional *kantok* tables—no chairs, just floor cushions.

➡ [M]Passeig de Gràcia. Walk along Passeig de Gràcia away from Plaça Catalonia. Turn right onto C. de la Diputació. [$] Appetizers €8.35-12.15; entrees €15.90-18.80. Daily lunch menú €15. ⏰ Open daily 1-4pm and 8-11:30pm.

CAMPECHANO 🚬♿🍸⛅ GRILL [3]

C. Valencia, 286 ☎93 215 62 33 🖥www.campechanobarcelona.com

The great outdoors comes indoors at Campechano, which offers *carnes a la brasa* with a campfire setting to match. If you ever wondered what it was like to picnic at a '30s Barcelona *merendero*, Campechano may not satisfy your curiosity, but it'll try. Peek through the painted trees to peep at mountainside campers while saddling up and preparing to chow down on relatively cheap eats at picnic tables.

➡ [M]Diagonal. Walk to Passeig de Gràcia and take a right. Walk 3 blocks and take a left onto C. Valencia. [$] Lunch menú €9.95. Salads €4-6. Entrees €6-15. ⏰ Open M-W 9am-4pm, Th-Sa 9am-4pm and 9pm-2am.

LA MUSCLERIA 🚬🍸❄⛅ SEAFOOD [2]

C. Mallorca, 290 ☎93 458 98 44 🖥www.muscleria.com

Would you eat them in a can, would you, could you, in a van? Would you eat them in a boat, could you eat them on a float? Although you probably won't be able to answer these questions, La Muscleria will let you try—they offer up more mussel options than a single mind can muster, though you'll have to order takeout (at a 20% discount) to experiment with eating locales. Ordering in gets you a bucket of mussels and a smaller dish of fries. Other seafoods (calamari and oysters, to name a few) round out the menu.

➡ [M]Girona. Walk along C. de Girona toward C. d'Aragó and take a left onto C. Mallorca. La Muscleria is located on the left, in a basement. ℹ 20% discount for takeout. [$] Salads €6.75-7.05. Mussels €8.95-10.85. ⏰ Open M-Sa 1-4pm and 8:30-11:30pm, Su 1-4pm.

KIRIN 🚬♿🍸❄ JAPANESE, BUFFET [2]

C. Aragó, 231 ☎93 488 29 19

One of many Japanese all-you-can-gorge buffets in the area, only with two main advantages: the ambience doesn't feel like you're back in a high school cafeteria, and you don't even have to leave your seat to eat. Little conveyor belts bring around an array of sushi, dumplings, and edamame for you to snag when hunger strikes, though you'll have to leave your seat to assemble a dish of raw meat, veggies, and seafood if you want a stir fry. Don't worry, though—the DIY aspect ends there, and their able chefs will take the plate off your hands and whip up a tasty dish in front of your eyes.

➡ [M]Universitat. Walk on the road to the right of the university, C. Balmes. Take a right onto C. d'Aragó. [$] Buffet lunch M-F €8.60; Sa-Su €11.60; nights €12.90. ⏰ Open daily 1-4pm and 8pm-midnight.

CAN CARGOL 🚬♿🍸❄ CATALAN [3]

C. València, 324 ☎93 458 96 31 🖥www.cancargol.es

A fun selection of snail dishes *(including "grandfather" or "mother-in-law" style; each €9.25)* are complemented with a range of charcoal grilled veggies and meat-centric entrees, ranging from pig's feet *(€5.25)* to *bacalau* with garlic mousseline *(€7.50)*. Though obviously nicer than your average kebab stand, the relatively laid-back atmosphere with exposed rafters and blackened wine bottles won't make you feel too out of place when you show up in your shirt and cargo shorts.

⚡ Ⓜ*Girona. Walk along C. de Girona toward C. d'Aragó and take a left onto C. de Valencia.* **i** *Reservations recommended F-Su.* Ⓢ *Appetizers €3.75-8.75; entrees €5.75-18.25.* ⓒ *Open daily 1:30-4pm and 8:30pm-midnight.*

SON HAO
C. Muntaner, 66

♥⊗ℽ❀ CHINESE, THAI ❷

☎93 453 83 03

An army of rainbow-colored Buddhas waits to usher you into the dragon-and-gold-bedecked shrine to Chinese stereotypes. Kitschy oriental paintings, Buddha heads, dangling red tassles, and lots of red predict a menu of pork stew in *huko* (€8) and shark fin soup (€4), as well as noodle dishes, veggie-friendly platters, and other standard items for those sick of *jamón serrano*.

⚡ Ⓜ*Universitat. Face the university. Take a left onto Gran Vía and a right onto C. Muntaner. Son Hao is before you reach C. d'Aragó.* Ⓢ *Soups €2.50-8. Salads €4-6.60. Entrees €5-14. Weekday lunch menú €12.* ⓒ *Open M-Sa 1-3:45pm and 8-11pm, Su 1-3:45pm.*

MOON CAFE
C. Provença, 213

♥Ġℽ CAFE ❷

☎93 488 17 21

One of the few places to find a veggie burger this side of Gran Vía (before hitting Gràcia, anyway), it's also one of the few places you'll find where said burger can live in peace with its veal counterpart on the menu. This brick-walled downstairs cafe stays dark, lush, and romantic at any hour of the day, but gets especially suave later in the evening.

⚡ Ⓜ*Diagonal. Walk on C. del Rosselló away from Passeig de Gràcia. Take a left onto C. Balmes. Moon Cafe is a small door on the corner.* Ⓢ *Tapas €2.50-7. Salads €8-9. Sandwiches and rolls €3.50-7.50. Cocktails €6-7.* ⓒ *Open M-Th 9am-2am, F-Sa 9am-3am, Su 9am-2am.*

LA RITA
C. Aragó, 279

♥Ġℽ❀ CATALAN ❸

☎93 487 23 76 🖳www.laritarestaurant.com

The stomping ground of locals looking for an unbeatably priced midday meal. The cuisine spans a small range of traditional items with a twist, including potatoes and black sausage, duck breast with apples, raspberry *coulis*, and mango chutney. Though the price is near dirt cheap for the quality, the interior is anything but; expect an upscale but relaxed ambience that will make you question wearing that T-shirt—but not quite regret the decision.

⚡ Ⓜ*Girona. Walk toward C. d'Aragó and take a left onto the street. La Rita is a flew blocks down on your right.* Ⓢ *Appetizers €4.75-7, entrees €7-11.* ⓒ *Open daily 1-3:45pm and 8:30-11:30pm.*

TAPAS, 24
C. Diputació, 269

♥⊗ℽ❀♨ TAPAS ❷

☎93 488 09 77 🖳www.carlesabellan.com

Climb down the stairs and into the den of delicious tapas. Chef Carles Abellan, formerly of El Bulli, serves up food that you can actually afford at this alternative to his acclaimed Comerç 24. Marble countertops and colorful paintings of the menu spruce up this cafeteria-esque alcove. Try a plate of *patatas bravas* (€3.75) with either a glass of *cava* (€3) or their house *sangría* (€3.75).

⚡ Ⓜ*Passeig de Gràcia. Walk away from Plaça Catalonia. Tapas, 24 is on the corner of C. Diputació and Pg. de Gràcia.* Ⓢ *Tapas €2.50-8. Raciones €9-12. Wine and cava €3.* ⓒ *Open daily 9am-midnight.*

TXAPELA (EUSAKI TABERNA)
Psg. de Gràcia, 8-10

♥Ġℽ❀ TAPAS ❶

☎93 412 02 89 🖳www.angrup.com

If you're looking for tapas then Txapela's got' em, along with enough seating to fit however many people may be in your entourage. Two floors of warm-colored wood floors and tinted walls let you have some of the perks of a small mom-and-pop place (cheap, interesting tapas) without all of that small talk and physical contact.

food · l'eixample

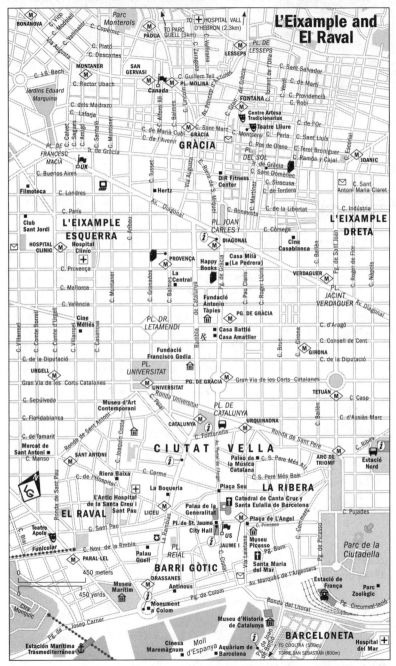

L'Eixample and El Raval

ⴲ ⓂPasseig de Gràcia. Walk toward Plaça de Catalonia on Pg. de Gràcia. Txapela is on the left. Ⓢ Tapas €1.40-2. Wines by bottle €5.25-18.10. Cava by bottle €19.35-26.20. 🕐 Open M-Th 7:45am-1:30am, F 7:45am-2am, Sa 8:45am-2am, Su 10:45am-1am.

RODIZIO GRILL
🍴♿❣❀ BRAZILIAN GRILL, CATALAN ❸

C. Consell de Cent, 403 ☎93 265 51 12

Not only is this buffet food delicious, fresh, and of high-quality, but some of the fare, including Brazilian meats, make their way around to each of the tables. The buffet will cost you €18-20, so come hungry enough to eat the entire blue-and-white cow looking down from overhead.

ⴲ ⓂGirona. Walk along C. de Girona toward C. Consell de Cent and turn right onto the road. Rodizio Grill is to the left. Ⓢ M-Th lunch buffet €18.20; nights and F-Sa €20.50. Desserts €3.24-4.30. Cocktails €5. 🕐 Open M-Th 1-4:30pm and 9pm-midnight, F-Sa 1-4:30pm and 9pm-1am, Su 1-4:30pm and 9pm-midnight.

EL RAIM
🍴♿❣❀ TAPAS, CAFE ❷

C. Muntaner, 75 ☎93 453 59 53

Authentic Catalan tapas and *bocadillos* without any affectation. Bare walls and ceramic tile paintings remind you of your favorite outdated, rock-studded hole-in-the-wall back home, with prices to match. If you're sick of building a meal out of little orders of stuffed eggplant and chicken legs with stewed plum *(€2-3)*, then feel even more eerily close to home with a platter of bacon, eggs, and potatoes *(€5.65)*.

ⴲ ⓂUniversitat. Face the university. Take a left onto Gran Vía and a right onto C. Muntaner. Walk for 3 blocks, El Raim will be on the left. Ⓢ Entrees €5.45-9.75. Sandwiches €2.90-6.40. 🕐 Open M-Sa 9am-1am.

YAMAMOTO
🍴♿❣❀ JAPANESE, BUFFET ❸

C. Aragó, 197 ☎93 451 87 02

One of the many buffet-style Japanese restaurants in this area of the Eixample, Yamamoto is pretty similar to its horde of competitors. White walls and cafeteria-style seating let you gorge your face in the appropriate setting as you return plate after plate to the buffet to grab sushi, croquettes, dumplings, and maybe even some fruit so your bowels don't hate you. You can also assemble your own mix of fresh seafood, meats, and veggies before sending it off to the chef to be stir-fried.

ⴲ ⓂUniversitat. Walk down C. Aribau, to the left of the University, and take a left onto Aragó. Ⓢ Buffet only: M-F midday €8.80, M-Th night €13.25; F night, Sa-Su all day €14.25. 🕐 Open daily 1-4pm and 8:30pm-midnight.

BARCELONETA

🔲 BOMBETA
◉♿❣ TAPAS ❸

C. Maquinista, 3 ☎93 319 94 45

Take heed of the warning scrawled above the bar, "No hablamos inglés, pero hacemos unas bombas cojonudas"—or, for the non-Spanish speaking set, "We don't speak English, but we make *bombas* that are out of this world." A retro facade with windows plastered with menu listings offers typical Spanish fare like *tostadas*, tortillas, and tapas, but really—just get the *bombas*.

ⴲ ⓂWalk down Pg. Juan de Borbó (toward the beach) and take a left onto C. Maquinista. Ⓢ Appetizers €3-9.50; entrees €5-18. 🕐 Open M-Tu 9am-11:45pm, Th-Su 9am-11:45pm.

SOMORROSTRO
🍴♿❣❀ SEAFOOD ❸

C. Sant Carles, 11 ☎93 225 00 10 🔲www.restaurantesomorrostro.com

This eatery is one of the few restaurants that is a part of Barceloneta's restaurant association, a recently established organization dedicated to making the inflated prices of Barceloneta actually worth the cost while bringing the best of the port to its tables. Somorrostro is also one of the best priced of this group, with reasonable seafood dishes, paella, and curries *(€13-19)* and a nighttime *menú (€15)*.

The real draw for the restaurant comes midday on weekdays—a seafood buffet lets you pay for fish, prawns, and more fresh from the port and cooked to your liking for unbelievably cheap prices *(€13 per kg)*.

➜ Ⓜ Barceloneta. Walk on Pla del Palau over Ronda Litoral to follow the harbor. Take the 5th left after crossing Litoral, onto C. Sant Carles. $ Weekday lunch buffet €13 per kg. Dinner menú €15. Appetizers €5.50-10; entrees €13.60-18.50. ⏰ Open Tu-Sa 8pm-11:30pm, Su 2-4pm and 8-11:30pm.

CAN MAÑO ⊛ ♿ 🍸 SEAFOOD [2]

C. Baluart, 12 ☎93 319 30 82

A no-frills bar-restaurant that has been serving fresh seafood for good prices to a never ending crowd of locals for years. Tile floors, white paint, and a random assortment of old framed newspaper clippings provide a refreshing break from those restaurants that make any attempt at interior decoration. If you had any doubts about just how little pretension this place harbors, just ask ☑ Tommy the Trout to start singing, "Take Me to the River" to you from his wall plaque.

➜ Ⓜ Barceloneta. Walk on Pla del Palau over Ronda Litoral to follow the harbor. Take the first left after crossing Litoral, onto C. Balboa. Take the 2nd right onto C. Baluart. $ Meat and fish dishes €3-10. Combination plates €6-8. ⏰ Open M-F 8am-5pm and 8-11pm, Sa 8am-5pm.

SEGONS MERCAT 💳 ♿ SEAFOOD [2]

C. Balboa, 16 ☎93 310 78 80 💻www.segonsmercat.com

Don't be misled by the cartoonish kitchen disasters painted all over its walls—Segons Market serves seriously fresh seafood for reasonable prices, with no worry of a culinary catastrophe. Dark wooden floors paired with orange and white school-style plastic chairs may make you feel as if you're in a child's version of a classy restaurant, but the food is nothing but refined.

➜ Ⓜ Barceloneta. Walk on Pla. del Palau over Ronda Litoral to follow the harbor. Take the 1st left after crossing Litoral, onto C. Balboa. $ Tapas €3.90-7.50. Entrees €7.90-16.90. ⏰ Open M-Sa 1-4pm and 9pm-midnight.

GRÀCIA

👍 LA NENA ⊛ ❄ CAFE, ORGANIC [1]

C. Ramon i Caja, 36 ☎93 285 14 76

An extensive menu of gourmet chocolates, ice creams, crepes, sandwiches, and quiches with ridiculously low prices. Don't try ordering a cold beer to beat the heat, though—the huge banner overhead alerts visitors that they may be the only spot in Barcelona that doesn't serve alcohol. Chill jazz plays over the speakers and kids' games and books line the tall, bright walls. For a filling treat, try one of their *tostadas*, like the goat cheese (goat cheese, tomato, and mushroom on bread), that will have you wishing you too had an extra stomach for more room.

➜ Ⓜ Follow C. d'Asturies, the one-way road leading from the metro stop and take a right onto Torrent de l'Olla. Walk a few blocks and take a left onto C. Ramon i Caja. $ Sandwiches €3.50. Quiches €5.50. ⏰ Open daily 1pm-1am.

👍 GAVINA 💳 ♿ 🍸 ❄ PIZZA [2]

C. Ros de Olano, 17 ☎93 415 74 50

Although there's not yet a market for pizza places where you can dine under life-sized patron saints, Gavina is just ahead of the curve. Don't misinterpret their slant, though—George Washington and a plethora of other nations' money serve to secularize this sanctuary of informal Italian cooking. The big draw is the gigantic, delicious pizzas. Try their namesake the Gavina (potatoes, ham, onion, and mushrooms), but be sure to bring friends or an otherworldly appetite.

➜ Ⓜ Fontana. Walk on Gran de Gràcia away from C. d'Asturies and take a left onto C. Ros de Olano. $ Pizza €6.50-14. Wine €8.50-15. ⏰ Open M-Th 1pm-1am, F-Sa 1pm-2am, Su 1pm-1am.

L'ILLA DE GRÀCIA 🍴♿🍸❄ VEGETARIAN ❷

C. St. Domenec, 19 ☎932 38 02 39 💻www.illadeGràcia.com

A haven for vegetarians, this classy modern eatery serves real meatless meals worlds away from the *queso bocadillos* you've been downing when your friends had *jamón.* The restaurant offers vegetarian versions of Catalan classics, including spinach *cannoloni* and delicious seitan dishes served in personal crocks *(€6-7).* Expect more Whole Foods than bohemian chic—this restaurant's decor is slick, minimal, and modern.

➜ [M]Fontana. Take a right onto C. Gran de Gràcia and walk about 5min. Left onto L'illa de Gràcia. $ Salads €5-6. Entrees €3.60-7.80. ⏰ Open M-Th 1-4pm and 9pm-midnight, F-Su 2-4pm and 9pm-midnight.

IKASTOLA ⊗♿🍸❄☀ BAR, CAFE ❶

C. Perla, 22

If you don't like the specials, just make your own alternate menu on their blackboard—but don't expect the cook to take heed. Every night young locals gather at Ikastole (Basque for "nursery school") to chat, pound out tunes on the upright piano, and scribble everything from love notes to apartment listings on the walls of this laid-back nighttime cafe. Lively, bright, and quick with cheap *bocatas*, Ikastola is the perfect place to start the night before embarking on more mature shenanigans.

➜ [M]Fontana. Follow C. Asturies, the one-way road leading from the metro stop. Take a right onto C. Torrent de l'Olla and a left onto Perla. $ Sandwiches €4.50, half €3. Salads €7. Beer €1.70-2.30. Wine €2. ⏰ Open M-Th 7pm-midnight, F-Sa 7pm-1am, Su 7pm-midnight.

CAFE DEL TEATRE ⊗♿📶🍸❄ CAFE, BAR ❷

C. Torrijos, 41 ☎93 416 06 51

If all of the gardens of earthly delights were to be contained in one bowl, it would look and taste like a Cafe del Teatre salad. Pictures of Gràcia line the red walls, while stained-glass windows cast patterns over a chill but perky intellectual clientele. Drop by for dinner and grab a Cocktail del Cafe del Teatre *(€6)* as you wait to start off the night.

➜ [M]Joanic. Take a right onto C. de l'Escorial and a left onto C. de Sant Lluis after a block. Cafe del Teatre is in the plaça after C. del Torrent d'en Vidalet. $ Entrees and sandwiches €4.90-6.50. Menú €5.80-6.50. ⏰ Open daily until 3am.

CHIDO ONE 🍴♿🍸 MEXICAN ❷

C. Torrijos, 30 ☎93 285 03 35 💻www.chidoone.es

This Mexican restaurant has more *luchador* mettle than Strong Bad, complete with brightly painted walls splattered with murals, crafty animals, and other knickknacks brought from the homeland. Try one of their handmade tortillas in their delicious quesadillas *(€8.50-10),* and grab a Mexican beer to wash them down.

➜ [M]Joanic. Take a right onto C. de l'Escorial and a left onto C. de Sant Lluis after a block. Left onto C. Torrijos. $ Appetizers €8.50-9.50; entrees €9.50-11. ⏰ Open M-Th 1-5pm and 7pm-midnight, F-Su 1pm-2am.

L'ARMARI ⊗♿🍸❄ FRENCH ❷

C. Montseny, 13 ☎93 368 54 13

Relaxed French cuisine including foie gras, truffles, cheeses, and a range of tartars fill this bistro. Young locals gather under delicate lighting for a midday meal with friends on mismatched chairs (some of which are somehow sporting a classy zebra stripe), while the black-and-white photos and French books on the walls set an appropriately refined scene. But with €4 mixed drinks before 10pm, don't feel as if you need to stay straight-laced.

➜ [M]Fontana. Walk on Gran de Gràcia away from C. d'Asturies and take a left onto C. Montseny. $ Tapas €3.50-6. Entrees €5.50-12. Cocktails €4, after 10pm €5.50. ⏰ Open M-F 9am-2:30am, Sa-Su 6pm-2:30am.

BARCELONA REYKJAVÍK

⬤♿ BAKERY ❶

C. Astúries, 20   ☎93 237 69 18 ▪www.barcelonareykjavik.com

This difficult-to-pronounce bakery is perfect for the discerning backpacker that's tired of white bread and sugary, mass-produced *magdalenas*. This eatery bakes mindblowing breads—if you've been in Spain long enough you'll find their sourdough a godsend—as well as delicious muffins, brioche, and other baked goods. Ingredients and potential flags for each are listed, making people with dietary restrictions' lives a little easier, if only for a short second before they venture back out into the world of meat, cheese, sugar, and gluten. Be prepared to eat on your feet or save it for later—this little storefront has no seating.

✈ Ⓜ*Follow C. d'Asturies, the one-way road leading from the metro stop.* ⓲ *Each item labeled for gluten, dairy, eggs, sugar.* Ⓢ *Items sold by weight. Breads normally €3-5. Baked goods €1-2.* ⏰ *Open M-Sa 11am-9:30pm.*

LAILA

⬤♿Ⓨ LEBANESE, PIZZA ❷

C. d'Asturies, 17   ☎93 415 52 70

Gourmet pizzas and a selection of tasty Lebanese dishes draw in a young and hip crowd, while low, black couches and comfy pillows keep them around. Expect to see a forest of laptops during the chill daytime hours, with the sunset ushering in groups of friends here to literally get their fill.

✈ Ⓜ*Fontana. Follow C. d'Asturies, the one-way road leading from the metro stop.* Ⓢ *Salads €8.90-10.50. Entrees and pizzas €7.90-10.90. Menú €9.80.* ⏰ *Open daily 10am-midnight.*

DIAMANT

⬤♿Ⓨ❄☼ CAFE ❶

C. Asturies, 67   ☎93 217 02 18

A student-laden cafe offering cheap meals, chill atmosphere, and interesting bocadillos—try the chicken and vegetable curry (*€3.80)* or the *cabra*, a mix of goat cheese, lettuce, tomato, and eggplant *(€3.50)*. Not hungry? Feel free to whip out your David Foster Wallace and kick back with a *cafe con leche* to pass the afternoon.

✈ Ⓜ*Fontana. Follow C. d'Asturies, the one-way road leading from the metro stop, for a few blocks. Diamant is located on your right as you enter Plaça d'Or.* Ⓢ *Salads €5.80. Sandwiches €3-4. Tapas €2.10-3.50.* ⏰ *Open daily 9am-3am.*

ASKA DINYA

⬤❄ MIDDLE EASTERN ❸

C. Verdi, 28   ☎93 368 50 77

Garden views abound in this crumbling rock-walled oasis. Pesky cats look down from overhead as an intoxicating smell of incense fills the nostrils. Afraid of a feline messing with your meal? Well, don't fear—it's all a painted ruse (or at least the cats are), but the serious quality of their food isn't. Loads of Palestinian-inspired options fill the menu, including *babaganoush (€6.50)*, hummus, falafel, and tons of vegetarian options. In fact, this is one of the few places where you're given the option to *add* meat to your liking instead of trying to keep it out.

✈ Ⓜ*Follow C. d'Asturies, the one-way road leading from the metro stop and take a right onto C. Verdi after crossing Torrent de l'Olla.* Ⓢ *Appetizers €6.50-8.50; entrees €9-13.50. Menú €8.* ⏰ *Open daily 1pm-1am.*

nightlife

BARRI GÒTIC AND LAS RAMBLAS

⬛ BARCELONA PIPA CLUB

⬤⊗Ⓨ BAR, CLUB

P. Reial, 3   ☎933 02 47 32 ▪www.bpipaclub.com

With pipes from four continents, smoking accoutrement decorated by Dalí, and even an "ethnological museum dedicated to the smoking accessory," the only

barcelona

pipe-related article missing from this club—albeit somewhat appropriately—is René Magritte's *"Ceci n'est pas une pipe."* Despite its cryptic lack of signage and an ambience of a secret society, the combination bar, pool room, and music lounge boasts a surprising number of travelers. The dark wood, low lights, and provincial furnishings make for a perfect place to transport yourself from the more collegiate nightlife of the Plaça Reial, even if the only experience you have with smoking is toting a candy cigarette.

⇆ [M]Liceu. Walk on Las Ramblas toward water. Left onto C. Ferran and first right to enter Plaça Reial. Pipa Club is an unmarked door to the right of Glaciar Bar. To enter, ring the bottom bell. ℹ Rotating selection of tobacco available for sale. Special smoking events. Tango and salsa lessons M and Tu 8:30-10:30pm. Jam session Su 8:30pm. $ Beer €4-5. Wine €4-5. Cocktails €7.50-9. ⏰ Open daily 6pm-6am.

★ HARLEM JAZZ CLUB — MUSIC CLUB, BAR

C. Comtessa de Sobradiel, 8 ☎933 10 07 55 🖥www.harlemjazzclub.es

With two live music performances each night and a drink included with admission, Harlem Jazz Club promises to beat those empty-wallet blues. A performance schedule online and on their door lets you choose whether you'll drop in to hear lovesick English crooning or a little saucier Latin flavor. With acts ranging from Bossa Nova to gypsy punk, blues to funk, and soul to salsa, the club is a fantastic place for any music lover to spend the evening.

⇆ [M]Liceu. Walk toward the water on Las Ramblas. Left onto C. Ferran. Right onto C. Avinyó. Left onto C. Comtessa de Sobradiel. ℹ Live music M-Th 11:30pm and midnight, F-Sa 11:30-m and 1am, Su 11:30pm and midnight. Calendar of events for the month available online or at door. $ Cover M-Th €5, includes 1 drink; F-Sa €8, includes 1 drink; Su €5. Beer €3.80. Cocktails €7.80. ⏰ Open M-Th 9pm-4am, F-Sa 9pm-5am, Su 9pm-4am.

SMOLL BAR — BAR

C. Comtessa de Sobradiel, 9

The chic '60s decor and friendly, burly bartenders combine to please an ever-present hip, gay-friendly, and young crowd. When there's room at the bar, squeeze in tight and try one of over 25 cocktails or a signature shot. The Rasmokov (vodka shot with a lime wedge topped in sugar and espresso powder) will leave you caffeinated, sugar-buzzed, and full of fuzzy, extroverted feelings.

⇆ [M]Liceu. Walk toward the water on Las Ramblas. Left onto C. Ferran. Right onto C. Avinyó. Left onto C. Comtessa de Sobradiel. $ Beer €3.50. Cocktails €5.60. ⏰ Open M-Th 9:30pm-2:30am, F-Sa 9:30pm-3am.

MANCHESTER — BAR

C. Milans, 5 ☎663 07 17 48 🖥www.manchesterbar.com

The long listing of bands on the exterior—Joy Division, The Cure, Arcade Fire, The Smiths, and many, many more—leaves little to the imagination. After passing the turning record table on the interior, you'll find a dark world of intimate seating, band references, and people who love both chatting and drinking the night away. A 7-10pm happy hour with €1.50 Estrellas gets the night started off right, and a vending machine selling tobacco is open until closing.

⇆ [M]Liceu. Walk toward the water on La Rambla, left onto C. Ferran. Right onto C. d'Avinyó. Left onto C. Milans before hitting C. Ample. Manchester is located where the street curves. ℹ Happy hour beer €1.50. $ Beers €2-4. Shots from €2.50. Mixed drinks €6. ⏰ Open M-Th 7pm-2-:30am, F-Sa 7pm-3am, Su 7pm-2:30am. Happy hour daily 7-10pm.

TRECE — BAR

C. Lleona, 13

If you can fight your way through the crowd of international 20-somethings into this pocket-sized hangout, Trece offers some of the best mojitos in Barcelona *(€6)*. Bare walls with exposed brick show off local artwork and an assorted selection of dismembered body parts, including a set of mannequin legs sticking out over the restroom door and a torso functioning as the primary light source. Hits from the '80s abound, and a projector plays a selection of music videos and YouTube clips over the heads of the clientele.

➜ [M]Liceu. Walk on Las Ramblas toward the sea, left onto C. Ferran. Right onto C. d'Avinyó and left onto C. de la Lleona. $ Beer €3. Cocktails €6-7. ⏰ Open M-Th 7pm-3am, F-Sa 7pm-5:30am, Su 7pm-3am.

SINCOPA 🍸 BAR

C. Avinyò, 35

At night this music-themed bar plays hosts to as many nationalities as it has currencies and secondhand instruments on its walls. Stop by midday for a change of pace—mostly filled with locals, the house boasts a big screen dedicated solely to *fútbol.* On slow days, the sculpture band of musicians hanging from the ceiling provides heartwarming company.

➜ [M]Liceu. Walk on Las Ramblas toward the water and take a left onto C. Ferran. Right onto C. d' Avinyò. $ Beer €2-3. Cocktails €7. Juices €2.50. ⏰ Open M-Th 6pm-2:30am, F-Sa 6pm-3am.

SOUL CLUB ♿ 🍸 ❄ BAR, NIGHTCLUB

C. Nou de Sant Francesc, 7 ☎93 302 70 26 🖥www.soulclub.es

Pink mood lighting and a soundtrack of soul, blues, and jazz will leave even the most painfully awkward social outcast feeling as suave and overtly sexual as the voice of Barry White. A small dance floor boosts the intimacy, and leather couches and chairs give you a classy place to court your dance partner (or just sit down for a breather after the music picks up).

➜ [M]Drassanes. Walk on Las Ramblas toward Plaça Catalonia. Turn right onto C. Escudellers, and then right onto C. Nou de Sant Francesc. $ Cover F-Sa €5. Beer €3.50. Cocktails €7.50. ⏰ Open M-Th 10pm-2:30am, F-Sa 10pm-3am, Su 10pm-2:30am.

ANDÚ ♿ 🍸 BAR

C. Correu Vell, 3 ☎646 553 930

A wall of well-stocked wine nestled in a wrought-iron grid lies underneath a bare brick arch behind the bar, perfectly summing up what this bar aims to project. Reliquaries of vintage instruments, tennis rackets, and armarios create a stage setting for refined 20-somethings to imbibe from their fine selection of vino *(€4 for a glass, or by bottle up to €21)* in class.

➜ [M]Jaume I. Walk on Via Laietana towards the water. Turn right onto C. d'Àngel Baixeras. $ Wine by the glass €4. Cocktails €6. Tapas €3-5. ⏰ Open M-Th 6pm-1am, F-Sa 6pm-3am, Su 6pm-1am. Kitchen open until 1am.

OVISO 🍸 CAFE, BAR

C. Arai, 5 🖥www.barnawood.com

Cafe Oviso is where ancient Roman villa meets bohemian dive bar. A myriad of frescos adorn the walls, including images of peacocks, myths, and a curious scene in which a man appears to be putting the moves on a lion. Benches and larger tables invite clients to continue the theme and lounge at their discretion like a drunken Bacchus. A delicious variety of food and juices are served during the day, while at night the bar fills up quickly with a mix of locals from the Plaça Trippy.

➜ [M]Liceu. Walk toward the water on Las Ramblas. Left onto C. Ferran. Right onto C. Avinyó. Left onto C. Arai; Oviso is on the right as you enter the plaça. ℹ Food and juice served during the day. $ Beer €3. Cocktails €7. ⏰ Open M-Th 10am-2:30am, F-Sa 10am-3am, Su 10am-2:30am.

LA RIA ♿ 🍸 TAVERN

C. Milans, 4

Bright white interior, upright seating, and an almost-entirely Catalan clientele makes for cheap booze, cheap food, and a refreshing—albeit grittier—alternative to the dressed up faces in the Plaça Reial. Relaxed and refreshingly authentic, La Ria is exactly the tavern it claims to be.

✚ ⓜJaume I. *Walk on Via Laietana towards the water and take a right onto C. d'en Gignàs. La Ria will be on the corner of Gignàs and C. Milans.* ⑤ *Beer €1-2.50. Wine €1.50-1.80. Copas €3. Tapas €4-12. Menú €4.* ☪ *Open M-Th 6:30pm-2am, F-Sa 6:30pm-3am.*

JAMBOREE   ●✦♈❀ NIGHTCLUB, MUSIC CLUB
P. Reial, 17   ☎933 19 17 89 ▣www.masimas.com/jamboree/

A hall-of-fame assortment of jazz musicians on the walls of the lower level will leave you with no guesses as to where this club's allegiances lie, even when its grotto-like halls are filled with Americans singing Aaliyah. The club offers nightly performances by jazz and blues musicians and opens to a younger set after these shows end at midnight. After this witching hour, be prepared for everything from hip hop to Shania Twain.

✚ ⓜLiceu. *Walk on Las Ramblas toward the water. Left onto C. Ferran, then right to enter Plaça Reial.* ⓲ *Music club performances usually daily 9pm and 11pm. Full list of upcoming events and concerts on website. Flyers provide discounts.* ⑤ *Event tickets €4-12. Dance club cover €10. Beer €5. Cocktails €9-10. Tarantino (upstairs, mostly flamenco) cover €6.* ☪ *Nightclub open M-Th 12:30-5am, F-Sa 12:30-6am, Su 12:30-5am. Music club open daily 9pm-1am. Tarantino open daily 8-11pm.*

SHANGÓ   ●⊗✦❀ BAR
C. d'en Groch, 9   ☎662 10 51 65 ▣www.shangolatinbar.com

Tucked down a poorly lit alley, Shangó's bright yellow-and-black door provides a warm, sunny beacon that beckons to revelers throughout the night. Free salsa lessons and a neverending supply of saucy Latin tunes complement the cheap mojitos (€4.50) and beer. Meanwhile, the comfortably full level of chairs and couches provides a relaxing place to grab a drink, meet some strangers, and soak in the sensation of being inside a big, sugary lemon.

✚ ⓜJaume I. *Walk down Via Laietana toward the water. Take a right onto C. d'En Gignàs and right onto C. d'En Groch.* ⓲ *Free salsa lessons Tu-W.* ⑤ *Beer €1.50-3. Mojitos €4.50. Cocktails €5-6.* ☪ *Open daily 9pm-3am.*

MARGARITA BLUE   ●ᕗ✦ BAR
C. Josep Anselm Clavé, 6   ☎934 12 54 89 ▣www.margaritablue.com

Surprisingly, Margarita Blue has margaritas and—surprise #2!—they're blue. Mexican platters complement the vaguely Mexican drink selection as colorful paintings of musicians paired with a mirrored wall keep loving watch over the bar. For those not needing supervision, a bright blue daisy wall in the back offers fluorescent cheer.

✚ ⓜDrassanes. *Walk toward the water on Las Ramblas and take a left onto C. Josep Anselm Clavé.* ⓲ *Magic show W and Su 10pm.* ⑤ *Food €5.80-9, cocktails €7-8.* ☪ *Open M-W 7pm-2am, Th-Sa 7pm-3am, Su 7pm-2am.*

EL BOSQ DE LES FADES   ●ᕗ✦❀ CAFE, BAR
Pg. de la Banca, 16   ☎933 17 26 49 ▣www.museocerabcn.com

If you have ever wondered what it's like to be a hobbit and drink a whole pitcher of sangria (€12), Bosq de les Fades provides the perfect opportunity to settle your burning curiosity. A wooded canopy creates an enchanted forest deserving of the bar's name. If you're not the outdoorsy type and prefer something more domestic, you can hang out in a haunted bedroom, so long as you don't mind a woman behind a false mirror dropping in on your conversation. Be prepared for as many gawkers as diners, as the fantastical facade across from the Wax Museum is a popular photograph point.

✚ ⓜDrassanes. *Walk briefly along Las Ramblas toward the water. Turn left onto Pg. de la Banca. El Bosq de les Fades is at the end of the road, in front of the Museu de Cera.* ⑤ *Cava glass €3, bottle €16. Sangria €3.50, pitcher €12. Wine €2.30. Cocktails €6.10-7.20.* ☪ *Open M-Th 10:30am-1-am, F-Sa 10:30am-1:30am, Su 10:30am-1am.*

nightlife • barri gòtic and las ramblas

BOULEVARD CULTURE CLUB

☻❣ NIGHTCLUB

Las Ramblas, 27 ☎933 01 62 89 🌐www.boulevardcultureclub.com

With three rooms, dizzying lights, and a clientele that borders on barely legal, Boulevard Culture Club plays host to the nightclubbers of the traveler-laden Las Ramblas. Promoters draw in dancers with discount fliers along the street. If you don't like the techno playing in the first room, just move on to the next to hear some Missy Elliott instead.

❣ Ⓜ*Liceu. Walk on Las Ramblas toward the water, destination on right.* ⓘ *Reduced admission with flyer distributed along Las Ramblas. Calendar of special events and theme nights on website.* Ⓢ *Cover €15; includes one drink.* 🕐 *Open daily midnight-6am. Free for men before 1am and women before 2:30am.*

KARMA

❣ NIGHTCLUB, BAR

Pl. Reial, 10 ☎933 02 56 80 🌐www.karmadisco.com

Karma: for those who dream of disco in a partified subway station. A bizarre mix of blues, soul, and '80s music plays for a largely uninterested older set while rainbow lights wrap around two barrel vaults that mark the bar and dancefloor. You may be better off living your actual dream by grabbing a boombox, some streetside beer, and a metro ticket—not that *Let's Go* suggests (illegally) drinking in public.

❣ Ⓜ*Liceu. Walk on Las Ramblas toward the water. Left onto C. Ferran, Right to enter Plaça Reial.* Ⓢ *Club cover €10; includes 1 drink. Beer €4. Cocktails €6-8.* 🕐 *Club open Tu-Th and Su 12am-5am, F-Sa 12am-6am. Bar open daily 6pm-2:30am.*

LA RIBERA

▩ ALMA

♥👌❣❄ BAR

C. de Sant Antoni dels Sombrerers, 7 ☎933 19 76 07

A quieter alternative for those too cool to bother with the packed houses and inflated prices of nearby Passeig del Born. Cheap drinks provide bait for any traveler, while relaxed seating, rotating art exhibitions, and a bartender that stays surprisingly laidback even when drunkenly berated about the lack of mojitos give solid reasons to stay for the night.

❣ Ⓜ*Jaume I. Walk down C. de la Princesa and take a right onto C. Montcada. Upon entering Psg. del Born, take a right onto C. dels Sombrerers and then take a right again onto the 1st street on your right, C. de Sant Antoni dels Sombrerers.* Ⓢ *Cava €1.80. Beer €2. Cocktails €6.* 🕐 *Open Tu-Th 8:30pm-2:30am, F-Sa 8:30pm-3am.*

EL BORN

♥👌❣ BAR

Pg. del Born, 26 ☎933 19 53 33

Shed the pretense and shabby themes and stop in to El Born for a straight-up bar—no more, no less. Marble tables and a green palette provide gametime seating and trenches for those brave enough to claim them on weekend nights. With cheap beer *(€2-2.50)* and ambient music, it's no wonder this place is always full.

❣ Ⓜ*Jaume I. Walk down C. Princesa and take a right onto C. Montcada. Follow until you hit Psg. del Born.* ⓘ *Free Wi-Fi.* Ⓢ *Beer €2-2.50. Mixed drinks €6.* 🕐 *Open Tu-Su 10am-2:30am.*

LA FIANNA

♥👌❣❄ BAR

C. Banys Vells, 15 ☎933 15 18 10 🌐www.lafianna.com

A glass partition divides the restaurant and bar, but be prepared to push your way through on weekend nights no matter where you choose to stay. Unlike in most places in the area, finding a seat at the bar is a distinct possibility. Patience pays off with mojitos as large as your fist, made with special bitters to set it apart *(€7)*. An elevated lounge area keeps it loose—stretch out on the pillows and survey the pack.

❣ Ⓜ*Jaume I. Walk down C. de la Princesa and take a right onto C. Montcada. Upon entering Psg. del Born, take a right onto C. dels Sombrerers and then take a right onto C. dels Banys Vells.* Ⓢ *Beer €2.50-3.40. Cocktails €4-7. Tapas €2-4.75.* 🕐 *Open M-W 6pm-1:30am, Th-Sa 6pm-2:30am, Su 6pm-1:30am. Happy hour with discount tapas on M-Th 7pm-12:30am, F-Sa 7pm-11:30pm, Su 7pm-12:30am.*

BERIMBAU ♿🍸 LATIN BAR

Pg. del Born, 17 ☎933 19 53 78

This Brazilian *copas* bar, reportedly the oldest Brazilian bar in Spain, offers a range of drinks you won't easily find this side of the Atlantic. Try the *guarana* with whiskey *(€8)* or an orange and banana juice with vodka *(€9)*. Relaxed, beachy beats fill the air, with wicker chairs to let you live out the summer dream.

🚏 [M]Jaume I. Walk down C. Princesa and take a right onto C. Montcada. Follow to Psg. del Born. $ Cocktails €8-10. ⏰ Open M-Th 6pm-2:30am, F-Sa 6pm-3am, Su 6pm-2:30am.

CACTUS BAR ♿🍸 BAR

Passeig del Born, 30 ☎933 10 63 54 💻www.cactusbar.cat

This little bar thankfully bears little resemblance to its vaguely Mexican-themed name. Instead, expect a packed house and an interior like a subdued carnival. A huge selection of gin and tonics and overtly friendly staff light up the night, while a calmer crowd and all-day breakfast specials create a vibrant atmosphere even before happy hour kicks in at 6pm.

🚏 [M]Jaume I. Walk down C. Princesa and take a right onto C. Montcada. Follow until you hit Psg. del Born. $ Breakfast €1.50. Sandwiches €2.50-3.70. Tapas €1.80-6.50. Beer €3. Cocktails €8. ⏰ Open M-Th 9am-2pm, F-Sa 11am-3pm. Happy hour daily 6-8pm.

NO SÉ 💳♿🍸 BAR

Psg. del Born, 29 ☎67 148 59 87

One of the many popular bars along Passeig del Born, No Sé aims for nothing in particular. Artwork lines the walls and a young crowd fills its floor, but don't expect a theme. Shiny vinyl paintings, bright walls, scattered seating, and loud electronic music make the potential for an upbeat dance floor on weekday nights when there's actually room to breathe.

🚏 [M]Jaume I. Walk down C. Princesa and take a right onto C. Montcada. Follow until you hit Psg. del Born. $ Mixed drinks €8-10. ⏰ Open daily 8pm-2:30am.

PITIN BAR 🌐♿🍸⛅ BAR

Pg. del Born ☎93 319 59 87 💻www.pitinbar.com

With copious outdoor seating and a lounge upstairs, Pitin Bar offers a more relaxed and mature alternative to the nightclub-in-your-pocket bars that dot the Passeig del Born. This is where the non-20-somethings come out to play, so expect a more relaxed and mature audience.

🚏 [M]Jaume I. Walk down C. Princesa and take a right onto C. Montcada. Follow to Psg. del Born. $ Beer €2.50-4. Cocktails €6.50-7. ⏰ Open M-Th noon-2:30am, F-Sa noon-3am, Su noon-2:30am.

BARROC CAFE 💳♿🍸❄⛅ BAR

C. del Rec, 67 ☎932 68 46 23 💻www.barroc-cafe.com

Velvet heart-shaped booths, baroque golden frames, and medieval ironwork set the sight for romance while flying cherubim lining the walls move in for the kill. Throbbing techno produces a little confusion, but a little of the house special *mojito barroc (€8)* will clear away any doubts (or inhibitions).

🚏 [M]Jaume I. Walk down C. de la Princesa and take a right onto C. Flassanders. Follow over the Passeig del Born as it becomes C. del Rec. $ Beer €3-3.20. Cocktails €8. ⏰ Open M-Th 3pm-2:30am, F-Sa 3pm-3am, Su 3pm-2:30am.

LA HACIENDA 💳♿🍸❄ BAR, MEXICAN

C. del Rec, 69

This Mexican bar serves semi-authentic Mexican food and drink under plaster walls, colorful Christian flags, and a vividly colored Aztec mural. Cool the spices of the burritos and *enchiladas (€6.95)* with a Mojito Mexicano *(€4)*. Although most come to dine more than wine, the place still gets busy and bumping on weekend nights.

🚏 [M]Jaume I. Walk down C. de la Princesa and take a right onto C. Flassanders. Follow over the Passeig del Born as it becomes C. del Rec. $ Appetizers €3.50-6.50; entrees €7. Mixed drinks €4-6. ⏰ Open daily noon-3am.

EL RAVAL

MARSELLA BAR

BAR

C. de Sant Pau, 65 ☎93 442 72 63

Walls lined with antique mirrors, cabinets, old advertisements, and dusty bottles will have you waiting to witness your first saloon brawl. Luckily, the crowd is genial and friendly, even after a few absinthes *(€5)*—not that there's room to fight in this crowded place anyway. Crackling paint and fuzzy chandeliers will have you feeling every month of the bar's 190 years of business.

[M]Liceu. Walk down C. Hospital and take a left onto C. Junta de la Comerç. Take a right at the end of the street onto C. de Sant Pau. $ Beer €3.50. Absinthe €5. Mixed drinks €5-6. ⏰ Open M-Th 11pm-2am, F-Sa 11pm-3am.

PLASTIC BAR

BAR

C. Sant Ramón, 23 www.myspace.com/plasticobar

This hip bar is big enough to host as many people as are cool enough to enter. Dark paisley walls with a green lit bar let you squeeze through to the back portion, where the real life awaits. The upper level is for lounging, while the scratchy soundsystem of the lower portion pumps a mix of modern indie and '60s rock to a crowd excited to dance the night away.

[M]Liceu. Walk on Las Ramblas toward the Sea. Take a right onto C. Nou de la Rambla and right onto C. de Sant Ramón. $ Shots €3. Beer €3-3.50. Mixed drinks €6. ⏰ Open M 11pm-2:30am, W 11pm-2:30am, Th 11pm-2:30am, F-Sa 11pm-3am.

BAR BIG BANG

BAR, MUSIC CLUB

C. Botella, 7 www.bigbangbcn.net

The back room attracts a collegiate crowd to watch free nightly performances like the jazz acts, standup comedy, and vaudeville-esque theater. Out front, customers are serenaded by big band favorites—both local and national—over the stereo and black-and-white projector screen. Creepy eyes look down from every corner, whether from the frames of outsider art or from the jazz star photos lining the dark walls.

[M]Sant Antoni. Walk down C. de Sant Antoni Abad (in the corner of the square where C. del Comte d'Urgell and C. de Manso meet) and take a hard right onto C. Botella. i Schedule of performances and special events on website. Variety show on Tu, DJ on F and Sa at midnight. $ Shots €3. Beer €3-4. Cocktails €6.50. All cheaper before 11pm. ⏰ Open Tu-Sa 9:30pm-2:30am, Su 10:30pm-2:30am.

VALHALLA ROCK CLUB

BAR, MUSIC CLUB

C. Tallers, 68 www.myspace.com/valhallaclubderock

Be prepared to see burly men air-guitaring Slayer in the place where a normal dance floor should be. At times serving as a concert hall, this dark and industrial-esque nightclub is a haven for those sick of flashing lights and throbbing techno. Free cover on non-show nights means you can use the saved cash to try their entire selection of *chupitos del rock*, specialty shots named after bands from Elvis to Whitesnake *(€1)*.

[M]Universitat. Walk down C. Tallers. i Draught beer €1.50-2.50 daily until 10pm. Check MySpace for calendar of concerts and special events. $ Shots €1-2. Sangria €2.50. Beer €2.50-5. Mixed drinks €6-7. ⏰ Open daily 6:30pm-2:30am.

SANT PAU 68

BAR

C. Sant Pau, 68 ☎934 41 31 15

An absurdist bar with an identity crisis. The Van Gogh-esque wall of ears is paired with gas tank-inspired lights and a metal chandelier with circuit board cutouts casting geeksheek patterns of light across the stairwell. If you're looking to get away from the crowd, grab a Bloody Mary *(€6)* and head upstairs to scrawl your regards on the graffiti wall.

⇆ [M]Liceu. Walk down C. Hospital and take a left onto C. Junta de la Comerç. Take a right at the end of the street onto C. de Sant Pau. $ Beer €2. Mixed drinks €6. ⏰ Open M-Th 8pm-2:30am, F-Sa 8pm-3:30am, Su 8pm-2:30am.

BETTY FORD 🍴♿🍸❄ BAR

C. Joaquín Costa, 56 ☎933 04 13 68

This small bar and restaurant hosts local students coming in to chow down on their relatively cheap burgers. Join in and listen to a mix of funky music while being surrounded by '20s flapper flair. Happy hour (6-9pm) provides cheap drinks, and the bathroom size guarantees some intimate encounters.

⇆ [M]Universitat. Walk down Ronda de Sant Antoni and take a slight left onto C. de Joaquin Costa. Happy hour mixed drinks €4. $ Burgers €6.50. Fries €2. Shakes €3.50. Beer €3. Mixed drinks €5-6. ⏰ Open M-Th 2pm-1:30am, F-Sa 2pm-2:30am, Su 8pm-1:30am. Kitchen open M-Sa 2-4pm and 7-10pm, Su 7-11pm. Happy hour daily 6-9pm.

ODDLAND 🍴♿🍸❄ BAR

C. Joaquín Costa, 52 ☎934 12 00 49

Not as alienatingly bizarre as the name would imply, this quirky bar gets dancier as the night goes on, thanks to a live a DJ playing electro hits. Painted butteflies cover the walls and a trippy blacklit wonderland at the bar allows for an otherworldly experience. Stop in for a weekday cocktail—at only €3.50-4, you might get to see the butterflies take flight.

⇆ [M]Universitat. Walk down Ronda de Sant Antoni and take a slight left onto C. de Joaquin Costa. $ Snacks €1-4.50. Beer €2.30-4. Cocktails M-F €3.50-7. ⏰ Open M-W 7pm-2am, Th-Sa 7pm-2:30am, Su 7pm-1am.

CAFÈ DE LES DELÍCIES 🍴♿🍸❄☁ CAFE, BAR

Rambla del Raval, 47 ☎934 41 57 14

Light from the Rambla outside filters in through the French-doors-turned-windows, and after a few drinks the fully furnished house jutting out over the bar will have you wondering whether you're actually inside. Serving a small selection of *bocadillos* during the day to a sparse crowd, the cafe's book and art-lined walls fill up quickly at night.

⇆ [M]Liceu. Walk on C. L'Hospital and take a left onto Rambla del Raval. Cafè de les Delícles will be on the righthand side of the Rambla. $ Sandwiches €1.50-3.50. Beer €2-3.50. Mixed drinks €5.50-6. ⏰ Open M-Th 9am-2:30am, F-Sa 9am-3am. Kitchen closes at 1am.

LA ROUGE 🍴♿🍸❄ BAR

Rambla del Raval, 10 ☎933 29 54 45

Push your way through the crowded bar area to lounge in the dark seating in back, or look down on the masses from its loft area. No matter where you stand, be sure to check out the chandelier made of little liquor bottles hanging above the entrance—just don't expect to drink them for free. Cocktails start at €5, while the house shot *chupito la rouge* will cost you €3.50. Electronic dance music plays over the stereo to please the younger crowd.

⇆ [M]Liceu. Walk on C. L'Hospital and take a left onto Rambla del Raval. La Rouge will be on the right side of the Rambla. $ Tapas €1.50-6.50. Appetizers €5-6. Cava €4. Cocktails €5-6. ⏰ Open M-Th 8pm-2am, F-Sa 8pm-3am.

L'OVELLA NEGRA 🍴♿🍸❄ BAR

C. Sitges, 5 ☎933 17 10 87 🖥www.ovellanegra.com

Think Viking beer hall without the possibility of a funeral pyre burning into the night. Cheap beer flows freely, which makes stomaching the kitsch—anyone care to take a picture with the drunken black sheep cutout?—possible. Split-log benches and a selection of foosball, pool tables, and TVs provide all the charm of a frathouse in Valhalla.

⇆ [M]Catalonia. Walk toward the sea on Las Ramblas and take a hard right onto C. dels Tallers.

Then take a hard left onto C. Sitges. ⑤ *Tapas €1.50-4. Shots €2.30-3. Beer €1.20-3.60. Pitchers of beer and sangria €10.70-12.50.* ☒ *M-Th 9am-2:30am, F 9am-3am, Sa 5pm-3am, Su 5pm-2:30am. Drinks cheaper before 11pm.*

TRA.LLERS
🖐️♿️🍴❄️ BAR

C. Trallers, 39-41
☎934 12 78 43

A mural of a foreboding, twisted desert paired with the accompanying spray-painting of a 🅰️**communist** woman soldier serve to supplement the tone that the heavily tattooed female owner and younger clientele have served to set. Multiple TVs, a wraparound bar, and an excellent selection of imported beer allow you to get surly the way it should be done—by the bottle.
♯ Ⓜ*Universitat. Walk down C. Tallers. Tra.llers is just past the intersection of C. Tallers and C. Ramelleres.* ⑤ *Sandwiches €2.50-3.80. Beer and wine €2.50-5. Mixed drinks €6.* ☒ *Open M-Th 11am-2am, F-Sa 11am-3am, and Su 11am-2am.*

RITA BLUE
♿️❄️☕ CAFE, RESTAURANT

Pl. Sant Agustí
☎934 81 36 86 🖥️www.ritablue.com

Bright rainbow chairs on the patio match the saturated interior, from the obnoxiously vibrant blue and pink walls to the orange Christmas lights. Rita Blue whips up a mix of cafe-style dishes with a Tandoori twist—try the *bacalao* or tandoori chicken fajitas (€9.70). A student *menú* (€6) keeps the crowd young, as if the strange mosaics and funky paintings of fat old ladies weren't enough to keep away the more mature set. Live house music and a mix of DJs, poetry slams, and other performances spice up the afterhours downstairs.
♯ Ⓜ*Liceu. Walk down C. l"Hospital and take a left onto C. Junta de la Comerç to enter the plaza.* 𝒊 *Live house music M-Sa 11pm.* ⑤ *Entrees €9.70-18. Salads and starters €4-8. Lunch menú €5.90, dinner menú 9.90. Beer €2.20. Mixed drinks €5.50-8.* ☒ *Open M-Th 6pm-2am, F-Sa 6pm-3am, and Su 6pm-2am.*

CAFE-BAR CENTRIC
🖐️♿️🍴 CAFE, BAR

C. Ramelleres, 27
☎933 01 81 35

Bar Centric serves cheap comfort foods during the day, including pork sticks, french fries, pastas, and tapas. In the evening, the dark wooden, parlor-like interior fills up with locals looking to chat or catch the game. Come early, but don't expect to stay late—get your fill of the €2 beers and €5-9 mixed drinks while they last, as this bar only stays open until 10:30pm at the latest.
♯ Ⓜ*Universitat. Walk down C. Tallers. Bar Centric will be on the corner of C. Tallers and C. Ramelleres.* ⑤ *Tapas €1-6. Specials €4.50-9.50. Beer and wine €2-2.50. Mixed drinks €5-9.* ☒ *Open M-F 8:30am-10pm, Sa 11am-10:30pm.*

MOOG
🖐️♿️🍴❄️ CLUB

C. Arc del Teatre, 3
☎933 01 72 82 🖥️www.masimas.com/moog

One of Spain and Europe's premiere clubs for electronic music, Moog caters both to electrotrash afficionados and lost souls just trying to find a place to dance in Raval. Come on Wednesdays and weekends for the crowd, or drop in earlier during the week for house DJ sets. If you're looking for older hits or just want to get away from the throbbing mass on the dancefloor, check out the upper portion, which plays a mix of older electro, disco, and techno.
♯ Ⓜ*Drassanes. Walk away from the water on C. de Guardia and take a right onto C. de l'Arc del Teatre.* 𝒊 *Discount flyers often available on Las Ramblas.* ⑤ *Cover €10.* ☒ *Open M-Th midnight-5am, F-Sa midnight-6am, Su midnight-5am.*

BAR RESTAURANT ELISABETS
🖐️♿️🍴 BAR, RESTAURANT

C. Elisabets, 2-4
☎933 17 58 26

Serving a delicious array of tapas and homemade dishes during the day, Bar Restaurant Elisabets gets to business on weekend nights. Get the night started early for cheap drinks with a younger, mostly local clientele, and soak in the bar's

barcelona

history as an agricultural cooperative by looking at pictures along the wall.

↱ *Ⓜ Universitat. Walk down C. Tallers and take a right onto C. Elisabets.* [$] *Starters and sandwiches €2.40-3.45. Tapas €2-3.55. Lunch menú €8.50. Entrees €6-12. Beer €1.40-2.15. Mixed drinks €5-7.* ⏰ *Open M-Th 7:30am-11pm, F-Sa 7:30am-2am.*

L'EIXAMPLE

👍 LES GENTS QUE J'AIME

💳🚫♿🍸 BAR

C. Valencia, 286 ☎93 215 68 79

Come down the stairs into this sultry red velvet underworld for antique photographs, jazz covers of "Tainted Love," and vintage chandeliers that set the mood for you to partake in their sinful pleasures. Not sure where to head for the rest of the night? Cozy up next to the palm-reader, or have your tarot cards read to keep from indecision.

↱ *Ⓜ Diagonal. Turn right onto Passeig de Gràcia and walk for 3 blocks. Take a left onto C. Valencia. Les Gents is downstairs next to Campechano.* ***i*** *Palm reading and tarot cards M-Sa, €30 and €25.* [$] *Wine €3. Beer €3.50. Cocktails €7.* ⏰ *Open M-Th 7pm-2:30am, F-Sa 7pm-3am, Su 7pm-2:30am.*

👍 LA FIRA

🚫💳🚫♿🍸 CLUB

C. Provença, 171 ☎65 085 53 84

Decorated entirely with pieces from the old Apolo Amuseument Park in Barcelona, this club is like a debaucherous family reunion without having to worry about the faux pas of incest. The walls act as a mausoleum to innocent years past, sporting dioramas of the fair, fortune tellers, and masks of questionable racial politics. Dance away under the big top, and try not to get too creeped out while downing *Espit Chupitos* under the glare of the knowing sphynx.

↱ *Ⓜ Hospital Clinic. Walk away from the engineering school on C. del Rossello and take a right onto C. de Villarroel when it dead-ends. Take the first left onto Provença; La Fira is a few blocks down.* ***i*** *Often hosts shows or parties, sometimes with entrance fee or 1-drink min.* [$] *Beer €5. Cocktails €8.* ⏰ *Open Th-Sa 11:30pm-3am.*

ZELTAS

💳♿🍸❄▼ BAR

C. Casanova, 75 ☎93 450 84 69 🖥www.zeltas.net

Like a story lifted from a sultry romance novel about an all-male harem with impeccable taste, Zeltas pleases the eyes in more ways than one. An all black interior draped in white, flowing fabric sets the tone, while chic white couches and a bar seemingly dedicated to those looking to dance shirtless sets the mood. Musky cologne floats through the air, and beefy male dancers in tight black spankies make the air somehow thicker.

↱ *Ⓜ Universitat. Face the University building and walk left on Gran Vía. Turn right onto C. Casanova. Zeltas is down 2 blocks.* ***i*** *Male dancers nightly.* [$] *Beer €5. Cocktails €7.50.* ⏰ *Open daily 11pm-6am.*

LA CHAPELLE

💳♿🍸❄▼ BAR

C. Muntaner, 67 ☎93 453 30 76

A wall of devotional figurines and paintings with mostly nude men in front allows La Chapelle to show a gayer side of the sacrament. Solemn red lighting mixed with modern bubble lights cut through the veil of testosterone—apparently debaucherous religious imagery is bait for bears. Get a little closer to God while getting a lot closer with some grizzly guys.

↱ *Ⓜ Universitat. Face the University building and walk left on Gran Vía. Turn right onto C. Muntaner. La Chapelle is 2 blocks down.* [$] *Beer €2.50. Mixed drinks €5.* ⏰ *Open daily 4pm-2:30am.*

ATAME

💳♿🍸❄▼ BAR

Consell de Cent, 257 ☎93 434 92 73 🖥www.facebook.com/bar.atame

Dietrich Gay Teatro Cafe's life partner, Atame's sleek minimalist interior pulses with '80s hits and a mostly male crowd that loves to sing along (and encourage you to sing with them). The dance floor in back is packed when drag shows aren't in session, while the front of the bar provides a lush hunting ground with diverse prey for those on the prowl.

✈ ⓜUniversitat. *Face the University building and walk left on Gran Vía. Turn right onto Aribau and walk 2 blocks. Take a left onto Consell de Cent. Atame is a block away.* ⓲ *Happy hour mixed drinks €4. Drag shows and other events nightly. Call for more info.* ⓢ *Mixed drinks €5.* ⓞ *Open daily 7pm-3am. Happy hour 6pm-11am.*

DOW JONES

⛟&♿✿ BAR

C. Bruc, 97   ☎93 476 38 31 ▦www.bardowjones.es

During the day this English-centric bar has enough television screens to keep every fútbol fan happy, no matter his allegiance. At night, the bar lights up with raucous foreigners trying desperately to order their favorite drink before the price spikes—like the stock market, drinks' prices vary based on their popularity during the day. Wait for the prices to crash if you're counting on a winner, or keep buying low and be glad the staff speaks English fluently for when you're slurring your Spanish.

✈ ⓜGirona. *Walk toward C. Aragó on C. Girona and take a left onto C. Valencia after passing Arago. Walk 1 block and take a left onto C. del Bruc. Dow Jones is close to the corner.* ⓢ *Food €2.75-7.50. Beer €2-5.50. Cocktails €4-7.* ⓞ *Open M-F 7am-2:30am, Sa-Su noon-3am.*

AIRE

⛟⊗♿✿▼ CLUB

C. Valencia, 236   ☎93 454 63 94 ▦www.arenadisco.com

If you're looking for a queer-centric party spot that isn't overwhelmingly male (i.e. the rest of l'Eixample), check out Aire for all of the non-guy company the neighborhood seemed to be lacking. This huge club is packed nearly as soon as its doors open and continues to party with a mix of pop hits, R and B, and electronica well into the night. Don't worry about feeling left out—no matter your gender or orientation, unless you show up at one of their Women-only strip shows *(6-10pm one Su each month)*—the owner says the club is, "for girls...and friends."

✈ ⓜUniversitat. *Face the university building and walk down the street that runs along its right side, C. Balmes. Turn left onto C. Valencia, 1 street after crossing Arago.* ⓲ *Women-only strip show 6-10pm 1st Su of every month.* ⓢ *Cover €5-10; includes 1 drink.* ⓞ *Open Th-Su 11:30pm-3am.*

PLATA BAR

⛟&♿✿⊘▼ BAR

C. Consell de Cent, 233   ☎93 452 46 36 ▦www.facebook.com/platabar

Four flatscreens play a simulcast of Lady Gaga videos in an interior chic enough that sculptural water bottles can parade convincingly as art. Colored lights spice up the chic interior with rainbow flags in the window to match. Order a mojito *(€9.50)* from one of the ripped bartenders, and settle into this classy gay bar before heading over to shake your tail elsewhere.

✈ ⓜUniversitat. *Face the University building and walk down the road that runs along its left side. After 2 blocks, turn left onto C. Consell de Cent. Plata Bar is 2 blocks down.* ⓢ *Beer €3.50. Cocktails €9.50.* ⓞ *Open daily 7pm-3am.*

ESPIT CHUPITOS (ARIBAU)

⛟&♿✿ BAR

C. Aribau, 77   ▦www.espitchupitos.com

If you want shots, they've got 'em—580 different delectable little devils will let you party as if you'd gone to Cancun on vacation instead of the Mediterranean. Be prepared for a little more than just drinking, though. Spectacle shots such as the *Harry Potter* literally light up the night, while others have the bartenders getting down and dirty. If you can't get enough, Espit Chupitos has gotten so popular that it now has two other locations in the city, a sister store in l'Eixample called Gato Negro, and an outpost inside La Fira.

✈ ⓜUniversitat. *Walk on C. Aribau to the left of the university building. Espit Chupitos is 4 blocks down.* ⓢ *Shots €2. Cocktails €8.50.* ⓞ *Open M-Th 8pm-2:30am, F-Sa 8pm-3am, Su 8pm-2:30am.*

MOJITO CLUB

♥ ⏲ ❀ CLUB

C. Rosselló, 217   ☎65 420 10 06 ▨www.mojitobcn.com

A salsa-inspired club for the younger set, Mojito can't be as easily defined as its Latin beat-blasting genre-mates. Low black leather couches and semi-private alcoves dot the foyer, while the dance floor pulses to everything from hip hop to rumba, depending on the night. Stop by during the day to take a salsa lesson from the **Buenavista Dance Studio** *(☎93 237 65 28)* or go for a cheaper option on Wednesday nights with free Samba lessons during their Brazil party, starting at 11:30pm.

⚘ ⓂDiagonal. Walk away from Passeig de Gràcia on C. Rossello. Mojito is near the intersection of C. Balmes, on the far side. i Th salsa night, F-Sa salsa until 1:30am. Special events info on website. ⓢ Cover F-Sa €12; includes 1 drink. Th and Sa 1-drink min. Beer €7. Cocktails €9. ⌚ Open Th 11:pm-4:30am, F 11pm-4:30am, Sa 11pm-3:30am, Su 8:30pm-4:30am.

LUZ DE GAS

♥ ♿ ⏲ ❀ CLUB, CONCERT HALL

C. Muntaner, 244-256   ☎93 209 77 11 ▨www.luzdegas.com

The most well-known club in the city, and for good reason. Red velvet walls, gilded mirrors, and sparkling chandeliers will have you wondering how you possibly got past the bouncer. Big name jazz, blues, and soul performers occasionally take the stage during the evening hours, while after 1am it becomes overrun by swanky partygoers. Ritzy young things dance to deafening pop, from Outkast to Nancy Sinatra, pounding through the lower area, while the upstairs lounge provides a much-needed break for both your feet and ears.

⚘ ⓂDiagonal. Take a right onto Rambla de Catalonia, walk 1 block and take a slight left onto Av. Diagonal. Walk 5min. and take a right onto C. de Muntaner. i For show listings and times check the Guía del Ocio or their website. ⓢ Club cover €18. Beer €7. Cocktails €10. ⌚ Dance club open daily 11:30pm-5:30am.

DBOY/LA MADAME/DEMIX

♥ⓧ⏲❀ CLUB

Ronda Sant Pere, 19-21   ☎93 453 05 82 ▨www.matineegroup.com

Three clubs in one, this single spot hosts a downright confusing variety of nightlife options depending on the night. **DBoy** is no-girls allowed, with a young and lively gay crowd dancing in a laser-lit wonderland. **La Madame** fems it up, offering a hetero-centric alternative geared mostly towards women, and **Demix** supplies just like what it sounds—a mixed crowd. Check the website beforehand to see which way the club swings.

⚘ ⓂUrquinaona. With your back to Plaça Urquinaona, Ronda Sant Pere runs to the right from the Plaça. Follow it a few short steps and look for the LED sign. ⓢ Cover varies €10-15. ⌚ DBoy open in summer F-Sa midnight-6am. La Madame open in summers Su midnight-5am. Demix open Jan-July F-Su midnight-6am; Sept-Dec F-Su midnight-6am.

DIETRICH GAY TEATRO CAFE

♥♿⏲❀▼ BAR

C. Consell de Cent, 225   ☎93 451 77 07 ▨www.facebook.com/dietrichcafe

Rainbow flags, a cheery staff, and an unquestionably classy portrait of an old, saggy, fishnet-clad Marlene Dietrich wait to greet you as you walk in the door. Despite the cheery atmosphere, a serious dance floor lies waiting in back, complete with a Bacardi-cooler-turned-sculpture along the bar. Some nights are hit or miss—a packed house during their special events is countered by an echoing shell on nights off. If the bar seems too empty for your tastes, hop next door to the club's other portion, Atame, for a guaranteed full house.

⚘ ⓂUniversitat. Face the University building and walk left on Gran Vía. Turn right onto Aribau and walk 2 blocks. Take a left onto Consell de Cent. Dietrich is 1 block away. i Drag shows, acrobatics, and dancing on some nights. Check with restaurant for event schedule. ⓢ Beer €3.50. Mixed drinks €4.50-7.50. ⌚ Open Th-Sa 10:30pm-2:30am.

BAR CENTRIK ⊛ & ☝ ❄ ▼ BAR
C. Aribau, 30

One of the newest additions to gay-friendly nightlife in l'Eixample, Bar Centrik caters to a mix of sexualities about as convoluted as its interior decoration—prepare to be engulfed by lush purple walls clad with '60s logos sitting under the bar's straw hut overhang. Super friendly regulars will have you sharing your secrets in no time (as well as listening to some of their own), and just one of their delicious but potent cocktails will have you confessing more than you may have wanted.

✦ Ⓜ*Universitat. Face the University building and walk left on Gran Vía. Turn right immediately onto C. Aribau. Bar Centrik is 1 block away.* Ⓢ *Beer €4. Cocktails €6-8.* ☼ *Open daily 11pm-3am.*

EL GATO NEGRO & ☝ BAR
Consell de Cent, 268 ☎69 977 36 74 🖳www.espitchupitos.com

All of the shocking variety of Espit Chupitos, now with half-hearted attempts at a spooky theme (look for the black cat in the corner). Luckily, this young and bustling bar is a favorite for lively travelers, and the atmosphere (paired with the cheap, often incredibly amusing, shots) makes up for its lack of ambience. Check out Espit Chupitos just down the street if the pocket-sized bar gets too packed for your refined tastes.

✦ Ⓜ*Universitat. Face the University building and walk left on Gran Vía. Turn right onto Aribau and walk 2 blocks. Take a right onto Consell de Cent and it's 1 block away.* Ⓢ *Shots €1.50-3. Beer €1.60-2. No credit cards after 11pm.* ☼ *Open M-Th 8am-2:30am, F-Sa 8am-3am, Su 8am-2:30am. Kitchen closes at 11pm.*

SNOOKER BAR ✈ & ☝ ❄ BAR
C. Roger de Llúria, 42 ☎93 317 97 60 🖳www.snookerbarbarcelona.com

With award-winning interior decoration in front and an equally impressive pool hall in back, Bar Snooker is like what your smokey-bowling-alley-pool-hall back home would look like after an episode of "Pimp My Snooker." Sit back in one of the red velvet chairs with one of their many scotches and try to figure out why anyone ever decided that pool tables should be neon-lit.

✦ Ⓜ*Passeig de Gràcia. Face Plaça Catalonia and walk left on Gran Vía for 2 blocks. Take a left onto C. Roger de Lluria.* 𝑖 *Singles night W 8pm.* Ⓢ *Mixed drinks €8.* ☼ *Open M-Th 6pm-2:30am, F-Sa 6pm-3am, Su 6pm-2:30am.*

MOMO'S BAR Y COPAS ⊛ & ☝ BAR
C. Consell de Cent, 268 ☎93 487 33 14

A sleek interior lit with old Victorian lanterns and a more upbeat string of rainbow-colored lights around the bar. Candles along the bar warm the place up, while low couches along the back provide ample seating for the young crowd that trickles in later during the night. Don't come here expecting a rager—a calm and sparse clientele keeps it classy.

✦ Ⓜ*Universitat. Face the University building and walk down the road that runs along its lefthand side. After 2 blocks, turn right onto C. Consell de Cent.* Ⓢ *Beer, wine, and shots €3. Mixed drinks €7.* ☼ *Open M-Th 8pm-2:30am, F-Sa 8pm-3am, Su 8pm-2:30am.*

BARCELONETA

▨ ABSENTA ✈ & ☝ BAR
C. Sant Carles, 36

Not for the easily spooked, Absenta is like an episode of *The Twilight Zone* if you were trapped inside the television looking out. Staticky TV sets with flickering faces dot the walls, and a life-sized angel hovers above while you sinfully sip your absinthe (€4-7). A young crowd brings this *modernisme*-inspired beauty up-to-date in an appropriately artsy manner.

✦ Ⓜ*Barceloneta. Walk down Pg. Joan de Borbó toward the beach and take a left onto C. Sant Carles.* Ⓢ *Beer €2.30. Mixed drinks €7. Absinthe €4-7.* ☼ *Open Tu-F 11pm-2am, Sa 11am-3am, Su 6pm-2am.*

barcelona

KE?

⊜&♈ BAR

C. del Baluart, 54   ☎93 224 15 88

Pull up a keg chair—they're comfier than they sound. This small bar attracts a gathering of internationals and provides a literal alterative to the crowded beaches and throbbing bass of the *playa*. Shelves hanging as tables, fruit decals along the bar, and a playful group of faces peering down from overhead may not be weird enough to have you wondering "whaaat?" but they'll at least remind you not to take yourself too seriously.

✚ ⓂBarceloneta. Walk down Pg. Joan de Borbó toward the sea and take a left onto C. Sant Crles. Take a left once you enter the plaza onto C. del Baluart. ⓢ Beer €2.50. Cocktails €6. ⌚ Open M-Th 11:30am-2:30am, F-Sa 11:30am-3am, Su 11:30am-2:30am.

CATWALK

⟟⊗♈❀♧ NIGHTCLUB

C. Ramón Trias Fargas, 2-4   ☎69 264 14 29 █www.clubcatwalk.net

Though you'll only get access to the ritzy elevated walk above if you're a VIP, there's enough glam below to ward off your jealousy, so be sure to leave your T-shirts and sneakers back in your hostel. Beautiful people deck the lounges and dancefloor, while the brave (or possibly drunk) take advantage of the lit dancing boxes to strut their stuff to a mix of pop, electro, and R and B.

✚ ⓂPort Olímpic. ⓘ No T-shirts, torn jeans, or sneakers permitted. Events listing on website. ⓢ Cover €18. Beer €7. Mixed drinks €12. ⌚ Open Th midnight-5am, F-Sa midnight-6am, Su midnight-5am.

OPIUM MAR

⟟&♈♧ NIGHTCLUB, RESTAURANT

Pg. Marítim de la Barceloneta, 34   ☎90 226 74 86 █www.opiummar.com

Slick restaurant by day and an even slicker nightclub by night, this lavish indoor and outdoor party spot still knows how to kick it up a notch despite its facade of decorum. Seafood is served until 1am, after which a mix of electronica and American pop pounds from the stereo and lures dancers off of the fashionable white chairs and onto the dance floor.

✚ ⓂPort Olímpic. ⓘ Events listing on website. DJs every W. ⓢ Cover €20; includes one drink. ⌚ Restaurant open daily 1pm-1am. Club open M-Th midnight-5am, F-Sa 1-6am, Su midnight-5am.

GRAN CASINO

⟟&♈❀ CASINO

C. Marina, 19   ☎93 225 78 78 █www.casino-barcelona.com

The most beautiful casino in Barcelona, nestled within the requisite amount of glitz and glam surrounding Port Olímpic. Slot machines above in the Sala Americana start the night off slowly, while things get more serious (and addictive) below with tables of blackjack, American and French roulette, a theater hosting Vegas-esque shows, and a killer buffet. Admission to the main floor will cost you (€4.50) unless you bring a flyer, but that's nothing compared to the money you'll be lured into gambling away the entire night anyway.

✚ ⓂPort Olimpic. Under the Fish. ⓘ Must be 18 to play. No sneakers or beach clothes allowed; collared shirt recommended for men. Passport required. Live jazz in Sala Principal F-Sa. ⓢ Entrance to Sala Principal €4.50 ⌚ Sala Americana (slot machines and bar) open M-Th 10am-5pm, F-Sa 10am-5:30pm, Su 10am-5pm. Sala Principal (theater, game tables) open daily 3pm-5am.

MONTJUÏC AND POBLE SEC

▨ ROUGE CAFE

⟟❀ BAR

C. Poeta Cabanyes, 21   ☎93 442 49 85

When you walk into a sultry rouge-lit lounge decked in leather chairs and a cavalcade of vintage decor (including a shoddy copy of the Arnolfini wedding portrait), you know you're doing something right. Luckily, a crowd of hip, friendly locals are there to join you. The prettiest, most stereotypically girly drinks in the city are some of the most delicious, so try the melon Absolut Porno (€6) or the vodka-based Barcelona Rouge (€6.50).

🚏 Ⓜ Parallel. With Montjuïc to your left, walk along Av. Parallel. Take a left onto C. Poeta Cabanyes. Rouge Cafe will be on your left before Mambo Tango Youth Hostel. ⏰ Open daily in summer 7pm-3am; in winter 8pm-3am.

👍 TINTA ROJA — 💳♿🍸❄ BAR

C. Creu dels Molers, 17 — ☎93 443 32 43 💻www.tintaroja.net

Named after the 1941 tango "Tinta Roja" by Cátulo Castillo and Sebsatián Piana, this cafe-bar mixes literal Latin flavor with the flair of the theater. Argentine drinks are their specialty, ranging from a little boost of maté *(€4.80)* to a full range of the country's liquors and beers. Scattered seating under questionably erotic Impressionistic paintings populate the front, while a back stage plays host to popular tango classes on Wednesday nights at 9pm. Don't mind the mannequins looking down over your footwork—chances are they're just admiring your work.

🚏 Ⓜ Poble Sec. With Montjuïc to your right, walk along Av. Parallel. Take the second right onto C. de la Creu dels Molers; Tinta Roja will be on the left. ℹ Tango classes W 9-11:30pm. $ Beer €2.30-4. Wine €2.50-3.70. Maté €4.80. Argentinian liquors €5.50-6. Mixed drinks €7. ⏰ Open Th 8:30pm-2am, F-Sa 8:30pm-3am.

242 — 💳 CLUB

C. Entença, 37 — ☎932 28 90 73 💻www.myspace.com/club242

Fearing a hangover after that massive night of partying? One of the longest running after-hours clubs in the city of Barcelona, 242 lets you skip right over those painful waking hours and relive the night you already enjoyed. A crowd trickles in after 6am as the other clubs close to enjoy drinks, electronica, air conditioning, and movies. If you find yourself winding down, they even have food for breakfast.

🚏 Ⓜ Espanya. Walk away from Montjuïc on Gran Vía and take a right onto C. de' Entença. 242 is right before the intersection with Sepúlveda. ℹ Special events listed on Myspace. $ Cover €15; includes 1 drink. Beer €5. Mixed drinks €10. ⏰ Open F-Su 6am-whenever the party stops.

MAU MAU — 💳♿🍸 BAR

C. Fontrodona, 35 — ☎93 441 80 15 💻www.maumaunderground.com

The ground zero of the cultural underground in Barcelona, Mau Mau is best known for its online guide to art, film, and other hip happenings around the city. Expect to see artsy 20-somethings lounging on this warehouse-turned-lounge's classy couches before and after concerts at the nearby Sala Apolo, or maybe for the screening of a Herzog flick *(movies every Th-Sa at 10pm)*.

🚏 Ⓜ Parallel. When facing Montjuïc, walk right along Av. Parallel and take a left onto C. Fontrodona. Follow the street as it zigzags—Mau Mau is just a few blocks down. $ Year-long membership €12. Visitors free. Beer €2-3. Mixed drinks €6-8. ⏰ Open Th-Sa 11pm-2:30am. Open other days of the week for special events.

SALA APOLO — 💳♿🍸❄ CLUB

Nou de la Rambla, 113 — ☎93 441 40 01 💻www.sala-apolo.com

Looking for a party, but lamenting that it's Monday? Sulk no longer—for the last number of years Sala Apolo has been drawing locals to start the week off right with Nasty Mondays, featuring a mix of rock, pop, indie, garage, and '80s *(€11)*. In fact, the night is so popular that it spawned an equally persuasively named Crappy Tuesdays *(indie and electropop; €10-12)*, which take over after the American one-woman Broadway-esque show "Anti-Karaoke." Stop by later in the week to catch a varied crowd, and check the website for the latest bigger name indie concerts rolling through the venue.

🚏 Ⓜ Paral-lel. Walk along Parallel with Montjuïc to your right. Take a hard right onto Nou de la Rambla. Not to be confused with Teatre Apolo, which is on Av. Parallel. $ Anti-karaoke €8. Nasty M €11. Crappy Tu €10-12. W Rumba €6-10. Other tickets €15-23.

GRÀCIA

EL RAÏM
BAR

C. Progrés, 48 www.raimbcn.com

Though a little farther from Gràcia's roaring plazas, this time capsule with an identity crisis is well worth the short trek. A mix between a Catalan bodega and '50s Cuban bar, this traditional winery has been in business since 1886, when it served as the diner for the old factory across the street. Since then, the owner has transformed the place into a shrine to Cuban music and memorabilia, rum, and incredible mojitos. It consistently attracts a flock of down-to-earth locals looking for one (or all) of the three.

[M]Fontana. Walk down C. Gran de Gràcia and make a left on C. Ros de Olano. Walk for about 4 blocks and take a right onto C. Torrent de l'Olla. Take the 4th left onto Siracusa, and El Raïm is on the corner of its intersection with C. del Progrés. $ Beer €2-3. Mixed drinks €5.50. Open daily 8pm-2:30am.

VINIL
BAR

C. Matilde, 2 ☎66 917 79 45 www.vinilus.blogspot.com

Those expecting a fetish club—whether for LPs or something of a kinkier persuasion—may be disappointed. Though this is certainly no shrine to a musical era past (or present), the warm lighting and comfy pillows make the perfect place to kick back and watch their daily screened movie. Feel free to geek out over their giant phonograph or the Velvet Underground song playing over the speakers—chances are the hip clientele will perfectly understand.

[M]Diagonal. $ Beer €3-3.50. Mixed drinks €5. Open in summer M-Th 8pm-2am, F-Sa 8pm-3am; in winter M-Th 8pm-2am, F-Sa 8pm-3am, Su 8pm-2am.

ASTROLABI
BAR

C. Martinez de la Rosa, 14

Pirate decor with bartenders to match. Maps, clocks, and miniature ships all help to explain away your drunk dizziness as "seasickness." Drop in earlier in the night for some entertainment, with a small and dedicated following cozying up in the watering hole to watch acoustic acts croon over lost loves and anachronisms. If you need an ear to listen, shrunken heads dangle over the bar for your disposal.

[M]Diagonal. Walk toward Passeig de Gràcia and take a left onto it. Follow the street as it crosses Av. Diagonal and becomes Passeig de Gràcia. Turn right onto C. de Bonavista before Passeig de Gràcia turns into C. Gran de Gràcia. Left onto C. Martinez de la Rosa. i Live music daily at 10pm. $ Beer €2.60. Wine €1. Mixed drink €6. Open M-Th 8pm-2:30am, F-Sa 8pm-3am, Su 8pm-2:30am.

LA CERVERSERA ARTESANA
BAR, BREWERY

C. Sant Agustí, 14 ☎93 237 95 94 www.lacervesera.net

When you visit the only pub in Barcelona that makes its own beer, you better order their beer no matter what vows you've taken with PBR. With a huge variety of brews—dark, amber, honey, spiced, chocolate, peppermint, fruit-flavored, and more—there's literally something for everyone, along with seasoned bar snacks to encourage your thirst. If beer isn't your thing, at least come to hear the music—you probably won't hear Pink Floyd and Phil Collins played back-to-back anywhere else in the city.

[M]Diagonal. Take a left onto Psg. de Gràcia and a right (exact right, 90 degree angle) onto C. Corsega at the intersection of Psg. de Gràcia and Via Diagonal. C. Sant Agustí is the 3rd street on the left. $ House brews €4.80-5. Open M-Th 6pm-2am, F-Sa 6pm-3am, Su 6pm-2am.

DEDUES COCKTAIL AND BAR
BAR

C. Torrent de l'Olla, 89 ☎93 416 14 96 www.dedues.es

Cheap beer, free bar snacks, daily specials, and incredible €4 cocktails will keep you in your cups and in the money at this snazzy orange floral-clad *cocteleria*, whether you're looking for a day drink or a nightcap. Drop by with a new friend during weekday evenings *(M-Th 9-11pm)* to grab two cocktails with natural fruit juice for €8, though they're so good that you may just want them both for yourself. ⚉ Ⓜ*Fontana. From the metro, walk down C. Asturies until you hit C. Torrent de l'Olla. Walk 5½ blocks down C. Torrent de l'Olla.* Ⓢ *Sandwiches €1.80-4. Food €3-4. Cañas of beer €1 daily 4-7pm. Cocktails €4.* Ⓒ *Open M-Th 4pm-2:30am, F 4pm-3am, Sa 6pm-3am.*

VELCRO BAR ✈♿♀ BAR
C. Vallfogona, 10 ☎61 075 47 42

Though Velcro Bar is a bit farther from Gràcia's popular plazas, its screenings of nightly movies attract a young and hip clientele that ends up paying little attention to the moving pictures. True to its name, this is a bar where bright green and pink velcro waits to hold the bottom of your drink. ⚉ Ⓜ*Fontana. Follow C. Asturies to C. Torrent de l'Olla and make a right. Follow for three blocks, make a left onto C. Vallfogona.* Ⓢ *Mixed drinks €5-8.* Ⓒ *Open daily 7pm-2:30am.*

LA BAIGNOIRE CAFE ✈♿♀❀ BAR, CAFE
C. Verdi, 6 ☎60 633 04 60

More cafe-bodega than bar, the vintage chic interior of this dollhouse-sized establishment attracts a sophisticated younger crowd unafraid of sporting T-shirts. Treat yourself to some fancy wine and a cheese platter before heading back to the life of drinking six-packs of Estrella in the plaza. ⚉ Ⓜ*Fontana. Take a right onto C. Gran de Gràcia toward C. Montseny. Take the 3rd left onto C. Ros de Olano and follow as it changes into C. Terrol. Take a left onto C. Verdi and it'll be on your right.* Ⓢ *Wine from €2.70. Cheeses €3.60-3.90.* Ⓒ *Open M-Th 7pm-1:30am, F-Sa 7pm-2am, Su 6pm-1am.*

FLANN O'BRIEN'S ✈♿♀❀ BAR
C. Casanova, 264 ☎93 201 16 06 🖳www.flannobrienbcn.com

One of Barcelona's thousands of Irish Bars and one of the few in which you'll actually find any Irish, this sprawling den has been a local and English-speaking favorite for almost 20 years. Nightly live music draws a crowd around 9pm, but grab a Guinness, throw on your rugby shirt, and stick around after the show to see if the ex-pats to get surly. ⚉ Ⓜ*Diagonal. Walk for 10min. on Av. Diagonal away from Psg de Gràcia. Take a right onto Casanova before the round Placa de Francesc Macia.* 𝒊 *Live music nightly 9pm.* Ⓢ *Beer €3.50-5. Mixed drinks €6.* Ⓒ *Open daily 5:45pm-3am.*

OTTO ZUTZ ✈⊗♀❀ CLUB
C. Lincoln, 15 ☎93 238 07 22 🖳www.ottozutz.com

Like a tiered layer cake with an impeccably designed party inside (or maybe a portion of Dante's Inferno, depending on the night), three floors of dancing and drinks await. At least four different DJs pound out a huge variety of music to a chic and shiny crowd, with a reprieve from the throbbing masses only available up top. Watch out—during the summer this heaven gets hellishly hot. ⚉ Ⓜ*Fontana. Walk along Rambla de Prat and take a right as it dead-ends into Via Augusta. Take the first right onto C. Laforja and the first right again to reach C. Lincoln.* Ⓢ *Cover €10-15; includes 1 drink. Beer €6. Mixed drinks €6-12.* Ⓒ *Open W-Su midnight-6am.*

KGB ⊛⊗♀ CLUB ❸
C. Alegre de Dalt, 55 ☎93 210 59 06 🖳www.salakgb.net

In Soviet Russia, KGB dances you. No, but really—the only indications of the eastern block are the oppressive KGB posters hanging from the walls like propaganda and the sheer utility of the decorations—expect lots of black, lots of metal, and little glitz or bourgeois sparkle. Scrappy youth join the bartenders and live DJ and VJ in a sweaty countdown to get down. Entrance is free with a flyer; otherwise you'll be paying €12-15 to join this Communist party. ⚉ Ⓜ*Joanic. Walk along C. Pi i Maragall and take the 1st left. To get a cab home, come back to Pi i Maragall.* Ⓢ *Cover €12 with 1 drink, €15 with 2 drinks until 3am. Free with flyer.* Ⓒ *Open Th 1-5am, F-Sa 1-6am.*

MI BAR 🚭♿🍸❄ BAR

C. de les Guilleries, 6

With chill alternative tunes and a graffitied walls lit by crystal chandeliers, it's only fitting that one of Mi Bar's fans has scrawled in Spanish, "it's better that I stay here." A pool table and cheap drinks keep locals coming back to this steadfast hangout.

✣ [M]Fontana. Walk down C. Gran de Gràcia and make a left onto C. Montseny. Continue for 6 blocks, then make a right onto C. de les Guilleries. $ Wine €1. Beer €1.50-2. Mixed drinks €5-7. ⏰ Open M-Th 10pm-2am, F-Sa 10pm-3am.

CAFE DEL SOL 🍴❄🍸 CAFE, BAR

Pl. del Sol, 16 ☎93 237 14 48

One of the many tapas bars lining the Plaza del Sol, the Cafe del Sol offers cheap and delicious eats in an ambience well-suited to the square's unbeatably chill nightlife. Giacommeti-esque figures line the wall along the bar, while a back room provides a cozy shelter for those looking for respite from the square.

✣ [M]Fontana. Walk down C. Gran de Gràcia, make a left on C. Ros de olano and the a right on C. Cano/C. Leopoldo Alas. $ Beer €2.20-2.80. Tapas €3.50-7.50. Entrees €3.50-5.80. ⏰ Open M-Th noon-2:30am, F-Sa noon-3am, Su noon-2:30am.

EL OTRO BAR 🍴♿🍸🍴 BAR, CAFE

Travessera de Gràcia, 167 ☎93 323 67 59

Hopping cafe-restaurant by day and a popular local hangout at night, El Otro Bar has industrial metal walls in back that fade into a cheerier Tetris-like bar up front. Otherworldly dioramas decorate each of the tables, with a neon color palette that might distract you from your conversation.

✣ [M]Fontana. Walk down C. Gran de Gràcia until you reach Trav de Gràcia. Take a left—El Otro Bar is on the corner. $ Wine and beer €2.50-3. Mixed drinks €6.40. Food €2.10-4.50. ⏰ Open M-Th 8:30am-2:30am, F 8:30am-3am, Sa 9:30am-3am, Su 10:30am-1:30am.

MOND BAR 🚭♿🍸 BAR

Pl. del Sol, 21 ☎93 272 09 10

Tattoos, v-necks, and fedoras form the trifecta of hip gear you'll need to fit in here. A well-stocked jukebox lets you pick the hits without bartender intervention, with space to sprawl out on the amphitheater-style stacked benches in back.

✣ [M]Fontana. Take a right onto C. Gran de Gràcia toward C. Montseny. Take the third left onto C. Ros de Olano until you reach Plaza del Sol. $ Beer €2-4. Mixed drinks €5-6. ⏰ Open M-Th 7pm-2:30am, F-Sa 7pm-3am, Su 7pm-2:30am.

NICTALIA 🍴♿🍸❄ BAR

C. St. Domenec, 15 ☎93 237 23 23

A 13-year-old girly-girl's dream—lilac purple walls, white furniture, and colorful chalkboards create a more innocent-feeling place to knock back a few, while some chic modern touches make it feel mature enough for your imbibing not to be debaucherous. Settle in for a few cheap shots *(€2)* with the locals.

✣ [M]Fontana. Walk down C. Gran de Gràcia to C. St. Domenec and make a left. Nictalia is 2 blocks down on the left. $ Shots €2. Beer €2.50. Cocktails €5-7. ⏰ Open M-Th 8:30pm-2am, F-Sa 8pm-3am.

CAFE DEL TEATRE ♿📶🍸❄ CAFE, BAR

C. Torrijos, 41 ☎93 416 06 51

Black cats, white, french doors, stained glass, big green bubble lights, and lots o' locals dot this bustling creep-meets-provincial cafe-bar day and night. Order a mindblowing salad to pad your stomach before downing their signature *Cocktail del Cafe del Teatre* (€6).

✣ [M]Joanic. Take a right onto C. de l'Escorial and a left onto C. de Sant Lluis after a block. Cafe del Teatre is in the plaça after C. del Torrent d'en Vidalet. $ Beer €1.50-3.60. Shots €2.50-4. Sandwiches €5-6. ⏰ Open M-Sa 8am-3am, Su 5pm-3am.

TIBIDABO

▧ MIRABLAU

♥♿⅋⌂ BAR, NIGHTCLUB

P. Dr. Andreu ☎934 18 58 79 ▣www.mirablaubcn.com

With easily the best view in Tibidabo and arguably the best view in Barcelona, Mirablau is a favorite with posh internationals and the younger crowd. It also happens to be near the top of Collserola mountain range's highest peak. Reasonable drinks for the area *(cocktails €7-9.50)* and a view that will leave you feeling like you've ascended to heaven—a heaven that plays the Village People—earns this bar a *Let's Go* thumbpick. A relaxed bar and lounge area upstairs changes into a energy-filled dance floor on the lower level, leaving those with two left feet room to spill out onto the terrace.

⚑ *Take the L7 to* Ⓜ*Avinguda de Tibidabo or the Tramvia Blau to Pl. del Doctor Andreu. From the metro, walk up the mountain on Av. de Tibidabo to Plaça Dr. Andreu. From the tram, it's to your left when facing the city.* ⓲ *Credit card minimum Th-Sa €4.70. Drinks discounted M-Sa before 11pm, Su before 6pm.* Ⓢ *Beer and wine €1.80-6. Cocktails €7-9.50.* ☒ *Open M-Th 11am-4:30am, F-Sa 11am-5:45am.*

MERBEYÉ

♥♿⅋⌂ BAR

Plaça Dr. Andreu ☎934 34 00 35

More like a den than the clifflike Mirablau on the opposite side of the road, Merbeyé provides a classy, red-velvet atmosphere for those looking to embrace the romantic side of the picturesque surroundings. With a lounge whose lights are so low that seeing your companion may be a problem, Merbeyé creates the perfect setting to bring a date or possibly find another at the seemingly neverending bar. Smooth jazz serenades throughout, and with just one Mirabeye *(Cava Brut, cherry brandy, and Cointreau; €9-10)* you'll be guaranteed to find yourself at the requisite level of chill.

⚑ *Take the L7 to* Ⓜ*Avinguda de Tibidabo or the Tramvia Blau to Pl. del Doctor Andreu. From the metro, walk up the mountain on Av. de Tibidabo to Plaça Dr. Andreu. From the tram, it's to your back when facing the city.* Ⓢ *Non-alcoholic drinks €8-9. Cocktails €9-10. Food €2-7.60.* ☒ *Open W 7pm-1am, Th noon-2am, F-Sa noon-4am, Su noon-2am.*

arts and culture

MUSIC AND DANCE

For comprehensive guides of large events and information on cultural activities in the city, contact the **Institut de Cultura de Barcelona (ICUB)** *(Palau de la Virreina, La Rambla, 99* ☎*93 316 10 00* ▣*www.bcn.cat/cultura* ☒ *Open daily 10am-8pm)* or the **Guía del Ocio** *(*▣*www.guiadelociobcn.com)*.

More guide options exist online for those able to glean basic information from Catalan: ▣**www.butxaca.com** is the best of the bunch, with comprehensive bimonthly agenda with film, music, theater, and art listings. The website ▣**www.maumaunderground.com** lists local music news, reviews, and a daily agenda of shows and events, while ▣**www.infoconcerts.cat/ca** provides even more concert listings. For tickets, check out **ServiCaixa** *(*☎*90 233 22 11* ▣*www.servicaixa.com* ☒ *Open M-F 8am-2:30pm)*, available at any branch of the Caixa Catalonia bank, **TelEntrada** *(*☎*90 210 12 12* ▣*www. telentrada.com)*, or **Ticketmaster** *(*▣*www.ticketmaster.es)*.

Although a destination for musicians year-round, Barcelona especially perks up during the warmer months with an influx of touring bands and impressive music festivals. The biggest and arguably baddest of these is the three-day electronic music festival **Sónar** *(*▣*www.sonar.es)* taking place in mid-June, which attracts internationally renowned DJs, electronica fans, and party people from all over the world. The **Grec** summer festival *(*▣*www.bcn.cat/grec)* takes place throughout the summer months, using multiple venues throughout the city to host international music, theater, and dance. The indie-centric **Primavera Sound** *(*▣*www.primaverasound.com)* at the end of May is also quickly becoming a regional must-see. More information on local festivals is available in the *Mondo Sonoro*, which lists happenings across the world.

High Class(ical) and Opera

PALAU DE LA MÚSICA CATALANA
🎫♿❄ L'EIXAMPLE

St. Francesc de Paula, 2 ☎90 244 28 82 💻www.palaumusica.org

Although the Bach- and Verdi-studded stage still hosts primarily classical concerts, this *modernista* structure also hosts a surprising variety of musical acts almost every night. Over 300 performances of choral and orchestral pieces, pop, acoustic, jazz, and flamenco grace its stage every year, including those from its very own **Orfeo Català** (Catalan choir) for which the building was constructed. If you're just looking for an excuse to see the breathtaking Secret Garden-esque interior without a tour (or you really like giant air-driven, tubed instruments), drop by for one of their frequent and cheap organ performances—they need them to keep the organ pipes clean.

⇄ [M]Jaume I. Facing Via Laietana from the Plaça de l'Angel exit, take a left onto the road. Walk for 10min. and take a right onto the plaza-like C. Sant Pere Mas Alt. ℹ Check the Guía del Ocio for listings. $ Concert tickets €8-175. ⏰ Box office open M-Sa 10am-9pm, Su from 2hr. before show time. No concerts in Aug.

L'AUDITORI
🎫♿❄ GRAN VÍA

C. Lepant, 150 ☎93 247 93 00 💻www.auditori.com

Built in 1999 by world-renowned architect Rafael Moneo, this modern auditorium is now home to the Symphonic Orchestra of Barcelona (OBC). Glass, steel, and concrete house a variety of music types, including classical, chamber, world music, contemporary, and more. Check the website to browse the performances by type. A number of festivals are held here throughout the year in addition to their regular programming, including the World Music Festival, International Percussion Festival of Catalonia, Festival of Old Music of Barcelona, and even the electronic Sònar for those tired of actual instruments.

⇄ [M]Monumental. Walk on C. Marina toward Gran Vía. Walk 2 blocks and take a left onto C. d'Ausiàs March, then take the 1st right onto C. Lepant. ℹ Tickets available by phone, through ServiCaixa or TelEntrada, or at box office. $ Tickets €4-40. ⏰ Box office open M-Sa noon-9pm, Su 1hr. before show starts.

GRAN TEATRE DEL LICEU
🎫♿🍸❄ LAS RAMBLAS

La Rambla, 51-59 ☎93 485 99 13 💻www.liceubarcelona.com

A Barcelona institution since its founding in 1847, the Gran Teatre del Liceu is actively reclaiming its role as the premier venue for upscale performances after being closed due to fire in 1994. Classical, opera, and ballet grace the stage of its impressively restored auditorium, while a smaller reception room hosts discussions about the pieces and smaller events. If you're afraid of committing to a ticket, drop in for a tour and hope to catch a sneakpeak of the rehearsal for the night's performance.

⇄ [M]Liceu. Face the plaza and the house with umbrellas on its side and walk to your right down La Rambla. Teatre is about a block away. ℹ Tickets available at box office, online, or through ServiCaixa. ⏰ Box office open M-F 1:30-8pm.

Pop and Rock 'n' Roll

RAZZMATAZZ
🎫🍸❄ LAS RAMBLAS

C. Pamplona, 88 and Almogàvers, 122 ☎93 272 09 10 💻www.salarazzmatazz.com

This massive, converted warehouse hosts big-name popular acts from reggae to electropop and indie to metal. The big room packs the popular draw (bands like Motorhead, Alice in Chains, and Gossip), while the smaller rooms hide up-and-comers like the Vivian Girls. Wherever there isn't a throng of people for the concerts, you'll find a young crowd pulsing to the beat of one of their nightly DJs. The labyrinthine nightclub spans across multiple floors in two buildings, connected by industrial stairwells and a rooftop walkway—definitely not intended for the navigationally deficient.

✦ Ⓜ*Bogatell. Walk down the diagonal street (C. Pere IV) away from the plaza and take the 1st slight left onto C. Pamplona. Razzmatazz is immediately on the right.* *i* *Tickets available online through website, TelEntrada, or Ticketmaster.* Ⓢ *Tickets €12-22.*

SIDECAR
⊕♿♈☀☂ LAS RAMBLAS

Plaça Reial, 7   ☎93 317 76 66 ▣www.sidecarfactoryclub.com

Though bigger indie bands may tour here from time to time, Sidecar's real specialty is local fare. Pop, rock, punk, and alternative acts with an edge grace the smallish stage downstairs in a setting much more intimate than other clubs of the same caliber in town.

✦ Ⓜ*Liceu. Facing the house with the ▨dragon and umbrellas on it, walk down La Rambla to your right and take a left onto C. Ferran. Take the 1st right to enter Plaça Reial. Sidecar is in the corner to your left.* *i* *Tickets often available through Ticketmaster via the club's website, or* ▣*www. atrapalo.com.* Ⓢ *Tickets from €12.*

Folk and all that Jazz

JAMBOREE
⊕⊘♈☀ LAS RAMBLAS

Plaça Reial, 17   ☎93 319 17 89 ▣www.masimas.com

The black-and-white portraits of jazz musicians lining the walls tell of the club's long-standing history. Jamboree has been hosting jazz acts for over 50 years, and manages to mix this rich history with a surprising dose of relevant contemporary artists—expect to hear a Billie Holiday tribute one night and the Markus Strickland Quartet the next. If you're looking for something a little less predictable, their WTF Jam Sessions are popular with local musicians and will only cost you €4 to peep.

✦ Ⓜ*Liceu. Facing the house with the ▨dragon and umbrellas on it, walk down La Rambla to your right and take a left onto C. Ferran. Take the 1st right to enter Plaça Reial. Jamboree is in the far corner to your right.* *i* *Tickets available through TelEntrada.* Ⓢ *Jazz tickets €10-25 (normally €10-15), Su jam session €4, flamenco €6.* ⏰ *Jazz performances Tu-Su 9 and 11pm, check site for exact times as some performances start at 8pm. WTF Jam Sessions M 9pm-1:30am. Upstairs Tarantos holds flamenco shows daily 8:30, 9:30, and 10:30pm.*

HARLEM JAZZ CLUB
⊕♿♈ LAS RAMBLAS

C. Comtessa de Sobradiel, 8   ☎933 10 07 55 ▣www.harlemjazzclub.es

With two live music performances each night and a drink included with admission, Harlem Jazz Club promises to beat those empty-wallet blues. A performance schedule online and on their door lets you choose whether you'll drop in to hear crooning in English over a lost love or a little saucier Latin flavor. With acts ranging from Bossa Nova to gypsy punk, blues to funk, and soul to salsa, the club is a perfect place for any music lover to spend the evening.

✦ Ⓜ*Liceu. Walk toward the water on Las Ramblas. Left onto C. Ferran. Right onto C. Avinyó. Left onto C. Comtessa de Sobradiel.* *i* *Calendar of events for month available online or at door.* Ⓢ *M-Th €5, includes 1 drink. F-Sa €8, includes 1 drink. Su €5. Beer €3.80, mixed drinks €7.80.* ⏰ *Open M-Th 9pm-4am with live music at 11:30pm and midnight; open F-Sa 9pm-5am with live music at 11:30pm and 1am, Su 9pm-4am.*

CENTRE ARTESÁ TRADICIONÀRIUS
♥♿ GRÀCIA

Tr. de Sant Antoni, 6-8   ☎93 218 44 85 ▣www.tradicionarius.com

A mini-convention center of sorts that serves as a one stop shop for traditional Catalan music in a relaxed setting. Whether you're looking to drop in for a Barcelonan singing on a ukelele, or just to track down the next outdoor rumba session or Catalan folk festival, C.A.T. can provide. Each winter they help to organize the Festival Tradicionàrius, which highlights a smorgasbord of Catalan music, dance, and art over the course of January to March.

🚇 ⓂFontana. Take a right onto C. Gran de Gràcia, then turn left onto C. del Montseny. Take a left onto Travessia de Sant Antoni. *i* Events often located in other locations throughout the city, check site for details. Ⓢ Events €6-20. 🕐 Office open M-F 11am-2pm and 5-9pm.

Flamenco

GUASCH TEATRE
🚶‍♂️♿❄ LAS RAMBLAS

C. Aragó, 140 ☎93 323 39 50 or 93 451 34 62 🖥www.guaschteatre.com

If you stop by during the early evening hours, chances are you'll wonder why all the spectators are pint-sized. Half children's theater and half adult shows, the Guasch's stage shows everything from Heidi to the comedic Sex and Jealousy. If the dramatic arts aren't your thing, they frequently showcase *flamenco*—just check the website or call to learn about upcoming events.

🚇 ⓂHospital Clinic. Face the engineering school and walk right down C. Comte d'Urgell for 5min. Cross the diagonal Av. de Roma and take the next left onto C. Aragó. *i* Tickets available through TelEntrada or box office. Ⓢ Adult tickets €18-20. 25% student discount available. 🕐 Children's theater generally shown Th 6pm, F-Sa 12:30pm, Su 5:30pm; adult theater Th 9pm, F-Sa 10pm, Su 7:30pm. Box office opens 2hr. prior to performance.

EL PATIO ANDALUZ
🚶‍♂️🍸🎭 L'EIXAMPLE

C. Aribau, 242 ☎93 209 33 78

Rumba, *flamenco*, *sevillano*—El Patio provides dinner and an authentic and saucy show, no matter what southern flavor you choose. Entrance includes your choice of drink, tapas, or a full *menú* (depending on which option you choose), with the earlier show lasting about an hour and the later show normally approaching 2hr. Sick of sitting by the sidelines? Performers often encourage diners to try their luck at the floor, so be sure to wear your dancing shoes and most eager expression.

🚇 ⓂDiagonal. Take a left onto Av. Diagonal and walk for 10 min., then take a right onto C. Aribau. Patio Andaluz is before the next block. *i* Call 9am-7pm for reservations or buy tickets at 🖥www.flamencotickets.com. Ⓢ Show and 1 drink €30; show and menú €54-67. 🕐 Daily shows at 8pm and 10pm.

THEATER

TEATRE LLIURE
🚶‍♂️♿❄ LA RIBERA

Plaça Margarida Xirgu, 1 ☎93 218 92 51 🖥www.teatrelliure.com

Established in 1976 by the artsy inhabitants of Gràcia, the Teatre Lliure has become known for presenting works in Catalan, including contemporary pieces and classics from around the globe, and many original Catalan pieces birthed from its own theater cooperative. The present location at the foot of Montjuïc has housed the theater since 2001 but still maintains the feel of its bohemian homeland. Most tickets are more than reasonably priced, and many include entrance to a discussion after the show with the crew and theater critics.

🚇 ⓂEspanya. Face Montjuïc and go right on Av. Parallel. Take a right onto C. de Lleida and a left through the gate to enter the plaza. *i* Tickets available by box office or ServiCaixa. Some original productions include talk with the artists and critics afterward; check website for info. Language of performance listed on website. Art exhibitions relating to current shows. Ⓢ Tickets €15-24. 🕐 Art exhibitions on view on days of performances Tu-F 6-8:30pm, Sa-Su 4-6pm.

TEATRE GREC
🎭 LA RIBERA

Passeig de Santa Madrona, 36 ☎93 316 10 00 🖥www.bcn.cat/grec

No, this theater isn't left over from the good ol' days, no matter what its name may imply. This open-air Grecian-style amphitheater instead dates just from 1929, when it was carved out of an old stone quarry for the International Exhibition that gave birth to many of Montjuïc's existing spectacles. These days the theater hosts a range of theater, opera, dance, and music performances during the summer months and is the main venue of the city's annual Festival Grec, which takes place from mid-June to early August. Be sure to bring mosquito repellent—being nestled in the Jardins Amargós comes with a price.

✣ ⓜ*Espanya. Head through the 2 bell towers marking the entrance to Montjuïc and follow the escalators to the top. When facing the palace-like art museum, walk along the street to the left and be sure to stay left as it breaks. Teatre Grec is on this road (Passeig de Santa Madrona) just after the Ethnological Museum.* ⓘ *Tickets available at Tiquet Rambles (Rambla, 99 ☎93 316 11 11) ⓘ Tiquet Rambles open daily 10am-8:30pm), Telentrada, and ServiCaixa. Most theater performances in Catalan or Spanish.*

TEATRE NACIONAL DE CATALONIA
🏄♿ BARCELONETA

Plaça de les Arts, 1 · · · ☎93 306 57 00 ▣www.tnc.es

This modern structure designed by Ricardo Bofill is a confusing steel and glass nod to the Parthenon. Inaugurated on September 11, 1997, the National Day of Catalonia, it has since been posed as the next cultural center of Barcelona, with an adjacent auditorium with a capacity of 36,000 slated to be completed in the near future. The two performance halls of the main building host contemporary Catalan and foreign plays, classics, and traditional Catalan dances and music from time to time, while the second building of the complex houses all of the workshops that make the stage tick. Take advantage of youth, if you have it—tickets for shows start from €12 if you're under 25.

✣ ⓜ*Glories. Face the rocketshaped Torre Agbar and take the 1st road to your right, Av. Meridiana. Teatre Nacional de Catalonia will be on your right.* ⓘ *Tickets available through TelEntrada, ServiCaixa, Tiquet Rambla, and box office.* ⓢ *Tickets €15-32, under 25 from €12.* ⓘ *Box office and info open W-F 3-8pm, Sa 3-9:30pm, Su 3-6pm.*

CINEMA

CINEMA VERDI
🏄♿❀ GRÀCIA

C. Verdi, 32 · · · ☎93 238 78 896 ▣www.cines-verdi.com/barcelona/

This is Barcelona's first theater to run movies in their original language and still the most popular of the few. Together, the cinema and its annex a few streets over make a cinephile's mecca in the city, with 10 screens featuring independent and foreign films. Perfect for any aspiring Ebert, or just a lonely American who's sick of subtitles.

✣ ⓜ*Fontana. Walk down C. d'Asturies for 5min. and take a right onto C. Verdi.* ⓘ *Movie and special events schedule available on website.* ⓢ *Tickets €5-7.50; special events €12-16.*

FESTIVALS

Barcelona loves to party. Although *Let's Go* fully supports this endeavor to its fullest extent, we still need to include some nitty-gritty things like accommodations and, you know, food, so we can't possibly list all of the annual festivals around Barcelona. For a full list of what's going on during your visit, be sure to stop by the **tourist information office** once you arrive in the city. As a teaser, here are a few of the biggest, most student-relevant shindigs:

FESTA DE SANT JORDI
La Rambla

This provides a more intelligent, civil alternative to Valentine's Day. Celebrating both St. George (the city's patron saint) and the deaths of Shakespeare and Cervantes, Barcelona gathers along Las Ramblas in search of flowers and books to gift to lovers.
ⓘ *April 23.*

FESTA MAJOR
Plaza Rius i Taulet

Festa Major is a community festival in Gràcia in which the artsy intellectuals put on performances and fun happenings in preparation for the Assumption of Mary. Expect parades, concerts, floats, arts and crafts, live music, dancing, and parties.
ⓘ *End of Aug.*

LA DIADA

Fossar de les Moreres

This festival is Catalonia's national holiday celebrating the end of the city's siege in 1714 as well as of reclaiming national (whoops, we mean regional) identity after Franco. Celebrations will be had and flags will be waved.

🕜 *Sept 11.*

FESTA DE SANT JOAN

The beachfront

These days light a special fire in every pyromaniac's heart as fireworks, bonfires, and torches light the city and waterfront in celebration of the coming of summer.

🕜 *June 23-24.*

FESTA MERCÈ

Placa de Sant Jaume

This multi-week celebration of Barcelona's patron saint Our Lady of Mercy, it is the city's main annual celebration. More than 600 free performances and 2000 entertainers cloak the city in multiple venues, all of which are free. There is a contest in the Placa de Juame every year in which contestants have to build a human tower and have a small child climb up it.

🕜 *Weeks before and after Sept 24.*

BARCELONA PRIDE

Parade ends in Avinguda Maria Cristina

This week is the Mediterranean's biggest GLBT celebration and takes place throughout Catalonia. Multiple venues throughout the city and surrounding region take active part throughout the festival, culminating with a parade and festival on the final weekend.

🕜 *Last week of June.*

FOOTBALL

Although Barcelona technically has two football teams, **Futbol Club Barcelona (FCB)** and the **Real Club Deportivo Español de Barcelona (RCD),** you can easily pass a stay in the city without ever hearing about the latter. It is impossible to miss the former, however, and for good reason. Besides being a really incredible athletic team, FCB lives up to its motto as "more than a club."

During the years of Francisco Franco, FCB was forced to change its name and crest in order to banish any nationalistic references to Cataluña, and thereafter became a rallying point for oppressed Catalan separatists. Once the original name and crest were reinstated after Franco's fall in 1974, the team retained its symbolic importance and is still seen as a sign of democracy, identity, and pride for the region.

This passion is not entirely altruistic, however—FCB has been one of the best teams in the world in recent years. In 2009 they were the first team to win six out of six major competitions in a single year. Their world-class training facilities (thanks in part to the 1992 Olympics) supply many World Cuppers each year, leaving many Barcelonans annoyed that they are not permitted to compete as their own nation, similar to Ireland or Wales in the United Kingdom. Much to the chagrin of some hardheaded FCB fans, Spain won the World Cup in 2010.

Because FCB fervor is so pervasive, you will not need to head to Camp Nou to join in the festivities—almost every bar off the tourist track boasts a screen dedicated to their games. Sit down, kick back with a brew, and just don't root for the competition.

arts and culture . football

essentials

PRACTICALITIES

barcelona

- **TOURIST OFFICES: Plaça de Catalonia** is the main office along with Pl. de Sant Jaume. *(Pl. de Catalonia, 17S ☎93 285 38 34* 🖳*www.barcelonaturisme.com* ⚓ Ⓜ*Catalonia, underground across from El Corte Inglès. Look for the pillars with the letter i on top.* *i* *Free maps; brochures on sights, transportation, tours, and about everything else you could want to find; booking service for last-minute accommodations; gift shop; money exchange; and box office (Caixa de Catalonia).* ⏰ *Open daily 9am-9pm.)* **Plaça de Sant Jaume** *(C. Ciutat, 2 ☎93 270 24 29* ⚓ Ⓜ*Jaume I, located in the Ajuntament building in Plaça Sant Jaume.* ⏰ *Open M-F 9am-8pm, Sa 10am-8pm, Su and holidays 10am-2pm. Closed Jan 1 and Dec 25).* **Oficina de Turisme de Barcelona** *(Palau Robert, Pg. de Gràcia, 107 ☎93 238 80 91, ☎012 in Catalonia* 🖳*www.gencat.es/probert* ⚓ Ⓜ*Diagonal.* ⏰ *Open M-Sa 10am-7pm, Su 10am-2pm. Closed Dec 25 and 26, and Jan 1 and 6).* **Institut de Cultura de Barcelona (ICUB)** (Palau de la Virreina, La Rambla, 99 ☎93 316 10 00 🖳www.bcn.cat/cultura ⚓ Ⓜ Liceu. ⏰ Info office open daily 10am-8pm). **Estació Barcelona-Sants** *(Pl. Països Catalans☎90 224 02 02* ⚓ Ⓜ*Sants-Estació* *i* *Info and last-minute accommodation booking.* ⏰ *Open June 24-Sept 24 daily 8am-8pm; Sept 24-June 23 M-F 8am-8pm, Sa-Su 8am-2pm).*

- **TOURS: Self-guided tours** of Gothic, Romanesque, *modernista*, and contemporary Barcelona available; pick up pamphlets in tourism offices. A wide variety of **paid walking tours** also exist, with information available in the brochures at the tourism office. The **Pl. de Catalonia tourist office** hosts its own walking tours and has information about bike tours. *(☎93 285 38 32.* Ⓢ *€12, ages 4-12 €5.* ⚓ Ⓜ*Catalonia, underground across from El Corte Inglès. Look for the pillars with the letter i on top.* *i* *2hr. walking tour of the Barri Gòtic.* ⏰ *Tours daily at 10am (English) and Sa at noon (Catalan and Spanish).)* **Picasso tours** *(☎93 285 38 32)* of Barcelona. ⚓ Ⓜ Catalonia *i* Check for English, Spanish, and Catalan tour availability. Tour includes entrance to **Museu Picasso.** *(*Ⓢ *€19, ages 4-12 €7* ⏰ *Tu, Th, Sa 4pm (English) and Sa at 4pm (Spanish or Catalan with pre-booking).)*

- **LUGGAGE STORAGE: Estació Barcelona-Sants** *(*⚓ Ⓜ*Sants-Estació.* Ⓢ *Lockers €3-4.50 per day.* ⏰ *Open daily 5:30am-11pm).* **Estació Nord** *(*⚓ Ⓜ*Arc de Trimof.* Ⓢ *Lockers €3.50-5 per day, 90-day limit).* **El Prat Airport** *(*Ⓢ *€3.80-4.90 per day).*

- **GAY AND LESBIAN RESOURCES: GLBT tourist guide** includes a section on GLBT bars, clubs, publications, and more *(Pl. de Catalonia tourist office).* **GAYBARCELONA** *(*🖳*www.gaybarcelona.net)* and **Infogal** *(*🖳*www.colectiugai.org)* have up-to-date information. **Barcelona Pride** has annual activities during the last week of June *(*🖳*www. pridebarcelona.org/en).* **Antinous** specializes in gay and lesbian books and films *(C. Josep Anselm Clavé, 6 ☎93 301 90 70* 🖳*www.antinouslibros.com* ⚓ Ⓜ*Drassanes* ⏰ *Open M-F 10:30am-2pm and 5-8:30pm, Sa noon-2pm and 5-8:30pm).*

- **INTERNET ACCESS: Barcelona City Government** offers free Wi-Fi access at over 500 places including some museums, parks, and sports centers. *(*🖳*www.bcn.es.)* **Easy Internet Cafe** *(La Rambla, 31 ☎93 301 75 07* ⚓ Ⓜ*Liceu.* Ⓢ *Decent prices and around 300 terminals. €2.10 per hr., min. €2. 1-day unlimited pass €7; 1wk. €15; 1 mo. €30.* ⏰ *Open daily 8am-2:30am).*

- **POST OFFICE:** *(Pl. d'Antoni López ☎90 219 71 97* 🖳*www.correos.es* ⚓ Ⓜ*Jaume I or* Ⓜ*Barceloneta.* Ⓢ *Open M-F 8:30am-9:30pm, Su noon-10pm.)*

- **POSTAL CODE:** ☎08001.

EMERGENCY!

- **EMERGENCY NUMBERS:** ☎061.
- **POLICE: Local police:** ☎092. **National police:** ☎091. **Tourist police** *(La Rambla, 43 ☎93 256 24 30 ✈ ⓂLiceu. 🕐 Open 24hr).*
- **LATE-NIGHT PHARMACY:** Rotates. Check any pharmacy window for the nearest on duty, contact the police, or call **Información de Farmacias de Guardia** *(☎93 481 00 60).*
- **HOSPITALS/MEDICAL SERVICES: Hospital Clínic i Provincal** *(C. Villarroel, 170* ☎93 227 54 00 ✈ ⓂHospital Clínic. Main entrance at C. Roselló and C. Casanova). **Hospital de la Santa Creu i Sant Pau** *(☎93 291 90 00; emergency ☎91 91 91 ✈ ⓂVall d'Hebron).* **Hospital del Mar** *(Pg. Marítim, 25-29 ☎93 248 30 00 ✈ ⓂCiutadella or ⓂVila Olímpica).*

GETTING THERE

By Plane

AEROPORT DEL PRAT DE LLOBREGAT BCN

☎93 478 47 04 for Terminal 1, ☎93 478 05 65 for Terminal 2B
To get to Pl. Catalonia, take the **Aerobus** *(☎92 415 60 20)* in front of terminals 1 or 2 *(Ⓢ €5, round-trip ticket valid for 9 days €8.65. 🕐 35-40min.; every 6-15min. to Pl. Catalonia daily 6am-1am, to airport 5:30am-12:14am).* To the airport, the A1 bus takes you to Terminal 1, A2 bus to Terminal 2. For early morning flights, the Nitbus **N17** runs from Pl. Catalonia to all terminals *(Ⓢ €1.40. 🕐 from Pl. Catalonia every 20min. daily 11am-5am, from airport every hr. 9:50pm-4:50am).* Cheaper, and usually a bit faster, than the Aerobus is the **RENFE train** *(☎90 224 34 02 Ⓢ €1.40 or free with T10 transfer from metro. 🕐 20-25min. to Estació Sants, 25-30min. to Pg. de Gràcia; every 30min., from airport 6am-11:38pm, from Estació Sants to airport 5:35am-11:09pm).* To reach the train from Terminal 2, take the pedestrian overpass in front of the airport (it's on the left when your back is to the entrance). For those arriving at Terminal 1, a shuttlebus is available outside the terminal to take you to the train station.
✈ ⓂSants-Estació. *i Info and last-minute accommodation bookings, as well as transport connections from the airport to the city center and other locations. 🕐 Open daily 9am-9pm.*

AEROPORT DE GIRONA GRO

☎90 240 4704 ▇www.girona-airport.net
Transport to Barcelona is available from the airport by **Barcelona Bus** *(Ⓢ €12, round-trip €21. 🕐 1hr. 10min. from Girona to Estacio d'Autobusos Barcelona Nord i Buses from the airport to Estacio d'Autobusos Barcelona Nord are timed to match flight arrivals. Buses from Estacio d'Autobuses arrive at Girona Airport approximately 3hr. before flight departures. 🕐 Open 24hr.)*

By Train

Depending on the destination, trains can be an economical option. Travelers may find trains at **Estació Barcelona-Sants** in Pl. Països Catalans (ⓂSants Estació) for most domestic and international traffic, while **Estació de Franca** on Av. Marques de l'Argentera (ⓂBarceloneta) serves regional destinations and a limited number of international locations. Note that trains often stop before the main stations; check the schedule. **RENFE** *(reservations and info ☎90 224 02 02, international ☎24 34 02 ▇www.renfe.es)* runs to **Bilbao, Madrid, Sevilla,** and **Valencia** in Spain. Trains also travel to **Milan** (via **Turin** and **Figueres**) in Italy and **Montpellier** in France, with connections to Geneva, Paris, and the French Riviera. There's a 20% discount on round-trip tickets. Call or check website for train times and seasonal schedules.

By Bus

Buses are often considerably cheaper than the train and should be considered for those traveling within the region on a budget. The city's main bus terminal is **Barcelona Nord Estació d'Autobuses** *(☎902 26 06 06 🖳www.barcelonanord.com ⇟ [M]Arc de Triomf or #54 bus)*, with buses also departing from the Estació Sants and the airport. **Sarfa** *(ticket office at Ronda Sant Pere, 21 ☎90 230 20 25 🖳www.sarfa.es)* is the primary line, but **Eurolines** *(☎93 265 07 88 🖳www.eurolines.es)* also goes to **Paris** via **Lyon** and offers a 10% discount to travelers under 26 or over 60. **ALSA/ENATCAR** *(☎90 242 22 42; 🖳www.alsa.es)* goes to **Alicante, Bilbao, Madrid, Sevilla, Valencia,** and **Zaragoza.**

By Ferry

Ferries to the **Baleares Islands, Majorca,** and **Ibiza** leave daily from the port of Barcelona at **Terminal Drassanes** *(☎93 324 89 80)* and **Terminal Ferry de Barcelona** *(☎93 295 91 82 ⇟ [M]Drassanes)*. The most popular ferries are run by **Transmediterránea** *(☎902 45 46 45 🖳www.transmediterrana.es)* in Terminal Drassanes.

GETTING AROUND

By Metro

The mode of transportation used most in the city is the Barcelona **Metro** *(☎93 318 70 74 🖳www.tmb.cat)*. Get to know it well—the extensive train and bus system provides cheap, easy access to nearly the entire city. Different lines are identified by L and then their number *(L1, L2, L3, L4, L5, L8, L10, L11)*. **Trains** run Monday through Thursday and Sundays from 5am to midnight, Friday and days prior to holidays 5am to 2am, and Saturday all day. Stops are marked by a red sign with a white capital M.

By Bus

For more remote or hard-to-access places, the bus may be an important complement to the metro during your journey. Barcelona's tourist office also offers a **Tourist Bus** *(🖳bcnshop.barcelonaturisme.com $ 1 day €22)* that frequents sights of particular interest in the city and allows riders to hop on and off for a 24hr. period. Depending on how much you plan to use the route (and how much you loathe hopping off of a red double decker labeled "Tourist Bus" when you're traveling), the bus may be a worthwhile investment upon arriving in the city.

Rentals

Motocicletas (motos for short—scooters, and less frequently motorcycles) are a common sight, and **bicycles** are also becoming more popular. Many institutions rent motos by hour, day, and month, but you need a valid driver's license recognized in Spain in order to rent one for personal use. Many places also offer bike rental. If you will be staying in the city for an extended period, it is possible to buy a bike secondhand or register for **Bicing** (*☎902 31 55 31 🖳www.bicing.cat)*, the municipal red and white bikes.

By Taxi

When all other cheaper and more exciting options fail, Barcelona offers a taxi service to get you back home safely on those nights when revelry lasts after metro hours. The official taxi service is **Radio Taxi** *(☎93 225 00 00)* and is identifiable by the black and yellow cars.

SITGES

There is a reason why this tiny town (pop. 27,000) has a population like an elastic waistband. Situated just 50km south of Barcelona, the town's sandy beaches serve as a refuge for those fleeing the city to seek crystalline water, 300 days of sun, and rocky alcoves. However, the city is much more than a sandy second. Its gorgeous architecture tells the story of a time of farming and fishing long past, while the lush interiors of its museums hint at its rise to prominence in the late 19th century as a center of the *modernisme* art movement. This bohemian flavor still remains in spirit with its thriving arts community, and its role as a premier gay destination in the Mediterranean.

greatest hits

- **CARNE-VALE.** Before Lent kicks in and all good Catholics have to give up meat on Fridays, pig out and thrown down at Sitges's crazy Carnivale (p. 297).
- **A PROFUSION OF PLAYAS.** There are fifteen beaches in Sitges. *Fifteen* (p. 295).
- **MOVE OVER, BARCELONA.** Yeah, yeah, the capital of Catalonia's covered in Gaudí's works, but Sitges has just as much modernisme to offer (p. 295).

orientation

Most people arrive at Sitges by train or bus, and both methods of transportation let off at different spots along **C. Carbonell/Passeig de Vilanova**—buses to the east, at the intersection of Psg. de Vilanova and Psg. de Vilafranca, and trains at the train station to the east on C. Carbonell. Going left along C. Carbonell from the bus stop or right from the train station, turn onto **C. Sant Francesc** and walk for 5min. to find the heart of the old town, intersected by **C. de les Parellades.** Any street off **Parellades** will land you at the waterfront after a 5min. walk, with **Passeig de la Ribera** wrapping around the closest (and most popular) beaches.

accommodations

HOSTAL PARELLADES
HOSTAL ③

C. Parellades, 11 ☎93 894 08 01

Ceilings that reach to the sky house bed-and-breakfast-worthy rooms just big enough to get around in comfortably. Singles are the cheapest in the area, and the sunny terrace with a shaded arcade provides a nice place to curl up with a book after a day spent a block away on the beach. For those musically inclined, a piano awaits your fingertips in the sunny common room.

On C. Parelledes between C. San Pedro and San Pablo. i Sheets included. $ Singles €30; doubles €60; triples €75.

HOSTAL BONAIRE
HOSTAL ③

C. Bonaire, 31 ☎93 894 53 26 www.bonairehostalsitges.com

With the beach in full view at the end of the street, chances are that you won't want to spend too much time lounging in front of the TV. If you do, though, or if you prefer A/C, or even a terrace, just ask—the hostal contains a mix-and-match assortment of amenities fitting the laid-back, house-like feel.

From C. Parellades, walk toward the beach on C. Bonaire. i Complimentary Wi-Fi. $ Singles €30-42; doubles €45-70; triples €65-90.

HOSTAL ESPALTER
HOSTAL ③

C. Espalter, 11 ☎93 894 28 63 www.pensionespatler.com

Nestled inside the Sauna Sitges behind a door framed by rainbows, this pension offers cheap rooms near the heart of Sitges' (specifically gay) nightlife. Those rooms that don't have balconies have a fullblown patio-size terrace, a fact that'll distract you from the questionable taste in bright pink and blue wall coloring. Have any questions? The super friendly owners and staff will be more than happy to enthusiastically help you with whatever you may need.

Take a right onto Carbonell from the train station and a right onto C. San Francesc at the round-about. Take a left onto C. Espalter. Hostal Espalter is in the Sauna Sitges. i Free Wi-Fi. Each room has fridge and ensuite bathroom. $ Singles €35; doubles €60.

HOTEL CID
HOTEL ④

C. Sant José, 39 ☎93 894 18 42 www.hotelsitges.com

A cheap hotel with an ambience appropriate to its name—good-sized rooms are furnished with pieces that scream of the Inquisition, with large impressionistic paintings to keep you from feeling oppressed. It's not often you'll be offered a view over a pool for the price, much less be able to use the pool it overlooks. Wi-Fi is only available in the lower level, but luckily it's decked with enough leather couches, stone pillars, iron fixtures, and even a piano, making it worth some of your time.

Take a right onto C. Carbonell from the train station, pass the rotunda, and take the 4th left off C. Carbonell. $ Singles €54-60; doubles €68-79; triples €99-115. Rooms with pool view more expensive. ⏰ Open May-Oct.

CAU FERRAT MUSEUM, MARICEL MUSEUM, ROMANTIC MUSEUM ART

C. Fonollar; C. Sant Gaudenci, 1 ☎93 894 03 64 www.diba.es/museus/sitges.asp

Although Sitges' museums may not all be housed under one roof, the city couldn't have made visiting them any easier: all have the same hours and ticket prices, and the combination tickets providing entrance to all three museums are a deal. Overlooking the waterfront by the church, on C. Fonollar, the **Cau Ferrat Museum** is the former home of *modernista* big shot Santiago Rusiñol (1861-1931) and provides a snapshot into the area's artistic, star-studded past with works from Picasso, Zuloaga, Casas, and more.

Next door sits the **Maricel Museum,** a palace built in 1910 for the American millionaire Charles Deering. True to the American way, the interior is nothing short of sumptuous, with incredible halls and rooftop terraces. Art from medieval to modern decks the walls, providing a chronology of Catalan art and influences from the romantic period onward for those willing to make the mental leap. These museums are currently undergoing renovations, so you should call ahead or sneak a peak at the website to check opening information.

The **Romantic Museum** is located a bit further inland at C. Sant Gaudenci, 1, off C. de les Parellades, and provides a literal snapshot of the town's past where the other museums only hint around it. This perfectly preserved 19th-century house is filled with ceramics, music boxes, and fantastic furniture, and the special collections boast over 400 antique dolls from around the world and over 25 intricate, though somewhat creepy, dioramas of life at the time in Sitges.

i Cau Ferrat Museum and Maricel Museum currently undergoing renovations. $ Single tickets €3.50, students and seniors €1.75; combined ticket for all museums €6.40/3.50. ⏰ Open July-Sept Tu-Sa 9:30am-2pm and 4-7pm, Su 10am-3pm; Oct-June Tu-Sa 9:30am-2pm and 3:30-6:30pm, Su 10am-3pm. Hourly guided tours in Museu Romàntic.

BEACHES

Fifteen different beaches and over 3km of coast along the city center make Sitges a clear alternative to Barcelona's nearby crowded shores. That being said, don't expect to find your own spot near the beaches close to downtown during the summer months. To flee the crowds, try **Platja de la Barra** and **Platja de Terramar** a few kilometers away or take the L2 bus from the train station to the stop next to Hotel Terramar, and walk for a few minutes back towards the city center *($ €1. ⏰ Every 30min. 9am-9pm).*

What with Sitges being a top gay resort, it only makes sense that there are some beaches catering to the crowd—**Platja de la Bassa Rodona** is the most popular and just a short walk from downtown, located in front of Hotel Calipolis, though in the past years its tight bronzed bodies and little Speedos have been infiltrated by a more mixed crowd. A rocky outcropping makes for a shallow bathing area secluded from the waves. For some clear water ideal for snorkeling and just gawking, head to **Platja de las Balmins.** To get there, take a left and pass the church and **Platja Sant Sebastia.** Go around the first restaurant you come to, and then take the dirt walkway between the coast and walls of the cemetery—the beach is the quiet cove before the port right after the little hill.

If tan lines aren't your thing, try one of Sitges' many renowned nude beaches—the farther out they are, the less likely getting your picture snapped will be. A 50min. walk to the right along the seafront past Terramar, rocks, and a golf course (or, conversely, taking a cab to Club Atlàntida and walking 10min.) will get you near **Platja de l'Home Mort,** though the small cove itself is located just behind the hills where the train tracks run along the coast. This cove also houses Sitges' only exclusively gay beach, with a neighboring forest known for its debauchery. Literally on the other side of the track (and the city) is **Caia Morisca**—to get there, just walk past the church and **Platja d'Aiguadolç.**

food

👍 IZARRA — 💳♿🍸 BASQUE TAPAS [2]

C. Major, 24 ☎93 894 73 70

Izarra offers some of the best Basque food this side of Catalonia with surprisingly reasonable prices, especially for the area. Miniature stools line the walls and bar, but don't expect to get a seat unless you show up early. Order from their daily *menú* or snag a white plate from the back and pile on the tapas yourself.

➜ Walk down C. Major from C. Parralledes. Izarra will be on your left. [$] Tapas €3-11. ⏰ Open daily 8:30am-midnight. Menú available 1:30-4pm and 8:30-11pm.

👍 CAFE DEL MON — 💳♿🍸❄⛅ CAFE [1]

C. Francesc Gumá, 7 ☎93 811 11 04

An all-day cafe harboring two rarities near the Sitges center—local youth and cheap prices. Sunny yellow walls and rainbow mosaiced cafe tables capture a glowing crowd of sunbathed shoulders serenaded by beats from around the world. A menu of cheap *bocadillos*, pizza, and filing *platos* even caters to vegetarians—try the *bocadillo completo* with lettuce, tomato, carrot, asparagus, and cheese *(€4)*. Spice up your meal with one of its cocktails *(€4.50)*.

➜ Walk along Parellades away from Plaça Espanya and veer left to stay on C. Jesús. Turn left onto C. Francesc Gumá; the cafe is on the left before the next street. [$] Salads €4.50. Platos €5.80-7.50. Tapas and bocadillos €1-7. Cocktails €4.50. ⏰ Open daily 9am-10pm.

ALFRESCO CAFE — 💳♿ MEDITERRANEAN [3]

C. Major, 33 ☎93 894 73 70

Pull up a white modern bowl stool under the stained glass and geometric tile and whip out one of their *Sotheby's* or *Barcelona Style* magazines for some light reading. This bright, stylish cafe mixes Mediterranean sun with modern chic, both in ambience and in cuisine. Chalkboard menus change regularly and consistently offer fresh, exciting options. Although entrees start at €16 and salads at €15, you'll certainly get your money's worth.

➜ Walk down C. Major from C. Parralledes. Alfresco Cafe will be on your right. [$] Appetizers €15; entrees €16. Midday menú €17.50; night menú €22. ⏰ Open daily 9am-11pm.

nightlife

👍 TRAILER — 💳♿🍸❄▼ CLUB

C. Àngel Vidal, 36 ☎69 355 94 40 💻www.trailerdisco.com

Shed those heavy clothes, shoes, and inhibitions for Trailer's incredibly popular Wednesday foam parties, and don't be surprised if you see fellow revelers (or pairs of revelers) with nothing to hide. One of the oldest gay danceclubs in Spain, Trailer boasts 30 years in the game and will easily have you understanding why. Though a sausagefest most nights, this club becomes nothing but men on Thursdays—during "After Dark" the colored lights are flipped off and anything goes.

➜ Take a left onto C. de l'Hort Gran from the train station and take a right onto C. de Sant Sebastién right before the elbow. Take the 3rd right onto C. San Damian and the 90° right at the 1st intersection onto C. de Angel Vidal. ℹ Foam parties on W, After Dark on Th. [$] Cover €15; includes 1 drink. Use a flyer for free admission. ⏰ Open May-Sept daily 1-6am; Oct-Apr Sa 1-6am.

ATLÁNTIDA — 💳⛅ CLUB

Platja les Coves ☎93 453 05 82 💻www.clubatlantida.com

This expansive beach-bar and nightclub has it all—beautiful sand, chic lighting, and a crowd not afraid to take it off. Sweaty bodies slide past each other to electronic hits during the summer months, spilling into the open air in a half-hearted attempt to cool down. Regular themed nights abound—check the events schedule to see which way the night swings.

➜ Free bus runs from Calipolis hotel in Sitges center. ℹ Listing of events on website. VIP list available on facebook page. [$] Cover €15-20. ⏰ Open June-Sept M-Th midnight-5am, F-Sa midnight-6am.

arts and culture

In the 19th century, Sitges was a hangout of *modernisme* artists ranging from Rusiñol to Picasso; however, you won't need to visit the Cau Ferrat Museum to be reminded of their influence. Morell's **Modernista Clocktower** *(corner of C. d les Parellades and C. Sant Francesç)* looms over a city that has embraced a vibrant cultural community in its own right, with the **Sitges Music Festival** *(July and Aug)* and **Sitges Film Festival** *(Oct)* attracting thousands to its sandy shores every year. Almost nearly as long as the city has been known for its arts, it has also been known as a gay mecca. The **Sitges Gay Pride** *(mid-July)* attracted over 60,000 people from across the world in its first year in 2010, packing the beaches and over 20 gay bars in the city. True to its (arguably) Spanish roots, **Corpus Christi** clothes the streets with flower blankets, while the **Festa Major** *(week of Aug 23)* unites the city under flames and fireworks to celebrate Sant Bartolomé, the city's patron saint. The city's **Carnivale** *(1st week of Lent)* celebrations are some of the most famed in the region. True to Mediterranean fashion, Sitges is also proud of their booze—Sept. brings the **Festa de la Verema,** or grape harvest, where competitors fight to squash grapes along the beach. Despite its small size, Sitges knows how to party hardy, and the rest of the world knows it should follow.

Film Festival

Since 1968, sci-fi geeks, scary movie buffs, and really, really famous people have flocked to the sandy shores of Sitges in early October to catch the world's foremost film festival specializing in fantasy and horror. This 10-day extravaganza has seen the special screening of movies from *Final Fantasy VII (2005)* to ▶*Hellraiser (1987), The Bourne Identity (2002)* to *Aliens (1986),* and *Kill Bill (2003)* to *Mulholland Drive (2001),* the best of which each year receive the **Midnight X-Treme Award.** Besides being a fantastic place to catch a flick, the festival also attracts a star-studded crowd of directors, actors, and producers ready to receive their awards, known as **Marias,** for the best of their categories, as determined by international jury. Like a doomsday scene from one of the movies being screened, the city becomes swarmed with a sea of the living undead during the festival's annual **Zombie Walk.**

Carnivale

By now, it should come as no surprise that Catalonians know how to party. So, what can you expect when the somber legacy of Lent threatens to take away revelry for 40 days? One giant, ridiculous party. Boasting one of the biggest and baddest Carnivales in all of Europe, the small town of Sitges fills with over 250,000 visitors for the week's festivities, held the seven days preceding Lent during February. The week kicks off with *Dijous Gras* (Fatty Thursday), with the King of the Carnival marking the start of the party. Other highlights of the week include Sunday's **Rua de la Disbauxa** (Debauchery Parade), which includes over 40 floats and 2500 participants. Masked and masqueraded festivities continue throughout the week, with Tuesday's **Rua de l'Extermini** (Extermination Parade) solemnly marking the end of the party week with drag queens dressed in mournful black to grieve of the death of the King of the Carnival. After nearly a full week of revelry, Carnivale is symbolically put to rest with Wednesdays' **Burial of the Sardine,** where a large effigy of the little fish is buried along the beach to mark the end of debauchery and the start of more somber ways. Get your hotel reservations early if you prefer not to sleep on the beach—not surprisingly, this is the local hotel industry's busiest time of year.

essentials

PRACTICALITIES

- **TOURIST OFFICES:** Contact the **Sitges tourist office** for free maps, the monthly agenda of events **Sitges Agenda,** and help booking accommodations. *(Pl. Eduard Maristany, 2* ☎93 810 93 40 ▣*www.sitgestur.com* ⚓ *From station, turn right onto the street*

essentials · practicalities

running in front of the station, C. Carbonell, and take the next right at the roundabout, onto Pg. de Vilafranca. The office is 1 block up on the left. **i** *Additional branches at the train station and near the beach, below the church.* ⏰ *Open mid-June to mid-Sept M-Sa 9am-8pm; late Sept-early June M-F 9am-2pm and 4-6:30pm.)*

- **LAUNDRY: Net i Sec** provides the opportunity for you to wash that 2-week-old T-shirt, if you wish. No pressure. *(C. Artur Carbonell, 8 ☎93 894 98 11* ⇄ *Take a right onto Carbonell from the train station. Net i Sec will be on your left.* ⏰ *Open daily 7am-midnight.)*
- **INTERNET: Cafe Cappuchino** provides internet access and phone services. *(C. Sant Francesc, 44* ⇄ *Turn right onto Carbonell from the train station and take the 3rd left onto C. San Francesc.* $ *€1 per 15min.* ⏰ *Open daily 9am-11pm.)*
- **POST OFFICE:** *(Pl. d'Espanya ☎93 894 12 47 💻www.correos.es* ⇄ *Take a right onto Carbonell upon exiting the train station. Continue through the roundabout as it turns to Psg. de Vilanova and take a left onto C. d'Europa. Follow as it takes a slight right and take a slight right onto Espatler to enter the plaza.* ⏰ *Open M-F 8:30am-2:30pm, Sa 9:30am-1pm. No package pickup Sa.)*
- **POSTAL CODE:** 08870

EMERGENCY!

- **EMERGENCY NUMBER:** ☎112.
- **POLICE: Local police** love 'em or hate 'em, they're there for you when you need 'em. *(Pl. Ajuntament ☎93 811 00 16;93 810 97 97.)*
- **HOSPITAL/MEDICAL SERVICES: Hospital Sant Camil** provides medical assistance so your friends don't have to *(Ronda De Sant Camil ☎93 896 00 25 💻www.hrsant-camil.es).*

GETTING THERE

By Train

Cercanías RENFE trains *(☎90 224 02 02 💻www.renfe.es/cercanias)* run from **Estació Barcelona-Sants** to **Sitges** *(*$ *€3* **i** *Line 2 toward St. Vicenç de Calders or Vilanova. Use machines to left of ticket queue to shorten your wait. Ticket booth open until 10pm* ⏰ *45 min., every 25-40min. 7:05am-10:21pm).* From Sitges to **Barcelona** *(*$ *€3* ⏰ *Every 25-40min., 6:15am-10:54pm).* Trains also run from **Sitges** to **Cambrils** *(*$ *€5.70* ⏰ *1hr. via* **Tarragona***).*

By Bus

Mon Bus *(☎93 893 70 60 💻www.monbus.cat)* connects the Barcelona **airport** to Pg. de Villafranca in Sitges. *(*$ *€3* ⏰ *Every hr. M-F 7:40am-11:40pm.)* Late-night buses operate from Pg. de Villafranca to Ronda Universitat in Barcelona and back *(*$ *€3* ⏰ *Every hr. 12:13-3:13am).*

By Taxi

Taxis *(☎93 894 13 29)* run between **Barcelona** and **Sitges** *(*$ *€50-60).*

GETTING AROUND

Sitges is first and foremost a walking city with the main sites being just a 5-10min. walk from each other. If you're adventurous and looking to head to **Atlántida** for some partying, a **free bus** runs from the center of Sitges to the Platja de les Coves, right in front of the club.

If you're looking to venture outside the center, **Bus Urbà** operates within the city. All three lines start their route at the train station and travel outward, with the **L1** covering the north, **L2** covering the west (both ending at Passeig Vilafranca), and **L3** covering the east, ending at C. Emili Picó. *(☎93 814 49 89* $ *1 ride €1.40, 10-ride pass €7.85* ⏰ *Every 30min. M-F 6:45am-8:45pm, Sa-Su and holidays 8:45am-8:45pm.)*

Taxis provide a safe ride home for tired feet and drunken bodies. *(☎93 894 35 94, ☎93 894 13 29 or ☎088.)*

PAÍS VASCO
Euskadi

Celebrated Basque artist Eduardo Chillida once said, *"Euskal Herrian nire tokian sentitzen naiz, bere lurrari moldatutako zuhaitza bezala, baina besoak mundura zabalik."* If you spoke Basque, or *euskara*, you would know that his words roughly translate to English as "In the Basque homeland, I feel I am in my proper place, like a tree that is right for its spot, but with its arms open, toward the world." The Basques, whose ancestors were supposedly one of the first groups in Europe, are certainly rooted to their homeland, where they have maintained their language and traditions despite opposition from Romans, Moors, and fascists.

The Autonomous Community of País Vasco technically consists of the provinces of Guipúzcoa, Vizcaya, and Álava, but the traditional Basque homeland, *Euskal Herria*, includes parts of Navarra (including Pamplona) and France. So proud are the Basques of their diverse and culturally rich homeland that many want complete independence from Spain, including the now unpopular terrorist organization *Euskadi ta Askatasuna* (ETA: "Basque Country and Freedom").

Since Franco's death in 1975, Basque culture has flourished. Though the *euskera* spoken by those who lived through the Fascist regime and the *euskara* spoken by those who have since learned it in schools are at times mutually unintelligible, the Basques are nevertheless united by this distinct language (*euskara* is believed to be unrelated to any other language spoken today). País Vasco is also the homeland of some rich (if salty) cuisine and the birthplace of the dangerous sport of *pelota vasca*, or *jai alai*, which sort of looks like squash with live ammunition.

greatest hits

- **EUREKA! EUSKARA!** The native Basque language has flourished since Franco's death. Come experience the oddity and beauty of this unclassifiable language for yourself.

- **GET UP, GET OUT.** Dive into the outdoor opportunities in San Sebastián (p. 304).

- **GAWK AT THE GUGGENHEIM.** Take a look the museum that put Bilbao on the map (p. 311).

san sebastián *donostia* ☎943

San Sebastián's history is quite different from that of many neighboring cities in Spain's northeast, giving the city a distinct character. Formed by combining three Basque fishing and whaling towns along the bay into one mega-port city, San Sebastián (pop. 180,000) thrived and became a major seaport but was **burned to the ground** in 1813 by Anglo-Portuguese forces. And so, instead of a *casco antiguo* filled with medieval buildings, San Sebastián's historic center is the **parte vieja,** whose older constructions come from the French Beaux-Arts and Art Nouveau styles, popular at the end of the 19th century when the city was rebuilt. Even the cathedral is new (relatively speaking—it's from the 1890s), and the narrow streets of the old quarter are basically on a grid. This newly built city attracted tourists from all over Europe with its sunny beaches (made popular by Queen Isabel II), helping it to become the **resort town** that it is today. There are still neighborhoods (particularly on the east side of the river) where one can escape the occasionally overwhelming feel of turn-of-the-century opulence, but the beaches are free, so even those traveling on a budget can **bask in the sunny luxury** of San Sebastián.

ORIENTATION

San Sebastián's relatively tiny but bustling **parte vieja** ("old part") is only about eight blocks by eight blocks in size and sits at the northern end of the central part of the city bordered by **La Concha** bay to the west, **Monte Urgull** to the north, **Río Urumea** to the east, and the broad **Alameda del Boulevard** to the south. South of that is **El Centro,** a newer district that is the city's center for shopping and business that contains the **cathedral.** To the east, across the Río Urumea, lies the **Gros** neighborhood, which has a **surf beach** (Playa de Zurriola) and tends to be slightly trendier and cheaper than the *parte vieja.* On the other side of the tracks to the south of Gros is **Egia,** where you're unlikely to find any tourists but is one of the coolest parts of town. To the west of El Centro is the **Playa de la Concha,** which is not nearly as exciting as the surf beach but enjoys a longer and richer history as a resort hangout. The city is divided by the beaches and mountains that line the coast: from west to east, **Monte Igueldo,** Playa de Ondarreta and Playa de la Concha, Monte Urgull (and the *parte vieja*), Playa de Zurriola, and **Monte Ulia.**

ACCOMMODATIONS

Though San Sebastián is hardly limited to its **parte vieja** and **El Centro** neighborhoods, these locales tend to be the hub of hotels and hostels. Thankfully, it's a small city and easy to walk, so the limited range of location options shouldn't hold you back.

HOSPEDAJE KATI　　　　　　　　　　　　　　　　●⊗⁽ᵞ⁾⊰ HOSTEL ❷

C. Fermín Calbetón, 21, 5C　　　　　　　　　☎677 06 69 00 ■www.hospedajekati.com

An elderly couple rents beds (five crammed into one room) in their fifth-story apartment in the *parte vieja.* They do a great good-cop, bad-cop routine: Kati comes in to say good night, then Luis follows to scold you for using the big light

país vasco

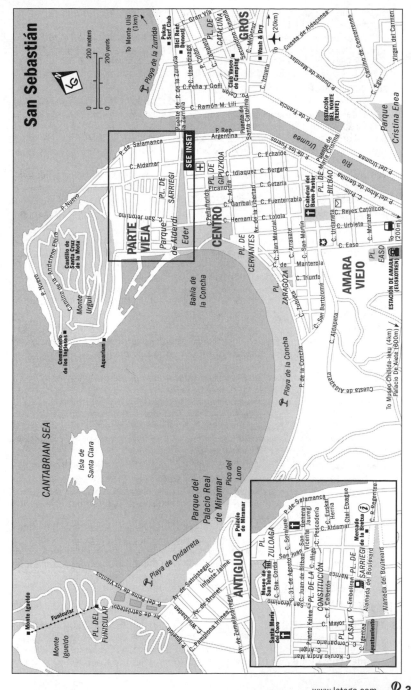

San Sebastián

GROS

To Monte Ulia (1km)

Pukas
Surf Club
Bici Rent
Benosti

C. Gran Vía
PL. DE
CATALUÑA

To (20km)

Club Vasco
de Camping

Wash & Dry

ESTACIÓN
DEL NORTE
(RENFE)

Parque
Cristina Enea

P. de la Zurriola

Playa de la Zurriola

Puente de
la Zurriola

P. Rep.
Argentina

SEE INSET

PARTE
VIEJA

Parque
de Aiderdi
Eder

Bahía de
la Concha

CANTABRIAN SEA

Isla de
Santa Clara

Playa de la Concha

Parque del
Palacio Real
de Miramar

Palacio
de Miramar

Pico del
Loro

Playa de Ondarreta

Monte Igueldo

Funicular

PL. DEL
FUNICULAR

Monte
Igueldo

ANTIGUO

CENTRO

AMARA
VIEJO

ESTACIÓN DE AMARA
(EUSKOTREN)

To Museo Chillida-leku (4km) /
Palacio De Aiete (600m)

Catedral del
Buen Pastor

PL. DE
BILBAO

PL. DE
GIPUZKOA

(six bulbs) instead of the single-bulb lamp by the bed. There's a large, lovely terrace as well, just off the bedroom. During the high season, the place is full; during the low season, you may have the largest, cheapest single in town.

✦ *From Alameda del Boulevard, head north onto C. de San Juan 3 blocks, then turn left onto C. Fermín Calbetón.* ℹ *Breakfast included. TV and shared bath.* Ⓢ *Dorms July 16-Sept 14 €25-30; Sept 15-July 15 €18-22.* 🕐 *Reception 10am-10pm.*

PENSIÓN AMAIUR
◉⊗ PENSIÓN ❹

C. 31 de Agosto, 44 ☎943 42 96 54 🖳www.pensionamaiur.com

Situated on one of the *parte vieja's* main tapas bar streets, this little *pensión* is colorfully cozy. The beds are big, the rooms clean with lots of closet space, and the shared kitchens well stocked (though breakfast is not included). Lovely views through flowery balconies onto the street below are available in the exterior rooms for just €5 extra.

✦ *From Alameda del Boulevard, head north on C. de San Juan 7 blocks, then turn left onto C. 31 de Agosto.* ℹ *TV and kitchen.* Ⓢ *July-Aug doubles €60-65; triples €80; Sept-June singles €32; doubles €50; triples €75. Family lodging €100.* 🕐 *Reception 24hr.*

HOSTEL SAN FERMÍN
➥⊗⑴⛵ HOSTEL ❶

C. Fermín Calbetón, 23 ☎943 42 54 91

This hostel offers no-frills, dormitory-style lodging at some of the *parte vieja's* lowest rates. It attracts a fun, youthful crowd that is always down to party. The staff is young and helpful, and they often go out with the guests to show them the best nightlife and hidden restaurants.

✦ *From Alameda del Boulevard, head north onto C. de San Juan 3 blocks, then turn left onto C. Fermín Calbetón.* ℹ *Lockers available. Surfboard and wetsuit rental.* Ⓢ *Dorms July-Aug €20-25; Sept-June €15-20.* 🕐 *Reception 8am-midnight, but guests get keys.*

PENSIÓN IZAR BAT
◉⊗⑴ PENSIÓN ❹

C. Fermín Calbetón, 6 ☎943 43 15 73 🖳www.pensionizarbat.com

This *pensión's* prices tend to get a little steep during the *temporada alta (July-Sept)* but this place is great if you're looking for a clean, cheery room with a private bathroom (an amenity you start to miss after extensive travel). Just steps from the Alameda del Boulevard, Izar Bat is easily spotted from C. San Juan due to its flowering balconies overlooking the beginning of C. Fermín Calbetón.

✦ *From Alameda del Boulevard, head north onto C. de San Juan 3 blocks, then turn left onto C. Fermín Calbetón.* ℹ *TV, radio, and fridge. Private bath with hair dryer.* Ⓢ *July-Sept singles €50-60; doubles €60-65. Oct singles €30-35; doubles €40-45. Nov-Apr singles €20-25; doubles €25-30. May-June singles €30-35; doubles €40-45.* 🕐 *Reception 24hr.*

PENSIÓN LA PERLA
◉⊗⑴ PENSIÓN ❹

C. Loiola, 10, 2nd fl. ☎943 42 81 23 🖳www.pensionlaperla.com

This *pensión's* rooms are small, but its beds are big and comfy, and the spaces are quite bright during the day—except for the almost daily 20min. rainstorms that plague San Sebastián. Sandwiched between a modern shopping center and the cathedral, there's something for devout Catholics and capitalists alike (those who fall into the center of that Venn diagram will be on cloud nine).

✦ *On the street directly in front of the cathedral that heads north, away from the cathedral.* ℹ *Private bath and TV. Laundry service available.* Ⓢ *June 21-Sept 30 singles €50; doubles €60; triples €75. Oct-May singles €30-40; doubles €38-50; triples €53-60. June 1-21 singles €40; doubles €50; triples €60.* 🕐 *Reception 24hr.*

SIGHTS
◉

🖼 MUSEO CHILLIDA-LEKU
➥♿ MUSEUM, GARDEN

Barrio de Jauregi, 66, Hernani ☎943 33 60 06 🖳www.museochillidaleku.com

Just a quick bus ride from *El Centro* is the Museo Chillida-Leku, a sculpture-garden-cum-farmhouse filled with the abstract works of the Basque country's

país vasco

most renowned modern artist, designed in large part by the late artist himself. **Eduardo Chillida's** work can be found in public spaces all over San Sebastián, most prominently at the promontories at the far ends of the beaches. This museum's approach is more holistic than most: there is no set path, so visitors are supposed to wander as they wish and are even supposed to touch the outdoor sculptures.

➔ Take Lurraldebus G2 from C. de Okendo, in front of Teatro Victoria Eugenia to Museo Chillida-Leku stop. **ℹ** *Visitors allowed and encouraged to touch outdoor sculptures with hands. $ €8.50, students and seniors €6.50, under 12 free. Reduced price M. Guided tours €5.50. ⏰ Open July-Aug M-Sa 10:30am-8pm, Su 10:30am-3pm; Sept-June M 10:30am-3pm, W-Su 10:30am-3pm. Guided visits M-Sa 10:30am-6pm, Su 11am-1pm.*

MONTE URGULL AND CASA DE LA HISTORIA 👍⊗ MUSEUM, HISTORICAL SITE

Castillo de la Mota de Urgull ☎943 42 84 17

Monte Urgull, the big mountain next to the *parte vieja* with the **Jesus statue** on top, is not a strenuous enough walk to make it into the hiking listings. The trek is still a lovely escape from the city, despite being just meters away—up, up, and away, of course. As you ascend, you'll pass castle after castle and be rewarded for your shin splints with breathtaking views of the city and bay (though the breathtaking part could also be chalked up to the climb). At the very top is the **Castillo de la Mota,** which houses the **Casa de la Historia** and a comprehensive exhibit of San Sebastián's history. Take the north side of the mountain back down and pass the hauntingly beautiful 1837 **English Cemetery,** whose headstone carvers must not have been English, as names that are memorialized include misspelled ones like "Whiliam."

➔ Head uphill to the left of Iglesia de Santa María on C. 31 de Agosto. $ Free. ⏰ Monte Urgull open daily May-Sept 8am-9pm; Oct-Apr 8am-7pm. Casa de la Historia open daily May 2-Sept 14 11am-8pm; Sept 15-30 11am-7:30pm; Oct-Apr Tu-F 10am-2pm and 3-5:30pm, Sa-Su 10am-5:30pm. Castillo de la Mota open daily May-Sept 8am-8pm; Oct-Apr 8am-6pm.

MONTE IGUELDO 👍⊗ VIEWS

☎943 21 35 25 🖥www.monteigueldo.es

Take the **funicular** *(Pl. del Funicular, 4 ☎943 21 35 25 $ Round-trip €2.60, under 7 €1.90)* to the top of the mountain on the far western end of town for amazing views and creepy-looking carnival rides. Mostly for the views, though.

➔ Funicular leaves daily every 15min. 10am-9pm. $ Free. ⏰ Panoramic terraces open 10:30am-dusk.

IGLESIA DE SAN VICENTE ♿ CHURCH

C. Narrica, 26

This massive church is one of the city's oldest remaining structures, built in the early 16th century. The interior is gorgeous and often redolent of the lilies by the altar, and there are plenty of holy-water fonts for impromptu exorcisms. You can also walk up to the balcony for a better view of the church and the stained glass.

➔ Walk up C. Narrica from Alameda del Boulevard. $ Free. ⏰ Open M-Sa 9am-1pm and 5-8pm.

CATEDRAL DEL BUEN PASTOR ♿ CHURCH

Pl. del Buen Pastor

This Neo-Gothic cathedral in the newer part of town dates from the last years of the 19th century and has a direct view of the Baroque Iglesia de Santa María del Coro up the long street into the *parte vieja*. The 250 ft. high belfry towers over San Sebastián and is visible from most of the city and bay. It was built as a mere church, but it got called up to the big leagues in 1949 when the diocese of San Sebastián was formed and it became a **cathedral.**

➔ From Alameda del Boulevard, take C. de Hernani south from the western end; the cathedral is at the end. $ Free. ⏰ Open M-Sa 8:30am-12:30pm and 5-8pm.

THE GREAT OUTDOORS

Hiking

TXINDOKI

This peak in the Aralar range stands at just over 4400 ft. and is considered one of the best hikes around. It's challenging but requires no particular expertise. The only problem is that it's difficult to reach without a car; some travelers say that hitchhiking (which *Let's Go* does not recommend) is an option, but renting a car is always safer.

➔ Best reached by car. Take the A-8 to the E-5, then take exit 431 onto the GI-2131 toward Alegia, and follow signs toward Amezketa. $ Free. ⏰ Don't start later than noon if you want to make it to the peak and down before dark.

CAMINO DEL NORTE

The second stage of the Camino del Norte, which runs from Irún to Santiago de Compostela, goes from San Sebastián to Zarautz and is about 14 mi. Take the highway up Monte Igueldo and then follow the signs; turn back whenever you feel like it, since there's no pressure to make it all the way to Zarrautz, unless you're meeting up with someone to go surfing.

➔ Keep walking west along the bay until you see signs for the Camino.

Beaches

PLAYA DE ZURRIOLA

This is the **surf beach,** located to the east of the river and along the Gros neighborhood. Though not exclusively for surfing, this beach tends to draw a much younger crowd than its more historic neighbor to the west. Bikini tops optional; bikini bottoms encouraged. If you have a problem with nudity, avoid this beach—or just about any beach in Europe, actually.

➔ East of Río Urumea, on the waterfront. $ Free. ⏰ Open dawn-dusk.

PLAYA DE LA CONCHA

This was the beach around which San Sebastián cultivated its reputation as a resort town for the vacationing European bourgeoisie; today it tends to be frequented mostly by an older crowd (and their grandchildren).

➔ Just west of the parte vieja and El Centro; it's the big strip of land with sand and water—you can't miss it. $ Free. ⏰ Open dawn-dusk.

PLAYA DE ONDARRETA

Just to the west of Playa de la Concha but east of Monte Igeldo, this beach is a little less crowded, simply by virtue of its slightly greater distance from the center of town. During the high season, though, it's as packed as the rest of the beachfront.

➔ Follow Paseo de la Concha west. ℹ Currently undergoing intermittent rehabilitation to prevent beach erosion. $ Free. ⏰ Open dawn to dusk.

PLAYA DE ZARAUTZ

About 30min. from San Sebastián via Euskotren is **Zarautz,** a tiny town with a huge beach, almost completely tourist-free and home to some gnarly waves. Pukas surf shop, below, rents boards and gives lessons.

➔ From the Euskotren station, take the train toward Zumaia. Once there, head toward the water. $ Free. ⏰ Open dawn-dusk.

Kayaking

ALOKAYAK — KAYAKING [2]

Playa de Ondarreta ☎646 11 27 47 💻www.alokayak.com

This stand is set up on the Playa de Ondarreta during the high tourist season (June 15-Sept 15) and rents kayaks for solo excursions in the bay and surrounding area.

➔ Walk west along Playa de la Concha to Playa de Ondarreta; it's the shack that says "aloKAYAK." ℹ Group rates available. $ Kayaks €6-7 per 30min., €10-12 per hr., €16-19 per 2hr. 2-person kayaks €10 per 30min., €15 per hr., €25 per 2hr. ⏰ Open June 15-Sept 15 daily 9am-8pm.

Surfing

⬛ PUKAS
Av. de Zurriola, 24

☞943 32 00 68 💻www.pukassurfeskola.com

⬛ SURFING ❷

This is the Playa de Zurriola's go-to spot for surf gear, rentals, and lessons; in a world of slackers, these guys are pros. Try to get three other novices and go for a 3hr. group lesson over a weekend (€53), or if you're more experienced, rent a board for a day (€25).

🏄 *On Av. de Zurriola across from the surf beach.* 🛈 *Passport and credit card required for rentals.* ⑤ *Surfboards €10 per hr., €15 per 2hr., €17 per 4hr., €25 per day. Wetsuit rental €5 per hr., €9 per 2hr., €11 per 4hr., €20 per day. Stand-up-paddle course €23 per hr. Private surf lessons €52 per hr.* 🕙 *Open M-Sa 11am-2pm and 4-8pm, Su 10am-2pm.*

FOOD

Foodies the world over know San Sebastián for its outstanding culinary reputation. But you don't have to go to **Arzak** (average price €155 per person) to have some of the best meals of your life. The city's best **tapas bars** are all affordable and can be found in the *parte vieja*, especially along **Calle 31 de Agosto** and **Calle Fermín Calbetón**. Many restaurants tend to be concentrated in this area as well, but for better prices (and, often, better food) check out the restaurants in **Gros** to the east of the river, particularly on Paseo Colón. Those looking to do some exploring can look for hidden gems in the not-yet-gentrified **Egia** neighborhood.

⬛ ITXAS MAGALEAN
Av. Navarra, 2

🍴👤🍷❄ SEAFOOD ❸

☞943 32 12 25

Across from the far eastern end of the surf beach, just before the sand ends and the mountain begins, sits Itxas (pronounced "EET-chas") Magalean, home to San Sebastián's best squid-ink pasta *(spagueti tintados de sepia con langostinos; €9.80)* and a cool, beachy feel. The *calamares   (fried squid; €7)* are just like what you get at restaurants back in the good old US of A, except they don't taste like fried rubber, but rather of ocean and goodness. The ingredients are always fresh, and they come together to make some of the best meals you're likely to find anywhere.

🏄 *Follow Av. de Zurriola east along the surf beach (Playa de Zurriola) to the rotary at the end; the entrance is across the street from the beach on the southwest corner, facing the mountain.* 🛈 *Reservations necessary Th-Su, especially during summer.* ⑤ *Appetizers €4-16; entrees €8.50-16.* 🕙 *Open daily 8am-midnight.*

⬛ GARRAXI
C. Tejería, 9

🍴👤🍷🥗 VEGETARIAN ❷

☞943 27 52 69

While omnivores will have no issues eating their way through San Sebastián's incredible culinary offerings, some vegetarians may feel a bit left out amid all the *jamón* and *mariscos*. For those adventurous enough to trek away from the Cantabrian coast and into the Egia neighborhood, there's a vegetarian option that's right up there with the best of the restaurants in the *parte vieja* and Gros. The inexpensive food at this laid-back restaurant is so delicious that even the most ardent meat eater won't notice its absence. The *bolitas de patatas y cebollas   (potato and onion balls; €6)* are the best-tasting misshapen *latkes* you'll ever eat, and they're served in a curry sauce that gives them a little kick that will send you straight to veggie heaven.

🏄 *From the Gros neighborhood (east of the river), take C. Iparraguirre south, under the train tracks, then turn left at C. Iztueta, which bends to the right and becomes Paseo de Duque de Mandas. Next, turn left at C. Egia, then take a left again onto C. San Cristobal for 1 block.* 🛈 *Menu available in English.* ⑤ *Entrees €4-9. Menú del día €10.60.* 🕙 *Open daily 1:30-3:30pm and 8:30-11pm.*

A FUEGO NEGRO
C. 31 de Agosto, 31

🍴👤🍷 TAPAS ❸

☞650 13 53 73 💻www.afuegonegro.com

This place knows how to do tapas with some 'tude: it's definitely the most bad-ass tapas bar in the *parte vieja*. Instead of the rapid-fire, unintelligible *castellano* that

san sebastián • food

forms the soundtrack for most bars, A Fuego Negro plays modern Spanish rock and even some 🏆 **reggaetón.** The customers tend to be on the younger side of the tapas spectrum. It's a little pricey—the €15 plates to share don't come with nearly as much as one might expect, and the single *pinchos* (which are certainly worth it) run about €0.50-1 more expensive than elsewhere. The best deal in the place is a bottle of *sidra* (cider), a very popular drink in this region, for €5. Make sure you have the bartender pour it for you, as it is quite a spectacle (warning: first few rows may get wet).

➡ From Alameda del Boulevard, head north onto C. Mayor for 4 blocks, then turn right at C. 31 de Agosto. $ Pintxos €3-6. Plates to share €15. Mixed drinks €7. ⏰ Open daily 11am-midnight. Kitchen open 11am-4pm and 8pm-midnight.

BAR MARTÍNEZ — 🥦♿🍸 TAPAS ❶

C. 31 de Agosto, 13 — ☎943 42 49 65

This traditional tapas bar in the *parte vieja* has an enormous selection of *tapas* and *pinchos:* there is barely a square inch of space on the bar, completely covered with overlapping plates. The alcachofas con Ibérico *(fried artichokes with ham; €2)* are wonderful, and the salmon *(€2)* is salty and fresh (though you may want to scrape off a bit of the heap of onions sitting on top, especially if you've brought along a date). The specialty here is red peppers filled with *bacalao (cod; €1.75).*

➡ From Alameda del Boulevard, turn north onto C. San Juan, then turn left at C. 31 de Agosto. $ Tapas €1.50-5. ⏰ Open M-W 11:30am-3:30pm and 6:30-11:30pm, F 6:30-11:30pm, Sa 11:30am-3:30pm and 6:30-11:30pm.

CAMPERO — 🥦♿🍸 SANDWICHES ❶

Paseo José Miguel Barandiarán, 8 — ☎943 27 14 95

Amazing, big, inexpensive sandwiches right across from the beach. The "Campero" *(ham, cheese, lettuce, sautéed onions, tomato, alioli; €3.50)* will fill you up for the whole afternoon. They also have burgers and traditional sides like *patatas bravas.*

➡ At the far eastern end of the surf beach, across the street from the basketball courts. i Dogs welcome. $ Sandwiches €3-6.50. ⏰ Open M-Th 12:30-11pm, F-Sa 12:30pm-midnight. □am-midnight, Sa 8am-1am, Su 8am-10:30pm.

NIGHTLIFE

The most tourist-frequented nightlife scene in San Sebastián is unsurprisingly in the **parte vieja,** where the bars that served noisy tapas in the afternoon become bars that serve even noisier drinks at night. One bar is pretty much the same as the next, but a few have their own distinct character. The nightlife options listed here are a little less obvious to the average tourist and are slightly further off the beaten track.

🏆 ETXEKALTE — 🥦♿🍸 BAR, CLUB

C. de Mari, 11 — ☎943 42 97 88

As with most Spanish bars outside of the major cities, the *entre semana* (midweek) tends to be a bit quiet, though the place gets livelier each night as the weekend approaches. The place explodes on Thursday through Saturday nights, when there's a DJ spinning in the club downstairs, and the party doesn't end until just before dawn.

➡ Take Alameda del Boulevard west to the bay, then turn right onto C. de Mari. $ Beer €2.20. Vino tinto €2.50. Mixed drinks €4-8. ⏰ Open Tu-Th 6pm-4am, F-Sa 6pm-5am, Su 6pm-4am.

LE BUKOWSKI — 🥦⊗🍸 CLUB

C. Egia, 18 — 💻www.lebukowski.com

Six or seven years ago, this was the center of San Sebastián's punk scene. It's unclear whether the punks have disappeared or simply moved on, but today it's more of a hipster hangout, with live music Friday and Saturday nights.

➡ Take Av. de la Libertad east across the river and follow the road at about 2 o'clock for 1 block, then cut through the park under the train tracks. Turn right at Paseo del Duque de Mandas and left when you pass the big park onto C. Egia. $ Drinks €2-7. ⏰ Open M-Th 5pm-1:30am, F-Sa 5pm-3am, Su 5pm-1:30am.

BE BOP BAR
Paseo de Salamanca, 3   ❸⊗⑤❡ BAR, CLUB   ☎943 42 98 69

This place doesn't start getting exciting until around 2:15am during *entre semana*, once every place besides Etxekalte and Be Bop has closed. Before 2am, the bar is not terribly exciting, but once the competition closes, this place is definitely in demand.

❖ *On the Paseo de Salamanca in the parte vieja, along the river.* ℹ️ *Bouncer may not let you in if it's too crowded and you don't look like the type of person he wants to let in (i.e., female), so get there before it fills up.* ⑤ *Mixed drinks €2-6.* 🕐 *Open M-Th 3pm-4am, F-Sa 3pm-5:30am, Su 3pm-4am.*

FESTIVALS

INTERNATIONAL FILM FESTIVAL
Av. de Zurriola, 1   🖳www.sansebastianfestival.com

For a week in September every year since 1953, the international film scene has descended on San Sebastián for the film festival, largely responsible for putting San Sebastián on the tourism industry's map. Shell out the big bucks and attend the festival, or just admire the celebrities from afar. Better yet, get a couple of friends to crowd around you and take pictures, and see how long it takes before the real paparazzi start calling your name and stealing your pictures.

❖ *Ticket sales and most events at the Kursaal (Av. de Zurriola, 1).* ⑤ *Most screenings €6-8; tickets for awards ceremonies and galas €60-235.* 🕐 *Dates change annually.*

JAZZALDIA
Select venues throughout the city   ☎943 48 19 00 🖳www.heinekenjazzaldia.com

San Sebastián's annual jazz festival takes place in the fourth week in July, with performances at Teatro Victoria Eugenia, Pl. de la Trinidad, and Kursaal Auditorium. Concerts at the historic Pl. de la Trinidad have an amazing atmosphere (especially at night) and shouldn't be missed.

❖ *Teatro Victoria Eugenia is just south of the far eastern end of Alameda del Boulevard; Pl. de la Trinidad is at the far north end of the parte vieja; Kursaal Auditorium is just east of the river, on the bay.* ⑤ *Tickets for 3-4 shows €40-105.* 🕐 *Late July.*

SEMANA GRANDE
🖳www.donostia.org

This week of festivities occurs the third week of August and is marked by spectacular displays of fireworks and 15 ft. tall puppets. A detailed schedule of all the festivities (and there are many) can be found at www.donostia.org.

🕐 *See schedule at www.donostia.org for times and locations.*

ESSENTIALS

Practicalities

- **TOURIST OFFICE:** The tourist office has representatives who speak English, French, and German and is located just outside the *parte vieja. (Alameda del Boulevard, 8* ☎*943 48 11 66* 🖳*www.sansebastianturismo.com* 🕐 *Open M-Th 9:30am-1:30pm and 3:30-7pm, F-Sa 9:30am-7pm, Su 10am-2pm.)*

- **LUGGAGE STORAGE:** Luggage storage is available at the **Continental Auto** ticket office just north of the bus station. *(Av. de Sancho el Sabio* ⑤ *€2.* 🕐 *Open 7am-2pm and 3-8pm.)*

- **INTERNET:** The **Biblioteca Central** *(Pl. Ayuntamiento* 🕐 *Open M-F 10am-8:30pm, Sa 10am-2pm and 4:30-8pm)* has **free Wi-Fi** and 45min. of **free internet access** when you sign up at the front desk.

- **POST OFFICE:** The main post office *(C. Urdaneta* ☎*902 19 71 97* 🕐 *Open M-F 8:30am-8:30pm, Sa 9:30am-2pm)* is right behind the cathedral.

Emergency!

- **POLICE:** *(☎092)*
- **HOSPITALS/MEDICAL SERVICES: Casa de Socorro.** *(C. Bengoetxea, 4 ☎943 44 06 33)*

Getting There

By Bus

The easiest and cheapest way to get to San Sebastián from any nearby city is **bus,** at least while the high-speed train from Madrid is still under construction. The bus station is a decent walk from the center of town, on the south side of the city, but the #21, 26, and 28 buses run from the bus station to Alameda del Boulevard. Buses arrive from: **Barcelona** (Ⓢ €30. 🕐 5-6hr., 3-4 per day 7:30am-11pm); **Bilbao** (Ⓢ €7. 🕐 1¼hr., 10 per day 5:15am-1:15am); **Bilbao airport** (Ⓢ €15. 🕐 1½hr., 17 per day 7:45-11:45); **Burgos** (Ⓢ €15.50. 🕐 3hr., 7 per day 3:15am-midnight); **Granada** (Ⓢ €50. 🕐 12hr., 5 per day 8am-6pm); **Madrid** (Ⓢ €32. 🕐 6hr., 9-11 per day 7:30am-12:30am); **Pamplona** (Ⓢ €7. 🕐 1-1¼hr., 18 per day 7am-10:45pm); **Salamanca** (Ⓢ €30.50. 🕐 7hr., M-F 4 per day 2:45pm-midnight, Sa 1 per day at noon, Su 4 per day 2:45pm-midnight); and **Santiago de Compostela** (Ⓢ €57-72. 🕐 13hr.; M-Sa 2 per day 8:30am-6pm, Su 3 per day 8:30am-6pm).

By Train

Euskotran (☎902 54 32 10 🖥www.euskotren.es) runs trains from **Bilbao.** (Ⓢ €4.80. 🕐 2½hr., 16 per day 6am-10:30pm.) The **RENFE train** (☎902 10 94 20 🖥www.renfe.es) has trains from **Barcelona** (Ⓢ €37-61. 🕐 5½hr., 2 per day 7:35am-3:35pm) and **Madrid** (Ⓢ €31-52. 🕐 5½hr., 2 per day 8am-4:10pm); check the RENFE website for other points of departure.

By Plane

Frequent flights arrive at the airport in Hondarribia (☎943 66 85 00 🖥www.aenea.es) 15mi. east of San Sebastián from Madrid and Barcelona and less frequently from other destinations. Buses run from the airport every 30min. (Ⓢ €1.75. 🕐 45min.; M-Sa Sept-June 7:35am-9:45pm; July-Aug M-Sa 7:35am-9:45pm, Su 8:45am-9:45pm.) A taxi to the airport costs about €30.

Getting Around

By Bus

The best way to get around San Sebastián is to **walk,** though for really long trips the **city bus system** (☎943 00 02 00 🖥www.dbus.es Ⓢ €1.35) is fast and efficient. Buses #21, 26, and 28 go from the bus station to the Alameda del Boulevard next to the *parte vieja.* There is also another bus system called **Lurraldebus** (☎943 00 01 17 🖥www. lurraldebus.net Ⓢ €1-3), whose routes go to the smaller towns outside San Sebastián.

By Bike

Bikes are another popular way to get around, and there are actually a fair number of bike paths and lanes. Rent one at **Bici Rent Donosti.** *(Av. Zurriola, 22 ☎639 01 60 13 Ⓢ €4 per hr., €13 per 4hr., €21 per day. 🕐 Open daily 10am-2pm and 4-8:30pm.)*

By Taxi

The **taxi** companies are Radio Taxi Donosti (☎943 46 46 46 🖥www.taxidonosti.com) and Vallina Teletaxi (☎943 40 40 40 🖥www.vallinagrupo.com).

bilbao *bilbo*   ☎944

Bilbao (pop. 350,000) is for the most part a modern city that has not forgotten its historic roots. The city thrived during the Middle Ages, as it was on both a major 🢒**sea route** and on the 🅽**Camino de Santiago.** After a couple of fairly quiet centuries, nearby lucrative mineral deposits were discovered in the 19th century, and the city grew as both a seaport and an **industrial center,** known mainly as a producer of steel

país vasco

and the Basque country's economic hub. In the late 20th century, the steel industry declined and Bilbao began to experience some urban decay; it was lovingly known as **"the Pittsburgh of Spain."** Over the last couple of decades, Bilbao has been thoroughly revitalized, due mostly to the transformation of industrial zones into parks and cultural spaces like Frank Gehry's architecturally marvelous **Guggenheim Museum.** The "Guggenheim Effect" has propelled Bilbao back to the top of the proverbial heap economically and as a tourist destination.

ORIENTATION

The **casco viejo,** or old quarter, sits on the east side of the city, to the east of the **Ría de Bilbao** (also known as the Río Nervión), which makes a sort of upside-down "U" as it cuts through the city. The *casco viejo* contains the cathedral and **siete calles** (the original seven streets of Bilbao) and has the highest concentration of bars and accommodations. Across the river from the *casco viejo* are the neighborhoods of **Abando** to the north (where the museums are), **Indautxu** further south (where the nightlife is after 2am), **Basurtu** to the southwest (where the bus terminal is), and **Deusto** all the way west, across the river.

ACCOMMODATIONS

The *casco viejo* is brimming with cheap *pensiónes*, most on the upper floors of residential buildings; you can just walk down any street, look for a "Pensión" sign on the side of a building, and ring up asking for a room. In the high season, it's better to reserve a place in advance, though. *Pensiónes* outside the *casco viejo* tend to be quieter and less expensive. Rates may be higher during *Aste Nagusia* (mid- to late August).

BILBAO AKELARRE HOSTEL
C. Morgan, 4-6

♨ ⓺ ⒨ HOSTEL ❶

☎944 05 77 13 🖳www.bilbaoakelarrehostel.com

The only privately run hostel in Bilbao is located a bit far from most of the city's sights, though it's only a 5min. walk from the Metro station and a 10min. walk from the Euskotran, both of which will speedily take you wherever you need to go. The dorm-style rooms are simple but clean, and you can fill your pockets with *magdalenas* (individually packaged mini-muffins, a staple of Spanish breakfast cuisine) before heading out for the day.

✦ *Take Bilbobus #11 to Deusto to the last stop, Madariaga/Basabe, and turn left onto C. Morgan. Or take Euskotran tram to Euskalduna, then walk across the Puente Euskalduna (the bridge that curves to the left), and follow C. Morgan (the 1st street after the bridge) west. Or take Metro to* Ⓜ*Deusto (Iruña exit) and follow C. Iruña south to the river, then turn right onto C. Morgan.* **i** *Shared bath. Breakfast included. Lockers available. Common area with TV. English, French, and Spanish spoken.* ⑤ *12-bed dorms €17; 8-bed €18; 6-bed €19; with private bath €20. Doubles €42.* ⓩ *Reception 8am-11pm. Guests receive keycards with 24hr. access.*

PENSIÓN MÉNDEZ I
C. Santa María, 13, 4 (5th fl.)

⊛⊘ PENSIÓN ❷

☎944 16 03 64 🖳www.pensionmendez.com

Though not quite as comfortable as the affiliated Pensión Méndez II downstairs (which is €15-20 more expensive), these austere but good-sized rooms are located five stories above one of the busiest tapas- and bar-hopping streets in the *casco viejo*. It's right in the center of one of the liveliest spots in town—be careful when you open the front door to leave on a weekend evening, as you might trip over (or, better yet, get invited to) a *botellón* taking place on the doorstep.

✦ *From bus station, take Euskotran tram to Arriaga station and walk south along the river for 1 block, then turn left onto C. Santa María. Or take the Metro to* Ⓜ*Casco Viejo (Pl. Unamuno exit) and follow C. Sombrerería before making a left at C. Santa María.* **i** *5th-fl. walk-up. Reservations by phone only.* ⑤ *Singles €20-25; doubles €30-35; triples €45-50.* ⓩ *Reception 24hr.*

PENSIÓN LADERO
C. Lotería, 1 (5th fl.)

⊛⊘ PENSIÓN ❷

☎944 15 09 32

This family-run *pensión* has bright rooms with balconies in the center of the

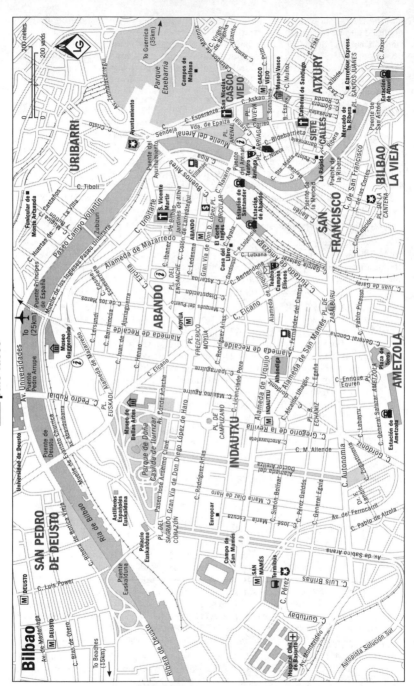

país vasco

Bilbao

casco viejo. There are two enormous triples (which can become quadruples for an extra €10), and several smaller doubles.

 # From Ⓜ Casco Viejo (Pl. Unamuno exit), follow C. de la Cruz south 1 block, then turn left onto C. España, which bevomes C. Lotería. i Shared bath. TV. $ Singles €24; doubles €36; triples €53. Extra bed €10. ⏰ Reception 8am-11pm.

SIGHTS

MUSEO GUGGENHEIM BILBAO

MUSEUM ❷

Av. Abandoibarra, 2 ☎944 35 90 80 www.guggenheim-bilbao.es

It is hardly an exaggeration to say that **Frank Gehry** put Bilbao on the map. Since the Guggenheim opened in 1997, Bilbao has become an internationally known cultural center—a far cry from its former reputation as "the Pittsburgh of Spain"—and there is no doubt that this owes much more to the building itself than to the artwork it houses. While the art should certainly not be overlooked—**Richard Serra's** installation *The Matter of Time* is truly a sublime experience that undermines perceptions of space and context, and **Jeff Koons's** *Puppy* is enormously adorable—they might hardly have been noticed in a less architecturally remarkable home. Everybody sees the enormous titanium, limestone, steel, and glass building as resembling something different, but perhaps most impressive is how different it appears from each possible angle and location at different times of the day; Monet would have had a field day with this place.

 # Exit the Euskotran at the Guggenheim stop. i Free audio tour with admission. $ €13, students and seniors €7.50, under 12 free. Bono Artean, which provides admission for both the Guggenheim and the Museo de Bellas Artes, can be purchased for €13.50. ⏰ Open July-Aug daily 10am-8pm; Sept-June Tu-Su 10am-8pm. Guided tours daily at 11am, 12:30, 4:30, 6:30pm. Cafeteria open Tu-Su 9:30am-8:30pm. Cafe open Tu-Su 1-3:15pm. Restaurant open Tu 1:30-3:30pm, W-Sa 1:30-3:30pm and 9-10:30pm, Su 1:30-3:30pm.

MUSEO DE BELLAS ARTES

MUSEUM ❶

Pl. del Museo, 2 ☎944 39 60 60 www.museobilbao.com

While this museum's building is an interesting one—a century-old brick structure sheathed in a modern renovation—the main attraction here (in contrast to its neighbor the Guggenheim) is the actual artwork. Some 33 rooms house a collection that's essentially a basic survey course in Western European art history since the Middle Ages; these are the best examples from each period that you've never heard of. Don't let lack of name recognition turn you away; though there are works by El Greco (born Domenikos Theotokopoulos—say that five times fast), Ribera, Zurbarán, Goya, and Cassatt, the ones that catch your eye may be by artists you'll discover for the first time.

 # From casco viejo, take Puente de Arenal bridge across the river and follow Gran Vía Don Diego López de Haro to Pl. Moyua, then turn right and follow C. Elcano to Pl. del Museo. Or, by Metro, head to Ⓜ Moyua, then follow C. Elcano to Pl. del Museo. $ €6, students and seniors €4.50, under 12 free; free on W. Audio tour €1. Bono Artean, which provides admission for both the Guggenheim and the Museo de Bellas Artes, €13.50. ⏰ Open Tu-Su 10am-8pm; guided tours Su at noon.

FOOD

The **casco viejo** is the best place to go **tapas-hopping; Calle Santa María, Barrenkale Barrena,** and **Calle Barrenkale** are some of the most crowded streets with some of the best bars. There are also a number of good, affordable restaurants in the **Abando** neighborhood, which has flourished with the opening of the Guggenheim Museum and the subsequent boost to the neighborhood's economy.

GATZ

TAPAS ❶

C. Santa María, 10 ☎944 15 48 61

The Great Gatsby (born James Gatz) may have been a sham, but this place is the real deal. Its various *pintxo* prizes are displayed on the wall behind the bar, and no diner there will disagree that they are well deserved. Though the average price is only a few cents higher than the neighboring bars, this one is a cut above the rest. The fried foie and potato *pintxo* *(€1.50)* is so rich you won't have to eat another meal for the rest of the day, and the smoked salmon wrapped around cream cheese and capers *(€1.50)* is perfect for anyone pining for a nice nova and a schmear.

On C. Santa María in the casco viejo, between C. Jardines and the river. $ Pintxos €1.50-2. ⏰ Open M-Th 1-3pm and 7-11pm, F-Sa 1-3pm and 7pm-midnight, Su 1-3pm.

ZAZPI BIDE TABERNA — TAPAS 1

C. Barrenkale Barrena, 18, bajo 2 — ☎944 79 58 17

This bar in the *siete calles* ("seven streets") district of the *casco viejo* has one of the liveliest atmospheres and some of the most reasonable prices of any establishment in town (one assumes these two factors do not exist independent of each other). It takes its name from its menu: *zazpi* means "seven" in Basque (as in the *siete calles* district), and *bide* means "euro fewer than you would have spent for the same food in San Sebastián."

At the north end of the street 1 block east of Barrenkale Barrena. $ Pintxos €1-1.50. Beer €1.70. Mixed drinks €3.50. ⏰ Open M-Th noon-4pm and 7pm-midnight, F-Sa noon-4pm and 7pm-1am, Su noon-4pm and 7pm-midnight.

LAMIAK — TAPAS 1

C. Pelota, 8 — ☎944 15 96 42

A cafe/bar in the *casco viejo* that's a little quieter than its neighbors early in the evening and a little louder later on, Lamiak serves *pintxos* in a more open, lounge-style atmosphere: there's more seating than in most bars and a trendier area upstairs that looks down onto the bar.

Between C. Santa María and the river, in the casco viejo. $ Pintxos €1-2. ⏰ Open Tu-Sa 4pm-midnight, Su 4-11:30pm.

NIGHTLIFE

The nightlife in Bilbao is simple: most revelers do a fairly standard **bar crawl** in the **casco viejo** until every place closes down, then head over to the **newer part of town** for more club-type places. The main spots are **Calle Licenciado Poza,** particularly around **Calle Aranzadi, Calle Simón Bolívar,** and **Calle Manuel Allende** farther west. There are also a few clubs on **Calle Dos de Mayo** and **Calle Hernani,** closer to the *casco*.

IRRINTZI — BAR

Santa María, 8 — ☎944 16 76 16 www.irrintzi.es

A good place to begin your night hopping from bar to bar in the *casco*, sampling *cervezas*, *sidras*, and whatever other type of *bebida* suits you; maybe even a *pintxo* or two as well. Make what you will of the slightly hipstery faux-ironic Japanese manga-anime theme, but the establishment calls itself a *"bar emblematico de Bilbao."*

[M]Casco Viejo. Follow C. Sombrerería to C. Victor to C. Jardines, then right on C. Santa María. $ Pintxos €1.50. Beer €2. Cider €2.50. ⏰ Open M-Th 10am-11pm, F-Sa 11am-midnight, Su 11am-10pm.

COTTON CLUB — CLUB

C. Gregorio de la Revilla, 25 — ☎944 10 49 51 www.cottonclubbilbao.es

This place may be a little hard to find, but once you see it, you'll know—it's the one with the **animatronic polar bears** in the window. The walls are covered with tens of thousands of bottle caps and the dance floor with dozens and dozens of partiers. The place is jammed on Friday and Saturday nights and occasionally has live music with bands from Spain and farther afield; it's a bit calmer during the week.

From [M]Indautxu, exit to the right through the shopping area, then make a right at the elevator. Then make an immediate left once outside; entrance is on C. Simón Bolívar. $ Beer €2.50. Mixed drinks €6. ⏰ Open M-Th 5pm-3:30am, F-Sa 5pm-6am, Su 6:30pm-3:30am.

FESTIVALS

ASTE NAGUSIA (SEMANA GRANDE) — PL. ARRIAGA

☎94 420 42 00 www.astenagusia.com

Nine beloved and anticipated days of fireworks, music, theater, and bullfights

in late August. It's nothing on the scale of Pamplona's *San Fermín*, but it begins with a *txupin* (rocket) all the same and takes over the city for over a week. Aste Nagusia came in first in a competition of Spain's best intangible cultural treasures. Get a *Bilbao Guide* from the tourist office for a schedule and more information.
⇆ Events centered on Pl. Arriaga, but the festival is located throughout the whole city. $ Free. ⏰ Begins the 1st Sa after Aug 15.

INTERNATIONAL FESTIVAL OF DOCUMENTARY AND SHORT FILMS CITYWIDE
☎944 24 86 98 💻www.zinebi.com
The Festival Internacional de Cine Documental y Cortometraje de Bilbao began as a documentary film competition in 1959, then began screening short films as well in 1971. It managed to survive Generalísimo Franco, a complete lack of money, and controversy (the true sign of good art) to become one of Spain's leading film festivals. The main festival is the last week in November, but there is related programming earlier in the month and an affiliated fantasy film festival at the beginning of May.
⏰ Nov.

ZINEGOAK ▼ CITYWIDE
☎94 415 62 58 💻www.zinegoak.com
Zinegoak, the Bilbao international gay, lesbian, and transgender film festival, runs for a week from the end of January through the beginning of February. So, if you can't find a bar to watch the Super Bowl, here's an alternative.
⇆ Check website or check with tourist office for venues and schedule. $ Opening ceremony €7, screenings €5. ⏰ Late June to early Feb.

LOS DULCES DEL CONVENTO CASCO VIEJO
Pl. de la Encarnación ☎944 32 01 25
The last weekend in May every year, the Diocesan Museum of Religious Art houses a sweets fair in their usually quiet cloister. All the *dulces* are made by cloister nuns and monks, mostly with raw materials they grow themselves. The fair draws approximately 10,000 visitors annually.
⇆ In the casco viejo, follow C. Ribera to C. Atxuri, or take the Euskotran to Atxuri and walk 1 block back along the track, then make a right. $ Free. Sweets €2-12. Museum tours €1. ⏰ Last weekend in May F-Su 10:30am-8pm.

ESSENTIALS [i]

Practicalities

- **TOURIST OFFICES:** The tourism office's main branch is in **Abando** *(Pl. del Ensanche ☎944 79 57 60 💻www.bilbao.net/bilbaoturismo ⏰ Open June-Sept M-Sa 10am-7pm, Su 10am-6pm; Oct-May M-F 9am-2pm and 4-7:30pm)*, but that branch is not open on weekends during the low season; instead, go to the branch at **Teatro Arriaga** in the *casco viejo* *(Pl. Arriaga ⏰ Open daily June-Sept 9:30am-2pm and 4-7:30pm; Oct-May M-F 11am-2pm and 5-7:30pm, Sa 9:30am-2pm and 5-7:30pm, Su 9:30am-2pm)* or the branch at the **Guggenheim Museum** *(Av. Abandoibarra, 2 ⏰ Open June-Sept M-Sa 10am-7pm, Su 10am-6pm; Oct-May Tu-F 11am-6pm, Sa 11am-7pm, Su 11am-3pm).*
- **TOURS:** Guided walking tours *($ €4.50 per person. ⏰ 1½hr.)* leave from the Guggenheim tourism office at noon for the tour of Ensanche and Abandoibarra, and from the Arriaga Theater at 10am for the tour of the *casco viejo.*
- **CURRENCY EXCHANGE: Caja Laboral** *(Pl. Circular ⏰ Open June-Sept M-Th 8:30am-2:15pm and 4:15-7:45pm, F 8:30am-2:15pm; Oct-Mar M-F 8:30am-2:15pm and 4:15-7:45pm, Sa 8:30am-1:15pm)* or any of the banks along the Gran Vía.
- **LUGGAGE STORAGE:** Lockers are available in the **Termibús** bus station near the information booth. *($ €1. ⏰ Open M-F 7am-10pm, Sa-Su 8am-9pm.)*
- **POST OFFICE:** The main post office is in Abando, but there are branches all over the city. *(☎944 70 93 38 ⏰ Open M-F 8:30am-8:30pm, Sa 9:30am-2pm.)*

Emergency!

- **MUNICIPAL POLICE:** (*C. Luis Briñas, 14* ☎092)
- **MEDICAL SERVICES: Hospital de Basurto.** (*Av. Montevideo, 18* ☎112)

Getting There

By Bus

The **Termibús** bus station (*C. Gurtubay, 1* ☎944 39 50 77 *www.termibus.es*) is on the west side of Bilbao and has connections to the Euskotran, Metro, and city bus. Buses arrive from **Barcelona** (Ⓢ €42. ⏱ *7hr., at least 4 per day 7:15am-10:30pm*), **Burgos** (Ⓢ €11.50. ⏱ *2hr.; M-Sa 7-10 per day 7:15am-7pm, Su 8 per day 10:30am-10:30pm*), **Madrid** (Ⓢ €27.20. ⏱ *5hr.; M-Sa 13 per day 7am-1:30am, Su 15 per day 9am-1:30am*), and **Santiago de Compostela** (Ⓢ €50. ⏱ *9-12hr.; M-Th and Sa 3 per day 8:30am-11:15pm, F and Su 5 per day 8:30am-11:15pm*).

By Train

Bilbao has three train stations: **Euskotren** (☎902 54 32 10 *www.euskotren.es*) arrives at **Estación de Atxuri**, just east of the *casco viejo;* **FEVE** trains (☎944 24 45 12 *www. feve.es*) arrive at **Estación de Santander,** across the river from the *casco viejo;* and **RENFE** (☎902 10 94 20 *www.renfe.es*) trains arrive at **Estación de Abando.** The Euskotren runs to Bilbao from **San Sebastián.** (Ⓢ €6.20. ⏱ *2hr.; 17-18 per day M-F 6am-8:30pm, Sa-Su 7am-8:30pm.*) FEVE arrives at Bilbao from **León.** (Ⓢ €22. ⏱ *7½hr.; daily 2pm.*) **RENFE** goes to Bilbao from **Barcelona** (Ⓢ €40. ⏱ *6½hr.; M-Sa 2 per day 7:30am and 3:30pm, Su 3:30pm*), **León** (Ⓢ €18-29. ⏱ *5hr.; daily 3pm*), **Logroño** (Ⓢ €13-21. ⏱ *2½hr.; M-Sa 11:24am and 7:25pm, Su 7:25pm*), **Madrid** (Ⓢ €29-49. ⏱ *5hr.; M-F 8am and 4pm, Sa 8am, Su 4pm*), and **Salamanca** (Ⓢ €19-32. ⏱ *6hr., daily 10:30am*).

By Plane

Loiu Airport (*www.aena.es*) has about 25 flights per day from Barcelona and Madrid and other flights from all over Europe. The airport is about 6 mi. out of Bilbao; **BizkaiBus** (Ⓢ €1.10. ⏱ *25min., every 30min. 6:15am-midnight*). from **Pl. Moyúa** goes to the airport, and **taxis** to the airport usually run about €20.

Getting Around

While **walking** is always the cheapest way to get around, Bilbao is not a small city, and getting from the *casco viejo* to the Guggenheim on foot can be a schlep. Fortunately, Bilbao has some very convenient alternatives.

By Light Rail

If you're going to be in Bilbao for longer than a day, get a **creditrans** card, which cuts the price of all public transportation nearly in half. The **EuskoTran** (☎902 54 32 10 *www.euskotren.es/ euskotran* Ⓢ €1.25), a futuristic light rail line, runs along the river. Its stops include the bus terminal, Guggenheim Museum, *casco viejo,* and Atxuri EuskoTren station.

By Metro

The brand-new Metro (☎944 25 40 00 *www.metrobilbao.net* Ⓢ €1.40) is more suited for travel between the city center and the suburbs, but it's a very quick way to get from one side of town to the other. Stops include Deusto, San Mamés (bus terminal), Indautxu, Moyua, Abando, and Casco Viejo. Don't lose or throw away your ticket, as you'll need it to exit.

By Bus

The **Bilbobús** (☎944 79 09 81 *www.bilbao.net* Ⓢ €1.20, €0.60 with creditrans card) goes all over the city; check their online map for route information. **BizkaiBus** (☎902 22 22 65) goes between Bilbao and the airport and to some other suburbs.

By Taxi

Taxi services include **TeleTaxi Bilbao** (☎944 10 21 21 *www.teletaxibilbao.com*) and **Radio Taxi Bilbao** (☎944 44 88 88 *www.taxibilbao.es*). Taxi stands can be found in the *casco viejo* at the Puente de Arenal and Puente de San Antón bridges as well as at the northwest and southeast corners of the *casco.* On the other side of the river, stands can be found at the Museo de Bellas Artes, Museo Guggenheim, and various points throughout the city.

THE CAMINO

Many travelers, particularly those who do not hail from Europe, have never heard of the Camino—or if they have, they know it mainly as something from their medieval history textbooks. But the ▨**Camino de Santiago** (St. James' Way), the **pilgrimage route to Santiago de Compostela** from starting points all over Europe, has been a constant phenomenon from the Middle Ages to the present day. In recent years it has experienced a remarkable resurgence, bolstered by efforts from the European Union and Spanish governments, as well as by its appearance in popular novels from Brazil to South Korea. The most popular route is the ▨**Camino Francés** (French Way), which begins in the French Pyrenees and cuts across the Castilian plain, but the **Camino del Norte** (Northern Way) along the Cantabrian coast is also well traveled. Travelers use their feet, their bikes, or their ▨**horses** to go hundreds of miles the old-fashioned way; some do it for the spiritual journey, others simply for the **adventure**. The Camino is most heavily traveled in years in which St. James' Day (July 25) falls on a Sunday, which means it's a **Holy Year**—in Holy Years, pilgrims who have their official credentials (passport-like books stamped and dated at each stop along the way), have walked the last 100km or biked the last 200km, profess a spiritual motivation, attend mass at Santiago de Compostela, confess, and do a work of charity receive a full indulgence for their sins. The last Holy Year was 2010; the next will be in 2021. Of course, all the cities along the way are worth seeing even if you're not looking for pardon from the church for your sins, or if you're taking a bus instead of getting there using the power of your own ▨**feet,** though you may draw some ▨**dirty looks** from the die-hard **pilgrims.**

greatest hits

- **PAPAL BULLS.** Follow the steps of many a *papa* and make a pilgrimage down the Camino. You get cheaper lodging, better street cred, and maybe even an eternal reward.
- **RUNNING BULLS.** You've heard the stories, you've seen the news stories, but you have to experience Pamplona's fiesta for yourself (p. 321).
- **IN THE BULL PEN.** Should Spain ever need his swordfighting services again, El Cid is resting in the Catedral de Burgos (p. 331).

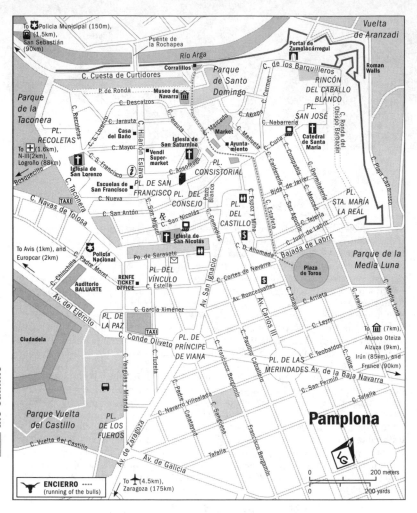

To ✚ Policia Municipal (150m),
🚌 (1.5km),
San Sebastián
(90km)

Puente de
la Rochapea

Río Arga

Corrallilos

Vuelta
de Aranzadi

C. Cuesta de Curtidores

Portal de
Zumalacárregui

Roman
Walls

Parque
de Santo
Domingo

C. de los Barquilleros

RINCÓN
DEL CABALLO
BLANCO

P. de Ronda

Museo de
Navarra 🏛

Parque
de la
Taconera

C. Descalzos

C. Jarauta

C. Jarauta

C. Attapa

C. Carmen

C. Mercado

PL.
SAN JOSÉ

C. Ronda del
Obispo Barbazán

PL.
RECOLETAS

C. Recoletas

Casa
del Baño

Iglesia de
San Saturnino

Market

C. Nabarrería

Catedral
de Santa
María

C. Mayor

Vendi
Super-
market

C. Ansoleaga

C. Mañueta

Ayunta-
miento

C. Cuña

C. Plaza Caparroso

To ✚ (1.6km),
N-III(2km),
Logroño (88km)

C. S. Francisco

Iglesia de
San Lorenzo

PL.
CONSISTORIAL

C. Compañía

C. Calderería

Bjda. de Javier

C. Dormitalería

PL.
STA. MARÍA
LA REAL

Bosquecillo

C. Taconera

Escuelas de
San Francisco

PL. DE SAN
FRANCISCO

PL. DEL
CONSEJO

C. San Agustín

C. Mercado

C. Navas de Tolosa

TAXI

C. Nueva

C. San Miguel

C. San Nicolás

PL.
DEL
CASTILLO

C. Espoz y Mina

C. Estafeta

C. San Agustín

C. Tejería

C. San Antón

℞

C. San Nicolás

C. Comedias

Iglesia de
San Nicolás

C. D. Ahumada

C. Juan de Labrit

To Avis (1km), and
Europcar (2km)

C. Chinchilla

C. Padre Moret

Po. de Sarasate

Bajada de Labrit

Parque de la
Media Luna

Policia
Nacional

PL. DEL
VÍNCULO

Plaza
de Toros

C. Media Luna

Auditorio
BALUARTE

RENFE
TICKET
OFFICE

C. Estella

C. Cortes de Navarra

Av. Roncesvalles

C. Arrieta

C. Arga

Av. del Ejército

C. García Ximénez

C. San Ignacio

Av. Carlos III

C. Anaya

C. Leyre

To 🏛 (7km),
Museo Oteiza
Alzuza (9km),
Irún (85km), and
France (90km)

Ciudadela

PL. DE
LA PAZ

C. Conde Oliveto

TAXI

PL. DE
PRÍNCIPE
DE VIANA

C. Francisco Bergamín

C. Paulino Caballero

C. Teobaldos

C. Olite

PL. DE LAS
MERINDADES

Av. de la Baja Navarra

the camino

C. Yangüas y Miranda

C. Tudela

C. San Fermín

C. Tafalla

Parque Vuelta
del Castillo

PL.
DE LOS
FUEROS

C. Navarro Villoslada

C. Padre Calatayud

C. Sanduesa

C. Francisco Bergamín

Pamplona

C. Vuelta del Castillo

Av. de Zaragoza

Tafalla

Av. de Galicia

Tafalla

N

0   200 meters

0   200 yards

🐂 ENCIERRO ····
(running of the bulls)

To ⚓ (4.5km),
Zaragoza (175km)

While being a pilgrim comes with certain negative aspects (you smell, you're tired), one benefit is staying in the pilgrim-exclusive hostels that line El Camino and are oh-so-wonderfully cheap. These hostels have seen thousands of other travelers that also smell and are tired, so they know how to take care of you. All you have to do is show your Camino pilgrim passport, which you can obtain when you begin your route. These hostels, called *refugios* in Spain, are great places to meet other travelers and maybe find a couple of students from another country with whom you can hike to the next town. The Camino is all about solidarity, so don't be surprised by communal meals and offers of help—it's all part of the experience.

pamplona *iruña* ☎948

If people know one thing about Pamplona (pop. 200,000), it's the **Running of the Bulls.** If they know two things about Pamplona, it's the **Running of the Bulls** and the **earth-shattering week of partying** that accompanies the former. Hemingway may have made this town famous in *The Sun Also Rises*, but Pamplona has had no trouble keeping itself in the headlines. The week of *los Fermines* fills the city to the gills with revelers, and the high demand leads to skyrocketing prices. Pamplona takes its name from the Roman general Pompey, who is said to have founded the town in the first century BCE, after which it grew and developed under the Romans and later the Visigoths. Despite its Roman history, though, Pamplona has a strong sense of its **Basque heritage:** almost all public signage in Pamplona (*Iruña* in Basque) is in both *castellano* and Basque (*euskera* in Basque). The heavily fortified Pamplona has been a border city since the eighth century, caught between various Iberian kingdoms, France, and Spain. Since the Middle Ages, the *Camino de Santiago* has connected Pamplona with the rest of Europe across the Pyrenees and has kept it economically and culturally prosperous. The *casco antiguo* and nearby areas are largely tourist-oriented, but are still heavily frequented by locals in the low season.

ORIENTATION

Most of the action in Pamplona takes place east of the parks (**la Ciudadela** and Parque de la Taconera) and to the south and west of the río Arga. At the north end of this area is the *casco antiguo*, the old quarter, which has narrow streets lined with shops, bars, and plazas. The **Catedral** is in the *casco's* northeast corner; the massive **Pl. del Castillo** is in the center at the south end. The wide, pedestrian *Av. Carlos III* connects the *casco* to the *segundo ensanche*, an urban zone certainly newer than the *casco*, but not without its own charm. The **Av. de la Baja Navarra** is the city's main thoroughfare, and it cuts east-west through the *segundo ensanche*, with the **bus station** at its western end.

ACCOMMODATIONS

Most of the accommodations in Pamplona are in the *casco antiguo*. Cheaper and quieter places can be found in the **segundo ensanche.** The city's just not big enough to worry about being 3 blocks away from all the action.

HOSTEL HEMINGWAY ✆⊗(ᵠ) HOSTEL ❶

C. Amaya, 26, 1izq. (2nd fl., on the left)   ☎948 98 38 84 www.hostelhemingway.com

Traveling alone and looking for a group to go tapas-tasting or barhopping with? This recently opened hostel's communal spaces (like its common area with a giant TV) create instant bonds among the young crowds that stay here, facilitated

pamplona · accommodations

by the fact that English is Hemingway's *lingua franca*. The hostel was opened in 2009 by three young friends traveling through Pamplona who realized there wasn't a hostel in town save those for pilgrims, so they decided to open their own. The shared bedrooms aren't exactly spacious, and it's in the *segundo ensanche*, a short walk from the *casco antiguo*, but the free breakfast and camaraderie among guests and hosts more than make up for it.

✠ *From bus station, take Av. de la Baja Navarra east 8 blocks, then right on C. Amaya for 3 blocks.* **i** *Breakfast included. Laundry €3 wash, dry €4. Kitchen available. All rooms with shared bath. Computers with internet €0.50 per 15min.; €1.50 per hr.* Ⓢ *6-bed dorms €19; 4-bed €20. Singles €21; doubles €22; Su-Th €15 for pilgrims with accreditation. During San Fermín €55/€65/€14. Bike rental €2 per 2hr., €3 per 4hr.* Ⓣ *Reception 8am-midnight, but keys are available to guests with a €10 deposit.*

PENSIÓN ARRIETA
⦿⊗ PENSIÓN ❹

C. Arrieta, 27., 1izq. 2nd fl. on the left ☎948 22 84 59 🖳www.pensionarrieta.net

Though it's located a few blocks out of the *casco antiguo* in a more modern part of town, this *pensión* is close to both the wide, pedestrian Av. de Carlos III, and the bus station. The rooms are large and bright, and don't worry about that squawking noise—the house parrot goes to sleep at night, so he won't keep you up.

✠ *From bus station, take Av. de la Baja Navarra east, then left onto C. Caballero, then right onto C. Arrieta. From casco antiguo, take Av. de Carlos III south, then right onto C. Arrieta.* **i** *Laundry service. English spoken.* Ⓢ *July 5-14 doubles €150, with bath €200; triples €200. Jul 15-Sept 15 singles €40; doubles €50; triples €60. Sept 16-July 4 €35/45/55.* Ⓣ *Reception 9am-8pm.*

PENSIÓN ESLAVA
⦿⊗ PENSIÓN ❶

C. Eslava, 13, 2nd fl. ☎948 22 15 58

A shrewd old woman operates this *pensión* on the second floor of a purple-painted building at the end of C. Eslava. The rooms are bare-bones: beds, closets, and windows. Some rooms come with a sink, while others have balconies looking onto one of the few relatively quiet streets in the *casco antiguo*. The few rooms here fill up quickly in the summer.

✠ *From Pl. San Francisco, take C. Eslava 3 blocks north.* **i** *Shared baths.* Ⓢ *Singles €15; doubles €20-25. During San Fermín singles €60-70; doubles €100.*

SIGHTS
👁

Walk around the **old quarter** enough and you're bound to see some historic sight that catches your eye. The northeast corner of the *casco*, by the cathedral, is one of the most beautiful areas of the town. Don't miss the **Pl. Consistorial,** with its unbelievably florid **city hall.**

CATEDRAL DE SANTA MARÍA Y MUSEO DIOCESANO
⦿⅊ CHURCH

C. Dormitalería, 3-5 ☎948 21 25 94 🖳www.catedraldepamplona.com

This Gothic cathedral was built over the course of the 15th century on and around the ruins of its 12th-century Romanesque predecessor, whose larder still stands. The larder is currently part of the museum, and may contain more silver and jewel-encrusted crosses than the entire rap music industry. The facade was added later, completed in 1799. The cloister is considered one of Europe's most beautiful, though it hides a dark secret: the numbers on the floor tiles correspond to tombs beneath them.

✠ *From Pl. del Castillo, head east on Bajada Javier 3 blocks, then left onto C. Dormitalería.* **i** *Facade undergoing renovations due to be completed in 2012, but the sides and rear of the cathedral are unaffected and can still be seen in all their Gothic splendor. Free information pamphlets with plenty of pictures available in English.* Ⓢ *€4, children €2.50, pilgrims €2, groups €3.35 per person.* Ⓣ *Mar 16-Nov 14 M-Sa 10am-7pm; Nov 15-Mar 15 M-Sa 10am-5pm.*

LA CIUDADELA
    ♿ PARK, HISTORIC SITE

Av. del Ejército
    ☏948 22 82 37

What would you do if you had an unused medieval fortress half the size of the *casco antiguo* just sitting around? If you were Pamplona, you'd make it a public park. *La Ciudadela* is a fascinating mix of vegetation and crumbling fortifications. Its a great place to lounge during the *siesta*, or while waiting until your bus leaves from the station next door.

⍒ *From Pl. del Castillo, take Paseo de Sarsate to C. Taconera, then left onto C. Chinchilla; the entrance is on the other side of Av. del Ejército.* Ⓞ *Free.* ☉ *Park open M-Sa 7:30am-9:30pm, Su 9am-9:30pm. Rotating art exhibitions open M-F 6-8:30pm, Sa 11am-2pm and 6-8:30pm, Su 11am-2pm.*

IGLESIA SAN LORENZO
    ♿ CHURCH

C. Mayor, 74
    ☏948 22 87 90

It's easy to forget amongst the constant flow of alcohol and adrenaline, but *San Fermín* is a religious festival, and the Capilla de San Fermín at the Iglesia San Lorenzo is where it all begins. This is the starting point of the procession in honor of San Fermín, whose 16th-century effigy can be found in a chapel inside.

⍒ *From Pl. del Castillo, take C. San Nicolás west to C. Taconera. Church is up 1 block on the right.* i *Be sure remain quiet while entering, as religious services may be taking place.* Ⓞ *Free.* ☉ *Open M-Sa 8am-12:30pm and 5:30-8:30pm, Su 8:30am-1:45pm and 5:30-8pm.*

FOOD
⌧

MESÓN PIRINEO
    🕬♿♿ TAPAS ❶

C. Estafeta, 41
    ☏948 20 77 02

This bar serves up great tapas and *pinchos* at some of the lowest prices around. Just look at the counter, find something you like, and order it; all the *tapas* are delicious and under €2. The *pincho* with mushrooms and ham and the *tapa* with *bacalao* (cod) are particularly tasty.

⍒ *From the Pl. del Castillo, head east one short block on Bajada Javier, then left onto C. Estafeta.* Ⓞ *Tapas and pinchos €1.80-5.* ☉ *Open daily 11am-3:30pm and 5:30pm-midnight.*

LA MEJILLONERA
    🕬♿♿ TAPAS ❶

C. Navarrería, 12
    ☏948 22 91 84

This *cervecería* and tapas bar is a favorite among locals who come to enjoy the *mejillones (mussels; €2.50-3)* from which the bar takes its name. The drinks cost about half what you could expect to pay a couple of blocks away at the Pl. del Castillo—€1.20 for a *caña* of beer, €1.50 for a sangría. The tapas selection is mostly seafood-based, but still varied. They also claim "the best *patatas bravas* in Pamplona."

⍒ *From Pl. del Castillo, head east on Bajada Javier, then left onto C. Calderería, then right onto C. Navarrería.* i *Standing room only.* Ⓞ *Tapas and mussels €2-5.* ☉ *Open M 6:30-11pm, Tu-Su 12:30-3pm and 6:30-11pm.*

CAFE-BAR IRUÑA
    🕬♿♿♿ CAFE ❸

Pl. del Castillo
    ☏948 22 20 64

This cafe, a staple of Pamplona's enormous central square since 1888, is a truly lovely place to sit outside, enjoy a drink, and peoplewatch. Their affordable *menú (€13)* is worth the slightly higher prices (*€2.50 for a caña of beer; €0.50 extra to be served outside*). Make sure to try their *bocadillos*, which put Jared and his Subway sandwiches to shame.

⍒ *In the center of the north side of the Pl. del Castillo.* Ⓞ *Entrees €7.50-11. Menú €13.* ☉ *Open M-Th 8am-10pm, F-Su 8am-2am; during San Fermín bar open daily 11am-10:30pm.*

pamplona • food

CASA PACO ⊘♿🍸 RESTAURANT ❸

C. Rincón de San Nicolás ☎948 22 51 05

The main draw of this restaurant, tucked away behind the Iglesia San Nicolás, is the *menú (€13),* which comes with *vino tinto* and bread (most places charge for the bread basket they give you, whether you've requested it or not). It's a great deal, as long as you stick to the basics: pasta for the first course, *lomo* (pork) or *bistec* (steak) with fries as the next, and *flan* for dessert.

➜ From the Pl. del Castillo, head west on C. San Nicolás for 2 blocks, then make 2 subsequent lefts. Ⓢ Entrees €10-17. Menú €13 including bread and wine. ⏰ Open M 9:30am-5pm, Tu-Th 9:30am-5pm and 7:30-10pm, F-Sa 9:30am-5pm and 7:30-11pm; during San Fermín open daily 8:30am-6pm and 9pm-1am.

NIGHTLIFE 🌙

The claustrophobic streets of the **casco antiguo** are the main arteries of the Pamplona nightlife scene. Most of the bars are more or less the same, and after a couple of minutes of wandering around to find one with the kind of crowd you're looking for (younger, older, loud, mellow—they often change from weekend to weekend and vary by night), head in and order. The main locales for this type of barhopping are C. San Nicolás, C. San Gregorio, C. Caldereria, C. Navarrería, and C. San Agustín, but **following the shouts** echoing down the streets can also help you start your night. Fair warning: things are dead around here on Sunday or Monday nights. But of course, during *los Sanfermines*, the party practically never stops.

BISTROT CATEDRAL 💳♿🍸 BAR, LOUNGE

C. Navarrería, 20 ☎948 21 01 52 💻www.bistrotcatedral.com

This bar and lounge near the cathedral tries to be a little trendier than it actually is—the super-hip décor is a couple of notches cooler than its clientele—but it's still a good change of pace from its neighbors. It's less of a bar than the establishments nearby—come to hang hip rather than drown in your cups.

➜ From Pl. del Castillo, take Bajada de Javier east 4 blocks, then left on C. Dormitalería, then left on C. Navarrería. Ⓢ Mixed drinks €4-9, beer €2. ⏰ Open Su-W 10am-midnight, Th 10am-1am, F 10am-2:30am.

DISCOTECA REVERENDOS 💳⛔🍸 CLUB

C. Monasterio Velate, 5 ☎948 26 15 93 💻www.reverendos.com

For those who don't mind a little evening stroll (20-30min. from *casco antiguo*), head to the *barrio de San Juan.* This futuristic *discoteca* tends to draw a big student crowd from the nearby university and pumps house music and hip hop until the early morning.

➜ Follow Av. de la Baja Navarra west, then follow Av. del Ejército along the northern edge of la Ciudadela, then take a slight left onto Av. de Bayona, then stay right at the fork onto C. Monasterio Velate for 2 blocks; Reverendos is on the left. Ⓢ Mixed drinks €6-11. ⏰ Open M-Th 12:30-6am, F-Sa 12:30-6:30am, Su 12:30-6am.

FIESTA DE SAN FERMÍN 🎆

Las Fiestas de San Fermín, also known as **los Sanfermines,** is considered by many the greatest, **wildest week of partying in Europe** (or anywhere, for that matter). The nine-day festival encapsulates two crucial facets of Navarra's culture: millennia-old religious conservatism and a fervent desire to **party like it's going out of style.** The festival celebrates the third-century Saint Fermin *(San Fermín)* of Amiens, Navarra's patron saint and first bishop of Pamplona, whose mentor, Saint Saturninus, was martyred by being dragged to death after having his feet tied to a bull. The religious components of the *fiesta* take place alongside the nonstop debauchery of the red-scarved revelers, and despite the city's relatively small size, the two manage to coexist.

The *Sanfermines* begin the morning of July 6, when the entire city of Pamplona and visitors from around the world gather at the Pl. Consistorial. At noon (though the plaza is too crowded to get into by 10am), the mayor appears amid shouts and traditional *San Fermín* cheers and songs, such as the famous *"Uno de enero, dos de febrero, tres de marzo, cuatro de abril, cinco de mayo, seis de junio, siete de julio, ¡San Fermín! A Pamplona hemos de ir, con una media, con una media, a Pamplona hemos de ir, con una media y un calcetín."* ("January 1, February 2, March 3, April 4, May 5, June 6, July 7, San Fermín! To Pamplona we must go, with a stocking, with a stocking, to Pamplona we must go, with a stocking and a sock!") The mayor then fires a rocket from his balcony and yells in Spanish and Basque, "People of Pamplona! Long live *San Fermín!*" Whatever can be found (food, clothing, trash, small animals) is then thrown up in the air and rained down on the partiers, as the *fiesta* begins and everyone fans out from the Pl. del Consistorial to fill the streets of the *casco antiguo*, which won't empty again for another nine days. The religious side of the festival makes an appearance with the **procession of San Fermín** at 10am on July 7, when church and city officials march the 16th-century statue of *San Fermín* from its home in the **Iglesia de San Lorenzo** through the *casco antiguo*, in the hope that it will protect the runners in return for the extravagant adulation.

THE RUNNING OF THE BULLS
Encierro route

The most famous component of *los Sanfermines* is the *encierro*, the running of the bulls each day July 7-13 at 8am. The *encierro's* roots lie in the Middle Ages, when the bulls would be driven at dawn from the *corralillos* outside the city walls to certain death at the *plaza de toros*. At some point, young men began a tradition of running in front of the bulls during this daily routine, an act of lunacy and courage much like riding on top of subway cars today. Though the authorities tried to stop this dangerous ritual for the first couple of centuries of its establishment, they eventually decided to embrace it. In 1776, the Pamplona City Council passed a law that fences must be put up along the whole route, and thus began the centuries-old tradition. The route used for the *encierro* today has been in place since 1927. At exactly 8am the first *txupinazo* (rocket, pronounced and sometimes spelled *chupinazo*) is set off and the *encierro* begins. The first segment is a steep uphill section that is quite dangerous, as the bulls handle the incline much better than the bipedal humans. Once all the bulls are in the street, the second *txupinazo* is set off. The runners—who have just finished praying for San Fermín's blessing—and bulls then go through the Pl. Consistorial, past the *Ayuntamiento* (town hall), and make a left turn and then a 90° right turn. At this last turn, the Mercaderes bend, and the speeding bulls tend to skid and pile up against the wall; the runners who aren't pinned use this brief distraction to get away. After another few hundred yards, they all enter the bullring (cue *txupinazo* number three), where the bulls are rounded up and put into holding pens (final *txupinazo*) for bullfights later in the day. For those who think about running with the bulls and hear their mother's voice unbidden in the back of their heads shrieking, **"You're going to do WHAT?"** the *encierro* can be watched from a safe distance, in the bullring or behind the fences. Those who wish to watch the spectacle at the *plaza de toros* should arrive no later than 6:30am, as tickets (€4.50-6) go on sale at 7am at the bullring box office. There is a free section, but the danger of suffocation and trampling is significantly higher. To watch from behind the fences, arrive as early as you can get up (or as late as you can stay up, as the case may be), around 6am to get a decent spot. If you want to see one of the bullfights *(Jul 7-13, 6:30pm)*, chances are pretty slim that you'll get in, as only a few tickets are on sale each day; the rest belong to season ticket-holders. Some travelers purport that the easiest way to procure tickets is to buy them from scalpers *(usually €50 or higher; lower as the start of the fight approaches)*.

pamplona · fiesta de san fermín

THE PARTY.
Plaza del Castillo

Seriously. This is The Party, capital T. Nine days of chaos, shennanigans, fireworks, dancing, singing, music, drinking, and just about anything else you can think of adding to make things crazier. Sleeping often occurs (when it does occur, that is) in streets, parks, or any free square inch that can be found in the packed city. Many of the bars are open 23hr. per day—they are legally obligated to close 1hr. each day to clean up a bit—or at least give the drunken masses a second to breathe between beers. The Pl. del Castillo, in the heart of the *casco antiguo* but close to the *segundo ensanche*, is the center of this orgiastic glory. The plaza becomes one massive 24hr. *discoteca*, with the ever-swelling sea of partiers dressed in white with red *fajas (sashes; about €6)* and *pañuelos (handkerchiefs; €2-5)*, which can be bought at stands throughout Pamplona. At midnight on July 14, the festival officially ends, as the revelers that remain sing the *Pobre de mí: "Pobre de mí, pobre de mí, que se han acabado las Fiestas de San Fermín."* ("Woe is me, woe is me, *San Fermín* has ended.")

ESSENTIALS   🔢
Practicalities

- **TOURIST OFFICE:** The tourist office has excellent maps and information on the city of Pamplona, as well as on the region of Navarra and *camino*-specific sights. It also offers an essential **San Fermin Fiesta Programme** guide, with just about everything you would want to know about the *encierro* and festivals. Ask about guided tours. English, French, and ⛰**Basque** spoken. *(C. Eslava, 1, on northwest corner of Pl. San Francisco* ☎*848 42 04 20* 💻*www.turismo.navarra.es* 🕐 *Open Sept 22-June 20 M-Sa 10am-2pm and 4-7pm, Su 10am-2pm; June 21-Sept 21 M-F 9am-6pm, Sa 9am-2pm and 4-6pm, Su 10am-2pm; San Fermín daily 9am-2pm and 3-5pm.)*

- **CURRENCY EXCHANGE:** The **Banco Santander Central Hispano** has a 24hr. **ATM** and will exchange American Express travelers checks commission-free if they are for euros. *(Pl. del Castillo, 21, and Paseo Sarasate, 15* ☎*948 20 86 00* 🕐 *Open daily Apr-Sep M-F 8:30am-2pm; Oct-Apr M-F 8:30am-2pm, Sa 8:30am-1pm; during San Fermín open M-F 9:30am-noon.)*

- **LUGGAGE STORAGE:** is available at the bus station for €5.10 per day. *(🕐 Open M-Sa 6:15am-9:30pm, Su 6:30am-1:30pm and 2-9:30pm; closed for San Fermín, when the* **Escuelas de San Francisco,** *across Pl. San Francisco from the library, is open instead.* ***i*** *Passport or ID required.* 🕐 *Open 24hr. Jul 4-Jul 16 8am-2pm.* 💲 *€3.40 per day.)*

- **LAUDROMAT AND PUBLIC BATHS:** The **Casa del Baño** offers wash-and-dry services as well as showering facilities. *(C. Eslava, 9* ☎*948 22 17 38* 💲 *Wash and dry €10.60. Showers €1.10.* 🕐 *Open M-Sa 8:30am-8pm, Su 9am-2pm. Wash and dry not offered during San Fermín.)*

- **INTERNET ACCESS:** For **free internet access,** go to the **library** on Pl. San Francisco. *(🕐 Open Sept-May M-F 8:30am-8:45pm, Sa 8:30am-1:45pm; Jun-Aug M-F 8:30am-12:30pm. During San Fermín open M-F 12:15-1:45pm.)*

- **POST OFFICE:** The **post office** is just a couple minutes' walk from the Pl. del Castillo. *(Paseo de Sarasate, 9* ☎*948 20 68 40* 🕐 *Open M-F 8:30am-8:30pm, Sa 9:30am-2pm. Jul 6 9am-2pm. Closed Jul 7.* ***i*** *If you're walking the camino, it will send any excess luggage—up to 20kg—to Santiago to await your arrival (up to €13.40.)*

- **POSTAL CODE:** 31001.

Emergency!

- **EMERGENCY NUMBERS: Municipal police** are at C. Monasterio de Irache, 2 *(☎092 or 948 42 06 40).* **National police** are at C. General Chinchilla, 3 *(☎091).*
- **24HR. PHARMACIES: Farmacia Yangüas** is located opposite the bus station. *(C. Yangüas y Miranda, 17 ☎948 24 50 30 🖳www.farmayanguas.com ⏰ Open 24hr.)*
- **MEDICAL SERVICES:** The **Hospital de Navarra** is at the corner of C. Irunlarrea and Av. de Pío XII *(C. Irunlarrea, 3 ☎848 42 22 22 or ☎112 for emergencies).* During *San Fermín*, the **Red Cross** sets up stations at the bus station, along the *corrida*, and at various points in the *casco antiguo.*

Getting There

By Bus

The bus station is located along the eastern edge of la Ciudadela *(Av. de Yangüas y Miranda ☎948 20 35 66 🖳www.estaciondeautobusesdepamplona.com ⏰ Open daily 6:30am-11pm).* Buses arrive from: **Barcelona** *($ €31-37. ⏰ 6hr.; M-Sa 3 per day 7:30am-3:35pm, Su 5 per day 7:30am-11:30pm);* **Bilbao** *($ €13. ⏰ 2½-3hr.; M-Sa 6 per day 7am-8:30pm, Su 5 per day 8:30am-8pm);* **Irún** *($ €7. ⏰ 2hr.; 1 per day M-Sa 8am, Su 9am);* **Logroño** *($ €8. ⏰ 2hr.; M-F 9 per day 6:45am-8pm, Sa 7 per day 7:45am-8pm, Su 5 per day 10am-8pm);* **Madrid** *($ €38. ⏰ 5¾hr., M-Th 6 per day 1am-7:30pm, F 7 per day 1am-7:30pm, Sa-Su 6 per day 1am-7:30pm);* **San Sebastián** *($ €7. ⏰ 1¼-2hr.; M-Th 13 per day 7am-8:15pm, F 17 per day 7am-9:15pm, Sa 13 per day 7am-8:15pm, Su 15 per day 7am-9:15pm).*

By Train

The RENFE train station *(☎902 24 02 02 ⏰ Open M-Sa 6am-11:30pm, Su 8am-11:30pm)* is a bit far away from the *casco antiguo*, but is serviced by bus #9 *(€1.10)*, which goes to the center of town in about 15min. Trains arrive from **Barcelona** *($ €56, if booked a week in advance €34. ⏰ 3¾hr.; M, Tu, Th, Sa 3 per day 7:35am-3:35pm, W, F, Su 4 per day 7:35am-4:35pm)* and **Madrid.** *($ €56, if booked a week in advance €33. ⏰ 3hr.; M-F 4 per day 7:35am-7:35pm, Sa 3 per day 7:35am-3:05pm, Su 3 per day 10:35am-7:35pm.)*

By Plane

Aeropuerto de Pamplona-Noáin *(☎902 40 47 04 🖳www.aena.es)*, about 4mi. out of town, is serviced by bus #21 *(€1.10).* Planes arrive from destinations throughout Spain; check **Iberia's** website *(🖳www.iberia.es)* or **TAP-Air Portugal's** *(🖳www.flytap.com)* for prices and schedules, as they vary.

Getting Around

The easiest way to get around Pamplona is **by foot.** The *casco antiguo* is tiny, and the *segundo ensanche* is not so big that you can't walk from one end to the other in 10min. There is a **bus** system *(☎901 50 25 03 🖳www.mcp.es/tuc/index.asp $ €1.10, with tarjeta monedero €0.56; free transfers. Wheelchair-accessible except lines #13, 21, and 23).* The #4, 10, 12, 13, and 18 buses go to the **bus station;** bus #9 goes to the **RENFE train station,** and bus #21 goes to the **Aeropuerto de Pamplona-Noáin. Taxi** stands near the *casco antiguo* and *segundo ensanche* can be found at Hotel 3 Reyes (C. Navas de Tolosa, 25), Pl. del Vínculo (intersection of C. de Estella and C. de Sancho "El Mayor"), Pl. Duque de Ahumada (just south of Pl. del Castillo, on east edge of Av. Carlos III), C. Amaya between Av. de la Baja Navarra and C. Teobaldos, Pl. de la Cruz (Bergamín, 6), inside and outside the bus station, and at Pl. Conde Rodezno; there is also a stand at the RENFE station. Alternatively, call Teletaxi San Fermín *(☎948 23 23 00 or ☎948 35 13 35).*

logroño ☎941

The Roman town that stood where Logroño is today (if it's a town and it's in southern or western Europe, it's safe to assume the Romans founded it) was destroyed by the Visigoths in the sixth century; the city's current incarnation began around that time. The name Logroño most likely comes from the Latin *illo* ("that") and the Germanic *gronio* ("river's ford"); in a similar multicultural mishmash, the Romance culture in Logroño has grown and flourished out of the ruins left by the Goths. The city owes much of its local prominence to its location along the pilgrimage route known as the **Camino de Santiago,** which has made Logroño a hub of travel and commerce since the Middle Ages. This town was also strategically important in the Middle Ages, as it was located near the border between Castile, Navarre, and Aragón. Today, Logroño is the capital of the **Comunidad Autónoma de La Rioja** and is home to over 150,000 citizens. The region is famous for its 👍**wines,** which make up a large portion of the region's economy and draw oenophiles from around the world. Since Logroño tends to be a bit off the typical tourist's path, there is more of a focus on commerce than on tourism, and it is clear that this is a modern, growing city that is open to tourism but not driven by it.

ORIENTATION ✴

Logroño can essentially be divided into two sections: the **casco antiguo** (old quarter) and **everywhere else.** The *casco* is bordered by the Río Ebro to the north and the **Paseo del Espolón** (a large open area, somewhere between a park and a plaza) on the south, and it is cut into quarters by the C. Sagasta (north-south) and the C. Portales (east-west). The **Gran Vía Rey Juan Carlos I,** lined with tall apartment and office buildings, is the main east-west thoroughfare and is generally seen as the old town's southern border. The **Calle del General Vara de Rey** is the major north-south avenue and goes past the **bus station** and **train station**. The train station's entrance is temporarily on the side of the tracks away from the center of town; from the station, head right on C. Marqués de Larios, which bends left and becomes C. Hermanos Hircio; then turn right at C. Poeta Prudencio and right on C. del General Vara de Rey, which goes to the Paseo del Espolón.

ACCOMMODATIONS 🏠

Most hotels and *hostals* in Logroño can be found in the **casco antiguo,** but the more modern living areas have better prices and aren't too far away. Besides, living in an apartment building in a residential neighborhood where it seems like only five tourists have been since the city's founding in the 11th century makes you really 👍**feel like a badass local.**

👍 PENSIÓN REY PASTOR — 💳🚭📶 PENSIÓN [2]

C. Marqués de Murrieta, 35, 1D, 2nd fl. ☎630 50 23 50 🖥www.pensionreypastor.com

About a 10min. walk from the *casco antiguo*, this *pensión* is in an apartment building in a more modern part of town, across the street from two supermarkets and surrounded by shops and restaurants. The affordably priced rooms with free Wi-Fi and a TV are spacious and cheerfully decorated with orange walls and rainbow-colored comforters.

➜ From the casco antiguo, follow C. Portales to Pl. Alférez Provisional, then take C. Marqués de Murrieta, passing through the Gran Vía. From the bus or train stations, take C. del General Vara de Rey to the Gran Vía, then make a left; make another left at the C. Marqués de Murrieta. ℹ Shared baths. $ Singles €20; doubles €30; triples €55. F-Sa €25/49/69. ⏰ Reception 8am-midnight.

HOSTAL LA NUMANTINA — 💳🚭📶 HOSTAL [3]

C. Sagasta, 4, 2nd fl. ☎941 25 14 11 🖥www.hostalnumantina.com

Just around the corner from the Cathedral and the Paseo del Espolón, La Numantina's rooms are comfortable and convenient. The lounge, with soft sofas and a flatscreen TV, is a great place to plan the day ahead or crash after furious sightseeing. The private bathrooms have bathtubs to soak away the stress of travel, but big spenders can splurge on a massage as well *(€45).*

On C. Sagasta in the casco antiguo, one block north of the Paseo del Espolón. ℹ Private baths, common area with sofas, fridge with drinks (€1). $ Singles €35; doubles €58. ⏰ Reception 24hr.

ASOCIACIÓN RIOJANA DE AMIGOS DEL CAMINO DE SANTIAGO ALBERGUE [1]

Ruavieja, 32 (enter on Travesado Palacio) ☎941 26 02 34 or 941 23 92 01 🖥www.asantiago.org

This is probably the cheapest place you'll find to spend a night in Logroño (€3), but it's just for pilgrims walking the Camino de Santiago. If you don't have a stamped pilgrim passport and a backpack, you will be turned away. To stay in one of their 88 beds (you share a room with 21 of your closest new friends), you must come *"andando, a caballo, o en bicicleta* " ("on foot, on horse, or on bicycle"), and beds are given on a first-come, first-served basis.

Head north on C. Sagasta, then right at C. Ruavieja. ℹ Must have pilgrim passport (available at Federación Española Asociaciones de Amigos del Camino de Santiago, C. Ruavieja, 3 bajo, open M-F 8am-3pm) and stamp from Logroño (available at tourism office or cathedral). $ €3. ⏰ Backpack pickup and showers noon-4pm. Reception open 4-10pm. Lights-out 10pm.

FONDA BILBAÍNA HOSTAL [2]

C. Capitán Eduardo Gallarza, 10, 2nd fl. ☎941 25 42 26 or 616 72 40 85

This *hostal* is right in the center of town and can get a bit noisy (though the stalled construction going on down the street won't be much trouble while the recession keeps up). After climbing up from the dimly lit but elegantly tiled entryway, travelers are greeted with bright rooms, big beds, and TVs. Don't stay here, however, if you can't stand the smell of cigarette smoke—many rooms smell like the Marlboro Man.

Take C. Sagasta into the casco antiguo, turn left on C. Hermanos Moroy, and then right on C. Capitán Eduardo Gallarza. ℹ Private bath available. Washing machines €3. $ Singles €25; doubles €36-40. ⏰ Reception 24hr.

SIGHTS

MUSEO WÜRTH ♿ MUSEUM

Av. de los Cameros, 86-88 ☎941 01 04 10 🖥www.museowurth.es

Don't let this museum's location (in an industrial park in Agoncillas, 15min. by car from Logroño) drive you away; instead, let the museum drive you to it with its complimentary bus service. Opened in 2007 by industrial manufacturing company Würth Spain, the Museo Würth's architecturally stunning white cement, red steel, and tinted glass building stands in stark contrast to the cheaply made industrial buildings of the surrounding *polígono industrial.* Inside, bright and spacious galleries display works from the Würth collection—mostly 20th-century European art, including works by Picasso and Braque—and exhibitions by contemporary artists based in Spain and around the world.

Free bus provided by museum (large white coach, not a city bus) on M, W, F at 6pm (returns 8pm); Tu, Th varies, check schedule; Sa at 11:30am and 6pm (returns 2pm and 8pm), Su at 11:30am (returns 2pm). Bus leaves from Logroño's Glorieta del Doctor Zubía bus stop $ Free. ⏰ Open M-Sa 10am-8pm, Su 10am-3pm. Guided visits M-Sa 6:30pm, Su noon.

EL CUBO DEL REVELLÍN ♿ MUSEUM, HISTORICAL SITE

C. Once de Junio, 6 ☎941 50 31 16 🖥www.logro-o.org/cubo_revellin/index.htm

El Cubo, the artillery fortification at the northwest corner of Logroño's city walls, was built in the 1520s when Logroño was Castile's main stronghold on the border with Navarre. Today, it houses a museum opened in 2006 after renovations and restoration. The old structure's architecture represents a middle phase between medieval and more modern building techniques, while the recent glass, metal, and faux-old-wood additions highlight the best of modern design.

*⇢Just up C. Once de Junio from the tourism office. **i** Call ahead or email cubodelrevellin@logro-o.org for tours. Free 6min. film every 15min. $ Free. ⏰ Open W 10am-1pm; Th-F 10am-1-pm and 5-8pm, Sa 11am-2pm and 5-8pm; Su 11am-2pm.*

SALA AMÓS SALVADOR ♿ MUSEUM

C. Once de Junio ☎941 25 92 02 🖥www.logro-o.org/culturalrioja/sala_amos.htm

On the northwestern edge of the *casco antiguo* is a building that has been a convent, military hospital, barracks, warehouse, jail, tobacco factory, and, most recently, a space for art exhibitions. It still says "Fábrica de Tabacos" above the entrance, but the building is now 640 sq. ft. of exhibition space where tourists and locals can come for free to browse an exhibition of photography, sculpture, or whatever is on display at the time; there is usually a new exhibition every couple of months.

*⇢ Head north on C. Sagasta, then left at C. Portales, then right at C. Once de Junio. **i** Closes occasionally to take down and install exhibitions; check website to make sure it will be open. $ Free. ⏰ Open Tu-Sa 11am-1pm and 6-9pm, Su noon-2pm and 6-9pm.*

MUSEO DE LA RIOJA ♿ MUSEUM

Pl. de San Agustín, 23 ☎900 70 03 33 🖥www.larioja.org

Though closed while the museum's ambitious expansion continues, when the Museo de La Rioja reopens it will lead visitors through the region's history from *el hombre cazador* (the hunter) and *la primera producción de alimentos* (the earliest food production) to *el sistema métrico decimal* (the metric system) and *el arte contemporáneo en La Rioja* (contemporary art in La Rioja). The museum will be housed in two adjacent buildings, one a baroque palace from the 18th century, the other a modernist, minimalist block from the 21st.

*⇢ From C. Sagasta, turn left onto C. Peso, then right onto C. Capitán Gallarza, then left on C. San Agustín. **i** Closed indefinitely for renovation and expansion. $ Free. ⏰ Open Tu-F 9am-2:30pm and 4-9pm.*

IGLESIA DE SAN BARTOLOMÉ ♿ CHURCH

C. San Bartolomé, 2 ☎941 25 22 54

This church, located on the pleasant and open Plaza San Bartolomé, dates back to the 12th century, though much of what is currently visible consists of 16th-century renovations (practically new, by European standards). The ornately decorated portico, from the late 13th century, depicts scenes from (surprise!) the Bible, with Christ over the doorway and St. Bartholomew on the sides (he's the one having his skin pulled off). During the late afternoon, find silence, incense, and reverence illuminated by a divine light streaming in through a small window.

⇢ From C. de los Portales, head north on C. Juan Lobo, then right onto C. Caballerías, then left onto C. San Bartolomé. $ Free. ⏰ Open to public M-Sa 10am-noon and 6-8pm. Religious services M-Sa 8am-2pm and 6-9pm, Su 9am-2pm and 6-9pm.

CATEDRAL DE SANTA MARÍA DE LA REDONDA ♿ CHURCH

Pl. del Mercado (enter on C. de los Portales)

Logroño's cathedral is one of the city's most emblematic sights, its twin 18th-century spires rising over the *casco antiguo* (most of the cathedral was built in the 15th century). As with most cathedrals, Logroño's is massive and awe-inspiring, with stone pillars climbing up to high, vaulted ceilings. Dimly lit chapels line the cathedral's sides with religious artworks and tombs. The cathedral is also home to a painting of the crucifixion, the *Calvario*, attributed to Michelangelo, hidden in a chapel in the back.

⇢ Take C. Sagasta into the casco antiguo, then right onto C. Portales for 1 block. $ Free. To view the Calvario €0.50. ⏰ Open daily 9am-1pm and 6-9pm.

THE GREAT OUTDOORS

If the tree-lined Paseo del Espolón and the thrilling mile or so of Camino that runs through Logroño don't satisfy your thirst for natural beauty and adventure, just keep following the **Camino de Santiago.** You can head northeast, crossing the Ebro via the Puente de Piedra and heading up into the hills. All the pilgrims heading west will think you're quite lost, though, since Santiago de Compostela is in the other direction. To take the Camino westward, you can find a backpacker and follow him, or you can follow the **yellow arrows and signs,** which will lead you along C. Marqués de Murrieta and C. Duques de Nájera, and into the Parque San Miguel. From there, the route goes across the highway and into the countryside, through fields and toward Santiago de Compostela. The next stop on the Camino after Logroño is Navarrete (7½ mi.), then Nájera (another 9½ mi.).

FOOD

JUAN AND JUAN — BAR, RESTAURANT ❶

C. Albornoz, 5 ☎941 22 99 83

Juan and Juan, owned by brothers Juan Manuel and Juan Marcos, is a lively bar and restaurant hidden in the winding streets of the *casco antiguo*. You may have to push your way through the throng of locals to get to the bar, but it's worth the trouble for the affordable and salty *panceta (€2)* or *chuletilla de cordero (lamb chop; €2.50)*, which go great with a glass of local Rioja *vino tinto (€0.70)*. For a full meal, try the 3-course lunch *menú (€14)* or an entrée *(€9-15)*; there are also plenty of vegetarian options *(€6)*.

Head west on C. Portales, then left onto C. Capitán Gallarza, then right onto C. San Agustín, and then left onto C. Albornoz. $ Entrees and tapas €2-15. Open daily noon-4pm and 8pm-midnight.

EN ASCUAS — SPANISH ❷

C. Hermanos Moroy, 22 ☎941 24 68 67

The name En Ascuas literally "In the Embers," is a reference to the open flame in the kitchen that diners can see through a large glass pane in the back of the restaurant. This establishment is much more clean-cut and modern-looking than some of its neighbors but has no problem serving up traditional dishes like the savory *revuelto de hongos y jamón ibérico*, scrambled eggs with mushrooms and Iberian ham—don't let the runny texture scare you away *(€10.85)*. And, as befits any self-respecting restaurant in the heart of La Rioja, the wine selection is extensive.

Take C. Sagasta north from Paseo del Espolón, then left onto C. Hermanos Moroy. $ Entrees €8-15. Side dishes €4-7. Open Tu-Su 1:30-3:30pm and 8:30-11:30pm.

LOS ROTOS — FAST FOOD ❶

C. San Juan, 14 ☎941 23 65 67

This place's specialties are its namesake *rotos* (€2.30)—hollowed-out half-loaves of bread filled with scrambled eggs and just about anything you can think of: mushrooms, cod, Basque sausage, blood sausage, chicken, cheese, and more. These *rotos* are messy and wonderful, perfect for a late lunch or for a quick refueling stop before tearing up the nightlife.

From Pl. del Mercado, head south on C. Marqués de Vallejo, then left onto C. San Juan. $ €2-6. Open Tu-Su noon-4pm and 6:30pm-1am.

MERCADO DE SAN BLAS — MARKET ❶

C. Sagasta, 1 ☎941 22 04 30 www.eabastos.com

This market, or "La Plaza" as it's known locally, offers fresh fruits and vegetables at low prices, and a great selection of meat and fish (excellent deals if wherever you're staying has a kitchen). A sign out front and a huge banner inside remind visitors that this *mercado* won first prize in the 1994 Alimentos de España competition, but you probably already knew that. Don't forget to wash anything you buy with bottled water before chowing down. No offense to the market, it's just being careful.

Enter on C. Sagasta or C. del Capitán Gallarza. ⏰ Open M-F 7:30am-2pm and 4-8pm, Sa 7:30am-2pm.

NIGHTLIFE

Logroño's really not known for its club scene—to be honest, in most places it's not known at all. The main streets for nightlife are in the *casco antiguo:* **Calle de los Portales, Calle del Laurel, C. del San Agustín,** and **Calle de San Nicolás** tend to be the best for bar hopping, and there are a couple of places with older crowds along C. del Marqués de Murrieta.

JUAN Y PÍNCHAME — BAR

C. Laurel, 9 ☎678 58 96 33

This bar, whose name is a clever pun—*pinchos* are a type of tapas, and *Juan y Pínchame* is a classic joke (Question: "Juan and Pínchame are in a boat. Juan falls out. Who's left?" Answer: *"Pínchame,"* which means "stick me")—is a popular place for tapas in the afternoon and drinks at night. If you can push your way up to the bar, their specialty is a juicy *brocheta de langostino y piña,* a skewer with pineapple and prawns *(eight for €4).*

From C. Sagasta heading north, turn left at C. Hermanos Moroy, then left at C. del Capitán Gallarza, then right onto C. Laurel. $ Drinks and tapas €6-11. ⏰ Open Tu-Th 1-3:15pm and 8pm-12:30am, F-Su 1-3:15pm and 8-11:30pm.

LA GRANJA — CLUB

C. Sagasta, 9 ☎941 23 02 62

La Granja does morning breakfast and *cafe,* midday lunch, and afternoon tapas and then livens up again as a trendy dance club that starts to fill up around 1am on weekends. Strobe lights and heavy bass pour out onto the street as the mullet-sporting men and mini-skirted women get down.

On C. Sagasta 2 blocks north of the Paseo del Espolón. $ Drinks €4-13. ⏰ Open M-Th 7am-12:30am, F-Su 8am-3am.

ESSENTIALS

Practicalities

- **TOURIST OFFICES:** Logroño's **tourism office** offers information in English, French, and German and excellent (as well as necessary) maps of the city. Call for information about tours. *(C. Portales, 50 ☎941 27 33 53 www.logroturismo.org. $ Tours €3 ⏰ Open Jul-Sep daily 10am-2pm and 5-8pm, Oct-Jun M-Sa 10am-2pm and 4:30-7:30pm, Su 10am-2pm.)*
- **CURRENCY EXCHANGE:** You can use any of the banks that line the Av. de La Rioja on the western edge of the Paseo del Espolón *(⏰ Most open M-F 9am-2pm, though hours vary depending on the bank).*
- **LUGGAGE STORGAE:** This is available at the **bus station** ($ €2 ⏰ Open M-Sa 6am-11pm, Su 7am-11pm) and **train station** ($ €3 $ Open 24hr.).
- **POST OFFICE:** The **post office** or *correos* is four blocks west of the bus station on C. Pérez Galdós–don't forget to send everyone postcards (C. Pérez Galdós, 40. ⏰ Open M-F 8:30am-8:30pm, Sa 8:30am-2pm).
- **POSTAL CODE:** 26001.

Emergency!

- **EMERGENCY NUMBERS:** ☎112. **Medical Emergency:** ☎061.
- **POLICE:** To get to the **local police station** take C. Sagasta toward the river and turn right at C. Ruavieja; the police station is on the left after 2 blocks *(☎092).*
- **MEDICAL SERVICES:** Go to **Hospital San Pedro** *(C. Piqueras, 98, on Pl. de San Pedro, ☎941 29 80 00.)*

Getting There

By Bus

The **bus station** *(Av. de España, 1 ☎941 23 59 83)* is a couple of blocks north of the train station. Buses from: **Barcelona** *($ €28. ⏰ 2½hr., 5 per day 8am-11pm);* **Bilbao** *($ €13. ⏰ 2½hr.; M-F 5 per day 7:30am-8pm, Sa 4 per day 8:30am-8pm, Su 4 per day 8:30am-9pm);* **Burgos** *($ €10. ⏰ 1¼hr.; M-F 7 per day 8:30am-9:30pm, Sa 5 per day 8:30am-7:45pm, Su 4 per day 2-7:45pm);* **Madrid** *($ €16-21. ⏰ 4½hr.; M-Sa 13 per day 7am-1am, Su 18 per day 7am-1am);* **Pamplona** *($ €8. ⏰ 1¾hr.; M-F 8 per day 6:45am-8pm, Sa 7 per day 7:30am-8pm, Su 5 per day 10am-8pm).*

By Train

The **train station** *(Pl. de Europa, ☎902 24 02 02)* is located on the south end of town, a 15min. walk from center. Daily RENFE Alvia trains *($ €56; if booked more than a week in advance €33)* leave from **Madrid's** Atocha Station *(⏰ 3½hr.; M-F 6:30pm, Su 6:30pm)* and goes back to Madrid *(⏰ 3¼hr.; M-Sa 7:50am).* Trains from: **Barcelona** *(⏰ 4hr., 5 per day, 7:30am-10:45pm. $ €40-64);* **Bilbao** *(⏰ 2½hr., 7:45am and 3:30pm $ €21);* **Burgos** *(⏰ 1¾hr., 3 per day, 1:20-9am. $ €19-21);* **Zaragoza** *(⏰ 2hr., 8 per day 3am-10:15pm. $ €12-22).*

By Plane

Iberia *(☎902 40 05 00 💻www.iberia.com)* offers daily flights from **Madrid** *($ If purchased 6 days in advance €85. ⏰ 50min.; 8-9pm),* which arrive at **Aeropuerto de Logrono-Agoncillo** *(Carretera LO-20, 15km from city center ☎941 27 74 00).*

Getting Around

Logroño is a great city to **walk:** the *casco antiguo* is almost entirely car-free, leaving it a pedestrian paradise. While it's nice to *callejear* ("meander through the streets," a wonderful word for which there's no accurate English equivalent) a bit sometimes, if you're in a rush to get somewhere or simply enjoy walking with purpose, make sure you plan your route beforehand, as many of the older streets are narrow and confusingly unmarked. For those interested in exploring parts of the city farther from the center or too lazy to walk to the train station, there is a **bus** system *(€0.60, 10-trip bonobús €4.52, 1-month bonobús €29).* **Taxis** can be found at the **bus station** *(☎941 23 75 29)* or can be called: Radio-taxi *(☎941 22 21 22)* and Tele-taxi *(☎941 50 50 50)* are the main companies.

burgos ☎947

Burgos (pop. 180,000) has one of the most spectacular city entrances anywhere, and this breathtaking first impression accurately introduces this northern gem. After walking through the large and ornate **Arco de Santa María** to the mind-bogglingly massive **Catedral** on the Pl. del Rey San Fernando, it doesn't take much imagination to understand why this was a favorite seat and burial place of Castilian and Leonese royalty. Though the Catedral is undoubtedly Burgos's centerpiece, the city is filled with dozens of other churches, from the 9th-century *Castillo* up the hill to the medieval monasteries on the city's outskirts. In the evening, plazas fill with friends and families enjoying their *paseos*, and as the clock strikes midnight they buzz with partiers on their way to the bars along the Camino de Santiago and the *discotecas* in the shadow of the Catedral.

ORIENTATION

Burgos is a simple city, but the streets run in ridiculously complicated directions. Before traversing this area, pick up a map from the tourist office. The **bus station, post office, Museo de Burgos,** and **Monasterio de las Huelgas** are pretty much the only important things south of the east-west-running **Río Arlanzón**. Most of the *centro histórico* is to the north of the river, with the **Catedral** on the west end, the **Castillo** up the hill to the north, and various winding streets and **magnificent, open plazas** throughout the city. The **Plaza de España,** a hub for most city buses, is east of the centro, and the **train station** is outside of the city to the northeast.

ACCOMMODATIONS

HOSTAL CARRALES — HOSTAL ❷

C. Puente Gasset, 4 ☎947 20 59 16 www.hostalcarrales.com

A couple of blocks from the *centro histórico* and about 15min. on foot from the bus station, this quiet *hostal* has basic rooms, full baths, and a very affectionate cat who lives in the reception (on a different floor from the rooms, allergy sufferers).

Just on the north side of the river, between C. de Vitoria and Av. del Arlanzón, 4 blocks east of Pl. del Cid. ℹ *Private baths available.* $ *Singles €25-40; doubles €35-50.* ⏰ *Reception 8am-11pm.*

PENSIÓN VICTORIA — PENSIÓN ❷

C. de San Juan, 3, 2der. (3rd fl., right) ☎947 20 15 42

This sunny *pensión* sits smack dab on the Camino de Santiago. Affordable rooms have balconies over the pilgrimage route and are a few blocks down the road from the Catedral and the nightlife. Deal-finders with claustrophobia take note: doubles are the same size as singles but hold two twin beds.

From Pl. de Santa María (in front of cathedral), go up the stairs and to the right; head straight, following C. de Fernán González to C. de Avellanos to C. de San Juan. ℹ *Shared bath but some rooms have sinks..* $ *Singles €20; doubles €32.* ⏰ *Reception 8am-11pm.*

CAMPING FUENTES BLANCAS — CAMPING ❶

Ctra. Burgos-Cartuja de Miraflores, Km. 3.5 ☎947 48 60 16 www.campingburgos.com

Located in the Fuentes Blancas park a 10min. bus ride from the *centro*, Camping Fuentes Blancas is a beautiful municipal campsite. Campers can save money with this cheaper overnight option, and outdoorsy backpackers can explore the many hiking trails—they can even walk here along a scenic river from Burgos itself.

#27 bus leaves from northwest side of Pl. de España and runs to Fuentes Blancas ("Camping" stop). 4 per day 9:30am-7:15pm, returns to Pl. de España 4 per day 9:45am-7:30pm. #26 bus runs **only from Jun 29-Aug 31** *and leaves from the same stop, 10 per day 11am-9pm, returns to Pl. de España 10 per day 11:15am-9:15pm.* ℹ *Shop, restaurant, bar, lounge, pool, beach, mini-golf (€4), common showers.* $ *€4.65 per person, ages 2-10 €3.20, €3.72-7.55 per tent, €4.65 per car. Electricity €4. Bungalows with private bath €35-85.* ⏰ *Open in summer daily 7am-midnight; in winter 8am-11pm.*

SIGHTS

Turn any corner in Burgos' *centro histórico* and you're likely to stumble across a 14th-century church or the building where Ferdinand and Isabella met with Columbus upon his return from his second voyage to the New World. (If *Let's Go* told you where it was, you wouldn't be able to stumble across it, now would you?) The **Catedral** is the city's main attraction, but Burgos has dozens of other sites that shouldn't be missed.

👍 CATEDRAL DE BURGOS 💳🚫 CHURCH [1]

Pl. del Rey San Fernando ☎947 20 47 12 💻www.catedraldeburgos.es

The **Catedral,** a UNESCO World Heritage site, is one of the most impressive churches in the world. Whether you first approach it from behind, by following the Camino de Santiago, or from the front via the magnificent Arch of Santa María, its incredible size and detailed stone carvings will blow your mind. What began in the early 13th century as a Romanesque church has been transformed over the intervening centuries into a Gothic marvel, and recent restorations (which some consider a bit excessive) have returned its original vivid colors and gilded finish. The Capilla de los Condestables is covered with incredible carvings in wood and stone; be sure to look up at the intricate skylight, and look to the right as you walk in for carved 🐇**dragons.** Just off the stained-glass-enclosed upper cloister (built 1260-1280) is the 👍**Capilla de Santa Catalina,** whose walls are covered from floor to high ceiling with portraits of the clergy, and which houses the Visigothic Bible of Cardeña (c. 915) and **El Cid's** nuptial documents (1074); **El Cid** himself is in the transept. The museum's extensive collection includes reliquaries containing the remains of many saints as well as an artist's rendition of a stunningly handsome El Cid that looks more like the cover of a romance novel than anything else.

🧭 Take the Puente de Santa María bridge from the south side of the river; through the arch. $ €5, seniors €4, students €3, pilgrims €2.50, ages 7-14 €1. ⏰ Open in summer M 9:30am-6:30pm, Tu 9:30am-3pm and 3:30-6:30pm, W-Su 9:30am-6:30pm; in winter M 10am-6pm, Tu 10am-3pm and 3:30-6pm, W-Su 10am-6pm.

👍 MONASTERIO DE SANTA MARÍA LA REAL DE LAS HUELGAS 💳♿ CHURCH [1]

Compases de Huelgas ☎947 20 16 30

Built in 1187 by King Alfonso VIII, the Monasterio de las Huelgas was a summer palace for Castilian kings and a Cistercian convent for princesses and nobles. Though the Cistercians preferred a no-frills attitude toward interior decorating, the monastery's royal status allowed it to break some of the order's strict rules against signs of opulence. The Romanesque cloister dates all the way back to the monastery's founding in the 12th century, and the colors on the ceiling of the Capilla de Santiago (which looks like it belongs more in the Alhambra of Granada than in a Castilian monastery) are original and from the 13th century. The museum contains the Pendón de las Navas de Tolosa, the Moors' flag captured by the re-conquering Castilians in 1212, which you can also see depicted on the far right of the huge 17th-century mural in the first room.

🧭 Take the "Barrio del Pilar" bus (€0.85) from Pl. de España to Barrio de las Huelgas; or, walking (approx. 20min. from cathedral), follow Paseo de la Audiencia west along the river, then turn left across the bridge at Pl. de Castilla roundabout. Take a right along Av. de Palencia and a slight left onto Av. Monasterio de las Huelgas; monastery is at the end of the avenue. $ €5, students, seniors, ages 5-16 €2.50, under 5 free. ⏰ Open Tu-Sa 10am-1pm and 3:45-5:30pm, Su 10:30am-2pm. Mandatory tours (1¼hr.) given in Spanish every 30min.

FOOD 🍎

Queso de Burgos and *morcilla* sausage are staples of the Burgalese kitchen and can be found throughout the *centro histórico*, mainly near the Catedral. For tapas, the C. San Lorenzo off the Plaza Mayor is overflowing with bars; the streets parallel to C. San Lorenzo are good for nightlife as well.

CERVECERÍA MORITO 💳♿🍸 BAR, RESTAURANT [1]

C. Porcelos, 1 ☎947 26 75 55

Even during the low season, the line for this *cervecería's* deliciously cheap fare runs out the door and around the block. Pair their sangria *(€1.50)* with the *ración of champiñones* *(mushrooms served with ham; €4),* or get adventurous and try something with *gulas* (baby eel).

From Pl. del Rey San Fernando (next to cathedral), follow C. de la Virgen de la Paloma 1 block, then right onto C. Porcelos. $ Raciones €1.50-6. Sandwiches €3-6. Beer €1. Sangria €1.50. ⏰ Open daily noon-3:30pm and 7pm-midnight. Kitchen open 1-3:30pm and 7pm-midnight.

LA TAPERÍA DEL CASINO CAFE, RESTAURANT [2]

Pl. Mayor, 31 ☎947 27 81 56

Right on the Plaza Mayor, this place offers traditional Spanish food, from paella *(€9-10)* to *patatas bravas* *(€2)*. There's a €0.40 surcharge to sit outside on the Plaza, but the shaded seating area is worth every cent. Make sure not to miss (or pay for) the free olives.

On the south side of the Pl. Mayor. $ Appetizers €1-2. Raciones €5.60-15.60. Salads €7.60-9.60. Sandwiches €3-4.10. Pizza €9.60. Menú del día €12. ⏰ Open daily 9am-midnight.

NIGHTLIFE

Locals start off the night with tapas and *tinto* in the crowded bars along **C. de San Lorenzo,** then head to the bars along **C. de San Juan** and **C. de la Puebla** for some liquid courage before hitting the **discotecas** on **C. del Huerto del Rey** and **C. de Fernán González** behind the Catedral.

EL BOSQUE ENCANTADO BAR, CLUB [1]

C. de San Juan, 31 ☎947 26 12 66

For an undoubtedly unique (this bar is so funky *Let's Go* even uses a grammatically incorrect qualifier before "unique"!) experience, head to this bar along the busy C. de San Juan, where trance music floats around strangely placed dollhouses—yeah, we don't get it either. The establishment takes its name from the enormous fake tree that sits at the bar, illuminated by lighting reminiscent of a high school theater production. No matter how kitschy this bar may sound, it offers a great deal on beers and teas *(€1.50-2.50)*.

On C. de San Juan west of C. Santander. $ Tea €1.50-2.50. Beer €2. ⏰ Open M-W 5pm-midnight, Th 5pm-12:30am, F-Sa 5pm-4am.

EL PEREGRINO CLUB [2]

C. Fernán González, 48

Situated just behind the Catedral on the Camino de Santiago, this bar (whose name means "the pilgrim") draws a young crowd that knows how to party. It's less Euro-pop than the clubs on C. del Huerto del Rey and more Euro-rock like the other spots along C. Fernán González. El Peregrino's mixed drinks *(€4-8)* can be pricey, so be the conservative pilgrim and order beers *(€2)*.

From Pl. Mayor, head north on C. Cardenal Segura, then left at C. Fernán González. $ Beer €2. Mixed drinks €4-8. ⏰ Open M-Th 6pm-midnight, F-Sa 6pm-4am.

ESSENTIALS

Practicalities

- **TOURIST OFFICES:** The **tourist office** has excellent maps that are necessary for navigating the city's jumbled streets. *(Pl. Alonso Martínez, 7 ☎947 20 31 25 🖥www.turismocastillayleon.com ⏰ Open Sep 16-Jun 30 M-Sa 9:30am-2pm and 4-7pm, Su 9:30am-5pm; Jul 1-Sep 15 daily 9am-8pm.)*
- **TOURS:** Contact the tourist office for guided tours of the *centro histórico. (12:15pm $ €10, ages 7-14 €3.)*
- **CURRENCY EXCHANGE: Banco Santander** offers currency exchange and ATMs. *(Pl. de Mío Cid, ☎902 24 24 24 ⏰ Open Apr-Sept M-F 8:30am-2pm; Oct-Mar M-F 8:30am-2pm, Sa 8:30am-1pm.)*
- **LUGGAGE STORAGE:** The bus station offers storage. *(C. Miranda, 4 ☎947 28 88 55 $ €2 per day.)*

- **INTERNET ACCESS: Biblioteca del Teatro Principal** has 30min. free Wi-Fi. *(Paseo del Espolón ☎947 28 88 73 Open July M-F 8:30am-2:30pm; Aug M-F 8:30am-9pm; Sept-June M-F 9am-9pm, Sa 9:30am-2pm.)*
- **POST OFFICE:** *(Pl. Conde de Castro ☎947 26 27 50 Open M-F 8:30am-8:30pm, Sa 9:30am-4pm.)*

Emergency!

- **EMERGENCY NUMBERS:** ☎092.
- **POLICE:** *(Av. Cantabria☎947 28 88 39)*
- **HOSPITALS/MEDICAL SERVICES: Hospital General Yagüe** *(Av. del Cid, 96 ☎947 28 18 00)*

Getting There

By Bus

The best way to get to Burgos is by bus; the bus station *(C. Miranda, 4 ☎947 28 88 55)* is one block south of the river and just across the bridge from the cathedral. Buses arrive from **Barcelona** *(8hr., 5 per day 8:45am-11pm €35)*, **Bilbao** *(2hr., 12 per day 6:30am-8:30pm €11.50)*, **Carrión de los Condes** *(1¼hr., M-Sa 5:10pm €5.50)*, **León** *(2hr., 3-4 per day 10:15am-9:15pm €14)*, **Logroño** *(2hr., M-Sa 8 per day 9:30am-9:30pm, Su 4 per day 1-11:45pm €10)*, **Madrid** *(3hr., M-Th, Sa 16 per day, F 24 per day, Su 17 per day 7am-12:30am €16)*, **Salamanca** *(3-4hr., M-Sa 4-5 per day 9:30am-3:15am, Su 2 per day 9:30am-3:30pm €15-22)*, **San Sebastián** *(3hr., 6-8 per day 7:40am-12:30am €15.50)*, **Santiago de Compostela** *(7-9hr., 2 per day 2-11:15pm €37-40)*.

By Train

The new RENFE train station *(Av. Principe de Asturias ☎902 24 02 02)* is about 3mi. from the *centro histórico.* **Trains** arrive from **Barcelona** *(6hr., 4 per day 9:20am-8:45pm €63-78)*, **Bilbao** *(3hr., M-F 4 per day 8:55am-5:10pm, Sa 3 per day 8:55am-2pm, Su 3 per day 8:55am-5:10pm €13-19)*, **León** *(2hr., 4 per day 1:12pm-12:14am €20-37)*, **Lisbon** *(11hr., daily 4:30pm €61)*, **Logroño** *(2hr., M 4 per day 7:36am-1:59am, Tu-Su 3 per day 4:06pm-1:59am €18-21)*, **Madrid** *(2-4hr., M-F 6 per day 8am-5:30pm, Sa 4 per day 8am-4:10pm, Su 3 per day 8:am-4:10pm €25-40)*, **Pamplona** *(2hr., daily 1:10pm €23.50)*, **Paris** *(10hr., M-F, Su 7:47pm €150)*, **Salamanca** *(2½hr., 3 per day 6:40am-12:35am €21-23)*, and **San Sebastián** *(3hr., 5 per day 8:42am-10:40pm €21-27)*.

By Air

The **Aeropuerto de Burgos-Villafría** *(☎902 40 47 04 ▪www.aena.es)* is about 2½mi. outside the *centro;* **flights** arrive daily from **Barcelona.** *(1½hr., 12:20pm. €62.)*

Getting Around

Burgos is a small city with an almost entirely pedestrian *centro histórico,* so the best way to get around is to **walk.** For sites outside the *centro,* the **bus** system *(€0.85)* is quick and easy to use; most buses run through the Pl. de España to the northeast of the *centro.* Buses #25 and #43 go from the Pl. de España to the RENFE station; bus #24 goes from the Pl. de España to the **airport.** For **taxis,** call Radio Taxi *(☎947 27 77 77)*.

carrión de los condes ☎979

Carrión de los Condes (pop. 2,328) is a tiny *pueblo* in the province of Palencia, the heart of Castilla y León. It's the sort of place where you wake up to the sounds of church bells and roosters and spend the day meandering through the quiet streets under darting swallows and swooping storks. It is a mandatory stop—one of the most impressive—along the Camino de Santiago, and is renowned for its incredible Romanesque churches and the Renaissance cloister of San Zoilo across the river.

ORIENTATION

Rising above the surrounding plains and farmland, Carrión is located above its namesake Río Carrión, midway between Burgos and León. The **Camino de Santiago** runs east-west through the town and goes by most major sights, following the main roads and passing through the main plazas: C. de Santa Clara, Pl. Piña Merino (home to the bus stop), the beautiful Pl. de Santa María, C. de Santa María, Pl. Mayor (still "Plaza del Generalísimo" on many maps), and C. de Esteban Collantes, before heading across the river to the monastery of San Zoilo. Just follow the Camino up **C. Santa María** to get to the center of town from the bus stop. The northwest corner of town has several lovely churches but used to be the *judería* (Jewish quarter), hence the C. de Rabí Don Sem Tob. Interestingly, the Ermita de la Cruz was once the synagogue. Take note: on the tourist office's map and the map at the Pl. de Santa María, North is oriented about 45 degrees to the right.

ACCOMMODATIONS

Accommodations in Carrión are generally less expensive than their equivalents in larger cities but can fill up during the summer as pilgrims flood the town. Location is not crucial in a town this small, but most lodging is located on or just off the C. de Santa María.

PENSIÓN EL RESBALÓN — PENSIÓN [1]

C. de Fernán Gómez, 19 — ☎979 88 04 33

This *pensión* in the heart of the village offers little more than a bed, a window, and a lightbulb, but for these prices it's a steal. However, don't stay here if you're looking for a good night's sleep after a long day of pilgrimages or sightseeing—it's right next to the main nightlife street, and what the local youth may lack in numbers, they make up for in volume.

➜ From C. de Santa María heading toward the Pl. Mayor, turn right onto C. de Fernán Gómez. i Shared bath. $ Singles €15; doubles €22; triples €27. ⏰ Reception 8am-11pm.

CAMPING EL EDÉN — ♿ CAMPING [1]

Parque Municipal — ☎979 88 01 95

Sick of always having to take a bus or a 3mi. hike into town from the campsite? Not in Carrión: El Edén, right down by the river, is no more than a 2min. walk from the Pl. Mayor (though, to be fair, few things in this town are more than a 2min. walk from the Pl. Mayor).

➜ On the southwest side of town. Follow C. de Enrique Fuentes Quintana down from the Pl. Mayor, then left through the park. i Shared bath. Restaurant and bar. $ €4 per person; €3.50-3.90 per tent; €4 per car. Electricity €3.50. ⏰ Reception 9am-10pm.

SIGHTS

Though small in population and area, Carrión is full of historic religious buildings put up over the course of the last millennium. Many of them, such as Carrión's oldest church, the **Iglesia de Santa María del Camino** *($ Free. ⏰ Open in summer daily 9am-2pm and 4:30-6pm; in winter M-Sa 11am-1:30am and 6-9pm, Su noon-1:30pm.),* lie on the Camino de Santiago, but a quick walk through town reveals churches, monasteries, and *ermitas* of all eras and architectural styles.

REAL MONASTERIO DE SAN ZOILO — CHURCH

C. de San Zoilo ☎979 88 00 50

Though the date of its founding is unknown, monks lived here as early as 948 CE. Throughout the Middle Ages it was a center of political and religious power, and a key point along the Camino de Santiago. The monastery features Romanesque elements dating to the 11th century and is perhaps best known for its glorious Renaissance cloister.

Follow the well-marked Camino de Santiago: from the Pl. Mayor, head northwest on C. de Esteban Collantes, then left at C. de Piña Blasco, and across the bridge and to the right. $ €2, pilgrims and groups of over 20 people €1.50, ages 9 and under free. ⏰ Open daily 10:30am-2pm and 4:30-8pm.

IGLESIA DE SANTIAGO AND MUSEO PARROQUIAL — CHURCH

Pl. Mayor ☎902 20 30 30

Though it had fallen into ruin after being badly damaged during the 1811 War of Independence, this recently restored 12th-century church exhibits some of the most incredible examples of Romanesque facades like its heavily decorated doorway and ornately elegant frieze of the Last Judgment. Inside, the church is filled with the religious objects and artwork of the Museo Parroquial.

On the Pl. Mayor. $ €1. ⏰ Open daily 11am-2pm and 4:30-8pm.

FOOD

For standard but inexpensive meals, hit the bars near the bus stop and along the Pl. Mayor. Otherwise, get your grub on at eateries along the Camino.

RESTAURANTE LA CORTE — CASTILIAN 2

C. de Santa María, 34 ☎979 88 01 38 www.hostallacorte.com

Across from the Pl. de Santa María next to the affiliated *hostal*, this traditional Castilian restaurant has an affordable *menú* and a salty but filling *sopa castellana*. Stop here for breakfast as early as 6am to try the *café*, *pan tostada*, and fresh orange juice *(€3)* before an early trip to the Camino.

Up C. de Santa María 1 block from the bus stop. $ Entrees €6-17. Menú €10. Breakfast €3. ⏰ Open daily 6-10am, 1:30-4pm, and 7-11pm (closing times approximate).

BAR ABEL — BAR 1

C. de Esteban Collantes, 15 ☎979 88 03 25

This welcoming bar is where locals come to hang out before their *siestas*. Don't worry, though: they won't make you feel left out, even though you're the only one who doesn't know that story about Don Ronaldo and the donkey.

2 blocks north of Pl Mayor, up C. de Esteban Collantes. $ Menú €11, Sa-Su €17. ⏰ Open daily 1-3:30pm, F-Su also 8:30-10:30pm.

NIGHTLIFE

CAFETERÍA CARRIÓN — BAR, LOUNGE

C. de Esteban Collantes, 8

If this establishment's name were in English instead of Spanish, it would sound quite unappealing. Fortunately, the false cognate doesn't seem to drive away any of the locals. Most get their *cañas* and *kalimotxos* at the bar and take them out to the street, but some stay in the smoky and surprisingly large drinking space to play cards, *futbolín* (foosball) or *billar* (pool) before heading out to the *discotecas*.

1 block north of the Pl. Mayor on C. de Esteban Collantes. $ Beer €1.50. Kalimotxos €2.50. ⏰ Open M-Th 9am-1am, F-Sa 9am-2am.

ADARVE — CLUB

Pl. de los Regentes

If you can pick your way through the sometimes menacing crowd of *jóvenes* outside (approach from the Pl. Mayor rather than C. de Fernán Gómez, where the *botellones* and *lucha libre* tend to take place), this disco-pub is where Carrión's nightlife can be found. The party pours out onto the Plaza de los Regentes in front, and often down the adjacent streets. Watch out for flying bottles: smashing is the preferred method of glass disposal, as recycling hasn't completely caught on yet.

From C. de Santa María, take C. de Fernán Gómez one block north, then left at Pl. de los Regentes. Or (the more dramatic route) from Pl. Mayor, go through the arch to the right of the Iglesia de Santiago, down the narrow alleyway past the museum, which leads right to the Pl. de los Regentes. $ Shots €1. Beer €1.50. ⏰ Open M-Th 10pm-2am, F-Sa 10pm-3:30am.

ESSENTIALS

Practicalities

- **TOURIST OFFICES:** For information and brochures on the area, head to the office across from the bus stop *(☎979 88 02 50 Across from the bus stop. ⏰ Open Sept-June Sa-Su 10am-2pm and 5:30-7:30pm; July-Aug daily 10am-3pm and 5-7:30pm)* or in Pl. Mayor (In the Museo de Arte Contemporáneo. ⏰ Open Tu-Su 11am-2pm and 5-7pm).
- **CURRENCY EXCHANGE: Banco Santander** *(Pl. Primer Marqués de Santillana, 4 ⏰ Open M-F 8:30am-2:30pm.)*
- **INTERNET ACCESS: Cafetería Yadira** *(Across from Bar España and the bus stop. $ €1 for 20min.)*
- **POST OFFICE:** *(C. José Antonio Girón ☎979 88 03 45 ⏰ Open M-F 8:30am-2:30pm, Sa 9:30am-1pm).*

Emergency!

- **EMERGENCY NUMBER:** ☎092.
- **POLICE:** Police are located at the Ayuntamiento. *(Pl. Mayor ☎979 88 02 59)*
- **LATE-NIGHT PHARMACIES:** Pharmacies are located on Pl. Mayor *(Pl. Mayor, 14 ☎979 88 02 59)* and C. la Rúa *(C. la Rúa, 4 ☎979 88 03 33).*
- **MEDICAL SERVICES: Centro médico** *(Pl. Conde de Garay ☎979 88 02 45)*

Getting There

By Bus

Buses stop in front of Bar España in the town's eastern end, a 2min. walk up C. de Santa María from the Plaza Mayor. Buses arrive from **Bilbao** *(⏰ 3½hr., M-Sa 9:15am $ €15.26),* **Burgos** *(⏰ 1¼hr., M-Sa 11:30am $ €5.36),* **León** *(⏰ 2hr., Su-F 3:15pm $ €8.49),* and **San Sebastián** *(⏰ 5½hr., M-F 7:10am, Su 7:10am $ €13.89).*

Getting Around

Walking is the easiest way to get around this small town. There is also a **taxi** stand at Pl. de Santa María *(}979 88 04 14).*

león ☎987

León (pop. 165,000) is the last major city along the Camino de Santiago before the final stop of Santiago de Compostela itself. Though the old city retains vestiges of the Romans and the Middle Ages, the modern city that surrounds it has broad avenues and a cosmopolitan feel. The city's name (originally *Legio* in Latin, but changed over time to *León*) means "lion," and its inhabitants are appropriately proud of their city and identity, having been known to take down the occasional gazelle. The Roman walls still stand in part today, and the once heavily fortified city was a launching point for the knights of the *Reconquista.* The city is best known for its spectacular cathedral and its infamously boisterous nightlife.

ORIENTATION

León's **bus** station and RENFE **train** station are located on the west side of the Río Bernesga, while the rest of the city is to the east. **The Avenida Ordoño II** runs directly east from the river to the mainly pedestrian **casco antiguo,** where it goes through the **Plaza Santo Domingo** and becomes **Calle Ancha,** the *casco's* main street. To the north of C. Ancha is the walled part of the city, with the **Cathedral** and **Basílica de San Isidoro.** To the south is the **barrio húmedo** ("humid neighborhood") the main nightlife area, where the **Plaza Mayor** and **Plaza San Martín** can be found.

ACCOMMODATIONS

León has a fair number of inexpensive *hostals* and *pensiones* located between the old town and the river, especially around Av. de Roma, Av. de Ordoño II, and Av. de la República Argentina. They tend to fill up very quickly from June-Sept, so try to **reserve rooms in advance,** especially on weekends.

👍 PENSIÓN BLANCA — 💳⊗🖥 B and B ❷

C. Villafranca, 2, 2A (3rd fl.) ☎987 25 19 91 🖥www.pensionblanca.com

Large, brightly decorated rooms with high ceilings and clean wooden floors just steps from the main street between the river and the *casco antiguo.* Free breakfast and internet access keep guests happy, and daily newspapers will keep you up on current events in Spain and abroad.

⇟ Just off Av. de Ordoño II, 2 blocks from the river. ℹ Breakfast included. Shared bath. Kitchen. Laundry €7. $ Singles €22, with bath €27; doubles €35, with bath €43; triples €55, extra bed €12. ⏰ Reception open daily 9am-11pm.

HOSTAL DON SUERO — 💳⊗🖥 HOSTAL ❷

Av. del Suero de Quiñones, 15 ☎987 23 06 00

This *hostal's* size (8 floors of rooms complete with elevator) means it's your best shot if you're rolling into town without a reservation. That said, *Let's Go* does not advise rolling into town without a reservation. Don't forget to bring your bubbles—Don Suelo's standard-sized rooms have tiny private baths but relatively spacious bathtubs.

⇟ From Pl. de Santo Domingo, follow Av. de Padre Isla 7 blocks, then left onto Av. del Suero de Quiñones. ℹ All rooms with private bath. Cafe downstairs. $ Singles €24; doubles €40. ⏰ Reception 24hr.

PENSIÓN PUERTA SOL — ⊛⊗ PENSIÓN ❶

C. Puerta del Sol, 1, 3rd fl. ☎987 21 19 66

This inexpensive *pensión* has decent rooms with low ceilings overlooking the large and beautiful Plaza Mayor in the *casco antiguo.* The plaza is scenic during the day and early in the week, but be weary of the loud commotion nearby on the weekend.

⇟ From Pl. Mayor, take C. Santa Cruz from southwest corner of plaza 1 block, then left onto C. Puerta del Sol. ℹ Shared bath. $ Singles €18; doubles €25. ⏰ Open 9am-10pm.

HOSTAL OREJAS — 💳♿ HOSTAL ❸

C. República Argentina, 28 ☎987 25 29 09 🖥www.hostal-orejas.es

Big, white rooms with large beds, private bathrooms, and cable TVs make this two-star *hostal* a pricier option but worth every penny. Make sure to book a room away from the seasonal construction directly across the street.

⇟ Entrance on C. Villafranca, 8. From Av. de Ordoño II heading toward casco antiguo, right onto C. Villafranca. ℹ All rooms with private bath. Laundry service available. $ Singles €26-45; doubles €43-56; triples €53-69. Breakfast in restaurant €2.50; lunch and dinner €10. ⏰ Reception 24hr.

SIGHTS

In addition to its Catedral—every Spanish city's mandatory sight—and the **Basílica de San Isidoro,** visitors to León can see the **Casa de Botines** *(at the far west end of C. Ancha, next to Pl. de Santo Domingo; now a bank),* one of Gaudí's few buildings outside of Catalonia, the **Convento de San Marcos,** a gorgeous palace on Pl. San Marcos converted into a luxury hotel, and several museums including the **Museo de León** *(Pl. Santo Domingo, open Tu-Sa 10am-2pm and 4-7pm, Jul-Sep also Su 10am-2pm, €1.20, free weekends)* and the **Museo de Arte Contemporáneo.**

CATEDRAL DE LEÓN AND MUSEO CATEDRALICIO — CHURCH

Pl. de la Regla ☎987 87 57 70 🖳www.catedraldeleon.org

This 13th-century cathedral in the middle of the old town is one of the finest examples of Gothic architecture you're likely to see anywhere. The stained glass windows sparkle in the sunlight from the outside, illuminating the interior with an eerie blue glow. The tremendous facade facing the Plaza de la Regla displays a rowdy group of demons enjoying a free *menú del día* consisting of damned souls, while saints float around them.

⇄ Keep following C. Ancha east. $ Full visit €5, partial visit €3, cloister €2. ⏰ Cathedral open M-Sa 8:30am-1:30pm and 4-7pm, Su 8:30am-2:30pm and 5-8pm; Oct-June M-Sa 8:30am-1:30pm and 4-7pm, Su 8:30am-2:30pm and 5-7pm. Museum open July-Sept M-Sa 9:30am-1:30pm and 4-7pm; Oct-June M-F 9:30am-1:30pm and 4-7pm, Sa 9:30am-1:30pm.

REAL COLEGIATA DE SAN ISIDORO — CHURCH

Pl. de Santo Martino, 15 ☎987 87 61 61 🖳www.sanisidorodeleon.org

The *Basílica de San Isidoro* is beautiful inside and out, but the real attraction here is the **Panteón Real,** dating back to the 11th century and housing some of the original **Kings of Leon.** The museum upstairs has an impressive collection of reliquaries and other religious artwork and paraphernalia, while the tombs downstairs are the final resting places of 23 kings and queens, 12 *infantas*, and 9 counts, watched over by the 12th-century Romanesque paintings on the ceiling. While the basilica offers a guided tour, *Let's Go* recommends picking up a pamphlet at the information counter, giving yourself a tour, and saving a ton of time.

⇄ From C. Ancha, left onto C. del Cid to Pl. de San Isidoro. $ Basílica free. Museum €4, free Th afternoon. ⏰ Open July-Aug M-Sa 9am-8pm, Su 9am-2pm; Sept-June M-Sa 10am-1:30pm and 4-6:30pm, Su 10am-1:30pm. Hourly guided tours in Spanish.

FOOD

The *casco antiguo* is jam packed with restaurants, bars, and cafes, especially around the **Pl. Mayor** and **Pl. de San Martín.** Outside the *casco*, there are plenty of restaurants along **C. Renueva,** the pedestrian **C. Burgo Nuevo** and **Pl. Pícara Justina,** and along Av. de los Reyes Leoneses near MUSAC. In most Leonese bars, you'll receive some **free tapas** with your drink, so many just bar-hop instead of ordering a *menú*—three or four drinks can usually get you the equivalent of a full meal—and maybe a buzz.

RÚA NOVA — LEONESE ❷

C. Renueva, 17 ☎987 24 4 61

This lively bar and restaurant is on the restaurant-lined C. Renueva just two blocks from the basílica de San Isidoro and the *casco antiguo*. Leonese cuisine tends to be heavy on the pork, and Rúa Nova follows suit by serving a mean *ración* of *jamón asado (grilled ham; €8.10).*

⇄ From Pl. de Santo Domingo, follow Av. de Padre Isla 7 blocks, then turn right on C. Renueva. $ Menú €11. Entrees €8-16. ⏰ Open M 7:30pm-midnight, Tu-Sa 12:30-4pm and 7:30-midnight, Su 12:30-4pm.

EL LLAR 💳♿🍸☀ LEONESE [2]

Pl. San Martín, 9 ☎987 25 42 87

El Llar serves traditional Leonese food in both the cozy bar inside and the open terrace on the Pl. de San Martín. Try to eat here on the early side, as the terrace gets chilly and the plaza's street vendors come looking for customers.

➔ From C. Ancha, head south on C. Varillas to C. Cardiles to C. Platerías, then turn right onto C. Plegaria, and left onto Pl. San Martín. $ Raciones €3-7. Entrees €5-14. ⏰ Open daily 1-3:30pm and 7pm-midnight.

NIGHTLIFE

León's best nightlife can be found in the casco antiguo, mainly around **Pl. San Martín** and **Pl. Mayor** in the neighborhood known as **el barrio húmedo** ("the wet neighborhood," for all the alcohol there) south of C. Ancha. The other side of C. Ancha tends to be a little more laid-back, but Spaniards do take a walk on the wild side around **Pl. Torres de Omaña, C. Cervantes,** and **C. del Cid.**

CAFE-BAR GALA ⚽♿🍸☀ BAR

C. del Cid, 20 ☎987 23 60 24

Gala is a great place to start your night, especially if there's a *fútbol* game on: an unimaginable crowd squeezes into the bar to watch the match on the **127in. TV.** If there's not a *fútbol* game on the big screen, hopefully you won't mind the **Godzilla-sized** face of Barbara Walters during the next rerun of *The View*.

➔ From C. Ancha facing the Cathedral, turn left onto C. del Cid. $ Beer €1.50. ⏰ Open Tu-Su 10am-3pm and 5pm-2am.

ECLIPSE ⚽🚭🍸 CLUB

C. Varillas, 5 ☎661 26 03 19 💻www.pubeclipse.es

This dance club in the *barrio húmedo* just off C. Ancha plays everything from Michael Jackson to Lady Gaga well into the morning. It's something of a starting point for partiers working their way from C. Ancha toward the Pl. San Martín and Pl. Mayor, so if it seems empty wait for the next wave of party animals to migrate inside.

➔ Follow C. Ancha toward the Cathedral, then turn right onto C. Varillas. $ Beer €2. Mixed drinks €3-8. ⏰ Open Th 11pm-3:30am, F-Sa 11pm-4:30am.

ESSENTIALS

Practicalities

- **TOURIST OFFICES:** The tourist office is hidden behind the Diputación on C. del Cid 1 block up C. Ancha toward the Catedral. *(C. del Cid, 1☎987 23 70 82 ⏰ Open Sept 16-June M-Sa 9:30am-2pm and 4-7pm, Su 9:30am-5pm; July-Sept 15 M-Sa 9am-8pm, Su 10am-8pm.)*
- **CURRENCY EXCHANGE: Banco Santander** *(Pl. de Santo Domingo ☎987 29 23 00 ⏰ Open Apr-Sept M-F 8:30am-2pm; Oct-Mar M-F 8:30am-2pm, Sa 8:30am-1pm.)*
- **LUGGAGE STORAGE:** Storage available at the RENFE train station *(€3)* and bus station *(€2)*.
- **INTERNET ACCESS: Locutorio La Rua** *(C. Varillas, 3 ☎987 21 99 94 ⏰ Open M-F 9:30am-9:30pm, Sa 10:30am-2:30pm and 5:30-9pm. $ €1 per hr.)*
- **POST OFFICE:** *(Jardín de San Francisco ☎987 87 60 81, open M-F 8:30am-8:30pm, Sa 9am-1pm).*

Emergency!

- **EMERGENCY NUMBER:** ☎112.

- **POLICE:** *(Paseo del Parque ☎987 25 55 00)*
- **HOSPITALS/MEDICAL SERVICES: Hospital San Juan de Dios** *(Av. San Ignacio de Loyola, 73 ☎987 23 25 00.)*

Getting There

By Bus

Buses arrive at the bus station *(Av. del Ingeniero Sáenz de Miera ☎987 21 10 00)* across the river from **Astorga** *(⏰ 50min., M-F 17 per day 7am-10:30pm, Sa 8 per day 8:30am-7:30pm, Su 6 per day 11:50am-11:50pm. $ €3.30),* **Barcelona** *(⏰ 10hr., 3 per day 8:45am-10pm. $ €45),* **Bilboa** *(⏰ 5½hr., M-Sa at 9:15am. $ €23.75),* **Burgos** *(⏰ 2-3hr., M-Sa 4 per day 6:35am-5:25pm, Su 3 per day 6:35am-5:25pm. $ €13.85),* **Logroño** *(⏰ 4hr., 3 per day 4:35am-3:15pm. $ €16-19),* **Madrid** *(⏰ 3-4hr., M-F 18 per day 9am-12:30am, Sa-Su 14 per day 9am-11:30pm. $ €21-26),* **San Sebastián** *(⏰ 7hr., M-Sa at 7:40am. $ €28.47),* and **Santiago de Compostela** *(⏰ 6hr., daily at 8am. $ €26.41).*

By Train

Trains arrive at the RENFE station *(C. Astorga ☎902 24 02 02),* also on the other side of the river, right next to the bus station, or at the FEVE station *(Av. del Padre Isla, 48 ☎987 22 59 19).* RENFE trains arrive from **Barcelona** *(⏰ 8hr., 3 per day 9:20am-8:45pm. $ €68),* **Bilbao** *(⏰ 5hr., daily at 9:15am. $ €30),* **Burgos** *(⏰ 2hr., 4 per day 12:10pm-4am. $ €20-37),* **Madrid** *(⏰ 3-4hr., 9 per day 6:50am-10:30pm. $ €33-43),* **San Sebastián** *(⏰ 5hr., daily at 9am. $ €33.20),* and **Santiago de Compostela** *(⏰ 8hr., daily at 9:25am. $ €31.40).* FEVE trains arrive from **Bilbao** *(⏰ 7hr., daily at 2:30pm. $ €22).*

By Plane

Flights arrive at León Airport 4mi. outside of the city from **Madrid** and **Barcelona.**

Getting Around

The easiest and cheapest way to get around is to **walk.** León has a **bus** system; bus #14 goes to the bus station, and #4 and #10 go to the RENFE train station. **Taxi stands** can be found at the Pl. Santo Domingo and along Av. Ordoño II, or call Radio Taxi *(☎987 26 14 15).*

astorga ☎987

Rising over the surrounding plain, Astorga (pop. 12,000) is the last major stop for Santiago-bound pilgrims before they hit the mountains like a caravan of steamrollers—or of tired pilgrims. Astorga has always been a crossroad: of silver-trading routes during Roman times, of pilgrimage trails during the Middle Ages, and of the A-6 and AP-71 today. The small old city is the renowned home of one of the few Gaudí buildings outside of Cataluña and also boasts a staggering rio of chocolate shops to square feet. In fact, Astorga may be the only city in Spain with more sweets shops than churches, and we bow down to its greatness. Those up to the challenge can try to eat one sugary treat from every store in town. C'mon. *Let's Go* double-dog dares you.

ORIENTATION

Astorga is a small city with Roman and medieval historic sights situated around the edges of its old city. The **Camino de Santiago** cuts through the center of town, passing the **Plaza de España,** the city's main square, at the eastern end and the **Plaza de Eduardo de Castro** at the northwest corner. The **bus station** *(Av. de las Murallas, 52 ☎987 61 91 00)* is just outside the northwest corner of the old city, and the **train station** *(Pl. de la Estación ☎987 84 21 22)* is about a 15min. walk to the northeast. Many accommodations are located a short walk west of the old city, about 15min. west of the bus station along **Av. de las Murallas,** which becomes **Av. de Ponferrada.**

ACCOMMODATIONS

Inexpensive lodging is tough to come by in Astorga: there's only one *hostal* and one *pensión* in the entire old city. However, there are three reasonably priced *hostales* and one *pensión* at the intersection of Av. de Ponferrada and the Carretera Madrid-Coruña, about a 15min. walk west of the historic center.

PENSIÓN GARCÍA — PENSIÓN [2]

Bajada del Postigo, 3 — ☎987 61 60 46

One of the only affordable accommodations in the old city itself, this *pensión* sits on a sloping street in the southeast corner of town, where several sights and much of the nightlife are located. The rooms have low but wide beds and are filled with the delicious aromas that waft up from the affiliated restaurant below.

➔ From Pl. de España, take C. de la Bañeza (to right of Ayuntamiento); it's across from the playground. ℹ All rooms have shared bath. Make reservations in advance. $ Singles €20; doubles €30. ⏰ Reception 8am-midnight.

HOSTAL SAN NARCISO — HOSTAL [2]

Ctra. Madrid-Coruña, km 325 — ☎987 61 53 70

About a 15min. walk from the old town, this *hostal* has huge rooms at very reasonable prices. Apparently, the builders were so set on making the rooms as big as possible for you that they made the walls as thin as they could to maximize living space, so you'd better hope your neighbors don't snore, smoke, or watch TV.

➔ From the bus stop, take a right onto Av. de las Murallas, which passes through Pl. del Aljibe and becomes Av. de Ponferrada. Follow Av. de Ponferrada 5 blocks, then turn left before the gas station, and the hostal is across the street. $ Singles €20, with bathroom €25; doubles €30, with bathroom €35. ⏰ Reception 24hr.

SIGHTS

Most of Astorga's must-sees are located within the small old city, where monumental **Roman walls** still surround some of the town. The partially excavated Roman **forum** and **baths** are in the southeast corner, and the **Museo Romano** *(Pl. San Bartolomé ☎987 61 69 37 ⏰ Open June-Sept Tu-Sa 10am-1:30pm and 4-6pm, Su 10am-1:30pm; Oct-May Tu-Sa 10am-1:30pm and 5-7:30pm, Su 10am-1:30pm. $ €2.50)* is just a couple of blocks away by the **Plaza de España.** The monumental **Cathedral** and **Palacio Episcopal** are in the northwest corner.

PALACIO EPISCOPAL AND MUSEO DE LOS CAMINOS — MUSEUM, PALACE

Pl. de Eduardo de Castro — ☎987 61 68 82

From outside, the Palacio Episcopal (one of the few buildings outside of Cataluña designed by architect **Antoni Gaudí,** though those who have been to León probably think they're everywhere) looks like a quirky medieval castle perched above the Roman wall. The interior is magnificent, including an open floorplan, ceramic-lined arches and doorways, and seemingly weightless walls that are in places made more of glass than of stone. Since 1963 Gaudí's palace has housed the **Museo de los Caminos,** whose collection contains Paleolithic, Roman, and modern artifacts.

➔ Just east of the Cathedral; from the bus station, cross the street, go through the small park and up the stairs, then turn left. $ €2.50, €4 combined ticket available for Palacio Episcopal and Cathedral Museum (also €2.50). ⏰ Open Oct-May Tu-Sa 11am-2pm and 4-6pm, Su 11am-2pm; June-Sept 10am-2pm and 4-8pm, Su 10am-2pm.

CATEDRAL DE ASTORGA AND MUSEO CATEDRALICIO

Pl. de la Catedral

♠& CHURCH

☎987 61 58 20

This Cathedral built between the 15th and 18th centuries rises over the city with an imposing amalgamation of Gothic, Renaissance, and Baroque motifs that reflect the periods over which it was constructed. Though there isn't much about the interior of the Cathedral that stands out apart from the flatscreen TV (so those with obstructed views can see Mass), the **Museo Catedralicio** has a phenomenal collection of manuscripts and documents from as early as 934 BCE as well as coins from the 16th century. Look for one from the king of León during the 12th century that sports an awesome hand-drawn lion.

⚎ From the bus station, cross the street, go through the small park and up the stairs, then turn right. ⑤€2.50, pilgrims €1, €4 entrada combinada available for Cathedral Museum and Palacio Episcopal. ۩ Cathedral side door open M-Sa 9-11am, Su 11am-1pm. Museum with Cathedral visit included open Tu-Sa 10am-2pm and 4-8pm, Su 10am-2pm.

FOOD

Astorga rose to prominence as the **chocolate capital of Spain** due to several factors: a cool, dry climate perfect for cocoa growth, an established network of trade routes, and, of course, the large local population of clergy and their notorious love of the sinful sweet. Since the 17th century, Astorga has been filled with chocolate factories (as many as 50 in 1914), and sweet shops line the streets of the old city today. Other local specialties are *cecina* (cured beef) and *Maragato* stew (chickpeas, potato, chorizo, cabbage, and various meats).

MUSEO DE CHOCOLATE

C. José María Goy, 5

⊗ DESSERT, MUSEUM ❶

☎987 61 62 20

The Museo de Chocolate falls somewhere between the world's most delicious museum and the world's most informative desserterie. Redolent of fresh chocolate throughout, the museum is full of artifacts from Astorga's historic chocolate industry and ends with a *degustación:* free samples of **dozens of different types of chocolate.** And they're damn good, too: who would know chocolate better than a museum dedicated to it?

⚎ From Pl. de Eduardo de Castro (in front of Palacio Episcopal), head east 3 blocks along C. de los Sitios to Pl. Obispo Alcolea, then right onto C. José María Goy. ⑤ €2, under 18 and over 65 €1, under 10 free. ۩ Open May-Sep Tu-Sa 10:30am-2pm and 4:30-7pm, Su 11am-2pm; Oct-Apr Tu-Sa 10:30am-2pm and 4-6pm, Su 11am-2pm.

CAFE BAR GAUDÍ

Pl. de Eduardo de Castro, 1

♠&Ɏ CAFE ❶

☎987 61 73 15

A nice little cafe right next to the Cathedral and Palacio Episcopal. The *bocadillos* are enormous, and the *tostas* (like toasted, open-faced sandwiches, only better) are fresh out of the oven and delicious.

⚎ On Pl. de Eduardo de Castro, on the corner closest to the Cathedral. ⑤ Bocadillos €3-5. Tostas €5.50. ۩ Open daily 8am-11pm.

RESTAURANTE SERRANO

C. Portería, 2

♠&Ɏ ASTORGAN ❸

☎987 617 866

This restaurant features *maragato* cuisine, the area's traditional home cookin'. The specialty is a *cecina con foie (cured beef with foie; €16)* that's big enough for at least two and best accompanied with plenty of bread to cut the overpowering richness.

⚎ Take C. Portería from Pl. de la Catedral. ⑤ Menú €12. Entrees €8-18. ۩ Open Tu-Su noon-4pm and 8-11pm.

NIGHTLIFE

Of the various things for which Astorga is known, nightlife cannot be considered one of them. What nightlife there is can be found on the east side of the old city, on **C. de Gabriel Franco** and **C. de Rodríguez de Cela**.

SIEMPRE

@⊗� CLUB, BAR ❶

C. de Gabriel Franco, 10 ☎987 61 58 78

Weary from walking here through the Pyrenees or just plain tired after the bus ride? Drown your pilgrims' sorrows in a massive cocktail made from seemingly random amounts of seemingly random liquors, topped off with a dash of 7 Up. Then reenergize yourself and dance the Astorgan night away.

✈ *From Pl. de España, head south on C. de Pietro de Castro, and take a left onto C. de Gabriel Franco.* ⑤ *Beer €1.50. Cocktails €3.50-7.* ☒ *Open Th-Sa 11:30am-5am.*

ESSENTIALS

Practicalities

- **TOURIST OFFICE: Oficina Municipal de Turismo** has detailed maps of the city and schedules for all major sights, buses, and trains. *(Pl. de Eduardo de Castro, 5 ☎987 61 82 22* ◼*www.ayuntamientodeastorga.com)* ✈ *From bus station, cross the street, walk through the small park and up the stairs; go between the Cathedral (the massive building to the right) and the Palacio Episcopal (the massive building to the left), and left in front of Palacio Episcopal. The office is across the street.* ☒ *Open Tu-Sa 10am-1:30pm and 4-6:30pm, Su 10am-1:30pm.)*

- **TOURS: Ruta Romana** offers tours of Roman Astorga *(⑤ €3.30.* ☒ *1¾hr., Tu-Sa 11am and 5pm, Su 11am)* that leave from in front of the tourist office.

- **CURRENCY EXCHANGE AND ATMS: Banco Santander** is right down the street from the tourist office, Cathedral, and Palacio Episcopal. *(P. Obispo Alcolea, 10 ☎902 24 24 24* ✈ *From Pl. de Eduardo de Castro follow C. de los Sitios east.* ☒ *Open M-F 8:30am-2:30pm.)*

- **INTERNET ACCESS: Ciberastor** offers internet access and printing. *(C. Manuel Gullón, 2 ☎987 61 80 17* ◼ *www.ciberastor.com* ✈ *From Pl. de España, take C. Pietro de Castro 1 block.* ⑤ *Internet access €2 per hr.* ☒ *Open daily 10am-2pm and 4-10pm.)*

Emergency!

- **EMERGENCY NUMBERS:** Police: ☎092.

- **MUNICIPAL POLICE: Policía Municipal** *(Pl. Arquitecto Gaudí, 6 ☎987 61 60 80* ✈ *From Pl. de España, head northeast on C. Ovalle 1 block, then across the street, on the right.)*

- **MEDICAL SERVICES: Centro de Salud** *(C. de Alcalde Carro Verdejo, 11 ☎987 61 66 88* ✈ *From bus station, turn right onto Av. de las Murallas, then turn right at the rotary onto C. de Alcalde Carro Verdejo.)*

- **POST OFFICE: Correos** *(C. Correos, 3 ☎987 61 54 42* ✈ *From Pl. de Eduardo de Castro, follow C. de los Sitios east through Pl. Obispo Alcolea, and keep straight on C. de la Cruz for 3 blocks; the post office is on the left.* ☒ *Open M-F 8:30am-2:30pm, Sa 9:30am-1pm.)*

astorga • essentials

Getting There

By Bus

ALSA runs **buses** from: **Bilbao** *($ €28.65. ⏰ 6½hr., daily 10:45am)*, **Burgos** *($ €17.15. ⏰ 4hr.; M-Sa 4 per day 6:35am-5:25pm, Su 3 per day 6:35am-5:25pm)*, **Barcelona** *($ €50. ⏰ 11-12hr., 4 per day 8:30am-8pm)*, **Gijón** *($ €13. ⏰ 2½-3hr., 3 per day 8am-6:30pm)* **León** *($ €3.30. ⏰ 50min.; M-F 20 per day 6am-9:30pm, Sa 8 per day 7:30am-8:30pm, Su 6 per day 10:30am-8:30pm)*, **Madrid** *($ €21-35. ⏰ 4-5hr.; M-F 10 per day 9:30am-12:30am, Sa-Su 8 per day 9:30am-12:30am)*, **Santiago de Compostela** *($ €20. ⏰ 4-5hr., 5 per day 8am-11:15pm)*, and **Sevilla** *($ €36. ⏰ 9½hr., daily 11:40pm)*.

By Train

Trains arrive from: **Bilbao** *($ €31.60. ⏰ 5¼hr., daily 9:15am)*, **Burgos** *($ €23-42. ⏰ 2½hr., 3 per day 12:11pm-2:49am)* **Barcelona** *($ €70-91. ⏰ 8-9hr., 2 per day 9:20am and 8:20pm)* **León** *($ €4-13. ⏰ 30min.; M-F 8 per day 7:10am-4:50am, Sa 6 per day 2:03pm-4:50am, Su 7 per day 2:03pm-4:50am)*, **San Sebastián** *($ €35.70. ⏰ 5½hr., daily at 9am.)*, and **Santiago de Compostela** *($ €29.30. ⏰ 5hr., daily 9:25am)*. The nearest **airport** is in León.

Getting Around

Astorga is a small city, and you can **walk** from one end to the other in under 30min. There is also a **taxi stand** at Pl. Obispo Alcolea *(☎987 61 60 00)*.

villafranca del bierzo

The tiny but beautiful town of Villafranca del Bierzo lies on the Camino de Santiago, hidden in the mountains and valleys of Spain's rugged northwest. Villafranca is beyond "cute." English does not have an adjective that adequately describes how adorable this village is. A little under 2hr. by bus from Astorga, Villafranca is full of ancient churches, narrow, cobble-stoned streets, and plazas from which you can see the town's medieval buildings silhouetted against the dramatic mountains that surround the village.

ACCOMMODATIONS

Try not to miss the last bus out of town, as cheap accommodations in Villafranca are practically non-existent. If you have to stay the night, **Hostal Burbia** is on a quiet street just a couple of blocks from the tourist office. *(C. de la Fuente de Cubero, 13 ☎987 54 26 67 💻www.hostalburbia.com ℹ Credit cards accepted. Breakfast included. All rooms with ensuite bath, Internet available. $ Singles €35-40; doubles €45-50. Extra bed €12. ⏰ Reception 8am-11pm.)*

SIGHTS

The **Iglesia de San Francisco** founded by St. Francis of Assisi himself according to legend, towers over the town with its 13th-century Romanesque doorway *(open Tu-Su 10am-1:30pm and 4-7pm, free admission; take the stairs from the southeast corner of Pl. Mayor)*. Up the hill at the southeast corner of town are the **Castillo de Villafranca** (you can't go in, but hey, a castle's a castle) and the 12th-century Romanesque **Iglesia de Santiago,** whose Puerta del Perdón is the Camino's end for those too ill to make it to Santiago de Compostela. *(Iglesia de Santiago $ Free admission. ⏰ Open daily 11am-1:30pm and 4:30-8:30pm.)* From the Iglesia de Santiago, you can **follow the Camino** along the postcard-like **C. de Ribadeo** and across the **Puente Medieval,** a majestic old bridge that takes westward pilgrims over the Río Burbia and on to Santiago.

FOOD

Restaurants and bars line the town's plazas and streets, especially **Pl. Mayor.** For something a little bit off the beaten track (in case Villafranca itself was too on-the-beaten-track for you), **El Padrino** has a €12 menú and a local feel. *(C. del Doctor Aren, 17 ☎987 54 00 75 ⏰ Open daily 1-3:30pm and 8-11pm)* Try not to miss the last bus out of town, as cheap accommodations in Villafranca are practically non-existent; if you have to stay the night, **Hostal Burbia** is on a quiet street just a couple of blocks from the tourist office. *(C. de la Fuente de Cubero, 13 ☎987 54 26 67 🖥www.hostalburbia.com ℹ Breakfast included, private bath, TV, internet. $ Singles €35-40, doubles €45-50. Extra bed €12. ⏰ Reception 8am-11pm.)*

ESSENTIALS

Before exploring Villafranca, pick up a map at the **tourist office;** the town is small, but its winding streets are very confusing. *(Av. de Bernardo Díez Ovelar, 10 ☎987 54 00 28 🖥www.villafrancadelbierzo.org ℹ English and French spoken. ⏰ Open daily 10am-2pm and 4-8pm.)*

Getting There

Buses leave from **Astorga** *(⏰ 2hr., 5 per day M-Sa 8:20am-5:15pm, Su 11:20am-6:20pm).* Many find it more convenient to change buses in Ponferrada, which allows for visits to Villafranca that don't have to end before 1pm. Buses leave for Ponferrada from Astorga (*$ €4.75. ⏰ 1hr.; M-F 14 per day 6:40am-10:10pm, Sa 6 per day 8:20am-9:10pm, Su 6 per day 11:10am-9:10pm*), and for Villafranca del Bierzo from Ponferrada (*$ €1.40 ⏰ 30min., M-F 11 per day 9:30am-8:30pm, Sa 4 per day 9:30am-5:30pm, Su 5 per day 9am-9:30pm; return M-F 11 per day 8am-7pm, Sa 4 per day 8am-5pm, Su 5 per day 10am-9pm*). Buses arrive in front of Hostal La Charola on Ctra. Madrid-Coruña; to get to the center of town from bus stop, cross the highway and follow Av. del Calvo Sotelo, which becomes C. del Campairo and leads to Pl. Mayor. Most buses leave from the same stop, but some buses leave from in front of tourist office on Av. de Bernardo Díez Ovelar; check with tourist office for bus locations.

santiago de compostela ☎981

If you've made it to Santiago after finishing the Camino, congratulations. Kick back with some local *tinto* or white *albariño* and give those tired pilgrims' feet a rest. If you flew here, give your stiff neck a rest and *Let's Go* will keep the congratulations. Santiago de Compostela (pop. 94,000) has grown with the centuries as its colonnaded streets have swollen with pilgrims from around the world. The **Cathedral,** which houses the remains of the city's namesake **St. James,** is the main attraction, and much of the city—from the be-crossed almond cakes to the multilingual *menús*—is geared toward its visitors. There's more to the city than pilgrims, though: the nightlife buzzes with students from USC (Universidade de Santiago de Compostela, not its sunnier Californian counterpart), and every restaurant's window is full of octupi and giant, Hershey's-kiss-shaped cheeses. Though it's known for its pilgrims, and it certainly embraces that identity, Santiago has its own, quirky character hiding beneath each arch of the ancient old city.

ORIENTATION

As soon as you arrive in Santiago, be sure to get a **map,** since the streets are very poorly marked. The main streets of the old city are **Rúa do Franco, Rúa do Vilar,** and **Rúa Nova,** which run (with some name changes, at times) from the **Praza do Obradoiro** and the **Catedral de Santiago de Compostela,** the old city's hub, to the **Praza de Galicia,** which sits between the old and new parts of town. The **bus station** *(Pr. de Camilo Díaz Baliño*

☎981 54 24 16 🕐 *Open daily 6am-10pm)* is to the northeast of the old city. To get to Pr. de Galicia, take bus # 2 or #5 *(💲 €0.90),* or head right on R. de Ánxel Casal, then left at the rotary onto R. da Pastoriza. Because this area is a living IQ test, this street subsequently turns into R. dos Basquiños, then R. de Santa Clara, and finally R. de San Roque. Next, turn left onto R. das Rodas which will turn into R. de Aller Ulloa, R. da Virxe da Cerca, R. da Ensinanza, and Fonte de Santo Antonio before reaching Pr. de Galicia. The **train station** *(R. de Hórreo ☎902 24 02 02)* is on the south end of the city; take bus #6 to get to Pr. de Galicia, or walk up the stairway across the parking lot from the main entrance and take R. do Hórreo uphill about 7 blocks.

ACCOMMODATIONS   🚩

HOSPEDAJE FONSECA   🚭⊗⊗⁽ᵞ⁾ PENSIÓN ❷
R. de Fonseca, 1, 2nd fl.   ☎646 93 77 65

The modern décor of this *pensión's* bright, high-ceilinged rooms contrasts with the ancient facade of the Cathedral, a literal stone's throw away across the street. These are just about the best prices you're going to find in the old city, and you couldn't dream of a better location.

🍴 *Take R. do Franco toward Pr. do Obradoiro, then turn right just before the Cathedral (1 block past little plaza) onto R. de Fonseca. Hospedaje Fonseca is on Rúa de Fonseca, not Praza de Fonseca or Travesa de Fonseca, which are all within 2 blocks of each other.* i *All rooms have shared bath.* 💲 *Jul-Sept singles €20-22; doubles €35. Oct-Jun €15-18 per person.* 🕐 *Reception 8:30am-11pm.*

A NOSA CASA   ➳⊗⁽ᵞ⁾ PENSIÓN ❸
R. Entremurallas, 9   ☎981 58 59 26 🖥www.anosacasa.com

This family-run *pensión's* comfortable rooms overlook a narrow, quiet street in the old town and are located a few blocks from the Cathedral and one block from the old city's main bus stop. The owners are more helpful and knowledge-able when it comes to Santiago than the tourist office, and they serve up a mean home-cooked breakfast every morning *(€3).*

🍴 *From main bus stop look up R. Entremurallas.* i *Breakfast €3. Laundry service available. All rooms with private bath.* 💲 *Singles €28-36; doubles €40-49; triples €52-62.* 🕐 *Reception 8am-10:30pm.*

HOSTAL PAZO DE AGRA   ➳⊗ PENSIÓN ❸
R. da Caldeirería, 37   ☎981 58 90 45

The rooms are not quite as palatial as the "Agra" part of the name might suggest (Agra is the Taj Mahal's hometown), but feel free to address your subjects from your room's balcony over the old city. Or ignore the plebes and just bask in the view. The bathrooms are private, but for singles they're outside the room across a narrow hallway, so you'll still need to cover up after a shower.

🍴 *From Pr. de Galicia, take R. das Orfas into old city; it becomes R. da Caldeirería after 3 blocks, and the hostal is on the right after 1 more block.* i *Private baths, but for singles are outside rooms.* 💲 *June-Sept singles €32; doubles €40. Oct-May singles €26; doubles €36.* 🕐 *Reception 24hr.*

PENSIÓN BADALADA   ➳⊗⁽ᵞ⁾ PENSIÓN ❸
R. de Xelmírez, 30   ☎981 57 26 18 🖥www.badalada.es

The rates are nearly as steep as the cobblestone street out front, but you could literally roll down the street to the Cathedral if you were so **inclined.** The rooms are small, but walls of stone decorated with vivid colors give them a cozy feel, and those on the top floor have views of the Cathedral.

🍴 *2 blocks up R. de Xelmírez from Pr. das Praterías.* i *Private bath, TV.* 💲 *Apr-Oct singles €35; doubles €47. Nov-Mar singles €40; doubles €59.* 🕐 *Reception 8:30am-11pm.*

the camino

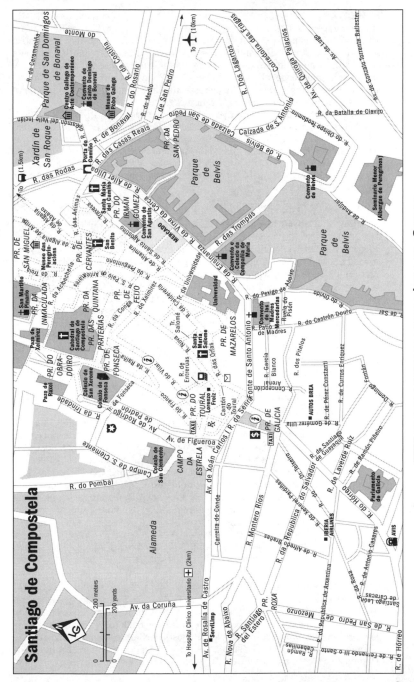

Santiago de Compostela

AS CANCELAS CAMPING [1]

R. do 25 de Xullo, 35 ☎981 58 02 66

Guests at this campsite can make the pilgrimage to Santiago de Compostela every day: the final 2km Camino runs just a couple blocks from the campsite toward the Cathedral, so guests can make the easiest and most brag-worthy part of the pilgrimage whenever they'd like. While As Cancelas is a campsite, it's hardly roughing it: there's a fancy restaurant and bar, and it's just a couple of blocks from a 5min. bus ride to the center of town.

 # Bus #4 (M-F every 30min., Sa-Su every hr.) runs from R. da Senra stop just west of Pr. de Galicia to As Cancelas. Or a 2km walk from old town north on R. de San Roque to Pr. da Paz to R. de San Caetano to Pr. de España, then right onto R. das Cancelas and right onto R. de 25 de Xullo. i Supermarket, cafeteria, restaurant, pool, and laundry service available. $ Sept-June €5 per person, under 12 €2.90; €5 per car; €5 per tent; 4-person bungalow €49, 5-person €59. July-Aug €6.40 per person, under 12 €4.70; €6.70 per car; €6.70 per tent; 4-person bungalow €80, 5-person €96. ⏰ Reception 9:30am-11:30pm.

SIGHTS

CATEDRAL DE SANTIAGO DE COMPOSTELA AND MUSEUM CHURCH, MUSEUM

Pr. das Praterías ☎981 58 11 55; 981 56 93 27 🖥www.catedraldesantiago.es

Pilgrims have arrived at this site for more than a millennia, walking here by following the well-trodden Camino de Santiago in order to gain personal fulfillment and their **plenary indulgence** from the Church. The Cathedral's towers speckled with mosses, lichens, and flowers rise from the center of the city, making the enormous holy site look as though it has spent the last couple of centuries at the bottom of the nearby ocean. It has been above water the whole time, though (unless you count the frequent Galician rains), and the site has been a destination of pilgrims since the **relics of James the Apostle** were discovered here in the 9th century. Work on the ancient Romanesque cathedral began in 1075 and was completed in 1211, though the cloister was added during the Spanish Renaissance and most of the facades are 17th- to 18th-century Baroque. Today, pilgrims and tourists line up to **embrace the jewel-encrusted statue** of the Apostle and see the silver coffer that contains his remains. The *botafumeiro*, the massive silver-plated censer swung across the altar to disperse thick clouds of incense in the Cathedral's most famous spectacle, is usually used during the noon service, though the schedule varies and is not made public. The Cathedral's bells are older than the Cathedral itself, taken to Córdoba in 997 by invading Moors. Fortunately, the reconquering Christians had the last laugh when they took Córdoba in the 13th century and made their prisoners carry the bells all the way back to Santiago. The **museum** includes the peaceful cloister, the library (the books that line the shelves are ancient, but many of those on display are facsimiles), and the crypt. That funky smell in the crypt is caused by the humidity, not by human remains—or at least that's the official line.

 # Enter Cathedral on Pr. das Praterías; the museum entrance is inside on the left. $ Cathedral free; museum €5, students, seniors and pilgrims €3. ⏰ Cathedral open daily 7am-9pm; museum open June-Sept M-Sa 10am-2pm and 4-8pm, Su 10am-2pm; Oct-May M-Sa 10am-1:30pm and 4-6:30pm, Su 10am-1:30pm.

MUSEO DAS PEREGRINACIÓNS MUSEUM [1]

R. de San Miguel dos Agros, 4 ☎981 58 15 58 🖥www.mdperegrinacions.com

This 14th-century palace has three stories of artifacts and historical information pertaining to pilgrimages of worldwide faiths going back to prehistory, but there is a predictable and understandable emphasis on Catholicism, particularly the Camino de Santiago route. Upstairs, there is an 18th-century map of Santiago de Compostela (try to map your own pilgrimage back to your hotel) and a room of artwork depicting James the Apostle slaying Moors like its his job.

Follow R. do Preguntoiro through Pr. de Cervantes as it becomes R. da Algalia de Arriba, then turn left onto R. de San Miguel dos Agros. $ €2.40, students €1.20, under 18, pilgrims, and seniors free. Free Sa 5-8 and Su. ⏰ Open Tu-F 10am-8pm, Sa 10am-1:30pm and 5-8pm, Su 10am-1:30pm.

GREAT OUTDOORS

Both of these sights are a good bus ride away from Santiago de Compostela.

CABO FINISTERRE (CABO FISTERRA) — CAPE

For some pilgrims, walking from the Pyrenees (or beyond) to Santiago is just not enough. The route continues beyond the Cathedral and keeps going until there's not another foot of dry land left to walk at **Cape Finisterre**—literally "the end of the earth," once believed to be just that. The wind-battered cape sticks out into the Atlantic, reaching toward the New World from the infamous **Costa da Morte** ("Coast of Death"; Costa de la Muerte in Spanish), so called because of its jagged shores treacherous to seafarers and those made queasy by long, winding bus rides. The tiny town of **Fisterra,** once a trading hub at a nexus of sea routes, has narrow, winding alleys down to a lively port with restaurants lining the boardwalk and exhausted backpackers sunning themselves on the rocks.

It's a 45min. walk uphill along the road to the **lighthouse** at the end of the cape *(follow signs for the faro),* the very end of the Old World. Stunning views of the town, ocean, and nearby coastline are the prize that greets those who make it to the end of the trail, and the route runs past the ruins of an 18th-century fortress near the edge of town. 45min. in the other direction from Fisterra are the town's best beaches, though the water's usually chilly. To get there, walk the 3mi. along the road back to Santiago or take the bus and ask the driver to stop at the beaches. A 1hr. hike inland takes you up **Monte San Guillermo** home to several odd rituals. Pilgrims burn their clothes, couples having trouble conceiving make love on the bed-shaped fertility rocks, and weaklings and strong men alike move boulders by rolling **As Pedras Santas** (the round rocks move effortlessly when pushed in the right spot).

The **Albergue de Peregrinos** *(C. Real, 2 ☎981 74 07 81 ⏰ Open Sept-May M-F 11am-2pm and 5-10pm, Jun-Aug 1-10pm)* has tourist information.

The bus stop is near the Albergue de Peregrinos, a couple of blocks uphill from the water. ⏰ Buses €11.85; round-trip €21.70. i Castromil/Monbus runs buses from Santiago to Fisterra. Last bus 7pm.

O CASTRO DE BAROÑA — BEACH, RUINS

An hour's bus ride to the sea and another 30min. on a local bus down the coast takes you to **O Castro de Baroña,** a beautiful, out-of-the-way site that holds the ruins of a **5th-century Celtic fortress** and a small but pristine crescent beach. A rocky, overgrown trail leads out to a lonely promontory sticking out into the crashing waves, with the remains of the castle close to the bluff and high above the sea. All that remain of the 1500-year-old structures are their foundations and low walls, but the site is great to explore and enjoy the views of the sea and coast. Another path goes down to a quiet beach, whose cold but calm waters are protected by the cove. Clothing is *"prohibido,"* but many beachgoers remain bathing-suited, and hostility toward the clothed is limited. There's little there beyond the fort, beach, and a bar, but a 45min. walk or 5min. bus back toward Noia (to the left as you face the road from the bar) is Porto do Son, which has inexpensive restaurants and accommodations near the bus stop.

To reach O Castro, you'll need to change buses in Noia. Castromil/Monbus runs buses from Santiago to and from Noia. (€3, round-trip €5.95). From Noia, Hefsel runs buses that stop at O Castro de Baroña (in front of Cafe-Bar O Castro) en route to Ribeira (€1.85) and return to Noia from the same stop. Check in the bar for the most up-to-date information and schedules, and take note of the last bus for each day. Be sure to tell the bus driver where you're going, as the stop for O Castro is easy to miss. From the bus stop, follow the signs to the fortress, downhill toward the water: at the fork with the two signs, the fortress is to the right, the beach to the left.

FOOD

👍 A TULLA — 💳🚭🍸☀ GALICIAN [2]

R. de Entrerrúas, 1 — ☎981 58 08 89

This is definitely the sort of place you have to know about in order to find—it's hidden down a crooked alley only a few feet wide—but those in the know just keep coming back. Pick just about anything off the handwritten menu (in Galego, of course), and it's bound to be delicious. Combine the *lentejas* (lentil stew; €3.50) with *chourizo á sidra* (spicy sausage cooked in cider; €4.50) to create one of the most delicious dishes in existence. They also have lots of vegetarian options, and a vegetarian *menú* (€10).

🧭 In narrow alley between Rúa Nova and R. do Vilar, just toward Cathedral from Pr. do Toural on R. Nova, and just toward Cathedral from Municipal Tourist Office on R. do Vilar. $ Menú del día €12, vegetarian menú €10. Soups/vegetables €3.50-7.50. Entrees €4.50-12.50. ⏰ Open June-July M-Tu 1-4pm and 8:30pm-midnight, Th-Su 1-4pm and 8:30pm-midnight; Aug-May M-W 1-4pm, Th-Sa 1-4pm and 8:30pm-midnight, Su 1-4pm.

👍 O DEZASEIS — 💳♿🍸 GALICIAN [3]

R. de San Pedro, 16 — ☎981 56 48 80 💻www.dezaseis.com

If you're willing to shell out just a few more euro, you can get a serious step up in quality. This basement restaurant has an earthy stone-and-wood feel and delicious regional cuisine at very affordable prices. The classics like *tortilla española* (€5.40) are superb, and if you want a dish that Santiago himself would approve of, try the *vieira a galega* (a huge scallop served in its own shell, like the ones that line the Camino; €4.20). If you keep the shell, clean it, paint a cross on it, and sell it to a pilgrim, and the dish will nearly pay for itself.

🧭 Take R. da Virxe da Cerca along the edge of the old city, then turn onto R. de San Pedro away from old city. $ Menú del día €12. Raciones €3.50-13.50. Entrees €12-14.50. ⏰ Open M-Sa 2-4pm and 8pm-midnight.

CASA MANOLO — 💳🚭🍸☀ SPANISH [2]

Pr. de Cervantes, 3 — ☎981 58 29 50

If you're even paying attention to how the food tastes after marveling at the portion-to-price ratio here, you're a true gourmand and will likely be a bit disappointed by the hit-or-miss *menú*, which has lots of options but only a few gems. The *chipirones* (cuttlefish), in particular, is adventurous but tasty, but many of the toher options are just OK. However, the peckish and the penniless aren't complaining: massive quantities of food at a great price sounds right on the money, so to speak.

🧭 From Pr. do Obradoiro facing Cathedral, go up through arch to left of Cathedral, straight across Pr. da Inmaculada, along R. de Acibechería, and across Pr. de Cervantes (the one with the column in the middle). $ Menú del día €8.50. ⏰ Open M-Sa 1-4pm and 8-11:30pm, Su 1-4pm.

OBRADOIRO — 🚫💳🚭🍸☀ CAFE, BAR [1]

R. do Pombal, 44 — ☎981 57 07 22

Pilgrims fill this bar and cafe for the daily €7 *menú*, which has huge portions and includes fresh bread and wine. With a patio for enjoying the rare but lovely Galician sun, this eatery offers one of the best-priced meals in town that isn't a kebab.

🧭 Just across the street from the Alameda (big park next to the old city); from Pr. de Galicia, follow R. da Senra to the left as you're facing the old city, then stay along the right side of the park down the hill. $ Menú del día €7. ⏰ Kitchen open daily 1-4pm and 8-10pm.

CAFE CASINO 💳♿🍸 CAFE, CONCERT [2]

R. do Vilar, 35 ☎981 57 75 03

Walk out of Santiago's medieval maze and into turn-of-the-century Paris. You could easily picture an arch Degas dashing off a pastel of the slinky-dressed singer as you sink into a plush armchair and enjoy a rich coffee *(€2.50-4)* and a local *tarta de Santiago* *(a not-sweet almond cake with a cross on it; €3.50).*

➜ On R. do Vilar, toward the Cathedral from Pr. do Toural. $ Coffee €2.50-4. Desserts €3.20-5. ⏰ Open M-Th 8:30am-2am, F-Sa 9am-3am, Su 9am-2am. Dinner daily 7:30-11pm.

NIGHTLIFE

Most of Santiago's nightlife is in the **old town** scattered around the **Cathedral,** but the area around the **Praza Roxa** has a more student-oriented scene.

CASA DAS CRECHAS 💳🚭🍸☀ BAR, LOUNGE, LIVE MUSIC [1]

Via Sacra, 3 ☎981 57 61 08 💻www.casadascrechas.com

Take a quick walk up the steps behind the Cathedral and descend into a Celtic witch's den that provides ample seating and beer. There are frequent jazz and Galician folk performances, so call ahead or check the website for the schedule; impromptu *foliadas* usually pop up on Wednesday evening, but you generally just have to be there when the right group of enthusiastic musicians comes in.

➜ From Pr. da Quintana with the Cathedral to your left, head up the stairs and to the right, then left onto Via Sacra. ⏰ Open daily in summer noon-4am; in winter 4pm-3am.

MODUS VIVENDI 💳🚭🍸 BAR, LOUNGE [1]

Pr. Feixóo, 1 ☎981 57 61 09 💻www.pubmodusvivendi.net

Welcome to the heart of Santiago's bohemia. Just about everyone will drop in at some point in the evening to mingle at the packed bar or push their way through to the more laid-back lounge. The trendy art and psychedelic lighting draw an eclectic crowd; the younger groups tend to gravitate to the back, so don't get scared off by all those graying male ponytails in front.

➜ From Pr. da Quintana with the Cathedral to your left, head out to the far left corner of the plaza, then left onto R. da Conga, and bear left. $ Beer €2. Mixed drinks €4.50-6. ⏰ Open July-Sept M-W 6:30pm-3:30am, Th-Su 6:30pm-4:30am; Oct-June M-W 4:30pm-3am, Th-Su 6:30pm-4:30am.

PUB LA CONGA 💳🚭🍸 DANCE CLUB [1]

R. da Conga, 8 ☎981 58 34 07

Come here to dance the night away, but step aside once the Latin dance pros hit the floor at this cool basement dance club. Shake-ira your hips to the salsa, or find a partner and try to keep up—just don't step on any toes.

➜ From Pr. das Praterías (with the fountain with the horses), take R. da Conga (to the right as you face the steps and Pr. da Quintana). $ Beer €2. Mixed drinks €4.50. ⏰ Open M-W 10pm-3am, Th-Sa 10pm-4:15am.

PUB TATOOINE 💳🚭🍸 CLUB, STAR WARS [1]

R. da República Argentina, 50

Far and away the most awesomely nerdy bar in town—if not along the entire Camino. Murals of stormtroopers and Darth Vader adorn this dark basement club, where clients are encouraged to show off their Jedi mind tricks and light sabers. Here, it's the cool kids who stand awkwardly against the wall.

➜ From Pr. de Galicia, take R. do Doutor Teixeiro (follow street on right side of plaza with your back to old town) 2 blocks, then turn right onto R. da República Argentina. $ Beer €1.50-2. ⏰ Open Th-Sa midnight-5am.

ARTS AND CULTURE 🎵

Festivals

APÓSTOLO

Santiago de Compostela celebrates its patron saint's feast day for a full two weeks known as **Apóstolo**, kicking off the party about a week before **el Día de Santiago** (St. James' Day, July 25—especially holy when it falls on a Sunday, which will next be in 2021), the peak of the festivities. On the night of the 24th, **las Vísperas de Santiago**, fireworks and *gaitas* (traditional Galician-Celtic bagpipes) fill the Praza do Obradoiro in front of the Cathedral, while the *botafumeiro* (a giant incense-burner) swings within. July 25 is also **Galicia Day** (*Día de la Patria Galega*), and traditional music and dance fill the city.

📅 *Apóstolo July 16-31; Día de Santiago July 25.*

ASCENCIÓN

Las Fiestas de la Ascención, which begin 40 days after Easter Sunday, is one of the city's biggest festivals, with events and revelry spreading to every corner of Santiago. *Ascención* lasts a week and draws much of its excitement from the participation university students who have just finished their exams. There are cattle markets, equestrian exhibitions, concerts, and a food fair (specializing in octopus) at the *Santa Susana* grove in the Alameda.

📅 *June 3-12, 2011.*

NOITE DE SAN XOÁN

The festival of **San Xoán** (pronounced *"hwan"*—it's the Galego equivalent of Juan, which is the Spanish equivalent of John) is essentially one massive peninsula-wide party, celebrated throughout Iberia with World-Cup-worthy vigor. In Santiago, the festival is marked by daredevils jumping over bonfires lit throughout the town on the night of June 23, as well as local street food in the parks and plazas and religious services in the Cathedral.

📅 *June 23-24.*

Traditional Music and Dance

Thought bagpipes were limited to the British Isles and St. Patty's Day parades? Not so. The **gaita** is a traditional **Galician bagpipe,** left by the Celts during their migration, and it's just as irritating as its Highland cousin. Often heard on Santiago's streets, particularly around the **Pr. do Obradoiro** (the archway to the left of the Cathedral is a popular spot) and in the **Alameda** park, these badboys are inescapable during every major **festival.** Galician folk music's Celtic influences are obvious to the ear, and the best chance to dive into the Galician music scene is **Festival del Mundo Celta de Ortigueira** (🖥*www.festivaldeortigueira.com),* a massive folk festival held every July in tiny Ortigueira. Throughout July, the **Via Stellae Festival de Música** (🖥*www.viastellae.es)* takes place in Santiago and surrounding towns along the Camino; free music of all genres occurs at various venues throughout the city. **ARTERIA Noroeste** *(R. das Salvadas, 2A, Parque Vista Alegre* ☎*981 56 90 82* 🖥*www.arteria.com)* performs music that generally slides along the jazz-to-Galician-folk spectrum. To get to the performance space, take bus #4 toward Cancelas or bus #C2 or C4 toward Fontiñas.

Traditional **Galician dance** is loud and lively and also reflects its Celtic origins—it looks sort of like a castanet-filled combination between an Irish jig and Andalusian flamenco. Demonstrations can be seen at the **festivals,** and sometimes at the **Teatro Principal** *(R. Nova, 21* ☎*981 54 23 47).*

the camino

ESSENTIALS

Practicalities

- **TOURIST OFFICE: Oficina Municipal de Turismo** has maps and thorough information on accommodations, as well as a 24hr. interactive information screen outside. *(R. do Vilar, 63 ☎981 55 51 29 💻www.santiagoturismo.com 🚏 On R. do Vilar 1 block toward Cathedral from Pr. do Toural. ℹ English, French, German, Portuguese, Italian, Galego, and other languages spoken. ⏰ Open daily June-Sept 9am-9pm; Oct-May 9am-2pm and 4-7pm.)* **Oficina de Turismo de Galicia** has information on the rest of Galicia, and on festivals. *(R. do Vilar, 30 ☎981 58 40 81 💻www.turgalicia.es 🚏 On R. do Vilar between Pr. do Toural and Cathedral, on opposite side of street from Municipal Tourism Office but closer to Cathedral. ⏰ Open M-F 10am-8pm, Sa 11am-2pm and 5-7pm, Su 11am-2pm.)* **Oficina del Xacobeo,** in the same building, provides information on the Camino de Santiago. *(R. do Vilar, 30 ☎981 58 40 81 ⏰ Open M-F 10am-8pm.)*
- **CURRENCY EXCHANGE:** Banco Santander has **Western Union** services and a 24hr. **ATM** outside, and cashes American Express Travelers Cheques commission-free. *(Pr. de Galicia, 1 ☎981 58 61 11 🚏 On side of Pr. de Galicia to the right with your back to the old town. ⏰ Open Apr-Sept M-F 8:30am-2pm; Oct-Mar Sa 8:30am-1pm.)*
- **INTERNET ACCESS:** Ciber Nova 50 has fast computers and pay phones. *(R. Nova, 50 ☎981 56 41 33 🚏 On R. Nova 1 block toward the Cathedral from Pr. do Toural. $ €0.45 for 12min., €2 per hour. ⏰ Open M-F 9am-midnight, Sa-Su 10am-midnight.)*
- **ENGLISH-LANGUAGE BOOKS:** Libraria Couceiro has several shelves of books in English. *(Pr. de Cervantes, 6 ☎981 56 58 12 💻www.librariacouceiro.com 🚏 From Pr. de Galicia take R. das Orfas into old city; it becomes R. da Caldeirería, then R. do Preguntoiro, and the bookstore is immediately to the left on Pr. de Cervantes. ⏰ Open M-F 10am-noon and 4-9pm, Sa 10am-noon and 5-9pm.)*
- **POST OFFICE:** Correos has a *Lista de Correos* and fax. *(R. das Orfas ☎981 58 12 52 💻www.correos.es 🚏 Take Cantón do Toural from Pr. do Toural 2 blocks to R. das Orfas. ⏰ Open M-F 8:30am-8:30pm, Sa 9am-2pm.)*

Emergency!

- **POLICE:** Policía Local. *(Pr. do Obradoiro, 1 ☎981 54 23 23 🚏 On Pr. do Obradoiro across from Cathedral.)*
- **MEDICAL SERVICES: Hospital Clínico Universitario** has a public clinic across from the emergency room. *(Tr. da Choupana ☎981 95 00 00 🚏 Take bus #1 from R. da Senra toward Hospital Clínico. ⏰ Clinic open M-Sa 3-8pm, Su 8am-8pm.)*
- **PHARMACY:** Farmacia R. Bescansa has been around since 1843—stop in to gawk at the classic 19th-century decor, even if you don't need anything. *(Pr. do Toural, 11 ☎981 58 59 40.)*

Getting There

By Bus

ALSA *(☎913 27 05 40)* runs buses from: **Astorga** *($ €20. ⏰ 5hr., 4 per day 4:15am-7:30pm);* **Barcelona** *($ €68.80. ⏰ 17hr., 3 per day 7am-8pm);* **Bilbao** *($ €50-53. ⏰ 9-11hr., 4 per day 10:30am-1:45am);* **Burgos** *($ €37. ⏰ 8½hr., daily at 1:15pm);* **León** *($ €26.50. ⏰ 6hr., daily at 4:45pm);* **Madrid** *($ €40-60. ⏰ 8-9hr.; M-Th 5 per day 7:30am-12:30am, F-Sa 4 per day 7:30am-12:30am);* and **Salamanca** *($ €29.20. ⏰ 6-7hr., M-F 3pm and 1:10am, Sa 5pm and 1:10am, Su 2 per day 3pm and 1:10am).*

By Train

RENFE trains arrive from: **A Coruña** (ⓢ €5-15. 🕐 40min., M-F 20 per day 5:45am-10:20pm, Sa 18 per day 6am-10pm, Su 17 per day 7am-10pm); **Bilbao** (ⓢ €44.90. 🕐 11hr., daily at 9:15am); **Burgos** (ⓢ €40. 🕐 8hr., daily at 12:11pm); and **Madrid** (ⓢ €49. 🕐 7-9hr. M-Sa 2 per day 2:20-10:30pm, Su 2 per day 1:22-10:30pm).

By Plane

Ryanair has inexpensive flights to Santiago's Lavacolla Airport (ⓢ €2.50. 🕐 30min. *bus from bus station or city center*) from: Alicante; Barcelona (El Prat); Barcelona (Reus); Madrid; Málaga; Frankfurt-Hahn; London-Stansted; and Rome. **Iberia** flies to Santiago from Bilbao, Sevilla, and Valencia.

Getting Around

Most of the old city is closed off to all but foot traffic, so the easiest way to get around is to **walk**. For those venturing farther afield, **buses** *(€0.90, €0.55 with bono)* are a good way to get around, though not particularly frequent on weekends. Bus #2 and #5 go to the bus station; bus #6 goes to the train station. **Freire** (☎981 58 81 11) runs buses *(30min., €2.50)* from R. do Doutor Teixeiro and the bus station to the airport. There are **taxi** stands at the bus and train stations and at Pr. de Galicia and Pr. Roxa. Otherwise, call Radio Taxi *(☎981 56 92 92)* or Eurotaxi *(☎670 53 51 54)*.

PORTUGAL

LISBON

Portugal's capital is divided into dozens of distinct neighborhoods, each of which feels like its own micro-city within the cohesive metropolis of Lisbon. Each district has its own indelible character, from the graffiti-covered party that is **Bairro Alto** to chic **Chiado,** to touristy **Baixa,** to the crumbling tiles of **Alfama**—cross a single street or descend one steep staircase and you're someplace new. The tired juxtaposition of the ancient and the modern is a common selling point for the travel industry, but this contrast of past and present can be seen and experienced in Lisbon like nowhere else. Colossal new *discotecas* sit on the **Tejo,** mere blocks from Moorish streets and homes that have stood since the Middle Ages, trendy cafes and luxurious hostels have taken over 19th-century palaces, and pre-WWI trams run over cobblestone streets alongside air-conditioned buses. The city stretches on and on, and there are enough sights and restaurants, enough parties and people, and enough sardines and *ginjinha* to keep you in Lisbon for years without getting bored. There's no city better—or easier—in which to get lost.

greatest hits

- **MAKE OUT LIKE A THIEF.** At the aptly named Feira da Ladra market, you can get all manner of knick-knacks on the cheap (p. 380).
- **LARGE AND IN CHARGE.** On the Belém waterfront, you can see tributes to the movers and shakers of the Age of Discovery while making your own moves toward the delicious ⬛Pasteis de Belém bakery (p. 368).
- **CHICKEN OF THE SEA.** For Americans, it's tuna. For the Portuguese, it's sardines. Be sure to try some in the capital city (p. 369).

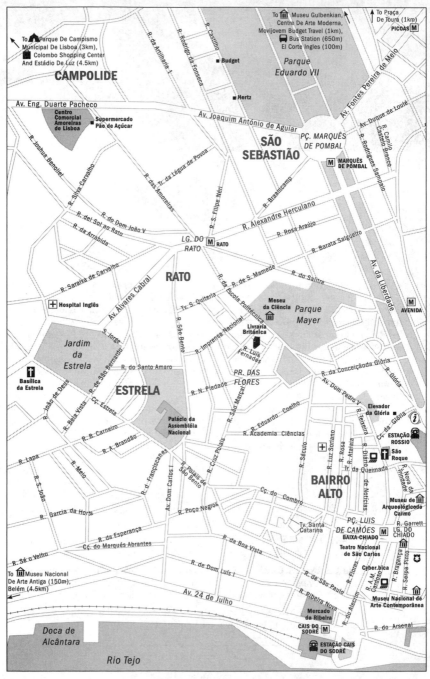

To 🏛 Museu Gulbenkian,
Centre De Arte Moderna,
Movijovem Budget Travel (1km),
🚌 Bus Station (650m)
El Corte Ingles (100m)

To ↑ Praça
De Toura (1km)
PICOAS Ⓜ

To 🏕 Parque De Campismo
Municipal De Lisboa (3km),
🏬 Colombo Shopping Center
And Estádio De Luz (4.5km)

■ Budget

Parque
Eduardo VII

CAMPOLIDE

R. da Artilharia 1

R. Rodrigo da Fonseca

R. Castilho

Av. da Antilharia 1

■ Hertz

Av. Fontes Pereira de Melo

Av. Duque de Loulé

Av. Eng. Duarte Pacheco

Centro
Comercial
Amoreiras
de Lisboa

■ Supermercado
Pão de Açúcar

Av. Joaquim António de Aguiar

R. Camilo
Castelo Branco

R. Joshua Benoliel

SÃO
SEBASTIÃO

PÇ. MARQUÊS
DE POMBAL

R. Rodrigues Sampaio

R. Silva Carvalho

R. das Amoreiras

Tr. da Légua de Povoa

Ⓜ MARQUÊS
DE POMBAL

R. do Dom João V

R. del Sol ao Rato

R. Braamcamp

R. da Arrabida

R. S. Filipe Néri

R. Alexandre Herculano

R. Rosa Araújo

R. Saraiva de Carvalho

LG. DO
RATO

Ⓜ RATO

R. Barata Salgueiro

Av. da Liberdade

R. da
R. de S. Mamede

R. do Salitre

RATO

✚ Hospital Inglês

Av. Álvares Cabral

Tv. S. Quiteria

Escola Politécnica

R. São Bento

Meseu
da Ciência
🏛

Parque
Mayer

Ⓜ
AVENIDA

S. Jorge

R. Imprensa Nacional

Livraria
Británica

Jardim
da
Estrela

R. de São Bernardo

R. do Santo Amaro

R. Luís
Fernades

PR. DAS
FLORES

R. da Conceiçãoda Glória

R. da Glória

✝ Basílica
da Estrela

R. Bela Vista

Cç. Estrela

João de Deus

ESTRELA

R. N. Piedade

R. São Marçal

R. Eduardo Coelho

Av. Dom Pedro V

R. Teixeira

Elevador
da Glória

Cc. da Glória

ⓘ

ESTAÇÃO
ROSSIO 🏛

R. B. Carneiro

Palácio da
Assembléia
Nacional

R. A. Brandão

R. Academia Ciências

R. Século

São
Roque
🏛

R. Nova da
Trindade

R. Lapa

R. Melo

R. Poais de
São Bento

R. Cruz Polais

R. Luz Soriano

R. Rosa

R. Ataíaia

R. Diario de Noticias

Tr. da Queimada

Museu de 🏛
Arqueológicode
Carmo

R. S. João

Av. Dom Carlos I

BAIRRO
ALTO

R. Garrett

LG. DO
CHIADO

R. Garcia da Horta

R. Poço Negros

PÇ. LUIS
DE CAMÓES
BAIXA-CHIADO

🏛

R. da Esperança

Tv. Santa
Catarina

Teatro Nacional
de São Carlos

R. Serpa Pinto

Cç. do Marqués Abrantes

R. da Boa Vista

Cyber.bica

R. Bragança

R. Sé o Velho

R. de Dom Luis I

R.A.M.
Carvalho

R. Flores

Museu Nacional de 🏛
Arte Contemporânea

To 🏛 Museu Nacional
De Arte Antiga (150m),
Belém (4.5km)
←

Av. 24 de Julho

R. de São Paulo

R. Ribeira Nova

R. do Alecrim

Mercado
da Ribeira

R. do Arsenal

Doca de
Alcântara

CAIS DO
SODRÉ Ⓜ

🚂 ESTAÇÃO CAIS
DO SODRÉ

Rio Tejo

lisbon

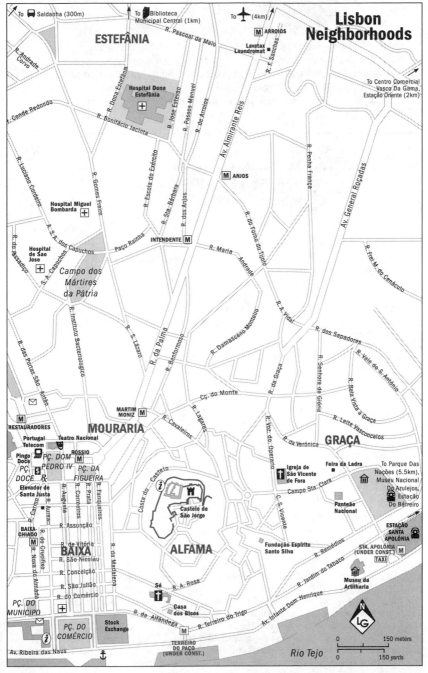

Lisbon Neighborhoods

To 🚉 Saldanha (300m)

To 📚 Biblioteca Municipal Central (1km)

To ✈ (4km)

ESTEFÂNIA

R. Pascoal de Melo

🅜 ARROIOS

Lavatax Laundromat

R. F. Sanches

To Centro Comercial Vasco Da Gama, Estação Oriente (2km)

R. Andrade Corvo

R. Dona Estefânia

Hospital Dona Estefânia ✚

R. Jose Estevão

R. Passos Manuel

R. de Arroios

Av. Almirante Reis

R. Conde Redondo

R. Bonifácio Jacinta

R. Penha França

R. Escola do Exército

🅜 ANJOS

Av. General Roçadas

R. Luciano Cordeiro

R. Gomes Freire

Hospital Miguel Bombarda ✚

R. Sta. Bárbara

R. dos Anjos

R. do Forno do Tijolo

R. Frei M. do Cenáculo

A. S.A. dos Capuchos

INTENDENTE 🅜

R. Maria Andrade

R. do Assunção

Hospital de Sao Jose ✚

Paço Rainha

Campo dos Mártires da Pátria

S.A. Capuchos

R. A. Vidal

R. Instituto Bacteriológico

R. S. Lázaro

R. da Palma

R. Benformoso

R. Damasceno Monteiro

R. dos Sapadores

R. Vale de S. António

R. das Portas Sao Antão

R. da Graça

R. Senhora da Glória

R. Bela Vista à Graça

Cç. do Monte

R. Leite Vasconcelos

MARTIM MONIZ 🅜

R. Cavaleiros

R. Lagares

🅜 RESTAURADORES

MOURARIA

R. Voz do Operário

R. da Verónica

GRAÇA

Portugal Telecom

Teatro Nacional

Pingo Doce

PÇ. DOM PEDRO IV

ROSSIO 🅜

Igreja de São Vicente de Fora

Feira da Ladra

To Parque Das Nações (5.5km), Museu Nacional Do Azulejos, Estação Do Bárreiro

PÇ. DOCE

PÇ. DA FIGUEIRA

Campo Sta. Clara

Elevador de Santa Justa

Costa do Castelo

ℹ

R. Augusta

R. Correeiros

R. Fanqueiros

Castelo de São Jorge

C. S. Vicente

Panteão Nacional

BAIXA-CHIADO 🅜

R. Aurea

R. Assunção

ESTAÇÃO SANTA APOLÓNIA

R. de Crucifixo

R. Nova da Almada

R. de Vitória

BAIXA

R. São Nicolau

ALFAMA

Fundação Espírito Santo Silva

R. Remédios

STA. APOLÓNIA (UNDER CONST.) 🅜

TAXI

R. Conceição

R. da Madalena

R. São Julião

Sé ✝

R. A. Rosa

R. Jardim do Tabaco

Museu da Artilharia 🏛

R. do Comércio

PÇ. DO MUNICÍPIO

✚

Casa dos Bicos

R. da Alfândega

R. Terreiro do Trigo

PÇ. DO COMÉRCIO

ℹ

Stock Exchange

TERREIRO DO PAÇO (UNDER CONST.) 🅜

Av. Infante Dom Henrique

N

Av. Ribeira das Naus ⚓

Rio Tejo

0   150 meters
0   150 yards

lisbon

orientation

Lisbon's historic center has four main neighborhoods: **Baixa,** where accommodations, shopping, and tourists galore can be found; **Chiado,** the cultural center just uphill west of Baixa; nightlife-rich **Bairro Alto,** still farther west; and ancient **Alfama,** on the east side of Baixa. The narrow, windy streets and stairways of Alfama and Bairro alto can be confusing and difficult to navigate without a good map. The **Lisboa Mapa da Cidade e Guia Turístico** (€3) has nearly every street in these neighborhoods labeled, and is a good investment if you're going to be exploring Lisbon for a few days. The maps at the tourist offices are reliable but do not show the names of many streets, particularly in Alfama and Bairro Alto. **Tram 28E** runs east-west, parallel to the river, and connects all these neighborhoods, with its eastern terminus in the inexpensive and off-the-beaten-path neighborhood of **Graça.**

BAIXA

Baixa, Lisbon's old business hub, is the most centrally located neighborhood, and its streets are lined with accommodations and clothing stores. This neighborhood is an absolute delight for travelers weary of getting lost in labyrinthine old cities: the entire neighborhood is flat and on a grid. The main pedestrian thoroughfare is the broad **Rua Augusta,** which runs from the massive riverside **Praça do Comércio** to Plaça de Dom Pedro IV, better known as **Rossio.** ⓂBaixa-Chiado has an entrance at the western end (to your right as you face the river) of R. da Vitória, which runs east-west and crosses R. Augusta. Connected to Rossio's northwest corner is **Praça dos Restauradores,** a huge urban transit hub where the Rossio train station (for trains to Sintra) and tourist office can be found; it is also the main drop-off point for airport

lisbon

buses. From Pr. dos Restauradores, **Avenida da Liberdade** runs away from Baixa to the **Praça do Marquês do Pombal** and its surrounding business district.

BAIRRO ALTO AND CHIADO

Bairro Alto (literally, "High Neighborhood") is a hilly stretch of narrow cobblestone streets with graffiti-covered walls and laundry-lined balconies, best known for its unique nightlife and its fado. The best way to get there is to take the Metro to Baixa-Chiado (Chiado exit), walk straight across Largo do Chiado and between the churches, and right up R. da Misericórdia (it becomes R. de São Pedro de Alcântara) before heading left into Alto's daytime slumber or nighttime madness.

    Chiado, slightly down the hill toward Baixa, is a little more clean-cut and cultured than its raucous neighbor to the west. The **Rua Garrett** cuts through the neighborhood, running between the **Largo do Chiado** and the stores and shopping center on R. do Carmo. The **Praça de Luís de Camões,** right next to Lg. do Chiado, connects the two neighborhoods.

ALFAMA

Alfama, Lisbon's hilly medieval quarter, was the only district to survive the 1755 earthquake, and those who have spent long, hot hours lost in its confusing maze of alleyways sometimes wish it hadn't. Many alleys are unmarked and take confusing turns and bends; others are long, winding stairways known as *escandinhas;* still others are dead ends. Expect to get lost repeatedly—with or without a detailed map. The **Castelo de São Jorge** sits at the steep hill's peak, with impressive views of the whole center; the **Sé** (cathedral) is closer to the river and to Baixa. The **Mouraria** (so called because it is where the Moors were forced to live after their expulsion from the castle in 1147) is on the north and west slope of the hill, away from the river; the old **Judiaria** (Jewish quarter, until their expulsion in 1492) is to the south, between the Sé and the river.

GRAÇA

Graça, a hilly, residential district, is one of Lisbon's oldest neighborhoods. An easy tram ride on 28E to the end of the line drops you off in **Largo da Graça:** on the side of the large white **Igreja da Graça** closest to the river is a shady park and spectacular *miradouro,* and on the side where the tram stops is a busy intersection lined with cheap eateries. It's an easy walk downhill from Graça into Alfama, or a less confusing tram ride back.

AROUND PRAÇA DO MARQUÊS DE POMBAL

The large Praça do Marquês de Pombal sits at the end of **Avenida da Liberdade,** opposite Pr. dos Restauradores. This is Lisbon's modern business district, which is full of department stores, shopping centers, office buildings, and some accommodations. To the north of Praça do Marquês de Pombal is the **Parque Eduardo VII,** and to the northeast of that in the **São Sebastião** district is the impressive **Museu Calouste Gulbenkian.**

accommodations

In recent years Lisbon has experienced an explosion of budget tourism, and new, low-priced accommodations have sprung up to cater to this crowd. The large number of hostels in **Baixa** and **Bairro Alto** means there is an impressive level of competition between them (one *Let's Go* researcher was even accused of being a spy for a different hostel), which keeps prices low and forces the owners to constantly attempt to improve to gain an edge. The hostels are all fairly similar—clean and brightly decorated, with mixed four- to eight-person dorms, shared bathrooms, a common kitchen and living room, and free internet and breakfast—but tend to differ slightly on amenities. Beds generally run €18-25 during the summer, with better rates for longer stays and larger groups.

accommodations

Lisbon has many cheap hotels and *pensões* as well, but if you don't see your room before paying, you may wind up in a funky-smelling closet with a cot. Swanky hotels cluster around Av. da Liberdade, while the less expensive rooms can be found in Bairro Alto and Baixa. Avoid the *pensões* on Rossio and the surrounding streets, where the rooms are overpriced; Baixa's **Rua da Prata, Rua dos Correios,** and **Rua do Ouro** have cheaper accommodations only about a 2min. walk from Rossio. Lodgings near the **Castelo de São Jorge** are quieter and closer to the sights but more difficult to find. You can usually find a room on little or no notice, but during mid-June the **Festa de Santo Antonio** fills Lisbon's accommodations.

Camping is fairly popular in Portugal, but campers can be prime targets for thieves. Stay at an enclosed campsite and ask ahead about security. There are 30 campgrounds within a 45mi. radius of the capital. The most popular, Lisboa Camping, is inside a 2,200-acre *parque florestal* and has the highest rating given to campsites in Portugal. They also have a hotel for dogs (€10 per day). Seriously. *(Parque Municipal de Campismo de Monsanto, Estrada da Circunvalação ☎217 62 82 00 ▣www.lisboacamping.com ⚕ Bus 714 runs from Pr. do Comércio to Parque de Campismo. ⑤ July-Aug €6.50 per person; €6-7 per tent; €4 per car; May-June and Sept €5.50/5-6/3.50; Oct-Apr €5/4.10-5/3.)*

BAIXA

Baixa doesn't offer much for the gourmand or party animal, but its location in the center of town and its easy navigability make it a prime spot for accommodations. Hostels here are trendy, chic, and fill up quickly in summer—way to go, internet. Baixa's *pensões* are by and large much less pleasant and much more expensive than its hostels, but they are more likely to have last-minute availability, even in summer.

▨ KITSCH HOSTEL   ⚕⊗⒲ HOSTEL ❶

Pr. dos Restauradoes, 65, 2nd fl.   ☎213 47 43 62 ▣www.kitschhostel.com

Eponymous kitsch covers the walls of this hidden hostel (you have to go through a back door in a tobacconist's to get there), which is a little rougher and edgier than its clean-cut counterparts on the other side of Rossio. The dorm rooms are simple and small, the private rooms not much better, but you're not going to spend too much time in bed if you're here anyway. The reception desk does double-duty as a lively bar for guests in the evenings who mingle among the pop-art before heading out.

⚕ ⓜRestauradores. On east side of Pr. dos Restauradores (to your right as you face the long, tree-lined Av. da Liberdade); enter through Tabacaria Restauradores, next to Santander Totta bank. *i* Breakfast and linens included. Free lockers. Laundry service available. Kitchen. Towels €1. Shared baths. ⑤ Oct-May 10- to 12-bed dorms €12; 8-bed dorms €14; 6-bed €16; 4-bed €18. Doubles €40; triples €60. June-Sept 12-bed dorms €14; 8- to 10-bed €16; 6-bed €18; 4-bed €20. Doubles €60; triples €75. ⚅ Reception 24hr.

▨ LISBON LOUNGE HOSTEL/LIVING LOUNGE HOSTEL   ⚕⊗⒲ HOSTEL ❶

R. de São Nicolau, 41   ☎213 46 20 61 ▣www.lisbonloungehostel.com

R. do Crucifixo, 116   ☎213 46 10 78

These nearby hostels, under joint ownership, have large common spaces and big rooms with the best interior design around, hostel or not. Staying here is really less like being in a hostel and more like staying in a nice hotel where you share bedrooms and bathrooms: if you reserve by 6pm, you can have a delicious traditional dinner in the dining room *(€8)*, you can hang out in the lounge, or you can get introduced to Lisbon on one of their free walking tours twice a week.

⚕ Lisbon Lounge: From ⓜBaixa-Chiado, take R. da Vitória exit, then immediate right onto R. do Crucifixo, then take the 1st left onto R. de São Nicolau and walk for 4 blocks. Living Lounge: From ⓜBaixa-Chiado, take R. da Vitória exit, then take an immediate left onto R. do Crucifixo. *i* Breakfast, towels, and linens included. Free lockers. Laundry €7. Kitchen. Free city tours Tu and F. ⑤ Lisbon Lounge: Oct 15-Apr 14 dorms €18; doubles €50. Apr 15-May 31 and Sept 16-Oct 14

lisbon

€20/60. Jun 1-Sep 15 €22/60. Living Lounge: dorms and doubles same rates as Lisbon Lounge. Singles Oct 15-Apr 14 €30; Apr 15-Oct 14 €35. ⏰ *Reception 24hr.*

GOODNIGHT BACKPACKER'S HOSTEL HOSTEL ❶

R. dos Correiros, 113, 2nd fl. ☎213 43 01 39 💻www.goodnighthostel.com

Four elevator-less floors of funky art, music, decor, and people include a book nook and more Andy Warhol posters than soup cans. Dorms and private rooms are snug but nicely decorated, and you can escape to the incredibly comfortable DVD lounge or one of the two large common rooms if needed. Fresh bread is delivered every morning for breakfast.

From [M]Baixa-Chiado, take the R. da Vitória exit and follow R. da Vitória for 4 blocks before turning left onto R. dos Correeiros. ℹ *Breakfast and linens included. Free lockers. Towels €1. Kitchen. Shared baths.* $ *Oct-Apr Dorms M-Th €16, F-Sa €17-18, Su €16. Doubles €25. May-Sept dorms €20. Doubles €25.* ⏰ *Reception 24hr.*

ROSSIO HOSTEL HOSTEL ❷

Cç. do Carmo, 6 ☎213 42 60 04

This brightly colored hostel has a cool feel, with exposed wooden beams and an impressive sound system that pumps bass. The location really can't be beat, and the price hardly reflects the fact that you're just steps from Rossio, Lisbon's heart. A hot breakfast of pancakes and eggs is served every morning, and every night there's a themed party.

[M]Rossio. Head west (to your left as you face the theater, coming from the river) on Cç. do Carmo a few yards. ℹ *Breakfast, towels, and linens included. Free lockers. Kitchen.* $ *Oct-Apr dorms €15-18; doubles €50. May-Sept dorms €20-25; doubles €50-70.* ⏰ *Reception 24hr.*

HOME LISBON HOSTEL HOSTEL ❷

R. de São Nicolau, 13 ☎218 88 53 12 💻www.mylisbonhome.com

The amenities that set this hostel apart are free laundry service (the Lisbon summer heat will make you go through clean clothes in record time), an elevator (it used to be called "Easy Hostel" for a reason), and Portuguese translations of useful English phrases painted on the common room wall—in case you left your dictionary at home. The rooms aren't huge but have classic wood floors and balconies with views over Baixa.

From [M]Baixa-Chiado, take the R. da Vitória exit, then turn right onto R. do Crucifixo. Take the 1st left onto R. de São Nicolau; it's 5 blocks down. ℹ *Breakfast, linens, lockers, and towels included. Kitchen. Free laundry service. Elevator.* $ *Dorms June-Sept €18-22.* ⏰ *Reception 24hr.*

BAIRRO ALTO AND CHIADO

Though not as centrally located as Baixa, the accommodations in the hipper neighborhoods of Bairro Alto and Chiado are closest to the nightlife and museums.

LISBON POETS HOSTEL HOSTEL ❷

R. Nova da Trinidade, 2, 5th fl. ☎213 46 10 58 💻www.lisbonpoetshostel.com

This hostel is flat-out luxurious. The dorm rooms, named for famous poets of various nationalities, are large and clean, and the common room is best measured in hectares. As the name suggests, a literary theme prevails: writers' quotes line the walls, there's a small book exchange, and there's even a typewriter—but you'll need to fix it first if you want to use it. Activities ranging from city tours to *fado* nights to cafe crawls take place daily and are free for guests.

From [M]Baixa-Chiado, take the Pr. do Chiado exit, and turn right up R. Nova da Trinidade. ℹ *Breakfast and linens included. Towels €1. Laundry €7. Free lockers. Kitchen. Shared bath. Elevator. Credit card min. €50.* $ *4- or 6-bed dorms €17-21; 2-bed €20-24. Private doubles €40-60. Discount with 5 nights total if 1 or more is in Oporto Poets Hostel.* ⏰ *Reception 24hr.*

OASIS BACKPACKERS MANSION HOSTEL ❷

R. de Santa Catarina, 24 ☎213 47 80 44 💻www.oasislisboa.com

This hostel is close to the nightlife of Bairro Alto and Cais do Sodré but in a quiet neighborhood just down the street from the pleasant Miradouro de Santa Catarina. It has its own nightlife, too, in the private patio bar *(open 6pm-1am)* just off the street, and the rooms are large and comfortable. Large, private doubles are located up the street on a lovely courtyard. This building also has a kitchen and trendily decorated common space.

✦ Ⓜ*Baixa-Chiado (Chiado exit). From Pr. de Luís de Camões, follow R. do Loreto (at far right side if entering plaza from direction of Metro station) 4 blocks, then left down R. Marechal Saldanha to the Miradouro de Santa Catarina (lookout point), then right; it's the big yellow house at the end of the street.* ⓘ *Breakfast, linens, and towels included. Kitchen. Free safe. Laundry €7.* Ⓢ *Dorms €18-22; doubles €45-56.* 🕐 *Reception 8am-midnight.*

BA HOSTEL
⊛⊗⒨❄ HOSTEL ❷

Tv. da Cara, 6 ☎213 46 81 26 💻www.hostelba-barrioalto.com

This hostel just opened in May 2010 and still has that new-hostel smell. It's no surprise that after only a couple of months there is already a group of regulars who keep coming back. The charismatic owners cook hot breakfast every morning because they enjoy the cooking and treat the guests like their own family. There are two TVs in the common room to avoid battles over the remote, and they also offer A/C, which is a must in Lisbon. Prices drop sharply with longer stays or a positive attitude. The only issue is the noise that comes up from the Bairro Alto sidewalks.

✦ *From* Ⓜ*Baixa-Chiado, take Pr. do Chiado exit, take a slight right out of the station and go straight between the white churches toward Pr. de Luís de Camões, then right up R. da Misericórdia 7 blocks, then left onto Travessa da Cara (right where park begins on right).* ⓘ *Breakfast, linens, and towels included. Kitchen.* Ⓢ *4- or 6-bed dorms €20-25; 2- to 3-bed €30. Singles €80.* 🕐 *Open 24hr.*

ALFAMA

Alfama's accommodations are expensive and limited but are perfect for those who can't resist the neighborhood's charm. The streets are steep and rarely well marked, so remember where you're staying before you head out. Just about the whole neighborhood is pedestrian, so if you usually go out, get smashed, and take a cab back to the hostel, Alfama's not for you.

LISBON AMAZING HOSTEL
➤⊗⒨ HOSTEL ❷

Beco do Arco Escuro, 17 ☎218 88 00 54

The rooms in this hostel certainly aren't the biggest, and it's more expensive than comparable accommodations in neighborhoods to the west, but stay in this hostel for the true Alfama experience. It's literally right above one of the ancient neighborhood's arches, one block from the cheap restaurants on R. dos Bacalhoeiros and the cathedral. The common areas are comfortable and have a television, and the neighborhood is much quieter at night than Bairro Alto, so you can actually get some sleep, if you want.

✦ Ⓜ*Terreiro Paço, tram 28E, or bus 737 to Sé. From the north side of Pr. do Comércio (farthest from the river), facing the river, head left along R. da Alfândega 3 blocks, then left, then left on R. dos Bacalhoeiros, then right through the arch and up the steps; follow signs for "LAHostels."* ⓘ *Breakfast, linens, and towels included.* Ⓢ *June-Sept dorms €30; doubles €55. Oct-May dorms €20-25; doubles €45-55.*

GUESTHOUSE BEIRA MAR
⊛⊗⒨ PENSÃO ❷

Lg. do Terreiro do Trigo, 16 ☎218 86 99 33 💻www.guesthousebeiramar.com

This guesthouse holds seven airy, brightly decorated rooms in a part of Alfama that's barely uphill from Baixa. Some rooms have balconies with views of the water while others look back into Alfama. Enter on R. da Judiaria, 3, to shorten the climb up to the guesthouse if you're coming from uphill or make it more scenic if you're coming from down below.

✦ Ⓜ*Santa Apolonia, or bus 28, 35, 206, 210, 745, 759, 794 to Alfândega. From Alfândega bus* stop, head 1 block away from river, then left to reach Lg. do Terreiro do Trigo. *i* Breakfast, linens, and towels included. Free lockers. Kitchen. $ Singles €20-25; doubles €35-45; triples €60. Prices lower in winter. ⏰ Reception 24hr.*

CASA DE HOSPEDES ESTRELA 🚭 PENSÃO [3]

R. dos Bacalohoeiros, 8 ☎218 86 95 06

Clean, simple rooms, some with views of the water, sit off an ancient, *azulejo*-covered stairway. It's very close to some of Alfama's sights—you can walk 2min. to the cathedral, or if you prefer you can go Shawshank on the place and break through the wall into the neighboring 16th-century Casa dos Bicos.

⇆ ⓂTerreiro Paço, or tram 28E. From the north side of Pr. do Comércio (farthest from the river), facing the river, head left along R. da Alfândega 4 blocks, then left across the plaza; it's right next to Casa dos Bicos, the spiky building. i Linens and towels included. $ Singles €25-40; doubles €30-45; triples €45-60. ⏰ Reception 24hr.

AROUND PRAÇA DO MARQUÊS DE POMBAL

BLACK AND WHITE HOSTEL 🚭📶 HOSTEL [1]

R. de Alexandre Herculano, 39, 1st fl. ☎213 46 22 12 💻www.costta.com

This hostel is in a slightly more upscale neighborhood (though less than a block from a supermarket), and staying here is like living in an artist's studio. Massive, colorfully bold murals and random pieces of art floating around the dorm rooms make the entire hostel feel like a large piece of performance art. The common spaces are large and comfortable, and the building itself feels charmingly worn.

⇆ ⓂMarquês de Pombal, or buses 1, 74, 202, 706, 709, 713, 720, 727, 738, 758, 773 to Rato. From ⓂMarquês de Pombal metro stop, take the exit toward R. de Alexandre Herculano, then walk down Av. da Liberdade away from the giant statue. Then turn right onto R. de Alexandre Herculano; the hostel is 4 blocks down on the left. i Breakfast and linens included. Towels €1. Kitchen. $ Dorms €15-20. ⏰ Reception 24hr.

POUSADA DE JUVENTUDE DE LISBOA ♿📶 HOSTEL [1]

R. de Andrade Corvo, 46 ☎213 53 26 96 💻www.pousadasjuventude.pt

This enormous hostel is a bit out of the way, but it's a good and reliably inexpensive alternative if the ritzier hostels in Baixa and Bairro Alto are all booked.

⇆ ⓂPicoas, or buses 30, 36, 44, 83, 91, 207, 727, 738, 745. Exit ⓂPicoas onto R. de Andrade Corvo; the hostel is marked by a large banner on the same side of the street. i Breakfast and linens included. Kitchen. $ Dorms €15-17; doubles €43-45. Must have cartão de alberguista (€6). ⏰ Reception open 8am-midnight.

sights

Lisbon's history can be seen on every street in the city, stretching from the present back 3,000 years. Moorish *azulejos* (painted and glazed tiles) line the ancient facades and interiors of Alfama; the fortress-like 12th-century Sé (cathedral) looms over the city with its imposing Romanesque presence; the 11th-century Castelo de São Jorge sits on a high hill over the center. The whole city is essentially one large sight to experience, from confusing Alfama to rigid and (more) modern Baixa. Those planning on doing a lot of sightseeing in a few days should consider purchasing the tourist office's Lisboa Card for a flat fee. Many museums and sites are closed Mondays and free Sundays and holidays before 2pm.

BAIXA

Baixa doesn't have many historical sights—the whole neighborhood was leveled and rebuilt after the earthquake of 1755. The pedestrian streets and *praças*, though, have their own newer brand of beauty and excellent people-watching.

Around Rossio

Rossio, known more formally as **Praça de Dom Pedro IV,** is Lisbon's heart. The city's main square has been used as a cattle market, public execution stage, bullring, and carnival ground—today it is home to tourists and the large central statue of Dom Pedro IV, with circling drivers making the plaza their own Indianapolis Motor Speedway. At the north end of the plaza is the magnificent Teatro Nacional de Dona Maria II, with a statue of Gil Vicente, Portugal's first great dramatist, peering down onto Baixa.

Around Praça dos Restauradores

In the long **Praça dos Restauradores,** just off the northwest corner of Rossio, a huge obelisk celebrates Portugal's independence from Spain, earned in 1640 after 60 years under the Spanish crown. The tourist office is in the Palácio da Foz on the west side of the plaza, and the gorgeous neo-Manueline **Estação Rossio** is in the southwest corner. From Pr. dos Restauradores, the long and straight tree-lined **Avenida da Liberdade,** modeled on Paris' Champs-Élysées, heads uphill 1 mi. to **Praça do Marquês de Pombal.** There, an 18th-century statue of the Marquês watches over the city he planned and put together two and a half centuries ago.

Around Praça do Comércio

If you think all European cities have centers with small, narrow, winding streets and ancient, crumbling buildings, think again. The area between Rossio and the Rio Tejo is a **perfect grid,** built in the late 18th century after the earthquake destroyed what was there before. Many of the straight streets are named for the professions once located on them: *sapateiros* (shoemakers), *douradores* (gold workers), and *bacalhoeiros* (cod merchants) all have their own avenues. The **Rua Augusta** runs through the center of Baixa, through the **Arco da Rua Augusta,** and into the enormous **Praça do Comércio,** at the edge of the Tejo. Dom João I watches over this huge, open space lined with shady colonnades; you can go down the steps that go right into the river and see the swarms of hungry fish at the banks. Just on the other side of the arch is the brandnew **Museu do Design e da Moda (MUDE),** which hosts exhibits of design and fashion history in a grand old bank building on the R. Augusta. *(Rua Augusta, 24 ☎218 88 61 17* ◨*www.mude.pt* Ⓢ *Free.* ✆ *Open Tu-Th 10am-8pm, F-Sa 10am-10pm, Su 10am-8pm.)*

BAIRRO ALTO AND CHIADO

The culture in Chiado is as high as its altitude, and the area is home to plenty of museums and historic sites. Neighboring Bairro Alto offers great views of the city from its *miradouros*.

MUSEU ARQUEOLÓGICO DO CARMO ⊛⊗ CHURCH, MUSEUM

Lg. do Carmo ☎213 47 86 29

Sick of those big, boring churches that all look the same? This archaeological museum is housed in a 14th-century Gothic church like any other, except it's **missing its roof.** The ruins became ruins in the 1755 earthquake and ensuing fire, and today they stand as an open courtyard under empty arches where the roof once stood. Highlights of the museum, whose collection spans four millennia and the entire globe, include mummies from Peru and Egypt, but the real sight here is the ruined building itself.

✦ ⓜBaixa-Chiado (Chiado exit) or bus #58, 100, or tram 28. From Rossio, walk (steeply) up Cç. do Carmo to Lg. do Carmo. Ⓢ €3.50, students and seniors €2, under 14 free. ✆ Open M-Sa June-Sept 10am-7pm; Oct-May 10am-6pm.

IGREJA E MUSEU DE SÃO ROQUE ⊛� CHURCH, MUSEUM

Lg. Trindade Coelho ☎213 23 54 44 ◨www.museu-saoroque.com

The Plague reached Lisbon in 1505, brought by an infested ship from Venice. King Manuel I was not too happy about this and requested a relic of São Roque from the Venetians in return, as this saint was supposed to have powers that could ward off disease. Well, he didn't, and thousands of Portuguese succumbed to the

Black Death. Nevertheless, the Jesuits put up this church in the saint's honor in the 16th century. The alms box on the left side of the nave echoes the awestruck words of many who enter: "Jesus, Maria, Jose" ("Jesus, Mary and Joseph"). The church is truly magnificent, with not a square inch left undecorated, so be sure to look up at the ceiling. The museum houses a collection of art pertaining to the Jesuits as well as a collection of Eastern art that includes a dazzling chest with glimmering inlay from Macau.

✴ Ⓜ*Baixa-Chiado (Chiado exit). Bus #758, 790, or tram 28. From Lg. do Chiado, head uphill on R. da Misericórdia; it's at the far side of the plaza on the right.* Ⓢ *Museum €2.50, students, under 14 and over 65 free; free to all Su before 2pm.* Ⓩ *Church open M 2-6pm, Tu-W 9am-6pm, Th 9am-9pm, F-Su 9am-6pm. Museum open Tu-W 10am-6pm, Th 2-9pm, F-Su 10am-6pm.*

ALFAMA

🏛 CASTELO DE SÃO JORGE   ✦⊗ CASTLE, HISTORIC SITE, VIEWS
Castelo de São Jorge   ☎218 80 06 20 ▪www.castelosaojorge.egeac.pt

Built by the Moors in the 11th century on the highest point in Lisbon, this hilltop fortress was captured by Dom Afonso Henriques, Portugal's first king, in 1147. Later Portuguese kings made it their residence, and today visitors can walk all around the ramparts to enjoy phenomenal panoramic views of Lisbon. There is a small museum of artifacts found at the site that date back to the sixth century BCE.

✴ *Bus 737, or trams 12E and 28E; follow signs to Castelo.* Ⓢ *€7, students and seniors €3.50, under 10 free.* Ⓩ *Open Mar Oct 9am-9pm; Nov-Feb 9am-6pm. Last entry 30min. before close. Museum has guided tours daily at noon and 4pm.*

🏛 SÉ CATEDRAL DE LISBOA   ✦⊗ CHURCH, MUSEUM
Largo da Sé   ☎218 86 67 52

Lisbon's 12th-century cathedral is massive and intimidating, built to double as a fortress, if needed. Its austere Romanesque style makes the few brightly colored stained-glass windows leap out of the walls, where the same ornamentation is often lost in a busy Gothic or Baroque church. The cloisters, an archaeological site perpetually under scaffolding, contain a collection of tombs with brilliant carvings of various scenes from daily life and the Bible. The treasury houses a small collection or religious objects and manuscripts.

✴ *Bus 737, or tram 28E. From Baixa, follow R. da Conceição east (to the left as you face the river) up past the church, then turn right onto R. de Santo António da Sé and follow the tram tracks; it's the large, simple building that looks like a fortress.* Ⓢ *Free. Cloister €2.50.* Ⓩ *Church open M 9am-5pm, Tu-Sa 9am-7pm, Su 9am-5pm. Treasury open M-Sa 10am-5pm. Cloister open May-Sept M 10am-5pm, Tu-Sa 10am-6pm; Oct-Apr M-Sa 10am-5pm. Mass Tu-Sa 6:30pm, Su 11:30am.*

GRAÇA

PANTEÃO NACIONAL   ✦♿ TOMBS, HISTORIC SITE
Campo de Santa Clara   ☎218 85 48 39 ▪www.igespar.pt

The Igreja de Santa Engrácia was started in the late 17th century, but once the architect died, the king lost interest in the project and the funding dried up, leaving the church unfinished for some 250 years. Eventually, General Salazar's regime took control of the construction and completed the dome, though the pinnacles the original architect intended for either side were never added. Salazar rededicated the building as the National Pantheon, a burial place for important statesmen, in 1966. However, when democracy was restored in 1975, the new government used the Panteão to house the remains of Salazar's most prominent opponents, while those who had worked with Salazar were prohibited from entering the building. The dome is a distinctive feature of the Lisbon skyline, and the much beloved Amália Rodrigues, queen of *fado*, is among those buried there.

✴ Ⓜ*Santa Apolonia, bus 12, 28, 34, 35, 704, 745, 759, 781, 782, or tram 28E. Get off tram 28E at Voz do Operário stop in front of Igreja e Mosteiro de São Vicente de Fora, then follow Arco*

Grande de Cima (to the left of church), then take the 1st right, 1st left, and then another right; you can't miss it. $ €3. Students and under 14 free. Seniors €1.50. Su before 2pm free for all. ⏰ Open Tu-Su 10am-5pm.

IGREJA E MOSTEIRO DE SÃO VICENTE DE FORA CHURCH, MONASTERY

Largo de São Vicente ☎218 85 56 52

The Church and Monastery of St. Vincent is dedicated to and named for Lisbon's official patron saint, though the city tends to favor its adopted patron, St. Anthony. The church's sanctuary is closed indefinitely for restoration and construction, but the attached monastery—a beautiful site in its own right—has a small museum dedicated to the church's history, with access to a tiny Baroque chapel.

[M]Santa Apolonia, bus 12, 28, 34, 35, 704, 745, 759, 781, 782, or tram 28E. Get off tram 28E in front of the massive white church at the Voz do Operário stop. $ €4, students and seniors €2. ⏰ Open Tu-Su 10am-6pm. Last entry 1hr. before close.

MUSEU NACIONAL DO AZULEJO ♿ MUSEUM

R. da Madre de Deus, 4 ☎218 10 03 40 🖥mnazulejo.imc-ip.pt

Enter this museum via its newly renovated entrance, passing by the incredible Manueline doorway of the Convento da Madre de Deus. The museum is devoted to the art of the *azulejo* (glazed and painted tile), one of Portugal's most famous and most ubiquitous forms of art. Some of the tiles are whimsical, others saucy, and the early-18th-century (pre-earthquake) panorama of the city of Lisbon is one of the world's largest works of *azulejo*. The faux-*azulejo* boards with cut-outs to stick your face in for a photo op detract from the cloister's beauty, but the rest of the museum is well laid out.

Take bus 28 or 759 from Santa Apolonia station bus stop (on the side of the road closest to the river, heading east); be sure to tell the driver where you're going. $ €5, seniors €2.50, under 14 free; Su before 2pm free for all. ⏰ Open Tu 2-6pm, W-Su 10am-6pm. Last entry 30min. before close.

BELÉM

The Belém waterfront, a couple of kilometers west of Lisbon's center, is one of the most majestic tributes to Portugal's Age of Discovery and its legendary seafaring spirit. This is where history-changing explorers Vasco da Gama and Prince Henry the Navigator left for distant lands, and the opulence of the new worlds they opened up can be seen today a short tram ride from Baixa. Almost as famous as the historic sights is **Pasteis de Belém,** a pastry shop with a reputation as rich as its pastries. *(R. de Belém, 84-92 ☎213 63 74 23 $ Pastries €0.90 each ⏰ Open daily 9am-11pm.)* The easiest way to get to Belém is by taking tram 15E from Pr. do Comércio (toward Algés) to Mosteiro dos Jerónimos stop, which is one beyond the stop labeled Belém.

MOSTEIRO DOS JERÓNIMOS ♿ CHURCH, MUSEUM

Pr. do Império ☎213 62 00 34 🖥www.mosteirojeronimos.pt

The Hieronymite Monastery was established in 1502 to honor Vasco da Gama's expedition to India. We're guessing the explorer's spirit is pleased with this ornate tribute. The Manueline building has the detail of its Gothic predecessors and the sweeping elegance of the oncoming Renaissance. In the '80s the monastery was granted World Heritage status by UNESCO, and it is in pristine condition inside and out. The church contains tombs (both symbolic and actual) of Portuguese kings and bishops. Symbolic tombs include areas of tribute to Vasco da Gama and Luís de Camões, Portugal's most celebrated poet. Entrance to the cloister is not cheap (€7, but free Su before 2pm), but it's worth it to see one of Lisbon's most beautiful spaces, which somehow retains its charm despite being filled with hordes of tourists.

Tram 15E, or bus 28, 76, 201, 204, 714, 727, 729, 751 to Mosteiro dos Jerónimos. $ Free. Cloister and museum €7, over 65 €3.50, under 14 free; F-Su before 2pm free for all. Combined ticket with Torre de Belém €10. ⏰ Open May-Sept Tu-Su 10am-6:30pm; Oct-Apr Tu-Su 10am-5:30pm. Last entry 30min. before close.

TORRE DE BELÉM

DEFENSE TOWER, HISTORIC SITE, VIEWS

Torre de Belém ☎213 62 00 34

Portugal's most famous tower has risen out of the water (except at low tide, when it's connected to the shore by a narrow, sandy isthmus) from the banks of the Tejo for nearly 500 years, gracing visitors' memories and souvenir stores' postcards since its completion in 1519. It's a short and lovely walk (if you walk along the river—the other side of the road is less scenic) from the Mosteiro dos Jerónimos. There is a shady park in front of it and a tiny strip of beach next to it. The tower has many levels to maximize artillery efficiency, as well as stunning 360-degree views of the Tejo and the city of Lisbon. Don't miss the detailed carvings shaped like a rhinoceros (there are signs pointing to it), and take a minute to relax in one of the shady turrets with stone window seats and stunning views.

From Mosteiro dos Jerónimos, take unmarked underground walkway in front of the monastery (from entrance, head toward the river; it's a small stairway) to other side of road and tracks and walk west along the river (to the right as you face the water) about 15min. Alternatively, walk in the same direction on the monastery's side of the road and take the pedestrian walkway over the road at the tower. [$] *€5. Students and under 14 free. Over 65 €2.50. Su before 2pm free for all. Combined ticket with Mosteiro dos Jerónimos €10.* ⏰ *Open May-Sept Tu-Su 10am-6:30pm; Oct-Apr Tu-Su 10am-5:30pm. Last entry 30min. before close.*

SÃO SEBASTIÃO

MUSEU CALOUSTE GULBENKIAN

♿ ART MUSEUM

Av. de Berna, 45A ☎217 82 30 00 💻www.museu.gulbenkian.pt

Want an art-history survey course for under €5? This museum has a large and eclectic collection of works from the ancient Mesopotamians and Egyptians through to the Impressionists and beyond. The collection belonged to native Armenian and oil tycoon Calouste Gulbenkian, who came to Portugal on vacation in 1942 and never left. His art didn't leave either: he left his artwork, some purchased from the Hermitage in St. Petersburg, Russia, to the Portuguese state, and it is now on display in Lisbon. The museum's building is an architectural site in its own right—a hideous international-style thing from the outside with incredible interior spaces surrounded by gardens. The illuminated manuscripts from the Middle East to France seem to have been dunked in molten gold, and the dark, quiet room with a garden view is a surprisingly lovely place to unwind.

[M]São Sebastião, or bus 15, 56, 718, 726, 742, 746. Exit [M]São Sebastião at Av. de António Augusto de Aguiar (north exit) and go straight uphill along the avenue until you reach the massive Pr. de Espanha, then turn right. It is not the building that looks like a castle in the park to your right; you need to keep going along the avenue. [$] *€5, students under 25 and seniors €2, under 12 free. Temporary exhibitions €3-5.* ⏰ *Open Tu-Su 10am-6pm.*

food

Lisbon has some of the best and best-priced restaurants this side of the Rhine, and some of the best wine to boot. Depending on the neighborhood, an average full dinner will usually run about €10-12 per person, with the *pratos do dia* often only €5-7. Some of the best and least expensive meals can be found in the ubiquitous **pastelarias:** don't be fooled by the name (it means pastry shop) or the appearance (the centerpiece is usually the counter with heaps of sweets), because these places can cook, too. That said, don't skip the pastries: **pasteis de nata** are generally less than €1 and are the city's most popular sweet. Local specialties include *caracois* (small snails; look for a restaurant with a sign that says "Há caracois" in the window), **lombo de porco com amêijoas** (pork with clams; much tastier than it sounds at first), and the Portuguese staples *alheira* (smoked chicken sausage), *sardinhas assadas* (grilled sardines), and *bacalhau*(cod) just about any way you can think of. Some of the best deals, in terms of getting a lot for a little, are the *tostas*, large grilled sandwiches that usually cost €2-3. The local traditional drink is **ginjinha** (pronounced "jee-JEE-nyah"; also often called *ginja*), a sour cherry liqueur served ice-cold in a shot glass and meant to be sipped. If it's bad, it tastes like cough syrup, but if it's good it's delicious and refreshing, particularly on hot Lisbon afternoons. It usually costs €1-1.50, and is sometimes served in a glass with chocolate for a little extra.

BAIXA

There are one or two places in Baixa worth trying, but most Baixa restaurants are quite forgettable. The restaurants that line the main pedestrian streets claim to offer typical Portuguese cuisine, but the menus out front posted in ten different languages seem to say otherwise. Look for places that have *pratos do dia* or lots of businessmen in them (generally locals on their lunch break who don't have time to go home and have no choice but to eat in Baixa).

👍 MOMA — 💳🚭🍸☀ RESTAURANT [2]

R. de São Nicolau, 47 — ☎914 41 75 36

A delicious oasis of good food in the desert that is Baixa. Moma's menu is printed new daily and posted in beautiful handwriting on a large slate out front. The dishes tend to be cool, light, and creative for the hot summer months, but heavier meals are there for the taking as well. The interior is simple and clean, but the outdoor seating is the place to enjoy your meal, in the middle of the R. de São Nicolau but separated from the touristic madness by umbrellas and bamboo blinds. Get there on the early side if you're going for lunch, though, as it tends to fill up quickly with local suits in the middle of their workday.

➡ [M]Baixa-Chiado (Baixa exit). Exit Metro station onto R. da Vitória, then right 1 block, and then left onto R. de São Nicolau. [$] Entrees usually €6-8. ⏰ Open M-Sa noon-7:30pm.

BONJARDIM — 💳🚭🍸☀ GRILL [2]

Tv. de Santo Antão, 12 — ☎213 42 74 24

A little bit past Rossio from the main part of Baixa, this restaurant just off the food-filled R. de Santo Antão serves massive portions of various styles of chicken, meat, and fish. Dine outside and enjoy your meal from the "king of chicken" while watching crabs and lobsters duke it out in the aquarium in the window, or the similarly bizarre spectacle of the plethora of lost tourists trying to get back to the main plazas and easily gridded streets to the south.

➡ [M]Restauradores or buses #36, 44, 90, 205, 207, 702, 709, 711, 732, 745, 746, 759. Take Travessa de Santo Antão from the east side of Pr. dos Restauradores. [$] Whole chickens €9. Grilled meats €8-12. ⏰ Open Tu 6-11:30pm, W-Su noon-11:30pm.

QUENTE AND BOM — 💳🚭☀ CAFE [1]

R. da Vitória, 46 — ☎213 46 71 35 🖥www.quenteebom.com

This ain't your granddaddy's *pastelaria*. It's got a clean, modern decor, though in an old building with some old stone arches still visible. This cafe is now a small chain with four other stores in the Lisbon area, but this is the original one.

➡ [M]Baixa-Chiado (Baixa exit). Follow R. da Vitória straight out of the Metro station. [$] Coffee €0.60-2.20. Pastries €1. Sandwiches €1.60-7. ⏰ Open M-F 8am-8pm, Sa-Su 9am-8pm.

TAO — 💳🚭 VEGETARIAN [2]

R. dos Douradores, 10 — ☎218 85 00 46

This self-service restaurant on one of the less trafficked streets in Baixa has inexpensive vegetarian options in a simple East-Asian-themed dining room. There's another dining room upstairs with seating on cushions on the floor, but this place is more appropriate for a quick bite than some kind of dining experience.

➡ [M]Baixa-Chiado (Baixa exit). Follow R. da Vitória to R. dos Douradores, then right. [$] Entrees €5-7.50. Soup of the day €1.50. ⏰ Open M 12:30-3:30pm, Tu-Sa 12:30-3:30pm and 7-9:30pm.

BAIRRO ALTO AND CHIADO

The narrow streets of Bairro Alto are lined with international restaurants and *fado* houses, sandwiched between the neighborhood's famous bars. Chiado's food tends toward the trendy, with sleek new restaurants and cafes. The side streets off Cç. do Combro (keep following R. do Loreto away from Pr. de Luís de Camões) have cheap, traditional hole-in-the-wall places, though most of the eateries in Chiado and Bairro Alto won't break the bank.

👍 CERVEJARIA TRINDADE — 💳🚭🍸⛅ TRADITIONAL [3]

R. Nova da Trindade, 20C — ☎213 42 35 06 🖥www.cervejariatrindade.pt

Cervejaria Trindade is famous all over Lisbon for the *molhos* (sauces) made from beer that were invented here. Eateries throughout the city will often offer a course "à trindade," named for this establishment. Cervejaria Trindade's location was occupied from the end of the 13th century by a convent and became one of Lisbon's first breweries at the start of the 19th century. Sagres, Portugal's second best-selling beer brand, came out with a beer called Bohemia 1835, created especially to celebrate the 170th anniversary of Cervejaria Trindade. The enormous dining rooms are covered with *azulejos* from this period, and the cloister of the convent is used for dining as well.

🧭 *From Ⓜ Baixa-Chiado, exit onto Lg. do Chiado, then take a sharp right up R. Nova da Trindade (to left of A Brasileira).* $ *Meat plates à trindade €9-18. Pratos do dia M-F €7.50.* ⏰ *Open daily noon-1:30am.*

KAFFEEHAUS — 💳♿🍸⛅ AUSTRIAN [2]

R. Anchieta, 3 — ☎210 95 68 28

It's understandable if you didn't come to Lisbon to order in German, but this sleek, chic cafe has great food for very reasonable prices. The outdoor seats are on the narrow (and thus shady and breezy) street outside, and the inside of the cafe is air-conditioned and filled with design magazines in English, Portuguese, and German. The drink selection is very impressive for an establishment that closes at midnight, and they have several refreshing homemade lemonades with unexpected but tasty additions like ginger. Come on Sunday morning for their brunch options *(€6.50-10).*

🧭 *From Ⓜ Baixa-Chiado, exit onto Lg. do Chiado, then take a very sharp right down R. Garrett 2 blocks, then head right down R. Anchieta.* $ *Sandwiches €4.20-5.20. Salads €4.10-9.80. Entrees €7.80-14.80. Vegetarian options €9. Coffees €1-2.40.* ⏰ *Open Tu-Sa 11am-midnight, Su 11am-10pm.*

ZAFFERANO — 💳🚭🍸 ITALIAN [3]

Lg. de Rafael Burdalo Pinheiro, 8 — ☎213 47 32 61 🖥www.zafferano.pt

This new Italian restaurant has a sharp design and chic clientele, but it's not expensive for the quality and quantity of the food. Very shareable pizzas *(€7-9)* and delicious pastas *(€9-12.50)* come in big portions that merit the prices. Zafferano also delivers for the lazy and has a takeout option for those in a hurry.

🧭 *From Ⓜ Baixa-Chiado, exit onto Lg. do Chiado, then sharp right up R. Nova da Trindade (to left of A Brasileira) 1 block, then take a right before taking the 1st left.* $ *Bruschette €2.30. Salads €7-9.50. Pizzas €7-9. Pastas €9-12.50. Meats €13.50.* ⏰ *Open M-Th noon-3pm and 7-11pm, F noon-3pm and 7pm-midnight, Sa 1-4pm and 7pm-midnight, Su 1-4pm and 7-11pm.*

JÜRGEN'S — 💳🚭🍸⛅ BAR [1]

R. do Diario de Noticias, 68 — ☎213 47 82 34

This small bar in the center of Bairro Alto's nightlife district becomes a happening drinking spot later on in the evening, but during the afternoon and around dinnertime, it's a great alternative to the pricey and touristy places up the street. The *tostas*, or grilled sandwiches *(€2-4),* are cheap, enormous, and very tasty, and the drinks are reliably strong.

⇄ Ⓜ Baixa-Chiado (Chiado exit), tram 28E, or buses 1, 202, 758, 790 to Lg. Trindade Coelho. From Lg. Trindade Coelho, cross R. da Misericórdia into Bairro Alto, then take the 3rd left down R. do Diario de Noticias. $ Tostas €2-4. Wine €2. Cocktails €5. ⏰ Open M-Th 3pm-2am, F-Sa 3pm-3am, Su 3pm-2am.

JARDIM DAS CEREJAS ♿ 🍸 VEGETARIAN, BUFFET ❷

Cç. do Sacramento, 36 ☎213 46 93 08

A lone island of vegetarian delights in a tumultuous sea of meat and fish. And of course, all-you-can-eat buffets are a great deal whether you're a vegetarian or not, and the fare here will satisfy meat-eaters as well.

⇄ From Ⓜ Baixa-Chiado, exit onto Lg. do Chiado, then take a very sharp right down R. Garrett 3 blocks, then turn left up Cç. do Sacramento. $ Lunch buffet €6.90; dinner buffet €8.90. ⏰ Open daily 8am-10:30pm.

ALI-A-PAPA 🍸 MOROCCAN, OPEN LATE ❷

R. da Atalaia, 95 ☎213 47 41 43

The enticing smell from the simple but tasty Moroccan dishes served here travels down the street into Bairro Alto. It draws hungry night owls looking for a good meal to fill their tanks before going to get tanked at the bars next door.

⇄ Ⓜ Baixa-Chiado (Chiado exit), tram 28E, or buses #1, 202, 758, 790 to Lg. Trindade Coelho. From Lg. Trindade Coelho, cross R. da Misericórdia into Bairro Alto, then take the 5th left. $ Entrees €6-12. ⏰ Open daily 7pm-2am. Kitchen open until 12:30am.

A BRASILEIRA DO CHIADO ♿ 🍸 CAFE ❷

R. Garrett 120-122 ☎213 46 95 41 💻www.abrasileira.pt

This beautiful cafe has been around for over a century, serving coffee, pastries and snacks in a gorgeous wood- and marble-filled space. It is most notable for being one of poet Fernando Pessoa's favorite haunts, and his statue sits outside today. Recently A Brasileira and its new ownership have come under fire for allegedly underpaying and mistreating their workers, and protests and banners can occasionally be seen outside.

⇄ Exit Ⓜ Baixa-Chiado (Chiado exit). Exit Metro station onto Lg. do Chiado, then turn right. $ Sandwiches €2-5. Entrees €8-20. Coffee €1-2.50. ⏰ Open daily 8am-2am.

ALFAMA

Alfama's maze of winding streets hides many small, traditional restaurants. The cheapest options tend to gather along **Rua dos Bacalhoeiros,** with the tastiest options located along **Rua de São João da Praça.**

lisbon

FLOR DA SÉ PASTELARIA ❶

Lg. de Santo António da Sé ☎218 87 57 42

This *pastelaria* is known throughout Lisbon for having the best pastries this side of Belém and for its cheap *pratos do dia* (around €5). Its location near the border between Alfama and Baixa makes it a good place to start or to end your tour of Alfama.

⇄ Take tram 28E to Sé, then walk back a block along the tracks toward Baixa; it's on the left. $ Pratos do dia €4.50-5.50 ⏰ Open M-F 7am-8pm, Su 7am-8pm.

CHURRASQUEIRA GAÚCHA ♿ 🍸 GRILL ❷

R. dos Bacalhoeiros, 26 ☎218 87 06 09

Great, traditional Portuguese fare in a simple but very large dining room. The meat and fish are displayed in a window on the street, so you can just walk by and pick what looks good.

⇄ From Baixa, follow R. do Comércio east (to the left as you face the water) until R. da Madalena, then slight right onto R. dos Bacalhoeiros. $ Main courses €7.50-14. ⏰ Open M-Sa noon-midnight.

POIS, CAFE 🍸 CAFE ❷

R. de São João da Praça, 93 ☎218 86 24 97 💻www.poiscafe.com

A new, trendy cafe right across from the massive stone walls of the ancient Sé.

Giant stone arches tower over the comfortable and relaxed seating in this chic cafe. Order something special (just don't ask for a "tall") from the hip baristas decked out in custom T-shirts.

Tram 28E to Sé. From plaza in front of cathedral, walk to the right of cathedral; the cafe is on the right. $ Lunch menu €5. Baked goods €2-7. ⏰ Open Tu-Su 11am-8pm.

ÓH CALDAS — TRADITIONAL ❸

R. de São Mamede, 22 ☎218 87 57 11

This traditional restaurant has favorites like *sardinhas assadas* *(grilled sardines; €6.50)*, *alheira* *(smoked chicken sausage; €6)*, and an ever-changing three-course daily menu *(€12)*. Its location on the scenic route between the Sé (cathedral) and the Castelo de São Jorge makes it a convenient Alfama stop.

From Baixa, follow R. da Conceiçao east toward Alfama (to left as you face the river), just past the Igreja da Madalena. Head left up Travessa d'Almada for 3 blocks, then left on R. de São Mamede. $ Daily menu €12. ⏰ Open daily noon-4pm and 8pm-midnight.

GRAÇA

The area around **Largo da Graça** is heaven for those looking for good, cheap meals. The *pastelarias* that line the square generally write their *pratos do dia* in magic marker on a paper tablecloth and post them outside; walk from one to the next and see what looks best and cheapest, though they all usually cost about €4-6. To get there, take tram 28E from the side of R. da Conceiçao that is closest to the river in Baixa, all the way to the end of the line. If you're looking for a drink or a light lunch with an amazing view, try the **Esplanada da Igreja da Graca,** a lovely lookout point with carts that serve cheap sandwiches and drinks. *(ℹ Cash only. ⏰ Open daily 11:30am-2am.)*

PASTELARIA ESTRELA DA GRAÇA — PASTELARIA ❶

Lg. da Graça, 98 ☎218 87 24 38

The pastry counter has more sweets than most have ever seen in one place, but don't get too distracted, because the daily specials are delicious and incredibly cheap. They usually come with all the fixings (rice, fries, small salad, sometimes an egg) and will leave you stuffed. A glass of the house wine costs less than €1 and is actually drinkable.

Take tram 28E to end of the line; it's across the street, next to the big church. $ Pratos do dia €4-6. ⏰ Open daily 7am-10pm.

RESTAURANTE JARDIM DA GRAÇA — TRADITIONAL ❷

Lg. da Graça, 20 ☎218 86 99 65

This small and noisy local favorite has delicious traditional fare inside and a very welcoming fake chef outside. It's something of a step up in quality from the *pastelarias* *(€0.50-1 extra per dish)*, but the price hardly reflects it.

Take tram 28E to the end of the line; it's right next to the tram stop, across from the big church. $ Main courses €6.50-7. Pratos do dia about €1-2 cheaper. ⏰ Open M-F 8am-11pm, Su 8am-11pm.

TASCA DO MANEL — TRADITIONAL ❷

R. de São Tomé, 20 ☎218 86 20 21

A small restaurant with walls covered in *azulejos* and an apparently random collection of black-and-white photographs. It's just down the road from Lg. da Graça toward Alfama, which makes it a very convenient stop. Expect a wait.

From Largo da Graça, go to the small park in front of the church, next to the lookout point, then follow Cç. da Graça straight; it becomes R. de São Tomé after a small plaza (stay to the right of the kebab place). $ Pratos do dia €6.50-9. Entrees €6.80-12. ⏰ Open Tu 11:30am-3:30pm and 6:30-10:30pm, W 6:30-10:30pm, Th-Su 11:30am-3:30pm and 6:30-10:30pm.

nightlife

Bairro Alto is one massive street party every night (even Sunday!) until 2am, and is where just about everyone in town starts their evening. Few people actually stay in the plethora of bars that line these narrow streets: you go into one of the places, get your massive beer or cocktail (generally about 9 parts alcohol and 1 part not), and take a seat on the **sidewalk.** Watch out for taxis, which have a difficult time navigating the crowds and whose roofs tend to become receptacles for empty drink containers. The main nightlife area here is bordered by R. da Atalaia to the west, Travessa da Queimada to the north, R. da Misericórdia to the east, and the Praça de Luís de Camões to the south; the major streets for bars are **R. da Atalaia, Rua do Diário de Notícias,** and **Rua do Norte,** all of which run north-south through the neighborhood. After these bars close around 2am (a little later F-Sa nights), there is a mass migration downhill toward **Cais do Sodré,** where bars gather under an overpass formed by R. do Alecrim. If these clubs are too crowded, or if people are looking for something a little flashier, they'll head west along to river to **Santos,** or even farther to **Alcântara** and the **Docas de Santo Amaro** at the foot of the 25 de Abril bridge. The area near the Santa Apolonia train station also has a couple of newer clubs, including the famous Lux. Though Bairro Alto tends to be quite casual, don't expect to get into any of the clubs if you're still in your swim trunks and your flippy floppies. Drinks inside tend to be expensive (beer is usually €3-5 early in the night, and rises as dawn approaches), and there is often a cover for the best clubs (usually €5-15, depending on the time and how you look, though often free for women; the cover usually includes a couple of free drinks as well). Don't show up before midnight, when the places feel like seedier versions of bad middle-school dances.

BAIRRO ALTO

👍 PORTAS LARGAS — 🎵⊗🍸 BAR, MUSIC

R. da Atalaia, 105 — ☎213 46 63 79

This staple of the Bairro Alto scene has live music every night (sometimes really good, other times unfortunate covers of '80s songs that are so bad they're good) and some of the biggest, strongest *caipirinhas* and mojitos around *(€4-6)*. It gets crowded inside, but you can enjoy the music and drinks just outside. Don't expect to be able to loiter inside and enjoy the music without buying a drink.

➜ [M]Baixa-Chiado (Chiado exit). Bus #1, 202, 758, 590, or tram 28E. Walk up R. da Misericórdia 4 blocks from Pr. de Luís de Camões, then left for 5 blocks. [$] Beer €2. Caipirinhas and mojitos €4. ⏰ Open Oct-June M-Th 8pm-2am, F-Sa 8pm-3am, Su 8pm-2am; July-Sept M-Th 7pm-2am, F-Sa 7pm-3am, Su 7pm-2am.

👍 BICA ABAIXO — 🎵⊗🍸 BAR

R. da Bica de Duarte Belo, 62 — ☎213 47 70 14

This bar is located on the steep slope of the shiny silver Elevador da Bica funicular, just to the south of the center of Bairro Alto. It's perfect for those making the trek down to the river or for those sick of Bairro Alto's cheaply made drinks: the native Brazilians who own and run this small bar make the best *caipirinhas* *(€3)* in town, crushed and mashed and mixed together right in front of you.

➜ [M]Baixa-Chiado (Chiado exit) or tram 28E to Calhariz-Bica. From Pr. de Luís de Camões, follow R. do Loreto (far-right corner of plaza, with your back to the Metro station) 3 blocks, then turn left down R. da Bica de Duarte Belo; it's on the left. [$] Beer €1.50. Mixed drinks €3-4. ⏰ Open daily 9pm-2am.

PAVILHÃO CHINÊS — 🎫⊗🍸 LOUNGE

R. de Dom Pedro V, 89 — ☎213 42 47 29

A little north of the main Bairro Alto scene, this nightlife spot is a little more laid-back (and indoors) than its raucous neighbors, but it's hardly boring. The brightly lit walls and ceilings are covered in decorations that range from the

lisbon

kitschy to the cool, with an East Asian theme. There is a huge menu of teas and classic drinks like the Sidecar—they're bringin' it back—presented in a 50-page menu-cum-graphic novel.

➜ Bus #1, 202, 758, 790. From Pr. de Luís de Camões, follow R. da Misericórdia up toward the miradouro, and keep following the same street as it bends to the left and becomes R. de Dom Pedro V. $ Teas €4. Drinks €6-9. ⏰ Open M-Sa 6pm-2am, Su 9pm-2am.

FRIENDS BAIRRO ALTO ⊛⊗📶🍸 BAR, BOOK EXCHANGE

R. da Rosa, 99 ☎213 43 24 19

In the afternoon, this is a cool and quiet reading lounge; at night it turns into a lively bar but loses none of its literary tendencies. Bring a book and exchange it for another one or for a drink, then mingle with the teen and 20-something hipster crowd.

➜ Ⓜ Baixa-Chiado (Chiado exit). From Pr. de Luís de Camões, follow R. do Loreto (far right corner of plaza with your back toward Metro station) 3 blocks, then turn right up R. da Rosa. $ Beer €1.50. Mixed drinks €3-5. ⏰ Open daily 3pm-2am.

PALPITA-ME ⊛⊗🍸 KARAOKE

R. do Diário de Notícias, 40B ☎965 41 94 19

Come sing pop songs you've never heard before in a language you don't quite know—it's a blast. This place gets packed to the gills with energetic young party animals singing their hearts out, and the room next door has live music every night.

➜ Ⓜ Baixa-Chiado (Chiado exit). From Pr. de Luís de Camões, head up R. do Norte (to the right near the far side of the plaza if your back is to the Metro station) 1 block, then left, then right up R. do Diário de Notícias. $ Shots €1-2. Beer €1.50. Cocktails €4-5. ⏰ Open M-Sa 8pm-2am.

SALTO ALTO 💳⊗🍸 BAR

R. da Rosa, 159 ☎916 52 21 07 💻www.saltoalto-bar.com

A new, hip bar that looks pretty much exactly how you would expect a new, hip bar to look: dim lighting, bright but solid-colored walls except for one with a trippy pattern, and shelves of drinks behind the bar lit from behind. Usually a bit quieter (though by no means quiet) than the streets in Bairro Alto's heart a few blocks southeast, but still a happening place.

➜ Ⓜ Baixa-Chiado (Chiado exit) or tram 28E to Calhariz-Bica. From Pr. de Luís de Camões, follow R. do Loreto (far-right corner of plaza, with your back to the Metro station) 3 blocks, then turn right up R. da Rosa. $ Cocktails €3-5. ⏰ Open W-Th 10pm-2am, F-Sa 10pm-3am, Su 10pm-2am.

PÁGINAS TANTAS ⊛⊗🍸 JAZZ, LOUNGE

R. do Diário de Notícias, 85 ☎917 60 03 29

A quieter sanctuary for those who need a brief break from the madness on the street outside, this bar is full of yuppies and jazz. There's live music on some weekend nights; recorded jazz is pumped through the impressive sound system the rest of the time.

➜ Ⓜ Baixa-Chiado (Chiado exit). From Pr. de Luís de Camões, head up R. do Norte (to the right near the far side of the plaza if your back is to the Metro station) 1 block. Turn left, then right up R. do Diário de Notícias. $ Beer €2. Mixed drinks €5.50. ⏰ Open daily 8pm-2am.

ALFAMA

★ LUX 💳⊗🍸 DISCOTECA ❸

Av. do Infante Dom Henrique ☎218 82 08 💻www.luxfragil.com

This club is known far and wide as one of the best clubs in Western Europe; Lisboans abroad will tell you that if you visit one *discoteca* in Lisbon, it has to be this one. The enormous riverside complex has three stories of debauchery. Chill on the calm rooftop with amazing views, start to get schwastey at a slightly more intense bar on the floor below that, then descend into the maelstrom on the lowest level to find a raging disco howling and shrieking with techno. The bouncers tend to be very selective, so just act cool and try to get on their good side by being polite and speaking Portuguese (even the most pathetic attempt at the difficult language is greatly appreciated, and it might even decrease your cover charge). Dress well—only wear jeans or sneakers if the jeans are super-skinny and the sneakers are canvas high-tops, since the stylin' hipster look tends to play well.

⚜ Ⓜ*Santa Apolónia, bus 12, 28, 34, 35, 206, 210, 706, 745, 759, 781, 782, 794. Just east of Santa Apolónia train station, on the side of the tracks closest to the river.* Ⓢ *Cover usually €12.* ☪ *Open Tu-Sa 11pm-6am.*

GINJA D'ALFAMA
GINJINHA ❶
R. de São Pedro, 12

Hidden in the heart of Alfama, this tiny hole-in-the-ancient-wall bar specializes in *ginjinha*, Lisbon's native wild-cherry liqueur, and serves it up cheap and ice cold (€1). You can take it outside to the small tables around the corner, which are much cooler than the stifling bar itself. It's a great place to start the night, serving sandwiches to carbo-load with before heading back out to hilly and confusing Alfama.

⚜ *Bus 28, 35, 206, 210, 745, 759, 794. Walk down R. de São João da Praça, to right of Sé Cathedral as you're facing it, and follow the same street (bear left at the fork 1 block past the cathedral) as it becomes R. de São Pedro; it's a small store on the left side.* Ⓢ *Ginjinha €1. Sandwiches €1.50-2.50.* ☪ *Open M 9:30am-midnight, W-Su 9:30am-midnight.*

THE RIVERFRONT
Once the bars in Bairro Alto close, the party walks down R. do Alecrim to Cais do Sodré, where there are more than a dozen clubs. The area looks pretty unsavory 7am-2am, but the lines for the clubs stretch around the block for the other five hours. Many party enthusiasts then continue westward toward the **25 de Abril bridge,** where the neighborhoods of Santos, Alcântara, and the newly redeveloped Docas de Santo Amaro have chic and exclusive clubs.

OP ART
DISCOTECA ❷
Doca de Santo Amaro ☎213 95 67 87 ▣www.opartcafe.com

During the daytime, this is a pleasant spot to sit by the water and watch the waves while listening to the hum of the cars passing over the bridge. On Friday and Saturday nights, it's a completely different story. Guest DJs rattle the panes of the all-glass structure, pumping hip hop and European techno until the sun starts to rise over the Tejo.

⚜ *Buses 1, 12, 28, 201, 714, 720, 732, 738, trams 15E and 18E. Head toward the bridge along the waterfront.* Ⓢ *Cover €5-10; includes 1 drink. Beer €2.50. Mixed drinks €5-7.* ☪ *Open Tu-Th 3pm-2am, F-Sa 3pm-6am, Su 3pm-2am.*

DOCK'S CLUB
DISCOTECA ❸
R. da Cintura do Porto de Lisboa, 226 ☎213 95 08 56

This disco near the bridge is famous for its Ladies' Nights on Tuesday (well, Wednesday mornings), when women not only get in free but also get €14 in free drinks. Spare the social commentary on this potentially sexist practice and enjoy the music blasting from the two different bars inside or the fresh air on the patio in back.

⚜ *Buses 1, 12, 28, 201, 714, 720, 732, 738, trams 15E and 18E.* Ⓢ *Cover €10-15. Beer €3. Mixed drinks €6.* ☪ *Open Tu midnight-6am, Th-Sa midnight-6am.*

KREMLIN
DISCOTECA ❸
Escadinhas da Praia, 5 ☎213 95 71 01 ▣www.grupo-k.pt

During the '80s, this club claimed to be the world's third best. It's run by the same management as **Kapital,** just around the corner on Av. 24 de Julho. While Kapital is the sort of place you go to just to get in and say you got in, Kremlin is a fun place to bounce to house music until dawn.

⚜ *Bus 1, 28, 60, 74, 201, 706, 714, 727, 732, 794 or tram 15E, 18E, or 25E to Santos. It's up a small alley off Av. 24 de Julho, on the side away from the river.* Ⓢ *Cover €10-20.* ☪ *Open F-Sa midnight-8am.*

arts and culture

FADO

A mandatory experience for visitors, Lisbon's trademark form of entertainment is the traditional *fado*, an art combining music, song, and narrative poetry. Its roots lie in the Alfama neighborhood, where women whose husbands had gone to sea would lament their *fado* (fate). Singers of *fado* traditionally dress in black and sing mournful tunes of lost love, uncertainty, and the famous feelings of *saudade* (to translate *saudade* as "loneliness" would be a gruesome understatement). However, many *fado* venues will have less melancholy songs and even some comedic crowd-pleasers (if you understand Portuguese, at least). Many *fado* houses can be found in Bairro Alto and in Alfama between the cathedral and the water. Many small restaurants on side streets have performances for low prices or for free, and snippets can be heard along the streets almost every night. Almost all *fado* houses are rather touristy, since not all that many Portuguese want to hear *fado* sung by anyone other than the beloved Amália Rodrigues. Expensive *fado* houses with mournfully high minimums include **Cafe Luso** *(Tv. da Queimada, 10 ☎213 42 22 81 ☐www.cafeluso.pt⑤ $25 min. ☒ Open daily 7:30pm-2am)* and **Adega Machado** *(R. do Norte, 91 ☎213 22 46 40 ⑤ €16 min. ☒ Open Tu-Su 8pm-2am)* There are also some well-marked and easy-to-find places on **Rua de São João da Praça** in Alfama, including one called **Clube de Fado** with road signs pointing to it all the way from Baixa. The places listed below are either free or truly worth the money.

VOSSEMECÊ   ⊛♿✿ ALFAMA
R. de Santo António da Sé, 18   ☎218 88 30 56

This *fado* joint, conveniently located near Baixa, is housed in a beautiful, if oddly shaped, stable; arched ceilings and heavy stone columns run farther than the eye can see into the darkness of the ground-level restaurant. The *fadistas* rotate, each singing a couple of songs ranging from lively and funny to mournful. There's no cover charge or drink minimum, but the drinks are reasonably priced *(€3.50-6.50)* and quite good.

✈ Ⓜ*Baixa-Chiado (Baixa exit), OR tram 28E. Follow R. da Conceiçao east toward Alfama (to the left as you face the river) past Igreja da Madalena; it's on the corner across the street to the left. ⑤ Drinks €3.50-6.50. Main courses €8-15. ☒ Open M-Tu noon-4pm and 8:30pm-midnight, Th-Su noon-4pm and 8:30pm-midnight; fado 9pm-midnight.*

A TASCA DO CHICO   ⊛⊘✿ BAIRRO ALTO
R. do Diário de Notícias, 39   ☎965 05 96 70

This Bairro Alto *fado* location is popular with locals and has no cover charge or drink minimum. You're going to want a cold drink, however, as it gets crowded and stiflingly hot early on. Many choose to grab a spot at the open window and watch from the cool(er) street outside. Pretty much any amateur *fadista* who wants to take a turn can sing, so on a given night you could hear something you'd rather forget immediately, followed by the next big thing in *fado*.

✈ Ⓜ*Baixa-Chiado (Chiado exit). From Pr. de Luís de Camões, head up R. do Norte (to the right near the far side of the plaza if your back is to the Metro station) for 1 block, then take a quick left. Next, turn right up R. do Diário de Notícias. ⑤ Beer €1.50. ☒ Open M-Sa 8pm-2am. Fado starts around 9:30pm, but arrive much earlier to get a seat.*

BULLFIGHTING

Portuguese bullfighting differs from the spectacle practiced across the border in Spain in that the bull is not killed in the ring; instead, it's butchered afterward. At first blush, the Portuguese variety of *tauromaquia* seems a much fairer match between man and beast: rather than one *matador* with a sword like in Spain, five unarmed *forcados* line up in front of the bull and take him down with their bare hands. However, once you remember that the bull has been poked, prodded, and stabbed for the previous 15-20min., the justness of the final battle becomes a little less impressive. Most bullfights take place on Thursday nights at the newly renovated **Praça de Touros de Lisboa** at Campo Pequeno. *(☎217 99 84 50 💻www.campopequeno.com $ €23-75.)* True fans of the sport, however, will want to make a pilgrimage to **Santarém,** Portuguese bullfighting's capital and home to the best matches. *(Praça de Touros Monumental Celestino Graça, Campo Emílio Infante da Câmara ☎243 32 43 58 $€11 ⏰ 45min. by train. Trains run to Santarém from Lisbon's Santa Apolónia station 15 per day 7:30am-9:30pm.)*

FUTEBOL

For many Portuguese, *futebol* (known in many Anglophone countries as "football," and in the United States as "soccer" or "that sport we care about for two weeks once every four years") is a way of life. The Portuguese side returned from the 2006 World Cup as national heroes after reaching the semifinal round for the first time in 40 years. They had a strong showing in the 2010 World Cup as well, though they lost in the quarterfinal round to eventual champion Spain in a lackluster performance that left many a Portuguese citizen in tears. If you're in Lisbon when Portugal is playing, head to one of the **giant TV screens** set up around town, usually located at **Praça do Marquês de Pombal, Praça da Figueira,** or just off **Praça dos Restauradores,** next to the Rossio train station. Portugal's two most renowned clubs are located in Lisbon: **Benfica** won the league championship in 2010, and **Sporting** has some of the best footballers in the world. Benfica plays at **Estádio da Luz,** known to fans as the *catedral (Av. do General Norton de Matos ☎217 21 95 00 💻www.slbenfica.pt),* and Sporting plays at **Estádio José Alvalade** *(Av. de Padre Cruz ☎707 20 44 44 💻www.sporting.pt).* The season begins in mid-August and ends in mid-May. These two sides are bitter rivals, so be careful whom you're supporting and where.

THEATER, MUSIC, AND FILM

Teatro Nacional de Dona Maria II in Rossio stages performances of classical and foreign plays. *(Pr. de Dom Pedro IV ☎213 25 08 00 💻www.teatro-dmaria.pt 🚏 [M]Rossio.)* At Lisbon's largest theater, **Teatro Nacional de São Carlos,** opera and classical music hold sway. *(R. Serpa Pinto, 9 ☎213 25 30 00 💻www.saocarlos.pt 🚏 [M]Baixa-Chiado, tram 28E.)* From the end of June to the end of July, this theater fills the neighboring **Largo de São Carlos** with free music and dance performances in the open-air Chiado evening. *(Lg. de São Carlos 💻www.festivalaolargo.com.)* The **Cinema São Jorge** is one of Portugal's grandest and oldest movie theaters. *(Av. da Liberdade, 175 ☎213 10 34 00 💻www.cinemasaojorge.pt 🚏 [M]Avenida.)* Other cinema complexes can be found at the **Amoreiras** shopping center *(Av. do Engenheiro Duarte Pacheco ☎213 81 02 40 💻www.amoreiras.com 🚏 Buses 207, 711),* the **Colombo** shopping center *(Av. Lusíada ☎217 11 36 36 💻www.colombo.pt 🚏 [M]Colégio Militar-Luz),* the **Centro Vasco da Gama** *(Av. de Dom João II ☎218 93 06 00 💻www.centrovascodagama.pt 🚏 [M]Oriente),* and **El Corte Inglés** *(Av. António Augusto de Aguiar, 31 ☎217 95 64 38 💻www.elcorteingles.pt 🚏 [M]Marquês de Pombal).*

FESTIVALS

June is Lisbon is essentially one month-long festival, with food, drink, music, and dancing filling the streets from Bairro Alto to Graça and far, far beyond. The night of June 12 is the peak of the festivities, when Lisbon's adopted patron Saint Anthony is celebrated during the **Festa de Santo António.** Banners, streamers, and colored lights criss cross the streets and streetlamps, and confetti falls by the metric ton on the **Avenida da Liberdade** during the parade. The crowded streets of Alfama, particularly around the **Igreja de Santo António da Sé,** erupt with zealous revelry, and everyone consumes *sardinhas assadas* (grilled sardines) and *ginjinha* (wild cherry liqueur). Decorations hang in Alfama for months after the **festas de Lisboa** end, and serve as reminders of the crazy month. For three days during the second week in July, the **Optimus Alive** music festival takes over the Algés waterfront, drawing some of the world's most popular artists and fans from across the globe *(☎213 93 37 70 💻www.optimusalive.com).*

festival of san antonio

What do green wigs, sardines, streamers, and being drunk in the street cerca 6:30am have in common? All are part of Lisbon's biggest festival of the year, the Festival of Santo Antonio (called "Santos" by those in the know) which takes place the night before June 13th annually.

The Portuguese owe this celebration to Saint Anthony, also known as Fernando Martins de Bulhões, who is known in Portugal as the marriage saint. Couples who are married on June 13th are said to receive his blessing. This is no Vegas-style free-for-all wedding, however, as only a lucky group of couples get married in a group ceremony called "Santo Casamenterio" at the Sé Cathedral in the Almalfa neighborhood.

The festivities truly start, however, with a giant parade held on Avenida da Liberdade called "Marchas Populares," in which each Lisbon neighborhood prepares its own unique costumes and folk dance as part of a competition for best march that has been a tradition since 1932. These dances are actually fiercely competitive, and preparation for these marches, including costume selection and dance choreography, starts months in advance. Although the parade does not start until around 9:30pm the night before Santos, many start lining up over an hour before the parade's start in order to ensure that they grab the best viewing spot of the folk dances. The parade is no short affair either—there are often long spaces of time between neighborhood acts, and the parade does not wrap up until around midnight.

After you've got your share of parade viewing and a decent amount of Super Bock in your system, it's time to head over to one of the Barris in order to eat the festive meal of sardines. Those salty-fish averse be warned: sardines are often the only option served at some of the more authentic restaurants in the historic Almalfi district where the festival is in its fullest swing.

After you've had your fishy fill, head to the streets. Most of the bars and restaurants locate outside and sell beers and other drinks for usually between 1 to 2 euros. From then on, each street has its own adventure to offer. Some streets feature circles of dancers with one dancer breaking it down in the middle, other streets are more reminiscent of a frat party on a Saturday night, while others still have that "olde towne" traditional flare. Be sure to try some "Ginja," a cherry liquor somewhat reminiscent of super-condensed (and super-strong) red wine. No matter what street-side adventure you find, be forewarned that there are little to no bathrooms available outside anywhere—many restaurants will not let you enter at all or will charge you an under-the-table fee to use their facilities.

arts and culture . feiras

FEIRAS *Markets*

Most of Lisbon's shopping districts and malls don't have anything that you couldn't find elsewhere, but the *feiras* can be great places to pick up one-of-a-kind souvenirs and other items on the cheap. *Feiras* that take place regularly include the **Feiras das Velharias,** antique fairs held in Lisbon's western suburbs (in **Oeiras** and **São Julião da Barra** on the first Sunday of the month, in **Caxias** on the second Sunday of the month, in **Paço de Arcos** on the third Sunday of the month, and in **Algés** on the fourth Sunday of the month) and the **Feira de Carcavelos,** one of the area's oldest markets that carries cheap clothing, which takes place in Carcavelos every Thursday. The **Feira de Artesano de Estoril,** which celebrates Portuguese pottery, takes place every July and August and is a 30min. train ride west of Lisbon in Estoril, in front of the casino.

🛍 **FEIRA DA LADRA** GRAÇA

Campo de Santa Clara

The so-called "thief's market" is Lisbon's best known, held in Graça near the edge of Alfama. The stalls at this market, which takes place every Tuesday and Saturday, stretch from the Mosteiro de São Vicente da Fora to the Panteão Nacional, with vendors selling antique books, vintage vinyls, old postcards, and just about anything else you might want. Prices are flexible and bargaining is encouraged, but initially posing too low of an offer can be thought of as an insult. Get there early before the tour groups pick the place clean.

🚏 Take tram 28E to Igreja e Mosteiro de São Vicente de Fora, then walk to the left of the big white church. ⏰ Open Tu 7am-2pm, Sa 7am-2pm.

days of the week

In Portuguese, the days of the week Monday through Friday (segunda feira, terça feira, quarta feira, quinta feira, and sexta feira, often abbreviated 2a, 3a, 4a, 5a, and 6a), take their names from the markets (feiras) held on those days.

essentials ℹ

PRACTICALITIES

- **TOURIST OFFICE:** The Tourist Office on Pr. dos Restauradores has information for Lisbon and all of Portugal. *(Pr. dos Restauradores, 1250 ☎213 47 56 60 💻www.visitlisboa.com 🚏 [M]Restauradores, or bus 36, 44, 91, 205, 207, 702, 709, 711, 732, 745, 746, 759. On west side of Pr. dos Restauradores, in Palácio da Foz. ⏰ Open daily 9am-8pm.)* The **Welcome Center** is the city of Lisbon's main tourist office where you can buy tickets for sightseeing buses and the Lisboa Card, which includes transportation and discounted admission to most sights for a flat fee *(R. do Arsenal, 15 ☎210 31 27 00)*. The **Airport branch** is located near the terminal exit. *(☎218 45 06 60 ⏰ Open daily 7am-midnight.)* There are also information kiosks in Santa Apolónia, Belém, and on R. Augusta in Baixa.
- **TOURS: CARRISTur** provides 1½hr. tours of the historic center in pre-WWI tram cars. *(Pr. do Comércio ☎213 58 23 34 💻www.carristur.pt 🚏 [M]Baixa-Chiado, buses 7, 28, 35, 36, 40, 44, 60, 74, 91, 92, 205, 206, 207, 208, 210, 706, 709, 711, 714, 732, 745, 746, 759, 781,782, 790, 794, or trams 15E, 18E, 25E. Trams leave from Pr. do Comércio, the giant plaza by the water at the end of R. Augusta in Baixa. [$] €18, ages 4-10 €9. ℹ Available in Dutch, English, French, German, Italian, Japanese, Portuguese, and Spanish. ⏰ Tours depart from Pr. do Comércio every 30-40min. 10am-8pm.)*
- **CURRENCY EXCHANGE: NovaCâmbios** in Rossio provides currency exchange. *(Pr. de Dom Pedro IV, 42 ☎213 24 25 53 💻www.novacambios.com 🚏 [M]Rossio or buses 36, 44, 91, 205, 207, 709, 711, 732, 745, 746, 759. On west side of Rossio plaza. ⏰ Open M-F 8:30am-3pm.)*
- **INTERNET: Biblioteca Municipal Camões** has free internet access. *(Lg. do Calhariz, 17 ☎213 42 21 57 💻www.blx.cm-lisboa.pt 🚏 [M]Baixa-Chiado, tram 28E OR bus 58, 100. From Pr. de Luís de Camões, follow R. do Loreto for 4 blocks. ⏰ Open Sept 16-July 15 Tu-F 10:30am-6pm; July 16-Sept 15 M-F 11am-6pm.)*
- **POST OFFICE: Correios** main office is on Pr. dos Restauradores, but the Pr. do Comércio branch *(⏰ Open M-F)* is less crowded. *(Pr. dos Restauradores, 58 ☎213*

23 89 71 🖥www.ctt.pt 🪧 [M]Restauradores OR bus 36, 44, 91, 205, 207, 702, 709, 711, 732, 745, 746, 759. ⏰ Open M-F 8am-10pm, Sa-Su 9am-6pm.)

EMERGENCY!

- **POLICE: Tourism Police Station** provides police service for foreigners. *(Pr. dos Restauradores, 1250 ☎213 42 16 24 🪧 [M]Restauradores OR bus 36, 44, 91, 205, 207, 702, 709, 711, 732, 745, 746, 759. On west side of Pr. dos Restauradores, in Palácio da Foz next to the tourist office.)*
- **LATE-NIGHT PHARMACIES: Farmácia Azevedo and Filhos** in Rossio posts a schedule of pharmacies open late at night, as do most other pharmacies, or just look for a lighted, green cross. *(Pr. de Dom Pedro IV, 31 ☎213 43 04 82 🪧 [M]Rossio or buses 36, 44, 91, 205, 207, 709, 711, 732, 745, 746, 759. In front of metro stop at the side of Rossio closest to river. ⏰ Open daily 8:30am-7:30pm.)*
- **HOSPITAL/MEDICAL SERVICES: Hospital de St. Louis** is in Bairro Alto. *(R. de Luz Soriano, 182 🪧 [M]Baixa-Chiado. From Pr. de Luís de Camões, follow R. do Loreto 4 blocks, then right up R. de Luz Soriano. ⏰ Open daily 9am-8pm.)* Lisbon's main hospital is **Hospital de São José.** *(R. de José António Serrano ☎218 84 10 00 🪧 [M]Martim Moniz or bus 8, 799. ⏰ Open 24hr.)*

GETTING THERE ✈

By Plane

All flights land at **Aeroporto de Lisboa** *(☎218 41 37 00)*, near the northern edge of the city. Major airlines have offices along Av. da Liberdade and at the Pr. do Marquês de Pombal. **Vueling** has inexpensive flights from Spain, and **easyJet** has cheap direct flights from various locations in western Europe, including Barcelona, Berlin, London, Madrid, Milan, Paris, and Rome. The cheapest way into town from the airport is by **bus:** to get to the bus stop, walk out of the terminal, turn right, and cross the street to the bus stop, marked with yellow metal posts with arrival times of incoming buses. Buses 44, 91, and 745 *([$] €1.45. ⏰ 15-20min., every 12-25min. 6am-12:15am)* run to Pr. dos Restauradores, where they stop in front of the tourist office. The express AeroBus 91 runs to the same locations *([$] €3.50. ⏰ 15min., every 20min. 7am-11pm)* and is a much faster option during rush hours. A **taxi** downtown costs about €10-15, but fares are billed by time, not distance, so watch out for drivers trying to take a longer route.

By Train

Those traveling in and out of Lisbon by train are regularly confused, since there are multiple major train stations in Lisbon, all serving different destinations. The express, inexpensive **Alfa Pendular** line runs between Braga, Porto, Coimbra, and Lisbon. Regional trains are slow and can be crowded; buses are slightly more expensive but faster and more comfortable. **Urbanos** trains run from Lisbon to Sintra and to Cascais, with stops along the way, and are very cheap and very reliable; make sure you go to the right station, though. Contact **Comboios de Portugal** for more info *(☎808 20 82 08 🖥www.cp.pt)*. **Estação do Barreiro** is across the Rio Tejo from Lisbon and runs trains to destinations to the south of the city; to get there, take a ferry from Terreiro do Paço dock, just east of Pr. do Comércio. *([$] €2.15. ⏰ 30min., 2 per hr.)* Urbanos trains run to Praias do Sado *(⏰ Every hr. 6:25am-12:30am)* with stops at Pinhal Novo *([$] €1.35)* and Setúbal *([$] €1.75)*. **Estação Cais do Sodré** is right at the river, a 5min. walk west from Baixa or a quick Metro ride to the end of the green line. Urbanos trains leave every 15-30min. and service the suburbs (and beaches) to the west of the city, with the line ending in Cascais. Take trains labeled "Oeiras" or "Cascais Todos" to get to Belém *([$] €1.25)* and trains labeled "Cascais" or "Cascais Todos" to Estoril *([$] €1.75)* and Cascais *([$] €1.75)*. **Estação Rossio** is the gorgeous neo-Manueline building between Rossio and Pr. dos Restauradores and services the northwestern suburbs, with the line ending in Sintra. *([$] €1.75. ⏰ 40min., every 10-20min.)* **Estação**

Santa Apolónia is one of the main international and inter-city train stations in Lisbon, running trains to the north and east. It is located on the river to the east of Baixa; to get there, take the blue Metro line to the end of the line. Trains between **Santa Apolónia** and **Aveiro** (Ⓢ €16.50-25. 🕐 2½hr., 16 per day 6am-10pm), **Braga** (Ⓢ €31. 🕐 3½hr., 4 per day 6am-10pm), **Coimbra** (Ⓢ €20-31. 🕐 2hr., 20 per day 6am-10pm), **Porto** (Ⓢ €20-28.50. 🕐 3hr., 16 per day 6am-11pm), and **Madrid** (Ⓢ €59. 🕐 10hr., daily at 10:30pm). **Estação Oriente** runs southbound trains. The station is near the Parque das Nações, up the river to the east of the center; take the red Metro line to the end of the line. Trains run between Oriente and Faro (Ⓢ €18.50-21. 🕐 3½-4hr., 6 per day 8am-8pm) with connections to other destinations in the Algarve.

By Bus

Lisbon's bus station is close to Ⓜ Jardim Zoológico, but it can be hard to find. Once at the Metro stop, follow exit signs to Av. C. Bordalo Pinheiro. Exit the Metro, go around the corner, and walk straight ahead 100m; then cross left in front of Sete Rios station. The stairs to the bus station are on the left. Rede Expressos (☎707 22 33 44 ▪www.rede-expressos.pt) runs buses between Lisbon and **Braga** (Ⓢ €19. 🕐 4-5hr., 14-16 per day 7-12:15am), **Coimbra** (Ⓢ €13. 🕐 2hr., 24-30 per day 7am-12:15am), and **Lagos** (Ⓢ €18.50-19. 🕐 4hr., 14-16 per day 7:30am-1am).

GETTING AROUND   🚩

By Public Transportation

Carris (☎213 61 30 00 ▪www.carris.pt) is Lisbon's extensive, efficient, and relatively inexpensive transportation system that is the easiest way to get around the city of Lisbon. The city is covered by an elaborate grid of subways, buses, trams, and *elevadores* (funiculars, useful for getting up the steep hills). Fares purchased on board buses, trams, or *elevadores* cost €1.45; the subway costs €0.85 but you must first purchase a rechargeable *viva viagem* card (Ⓢ €0.50). The easiest and most cost- and time-effective option for those who will use a lot of public transportation is the unlimited 24hr. **bilhete combinado** (Ⓢ €3.75), which can be used on any Carris transport and means you don't have to go into a Metro station to recharge your card before getting on a bus or tram. You can buy the *bilhete combinado* in any Metro station, and you can fill it with up to seven days' worth of unlimited travel. You can also put money on the €0.50 *viva viagem* card and use that; fares are €0.81 this way.

By Bus

Carris buses (Ⓢ €1.45, with viva viagem card €0.81) go to just about any place in the city, including those not serviced by the Metro.

By Metro

The Metro (Ⓢ with viva viagem card €.81) has four lines that cross the center of Lisbon and go to the major train stations. Metro stations are marked with a red "M" logo. Trains run daily 6:30am-1am.

By Tram

Trams (Ⓢ €1.45, with viva viagem card €.81) are used by tourists and locals alike to get around. Many vehicles predate WWI. Line 28E runs through Graça, Alfama, Baixa, Chiado, and Bairro Alto; line 15E goes from the Pr. do Comércio to Belém, passing the clubs of Santos and Alcântara.

By Taxi

Taxis in Lisbon can be hailed on the street throughout the center of town. Good places to find cabs include the train stations and main plazas. Bouncers will be happy to call you a cab after dark. Rádio Táxis de Lisbon (☎217 93 27 56) and Teletáxis (☎218 11 11 00) are the main companies.

CASCAIS AND SINTRA

Sometimes you just need to get away—but you're already vacationing in Portugal, so we don't know what you're complaining about. However, if Lisbon's urban atmosphere is feeling too modern at the moment, come to Cascais or Sintra for the decidedly medieval combination of ◣**castles** and ◤**caves.** Neither is farther than a train ride from Lisbon, and both are connected to each other by bus, so you won't need a time machine to reach your pre-20th-century paradise.

Hike in the footsteps of Hans Christian Andersen; play hide-and-seek with your new Portuguese pals at the Praia da Rainha; surf some serious waves. Explore the playground of a Bavarian prince—or of the Prince of Darkness, if that's more your thing. Mosey from beach to beach or hike from trail to trail. Whatever outdoorsy escape you want to pursue, these daytrips will have something to suit your taste.

greatest hits

- **ROBBER BARONS AND ROYAL BAVARIANS.** Between the contributions of the *nouveau riche* and old money, Sintra's stacked with perfect palaces (p. 387).

- **BETWEEN A ROCK AND A HARD PLACE.** At Cascais's Praia da Rainha, the funky rock formations and crazy-shaped stones make for a wild experience (p. 385).

cascais ☎214

A quick train ride (or longer swim) from Lisbon takes you away from the frenzied metropolis, past the historic sites of Belém and the ritzier resort of Estoril, and into the beach town of Cascais. Once a strategic outpost for sea trade and defense, Cascais became popular with the Portuguese aristocracy at the end of the 19th century; their palatial homes still dot the coastline. Today, Cascais attracts a much more varied crowd, consisting of international beach-lovers and Lisbon residents escaping the city for a day.

ORIENTATION

The Cascais **train station** is at the eastern edge of town; the **bus terminal** is beneath the large blue shopping center to the right as you exit the train station. From the train station, head along Av. Valbom (just to the right of the McDonald's) to the end of the street to reach the **tourism office,** a yellow building with a sign reading *"turismo."* Facing the tourist office, head left down **Avenida dos Combatentes da Grande Guerra** to reach the **beaches; Praia da Ribeira** is to the right, **Praia da Rainha** and **Praia da Conceiçao** are to the left. **Praça 5 de Outubro** and **Largo de Luís de Camões** are the town's main plazas, both just west (right while facing the water) of Av. dos Combatentes da Grande Guerra. The streets around the beaches are full of tourists and shops selling schlock to them; those farther west (to the right as you face the beach) tend to be quieter and are lovely to explore.

ACCOMMODATIONS

Inexpensive accommodations are hard to come by in Cascais; it's far more practical to stay in Lisbon, a short and cheap train ride away. If you do want to spend the night, there are a couple of good options.

👍 CASCAIS BEACH HOSTEL — HOSTEL ❶

R. da Vista Alegre, 10 ☎309 90 64 21 💻www.cascaisbeachostel.com

This is far and away the most affordable and most fun place to stay in Cascais. It's located on a shady residential street a short walk from the beach, but if you're too lazy to make it to the shore you can take a dip in the hostel's **pool**—or just lounge on a deck chair next to it. The four-, six-, and seven-bed rooms are big and clean, with a trendy lime-green and white color scheme, and the indoor common area has a TV and beanbags.

*# From train station, head straight down Av. Valbom to the tourist office, then right up R. Visconde da Luz with the park on the right, then left onto R. Manuel Joaquim Avelar, which becomes R. da Vista Alegre after 4 blocks; the hostel is 1 block up on the right. **i** Breakfast €3. Linens included. Kitchen. $ Dorms €18-20; doubles €49-69. Extra bed €10. ⏰ Reception 24hr.*

PARSI — PENSÃO ❸

R. Afonso Sanches, 8 ☎912 36 35 22

Large colorful rooms with walls covered in freshly painted designs overlook the Pr. 5 de Outubre and the beach. It can get a bit noisy in the evening when the pub downstairs fills up, but the location can't be beat. The rooms are all different in size and layout (one triple involves a kind of skewed bunk bed affixed to the wall), so ask to see all your options before choosing.

 # Just off Pr. 5 de Outubro, in the far-left corner with your back to the beach. $ Singles with shared bath €30; doubles €40, with ensuite bath €50-80; triples €60. ⏰ Reception 24hr.

SIGHTS

👍 BOCA DO INFERNO — CAVE

At this massive open cave, you can supposedly hear the devil's whisper resounding from the crashing surf. If you record the sound and isolate the correct wavelength, then play it backward, you'll hear the Satanic message, "You have way too much free time on your hands." (Idol hands are the devils tools, as they say.)

 # Follow the road along the water west (to the right as you face the water) about 1km. $ Free.

THE GREAT OUTDOORS

Cascais has a few beaches suitable more for surfing than sunbathing. **Guincho,** a 25min. bus ride away, is located on the Atlantic coast. To call this beach windswept or even wind-battered would be an understatement: Guincho is wind-beaten-to-within-an-inch-of-its-life-and-then-punched-in-the-kidneys. Gnarly waves and gale-force winds make it a major destination for all kinds of surfers: wind, kite, and regular. To get to Guincho, take ScottURB bus #405 (🕐 *1 per hr. M-Sa 6:50am-7:50pm, Su 6:50am-6:50pm)* or #415 (💲 *€2.80.* 🕐 *1 per hr. M-Sa 6:30am-8:30pm, Su 6:30am-7:20pm),* which run from the Cascais bus terminal (below shopping center next to train station). From the Guincho bus stop, head to the right as you face the water to get to the beach.

Surfing

GUINCHO SURF SCHOOL
SURF SCHOOL

Praia do Guincho ☎917 53 57 19 🖥www.guinchosurfschool.com

This surf school offers lessons for surfers of all ages and skill levels *(€25)* and will take you to another beach free of charge if conditions at Guincho are not suitable for surfing.

⚑ *Take ScottURB bus #405 or #415 to Guincho, then head to the right (as you face the water) to get to the beach; follow the sign down to the "Estalagem" and walk around it to the far side and down to the beach. The surf shop is in the same building, immediately to the left.* **i** *Reservations recommended; book a day in advance (by 7pm).* 💲 *1 lesson €25; 4 €80; 8 €120; 12 €150.* 🕐 *Open daily 9am-7pm.*

Beaches

There are three main beaches in Cascais, all side by side near the city center. **Praia da Ribeira,** the westernmost, is small but the most centrally located (right next to the Pr. 5 de Outubro), and it tends to get packed. **Praia da Rainha** is also small, but it has interesting and beautiful rock formations that make it seem like a wild, undiscovered coastline, with hiding places and coves behind every boulder. It tends to attract a younger crowd and is better for socializing than swimming. **Praia da Conceição,** east of both other beaches, is much larger and looks like any other beachgoer-filled shoreline.

FOOD

Restaurants line **Av. dos Combatentes da Grande Guerra,** and cheap sandwiches and fast food can be found on the main drags running from beach to beach.

O VIRIATO
⬤⊗♈ TRADITIONAL ❸

Av. de Vasco da Gama, 34 ☎214 86 81 98

This is a locals-only joint in an otherwise tourists-only town, which is refreshing if you can endure the leery glances and whispered comments from the regulars. The food is traditional, which means you'll have to skin, gut, and bone your fish yourself unless you request otherwise—but everything's delicious. Look into the kitchen via the big window on the adjacent street to see what looks good.

⚑ *From tourist office, follow R. de Alexandre Herculano (to the right of the office as you face it) which becomes Beco das Terras, then turn left onto Av. de Vasco da Gama.* 💲 *Entrees €7.80-16.* 🕐 *Open M noon-3pm and 7-11pm, Tu noon-3pm, W-Su noon-3pm and 7-11pm.*

RESTAURANTE DOM PEDRO I
⬤⊗♈⊿ TRADITIONAL ❷

Beco dos Inválidos, 32 ☎214 83 37 34

Sick of all the tourists and sunbathers on the beach and surrounding streets? Take a hidden alleyway off the Pr. do 5 de Outubro and have a quiet lunch under a short but broad and shady tree to escape the maddening crowds.

⚑ *Take narrow Beco dos Inválidos from left side of Pr. 5 de Outubro, with your back to the beach.* 💲 *Entrees €8.50-10.50.* 🕐 *Open M-Sa noon-3pm and 7-10pm.*

NIGHTLIFE

Nightlife in Cascais is simple: around 10:30pm, the side-by-side bars along **Largo de Luís de Camões** fill up with partiers, and the few establishments compete with each other to be the loudest. If they're too crowded and you can't get in, try the back

cascais · nightlife

entrances on Av. dos Combatentes da Grande Guerra. **Pr. 5 de Outubro** also has some action. At 2am, the party migrates down to the **waterfront,** where there are a couple of clubs along **Av. de Dom Carlos I** and just off it. These establishments stay happening until 3 or 4am. Once these close, head back to **Lg. de Luís de Camões,** where a couple of places are open until 6am—it will be obvious which ones.

ARTS AND CULTURE

During the month of **July,** Cascais is filled with the syncopated notes of **Cascais Cool Jazz,** a month-long festival that in 2010 drew internationally renowned artists including Regina Spektor, Chris Isaak, Norah Jones, Corinne Bailey Rae, Diana Krall, and Elvis Costello. Check the festival's website *(🖥www.cooljazzfest.com)* for ticket prices *(usually €20-30),* schedules (most perfomances usually concentrated at the end of the month), and locations (public parks throughout Cascais).

ESSENTIALS

Practicalities

- **TOURIST OFFICE: Informação Turística** has maps and information. *(Av. dos Combatentes da Grande Guerra, 25 ☎214 82 23 27 ➜ From train station, take Av. Valbom (to the right side of the McDonald's) straight to the end of the street. ⏰ Open daily 10am-1:30pm and 2:30-6pm.)*

Emergency!

- **LATE-NIGHT PHARMACIES: Farmácia da Misericórdia** posts a schedule of pharmacies open late. *(R. do Regimento da Infantria 19, 69 ☎214 83 01 41 ➜ From Pr. 5 de Outubro with your back to the beach, take the street from the far right corner straight 2 blocks; it's on the left. ℹ Wheelchair-accessible. ⏰ Open M-F 8am-7pm, Sa 9am-2pm.)*

Getting There

Trains run to Cascais from **Lisbon's Cais do Sodré station** *(Ⓢ €1.75. ⏰ 30-40min., daily 5:30am-1:30am every 15-30min.).* ScottURB **buses** run from **Sintra.** *(Ⓢ €3.50. ⏰ 40min.-1hr.; M-F 11 per day 6:30am-7:25pm, Sa 12 per day 6:30am-8:35pm, Su 10 per day 7:45am-8:35pm.)*

Getting Around

Cascais is a small town, and it's easy to get around on **foot,** but there are **free bike rental stands** (ID and hotel information required) in front of the train station and at the Cidadela fortress's parking lot, along Av. de Dom Carlos I from Pr. do 5 de Outubre. *(⏰ Apr-Sept daily 8am-7pm; Oct-Mar M-F 9am-4pm, Sa-Su 9am-5pm.)* There is also a taxi stand outside the train station *(☎214 66 01 01).* Buses are necessary to get to **Praia do Guincho.**

sintra ☎219

The tiny town of Sintra sits at the foot of the mountains, a 45min. train ride west of Lisbon. Quirky romantic castles and ancient fortresses look down on the small city from the surrounding hillsides, with more palatial residences a couple of kilometers away. Sintra and the stretch of mountain range just west of it are classified as a World Heritage Cultural Landscape by UNESCO, and castle-hopping visitors will surely understand why.

ORIENTATION

Sintra has three main neighborhoods: **Estefânia,** where the train station, bus stop, and several inexpensive restaurants and accommodations can be found; **São Pedro,** a bit farther uphill, which has some shops and government offices; and the **Historic Center,** where most of the town's sights are located. To get to the Historic Center, take a left out of the train station onto **Av. do Doutor Miguel Bombarda** and follow it 150m to the intersection, at which point the curving **Volta do Duche** veers to the left. This statue-lined road hooks around the valley between Estefânia and the center and is about a 15min. walk to the center. Stay to the right for the **Palácio Nacional de Sintra** or keep straight to get to the **tourist office.** Sintra itself is small and easy to get around, but several sights lie outside of town and are best reached by bus or taxi.

ACCOMMODATIONS

Accommodations in Sintra tend to be pricey, especially in the Historic Center. The only inexpensive accommodations are near the train station, so you might as well stay someplace less expensive in Lisbon and take a 45min. train ride. The tourist office in the center of town has a list of private accommodations that are usually about €5 cheaper than the *pensões* but are often located farther from both the train station and the center of town.

2 AO QUADRADO HOSTEL   ⊛⊛⑽⌘ HOSTEL ❶
R. de João de Deus, 68   ☎219 23 45 07

This hostel, the best budget accommodation in Sintra, is run out of the very hip bar and cafe downstairs, whose exterior is plastered with posters and artwork. The rooms are large and colorful, though some face the noisy train tracks.

⚑ *On opposite side of tracks from train station exit.* ⓘ *Private lockers in each room.* ⓢ *Dorms €15; doubles €35.* ⌚ *Reception M-Sa 2pm-midnight.*

SIGHTS

📷 PALÁCIO E QUINTA DA REGALEIRA   ✐⊛◎⛆ PALACE, GARDENS ❷
Quinta da Regaleira   ☎219 10 66 56 ▪www.cultursintra.pt

This UNESCO World Heritage Site was built in the first years of the 20th century as a neo-Manueline paradise for its eccentric owner, wealthy Brazilian capitalist António Augusto de Carvalho Monteiro, who wanted to create a magical and mysterious castle home. Italian architect Luigi Manini, who had worked as a set designer in theaters all over the world, was certainly up to the task, and the finished product looks nothing short of fictional. It is decorated all over with hidden mythological and occult motifs, and the 📷**library** upstairs is possibly the **world's trippiest room.** The surrounding gardens are a masterpiece in their own right and are intended to be a transcendent microcosm of the universe—or something like that. You can explore an extensive tunnel system that goes below the castle and gardens or descend the spiral stairway into the **Poço Iniciatico** (Initiation Well), which was inspired by the rituals of the Knights Templar.

⚑ *Bus #435 stops at the train station and Historic Center. On foot, turn right out of the tourist office and follow R. de Consiglieri Pedroso as it turns into R. de M. E. F. Navarro.* ⓢ *€5, seniors and students €4, ages 9-14 €3, under 9 free. Guided visits €10/8/5/free.* ⌚ *Open daily Apr-Sept 10am-8pm (last entry 7pm); Oct 10am-6:30pm (last entry 6pm); Nov-Jan 10am-5:30pm (last entry 5pm); and Feb-Mar 10am-6:30pm (last entry 6pm).*

📷 PALÁCIO DA PENA   ✐⊛ PALACE ❸
Parque da Pena   ☎219 10 53 40 ▪www.parquesdesintra.pt

Built during the 1840s on what was left of a medieval monastery by Prince Ferdinand of Bavaria and his wife Dona Maria II, this colorful royal retreat is one funky castle. It has neo-just-about-any-style-you-can-think-of architecture, and the neo-Mudejar entrance gate has 📷**alligator gargoyles** at the top. The archway over the entrance to the purple building (not really purple; get a close look at the tiles) is spectacular in the weirdest, most ornate way, and views from the various terraces (the Queen's Terrace has the best) stretch all the way to Lisbon. The use of materials is truly creative: the Capela de São Jerónimo is decorated with shells, stones, and porcelain, while the Arab Room is decorated with paint, and its ceiling is entirely *trompe-l'oeil.*

⚑ *Bus #434 (€2.50) runs from the tourist office to the palace daily every 15min. 9:15am-7:50pm; from entrance, either walk up to the palace or take shuttle bus.* ⓢ *€12, students and seniors €8. Guided tours €5 more; €4 9:30-11am.* ⌚ *Palace open daily Apr-Sept 9:45am-7pm (last entry 6:30pm); Oct-Mar 10am-6pm (last entry 5pm). Surrounding Parque da Pena open daily Apr-Sept 9:30am-8pm; Oct-Mar 10am-6pm.*

cascais and sintra

THE GREAT OUTDOORS

Sintra-Cascais Natural Park *Parque Natural de Sintra-Cascais*

The **Sintra-Cascais Natural Park** contains miles and miles of beautiful landscape, stretching from the *serra* on which Sintra sits all the way down to the coast, including Cabo da Roca, Europe's westernmost point. It has been a protected area for 30 years and contains many trails, though some are accessible only by car. One of the best hikes begins at the tourist office in **Cabo da Roca** and heads inland up into the hills before coming back along the dramatic beach (about 10km total). There are many shorter hikes just around **Sintra,** which are by no means walks in the park. The 4.5km **Percurso da Pena,** which runs from the **Palácio Nacional da Sintra** up to the **Palácio da Pena,** will leave you a sweaty mess, but it goes up past the Igreja de Santa Maria, the Casa do Adro where Hans Christian Andersen once lived, the Convento da Santíssima Trinidade, and the Castelo dos Mouros.

FOOD

Pastelarias and restaurants crowd the end of **Rua de João de Deus** and **Avenida de Heliodoro Salgado.** In the old town, **Rua das Padarias** (near the **Palácio Nacional**) is lined with lunch spots. On the second and fourth Sundays of every month, take bus #433 from the train station to São Pedro *(15min.)* for the **Feira de São Pedro,** which features local cuisine, music, clothes, flowers, and antiques.

APEADEIRO CAFE, BAR [1]

Av. do Doutor Miguel Bombarda, 3A ☎219 23 18 04

This cafe has a welcoming atmosphere that makes it feel like home—only in Portugal. The flag on the wall and soccer ball hanging over the bar act as reminders of this fact. The creepy animatronic little girl dressed as a mustachio-ed chef standing on the bar acts as a reminder that...well, we don't really know.

Left out of the train station and slightly down the hill. $ Entrees €5.50-13. Open M-W noon-midnight, F-Su noon-midnight.

FESTIVALS

FESTIVAL DE SINTRA MUSIC, DANCE, ART

☎219 10 71 10 www.festivaldesintra.com

Every June for the last half century, Sintra has been filled with the music, dance, and "counterpoints" (miscellaneous performances and exhibitions) of the Festival de Sintra. Events, which range from children's movies to avant-garde theater performances, often spill over on either end into May and July. Performances take place all over town, from public plazas to the massive *palácios* just up the mountain, and usually take place a few times a week.

Events held at various venues throughout Sintra. $ Tickets for music and dance performances €15-20, under 18 and over 65 €10-12.50. Most other events under €10. June.

ESSENTIALS

Practicalities

- **TOURIST OFFICE: Posta de Turismo** is in the Historic Center, just up the street from the Palácio Nacional de Sintra. *(Pr. da República, 23 ☎219 24 78 50 www.cm-sintra.pt Open daily Jun-Sep 9am-8pm; Oct-May 9am-7pm.)* There is also a **branch** in the train station with the same hours. *(☎219 24 16 23.)*
- **INTERNET ACCESS: Sabot** also offers luggage storage and has pizza. *(R. do Doutor Miguel Bombarda, 57 ☎219 23 08 02 Just across from the train station, to the right. $ €1 per 15min., €1.60 per 30min., €2.50 per hr. Open M-Sa 1pm-midnight, Su 7pm-midnight.)*
- **POST OFFICE: Correios** is on the Pr. da República, on the way to the tourist office. *(Pr. da República, 26 ☎219 10 67 91 Open M-F 9:30am-12:30pm and 2:30-6pm.)*

Emergency!

- **POLICE: Guardia Nacional Republicana.** *(R. de João de Deus, 6 ☎219 24 78 50 ⇄ Exit the train station, and keep left around the station; the Guardia Nacional building is across the street.)*
- **LATE-NIGHT PHARMACIES:** Pharmazul is right across from the train station. *(Av. do Doutor Miguel Bombarda, 37 ☎219 24 38 77 ⏰ Open M-F 9:30am-7pm, Sa 10:30am-7:30pm.)*

Getting There

The easiest way to get to Sintra from Lisbon is by **train.** Trains run from **Lisbon's Rossio** station in Baixa. *($ €1.75. ⏰ M-F every 10min. 6:11am-8:21pm, every 20min. 8:21-10:01pm, every 30min. 10:01pm-1:31am, Sa-Su every 20min. 6:01am-9:21pm, every 30min. 9:51pm-1:21am.)* ScottURB runs **buses** from Cascais. *(Bus 417 $ €3.25. ⏰ 40min.; every hr. M-F 7am-9pm, Sa 8am-8pm, Su 9am-9pm.)*

Getting Around

The best way to get around within Sintra is to **walk.** To get to the sights, either take a **bus** from in front of the tourist office or train station or a **horse-drawn carriage** from next to the Palácio Nacional de Sintra *(Sintratur, R. de João de Deus, 82 ☎219 24 12 38 💻www.sintratur.com $ Fixed rates of €30-70 depending on time and distance).* **Taxis** are also relatively inexpensive and can be a good option if you've just missed the bus and have more than one person. *(☎219 23 02 05 ⇄ Stands in Historic Center across from Palácio Nacional and at train station.)*

ALGARVE

The North Atlantic has never looked so lovely. If you ever thought the Mediterranean had a monopoly on the European summer, think again. The warm southwest of Portugal is banded by big beautiful beaches and craggy cottage-cheese-shaped cliffs; it's dotted with caves and branched into cabos, popular with tourists and well-loved by locals. In short, this big blue sea may be officially west of the Strait, but it's unofficially awesome, with a lot less Perfect Storm and a lot more perfect summer than you'd expect from the intimidating ocean Magellan once crossed.

Lagos is your destination for boozing and bronzing. It's got a pack of pretty praias along the shore and a solid party atmosphere, along with enough surf classes and grotto tours to get the party people out of the club and into the sunshine. And if the pretty scenery's not enough to tempt them? Well, there's a ⚑booze cruise. Sagres is quieter and calmer, but it's by no means a ghost town. This means it must have livened up considerably since the 1400s: it was once considered the marker of "the end of the world." (No, seriously.) But if the current scene still doesn't have enough drama for you, check out the sheer cliffs on which the Fortaleza de Sagres rests. Now that's a dramatic drop.

greatest hits

- **TOUR DE FORCE.** You may not like tour groups, but we bet you like drowning less. So leave your flippers at home and take a grotto tour in Lagos. You'll thank us when you sail into some seriously stunning scenery (p. 394).
- **PIRATES OF THE CARIBBEAN: AT WORLD'S END.** OK, there aren't any pirates, and we admit this isn't the Caribbean. But the Cabo de San Vicente is a dazzlingly final ridge that really does look like the world's end. Makes you understand why they thought that Columbus guy was so brave (p. 396).

lagos ☎282

You'll have an insane time in Lagos...if you can remember it. This tiny beach town in the south of Portugal proves that life's a beach *and* a party. During the day, go to one of the city's beautiful white sand beaches and see the stunning grottos that make this coast famous. If lounging isn't your idea of fun, there are dozens of recreational activities to keep you busy, including sailing, scuba diving, surfing, and biking. If you've worked up an appetite, hit one of the city's many fusion restaurants, or try an authentic Portuguese meal. After your siesta, prepare for a rowdy time hopping between this town's tightly packed bars.

ORIENTATION ✷

From the train and bus stations, the center of town will be a 10min. walk west. You'll know you're there when you see the children's carousel and clothing shops. From there, the center of town is a labyrinth of winding streets that can be confusing, but the entire area is so tiny you're bound to find your bearings fast. A little past the center of town (about a 2min. walk) is the closest and most packed beach, **Batata.** To get to more secluded beaches like beautiful **Pinhão,** walk along the cliff road and make your way down when you see direction signs. Alternatively, you can take the tiny ferry across the boat channel to **Meia Praia,** the area's largest beach. Be sure to pick up a free Lagos map from your hostel.

ACCOMMODATIONS 🏠

👍 RISING COCK — 🎉⊗ HOSTEL ❶

Travessa do Forno 14 ☎968 75 87 85 💻www.risingcockhostel.com

We don't mean to be "fowl," but with signs like "Are you wet?" and a name like Rising Cock, you know you'll have a good time here. Come to this legendary party hostel for a rowdy, messy time. The name actually originates from a story about a prisoner who was accused of theft. As the story goes, the magistrate said that if the nearby cock crowed, it would prove the man innocent. Well, the cock crowed, and the man was let free. A former preschool, the Rising Cock has colorful rooms (think lime green walls and Thomas the Tank Engine sheets), and crowd of raucous backpackers and students ready for a good time. If you're looking for a good night's sleep, don't come here to get it. Guests pre-game until late in the night on the outdoor patio and come stumbling home at all hours of the night. If you're a girl, request the girls-only "castle" room with Disney princesses on the wall. The beloved Mrs. Ribeiro, the "Mama" of the house, makes crepes and "magic juice" for breakfast.

⇞ *Walk through Marina and cross the pedestrian suspension bridge and turn left onto the main avenue (Avenida dos Descobrimentos). Take a right once you get to the main avenue of Lagos (Av. dos Descobrimentos). Take a right after the parking lot and walk to the end of the street. Turn right and walk straight until you reach The Snack Bar on the left. Cross the street and take the pedestrian walkway. Continue up the street, you will see Three Monkeys Bar up on your right. Turn left onto the street before 3 Monkeys. You will pass a hemp shop and take a right after passing a small bakery on the corner. Turn to your left and you will see a road going up a hill, do not go up here. Turn right and go up the other street. There will be a small supermarket, and the hostel is after this on the right, just press the buzzer and reception will let you in.* $ *Dorms €17-25.* ⏰ *Reception 24hr. Common room closes at midnight.*

👍 STUMBLE INN — 🎉⊗ HOSTAL ❷

Rua Soeiro de Costa 10-12 ☎351 28 20 81 607 💻www.stumbleinnlagos.com

Perfectly located among Lagos' beaches, restaurants, and nightlife, the Stumble Inn is a new accommodation developed from a row of converted Portuguese houses. With only triples and quads, you'll feel like you're living in a room in a house rather than an overcrowded messy hostel. While not as rowdy or social as some other nearby options, it's a great place to come back and recuperate after a hard day's night of barhopping. The owner, Jamie, is one of the nicest guys in Lagos, and he's full of suggestions for excellent restaurants and bars.

🧭 *From the information office, walk west down R. 25 de Abril, then north up R. Soeiro de Costa.* $ *Beds €20-30.* ⏰ *Reception 24hr.*

GREAT OUTDOORS

Beaches

BATATA

The closest beach to the center of town is also the most popular, teeming with tourists and locals staking out their piece of sand. Many families come here during the day, so don't expect a boozin' party. Sands are smooth, although the water gets filled with seaweed fast. There's a nearby snack bar and restaurant in case you get the munchies.

🧭 *The second beach past the Lagos fortress.*

MEIA PRAIA

Although a little harder to get to compared to the other beaches, the endless sands of Meia Priaia make it worth it. To get there, take the tiny ferry across the harbor, or just walk across the footbridge towards the train station. Bigger than the tiny beaches along the coastline, Meia Praia has more of a California vibe.

🧭 *Walk towards the harbor where you'll see the tiny ferry that takes you to the beach.*

Water Sports

SURF EXPERIENCE

💳 SURFING

R. dos Ferreiros, 21 — 🖥www.surf-experience.com

To live out your *Blue Crush* dreams, go on the Surf Experience for one- to two-week surfing trips with lessons, transportation, and accommodations in a Lagos surf house. All levels welcome. There are also one- to three-day lessons available as well.

$ *Board rental €75; wetsuit rental €114. Apr-Nov boards €525 per week, €881 per 2 weeks; Dec-Mar €473/836.*

THE BOOZE CRUISE

💳 BOATING

☎969 41 11 31

For a water sport of a different sort, go on the booze cruise—basically, a frat house on water. Be prepared to chug (or skull, as the Aussies call it) down your beer or sangria if you don't comply with the cruise rules like only drinking with your left hand, or you'll get pegged with a clothespin. Midway through the trip, anchor drops and partygoers jump into the water. There are two cruises: one that leaves from Joe's Garage and one that includes lunch and leaves from Nah Nah Bah. Although more expensive, the latter is supposed to be the best.

🧭 *Boats depart from Joe's Garage and Nah Nah Bah.* ℹ *Get information like times and availability at local hostels.* $ *Joe's Garage cruise €25; Nah Nah Bah tour €40.*

GROTTO TOURS

💳 TOUR

When you walk from the train or bus station into town, you'll see tons of stands advertising grotto tours. Definitely a must-see while you're in Lagos, the tiny tour boats take you on a 30min. trip along the Lagos coastline, sailing into some of the caves and grottos. Prepare for absolutely stunning views.

$ *Around €10.* ⏰ *Boats typically leave every 30min.*

FOOD

MEU LIMÃO

💳 🍸 TAPAS [1]

Rua Silva Lopes, 40-42 — ☎282 76 79 46

For excellent tapas and a taste of authentic Portuguese food, stop by Meu Limão on your way to the beach. This tapas joint is decorated with high white chairs and yellow walls and features various kinds of tapas. Their special is a ½kg dish of mussels, which you can order with different seasoning.

➡ *Right outside of the Golden Chapel.* Ⓢ *€4-6.30 for a tapas dish.* ⏰ *Open daily 11am-11pm.*

NAH NAH BAH
💳🚫♿🍸⛅ SOUL FOOD ❷

Travessa do Forno, 11 ☎966 207702 💻www.risingcock.com/nahnahbah

Promising good times, good food, and good grooves, Nah Nah Bah delivers all three. Come to this Havana-themed restaurant for flavorful soul food made with fresh ingredients. Check ahead of time for their themed parties, or just show up on Saturday for a sweaty salsa night.

➡ *Across the street from the Rising Cock.* Ⓢ *Entrees €5-15.* ⏰ *Open daily 6pm-midnight.*

NIGHTLIFE 🌙

THREE MONKEYS
🚫💳🚫♿🍸 BAR

R. Lancarote de Freitas, 26 ☎282 762 995 💻www.3monkeys.me.uk

With cheap drinks, a friendly staff, and rock and roll blasting on the stereo, Three Monkeys brings the party starting at the beginning of the night: get two-for-one cocktails from 7-11pm.

➡ *From the youth hostel, walk towards the ocean.* Ⓢ *Drinks €3-6.* ⏰ *Open daily 1pm-2am.*

JOE'S GARAGE
🚫💳🚫♿🍸 BAR

Rua de Maio, 1 💻www.risingcock.com/joes

With a name like "Joe's Garage," this place certainly has a manly vibe. Get cocktails and pints until 11pm *(€2; large drinks €6)*. At night, it becomes a pop music hotspot complete with girls dancing on tabletops. Be forewarned: this place doesn't have A/C, so the dance floor becomes sauna-like fast.

Ⓢ *Drinks €2-6.* ⏰ *Open daily 9am-2am.*

INSIDE OUT
🚫💳🚫♿🍸 BAR

R. Cândido dos Reis, 119 💻www.insideoutbar.com

The newly opened Inside Out bar keeps the jams and good times rolling with sassy, dancing bartenders and good strong drinks. Try the fishbowl *(€25)*, a house specialty mixture of questionable alcohols.

➡ *At the end of the main drag of bars.* Ⓢ *Shots €3-3.50. Beer €3-4.50. Mixed drinks €5-6.50.* ⏰ *Open daily 8pm-4am.*

ESSENTIALS ℹ

Practicalities

- **CURRENCY EXCHANGE: Cotacâmbios** *(Pr. Gil Eanes, 11 ☎282 76 44 52)*
- **LAUNDROMAT: Lavanderia Míele** *(Av. dos Descobrimentos, 27 ☎282 76 39 69. Ⓢ Wash and dry €7 per 5kg. ⏰ Open M-F 9am-1pm and 3-7pm, Sa 9am-1pm.)*
- **INTERNET ACCESS: Snack Bar Ganha Pouco** *(➡ 1st right after the footbridge coming from the bus station. Ⓢ €2.50 per hr. ⏰ Open M-Sa 8am-7:30pm, Su 9am-7:30pm.)*

Emergency!

- **POLICE:** ☎282 762 930
- **HOSPITAL/MEDICAL SERVICES:** ☎282 770 100
- **LATE-NIGHT PHARMACIES: Farmácia Silva.** *(R. 25 de Abril, 9☎282 76 28 59)*

Getting There ✈

To reach Lagos from northern Portugal, you must go through Lisbon. Trips originating in the east generally transfer in Faro.

By Train
Trains come from **Lisbon** *($ €15.50. ⏰ 3-4hr., 7 per day 6:11am-6:12pm).*

By Bus
The EVA bus station *(Av. dos Descobrimentos ☎282 76 29 44)* has buses arrive from **Lisbon** *($ €19. ⏰ 5hr., 6 per day 5:30am-6:15pm)* and **Sagres** *($ €3.40. ⏰ 1hr., 16 per day 7:15am-8:30pm).*

Getting Around
You can reach anything in Lagos by foot. If you have a lot of luggage, you might want to get a taxi to the bus or train stations.

sagres ☎282

With a calmer atmosphere than nearby Lagos, Sagres is a great tiny beach town to escape to for the day. Come for a relaxing day on the beach with stunning views of incredible cliffs. Enjoy some excellent snacks and drinks in bars along the main street and stay for a good time with friendly locals.

ORIENTATION
It isn't hard to get around Sagres, as there isn't much of it. Almost all of the city's best restaurants and bars are on the main street, **Avenida Comandante Matoso** which you can walk the length of in around 15 minutes or less.

ACCOMMODATIONS

CASA AZUL — 💳🚭📶❄ GUEST HOUSE [2]
Rua Patrao Antonio Faustino ☎282 624 856 💻www.casaazulsagres.com

Come to the Casa Azul guest house for a hotel experience at hostal prices. With brightly colored modern furniture, lots of space, and friendly service, the Casa Azul is one of your best options for a weekend in Sagres. While cheaper than some of the five-store resorts nearby, you'll still have a pampered experience.

🧭 At the very end of the main street towards the harbor. $ Quads for €106. ⏰ Reception 24 hr.

GOOD FEELING — 💳🚭📶❄ HOSTEL [1]
Raposeira, Vila do Bispo, Portugal ☎91 465 88 07 💻www.thegoodfeeling.com

While not a party hostel, the Good Feeling is an excellent hostel in which to kick back, relax on their hammocks hanging out front, and chill out with people on the front porch. A 15min. bus ride from Sagres makes it a little inconvenient to get to the beach, but the secluded feel is nice for people wanting to get away from the hustle and bustle of constant traveling. At night, the hostel owners make a delicious dinner *(€4)* and often take group trips to get coffee at the bar down the road or drinks in Sagres.

🧭 From the Raposeira bus stop, step off the bus, make a left, and keep walking until you see it on your right (5min. walk). $ June 1-Sept. 30 dorms €20; Oct 1-May 31 dorms €15. ⏰ In your reservation, let them know what time you'll be there and they'll be sure to have someone to let you in.

SIGHTS

👍 CABO DE S. VICENTE (SAINT VINCENT'S CAPE) — LIGHTHOUSE, VIEWING POINT
Once considered "the end of the world," before Columbus up and discovered a little place called America, Saint Vincent's Cape is the main attraction in Sagres. The cape has been famous since the age of discovery and is a famous landmark on the sea routes linking Europe, Africa, an Asia. Come on a clear day for spectacular views and a beautiful sunset. Some overeager tourists have been known to walk to the very edge of the dangerous cliffs for their kodak moment. Wiser locals know that the rocks near the edge are fragile and not to be tested.

Two buses generally transport tourists from the main bus stop in Sagres to the cape. Ask at the tourist office for times. $ Free. Open daily May-Sept. 9:30am-8pm; Oct.-Apr. 9:30am-5:30pm. Closed May 1 and Dec. 25.

FORTALEZA DE SAGRES — FORT

This site was supposedly where Henry the Navigator founded his "naval school" and it has been used for protection since the 15th century. Less touristed than St. Vincent's cape, this is a great place for snapping pictures without other tourists milling around. On the way you'll also see a bizarre large geometrical sand design dating back to Henry's days called "wind rose." Nobody really knows what it is, although there is speculation that it was used as a sun dial.

$ €3, under 25 or retired €1.50, youth cardholders €1.20. Free 30min. guided tours at noon, 4, 5pm. Max. 20 people. Meet near compass. Open daily May-Sept 9:30am-8pm; Oct-Apr 9:30am-5:30pm. Closed May 1 and Dec. 25.

THE GREAT OUTDOORS

With dramatic jaw-dropping cliffs, smooth white sands, and crystal clear blue water, Sagres is the perfect place for a day of relaxation and a surfer's paradise. More adventurous sorts head to one of the area's surf shops, where you can rent a bike, surf equipment, kayak, or bodyboard. If you want to go all out, ask about the international surf school camp (www.sagres-surfcamp.com) where you eat, drink, and sleep surfing for a week—really though, you eat with fellow surfers, sleep in hostel-like accommodations, and surf until your toes fall off.

SURF PLANET

Estrada Nacional, 268 — ☎282 624815 www.surfplanet.pt

With beachwear galore, wetsuits, body boards, swimming fins, kayaks, surfboards, skim boards, and more, Surf Planet is a one-stop shop for everything you need to get ocean bound. Ask about their surf lessons and one-week surf camp, where beginnings to intermediate surfers can eat, drink, and sleep (literally, you sleep in a hostel-like guest house with other surfers) waves all week.

FOOD

O TELHEIRO DO INFANTE — SEAFOOD [2]

Praia de Mareta — ☎282 624 179 www.telheirodoinfante.com

The real draw of this seaside spot is the spectacular view of the ocean and dizzying nearby cliffs. Sit out on the balcony and enjoy their menu of fresh seafood including the lobster ricepot, monkfish and shellfish cataplana, and special Sagres fish. Although it is a bit out of the way, there are signs on the major street pointing you in the right direction.

$ Fresh fish €10-12. House specials for two €30-45. Mixed salads, cold dishes, eggs, spaghetti, fish, and meat €6-15.

VILA VELHA — PORTUGUESE, INTERNATIONAL, VEGETARIAN [3]

Rua Patrão Antonio Faustino — ☎282 624 788 www.vilavelha-sagres.com

One of the fancier restaurant options in Sagres, this is your stop for genuine Portuguese food. With wicker chairs, white tablecloths, and homey but fancy decoration, Vila Velha manages to walk the thin line between upscale and comfortable. Be prepared to spend a decent amount on your meal, but expect your money's worth. Try the delicious lamb *(€15)*.

From the bus station, walk east towards the harbor on Av. Comandante Matoso. Make a right onto R. Patrão Antonio Faustino. $ Entrees €15-25. Open daily 6:30-10pm.

NIGHTLIFE

MITIC

BAR

Av. Comandante ☎964139350 🖳mitic.sagres@gmail.com

One of the newest in the series of bars lining Avenida Comandante Matoso, Mitic is a modern, fun place to grab a drink or a snack before heading out to the beach. Sit out on their second floor terrace for great views of the beach. With a huge selection of smoothies, fresh-squeezed juices, coffees, teas, beers, and cocktails, Mitic has pretty much every drink you could want for any time of day. If you're feeling like a snack, have one of their crepes, salads, toasts, sandwiches, or hamburgers. At night, Sagres residents and tourists gather here to watch the game or listen to live music. Try their tequila sunrise, made with fresh squeezed orange juice and a lot of liquid courage.

From the bus station, walk down Avenida Comandante Matoso. Bar will be on your left. $ *Drinks €4-10.* ⏰ *Open daily 10am-3am.*

DROMEDARIO

BAR

Avenida Comandante Matoso ☎282 624219 🖳www.dromedariosagres.com

Established in 1985, Dromedario is one of Sagres' oldest favorites. Despite its cheerful yellow walls, a camel mascot, and desert-themed decor, Dromedario is more of an oasis providing visitors with an awesome selection of refreshing drinks like smoothies and milkshakes. During the day come for a bite of their mouth-watering snacks, crepes, hamburgers and by night come for their big and fruity mixed drinks.

From the bus station, walk down Avenida Comandante Matoso. Bar will be on your left. $ *Drinks €4-10.* ⏰ *Open daily 10am-3am.*

ESSENTIALS

Practicalities

Since Sagres is a small beach town and often visited as a daytrip from Lagos, it doesn't have the infrastructure of a city. For a free map and information about the area, head to the **tourist office** which is to your left when you get off the bus *(Rua Comandante Matoso ☎282 624873).* **Bike** rentals at Surf Planet *(€5 per hr., €10 per 4hr., €15 per 8hr.)* and Sagres Natura *(€15 per day).* Free **internet** at Água Salgada and neighbor O Dromedário.

Getting There

EVA **buses** *(☎282 76 29 44)* run from **Lagos** ($ *€3.40* ⏰ *1hr.; M-F 14 per day 6:10am-7:35pm, Sa 9 per day 6:10am-7:10pm, Su 7 per day 7:15am-7:10pm*). Buses also run to Lisbon *(⏰ 5hr., July-Sept. daily 4pm. $ €18).*

Getting Around

Getting around in Sagres is super easy, as almost all of the city's bars and restaurants center around the main street, Avenida Comandante Matoso, which is steps away from the beautiful main beach. If you're staying in a different area, check the tourist office (right next to the bus station) for **bus** times. If it's too late and the last bus has left, you can call a **taxi**, although you'll have to book in advance and it will be rather expensive.

NORTHERN PORTUGAL

Whether you're the sort who's always looking to escape civilization or the type who needs to be thoroughly entrenched in it—or somewhere in between—northern Portugal is the place to be. Traverse rugged mountain trails whose stones are graced more frequently by the paws of the Iberian wolf than the soles of human feet, or head off in search of an empty beach with perfect waves. Explore some of the world's most complex cities—true jungles in their own right—where ancient castles loom over modern discotheques and where crumbling arches hide trendy cafes. This country by the sea certainly welcomes tourism but doesn't bend over backwards to attract the camera-armed hordes, and for this reason it is a favorite of many experienced travelers. The historic city centers aren't tidied up and covered with a fresh coat of paint: they're living cities. The national parks have trails marked but little else: you just walk to the start of your path and go. In the marvelous cities and breathtaking wilds of this nation renowned for its explorers, there are still adventures to be found.

greatest hits

- **GET AHEAD OF THE (SIX) PACK.** Ditch that Natty Light for a classier beverage: port enjoyed in its native atmosphere (p. 401).

- **RUN WITH THE WOLVES.** Or not. Hiking the glorious forest trails at Parque Nacional de Peneda Gerês is a lot more fun at your own pace and without hungry Iberian wolves following you (p. 405).

- **HOWL AT THE MOON.** Sing the famously mournful *fado* in Coimbra. You'll definitely be out late enough, especially if school's in session at the university (p. 411).

Northern Portugal's most famous export, port, is named after the city of Porto, and guess what the entire country is named after? It really all centers on this delicious alcoholic beverage made from wine that, by virtue of residual sugar, has become more than four times as alcoholic as regular wine. With half the proof of vodka and more than twice its tastiness, port can be quite the temptress, and before you know it, you're passed out at the tasting. Port is no old-person's drink either—students at Coimbra are just as likely as seniors playing cards to be imbibing the ruby drink.

porto *oporto* ☎22

northern portugal

Visitors' first impression upon arriving in Portugal's second-largest city is of the broad avenues and Beaux Arts buildings in the plazas near São Bento train station. But a descent into the oldest part of the city toward the river is a clear reminder: this ain't Paris. Crumbling buildings hang over tiny and confusing streets covered with hanging laundry and echoing with the conversations of residents. Though the historic center of Porto is a UNESCO World Heritage site and the area right by the river is lined with shops and restaurants aimed at visitors, there's no question that the old city is not a pristine, Disney-esque tourist town but a living *bairro*. Porto has the gritty beauty of a true city, built and currently thriving on commerce, not tourism—and it's got the history (and port wine) to go along with it.

ORIENTATION

Porto's **insane maze of steep streets** can be very difficult to navigate; at times it seems a topographic map would be more useful than the one available at the tourist offices. At the center of town is a massive, sloping plaza formed by **Praça da Liberdade, Avenida dos Aliados,** and **Praça do General Humberto Delgado.** East of this plaza is the **Rua de Santa Catarina, Mercado de Bolhão,** and the main shopping district; just off the southeast corner is the **São Bento train station,** and to the west is **Vitória,** a hilly, trendier area. The oldest part of town is the **Ribeira** district, which lies to the south of the city center and goes down to the banks of the **Río Douro,** where confusing streets contain many historic sights and much of Porto's nightlife. The two level **Ponte de Dom Luís** connects Porto to **Vila Nova de Gaia** on the other side of the river, where the port wine cellars can be found. The **Foz** district, several kilometers west of the center where the Douro meets the Atlantic, is a popular nightlife neighborhood, as is the **industrial area** 4-5km northwest of the center.

ACCOMMODATIONS

🖌 OPORTO POETS HOSTEL

 HOSTEL ❶

R. dos Caldeireiros, 261   ☎223 32 42 09 www.oportopoetshostel.com

This hostel, decorated with literary art and trendy decor, is the hippest place to stay in Porto. The dorms and reception are in a building on R. dos Caldeireiros (right behind the church with the tall tower) that has common spaces that will put your living room to shame, and the private rooms are located down an adjacent alley in a lovely little house with a patio, garden, 🖌**hammock,** and cathedral views.

✈ Ⓜ*São Bento. Buses #202, 500 to Loios; #507, 601, 602 to Cordoaria; or #305, ZH, 703 to Cordoaria. From Ⓜ São Bento, walk up R. dos Clérigos past Torre dos Clérigos, then turn left down toward the river 2 blocks, then veer left on R. dos Caldeireiros.* ***i*** *Breakfast included. Shared baths. Kitchen.* Ⓢ *Dorms €16-20; singles €42-50. 10% discount for stays of 5 nights or longer.* ⏰ *Reception 24hr.*

SIGHTS 👁

PALÁCIO DA BOLSA 💳⊗ HISTORIC SITE

R. de Ferreira Borges ☎223 39 90 00 💻www.palaciodabolsa.pt

The enormous and elegant Palácio da Bolsa (Stock Exchange) sits over Ribeira's main plaza and is one of Porto's most visited sites. Upon entering, visitors walk into the massive, bright, and beautifully decorated market floor, then up the granite stairs whose construction delayed the building's completion by almost a half century. One room has a table with intricate wooden inlay, done entirely with a pen-knife, while another looks to be decorated with wood, bronze, and marble but is actually all just painted plaster, designed to show off the local painters' craftsmanship. The Palácio da Bolsa's most spectacular room is the Sala Árabe, whose sole purpose was to impress foreign businessmen who were received there. Its walls and ceilings proclaim the odd combination of the phrases "Glory to Allah" and "May Allah protect Dona Maria II," Portugal's Catholic queen.

⇆ *ⓂSão Bento. Buses ZH, ZM. From ⓂSão Bento, follow R. Mouzinho da Silveira downhill to Pr. do Infante Dom Henrique—it's the massive building on the right side of the plaza.* ***i*** *Guided tours available in English.* Ⓢ *€6, students and seniors €3.* ⏰ *Open daily Apr-Oct 9am-7pm; Nov-Mar 9am-1pm and 2-6pm. Last tour 30min. before close.*

WINERIES 🍷

If you're in Porto, at least one visit to a winery is mandatory. They're either free or very cheap *(under €4),* and tours usually run about 30-40min. Most of the tasting occurs across the Douro in **Vila Nova de Gaia** and its 17 massive **port lodges,** and the best way to get to this port authority is to walk across the bottom level of the Ponte de Dom Luís from Ribeira.

👍 SOLAR DO VINHO DO PORTO 💳⊗🍸⛅ JARDINS DO PALÁCIO DE CRISTAL [1]

R. de Entre Quintas, 220 ☎226 09 47 49

Sit on the terrace of a fancy mansion and sip your sweet, sweet port. Pretend the whole place is yours (including the gigantic park in which the winery is located) and that the other diners are your guests—unless of course you actually own the place.

⇆ *Buses ZM, 200, 201, 207, 303, 501, 601, 602. From ⓂSão Bento, head up R. dos Clérigos, go right up R. das Carmelitas, head straight toward Hospital Santo António, go around it to the right, then forge straight ahead on R. de Dom Manuel II, around park to end of R. de Entre Quintas.* Ⓢ *Port €1.50-16.* ⏰ *Open M-Sa 4pm-midnight.*

CROFT 💳⊗🍸⛅ GAIA [1]

Lg. de Joaquim Magalhães, 23 ☎223 74 28 00 💻www.croftport.com

Wet your whistle before the tour with a free tasting, then learn more about port than anybody outside the wine industry would ever need to know. This winery has been around since 1588, and they know their stuff. Visits must be guided, lest tourists attempt to make off with one of the massive aging vats.

⇆ *ⓂJardim do Morro; buses #900, 901, 906. From Gaia waterfront, follow R. Dom Alfonso III 2 blocks, then right.* Ⓢ *Tours and tasting free.* ⏰ *Open daily July-Aug 10am-8pm; Sept-June 10am-7pm. Last tour starts 45min. before close.*

FOOD 🍴

The areas around **Pr. da Batalha** and uphill west of Av. dos Aliados have cafes with inexpensive meals, as do the tiny restaurants that line the waterfront in **Ribeira.** The best deal around is a **francesinha:** a cheap sandwich available at most cafes that's essentially several types of meat squeezed between two pieces of bread smothered in cheese and a tomato-like gravy. What's a calorie when you're on vacation?

BRASA DOS LEÕES — GRILL [1]

Pr. de Guilherme Gomes Fernandes, 7 ☎222 05 11 85

Big appetite? Small budget? Get a whole grilled chicken for only €6 with a liter of sangria for another €4.50. Outdoor seating on a shady plaza just up the street from the Torre dos Clérigos.

➔ *[M]Aliados; buses #207, 300, 302, 304, 305, 501, 703. From Pr. da Liberdade facing uphill, head up Av. dos Aliados, then left onto R. de Elísio de Melo, which becomes Pr. de Filipa de Lencastre and then R. de Ceuta. Turn left onto Pr. de Guilherme Gomes Fernandes.* $ *Entrees €4-7.* 🕐 *Open daily 10am-10pm.*

GALERIA DE PARIS — CAFE, BAR [3]

R. da Galeria de Paris, 56 ☎222 01 62 18

The vintage paraphernalia that line the shelves behind the bar and are scattered throughout this restaurant fall somewhere between kitsch and awesome, and the atmosphere is decidedly cool. There's an old motorcycle in the corner and a host of bicycles hanging from the ceiling downstairs near the bathrooms. The food isn't cheap, but it's delicious, and there's live music on Friday and Saturday nights.

➔ *[M]São Bento; buses #200, 201, 207, 300, 302, 304, 305, 507, 601, 602. From [M]São Bento, head up R. dos Clérigos, then right up R. das Carmelitas, then right up R. da Galeria de Paris.* $ *Daily special €10. Entrees €8-13.* 🕐 *Open M-Sa 9am-2am, Su 7-9pm.*

NIGHTLIFE

Porto's nightlife is mostly centered on the **Ribeira** district down by the water, though recently some great nightlife has sprung up in **Vitória,** particularly along R. da Galeria de Paris. After 2am, the scene moves farther afield, to **Foz** along the riverfront and the industrial areas farther inland near [M]Viso. Public transportation to these areas does not run after 1am, which means you can't get there when you want unless you take a cab *(€5-6)* or have a car. Gaia, just across the river, is a much more easily accessible option; just cross the Ponte de Dom Luís from Ribeira, or take a €3 cab.

SAHARA — BAR

Cais da Estiva, 4 ☎969 20 60 37

This laid-back bar has a loungey feel and seating (well, cushions and carpets) outside by the river. The *não fumadores* sign and the hookahs inside make for an odd paradox. The creative coffees will give you the boost of caffeine you need for the rest of the night.

➔ *[M]São Bento; buses ZR, 900, 901, 906. From Pr. do Infante Dom Henrique (in front of Palácio da Bolsa), head down toward water along R. da Alfandega, then left at waterfront.* $ *Coffee €1-3. Mixed drinks €2-6.* 🕐 *Open daily 3pm-2am.*

FESTIVALS

NOITE DE SÃO JOÃO — SUMMER

On the evening of June 23 each year, the citizens of Porto run through the streets hitting complete strangers on the head with leeks (not what they look like when you eat them—these are long stalks with round purple flowers at the end) and toy mallets, while stopping at bars and restaurants to eat whole schools of grilled sardines and herds of baby goats. At midnight, the town goes down to the riverside to watch the fireworks, after which the under-25 population walks 8 mi. to the beach for a massive techno concert that goes until dawn. Celebrants jump over bonfires for luck, and women roll in the morning dew to ensure fertility. The next day is much sleepier, but in the early afternoon there is a sailboat race between all the port wineries from the mouth of the Douro to the city; the competition was originally meant to determine which winery had the fastest boats and could thus ship the most port.

$ *Mallets about €1.50.* 🕐 *June 23-24, with festivities and free events throughout June.*

SHOPPING

Porto's main shopping area is around the **Rua de Santa Catarina,** which is lined with stores and has the Via Catarina shopping center, for those pining for an American-style mall.

◪ LIVRARIA LELLO E IRMÃO
◆❀ VITÓRIA

R. das Carmelitas, 144   ☎222 01 81 70 ▣www.lelloprologolivreiro.com.sapo.pt
This magnificent Art Nouveau bookstore on R. das Carmelitas is a masterpiece and truly an experience. The white facade draws tourists and book-lovers to ornate wooden shelves holding books from every genre and era. The twisting staircase in the middle leads up to a second floor, where there are more books, a cafe, and memorabilia from the bookstore's history. Don't forget to look up at the marvelous stained-glass on the ceiling.

♯ ⓂSão Bento; buses #200, 201, 207, 300, 302, 304, 305, 507, 601, 602. From ⓂSão Bento, head up R. dos Clérigos, then right up R. das Carmelitas. ⏱ Open M-F 10am-7:30pm, Sa 10am-7pm.

ESSENTIALS
◪

Practicalities

- **TOURIST OFFICES: Postos de Turismo Municipais** are located throughout the center of town and sell **Porto Cards,** which give discounts at museums, monuments, shops, and restaurants and provide unlimited access to public transportation systems. Locations in the **Centro.** (R. do Clube dos Fenianos, 25 ☎223 39 34 70 ♯ ⓂAliados; bus #904. From Pr. da Liberdade, walk up left side of Av. dos Aliados 3 blocks. ⏱ Open daily June-Sept 9am-7pm; Oct-May 9am-5:30pm.) **Ribeira** (R. do Infante Dom Henrique, 63 ☎222 06 04 12 ♯ ⓂSão Bento; buses ZR, 900, 901, 906. On side of Pr. do Infante Dom Henrique closest to the river. ⏱ Open daily June-Sept 9am-7pm; Oct-May 9am-5:30pm). **Sé** (Terreiro da Sé ☎223 32 51 74 ♯ ⓂSão Bento; bus ZH. Next to cathedral; from ⓂSão Bento, follow Av. de Vimara Peres toward the river (left with your back to the train station) and bear right uphill. ⏱ Open M-F 9am-5:30pm).

- **POST OFFICES: Correios** has a **Poste Restante.** (Pr. do General Humberto Delgado ☎223 40 02 00 ♯ ⓂAliados; bus 904. From Pr. da Liberdade, walk up right side of Av. dos Aliados 3 blocks. ⏱ Open M-F 8:30am-7:30pm, Sa 9:30am-3pm.)

Emergency!

- **POLICE:** Polícia Municipal are located uphill from Pr. da Liberdade. (R. do Clube dos Fenianos, 11 ☎222 08 18 33 ♯ ⓂAliados; bus #904. From Pr. da Liberdade, walk up left side of Av. dos Aliados 3 blocks.)

- **LATE-NIGHT PHARMACIES:** Farmácia Santa Catarina posts a 24hr. pharmacy schedule. (R. de Santa Catarina, 141 ☎222 00 21 45 ▣www.fscatarina.com ♯ ⓂBolhão; bus #302. Just up R. de Santa Catarina from Pr. da Batalha. ⏱ Open M-Sa 9am-8pm, Su 10am-7pm.)

- **HOSPITALS/MEDICAL SERVICES: Hospital Geral de Santo Antonio.** (Lg. do Profesor Abel Salazar ☎222 07 75 00 ♯ ⓂSão Bento; buses #18, 200, 201, 207. From ⓂSão Bento, walk up R. dos Clérigos, then right at R. das Carmelitas, then straight along R. do Carmo.)

Getting There
▣

By Plane

Aeroporto Francisco de Sá Carneiro (☎229 43 24 00) is 13km from downtown. The Metro E (violet line) subway goes to the airport and is the fastest and cheapest option. (Ⓢ €1.35. ⏱ 25min.) Buses #601 and 87 run from the airport to R. do Carmo, but make multiple stops. (ⓢ €1.50. ⌚ 1hr.) The aerobus (☎225 07 10 54) to Av. dos Aliados is more efficient. (ⓢ €4. ⌚ 40min., every 30min. 7am-7pm. Free for TAP passengers.) Buy tickets on board. Taxis are even faster, but predictably more expensive. (ⓢ €18-20. ⌚ 15-20min.) **TAP Air Portugal** (Pr. Mouzinho de Albuquerque, 105 ☎226 08 02 31), flies to Lisbon from major European cities, with six daily shuttles from Lisbon. (ⓢ €100-150. ⌚ 35min.)

By Train

Trains to Porto arrive at **Estação de Campanhã** (Pr. Almeida Garrett ☎808 20 82 08 ▣www. cp.pt); some trains continue on to **Estação de São Bento** in the center of town. Otherwise, transfer to a free train that does. Trains arrive at Campanhã from: **Braga** (ⓢ €13. ⌚ 41min., 4 per day 6am-8pm); **Coimbra** (ⓢ €11-15.50. ⌚ 1hr., 18 per day 7:45am-11:35pm); **Lisbon** (ⓢ €20-28.50. ⌚ 3hr., 16 per day 6am-9:30pm).

By Bus

There are several bus companies that operate in the downtown area. Try to find out ahead of time where your bus will stop, since there is no central bus terminal. **Internorte** (Pr. de Galiza, 96 ☎226 05 24 20 ▣www.internorte.pt) runs buses from Madrid. (ⓢ €48. ⌚ 10hr., 1-2 per day.) Book at least 3 days in advance. **Rede Expressos** (R. de Alexandre Herculano, 366 ☎707 22 33 44 ▣www.rede-expressos.pt) runs buses from **Braga** (€5.90. ⌚ 1hr., 20-25 per day 5am-11:30pm), **Coimbra** (ⓢ €11.50. ⌚ 1½hr., 11-13 per day 8:30am-3am), and **Lisbon** (ⓢ €18. ⌚ 3½-4hr., 20-24 per day 7am-12:15am). **Renex** (Campo Mártires da Pátria, 37 ☎222 00 33 95 ▣www.renex.pt) runs express buses from Lagos (ⓢ €26. ⌚ 4½hr., 8 per day 5:30am-12:30am).

Getting Around

Though Porto is a large city, it's quite **walkable,** and many streets in the old part of town are pedestrian-only. The main issues with walking around Porto are the steep hills; many prefer to walk downhill and take public transportation uphill. The Metro system is mostly for transport between Porto and its suburbs, but the **D** (orange) line stops at **Av. dos Aliados** and **São Bento,** among other locations, and the other lines stop at convenient locations as well. With service to just about every corner of the city, the bus and tram system is massive and one of the best ways to get across town. You can pick up a detailed bus and Metro map from the tourist offices. If you take a taxi, make sure it has a meter. Otherewise, you may get ripped off.

parque nacional da peneda-gerês ☎253

Portugal's mountainous border with Spain is pure Eden for those who love the outdoors: kilometer after kilometer of **forest trails** meander through the densely wooded serras and along teal-blue lakes, past ruins from the Iron Age and Roman period, and through modern villages. The Parque Nacional da Peneda-Gerês, which became Portugal's first protected wilderness area in 1971, is also home to the endangered ▣**Iberian wolf,** so be wary of this little doggie coming by your camp.

ORIENTATION

The roughly c-shaped park covers 270 sq. mi. of mountains and forests along Portugal's border with Spain, with the **Serra da Peneda** mountain range making up the wilder northern part and the **Serra do Gerês** encompassing much of the south. The most popular point of entry for the park is **Vila do Gerês** (pronounced "VEE-luh doo j-RESH," also called **Caldas do Gerês**), a small spa town. This valley town essentially has **one circular one-way road;** the **bus stop** is just below the bottom of the circle, and the **tourist office** is uphill along the road to the right (where just about everything is), at the far end.

ACCOMMODATIONS

The town of Gerês is full of hotels and *pensões*—there may be more accommodations there than full-time residents. Fancier hotels line the **Av. Manuel Francisco da Costa,** while the less expensive places are on a ridge overlooking the town. From the bus stop, head toward the town, turn left after the roundabout, and then take either the first **(R. de Miguel Torga)** or second **(R. de Arnaçó)** left; both roads have cheap accommodations.

PENSÃO-RESIDÊNCIAL O HORIZONTE DO GERÊS — PENSÃO ❷

R. de Arnaçó, 19 ☎253 39 12 60

These simple rooms have lovely views over the town and into the surrounding mountainside, as well as private bathrooms and TVs. Nothing's especially far from anything in Gerês, but this *pensão* is particularly close to the bus stop heading back toward Braga.

From the bus stop, head uphill toward town, then turn left downhill after the roundabout. Go straight about 5min., then left again up R. de Arnaçó. From tourist office, follow the road around the top part of town and back toward the bus stop and make the second right. $ Singles €25; doubles €30; triples €35. ⏰ Reception 24hr.

PARQUE DE CAMPISMO DO VIDOEIRO — CAMPGROUND ❶

Vidoeiro, Caldas do Gerês, Terras de Bouro ☎253 39 12 89 🖥www.adere-pg.pt

If you've come to the park to get in touch with nature, this is the place to stay. Surrounded by forest, this campground is over a kilometer from the nearest small town and is right beside a bubbling brook. Hop out of bed and onto one of the nearby trails to turn your morning into a workout.

From Vila do Gerês, follow the road uphill past the tourist office 1km, past the tinier town of Vidoeiro and up the bends in the road. Turn left at the sign for "campismo." $ €3.25 per person; children 5-10 €2.35; under 5 free. Spaces €3.15-4.80. Cars €3.15; trailers €2.65. Electricity €1.20. ⏰ Reception Aug 8am-10pm; Sept-July 8am-noon.

THE GREAT OUTDOORS

Hiking

The Parque Nacional da Peneda-Gerês is renowned throughout Portugal as one of the country's best hiking destinations. Kilometers of trail stretch through the park and across the border into Spain's **Baixa Limia-Serra do Xurés park,** with panoramic vistas and pre-Roman ruins along the way. The less challenging—though no less fulfilling—trails are in the southern part of the park near **Vila do Gerês,** while the **Serra da Peneda** in the north has trails for serious trekkers. These southern trails showcase petroglyphs, waterfalls, and tiny villages. The **Trilha da Preguiça** (Lazy Trail, 5.5km) begins 3km north of Vila do Gerês and follows the Gerês River; the longer **Trilho dos Currais** (10km) runs just north of Vidoeiro, 1km north of Vila do Gerês. The **tourist and park offices** are the best resources for recommending trails and giving directions.

Unwinding

Vila do Gerês grew as a spa town around its hot springs (*caldas*), which are now owned by **Empresa das Águas do Gerês** *(Av. Manuel Francisco da Costa, 133 ☎253 39 11 13 🖥www.aguasdogeres.pt).* The spa and healing waters are located in the pink building in the center of town, and they offer so many spa treatment options your head will spin faster than their jacuzzi water *(⏰ Thermal spring open daily 7:30am-noon and 3:30-6pm. Spa open M-Sa 8am-noon and 4-6pm. Pool and massages open M-F 8am-1pm and 4-7pm).* The **Parque das Termas,** owned by the same company and located across the street from the tourist office, has swimming pools for those who prefer their water a little less therapeutic and a little more child-friendly. *(☎253 39 11 13 $ Park entrance €1, under 12 €0.50. Pool M-F €4, Sa-Su €6. ⏰ Park open daily 9am-7pm; Pool open daily July-Sept M-F 10am-7pm, May-Jun Sa-Su 9am-6pm.)* Parque das Termas also has tennis *($ €3 per hr.)* and canoeing *($ €3 per 30min.).*

FOOD

Vila do Gerês is full of restaurants, cafes, and bars along **Av. Manuel Francisco da Costa.** Prices tend to increase with altitude: food gets more expensive as you move from the roundabout at the south end of town uphill to the tourist office at the north end.

VAI...VAI   ⚈⊗⫙⏦⌁ CAFE ❶

R. de Augusto Sérgio Almeida Maia, 1   ☎352 39 20 48

This small cafe in the middle of town gets packed around 1:30-2pm, so get there on the early side for lunch during the high season. The sandwiches are cheap and the *cachorros (similar to cut-up hot dogs covered in cheese on buns: €2.50-6)* come bathed in fries and hot sauce.

⫙ *On the main road across from spa and hotel (pink buildings).* ⓢ *Tostas €0.40-4.50. Sandwiches €2.50-3. Hamburgers and cachorros €2.50-6. Combinados €2.50-7.* ⌁ *Open M-Sa 10am-10pm.*

GARRAFEIRA E FUMEIRO DO GERÊS   ⚈� SUPERMARKET ❶

Av. Manuel Francisco da Costa   ☎253 39 13 50

Stock up on food and wine and head off into the park with your picnic basket. Don't worry about Yogi and Boo-Boo; they only bother the rangers. Even if you aren't camping, buying produce and sandwich fixins at this supermarket can save you some serious coin.

⫙ *On the left side of Av. Manuel Francisco da Costa (bear right after the roundabout heading into town from the bus stop).* ⌁ *Open daily 9am-noon and 2-6:30pm.*

ESSENTIALS   ◪

Practicalities

- **TOURIST OFFICES: Delegaçao de Turismo** has maps of the area and information on the town of Gerês and trails. *(Av. Manuel Francisco da Costa ☎253 39 11 33⫙ From the bus stop, head uphill past the roundabout, bearing right to follow Av. Manuel Francisco da Costa; the tourist office is at the end, to the right just before the colonnaded area. i Tours available in English. ⌁ Open M-W 9:30am-12:30pm and 2-5:30pm, F-Sa 9:30am-12:30pm and 2-5:30pm.)* **Centro de Educação Ambiental do Vidoeiro,** has information about the national park. *(☎253 39 01 10 ⫙ Located in a large white building on the left side of the road past Vidoeiro 1km up the road from Vila do Gerês. ⌁ Open July 15-Sept 15 daily 9am-noon and 2-5:30pm; Sept 16-July 14 M-F 9am-noon and 2-5:30pm.)* The **Park Office** is located in **Braga** on Av. António Macedo. *(☎253 20 34 80 ⫙ Take R. Boavista to Av. António Macedo, cross the street, and then take a right. ⌁ Open M-F 9:30am-12:30pm and 2:30-5:30pm.)*

- **INTERNET: Espaço Internet** in the Biblioteca Municipal has free internet access. *(Av. Manuel Francisco da Costa ☎253 39 17 97 ⌁ Open M-F 9:30am-1pm and 2-5:30pm, Sa 9am-12:30pm.)*

- **POST OFFICE: Correios** is near the bus stop. *(☎253 39 00 10 ⌁ Open M-F 9am-12:30pm and 2-5:30pm.)*

Emergency!

- **POLICE:** Polícia *(Av. Manuel Francisco da Costa ☎253 90 00 10).*

- **MEDICAL SERVICES:** Cruz Vermelha Portuguesa (Red Cross) *(R. Chã de Ermida ☎253 39 16 60).*

Getting There

Empresa Hoteleira do Gerês *(☎253 26 20 33)* runs **buses** between **Braga** and **Gerês.** *(ⓢ€3.90. ⌁ 1½hr.; M-F 10 per day 7:10am-7:10pm, Sa 6 per day 7:55am-7:10pm, Su 4 per day 9:15am-7:10pm.)* Gerês-Braga buses stop at the bus stand on the street that runs from

northern portugal

the tourist office to the roundabout, parallel to the main street that runs in the other direction. Tell the bus driver you're getting off at Vila do Gerês, or he'll continue on to Vidoeiro. (ⓢ €3.90. 🕐 M-F 10 per day 6:20am-6:05pm, Sa 6 per day 6:20am-5pm, Su 4 per day 7:05am-5pm.)

Getting Around

The town of Vila do Gerês is one small loop, and the rest of the park is mainly narrow roads and dirt trails. **Walking** is the easiest option, but some may choose to bike some of the roads and trails. **Taxis** are also available (☎253 39 12 14).

braga ☎253

Braga has an odd but charming mixture of cosmopolitan urbanity and ancient allure. Expensive clothing stores sit next to fruit stalls beneath crumbling tiled palaces, massive flat-screen TVs adorn the walls of otherwise rustic courtyard restaurants, and the expanding city's newer, car-filled avenues are lined with stalls selling cheap goods to the passersby. The city is small enough to be manageable but big enough to be interesting, allowing for excellent wandering opportunities as well as a great launching point for a visit to the nearby **Parque Nacional da Peneda-Gerês**.

ORIENTATION

Braga's center is mostly pedestrian, with the **Rua do Souto** cutting east-west through the city center with smaller streets leading off it. The pleasant **Jardim de Santa Barbara** and the **Praça do Municipio** lie to the north, and the **Cathedral** lies to the south. At the east end of R. do Souto is the **Largo Barão de São Martinho,** a massive plaza from which the store-lined **Avenida Central** leads east and the pedestrian thoroughfare **Avenida da Liberdade** leads south. The **tourist office** is at this intersection, and the **bus station** is a few blocks north of the oldest part of town. To get from the bus station to R. do Souto, turn right onto **Av. de General Norton de Matos,** then right again onto **R. de Gabriel Pereira de Castro,** and then a slight left at **R. do Carmo.** From the **train station** a few blocks west, take **R. de Andrade Corvo** past the plaza and through the old gate.

ACCOMMODATIONS

RESIDÊNCIAL AVENIDA ⟡⊛⑨❄ PENSÃO ❷

Av. Liberdade, 738, 3rd fl.   ☎253 60 90 20 📧www.residencialavenida.net

Right next to the tourist office in the center of town, this is Braga's easiest place to find. The rooms have balconies over the broad Av. da Liberdade, which is a bonus except during loud festivals. With breakfast included, shower water hot enough to boil pasta, and TVs with more channels than you can shake a remote at, Residêncial Avenida is *Let's Go's* idea of a backpacker's steal—just be wary of the private baths, which are more ad-hoc cubicle structures in the corner of rooms than ritzy washrooms.

⚐ On Av. da Liberdade, next to tourist office. ⓘ Breakfast included. English spoken. Elevator closed midnight-8am. ⓢ June 15-Sept 15 singles €35-42; doubles €35-52. Extra bed €10. Sept 16-June 14 singles €23.50-40; doubles €28-45. Extra bed €7.50. 🕐 Reception 24hr.

HOTEL RESIDÊNCIAL SÃO NICOLAU ⊛⊗ PENSÃO ❷

Av. João XXI, 732   ☎253 61 94 63 📧www.hotelresidencialsaonicolau.com

Simple, inexpensive rooms in a newer part of town that's just a short walk from the pedestrian center and even closer to the town's Roman ruins. Also, its name rhymes. *Let's Go* enjoys rhymes—especially in foreign languages.

⚐ Follow Av. da Liberdade away from Lg. Barão de São Martinho 4 blocks, then left onto Av. João XXI. ⓢ Singles €25-28; doubles €30-35; triples €35-40. 🕐 Reception 24hr.

SIGHTS

CATEDRAL DE SANTA MARIA DE BRAGA — CHURCH, MUSEUM

R. do Cabido ☎253 26 33 17 🖥www.se-braga.pt

Braga's cathedral, *Sé de Braga*, founded in the late 11th century, is the oldest in Portugal. Its twin spires are typical of the Portuguese style that can be seen throughout Braga. Drop in Sundays and listen as the sounds of mass fill the sparkling Baroque interior.

➔ From Lg. Barão de São Martinho, follow R. do Souto 5 blocks, then left. $ Cathedral free. Museum €3. ⏰ Cathedral open daily 8am-6:30pm. Museum open Tu-Su 9am-12:30pm and 2-6:30pm.

FOOD

There are dozens of cafes and pastry shops that serve inexpensive meals scattered throughout the pedestrian part of town along **R. do Souto** and **R. de Dom Afonso Henriques.** The **Campo das Hortas,** just beyond the gate at the far west end of R. do Souto, is lined with restaurants, and the **Parque do Conde de Agrolongo** (head away from Lg. Barão de São Martinho on R. do Souto 3 blocks, then right at R. de Cidade do Porto 1 block past the garden, then left) has some reasonably priced options as well.

ADEGA MALHOA — ❁♿🍸 TRADITIONAL ❶

R. de Dom Paio Mendes, 19 ☎964 00 59 71

This colorful, dimly lit but brightly decorated den serves a €6 menu that includes 2 courses, bread, wine, and coffee. House specialties are traditional regional dishes like *Rojões à moda do Minho* *(spiced and marinated cubes of pork, €6)* and various *bacalhau* (cod) dishes.

➔ Follow R. do Souto 6 blocks away from Lg. Barão de São Martinho. Take a left in front of the Catedral, then turn right onto R. de Dom Paio Mendes. $ Entrees €5-9. Daily menu €6. ⏰ Open Tu-Su noon-3pm and 6-10pm.

ESSENTIALS

Practicalities

- **TOURIST OFFICE:** The **Posto de Turismo** has maps and information on tourist sights. *(Av. da Liberdade, 1 ☎253 26 25 50 🖥www.cm-braga.pt ➔ At intersection of R. do Souto, Av. da Liberdade, and Av. Central. ⏰ Open M-F 9am-12:30pm and 2-6:30pm, Sa-Su 2-5:30pm.)*
- **LAUNDROMAT: Lavandería Bracarense** *(R. de S. Marcos, 117 ☎253 11 35 54 $ 4kg wash and dry €12. ⏰ Open M-F 8am-7:30pm, Sa 8am-2pm.)*
- **POST OFFICE:** Correios *(Travessa Praça da Justiça ☎253 20 83 30 ⏰ Open M-F 9am-12:30pm and 2-5:30pm, Sa 9am-1pm.)*

Emergency!

- **POLICE:** Polícia Municipal *(Largo do Rossio da Sé, 12 ☎253 60 97 40)*
- **MEDICAL SERVICES:** The **Centro de Saúde de Braga I** offers healthcare services. *(Largo Mercado do Carandá ☎253 20 15 00.)*

Getting There

Alsa runs **buses** from **Santiago de Compostela** (*$ €29. ⏰ 2hr.; daily at 10:30am, Su 10pm)* via Pontevedra and Vigo. Rede Nacional de Expressos *(☎253 20 94 01 🖥www.rede-expressos.pt)* runs **buses** from: **Coimbra** *($ €12.70. ⏰ 3hr.; M-Sa 10 per day 8:30am-3am, Su 8 per day 10am-3am);* **Lisbon** (*$ €18. ⏰ 5hr., 13 per day 7am-12:15am);* and **Porto** *($ €5.70. ⏰ 1hr.; 20-33 per day M 8:45am-4:30am, Tu-Sa 10am-4:30am, Su 10:30am-4:30am)* CP runs **trains** from **Porto** *($ €13. ⏰ 45min., 4 per day 9:46am-9:46pm).*

Getting Around

Since the city isn't large and most of it is accessible only to pedestrians, the best way to get around the old part of Braga is to **walk.** There is a **bus** system *(💻www.tub.pt)* and a 24hr. **taxi** service, Braga Táxis *(☎253 253 253).*

coimbra ☎239

Coimbra is best known for its hilltop **university** and its famous **fado,** or folksongs. The university has been around for over 700 years, and Coimbra's mournful *fado,* whose distinct northern brand is usually sung by men, sounds something like a musical embodiment of Death, but in the most beautiful way possible. The different zones of the city have very different feels, and this variation can even be discerned from one hilly, ancient street to the next. Unlike many cities, which are at their liveliest in the summer months, Coimbra is at its most vibrant during the school year when the students run wild.

ORIENTATION

Coimbra's historic upper city, **Alta,** once reserved for students by royal decree, has steep streets and stairways, with the **university** at the top; the lower part of town forms a crescent around the upper city's hill. In **Baixa,** the lower part of Coimbra, the **Coimbra-A train station** is right on the river. From the station's main entrance, head left one block to reach the wide **Av. de Fernão de Magalhães,** which runs parallel to the river. To the right, Av. de Fernão de Magalhães becomes the narrower R. da Sota and goes to **Largo da Portagem,** a big plaza where there is a **tourist office.** Continuing along the river is a park with some restaurants and accommodations across the street. In the other direction, the pedestrian **Rua de Ferreira Borges** goes from Lg. da Portagem straight to the **Praça 8 de Maio,** with two sets of stairs along the way on the left side that lead down to **Praça do Comércio.** This street and these two plazas are the heart of Baixa, with narrower capillaries leading off them. Continuing to the right after Pr. 8 de Maio will take you around the old city's hill to the huge, tree-lined **Av. Sá da Bandeira,** which ends at the **Pr. da República.**

ACCOMMODATIONS

Most accommodations are packed along the **Av. de Fernão de Magalhães** and the streets just off it around the **Coimbra-A train station,** while the youth hostel is a 30min. walk (largely uphill), 10min. bus, or €4 cab ride away from the station.

RESIDÊNCIAL VITÓRIA — PENSÃO [2]

R. da Sota, 11 ☎239 82 40 49

Inexpensive rooms on a nice, narrow street just two blocks from the train station and the river. Rooms are simple but come with A/C and TV.

➔ From Coimbra-A train station, head 1 block away from river to Av. de Fernão de Magalhães, then right to reach R. da Sota. $ Singles €20, with ensuite bath €30; doubles €30/45; triples with ensuite bath €60. Breakfast €5. ⏰ Reception 24hr.

SIGHTS

UNIVERSIDADE DE COIMBRA — UNIVERSITY

Lg. da Porta Férrea ☎239 85 98 84 💻www.uc.pt

The walk to the university from Baixa takes you through the ancient part of town, up streets with names like "Quebra-Costas" (Backbreaker) that were clearly meant to be conquered via mule. The university, for centuries the country's only one and still among its most prestigious, is at the very top of the hill. Much of the university suffers from brutal Salazar-era architecture, but there are some true gems, particularly in the panoramic **Paço das Escolas.** The **Biblioteca Joanina,** a Baroque library (Portugal's oldest) whose building dates from the start of the 18th century but whose collection goes back centuries earlier, is a truly splendid book-lover's paradise, trimmed with gold and filled with three stories of ancient tomes. Listen for the squeaks of the **bats** that live here and protect the collection by feasting on evil papyrophagi (paper-eating insects). Next door, the **Capela de São Miguel** is a Manueline masterpiece, with incredible decorations and a 3000-tube organ from 1737 that is still played regularly. The **Sala dos Capelos** (Room of Cowls, a reference to the academics' garb) or Sala dos Actos (Room of Acts) is one of the university's most important rooms, in which doctoral candidates take their examinations and later (depending on the examination, of course) receive their caps and velvet cowls. This room was once the Royal Palace's **throne room,** where the first kings of Portugal held court from 1143-1383.

Buses 1A, 34, 60, 103, or market elevator from Mercado de Dom Pedro V. ℹ *Tickets can be purchased in the Biblioteca Dom João V, on Pr. da Porta Férrea.* [$] *Combined admission (includes visit to Biblioteca Joanina, Sala dos Capelos, Capela de São Miguel, and Academic Prison) €7, students and seniors €5, under 12 free. Biblioteca Joanina €5, students and seniors €3.50. Sala dos Capelos (includes Capela de São Miguel) €5, students and seniors €3.50. Capela de São Miguel €3, students and seniors €2.10. Academic Prison €2, students and seniors €1.40.* ⏰ *Open Apr-Oct daily 9am-7pm; Nov-Mar M-F 9:30am-5:30pm, Sa-Su 10:30am-4:30pm.*

FOOD

The side streets off Pr. do Comércio and Pr. 8 de Maio tend to be good locations for inexpensive meals, as is the area around Pr. da República on the other side of the hill. Local specialties include gamey but tasty *cabrito* (kid goat) and the not-terribly-appetizing-looking *arroz de lampreia* (rice with lamprey eel). The **Mercado de Dom Pedro V** on R. Olímpio Nicolau Rui Fernandes *(⏰ Open M-Sa 8am-1pm)* is a great place for fresh bread, produce, and just about everything else, with the fish in a separate room so the whole place doesn't stink by the afternoon. The supermarket **Pingo Doce** is at R. de João de Ruão, 14, a 3min. walk up R. da Sofia from Pr. 8 de Maio *(☎239 85 29 30 ⏰ Open daily 8:30am-9pm).*

coimbra traditions

Without our traditions, our lives would be as shaky as a fiddler on a roof—and a fall from one of the roofs of the Universidade de Coimbra would mean a long, long tumble down to Baixa. Thankfully, the university, founded in 1290, has an elaborate and amazing set of traditions, known as the Praxe Académica. The Festa das Latas (Festival of the Cans) occurs when the students return from their summer vacations at the beginning of the school year, as freshmen are led through town and forced by their seniors to perform ridiculous initiation tasks. The festival and procession, or latada, whose origins are in the 19th century, take their names from the noisy latas (cans) that the students wear on their feet. The Queima das Fitas (Burning of the Ribbons), which goes back as far as the 14th century, takes place at the end of the school year in May. Students tear up and burn their traditional uniforms, including their cloaks, which are supposed to represent their collected academic experiences. These cloaks are also supposed to remain unwashed, which could explain the burning part. The festivities last eight days (one day for each of the faculdades) when the whole town buzzes with processions and concerts and performances, including the serenata monumental, in which students sing a nighttime fado on the steps of the Sé Velha.

👍 ADEGA PAÇO DO CONDE 💳♿🍸☀ GRILL [1]

R. Paço do Conde, 1 ☎239 82 56 05

This restaurant, which has indoor and outdoor (well, tin-roof-covered) seating, is loved by locals and budget travelers alike. You can get huge portions for €5-6—the shareable *costeleta de porco* (pork ribs/chops) is a great deal for €5.20 and comes with tons of fries, rice, and salad.

➜ *From Pr. do Comércio, take R. de Adelino Veigo (directly across from Igreja de São Tiago) 2 blocks, then turn right.* $ *Entrees €4.15-10.* ⏰ *Open M-Sa noon-3pm and 7-10pm, Su noon-3pm.*

NIGHTLIFE

Coimbra's nightlife is at its best from October through June, when the students are around and crazy. The bars below the university around Pr. da República tend to be good spots earlier in the night, with the bars and clubs on the hill on the other side of R. Sá da Bandeira becoming more popular, as well as the four new side-by-side bars along the Río Mondego. Many choose to take a train to Figueira da Foz, an hour away on the coast, and party all night before heading back on the first train in the morning.

👍 A CAPELLA 🚬⊘🍸☀ FADO

R. do Corpo de Deus ☎918 11 33 07 🖥www.acapella.com.pt

Built as a 14th-century church, this small chapel now houses a smoky *fado* club with professional *fadistas* and loads of tourists. The acoustics are phenomenal, and anyone who has ever visited a stone church during a service and had to sneeze will understand why. There is also a cafe with outdoor seating on the cobblestone plaza.

➜ *From Pr. 8 de Maio, head toward Lg. da Portagem along R. do Visconde da Luz, then take the 1st sharp left up R. do Corpo de Deus; it's on the left after a small plaza.* $ *Cover €10; includes 1 drink.* ⏰ *Open daily 9pm-2am. Performances at 9:30, 10:30, 11:30pm.*

DILIGÊNCIA BAR 💳⊘🍸 FADO

R. Nova, 30 ☎239 82 76 67 🖥www.diligenciabar.com

Also a pretty touristy joint, in case the signs in English out front don't tip you off, but it's easy to get to and has a nice, traditional feel inside. Much of the *fado* performed here is sung by caped students or by nightly regulars.

➜ *From Pr. 8 de Maio, head along R. Direita (far-right corner with your back to Igreja de Santa Cruz) 1 block, then turn right on R. Nova.* $ *Entrees €9.50-13.50. Sangria €10 per jug. €5 credit card min.* ⏰ *Open daily 7pm-2am.*

ESSENTIALS

Practicalities

- **TOURIST OFFICE: The Regional Office** has information about Coimbra, though it specializes in information about the region rather than the city itself. *(Lg. da Portagem* 🖥*www.turismo-centro.pt* ➜ *From Estação Coimbra-A, walk along the river with the water to your right until Lg. da Portagem; the office is on the far side.* ⏰ *Open June-Sept M-F 9am-6pm, Sa-Su 9am-1pm and 2:30-6pm; Oct-May M-F 9am-5pm, Sa-Su 9am-noon and 2:30-5pm.)* The **Municipal Office** has a desk in the Biblioteca de Dom João V at the University. *(Pr. da Porta Férrea* ☎*239 83 41 58* ⏰ *Open M-F 10am-5pm, Sa-Su 10am-6pm.)*
- **CURRENCY EXCHANGE: Montepio** will exchange money under €50 commission-free. *(Lg. da Portagem* ☎*239 85 17 00* ⏰ *Open M-F 8:30am-3pm.)*
- **LAUNDROMAT: Lavandaria Lucira** will wash and dry 6kg for €6. *(Av. Sá da Bandeira, 86* ☎*239 09 06 15* ⏰ *Open M 9am-7pm, Tu-F 9am-8:30pm, Sa 9am-5:30pm.)*
- **POST OFFICE:** Correios *(Lg. Mercado Municipal de Dom Pedro V* ☎*239 85 18 70* ⏰ *Open M-F 8:30am-6:30pm, Sa 9am-12:30pm.)*

Emergency!

- **POLICE:** Polícia Municipal *(Av. Elísio de Moura, 155* ☎*239 85 35 00* ⚔ *From Pr. 8 de Maio with the church to your right, head right and cross the street.)*
- **HOSPITAL:** Hospital da Universidade de Coimbra. *(*☎*239 40 04 00* ⚔ *At Pr. do Professor Mota Pinto and Av. do Doutor Bissaya Barreto. Take bus #6, 7, 7t, 29, 35, 36 or 37.)*
- **LATE-NIGHT PHARMACIES: Farmácia Universal** is right on the Pr. 8 de Maio and has a schedule of pharmacies open at night and on Sundays in the window. *(Pr. 8 de Maio, 35* ☎*239 82 37 44* ⓩ *Open daily 8am-7pm.)*

Getting There

By Train

There are two train stations in Coimbra. **Estação Coimbra-A (Nova)** is right beside the river near the center of Baixa; **Estação Coimbra-B (Velha)** is 3km northwest of town. *(*▣*www.cp.pt)* All trains stop at Coimbra-B, but long-distance trains do not continue on to Coimbra-A. If your train will not go to Coimbra-A, get off at Coimbra-B and take a free connecting train to Coimbra-A to reach the city. Trains arrive from: **Lisbon's Sta. Apolonia Station** *(*⑨ *€12-30.* ⓩ *2-3hr., 17 per day 5:30am-8:46pm)* and **Porto's Campanhã Station** *(*⑨ *€8.10-15.50.* ⓩ *1-2hr., 19 per day 5:45am-1:30am).*

By Bus

Buses *(*▣*www.rede-expressos.pt)* arrive at the river, next to Estação Coimbra-A from: **Braga** *(*⑨ *€13.20.* ⓩ *3hr., 9-12 per day 6am-11:30pm)*, **Lisbon** *(*⑨ *€13.* ⓩ *2½hr., 25 per day 7am-12:15am)*, and **Porto** *(*⑨ *€11.50.* ⓩ *1½hr., 12-15 per day).*

Getting Around

The **bus** system is the easiest way to get to the university without breaking a sweat. SMTUC buses *(*▣*www.smtuc.pt)* run there. *(*⑨ *One-way ticket €1.50, 3-trip ticket €2, 11-trip €6.10, one-day €3.20.)* These can be purchased at vending machines in Lg. da Portagem, Pr. da República, and small shops throughout town. There is a **taxi** stand outside Estação Coimbra-A, or call Politáxis *(*☎*239 49 90 90; 239 82 22 87).*

northern portugal

MOROCCO

TANGIER

Like a coy mistress, the port city of Tangier (*Tanger* in French and Spanish) is at once irritating and alluring. If you're going to visit, be prepared to tolerate her whims. Only 14km by ferry from Tarifa, Spain, travelers to Tangier must navigate the chaotic medina (the old Arab quarter), steer clear of hustlers feigning hospitality, and confront the tentative supsicion of locals. Put on a brave face, learn to say *Salaam*, and Tangier's allure can redeem its challenges.

While the city used to be famous for its vibrant party life, Tangier is better known these days for its rich history, art, and culture, in addition to its many cafes and gorgeous views of the sea. In 1923, the city was declared an "interzone" loosely governed by the US and eight other European countries. The lack of law enforcement made it a hotspot for partying heiresses, artists, drug users, spies, and Beat Generation poets. Since Moroccan independence in 1956, the government has closed down the brothels and clubs of yesterday in an effort to reclaim Tangier for Moroccans. Today, the city is a growing commercial center that retains the evidence of its cosmopolitan history.

For confident daytrippers from Spain or backpackers traveling into the heart of Morocco, Tangier is certainly worth a one-day visit. Find a bargain in the medina, sit in the awe-inspiring garden of the **Dar al-Makhzen Museum** in the **Kasbah** (fortress), and drink a piping hot mint tea at **Cafe Paris.** If you're staying the night, hit up the party at **Tangier Inn.** And remember: keep your guard up and don't get suckered.

greatest hits

- **THE LION'S SHARE.** Or the sharing of lions, if you happen to be a Moroccan sultan. Find out how the exchange of these carnivorous cats affected American-Moroccan relations at the Old American Legation (p. 418).

- **JUST MY CUP OF TEA.** No, seriously, *just* a cup of a tea—mint tea is all you need for a good time in Tangier (well, that and a cafe in which to drink it) (p. 420).

- **EAT LIKE A KING.** Head to Brahim Abdelmalek, a fast-food joint that King Hassan II ate at in the '70s (p. 420).

orientation

call me

The phone code for Tangier is ☎05 39.

Av. d'Espagne (also known as **Av. Mohammed VI**) is the large boulevard along the beach that forms the western border of Tangier. If you're coming from Spain on the ferry, you'll step onto Av. d'Espagne as you leave the port entrance; if you are coming from the train station or the airport, Av. d'Espagne is one of the main roads into the city. Many of the *ville nouvelle* hotels are located just uphill from Av. d'Espagne, 1km away from the ferry terminals.

Grand Socco, a large outdoor market with fruit and sandwich vendors that is the nexus of the **ville nouvelle** and the **medina,** and the ideal landmark for travelers. To get there from the port entrance, turn right at the **CTM bus station** on Av. d'Espagne and go up **Rue du Portugal.** Continue climbing with the medina's walls to your right. Turn right on **Rue Salah Idine al-Ayoubi** and with just a bit more climbing you'll reach the Grand Socco's fountain.

The **medina,** or walled Arab quarter, can be reached from the port by turning all the way to the right at the CTM station, and following **Rue Moulay Rachid** until you see stairs into the medina. Walk up the stairs and take either **Rue Mokhtar Ahardan** or **Rue de la Marine** to the **Petit Socco,** a small open space in the medina. Both streets are lined with inexpensive *pensions* to stay the night (50-100dh). Alternatively, walk from the Grand Socco through the central gate, **Bab el Fahs,** directly below the main fountain, onto **Rue d'Italie,** which continues all the away along the medina's western wall. To enter the medina, turn right into the first gate off of rue d'Italie and walk downhill on **Rue Al-Siaghin** until you reach the Petit Socco. Note that continuing straight on rue d'Italie will take you to the northwest tip of the medina where the **Kasbah** is located.

To get the fun parts of the *ville nouvelle*, orient yourself in the Grand Socco and walk away from the medina up **Rue de la Liberté.** When you reach the taffic circle, welcome to **Place de France.** Turn right on **Blvd. Pasteur,** Tangier's main street, and stroll past the **Terrace des Parraseux** (Idler's Terrace), with its canons and lovely views of Spain, until Pasteur becomes **Blvd. Mohammed V.** On the boulevards, you will find banks, cafes and the post office.

tangier

accommodations

Tangier has an abundance of cheap and clean accommodations; score 1 for you, intrepid traveler. You can either choose to stay in the medina or the **ville nouvelle,** depending on how much comfort you require and how much courage you have. On the whole, the *ville nouvelle* accommodations offer more amenities (read: toilet paper), while the medina's accommodations put you right in the heart of darkness, which is both exciting and kinda scary late at night.

MEDINA

The medina's many *pensions* are scattered in and around the Petit Socco along rue de La Marine or rue Mokhtar Aharden. At night, keep to the medina's largest streets since the smaller alleys can be unsafe.

PENSION PALACE — PENSION ❶

2 rue Mokhtar Ahardane ☎05 39 93 61 28

This might seem like an ordinary *pension*, but the two-story interior garden floods with natural light and belongs in a palace. Of course, the rooms aren't made for kings, but the well-kept double beds with communal showers charge do the trick. Toilets could use lids and toilet paper. Still, you won't find better value in the medina.

⇶ 20 ft. off the Petit Socco on rue Mokhtar Ahardane. i English spoken. $ Singles 50dh; doubles 100dh; triples 150dh; quads 200dh.

PENSION AMAR — PENSION ❷

Rue du Kadi no. 1 ☎05 39 93 71 27

Keep your eyes peeled for a sign on rue de la Marine above a dark alley. What? An alley? Don't be scared: 10ft. inside is a family-run home away from home with teenage receptionist Youssef to greet you. He'll take you up a beautifully-tiled staircase to your tidy room. Squat toilets upstairs. A single shower, *gratuit*, next to reception makes things *very* familiar.

⇶ 50 ft. off the Petit Socco on rue de la Marine. $ Singles 70dh; doubles 120dh; triples 160dh.

HOTEL MARHABA — HOTEL ❶

14 rue de la Poste ☎05 39 93 88 02

Midway between the Petit Socco and the medina wall, this place is built for travelers seeking a quieter place to hunker down. Spartan yet sufficient, this not-too-shabby hotel has the usual fare: dusty double beds, a table and sink in the room, clean communal showers for no extra charge and BYOTP toilets.

⇶ 200 ft. off the Petit Socco, tucked away in an alley that branches off rue Mokhtar Ahardan. $ Singles 50dh; doubles 100dh; triples 150dh.

VILLE NOUVELLE

You'll find many hotels on the Av. d'Espagne just opposite the beach, but the best value is slightly uphill towards Blvd. Pasteur and Blvd. Mohammed V.

HOTEL EL MUNIRIA — HOTEL ❷

1 rue Magellan ☎05 39 93 53 37

As hip as the Beat Poets who stayed here decades ago, this family-owned hotel has spacious color-themed rooms with luxurious beds and a private bath in each room. William Burroughs wrote *Naked Lunch* in room #9, and Jack Kerouac and Allan Ginsberg stayed in rooms #4 and #5. Check out the ocean view from the rooftop and smile at the Berber cleaning lady when she blows you a kiss. Ideal for travelers wanting to party, since **Tangier Inn** is right next door. Don't expect too much help from the laid-back owners, and don't expect the dance music to stop until 2am.

From Av. d'Espagne, head up the wide alley next to Hotel Biarritz and wind your way until you see a sign. Feels like you're lost but just keep taking the turns as they come. Trust in Let's Go and inshallah and you will arrive. $ Singles on 2nd fl. 200dh, on 3rd fl. (with a view) 250dh. ⏰ Hotel entrance has a doorbell. Reception closes at approx. 2am.

PENSION DAR OMAR KHAYAM PENSION ❷

26 rue Al Antaki ☎06 63 71 84 60

Old yellow-brick Moorish house just off Av. d'Espagne has modern tiled rooms furnished with single beds and serviceable communal baths. Hot showers are included.

Two blocks up rue Al Antaki off of Av. d'Espagne. $ Singles 100dh, with bath 120dh; doubles 150dh.

sights

During your trip to Tangier, you'll definitely hear a lot of hype about the **Kasbah.** Ever the explorer, you'll wander up rue d'Italie through **Bab Marshan,** and a hustler or two will try to tell you how to find it. Well my friend, you're already there. The word *Qasbah* refers to a high-walled fortress located in the medina of traditional Islamic cities. That means the Kasbah is a neighborhood, not a building. Now that you've got that under your belt, there are two ways to explore Tangier's Kasbah. Walk through the fortress' gate, turn right, and follow the diamonds in the street *into* the Kasbah's narrow passageways. Eventually you'll pass the impressive minarets of the **Mosque de la Kasbah,** followed by the **Dar al-Makhzen** museum and the **Place du Mechoir** or **Place de Kasbah**, which has open-air concerts at night. Alternatively, once you've passed through the Bab al-Marshan, walk straight until you have to turn right and follow the Kasbah walls for 200 ft. to the **Pl. du Mechoir's** open square and sweet view of the ocean. Be careful of friendly Moroccans who start showing you around. Most likely, they are looking for a fee.

ST. ANDREW'S CHURCH CHURCH

Built on land donated to Great Britain by Moulay Hassan I in 1883, St. Andrews's oasis of peace has a carefully tended garden, an English cemetery and a modest Anglican Church. Ask the gentle groundskeeper, Mustapha, to open the Church doors and you'll see an intricately carved wooden ceiling above the altarpiece as well as the Lord's Prayer inscribed in Arabic around the chancel arch. It's well-worth your time to appreciate St. Andrew's quietly beautiful fusion of English and Moorish architecture, and especially, to meet its lovely caretaker.

Logically located on rue d'Angleterre just up the hill from the Grand Socco. [i] Donations recommended. ⏰ Open M-F 9:30am-12:30pm and 2:30-4:30pm. Services Su from 8:30-11am.

OLD AMERICAN LEGATION HISTORIC MONUMENT

8 rue d'America ☎05 39 93 53 17

The old American embassy is probably the only place in Morocco where you'll find a picture of Barack Obama hanging next to an image of the current king, Mohammed VI. This quirky tidbit is just the latest installment in a long history of US-Morocco relations, which the Old American Legation examines through a series of entertaining exhibits. Historical artifacts include correspondence between George Washington and his "great and magnanimous friend" Sultan Moulay ben Abdelah, who was the first international leader to recognize American independence. The most hilarious piece in the collection is a letter from the consul, detailing his attempt to unsuccessfully refuse a gift of lions from the sultan. You can pay a special visit to the downstairs room dedicated to expat writer Paul Bowles, check out photos from Tangier's storied "interzone" days, or read an old favorite in the library of English fiction and poetry. The curator gives excellent tours upon request, but calling first is the polite thing to do.

✦ *Enter the medina through the white staircase on rue du Portugal, walk straight and look for the yellow archway emblazoned with the American seal.* ***i*** *Free. Donation suggested.* ⏰ *Open M-F 10am-1pm and 3-5pm.*

DAR AL-MAKHZEN
Pl. de Kasbah

🏛 MUSEUM ❶
☎05 39 93 20 97

As you stroll through the arches and columns of the Dar al-Makhzen museum, you can dream about what it would be like to rule Tangier from an opulent palace of your own, decked out with tapestries, intricate carvings and traditional music echoing through the halls. Since there are no more ruling pashas in Tangier—and since you are definitely not one of them—you'll have to settle instead for exploring the former palace's room-by-room exhibits of Tangier's fascinating history, from pre-Roman to Islamic times. Your inner archaeologist will delight in the lead sarcophagi, funerary urns, pottery, and the gorgeous Roman mosaic depicting the voyage of Venus, and your inner poet will want to sit for hours listening to the birds and the breeze in the massive interior garden.

✦ *Enter the medina through the Bab el Kasbah gate at the top of the hill on rue d'Italie. Walk straight until you must turn right. Follow the medina walls to the wide open space. Walk around to the right and voila!* 💲 *10dh.* ⏰ *Open M 9am-4pm, W-Th 9am-4pm, F 9am-12:30pm and 2:30-4:30pm, Sa-Su 9am-4pm.*

MARKETS

🏛 MARKET ❶

It's not too tough to find Tangier's nifty markets. If you haven't already wandered through them several times, simply make your way south of the **Grand Socco's** traffic circle down **Rue Salah Idine al-Ayoubi.** You'll pass vendors selling fresh fish, garlands of flowers, colorful robes (*jelbaab*), traditional shoes, giant watermelons, and spices from saffron to parsley. For a really local market farther from the tourist center, head up **Rue de Belgique** away from **Pl. de France** and turn left down **Rue Hollande.** At the corner of **Rue Ibn Baddis,** you'll descend steps into the dirty and fun **Spanish Market,** which caters to local food and livestock demand. The markets are worth wandering into, but not worth seeking out.

food

For a fabulous and cheap fast-food sandwich of *kefta*, egg and fries on a baguette, **Brahim Abdelmalek** is the place to go. If you're looking for an elegant Moroccan meal of couscous and *tajines*, and don't mind tourists or higher prices, then **Palace Mamounia** is the place for you. Whether you are in the *ville nouvelle* or the medina, you can eat very well for 50dh. For the tightest budgets, bargain the vendors down to 20dh for street food around the **Grand Socco.**

MEDINA

RESTAURANT HAMMADI
2 rue de la Kasbah

🏛🍽 TRADITIONAL, MOROCCAN ❷
☎05 39 93 45 14

Carpets, satiny cushions, and local musicians set the ambience for a dining experience that's as "authentically" Moroccan as any visitor can hope for. That means other tourists, but the specialty meat *tajines* and couscous are worth it. Beer and wine served.

✦ *Along rue d'Italie when it becomes rue de la Kasbah, just past the fork with rue Ibn Al Abbar. Entrance in a small alley. Restaurant 2 floors up.* 💲 *Harira soup 25dh. Entrees 55-75dh. 10% tax added.* ⏰ *Open daily 11am-3pm and 8pm-midnight.*

RESTAURANT EL AMRANI 🍴 MOROCCAN [1]

End of rue Smihi

El Amrani is ideal if you want to eat with Moroccan men in a place where no one speaks English. The bread (*khoubz*) is tough as leather and the *harira* comes out steaming. If you're in the medina, this hole-in-the-wall is equally cheap and better quality than the food vendors on the **Grand Socco.**

➜ Enter the medina through the 2nd gate off rue d'Italie and walk 50 ft. until rue Smihi ends. $ Harira 6dh. Entrees 20-30dh. Watermelon 6-8dh.

VILLE NOUVELLE

✓ BRAHIM ABDELMALEK 🍴 MOROCCAN, FAST FOOD, LATE NIGHT [1]

14 rue de Mexique

King Hassan II grabbed fast-food here in the '70s. You can too. Order a baguette with *kefta*, a fried egg, and french fries. Stellar sandwiches are a full meal and go down best with a coke.

➜ Walk straight up rue de Mexique off of Blvd. Pasteur. $ Entrees 15-25dh. Drinks 5dh. ⏰ Open daily 11am-1am.

SALON DE THÉ LIBERTÉ 🍴☀ MOROCCAN [2]

47 rue de La Liberté ☎05 34 25 90 15

This street cafe is great for people-watching in the late evening, but the secret terrace hidden in the back offers a better place to chow down on Moroccan and Western favorites.

➜ Along rue de la Liberté just off the Grand Socco. $ Entrees 25-50dh. ⏰ Open 7am-midnight.

nightlife

The most popular evening activity in Tangier is sipping mint tea in one of the city's many cafes. While most cafes are all-male, *Let's Go* picks cater to both genders. To drink something stronger than tea, make your way to the **Tangier Inn** next to **Hotel El Muniria.** If you want to go dance, hit up one of the discotheques along the beach on **Av. d'Espagne,** but be prepared to attract the attention of Moroccan women looking for more than a good time.

✓ TANGIER INN 🍸🍴 BAR

1 rue Magellan

An intimate basement bar that provides cold beer and hot hip hop. Attracts a cosmopolitan mix of men and women, both local and foreign. Known as the hippest place to party in town.

➜ Next to Hotel El Muniria. i Cash only. $ Beer 20dh. ⏰ M-Sa 10pm-2am.

CAFE DE PARIS 🍴 CAFE

1. Pl. de France ☎05 39 93 84 44

Famous for hosting countless meetings between spies during WWII—and more recently serving Matt Damon—Cafe de Paris couldn't be more central. Watch the crowds pass through Pl. de France, then go take in the view of Spain from the nearby **Terrace des Paresseux** after you've finished your tea or coffee.

➜ Corner of rue de la Liberté and Blvd. Pasteur. $ Tea/coffee 7-8dh. ⏰ Open daily 5-midnight.

shopping

If you're looking for traditional clothing, tapestries, and art, you'll find stalls and street vendors scattered throughout the markets of the **Grand Socco** and the **medina.** Bargain them down by quoting half the price initially offered, and be poised to walk away if it's refused.

essentials

Most essentials can be found in the *ville nouvelle* along **Blvd. Pasteur and Blvd Mohammed V,** which includes many banks, internet cafes, pharmacies and general stores.

PRACTICALITIES

- **TOURIST OFFICE:** The office at 29 Blvd. Pasteur gives out pocket guides to Tangier full of accommodations, listings, and attractions, along with train schedules and emergency numbers upon request. (☎ *05 39 94 80 50* ⇄ *On the right-hand side of the street as you walk towards Place de France.* ℹ *French, Spanish and a bit of English spoken.* ⏰ *Open M-F 8:30am-4:30pm.)*
- **CURRENCY EXCHANGE:** Several banks can be found on Blvd. Pasteur and Blvd. Mohammed V, including **BMCI - BNP Paribas** *(48 Blvd. Pasteur* ☎ *05 39 33 92 62* ⏰ *Open M-F 8am-4:30pm),* **BMCE** *(21 Blvd. Pasteur* ☎ *05 39 33 66 62* ⏰ *Open M-F 8:15am-3:45pm),* and the national Moroccan **Bank al-Maghrib** *(78 Blvd. Mohammed V* ☎ *05 39 34 95 50* ⏰ *Open M-F 8:30am-3pm).* No bank will accept traveler's checks, but all are equipped with **ATMs**. There are dozens of **Western Union** branches *(*⏰ *Open M-F 8am-9pm),* notably those across from BMCE and Bank al-Maghrib.
- **LUGGAGE STORAGE:** Luggage storage is available at the train station. *(*$ *15dh per bag.)* There is also a private *Consigne* to the right and up the hill from the CTM bus station that stores luggage for 15dh per bag per 24hr.
- **INTERNET ACCESS:** Several cafes in the *ville nouvelle,* including **Cyber Cafe Adam** *(2 rue ibn Roched, off Blvd. Pasteur.* ☎ *05 39 94 83 97.* $ *7 dh per hr for wireless and 8dh for internet. Open daily 9:30am-9pm).*
- **POST OFFICE:** The branch at 33 Blvd. Mohammed V, on the left-hand side of the street as you walk downhill on Mohammed V. coming from Blvd. Pasteur, has Poste Restante. *(*☎ *05 39 94 80 50* ℹ *For package pick-up, walk around the corner from the main entrance to the right side of the building.* ⏰ *Open M-F 8am-4:30pm, Sa 9am-noon.)*

EMERGENCY!

- **EMERGENCY NUMBERS: Ambulance:** ☎05 39 31 27 27.
- **POLICE:** ☎190. Stations are located at the port and main train station. At the port, ask for the **Brigade Touristique**, which deals with issues and complaints from travelers.
- **MEDICAL SERVICES: Red Crescent** *(6 rue al-Mansour Dahbi* ☎*05 39 94 25 17)* offers 24hr. medical services. The **hospital** also has an emergency line *(*☎*05 39 93 08 56).*

GETTING THERE

By Plane

The Tangier **airport** (☎ 05 39 39 37 20) has domestic and international flights, including a daily route to **Madrid,** from **Royal Air Morac** (☎05 39 93 47 22) and **Iberia** (☎ 05 39 93 61 77). A *grand taxi* to the airport, 16km from Tangier, costs 100-150dh for up to 6 people.

By Train

The train station, **Tanger Ville,** (☎090 20 30 40) is a 10-15dh ride by *petit taxi* from the *ville nouvelle*. The station is brand new, impressive, and still pretty budget friendly. For certain destinations, the prices are comparable to bus fares, if only slightly more expensive. Trains run to: **Meknes** (ⓈOU 81dh. ⓉXI 4 hr.; 11:15 am, 5:15pm and 9pm); **Rabat** (Ⓢ 95dh. ⓉXI 5 hr.; 8am, 11am, 2pm and 5pm); **Fes** (Ⓢ 105dh. ⓉXI 5 hr.; 11:15am and 5:15pm); **Casablanca** (Ⓢ 125 dh. ⓉXI 6 hr., 8am, 11am); **Marrakech** (Ⓢ 205dh. ⓉXI 10hr., 2 per day 8am and 2pm).

By Bus

There are two bus stations in Tangier—the **CTM Station** at the port entrance, and a cheaper **non-CTM station** with multiple bus lines in Pl. Jamia al-Arabia. The **CTM Station** (☎05 39 93 11 72) runs buses to: **Tetouan** (Ⓢ 22dh. ⓉXI 1 hr.; 10am, noon, and 8pm); **Fes** (Ⓢ 110dh. ⓉXI 6 hr.; 10am, 12:15pm, 3:15pm, 7:15pm, 9:15pm, 11:15pm); **Rabat** (Ⓢ 100dh. ⓉXI 5:30am, 11:15am, 2:45pm, 4:30pm); **Casablanca** (Ⓢ 130dh. ⓉXI 6hr.; 5:30am, 11:15am, 2:45pm, 4:30pm); **Marrakech** (ⓉXI 10 hr., 4:30pm and 2:30am).

The non-CTM station is a 7dh ride by *petit taxi* from the *ville nouvelle* and houses multiple bus lines. Compare prices on the ticket windows and expect representatives to actively recruit your business. From window #2 of 11: to **Casablanca** (Ⓢ 90dh. ⓉXI 4 hr., 10 per day 5am-10:30am) and **Marrakech** (Ⓢ 150dh. ⓉXI 12 hr., 6 buses per day 6:45am-1:30am).

By Ferry

The ferry terminal is located at the end of the port and is a 7min. walk from the entrance. Fast ferries travel to and from **Tarifa, Spain** every 2hr. Walk past the other ticket agencies and find an **FRS** office (☎05 39 94 26 12 Ⓢ *Ferries 370dh per person, 930dh per car.* ⓉXI *Open 8am-11pm)* just before you enter the terminal. Make sure to get your customs form from a uniformed officer inside the terminal, and not from the men outside who will charge you 10dh.

GETTING AROUND

By Taxi

You can walk almost everywhere you want to go, but for faster jaunts in and around the city, take a **petit taxi** (small blue hatch-backs) and for longer distances like the airport, take a **grand taxi** (larger beige sedans). Since Moroccans share their *petit taxis,* don't be surprised if your driver pulls over to pick up passengers while you're in the car, and feel free to hail an already-occupied cab; if the passengers are heading in your direction, climb on in. But remember, in a *petit taxi,* passengers each pay the full fare. Make sure the *conteur* (meter) is running and don't pay more than 10-15dh for the farthest rides (e.g., 4km away) to the train station. The fare in a *grand taxi,* on the other hand, can be shared; in a *grand taxi* filled to capacity with six people, aim to bargain for a price of 20dh per person. There are *grand taxi* stands everywhere, especially by the **Grand Socco** and the intersection of **Blvd. Pasteur and Blvd. Mohammed V.**

FÈS AND MEKNÈS

It's time get royal. Like Marrakesh and Rabat, Fès and Meknès were once pretty big deals. As the tour guides and street venders here will constantly tell you, these are Imperial Cities. Fès was the capital of both the Idrisid and Marinid dynasties, and today it's the site of the Merenid tombs. To the southwest, Meknès was chosen by Sultan Moulay Ismail as his capital in the 17th century. He outfitted his kingly crib with the grand Bab al-Mansour gate, miles of imposing ramparts, and a royal palace—all of which still stand today.

However, while Meknès might have the most bureacratic bling to show for its time as a capital city, in a game of "My Medina is Better Than Yours," Fès wins. Every damn time. It truly is a site for sore eyes (UNESCO certainly thinks so), but don't discount the medina in Meknès. It was once the capital of the Moroccan empire, and sultans aren't known for keeping things simple. As with all parts of Morocco, this region has something for everybody, from camels to cocoa—get after it.

greatest hits

- **WORK THAT SHIT.** That's quite literally what they do at the ⬛Tanneries in Fez, where fecal matter, cow hides, and pee are only part of the cocktail that goes into making those leather pumps you love so much (p. 429).
- **THE SUN NEVER SETS ON MOULAY'S EMPIRE.** Well, actually, it does—the sunset on Bab al-Mansour gate is absolutely stunning (p. 437).
- **I'LL HAVE THE PU-PU PLATTER.** Actually, if you're eating at Restaurant Milles Nuits et Une Nuit, you'll probably want to try something a little more Moroccan like their *pastillas* or *tajines* (p. 439).

It's 9pm, and you're walking along **ave. Hassan II** in Fès. A warm breeze passes through the palm fronds as you stroll past young couples and families. It's not your traditional nightlife scene, but this is Fès. If you (and hopefully that special someone) get tired of strolling, pop into one of the many budget friendly cafes in the *ville nouvelle* before heading back to your hostel. You may not be dancing the night away, but if you're with the right person, we're sure you'll find something to keep you busy. When you're done with that and looking for some time outside the city, the Middle Atlas region has great towns like Ifrane that will make you forget you're in Africa. Roman ruins, and ski chalets—certainly a change of pace.

fès *fez* ☎05 35

Fès's medina is sensory overload at its finest. Enter through the cobalt blue gates of the **Bab Boujeloud** and **marhaba**, and submerge yourself in an eighth-century medieval maze that is as complex as it is spectacular. Donkeys rush by with refrigerators on their backs, old men weave carpets and dance around dye pits with huge stacks of leather, children lead bewildered tourists out of alleyways, and everyone is selling something.

    Of course, the medina isn't the only reason to visit Fès, although it's definitely the best one. Known historically as the spiritual, artistic, and intellectual capital of Morocco, Fès is an imperial city that boasts a massive royal palace, world-renowned music festivals, and a growing *ville nouvelle* that combines cosmopolitan boulevards, ancient ruins and gorgeous public gardens. Whether you are looking for chaotic or peaceful, medieval or modern, Fès packs it all into what is certainly one of Morocco's most enjoyable and least navigable cities.

ORIENTATION

Fès is divided into three main areas: the French-built **ville nouvelle**, the Arab-built **Fez al-Jdid** (New Fès) with the royal palace of King Hassan II and the old Jewish quarter, and the medina of **Fez al-Bali** (Old Fès).

Ville Nouvelle

The two most important streets that intersect the *ville nouvelle* are **Av. Hassan II** and **Blvd. Mohammed V.** Hassan II is a grand four-lane road split in two by rows of trees; Fassi families habitually stroll by its fountains in the evening. It crosses Blvd. Mohammed V at the *ville nouvelle's* central hub, **Pl. de Florence.** Most of the best budget accommodations, restaurants, and services in the *ville nouvelle* are to be found along Blvd. Mohammed V as it stretches away from Pl. de Florence and toward the next city square (which is actually a circle) called **Pl. Mohammed V.**

Fès al-Jdid

Heading north along Av. Hassan II toward Fès al-Jdid leads to **Pl. de la Resistance.** Continuing to the left along **Av. Moulay Youssef** brings you to **Pl. Alaouites** directly in front of the imposing and heavily guarded royal palace, **Dar al-Makhzen,** with bronze gates. Fès al-Jdid is dominated by this royal palace, which is neighbored by the old Jewish quarter, or **mellah,** with its cemetery of white gravestones overlooking the surrounding hills. Enter the *mellah* to the right of the royal palace and take **Rue des Merinides** until it hits the gate of **Bab Smarine.** Once past this gate, **Rue Fez al-Jdid** follows

fès and meknès

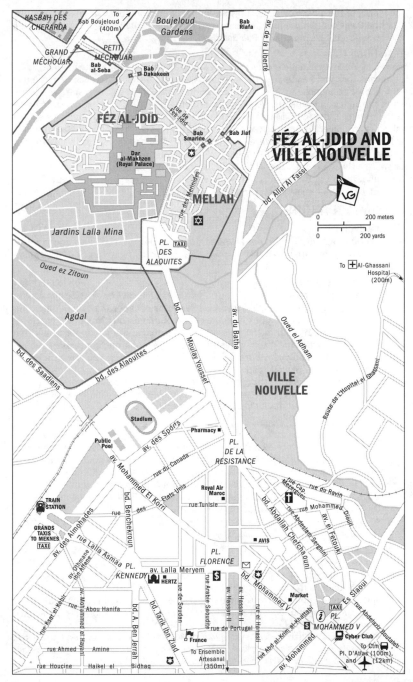

KASBAH DES CHERARDA

To Bab Boujeloud (400m)

Bab Boujeloud

Boujeloud Gardens

Bab Riafa

av. de la Liberté

GRAND MÉCHOUAR

PETIT MÉCHOUAR

Bab al-Seba

Bab Dakakeen

rue de Fès-Jdid

FÉZ AL-JDID

Bab Smarine

Bab Jiaf

FÉZ AL-JDID AND VILLE NOUVELLE

Dar al-Makhzen (Royal Palace)

rue des Merinides

MELLAH

bd. Allal Al Fassi

N

0   200 meters
0   200 yards

Jardins Lalla Mina

Oued ez Zitoun

PL. DES ALAOUITES

TAXI

To ✚ Al-Ghassani Hospital (200m)

Agdal

bd. des Saadiens

bd. des Alaouites

Moulay Youssef

bd.

av. du Batha

Oued el Adham

Route de l'Hôpital el Ghassani

VILLE NOUVELLE

Stadium

Public Pool

av. des Sports

Pharmacy

PL. DE LA RESISTANCE

rue du Canada

rue Cap. Mézergues

rue du Ravin

av. Mohammed El Korri

bd. Benchekroun

des

rue

rue Tunisie

Royal Air Maroc

bd. Abdallah Chefchaouni

rue Mohammed Diouri

rue Abdeslem Serghini

av. el Fetouki

TRAIN STATION

GRANDS TAXIS TO MEKNES

TAXI

av. des Almohades

rue Lalla Asmaa

PL. KENNEDY

av. Othmane ibn Affane

AVIS

PL. FLORENCE

av. Lalla Meryem

HERTZ

rue Arabie Saoudite

bd. Mohammed V

av. Hassan II

av. Mohammed V

Market

TAXI

i

PL. MOHAMMED V

Cyber Club

To Ctm

rue Es Siaoui

rue Abdelaziz Boutaleb

rue Ahmed

rue Ksar el Kebir

rue Mohammed el Hayani

Amine

Abou Hanifa

bd. A. Ben Jerrah

bd. Tarik Ibn Ziad

rue de Soudan

rue de Portugal

av. Hassan II

rue el Hanashi

rue Abd al-Krim al-Khattabi

av. Mohammed

France

To Ensemble Artesanal (350m)

Haikel el Bidhaq

rue Houcine

To Pl. D'Atlas (100m), and ✈ (12km)

the length of the palace on the left. At its end, a right through **Bab Dakakeen** takes you past the **Boujeloud gardens** and brings you to the wide **Pl. Boujeloud.** Downhill on the right is the medina's main gate, **Bab Boujeloud.**

Fès al-Bali (Medina)

Here's a tip: down usually means that you are heading deeper into the medina, while up means that you heading to its periphery. Other than this general advice, the medina is best conquered by knowing three main routes. The first two start when you enter through Bab Boujeloud. Right at the Bab, there's a fork in the road; **Tala'a Kebira** is the road to the left, and **Tala'a Seghira** is the road to the right. Whichever way you take, the two meet up again at a stretch of medina known as the **Attarine Market,** which is famed for the spices that were once sold there. Past the market is the **Qaraouiyine Mosque,** which is closed to non-Muslims. Whether you turn left or right at the Mosque or stick to the main drag (the widest and most crowded street), you'll make a circuit through a region of the medina known as **el Blida,** where many leather tanneries are located. Other than these basic directions, good luck.

ACCOMMODATIONS

Ville Nouvelle

Accommodations in the *ville nouvelle* tend to offer more cleanliness and comfort for your money, but are also a hike or *petit taxi* ride away from the medina's excitement.

👍 AUBERGE DES JEUNES HOSTEL [1]

18 rue de Abdeslam Serghini ☎05 35 62 40 85 💻www.fesyouth-hostel.com

For the young and weary, it doesn't get better or cheaper than this. A little out of the way, this hostel has immaculate beds, complimentary breakfast, sparkling showers that are cold in the hot summer months, and a shady garden with a neighborly turtle. Important rules like the 11pm lock-out constrain your autonomy, but the engaging staff is committed to welcoming you. There are only 37 beds, so reserve well in advance.

➜ From Pl. de la Resistance, it's down rue Abdeslam Serghini on the left. ℹ Breakfast and showers (hot Oct-May) included. Member of Youth Hostelling International. $ Dorms 55dh; singles 65dh. ⏰ Lockout 10am-noon. Curfew 11pm. Showers for men 8-9am, for women 9-10am.

HOTEL AMOR 🍸 HOTEL [2]

31 rue Arabie Saoudite ☎05 35 62 27 24

Hotel Amor gives you everything you need: decent decor, solar-powered showers with shockingly good water pressure, toilets, and comfy double beds even in singles. Showers are hottest in the evenings, and the three lightbulbs are somehow not enough to properly light up the rooms. You might pay a few dirhams extra, but the amenities and near-perfect location in Pl. de Florence are worth it. Oh, and there's a bar downstairs. Enough said.

➜ One street off Pl. de Florence. $ Singles 161dh; doubles 185dh. Prices may vary according to the season. ⏰ Reception closes at midnight.

HOTEL ROYAL HOSTEL [1]

36 rue de Soudan ☎ 05 35 62 46 56

Centrally located just off Pl. de Florence and directly across from a *lycée* where you can hang with Fès's rowdy high schoolers. Yellowing rooms are comfortable and spacious enough for you and the occasional cockroach. As a plus, there are showers in the rooms, with communal European toilets and toilet paper just down the hall.

➜ 5min. from the train station. Heading towards Pl. de Florence along Av. Lalla Meryem, turn left up the first street past the Mosque. Hotel on your right. ℹ Pay upfront. $ Singles 100dh; doubles 140dh. ⏰ Reception closes at midnight. Showers hot 7-11am.

Fès al-Jdid

Although there's less going on in Fès al-Jdid than in the medina and the *ville nouvelle*, the location is an ideal base of operations for travelers that want to be equidistant from Fès's modern and medieval attractions.

HOTEL AGADIR

92 Bab Jief

🌐 HOTEL ❶

☎05 35 94 27 25 92

Six well-scrubbed rooms near the royal palace. Communal toilets without toilet paper, but the showers are hot. The tin roof in places provides natural lighting and sets low expectations. It ain't royal, but the rooms are cheap and situated neatly between the medina and the *ville nouvelle*. Call to reserve.

🍴 *Just to the right of Barb Smarine outside of the Mellah.* Ⓢ *Singles 55dh; doubles 100dh; triples 130dh.* 🕑 *Receptions closes midnight-2am depending on the season.*

Fès al-Bali

Like the medina itself, accommodations here can sometimes be run-down, but they usually do the trick. Budget hostels cluster around **Bab Boujeloud,** although *pensions* can be found everywhere in the medina's narrow streets. Some travelers report successfully bargaining for prices, especially in the late afternoon when it's less likely that a vacant room will be filled. However, vacancies can be hard to come by in the high season, so making a reservation beforehand is safer.

PENSION TALAA

14 Talaa Seghira

🌐 HOSTEL ❶

☎05 35 63 33 59

This immaculate pension is a tight squeeze, with narrow halls, vertigo-inducing stairs, and rooms the size of the beds. But the warm-hearted staff, cozy bedding, and perfect distance from the tourist mobs are more than worth it. Add in spiffy new showerheads that make you actually want to clean yourself, and you've got a real diamond in the rough. However, like most shiny objects in the sand, this place is small and in high demand—reserve ahead of time.

🍴 *Enter the medina through Bab Boujeloud and follow the right fork (Talaa Seghira, not the left-hand Talaa Kebira) for 5-10min. Look for the Pension's sign on your right.* 𝒊 *Reservations recommended.* Ⓢ *Singles 75dh; doubles 150dh; triples 225dh.*

HOTEL CASCADE

26 Serrajine Boujeloud

🌐 HOSTEL ❶

☎05 35 63 84 42

Designed for true backpacker types who can sleep just about anywhere and have the knotted dreads to prove it, this huge and slightly crumbling hotel located right on Bab Boujeloud is a social hub for travelers from the world over. Bare-bones rooms come with toilets *sans* toilet paper and hot communal showers. If you really want to rough it, you can sleep in the makeshift cafe/restaurant on the terrace *(tea 5dh, fixed menu 60dh)* for a mere 50dh.

🍴 *Just inside Bab Boujeloud.* Ⓢ *Terrace 50dh. Singles 80dh; doubles 160dh; triples 240dh.*

HOTEL BAB BOUJELOUD

49 Pl. Iscesco Kasbat Boujeloud

🌐((•))❄ HOTEL ❷

☎05 35 63 31 18 📧www.hotelbabboujeloud.com

Less than a year old, and an absolute luxury given the price. Singles are big enough for two and come with a bath, TV, A/C, Wi-Fi, and overwhelming tan decor. Built around a small interior courtyard with a rooftop terrace for lounging, this first-class hotel is as refreshing as the cold drinks on offer at reception.

🍴 *50m down the street from Bab Boujeloud. Big blue sign, so you can't miss it.* 𝒊 *Free Wi-Fi.* Ⓢ *Singles 200dh; doubles 350dh; triples 450dh.*

SIGHTS

Fès Al-Bali

The Medina

No one ever said that conquering Fès al-Bali's famed medina would be easy. In this nest of 9000 unmarked streets, many of them more like alleys, the ordinary and extraordinary sights are only half the experience. Getting lost and finding your way is the other half. The easiest way to get to know the medina is with an official multilingual guide, who can be hired at the **Syndicat d'Initiative.** An experienced guide will save you time, discourage hustlers, and provide detailed information about the medina. *($ half-day 150dh, full-day 250dh.)* Unofficial or faux guides are officially illegal, and they are generally a much less reliable source of information. Whomever you hire, know the price right off the bat and nail down an itinerary that interests you, since guides will often take visitors to stores where they receive commission. The more intrepid among you will find that with a little research, the medina can be conquered (well, explored) without a guide. To keep hustlers at bay, ignore the cat calls and hisses and simply say *non, merci* or *la shukran* to those who approach you directly. Remember: generally speaking, walking downhill will take you farther into the medina, while trekking uphill will lead you out. The madness abates somewhat under the noonday sun, and beware wandering the streets at night.

TANNERIES — TANNERY

What process uses cobalt oxide, cedarwood, pigeon poop, cow urine, water, and weeks of human labor? You got it: tanning and dying leather. Fès al-Bali's leather tanneries are some of the most popular attractions in the medina, and offer a window into a painstaking practice that has remained the same for more than a millennium. Pay a few dirhams to climb up the stairs of a leather shop (and a little extra for a sprig of mint to mask the smell of decaying animal parts) and you can look down at old men standing knee deep in a catacomb of red and white pits, working arduously with sheep hides. Dyes are all *au naturel*, coming from poppy flowers, indigo, henna, and grapeskins. Feel free to take pictures of this unbelievable spectacle. When you try to leave, be prepared for a salesman to pounce. Unless you're armed for a bargaining battle, find the nearest exist.

There are 2 regions to find leather tanneries. The first is a small tannery located just around the corner from the Nejjarine Art Museum. Follow the signs outside of the museum. The second is the large stretch of Chouara tanneries. To get there, turn left at the end of Tala'a Kebira and follow the winding road until you reach a T-junction. Turn right and follow the signs to the Chouara tanneries, or wait to be accosted by a tannery "guardien," who will lead you up to the terraces of a leather store. $ Haggle for the price; 2-20dh depending on the season. ⏰ Open daily.

BOU INANIA MEDERSA — ISLAMIC SCHOOL,

It is said that when Sultan Abu Inan was given the bill for the *medersa's* construction, he tore it up and threw it into the river that crossed the courtyard, claiming that no price could be put on such beauty. And indeed, this 14th-century *medersa* (a.k.a. madrasa, or religious school), built between 1350 and 1356, is Morocco's finest. Stunning stucco, glorious *zellij* tilework, complex carved-cedar craftsmanship, and flowing Qur'anic inscriptions—the *medersa's* captivating courtyard is decked out in invoice-inducing luxuries that you truly shouldn't put a price on (if only because the number of zeroes would make you rip up the bill, too.) It's still a functioning mosque, and one of the few that allows non-Muslims inside.

As you walk down Tala'a Kebira from Bab Boujeloud, Bou Inania will be on your right in 100m. $ 10dh. ⏰ Open daily 9am-6pm.

ATTARINE SOUQ (MARKET)   MARKET

Named for a word that denotes fragrance and spice, this 600m stretch of medina once housed 150-170 shops brimming with medicinal products. These remedies were sold to physicians at the Maristan Sidi Frej, located in the Henna *Souq* at the beginning of the Attarine *Souq*, where depressed people were treated with music, spices, and sex (we approve). In fact, the first psychiatric hospital in the Western world, opened in Valencia in 1410, was modeled on this treatment plan. The Henna *Souq*, named for the dye that local women wear on their hands and feet for weddings, still sells a little of its namesake, but both the Henna and Attarine *Souq*s are dominated today by less exciting modern shops selling knock-off watches.

⚡ *Take Tala'a Kebira past its junction with Tala'a Seghira and you'll have to run into the market.*

Fès al-Jdid

Located squarely between the medina and the *ville nouvelle*, the Fès al-Jdid was built in the 13th century by the Merenid sultan Youssef Yacoub to fortify himself against the world. The enormous **Dar al-Makhzen,** the royal palace, is the gargantuan legacy. One of King Mohammed VI's homes, the palace is heavily guarded and not open to the public. Nevertheless, you should go right up and examine the gorgeous brass doors at the end of the plaza. An icon of Morocco, they were made by artisans of Fès in 1968 and the prevalence of cobalt blue represents Fassi pride.

To the right of the palace is the **mellah,** the old Jewish quarter of Fès. In the 14th century, the city's Jews were relocated here to offer them greater protection—and to more easily tax them. Just before the entrance to the *mellah* is the ▨**Jewish cemetery,** which is the final resting place of over 2000 people. (Ⓢ *Donations recommended.* ▢ *Open dawn-dusk.*) The rows of white tombstones overlooking the hills, and the candles lit by visitors, mark the site as a spiritually significant relic of the once impressive Jewish presence in Fès. Among some families, it is still customary for Moroccan Jews living on foreign soil to be buried with their ancestors in the cemetery. Look out especially for the mausoleum of Soulika, a 14-year-old Jewish woman who was assassinated after refusing to marry the local prince and convert to Islam. After visiting the cemetery, the *mellah* is best explored along **Rue des Merinides.** To the right along rue des Merinides is the recently restored **Ibn Danan Synagogue** with its own Torah scroll and ritual bath, or *mikveh*, still occupied by rain water. (*Knock during the day for the guardian to open the synagogue. 20dh to enter.*)

At the end of the *mellah* is **Bab Smarine,** the gate to **Rue de Fez al-Jdid,** which is a sight in and of itself. Choked with clothing stories, locals flood the area in the evening, and the gateway quickly becomes an impassable mass of women bargaining for robes and young men calling out their wares like auctioneers. Turn left at the end of rue de Fès al-Jdid ino the **Pétit Méchouar.** On the left is **Bab Dakakeen,** the back entrance to the Dar al-Makhzen. Out Bab Dakakeen and to the right is **Av. Moulay Hassan**, which leads to the massive **Boujeloud Gardens.** Past **Bab Chems** is the open square of **Pl. Boujeloud** and finally, the blue gate to the medina.

Beyond the Medina

▨ **BORJ NORD AND THE MERENID TOMBS**   ◉ MUSEUM, RUINS

☎Museum: 05 35 64 75 66

The hills above Bab Boujeloud are, without a doubt, one of the best spots in all of Fès. For a museum experience, you can head to the Borj Nord, a 16th century fortress that displays suits of armor, sabers, cannons, and all kinds of arms from Morocco and 35 other countries. But better than the museum is scrambling up on the hills beyond the Borj to the Merenid Tombs, ruins dating from the collapse of the Merenid dynasty in 1415. Spectacularly old and neglected, the decaying red arches, pillars, and slabs are amazingly accessible. From the hills,

Fès and meknès

the panorama of the city is stunning in the half-light of dusk and during calls to prayer, when over a hundred *muezzin* summon the faithful, the experience is almost mystical.

Take a petit taxi from Bab Boujeloud for 5dh or walk uphill away from Bab Boujeloud. When you reach the traffic circle at the highway, continue straight uphill. At the next intersection turn right and walk beside the strip of park until the Borj. You'll know it as the giant fortress. The Merenid Tombs are further along the road on the other side of the resort hotel Les Merinides. $ Museum 10dh. ⏰ Museum open in summer T-Su 8:30am-6:30pm; in winter Tu-Su 8:30am-5pm.

MUSÉE DAR BATHA MUSEUM, GARDENS

Pl. Batha

The Dar Batha Museum is a massive 19th century Andalusian mansion that is 60% gardens. With a comparatively small collection of "ethnographic art" (read: clothes, instruments, and Qur'anic inscriptions that people used in their ordinary lives a long time ago), it's the architecture and greenery that are worth the price of admission. The grand building hosted Sultan Hassan I and his son, Moulay Abd al-Aziz, during the last years of decadence before the French occupation. The magnificent gardens contain old and immense trees labeled according to their genus and species, including cypresses, myrtles, and palms and among the art, pottery displaying the signature cobalt "Fès blue" are most striking.

Start at Bab Boujeloud and take Av. de la Liberté. Turn right at the street with Hotel Batha on the corner and head to the archway below the single Moroccan flag. $ 10dh. ⏰ Open M 9am-6pm, W-Su 9am-6pm.

FOOD

Ville Nouvelle

Yummy and low-cost food is plentiful in the *ville nouvelle*, especially along **Blvd. Mohammed V.** You'll find pastry and sandwich shops, as well as the occasional Italian joint. To buy your own food there is a daily market (*8am-2pm*) on Blvd. Mohammed V that sells fruits, vegetables, flowers, meat, and some giant fish.

CAFE CENTRAL PARC CAFE 2

Jardin Lalla Amina ☎ 05 35 65 06 61

Situated in the center of the lovely *Jardin Lalla Amina*, tall palms and spreading flowers surround this cafe. Local and international students take advantage of the free Wi-Fi and tourists come for the tasty food. Perfect for a meal, a strong cup of Moroccan coffee, or riding your tricycle with the other kids in the park.

Walking down Blvd. Mohammed V toward Pl. Mohammed, turn left on the street past the Market and continue straight until the park. $ Coffee 9dh. Breakfast 22dh. Sandwiches 30dh. Tajine 40dh. Ice cream 9dh per scoop. ⏰ Open daily 7:30am-11pm.

PIZZERIA CHEZ VITTORIO ITALIAN, BISTRO 2

21 rue Brahim Roudani ☎ 05 35 62 47 30

This pizzeria provides delicious Italian and a guilty break from routine *tajines*. Hearty tomato sauce, plentiful Parmesan, cheesy goodness, or a sizzling steak if you can afford it. Red curtains allow the *vino* to flow freely without detracting from the family feel.

Next door to Snack Chez Hamza. $ Pizza or pasta 60-75dh. Entrees 100-130dh. Beer 25dh. 10% service charge. ⏰ Open daily noon-3pm and 7pm-midnight.

Fès al-Bali

Quite simply, you'll never go hungry in the medina. There are palatial restaurants, cheap *tajines*, camel-kebab stalls and mobile cantaloupe carts all over the place. *Harira* (*spicy lentil soup 10dh*) typically comes with potatoes and bread, and you can always play it safe with sandwiches (*15-20dh*). Just like everything else in the medina, food prices are up for bargaining.

Many of the medina's food stalls can be found on **Tala'a Kebira** and **Tala'a Seghira,** while some of Morocco's cheapest grub is in and near the **Attarine Market.** To leave the beaten path and get away from the other tourists, you can always wander down an alley in search of someplace really local. Just be prepared to get lost.

👍 CAFE LA NORIA — 🍴⛅ MOROCCAN, CAFE ❷

food you can stomach

Between the mix of French and Arabic, it can be sometimes confusing to decipher a menu in Morocco. Here are the basic foods that you can order without your stomach punishing you.

Tajin: This dish is a meat combo with cooked dates and vegetables. Its slow roasted over coals in a pointed ceramic dish. You may be confused what a pointed dish looks like, until you see one. Trust us, you'll know. Local meats such as beef and lamb go well with the dish, but be careful since its served hot enough to melt flesh.

Pastilla: This is pronounced "bastiyya" and its an elaborate meat pie. Its usually made with, um... how do we put this gently? [?] **baby pigeons**, but its also made more commonly with chicken. The top of the pie is covered in powdered sugar and cinnamon, making it a strange, but oddly tasty meal.

Couscous: For the vegetarians, this is a safe option that lacks weird meat, unless you order it with sausage. Its made with spherical granules made by rolling semolina wheat. A **Couscous Royale** is one with everything plus the kitchen sink.

Börek: Not like the Kazak movie star, this is a filled pastry. The flaky crust will get everywehre and so will its filling of either cheese, meats, or veggies.

43

Btatha, Fès al-Jdid — ☎05 35 65 42 55

With a trellis weighed down by bushels of grapes and a brook flowing beneath the stone floor, La Noria is more like a secret garden than a cafe. You can sip mint tea at outdoor tables beside chatting Japanese tourists or dine on Moroccan specialties in the attached restaurant. You'll pay a bit more for the idyllic scenery, but the peace and quality are a refreshing respite from the medina's bazaars.

🧭 Heading towards the medina at the end of rue Fès al-Jdid just past Bab Dakakeen. Turn right at the black sign pointing into a side street and the cafe is 100 meters up on the left. $ Drinks 6-10dh. Prix fixe menu 80-200dh. Entrees 55-120dh. ⏰ Open daily 6pm-midnight.

RESTAURANT BOUANANIA — 🍴⛅ MOROCCAN ❶

8-6 Tala'a Kebira — ☎05 35 74 04 69

Once a cafe where old men played Moroccan card games, this heavily carpeted restaurant offers the same fare as other eateries by the Bab, but is happily shielded around the corner from the chaos of the tourist mobs. It offers the usual *tajines* or couscous, an unusual chicken coop outside, and a terrace upstairs.

🧭 Enter through Bab Boujeloud, turn left onto Tala'a Kebira and the restaurant is on your left. $ Prix fixe menu for 60dh. Tajine, Coucous 40dh. ⏰ 10am-11pm.

ARTS AND CULTURE 🎵

Pottery, Carpets, and Metalwork

👍 KHAYAR DRISS'S BRONZES — 🛍 CHINA

30 Souiket Dehbane — ☎06 62 48 18 35

If you manage to find it, this shop in the middle of the medina is nothing short of extraordinary. Cross the threshold and you'll find local artisan Omar hunched over a bronze plate, his eyes fixed on the metal as he painstakingly engraves intricate designs with a small hammer. The labor is so intense that it can only be humanly sustained for three to four hours each day. As the ebullient owner, Khayar Driss, will quickly explain, each of Omar's plates takes two weeks to complete. It was supposedly his father who created the doors to the royal palace. The way these works of art shine, it wouldn't be surprising.

Good luck. This small shop is located just off the Achabine Market in the Fondouq Lihoudi (the old Jewish neighborhood) of the medina. The easiest way to get there is to start at Bab Guissa. At the gate, take middle fork of three several hundred feet downhill to an open market. This is Achabine. Turn left and keep your eyes absolutely peeled for the next right turn. You'll see metal wares in a shop with no sign. Alternatively, take Tala'a Kebira until the Attarine Market. At the T turn left and ask someone for "Souq Laghzal." Turn left into this Souq and the store is a few feet in. $ Prices from 100-800dh.

QUARTIER DES POTIERS POTTERY

Charcoal-black smoke wafts above the Pottery Quarter, an artisan's neighborhood located to the east of Fès just inside Bab al-Ftouh. The smoke is produced by burning ground olive pits to temperatures of 1200 degrees Celsius; these extreme temperatures heat the kilns that bake soft gray clay into Fès's gorgeous ceramic wares. Inside the quarter is a massive government cooperative called **Poterie de Fes** (*32 Ain Noukbi, ☎ 05 35 76 16 29*). Ask for a tour of the facility, and you can watch potters gently mold *tajine* vessels on their wheels, or hammer away at multi-colored tiles to create mosaics. At the back of the factory is an exhibit room filled floor to ceiling with ceramics; everything from miniature sugar bowls to mosaic fountains.

The Pottery Quarter is located to the east of Fès towards Taza. It is best reached by taking a petit taxi for 15 dh from the ville nouvelle. i Prices are fixed. $ 50-500dh. ⏰ Open daily 8:30am-7pm.

he called me a berber!

The Berbers were natives of Morocco, before the Arabs took over in the 1300s. The Moroccans have hypocritical feelings about Berbers, since most of the population is Berber, and even the King is half Berber, yet they still look at Berbers as inferior. As a manner of public relations, the King always takes at least one full-blooded Berber wife. How does this relate to you? Well, if after a vigorous haggling for that rug/teapot/useless thing, you are called a Berber, they are calling you cheap and shifty. Congrats. You are a decent negotiator.

SHOPPING

As anyone hawking goods in the medina will tell you, Fès is the artisanal capital of Morocco, and the city is especially famous for cobalt blue pottery, Berber rugs and carpets, intricate metalwork, and fine leather from the stinky tanneries. You can get just about anything here from henna to herbal remedies for aging and impotence, daggers to brass tea services. Quality ranges from handmade artisanry to shoddy, mass-produced stuff, but discerning the difference can be difficult for the untrained eye. In general, the stores along **Tala'a Kebira** offer cheaper but lower-quality items, while the *funduqs* (old *caravanserais* or hotels for traveling merchants) that are now specialty stores selling much better goods at higher prices. Bargain at a few stores before buying anything to get an idea of what something is worth. The first offer is always too high, and usually twice what the item is actually worth; you normally won't get a good deal until the price is lowered a third or fourth time.

ESSENTIALS

You'll have no trouble finding essentials in Fès, since even the medieval medina is fully wired with ATMs and internet cafes. For late-night practical needs (not those romantic ones), the *ville nouvelle* is the place to go.

Practicalities

- **TOURIST OFFICE: Syndicat d'Initiative**. Worth a visit if you're willing to probe for information. Excellent map of Fès's labyrinthine medina with color-coded thematic walking tours. Colors happily correspond to signage on the actual routes. (*Pl. Mohammed V.* ☎*05 35 62 34 60.* Ⓢ Official guides on hire 150dh per half-day, 250dh per day. *i It is advisable to pay for an experienced official guide, especially if you split the bill with friends. Just make sure to read up on the medina first, so that you can be in charge of your own tour. Ⓣ Open M-F 8:30am-4:30pm.*)

- **CURRENCY EXCHANGE: BMCE.** Handles MC/V and traveler's check transactions. Has **ATMs.** (*Pl. Mohammed V, opposite the Syndicat d'Initiative and to the right of the main bank entrance. Ⓣ Open M-F 8:15am-3:45pm. Pl. de forence has branches of most Moroccans banks and ATMs can be found frequently throughout the ville nouvelle and the medina.*)

- **LUGGAGE STORAGE:** There is a *Consigne* for storing luggage at the **Private Bus Station.** (Ⓢ *3dh per day until 9am the next morning. Ⓣ Open 6am-11pm.*)

- **INTERNET ACCESS:** Just look for a "Cyber" sign. **Cyber Club** (*1 block south of Pl. Mohammed V above the teleboutique. Ⓣ 10dh per hr. Ⓣ Open daily 10am-11pm.*)

- **POST OFFICE:** The main office is at the corner of Av. Hassan II and Blvd. Mohammed V in the *ville nouvelle* with branch offices in Fès al-Jdid and Fès al-Bali. Western Union inside the post office. (☎*05 35 62 24 60* Ⓣ *Open M-F 8am-4pm, Sa 8:30-11:30am.*)

Emergency!

- **EMERGENCY NUMBERS: Police:** ☎19. **Ambulance:** ☎15.

- **POLICE:** One station located at the corner of Av. Mohammed V and rue Allal Laoudiyi.

- **LATE-NIGHT PHARMACY: Pharmacie Liberté.** (*Av. Moulay Youssef at Pl. de la Résistanc.* ☎ *05 35 62 19 73* Ⓣ *Open M-F 8:30am-12:30pm and 4:30-8:30pm, Sa 8:30am-1:30pm. Just outside the door on the left wall is a list of rotating pharmacies that stay open 24 hours.*)

- **HOSPITAL: Al-Ghassani.** (*In the Dar al-Mahrez district east of town. From Pl. Mohammed V, walk down Av. Mohammed Siaoui as it becomes Ben Arbi Alaoui for 15 min., and then turn left on Av. al-Ghassani.* ☎ *05 35 62 27 77.*)

Getting There

By Plane

Aéroport de Fès-Saïs. (☎*05 35 62 48 00* ✈ *16km out of the city.*) Bus **#16** leaves from Pl. Mohammed V to the airport (Ⓢ*3dh*). *Grand taxis* 120dh. Flights daily to **Casablanca, Tangier, Marrakesh, Marseilles, London,** and **Paris.**

By Train

Gare Ferrovière or **Gare de Fes,** at the intersection of **Av. Almohades** and **Av. Leila Meryem,** 10min. walk from **Pl. de Florence** (☎*05 35 93 03 33 for station; for national ONCF line* ☎*08 90 20 30 40).* A 4dh *petit taxi* ride to the *ville nouvelle*, or 10dh to the medina's **Bab Bou-**

jeloud. Second-class tickets are a bit pricier than bus fare, but offer relative comfort and style. To: **Meknes** (Ⓢ 20dh. ⏰ 45min., every hr. 4:50am-10:50pm); **Rabat** (3hr., every hr. 4:50am-10:50pm, 80dh) **Casablanca** (4hr., every hr. from 4:50am-6:50pm, 110dh); **Marrakesh** (Ⓢ 195dh. ⏰ 7hr., every 2hr. 2:30am-4:50pm); **Tangier** (Ⓢ 105dh. ⏰ 5hr., 4 per day).

By Bus

CTM ☎05 35 73 29 92. At **Pl. d'Atlas**, a 15min. walk down Blvd. Mohammed V away from the center of the *ville nouvelle*. Turn left at Av. Youssef ben Tachfine and take the first right at Pl. d'Atlas. To: **Casablanca** (Ⓢ100dh ⏰ 4hr., 8 per day 7-2am); **Rabat** (Ⓢ 70dh ⏰ 4hr., 8 per day 7-2am); **Meknes** (Ⓢ 20-25dh ⏰ 1hr., 5 per day 10:30am-11pm); **Tanger** (Ⓢ100-110dh ⏰ 6hr., 4 per day 10:30am-11pm); **Marrakesh** (Ⓢ 150dh ⏰ 9hr.; 6:30am and 8pm). The **private bus station** of **Gare Routière** is located just outside of the medina near **Bab Boujeloud** and beneath the **Borj Nord**. It seems to have been designed to generate maximum confusion, with few signs, no centralized schedules, multiple windows for different destinations and last-minute passengers running to catch moving buses. But for the spendthrift traveler, the prices are lower than **CTM**.

Getting Around

By Taxi

As in other Moroccan cities, *grand taxis* are used to travel beyond the city limits, while *petit taxis* travel everywhere within the city. *Grand taxis* to the airport cost 120dh, to **Meknes** 20dh per person, and to **Rabat** 70dh per person. Fès's red *petit taxis* are an inexpensive and abundant resource for getting anywhere the average visitor needs to go. Hail a *petit taxi* on the street, or visit *grand taxi* stands located at the train station in the *ville nouvelle* and the private bus station by the medina. For *petit taxis*, ensure that the *conteur* (meter) is used, and note that fares increase 50% after 8pm in the winter, and 50% after 9 pm in the summer.

By Public Transit

You should be able to walk or take a *petit taxi* wherever you need to go, but for frequent bus service, important routes include: **#9** from the **Syndicat d'Initiative** to **Dar Batha; #11** from the Syndicat d'Initiative to **Bab Boujeloud; #19** from the train station to **Pl. Rcif** in the middle of Fès al-Bali; and **#47** from the train station to **Bab Boujeloud.** Fare is 3dh per person.

meknès

Maybe it's the Meknesi friendliness. Maybe it's just the air. But despite a population approaching one million, Meknes welcomes its visitors like a small town. When compared to its bigger and better-known brothers, Meknes has the best of both worlds: small town warmth and tranquility with vibrant big city attractions.

Meknes epitomizes Moroccan living, from the golden alleys of the medina to the classy boulevards of the *ville nouvelle*. Enjoy the merrymaking crowds of Place el-Hedim in the evening, the jaw-droppingly gorgeous Mausoleum of Moulay Ismail in the Imperial City, the nightlife on Av. Mohammed V and, of course, the medina's madness and fresh food bazaars. If you have time, a side-trip to the Roman ruins of Volubilis, only 33 km north of the city, makes for a sweet archaeological escapade.

ORIENTATION

Meknès is split into three main areas: the cosmopolitan *ville nouvelle*, which provides travelers with essentials, restaurants, and nightlife; the old-world **medina's** markets and eateries; and the **Imperial City** of Sultan Moulay Ismail. The medina and Imperial City are on one side of Meknes, and the *ville nouvelle* is on the other. The areas are connected by the central road of **Av. Moulay Ismail.**

Ville Nouvelle

The *ville nouvelle* is comprised of a grid of main streets. **Rue Emir Abdelkader,** where the **train station** is located, **Av. Mohammed V,** and **Blvd. Allal ben Abdellah** are three parallel roads filled with budget hotels and restaurants. At one end, they are bounded by the highway of **Av. des FAR.** The CTM station is located several blocks along this avenue away from the city center. At the other end, they meet **Av. Hassan II,** which is the *ville nouvelle's* central line leading to the medina. Av. Hassan II becomes **Av. Moulay Ismail** as it descends past public gardens to the medina. Towards the medina on Av. Hassan II, the administrative hub of **Pl. de l'Istiqlal** with the Tourist Office, banks and post office are on the left, while the youth hostel is a ways up on the right.

Medina

Past the public gardens and traffic circle, Av. Moulay Ismail meets with **Rue Rouamzine,** which curves to the right, then left and finally opens up at **Place el-Hedim.** This is the medina's main square and a traveler's main landmark. It is a fabulous and popular spot in the pink hues of evening time. At the end of Pl. el-Hedim is the entrance to Meknes' medina. Immediately across from the square is the imposing **Bab al-Mansour** gate to the Imperial City, although the actual entrance is a side gate earlier along rue Rouamzine. Once inside the City, the main road is **Rue Palais**. If you continue along Rouamzine past Bab al-Mansour you will hit the mellah, or old Jewish quarter. To the left is the **Gare Routière**.

ACCOMMODATIONS

Meknes' best budget options are predominantly in the *ville nouvelle.* Although the medina has the excellent **Hotel Maroc,** otherwise it can be slim pickings. **Hotel Touring** is central and extremely well-priced, while the **Auberge de Jeunes** is the place to make friends.

Ville Nouvelle

HOTEL MAJESTIC — HOTEL ❸

19 Av. Mohammed V — ☎05 35 52 20 35

It's majestic, even for the price tag, and an old *Let's Go* favorite that's been maintained with care over the years. The dark wood in the lobby exudes elegance, and the refinement just keeps going as you move up the grand staircase to halls with high ceilings and spotless rooms. There's a giant rooftop clothesline that bakes wet laundry in the sun, and a complimentary breakfast is served in the lobby restaurant.

On Av. Mohammed V 3 blocks from the train station. ℹ Breakfast included. $ Singles 191dh, with shower 241dh, with full bath 271dh; doubles 272dh/322/342; triples with full bath 479dh. Let's Go readers receive a 5% discount.

AUBERGE DE JEUNES — HOSTEL ❶

Rue Okba Ben Nafae — ☎05 35 52 46 98 www.hihostels.com

A 30min. walk to the medina isn't nothing, but Meknes' youth hostel is still *the* social hub of the *ville nouvelle* for young travelers passing through the Imperial city. Bungalow-style dorm rooms surround a garden of fruit trees. There's a lounge and a kitchen for communal bonding. The gracious staff fulfills their promise to help with sight-seeing and Moroccan living. It's best to reserve in advance.

Coming from the train station, turn right on Av. Mohammed V and walk straight until the second large traffic circle. Take the second road coming off the circle on your left, Av. al-Amir Moulay Abdallah. At the next confusing multiple intersection, turn 45 degrees right onto rue Okba Ben Nafae. Or, take a petit taxi for 5-10dh. ℹ Breakfast included. 60-person capacity. $ Dorms 55dh; doubles 140dh; triples 195dh; quads 240dh. Hot showers 7dh. ⏰ Open daily 8am-midnight. No lockout.

Medina

👍 HOTEL MAROC — HOTEL [2]

7 Av. Rouamzine — ☎05 35 53 00 75

Hotel Maroc rolls out the red carpets in its hallways for backpackers from around the world. Some of the paint may be peeling, but the colorful bedspreads are still vibrant and orange leaves burst through windows from the quiet courtyard. Mattresses on the terrace are there for the most budget conscious, and it's just a 5min. walk from Place al-Hedim.

➜ Walking towards the medina alone rue Rouamzine, look for an alley with the Hotel Maroc sign on your left. ℹ Breakfast 20dh. Toilet paper 4dh. $ Terrace 50dh; singles 100dh; doubles 200dh; triples 270dh.

SIGHTS

Medina

The golden walls, friendly faces, and manageable maze of Meknes' medina make for a wonderful few hours of ambling. Although there are sections stuffed with shops selling everything from *babouches* to DVDs, there are also stretches of simple neighborhood houses and schools. In fact, the best flea markets in Meknes are outside the medina. Head up **Rue Sekkakine** veering off to the left of **Pl. el-Hedim** and continue straight to the sales. Eventually, you'll hit **Bab el-Jdid gate** and re-enter the medina to find fish guts and other yummies everywhere. To locate **Medersa Bou Inania,** double-back to **Pl. el-Hedim** and enter the arch to the left of **Musée Dar Jamai.** Turn right at the T-junction with rue Najjarine until you reach the doors of the **Grande Mosquée,** which is off-limits to non-Muslims. Just down the street is the Bou Inania Medersa. This is prime wandering area, as there are various *souqs* and covered markets.

MEDERSA BOU INANIA — MADRASA

If you've seen the *medersa* in Fès al-Bali that bears the same name, you'll recognize much of the same gorgeous wood carving and *zellij* tilework. Both built by Sultan Bou Inan, Meknes' version was completed in 1358. On a good day, you might be the only one in the tranquil courtyard. You can sit down and read just as the 8 to 10 year olds once did in the sacred schoolhouse, or climb upstairs to check out their dorm rooms. Modern dorms might be bigger, but we've lost some of that magical architecture.

➜ Facing Musée Dar Jamai (next to the BMCI bank), turn right and enter the medina. At the next opportunity, turn left and continue to the Grand Mosqué. At the T-junction, turn left and the madrasa is straight ahead. $ 10dh. ⏰ Open daily 9am-5:30pm.

MUSÉE DAR JAMAI — CRAFTS MUSEUM

Pl. el-Hedim

Like the ragged cats that sunbathe in its courtyard, this building is on the fourth of its nine lives. It was first built as a home to the powerful Jamai family in 1889. Under the French protectorate it became a military hospital, then it did a brief stint as a judicial court. Now, in its latest incarnation, the palace and Andalusian gardens serve as a museum for Meknesi crafts of old. You can wander from room to room to see embroidery, Qur'anic manuscripts, horse-saddles and an entirely recreated traditional salon. Although fun for craft-lovers, the collection is comparatively small, as are the enclosed gardens.

➜ At the end of Pl. el-Hedim opposite Bab al-Mansour. $ 10dh. ⏰ Open M-Tu 9am-3pm, Th-Su 9am-3pm.

Imperial City

The beautiful gate of **Bab al-Mansour** looks best in the setting sun. At any time of day, it marks the entrance to Meknes' **Imperial City,** founded by Sultan Moulay Ismail in the 17th century. Although you can't walk through the Bab, you can enter through a modest gate next-door. The 25km ramparts contain everything from a royal palace to a golf course.

MAUSOLEUM OF MOULAY ISMAIL TOMB

Rue Palais

With only a small signpost 20ft from the entrance, and no one guarding the door, it's hard to know you're in the right place. Room after beautiful room of nothing makes things more confusing. Don't fear. You are walking through empty courtyards, intended to instill a clear mind and calm heart. And it works. By the time you reach the mausoleum and take off your shoes to enter, the grandeur makes an impact. With regal red carpeting, marble pillars, a chandelier positioned between two grandfather clocks, and of course, the tombs of Sultan Moulay Ismail and his family are the definition of silent majesty. You can't enter, but you and the other hushed tourists can peer inside.

Walk into the imperial city through the smaller gate next to Bab al-Mansour. Heading to your right, pass an open plaza and turn up rue Palais on your left. The mausoleum is through an unguarded and open door. ***i*** *Donations recommended.* ⏰ *Open M-Th and Sa-Sun 9am-1pm and 3-6pm.*

KOUBBAT AS-SUFARA HISTORIC MONUMENT

Pl. Lalla Aouda

Diplomacy was boring then and it still is, there's not much to see in this historical reception hall for foreign ambassadors. But the giant crypt next door is creepily awesome. It's unclear whether entrance to the crypt is free or not, even though you pay for the diplomatic tedium upstairs. See what happens. Informal guides will tell you elaborate stories about the crypt's history as a dungeon for Sultan Moulay Ismail's thousands of slaves. Unfortunately, the reality of one big pantry is less exciting than their tall tales.

Just inside the Imperial City and to the right. At the far edge of the open plaza you'll see before turning up rue Palais. $ *10dh.* ⏰ *Open daily 9am-6pm.*

fès and meknès

FOOD

Ville Nouvelle

The *ville nouvelle*'s culinary treats are distributed along the main streets of **Av. Mohammed V, Blvd. Allal ben Abdallah,** and **Av. Hassan II.**

MARHABA RESTAURANT MOROCCAN, GRILL [1]

23 Av. Mohammed V ☎05 35 52 16 32

Laundry baskets of *khoubz* and rotisserie chickens beckon you into this local favorite. Once inside, the restaurant showcases more than good food. Qur'anic chants make waves in the background, and a beautiful Amazigh woman keeps you company from a giant portrait on the wall. Whether you want *tajines*, roast chicken, or an old-fashioned hamburger, this restaurant says a big *marhaba*.

On Av. Mohammed V just off the intersection with. $ *Plates 30dh, Tajines 25dh.* ⏰ *Open daily noon-10pm.*

LE PUB 🍸 PUB [2]

20 Blvd. Allal Ben Abdellah ☎05 35 52 42 47

Don't let the bouncers at the door scare you away. The upstairs is a sit-down restaurant featuring European cuisine with an adjacent bar-lounge, but that's just the beginning. Downstairs is where the fun really gets going, in an immense piano bar that holds live music concerts every night of the week. The red hues, eclectic eats, and liberal drinks take you and the locals away from Meknès for a night.

A corner building on Av. Allal ben Abdellah before Av. Hassan II. $ *Entrees 90-110dh. Speciale 20dh. Martini 25dh.* ⏰ *Open daily 9am-1:30am.*

Medina

Much of the medina's savory and inexpensive food is actually found on the roads surrounding the medieval quarters. **Rue Rouamzine** has dozens of snack places, **Pl. ed-Hedim** is lined with touristy cafes and just down from the covered market on the road to the **Gare Routière,** you'll find street vendors frying up onions in the evening.

[✓] RESTAURANT MILLES NUITS ET UNE NUIT — 🍴 MOROCCAN ❷

3 rue Sidi Amar Bouawada ☎05 35 55 90 02

It might be called a restaurant, but you're actually dining in a family's home. The toys lying around and the cute kids that accompany them make the spectacular *pastillas* or *tajines* taste all the better. Best of all, of you show the generous proprietors your *Let's Go* guide, they'll offer a large discount. Here's your chance to taste home-cooked Moroccan. You won't find better.

➜ With your back to Bab el-Mansour, enter the medina at the top-right corner of Pl. el-Hedim, to the right of the BMCI bank. Walk up this road and look for a sign on the right. ℹ Discount for Let's Go readers. $ Harira 15dh. Tajines 85-90dh. Pastilla 90dh. Student prices for all entrees 50-65dh. ⏰ Open daily 11am-2pm and 7-10pm.

[✓] COVERED MARKET — 🍴 MARKET ❶

Pl. ed-Hedim

A patchwork tin roof, light bulbs hanging on shoe strings, and food so plentiful it makes COSTCO look like a corner store. Avoid getting stung by the wasps that swarm the sweets' aisle, and don't tell PETA about the one or two cow's heads you stumble across. The aisles are easy enough to navigate, and are arranged according to categories of food item such as fruits, vegetables, spices, and meats. This awesome market is worth visiting even if you're not planning to cook dinner. If you smile, you might get a free candy or two out of the experience.

➜ With your back to Bab el-Mansour, through an entrance on the left of Pl. ed-Hedim, just before the string of tourist cafes. $ Prices are listed on a chalkboard inside that you probably can't read. Ask for local help. ⏰ Open M-Th and Sa-Su 9am-10pm.

ESSENTIALS [i]

Practicalities

- **TOURIST OFFICE: Délégation du Tourisme** Staff only speaks French or Arabic. (*Pl. Administratif, next to the Main Post Office. ☎05 35 51 60 22 ⏰ Open M-F 9:30-4:30pm.*)
- **CURRENCY EXCHANGE: BMCI**. (*Rue Union Africaine. Next to the Main Post Office ☎ 05 35 40 46 48 ℹ Traveler's checks not accepted. ⏰ Open daily 8:15am-3:45pm.*) **BMCE**. (*66 rue Rouamzine in the medina ℹ* Traveler's checks accepted at the main BMCE branch in the *ville nouvelle* on Ave. des FAR, near the CTM station. *⏰ Open daily 8:15am-3:45 pm.*)
- **LUGGAGE STORAGE:** There is a *Consigne* at the Gare Routière. (*$ 6dh per bag until midnight that day. ⏰ Open 24hr.*)
- **INTERNET: Cyber Cafe Quicknet**. (*28 rue Emir Abdelkader in the ville nouvelle $ 6 dh per hr. ⏰ Open daily 9am-11pm.*) There is an abundance of Cyber Cafes through the city.
- **POST OFFICE:** Main office at Pl. de L'Istiqlal in the *ville nouvelle*. (*☎05 35 52 25 00 ⏰ Open daily 8am-4:30pm.*)

Emergency!

- **EMERGENCY NUMBERS: Police:** ☎190. **Ambulance:** ☎15.
- **PHARMACY: Pharmacie Nouvelle**. (*18 Av. Hassan II in the ville nouvelle ☎05 35*

52 06 68 ⏰ Open daily 8:30am-1pm and 4-8:30pm.) Rotating 24hr. pharmacies are open every night of the week. Updated lists are posted outside all pharmacies.

- **HOSPITAL: Hopital Moulay Ismail.** (*Off Av. des FAR as it curves towards the medina ☎05 35 52 28 05*)

Getting There

By Train

El Amir Abdelkader Train Station is one block from the intersection of **Rue Emir Abdelkad-er**and **Rue Atlas.** An easy walk to anywhere in the *ville nouvelle* and a 7 dh *petit taxi* to the medina. National ONCF Reservation Number ☎ 08 90 20 30 40. To: **Fez** (*$ 20dh ⏰ 45min., 9:30-1:30am every 2 hr.);* **Rabat** (*$ 65dh. ⏰ 2hr., 5:30am-7:30pm every 2hr.);* **Marrakech** (*$ 174dh. ⏰ 6½hr., 5:30am-5:30pm every 2hr.);* **Casablanca** (*$ 110dh. ⏰ 3½hr., 5:30am-5:30m every 2hr.);* **Tanger** (*$ 85dh. ⏰ 3-4hr.; 4 per day).*

By Bus

There's a **CTM Station** on Av. des FAR away from the center of town. *(☎05 35 51 46 18 ⇄ A 5dh petit taxi ride to the ville nouvelle; 10dh to the medina.)* Buses from here to: **Fez**: *($ 25dh. ⏰ 1hr., 5 per day);* **Rabat** *($ 55dh. ⏰ 2½hr., 3 per day);* **Marrakech** *($ 150dh. ⏰ 8hr., daily 7pm);* **Casablanca** *($ 85dh. ⏰ 4 hr., 4 per day);* **Tanger** (*$ 90dh. ⏰ 5hr.; 3 per day*).

Gare Routière is outside Bab el-Khem on Av. Ibn Zaydounn beyond the medina. *(☎05 35 53 26 49 ⇄ A 10min. walk to Pl. el Hedim or 7dh petit taxi ride to the ville nouvelle.)* Like other private bus stations, it's organized chaos. Bypass the aggressive vendors outside and head straight to a ticket window. Buses to: **Fez** (*$ 13dh. ⏰ 1 hr., 5am-10pm every hr.);* **Rabat** *($ 30-40dh. ⏰ 2½hr., every hr.)*; **Marrakech** *($ 100dh. ⏰ 8-10hr.; 5:30am, 6:30am, 9:35am, 4:30pm)*; **Casablanca** *($ 60dh. ⏰ 4hr., every hr. 7am-4pm)*; **Tanger** (*$ 60dh. ⏰ 5hr., 4:45am-5pm every hr.*). No surcharge for baggage.

Getting Around

By Taxi

With abundant *petit taxi* drivers who are good about using their meters, you'll never want for a cab. Fares increase 50% after 8pm or 9pm, depending on the season. *Grand taxis* can be found at the **Gare Routière** near the medina, and outside the **El Amir Abdelkader Train Station.**

CASABLANCA
AND RABAT

This chapter focuses on Morocco's two largest cities, both its most famous and its most important. Casablanca, made famous by the movie—you guessed it—*Casablanca*, is the first place most English speakers think of when they hear "Morocco." However, although Rick and Ilsa did their dramatic song-and-dance here, today's Casablanca is an urban entity with slums, clubs, and a lot more going on than a battle of the bands in Rick's Cafe.

Rabat, on the other hand, isn't exactly famous. It doesn't have a UNESCO World Heritage Medina like Fès, it can't cash in past Beat Poets or international heiresses like Tangier, and the snake-charmers of Marrakesh's **Djema'a al-Fna** are conspicuously absent. All the better. Rabat isn't a tourist trap—it's Morocco's political capital, with fabulous food, culture, and nightlife. Here, the country's bureaucrats, a large population of university students, and none other than King Mohammed VI himself do their day-to-day thing.

greatest hits

- **HASSAN II FAST, II FURIOUS.** The $800 million Hassan II mosque doesn't play games, with a location over the ocean and an interior that's shinier and swankier than any sports car (p. 444).
- **IT REMAINS TO BE SEEN.** The Roman temple may have nearly disappeared, but the Chellah ruins in the sprawling Merenid complex in Rabat is here to stay and be seen (p. 449).

We could make plenty of Humphrey Bogart and Ingrid Bergman jokes. We could tell you that you have to eat at **Rick's Cafe,** just for the novelty. But *Let's Go* is above cheap puns. We'd rather tell you to go to **Le Taverne du Dauphin** for their winning fish plates. We could tell you to tell the DJ to "play it again" at **Calypso,** but you'll be too busy dancing to make requests. Here's to looking at you, kid, having a good time (insert groan here).

casablanca

Travelers to Casablanca (a.k.a. Casa) expecting romance might be a bit disappointed. Contrary to the movie, the sprawling city is less appealing than other Moroccan destinations. A small town at the turn of the 20th century, Casablanca became an economic center under French rule, when the colonial authorities built its wide boulevards and crumbling Art Deco buildings. Africa's largest port is a discordant mixture of urban high-rises and desperately poor slums. Decaying colonial facades give the impression of decline, while the daily bustle of professional men and women wearing the latest Western fashions testify to a modern dynamism. Other than the decadent club scene on **Blvd. da la Corniche,** which ranges from sophisticated to seedy, the city's true highlight is the Hassan II Mosque. The third largest in the world and one of the few to allow members of any faith inside, the mosque is absolutely spectacular. Stay in Casablanca just long enough to feel your jaw drop as you enter the prayer hall.

ORIENTATION

Casablanca has two main squares. The first, **Place Nations Unies,** is a major traffic hub 10min. south of the port and an easy walk from either **Casa Port train station** or the **CTM bus station.** (Note that **Casa Voyageur,** Casablanca's second train station, is a 30min. walk east of the center on Blvd. Mohammed V.) In one corner of the Pl. Nations Unies is the clocktower entrance to Casblanca's tiny **medina.** The Hyatt Regency is another straightforward landmark. Another 10min. south along Av. Hassan II from Pl. Nations Unies is the second main square, **Place Mohammed V,** which is lined by various administrative buildings, including the Principal Post and the Court House. Just south of Pl. Mohammed V are the palm-filled gardens of the **Parc de la Ligue Arabe,** a beautiful spot for a stroll during the day and early evening.

Conveniently, all of the useful arteries for travelers radiate out from Pl. Nations Unies and Pl. Mohammed V. At the far north and closest to the port is **Av. des F.A.R.,** which moves past the Hyatt Regency and cuts through the top of Pl. Nations Unies. Popular banks, travel agencies, and airlines are located here. Farther south is the thoroughfare **Blvd Mohammed V,** and just before Pl. Mohammed V is the especially pretty **Blvd. de Paris.** Most restaurants, hotels, and essential services are located on Blvd. Mohammed V, Blvd. de Paris, and the many cross-streets that intersect them. Connecting Pl. Nations Unies, Pl. Mohammed V and downtown Casa to the south is the city's largest artery, **Av. Hassan II.** The spectacular **Hassan II Mosque** is northwest of the city center, 20min. on foot along **Blvd. des Almohades,** the highway, with the medina walls on one side and the port on the other. Casa's hopping club district, **Blvd. de la Corniche,** is significantly further west on this route, and is best reached by *petit taxi* for 30-40dh at night.

casablanca and rabat

ACCOMMODATIONS

Casa's glory days are sadly past, and it shows in the grayed facades and worn feel of many budget accommodations, that have seen better times. Nevertheless, there are still some gems here, especially 👍**Hotel Gallia.** Most other cheap and central accommodations are found in the streets just southeast of Pl. des Nations Unies, up and down the side streets in between Blvd. Mohammed V and Blvd. de Paris. Casa traffic can be very noisy, so ask for a room offset from the street.

👍 HOTEL GALLIA — @📶 BOUTIQUE HOTEL [2]

19 rue Ibnou Batouta ☎05 22 48 16 94 💻www.hotelgalliacasa.com

It doesn't get better. Gallia is a stylish boutique hotel and backpacker haven. You'll sleep like a baby in soft double beds surrounded by light-blue walls, tall windows and legit art, for once. The staff exudes warm hospitality, and maintains a dining area and lounge for breakfast with a flatscreen TV. The only downside is the smelly walk home since the decaying buildings opposite the Central Market and near the hotel are used as a public toilet.

📍 From Pl. des Nations Unies, walk down Blvd. Mohammed V. Turn right 2 streets past the Post Office and across from the Central Market. The hotel is past some decaying buildings on your left. ℹ Free internet and Wi-Fi in the lobby. $ Singles 150dh, with shower 170dh; doubles 220dh, with shower 250dh, with bath 270dh; triples 295/330/350dh. ⏰ Reception 24hr.

AUBERGE DES JEUNES — @📶 HOSTEL [1]

6 Pl. Ahmed El Bidaoui ☎05 22 22 05 51 💻www.hihostel.com

Other than the Moroccan pop that wakes you up at 8am, Casa's souped-up youth hostel is relative luxury given the price. Its single beds in semi-private dorm rooms are a step up from the usual rows of bunks, and the internet cafe is a sweet convenience (*5dh*). The hostel's flexible staff are used to accommodating all kinds of travelers and large groups. Spacious central lounge, TV, and bright blue-tiled communal bath with newly installed solar-heated showers. Private rooms are also available, if you're hoping to avoid the smells and sounds of other travelers. But sometimes that's half the fun.

📍 There are blue signs directing hostel-goers from the CTM bus station and the train station. Walk along Blvd. Almohades towards the medina. At the second entrance, turn left and the Auberge is in the square up the ramp-like street. Breakfast included. ℹ Breakfast 8-9am. Cleaning 10am-12pm. $ Dorms 60dh; doubles 135dh, with shower 200dh; triples with shower 200dh; quads with shower 260dh. ⏰ Lock-out 11pm-midnight.

HOTEL LAUSANNE — @ HOTEL [2]

24 rue Tata (ex. Poincaré) ☎05 22 22 26 86 90 💻hotellausanne@voila.fr

A glass peacock welcomes you at hotel Lausanne's reception. If that's not a good enough reason to stay here, maybe the ancient two-person elevator will convince you. The place is a historic melange of French Art Deco and Moroccan style. Picturing brass plates and portrayals of desert scenes? Good. Long hallways lead to roomy digs with full baths and tiny TVs. Although the building is on the older side, it's clean, comfortable, and well-situated, with an ice cream parlor and cafe next door.

📍 From Blvd. de Paris at Pl. Mohammed V, turn left on rue Tata and the hotel is on your left. $ Singles 225dh; doubles 270dh; triples 470dh.

HOTEL COLBERT — @ HOTEL [1]

28 rue Chaouia (ex. Colbert) ☎05 22 31 82 75 💻www.hotelcolbert.ma

Less exciting than Stephen Colbert, but one step up from a dirty cardboard box or other cheap options, Hotel Colbert's potted plants, leather couches in the reception area, and friendly concierge add a little comfort to an otherwise budget experience. Five floors of endless pink and cream hallways lead to sparse clean rooms with just a bed, a light bulb, and sink. The communal showers have new plastic nozzles. Concierge will help you with your luggage.

At the corner of Blvd. Mohammed V and rue Chaouia next to the Central Market. $Single without shower 90dh; doubles without shower 130dh, with shower 210dh; triples without shower 170dh, with shower 250dh.

SIGHTS

The awe-inspiring Hassan II Mosque alone makes a trip here worthwhile. After that, though, there's not too much to see in commercial Casablanca.

HASSAN II MOSQUE — MOSQUE

Inspired by the Qur'anic verse stating that the throne of God is built upon the water, King Hassan II built his mosque to hang dramatically over the Atlantic. The 210m minaret is the tallest in the world, and quite literally testifies to the heights of human creativity. The mosque itself is the third largest in the world, outdone only by the wonders of Mecca and Medina. Designed by Frenchman Michel Pinseau, construction began in 1986 and continued for six years, as 2500 craftsman carved, painted, and gilded the masterpiece. All the materials were locally produced, except for the 56 Venetian glass chandeliers and the Carrera marble that surrounds the *mahrib*, the prayer niche that points to Mecca. The construction bill came to a total of US$800 million, much of it collected through public taxes, and the mosque first opened its doors in 1993 to Muslims and non-Mulsims alike. Inside, the prayer hall accommodates 25,000 worshippers, and is adorned with a fabulously intricate design. The mosque has a retractable cedar roof that opens to the sky when the weather is good, and in the winter the floor is electrically heated. At one end of the prayer hall gates weighing over 34 tons open once a year during the birthday celebration of the Prophet for a grand entrance by one of his living descendants, the King himself. Downstairs, the ablution rooms for men and women each contain *hammams* and no less than 41 fountains. The plaza outside accommodates another 80,000 worshippers. Despite its formidable size, both the mosque and its plaza quickly fill to capacity during Ramadan. If that doesn't give you goosebumps, the views of the minaret will. All guests must be modestly attired; women must cover their legs and shoulders, and you'll have to take off your shoes before entering the prayer hall.

*From Blvd. Félix Houphouet-Boigny, walk along the coastal road (Blvd. des Almohades and subsequently Blvd. Sidi Mohammed ben Abdellah) with the medina walls on your left for 20 minutes. The minaret will guide your way. Or, take a petit taxi for 10-15. Tickets are sold to the left of the minaret down the stairs. **i** Hassan II souvenir shop inside. $ Tours: 120dh, student with card 60dh, child 30dh. ⏰ Daily tours 9am, 10am, 11am, noon, 3pm and Friday 9am, 10am, 3pm.*

FOOD

Casablanca offers every type of cuisine under the sun, from McDonald's to Mexican, for those willing to look. The center is dominated by seafood places, sandwich joints, *patisseries* and pizzerias. A hub of cheap eats is centered around the Central Market, a few blocks south-east of Pl. Nations Unies on Blvd. Mohammed V. **Rue Chaouia** (ex. Colbert) hosts the crowded seafood restaurant **Snack Amine,** as well as the inexpensive, greasy, and delicious **Rotisserie Centrale.** Fresh meats, produce and preserved foods can be found in the modernized Central Market (open daily 7am-3pm).

LE TAVERNE DU DAUPHIN — SEAFOOD [1]

115 Blvd. Félix Houphouet Boigny ☎05 22 22 12 00

Don't be surprised if the British tourist two tables down sounds like they're having a *When Harry Met Sally* deli moment—Dauphin's fish is just that tasty. The sophisticated menu offers artichoke hearts in the nicoise salad, a specialty of mixed ocean-dwellers from ombrine to shrimp served up whole and crispy, and schools of other fish including salmon and sea bass. Better than the captain's wheels on the walls, the underwater-themed stained glass, or the delicious four-course set menu, is the fact this elegant restaurant is recommended by "Best Restaurants Maroc" iPhone app.

❦ *On Blvd. Félix Houphouet Boigny one block from Blvd. des Almohades.* ⓘ *Non-smoking upstairs.* Ⓢ *Fish plates 44-120dh. 4-course set menu 115dh.* ☑ *Open M-Sa 12am-11pm.*

ROTISSERIE CENTRALE   🍗 CHICKEN ❶
35 rue Chaouia

Picture rows of chickens rotating in a glass case above other chickens. Add fire. Now imagine grease-covered waiters spooning the fat and gravy from all those rotating birds into little bowls. Are you licking your lips? Are you wretching into this guidebook? This is precisely the artery-clogging scene that comes with your ¼-roast chicken, fries, and coke at Rotisserie Centrale. And all for 25dh. The cheapest way to stuff yourself any time of day or night. For your cardiologist's sake, you can always choose to abstain from your bowl of gravy. The white meat will still be succulent, and crispy fries are delicious in Dijon mustard.

❦ *On rue Chaouia next to Snack Amine and across from the flower vendors.* Ⓢ *Prix-fixe 25dh.* ☑ *Open daily until 1am.*

SNACK AMINE   🍤 SEAFOOD ❷
rue Chaouia (ex. Colbert)   ☎05 22 54 13 31

Follow the locals and you'll end up at Snack Amine for a delicious seafood meal—that is, if you can find a table. Waiters scurry across the floors, grabbing bread from buckets, pre-made salads from behind glass counters, and sizzling plates of fried and pan-seared fish from chefs who work frantically. (Caution: this place is not to be confused with Snack Amine Adam down the street or the defunct Snack Yamina sign above Rotisserie Centrale. Confusing, isn't it?)

❦ *Just off Blvd. Mohammed V on rue Chaouia.* Ⓢ *Plates 67-126dh.* ☑ *Open daily 11:30am-11pm.*

RICK'S CAFE   ✒((ɣ))✲ CAFE ❸
248 Blvd. Sour Jdid   ☎05 22 27 42 07

A shrine to the movie *Casablanca*, this nod to American culture has Fès-capped waiters serving pricey and decadent dishes to swarms of tourists. During the day, the beautiful cafe is a Wi-Fi hotspot; the live piano music starts after dinner, and the lounges and terrace stay open for the crowd to enjoy themselves. The giant bottle of Veuve Cliquot is a tip-off that the alcohol flows very liberally here. Although Rick's famous cheesecake is a let-down, you'll tip your fedora, or your Fez hat to the ambience. Play it again Sam, indeed.

❦ *Follow the port road away from the center until the end of the medina walls. Signs point to Rick's on the left.* Ⓢ *Mains 125-160dh, cheesecake 55dh.* ☑ *Open daily noon-2:30pm and 6:30pm-1am.*

NIGHTLIFE

Casa's Western feel might leave you hoping for a club scene, and the city doesn't disappoint. The center has its share of male-dominated bars as well as the upscale night-club in the **Hyatt Regency,** but most of the action is in **Ain Diab,** a wealthy neighborhood on the beach 4km west of the city center. The young and sexy flock to the bars and discos along **Blvd. de La Corniche** to flirt, drink, and show a little skin (or a lot). Most places get going around 2am. Dress codes require you to look the part, which means nice shoes and a collar for men and a dress or skirt for women. It's both more fun and safer to go out in groups, especially for female travelers. Take a break from dancing to grab a sandwich at **Snack Taghazout,** open until 5am. Expect to pay a 100-150dh cover and 30-40dh for a cab each way from the center.

🖼 CALYPSO   ✒✲ CLUB
Black lighting looks great on hot bods in an unpretentious club, where the young and energetic go for an unadulterated good time on the Corniche. Locals and

tourists alike rev up on the dance floor to house, Latin, R and B, hip hop and other beats upon request, but the party only really starts after 2am.

In the middle of the Corniche on a corner just past Balcon 33. $ Cover 100dh. Drink 100dh. Bottle 1000dh. ⏰ Open until 4am.

BACLON 33 — CLUB, EXCLUSIVE

Make sure you look the part of a well-dressed Casablancais yuppie if you're going to Balcon 33. A restaurant and bar with sexy red lighting, the place turns into an exclusive club after midnight, with an intimate dance floor that gradually takes over the bar. On a Saturday night, there's barely room to move among the 20- and 30-somethings.

One of the first clubs you will hit along Blvd. de la Corniche coming from the center of town. $ Cover 150dh. Drink 100dh, bottle 1000dh. ⏰ Open until 3am.

LE VILLAGE — CLUB

One of the Corniche's older venues, anything goes in the liberal Le Village. The circular dance floor is surrounded by candle-lit tables, pleated mirrors, two bars and a DJ booth with live music on the weekends and French tunes during the week. The motley crowd doesn't show up 'til 2am, but if you're there on a prime night, the party keeps going until sunrise.

The first club on Blvd. de la Corniche coming from the center of town. Number 11. $ Cover 150dh. Drink 50dh. Bottle 800dh. ⏰ Open until 4 am.

JOY — CLUB

One of the Corniche's larger clubs, the discoball and seizure-inducing lighting make for more hardcore gyrating on stone floors among the mob of sexy 30-somethings. You'll have to yell at the top of your lungs for a drink, but you're likely to find a dance party past 2am, especially if there's a line-up out the door. Tuesdays are 80s and 90s night, Wednesdays Latin, Thursdays Oriental and live Moroccan, while Saturdays and Sundays international DJs perform.

This is the last club you'll hit along the Corniche coming from the center of the city. It's at the traffic circle next to Hotel Suisse. $ Cover 150dh. Drinks 100dh. Bottles 1000dh. ⏰ Open until 4am.

SHOPPING

Some of the best shopping for Moroccan arts and crafts can be done in the **Quartier Habous,** a "new medina" built by the French in the 1920s. The pedestrian-friendly streets are wide, the green lawn in front of the mosque is welcoming, and the commercial arcades are hemmed by orderly stalls selling teapots, trays, carpets, clothing, and the typical array of Moroccan specialties. Shopping here is a more tranquil experience than new traditional medinas, but it doesn't merit a trip for more than souvenirs. If you're craving designer brands, head to the **Maarif** neighborhood in the downtown core southwest of the **Parc de la Ligue Arabe.** The shopping mall in the Twin Center will partly satisfy your craving with the occasional **Guess** or **Zara,** but it's a far cry from Paris.

ESSENTIALS

Practicalities

- **TOURIST OFFICE: Conseil Régional du Tourisme.** More tourist-friendly than the Syndicat d'Initiative. One kiosk outside Hassan II Mosque and another at Pl. Mohammed V. Look for a kiosk with a big "i". (☎ *05 22 20 62 65. Open daily 8:30am-12:30pm and 2:30-6pm.*) Excellent maps and helpful information. Brochures in French and English. **Syndicat d'Initiative.** (*98 Blvd. Mohammed V.* ☎ *05 22 22 15 24.* ⏰ *Open M-F 8:30am-4:30pm, Sa 8:30am-12pm.*) Provides a somewhat useful pocket guide to Casablanca that lists restaurants, accommodations, and phone numbers. Guides on hire, but don't be bamboozled into a tour if you don't want one.

- **CURRENCY EXCHANGE: BMCI** has a bank on the first floor. *(Pl. des Nations Unis. ➡ Located at the corner of Av. Hassan II and Blvd. Mohammed V.)* There is a *bureau de change* to the right of the main bank entrance and a Western Union. The **Hyatt Regency** at Pl. des Nations Unis has a **currency exchange desk.** *(⏰ Open M-F 8am-11:30pm and 4-11pm, Su 6-11pm.)*
- **ATMS:** There is an ATM in **BMCI.** *(⏰ Open M-F 8:15am-6:30pm, Sa-Su 9am-6pm.)* **BMCE,** at Pl. Mohammed V across the Principal Post Office, also has an ATM. *(⏰ Open M-F 8:15am-3:45pm.)* As well, the **Hyatt Regency** at Pl. des Nations Unies has a currency exchange desk open M-F from 8am-11:30pm and 4-11pm. Su 6-11pm.
- **INTERNET:** There are plenty of internet cafes along Blvd. de Paris and Blvd. Mohammed V, including **Cyber Marocondia,** 71 Blvd. de Paris. It shares its storefront with a perfume shop. The computers are upstairs. *($ 6dh per hr. ⏰ Open daily 8:30am-11:30pm.)*
- **POST OFFICE: Principal Post Office.** *(Blvd. Paris at Av. Hassan II. ⏰ Open M-F 8am-4:15pm, Sa 8am-noon.)* Poste restante can be picked up in a separate office on the side of the building. Western Union inside. There is another branch with the same hours located on Blvd. Mohammed V next to the Syndicat d'Initiative.

Emergency!

- **EMERGENCY NUMBERS: Police:** ☎ 19. **Ambulance:** ☎15.
- **POLICE: Poste Police Touristique.** Tourist brigade at the corner of Blvd. Houphouet-Boigny and Blvd. des Almohades open 24/7. Another post on Av. Hassan II one block past Pl. Mohammed V.
- **LATE-NIGHT PHARMACIES:** Many pharmacies can be found along Blvd. de Paris. **Pharmacie des Ecoles.** *(12 Av. Hassan II, off Pl. des Nations Unies. ☎05 22 27 53 11 ℹ There is a list of rotating 24hr. pharmacies posted outside. ⏰ Open M-F 9am-12:30pm and 4-8:30pm, Sa 9am-1pm.)*
- **HOSPITAL: Hospital Ibnou Rochd.** *(☎05 22 22 41 09 ➡ Walk south on Hassan II past the Parc de la Ligue Arabe and continue straight through the next traffic circle. 4 blocks later, turn left and continue straight. The complex is one block up on the right. Served by bus #59 along Av. Hassan II.)* **S.O.S. Medecins Maroc** *(☎05 22 44 44 44).*

Getting There

By Plane

Aeroport Mohammed V. *(☎05 22 53 91 03)* There are 45min. trains from **Casa Voyageurs** to the airport terminal every 30min. for 42dh.

By Train

Casablanca has two train stations. **Casa Port** is on the waterfront close to the city center. It is a 10-15min. walk from Pl. des Nation Unies, right off the port highway. **Casa Voyageurs** is 4km outside of the center on Blvd. Ba Hammed and a 10-15dh *petit taxi* ride from the center. Trains run from **Casa Port** to: **Fez** *($ 110 dh. ⏰ 4 hr., every hr. 5:15am-11:30pm);* **Meknès** *($ 90dh. ⏰ 3hr., every hr. 5:15am-11:30pm);* **Rabat** *($ 35dh. ⏰ 1hr., every 30min. 6:30am-10:30pm).* From **Casa Voyageurs** to: **Marrakech** *($ 90dh. ⏰ 3½hr., every 2hr. 6:50am-8:50pm);* **Essaouira** *($ 140dh. ⏰ 3½hr., every 2hr. 6:50am-8:50pm);* **Tangier** *($ 125dh. ⏰ 6hr.; daily 6:45 am, 9:45am, 4:45pm).*

By Bus

Buses leave from the **CTM Station,** 23 rue Léon L'Africain, which is a 10min. walk from Pl. des Nations Unies. *(☎05 22 54 10 10 ➡ Walk away from the Place on Av. des F.A.R. Turn right at Rue Chaouia and make the next left. the station is at the end of the block.)* Buses to: **Fez** *($ 100 dh. ⏰ 4hr., every 2hr. 7am-9pm);* **Meknès** *($ 90dh. ⏰ 3½hr., 7 per day);* **Marrakech** *($*

90dh. 🕐 *3½hr., 10 per day);* **Essaouira** *(💲 140 dh.* 🕐 *6hr., 7am and 3pm);* **Tanger** *(💲 145dh.* 🕐 *5½hr.; daily 5:30am, 11am, 2:30pm, 5pm and 11:45pm).*

Getting Around

By Car

Avis. *(19 Av. des F.A.R.* ☎05 22 31 24 24. *Daily rental rates from 816dh. Drivers 25+ with 2 years on their permit. Open M-F 8am-7pm, Sa 8am-12pm and 2-7pm, Su 8am-12pm.)* **Hertz.** *(25 rue de Arabi Jilali.* ☎05 22 48 47 10. *Low-season from 570dh per day; high-season from 716dh. 240dh surcharge for drivers ages 21-23. Open M-F 8am-noon and 2:30-6:30pm, Sa 9am-noon and 3-6pm, Su 9am-noon.)*

By Public Transit

Pl. des Nations Unies is the hub for Casa's public transportation system, which centers on buses. *(💲 4dh.)* Bus **#9** goes to the Blvd. de la Corniche in Ain Diab, **#2** traverses Av. des F.A.R. to Casa Voyageur train station, **#40** heads to Quartier Habous and **#59** goes south on Av. Hassan II to the hospital. Morocco, Tunisia and Algeria are known in French collectively as le Maghreb, stemming from the Arabic "al-Maghribiya" meaning "place of sunset," or the west. Morocco's full name is "Al-Mamlaka al-Maghribiya" which means "The Western Kingdom." What's in a name?

rabat *ar-rabāt* ☎537

For the traveler who wants to see Morocco, Rabat is seriously worthwhile, especially for the grub. The orderly medina has some of the tastiest street food in the *Maghreb.* The blue-and-white Kasbah of Oudaya gives way to a refreshing strip of the Atlantic, and there's a stellar playground of ruins and overgrown jungle at **Chellah.** You can find just about anything in the clean and attractive city streets, including fine dining, bars, and clubs in *centre ville* and the surrounding neighborhoods. And, as a huge bonus, there are no faux guides or hustlers. Come to Rabat and you'll want to come back.

ORIENTATION

Although Rabat is a sprawling modern city with a population nearing two million, the *centre ville* is relatively straightforward and easy to navigate on foot. There are two main streets that any newbie should know: **Av. Hassan II** and **Av. Mohammed V.**

The highway from Casablanca turns into Av. Hassan II as it enters the wealthy suburbs of Rabat from the south. It subsequently passes through the 'burb of **Agdal,** where the **CTM station, Gare Routière,** and hospitals are located, and progresses into the center of the *ville nouvelle.* Eventually Av. Hassan II hits an essential landmark, **Bab al-Had,** one of the main gates to the imperial city. The hub for public buses is just outside the Bab, in addition to Rabat's welcoming **Auberge de Jeunes**. Once through the gate, the 17th century walls of the **medina** are to one side, while the happening avenues of the *ville nouvelle* are to the other.

Two blocks through the Bab, and Av. Hassan II hits **Av. Mohammed V.** This hopping avenue cuts right through the middle of *centre ville* to the Royal Palace and has banks, pharmacies, the **Gare Rabat Ville** train station, as well as restaurants, cafes and bars galore. The next parallel street, **Av. Allal ben Abdallah,** is another important street for the munchies, while many budget hotels are found on perpendicular side streets. In the other direction, Av. Mohammed V enters the medina and serves as a main street filled with succulent street food, markets, and several budget hotels. To get to the **Kasbah** (also called **Oudaya**), go to the end of Av. Mohammed V and turn right past the cemetery until the main gate of **Bab Oudaia.** Past the Kasbah is the beach.

Finally, Rabat's awesome historic sights, including the landmark **Tour Hassan** and the archaeological wonder of **Chellah,** are best reached with a 10 to 15dh *petit taxi* ride from *centre ville*, although the intrepid traveler can certainly walk the distance.

ACCOMMODATIONS

Budget accommodations in Rabat tend to offer greater cleanliness than similarly priced options in other Moroccan cities. Some of the best options don't have huge capacity, so it's best to reserve in advance or arrive early in the day.

👍 AUBERGE DES JEUNES — 🌐 HOSTEL [1]

43 rue Marassa, Bab al-Had — ☎05 37 72 57 69 💻www.hihostels.com

Like summer camp in Rabat, this welcoming hostel is a home away from home for travelers and locals alike. Whether you're playing cards in the leafy courtyard, watching American horror movies on TV, or shooing away the adorable kitten on your bed in the tidy dorms, Rabat's hostel managers will take great care of you. It also happens to be ideally located within walking distance of the medina and *centre ville.* Make sure to reserve in advance.

🧭 From Bab al-Had, walk through the plaza past the fountain. Look in front of you and slightly to the left. The Auberge is white with a blue sign. ℹ Breakfast 8am. $ 65dh for a bed including breakfast and hot showers. ⏰ Doors close around 11pm.

HOTEL DOGHMI — 🌐 HOTEL [1]

313 Av. Mohammed V, Pl. Marché Central, Medina — ☎05 37 72 38 98

Walk up the stairs and follow the big doormats onto sunny white and blue balconies, with 10 simple rooms arranged around a courtyard. Proprietor Kenza will graciously show you to your quarters or open up the spacious, bizarrely triangular shower for an extra 10dhs of cleanliness. Best of all, you're only 100ft from where the medina street food start.

🧭 On the right, just inside the medina on Av. Mohammed V. ℹ Washing machine 80dh. Showers 10dh. $ Singles 90dh; doubles 130dh; triples 195dh; quads 260dh. ⏰ Best to arrive before noon or reserve in advance.

HOTEL SPLENDID — 🌐 HOTEL [2]

8 rue Ghazza, Ville Nouvelle — ☎05 37 72 32 83

From the distinctly French vibe to the ubiquitous floral tiling, this hotel is splendid given its price and location. The linens on the double beds manage to stay crisp and white in spite of the dusty Moroccan heat. An easy walk to the medina in one direction or the bars and restaurants of *centre ville* in the other. When you're not sleeping, there's a patio for chillin'.

🧭 Walk along Av. Mohammed V toward the palace and turn left on rue Ghazza. $ Singles 125dh; doubles 230dh; triples 300dh.

SIGHTS

👍 CHELLAH — 🌐 RUINS

While you're looking at what's left of a mosque amid the Chellah ruins, a hefty stork is probably leering at you from his nest on top of the minaret. Although the birds own the place, it did once belong to the Romans for almost a thousand years. While the Roman ruins are hard to make out, including the epically named **Jupiter Temple**, the Islamic complex of the 14th century Merenid inhabitants is still standing. There's a **mosque, medersa, tombs** and the lushest **gardens** in Rabat. Much of the historical detail will be lost on visitors who don't read French or Arabic, but you can enjoy wandering through these stone structures overgrown with the flowers and trees of Moroccan jungle for hours.

🧭 Beyond the southwest ramparts of the ville nouvelle. Take Av. Mohammed V until the Royal Palace. Then follow Av. Yacoub al-Mansour along the Palace walls until it exits the ramparts. Chellah is beyond the highway (Blvd. ad-Doustour). ℹ No tours. $ 10dh. ⏰ Open daily 8:30am-6:30pm.

MEDINA NEIGHBORHOOD

It's not a maze, but it's a-maz-ing. Without any *faux guides* to lead you astray, Rabat's grid-like medina is Moroccan living at its finest. Finest food, that is. The place is bubbling over with delicious eats, including specialties like egg and potato sandwiches, grilled corn on the cob, and mouth-watering fried eggplant. The best street food is on **Av. Mohammed V** and **Rue Sidi Fateh,** which run parallel to one another. When you're not stuffing your face, you can browse bootleg DVD from basket-vendors—so long as they're not scurrying away to avoid the cops—or wander past the clothing bazaars on the perpendicular **Rue Soulika.** Turn left at **Rue Des Consuls** and at the northern end you'll hit **Souq Tahit** with the best *jellaba*,, ceramics, leather and other crafts, including hookahs.

Depends on your bargaining skills. Open 24hr., but best explored during the day and then again in the evening until midnight.

KASBAH NEIGHBORHOOD

The salty sea breeze, rivers of ice cream, and a calm neighborhood vibe await your roaming pleasure as you pass through a side-door into **Bab Oudaia,** the impressive 12th century gate to the Kasbah. Follow **Rue Jamaa,** the main street, until the **Plateforme du Sémaphore** and you'll get a wicked view of the water from the ramparts. If you double-back and turn left down **Rue Bazzo,** there is overpriced mint tea at **Café Maure** and the peaceful **Andalusian Gardens** right next door, open daily 8am-8pm. An ice cream on the platform is better than tea in the gardens.

MAUSOLEUM OF MOHAMMED V AND LE TOUR HASSAN ROYAL TOMB

This mausoleum's golden dome and hushed interior is fit for the monarchs buried below: King Mohammed V and his son, the late King Hassan II. Opposite the mausoleum is the minaret of an immense mosque commissioned by Sultan Yacoub al-Mansour in the 12th century. The tower was supposed to be twice as tall, but construction stopped at 44m when the sultan died. He probably wouldn't have been too thrilled to know that. The stone pillars in the plaza are the remains of his mosque, which was destroyed by an earthquake in 1755. Poor sultan. Even though you can't go inside, the tower is one landmark to photograph. It's virtually synonymous with Rabat. Caution: Unless you're looking for a tattoo, keep your arms and legs close to your body as you leave the plaza, since henna girls are known to lie in wait for tourists.

45min. walk through Bab al-Had on Av. Hassan II. At rue Moulay Ismail turn right and make a left at rue al-Mansour ad-Dahbi. Keep going as the road curves to your right. With the ocean on your left, the main gates to the Mausoleum are past the gardens and up the hill. Or, take a 6dh petit taxi from centre ville. ***i*** *Free. From the 1st call to prayer until the 4th: sunrise to sunset.*

THE BEACH BEACH

Rabat ain't the Bahamas. For pristine sand and crystal waters, you'll have to leave the city and motor 10-20km along the coast. Here in town, you'll need to settle for sand that serves the dual purpose of playground and trash heap. But if you don't mind a little refuse, the Rabat beach just north of the Kasbah is a sunny spot to meet fun-loving locals. (Note that it is mostly men who swim due to Islamic customs of modest dress, although women definitely frequent the beach too.) The air off the Atlantic is refreshing, and the sunsets are fluorescent beauties. After you've joined the fun for a time, you can surf the waves at **Oudayas Surf Club,** with more intense waves at the beach next door.

From Bab al-Had walk on Av. de l'Egypte with the medinal walls on your right. Turn left into Bab al-Alou gate and walk along Blvd. al-Alou. Pass the cemetery on your left. Turn left at the four-lane highway right before the Kasbah and walk along the highway until the beach appears down to your right. Oudayas Surf Club is on the highway. ***i*** *Oudayas Surf Club takes cash or checks. They arrange weekly excursions along the coast. 150dh for a 1½hr. surfing lesson. Surfboard included. Surf courses Tu-Su 10am, 3pm, 6pm.*

FOOD

Medina

If you don't do anything else on your visit to Rabat, try the medina street food. It's some of the best in Morocco. Depending on the season, you'll find liver and onions, fried sardines, grilled corn on the cob, a Rabati specialty of egg and potato sandwiches, breaded eggplant, snails in garlic broth, coconuts, and delicious Moroccan sweets like *shebakia* (a kind of honey pretzel). You can have a veritable feast for 5 to 15dh. Vendors are most prevalent on **Av. Mohammed V** and **Rue Sidi Fateh,** which is the continuation of **Av. Allal ben Abdellah.**

SNACK FDARNA — 🍴 FAST FOOD, MOROCCAN [1]

20 rue Sidi Bourazzouk — ☎05 37 72 74 51 💻www.fdnarna.ma

Fdarna is awesome. Period. Quite possibly the only snack place in the whole medina to be recently renovated, you might not go for the lime and fuschia walls, but you'll stay for the fast and liberally-spiced Moroccan favorites. Take in a soccer game on the flatscreen or meet medina-dwellers. If you're up for it, you even can buy an entire rotisserie chicken to-go for 45dh.

⇄ To the left off Av. Mohammed V in the medina. Look for the sign on Mo. V. $ Pizza 5dh. Sandwiches 8-20dh. Tajines 15-22dh. Couscous 20dh. ¼-chicken 22dh. ⏰ Open daily 10am-11pm.

RESTAURANT DE LA JEUNESSE — 🍴 MOROCCAN [1]

305 Av. Mohammed V — ☎06 61 47 60 06

Contrary to what the name suggests—Restaurant of Youth—the aging plastic chairs and tablecloths have been well-used over many years. But the name isn't completely a lie. Due to its convenient location near the entrance to the medina, young backpackers love to grab a brimming bowl of *harira* or well-priced, heaping plate of couscous. Nobody but locals realize that the second floor has giant windows for medina-watching, which is especially beautiful in the evening.

⇄ On the right side of Av. Mohammed V past the Central Market. $ Harira 4dh. Tajines 20-23dh. Couscous 20dh. ⏰ Open daily 11am-11pm.

EL JAOUHORI — 🍴 YOGURT SHOP [1]

Rue Souika

If you can find space in between the people slurping and ordering here, the *Raib aux fruits* (fruit and yogurt parfait) is out-of-this-world. Peaches, melon, banana, apple, plum, papaya, and other freshies on top of yogurt in a big plastic container. Two warnings: the sweet red syrup they pour over the parfait will dye your fingers, and your sensitive stomach might complain a little (or a whole lot) after consuming this Moroccan Ambrosia. The memory is arguably worth it and for those with iron tummies, don't worry about it.

⇄ At the corner of rue Souika and Av. Mohammed V. $ 10dh. ⏰ Open daily 7am-10pm.

Ville Nouvelle

A little less colorful than the medina but still a gourmand's delight, *Centre ville* is the spot to go for a sit-down meal of upscale Moroccan or international cuisine.

LA MAMMA — 💳🍸 ITALIAN [2]

6 rue Tanta — ☎05 35 70 73 29

Your body will say *grazie* after carbo-loading on pretty darn tasty pastas and pizzas, including Hawaiian for those nostalgic Americans. Although dark and foreboding from the outside, the tinted glass wall filters pretty red, blue, green, and yellow light onto your table and hearty portions. Techno beats are too loud, but the house red wine is a treat you deserve after a dusty day in the heat.

⇄ Walk through the underpass of Hotel Balima and the restaurant is on your left. The red sign lights up between 7:30 and 8pm. $ Pasta 47-63dh. Grilled dishes 83-117dh. Pizzas 50-70dh. House red wine 26dh. ⏰ Open daily noon-3pm and 7:30pm-midnight.

LE PETIT BEUR - DAR TAJINE
🍴🍸 MOROCCAN ❸

8 rue Damas ☎05 37 73 13 22

Here's the scenario. You're a student studying abroad and your family is visiting. You're trying to impress them with your knowledge of elegant, reasonably priced Moroccan restaurants. You take them to Le Petit Beur and are showered with praise and a garland or two of flowers. Here's why: not only was the bistro designed by a talented interior decorator, with blue tiling and painted wood like any ancient *medersa*, but the portions are large and succulent. Ten times the price of medina street food, but it's worth it for the ambience and the beer on tap.

➜ On rue Damas one block down from the McDonald's. You could always go there... $ Harira 25dh. Appetizers 60-80dh. Plates 100-230dh. ⏰ Open M-Sa 11:30am-2pm, 6:30-11pm.

TOP BATIDO
🍴 SMOOTHIES, SANDWICHES ❶

Av. Mohammed V ☎05 37 70 04 29

Imagine you died and went to a heaven where you could order any smoothie that ever existed. Top Batido is that heaven. The small shop has smoothies from celery to carob, including the Batido special made from cherries and mangoes. In spite of the pukey pink walls, the drinks are yum-tacular and travelers claim that the egg-and-cheese sandwiches are ideal Moroccan comfort food.

➜ Next to the Hertz Rental agency on Av. Mohammed V towards the royal palace. $ Sandwiches 12-20dh. Smoothies 20-30dh. ⏰ Open daily 5:30am-midnight.

NIGHTLIFE

Unlike Tangier or Fès, where you're guaranteed to meet prostitutes working the club scene, Rabat has a vibrant night life for its young university students. There are popular bars and clubs in *centre ville* and in **Souissi,** a wealthy suburb of the city.

EL PALATINO
🍸 BAR

73 Av. Allal Ben Abdellah ☎05 37 70 81 32

Like Morocco, this tapas restaurant and bar is an eclectic mix of East and West: Muhammad Ali, a Red Bull sign, and Che Guevara line the red and black walls. Dark, smoky, and hoppin' at night, you can order an equally diverse selection of tapas like paella and beef tongue, or drink until you're lost on the map. Cocktail menu is thicker than your wallet. Don't mind the big bouncers.

➜ On Av. Allal ben Abdallah walking away from the medina walls. $ Tapas menu A, 4 for 140dh. Menu B 4 for 160dh. Appetizers 65-80dh. Entrees 90-140dh. Beer 30- 50dh. ⏰ Open daily 7:30pm-1:30am.

HAROLD'S
🍴🍸 CLUB

Corner of Av. Mohammed V and rue Ahmed Rifai, Centre Commercial Presite, Souissi ☎06 61 44 55 53

Harold, will you please party with me? Yes, *Let's Go* reader, he will. With what seems like hundreds of tables for drinking with old or new friends, many of them teens, this hip club among Rabat's wealthy youth keeps the bottles coming. For a price, that is. The nightly trance and house music are fire to burn on the dancefloors, especially Thursday through Saturday.

➜ At the intersection of Av. Mohammed V and rue Ahmed Rifai in the suburb of Souissi. At night, it costs 35dh to get there by petit taxi. $ Cover 100dh. Bottles 700dh. Deluxe 1300dh. Glasses 40-50dh before midnight and 60dh after. ⏰ Open daily 9pm-4am.

LE CLUB PRIVÉ
🍸 CLUB

Av. Ahmed Rifia, Centre Claridge, Souissi ☎06 61 68 30 82

The club may look like a ballroom spray-painted silver, but Rabat's young, beautiful, and wealthy definitely aren't dancing to Mozart. Live DJs spin beats every night while you drink and gyrate. If the prices are any indication, Privé is even more exclusive than Harold's, and more progressive too. Wednesday is ladies' night. You might have to wait in line for the best nights, Thursday through Saturday.

➜ 50 meter away from Harold's, next to Lenotre. $ Cover 150dh on weekends. Free weekdays. Bottle 1100dh. Deluxe 1300dh. Glass 50-60 dh before 1:30am, 90 dh after.

HENRY'S BAR 🍸 BAR

Av. Mohammed V ☎05 37 70 80 20

The epitome of an all-male dive bar: 14dh Speciale, a pinball machine, brown everything, and friendly cockroaches. Should be called Henry and Friend's Bar. You won't find cheaper booze in *centre ville* and despite the local crowd, groups of women are welcomed (but it's better to come with male company.) Try the pastis, but don't cry when the lights come on at 10pm. Locals need to work tomorrow.

➜ Av. Mohammed V past the train station, on the opposite side of the street. ℹ Cash only. $ Beer 14 dh. ⏰ Open daily 6am-10pm.

SHOPPING

Specialty Items

The best budget shopping in Rabat is found, not surprisingly, in the medina. But the best of the best is tucked away from the main entrance in the medina's north corner at the end of **Rue des Consuls.** Where old embassies used to be, you can now find **Souq Tahti,** with arts and crafts shops galore. There are specialty stuffs like carpets, shawls, leather goods, metal lamps, handpainted ceramics, a leather jacket store, *jellaba*, jewelry and, of course, hookahs.

ESSENTIALS

Practicalities

- **TOURIST OFFICE: Office National du Tourisme.** Houses the fancy bureaucracy that organizes Moroccan tourism at the national level. Ironically, not at all designed for tourist drop-ins. (*At the corner of rue Oued al-Makhazine and rue Zellaka in the suburb of Agdal. Located past the Rabat-Agdal Train Station in a maze of side-streets off of Rue Ibn-Sina. Best found in a petit taxi. ☎ 05 37 7 40 13 ⏰ Open daily 9am-4pm.*) **Direction Régionale du Tourisme.** Equipped with an inconsistently staffed welcome desk, maps from 2006 and flashy brochures. (*22 rue D'Alger Hassan ☎ 05 37 66 06 63 💻www.visitrabat.com ⏰ Open daily 9am-4pm.*)
- **CURRENCY EXCHANGE: BMCE Agence Central** has **ATMs** and handles traveler's checks. (*260 Av. Mohammed V along the first block away from the medina and towards the royal palace ☎05 37 21 61 40 ⏰ Open M-F 8:15am-3:45pm.*) In general, there is no shortage of banks or ATMs, especially along Av. Mohammed V in the center of town.
- **LUGGAGE STORAGE:** *Consigne* at the **Gare Routière** (*3km away from the city center on Av. Hassan II. 15-20dh in a petit taxi, 4-5dh in a grand taxi, or 3.5 dh on bus # 52. $5 dh per piece of baggage for one day. Bags can be left for up to 3-months. ⏰ Open daily 6am-midnight*).
- **INTERNET: Arab Cafe.** (*4 Av. Allal ben Abdellah around the corner from Av. Hassan II. ☎ 05 37 73 22 08. Limitless Wi-Fi and a complimentary drink for 15dh. ⏰ Open daily 5am-10pm.*) Otherwise, **Cyber Chahrazad.** (*Av. Hassan II one block in from Bab al-Had $ 6dh per hr. ⏰ Open daily 8:30am-10:30pm.*)
- **POST OFFICE:** Principal Post Office of Rabat. (*Corner of Av. Mohammed V and rue Soekarno as you walk towards the royal palace ☎05 37 21 01 28 ⏰ Open M-F 8am-6pm and Sa 8am-2pm. Poste restante is through a separate entrance to the right of the main doors on Av. Mohammed V. Western Union inside.*)

Emergency!

- **POLICE:** ☎19. There is a police station at the entrance to the medina on Av. Mohammed V across from the **Central Market** as well as an outpost at the **Gare Routière.**
- **LATE-NIGHT PHARMACY: Pharmacie Renaissance** *(356 Av. Mohammed V. ☎05 37 72 24 22. Open M-F 9am-1pm, 3-7:30pm).* Rotating 24-hr pharmacies are open every night of the week. Updated lists are posted outside all pharmacies in Rabat.
- **HOSPITAL: Hospital ibn Sina** (also known as Hopital Avicennes. Pl. Ben Iznasen 20 dh by *petit taxi* from *centre ville.* *☎05 37 67 44 03).* **Ambulance** ☎ 05 37 20 20 20.

Getting There

By Plane

Aeroport Rabat-Sale *(☎05 37 80 80 90),* 9km northeast of Rabat, is the arrival point for all flights into Rabat. A *grand taxi* from *centre ville* costs 150dh. **Royal Air Maroc** is located at Pl. des Alaouites on Av. Mohammed V, diagonally opposite the **Rabat Ville** train station. *(☎05 37 21 92 20 ⏰ Open M-F 8:30am-12:15pm and 2:30-7pm.)*

By Train

The train station, **Gare Rabat-Ville,** is on Av. Mohammed V at Pl. des Alaouites. *(☎ 08 90 20 30 04 ➡ A 10min. walk from Bab al-Had. ⏰ Ticket office open M-F 6:30am-8:30pm, Sa 8am-4pm, Su 11am-7pm.)* Trains run to: **Fez** *([$] 100dh. ⏰ 3½hr., every hr. 6am-11pm);* **Mèknes** *([$] 65 dh. ⏰ 2½hr., every hr. 6am-11pm);* **Marrakesh** *([$] 120dh. ⏰ 4½hr., every 2hr. 5:45am-7:45pm);* **Casablanca** *([$] 95dh. ⏰ 1hr., every 2hr. 6:30am-9pm);* **Tangier** *([$] 95dh. ⏰ 4½hr., approx. every 3hr. 7:45am-5:45pm).*

By Bus

CTM Station, two blocks past Pl. al-Qamra on Av. Hassan II towards Casablanca. *(☎05 37 28 14 86.)* To: **Fez** *([$] 75dh ⏰ 3hr., 8:30am, 9:10am, 1:10pm, 6:40pm, 8:15pm, 9:45pm, 10:10pm, and 10:30pm);* **Marrakech** *([$] 135dh ⏰ 4.5hr., 1:30pm, 9:30pm and 9:35 pm);* **Tanger** *([$] 110dh ⏰ 4hr., 7:30am, 12:30pm, 4pm, 6:45pm, 1:15am);* **Essaouira** *([$] 185dh ⏰ 7hr., 5am, 12:30pm);* **Casablanca** *([$] 35dh ⏰ 1-1.5 hr., 4am-9:30pm almost every half-hour);* **Meknes** *([$] 55dh ⏰ 2hr., 7am, 11:40am, 2:40pm, 8:15pm, 9pm and 9:45 pm).*

Gare Routière at Pl. al-Qamra on Av. Hassan II towards Casablanca. *(☎05 37 79 58 16).* As is the case with other private bus stations in Morocco, there are 15 ticket windows representing various bus companies. Roughly speaking, #1-7 serve the Moroccan north, while 1-8 serve the south. The fares are consistent throughout and are cheaper than CTM prices. To: **Fez** *([$] 40dh ⏰ 4hr., 5am-7pm, every half-hour);* **Marrakech** ([$] 70dh *⏰ 4hr., 5:30am-midnight, every hour);* **Casablanca** *([$] 20dh. ⏰ 1 hr., every 10min.);* **Essouira** *([$] 80-90dh. ⏰ 5-6hr., 4 per day);* **Tanger** *([$] 110dh. ⏰ 3hr.; 5:30am, 6:30am, 7:15am-10:15 every hour);* **Meknes** *([$] 30-35dh. ⏰ 2½hr., 5am-7pm every 30min).* For both the CTM and main stations, it costs 20dh by *petit taxi* from the center of town, 4-5dh per person in a *grand taxi* or 3.50dh on bus #52.

Getting Around

Grand and *petit taxis* can be found at **Bab al-Had** and **Gare Rabat Ville**. The price of a *grand taxi* to the airport is 150 dh. *Petit taxi* meters increase by 50% after 8 or 9pm, depending on the season. If your time of arrival doesn't need to exact, head to Av. de l'Egypte at Bab al-Had, the central hub for Rabat's public transportation. In spite of snazzy buses, it's anyone's guess where to find a schedule. Fares are 3.50dh per person. Bus **#21** goes from Bab al-Had to **Chellah.** Buses **#17, 30,** and **41** go from Bab al-Had to the bus stations, and **#52** goes from the **Gare Routiière** to *centre ville* along Av. Hassan II.

MARRAKESH AND ESSAOUIRA

Did you come to Morocco for sand, *souqs*, and *skalas*? Did you set off to lose your way navigating a bazaar and lose your breath hiking the Atlas Mountains? Then forget that 1940s movie and drop that little red hat—it's Marrakesh and Essaouira that you want.

It's no wonder that Marrakesh is the tourist capital of Morocco. There's the medina's world-famous **Djema'a al-Fna**, an extraordinary open-air spectacle of snake charmers, performing artists, charlatans, mystics and more, not to mention some of the most mouth-watering food in all of Morocco. On the other side of town is the *ville nouvelle*, a cosmopolitan city with luxurious hotels, gourmet restaurants, and off-the-hook nightlife. The abundance of lush gardens are a welcome respite from the heavy heat, and hikes into the nearby Atlas Mountains are only a jaunt away.

Right along the coast, Essaouira is less popular with tourists, but its cool ocean breezes, soft beaches, and laid-back lifestyle are enough to make anyone want to go native. Jimi Hendrix and Cat Stevens liked the vibe in '69, and it hasn't changed much since, except for a steady increase in tourists eager to breathe Morocco's freshest air. Give yourself more than a day and you might find your visit slipping into weeks, months, and even years.

greatest hits

- **DEAD CENTER.** The bustling bazaar at Djema'a al-Fna is the most happenin' "assembly of the dead" this side of the Last Judgment (p. 457).

- **AIN'T NO MOUNTAIN HIGH, AIN'T NO VALLEY LOW...** From the summit of Mt. Toubkal to the lowlands of Marrakesh, and with the Seven Waterfalls to boot, there ain't even a river wide missing in this area of Morocco (p. 459).

- **JUST DESERTS.** Just about the only stretch of sand in Morocco that isn't deadly, Essaouira's little slice of non-Saharan real estate is a beach resort done Moroccan style—camels *will* be joining you while you tan (p. 466).

When in Marrakesh, do as the marrakchi do—charm smoke some hookah, dance to local music, and sip some cocktails. Now if only there were a place to do all of those things...Oh that's right, **African Chic.** The name says it all, but if you'd like a more laid-back experience, try grabbing a meal with friends at Restaurant Toubkal; the prices are more than reasonable, and they're open late. If you're aching for the feel of sand between your toes, a daytrip to Essaouira is just what the doctor ordered. It's the student-beach destination of Morocco, with prices and nightlife to match.

marrakesh   ☎05 24

Marrakesh has been a thriving city for almost a thousand years. The Red City was founded in 1062 by the Almoravid dynasty, and its mosques and *medersas* quickly became a cultural and intellectual epicenter of North Africa. The Almohads destroyed much of the city upon succeeding the Almoravids, but rebuilt Marrakesh using Andalusian artisans, who instilled the city with its characteristic Spanish flare. Marrakesh subsequently served as Morocco's capital under various sultanates, and today is, without a doubt, one of the nation's most beautiful big cities. As a hybrid of old world mysticism and new world momentum, Marrakesh will remain so for many years to come.

ORIENTATION

The famed **Pl. Djema'a al-Fna** is right at the heart of things; to the west of Djema'a al-Fna, past the horses of the *calèche* stands, is the landmark **Koutoubia Mosque.** Put this action-packed plaza at the center of your mental map. There are several important thoroughfares that radiate from Pl. Djema'a al-Fna. To the west, **Av. Mohammed V** is the main avenue out of the Djema'a al-Fna and the medina to the *ville nouvelle.* To the south, the central **Rue Bab Agnou** leads to budget hotels and the **Kasbah. Rue Moulay Ismail** runs roughly parallel to rue Bab Agnou and hosts the post office and a series of banks. To the east (opposite the mosque), two main streets exit the Pl. Djema'a al-Fna: **Rue Riad Zitoun El Kedim,** which is right by **Restaurant Toubkal,** and **Rue Riad Zitoun El Jdid,** which is by **Chez Chegrouni.** Finally, at the north end of the plaza is **Rue Souq Smarine,** which winds through the medina's bustling markets and arrives at museums and worthwhile sights. With **Pl. Djema'a al-Fna** and the **Koutoubia Mosque** as your landmarks, you can tackle the medina.

The *ville nouvelle* is 30min. by foot, 10dh by *petit taxi* or 4dh on bus **#1** away from the medina along **Av. Mohammed V.** The cosmopolitan neighborhood you'll want to visit is called **Guéliz.** This is where many of the city's eclectic restaurants, night clubs, and bars are found, in addition to essential services like hospitals, banks, car rental agencies, the principal post office and a Mickey D's. The center of Guéliz is the traffic circle **Pl. du 16 Novembre** on Av. Mohammed V. The **Gare Ferrovière** is several blocks down **Av. Hassan II** off of Pl. du 16 Novembre. The **Gare Routière** is just beyond the medina outside of **Bab Doukkala** gate (See "Getting There" for directions).

ACCOMMODATIONS

Marrakesh's inexpensive accommodations are in abundant supply near Pl. Djema'a al-Fna. The best in budget hotels clump along the *derbs* (side streets) off of **Rue Bab Agnou** and **Rue Riad Zitoun Qedim,** as do *riads,* opulent restored medina accommodations with lovely terraces and home-cooked meals. On the other end of the spectrum, many hotels will allow you to sleep on their terrace for 40dh, a good option if you can't find a room, are desperately broke, or don't mind sleeping in the summer heat.

HOTEL SINDI SUD — HOTEL ❶

109 Derb Sidi Boloukate ☎05 24 44 33 37 💻sindisud@hotmail.com

A budget masterpiece. Beautiful blue tiling, intricate painted doors to every room, colored glass windows that open into the echoing interior courtyard, and immaculate rooms with single and double beds. You might expect this kind of comfort for an upscale *riad*, but not a backpacker haven. Although you'll have to bring your own toilet paper and pay 5dh for a hot shower, the communal baths are modern and spotless. This official Peace Corps volunteer favorite also has a lovely terrace for relaxing in the evening. The only downside is that all that tiling and open space means you might hear more of your neighbors at night than you'd hope for.

From rue Bab Agnou walking towards Pl. Djema'a al-Fna, turn right onto the last alley before the Place. Go straight then wind right, left and right. You will pass multiple hotels. Head underneath a small tunnel and continue straight to the hotel in front of you. $ Singles 60dh; doubles 100 dh; triples 150dh. Shower 5dh; breakfast 20dh. Inquire about sleeping on the terrace for around 30dh. ⏰ Reception 24hr. but the doors lock around 1am. Knock afterwards.

RIAD PETIT DARKOUM — RIAD ❷

12 Derb Kennaria El Jadida ☎05 24 37 82 91 💻www.riad-petitdarkoum.com

If you can navigate the twisting alleys to find this home in the heart of the medina, you'll be showered with warm hospitality by Saadia, a former Professor of Sociology at the Sorbonne and as sophisticated a woman as they come. But this hidden gem isn't for just anyone. It's for those willing to sit up late into the night exchanging ideas with a true savante in the salon before retiring to the beautifully decorated rooms or the breezy terrace; mind you it's also for those with fluent enough French to appreciate Saadia's stories. A study-abroad or thesis-writers's paradise. Reserve in advance.

Head away from Pl. Djema'a al-Fna on rue Riad Zitoun El Jdid for 10min. then turn right at Alabnak, a small alley. Make another right to enter Derb Kenaria Jdida which you follow until the Riad Petit Darkoum #12. The black door with brass bolts is the second to last as the Derb ends shortly after. $ Normally 300dh per night, but 150dh per Let's Go student interested in more than tourism, and negotiable.

HOTEL ALI — ❄ HOTEL ❶

Rue Moulay Ismail ☎05 24 44 49 79 💻wwww.hotelali.com

A small mall of essential services with a buffet restaurant, cafe, 24hr. currency exchange, hostel-style dorms, private rooms and a sunny terrace, just steps away from Djema'a al-Fna. The rooms are just as service-friendly, with bouncy double beds, fresh towels for the full baths and A/C (woah!). Made for travelers, this hotel attracts many of them, so it's best to reserve in advance.

From Djema'a al-Fna, walk down the rue Moulay Ismail, the road with the Post Office. ℹ Breakfast always included. $ Dorms or terrace room 70dh; singles 200dh; doubles 300 dh; triples 400dh; quads 500dh. ⏰ 24hr. currency cxchange in the lobby.

SIGHTS

If you ever get tired of exploring Djema'a al-Fna (trust us: you won't), Marrakesh has more old palaces, *medersas*, monuments and museums than it knows what to do with. When you're finished learning about Marrakshi history, escape the heat and turn off your brain in one of the city's lush gardens.

DJEMA'A AL-FNA — SQUARE

Djema El-fna Plaza

Welcome to Djema'a al-Fna (Assembly of the Dead), one of the most extraordinary open-air spectacles in the world. Once the sight of public executions, this enormous plaza has been given over to a loose fraternity of artists, storytellers, musicians, dancers, and entertainers. By day, women will tattoo you with henna or read your fortune in tarot cards, while Barbary apes dance on chains next to oboe-players charming snakes. But the real show starts at night, when food stalls open, smoke clouds the air, and Marrakshis of all ages visit Djema'a to be entertained and delighted. Amid the incredible commotion, you can eat a mouth-watering *tangia*, listen to men spinning stories in a language you regrettably don't understand, dance, or follow a boxing match or two. Throw a few dirhams to performers who enchant you and, as always, keep your wits about you.

LA MAISON DE LA PHOTOGRAPHIE — ART GALLERY

46 rue Ahal Fes ☎05 24 38 57 21 www.maison-delaphotographie.com

Look closely at a 1927 photo of Djema'a al Fna, and you can just make out the orange specks on vending stalls in the center of the square. Learning that fresh OJ has been sold for nearly 100 years here is just the beginning of a fascinating and striking exhibit of Moroccan history. This *riad*-turned-museum contains over 4000 photos taken from 1817-1950. Although Europeans were behind the camera lens, the images explore Morocco's myriad faces, including its Berber, Jewish, Arab, and Tuareg communities. Highlights are silhouetted camels in the desert and intensely expressive portraits of young men and women. *La Maison* also boasts one of the earliest color photographs taken by the French cinematographers, *Les Frères Lumière*, in 1907. After watching Berbers of the High Atlas dance and sing in the 1957 French documentary playing on loop, climb up to the terrace for a panorama of the medina.

From the Musée de Marakech, continue around the corner to the Medersa Ben Youssef. Keep going straight past the medersa and head left when the road forks. The maison is ahead on your left past the Restaurant Le Fondouq. i French skills will enhance the experience. $ 40dh. ⏰ Open daily 9am-7pm.

MEDERSA BEN YOUSSEF — SCHOOL

Place Ben Youssef ☎024 43 90 91

In 1565, Sultan Moulay Abdallah al-Ghalib built the *Medersa Ben Youssef* in the medina center, and it remained the largest Qur'anic school in the Maghreb until it closed in 1960. The *medersa* is an absolutely glorious example of the Merenid style, with *zellij* tile, ornate stucco work, and carved cedar on the courtyard walls. A huge arch opens on the *mihrab* (prayer niche) and the prayer room. Upstairs there are 132 cells which once accommodated all 900 of the students. Of all those cells, two have been recreated with writing desks, candles, and copies of the Qu'ran. Don't you wish your dorm room looked like this?

Exiting the Museum of Marrakesh, turn right and round the corner. $ Medersa 50dh. Museum of Marrakesh and Medersa Ben Youssef 60dh. ⏰ Open daily 9am-4:30pm.

GARDENS — FLOWERS, TREES, NORTH-AFRICAN FASHION DESIGNER

Despite the heavy heat, Marrakesh blooms with lush gardens. Starting at the top, the **Majorelle Gardens** are at the height of green fashion. The bamboo forests, flowers, and koi ponds were designed by French painter Jacques Majorelle in the 1920s, and are owned today by the Yves Saint-Laurent Foundation. Past the bamboo is a lone column fragment, a memorial to the famous French designer who was born in North Africa in 1936. Taking their cue from the memorial, travelers have carved their initials in the bamboo trunks over the years. Caretakers won't be too happy if you do the same. Next, there are the **Menara Gardens,** where Moroccan couples and families go to picnic, romance, and play. Even though the rows of olive trees don't rival the aesthetic of Majorelle, sitting in the Menara is a window into local life. If you'd rather be exclusive, the backyard of **La Mamounia** is for you. You might not be Winston Churchill or King Mohammed VI, but you can at least walk through the gardens of the posh hotel where they stayed. Just make sure to dress the part, which means closed-toed shoes, slacks for men, and skirts for women. Wherever you wind up, from *haute couture* forests to public orchards, there's bound to be shade and refreshment.

*🚶 **Majorelle**: Exit the medina through Bab Doukkala and walk straight past the traffic circle on Av. Moulay Youssef. Turn right at Av. Yacoub El Mansour and left at the sign for the gardens. **Menara**: From Pl. Djema'a al-Fna, walk down rue Moulay Ismail until Av. Bab Jdid. Exit the medina through Bab Jdid and continue straight on Av. de la Menara until the gardens. It's a hike so you might want to take a petit taxi for 10 dh. **La Mamounia**: On Av. Bab Jdid before it leaves the medina through Bab Jdid. ℹ Cash only for various entrances fees. $ **Majorelle** 30dh. **Menara** free. **La Mamounia** free. ⏰ **Majorelle** open daily 8am-5:30pm although hrs change slightly during the winter and Ramadan. **Menara** open daily 9am-8pm. **La Mamounia** open M-F 11am-5pm.*

KOUTOUBIA MOSQUE — MOSQUE

Avenue Mohammed V

The Koutoubia Mosque is like the north star; wherever you are in Marrakesh, it's 70m minaret will lead you home. Legend has it that Sultan Yacoub al-Mansour's wife melted her jewelry to gild one of the four golden lanterns atop the minaret. The beautiful product was the model for its sisters, one in Rabat and the other—*the Giralda*—in Sevilla. In addition to sending out calls to prayers that miraculously overpower Djema'a's tumult, the minaret looks most impressive backlit against the night sky. As at most Islamic prayer halls, entrance is forbidden to non-Muslims. Admire the Koutoubia and learn to love this Marrakchi icon as your traveler's compass.

ℹ Entrance is limited to Muslims.

THE GREAT OUTDOORS

The rocky heights of **Mt. Toubkal,** North Africa's tallest peak, are only a short trip from Marrakesh's pink flatness. The best way to visit this national park and climb its peak is, of course, with a guide. You can consult the **Conseil Régional du Tourisme** to arrange your mountain adventure, or take a *grand taxi* from **Bab er-Rob** directly to the village of **Imlil** where Berber guides and their mule companions are available for hire. Expect the adventure to take two days: one night at the mountain refuge followed by the 6-7hr. ascent and descent the following morning. There is also an easy and rewarding daytrip from Marrakesh to the village of **Setti Fatma** in the lush **Ourika Valley.** At Setti Fatma, hire a local guide or just ask for directions to visit the **Seven Waterfalls.**

FOOD

The nightly food in Pl. Djema'a al-Fna is so unquestionably amazing and so unbelievably inexpensive that you have no good reason to eat dinner in a restaurant. Food vendors wheel their stalls and tables onto the square beginning at 6pm and the fire doesn't stop burning until midnight, at least. Whet your appetite with hot *harira*, a lentil and tomato soup served with dates (*3dh*). If you're a vegetarian, chow down on lentils and beans (*5-6dh*), or the oily and amazing egg and potato sandwiches (*10dh*) at **stall #66.** For Marrakesh's specialty, visit **stall #44** and order *tangia* (*15-20dh*). Cooked with oranges and spices in a clay vessel that sits for hours in the 1000 degree heat of the public *hammam* furnace, *tangia* might very well be Morocco street food's *pièce de la resistance.* If there's any change left in your pocket, climb the stairs to **Cafe Glacier** or **Cafe Argana** for tea (*10-14 dh*) and views of the square that are the stuff of dreams and memories.

ABDESSADEQ'S BARBECUE — BARBECUE 1

Rue de la Kasbah

To feast on what can confidently be called the best barbecue in the medina, follow these instructions carefully: after finding a restaurant that has no name or sign (Abdessadeq is the owner), walk up to the smoking grill. Whatever you do, don't tear up from the thick cloud of smoke, since this is a sign of weakness.

Confident and strong, order 5-6 kebab per person in French, Arabic, or sign language. They're usually red meat, so if you want some variety ask for chicken too. Make sure to get your appetizer of *shlada*, a refreshing dip similar to gazpacho, with diced onions that you scoop up with pieces of steaming hot *khoubz* in your right hand. Take a seat if you can find one (unlikely around 9 or 10pm), enjoy the olives and wait for someone to call your order. Follow these time-honored instructions and your reward is unimaginable deliciousness.

Walk 10min. away from Pl. Djema'a al-Fna on rue Bab Agnou. Enter the Kasbah through the main gate and follow the road as it curves to the right. Pass the minaret of the Kasbah Mosque and the entrance to the Saadian Tombs. The restaurant is immediately ahead on your left next to the "Global Cash" sign. It has red Coca Cola drapes in front and a smoking grill. It might be a little far from Djema'a al-Fna, but boy is it worth it. $ 20dh per person. ⏰ Open 10am-midnight.

EARTH CAFE — VEGETARIAN ❷

2 Derb Zouak ☎06 61 28 94 02 www.earthcafemarrakech.com

Hidden down an unassuming alley in the medina, Earth Cafe is an oasis of vegetarian delights. Marrakesh might be hot, but thankfully this hipster hideout is no mirage. Start your meal off with multi-grain *khoubz* dipped in Marrakesh's famous argan oil (good for your skin and your stomach!) while sipping on one of a dozen smoothies with exotic ingredients from beetroot to ginger. Next, sink your teeth into one of the enormous plates, like the filo pastry stuffed with vegetables and goat cheese. The veggie vibe and the foreign crowd are straight out of Cali, but don't worry—the *riad* design with tranquil upstairs seating and the chef sporting a *hijab* say Morocco.

From Djema'a al-Fna, walk down Riad Zitoun El Qedim for 5min. and look for orange signs directing you to "Earth Cafe." After a well-signed right turn onto Derb Zouak - a medina alley - the cafe is immediately on the right. $ Drinks 15-20dh. Vegetable plates 60dh. ⏰ Open daily 11am-10pm.

RESTAURANT LE FONDOUQ — MOROCCAN ❸

55 Souq Hal Fassi ☎05 24 37 81 90

Put on your fancy pants and wind your way past the *Medersa Ben Youssef* to the medina's most elegant restaurant. In this converted riad, the evening light plays against dark wood and candelight as you play gourmand with your most sophisticated table manners. But the food is so fine that you'll need every bit of restraint to resist tossing your fork aside and plunging your forehead into the couscous. Cocktails and other alcoholic goodies are offered in the moody bar on the ground floor, and the terrace boasts a glorious view of the sunset beside trellises of climbing flowers. If the price is stressing you out, just meditate beside the zen fountain. When's the next time you're going to be here again, anyway?

From the Musée de Marakech, continue around the corner to the Medersa Ben Youssef. Keep going straight past the medersa and head left when the road forks. $ Appetizers 65-110dh. Plates 120-150dh. Special 35dh. Cocktails 85dh. ⏰ Open Tu-Su noon-midnight.

NIGHTLIFE

Marrakesh nightlife is cool, sexy, and fun. The catch is you have to go to Guéliz, a neighborhood just outside of the *ville nouvelle* and well outside of the medina. Dress up, bring 100-150dh in cover, and don't be surprised if you dish out more dirhams for the cab ride home, since late-night *petit taxi* drivers often refuse the meter. Still, you get what you pay for: open-air aromatic hookah bars, famous international DJs, bursting dance floors, and beautiful people.

AFRICAN CHIC — BAR

6 rue Oum Errabia ☎05 24 43 14 24 www.african-chic.com

If you're not swinging to the live band under black lighting, or slurping up the "African chic" mixed drinks of vodka, Malibu, orange, peach, and grapefruit juices, then you're probably transfixed by the bootylicious music videos playing on flatscreen TVs. Better yet, maybe you're flirting with bootylicious locals on tiger or leopard print couches, or at one of the tables. If not there, try the dance floor or bar. All in, African Chic lives up to its name, with classy vibes that offer a good-looking good time, especially on the weekends. Sundays, there's a DJ and bellydancers.

☀ *Leave the medina on Av. Mohammed V. rue Oum Errabia is a right turn one major street past the traffic circle at Pl. de la Liberté. Within walking distance or a 10 dh metered ride by petit taxi from the medina.* *i Happy hour 7-10:30pm, drinks 30dh.* Ⓢ *Beers 50dh. Cocktails 90-120dh. Bottles 100dh.* Ⓣ *Open daily 4:30pm-2am.*

MONTECRISTO
⚑🍸 HOOKAH, BAR
20 rue Ibn Aicha
☎05 24 43 90 31

Montecristo is comprised of four different venues. The restaurant is decent but not what you came here for. The bar is more like it, with bright lighting, plush couches, and live local bands performing every night. Grab a *speciale* and jam to start your night off. If you'd rather channel your inner John Travolta, strut past a traditional *zellij* fountain with not-so-traditional red lighting and head upstairs to the disco. Things get a lot darker, louder, and more scantily clad. The real highlight, though, is the skybar, its tantalizing aromas wafting from all the young people puffing on hookahs. This is just about as sweet as it gets.

☀ *In side-streets off of Av. Mohammed V past Pl. du 16 November. Best reached with a petit taxi from African Chic or anywhere in Guéliz for 10dh on the meter. 20dh from the medina.* Ⓢ *Shisha per night 120dh; drinks 80dh; bottles 1,100dh.* Ⓣ *Open 8pm-2am.*

THEATRO
⚑🍸🎴 CLUB
Hotel Es Saadi
☎06 64 86 03 39

On Theatro's raging dancefloor, massive screens flash "Dance Like Never Before." Subliminal message or not, it works. To use a well-worn and cheesy adage: Theatro is off-the-hook, yo. Lots of young Moroccans and travelers go wild to the house, techno and R and B for a party that starts spinning at 2am. Between the crinkled tin-foil walls and the massive, padded entrance doors to get in, you'll feel like you're in another world. And by traditional Moroccan standards, you definitely are. Security is tight but if you look the part, you'll pass.

☀ *Down rue Echouhada from Pl. de la Liberté. At the taffic circle, turn left. The club is next to the Casino. Best reached in a 10-20dh petit taxi using the meter from Guéliz or the medina.* *i Security is tight, expect your bag to be checked.* Ⓢ *Cover 150 dh. Drinks 90 dh. Bottles 1200 dh.* Ⓣ *Midnight-5am.*

DIAMANT NOIR
⚑🍸 CLUB
Hotel Le Marrakesh, Pl. de la Liberté
☎05 24 44 63 91

You might not be able to see the dark and beautiful figure you're dancing with, but all rules are off in a different country, right? Yes, it might be a bit scandalous, but say the name Diamant Noir and all Marrakshis will know what you're talking about. The party is best on weekends and doesn't start until 2am.

☀ *Next to African Chic on rue Oum Erabia. Easy, right?* Ⓢ *Cover M-Th and Sun 100dh, Fri-Sat 150dh. Drinks 80-120dh; Bottles 900-1200dh.* Ⓣ *Open daily 11am-dawn.*

Souqs

🏯 MEDINA SOUQS
🎴

The *souqs* of Marrakesh's medina are only slightly less overwhelming than Fès. A shopping trip begins at the entrance to **Rue Souq Smarine** at the back of Pl. Djema'a al-Fna (prime time for crowds is between 5-8pm). Enter the medina to the right of **Cafe Argana** and walk through the archway to enter rue Souq Smarine, the main thoroughfare through the markets. This street is home to the **fabric souq** with gorgeous silky woven blankets, and their owners, calling out to you to buy them. There are also lamps, hookahs, scented candle and leather stores. A few minutes later, you'll come to an alley to the right heading into the **Rahba Kedima.** You might smell it first: the avenue is full of stalls selling herbs, spices and sops for all variety of cuisines and illnesses. The path quickly opens to a square called **La Criée Berbère,** which was once home to a slave auction. It is now of spice shops, an open-air basket market, and the lovely **Cafe des Epices.** Back on **Rue Souq Smarine,** the road quickly forks. The right fork leads to more shops and eventually to the **Museum of Marrakech** and the **Medersa Ben Youssef.** The left fork is the **babouche souq.** In spite of its name, these stalls sell more than just the traditional Moroccan slipper, although there certainly are a lot of *babouches.* When you reach a sharp left turn, head down it to find the **dyers' souq.** Pushing through the bubbling vats will lead you to the 16th-century **Mouassine Fountain,** a grimy but character-laden sight. Those with strong stomachs can visit the tanneries: continue straight through the markets and take a right after the **Medersa Ben Youssef.** Head straight for 10min through a run-down section of the medina and the tanneries are on your right. If you get lost, ask a merchant for directions.

ESSENTIALS

Practicalities

- **TOURIST OFFICE: Délégation du Tourisme**. Welcome desk that offers maps of Marrakesh and will connect tourists to official guides, often through hotels. (*Av. Mohammed V at Pl. Abdelmoumen Ben Ali ☎05 24 43 61 31 ➡ Several blocks from Pl. du 16 Novembre away from the medina. 🕒 Open M-F 8:30am-4:30pm.*) **Conseil Regional du Tourisme** provides a simple and excellent map. (*Pl. Yousef Ben Tachfine.* ☎05 26 38 52 61. *🕒 Open M-F 8am-noon and 3-6pm.*)
- **CURRENCY EXCHANGE:** Most major banks in the medina are off rue Moulay Ismail, off Djema'a Al-Fna. **BMCi**. (*☎05 24 38 81 90 🕒 Open M-F 8:15am-4pm.*) **BMCE**. (*🕒 Open M-F 8:15am-3:45pm.*) In the ville nouvelle there are branches of all major banks on Av. Mohammed V in Pl. 16 Novembre. **BMCI** (*➡ Next to McDonald's. 🕒 Open M 12:45-4pm, Tu-F 8:15am-4pm, Sa 9:15am-12:30pm.*) **BMCE.** (*➡ Further along Av. Mohammed V away from the medina, 🕒 Open M-F 8:15am-3:45pm.*) All banks have 24hr. ATMs.
- **INTERNET: Téléboutique/Cyber**. (*48 rue Bab Agnou, 20m from Pl. Djema'a al-Fna $ 8dh per hr. 🕒 Open daily 9am-midnight.*) There are a good number of cyber cafes on the streets radiating from Djema'a al Fna.
- **POST OFFICE: Principal Post Office,** Pl. 16 Novembre in the *ville nouvelle,* has poste restante. (*☎05 24 43 19 63 🕒 Open M-F 8am-4:30pm, Sa 8:30am-noon.*) **Western Union** inside is open daily 8am-7pm. There is also a Post Office in Djema'a al-Fna at the top of rue Moulay Ismail with the same hours.

Emergency!

- **POLICE:** General phone number: ☎19. **Police Touristique**. Right in Pl. Djema'a al-Fna across from the Post Office. ☎05 24 38 46 01. Open 24hr. There is a police outpost at the **Gare Routière**.
- **MEDICAL: S.O.S. Medecins Maroc**. ☎05 24 40 40 40. Emergency doctors on-call. **Croissant Rouge** ambulance service: ☎05 24 44 54 27. **Polyclinique du Sud**, 2 rue Yugoslavia, Guéliz is a private medical clinic with 24hr. emergency services and a range of specialists available (*☎05 24 44 79 99).* The **public hospital,** Hopital Civil Ibn Toufail, is 2 blocks away from Polyclinique du Sud (*☎05 24 44 80 11).*
- **PHARMACY: Pharmacie du Progres**. (*56 Pl. Djema'a al-Fna. ☎05 24 44 25 63 🕒 Open M-F approximately 9am-6pm with a lunch break.*) There is a list of rotating 24hr. *de garde* pharmacies posted outside all pharmacies in Marrakesh.

Getting There

By Plane

Aeroport de Marrakech Menara is 5km southwest of Djema'a al-Fna (☎05 24 44 78 65). A *petit taxi* to and from the airport costs 50dh. Better yet, there is an airport shuttle run by ALSA. (ⓢ *One-way 20dh, round-trip 30dh.* ⏰ *15-25min., every 30min. 6:15am-9:15pm.)* It takes 15min. to go *from* the airport to Djema'a al-Fna, but 25min. in the other direction, since the shuttle passes the **Gare Routière, Pl. du 16 November** in Guéliz, and the train station, before heading to the airport.

By Train

Gare Ferrovière is at the intersection of Av. Mohammed VI and Av. Hassan II. Walking along Av. Mohammed V from the medina, at Pl. 16 du Novembre turn left on Av. Hassan II. 40min. by foot from the medina or a 13dh *petit taxi* ride with the *conteur*. Buses to: **Casablanca** (ⓢ *90 dh.* ⏰ *3hr., 5am-9pm every 2hr.)*; **Rabat** *(*ⓢ *120dh.* ⏰ *4hr., 5am-9pm every 2hr.)*; **Fez** *(*ⓢ *195dh.* ⏰ *7hr., 5am-7pm every 2 hr.)*; **Meknes** *(*ⓢ *174dh.* ⏰ *6½hr., 5am-7pm every 2hr.)*; **Tanger** *(*ⓢ *205 dh.* ⓢ *10 hr., 4 per day)*. Next to the train station, there is frequent and reliable bus service to **Essaouira** with **Supratours** *(*ⓢ *65dh. 5dh for large luggage.* ⏰ *3½hr., 5 per day)*. But tickets one day ahead, since they are always oversold.

By Bus

Gare Routière is at Bab Doukkala immediately beyond the medina walls. Walk towards the *ville nouvelle* along Av. Mohammed V and turn right onto rue El Adala past the **Complexe Artisanal**. The first gate 10min. up on your left is Bab Doukkala *(*☎05 24 43 39 33)*. **CTM** *(*☎05 24 43 44 02)*, straight after you walk in the main doors, goes to: **Essaouira** *(*ⓢ *70dh.* ⏰ *2hr., 8am and noon)*; **Casablanca** *(*ⓢ *90dh.* ⏰ *3hr., 5 per day)*; **Rabat** *(*ⓢ *135dh.* ⏰ *4½hr., 5 per day)*; **Fez** *(*ⓢ *155dh.* ⏰ *8hr., 4 per day)*.

Getting Around

By Taxi

The public *grand taxi* station is a 20min. walk south of Bab Er-Rob, the southern gate exiting the medina next to the Kasbah. Depending on how you're feeling, it might be worth taking a 5dh *petit taxi* from Djema al'Fna'a to get there. From here, you can find taxis to **Setti Fatma** at 25dh per person. Remember that these prices are for a full and squishy cab of six people. There is a second *grand taxi* lot outside Bab Doukkala by the **Gare Routière**. Finally, private *grand taxis* line Av. Houmane El Fatouaki and can be hired at 100dh for daytrips.

By Bus

Marrakesh has an excellent public transportation system with frequent and reliable service. The main hub for buses is on Av. Houmane El Fatouaki at the corner with rue Moulay Ismail, just off Pl. Djema'a al-Fna. **#1** goes from Pl. Djema'a al-Fna to Gueliz, while **buses #8, 6, 10, 14** and **66** go from the Place to the **Gare Routière** and the Train Station. Fare is 4dh.

By Moped/Scooter

Rental stands dot the sidewalks around Pl. du 16 Novembre and back towards the medina. Rentals are approximately 300dh per day. Moped traffic in the city is always a little crazy, so drive at your own risk.

marrakesh · essentials

essaouira

The siren song of Essaouira is inescapable. A dye-producing colony in Phoenician times, the town has remained an important port throughout the ages, valued first for its secure ramparts, a later for its scrumptious sardines. The Gnaoua World Music Festival is held every year in June, and the town's numerous galleries flaunt its artistic riches, but for most of the year Essaouira's a quietly hip place.

ORIENTATION

Essaouira's gorgeous medina is a true pleasure to navigate. Even the few destinations outside of the ramparts, such as the bus station and the beach, are within easy walking distance. To get to the medina from the **Gare Routière,** turn right out of the station and walk along **Av. du 2 Mars** for 10-15min. until it ends. Turn left past the *calèche* stands and **Bab Doukala,** one of the main gates to the medina, is straight ahead.

Just to make your life easy, the medina is roughly a square with a main street that cuts diagonally from one corner to the other. At one corner is the **Bab Doukala** gate, while the **Bab El Mlnzah** gate is at the opposite corner beside the Atlantic Ocean. Even though the main street has two names, it's the widest avenue in town, so you can't miss it. At Bab Doukala, it's called **Av. Mohamed Zerktouni.** Moving towards the ocean, it passes beneath two gates and becomes **Av. L'istiqlal.** In between the first and second gates is the **Souq Jdid,** a square marketplace with shops and fried fish stalls. At the second gate, **Blvd. Mohamed Al Qouri** intersects with the main street perpendicularly, and leads to a third corner of the medina, which exits out of **Bab Marrakech.** In addition to the abundant fried fish stalls, Blvd. Mohamed Al Qouri is the fastest route to 🏠 **Hostel Essaouira.** The **Supratours** bus station is immediately outside of Bab Marrakesh.

Back on Av. L'Istiqlal, Essa's main drag, past a third gate and the landmark **Clock Tower,** the medina's main street opens into the **Place Moulay Hassan.** This plaza is crowded with fish vendors, banks, cafes, hotels, and stunning views of the crashing waves. With your eyes toward the water, the beach is a 5min walk to the left of the plaza. **Blvd. Mohammed V** is the road along the beach. To the right and inside the plaza are two useful streets: **Rue Skala,** which leaves Pl. Moulay Hassan in between **Banque Populaire** and **Taros Cafe,** and **Av. Sidi Mohamed Ben Abdellah,** which exits at the back of the plaza after the **BMCE.** Rue Skala follows the ramparts on the outside of the medina and leads to the **Skala de Ville** ramparts and the budget **Hotel Smara,** while Av. Sidi Mohamed Ben Abdellah runs parallel to the main street and has excellent restaurants and shops.

ACCOMMODATIONS

Hotels in Essaouira are a little pricier than elsewhere in Morocco, but that's because they're better, with tastefully decorated rooms, reliable hot water, and breezy roof terraces.

🏠 **HOSTEL ESSAOUIRA**   ⊛(((•))) ∀ ⚐   HOSTEL ❷

17 Derb Laghrissi   ☎05 24 47 64 81 ▪www.essaouirahostel.com

Grab a beer and make yourself at home with the young hip crowd in this super social hostel. Awesome staff and guests chill out in the bar/lounge downstairs, while the rooms upstairs are comfy dorms with names like Pink Floyd and Led Zeppelin. Psychedelic paint on every wall, great communal showers, and a terrace with couches and a fully stocked kitchen are just some of the perks. You pay more for the party, so if you want privacy and quiet, head elsewhere.

From the Supratour stations: head through Bab Marrakech onto Blvd. Mohammed El Qouri and look for the blue "Hostel Essaouira" sign in a few blocks on your upper right. Follow the successive signs straight and to the right but don't miss the unmarked entrance down an alley on your left. From Av. L'Istiqlal with your back to Bab Doukala, turn left down Av. Mohammed El Quori and look for the signs. ℹ *Free internet and Wi-Fi downstairs.* Ⓢ *10-bed dorms 131dh, 6-bed 153dh, 4-bed dorms 175dh. Doubles 600-650dh.*

HOTEL SMARA
⊕ HOTEL ❶

26 rue Skala ☎05 24 47 56 55

The best value in Essaouria and a backpacker favorite, this blue-and-white classic might be old, but it's still immaculate. Simple rooms and decent communal baths are complemented by stunning views of the sea in the slightly pricier rooms, but what a way to wake up in the morning. Mention *Let's Go* to win a smile and maybe even a bargain.

⚡ *At Pl. Moulay Hassan, turn down rue Skala next to Banque Populaire. Follow the road until the gate. Bypass the gate to the right and continue straight. The hotel is up ahead no the right.* Ⓢ *Singles 76dh; doubles 104dh, with view 134dh, with best view 196dh.* ⌚ *Reception 24hr.*

HOTEL CAP SIM
⊕ HOTEL❷

11 rue Ibnou Roch ☎05 24 78 58 34 ✉hotelcapsim@menara.ma

Budget accommodations don't get any snazzier than this hotel's wooden balconies, multi-colored glass windows, and luxurious Moroccan salon. More expensive rooms have Berber weaves and colorful tiles; more affordable digs go without showers are simpler but remain aesthetically pleasing. The communal showers are excellent, and so is the included breakfast. Reception is happy to negotiate prices for students and travelers staying for more than one night.

⚡ *At Pl. Moulay Hassan, turn down rue Skala next to Banque Populaire. Follow the road until the gate. Bypass the gate to the right and at the next opportunity, turn right. Walk through a mini-tunnel and turn right on the road as you emerge. The hotel is up ahead on your right.* ℹ *Breakfast included.* Ⓢ *Singles without shower 155dh, with bath 300dh; doubles 230/360dh; triples 350/400dh; quads 420/520dh.* ⌚ *Reception 24hr.*

HOTEL TAFRAOUT
⊕ HOTEL❷

7 rue Marrakech ☎05 24 47 62 76

This blue and white hotel has fluffy white pillows, Berber weaves on the beds, and bathrooms with brass sinks. There's also a terrace for laundry, and a spacious if slightly bare courtyard to liven the place up. The prices are on the high side for the value, but reception is willing to negotiate based on the season.

⚡ *In the back of Pl. Moulay Hassan turn left up rue Sidi Mohammed ben Abdellah past the BMCE bank. The hotel is down an alley on your right. Look for the sign.* Ⓢ *Singles 180dh, with bath 280dh; doubles 280/400dh.* ⌚ *Reception 24hr.*

SIGHTS
◉

In between relaxing on the beach and lolling in cafes, it's well worth your time to appreciate the artisan galleries of Essaouira's beautiful medina. Make sure to climb the ramparts of the Skala to get the best vantages of the Atlantic crashing against the fortress walls.

🏛 RAMPARTS AND PORT
⊕ FORTRESS, VIEW

Essaouira's two *skalas* sit dramatically at the edge of the violent Atlantic and offer spectacular views of the ocean and the isles. Their strange mixture of Moroccan and European military architecture is so striking that Orson Welles used it in his adaptation of *Othello*. Free to the public, **Skala de la Ville** has brass cannons to climb on and gorgeous views of the ocean crashing on the rocks below. The unoccupied nooks are popular with canoodling Moroccan couples, and it's easy to why. The other, **Skala du Port,** has a 10dh entrance fee that is more than worth the incredible oblique shots of the old medina walls. Don't forget your camera. On the sea side are the colorful old fishing boats and the beach melting away into the horizon.

➔ *To get to Skala de la Ville from Pl. Moulay Hassan, turn down rue Skala next to Banque Populaire. Continue straight through the gate. To get to Skala du Port walk to the fortress by the water at the end of Pl. Moulay Hassan.* $ *Skala du Port 10 dh.* ⏰ *Open M-Th 9am-6pm, F 9am-noon and 3-6:30pm, Sa-Su 9am-6pm.*

BEACHES ⛱ BEACH

One of Morocco's best beaches, Essaouira's sand feels great on bare feet. You can sunbathe on a recliner, swim in the refreshing Atlantic, kite surf with the wicked wind, or join in a game of beach soccer. Depending on the season and the time of day, the same breeze that makes Essaouria's climate so pleasant can also make sunbathing a little chilly. Lifeguards are always on duty during the day, and the beach is furnished with public restrooms and shower facilities. Surf clubs cluster along the boardwalk and rent boards by the hour or by the day. ➔

➔ *Facing the water, exit Pl. Moulay Hassan to the left and smile as the beach begins to stretch for miles in front of your eyes.*

MEDINA NEIGHBORHOOD

Beneath the ramparts of the **Skala de la Ville** are the wood-shops that produce some of Morocco's finest crafts. The lovely, deep aroma of *thuya* wood wafts down the street, where all sorts of hand-crafted finery are on display. The artisans inlay the *thuya* with cedar and ebony to produce cups, chess sets, drums, statues and masks which make for beautiful keepsakes. In addition to the wood, there's a vibrant local painting scene in Essaouira, and galleries line the medina streets. For other miscellaneous artwork, including silver jewelry, head to the *Souq Jdid* at the intersection of Av. L'Istiqlal and Blvd. Mohammed Al Qouri.

MUSEUM MOHAMMED BEN ABDELLAH 🏛 MUSEUM

Rue Lallouj ☎05 24 47 53 00

Essaouria's fine museum provides especially well-written accounts of the interesting stories behind traditional Moroccan wood carving, silver jewelry, calligraphy and clothing, in addition to detailing the history of the town and its people. Among the highlights of the collection is a 13th-century Qur'an. Somehow the glass case separating you and the sacred book does not detract from the power of seeing 800-year-old Islamic calligraphy. Unfortunately, for those who don't read French or Arabic, there is less to glean from the experience.

➔ *Looking at the clock tower from the third gate along Av. L'Istiqlal, turn right down Rue Attarine before walking through the gate. After a slight bend this becomes rue Lallouj. The museum is beside the post office on your left.* $ *10dh.* ⏰ *Open M 8:30am-6:30pm, W-Su 8:30am-6:30pm.*

FOOD 🍴

The cheapest dining can be found at the fish sandwich places along **Av. L'Istiqlal** and **Blvd. Mohammed Al Quori.** Pick any vendor and you can score a fish sandwich for 10-15dh. To eat unbelievably fresh and delicious fish, make a beeline for the blue huts at the port end of Pl. Moulay Hassan. Prices and selection are basically identical among the rows of blue huts, so just grab a table and dig in. For sit-down meals, Essaouria has some of the most eclectic eats in Morocco. Essa boasts especially fine French cuisine in addition to its hole-in-the-wall vegan joint.

👍 TAROS CAFE 🎫🍸⛱ CAFE ❸

Pl. Moulay Hassan ☎05 24 47 64 07

How can one place be so many incredibly cool things at once? Taros offers gourmet fish and fowl and a particularly juicy braised lamb shank (*90dh*), served by candlelight among local art displays. The prime view of the ocean, mouth-watering (albeit pricey) cocktails, and an unfailing crowd make this the hippest night spot in Essaouira.

➔ *In Pl. Moulay Hassan next to Banque Populaire.* $ *Appetizers 60-120dh; entrees 90-150dh. Beers 35-60dh. Cocktails 75-160dh.* ⏰ *Open daily until 1am or later, depending on the party.*

EARTH CAFE — 🍴 VEGAN ❷

Pl. Chrib Atai

You might not believe your eyes when you check out the entirely vegan menu inked in red onto the back mirror of this tiny oasis in meat-loving Morocco. Dig into veggies cooked to perfection in filo pastries while drinking vats of fresh OJ. Dried garlic and chilly garlands hang near rows of watermelons as appropriately earthy decor. The progressively named Burger Women with "mushed veggies," lentils and balsamic vinegar served on a heaping bed of squash, zucchini and other organics is so satisfying you just might give up on beef.

➜ Looking at the clock tower from the third gate along Av. L'Istiqlal, turn right down rue Attarine before walking through the gate. After a slight bend this becomes rue Lallouj. Immediately on your right is a tiny plaza with cafes and restaurants. Earth Cafe is inside on the far right. $ Heaping plate 60dh. ⏰ Open daily 10am-10pm.

CRÊPERIE MOGADOR — 🍴 CREPERIE, FRENCH ❶

4 rue Lallouj ☎05 24 78 30 96

Many people dream of opening up quaint restaurants in seaside paradises. The lovely French expat who owns this crêperie actually did it. Choose from a delicious selection of dinner and dessert crepes, filled with tomato, cheese, egg, leaks, mushrooms, honey, nutella, maple syrup, chocolate, almonds, and more. If you're not drooling by now, you're probably illiterate.

➜ Looking at the clock tower from the third gate along Av. L'Istiqlal, turn right down rue Attarine before walking through the gate. After a slight bend this becomes rue Lallouj. The restaurant is just ahead and on your left. $ Crepes 20-50dh. ⏰ Open M-Th noon-3pm and 7-1pm, Sa-Su noon-3-pm and 7-10pm.

RESTAURANT LAAYOUNE — 🍴 MOROCCAN ❷

4 rue El Hajjali ☎05 24 47 46 43

Candlelit and exquisite Moroccan dining. You'll get the full experience with one of four set menus, including *harira*, Moroccan cooked salads, *tajines* and couscous. The intimate interior is modeled on a Moroccan salon with traditional music and lovely windows onto the street. Fills up fast with the tourist crowd in the evenings, but the wait is worth the meal.

➜ At the back of Pl. Moulay Hassan walk straight past the BMCE bank and turn right when you have to. ℹ Cash only. $ Set menus 68dh, 78dh, 88dh. Spaghetti 45dh. Crepes 16dh. ⏰ Open M-Th noon-3pm and 7-10:15pm, Sa-Su noon-3pm and 7-10:15pm.

NIGHTLIFE

Just because Essaouira is a tranquil town by the sea, that doesn't mean there's no action to be found come nightfall. Start off your evening on one of two terrace bars in Pl. Moulay Hassan. **Casa Vera**, in the middle of the plaza, has a stellar view of the Skala du Port and hosts a live DJ every night until 1am. For more upscale crowd, head to **Taros Cafe** at the entrance to rue Skala. This multi-level terrace bar has delicious cocktails, a gorgeous view of the water, and a blue-and-white decor just like the medina. There are belly-dancers and live music on the weekends. When the terraces close down, walk towards the beach on Av. du Caire to hit up **Loubous** nightclub. 150 kinds of alcohol, 2 floors, 2 bars, and a combination of live music and DJs makes this the place to sweat away the sea-salt. The crowd varies with the season. Drinks start at 40dh.

ESSENTIALS

Practicalities

- **TOURIST OFFICE: Office du Tourisme.** *(Av. du Caire. ☎05 24 78 37 11 ➜ The street coming off of Av. L'Istiqlal opposite the clock tower. ℹ Excellent tourist brochures, helpful maps and warm welcomes. English spoken.)*

- **CURRENCY EXCHANGE:** In **Pl. Moulay Hassan** there's a **Banque Populaire** with an **ATM** and **Western Union** inside. *(🕐 Open M-F 8:15am-3:45pm.)* Nearby is a **Crédit du Maroc** *(☎05 44 47 58 19)* with the same hours that will accept traveler's checks. Around the back of the plaza is a **BMCE** with an **ATM** with the same hours.
- **INTERNET: Espace Internet Mogador.** *(Av. rue du Caire opposite the clock tower.* ☎*05 24 78 35 84.* 🟡 *Wi-Fi 10dh per hr.)*
- **LUGGAGE STORAGE:** There is a *Consigne* at the **Gare Routière** open 24hr. *(🟡 15dh per bag.)*
- **POST OFFICE: Post Principale Essaouira.** *(Av. Lalla Aicha* ☎*05 24 47 30 13* ✠ *The first left turn off of Blvd. Mohammed V along the beachfront where the BMCI bank is.* 🕐 *Open M-F 8am-4:15pm, Sa 8am-noon.) Poste Restante* available. There is also a **Western Union** inside.

Emergency!

- **POLICE:** ☎19. The police station is outside the medina in the **Quartier Azlef.** To get there, walk down Blvd. de l'Hopital and turn right at the highway. After the next left, the station is located in Pl. 11 Janvier.
- **LATE-NIGHT PHARMACIES Pharmacie Principale.** *(1 rue Boutouile* ☎*05 24 47 47 94* ✠ *Along Av. Mohamed Zerktouni, 1 block away from Bab Doukala.* 🕐 *Open in summer M-F 9:30am-1pm and 3:30-8pm, Sa 9:30am-1:30pm; in winter M-F 9:30am-1pm and 3:30-7:30pm.)* 24hr. pharmacies *en garde* are open on a rotating basis. Two 24hr. pharmacies are always open: one inside the medina and the other in the surrounding *ville nouvelle.* Lists are posted outside all pharmacies in Essaouira.
- **HOSPITAL: Hospital Sidi Mohammed ben Abdellah.** Blvd. de l'Hopital. From Bab Marrakech with your back to the medina, the hospital is straight across the open plaza and straight down the street slightly to the left and in front of you. *(☎05 24 47 27 16).* Emergency is through the gates and around the back of the main building.

Getting There

By Plane

Aéroport de Mogador is 15km south of town on the road to Agadir. *(☎05 24 47 87 04)*

By Bus and Taxi

Gare Routière *(☎05 24 78 52 41)* is 15min. from Bab Doukala along Av. du 2 Mars, and has various private bus companies including CTM. **CTM** runs to **Marrakesh** *(🟡 70dh.* 🕐 *3½hr.; 3 per day)* and **Casablanca.** *(🟡 145dh.* 🕐 *6hr., 7:45am and 11:30am).* For all other destinations, change at Marrakesh or Casablanca. **Private bus companies** run to **Marrakesh** *(🟡 40-50dh.* 🕐 *3½hr., 18 per day)* and **Casablanca** *(🟡 86dh.* 🕐 *6hr., 4:30am-3am 28 per day).* Other destinations are serviced by individual companies. **Supratours Bus Station** *(☎05 24 47 53 17* ✠ *From Bab Marrakech with your back to the medina, the bus station is 100m to your right)* runs to **Marrakesh** *(🟡 65dh.* 🕐 *3hr., 5 per day).* Large luggage usually costs 5-10dh extra. *Grand taxis* to Marrakesh leave from the **Gare Routière** and cost 80dh per person.

Getting Around

Walk! You can also take a *petit taxi* or ride in style in a horse-drawn *calèche* found outside of **Bab Doukala**.

SPAIN AND PORTUGAL ESSENTIALS

You don't have to be a rocket scientist to plan a good trip. (It might help, but it's not required.) You do, however, need to be well prepared, and that's what we can do for you. Essentials is the chapter that gives you all the nitty-gritty you need to know for your trip: the hard information gleaned from 50 years of collective wisdom (and that phone call to Spain the other day that put us on hold for an hour). Planning your trip? Check. Staying safe and healthy? Check. The dirt on transportation? Check. We've also thrown in communications info, meteorological charts, and a ▣phrasebook, just for good measure. Plus, for overall trip-planning advice from what to pack (money and as little underwear as possible) to how to take a good passport photo (it's physically impossible; consider airbrushing), you can also check out the Essentials section of ◼www.letsgo.com.

We're not going to lie—this chapter is tough for us to write, and you might not find it as fun of a read as 101 or Discover. But please, for the love of all that is good, read it! It's super helpful, and, most importantly, it means we didn't compile all this technical info and put it in one place for you (yes YOU) for nothing.

greatest hits

- **MO' MONEY, LESS PROBLEMS.** Credit, debit, ATM, traveler's checks. They all have their merits, but you don't want to be stuck exhanging money at a horrible rate because you didn't plan ahead (p. 471).

- **GET LEGAL.** Put getting a visa on your spring-cleaning list, since you'll need to apply six to eight weeks in advance (p. 470).

- **USE SKYPE TO STAY IN TOUCH.** So free, but only if you can teach your parents how to use it. (p. 479).

- **BUY A RAILPASS.** Want to traipse all over the country with no pesky reservations (p. 477)?

- **SHIP SOUVENIRS HOME BY SURFACE MAIL.** Our scintillating "By Snail Mail" section will tell you how. You'll laugh, you'll cry (p. 480).

planning your trip

entrance requirements

- **PASSPORT:** Required for visitors from all countries except EU citizens who can show their national ID.
- **VISA:** Required for those who wish to stay longer than 3 months.
- **WORK PERMIT:** Required for all foreigners planning to work in Spain or Portugal (see **Beyond Tourism**).

DOCUMENTS AND FORMALITIES

You've got your visa (especially if you're studying abroad) and your work permit, just like *Let's Go* told you to, and then you realize you've forgotten the most important thing: your passport. We're not going to let that happen. **Don't forget your passport!**

Visas

Citizens of Australia, Canada, Ireland, New Zealand, the UK, and the US do not need a visa for entrance into Spain or Portugal unless the stay will exceed 90 days over a period of six months. If you are going to be studying abroad in Spain or Portugal, and will thus stay for more than 3 months, you will need a visa. Visas cost $92.40 and allow you to spend up to six months in Spain or Portugal. Visas can be purchased at the Spanish Consulates in (US) Boston, Chicago, Houston, Los Angeles, Miami, New Orleans, New York City, San Francisco, Washington DC, (Canada) Ottowa, Toronto, Edmonton, Halifax, Montreal, Winnipeg, Quebec, St. John's (Australia) Melbourne, Sydney, Canberra (New Zealand) Christchurch. Portugal's consulates are located in (US) Washington DC, New York City, Boston, San Francisco, Newark, Philadelphia, Chicago, Houston, Los Angeles, Honolulu, (Canada) Ottowa, Toronto, (Australia) Canberra, Sidney, (New Zealand) Auckland, Wellington.

EU citizens do not need a visa to globetrot through Spain and Portugal. Citizens of Australia, Canada, New Zealand, and the US do not need a visa for stays of up to 90 days, but this three-month period begins upon entry into any of the countries that belong to the EU's **freedom of movement** zone. For more information, see **One Europe** (below). A visa allows the holder to spend 6 months in Spain or Portugal.

Double-check entrance requirements at the nearest embassy or consulate of Spain(listed below) for up-to-date information before departure. US citizens can also consult ◼http://travel.state.gov.

one europe

The EU's policy of freedom of movement means that most border controls have been abolished and visa policies harmonized. Under this treaty, formally known as the Schengen Agreement, you're still required to carry a passport (or government-issued ID card for EU citizens) when crossing an internal border, but, once you've been admitted into one country, you're free to travel to other participating states. Most EU states are already members of Schengen (excluding Cyprus), as are Iceland and Norway. For more consequences of the EU for travelers, see **The Euro** feature later in this chapter.

Work Permits

Admittance to a country as a traveler does not include the right to work, which is authorized only by a work permit. For more information, see the **Beyond Tourism** chapter.

TIME DIFFERENCES

Spain is 1 hr. ahead of Greenwich Mean Time (GMT) and observes Daylight Savings Time. During the summer, from the end of March until the end of October, time is shifted forward one hour (GMT + 2). This means that it is 6 hours ahead of New York City, 9 hours ahead of Los Angeles, 1 hour ahead of the British Isles, 8 hours behind Sydney, and 10 hours behind New Zealand.

Portugal is on Greenwich Mean Time (and is thus one hour behind Spain) and observes Daylight Savings Time. During the summer, from the end of March until the end of October, time is shifted forward one hour (GMT + 1).This means that it is 5 hours ahead of New York City, 8 hours ahead of Los Angeles, the same time as the British Isles, 9 hours behind Sydney, and 11 hours behind New Zealand.

money

GETTING MONEY FROM HOME

Stuff happens. When stuff happens, you might need some money. When you need some money, the easiest and cheapest solution is to have someone back home make a deposit to your bank account. Otherwise, consider one of the following options.

Wiring Money

Arranging a **bank money transfer** means asking a bank back home to wire money to a bank in Spain or Portugal. This is the cheapest way to transfer cash, but it's also the slowest and most agonizing, usually taking several days or more. Note that some banks may only release your funds in local currency, potentially sticking you with a poor exchange rate; inquire about this in advance. International bank transfers normally take 2-4 days to complete. Money transfer services like **Western Union** are faster and more convenient than bank transfers—but also much pricier. Western Union has many locations worldwide. To find one, visit ☐www.westernunion.com or call the appropriate number: in Australia ☎1800 173 833, in Canada 800-235-0000, and in the US 800-325-6000, in the UK 0800 735 1815, or in Spain 900 983273 and in Portugal 800 832 136. To wire money using a credit card in the US and Canada, call ☎800-CALL-CASH; in the UK, 0800 731 1815.

pins and atms

To use a debit or credit card to withdraw money from a cash machine (ATM) in Europe, you must have a four-digit Personal Identification Number (PIN). If your PIN is longer than four digits, ask your bank whether you can just use the first four or whether you'll need a new one. Credit cards don't usually come with PINs, so if you intend to hit up ATMs in Europe with a credit card to get cash advances, call your credit card company before leaving to request one.

Travelers with alphabetic rather than numeric PINs may also be thrown off by the absence of letters on European cash machines. Here are the corresponding numbers to use: 1 = QZ; 2 = ABC; 3 = DEF; 4 = GHI; 5 = JKL; 6 = MNO; 7 = PRS; 8 = TUV; 9 = WXY. Note that if you mistakenly punch the wrong code into the machine multiple (often three) times, it can swallow (gulp!) your card for good.

BACKPACKING
by the numbers:

117   **photos snapped**

41   **gelato flavors (3 lbs gained)**

23   **miles walked (in the *right* direction)**

6   **buses missed**

4   **benches napped on**

2½   **hostel romances**

1   **Let's Go Travel Guide**

0   **REGRETS.**

LET'S GO

www.letsgo.com

we'd rather be traveling, too.

spanish consular services

- **SPANISH CONSULATE IN AUSTRALIA: Consulate General.** *(Level 26, St-Martins Tower, 31 Market St., Sydney NSW 2000* ☎*+61 2 9261 2433* ▣*www.ambafrance-au.org* ☾ *Open M-F 9am-1pm.)*

- **SPANISH EMBASSY IN CANADA: Embassy.** *(74 Stanley Ave., Ottawa, Ontario, Canada, K1M 1P4* ☎*613 747 2252* ▣*www.mae.es/Embajadas/ Ottawa/en/Home* ☾ *Open M,T,W,Th 8:30am-5pm F 8:30am-2:15pm.)*

- **SPANISH EMBASSY IN IRELAND: Embassy.** *(3rd fl, Block E, Iveagh Court, Harcourt Road, Dublin Ireland* ☎*352 1 26 08 066* ▣*www.mae.es/Emba-jadas/dublin* ☾ *Open M-F 9:30am-1:30pm.)*

- **SPANISH CONSULATE IN NEW ZEALAND:** In Canberra, **Australia.**

- **SPANISH EMBASSY IN BRITAIN: Embassy.** *(39 Chesham Placve, London SW1X 8SB* ☎*20 7235 55 55* ▣*www.maec.es/Embajadas/Londres* ☾ *Open M-F 9:30am-12pm.)*

- **SPANISH EMBASSY IN USA: Embassy.** *(2375 Pennsylvania Ave., Washington DC 20037* ☎*+01 202 452 0100* ▣*www.maec.es/embajadas/ Washington.)*

in spain

- **AUSTRALIAN CONSULAR SERVICES: Embassy.** *(Torre Espacio, Paseo de la Castellana, 259D, Planta 24, Madrid 28046* ☎*34 91 353 6600* ▣*www. spain.embassy.gov.au* ☾ *Open M,T,W,Th 8:30am-5pm F 8:30am-2:15pm.)*

- **CANADIAN CONSULAR SERVICES: Embassy.** *(Torre Espacio, Paseo de la Castellana, 259D, Madrid 28046* ☎*34 91 382 8400* ▣*www.canadainter-national.gc.ca/spain-espagne* ☾ *Open M-Th 8:30am-2pm and 3-5:30pm F 8:30am-2:15pm, during August M-F 8:30am-2:15pm.)*

- **IRISH CONSULAR SERVICES: Embassy.** *(Ireland House, Paseo de la Cas-tellana 46-4, Madrid 28046* ☎*34 91 436 4093* ▣*www.irlanda.es* ☾ *Open M-Th 10am-2pm and F 8:30am-2:15pm.)*

- **NEW ZEALAND CONSULAR SERVICES: Embassy.** *(Pinar 7, 3rd Floo,r Madrid 28046* ☎*34 91 523 0226* ▣*www.nxembassy.com/spain* ☾ *Open M-F 9am-2pm and 3-5:30pm, during July and August M-F 8:30am-1:30 and 2-4:30pm.)*

- **BRITISH CONSULAR SERVICES: Embassy.** *(Torre Espacio, Paseo de la Castellana   259D, 28046 Madrid* ☎*34 91 714 6300* ▣*www.mae.es/ Embajadas/Ottawa/en/Home* ☾ *Open M,T,W,Th 8:30am-5pm F 8:30am-2:15pm.)*

- **USA CONSULAR SERVICES: Embassy.** *(calle de Serrano 75, Madrid 28006* ☎*34 91 587 2200* ▣*www.embusa.es* ☾ *Open M-F 8:30am-1pm.)*

money · getting money from home

- **PORTUGESE EMBASSY IN AUSTRALIA: Consulate General.** *(Level 9, 30 Clarence Street, Sydney NSW 2000, Australia* ☎*+61 2 926 221 99* ▣*www. secomunidades.pt/web/sidney* ☼ *Open M-F 9am-1pm.)*

- **AUSTRALIAN EMBASSY IN PORTUGAL: Embassy.** *(Avenida de Liberdade, 200, 2nd floor, 1250-147 Lisbon* ☎*21 310 1500* ▣*www.portugal.embassy. gov.au* ☼ *Open M,T,W,Th 8:30am-5pm F 8:30am-2:15pm.)*

- **PORTUGESE EMBASSY IN CANADA: Embassy.** *(7645 Island Park Drive, Ontario, Ottawa, Canada* ☎*613 729 0883* ▣*www.mae.es/Embajadas/ Ottawa/en/Home* ☼ *Open M,T,W,Th 8:30am-5pm F 8:30am-2:15pm.)*

- **CANADIAN EMBASSY IN PORTUGAL: Embassy.** *(Avenida da Liberdade, 198-200, 3rd Floor, 1269-121 Lisbon, Portugal* ☎*21 316 4600* ▣*www. canadainternational.gc.ca/portugal* ☼ *Open M-F 8:30am-12:30pm and 1:30pm-5pm.)*

- **PORTUGESE EMBASSY IN IRELAND: Embassy.** *(15 Leeson Park, Dublin 6, Ireland* ☎*01 412 7040* ▣*www.embaixadaportugal.ie* ☼ *Open M-F 10am-1pm.)*

- **IRISH EMBASSY IN PORTUGAL: Embassy.** *(Rua da Imprensa a Estrela, 1-4, 1200-684 Lisbon, Portugal* ☎*351 213 929 440* ▣*www.embassyofire-land.pt* ☼ *Open M-F 9:30am-12:30pm.)*

- **PORTUGESE EMBASSY IN NEW ZEALAND:** In Canberra, **Australia.**

- **NEW ZEALAND EMBASSY IN PORTUGAL:** Represented by the New Zealand Embassy in Rome, **Italy.**

- **PORTUGESE EMBASSY IN BRITAIN: Embassy.** *(11 Belgrave Square, London, United Kingdom* ☎*020 72355331* ▣*www.portuguese-embassy.org. uk* ☼ *Open M-F 8:30am-1pm.)*

- **BRITISH EMBASSY IN PORTUGAL: Embassy.** *(Rua de São Bernardo 33, Lisbon 1249-082* ☎*351 21 392 4000* ▣*ukinportugal.fco.gov.uk/en* ☼ *Open M-F 9am-1pm and 2:30-5pm.)*

- **PORTUGESE EMBASSY IN USA: Embassy.** *(2012 Massachusetts Ave. NW, Washington DC 20036 USA* ☎*1 202 350 5400* ▣*www.mne.gov.pt* ☼ *Open M-F 9am-4:30pm.)*

- **USA EMBASSY IN PORTUGAL: Embassy.** *(Avenida das Forças Armadas, 1600-081 Lisbon* ☎*351 21 727 3300* ▣*portugal.usembassy.gov* ☼ *Open M-F 8am-5pm.)*

US State Department (US Citizens Only)

In serious emergencies only, the US State Department will forward money within hours to the nearest consular office, which will then disburse it according to instructions for a US$30 fee. If you wish to use this service, you must contact the Overseas Citizens Services division of the US State Department *(☎+1-202-501-4444, from US).*

TIPPING AND BARGAINING

Native Spaniards rarely tip more than their spare change, even at expensive restaurants. However, if you make it clear that you're a tourist — especially an American one — they might expect you to tip more. Don't feel like you have to tip, the servers' pay is almost never based on tips. No one will refuse your money, but you're a poor student so don't play the fool.

Bargaining is common and necessary in open-air and street markets. Especially if you are buying a number of things, like produce, you can probably get a better deal if you haggle. However, do not barter in malls or established shops.

TAXES

Both Spain and Portugal have a 7-8% value added tax (IVA) on all means and accommodations. The prices listed in Let's Go include IVA unless otherwise mentioned. Retail goods bear a much higher 16% IVA, although the listed prices generally include this tax. Non-EU citizens who have stayed in the EU fewer than 180 days can claim back the tax paid on purchases at the airport. Ask the shop where you have made the purchase to supply you with a tax return form, but stores will only provide them for purchases of more than €50-100. **Taxes,** presently 21%, are included in all prices in Portugal. Request a refund form, an *Insenção de IVA*, and present it to customs upon departure.

the euro

Despite what many dollar-possessing Americans might want to hear, the official currency of 16 members of the European Union—Austria, Belgium, Cyprus, Finland, France, Germany, Greece, Ireland, Italy, Luxembourg, Malta, the Netherlands, Portugal, Slovakia, Slovenia, and Spain—is the euro.

Still, the currency has some important—and positive—consequences for travelers hitting more than one eurozone country. For one thing, money-changers across the eurozone are obliged to exchange money at the official, fixed rate (below) and at no commission (though they may still charge a small service fee). Second, euro-denominated traveler's checks allow you to pay for goods and services across the eurozone, again at the official rate and commission-free. For more info, check a currency converter (such as www.xe.com) or www.europa.eu.int.

safety and health

GENERAL ADVICE

In any type of crisis, the most important thing to do is **stay calm.** Your country's embassy abroad is usually your best resource in an emergency; registering with that embassy upon arrival in the country is a good idea. The government offices listed in the **Travel Advisories** feature at the end of this section can provide information on the services they offer their citizens in case of emergencies abroad.

Local Laws And Police

Travelers are not likely to break major laws unintentionally while visiting Spain or Portugal. You can contact your embassy if arrested, although they often cannot do much to assist you beyond finding legal counsel. You should feel comfortable approaching the police, although few officers speak English. There are three types of police in Spain. The **Policía Nacional** wear blue or black uniforms and white shirts; they deal with crime investigation (including theft), guard government buildings, and protect dignitaries. The **Policía Local** wear blue uniforms, deal more with local issues, and report to the mayor or town hall in each municipality. The **Guardia Civil** wear olive green uniforms and are responsible for issues more relevant to travelers: customs, crowd control, and national security. In Portugal, the **Policía de Segurança Pública** is the police force in all major cities and towns. The **Guarda Nacional Republicana** polices more rural areas, while the **Brigada de Trânsito** is the traffic police, that sport red armbands. All three branches wear light blue uniforms.

Drugs And Alcohol

Recreational drugs are illegal in Spain in Portugal, and police take these laws seriously. The legal minimum drinking age in both countries is 16. Spain and Portugal have the highest road mortality rates in Europe, and Spain has one of the highest rates of drunk driving deaths in Europe. Recently, Spanish officials have started setting up checkpoints on roads to test drivers' blood alcohol levels (BAC). Do not drive while intoxicated, and be cautious on the road.

travel advisories

The following government offices provide travel information and advisories by telephone, by fax, or via the web:

- **AUSTRALIA: Department of Foreign Affairs and Trade.** (☎+61 2 6261 1111 ▧www.dfat.gov.au)

- **CANADA: Department of Foreign Affairs and International Trade (DFAIT).** Call or visit the website for the free booklet *Bon Voyage...But.* (☎+1-800-267-8376 ▧www.dfait-maeci.gc.ca)

- **NEW ZEALAND: Ministry of Foreign Affairs.** (☎+64 4 439 8000 ▧www.mfat.govt.nz)

- **UK: Foreign and Commonwealth Office.** (☎+44 20 7008 1500 ▧www.fco.gov.uk)

- **US: Department of State.** (☎888-407-4747 from the US, +1-202-501-4444 elsewhere ▧http://travel.state.gov)

SPECIFIC CONCERNS

Natural Disasters

Apart from the occasional mild earthquake every 200 years, there is little to fear from nature in Spain. However, it is worth noting that if more than an inch of snow falls, many cities will shut down totally and driving will be incredibly slow, as Spanish drivers will be freaked from the weather conditions.

Terrorism

Basque terrorism concerns all travelers in Spain, with the active presence of a militant wing of Basque separatists called the Euskadi Ta Askatasuna (ETA; Basque Homeland and Freedom). In March 2006, ETA declared a permanent cease-fire that officially ended in June 2007. ETA's attacks are generally targeted politically and are not considered random terrorist attacks that endanger regular civilians. The March 11, 2004 train bombings linked to al-Qaeda are viewed by Spaniards in the same way that Americans view September 11, and there is a monument in Madrid to those who died. While terrorism is rarely an issue in Portugal, Spain has experienced more that its fair share of troubles in recent years.

spain and portugal essentials

PRE-DEPARTURE HEALTH

Matching a prescription to a foreign equivalent is not always easy, safe, or possible, so if you take **prescription drugs**, carry up-to-date prescriptions or a statement from your doctor stating the medications' trade names, manufacturers, chemical names, and dosages. Be sure to keep all medication with you in your carry-on luggage.

Pharmacists in Spain and Portugal often speak very good English and can help you find common over-the-counter drugs. The names for such drugs in Spanish are also quite similar to those in English.

Immunizations And Precautions

Travelers over two years old should make sure that the following vaccines are up to date: MMR (for measles, mumps, and rubella); DTaP or Td (for diphtheria, tetanus, and pertussis); IPV (for polio); Hib (for *Haemophilus influenzae* B); and HepB (for Hepatitis B). If you are reading this and are under the age of two, congratulations, you don't need vaccines and are entirely too literate for your age. For recommendations on immunizations and prophylaxis, check with a doctor and consult the **Centers for Disease Control and Prevention (CDC)** in the US or the equivalent in your home country (☎+1-800-CDC-INFO/232-4636 ▣www.cdc.gov/travel).

getting around

For information on how to get to Spain and Portugal and save a bundle while doing so, check out the Essentials section of ▣**www.letsgo.com.** (In case you can't tell, we think our website's the bomb.)

BY PLANE

Commercial Airlines

For small-scale travel on the continent, *Let's Go* suggests ▣**budget airlines** (above) for budget travelers, but more traditional carriers have made efforts to keep up with the revolution. **Iberia,** the flag-carrying airline of Spain, has reasonable rates all over the peninsula. The **Star Alliance Europe Airpass** offers low economy-class fares for travel within Europe to 220 destinations in 45 countries. The pass is available to non-European passengers on Star Alliance carriers, including Spanair *(*▣*www.staralliance.com).* **Europeby-Air's** snazzy FlightPass also allows you to hop between hundreds of cities in Europe and North Africa. *(*☎*+1-888-321-4737* ▣*www.europebyair.com* Ⓢ *Most flights US$99.)*

In addition, a number of European airlines offer discount coupon packets. Most are only available as tack-ons for transatlantic passengers, but some are standalone offers. Most must be purchased before departure, so research in advance.

BY TRAIN

Trains in Spain and Portugal are generally comfortable, convenient, and reasonably swift, and second-class compartments are great places to meet fellow travelers. Make sure you are on the correct car, as trains sometimes split at crossroads. Towns listed in parentheses on European train schedules require a train switch at the town listed immediately before the parentheses.

You can either buy a **railpass,** which allows you unlimited travel within a particular region for a given period of time, or rely on buying individual **point-to-point** tickets as you go. Almost all countries give students or youths (under 26, usually) direct discounts on regular domestic rail tickets, and many also sell a student or youth card that provides 20-50% off all fares for up to a year.

Renfe dominates the train services in Spain and Portugal and offers great rates if you book ahead on the web. Beware though, Renfe's English website is not as good as its Spanish version, and can often be difficult to navigate. You may be better off purchasing your ticket at the station.

budget airlines

The recent emergence of no-frills airlines has made hopscotching around Europe by air increasingly affordable. Though these flights often feature inconvenient hours or serve less popular regional airports, with ticket prices often dipping into single digits, it's never been faster or easier to jet across the continent. The following resources will be useful not only for crisscrossing Spain or Portugalbut also for those ever-popular weekend trips to nearby international destinations.

- **BMIBABY:** Departures from multiple cities in the UK to Paris, Nice, and other cities in France. *(☎0871 224 0224 for the UK, +44 870 126 6726 elsewhere 🖥www.bmibaby.com.)*
- **EASYJET:** London to Bordeaux and other cities in France. *(☎+44 871 244 2366, 10p per min. 🖥www.easyjet.com $ UK£50-150.)*
- **RYANAIR:** From Dublin, Glasgow, Liverpool, London, and Shannon to destinations in France. *(☎0818 30 30 30 for Ireland, 0871 246 0000 for the UK wwww.ryanair.com.)*
- **STERLING:** The first Scandinavian-based budget airline connects Denmark, Norway, and Sweden to 47 European destinations, including Montpellier, Nice, and Paris. *(☎70 10 84 84 for Denmark, 0870 787 8038 for the UK 🖥www.sterling.dk.)*
- **TRANSAVIA:** Short hops from Krakow to Paris. *(☎020 7365 4997 for the UK 🖥www.transavia.com $ From €49 one-way.)*
- **VUELING:** Many Iberian peninsula flights to all over Europe, especially the holiday islands like Tenerife and Ibiza. *(☎0906 754 754 1 for the UK 🖥www.vueling.com $ From €40 one-way.)*

BY BUS

Though European trains and railpasses are extremely popular, in some cases buses prove to be a better option. The bus network in Spain and Portugal is much more comprehensive than the train network and is often the best way to get to more rural destinations. Often cheaper than railpasses, **international bus passes** allow unlimited travel on a hop-on, hop-off basis between major European cities. **Busabout**, for instance, offers three interconnecting bus circuits covering 29 of Europe's best bus

rail resources

- **WWW.RAILEUROPE.COM:** Info on rail travel and railpasses.
- **POINT-TO-POINT FARES AND SCHEDULES:** 🖥www.raileurope.com/us/rail/fares_schedules/index.htm allows you to calculate whether buying a railpass would save you money.
- **WWW.RAILSAVER.COM:** Uses your itinerary to calculate the best railpass for your trip.
- **WWW.RAILFANEUROPE.NET:** Links to rail servers throughout Europe.
- **WWW.LETSGO.COM:** Check out the Essentials section for more details.

hubs. *(☎+44 8450 267 514 💻www.busabout.com $ 1 circuit in high season starts at US$579, students US$549.)* **Eurolines,** meanwhile, is the largest operator of Europe-wide coach services. We get misty-eyed just thinking about their unlimited 15- and 30-day passes to 41 major European cities. *(💻www.eurolines.com $ High season 15-day pass €345, 30-day pass €455; under 26 €290/375. Mid-season €240/330; under 26 €205/270. Low season €205/310; under 26 €175/240.)*

BY BOAT

Most European ferries are quite comfortable; the cheapest ticket typically still includes a reclining chair or couchette. Fares jump sharply in July and August. Ask for discounts; ISIC and Eurail Pass holders get many reductions and free trips. You'll occasionally have to pay a port tax (under US$10). You'll need a ferry to get to Ibiza or Majorca, and there are also ferries to Morocco from Spain and Portugal.

BY BICYCLE

Some youth hostels rent bicycles for low prices, and in many cities of Spain and Portugal, you can rent bicycles at ports all over the city and return them to any other bike port once you're finished.

keeping in touch

BY EMAIL AND INTERNET

Hello and welcome to the 21st century, where you can check your email in most major European cities, though sometimes you'll have to pay a few bucks or buy a drink for internet access. Although in some places it's possible to forge a remote link with your home server, in most cases this is a much slower (and thus more expensive) option than taking advantage of free **web-based email accounts** (e.g., **💻www.gmail.com**). **Internet cafes** and the occasional free internet terminal at a public library or university are listed in the **Practicalities** sections of cities that we cover . For lists of additional cybercafes in Spain and Portugal, check out 💻www.cybercaptive.com and 💻www.andalucia.com/internet/cybercafes/home.htm for Andalucia specifically. Also, sometimes you can steal Wi-Fi from hostels—just look like you're staying there and chill in the common area.

Wireless hot spots make internet access possible in public and remote places. Unfortunately, they also pose security risks. Hot spots are public, open networks that use unencrypted, unsecured connections. They are susceptible to hacks and "packet sniffing"—the theft of passwords and other private information. To prevent problems, disable "ad hoc" mode, turn off file sharing and network discovery, encrypt your email, turn on your firewall, beware of phony networks, and watch for over-the-shoulder creeps.

BY TELEPHONE

Calling Home From Spain/Portugal

Prepaid phone cards are a common and relatively inexpensive means of calling abroad. Each one comes with a Personal Identification Number (PIN) and a toll-free access number. You call the access number and then follow the directions for dialing your PIN. To purchase prepaid phone cards, check online for the best rates; 💻www.callingcards.com is a good place to start. Online providers generally send your access number and PIN via email, with no actual "card" involved. You can also call home with prepaid phone cards purchased in Spain.

If you have internet access, your best bet is probably **Skype** *(💻www.skype.com)*. You can even videochat if you have one of those new-fangled webcams. Calls to other

Skype users are free; calls to landlines and mobiles worldwide start at US$0.021 per minute, depending on where you're calling.

Another option is a **calling card,** linked to a major national telecommunications service in your home country. Calls are billed collect or to your account. Cards generally come with instructions for dialing both domestically and internationally.

Placing a collect call through an international operator can be expensive but may be necessary in case of an emergency. You can call collect without even possessing a calling card just by calling its access number and following the instructions.

Cellular Phones

The international standard for cell phones is **Global System for Mobile Communication (GSM).** To make and receive calls in Spain, you will need a GSM-compatible phone and a **SIM (Subscriber Identity Module) card,** a country-specific, thumbnail-size chip that gives you a local phone number and plugs you into the local network. For more information on GSM phones, check out ▪www.telestial.com. Companies like **Cellular Abroad** (▪*www.cellularabroad.com*) and **OneSimCard** (▪*www.onesimcard.com*) rent cell phones and SIM cards that work in a variety of destinations around the world.

international calls

To call Spain/Portugal from home or to call home from Spain/Portugal dial:

1. THE INTERNATIONAL DIALING PREFIX. To call from Australia, dial ☎0011; Canada or the US, ☎011; Ireland, New Zealand, or the UK, ☎00; Spain, ☎00; Portugal, ☎00.

2. THE COUNTRY CODE OF THE COUNTRY YOU WANT TO CALL. To call Australia, dial ☎61; Canada or the US, ☎1; Ireland, ☎353; New Zealand, ☎64; the UK, ☎44; Spain, ☎34; Portgual, ☎351.

3. THE CITY/AREA CODE. *Let's Go* lists the city/area codes for cities and towns in Spain and Portugal opposite the city or town name, next to a ☎, as well as in every phone number. If the first digit is a zero (e.g., ☎0981 for Santiago de Compostela), omit the zero when calling from abroad (e.g., dial ☎981 from Canada to reach Santiago de Compostela).

4. THE LOCAL NUMBER.

BY SNAIL MAIL

Sending Mail Home From Spain or Portugal

Airmail is the best way to send mail home from Spain or Portugal. **Aerogrammes,** printed sheets that fold into envelopes and travel via airmail, are available at post offices. Write "airmail" or *"por avion"* on the front. Note that most post offices will charge exorbitant fees or simply refuse to send aerogrammes with enclosures. **Surface mail** is by far the cheapest way to send mail. It takes one to two months for items to cross the Atlantic and one to three to cross the Pacific—good for heavy items you won't need for a while, like tacky souvenirs that you've acquired along the way.

Sending Mail To Spain or Portugal

In addition to the standard postage system whose rates are listed below, **Federal Express** handles express mail services from most countries to Spain or Portugal (☎+1-800-463-3339 ▪*www.fedex.com*). DHL serves the same purpose but serves more cities (☎+1-800-225-5345 ▪*www.dhl.com*). Sending a postcard within Spain costs €0.78 while sending letters up to 20g domestically requires €0.34. Sending a postcard from Portugal costs €0.74 while sending a letter domestically costs €0.80.

There are several ways to pickup letters sent to you while you are abroad. Mail can be sent via **Poste Restante** (General Delivery; *Lista de Correos* in Spanish and *Posta Restante* in Portuguese) to almost any city or town in Spain or Portugal with a post office, but it is not very reliable. Address Poste Restante letters like so:

Salvador DALÍ	Amalia RODRIGUES
Lista de Correos	Posta Restante
postal code	postal code
City, Spain	City, Portugal

The mail will go to a special desk in the central post office, unless you specify a post office by street address or postal code. It's best to use the largest post office, since mail may be sent there regardless. It is usually safer and quicker, though more expensive, to send mail **express or registered.** Bring your passport (or other photo ID) for pickup. If the clerks insist that there is nothing for you, ask them to check under your first name as well. *Let's Go* lists post offices in the **Practicalities** section for each city.

American Express has offices throughout the world that offer a free **Client Letter Service** (mail held up to 30 days and forwarded upon request) for cardholders who contact them in advance. Some offices provide services to non-cardholders (especially AmEx Travelers Cheque holders), but call ahead to make sure. For a complete list of AmEx locations, visit ◨www.americanexpress.com/travel.

climate

Much of Spain and Portugal has a Mediterranean climate, with hot dry summers and relatively mild winters. Northern Spain and Portugal have an Atlantic climate that is wetter and cooler than the south. The far northeast corner of Spain near the Pyrenees Mountains has an alpine climate.

AVG. TEMP.(LOW/ HIGH), PRECIP.	JANUARY			APRIL			JULY			OCTOBER		
	°C	°F	mm	°C	°F	mm	°C	°F	mm	°C	°F	mm
Madrid	2/9	35/49	39	7/18	54/65	48	17/31	63/88	11	10/19	50/66	53
Barcelona	6/13	43/56	31	11/18	52/65	43	21/28	70/83	27	15/21	59/70	86
San Sebastian	6/11	44/51	91	9/14	47/57	107	16/22	61/71	63	13/18	55/65	110
Santiago de Compostela	5/11	41/52	153	7/16	44/60	110	13/24	56/76	27	10/18	50/64	171
Lisbon	8/14	47/57	92	11/19	52/66	54	18/28	64/83	5	15/22	59/72	96

To convert from degrees Fahrenheit to degrees Celsius, subtract 32 and multiply by 5/9. To convert from Celsius to Fahrenheit, multiply by 9/5 and add 32. To learn how to multiply and divide, we recommend a math book.

°CELSIUS	-5	0	5	10	15	20	25	30	35	40
°FAHRENHEIT	23	32	41	50	59	68	77	86	95	104

measurements

Like the rest of the rational world, Spain and Portugal use the metric system. The basic unit of length is the meter (m), which is divided into 100 centimeters (cm) or 1000 millimeters (mm). One thousand meters make up one kilometer (km). Fluids are measured in liters (L), each divided into 1000 milliliters (mL). A liter of pure water weighs one kilogram (kg), the unit of mass that is divided into 1000 grams (g). One metric ton is 1000kg.

MEASUREMENT CONVERSIONS	
1 inch (in.) = 25.4mm	1 millimeter (mm) = 0.039 in.
1 foot (ft.) = 0.305m	1 meter (m) = 3.28 ft.
1 yard (yd.) = 0.914m	1 meter (m) = 1.094 yd.
1 mile (mi.) = 1.609km	1 kilometer (km) = 0.621 mi.
1 ounce (oz.) = 28.35g	1 gram (g) = 0.035 oz.
1 pound (lb.) = 0.454kg	1 kilogram (kg) = 2.205 lb.
1 fluid ounce (fl. oz.) = 29.57mL	1 milliliter (mL) = 0.034 fl. oz.
1 gallon (gal.) = 3.785L	1 liter (L) = 0.264 gal.

language

SPANISH

Thanks to a maniacal desire for gold and the fountain of youth (both on Earth and in the Catholic hereafter), Spain spread its titular language all across the world during its imperial heyday. Today, it is the third most widely spoken language in the world after English and Mandarin. However, Spain's Spanish still differs notably from the rest of the Spanish-speaking world by the tell-tale "theta": changing the pronunciation of *c*'s and *z*'s from an "*s*"-sound to a "*th*"-sound. Careful though, make sure not

spain and portugal essentials

to do this with *s*'s, because saying "Buenath Nocheth" will make people think you really do have a speech impediment. In general, Spanish is a very easy language to pronounce since all letters are pronounced and have a consistent sound.

Pronunciation

All of the phonetic sounds in Spanish are found in English but are represented differently. The *h* is silent in all words. An accent on a letter indicates that the emphasis of the word should be placed on that letter.

PHONETIC UNIT	PRONUNCIATION	PHONETIC UNIT	PRONUNCIATION
a	aw, as in "law"	u	oo, as in "boo"
e	ey as in "ray"	ll	y-, as in "year"
i	ee as in "fee"	j	h- as in "hat"
o	oh as in"oval"	v	a mixture of v/b

Phrasebook

ENGLISH	SPANISH	PRONUNCIATION
Hello!/Hi!	Hola!	Oh-law!
Goodbye!	Adiós!	Aw-dee-ose!
Yes.	Si.	See.
No.	No.	samesies
Please.	Por favor.	pohr fa-vohr
Sorry!/Excuse me!	Perdón!	peard-own!
Good morning	Buenos dias	booway-nos dee-as
Good evening	Buenas noches	booway-nas dee-as
How are you?	Cómo estás?	como ays-tas?
I'm fine, thanks, and you?	Bien, gracias, y tú?	Bee-ayn, gra-thi-as, ee too?
What time is it?	Qué hora es?	Kay ora es?
It's 5 o'clock	Son las cinco.	Sown las seen-ko
Wait!	Espera!	Ace--pear-a
EMERGENCY		
Go away!	Vete!	VAY-tay!
Help!	Socorro!	So-co-rro!
Call the police!	Llama la policia!	ya-ma la po-lee-see-a!
Get a doctor!	Llama el médico!	ya-ma el may-dee-co!
FOOD AND DRINK		
Waiter/waitress	camarero/a	Cama-ray-roh/rah
I'd like...	Me gustaría...	May goost-er-ee-a...
Is there meat in this dish?	Tiene carne este plato?	Tee-yen-ey car-nay es-tay plato?
salad	ensalada	
wine (sherry)	vino (jerez)	vee-no (hay-rayth)
shots	chupitos	choo-pee-tos
Spanish cured ham	jamon serrano	ha-mone serrano
Can I buy you a drink?	Te compro una copa?	Tay compro oo-na copa?
Is the bread free?	Está gratis el pan?	Es-TAH gra-tees el pan?

ENGLISH	SPANISH	ENGLISH	SPANISH
I am from (the US/ Europe).	Soy de (los Estados Unidos/Europa).	What's the problem, sir/ madam?	¿Cuál es el problema, señor/señora?
I have a visa/ID.	Tengo una visa/identificación.	I lost my passport/ luggage.	Se perdió mi pasaporte/ equipaje.
I will be here for less than three months.	Estaré aquí por menos de tres meses.	I have nothing to declare.	No tengo nada para declarar.
How much does a bed in the dorm (a single/ double/triple/quad room) cost?	Cuánto vale una cama en el dormitorio (una habitación individual, doble, triple, cuádruple)?	Are the towels/linens free?	Están gratis el uso de las toallas/las sábanas?

spain and portugal essentials

PORTUGUESE

Despite sharing a peninsula of origin and many linguistic similarities, Portuguese is nonetheless distinct from Spanish. The Portuguese are very proud of their linguistic heritage and will only begrudgingly understand if you speak to them in Spanish, so it might be better to just use English.

Pronunciation

Portuguese words are often spelled like their Spanish equivalents, although the pronunciation is different. In addition to regular vowels, Portuguese, like French, has nasal vowels: those with a *tilde* (*ã*, *õ*, etc.) or before an *m* or *n* are pronounced with a nasal twang. At the end of a word, *o* is pronounced "oo" as in "room," and *e* is sometimes silent (usually after a *t* or a *d*). The consonant *s* is pronounced "sh" or "zh" when it occurs before another consonant. The consonants *ch* and *x* are pronounced "sh," although the latter is sometimes pronounced as in English; *j* and *g* (before *e* and *i*) are pronounced "zh"; *ç* sounds like "es." The combinations *nh* and *lh* are pronounced "ny" as in "canyon" and "ly" as in "billion." The masculine singular definite article is "o" and the feminine singular definite article is "a."

Phrasebook

ENGLISH	PORTUGUESE	PRONUNCIATION
Hello!/Hi!	Olá!	oh-LAH!
Goodbye!	Até logo!	ah-TEH low-go!
Yes.	Sim	See.
No.	Não.	Now
Please.	Por favor.	pohr fa-VOHR
Thank you.	Obrigado/a.	oh-bree-GAH-doh/dah
Sorry!/Excuse me!	Desculpe!	dish-KOOL-peh!
Good morning	Bom dia	Bohm DEE-ah
Good evening	Boa noite	Boa no-EE-tee
How are you?	Como vôce está?	como vo-say es-TAH?
I'm fine, thanks, and you?	Eu bem, obrigado/a, e vôce?	Eh-oo baim obridgado/a, eh vo-say ?
What time is it?	Que horas são?	Kay orash saomm?
It's 5 o'clock	É cinco horas.	Ay seen-ko oras.
Wait!	Aguarde!	Ah-GWAR-dee!
EMERGENCY		
Go away!	Vá embora!	VAH ehm-bor-ah!
Help!	Socorro!	So-COH-hoh!
Call the police!	Chamar a polícia!	shamar a po-LEE-see-a!
Get a doctor!	Chamar um doutor!	shamar oom doa'tor!
FOOD AND DRINK		
Waiter/waitress	garçom/garçonete	gar-SOHM/gar-sohn-EH-tee
I'd like...	Gostaria...	Goh-star-ee-a...
Is there meat in this dish?	Este prato tem carne?	es-tey prah-toh tehm car-nay?
salad	salada	SAL-a-da
wine (sherry)	vinho (xerez)	veen-yoh (she-rayz)
shots	doses	do-say-s
seafood	frutos do mar	froo-tohs doh mar
Is the bread free?	Este pão de graça?	Estee pow day grah-sah?

ENGLISH	PORTUGUESE	ENGLISH	PORTUGUESE
My name is...	O meu nome é...	Do you speak English?	Fala inglês?
What's your name?	Como se chama?	I don't understand...	Não entendo.
How much does this cost?	Quanto cuesta?	Where is...?	Onde é...?
Who/what	quem/que	How do you get to...?	Como chego á...?

language · portuguese

let's go online

Plan your next trip on our spiffy website, www.letsgo.com. It features full book content, the latest travel info on your favorite destinations, and tons of interactive features: make your own itinerary, read blogs from our trusty Researcher-Writers, browse our photo library, watch exclusive videos, check out our newsletter, find travel deals, follow us on Facebook, and buy new guides. Plus, if this Essentials wasn't enough for you, we've got even more online. We're always updating and adding new features, so check back often!

MOROCCO
ESSENTIALS

You don't have to be a rocket scientist to plan a good trip. (It might help, but it's not required.) You do, however, need to be well prepared, and that's what we can do for you. Essentials is the chapter that gives you all the nitty-gritty you need to know for your trip: the hard information gleaned from 50 years of collective wisdom (and that phone call to Morocco the other day that put us on hold for an hour). Planning your trip? Check. Staying safe and healthy? Check. The dirt on transportation? Check. We've also thrown in communications info, meteorological charts, and a phrasebook, just for good measure. Plus, for overall trip-planning advice from what to pack (money and as little underwear as possible) to how to take a good passport photo (it's physically impossible; consider airbrushing), you can also check out the Essentials section of wwww.letsgo.com.

We're not going to lie—this chapter is tough for us to write, and you might not find it as fun of a read as 101 or Discover. But please, for the love of all that is good, read it! It's super helpful, and, most importantly, it means we didn't compile all this technical info and put it in one place for you (yes YOU) for nothing.

greatest hits

- **LEARN TO BARGAIN.** You'll be a sad camel indeed without this skill in the bazaar (p. 490).
- **FAKE DRUGS.** Don't buy drugs—you'll probably end up getting lawn clippings anyway (p. 490).
- **GET IMMUNIZED.** Don't want to get rabies? Us neither (p. 491).

planning your trip

entrance requirements

- **PASSPORT:** Required for citizens of United Kingdom, Canada, Australia, New Zealand, Ireland and the United States.
- **INTERNATIONAL DRIVING PERMIT:** Required if you plan to drive in Morocco, although foreign licenses with photo ID may be accepted.
- **WORK PERMIT:** Required for all foreigners planning to work in Morocco.

DOCUMENTS AND FORMALITIES

You've got your visa, your invitation, and your work permit, just like *Let's Go* told you to, and then you realize you've forgotten the most important thing: your passport. Well, we're not going to let that happen. **Don't forget your passport!**

Visas

Citizens of Australia, Canada, Ireland, New Zealand, the UK, the US do not need visas.

Double-check entrance requirements at the nearest embassy or consulate of Morocco (listed below) for up-to-date information before departure. US citizens can also consult ▥http://travel.state.gov.

Entering Morocco to study requires a special visa. For more information, see the **Beyond Tourism** chapter (p. 495).

Work Permits

Admittance to a country as a traveler does not include the right to work, which is authorized only by a work permit. For more information, see the **Beyond Tourism** chapter.

TIME DIFFERENCES

Morocco is on Greenwich Mean Time (GMT) and does observe Daylight Saving Time. This means that it is 5hr. ahead New York City, 8hr. ahead Los Angeles, on the same time as the British Isles, 9hr. behind Sydney, and 11hr. behind New Zealand.

money

GETTING MONEY FROM HOME

Stuff happens. When stuff happens, you might need some money. When you need some money, the easiest and cheapest solution is to have someone back home make a deposit to your bank account. Otherwise, consider one of the following options.

Wiring Money

Arranging a **bank money transfer** means asking a bank back home to wire money to a bank in Morocco. This is the cheapest way to transfer cash, but it's also the slowest and most agonizing, usually taking several days or more. Note that some banks may only release your funds in local currency, potentially sticking you with a poor exchange rate; inquire about this in advance. Money transfer services like **Western Union** are faster and more convenient than bank transfers—but also much pricier. Western Union has many locations worldwide. To find one, visit ▥www.westernunion.com or

embassies and consulates

- **MOROOCAN EMBASSY IN AUSTRALIA: Embassy.** *(17 Terrigal Crescent - O'Malley ACT 2606, Canberra ☎61 262 900 755 ■www.moroccoembassy. org.au ⏰ Open M-F 9am-3pm.)*

- **MOROCCAN EMBASSY IN CANADA: Embassy.** *(38 Range Road, KIN 8J4 Ottawa, Ontario ☎613 236 7391 ■www.ambamaroc.ca ⏰ Open M-F 9am-4pm.)*

- **MOROCCAN EMBASSY IN IRELAND: Embassy.** *(53 Raglan Road, Dublin 4 ☎353 1 660 9449.)*

- **MOROCCAN CONSULATE IN NEW ZEALAND: Consulate-General.** *(1 Garfield Street, Parnell, Auckland ☎64 09 520 3626.)*

- **MOROCCAN EMBASSY IN UK: Embassy.** *(49, Queens Gate Gardens London SW7 5 NE ☎0207 581 5001 ■www.moroccanembassylondon.org.uk ⏰ Open M-Th 9:30am-5pm, F 9:30am-3pm.)*

- **MOROCCAN EMBASSY IN UNITED STATES: Embassy.** *(1601 21st St. NW, Washington DC 20036 ☎202 462 7979 ■dcusa.themoroccanembassy. com ⏰ Open M-F 9am-5pm.)*

- **BRITISH EMBASSY IN MOROCCO: Embassy.** *(28 Avenue S.A.R. Sidi Mohammed, Soussi 10105 (BP 45), Rabat ☎212 0537 63 33 33 ■ukin-morocco.fco.gov.uk/en ⏰ Open M-Th 8am-4:15pm, F 8am-1pm.)*

- **AUSTRALIAN CONSULAR SERVICES IN MOROCCO:** Australia does not have an embassy in Morocco, but the Canadian Embassy in Rabat provides all services to Australian citizens except issuance of passports.

- **CANADIAN EMBASSY IN MOROCCO: Embassy.** *(13, bis rue Jaâfa-as-Sadik, Agdal, Rabat ☎212 537 68 74 00 ■www.moroccoembassy.org.au ⏰ Open M-Th 8am-12pm and 1:30-5:30pm F 8am-1:30pm.)*

- **IRISH CONSULATE MOROCCO: Consulate.** *(57, Bd Abdelmoumen, rue Salim Chrkkaoui, Résidence Al Hadi n.B, Casablanca ☎212 2882 1212 wwww.dfa.ie/home/index.aspx?id=5496.)*

- **NEW ZEALAND IN MOROCCO:** Handled by the embassy in Madrid.

- **UNITED STATES EMBASSY IN MOROCCO: Embassy.** *(2 Avenue de Mohamed El Fassi, Rabat ☎212 527 76 22 65 ■rabat.usembassy.gov ⏰ Open M-F 8am-5pm.)*

call the appropriate number: in Australia ☎1800 173 833, in Canada 800-235-0000, and in the US 800-325-6000, in the UK 0800 735 1815. To wire money using a credit card in Canada and the US, call ☎800-CALL-CASH; in the UK, 0800 833 833.

US State Department (US Citizens Only)

In serious emergencies only, the US State Department will forward money within hours to the nearest consular office, which will then disburse it according to instructions for a US$30 fee. If you wish to use this service, you must contact the Overseas Citizens Services division of the US State Department *(☎+1-202-501-4444, from US 888-407-4747).*

money · getting money from home

TIPPING AND BARGAINING

In restaurants tip around 10%, and in taxis round up to the nearest 5 dirhams. If someone guides you in the medina, give them 5-10 dirhams if your guide is a child and 10-20 dirhams if your guide is an adult, depending on the distance.

TAXES

Taxes are generally included in prices, though in malls and *grandes surfaces* (larger superstores) you will find a 7% value-added tax on food and a 20% tax on luxury goods.

safety and health

GENERAL ADVICE

In any type of crisis, the most important thing to do is **stay calm.** Your country's embassy abroad is usually your best resource in an emergency; registering with that embassy upon arrival in the country is a good idea. The government offices listed in the **Travel Advisories** feature at the end of this section can provide information on the services they offer their citizens in case of emergencies abroad.

Local Laws and Police

Homosexuality is a criminal offense in Morocco, and public displays of affection are not recommended. However, the cautious traveler will face little harassment or persecution. The Moroccan police, *La Direction Générale de la Sûreté Nationale* are responsible for enforcing civilian law. If you are harassed or are robbed, find the nearest police officer.

Drugs and Alcohol

Do not get involved with drugs, particularly hashish. You will be offered hashish in the medinas. Be aware that all narcotics and cannabis products are illegal, and some travelers report getting ripped-off or turned into the police as a result of hashish transactions. While alcohol is prohibited by Islam, you can buy wine in supermarkets and restaurants. Moroccan bars are generally entirely male and mainly populated by foreigners.

travel advisories

The following government offices provide travel information and advisories by telephone, by fax, or via the web:

- **AUSTRALIA: Department of Foreign Affairs and Trade.** (☎+61 2 6261 1111 🖳www.dfat.gov.au)

- **CANADA: Department of Foreign Affairs and International Trade (DFAIT).** Call or visit the website for the free booklet *Bon Voyage...But.* (☎+1-800-267-8376 🖳www.dfait-maeci.gc.ca)

- **NEW ZEALAND: Ministry of Foreign Affairs.** (☎+64 4 439 8000 🖳www.mfat.govt.nz)

- **UK: Foreign and Commonwealth Office.** (☎+44 20 7008 1500 🖳www.fco.gov.uk)

- **US: Department of State.** (☎888-407-4747 from the US, +1-202-501-4444 elsewhere 🖳travel.state.gov)

follow the rules

Morocco can have some odd rules (past and present). Here are some to both laugh at and make sure you never break.

Date Trees: One old rule that no longer exists in Morocco is the prohibition of the sale of Date Trees. Why, you ask? Well the date tree was sometimes the only source of wealth for a family, and this prevented sales in times of desperation, and was a good buster of monopolies.

Dirhams: Similar to few other countries, it is illegal to bring dirhams out of the country. Make sure you either spend it all, convert it, or hide it in the bottom of your bag. Don't empty your pockets at airport security to reveal a 100 dhs note, or you could be fined.

Jesus: Although Morocco is a secular state and religious practice is freely allowed, spreading the word of the Christian God is frowned upon in a big way. In March of 2010, nearly 40 foreigners were deported from Morocco and fined for proselytizing. Jesus may love everyone, but make sure to keep it to yourself.

SPECIFIC CONCERNS

Media Censorship

Morocco enthusiastically welcomes tourists, but public dissent in the media is not tolerated. In recent years, many newspapers and reporters have either been shut down or arrested for publishing "false information." While in Morocco, be very careful to be interviewed by reporters, even bloggers, especially on anything having to do with the Moroccan government. You don't want to end your trip with a stint in Moroccan prison or with a hefty fine, so keep your trap shut.

Terrorism

In 2003, 33 people were killed by 12 suicide bombers in Casablanca in the deadliest attack in Morocco's history. In 2007, there was another smaller attack. However, he Moroccan government has adopted an aggressive stance in response to terrorism, and monitors the activity of violent Islamist groups.

PRE-DEPARTURE HEALTH

Matching a prescription to a foreign equivalent is not always easy, safe, or possible, so if you take **prescription drugs,** carry up-to-date prescriptions or a statement from your doctor stating the medications' trade names, manufacturers, chemical names, and dosages. Be sure to keep all medication with you in your carry-on luggage.

Pharmacists often have a relatively good command of English, especially in relation to medicine, so ask for their help when looking for over-the-counter drugs.

Immunizations and Precautions

The CDC recommends getting vaccinated against typhoid fever and rabies, especially if traveling to more remote areas. Travelers over two years old should also make sure that the following vaccines are up to date: MMR (for measles, mumps, and rubella); DTaP or Td (for diphtheria, tetanus, and pertussis); IPV (for polio); Hib (for *Haemophilus influenzae* B); and HepB (for Hepatitis B). For recommendations on immunizations and prophylaxis, check with a doctor and consult the Centers for Disease Control and Prevention (CDC) in the US or the equivalent in your home country (☎+1-800-CDC-INFO/232-4636 ▪www.cdc.gov/travel).

safety and health · pre-departure health

STAYING HEALTHY

Diseases and Environmental Hazards

Travelers in Morocco face a different set of health issues than in Spain and Portugal; food and waterborne diseases in particular are a common cause of illness. The CDC recommends that travelers drink only boiled or bottled water, avoiding tap water, fountain drinks, and ice cubes. It is also advisable to only eat fruit and vegetables that are cooked or that you have washed yourself in clean water. Stay away from food sold by street vendors and check to make sure that dairy products have been pasteurized. There is only a slight risk of malaria in Morocco, but consult your doctor before leaving about the possibility of a vaccine or anti-malarial pills.

While there is a public health system in Morocco, travelers should seek out private clinics, which offer the most dependent and affordable care. There are few English-speaking doctors, though French is widespread; learn a few basic words of medical vocabulary in French in case of an emergency. Private clinics are found in large cities and university towns with medical schools, such as Casablanca and Rabat. Travelers with significant medical problems that might need sudden and immediate attention are advised to stay in larger cities.

getting around

For information on how to get to Morocco and save a bundle while doing so, check out the Essentials section of ◨**www.letsgo.com.** (In case you can't tell, we think our website's the bomb.)

petit taxi vs. grand taxi

With two distinct types of taxis in operation in Morocco, it's hard to know which ones to take and what they look like, and how much they cost. Here is a point-by-point comparison on average costs, description, and what to expect.

Petit Taxi: These taxis operate on a loose basis. They are often smaller, all color-codedaccording to their city: in Fès and Casablanca they are red, in Marrakesh they are yellow, and in Rabat and Tanger they are light blue. They are required to use a meter, and often have fixed rates for known distances, like to the airport. Stick with these if the distance is 20 min. or less.

Grand Taxi: These larger models are used for city-to-city transport, or between villages. Drivers will cram as many people as possible into a taxi at a stand before leaving. Because of this, you will not pay much for long distances of an hour or two's travel time. However, sometimes as many as 7 people (including the driver) are packed into a 4 door Mercedes without A/C, which is the kind of sauna you don't want. These taxis are light colored, and will gather at main squares. HEADS UP: Be insistent that you want a shared taxi, as the driver will try and make you hire the entire taxi and himself as a guide.

morocco essentials

BY PLANE

Royal Air Maroc is the national airline in Morocco. However, plane travel is much more expensive than any other kind of transport, so you're better off going by train or bus.

BY TRAIN

Trains in Morocco are generally comfortable, convenient, and reasonably swift . Especially in the hot summer months, trains are far more comfortable than buses. Second-class compartments, which seat eight people are great places to meet fellow travelers. Make sure you are on the correct car, as trains sometimes split at crossroads. Trains connect Casablanca, Fes, Tangiers, Rabat, and Marrakesh and run quite often. There is an overnight train from Tangier to Marrakesh.

BY BUS

Since trains don't run to popular destinations like Essaouira, so you'll likely have to take a bus at some point. The three main bus companies are Supratours, CTM, and SATAS. Most of the long-trip buses are air conditioned and fairly comfortable.

BY FERRY

Morocco is reachable from numerous ports in southern Spain (Algeciras, Almeria, Málaga, Tarifa). Most ferries are quite comfortable; the cheapest ticket typically still includes a reclining chair or couchette. Fares jump sharply in July and August. Ask for discounts; ISIC holders get many reductions and free trips.

keeping in touch

For internet and phone information, see **Spain and Portugal Essentials.**

international calls

To call Morocco from home or to call home from Morocco, dial:

1. THE INTERNATIONAL DIALING PREFIX. To call from Australia, dial ☎0011; Canada or the US, ☎011; Ireland, New Zealand, or the UK, ☎00; Morocco, ☎00.

2. THE COUNTRY CODE OF THE COUNTRY YOU WANT TO CALL. To call Australia, dial ☎61; Canada or the US, ☎1; Ireland, ☎353; New Zealand, ☎64; the UK, ☎44; Morocco, ☎212.

3. THE CITY/AREA CODE. *Let's Go* lists the city/area codes for cities and towns in Morocco opposite the city or town name, next to a ☎, as well as in every phone number.

4. THE LOCAL NUMBER.

BY SNAIL MAIL

In addition to the standard postage system, **Federal Express** handles express mail services from most countries to Morocco *(☎+1-800-463-3339 ▣www.fedex.com).*

There are several ways to arrange pickup of letters sent to you while you are abroad. Mail can be sent via **Poste Restante** (General Delivery) to many cities and towns in Morocco with a post office, and it is pretty reliable. Address Poste Restante letters like so:

Mohammad V
Poste Restante
Rabat, Morocco

The mail will go to a special desk in the central post office, unless you specify a post office by street address or postal code. It's best to use the largest post office, since mail may be sent there regardless. Bring your passport (or other photo ID) for pickup; there may be a small fee. If the clerks insist that there is nothing for you, ask them to check under your first name as well. *Let's Go* lists post offices in the **Practicalities** section for each city.

climate

Don't be fooled by Morocco's proximity to the Sahara desert. It's true that the country does have some desert regions, but the coastline of Morocco, where most cities are located, is kept cool by breezes from the Mediterranean and Atlantic. During the winter, the north gets quite a bit of rain and be aware that up in the Atlas Mountains temperatures frequently drop below zero.

AVG. TEMP. (LOW/ HIGH), PRECIP.	JANUARY			APRIL			JULY			OCTOBER		
	°C	°F	mm	°C	°F	mm	°C	°F	mm	°C	°F	mm
Marrakech	12/17	37/46	363	12/17	37/46	63	12/17	37/46	63	12/17	37/46	63
Fes	2/7	37/46	63	2/7	37/46	63	2/7	37/46	63	2/7	37/46	63

To convert from degrees Fahrenheit to degrees Celsius, subtract 32 and multiply by 5/9. To convert from Celsius to Fahrenheit, multiply by 9/5 and add 32.

°CELSIUS	-5	0	5	10	15	20	25	30	35	40
°FAHRENHEIT	23	32	41	50	59	68	77	86	95	104

language

Moroccan Arabic, a mixture of standard Arabic, Berber, French and Spanish, is unintelligible to an Arabic speaker from Egypt or the Gulf states. Because of the heavy Berber influence on grammar, it's best to learn a few simply phrases of Moroccan Arabic to get by. Helpfully, Moroccan Arabic is often transliterated and should be pronounced phonetically However, thanks to the decades-long French domination of Morocco, almost all Moroccans are fluent in French, so it's time to brush up on your middle school French knowledge.

PHRASEBOOK

ENGLISH	ARABIC	FRENCH
Hello!/Hi!	as salaam alaykum	Bonjour (bohn-ZHOOR)
Goodbye!	bessalama	Au revoir (oh ruh-VWAH)
Yes.	eeyeh	oui (wee)
No.	la	non (nohn)
Please	'afak (m)/'afik (f)	Si'l vous plaît
Thank you	shukran	merci (mehr-SEE)
Excuse me.	smeh leeyah	pahr-DOHN
Do you speak English?	wash kat'ref negleezeeya	Parlez-vous anglais? (par-lay-voo ahn-GLAY?)
Help!	'teqnee!	Au secours! (oh sek-OOR!)
I'm sick.	ana mreed	Je suis malade
bus/train	otubees/tran	bus/train (boos/tren)
I would like...	bgheet	Je voudrais...(jh'voo-DRAY)

SPAIN, PORTUGAL & MOROCCO 101

spain 101

facts and figures

- **POPULATION:** 46.6 million
- **AUTONOMOUS REGIONS:** 17
- **REGIONAL LANGUAGES:** Catalan, Basque, and Galicia
- **KILOMETERS OF BEACHES:** Over 8,000
- **NUMBER OF OLIVE TREES:** Over 300 million

HISTORY

When questioned about Spanish history, even the dimmest of schoolchildren can dutifully recite that back "in 1492 Columbus sailed the ocean blue." Indeed, the Age of Exploration (15th and 16th centuries) seems to be Spain's most well-known epoch. Knowledge of Spain's history following the destruction of the nation's Armada by English forces is not so ubiquitous, yet Spain deserves more attention; from Moorish colony to worldwide colonizer to Pyrenean pauper, the Spain of today has thrown off the shackles of Franco-era repression and is experiencing resurgence.

Please, Sir, May I Have Some Moors?

When a small force of Arabs, Berbers, and Syrians invaded Spain in AD 711 they easily defeated the ruling Visigoths and proceeded to govern for centuries from their capital at Córdoba. To this day, the Moorish legacy remains in the thousands of Spanish words that stem from the Arabic language, varying from aceituna (olive) to alacrán (scorpion).

Los Reyes Catolicos

The union of Fernando de Aragon and Isabel de Castilla in 1469 led to the unification of Spain's two most powerful Christian kingdoms, and paved the way for the momentous events of 1492, a banner year for the Spanish monarchy. In addition to the voyage of Christopher Columbus, this year marked the end of the Reconquista, with the capture of Granada from the Moors.

Hapsburgs Take the Stage

In 1516 the grandson of Fernando and Isabel, Carlos I, became Holy Roman Emperor Charles V (1516-1556). With Carlos as king, the Spanish empire prospered. However, under his successor Felipe II, Spain's power began to diminish. Of course, the ultimate downer was the 1588 defeat of the Spanish Armada. While Felipe III and IV managed to hold the country together, under Carlos II el Hechizado ("the bewitched"), the country slid into economic decline. When this Carlos failed to produce an heir, the War of Spanish Succession began.

The Reign in Spain

The 1713 Treaty of Utrecht ended the war, and Felipe V, the grandson of French king Louis XIV, gained the Spanish throne. His coronation ushered in the over 200 year-long reign of the Bourbon dynasty, which was broken up by Napoleon's *short*-lived occupation (1808-1813), and the establishment of the First Spanish Republic (1868-1875).

Rebellion and Franco's Regime

In 1931 the abdication of King Alfonso XIII brought about the creation of the Second Spanish Republic (1931-1939). Growing divisions between the liberal Republicans and conservative Nationalists led to the outbreak of the Spanish Civil War (1936-1939). In April 1939 the war ended with defeat for the liberal faction, as the fascist Generalisimo Francisco Franco emerged as victor. The oppressive dictatorship of Franco lasted until his death in 1975. At this point the Bourbon monarchy was restored under King Juan Carlos I, who remains ruling to this day, albeit in a much scaled-back role.

Democracy and Socialist Rule

In 1978 Spain adopted a new constitution and restored parliamentary government and regional autonomy. Since then, power has alternately shifted between the PSOE (Spanish Socialist Workers Party) and the more conservative Popular Party (PP). The PSOE has been in power since 2004, under the leadership of Jose Luis Rodriguez Zapatero. Under Zapatero, Spain withdrew its troops from Iraq in 2004 and legalized same sex marriage in 2005. A proponent of gender equality, there are currently more women than men in Zapatero's Cabinet, including Spain's first female Minister of Defense.

CUSTOMS AND ETIQUETTE

Spaniards are generally polite and courteous to foreigners. Even if your Spanish is a little rusty, do not be intimidated to speak in the native tongue – your efforts will be appreciated.

Taboos

Be aware that shorts and short skirts are not common in most parts of Spain, apart from the coasts. Wearing revealing clothing away from the beaches may garner unwanted attention or at the very least scream "I am a tourist!" Women with bare shoulders should carry a shawl to tour churches and monasteries, and it is considered disrespectful to wear shorts in these pious places.

Public Behavior

Spaniards tend to be very polite in mannerisms and social behavior, so in first encounters it's a good idea to be as formal as possible. Be sure to address those you meet as Señor (Mr.), Señora (Mrs.), or Señorita (Ms.), and don't be surprised if you get kissed on both cheeks in place of a handshake.

Tipping

Though a service charge is generally included in the check at bars and restaurants, an additional tip is common for good service: 5-10% will suffice. Taxi drivers and hotel porters will also expect small tips for their services.

FOOD AND DRINK

No immersion into Spanish culture would be complete without sampling the national cuisine, which is vibrant, varied, and inventive. Whether you're looking for a meal based on tradition or trendy culinary dishes, Spain is filled with epicurean delights. One dish all visitors are obligated to try at least

200 BC
The Roman Empire sets up camp.

409-711
Visigoths arrive in Iberia after sacking Rome, but fall to the Moors 300 years later.

1478
In an unexpected move, the Spanish Inquisition begins.

1519
Hernan Cortez lands in Mexico in search of gold, silver, and chocolate.

1588
The Spanish Armada proves to be as invincible as the Titanic was unsinkable.

1605
Cervantes publishes *Don Quixote* in Madrid.

spain 101 . food and drink

once is paella, a quintessentially Spanish mix of rice, vegetables, seafood, and meat. Along with oranges, the Mediterranean city of Valencia is known for its sumptuous *paellas*. Spain's Mediterranean climate has played an important role in its culinary development; notably, its climate allows it to be the number one producer of olive oil in the world.

For a country smaller than the state of Texas, Spain has a large number of distinct regions, each with its own specialties. From the cold, tomato-based gazpacho soup in the hot southern climate of Andalucía, to calamar en su tinta (squid in its own ink) in northern País Vasco, each locality has a proud culinary tradition. One universal favorite are the ubiquitous tapas, or small, savory dishes served hot or cold, typically with drinks at bars. If you're looking for something other than plain vino (wine) or cerveza (beer) to go with your tapas, a delicious Spanish option is sangria, a red-wine punch made with fruit, seltzer, and sugar.

THE ARTS

You don't need to be an art history major to appreciate the artistic and architectural treasures of Spain. From the intricate, geometric decoration of the 14th-century Alhambra in Granada to the unbridled imagination of Gaudí's unfinished La Sagraga Familia in Barcelona, many styles of architecture coexist within Spain, offering refreshingly new perspectives for visitors. Modern architectural interpretations are found in the buildings and bridges of Santiago Calatrava, and Frank Gehry's famous Guggenheim Museum in Bilbao.

Be sure to feast your eyes on the haunting, elongated figures of El Greco (1541-1614), the royal portraits of Diego Velázquez (1599-1660) and Francisco de Goya (1746-1828), the Surrealist expressions of Salvador Dalí (1904-1989), and, of course, the many paintings of Pablo Picasso (1881-1973).

A good way to initiate yourself with modern Spanish culture before traveling to Spain is through the medium of film. The Spanish film scene has exploded since the death of the repressive dictator Francisco Franco in 1979. Among the most highly acclaimed of today's Spanish directors is Pedro Almodóvar, whose career stretches back to the 1980s. His 1999 work Todo sobre mi madre won the Oscar for Best Foreign Language Film, and Volver (2006) won Best Screenplay at the Cannes Film Festival. His most recent film, Abrazos Rotos, starring Spanish actress Penélope Cruz, was released in 2009.

From **Enrique Iglesias** to **Placido Domingo** (one third of the **Three Tenors**), no exploration of the Spanish arts would be complete without delving into the world of music. When it comes to musical entertainment, there are few spectacles that can eclipse the pure passion and energy of live **flamenco**. Combining *cante* (song), *baile* (dance), and *guitarra* (guitar), flamenco has been an integral part of the Spanish musical tradition since the 18th century, when it was created by Andalusian gypsies. While flamenco heroes of the past include the singer **Antonio Mairena** (1909-1983), bands like the **Gypsy Kings** mix flamenco with the dance rhythms of salsa and rumba, creating an internationally acclaimed sound.

1808-1814
Napoleon occupies and rules Spain.

1898
Spain loses the Spanish-American War and the last of its colonies.

1923
Spain's first dictator, General Primo de Rivera, rises to power in a coup.

1939
Dictator Francisco Franco begins his reign.

1975
Franco dies; Spain rejoices.

2008
Zapatero is named Spain's first female Minister of Defense, pregnant upon being sworn in.

While film provides an excellent means to explore Spain's modern culture, those looking for a traditional cultural outlet should consider the Spanish art of **bullfighting**. Though most foreigners consider this classic Spanish activity (known locally as *toreo*) to be a sport, for aficionados it is an art form. Of course, animal rights activists view it in less lofty terms, calling it torture. *Toreo* has a long history in Spain; its modern form dates back to the 18th century. For anyone interested in experiencing this Spanish spectacle, do not expect to do so in the province of Catalonia; the Catalan Parliament has banned bullfighting within this region. While this may be due as much to Catalan nationalism as to cross-species sympathy, in a world of modern entertainment many contemporary Spaniards are losing interest in bullfighting. The steep price of attendance doesn't help. For good seats out of the sun, the cost can be on par with that of opera tickets. Still, whether you consider it to be barbaric or beautiful, bullfighting remains part of Spain's cultural heritage. To this day, visitors looking to experience the nine-day fiesta described in **Ernest Hemingway's** classic *The Sun Also Rises* can come to Pamplona in July for the annual Running of the Bulls.

portugal 101

facts and figures

- **OFFICIAL NAME:** Portuguese Republic
- **POPULATION:** 10.7 million
- **MOST FAMOUS INVENTION:** The Hot Air Balloon (1709)
- **AGE:** 871 in 2010
- **NUMBER OF CASTLES:** 101

HISTORY

Portugal's heyday came in the 14th and 15th centuries when the small Iberian realm harnessed its naval superiority to build an empire stretching from America to Asia, making it one of the most powerful nations in the world. While those days are emphatically over, national pride remains strong. Today, what Portugal lacks in global prominence it makes up for in cultural vibrancy.

The Birth of Portugal

A Portuguese victory over the Moors (who had been an established presence in Iberia since 711 AD) at the Battle of Ourique in 1139 led to the creation of the Kingdom of Portugal, ruled by Dom Alfonso Henriques (Alfonso I). His legacy, the boundary between Spain and Portugal, is the oldest established border in Europe.

Portugal Sails the Ocean Blue

Under Prince Henry the Navigator, Portugal was at the vanguard of exploration and trade. In 1488, Bartolomeu Dias sailed around the Cape of Good Hope, paving the way for Portuguese entry into the spice trade. One of the greatest feats of Portuguese navigation occurred when Fernao de Magalhaes, known as Magellan, completed the first circumnavigation of the globe in 1521.

Bring on the Bragança

As time went on, Portugal began to lose its predominance, and in 1580 Spanish king Felipe II, claimed the Portuguese throne. A mere 60 years later, the House of Bragança engineered a nationalist rebellion and wrested control away from Spain. The new rulers financed massive building projects, but the disastrous earthquake of 1755 devastated the country.

Back and Forth

The 19th century was a period of conflict and uncertainty in Portugal, as illustrated by the War of the Two Brothers (1828-1834), the "brothers" being the sons of King Dom João VI. This extreme case of sibling rivalry pitted the constitutionalists against the monarchists. The constitutionalists won the war, but tension between the two groups remained strong well into the 20th century. This tenuous political and financial situation paved the way for a former economics professor, Antonio de Oliveira Salazar, to become dictator in 1932. Salazar's repressive regime came to an end with his death in 1970, but his successor, prime minister Marcelo Caetano, was not much more popular.

You Say You Want a Revolution?

On April 25, 1974, a left-wing military coalition calling itself the Armed Forces Movement overthrew Caetano in a quick coup. The socialist government that resulted from this Carnation Revolution, as it came to be called, began to nationalize several industries, but soon backed off from blatantly Marxist policies. Since the first free and open elections in 1976, members of the Socialist party have predominantly ruled Portugal. In 1999 Portugal became a full member of the European Union, and ceded Macau, its last overseas territory, to the Chinese.

CUSTOMS AND ETIQUETTE

Like the Spanish, the Portuguese are generally friendly, easygoing, and receptive to foreigners. Any attempt on your part to speak in the native tongue will be appreciated.

Taboos

Though dress in Portugal is more casual in the hot summer months than in the cold of winter, strapless tops on women and collarless t-shirts on men are generally unacceptable; shorts and flip-flops may be seen as disrespectful in some public establishments and rural areas even during a heat wave. Skimpy clothes are always a taboo in churches, as are tourist visits during masses or services. Do not automatically assume that those you meet will understand Spanish; one of the best ways to offend a local is to tacitly suggest that Portugal is part of Spain.

Public Behavior

Politeness is key in Portuguese society. Be sure to address a Portuguese as *senhor* (Mr.), *senhora* (Ms.), *senhora dona* (Mrs.), followed by their first name. To blend in, it's a good idea to be as formal as possible at first impression. Introduce yourself in detail; you'll be welcomed openly if you mention

1139
Dom Afonso Henriques declares Portugal's independence from Spain.

1494
The Treaty of Tordesillas divides the New World between Spain and Portugal.

1498
Vasco de Gama lands in India.

1755
An earthquake destroys Lisbon.

1917
Three chilren claim to see the Virgin Mary in Fatima.

1976
First free and open election is held in Portugal.

who you are, where you're from, and what you're doing in Portugal. Don't be surprised if you get pecked on both cheeks by younger Portuguese, but handshakes are generally the standard introductory gesture by most of the population.

Tipping

In restaurants, a service charge (*serviço*) of 10% is usually included in the bill. When service is not included, it is customary to leave 5-10% as a tip. It is also common to barter in markets.

FOOD AND DRINK

Portugal is a paradise for fresh seafood. Whether you're a seasoned fan of nautical fare or a shellfish skeptic, the Portuguese offer up an enticing selection of marine cuisine. While bacalhau (cod) is by far the fish of choice for most in Portugal, peixe espada (swordfish) is also a popular option. When it comes to cephalopods, choco grelhado (grilled cuttlefish), polvo (boiled or grilled octopus), and lulas grelhadas (grilled squid) should not be missed. For those less enamored of seafood, don't fear—the Holy Trinity of Portuguese fare remains pork, potatoes, and pastries.

Many Portuguese pastry names have a distinctly religious air, from barriga de friera (nun's belly) to papos de anjo (angel's chins) to toucinho do céu (bacon from heaven). Despite its name, no pigs are harmed in the making of toucinho do céu; while the name derives from a time when bacon lard was used in its preparation, today all three of these divine treats are reliant upon egg yolks and sugar for their rich taste, providing a PETA-friendly pastry for the Portuguese.

LAND

For such a compact country (it's slightly smaller than Indiana), Portugal offers up an impressive amount of biodiversity and differing landscapes. There's no need to choose between mountains and beaches when traveling in this Iberian nation, as it's possible to experience them both. Cool and temperate in the mountainous region north of the Tagus River, and warm and dry in the rolling plains to the south, Portugal encompasses the best of both worlds. From sun-drenched interior towns to the dazzling coasts of the Algarve, mainland Portugal offers something for everyone.

morocco 101

facts and figures

- **CAPITAL:** Rabat
- **POPULATION:** 31 million
- **OFFICIAL LANGUAGE:** Arabic
- **SIZE:** 446,550 sq km
- **RELIGION:** 98% Muslim

HISTORY

Imperial Islam

Less than 50 years after the death of Muhammad in 632, Islam, along with the rule of the Umayyad Dynasty, had spread across North Africa to Morocco. Many local Berbers converted to Islam, setting the stage for the invasion of Spain in 711. Idris

Ibn Abd Allah founded the first Moroccan state in 789, and it was to Morocco that many Muslim immigrants fled in 1492, in order to escape the Spanish Inquisition.

European Contenders

Given its strategic location and wealth of resources, Morocco was disputed fought for by European powers for centuries. England, France, Portugal, and Spain all entered the fray. Under the 1912 Treaty of Fez, France laid claim to the majority of Moroccan land, though the Spanish were given the northern-most part, along with the southern Sahara.

Struggle for Independence

Morocco's nationalist movement began in 1944 with the founding of the Independence Party, Istiqial, which by 1947 had gained the support of the Moroccan sultan, Mohammad V. Though initially deported by the French, on November 18, 1955, Mohammad V was restored to his royal status. Morocco gained its independence from France and Spain the following year.

Modern Morocco

Today, Morocco is a constitutional monarchy, in which the king and his advisors make most important decisions. Under the current king, Mohammad VI, Morocco has undergone much modernization. For example, the new family code adopted in 2004, the Mudawana, aims to give women more power by equalizing laws on divorce, custody, and consent. Despite such efforts, Morocco still struggles with deeply entrenched social problems, including illiteracy and high infant mortality. When it comes to foreign travel, the terrorist attacks of September 11, 2001, were not exactly a boon to the Moroccan tourist market. While travelers to Morocco do not face a particularly elevated risk, given the unpredictable nature of terrorism, travel to the Western Sahara region is restricted.

CUSTOMS AND ETIQUETTE

Taboos

Modest clothing for both men and women is highly recommended, especially in rural areas. Even properly dressed non-Muslims are barred from entering many of Morocco's active mosques. Taboo topics to avoid in conversation with Moroccans include sex, Israel and Palestine, the royal family, and the Western Sahara.

Public Behavior

Tourists in larger areas are susceptible to the advances of Moroccans offering to guide them. If you refuse, be polite but insistent. Western women tend to attract attention from Moroccan men. In general, the best way to react is not at all. Toning down public visibility is always smart.

Table Manners

A traditional Moroccan meal begins with hand washing. Dinner may be served from a communal dish at a low, round table. Avoid directly using your left hand when eating, as this hand is

789
Idris Ibn Abd Allah founds first Moroccan state.

1884
Spain creates a protectorate along Moroccoan coast.

1963
First elections held.

1975
Spain leaves Spanish Sahara; Algeria and Morocco clash over the new territory.

1991
UN-monitored ceasefire begins in Western Sahara.

2007
Despite UN-sponsored talks, Morocco and the Polisario Front fail to come to any agreement.

traditionally reserved for personal hygiene. In more personal settings, such as in a Moroccan home, vocally praising the food is important.

FOOD AND DRINK

From decadent sweets to succulent meats, opportunities for epicurean adventurers in Morocco abound. Upon entering the country, you can banish "bland" from your culinary vocabulary – Moroccan cuisine incorporates a wealth of spices; turmeric, cumin, coriander, and saffron just scratch the surface of the aromatic delights to be found. The most widely known staple of Moroccan fare is couscous, a semolina-grain pasta, roughly the size of sesame seeds. While couscous is usually served with either beef or lamb, a great vegetarian option is couscous aux légumes (couscous with vegetables). Other popular dishes include tajine, a meat stew with vegetables and olives, harira, a chickpea soup, and pastilla, a sweet and savory meat pie comprised of pigeon or chicken, onions, almonds, eggs, butter, cinnamon, and sugar. If these options leave you looking for something slightly more, shall we say, unfamiliar, than sheep's eyes might be right up your ally. While the eye of the sheep is originally an Arabian delicacy, rest assured, cooked sheep's eye can be part of your Moroccan adventure. A more conventional sheep-based specialty is mechoui, lamb spitted over an open fire. Typical snacks and on-the-go eats include roasted almonds, dried chickpeas, and cactus buds.

In the realm of desserts, fresh seasonal fruits are a typical concluding treat for a meal. This is not to say Morocco suffers from a lack of baked goods. To the contrary, sweet-lovers will find themselves amidst honey-soaked pastries, including halwa shebakia, a fried, honey-infused sesame cookie. A perfect accompaniment to such treats is a cup of Moroccan mint tea, or green tea steeped in mint leaves and saturated with sugar. Those looking for something slightly stronger need not fear the Islamic prohibition against alcohol: Moroccan, French, and Spanish wines can be found in supermarkets and restaurants.

CRAFTS

Looking for the perfect Moroccan memento to commemorate your trip? From ceramics to woodwork, Morocco offers an abundance of cultural crafts. Known for its luxurious carpets, Morocco also has a long tradition in the leather industry; to this day leather tanners throughout the country continue to use medieval techniques. According to local legend, tanners are descended from demons whose spirits inhabit the tanneries. Even without the omnipresence of demons, tannery work can be quite unpleasant. In the process of creating salable leather, the hides are softened in pigeon droppings and later immersed in vats of water and blood. From start to finish, the tanning process takes around twenty days. Other traditional crafts include the colorful glazed tiles that make up a zellij, or mosaic. Often mosaics will incorporate **calligraphy**, particularly elegant illuminations of Qur'anic verses that meld religion with high art. Islamic mosaics portray rich geometric designs rather than people, animals, or plants. Moroccan souqs (markets) are brimming with local handicrafts. Bargaining is a serious business approached with vigor; a reasonable final price should be about 50% of your seller's original quote. If you hit a standstill, don't be afraid to simply walk out the door—the owner just may chase after you with a better offer.

BEYOND TOURISM

If you are reading this, then you are a member of an elite group—and we don't mean "the literate." You're a student preparing for a semester abroad. You're taking a gap year to save the trees, the whales, or the dates. You're an 80-year-old woman who has devoted her life to egg-laying platypuses and figuring out what the hell is up with that. In short, you're a traveler, not a tourist; like any good spy, you don't observe your surroundings—you become an active part of them.

Your mission, should you choose to accept it, is to study, volunteer, or work in Spain, Portugal, and Morocco as laid out in the dossier—er, chapter—below. More general wisdom, including international organizations with a presence in many destinations and tips on how to pick the right program, is also accessible by logging onto the Beyond Tourism section of ▣www.letsgo.com. We leave the rest (when to go, whom to bring, and how many changes of underwear to pack) in your hands. This message will ▓**self-destruct** in five seconds. Good luck.

greatest hits

- **BUST SOME MOVES.** Shake your tailfeather at the Taller Flamenco School in Sevilla, Spain (p. 510).
- **BUST SOME BALLS.** Work for womens' rights and advocate for female literacy in Rabat, Morocco (p. 511).
- **STOP FEELING BAD FOR BAMBI.** Save the wolves instead, at Portugal's Centro de Recuperação do Lobo Ibérico (p. 510).

studying

If you're looking to study abroad, there is no shortage of opportunities—this is especially true in Spain, one of the top study-abroad destinations for American students. However, researching your options is a must: academic requirements, cost, and duration are all factors to think about when choosing a destination. It is also a good idea to find out what types of students participate in each program. A lot of programs fail on the immersion factor, as they tend to bring together large groups of Americans who don't try to speak the native language. You may (understandably) decide that you feel more comfortable within this community; however, you may never again have the opportunity to practice the language or meet local students. If you are already fluent in Spanish, Portuguese, French, or Arabic, it may be more beneficial to enroll directly at a university, but make sure to check your home university's credit requirements. With any country or program you choose, there will be paperwork. If you intend to stay for longer than 90 days, you must obtain a visa from your destination's consulate. It is also essential that you check on the requirements for your chosen program, as many have their own requirements of GPA and language level.

Most Spanish study-abroad programs center around **Barcelona, Madrid** and **Sevilla**. To find out more, it's a good idea to directly contact US universities or youth organizations who regularly send students to the country. **Portugal** and **Morocco** are less popular study-abroad destinations, but programs do exist in these countries. Most Portuguese universities are open to foreign students, and Morocco is a dream destination for polyglots and linguists.

visa information

The visa is what makes you a legal, official person in your country, your "get out of jail free and don't get deported" card. The acquisition process can be complicated and requires more pieces of idetification than you knew existed, but often if you travel or study with a program rather than directly enrolling, the programs will help you with this process. For every country, the best and most up-to-date information can be obtained from your local consulate. Visa applications often have 💵**fees** attached to them, which can range from $30-$100.

UNIVERSITIES

Most universities in big European cities have opened their doors to English-speaking exchange students, either directly or through outside programs. While you'll still have to jump through lots of bureaucratic hoops and do your I'm-a-helpless-foreigner song and dance a few times, it is totally possible to enroll as an exchange student.

International Programs

ACADEMIC PROGRAMS INTERNATIONAL

301 Camp Craft Rd., Suite 100, West Lake Hills, TX ☎800-844-4124 🖥www.academicintl.com

Through this program you will be enrolled at a local university, but don't fret—there are some classes offered in English. With locations in Barcelona, Bilbao, Cadiz, Granada, Madrid, Salamanca, and Sevilla.

ℹ 18+. College or graduate students. Housing provided. $ $4800-21,500.

ACADEMIC STUDIES ABROAD

4 Belgrade Ave., Suite 5, Roslindale, MA ☎888-845-4272 🖥www.academicstudies.com

This small program provides lots of amenities including health insurance and a cell phone. Summer and semester-long programs offered in Barcelona, Madrid, Salamanca, and Sevilla.

i *Eligibility depends on the requirements of the host university.* Ⓢ *Semester $8495-13,495; summer $3995-5100; Prices depend on location and length.*

AMERICAN INSTITUTE FOR FOREIGN STUDY

River Plaza, 9 West Broad St., Stamford, CT ☎866-906-2437 💻www.aifs.com

Standard-fare American study abroad program, offering 4-6-week summer programs in Barcelona, Granada, and Salamanca and semester-long programs in Granada and Salamanca. All program fees include excursions to London and other Spanish cities. Scholarships available. Your school may be "affiliated," so check on their website!

i *2.7 min. GPA for Barcelona program.* 🎓 *Semester $13,495; summer $4995-7795, depending on location and length.*

ARCADIA UNIVERSITY FOR EDUCATION ABROAD

450 South Easton Rd., Glenside, PA ☎866-927-2234 💻www.arcadia.edu/abroad

Summer, semester- and year-long academic programs in Barcelona, Granada, Majorca (summer only), and Toledo. Some courses taught in English, some in Spanish. Toledo program fee includes four-day field study in Morocco. Internship program also offered in Toledo.

i *3.0 min. GPA for most but not all programs.* 🎓 *Semester $14,825-15,210.*

CENTRAL COLLEGE ABROAD

812 University, Pella, IA ☎800-831-3629 💻www.ciee.org

Offers term-time academic programs in Granada, in addition to service-learning opportunities and internships for students of intermediate or higher Spanish ability. Summer intensive language program, also in Granada. Four-day Morocco excursion included in all term-time programs.

i *Limited enrollment.* 🎓 *Semester $13,200-15,065; summer $3900. Program fees include homestay housing with 3 meals per day.*

COUNCIL ON INTERNATIONAL EDUCATION EXCHANGE (CIEE)

300 Fore St., Portland ME ☎207-553-4000 💻www.ciee.org

Well-established organization with several programs throughout Spain, ranging from internships to teaching opportunities to academic programs. Also offers semester and summer language programs in Rabat, Morocco with classes taught in English and French. Scholarships available. Opportunities for high school students also available.

i *Background in French and Arabic recommended for Morocco program.* Ⓢ *Spain costs vary depending on program and length. Morocco semester $13,700; summer $6400. Fee includes housing and most meals.*

INSTITUTE FOR THE INTERNATIONAL EDUCATION OF STUDENTS (IES)

33 N. LaSalle St., 15th flr, Chicago, IL ☎1-800-995-2300 💻www. iesabroad.org

Programs in Spain and Portugal. Check and see if your school is "affiliated" to apply.

i *US citizens and enrolled college student.* Ⓢ *Semester approx. $20,000.*

WORLD LEARNING SCHOOL FOR INTERNATIONAL TRAINING

Kipling Rd., PO Box 676, Brattleboro, VT ☎888-272-7881 💻www.sit.edu

For those interested in studying abroad with the goal of helping the locals. Programs in Spain and Portugal.

Ⓢ *Semester $15,000.*

studying · universities

Local Programs

AL AKHAWAYN UNIVERSITY

P.O. Box 104, Hassan II Ave., Ifrane, Morocco   ☎212 535 86 20 00 ▣www.aui.ma

This relatively young establishment, founded in 1995, is in the self-proclaimed "Little Switzerland" of Morocco. Yes, it has a ski resort. Sweet little red conical Fez hats not included.

$Semester 60,000 Dhs. Fees include room and board.

EUROPEAN UNIVERSITY BARCELONA

Ganduxer 70, Barcelona   ☎+34 93 201 81 7 ▣www.euruni.edu

One of the world's top business schools just happens to be in Barcelona. Perfect for all those future world-dominators out there.

Ⓢ *Semester approx. $7000.*

UNIVERSITAT DE BARCELONA

Gran Via de les Corts Catalanes 585, Barcelona   ☎+34 934 021 100 ▣www.ub.edu

Founded in 1450, boasting 18 "faculties" (majors, in America-speak), and eight graduate schools, *UB* gives you your pick of classes, and may even teach you to say "*Dondé está la biblioteca*" in *Catalá*!

UNIVERSIDAD COMPLUTENSE DE MADRID

Ciudad Universitaria, Madrid   ☎+34 91 394 7196/7194 ▣www.ucm.es

International enrollment available through the Moncloa campus. Their Office of International Programs emphasizes the "power of diversity," so you know they're eager to help out.

UNIVERSIDAD EUROPEA DI MADRID

☎+34 911 421 015 ▣ www.uem.es/en

One of the many institutions in this nation's capital, it even has programs for students over the age of 40. Some courses are offered in English.

Ⓢ 4-week summer course €2950. Price includes housing and full board.

UNIVERSIDAD DE LISBOA

Alameda da Universidade, Cidade Universitária   ☎+351 217 967 624 ▣www.ul.pt

Enroll directly to Portugal's oldest university. Today the institution has expanded far beyond its original four schools, boasting 11 different faculties and 9 "institutes" (graduate schools). Unlike other European universities, this one has school-sponsored sports teams, but classes are only offered in Portuguese.

LANGUAGE SCHOOLS

As renowned novelist Gustave Flaubert once said, "Language is a cracked kettle on which we beat out tunes for bears to dance to." While we at *Let's Go* have absolutely no clue what he was talking about, we do know that the following are good resources for learning **Spanish**, **Portuguese**, **Arabic**, or **Catalá**. However, keep in mind that language schools often may not give college credit.

ARABIC LANGUAGE INSTITUTE IN FEZ

B.P 2136, Fez, Morocco   ☎212 535 62 48 50 ▣www.alif-fes.com

Courses available in both modern Arabic and colloquial Moroccan Arabic. All courses are kept small, with around eight students in each class, and housing is available in ALIF housing, homestays, apartments, or hotels.

Ⓢ *Six-week course 9900dhs, three-week 5800dhs.*

CENTRO DE LINGUAS (CIAL)

Ave. da República, 41-8º, Lisboa   ☎217 940 448 ▣www.cial.pt

Portuguese language school in Lisbon. Caters to all levels, from the fluent to the forasteiros. Program length from two weeks to 1 year.

studying · language schools

CENTRO DE LENGUAS E INTERCAMBIO CULTURAL

Albareda 19, Sevilla ☎34 954 502 131 🖳www.clic.es

Spanish language school in Sevilla. Internship placement available after completion of courses.

DON QUIJOTE

c/Placentinos 2, Salamanca ☎800 518 0412 🖳www.donquijote.org

Schools in both Spain and Morocco. Courses range from 1-20wks. And yes, the "d" in "don" is actually lower-case—Don Draper disapproves.

$ *$300-10,000, depending on length of course.*

SPECIAL INTEREST SCHOOLS

"But, wait!" we hear you cry, "What if I don't want to study the history and culture of Lisbon? What if I couldn't care less about fulfilling my home school's requirements?" If your tastes are more specific than what a typical Iberian university can offer, here's some information on alternative schools.

- **ADENC:** For lovers of Spanish birds, this Association for the Study and Protection of Nature might be your (bird)calling *(☎937 171 887 🖳www.adenc.org).*
- **ESCUELA DE COCINA LUIS IRIZAR** For fans of Spanish cuisine, the Luis Irizar Cooking School in the Basque country offers cooking instruction and calories *(C. Mari 5, bajo San Sebastián ☎00 34 943 431540 🖳www.escuelairizar.com).*
- **TALLER FLAMENCO SCHOOL** If you want to brush up on those sexy Spanish dances, the Flamenco School in Sevilla teaches you the moves to impress your future lovers *(C. Peral, 49, 1st floor, Sevilla ☎+34 954 56 42 34 🖳www.tallerflamenco.com).*

volunteering

There's a saying in Spain: the further south you go, the better the food is, the better the weather is, and the less time they spend doing anything productive. Whether or not that's true, you can buck the traditional trend by volunteering all over the Iberian Peninsula—you're even needed south of the Strait in Morocco. The variety of opportunities is vast—from education to environmental conservation—but long-term programs are generally hard to come by, because most volunteers do so on a short-term or once-in-a-while basis.

ENVIRONMENTAL CONSERVATION AND ECOTOURISM

- **EARTHTRUST:** Interested in oceanographic research and conservation? Contact this group and make sure they're currently active in your area. *(☎808-261-5339 🖳www.earthtrust.org)*
- **EARTHWATCH:** This program takes on volunteers to help with fieldwork and data collection. Family and teen expeditions are available. *(3 Clock Tower Place, Suite 100, Box 75, Maynard, MA ☎800-776-0188 🖳www.earthwatch.org)*
- **QUERCUS:** This Portuguese environmental movement, the name of which means "oak," deals with issues including water contamination and nuclear waste. Caution! Website is in Portuguese only. Glory be to Google Translate. *(🖳www.quercus.pt/scid/webquercus)*
- **GO ECO:** Volunteer at the Portuguese Centro de Recuperação do Lobo Ibérico, a 42-acre sanctuary for the endangered Iberian wolf. Tasks include feeding and monitoring the wolves, cleaning the facilities, and preventing forest fires. Must be 18+ to volunteer. Also see **Grupo Lobo** *(🖳http://lobo.fc.ul.pt)* for in-Portuguese-only information on volunteering independently or adopting a wolf. *(🖳www.goeco.org $ 2-week $680, 3-week $780, 4-week $1060. Fees include accommodation, but not food or flight costs.)*

COMMUNITY BUILDING

- **CROSS-CULTURAL SOLUTIONS (CCS):** Program only available in Morocco. You'll be based in Rabat, working to "achieve important community objectives," which could be anything from helping health professionals to promoting women's rights. *(2 Clinton Place, New Rochelle, New York 💻www.crossculturalsolutions.org)*
- **HABITAT FOR HUMANITY INTERNATIONAL VOLUNTEER PROGRAM:** It's Habitat. They do everything. You'll have fun and work for a great organization. *(121 Habitat Street, Americus, GA ☎800-422-4828 💻www.habitat.org/ivp/Idealist)*
- **VOLUNTEER MOROCCO:** By working in association with several Moroccan and US organizations, this group helps struggling communities become economically stable. *(💻www.volunteermorocco.org)*

POLITICAL AND SOCIAL ACTIVISM

- **AMNESTY INTERNATIONAL:** Volunteer with the world's most well-established human rights organization. *(💻www.amnesty.org)*
- **STOP SIDA:** Works to increase AIDS prevention in Spain. *(Muntaner, 121 Entlo.1ª, Barcelona ☎902 10 69 27 💻www.stopsida.org)*

FOR THE UNDECIDED ALTRUIST

- **AMERISPAN:** AmeriSpan is a Study Abroad program that also offers volunteer placement opportunities in several countries. *(1334 Walnut St., 6th fl., Philadelphia, PA ☎800-879-6640, 215-751-1100 💻www.amerispan.com/volunteer_intern)*
- **SERVICE CIVIL INTERNATIONAL:** SCI is a "network of autonomous branches and non-profit partner organizations." Legal residents of Canada and the US assigned to a workcamp with tasks ranging from teaching English to farming. 2 weeks-1yr. *(☎434-336-3545 💻www.sci-ivs.org)*
- **VOLUNTEER ABROAD:** Part of Goabroad.com, this site is dedicated to covering volunteer abroad opportunities. *(💻www.volunteerabroad.com/search.cfm)*
- **VOLUNTEERS FOR PEACE:** Promotes International Voluntary Service projects (IVS). 2-3wks. Accommodations provided. *(1034 Tiffany Road, Belmont VT ☎802-259–2759 💻www.vfp.org $ Average cost $300.)*
- **WORLDWIDE HELPERS:** The Google of international volunteering programs. Use this in the search for other opportunities not listed here. *(💻www.worldwidehelpers.org)*

working

No matter what type of work you choose to look for while abroad, chances are you will need a work permit and a visa. If you are an EU citizen, you can work in any EU country; however, if you are from outside the EU, you will need a work permit. Make sure you have everything in order and understand what needs to be done to obtain the proper documentation, or else you can land yourself in some serious trouble.

LONG-TERM WORK

If you choose to seek long-term employment, it's best to do so well in advance of your arrival. If you are a college student, an internship would be the best way to segue into a real job. In terms of payment for these internships, let's just say the experience of working in a foreign country will be pay enough.

In Spain, if you're new to town, you can begin your job search at the **Oficinas de Empleo**, the national employment service that controls the job market. However, more seasoned travelers may go straight to the yellow pages or establishments themselves. In Portugal, you can look for job listings in the English-language newspaper, **Anglo-Portuguese News**. In Morocco, your consulate is the best place to inquire about employment openings.

more visa information

To work legally in any country as a non-citizen, more often than not you need a work permit or a work visa. Citizens of the EU may live and work in any EU country (you lucky ducks). For everyone else, a visit to your local Spanish or Portuguese consulate, a passport, and an official transcript of a job offer is a good start. For those interested in Morocco, a visit to the Morocco Ministry of Labor upon arrival is your best bet. Again, fees may apply, and may be anywhere from $30-$100. Note that all three of these countries tend to have high rates of unemployment.

Teaching English

More and more, English is becoming the dominant world language. You can make good use of your mastery of the English language by helping spread our vernacular abroad. Of the three countries discussed in this book, **Morocco** may be the hardest place to find a job, as the job market there is small. The easiest way to get an English-teaching job in any of these countries is to be a **private tutor.**

Teaching jobs, especially without a permit, tend not to be very well paid. Don't be put off by this. However, if you manage to land a job at an elite international or American school, those salaries can be much more competitive. If you're a college undergraduate, your best bet would be a temporary or summer position. If you desire something more permanent, bachelor's degrees are usually required. Many schools also require you to be certified in **Teaching English as a Foreign Language (TEFL)**, and/or to be certified in administering the **Test of English as a Foreign Language (TOEFL)**. Being certified isn't a prerequisite to teach, but lacking these credentials may mean you won't be paid as much.

The best way to find a teaching job in a school is to use placement agencies or contacts through the university. Alternatively, you can try contacting the school directly and testing your luck. If you attempt this approach, the best time to do so would be before the start of the school year. The agencies listed below may give you a leg up on your competition.

- **DAVE'S ESL CAFÉ:** The site may be difficult to navigate, but you're sure to find something in its long lists of opportunities in different countries. *(9018 Balboa Blvd. #512, Northridge, CA, USA* ✉*www.eslcafe.com)*

- **INTERNATIONAL SCHOOLS SERVICES:** This service finds placement at American schools abroad and is great if you don't speak the local language. *(15 Roszel Road, P.O. Box 5910, Princeton, NJ* ☎*609-452-0990* ✉*www.iss.edu/index.asp)*

- **MORE THAN ENGLISH** Specifically for those interested in teaching English to Spanish speakers. *(*☎*+34 913 913 400* ✉*www.morethanenglish.com)*

- **ONLINE TEACHING ENGLISH AS A FOREIGN LANGUAGE (TEFL):** Sets you up with the proper TEFL courses you need and has job listings for after certification. *(Woodside House, 261 Low Lane, Leeds, LS18 5NY, UK* ✉*www.onlinetefl.com)*

- **TEACHABROAD.COM:** Part of Go Abroad.com, as listed above. Lots of relevant pre-departure information. *(*✉*www.teachabroad.com)*

beyond tourism

- **TEACHERS OF ENGLISH TO SPEAKERS OF OTHER LANGAUGES-SPAIN (TESOL-SPAIN):** Contact your regional coordinator. Membership site for English teachers living in Spain. (⌨*www.tesol-spain.org*)

  - **TRANSITIONS ABROAD:** Check out the "Teaching English" link to find your best location to work abroad. (⌨*www.transitionsabroad.com/listings/work/esl/index.shtml*)

Au Pair Work

If you are a woman in her late-teens to late-twenties, au pairing is a definite possibility. If you're a man, this is not to say you shouldn't give it a shot, but au pairs are traditionally women who live with families and are provided room, board and a small salary to look after somebody else's children. Many parents are especially eager to hire native English speakers to teach their kids English. Again, this experience can really vary depending on the family with which you're paired. If you're interested, the agencies listed below can help. As you can see, there's no dearth of demand.

  - **AU PAIR.COM:** Families post listings directly to this site. (⌨*www.aupair.com*)

  - **AUPAIRCONNECT:** Potential au pairs and families can sign up to this service that matches these parties for free. (⌨*www.aupairconnect.com*)

  - **CHILDCARE INTERNATIONAL, LTD:** UK-based program. (☎*0800 652 0020* ⌨*www.childint.co.uk*)

  - **GREAT AU PAIR:** American website with au pair listings by location and country in English. (⌨*www.greataupair.com*)

  - **SUNNY AU PAIRS:** A cheery matching service that provides testimonials from previous users. (⌨*www.sunnyaupairs.com*)

  - **TRANSITIONS ABROAD:** General information site for everything you need to know about going abroad with specific listings for au pairs. (⌨*www.transitionsabroad.com*)

Internships

The best way to segue into a long-term, more permanent job abroad is through first finding an internship.

  - **INTERNATIONAL ASSOCIATION FOR THE EXCHANGE OF STUDENTS FOR TECHNICAL EXPERIENCE (IAESTE):** This program provides paid overseas inernships to full-time university students studying in technical fields. If you're unsure whether you're studying in a "technical field," see the website for a detailed list of eligible disciplines. Most programs run 8-12 weeks in the summer. Placement is available in Spain and Portugal, but you may not be placed in your preferred country. (⌨ *www.iaeste.org* Ⓢ *$1000 program fee for placement. Cost of covered by salary.*)

  - **INTERN ABROAD:** Part of the Go Abroad.com network that remains a jack-of-all trades. (⌨*www.internabroad.com*)

  - **GLOBAL EXPERIENCES:** Like a study abroad-type program for internships, meaning you get a support system and housing. Summer internships available for Spain. (⌨*www.globalexperiences.com* Ⓢ *Programs fees $7000-8000.*)

  - **WORLD ENDEAVORS:** Another study. Only available in Spain. Offers special "culinary internships." (⌨*www.worldendeavors.com* Ⓢ *Internships cost $4000-7000.*)

Other Long-Term Work

  - **ESCAPE ARTIST:** This craigslist-like listings website allows employers to post directly to its directory. (⌨*www.escapeartist.com/Overseas_Jobs*)

  - **TRABAJOS:** Spanish and spanish-language site for job posters and the job seekers. (⌨*www.trabajos.com*)

working · long-term work

- **BUNAC WORKING ADVENTURES WORLDWIDE:** UK-based program dedicated to helping you have a meaningful experience through work and/or volunteer programs. *(PO Box 430, Southbury, CT ☎800-GO-BUNAC▪www.bunac.org)*

- **IDEAL SPAIN:** Another move-to-Spain site with a limited "work" section, but good information on permits and other paperwork. *(▪www.idealspain.com)*

- **MOVING TO BARCELONA:** True to its name, this website gives helpful hints on employment and living to new city-dwellers. *(▪www.movingtobarcelona.com)*

- **SPAINEXPAT.COM:** A website for expats! In Spain! Imagine that. *(▪www.spainexpat.com)*

SHORT-TERM WORK

Budget stretched thin? Wallet sadly empty? Finding short-term work is your best bet. Keep in mind that working without a permit is illegal in the EU, but many establishments will hire people illegally for a short time. These jobs are especially popular in resort areas that have high turnover rates due to tourism. In these establishments, you can generally find work bartending, waiting tables or doing promotional work. Some hostels will hire you in exchange for free/discounted room and board. The easiest way to find these jobs is either by word of mouth or simple inquiry. *Let's Go* does not recommend working illegally.

- **TRANSITIONS ABROAD:** General site for moving abroad to the Iberian Peninsula. Lots of listings for student work, internships, and general short-term deals. *(▪www.transitionsabroad.com)*

- **EASY EXPAT:** This site offers diverse opportunities for the traveler looking to make some coin in the near future. *(▪www.easyexpat.com)*

- **BACK DOOR JOBS:** This site advertises "short-term job adventures." Make sure you navigate to the international page. *(▪www.backdoorjobs.com)*

- **RESORT JOBS:** Site with worldwide listings about recent resort openings and employment opportunities. *(▪www.resortjobs.com)*

- **SEASONWORKERS.COM:** Lots of different opportunities, from childcare to ski resort employment. Site also includes information on work visas and permits. *(▪www.seasonworkers.com)*

- **WORKAWAY:** Site includes listings for jobs, volunteering, and internships. *(▪www.workaway.info)*

- **WORLD WIDE OPPORTUNITIES ON ORGANIC FARMS:** Organizations like this thrive more on volunteers working for lodging than short-term workers, but it never hurts to ask about compensation. Not available in Morocco. *(▪www.wwoof.org)*

tell the world

If your friends are tired of hearing about that time you saved a baby orangutan in Indonesia, there's clearly only one thing to do: get new friends. Find them at our website, ▪www.letsgo.com, where you can post your study-, volunteer-, or work-abroad stories for other, more appreciative community members to read. There's also a Beyond Tourism section that elaborates on non-destination-specific volunteering, studying, and working opportunities. If you liked this chapter, you'll love it; if you didn't like this chapter, maybe you'll find the website's more general Beyond Tourism tips more likeable, you non-likey person.

beyond tourism

INDEX

index

MAP INDEX

map index

MAP LEGEND

▪	Sight/Service	♖	Castle	🖳	Internet Cafe	♣	Police
✈	Airport	⛪	Church	📙	Library	✉	Post Office
�Π	Arch/Gate	⚑	Consulate/Embassy	Ⓜ M	Metro Station	⛷	Skiing
$	Bank	✝	Convent/Monastery	⛰	Mountain	✡	Synagogue
⛱	Beach	⚓	Ferry Landing	☪	Mosque	☎	Telephone Office
🚌	Bus Station	(347)	Highway Sign	🏛	Museum	♥	Theater
✪	Capital City	✚	Hospital	℞	Pharmacy	ⓘ	Tourist Office
						🚂	Train Station

The Let's Go compass always points NORTH.

:::::::: Pedestrian Zone

\\\\\\\\ Stairs

 Park

 Water

 Beach

THE STUDENT TRAVEL GUIDE

These Let's Go guidebooks are available at bookstores and through online retailers:

EUROPE
Let's Go Amsterdam & Brussels, 1st ed.
Let's Go Berlin, Prague & Budapest, 2nd ed.
Let's Go France, 32nd ed.
Let's Go Europe 2011, 51st ed.
Let's Go European Riviera, 1st ed.
Let's Go Germany, 16th ed.
Let's Go Great Britain with Belfast and Dublin, 33rd ed.
Let's Go Greece, 10th ed.
Let's Go Istanbul, Athens & the Greek Islands, 1st ed.
Let's Go Italy, 31st ed.
Let's Go London, Oxford, Cambridge & Edinburgh,
     2nd ed.
Let's Go Madrid & Barcelona, 1st ed.
Let's Go Paris, 17th ed.
Let's Go Rome, Venice & Florence, 1st ed.
Let's Go Spain, Portugal & Morocco, 26th ed.
Let's Go Western Europe, 10th ed.

UNITED STATES
Let's Go Boston, 6th ed.
Let's Go New York City, 19th ed.
Let's Go Roadtripping USA, 4th ed.

MEXICO, CENTRAL & SOUTH AMERICA
Let's Go Buenos Aires, 2nd ed.
Let's Go Central America, 10th ed.
Let's Go Costa Rica, 5th ed.
Let's Go Costa Rica, Nicaragua & Panama, 1st ed.
Let's Go Guatemala & Belize, 1st ed.
Let's Go Yucatán Peninsula, 1st ed.

ASIA & THE MIDDLE EAST
Let's Go Israel, 5th ed.
Let's Go Thailand, 5th ed.

ACKNOWLEDGMENTS

JONATHAN ROSSI THANKS: In no particular order: Anna Boch, Marykate Jasper, the whole Let's Go office, Grace Sun, Michal Labik, Jocey Karlan, Mark Warren, Christa Hartsock, Elyssa Spitzer, my family, all the food establishments in Harvard Square, the Los Angeles Lakers, the Kevin & Bean radio show, Winthrop E-21, Winthrop G-42, Antoine Dodson, and coffee.

ANNA BOCH THANKS: In a very particular order: all the kick-ass RW's, Jonathan Rossi, Marykate Jasper, the Snuggie, Caturday, Iya Megre, honey-stung fried chicken, the Winthrop-Eliot Dramatic Society, Marcel Moran, friends-list, Lucy, Waffle, and Moustafa the smoothie guy in the T-stop.

DIRECTOR OF PUBLISHING   Ashley R. Laporte
EXECUTIVE EDITOR   Nathaniel Rakich
PRODUCTION AND DESIGN DIRECTOR   Sara Plana
PUBLICITY AND MARKETING DIRECTOR   Joseph Molimock
MANAGING EDITORS   Charlotte Alter, Daniel C. Barbero, Marykate Jasper, Iya Megre
TECHNOLOGY PROJECT MANAGERS   Daniel J. Choi, C. Alexander Tremblay
PRODUCTION ASSOCIATES   Rebecca Cooper, Melissa Niu
FINANCIAL ASSOCIATE   Louis Caputo

DIRECTOR OF IT   Yasha Iravantchi
PRESIDENT   Meagan Hill
GENERAL MANAGER   Jim McKellar

LET'S GO
masthead

ABOUT LET'S GO

THE STUDENT TRAVEL GUIDE

Let's Go publishes the world's favorite student travel guides, written entirely by Harvard students. Armed with pens, notebooks, and a few changes of clothes stuffed into their backpacks, our student researchers go across continents, through time zones, and above expectations to seek out invaluable travel experiences for our readers. Because we are a completely student-run company, we have a unique perspective on how students travel, where they want to go, and what they're looking to do when they get there. If your dream is to grab a machete and forge through the jungles of Costa Rica, we can take you there. If you'd rather bask in the Riviera sun at a beachside cafe, we'll set you a table. In short, we write for readers who know that there's more to travel than tour buses. To keep up, visit our website, www.letsgo. com, where you can sign up to blog, post photos from your trips, and connect with the Let's Go community.

TRAVELING BEYOND TOURISM

We're on a mission to provide our readers with sharp, fresh coverage packed with socially responsible opportunities to go beyond tourism. Each guide's Beyond Tourism chapter shares ideas about responsible travel, study abroad, and how to give back to the places you visit while on the road. To help you gain a deeper connection with the places you travel, our fearless researchers scour the globe to give you the heads-up on both world-renowned and off-the-beaten-track opportunities. We've also opened our pages to respected writers and scholars to hear their takes on the countries and regions we cover, and asked travelers who have worked, studied, or volunteered abroad to contribute first-person accounts of their experiences.

FIFTY-ONE YEARS OF WISDOM

Let's Go has been on the road for 51 years and counting. We've grown a lot since publishing our first 20-page pamphlet to Europe in 1960, but five decades and 60 titles later, our witty, candid guides are still researched and written entirely by students on shoestring budgets who know that train strikes, stolen luggage, food poisoning, and marriage proposals are all part of a day's work. Meanwhile, we're still bringing readers fresh new features, such as a student-life section with advice on how and where to meet students from around the world; a revamped, user-friendly layout for our listings; and greater emphasis on the experiences that make travel abroad a rite of passage for readers of all ages. And, of course, this year's 16 titles—including five brand-new guides—are still brimming with editorial honesty, a commitment to students, and our irreverent style.

THE LET'S GO COMMUNITY

More than just a travel guide company, Let's Go is a community that reaches from our headquarters in Cambridge, MA, all across the globe. Our small staff of dedicated student editors, writers, and tech nerds comes together because of our shared passion for travel and our desire to help other travelers get the most out of their experience. We love it when our readers become part of the Let's Go community as well—when you travel, drop us a postcard (67 Mt. Auburn St., Cambridge, MA 02138, USA), send us an email (feedback@letsgo.com), or sign up on our website (www. letsgo.com) to tell us about your adventures and discoveries.

For more information, updated travel coverage, and news from our researcher team, visit us online at www.letsgo.com.

THANKS TO OUR SPONSORS

HELPING LET'S GO. If you want to share your discoveries, suggestions, or corrections, please drop us a line. We appreciate every piece of correspondence, whether a postcard, a 10-page email, or a coconut. Visit Let's Go at **www.letsgo.com** or send an email to:

feedback@letsgo.com, subject: "Let's Go Spain, Portugal & Morocco"

Address mail to:

Let's Go Spain, Portugal & Morocco, 67 Mount Auburn St., Cambridge, MA 02138, USA

In addition to the invaluable travel advice our readers share with us, many are kind enough to offer their services as researchers or editors. Unfortunately, our charter enables us to employ only currently enrolled Harvard students.

Maps © Let's Go and Avalon Travel
Design Support by Jane Musser, Sarah Juckniess, Tim McGrath

Distributed by Publishers Group West.
Printed in Canada by Friesens Corp.

ISBN-13: 978-1-59880-705-9
Twenty-sixth edition
10 9 8 7 6 5 4 3 2 1

Let's Go Spain, Portugal & Morocco is written by Let's Go Publications, 67 Mt. Auburn St., Cambridge, MA 02138, USA.

Let's Go® and the LG logo are trademarks of Let's Go, Inc.

quick reference

YOUR GUIDE TO LET'S GO ICONS

⚲	Wheelchair-accessible	♨	Serves alcohol	⏱	Hours
⊛	Cash only	▲	Is GLBT or LGBT-friendly	$	Prices
💳	Takes credit cards	☂	Has outdoor seating	*i*	Other hard info
▣	Websites	(•))	Has internet access	✚	Directions
☎	Phone numbers	⊘	Not wheelchair-accessible	❄	Has A/C

PRICE RANGES

Let's Go includes price ranges, marked by icons ❶ through ❺, in accommodations and food listings. For an expanded explanation, see the chart in How To Use This Book.

SPAIN AND PORTUGAL	❶	❷	❸	❹	❺
ACCOMMODATIONS	under €20	€20-29	€30-37	€38-50	€ 50+
FOOD	under €6	€6-12	€13-17	€ 18-25	€25+

MOROCCO	❶	❷	❸	❹	❺
ACCOMMODATIONS	under 100dh	100-200dh	201-300dh	301-400dh	400dh+
FOOD	20-60dh	61-90dh	91-130dh	131-180dh	180dh+

IMPORTANT PHONE NUMBERS

SPAIN EMERGENCY: POLICE 091, FIRE 080, ANYTHING 112

Ambulance (Spain)	061	To Report a Crime (Spain)	902 102 112
Directory Assistance (Spain)	11822	Operator (Spain)	1008

PORTUGAL EMERGENCY: FOR ANYTHING 112

Directory Assistance (Portugal)	118	To Locate a Pharmacy (Portugal)	800 202 134
Tourism Information (Portugal)	808 781 212	Operator (Portugal)	171

MOROCCO EMERGENCY: POLICE 19, FIRE AND AMBULANCE 15

USEFUL PHRASES

ENGLISH	SPANISH	PORTUGUESE	MOROCCAN ARABIC
Hello!/Hi!	¡Hola!	Olá	es salaam aláykum
Goodbye!	¡Adiós!	Até logo!	bessalama
Yes.	Sí.	Sim.	eeyeh
No.	No.	Não.	la
Please.	Por favor.	Por favor.	'afak(m)/'afik(f)
Sorry!/Excuse me!	¡Perdón!	Desculpe!	smeh leeyah
Good morning	Buenos días	Bom dia	sabakh al-kheer
Good evening	Buenas noches	Boa noite	maseh al-kheer
How are you?	¿Cómo estás?	Como você está?	la bas?
I'm fine, thanks.	Bien, gracias.	Eu bem, obrigado/a.	la bas, barak.

MEASUREMENT CONVERSIONS

1 inch (in.) = 25.4mm	1 millimeter (mm) = 0.039 in.
1 foot (ft.) = 0.305m	1 meter (m) = 3.28 ft.
1 mile (mi.) = 1.609km	1 kilometer (km) = 0.621 mi.
1 pound (lb.) = 0.454kg	1 kilogram (kg) = 2.205 lb.